WORD
BIBLICAL
COMMENTARY

Volume 46

Pastoral Epistles

WILLIAM D. MOUNCE

THOMAS NELSON
Since 1798

NASHVILLE   DALLAS   MEXICO CITY   RIO DE JANEIRO

Word Biblical Commentary
PASTORAL EPISTLES
Copyright © 2000 by Thomas Nelson, Inc.

Library of Congress Cataloging in Publication Data
Main entry under title:

Word biblical commentary.

   Includes bibliographies.
   1. Bible—Commentaries—Collected works.
BS491.2.W67   220.7′7′ 81–71768
ISBN-10: 0-8499-0245-2 (v.46) AACR2
ISBN-13: 978-0-8499-0245-1

Printed in Mexico

The author′s own translation of the Scripture text appears in italic type under the heading *Translation*. Unless otherwise designated, Scripture quotations in the body of the commentary are the author′s own or are taken from the Revised Standard Version of the Bible, copyright 1946 (renewes 1973), 1956, and © 1971 by the Division of Christian Education of the National Council of the Churches of Christ in the USA, and are used by permission.

15 16 17 18 19 EPAC 15 14 13 12 11

To the women in my life:
Robin, my wife and best friend;
Rose and Rachel, who went on ahead to wait for me;
and Kiersten, who stayed behind with her dad.

Contents

Editorial Preface

The launching of the *Word Biblical Commentary* brings to fulfillment an enterprise of several years' planning. The publishers and the members of the editorial board met in 1977 to explore the possibility of a new commentary on the books of the Bible that would incorporate several distinctive features. Prospective readers of these volumes are entitled to know what such features were intended to be; whether the aims of the commentary have been fully achieved time alone will tell.

First, we have tried to cast a wide net to include as contributors a number of scholars from around the world who not only share our aims but are in the main engaged in the ministry of teaching in university, college, and seminary. They represent a rich diversity of denominational allegiance. The broad stance of our contributors can rightly be called evangelical, and this term is to be understood in its positive, historic sense of a commitment to Scripture as divine revelation and the truth and power of the Christian gospel.

Then, the commentaries in our series are all commissioned and written for the purpose of inclusion in the *Word Biblical Commentary*. Unlike several of our distinguished counterparts in the field of commentary writing, there are no translated works, originally written in a non-English language. Also, our commentators were asked to prepare their own rendering of the original biblical text and to use those languages as the basis of their own comments and exegesis. What may be claimed as distinctive with this series is that it is based on the biblical languages, yet it seeks to make the technical and scholarly approach to the theological understanding of Scripture understandable by—and useful to—the fledgling student, the working minister, and colleagues in the guild of professional scholars and teachers as well.

Finally, a word must be said about the format of the series. The layout, in clearly defined sections, has been consciously devised to assist readers at different levels. Those wishing to learn about the textual witnesses on which the translation is offered are invited to consult the section headed *Notes*. If the readers' concern is with the state of modern scholarship on any given portion of Scripture, they should turn to the sections on *Bibliography* and *Form/Structure/Setting*. For a clear exposition of the passage's meaning and its relevance to the ongoing biblical revelation, the *Comment* and concluding *Explanation* are designed expressly to meet that need. There is therefore something for everyone who may pick up and use these volumes.

If these aims come anywhere near realization, the intention of the editors will have been met, and the labor of our team of contributors rewarded.

General Editors: *Bruce M. Metzger*
David A. Hubbard†
Glenn W. Barker†
Old Testament: *John D. W. Watts*
New Testament: *Ralph P. Martin*

Author's Preface

The past thirteen years during which I have been immersed in this study have been a mixed blessing. It has been a joy to be devoted to God's word. 2 Timothy has always been my favorite book in the New Testament. It gives a personal look into Paul's heart as he writes to the one who I believe was his best friend, with words applicable especially to young pastors everywhere. These years for me have also seen their times of difficulty: sharp disagreement from those even within the evangelical camp in response to positions taken in my writing; personal tragedy in the death of my first two daughters; disappointment in discovering first hand that the answers of the academy often do not answer the real-life issues of the church. But God is good and sovereign, and to him I am thankful.

The target audience of the Word Biblical Commentary series is a broad one, and because the scope is so vast, I have chosen to focus on the needs of those involved in the life of the church. This is not to say that I have dismissed the issues critical to the scholar; indeed, I have struggled with them throughout the commentary. But my primary concern has been to be helpful to those in the pew and pulpit. With this in mind, I begin each verse with a discussion of its basic meaning and of Paul's flow of thought. Then I concentrate on word studies, and after that on the more technical issues.

I know that the tendency of some readers will be to judge this commentary on the basis of my views on authorship and the issue of women in ministry, but I hope that disagreements over these controversies will not keep readers from sharing my encounter with the Pastoral Epistles and from learning what Paul has to say about the ministry in general.

This commentary concentrates on an exposition of the text, and for tangential issues the reader is referred to other resources. My translations are idiomatic in order to reflect the nuances of the original Greek, even to the detriment of English usage. Words inserted into the translation, especially the article, are bracketed. I have tried to limit my word studies to the data in the PE, other Pauline literature, and the NT. I tended not to go outside this circle because of the problems inherent in using nonbiblical references even a century prior to or after Paul, unless the word clearly belonged to the Greco-Roman cultural milieu (excellent discussion of the broader ranges of meaning can be found in W. Lock, C. Spicq, and J. D. Quinn, as well as in standard dictionaries such as *TDNT* and *NIDNTT*). Unless otherwise stated, all biblical quotations are from the RSV or are my own translations. I discuss issues such as the meaning of words the first time they are mentioned in the text and thereafter make reference to that discussion. Questions of authorship have been restricted to the *Introduction*. In the *Explanation* sections I have summarized each passage and dealt with theological issues, including references to treatments of important themes in second- and third-century writings.

With regard to my predecessors, I found the commentaries by G. D. Fee, J. N. D. Kelly, and D. Guthrie to be the most helpful. C. Spicq, G. W. Knight III, and J. D. Quinn provided a rich source of details, and L. T. Johnson often had an interesting and helpful way of looking at the text. Although C. J. Ellicott published his commentary in 1856, I discovered it to be surprisingly contemporary (e.g., his recognition of the ad hoc nature of the instruction and its relationship to the historical situation in Ephesus). I also found that John Chrysostom has come at the text with a refreshing passion. Unfortunately, I. H. Marshall's commentary for the ICC series as well as those by W. L. Liefeld and J. D. Quinn (posthumously edited by W. C. Wacker) arrived too late for me to study. P. H. Towner's *The Goal of Our Instruction* is an excellent work, and I look forward to his commentary for the NICNT series. While I disagreed with A. T. Hanson's work almost constantly, I did appreciate his explanation of the more critical positions on the PE.

Of all the commentaries, I am most indebted to Fee's work, and in many ways see my contribution as an expansion of the road that he has paved, viewing the PE as letters written to specific historical situations. Most of the major commentaries (in English) in the last several decades have, like Fee, supported the authenticity of the PE. I hope that my efforts will help readers to appreciate the truly epistolary and ad hoc nature of these three books, addressed, like Paul's other letters, to real people in real-life situations, and to recognize the almost glaring differences between the PE and the Christian literature of the second century.

I am glad to express my thanks and indebtedness to the many people who have helped me in this endeavor. To Professors Tom Schreiner, Craig Blomberg, Robert Mounce, Aida Spencer, and Craig Keener, who read some or all of the commentary and were free with their criticisms and suggestions, I am profoundly indebted, especially as they helped me understand their positions that differ from mine. Thanks to my editors, Professor Ralph Martin, Dr. Lynn Losie, and Melanie McQuere, who improved the manuscript in many places and edited my text to conform to the style of the series. When I thought the task was simply too great, the Lord brought Ron Toews, Roger Smith, Foster Chase, and the Teknon Corporation into my life, through whose generosity I was enabled financially to finish the task. Thanks go to my church for its support, encouragement, and the opportunity to serve, especially to Richard Porter, Steve Yoell, and Doug Welbourn. Thanks also are due to my students Miles Van Pelt and Juan Hernández, Jr., for their months of library work on the text and on the indexes, to David and Carole Lambert for many hours of help, and to the members of my last seminar on the PE: Ted Kang, John Lin, Jim Cheshire, Tom Haugen, Ryan Jackson, Harold Kim, and Mathias Kuerschner. And while authors generally thanks their wives, let not the frequency of that sentiment ever question the value that my wife Robin has brought to my life and the study of this text. Without Robin's patience, support, love, and encouragement to leave a secure job and move to Spokane, Washington (where our only support would have to be from the Lord) so that I could finish this writing project and others, I probably would have given up years ago.

The PE are part of God's "two-edged sword," cutting deeply into the human heart. I am privileged to have been able to immerse myself in these chapters and so to have caught a clearer glimpse of Paul and the gospel, and for that I will be eternally grateful.

WILLIAM D. MOUNCE

March 1999
Garland Avenue Alliance Church, Spokane, Washington
Gordon-Conwell Theological Seminary, South Hamilton, Massachusetts

Abbreviations

A. General Abbreviations

c.	*circa*, about	OL	Old Latin
cf.	*confer*, compare	o.s	old series
chap(s).	chapter(s)	OT	Old Testament
DSS	Dead Sea Scrolls	par.	parallel
ed(s).	editor(s), edited by	PE	Pastoral Epistles
e.g.	*exempli gratia*, for example	PLond	London Papyri
		POxy	Oxyrhynchus Papyri
ET	English translation		
et. al.	*et alii*, and others	repr.	reprint
FS	*Festschrift*, volume written in honor of	rev.	revised, reviser, revision
Gk.	Greek	ser.	series
Heb.	Hebrew	tr.	translator, translated by, translation
id.	*idem*, the same		
i.e.	*id est*, that is	TR	Textus Receptus
lit.	literally	UP	University Press
LXX	Septuagint	vg	Vulgate
MS(S)	manuscript(s)	v, vv	verse, verses
MT	Masoretic Text	*v.l.*	*varia(e) lectio(nes)*, variant reading(s)
n.	note		
no.	number	vol.	volume
n.s.	new series	x	times (2x = two times)
NT	New Testament		

B. Abbreviations for Translations and Paraphrases

ASV	American Standard Version, American Revised Version (1901)	NEB	New English Bible
		NIV	New International Version
		NRSV	New Revised Standard Version
AV	Authorized Version = KJV		
GNB	Good News Bible	REB	Revised English Bible
KJV	King James Version (1611) = AV	RSV	Revised Standard Version
NASB	New American Standard Bible	Wey	Weymouth Translation

C. Abbreviations of Commonly Used Periodicals, Reference Works, and Serials

AB	Anchor Bible	BDF	F. Blass, A. Debrunner, and R. W. Funk, *A Greek Grammar of the NT*
ABD	D. N. Freedman (ed.), *Anchor Bible Dictionary*		
ACNT	Augsburg Commentaries on the New Testament	*BeO*	*Bibbia e oriente*
		BFCL	*Bulletin des Facultés Catholiques: Lyon*
AHDE	*Anuario de historia del derecho español*	BFCT	Beiträge zur Förderung christlicher Theologie
AJT	*American Journal of Theology*		
AnBib	Analecta biblica		
AnBoll	Analecta Bollandiana	BGU	Ägyptische Urkunden aus den königlichen Museen zu Berlin: Griechische Urkunden I–VIII
ANF	The Ante-Nicene Fathers		
Ang	*Angelicum*		
ANRW	*Aufstieg und Niedergang der römischen Welt*		
ANTC	Abingdon New Testament Commentaries	*BHH*	B. Reicke and L. Rost (eds.), *Biblisch-Historisches Handwörterbuch*
AsSeign	*Assemblées du Seigneur*		
ATANT	Abhandlung zur Theologie des Alten und Neuen Testaments	*BHK*	R. Kittel, *Biblia Hebraica*
		BHS	*Biblia Hebraica Stuttgartensia*
ATR	*Anglican Theological Review*	BHT	Beiträge zur historischen Theologie
ATW	*Am Tisch des Wortes*		
AusBR	*Australian Biblical Review*	*Bib*	*Biblica*
AUSS	*Andrews University Seminary Studies*	*BibInt*	*Biblical Interpretation*
		BibLeb	*Bibel und Leben*
		BibOr	Biblica et orientalia
BAGD	W. Bauer, W. F. Arndt, F. W. Gingrich, and F. W. Danker, *Greek-English Lexicon of the NT*	BibS(F)	Biblische Studien (Freiburg, 1895–)
		BibS(N)	Biblische Studien (Neukirchen, 1951–)
BARev	*Biblical Archaeology Review*	*BJRL*	*Bulletin of the John Rylands University Library of Manchester*
BBB	Bonner biblische Beiträge		
BBET	Beiträge zur biblischen Exegese und Theologie	BJS	Brown Judaic Studies
		BK	*Bibel und Kirche*
BBR	*Bulletin for Biblical Research*	*BLit*	*Bibel und Liturgie*
		BSac	*Bibliotheca Sacra*
BDB	F. Brown, S. R. Driver, and C. A. Briggs, *Hebrew and English Lexicon of the OT*	*BT*	*The Bible Translator*
		BTB	*Biblical Theology Bulletin*
		BTS	*Bible et terre sainte*

BVC	*Bible et vie chrétienne*	EKKNT	Evangelisch-katholischer
BWA(N)T	Beiträge zur		Kommentar zum
	Wissenschaft vom		Neuen Testament
	Alten (und Neuen)	*EM*	*Ephemerides*
	Testament		*Mariologicae*
BZ	*Biblische Zeitschrift*	*EnchBib*	*Enchiridion biblicum*
BZNW	Beihefte zur *ZNW*	*EstBib*	*Estudios bíblicos*
		EstEcl	*Estudios Eclesiásticos*
CB	*Cultura bíblica*	*ETR*	*Etudes théologiques et*
CBC	Cambridge Bible		*religieuses*
	Commentary	*EvQ*	*Evangelical Quarterly*
CBQ	*Catholic Biblical Quarterly*	*EvT*	*Evangelische Theologie*
CH	*Church History*	*Exp*	*The Expositor*
CivC	*Civiltà Cattolica*	*ExpTim*	*Expository Times*
ConB	Coniectanea biblica		
ConNT	*Coniectanea neotestamentica*	FB	Forschung zur Bibel
CP	*Classical Philology*	FFNT	Foundations and
CTJ	*Calvin Theological Journal*		Facets: New
CTM	*Concordia Theological*		Testament
	Monthly	FRLANT	Forschungen zur
CTQ	*Concordia Theological*		Religion und Literatur
	Quarterly		des Alten und
CTR	*Criswell Theological Review*		Neuen Testaments
CurTM	*Currents in Theology and*	*FV*	*Foi et Vie*
	Mission	*FZPT*	*Freiburger Zeitschrift für*
			Philosophie und
DACL	*Dictionnaire d'archéologie*		*Theologie*
	chrétienne et de liturgie		
DBSup	*Dictionnaire de la Bible,*	GH	B. P. Grenfell and A. S.
	Supplément		Hunt (eds.), *Greek*
DPL	G. F. Hawthorne and R.		*Papyri*, series II
	P. Martin (eds.),		(1897)
	Dictionary of Paul	*GL*	*Geist und Leben*
	and His Letters	*Greg*	*Gregorianum*
DTC	*Dictionnaire de théologie*	*GTT*	*Gereformerd theologisch*
	catholique		*tijdschrift*
DTT	*Dansk teologisk tidsskrift*		
		HBT	Horizons in Biblical
EBib	Etudes bibliques		Theology
EchtB	Echter Bibel	*HibJ*	*Hibbert Journal*
ED	*Euentes Doceta*	HNT	Handbuch zum
EDNT	H. Balz and G. Schneider		Neuen Testament
	(eds.), *Exegetical Dictionary*	HNTC	Harper's New Testa-
	of the New Testament		ment Commentaries
EDT	W. A. Elwell (ed.),	HTKNT	Herders theologischer
	Evangelical Dictionary		Kommentar zum
	of Theology		Neuen Testament
EETT	*Epistēmonikē epetēris*	*HTR*	*Harvard Theological*
	theologikēs scholēs . . .		*Review*
	Thessalonikēs		

HTS	Harvard Theological Studies	*JRS*	*Journal of Roman Studies*
HUCA	*Hebrew Union College Annual*	*JSNT*	*Journal for the Study of the New Testament*
HUT	Hermeneutische Untersuchungen zur Theologie	JSNTSup	*JSNT* Supplement Series
		JTS	*Journal of Theological Studies*
IB	*Interpreter's Bible*	KB	L. Koehler and W. Baumgartner, *Hebräisches und aramäisches Lexikon zum Alten Testament*
IBD	J. D. Douglas and N. Hillyer (eds.), *Illustrated Bible Dictionary*		
IBS	*Irish Biblical Studies*		
ICC	International Critical Commentary	*KD*	*Kerygma und Dogma*
ICR/C	*International Catholic Review/Communio*	KEK	Kritisch-exegetischer Kommentar über das Neue Testament
IDB	G. A. Buttrick (ed.), *Interpreter's Dictionary of the Bible*	*KR*	*Křest'anská revue*
IDBSup	Supplementary Volume to *IDB*	*LB*	*Linguistica Biblica*
IKaZ	*Internationale Katholische Zeitschrift/Communio*	LCL	Loeb Classical Library
		LEC	Library of Early Christianity
Int	*Interpretation*	*LQ*	*Lutheran Quarterly*
ISBE	G. W. Bromiley (ed.), *International Standard Bible Encyclopedia*, rev.	LSJ	H. G. Liddell, R. Scott, H. S. Jones, and R. McKenzie, *A Greek-English Lexicon*, 9th ed.
ITQ	*Irish Theological Quarterly*	*LTP*	*Laval théologique et philosophique*
JAAR	*Journal of the American Academy of Religion*	*MBG*	W. D. Mounce, *The Morphology of Biblical Greek*
JAC	Jahrbuch für Antike und Christentum		
JBC	R. E. Brown et al. (eds.), *The Jerome Biblical Commentary*	MM	J. H. Moulton and G. Milligan, *The Vocabulary of the Greek Testament*
JBL	*Journal of Biblical Literature*		
JEH	*Journal of Ecclesiastical History*	MNTC	Moffatt New Testament Commentary
JEKT	*Jahrbuch für evangelikale Theologie*	NCB	New Century Bible
JES	*Journal of Ecumenical Studies*	NCE	M. R. P. McGuire et al. (eds.), *New Catholic Encyclopedia*
JETS	*Journal of the Evangelical Theological Society*		
JJS	*Journal of Jewish Studies*	*NedTTs*	*Nederlands theologisch tijdschrift*
JQR	*Jewish Quarterly Review*		
JR	*Journal of Religion*	*Neot*	*Neotestamentica*
JRelS	*Journal of Religious Studies*	NGTT	*Nederduitse Gereformeerde Teologiese Tydskrif*

NICNT	New International Commentary on the New Testament	*PGM*	K. Preisendanz (ed.), *Papyri graecae magicae*, 2nd ed.
NIDNTT	C. Brown (ed.), *The New International Dictionary of New Testament Theology*	*PresR*	*Presbyterian Review*
		PRS	*Perspectives in Religious Studies*
NIDOTTE	W. G. VanGemeren (ed.), *The New International Dictionary of Old Testament Theology and Exegesis*	*PTR*	*Princeton Theological Review*
		QD	Quaestiones disputatae
		RAC	*Reallexikon für Antike und Christentum*
NIGTC	New International Greek Testament Commentary	*RB*	*Revue biblique*
		RBR	*Ricerche Bibliche e Religiose*
NJBC	R. E. Brown et al. (eds.), *The New Jerome Biblical Commentary*	*RechBib*	*Recherches bibliques*
		RelS	*Religious Studies*
		RelSRev	*Religious Studies Review*
NKZ	*Neue kirchliche Zeitschrift*	*ResQ*	*Restoration Quarterly*
NorTT	*Norsk Teologisk Tidsskrift*	*RevExp*	*Review and Expositor*
NovT	*Novum Testamentum*	*RevistB*	*Revista bíblica*
NovTSup	*Novum Testamentum, Supplements*	*RevistC*	*Revista Catalana de Teologia*
NPNF	Nicene and Post-Nicene Fathers	*RevistTL*	*Revista teologica, Lima*
		RevQ	*Revue de Qumran*
NRT	*La nouvelle revue théologique*	*RevThom*	*Revue thomiste*
NTAbh	Neutestamentliche Abhandlungen	*RGG*	*Religion in Geschichte und Gegenwart*
NTD	Das Neue Testament Deutsch	*RHE*	*Revue d'histoire ecclésiastique*
NTF	Neutestamentliche Forschungen	*RHPR*	*Revue d'histoire et de philosophie religieuses*
NTOA	Novum Testamentum et Orbis Antiquus	*RHR*	*Revue de l'histoire des religions*
NTS	*New Testament Studies*	*RivB*	*Rivista biblica*
		RNT	Regensburger Neues Testament
ÖBS	*Österreichische biblische Studien*	*RQ*	*Römische Quartalschrift für christliche Altertumskunde und Kirchengeschichte*
OCD [2]	*Oxford Classical Dictionary*, 2nd ed. (1975)		
OS	*Ostkirchliche Studien*		
OTL	Old Testament Library	RQSup	*Römische Quartalschrift, Supplements*
PG	J.-P. Migne, *Patrologia graeca*	*RSPT*	*Revue des sciences philosophiques et théologiques*
PGL	G. W. H. Lampe, *Patristic Greek Lexicon*	*RSR*	*Recherches de science religieuse*

RST	Regensburger Studien zur Theologie	Str-B	[H. Strack and] P. Billerbeck, *Kommentar zum Neuen Testament*
RTK	*Roczniki Teologiczno-Kanoniczne*		
RTR	*The Reformed Theological Review*	StudBib	Studia Biblica
		StudNeot	Studia neotestamentica
SacD	*Sacra Doctrina*	SUNT	Studien zur Umwelt des Neuen Testaments
SB	Sources bibliques		
SBLASP	Society of Biblical Literature Abstracts and Seminar Papers	*SUNT*	*Studien zur Umwelt des Neuen Testaments*
SBLDS	SBL Dissertation Series	*SWJT*	*Southwestern Journal of Theology*
SBLMS	SBL Monograph Series		
SBLSP	*SBL Seminar Papers*		
SBT	Studies in Biblical Theology	TANZ	Texte und Arbeiten zum neutestamentlichen Zeitalter
ScEs	*Science et esprit*		
Scr	*Scripture*		
ScrB	*Scripture Bulletin*	*TBei*	*Theologische Beiträge*
SD	Studies and Documents	TBT	*The Bible Today*
SE	*Studia Evangelica I, II, III* (= TU 73 [1959], 87 [1964], 88 [1964], etc.)	TCGNT[1]	B. M. Metzger, *A Textual Commentary on the Greek New Testament*, 1st ed. (1971)
SEÅ	*Svensk exegetisk årsbok*		
SEAJT	*South East Asia Journal of Theology*	TCGNT[2]	B. M. Metzger, *A Textual Commentary on the Greek New Testament*, 2nd ed. (1994)
SJT	*Scottish Journal of Theology*		
SKKNT	Stuttgarter kleiner Kommentar, Neues Testament		
SNT	Studien zum Neuen Testament	TDNT	G. Kittel and G. Friedrich (eds.), *Theological Dictionary of the New Testament*
SNTSMS	Society for New Testament Studies Monograph Series		
SNTU-A	Studien zum Neuen Testament und seiner Umwelt, Series A	*TF*	*Theologische Forschung*
		TGl	*Theologie und Glaube*
SNTU-B	Studien zum Neuen Testament und seiner Umwelt, Series B	THKNT	Theologischer Handkommentar zum Neuen Testament
SPap	*Studia papyrologica*	*TJ*	*Trinity Journal*
SR	*Studies in Religion/Sciences religieuses*	TLNT	C. Spicq, *Theological Lexicon of the New Testament*
ST	*Studia theologica*		
STK	*Svensk teologisk kvartalskrift*	TLZ	*Theologische Literaturzeitung*

TNTC	Tyndale New Testament Commentary
TPQ	Theologisch-praktische Quartalschrift
TQ	Theologische Quartalschrift
TRev	Theologische Revue
TS	Theological Studies
TSAJ	Texte und Studien zum antiken Judentum
TSK	Theologische Studien und Kritiken
TTKi	Tidsskrift for Teologi og Kirke
TTZ	Trierer theologische Zeitschrift
TU	Texte und Untersuchungen
TWAT	G. J. Botterweck, H. Ringgren, and H.-J. Fabry (eds.), Theologisches Wörterbuch zum Alten Testament
TWNT	G. Kittel and G. Friedrich (eds.), Theologisches Wörterbuch zum Neuen Testament
TWOT	R. L. Harris and G. L. Archer, Jr. (eds.), Theological Wordbook of the Old Testament
TynBul	Tyndale Bulletin
TZ	Theologische Zeitschrift
UBSGNT³	K. Aland et al. (eds.), United Bible Societies Greek New Testament, 3rd ed.
UBSGNT⁴	K. Aland et al. (eds.), United Bible Societies Greek New Testament, 4th ed.
UBSMS	United Bible Societies Monograph Series
USQR	Union Seminary Quarterly Review
VC	Vigiliae Christianae
VD	Verbum domini
VF	Verkündigung und Forschung
VS	Verbum salutis
VT	Vetus Testamentum
VTSup	Vetus Testamentum Supplements
WBC	Word Biblical Commentary
WC	Westminster Commentary
WD	Wort und Dienst
WMANT	Wissenschaftliche Monographien zum Alten und Neuen Testament
WO	Die Welt des Orients
WTJ	Westminster Theological Journal
WUNT	Wissenschaftliche Untersuchungen zum Neuen Testament
ZBNT	Zürcher Bibelkommentar/ Neues Testament
ZKNT	Zahn's Kommentar zum NT
ZKT	Zeitschrift für katholische Theologie
ZNW	Zeitschrift für die neutestamentliche Wissenschaft
ZTK	Zeitschrift für Theologie und Kirche
ZWT	Zeitschrift für wissenschaftliche Theologie

D. Abbreviations for Books of the Bible with Aprocrypha

OLD TESTAMENT

Gen	1–2 Kgs	Cant	Obad
Exod	1–2 Chr	Isa	Jonah
Lev	Ezra	Jer	Mic
Num	Neh	Lam	Nah
Deut	Esth	Ezek	Hab
Josh	Job	Dan	Zeph
Judg	Ps(s)	Hos	Hag
Ruth	Prov	Joel	Zech
1–2 Sam	Eccl	Amos	Mal

NEW TESTAMENT

Matt	Rom	Col	Heb
Mark	1–2 Cor	1–2 Thess	Jas
Luke	Gal	1–2 Tim	1–2 Pet
John	Eph	Titus	1–2–3 John
Acts	Phil	Phlm	Jude
			Rev

APOCRYPHA

1–2–3–4 Kgdms	1–2–3–4 Kingdoms	Ep Jer	Epistle of Jeremiah
1–2 Esdr	1–2 Esdras	S Th Ch	Song of the Three Children (or Young Men)
Tob	Tobit		
Jdt	Judith		
Add Esth	Additions to Esther	Sus	Susanna
4 Ezra	4 Ezra	Bel	Bel and the Dragon
Wis	Wisdom of Solomon	Pr Azar	Prayer of Azariah
Sir	Ecclesiasticus (Wisdom of Jesus the son of Sirach)	1–2–3–4 Macc	1–2–3–4 Maccabees
Bar	Baruch		

E. Abbreviations of Pseudepigrapha and Early Jewish Literature

Adam and Eve	*Books of Adam and Eve* or *Vita Adae et Evae*	*Apoc. Sedr.*	*Apocalypse of Sedrach*
Apoc. Abr.	*Apocalypse of Abraham*	*Apoc. Zeph.*	*Apocalypse of Zephaniah*
2–3 Apoc. Bar.	*Syriac, Greek Apocalypse of Baruch*	*Bib. Ant.*	Ps.-Philo, *Biblical Antiquities*

1–2–3 Enoch	Ethiopic, Slavonic, Hebrew *Enoch*
Ep. Arist.	*Epistle of Aristeas*
Jos. As.	*Joseph and Aseneth*
Jub.	*Jubilees*
Mart. Isa.	*Martyrdom of Isaiah*
Odes Sol.	*Odes of Solomon*
Par. Jer.	*Paraleipomena Jeremiou* or *4 Baruch*
Pr. Man.	*Prayer of Manasseh*
Pss. Sol.	*Psalms of Solomon*

Sib. Or.	*Sibylline Oracles*
T. Job	*Testament of Job*
T. Mos.	*Testament of Moses (Assumption of Moses)*
T. 12 Patr.	*Testaments of the Twelve Patriarchs*
T. Levi	*Testament of Levi*
T. Benj.	*Testament of Benjamin*
T. Reub.	*Testament of Reuben*, etc.

F. Abbreviations of Dead Sea Scrolls

CD	Cairo (Genizah text of the) *Damascus (Document)*
Hev	Naḥal Ḥever texts
Hev/Se	Naḥal Ḥever documents earlier attributed to Seiyal
Mas	Masada texts
MasShirShabb	*Songs of Sabbath Sacrifice,* or *Angelic Liturgy* from Masada
Mird	Khirbet Mird texts
Mur	Wadi Murabbaʿat texts
p	pesher (commentary)
Q	Qumran
1Q, 2Q, 3Q, etc.	Numbered caves of Qumran
QL	Qumran literature
1QapGen	*Genesis Apocryphon* of Qumran Cave 1
1QH	*Hôdāyôt* (*Thanksgiving Hymns*) from Qumran Cave 1
1QIsaᵃ,ᵇ	First or second copy of Isaiah from Qumran Cave 1
1QpHab	*Pesher on Habakkuk* from Qumran Cave 1
1QM	*Milḥāmâ* (*War Scroll*)
1QS	*Serek hayyaḥad* (*Rule of the Community, Manual of Discipline*)

1QSa	Appendix A (*Rule of the Congregation*) to 1QS
1QSb	Appendix B (*Blessings*) to 1QS
3Q15	*Copper Scroll* from Qumran Cave 3
4QFlor	*Florilegium* (or *Eschatological Midrashim*) from Qumran Cave 4
4QMess ar	Aramaic "Messianic" text from Qumran Cave 4
4QMMT	*Miqsat Maʿsê ha-Torâ* from Qumran Cave 4
4QPhyl	Phylacteries from Qumran Cave 4
4QPrNab	*Prayer of Nabonidus* from Qumran Cave 4
4QPssJosh	*Psalms of Joshua* from Qumran Cave 4
4QShirShabb	*Songs of Sabbath Sacrifice,* or *Angelic Liturgy* from Qumran Cave 4

4QTestim	*Testimonia* text from Qumran Cave 4	11QTemple	*Temple Scroll* from Qumran Cave 11
4QTLevi	*Testament of Levi* from Qumran Cave 4	11QpaleoLev	Copy of Leviticus in paleo-Hebrew script
11qMelch	*Melchizedek* text from Qumran Cave 11		from Qumran Cave 11
11QShirShabb	*Songs of Sabbath Sacrifice,* or *Angelic Liturgy* from Qumran Cave 11	11QtgJob	*Targum of Job* from Qumran Cave 11

G. Philo

Aet.	*De aeternitate mundi*	*Mos.*	*De vita Mosis*
Decal.	*De decalogo*	*Op.*	*De opificio mundi*
De Migr. Abr.	*De migratione Abrahami*	*Praem.*	*De praemiis et poenis*
De Vit. Cont.	*De vita contemplativa*		
Flacc.	*In Flaccum*	*Sacrif.*	*De sacrificiis Abelis et Caini*
Fug.	*De fuga et inventione*		
Her.	*Quis rerum divinarum heres sit*	*Somn.*	*De somniis*
		Spec. Leg.	*De specialibus legibus*
Leg.	*De legatione ad Gaium*		
Leg. All.	*Legum allegoriarum*		

H. Abbreviations of Early Christian and Greco-Roman Literature

Acts Pil.	*Acts of Pilate*	*Gos. Pet.*	*Gospel of Peter*
Acts Scill.	*Acts of the Scillitan Martyrs*	Herm. *Mand.*	Hermas *Mandate(s)*
Apoc. Pet.	*Apocalypse of Peter*	*Sim.*	*Similitude(s)*
Apost. Const.	*Apostolic Constitutions*	*Vis.*	*Vision(s)*
Asc. Isa.	*Ascension of Isaiah*	Ign. *Eph.*	Ignatius *Letter to the Ephesians*
Barn.	*Barnabas*		
1–2 Clem.	*1–2 Clement*	*Magn.*	*Letter to the Magnesians*
Clement of Alexandria		*Phld.*	*Letter to the Philadelphians*
Strom.	*Miscellanies*		
Corp. Herm.	*Corpus Hermeticum*	*Pol.*	*Letter to Polycarp*
Did.	*Didache*	*Rom.*	*Letter to the Romans*
Diogn.	*Diognetus*	*Smyrn.*	*Letter to the Smyrnaeans*
Ep. Lugd.	*Epistula ecclesiarum apud Lugdunum et Viennam* (= *Letter of the Churches of* ...ns)	*Trall.*	*Letter to the Trallians*
Eusebius *Hist.*	Eusebius *Historia*	Iren. *Adv. Haer.*	Irenaeus *Against All Heresies*
Eccl.	*Ecclesiastica*		
Praep.	*Praeparatio evangelica*	Jerome *Chron.*	*Catalogus sacrae ecclesiae* (= *Chronicon Eusebii*)
Gos. Eb.	*Gospel of the Ebionites*		
Gos. Heb.	*Gospel of the Hebrews*		
Gos. Naass.	*Gospel of the Naassenes*		

Jos. *Ag. Ap.*	Josephus *Against Apion*	Pol. *Phil.*	Polycarp, *Letter to the Philippians*
Ant.	*The Jewish Antiquities*	Prot. *Jas.*	*Protevangelium of James*
J.W.	*The Jewish War*		
Life	*The Life*	Tert. *Adv.*	Tertullian
Justin *1 Apol.*	Justin *1 Apology*	*Valent.*	*Against the Valentinians*
2 Apol.	*2 Apology*		
Dial.	*Dialogue with Trypho*	*Apol.*	*Apology*
		De Praesc. Haer.	*Prescription against Heretics*
Mart. Pol.	*The Martyrdom of Polycarp*		

I. Abbreviations of Orders and Tractates in Mishnaic and Related Literature

(Italicized *m.*, *t.*, *b.*, or *y.* used before name to distinguish among tractates in Mishnah, Tosepta, Babylonian Talmud, and Jerusalem Talmud.)

Abot	*Abot*	*Ket.*	*Ketubbot*
B. Bat.	*Baba Batra*	*Men.*	*Menaḥot*
Bek.	*Bekorot*	*Qid.*	*Qiddušin*
Ber.	*Berakot*	*Sanh.*	*Sanhedrin*
Ker.	*Keritot*	*Sot.*	*Soṭâ*

J. Abbreviations of Nag Hammadi Tractates

Acts Pet. 12 Apost.	*Acts of Peter and the Twelve Apostles*	*Great Pow.*	*Concept of Our Great Power*
Allogenes	*Allogenes*	*Hyp. Arch.*	*Hypostasis of the Archons*
Ap. Jas.	*Apocryphon of James*	*Hypsiph.*	*Hypsiphrone*
Ap. John	*Apocryphon of John*	*Interp. Know.*	*Interpretation of Knowledge*
Apoc. Adam	*Apocalypse of Adam*		
1–2 Apoc. Jas.	*1–2 Apocalypse of James*	*Marsanes*	*Marsanes*
Apoc. Paul	*Apocalypse of Paul*	*Melch.*	*Melchizedek*
Apoc. Pet.	*Apocalypse of Peter*	*Norea*	*Thought of Norea*
Asclepius	*Asclepius 21–29*	*On Bap. A–B–C*	*On Baptism A–B–C*
Auth. Teach.	*Authoritative Teaching*	*On Euch. A–B*	*On Eucharist A–B*
Dial. Sav.	*Dialogues of the Savior*	*Orig. World*	*On the Origin of the World*
Disc. 8–9	*Discourse on the Eight and Ninth*		
Ep. Pet. Phil.	*Letter of Peter to Philip*	*Paraph. Shem*	*Paraphrase of Shem*
Eugnostos	*Eugnostos the Blessed*	*Pr. Paul*	*Prayer of the Apostle Paul*
Exeg. Soul	*Exegesis on the Soul*		
Gos. Eg.	*Gospel of the Egyptians*	*Pr. Thanks.*	*Prayer of Thanksgiving*
Gos. Phil.	*Gospel of Philip*	*Sent. Sextus*	*Sentences of Sextus*
Gos. Thom.	*Gospel of Thomas*	*Soph. Jes. Chr.*	*Sophia of Jesus Christ*
Gos. Truth	*Gospel of Truth*	*Steles Seth*	*Three Steles of Seth*

Teach. Silv.	*Teachings of Silvanus*	*Tri. Trac.*	*Tripartite Tractate*
Testim. Truth	*Testimony of Truth*	*Trim. Prot.*	*Trimorphic*
Thom. Cont.	*Book of Thomas the*		*Protennoia*
	Contender	*Val. Exp.*	*A Valentinian*
Thund.	*Thunder, Perfect Mind*		*Exposition*
Treat. Res.	*Treatise on Resurrection*	*Zost.*	*Zostrianos*
Treat. Seth	*Second Treatise of the*		
	Great Seth		

Note: Some textual notes and numbers are drawn from the apparatus criticus of *Novum Testamentum Graece,* ed. E. Nestle, K. Aland, et al., 26th ed. (Stuttgart: Deutsche Bibelgesellschaft, 1979); from *Novum Testamentum Graece,* ed. E. Nestle, K. Aland, et al., 27th ed. (Stuttgart: Deutsche Bibelgesellschaft, 1994); and from *The Greek New Testament,* ed. K. Aland, M. Black, C. Martini, B. M. Metzger, and A. Wikgren, 4th ed. (New York: United Bible Societies, 1994). These three editions of the Greek New Testament are the bases for the *Translation* sections.

Commentary Bibliography

In the text of the commentary, references to commentaries on the Pastoral Epistles are by author's last name only.

Arichea, D. C., and **Hatton, H. A.** *Paul's Letters to Timothy and to Titus.* UBS Handbook Series. New York: United Bible Societies, 1995. **Barclay, W.** *The Letters to Timothy, Titus, and Philemon.* The Daily Study Bible Series. Rev. ed. Philadelphia: Westminster, 1975. **Barrett, C. K.** *The Pastoral Epistles in the New English Bible.* NCB. Oxford: Clarendon, 1963. **Bassler, J. M.** *1 Timothy. 2 Timothy. Titus.* ANTC. Nashville: Abingdon, 1996. **Berg, M. R. van den.** *De eerste brief van Paulus aan Timoteüs: Over Gods economie in zijn huishouding.* Zicht op de Bijbel 11. Amsterdam: Buijten & S., 1976. ————. *De tweede Brief van Paulus aan Timoteüs: Het testament van een ter dood veroordeelde.* Zicht op de Bijbel 13. Amsterdam: Buijten & S., 1977. **Bernard, J. H.** *The Pastoral Epistles.* 1899. Repr. Thornapple Commentaries. Grand Rapids, MI: Baker, 1980. **Blaiklock, E. M.** *The Pastoral Epistles: A Study Guide to the Epistles of First and Second Timothy and Titus.* Grand Rapids, MI: Zondervan, 1972. **Borse, U.** *1. und 2. Timotheusbrief, Titusbrief.* SKKNT 13. Stuttgart: Katholisches Bibelwerk, 1985. **Boudou, A.** *Les Épitres Pastorales.* VS 15. Paris: Beauchesne, 1950. **Bouma, C.** *De Brieven van den Apostel Paulus aan Timotheus en Titus.* Kommentaar op het Nieuwe Testament 11. Amsterdam: Bottenburg, 1946. **Bratcher, R. G.** *A Translator's Guide to Paul's Letters to Timothy and Titus.* Helps for Translators Series. New York: United Bible Societies, 1983. **Brown, E. F.** *The Pastoral Epistles: With Introduction and Notes.* Westminster Commentaries. London: Methuen, 1917. **Brox, N.** *Die Pastoralbriefe.* RNT 7. 4th ed. Regensburg: Pustet, 1969. **Bürki, H.** *Der erste Brief des Paulus an Timotheus.* Wüppertaler Studienbibel. Wüppertal: Brockhaus, 1974. ————. *Der zweite Brief des Paulus an Timotheus, die Briefe an Titus und Philemon.* Wuppertal Studienbibel. Wuppertal: Brockhaus, 1975. **Calvin, J.** *The Second Epistle of Paul to the Corinthians, and the Epistles to Timothy, Titus and Philemon.* Tr. T. A. Small. Grand Rapids, MI: Eerdmans, 1964. **Chrysostom, J.** "Homilies on the Epistles of St. Paul the Apostle to Timothy, Titus, and Philemon." NPNF 13. Ed. P. Schaff. 1889. Repr. Grand Rapids, MI: Eerdmans, 1956. **Cipriani, S.** *Lenere pastorali. 1–2 Timoteo–Tito: Intro & Notes.* Nuovissima Versione 42. Rome: Paoline, 1977. **Clark, G. H.** *The Pastoral Epistles.* Jefferson, MD: Trinity Foundation, 1983. **Cousineau, A.** *Les Pastorales: Traduction et Commentaire: Correspondance de St Paul.* Montréal: Éditions Panlines/Apostolat des Éditions, 1974. **Davies, M.** *The Pastoral Epistles.* Epworth Commentaries. London: Epworth, 1996. **De Ambroggi, P.** *Le Epistole Pastorali di S. Paolo a Timoteo e a Tito.* Torino: Marietti, 1953. **Demarest, G. W.** *1, 2 Thessalonians, 1, 2 Timothy, Titus.* The Communicator's Commentary. Waco, TX: Word, 1984. **Denzer, G. A.** "The Pastoral Letters." *JBC* 2 (1968) 350–61. **Dibelius, M.,** and **Conzelmann, H.** *The Pastoral Epistles.* Hermeneia. Tr. P. Buttolph and A. Yarbro. Philadelphia: Fortress, 1972. **Donelson, L. R.** *Colossians, Ephesians, First and Second Timothy and Titus.* Westminster Bible Companion. Louisville: Westminster John Knox, 1996. **Dornier, P.** *Les Épîtres Pastorales.* SB. Paris: Gabalda, 1969. **Duvekot, W. S.** *De Pastorale Brieven, 1 en 2 Timotheus en Titus.* Kampen: Kok, 1984. **Earle, R.** "1 Timothy, 2 Timothy." In *The Expositor's Bible Commentary,* ed. F. E. Gaebelein. Vol. 11. Grand Rapids, MI: Zondervan, 1996. 115–23. **Easton, B. S.** *The Pastoral Epistles.* New York: Scribners, 1947. **Ellicott, C. J.** *The Pastoral Epistles of St Paul.* 3rd ed. London: Longman, 1864. **Ensley, J. R.** *The Pastoral Epistles: A Commentary on I and II Timothy and Titus.* Hazelwood, 1990. **Erdman, C. R.** *The Pastoral Epistles of Paul.* Philadelphia: Westminster, 1923. **Fairbairn, P.** *The Pastoral Epistles.* Edinburgh: T. & T. Clark, 1874. **Falconer, R. A.** *The Pastoral Epistles.* Oxford: Clarendon, 1937. **Fausset, A. R.** "1–2 Timothy, Titus." In *A Commentary, Critical and Experimental, on the Old and New Testaments,* ed. R. Jamieson, A. R. Fausset, and D. Brown. Hartford, CT: Scranton, 1871. **Fee, G. D.** *1–2*

Timothy, Titus. Good News Commentary. San Francisco: Harper & Row, 1984. **Frede, H. J.** *Epistulae ad Thessalonicenses, Timotheum, Titum, Philemonem, Hebraeos.* Vetus Latina 25. Freiburg: Herder, 1983. **Freundorfer, J.** *Die Pastoralbriefe.* Lettre pastorale. Augsburg: Haas, 1954. Repr. Staten Island, NY: Alba House, 1965. **Galites, G. A.** *He pros Titon epistole tou Apostolou Paulou: Eisagoge, Hypomnema.* Thessalonike: Purnara, 1978. **Gealy, F. D.** "The First and Second Epistles to Timothy and the Epistle to Titus." *IB* 11 (1955) 341–551. **Groenewald, E. P.** *Die Pastorale Briewe.* Cape Town: Kerk, 1977. **Gromacki, R. G.** *Stand True to the Charge: An Exposition of 1 Timothy.* Grand Rapids, MI: Baker, 1982. **Grünzweig, F.** *Erster Timotheus-Brief.* Bibel-Kommentar 18. Neuhausen-Stuttgart: Hänssler, 1990. **Guthrie, D.** *The Pastoral Epistles: An Introduction and Commentary.* 2nd ed. TNTC 14. Grand Rapids, MI: Eerdmans, 1990. **Haapa, E.** *Timoteus ja Tiitus.* Helsinki: Sisälähetysseura, 1970. **Hanson, A. T.** *The Pastoral Epistles.* NCB. Grand Rapids, MI: Eerdmans, 1983. ———. *The Pastoral Letters: Commentary on the First and Second Letters to Timothy and the Letter of Titus.* CBC. Cambridge: Cambridge University Press, 1966. **Hasler, V.** *Die Briefe an Timotheus und Titus (Pastoralbriefe).* ZBNT 12. Zürich: Theologischer Verlag, 1978. **Hendriksen, W.** *I–II Timothy and Titus.* New Testament Commentary. Grand Rapids, MI: Baker, 1957. **Hiebert, D. E.** *First Timothy.* Everyman's Bible Commmentary. Chicago: Moody Press, 1967. ———. *Titus and Philemon.* Chicago: Moody Press, 1957. ———. "Titus." In *The Expositor's Bible Commentary,* ed. F. E. Gaebelein. Vol. 11. Grand Rapids, MI: Zondervan, 1981. 419-49. **Hillard, A. E.** *The Pastoral Epistles of St. Paul: The Greek Text with Commentary.* London: Rivingtons, 1919. **Hinson, E. G.** "1–2 Timothy and Titus." In *The Broadman Bible Commentary,* ed. by C. J. Allen. Vol. 11. Nashville: Broadman Press, 1973. 299–376. **Holtz, G.** *Die Pastoralbriefe.* THKNT 13. Berlin: Evangelische Verlagsanstalt, 1972. **Holtzmann, H. J.** *Die Pastoralbriefe, kritisch und exegetisch behandelt.* Leipzig: Engelmann, 1880. **Houlden, J. L.** *The Pastoral Epistles: I and II Timothy, Titus.* The Pelican New Testament Commentaries. Harmondsworth; New York: Penguin, 1976. Reprinted in TPI New Testament Commentaries. Philadelphia: Trinity, 1989. **Hughes, R. K.,** and **Chappel, B.** *Guard the Deposit.* Wheaton: Crossway, 2000. **Hültgren, A. J.** *I and II Timothy, Titus.* ACNT. Minneapolis: Augsburg, 1984. **Huther, J. E.** *Critical and Exegetical Hand-Book to the Epistles to Timothy and Titus.* Tr. D. Hunter. New York: Funk and Wagnalls, 1885. **Ironside, H. A.** *Timothy, Titus and Philemon.* New York: Loizeaux Brothers, 1948. **Jensen, I. L.** *1 and 2 Timothy and Titus.* Chicago: Moody Press, 1973. **Jeremias, J.** *Die Briefe an Timotheus und Titus.* NTD 9. Göttingen: Vandenhoeck & Ruprecht, 1975. **Johnson, L. T.** *Letters to Paul's Delegates: 1 Timothy, 2 Timothy, Titus.* The New Testament in Context. Valley Forge, PA: Trinity, 1996. **Johnson, P. C.** *The Epistles to Titus and Philemon.* Shield Bible Study Outlines. Grand Rapids, MI: Baker, 1966. **Jones, R. B.** *The Epistles to Timothy.* Shield Bible Study Series. Grand Rapids, MI: Baker, 1959. **Karris, R. J.** *The Pastoral Epistles.* New Testament Message 17. Wilmington, DE: Glazier, 1979. **Kelly, J. N. D.** *A Commentary on the Pastoral Epistles.* HNTC. New York: Harper & Row, 1964. Reprinted in Thornapple Commentary. Grand Rapids, MI: Baker, 1981. **Kent, H. A.** *Pastoral Epistles: Studies in I and II Timothy and Titus.* Chicago: Moody Press, 1958. **Knabenbauer, J.** *Commentarius in S. Pauli Epistolas.* Cursus Scripturae Sacrae. Paris: Sumptibus P. Lethielleux, 1923. **Knappe, W.** *Die Briefe an Timotheus und Titus, übersetzt und ausgelegt.* Hamburg: Schloessmann, 1937. **Knight, G. W., III.** *The Pastoral Epistles.* NIGTC. Grand Rapids, MI: Eerdmans, 1992. **Knoch, O.** *1. und 2. Timotheusbrief, Titusbrief.* Wüppertal: Echter, 1988. **Koehler, D.** *Die Pastoralbriefe.* Die Schriften des Neuen Testaments für die Gegenwart erklärt. 3rd ed. Tübingen: Mohr-Siebeck, 1917. **Kruijf, T. C. de.** *De Pastorale Brieven.* Het Nieuwe Testament. Roermond: Romen-Maaseik, 1966. **Läger, K.** *Die Christologie der Pastoralbriefe: Kommentar zum Titusbrief.* Hamburger theologische Studien 12. Münster: LIT, 1996. **Lea, T. D.,** and **Griffin, H. P.** *1, 2 Timothy, Titus.* New American Commentary 34. Nashville: Broadman, 1992. **Leaney, A. R. C.** *The Epistles to Timothy, Titus, and Philemon: Introduction and Commentary.* London: SCM Press, 1960. **Lenski, R. C. H.** *The Interpretation of St. Paul's Epistles to the Colossians, to the Thessalonians, to Timothy, to Titus, and to Philemon.* Minneapolis: Augsburg, 1937. **Liddon, H. P.** *Explanatory Analysis of*

St. Paul's First Epistle to Timothy. London: Longmans, 1897. **Lock, W.** *A Critical and Exegetical Commentary on the Pastoral Epistles.* ICC. Edinburgh: T. & T. Clark, 1924. **Luther, M.** *Lectures on Titus, Philemon, and Hebrews.* Luther's Works 29. St. Louis: Concordia, 1968. **Marcheselli-Casale, C.** *Le Lettere pastorali: Le due lettere a Timoteo e la lettera a Tito.* Scritti delle origini cristiane 15. Bologna: Dehoniane, 1995. **Meinertz, M.** *Die Pastoralbriefe übersetzt und erklärt.* Die Heilige Schrift des Neuen Testaments 8. 4th ed. Bonn: Hanstein, 1931. **Merkel, H.** *Die Pastoralbriefe.* NTD 9.1. Göttingen: Vandenhoeck & Ruprecht, 1991. **Moellering, H. A.,** and **Bartling, V. A.** *1 Timothy, 2 Timothy, Titus, Philemon.* Concordia Commentary. St. Louis: Concordia, 1970. **Molitor, H.** *Die Pastoralbriefe des Hl. Paulus.* Freiburg, 1937. **Neyrey, J. H.** *First Timothy, Second Timothy, Titus, James, First Peter, Second Peter, Jude.* Collegeville Bible Commentary 9. Collegeville, MN: Liturgical Press, 1983. **Oberlinner, L.** *Der Pastoralbriefe: Vol. 1. Kommentar zum ersten Timotheusbrief.* HTKNT 11.2. Freiburg: Herder, 1994. ———. *Der Pastoralbriefe: Vol. 2. Kommentar zum zweite Timotheusbrief.* HTKNT 11.2. Freiburg: Herder, 1995. ———. *Der Pastoralbriefe: Vol. 3. Kommentar zum Titusbriefe.* HTKNT 11.2. Freiburg: Herder, 1996. **Oden, T. C.** *First and Second Timothy and Titus.* Interpretation. Atlanta: John Knox, 1989. **Oosterzee, J. J. van.** "The Pastoral Letters." In *A Commentary on the Holy Scriptures: Critical, Doctrinal, and Homiletical,* ed. J. P. Lange. NT vol. 8. Tr. P. Schaff. 1865–80. Repr. Grand Rapids, MI: Zondervan, 1960. **Parry, R.** *The Pastoral Epistles.* Cambridge: Cambridge UP, 1920. **Plummer, A.** *The Pastoral Epistles.* 1891. Repr. Grand Rapids, MI: Eerdmans, 1943. **Quinn, J. D.** *The Letter to Titus: A New Translation with Notes and Commentary, and an Introduction to Titus, I and II Timothy, the Pastoral Epistles.* AB 35. New York: Doubleday, 1990. **Ramos, M. A.** *I Timoteo, II Timoteo y Tito.* Comentario Biblico Hispanoamericano. Miami: Editorial Caribe, 1992. **Reuss, J.** *The Epistles to Timothy, Titus and Philemon.* New Testament for Spiritual Reading 10. London: Sheed and Ward, 1979. ———. *The Two Epistles to Timothy.* Tr. B. Fahy. London: Burns Oates, 1969. ——— and **Stöger, A.** *Epistle to Titus and Epistle to Philemon.* New York: Sheed & Ward, 1971. **Ridderbos, H.** *De Pastorale Brieven.* Commentaar op het Nieuwe Testament. Kampen: Kok, 1967. **Riess, H.** *Der Philemon-, Titus- und 2. Timotheusbrief.* Stuttgart: Kreuz, 1956. **Roinerth K.** *Der erste Brief des Paulus an Timotheus, übersetzt und erläutert.* Hermannstadt: Honterus, 1943. **Roloff, J.** *Der erste Brief an Timotheus.* EKKNT 15. Zürich: Benziger, 1988. **Roux, H.** *Les Épîtres pastorales: Commentaire de I et II Timothee et Tite.* Geneva: Labor et Fides, 1959. **Sampley, J. P.,** and **Fuller, R. H.** *Ephesians, Colossians, 2 Thessalonians, the Pastoral Epistles.* Proclamation Commentaries. Philadelphia: Fortress, 1978. **Schierse, F. J.** *Die Pastoralbriefe.* Die Welt der Bibel: Kleinkommentare zur Heiligen Schrift 10. Düsseldorf: Patmos, 1968. **Scott, E. F.** *The Pastoral Epistles.* MNTC. New York: Harper and Brothers, 1936. **Siebeneck, R. T.** *Epistolas Pastorales de S. Pablo: 1 y 2 a Timoteo–a Tito.* Conoce la Biblia NT 11. Santander: Terrae, 1965. **Simpson, E. K.** *The Pastoral Epistles: The Greek Text with Introduction and Commentary.* Grand Rapids, MI: Eerdmans, 1954. **Smelik, E. L.** *De Brieven van Paulus aan Timotheus, Titus en Filemon.* De Prediking van het Nieuwe Testament. 3rd ed. Nijkerk: Callenbach, 1961. **Smith, J.** *The Pastoral Epistles.* Script. Disc. Com. 12. London: Sheed & Ward, 1972. **Soden, H. von.** *Die Briefe an die Kolosser, Epheser, Philemon; die Pastoralbriefe.* Hand-Commentar zum Neuen Testament 3.1. 2nd ed. Freiburg: Mohr, 1893. **Spain, C.** *The Letters of Paul to Timothy and Titus.* The Living Word Commentary 14. Austin, TX: Sweet, 1970. **Sparks, I. A.** *The Pastoral Epistles.* San Diego: Institute of Biblical Studies, 1985. **Spicq, C.** *Saint Paul: Les Épîtres pastorales.* 4th ed. 2 vols. EBib 29. Paris: Gabalda, 1969. **Stam, C. R.** *Commentary on the Pastoral Epistles of Paul, the Apostle.* Chicago: Berean Bible Society, 1983. **Stibbs, A. M.** "The Pastoral Epistles." In *The New Bible Commentary.* Rev. ed. Ed. D. Guthrie. London: Inter-Varsity Press, 1970. 1166–86. **Stott, J. R. W.** *Guard the Truth: The Message of 1 Timothy and Titus.* Downers Grove, IL: InterVarsity Press, 1996. ———. *Guard the Gospel: The Message of 2 Timothy.* Downers Grove, IL: InterVarsity Press, 1973. **Towner, P. H.** *1–2 Timothy and Titus.* IVP New Testament Commentary. Downers Grove, IL: InterVarsity Press, 1994. **Vine, W. E.** *Exposition on the Epistles to Timothy.* Every Christian's Library. London: Pickering, 1925. ———. *The Epistles to Timothy and Titus: Faith and Conduct.* Grand Rapids, MI: Zondervan,

1965. **Wallis, W. B.** "The First Epistle to Timothy, the Second Epistle to Timothy, the Epistle to Titus." In *The Wycliffe Bible Commentary*, ed. C. F. Pfeiffer and E. F. Harrison. Chicago: Moody Press, 1962. **Ward, R. A.** *Commentary on 1 and 2 Timothy and Titus.* Waco, TX: Word, 1974. **Weiss, B.** *Die Briefe Pauli an Timotheus und Titus.* 7th ed. KEK 11. Göttingen: Vandenhoeck & Ruprecht, 1902. **White, N. J. D.** "The First and Second Epistles to Timothy and the Epistle to Titus." In *The Expositor's Greek Testament*, ed. W. R. Nicoll. 5 vols. London: Hodder & Stoughton, 1897–1910. 4:55–202. **Wild, R. A.** "The Pastoral Letters." *NJBC.* 891–902. **Wilson, G. B.** *The Pastoral Epistles: A Digest of Reformed Comment.* London: Banner of Truth, 1982. **Wohlenberg, G.** *Die Pastoralbriefe.* 3rd ed. ZKNT 13. Leipzig: Deichert, 1923. **Woychuk, N. A.** *An Exposition of Second Timothy, Inspirational and Practical.* Old Tappan, NJ: Revell, 1974.

General Bibliography

Abbott-Smith, G. *A Manual Greek Lexicon of the New Testament.* Edinburgh: T. & T. Clark, 1937. **Adams, W. W.** "Exposition of 1 and 2 Timothy." *RevExp* 56 (1959) 367–87. **Albani, J.** "Die Bildersprache der Pastoralbriefe." *ZWT* (1903) 40–58. **Alexander, J. P.** "The Character of Timothy." *ExpTim* 25 (1914) 277–85. **Alford, H.** *The Greek New Testament.* 5th ed. 4 vols. 1875. Repr. Grand Rapids, MI: Guardian, 1975. **Allan, J. A.** "The 'in Christ' Formula in the Pastoral Epistles." *NTS* 10 (1963–64) 115–21. **Angus, S.** *The Environment of Early Christianity.* London: Duckworth, 1914. **Anton, P.** *Exegetische Abhandlung der Pastoralbriefe S. Pauli.* Halle, 1753–55. **Badcock, F. J.** *The Pauline Epistles and the Epistle to the Hebrews in Their Historical Setting.* London: S. P. C. K., 1937. **Bahr, G. J.** "Paul and Letter Writing in the First Century." *CBQ* 28 (1966) 465–77. **Banker, J.** *A Semantic Structure Analysis of Titus.* Ed. J. Callow. Dallas: Summer Institute of Linguistics, 1987. **Banks, R.** *Paul's Idea of Community: The Early House Churches in Their Historical Setting.* Grand Rapids, MI: Eerdmans, 1980. **Barclay, W.** *Educational Ideals in the Ancient World.* 1959. Repr. Grand Rapids, MI: Baker, 1974. **Bardtke, H.,** ed. *Gott und die Götter.* FS E. Fascher. Berlin: Evangelische, 1958. **Barnett, A. E.** *Paul Becomes a Literary Influence.* Chicago: University of Chicago Press, 1941. **Barrett, C. K.** *A Commentary on the First Epistle to the Corinthians.* HNTC. New York: Harper & Row, 1968. ———. *The Gospel according to St. John: An Introduction with Commentary and Notes on the Greek Text.* 2nd ed. Philadelphia: Westminster, 1978. ———. *The New Testament Background: Selected Documents.* Rev. ed. San Francisco: HarperSanFrancisco, 1987. ———. "Pauline Controversies in the Post-Pauline Period." *NTS* 20 (1973–74) 229–45. ———. "Titus." In *Neotestamentica et Semitica.* FS M. Black, ed. E. E. Ellis and M. Wilcox. Edinburgh: T. & T. Clark, 1969. 1–14. **Barsotti, D.** *Forti nella fede: Commento alla seconda Lettera a Timoteo.* Parola di Dio 15. Torino: Gribaudi, 1977. **Barth, M.** *Ephesians.* 2 vols. AB. New York: Doubleday, 1974. **Bartlet, V.** "The Historical Setting of the Pastoral Epistles." *Exp* 5–8 (1913) 28–36, 161–66, 256–63, 325–47. **Bartsch, H.-W.** *Die Anfänge urchristlicher Rechtsbildungen: Studien zu den Pastoralbriefen.* Theologische Forschung 34. Hamburg-Bergstedt: Reich, 1965. **Bauckham, R. J.** *Jude, 2 Peter.* WBC 50. Waco, TX: Word, 1983. ———. "Pseudo-Apostolic Letters." *JBL* 107 (1988) 469–94. **Bauer, W.** *Orthodoxy and Heresy in Earliest Christianity.* Tr. R. A. Kraft and G. Krodel. Philadelphia: Fortress, 1971. **Baughen, M.** *Chained to the Gospel.* Glasgow: Marshall Pickering, 1986. **Baumgarten, M.** *Die Ächtheit der Pastoralbriefe.* Berlin: Dehmigke, 1837. **Baur, F. C.** *Die sogenannten Pastoralbriefe des Apostels Paulus.* Stuttgart: Cotta, 1835. **Beker, J. C.** *Heirs of Paul: Paul's Legacy in the New Testament and in the Church Today.* Minneapolis: Fortress, 1992. ———. "The Pastoral Epistles: Paul and We." In *Text and Logos: The Humanistic Interpretation of the New Testament.* FS H. Boers, ed. T. W. Jennings. Atlanta: Scholars Press, 1990. 265–72. **Bengel, J. A.** *New Testament Word Studies.* Tr. C. T. Lewis and M. R. Vincent. 2 vols. 1864. Repr. Grand Rapids. MI: Kregel, 1971. **Berdot, D. N.** *Exercitatio theologica-exegetica in epistulam Pauli ad Titum.* 1703. **Berger, K.** "Apostelbrief und apostolische Rede: Zum Formular frühchristlichen Briefe." *ZNW* 65 (1974) 190–231. **Berkhof, L.** *Systematic Theology.* London: Banner of Truth Trust, 1960. **Bertrand, E.** *Essai critique sur l'authenticité des Épîtres Pastorales.* Paris: Librairie Fischbacher, 1888. **Bettler, J. F.** "Guidelines from II Timothy for Counseling People with Fears." *WTJ* 36 (1973) 198–208. **Bindley, T.-H.** "The Pastoral Epistles." *Interpreter* 9 (1913) 183–97. **Blight, R. C.** *A Literary-Semantic Analysis of Paul's First Discourse to Timothy.* Ed. J. Beekman. Dallas: Summer Institute of Linguistics, 1997. **Boehl, G.** *Über die Zeit der Abfassung und den paulinischen Charakter der Briefe an Timotheus und Titus.* Berlin, 1829. **Bordier, P.** *Les Épîtres Pastorales du Nouveau Testament: Étude sur leur authenticité.* Geneva, 1872. **Bourdillon, F.** *Titus in Crete, or Things Which Become Sound Doctrine.* London, 1906. **Bowman, J. W.** "The

Pastoral Epistles." *Int* 9 (1955) 436–55. **Brandt, W.** *Das anvertraute Gut: Eine Einführung in die Briefe an Timotheus und Titus.* Hamburg: Furche, 1959. ———. *Apostolische Anweisung für den kirchlichen Dienst: Eine Einführung in die Briefe an Timotheus und Titus.* Berlin: Furche, 1941. **Braun, W.** *Der zweite Timotheusbrief: Eine Einführung.* Barmen: Müller, 1922. **Brown, L. A.** "Asceticism and Ideology: The Language of Power in the Pastoral Epistles." *Semeia* 57 (1992) 77–94. **Brox, N.** "Amt, Kirche und Theologie in der nachapostolischen Epoche—Die Pastoralbriefe." In *Gestalt und Anspruch des Neuen Testament,* ed. J. Schreiner and G. Dautzenberg. Würzburg: Echter, 1969. 120–33. ———. "Historische und theologische Probleme der Pastoralbriefe des Neuen Testaments: Zur Dokumentation der frühchristlichen Amtsgeschichte." *Kairos* 11 (1969) 81–94. ———. "Die Kirche, Säule und Fundament der Wahrheit: Die Einheit der Kirche nach den Pastoralbriefen." *BK* (1963) 44–47. ———. "Προφητεία im ersten Timotheusbrief." *BZ* 20 (1976) 229–32. **Bruce, F. F.** *1 and 2 Thessalonians.* WBC 45. Waco, TX: Word, 1982. ———. *The Epistle to the Galatians: A Commentary on the Greek Text.* NIGTC. Grand Rapids, MI: Eerdmans, 1982. ———. *Paul, Apostle of the Heart Set Free.* Grand Rapids, MI: Eerdmans, 1977. **Bruggen, J. van.** *Die geschichtliche Einordnung der Pastoralbriefe.* Wuppertal: Brockhaus, 1981. ———. "Die geschichtliche Einordnung der Pastoralbriefe." *JETS* 25 (1982) 381–82. **Bultmann, R.** *Primitive Christianity in Its Contemporary Setting.* Tr. R. H. Fuller. New York: Meridian, 1956. **Bush, P. G.** "A Note on the Structure of 1 Timothy." *NTS* 36 (1990) 152–56. **Burtchaell, J. T.** *From Synagogue to Church: Public Services and Offices in the Earliest Christian Communities.* Cambridge: Cambridge UP, 1992. **Burton, E. D.** *A Critical and Exegetical Commentary on the Epistle to the Galatians.* ICC. Edinburgh: T. & T. Clark, 1921. ———. *Syntax of the Moods and Tenses in New Testament Greek.* 3rd ed. 1898. Repr. Grand Rapids, MI: Kregel, 1981. **Butterworth, G. W.,** tr. and ed. *Clement of Alexandria.* LCL. Cambridge, MA: Harvard UP, 1919. **Calvin, J.** *Sermons on the Epistles to Timothy and Titus: 16th Century Facsimile Editions, 1579.* Edinburgh: Banner of Truth Trust, 1983. **Campbell, R. A.** *The Elders: Seniority within Earliest Christianity.* Studies of the New Testament and Its World. Edinburgh: T. & T. Clark, 1994. ———. "Identifying the Faithful Sayings in the Pastoral Epistles." *JSNT* 54 (1994) 73–86. **Campenhausen, H. F. von.** *Ecclesiastical Authority and Spiritual Power in the Church of the First Three Centuries.* Tr. J. A. Baker. Stanford, CA: Stanford UP, 1969. ———. *Tradition and Life in the Church: Essays and Lectures in Church History.* Tr. A. V. Littledale. Philadelphia: Fortress, 1968. **Carrez, M.** "Les Épîtres pastorales." In *Introduction critique au Nouveau Testament* 3, ed. A. George. Paris: Desclée, 1977. **Chase, F.** *Confirmation in the Apostolic Age.* London: Macmillan, 1909. **Churchill, J. H.** "The Pastoral Epistles: A Problem for Preachers and Others." *SE* 7 (1982) 121–31. **Cipriani, S.** "La dottrina del 'depositum' nelle Lettere Pastorali." In *Studiorum Paulinorum Congressus internationalis catholicus 1961.* 2 vols. AnBib 17–18. Rome: Pontifical Biblical Institute, 1963. 127–42. ———. "La 'viva cristiana' nelle lettere pastorali." In *Una Hostia.* FS C. Ursi, ed. S. Muratore and A. Rolla. Napoli: D'Auria, 1983. 69–86. **Cohen, S. J. D.** "Was Timothy Jewish (Acts 16:1–3)? Patristic Exegesis, Rabbinic Law, and Matrilineal Descent." *JBL* 105 (1986) 251–68. **Coleman, T. H., Jr.** "Interpretation of the Pastoral Epistles and Some Selected Old Testament Wisdom Elements." Ph.D. Diss., Duke University, 1977. **Collins, R. F.** "The Image of Paul in the Pastorals." *LTP* 31 (1975) 147–73. ———. "Pastoral Ministry: Timothy and Titus." *Church* 3 (1987) 20–24. **Connolly, R. H.** *Didaskalia Apostolorum.* Oxford: Clarendon, 1929. **Cook, D.** "The Pastoral Fragments Reconsidered." *JTS* n.s. 35 (1984) 120–31. **Cothenet, E.** *Les épîtres pastorales.* Cahiers Évangile 72. Paris: Cerf, 1990. **Couser, G.** "God and Christian Existence in 1 and 2 Timothy and Titus." Ph.D. Diss., University of Aberdeen, 1992. **Cousineau, A.** "Le sens de 'presbyteros' dans les pastorales." *ScEs* 28 (1976) 147–62. **Cramer, M. J.** "Peculiarities of the Pastoral Epistles." *JBL* 7 (1887) 3–32. **Cranfield, C. E. B.** *A Critical and Exegetical Commentary on the Epistle to the Romans.* 2 vols. ICC. Edinburgh: T. & T. Clark, 1975, 1979. **Cranford, L.** "Encountering Heresy: Insight from the Pastoral Epistles." *SWJT* 22 (1980) 23–40. **Cremer, H.** *Biblico-Theological Lexicon of New Testament Greek.* Tr. W. Urwick. 4th ed. Edinburgh: T. & T. Clark;

New York: Scribner, 1892. **Cruvellier, Y.** "La notion de Piété dans les Épîtres Pastorales."
Études Évangéliques 23 (1963) 41–61. **Cuendet, J.** *La doctrine des Épîtres Pastorales.* Lausanne,
1883. **Cullmann, O.** *The Earliest Christian Confessions.* London: Lutterworth, 1949. ———.
The Early Church. London: SCM Press, 1956. **Daube, D.** *The New Testament and Rabbinic
Judaism.* London: Athlone, 1956. **Davies, M.** *The Pastoral Epistles.* New Testament Guides.
Sheffield: Sheffield Academic Press, 1996. **Dayton, M. W.** "Maintaining the True Doctrine:
An Analytical and Expositor Study of 1 Timothy." Th.M. thesis, Dallas Theological Seminary,
1953. **Deichgräber, R.** *Gottesshymnus und Christushymnus in der frühen Christenheit: Untersuchungen
zur Form, Sprache und Stil der frühchristlichen Hymnen.* SUNT 5. Göttingen: Vandenhoeck &
Ruprecht, 1967. **Deissmann, A.** *Bible Studies: Contributions, Chiefly from Papyri and Inscriptions,
to the History of the Language, the Literature, and the Religion of Hellenistic Judaism and Primitive
Christianity.* Tr. A. J. Grieve. 2nd ed. Edinburgh: T. & T. Clark, 1901. ———. *Light from the
Ancient East: The New Testament Illustrated by Recently Discovered Texts of the Graeco-Roman World.*
Tr. L. R. M. Strachan. 2nd ed. 1927. Repr. Grand Rapids, MI: Eerdmans, 1978. **Dibelius, M.**
Urchristentum und Kultur. Heidelberg: Carl Winters Universitätsbuchhandlung, 1928.
Dittberner, A. "Paul and Timothy." *TBT* 60 (1972) 787–90. **Dittenberger, W.,** ed. *Sylloge
Inscriptionum Graecarum.* 3rd ed. 4 vols. 1915–1924. Repr. Hildesheim: Olms, 1960. **Dornier,
P.** "Les Épîtres Pastorales." In *Le Ministère et les Ministères selon le Nouveau Testament,* ed. J.
Delorme. Paris: Seuil, 1974. **Draper, J. T.** *Titus: Patterns for Church Living.* Wheaton, IL:
Tyndale, 1978. **Dubois, A.** *Etude critique sur l'authenticité de la première Épître à Timothée.*
Strasbourg, 1856. **Dubois, J. D.** "Les Pastorales, la Gnose et l'hérésie." *FV* 94 (1995) 41–48.
Eichrodt, W. *Theology of the Old Testament.* 2 vols. OTL. Philadelphia: Westminster, 1961,
1967. **Elliott, J. K.** *The Greek Text of the Epistles to Timothy and Titus.* Ed. J. Geerlings. SD 36. Salt
Lake City: University of Utah, 1968. **Ellis, E. E.** "Die Pastoralbriefe und Paulus: Beobachtungen
zu Jürgen Roloffs Kommentar über 1. Timotheus." *TBei* 22 (1991) 208–12. ———. "Pastoral
Letters." In *Dictionary of Paul and His Letters.* Downers Grove, IL: InterVarsity Press, 1993.
659–66. ———. "The Pastorals and Paul." *ExpTim* 104 (1992) 45–47. ———. "Paul and His
Opponents: Trends in Research." In *Christianity, Judaism, and Other Greco-Roman Cults.* FS M.
Smith, ed. J. Neusner. Leiden: Brill, 1975. 264–98. ———. *Paul and His Recent Interpreters.*
Grand Rapids, MI: Eerdmans, 1961. ———. *Paul's Use of the Old Testament.* Edinburgh: Oliver
and Boyd, 1957. ———. "Traditions in the Pastoral Epistles." In *Early Jewish and Christian
Exegesis.* FS W. H. Brownlee, ed. C. A. Evans and W. F. Stinespring. Atlanta: Scholars Press,
1987. 237–53. **Evans, H.** "'Titus, My Partner': 2 Cor 8:23." *ExpTim* 90 (1978) 207–9. **Ewald,
P.** *Probabilia betreffend den Text des ersten Timotheusbrief.* Erlangen, 1901. **Eylau, D.** *Zur
Chronologie der Pastoralbriefe.* Landsberg: Schneider & Sohn, 1884. **Fanning, B. M.** *Verbal Aspect
in New Testament Greek.* Oxford: Clarendon, 1990. **Fee, G. D.** *The First Epistle to the Corinthians.*
NICNT. Grand Rapids, MI: Eerdmans, 1987. ———. *God's Empowering Presence: The Holy
Spirit in the Letters of Paul.* Peabody, MA: Hendrickson, 1994. ———. *Gospel and Spirit: Issues
in New Testament Hermeneutics.* Peabody, MA: Hendrickson, 1991. ———. "Hermeneutics
and Common Sense: An Exploratory Essay on the Hermeneutics of the Epistles." In *Gospel
and Spirit: Issues in New Testament Hermeneutics.* Peabody, MA: Hendrickson, 1991. 1–23.
———. *Paul's Letter to the Philippians.* NICNT. Grand Rapids, MI: Eerdmans, 1995. ———.
"Reflections on Church Order in the Pastoral Epistles, With Further Reflection on the
Hermeneutics of Ad Hoc Documents." *JETS* 28 (1985) 141–51. **Fernando, A.** *Leadership Life
Style: A Study of 1 Timothy.* Wheaton, IL: Tyndale, 1985. **Ferrua, A.** "Le reliquie di S. Timoteo."
CivC 98 (1947) 328–36. **Feuillet, A.** "Le dialogue avec le monde non-chretien dans les épîtres
pastorales et l'épître aux Hebréux." *Esprit et Vie* 98 (1988) 125–28, 152–59. ———. "La
doctrine des Épîtres Pastorales et leur affinités avec l'œuvre lucanienne." *RevThom* 78 (1978)
181–225. **Fiore, B.** *The Function of Personal Example in the Socratic and Pastoral Epistles.* An Bib
105. Rome: Biblical Institute Press, 1986. **Floor, L.** "Church Order in the Pastoral Epistles."
In *Ministry in the Pauline Letters.* Pretoria: New Testament Society of South Africa, 1976. 92–
109. **Foerster, W.** "Eusebeia in den Pastoralbriefen." *NTS* 5 (1959) 213–18. **Ford, J. M.** "A

Note on Proto-Montanism in the Pastoral Epistles." *NTS* 17 (1970) 338–46. **Freitag, J.** "Intransigeance et charité à la lumière de la Deuxième Épître à Timothée." Diss., Lateranensis Romae, 1958. **Friedrich, G.** "Lohmeyers These über das paulinische Briefpräskript kritisch beleuchtet." *TLZ* 81 (1956) 343–46. **Furnish, V. P.** *II Corinthians: Translation with Introduction, Notes and Commentary.* AB 32A. Garden City, NY: Doubleday, 1984. **Galtier, P.** "La réconciliation des pécheurs dans la Première Épître à Timothée." *RSR* 39 (1951) 317–20. **Getz, G. A.** *A Profile for a Christian Life Style: A Study of Titus.* Grand Rapids, MI: Zondervan, 1978. **Gonzalez Ruiz, J. M.** "Timoteo, Epistolas a." *EnchBib* 6 (1965) 1014–19. **Good, S. F.** *Authenticité des Épîtres Pastorales.* Montauban: Charles Forestie Fils, 1848. **Goodall, B.** *The Homilies of St. John Chrysostom on the Letters of St. Paul to Titus and Philemon: Prolegomena to an Edition.* Classical Studies 20. Berkeley: University of California Press, 1979. **Goodspeed, E. J.** *An Introduction to the New Testament.* Chicago: University of Chicago Press, 1937. **Goulder, M.** "The Pastor's Wolves: Jewish Christian Visionaries behind the Pastoral Epistles." *NovT* 38 (1996) 242–56. **Grech, P.** "Timoteo e Tito: modelli del vescovo nel periodo subapostolico." In *Il ministero ordinato nel dialogo ecumenico,* ed. G. Farnedi and P. Rouillard. Studia Anselmiana 92, Sacramentum 9. Rome: Pontifico Ateneo S. Anselmo, 1985. 67–75. **Greeven, H.** "Propheten, Lehrer, Vorsteher bei Paulus: Zur Frage der 'Amter' im Urchristentum." *ZNW* 44 (1952–53) 1–43. **Grudem, W.** *Systematic Theology: An Introduction to Biblical Doctrine.* Grand Rapids, MI: Zondervan, 1994. **Gunther, H.,** and **Volk E. D.** *Martin Luthers Epistel-Auslegung.* Vol. 5: *Timotheusbrief bis Jakobusbrief.* Göttingen: Vandenhoeck & Ruprecht, 1983. **Guthrie, D.** *New Testament Introduction.* 4th ed. Downers Grove, IL: InterVarsity Press, 1990. ———. *New Testament Theology.* Downers Grove, IL: InterVarsity Press, 1981. ———. *The Pastoral Epistles and the Mind of Paul.* London: Tyndale, 1956. **Hanson, A. T.** "The Domestication of Paul: A Study in the Development of Early Christian Theology." *BJRL* 63.2 (1981) 402–18. ———. *Studies in the Pastoral Epistles.* London: S. P. C. K., 1968. ———. "The Theology of Suffering in the Pastoral Epistles and Ignatius of Antioch." In *Studia Patristica.* Vol. 17.2. Elmsford, NY: Pergamon, 1982. 694–96. ———. "The Use of the OT in the Pastoral Epistles." *IBS* 3 (1981) 203–19. **Harnack, A. von.** *Die Briefsammlung des Apostles Paulus und die anderen vorkonstantinischen christlichen Briefsammlungen.* Leipzig: Hinrichs, 1926. ———. *Geschichte der altchristlichen Literatur bis Eusebius.* 2 parts. 4 vols. Leipzig: Hinrichs, 1958. ———. *Marcion: Das Evangelium vom fremden Gott: Eine Monographie zur Geschichte der Grundlegung der katholischen Kirche.* Leipzig: Hinrichs, 1921. ———. *Marcion: The Gospel of an Alien God.* Tr. J. E. Steely and L. D. Bierma. Durham, NC: Labyrinth Press, 1990. ———. *Die Zeit des Ignatius.* Leipzig: Hinrichs, 1878. **Hasler, V.** "Epiphanie und Christologie in den Pastoralbriefen." *TZ* 39 (1977) 193–209. ———. "Das nomistische Verständnis des Evangeliums in den Pastoralbriefen." *Studien und Texte zum Untersuchen* 28 (1958) 65–77. **Hatch, E.,** ed. *The Organization of the Early Christian Churches.* London: Longmans, 1895. **Haufe, G.** "Gnostische Irrlehre und ihre Abwehr in den Pastoralbriefen." In *Gnosis und Neues Testament,* ed. K.-W. Tröger. Gütersloh: Mohn, 1973. 325–40. **Hawthorne, G. F.** *Philippians.* WBC 43. Waco, TX: Word, 1983. ——— and **Martin, R. P.,** eds. *Dictionary of Paul and His Letters.* Downers Grove, IL: InterVarsity, 1993. **Hayden, E. V.** "Paul and Timothy." In *Essays on New Testament Christianity.* FS D. E. Walker, ed. C. R. Wetzel. Cincinnati: Standard, 1978. **Haykin, M. A. G.** "The Fading Vision: The Spirit and Freedom in the Pastoral Epistles." *EvQ* 57 (1985) 291–305. **Hegermann, H.** "Der geschichtliche Ort der Pastoralbriefe." In *Theologische Versuche* 2. Ed. J. Rogge and G. Schille. Berlin: Evangelische Verlagsanstalt, 1970. 47–64. **Hennecke, E.** *New Testament Apocrypha.* Ed. W. Schneemelcher. 2 vols. Philadelphia: Westminster, 1963, 1965. **Herzog, E.** *Über die Abfassungzeit der Pastoralbriefe.* 1872. **Hilgenfeld, A.** "Die Irrlehrer der Hirtenbriefe des Paulus." *ZWT* (1880) 448–63. **Hill, D.** *Greek Words and Hebrew Meanings.* Cambridge: Cambridge UP, 1967. **Hitchcock, F. R. M.** "Latinity in the Pastorals." *ExpTim* 39 (1928) 347–52. ———. "Philo and the Pastorals." *Hermathena* 56 (1940) 113–35. **Holmberg, B.** *Paul and Power: The Structure of Authority in the Primitive Church as Reflected in the Pauline Epistles.* Philadelphia: Fortress, 1978. **Holtzmann, H. J.** *Die Pastoralbriefe kritisch und exegetisch* *bearbeitet.* Leipzig: Engelmann, 1880. ————. "Der zweite Timotheusbrief und der neueste mit ihm vorgenommene Rettungsversuch." *ZWT* (1883) 45–72. **Hondius, J. J E.**, ed. *Supplementum epigraphicum Graecum.* 9 vols. Alphen aan den Rijn: Sijthoff & Noordhoff, 1923–38. **Horrell, D.** "Converging Ideologies: Berger and Luckmann and the Pastoral Epistles." *JSNT* 50 (1993) 85–103. **Hort, F. J. A.** *The Christian Ecclesia.* London: Macmillan, 1914. ————. *Judaistic Christianity.* 1894. Repr. Grand Rapids, MI: Eerdmans, 1980. **Hull, W. E.** "The Man—Timothy." *RevExp* 56 (1959) 355–66. **Hunt, A. S.**, and **Edgar, C. C.**, eds. and trs. *Select Papyri I.* LCL. Cambridge: Harvard UP, 1959. **Hunter, A. M.** *Paul and His Predecessors.* 2nd ed. London: SCM Press, 1961. **Jacoby, F.** *Die Fragmente der griechischen Historiker.* Leiden: Brill, 1954. **Jeremias, J.** *New Testament Theology: The Proclamation of Jesus.* New York: Scribner's, 1971. **Johnson, J.** "The Message of the Epistles: The Pastoral Epistles." *ExpTim* 45 (1933–34) 270–74. **Johnson, L. T.** *1 Timothy, 2 Timothy, Titus.* Knox Preaching Guides. Atlanta: Knox, 1987. ————. "II Timothy and the Polemic against False Teachers: A Reexamination." *JRS* 6–7 (1978–79) 1–26. **Kaiser, W. C., Jr.** *Toward an Exegetical Theology: Biblical Exegesis for Preaching and Teaching.* Grand Rapids, MI: Baker, 1981. **Karris, R. J.** "The Background and Significance of the Polemic of the Pastoral Epistles." *JBL* 92 (1973) 549–64. ————. "The Function and *Sitz im Leben* of the Paraenetic Elements in the Pastoral Epistles." Ph.D. diss., Harvard University, 1970. **Kasch, W.** "Pastoralbriefe." In *Evangelisches Kirchenlexikon: Kirchlich-Theologisches und Worterbuch.* 4 vols. Gottingen: Vanderhoeck & Ruprecht, 1961–62. **Käsemann, E.** *Essays on New Testament Themes.* Tr. W. J. Montague. SBT 41. London: SCM Press, 1964. ————. "Ministry and Community in the New Testament." In *Essays on New Testament Themes.* Tr. W. J. Montague. SBT 41. London: SCM Press, 1964. 63–94. ————. "Paul and Early Catholicism." In *New Testament Questions of Today.* Philadelphia: Fortress, 1969. 236–51. **Kelly, J. N. D.** *A Commentary on the Epistles of Peter and Jude.* 1969. Repr. Thornapple Commentaries. Grand Rapids, MI: Baker, 1981. ————. *Early Christian Creeds.* 2nd ed. London: Longmans, Green, 1960. **Kent, H. A.** "The Centrality of the Scriptures in Paul's First Epistle to Timothy." *JETS* 14 (1971) 157–64. ————. *The Pastoral Epistles: Studies in 1 and 2 Timothy and Titus.* Chicago: Moody Press, 1982. **Kertelge, K.** *Gemeinde und Amt im Neuen Testament.* Munich: Kösel, 1972. **Kidd, R. M.** *Wealth and Beneficence in the Pastoral Epistles: A 'Bourgeois' Form of Early Christianity?* SBLDS 122. Atlanta: Scholars Press, 1990. **Kinney, L. F.** "The Pastoral Epistles." *Int* 9 (1955) 429–35. **Kirk, J. S.**, and **Raven, J. E.** *The Pre-Socratic Philosophers.* Cambridge: Cambridge UP, 1957. **Klöpper, A.** "Zur Christologie der Pastoralbriefe." *ZWT* (1902) 339–61. ————. "Zur Soteriologie der Pastoralbriefe." *ZWT* (1904) 57–88. **Knight, G. W., III.** *The Faithful Sayings in the Pastoral Letters.* 1968. Repr. Grand Rapids, MI: Baker, 1979. **Kos, V.** "Fides personalitatis perfecte constitutae secundum S. Pauli Ep. ad Tim." *IB* (1957) 105–41. **Köstenberger, A. J., Schreiner, T. R.**, and **Baldwin, H. S.** *Women in the Church.* Grand Rapids, MI: Baker, 1995. **Kowalski, B.** "Zur Funktion und Bedeutung der alttestamentlichen Zitate und Anspielungen in den Pastoralbriefen." SNTU-A 19 (1994) 45–68. **Kretschmar, G.** "Der paulinische Glaube in den Pastoralbriefen." In *Glaube im Neuen Testament.* FS H. Binder, ed. F. Hahns and H. Klein. Biblisch-theologische Studien 7. Neukirchen: Neukirchener Verlag, 1982. **Kuehner, R.** "Pastoral Epistles." *NCE* 10 (1967) 1076–77. **Kühl, E.** "Die Gemeindeordnung der Hirtenbriefe." *ZWT* (1886) 456–72. ————. *Die Gemeindeordnung in den Pastoralbriefen.* Berlin: Hertz, 1885. **Ladd, G. E.** *A Theology of the New Testament.* Grand Rapids, MI: Eerdmans, 1974. **Lake, K.**, tr. *The Apostolic Fathers.* 2 vols. LCL. London; Cambridge, MA: Harvard UP, 1912–13. ————, tr. *Eusebius: The Ecclesiastical History.* 2 vols. LCL. Cambridge, MA: Harvard UP, 1926, 1932. **Läger, K.** *Die Christologie der Pastoralbriefe.* Hamburger theologische Studien 12. Munich: LIT, 1996. **Lampe, G. W. H.** *A Patristic Greek Lexicon.* Oxford: Clarendon, 1961. **Langkammer, H.** "Glówne tendencje doctrynalne Listow Pasterskich: Die wichtigsten Richtungen der Lehre in den Pastoralbriefen." *RTK* 25 (1978) 75–85. **Lategan, B. C.** "Die stryd van die evangeliedienaar: Enkele gedagtes oor die agon-motief in die Pastorale Briewe." *NGTT* 19 (1978) 237–48. **Lau, A.** *Manifest in Flesh: The Epiphany Christology of the Pastoral Epistles.* WUNT

2.86. Tübingen: Mohr, 1996. **Laughlin, T. C.** *The Pastoral Epistles in the Light of One Roman Imprisonment.* Inaugural Address, Pacific Theological Seminary, Berkeley, CA, January 23, 1905. San Francisco: Murdock, 1905. **Leal, J.** *Paulinismo y jerarquia de las cartas pastorales: Discurso inaugural.* Granada: Imp. de F. Roman Camacho, 1946. **Le Forte, P.** "Le responsabilité politique de l'Église d'après les Épîtres Pastorales." *ETR* 49 (1974) 1–14. **Lemaire, A.** "Pastoral Epistles: Redaction and Theology." *BTB* 2 (1972) 25–42. **Lemme, L.** *Das echte Ermahnungsschreiben des Apostels Paulus an Timotheus [2. Tim. 1,1–2,10. 4,6–22]: Ein Beitrag zur Lösung des Problems der Pastoralbriefe.* Breslau: Kohler, 1882. **Leo, P.** *Das anvertraute Gut: Eine Einführung in den ersten Timotheusbrief.* Berlin: Furche, 1935. **Lestapis, S. de.** *L'Énigme des Pastorales de Saint Paul.* Paris: Gabalda, 1976. **Lietzmann, H.** *The Apostolic Ministry.* London: Hodder & Stoughton, 1957. **Lightfoot, J. B.** "Additional Note on the Heresy Combated in the Pastoral Epistles." In *Biblical Essays.* New York: Macmillan, 1893. 411–18. ———. *The Apostolic Fathers: Revised Greek Texts with Introductions and English Translations.* Ed. J. R. Harmer. 1891. Repr. Grand Rapids, MI: Baker, 1984. ———. "The Chronology of St. Paul's Life and Epistles." In *Biblical Essays.* New York: Macmillan, 1893. 213–33. ———. "The Date of the Pastoral Epistles." In *Biblical Essays.* New York: Macmillan, 1893. 397–410. ———. *The Epistle of St. Paul to the Galatians.* 1884. Repr. Grand Rapids, MI: Zondervan, 1957. ———. *Saint Paul's Epistle to the Philippians.* 12th ed. 1913. Repr. Grand Rapids, MI: Zondervan, 1953. ———. "St. Paul's History after the Close of the Acts." In *Biblical Essays.* New York: Macmillan, 1893. 419–37. **Lips, H. von.** *Glaube–Gemeinde–Amt: Zum Verständnis der Ordination in den Pastoralbriefen.* FRLANT 122. Göttingen: Vandenhoeck & Ruprecht, 1979. ———. "Die Haustafel als 'Topos' im Rahmen der urchristlichen Paränese: Beobachtungen anhand des 1. Petrusbriefes und des Titusbriefes." *NTS* 40 (1994) 261–80. ———. "Von den Pastoralbriefen zum 'Corpus Pastorale': Eine Hallische Sprachschöpfung und ihr modernes Pendant als Funktionsbestimmung dreier neutestamentlicher Briefe." In *Reformation und Neuzeit: 300 Jahre Theologie in Halle,* ed. U. Schnelle. New York: de Gruyter, 1994. 49–71. **Lock, W.** "The Epistle to Titus and Its Practical Teaching." *Interpreter* 7 (1910–11) 149–57. ———. *Godliness and Contentment: Studies in the Three Pastoral Epistles.* Grand Rapids, MI: Baker, 1982. **Loewe, H.** *Die Pastoralbriefe des Apostles Paulus in ihrer ursprünglichen Fassung wiederhergestellt.* Cologne: Roemke, 1929. **Lohfink, G.** "Die Normativität der Amtsvorstellungen in den Pastoralbriefen." *TQ* 157 (1977) 93–106. ———. "Paulinische Theologie in der Rezeption der Pastoralbriefe." In *Paulus in den neutestamentlichen Spätschriften,* ed. K. Kertelge. QD 89. Freiburg: Herder, 1981. 70–121. ———. "Die Vermittlung des Paulinismus zu den Pastoralbriefen." *BZ* 32 (1988) 169–88. **Lohse, E.** "Das apostolische Vermachtnis—Zum paulinischen Charakter der Pastoralbriefe." In *Studien zum Text und zur Ethik des Neuen Testaments.* FS H. Greeven, ed. W. von Schrage. Berlin: de Gruyter, 1986. 266–81. ———. *The New Testament Environment.* Tr. J. E. Steely. Nashville: Abingdon, 1976. **Longenecker, R.** *Galatians.* WBC 41. Dallas: Word, 1990. **Löning, K.** "Epiphanie die Menschenfreundlichkeit: Zur Rede von Gott im Kontext städtischer Öffentlichkeit nach den Pastoralbriefen." In *Und dennoch ist von Gott zu reden.* FS H. Vorgrimler, ed. M. Lutz-Bachmann. Freiburg: Herder, 1994. 107–24. ———. "'Gerechtfertigt durch seine Gnade' (Tit 3,7): Zum Problem der Paulusrezeption in der Soteriologie der Pastoralbriefe." In *Der lebendige Gott: Studien zur Theologie des Neuen Testaments.* FS W. Thüsing, ed. T Söding. NTAbh n.s. 31. Münster: Aschendorff, 1996. 241–57. **Löwe, R.** *Ordnung in der Kirche im Lichte des Titusbriefes.* Gütersloh: Der Rufer, 1947. **Lütgert, W.** *Die Irrlehrer der Pastoralbriefe.* BFCT 13.3. Gütersloh: Bertelsmann, 1909. **Lyall, F.** *Slaves, Citizens, Sons: Legal Metaphors in the Epistles.* Grand Rapids, MI: Zondervan, 1984. **MacDonald, D. R.** *The Legend and the Apostle: The Battle for Paul in Story and Canon.* Philadelphia: Westminster, 1983. **MacDonald, M. Y.** *The Pauline Churches: A Socio-Historical Study of Institutionalism in the Pauline and Deutero-Pauline Writings.* SNTSMS 60. Cambridge: Cambridge UP, 1988. **Maehlum, H.** *Die Vollmacht des Timotheus nach den Pastoralbriefen.* Basel: Friedrich Reinhardt Kommissionsverlag, 1969. **Maestri, W. F.** *Paul's Pastoral Vision: Pastoral Letters for a Pastoral Church Today.* New York: Alba, 1989. **Maier, F.** *Die Hauptprobleme der*

Pastoralbriefe Pauli. Münster: Aschendorff, 1910. **Malherbe, A. J.** "Ancient Epistolary Theory." *Ohio Journal of Religious Studies* 5 (1977) 3–77. ————. "Hellenistic Moralists and the New Testament." *ANRW* II, 26:1 267–333. ————. "Medical Imagery in the Pastoral Epistles." In *Texts and Testaments: Critical Essays on the Bible and Early Church Fathers*. FS S. D. Currie, ed. W. W. March. San Antonio: Trinity UP, 1980 (repr. in *Paul and the Popular Philosophers* [Minneapolis: Fortress, 1989] 121–36). ————. *Paul and the Popular Philosophers*. Minneapolis: Fortress, 1989. ————. "Paulus Senex." *ResQ* 36 (1994) 197–207. **Mangold, W.** *Die Irrlehrer der Pastoralbriefe*. Marburg: Elwert'sche Universitäts-Buchhandlung, 1856. **Marcheselli-Casale, C.** "Veri e falsi profeti a Creta ed Efeso: Un problema pastorale sempre attuale." In *Una Hostia*. FS C. Ursi, ed. S. Muratore and A. Rolla. Naples: D'Auria, 1983. **Marcu, G. T.** "Insemnatatea Ep. Sf. Apostol Pavel catre Tit." *Mitropolia Ardealului* 13 (1968) 272–77. ————. "Sf. Ap. Pavel despre personalitatea religioasa-morala a pastorului de suflet . . . [. . . de personalitate religiosa et morali ad pastorem animarum]." *Studii Teologice* 7 (1955) 197–216. **Marshall, I. H.** *The Acts of the Apostles: An Introduction and Commentary*. TNTC 5. Grand Rapids, MI: Eerdmans, 1980. ————. "The Christian Life in 1 Timothy." *Taiwan Journal of Theology* 9 (1987) 151–64. ————. "The Christology of Luke-Acts and the Pastoral Epistles." In *Crossing the Boundaries*. FS M. D. Goulder, ed. S. E. Porter, P. Joyce, and D. E. Orton. Leiden: Brill, 1994. 167–82. ————. "The Christology of the Pastoral Epistles." SNTU-A 13 (1988) 157–78. ————. "Church and Ministry in 1 Timothy." In *Pulpit and People*. FS W. Still, ed. N. M. de S. Cameron and S. B. Ferguson. Edinburgh: Rutherford, 1986. ————. "Faith and Works in the Pastoral Epistles." SNTU-A 9 (1984) 203–18. ————. *The Gospel of Luke: A Commentary on the Greek Text*. NIGTC. Grand Rapids, MI: Eerdmans, 1978. ————. *The Origins of New Testament Christology*. Downers Grove, IL: InterVarsity Press, 1977. ————. "Prospects for the Pastoral Epistles." In *Doing Theology for the People of God*. FS J. I. Packer, ed. D. Lewis and A. McGrath. Downers Grove, IL: InterVarsity Press, 1996. 137–55. ————. "Recent Study of the Pastoral Epistles." *Themelios* 23 (1997) 3–29. ————. Review of *Luke and the Pastoral Epistles*, by S. G. Wilson. *JSNT* 10 (1981) 69–74. ————. "Salvation in the Pastoral Epistles." In *Geschichte—Tradition—Reflexion*. Tübingen: Mohr, 1996. ————. "Sometimes Only Orthodox? Is There More to the Pastoral Epistles?" *Epworth Review* 20 (1993) 12–24. **Martin, R. P.** *2 Corinthians*. WBC 40. Waco, TX: Word, 1986. ————. "Aspects of Worship in the New Testament Church." *Vox Evangelica* 2 (1963) 6–32. ————. *Colossians and Philemon*. NCB. 1974. Repr. Grand Rapids, MI: Eerdmans, 1981. ————. "A Footnote to Pliny's Account of Christian Worship." *Vox Evangelica* 3 (1964) 51–57. ————. *New Testament Foundations: A Guide for Christian Students*. 2 vols. Grand Rapids, MI: Eerdmans, 1975, 1978. ————. *Worship in the Early Church*. Westwood, NJ: Revell, 1964. **Maurer, C.** "Eine Textvariante klärt die Entstehung der Pastoralbriefe." *TZ* 3 (1947) 321–37. **McDermott, J. S.** "The Quest for Community Stabilization: A Social Science Interpretation of the Pastoral Epistles." Ph.D. diss., Drew University, 1991. **McEleney, N. J.** "The Vice Lists of the Pastoral Epistles." *CBQ* 36 (1974) 203–19. **McNeile, A. H.** *Introduction to the Study of the New Testament*. 2nd ed., rev. C. S. C. Williams. Oxford: Clarendon, 1953. **Médebielle, A.** "Les epîtres à Timothée et Tite." *DTC* 15 (1948) 1036–1121. **Meeks, W. A.** *The First Urban Christians: The Social World of the Apostle Paul*. New Haven, CT: Yale UP, 1983. **Meier, J. P.** "*Presbyteros* in the Pastoral Epistles." *CBQ* 35 (1973) 323–45. **Meinardus, O. F. A.** "Cretan Traditions about St. Paul's Mission to the Island." *OS* 22 (1973) 172–83. **Merk, O.** "Glaube und Tat in der Pastoralbriefen." *ZNW* 66 (1975) 91–102. **Metzger, B. M.** *Lexical Aids for Students of New Testament Greek*. Princeton, NJ: Theological Book Agency, 1969. **Michaelis, W.** *Das Ältestenamt der christlichen Gemeinde im Lichte der Heiligen Schrift*. Bern: Haller, 1953. **Michaels, J. R.** *1 Peter*. WBC 49. Dallas: Word, 1988. **Michel, O.** "Grundfragen der Pastoralbriefe." In *Auf dem Grunde der Apostel und Propheten*. FS T. Wurm, ed. M. Loeser. Stuttgart: Quell, 1948. 83–99. **Miller, J. D.** "The Pastoral Letters as Composite Documents." Ph.D. diss., University of Edinburgh, 1988. **Mingioli, R.** "The Idea of Christian Orthodoxy in the Pastoral Epistles." *ATR* 21 (1939) 186–89. **Moda, A.** "Le lettere pastorali e la biografia di Paolo: Saggio bibliografico." *BeO* 27 (1985)

149–61. **Moehlum, H.** "Dies Vollmacht des Timotheus nach den Pastoralbriefen." Diss., University of Basel, 1969. **Moffatt, J.** *An Introduction to the Literature of the New Testament.* 2nd ed. Edinburgh: T. & T. Clark, 1912. ———. *The New Testament: A New Translation.* Rev. ed. London: Hodder & Stoughton, 1935. **Molitor, J.** *Die georgische Version des 1 und 2 Timotheusbriefes und des Titusbriefes in Lateinische übertragen und nach Syriazismen untersucht.* Wiesbaden: Harrasowitz, 1977. **Moore, G. F.** *Judaism in the First Centuries of the Christian Era.* 3 vols. Cambridge, MA: Harvard UP, 1927–30. **Morgenthaler, R.** *Statistik des Neutestamentlichen Wortschatzes.* Zürich: Gotthelf, 1958. **Morris, J. E.** "The Use of the Pastoral Epistles in Relating Christian Faith to Selected Developmental Issues of Late Adulthood." D.Min. thesis, Drew University, 1982. **Morris, L.** *The Apostolic Preaching of the Cross.* 3rd rev. ed. Grand Rapids, MI: Eerdmans, 1965. ———. *The First Epistle of Paul to the Corinthians: An Introduction and Commentary.* 2nd ed. TNTC 7. Grand Rapids, MI: Eerdmans, 1985. ———. *New Testament Theology.* Grand Rapids, MI: Zondervan, 1986. **Moule, C. F. D.** *An Idiom-Book of New Testament Greek.* 2nd ed. Cambridge: Cambridge UP, 1959. ———. *Worship in the New Testament.* Ecumenical Studies in Worship 9. London: Lutterworth, 1961. **Moule, H. C. G.** *Studies in II Timothy.* Kregel Popular Commentary Series. Grand Rapids, MI: Kregel, 1977. **Moulton, H. K.** "Scripture Quotations in the Pastoral Epistles." *ExpTim* 49 (1937–38) 94. **Moulton, J. H., Turner, N.,** and **Howard, W. F.** *A Grammar of New Testament Greek.* 4 vols. Edinburgh: T. & T. Clark, 1908–76. **Müller, U. B.** *Zur frühchristlichen Theologiegeschichte.* Gütersloh: Mohn, 1976. **Mündel, H. O.** "Das apostolische Amt in den Deuteropaulinen." M.A. thesis, University of Göttingen, 1969–70. **Munro, W.** *Authority in Paul and Peter: The Identification of a Pastoral Stratum in the Pauline Corpus and 1 Peter.* SNTSMS 45. Cambridge: Cambridge UP, 1983. **Murphy-O'Connor, J.** "2 Timothy Contrasted with 1 Timothy and Titus." *RB* 98 (1991) 403–18. **Nauck, W.** "Die Herkunft des Verfassers der Pastoralbriefe: Ein Beitrag zur Frage der Auslegung der Pastoralbriefe." Diss., University of Göttingen, 1950. **Nielsen, C. M.** "Scripture in the Pastoral Epistles." *PRS* 7 (1980) 4–23. **Noack, B.** "Pastoralbrevenes 'troværdige tale.'" *DTT* 32 (1969) 1–22. **Oberlinner, L.** "Die 'Epiphaneia' des Heilswillens Gottes in Christus Jesus: Zur Grundstruktur der Christologie der Pastoralbriefe." *ZNW* 71 (1980) 192–213. ——— and **Vögtle, A.** *Anpassung oder Widerspruch: Von der apostolischen zur nachapostolischen Kirche.* Freiburg: Herder, 1992. **O'Brien, P. T.** *Colossians, Philemon.* WBC 44. Waco, TX: Word, 1982. **Okorie, A. M.** "Marriage in the Pastoral Epistles." Ph.D. diss., Southern Baptist Theological Seminary, 1988. **Oldfather, W. A.,** and **Daly, L. W.** "A Quotation from Xenander in the Pastoral Epistles?" *CP* 38 (1943) 202–4. **Oliveira, B. C. de.** "Tito." *EstBib* 3 (1984) 55–57. **Otto, C. W.** *Die geschichtlichen Verhältnisse der Pastoralbriefe aufs neue untersucht.* Leipzig: Teubner, 1860. **Oxford Society of Historical Theology.** *The New Testament in the Apostolic Fathers.* Oxford: Oxford UP, 1905. **Pate, C. M.** *The Glory of Adam and the Afflictions of the Righteous: Pauline Suffering in Context.* Lewiston, NY: Mellen, 1993. **Patsch, H.** "Die Angst vor dem Deuteropaulinismus: Die Rezeption des 'kritischen Sendschreibens' Freidrich Schleiermachers über den 1. Timotheusbrief im ersten Jahrfünft." *ZTK* 88 (1991) 451–77. **Peacock, H. F.** "A Commentary on the Epistle to Titus." Diss., Southern Baptist Theological Seminary, 1950. **Penny, D. N.** "The Pseudo-Pauline Letters of the First Two Centuries." Ph.D. diss., Emory University, 1980. **Perdue, L. C.** "The Social Character of Paraenesis and Paraenetic Literature." *Semeia* 50 (1990) 5–39. **Peretto, E.** "Il ruolo delle Lettere Pastorali di Paolo nella Regola di Benedetto." *Benedictina* 28 (1981) 485–503. **Pesch, R.** "'Christliche Bürgerlichkeit' (Titus 2,11–15)." *Am Tisch des Wortes* 14 (1966) 28–33. **Pfitzner, V. C.** "The Agon Motif in the Pastoral Epistles." In *Paul and the Agon Motif.* NovTSup 16. Leiden: Brill, 1976. 165–86. **Planck, H. L.** *Bemerkungen über den ersten Brief an Timotheus.* Göttingen: Rower, 1808. **Porter, R. K.** "A Study of the Pastoral Epistles." Diss., Glasgow, 1971–72. **Preisigke, F.** *Wörterbuch der griechischen Papyruskunden.* Completed by E. Kiessling. 3 vols. Berlin: Selbstverlag der Erben, 1925–27. **Prior, M.** *Paul the Letter-Writer and the Second Letter to Timothy.* JSNTSup 23. Sheffield: Sheffield Academic, 1989. ———. "Second Timothy: A Personal Letter of Paul." Ph.D. diss., London University, 1985. **Querdray, G.** "La doctrine des Épîtres pastorales:

Leurs affinités avec l'œuvre lucanienne: Remarques nouvelles." *Esprit et Vie* 88 (1978) 631–38. **Quinn, J. D.** "The Holy Spirit in the Pastoral Epistles." In *Sin, Salvation, and the Spirit,* ed. D. Durken. Collegeville, MN: Liturgical, 1979. 345–68. ———. "The Last Volume of Luke: The Relation of Luke-Acts to the Pastoral Epistles." In *Perspectives on Luke-Acts,* ed. C. H. Talbert. Danville, VA: Association of Baptist Professors of Religion, 1978. 62–75. ———. "Ministry in the New Testament." In *Biblical Studies in Contemporary Thought.* Somerville, MA: Grerno, Hadden, 1975. 130–60. ———. "On the Terminology for Faith, Truth, Teaching, and the Spirit in the Pastoral Epistles, A Summary." In *Teaching Authority and Infallibility in the Church,* ed. P. C. Empie, T. A. Murphy, and J. A. Burgess. Minneapolis: Augsburg, 1980. 232–37. ———. "Ordination in the Pastoral Epistles." *ICR/C* 8 (1981) 358–69. ———. "Paraenesis and the Pastoral Epistles: Lexical Observations Bearing on the Nature of the Sub-Genre and Soundings in Its Role in Socialization and Liturgies." *Semeia* 50 (1990) 189–210. ———. "The Pastoral Epistles." *TBT* 23 (1985) 228–38. ———. "Paul's Last Captivity." In *Studia Biblica* 3. Ed. E. Livingstone. JSNTSup 3. Sheffield: Sheffield Academic, 1980. 289–99. **Ramsay, W. M.** "A Historical Commentary on the Epistles to Timothy." *Exp* 7.8 (1909–11) 481–94; 7.8 (1909) 1–21, 167–85, 264–82, 339–57, 399–416, 557–668; 7.9 (1910) 172–87, 319–33, 433–40; 8.1 (1911) 262–73, 356–75. ———. *St. Paul the Traveller and Roman Citizen.* 16th ed. London: Hodder & Stoughton, 1927. **Rankin, D.** "Tertullian's Use of the Pastoral Epistles in His Doctrine of Ministry." *AusBR* 32 (1984) 18–37. **Redalié, Y.** *Paul après Paul: Le temps, le salut, la morale selon les épîtres à Timothée et à Tite.* Geneva: Labor et Fides, 1994. **Reed, J. T.** "To Timothy or Not: A Discourse Analysis of 1 Timothy." In *Biblical Greek Language and Linguistics: Open Questions in Current Research,* ed. S. E. Porter and D. A. Carson. JSNTSup 80. Sheffield: JSOT Press, 1993. 90–118. **Reicke, B.** "Les Pastorales dans le ministère de Paul." *Hokhma* 19 (1982) 47–61. **Reiser, M.** "Bürgerliches Christentum in den Pastoralbriefen?" *Bib* 74 (1993) 27–44. **Richardson, A.** *An Introduction to the Theology of the New Testament.* New York: Harper & Row, 1958. **Ridderbos, H. N.** *Paul and Jesus.* Philadelphia: Presbyterian & Reformed, 1958. ———. *Paul: An Outline of His Theology.* Tr. J. R. De Witt. Grand Rapids, MI: Eerdmans, 1975. **Rigaux, B.** *The Letters of St. Paul: Modern Studies.* Ed. S. Yonick. Chicago: Franciscan Herald, 1968. **Rinaldi, G.** *Lettera a Tito: Paolo, vita, apostolato, scritti, a cura di T. Ballarini.* Marietti, 1968. **Robertson, A. T.** *A Grammar of the Greek New Testament in the Light of Historical Research.* 6 vols. Nashville: Broadman, 1934. ———. *Word Pictures in the New Testament.* 6 vols. Nashville: Broadman, 1931. **Robinson, J. A. T.** *Redating the New Testament.* Philadelphia: Fortress, 1976. **Rogers, P.** "The Few in Charge of the Many: The Model of Ministerial Authority in the Pastoral Epistles, as a Positive Norm for the Church." Diss., Pontifical Gregorian University, 1977. **Roller, O.** *Das Formular der paulinischen Briefe: Ein Beitrag zur Lehre vom antiken Briefe.* BWA(N)T 4.6. Stuttgart: Kohlhammer, 1933. **Roloff, J.** *Apostolat—Verkündigung—Kirche: Ursprung, Inhalt und Funktion des kirchlichen Apostelamtes nach Paulus, Lukas und den Pastoralbriefen.* Gütersloh: Mohn, 1965. ———. "Der Kampf gegen die Irrlehrer." *BK* 46 (1991) 114–20. ———. *Die Kirche im Neuen Testament.* NTD 10. Göttingen: Vandenhoeck & Ruprecht, 1993. ———. "Pfeiler und Fundament der Wahrheit: Erwägungen zum Kirchenverständnis der Pastoralbriefe." In *Glaube und Eschatologie.* FS W. G. Kümmel, ed. E. von Gräßer and O. Merk. Tübingen: Mohr, 1985. 229–47. ———. "Der Weg Jesu als Lebensnorm (2 Tim 2,8–13): Ein Beitrag zur Christologie der Pastoralbriefe." In *Anfange der Christologie.* FS H. Hahn, ed. C. Breytenbach and H. Paulsen. Göttingen: Vandenhoeck & Ruprecht, 1991. 155–67. **Rordorf, W.** "Nochmals: Paulusakten und Pastoralbriefe." In *Tradition and Interpretation in the New Testament.* FS E. Ellis, ed. G. F. Hawthorne and O. Betz. Grand Rapids, MI: Eerdmans, 1987. 319–27. **Roux, H.** *Der Titusbrief.* Tr. H. H. Esser. Neukirchen: Neukirchen Verlag, 1964. **Rudolph, K.** *Gnosis: The Nature and History of Gnosticism.* Tr. R. M. Wilson. San Francisco: Harper & Row, 1983. **Rudow, T.** *Dissertatio de argumentis historicis, quibus recenter Epistolarum pastoralium origo Paulina impugnata est.* Göttingen: Typis expressit officina Academica Dieterichiana, 1852. **Saintes, A.** *Etudes critiques sur les trois lettres pastorales adressees à Timothée et à Tite et attribuées à l'apôtre Saint Paul.*

Paris: Ducloux, 1852. **Sanchez Bosch, J.** "Jesucrist, el Senyor, en les cartes pastorals." *RevistC* 14 (1989) 345–59. **Sand, A.** "'Am Bewährten festhalten': Zur Theologie der Pastoralbriefe." In *Theologie im Werden: Studien zu den theologischen Konzeptionen im Neuen Testament,* ed. J. Hainz. Paderborn: Schoningh, 1992. 351–76. ———. "Anfänge einer Koordinierung verschiedener Gemeindeordnungen nach den Pastoralbriefen." In *Kirche im Werden,* ed. von J. Hainz. Paderborn: Schöningh, 1976. 215–37. **Scharling, C.** *Die neusten Untersuchungen über die sogenannten Pastoralbriefe.* Jena: Hochhausen, 1846. **Schenk, W.** "Die Briefe an Timotheus I und II und an Titus (Pastoralbriefe) in der neueren Forschung (1945–1985)." *ANRW* II, 25/4:3404–38. **Schierse, F. J.** "Eschatologische Existenz und christliche Bürgerlichkeit." *GL* 32 (1959) 280–91. ———. "Kennzeichen gesunder und kranker Lehre: Zur Ketzerpolemik der Pastoralbriefe." *Diakonia* 4 (1973) 76–86. **Schille, G.** *Das älteste Paulus-Bild: Beobachtungen zur lukanischen und zur deuteropaulinischen Paulusdarstellung.* Berlin: Evangelische, 1979. ———. *Frühchristliche Hymnen.* Berlin: Evangelische, 1965. **Schlarb, E.** *Die gesunde Lehre: Häresie und Wahrheit im Spiegel der Pastoralbriefe.* Marburger theologische Studien 28. Marburg: Elwert, 1990. **Schlatter, A.** *The Church in the New Testament Period.* Tr. P. P. Levertoff. London: S.P.C.K., 1961. ———. *Die Kirche der Griechen im Urteil des Paulus: Eine Auslegung seiner Briefe an Timotheus und Titus.* Stüttgart: Calwer, 1958. **Schleiermacher, F.** *Über den sogenannten ersten Brief des Paulus an den Timotheos.* Berlin: Sendschreiben an J. C. Gass, 1807. **Schlier, H.** "Die Ordnung der Kirche nach den Pastoralbriefen." In *Die Zeit der Kirche: Exegetische Aufsätze und Vorträge.* Freiburg: Herder, 1958. 129–47. **Schlosser, J.** "La didascalie et ses agents dans les epitres pastorales." *RSR* 59 (1985) 81–94. **Schmithals, W.** "The Corpus Paulinum and Gnosis." In *The New Testament and Gnosis.* FS R. M. Wilson, ed. A. H. B. Logan and A. J. M. Wedderburn. Edinburgh: T. & T. Clark, 1983. 114–17. ———. "Die Gnostischen Elemente im Neuen Testament als hermeneutisches Problem." In *Gnosis und Neues Testament,* ed. K.-W. Tröger. Gütersloh: Mohn/Gütersloher Verlagshaus, 1973. 359–81. **Schmitt, J.** "Didascalie ecclésiale et tradition apostolique selon les Épîtres pastorales." *L'Année Canonique* 23 (1979) 45–57. **Schnackenburg, R.** "Christologie des Neuen Testaments." *Mysterium Salutis* 3.1 (1970) 277–388. ———. *Schriften zum Neuen Testament: Exegese in Fortschritt und Wandel.* Munich: Kösel, 1971. **Schoedel, W. R.** *Ignatius of Antioch.* Hermeneia. Philadelphia: Fortress, 1985. **Schöllgen, G.** "Hausgemeinde, OIKOS-Ekklesiologie und monarchischer Episkopat: Überlegungen zu einer neuen Forschungsrichtung." *JAC* 31 (1988) 74–90. **Schürer, E.** *The History of the Jewish People in the Age of Jesus Christ (175 B.C.–A.D. 135).* Rev. G. Vermes, F. Millar, et al. 4 vols. Edinburgh: T. & T. Clark, 1973–87. **Schüssler Fiorenza, E.** *In Memory of Her.* New York: Crossroad, 1984. **Schütz, E.** *Werdende Kirche im Neuen Testament: Eine Einführung in die Pastoralbriefe.* Kleine Kasseler Bibelhilfe. Kassel: Oncken, 1969. **Schwarz, R.** *Bürgerliches Christentum im Neuen Testament? Eine Studie zu Ethik, Amt und Recht in den Pastoralbriefen.* ÖBS 4. Klosterneuburg: Österreichisches Katholisches Biblewerk, 1983. **Sell, J.** *The Knowledge of the Truth—Two Doctrines: The Book of Thomas the Contender and the False Teachers in the Pastoral Epistles.* Frankfurt: Lang, 1982. ———. "'The Knowledge of the Truth' (CG II:138,13)." In *Acts of the Second International Congress of Coptic Studies.* Rome: CIM, 1985. 345–53. **Sellin, G.** "'Die Auferstehung ist schon geschehen': Zur Spiritualisierung apokalyptischer Terminologie im Neuen Testament." *NovT* 25 (1983) 220–37. **Selwyn, E. G.** *The First Epistle of St. Peter: The Greek Text with Introduction, Notes, and Essays.* 2nd ed. 1947. Repr. Thornapple Commentaries; Grand Rapids, MI: Baker, 1981. **Serra, A. M.** "'Servizio della parola' nelle epistole pastorali." *Servitium* 2 (1969) 325–37. **Sevenster, J. N.** *Paul and Seneca.* Leiden: Brill, 1961. **Sherwin-White, A. N.** *Roman Society and Roman Law in the New Testament.* Oxford: Clarendon, 1963. **Siebers, B.** "Ministerio y Carisma en las Cartas Pastorales." *RevistTL* 6 (1972) 9–23. **Simonsen, H.** "Christologische Traditionselemente in den Pastoralbriefen." In *Die paulinische Literatur und Theologie,* ed. S. Pederson. Arhus: Forlaget Aros; Göttingen: Vandenhoeck & Ruprecht, 1980. 51–62. **Simpson, E. K.,** and **Bruce, F. F.** *Commentary on the Epistles to the Ephesians and the Colossians.* NICNT. Grand Rapids, MI: Eerdmans, 1957. **Skarsaune, O.** "Heresy and the Pastoral Epistles." *Themelios* 20 (1994) 9–14. **Skeat, T. C.** "'Especially the

Parchments': A Note on 2 Timothy 4:13." *JTS* n.s. 30 (1979) 173–77. **Smith, R. E.**, and **Beekman, J.** *A Literary-Semantic Analysis of Second Timothy*, ed. M. F. Kopesec. Dallas: Summer Institute of Linguistics, 1981. **Smyth, H. W.** *Greek Grammer.* Rev. G. M. Messing. Cambridge, MA: Harvard UP, 1956. **Spicq, C.** "L'évêque selon les Epîtres Pastorales." *Témoignages* 8 (1955) 113–21. **Spitta, F.** *Über die persönlichen Notizen im zweiten Briefe an Timotheus.* Theologische Studien und Kritiken. Hamburg, 1878. ———. *Zur Geschichte und Literatur des Urchristentum.* Göttingen: Vandenhoeck & Ruprecht, 1893–1907. **Staab, E.**, ed. *Die Heilige Schrift in deutscher Übersetzung: Das Neue Testament.* 2nd ed. EchtB. Wurzburg, Echter, 1967–68. **Stauffer, E.** *New Testament Theology.* Tr. J. Marsh. New York: Macmillan, 1955. **Stecker, A.** "Dormen und Formeln in den paulinischen Hauptbriefen und in den Pastoralbriefen." Diss., Münster, 1966. **Stenger, W.** "Timotheus und Titus als literarische Gestalten (Beobachtungen zur Form und Funktion der Pastoralbriefe)." *Kairos* 16 (1974) 252–67. **Stewart, R.** "A Coptic Fragment of 2 Timothy." *SPap* 21 (1982) 7–10. **Stock, E.** *Practical Truths from the Pastoral Epistles.* Grand Rapids, MI: Kregel, 1983. **Stramare, T.** "Tito." *Bibliotheca Sanctorum (Lateran)* 12 (1969) 503–5. **Sweeney, M. L.** "From God's Household to the Heavenly Chorus: A Comparison of the Church in the Pastoral Epistles with the Church in the Letters of Ignatius of Antioch." Ph.D. diss., Union Theological Seminary, Virginia, 1989. **Swete, H. B.**, ed. "Theodore of Mopsuestia." In *Theodori episcopi Mopsuesteni: In Epistolas B. Pauli Commentarii: The Latin Version with the Greek Fragments.* Cambridge: Cambridge UP, 1880–82. **Szabo, C.** "Die liturgischen Elemente der Pastoralbriefe und des Hebraerbriefes." *Theologiai Szemle* 27 (1984) 72–76. **Thiessen, W.** *Christen in Ephesus: Die historische und theologische Situation in vorpaulinischer und paulinischer Zeit und zur Zeit der Apostelgeschichte und der Pastoralbriefe.* TANZ 12. Tübingen: Francke, 1995. **Thomas, W. D.** "Timothy." *ExpTim* 96 (1984) 85–87. ———. "Titus, the Good All-Rounder." *ExpTim* 96 (1984) 180–81. **Thörnell, G.** *Pastoralbrevens Äkthet.* Svensk arkiv for humanistiska avhandlingar 3. Göteborg: Eranos, 1931. **Tinnefeld, F. H.** *Untersuchungen zur altlateinischer: Ueberlieferung des l. Timotheusbriefes: Der lateinische Paulustext in den Handschriften DEFG und in den Kommentaren des Ambrosiaster und des Pelagius.* Wiesbaden: Harrasowitz, 1963. **Torm, F.** "Ueber die Sprache in den Pastoralbriefen." *ZNW* 17 (1918) 225–43. **Towner, P. H.** "Gnosis and Realized Eschatology in Ephesus (of the Pastoral Epistles) and the Corinthian Enthusiasm." *JSNT* 31 (1987) 95–124. ———. *The Goal of Our Instruction: The Structure of Theology and Ethics in the Pastoral Epistles.* JSNTSup 34. Sheffield: Sheffield Academic, 1989. ———. "Pauline Theology or Pauline Tradition in the Pastoral Epistles: The Question of Method." *TynBul* 46 (1995) 287–314. ———. "The Present Age in the Eschatology of the Pastoral Epistles." *NTS* 32 (1986) 427–48. **Trench, R. C.** *Synonyms of the New Testament.* Rev. ed. London: Macmillan, 1865. **Trummer, P.** "Corpus Paulinum— Corpus Pastorali: Zur Ortung der Paulustradition in den Pastoralbriefen." In *Paulus in den neutestamentlichen Spätschriften*, ed. K. Kertelge. Freiburg: Herder, 1981. 122–45. ———. "Gemeindeleiter ohne Gemeinden? Nachbemerkungen zu den Pastoralbriefen." *BK* 46 (1991) 121–26. ———. "Mantel und Schriften: Zur Interpretation einer persönlichen Notiz in den Pastoralbriefen." *BZ* 18 (1974) 193–207 (reprinted in *Paulus in den neutestamentlichen Spätschriften*, ed. K. Kertelge [Freiburg: Herder, 1981] 70–121). ———. *Die Paulustradition der Pastoralbriefe.* BBET 8. Frankfurt: Lang, 1978. **Turner, N.** *Grammatical Insights into the New Testament.* Edinburgh: T. & T. Clark, 1966. **Venter, C. J. H.** *Die Bediening van die versoening aan die bejaarde: 'n pastorale studie in die lig van die pastorale briewe.* Raad vir Geesteswetenskaplike Navorsing 57. Potchefstroom: Pro Rege, 1976. **Verner, D. C.** *The Household of God and the Social World of the Pastoral Epistles.* SBLDS 71. Chico, CA: Scholars Press, 1983. **Verzan, S.** "La première Épître du saint Apôtre Paul à Timothée: Introduction, traduction et commentaire." *Studii Teologice* 40 (1988) 2:9–122; 3:10–101; 4:10–115; 5:14–85; 6:30–108. **Villiers, J. L. de.** "Die opdrag van (aan) die Evangeliedienaar volgens de Pastorale Briewe." *NedTTs* 17 (1976) 191–96. **Vincent, M. R.** *Word Studies in the New Testament.* 2nd ed. 4 vols. 1902–3. Repr. Grand Rapids, MI: Eerdmans, 1946. **Vine, W. E.** *Expository Dictionary of New Testament Words.* 1939–41. Repr. Grand Rapids, MI: Zondervan, 1981. **Vögtle, A.** *Die Tugend- und Lasterkataloge im*

Neuen Testament: Exegetisch, religions- und formgeschichtlich Untersucht. NTAbh 16.4–5. Münster: Aschendorff, 1936. **Wagener, U.** *Die Ordnung des "Hauses Gottes": Der Ort von Frauen in der Ekklesiologie und Ethik der Pastoralbriefe.* WUNT 2.65. Tübingen: Mohr-Siebeck, 1994. **Waite, D. A.** "An Exposition of the Epistle of Paul to Titus." Diss., Dallas Theological Seminary, 1955. **Walder, E.** "The Logos of the Pastoral Epistles." *JTS* o.s. 24 (1923) 310–15. **Wallace, D. B.** *Greek Grammar beyond the Basics: An Exegetical Syntax of the New Testament.* Grand Rapids, MI: Zondervan, 1997. **Wanke, J.** "Der verkündigte Paulus der Pastoralbriefe." In *Dienst der Vermittlung,* ed. W. Ernst. Leipzig: St. Benno, 1977. 165–89. **Wansbrough, H.** "The Pastoral Letters." In *New Catholic Commentary on Holy Scripture.* London: Nelson, 1969. **Warfield, B. B.** "Some Exegetical Notes on I Timothy." *Presbyterian Review* 8 (1887) 500–508, 702–10. **Warren, M.** "Commentaries on the Pastoral Epistles." *Theology* 63 (1960) 15–19. **Wegenast, K.** *Das Verständnis der Tradition bei Paulus und in den Deuteropaulinen.* WMANT 8. Neukirchen: Neukirchener Verlag, 1962. **Weiser, A.** *Die gesellschaftliche Verantwortung der Christen nach den Pastoralbriefen.* Stuttgart: Kohlhammer, 1994. ———. "Die Kirche in den Pastoralbriefen: Ordnung um jeden Preis?" *BK* 46 (1991) 107–13. ———. "Titus 2 als Gemeindeparänese." In *Neues Testament und Ethik.* FS R. Schnackenburg, ed. H. Merklein. Freiburg: Herder, 1989. 397–414. **Weiss, J.** *The History of Primitive Christianity.* New York: Wilson-Erikson, 1937. **Wendland, P.** *Die urchristlichen Literaturformen.* HNT 1.3. Tübingen: Mohr, 1912. **Wengst, K.** *Christologische Formeln und Lieder des Urchristentums.* SNT 7. Gütersloh: Mohn, 1973. **Weninger, F.** "Die Pastoralbriefe in der Kanongeschichte zur Zeit der Patristik." Diss., Vienna, 1966. **Wettstein, J. J.** *Novum Testamentum Graecum.* 2 vols. 1751. Repr. Graz: Akademische Druck-und Verlagsanstalt, 1962. **Wickham, P.** *Segunda Timoteo y Tito. Las iglesias del NT:* Cuadernos de Estudio 9. Mexico: Literatura Biblica, 1981. **Wild, R. A.** "The Image of Paul in the Pastoral Letters." *TBT* 23 (1985) 239–45. **Wiles, G. P.** *Paul's Intercessory Prayers.* SNTSMS 24. Cambridge: Cambridge UP, 1974. **Wilson, R. M.** *The Gnostic Problem.* 2nd ed. London: SCM Press, 1964. **Wilson, S. G.** *Luke and the Pastoral Epistles.* London: S. P. C. K., 1979. ———. "The Portrait of Paul in Acts and the Pastorals." *SBLSP.* Missoula, MT: Scholars Press, 1976. 397–411. **Wimbush, V. L.** "I and II Timothy, Titus." *Books* 2 (1989) 319–26. **Windisch, H.** "Zur Christologie der Pastoralbriefe." *ZNW* 34 (1935) 213–38. **Wolfe, B. P.** "Paul, Scripture in the Pastoral Epistles: Pre-Marcion Marcionism?" *PRS* 16 (1989) 5–16. ———. "The Place and Use of Scripture in the Pastoral Epistles." Diss., University of Aberdeen, 1991. **Wolter, M.** *Die Pastoralbriefe als Paulustradition.* FRLANT 146. Göttingen: Vandenhoeck & Ruprecht, 1988. **Wuest, K. S.** *Wuest's Word Studies from the Greek New Testament.* 3 vols. Grand Rapids, MI: Eerdmans, 1973. **Yamauchi, E.** *Pre-Christian Gnosticism.* 2nd ed. Grand Rapids, MI: Baker, 1983. **Young, F.** "On EPISKOPOS and PRESBUTEROS." *JTS* n.s. 45 (1994) 124–48. ———. "The Pastoral Epistles and the Ethics of Reading." *JSNT* 45 (1992) 105–20. ———. *The Theology of the Pastoral Letters.* Cambridge: Cambridge UP, 1994. **Zedda, S.** *Le lettere Pastorali: Messaggio della Salvezza* 5. L. D. C., 1968. **Zerwick, M.** *Biblical Greek.* Tr. J. Smith. Rome: Scripta Pontificii Instituti Biblici, 1977. **Ziesler, J. A.** "Which Is the Best Commentary? XII. The Pastoral Epistles." *ExpTim* 99 (1988) 264–67.

Introduction

Bibliography

Aland, K. "Falsche Verfasserangaben? Zur Pseudonymität im frühchristlichen Schrifttum." *TRev* 75 (1979) 1–10. ———. "The Problem of Anonymity and Pseudonymity in Christian Literature of the First Two Centuries." *JTS* 12 (1961) 39–49 (reprinted in *The Authorship and Integrity of the New Testament*, ed. K. Aland [London: S.P.C.K., 1965] 1–13). **Ambroggi, P. de.** "Questioni sulle origini delle epistole pastorali a Timoteo e a Tito." *Scuola Cattolica* 79 (1951) 409–34. **Appel, N.** "The New Testament Canon: Historical Process and Spirit's Witness." *TS* 32 (1971) 627–46. **Bahnsen, G. L.** "Autographs, Amanuenses and Restricted Inspiration." *EvQ* 45 (1973) 100–110. **Baldwin, J. G.** "Is There Pseudonymity in the Old Testament?" *Themelios* 4.1 (1978) 6–12. **Balz, H. R.** "Anonymität und Pseudepigraphie im Urchristentum: Überlegungen zum literarischen und theologischen Problem der urchristlichen und gemeinantiken Pseudepigraphie." *ZTK* 66 (1969) 403–36. **Bardy, G.** "Faux et fraudes littéraires dans l'antiquité chrétienne." *RHE* 32 (1936) 5–23, 275–302. **Barr, J.** *Holy Scripture: Canon, Authority, Criticism.* Philadelphia: Westminster, 1983. **Bauckham, R.** "Pseudo-Apostolic Letters." *JBL* 107 (1988) 469–94. **Bauer, W.** *Orthodoxy and Heresy in Earliest Christianity.* Tr. R. A. Kraft and G. Krodel. Philadelphia: Fortress, 1971. **Baur, F. C.** *Die christliche Gnosis oder die christliche Religionsphilosophie in ihrer geschichtlichen Entwicklung.* 1835. Repr. Darmstadt: Wissenschaftliche Buchgesellschaft, 1967. **Bekes, G. J.** "La successione nella tradizione apostolica: Il problema del rapporto fra la successione del ministero e la paradosis apostolica nel documento." In *Il ministero ordinato nel dialogo ecumenico.* FS G. J. Bekes, ed. G. Farnedi and P. Rouillard. Studia Anselmiana 92, Sacramentum 9. Rome: Pontificio Ateneo S. Anselmo, 1985. **Bertrand, E.** *Critique sur l'authenticité de Épîtres Pastorals.* Paris: Fischbacher, 1887. **Binder, H.** "Die historische Situation der Pastoralbriefe." In *Geschichtswirklichkeit und Glaubensbewährung.* FS F. Müller, ed. F. C. Fry. Stuttgart: Evangelische Verlagswerk, 1967. 70–83. **Bird, A. E.** "The Authorship of the Pastoral Epistles—Quantifying Literary Style." *RTR* 56 (1997) 118–37. **Boer, M. C. de.** "Images of Paul in the Post-Apostolic Period." *CBQ* 42 (1980) 359–80. **Bowen, W. E.** *The Dates of the Pastoral Epistles.* London: Nisbet, 1900. **Braudel, F.** *The Mediterranean and the Mediterranean World in the Age of Philip II.* 2 vols. New York: Harper & Row, 1972. **Brockington, L. H.** "The Problem of Pseudonymity." *JTS* n.s. 4 (1953) 15–22. **Brown, R. E.** *The Churches Paul Left Behind.* New York: Paulist Press, 1984. **Brox, N.** *Falsche Verfasserangaben: Zur Erklärung der frühchristlichen Pseudepigraphie.* Stuttgarter Bibelstudien 79. Stuttgart: Katholisches Bibelwerk, 1975. ———. "Lukas als Verfasser der Pastoralbriefe?" *NTS* 15 (1969) 191–210 (reprinted in JAC 13 [1970] 62–77). ———. "Methodenfragen der Pseudepigraphie Forschung." *TRev* 75 (1979) 275–78. ———. "Pseudo-Paulus und Pseudo-Ignatius: Einige Topoi altchristlichen Pseudepigraphie." *VC* 30 (1976) 181–88. ———. "Religiöse Pseudepigraphie als ethisch-psychologisches Problem." *ZNW* 35 (1936) 262–79. ———. "Zu den persönlichen Notizen der Pastoralbriefe." *BZ* 13 (1969) 76–94. ———. "Zum Problemstand in der Erforschung der altchristlichen Pseudepigraphie." *Kairos* 15 (1973) 10–23. **Brox, N.,** ed. *Pseudepigraphie in der heidnischen und jüdisch-christlichen Antike.* Darmstadt: Wissenschaftliche Buchgesellschaft, 1977. **Bruce, F. F.** *The Epistle to the Hebrews.* Rev. ed. NICNT. Grand Rapids, MI: Eerdmans, 1990. ———. *New Testament History.* Garden City, NY: Doubleday (Anchor), 1972. ———. *Paul: Apostle of the Heart Set Free.* Grand Rapids, MI: Eerdmans, 1977. ———. "The Problem of Authorship: First and Second Timothy." *RevExp* 56 (1959)

343–54. ———. " 'To the Hebrews': A Document of Roman Christianity?" ANRW II, 25/4 (1987). **Calder, W. M.** "A Fourth-Century Lycaonian Bishop." *Exp* 7 (1908) 383–84. **Campenhausen, H. F. von.** "Polykarp von Smyrna und die Pastoralbriefe." In *Aus der Frühzeit des Christentums: Studien zur Kirchengeschichte des ersten und zweiten Jahrhunderts.* Tübingen: Mohr-Siebeck, 1963. 197–252. **Candlish, J. S.** "On the Moral Character of Pseudonymous Books." *Exp* 4 (1891) 91–107, 262–79. **Carrington, P.** "The Problem of the Pastoral Epistles: Dr. Harrison's Theory Reviewed." *ATR* 21 (1939) 32–39. **Carson, D. A., Moo, D. J.**, and **Morris, L.** *An Introduction to the New Testament.* Grand Rapids, MI: Zondervan, 1992. **Caulley, T. S.** "Fighting the Good Fight: The Pastoral Epistles in Canonical-Critical Perspective." *SBLSP* (1987) 550–64. **Clark, L. F.** "An Investigation of Some Applications of Quantitative Methods to Pauline Letters, with a View to the Question of Authorship." M.A. thesis, University of Manchester, 1979. **Collins, J. J.** "Pseudonymity, Historical Reviews and the Genre of the Revelation of John." *CBQ* 39 (1977) 329–43. **Collins, R. F.** "The Image of Paul in the Pastorals." *LTP* 31 (1975) 147–73. **Colson, F. H.** " 'Myths and Genealogies'—A Note on the Polemic of the Pastoral Epistles." *JTS* o.s. 19 (1917-18) 265–71. **Cook, D.** "The Pastoral Fragments Reconsidered." *JTS* n.s. 35 (1984) 120–31. **Dalton, W. J.** "Pseudepigraphy in the New Testament." *Catholic Theological Review* 5 (1983) 29–35. **Dassmann, E.** *Der Stachel im Fleisch: Paulus in der frühchristlichen Literatur bis Irenäus.* Münster: Aschendorff, 1979. **Dockx, S.** "Essai de chronologie de la vie de S. Timothée." In *Chronologies Néotestamentaires et vie de l'Eglise primitive: Recherches exegetiques.* Gembloux: Duculot, 1976. 167–87. **Donelson, L. R.** *Pseudepigraphy and Ethical Arguments in the Pastoral Epistles.* HUT 22. Tübingen: Mohr-Siebeck, 1986. ———. "The Structure of the Ethical Argument in the Pastorals." *BTB* 18 (1988) 108–13. **Doty, W. G.** "The Classification of Epistolary Literature." *CBQ* 31 (1969) 183–99. **Edwards, B. B.** "The Genuineness of the Pastoral Epistles." *BSac* 150 (1993) 131–39 (repr. from *BSac*, 1851). **Eichhorn, J. G.** *Historisch-kritische Einleitung in das Neue Testament.* Leipzig: Weidmannischen Buchhandlung, 1812. **Ellis, E. E.** "The Authorship of the Pastorals: A Résumé and Assessment of Current Trends." *EvQ* 32 (1960) 151–61 (reprinted in *Paul and His Recent Interpreters* [Grand Rapids, MI: Eerdmans, 1961] 49–57). ———. "The Problem of Authorship: First and Second Timothy." *RevExp* 56 (1959) 343–54. ———. "Pseudonymity and Canonicity of New Testament Documents." In *Worship, Theology and Ministry in the Early Church.* FS R. P. Martin, ed. M. J. Wilkins and T. Paige. JSNTSup 87. Sheffield: Sheffield Academic Press, 1992. 212–24. **Fenton, J. C.** "Pseudonymity in the New Testament." *Theology* 58 (1955) 51–56. **Finegan, J.** *Handbook of Biblical Chronology.* Princeton, NJ: Princeton UP, 1964. ———. "The Original Form of the Pauline Collection." *HTR* 49 (1956) 85–103. **Fischer, K. M.** "Anmerkungen zur Pseudepigraphie im Neuen Testament." *NTS* 23 (1976) 76–81. **Forbes, A. D.** "Statistical Research on the Bible." *ABD* 6:185–206. **Ford, J. M.** "A Note on Proto-Montanism in the Pastoral Epistles." *NTS* 17 (1970-71) 340. **Gilchrist, J. M.** "The Authorship and Date of the Pastoral Epistles." Diss., University of Manchester, 1967. **Goodspeed, E. J.** *An Introduction to the New Testament.* Chicago: University of Chicago Press, 1937. ———. "Pseudonymity and Pseudepigraphy in Early Christian Literature." In *New. Chapters in New Testament Study.* New York: Macmillan, 1937. 169–88. **Goppelt, L.** *Apostolic and Post-Apostolic Times.* Tr. R. A. Guelich. London: A. & C. Black; Grand Rapids, MI: Baker, 1970. **Grayston, K.**, and **Herdan, G.** "The Authorship of the Pastorals in the Light of Statistical Linguistics." *NTS* 6 (1960) 1–15. **Guthrie, D.** "The Development of the Idea of Canonical Pseudepigrapha in New Testament Criticism." *Vox Evangelica* 1 (1962) 43–59 (reprinted in *The Authorship and Integrity of the New Testament,* ed. K. Aland [London: S.P.C.K., 1965] 14–39). ———. "Early Christian Pseudepigraphy and Its Antecedents." Ph.D. diss., University of London, 1961. ———. *New Testament Introduction.* 3rd ed. Downers Grove, IL: InterVarsity Press, 1973. 583–634, 671–84. ———. "Tertullian and Pseudonymity." *ExpTim* 67 (1956) 341–42. **Haefner, A. E.** "A Unique Source for the Study of Ancient Pseudonymity." *ATR* 16 (1934) 8–15. **Harris, R. J.** "The Background and Significance of the Polemic of the Pastoral Epistles." *JBL* 92 (1973) 549–64.

Harrison, P. N. "Important Hypotheses Reconsidered, III: The Authorship of the Pastoral Epistles." *ExpTim* 47 (1955–56) 77–81. ———. "The Pastoral Epistles and Duncan's Ephesian Theory." *NTS* 2 (1956) 250–61. ———. *Paulines and Pastorals.* London: Villiers, 1964. ———. *Polycarp's Two Epistles to the Philippians.* Cambridge: Cambridge UP, 1936. ———. *The Problem of the Pastoral Epistles.* London: Oxford UP, 1921. **Haykin, M. A. G.** "The Fading Vision: The Spirit and Freedom in the Pastoral Epistles." *EvQ* 57 (1985) 291–305. **Heinrici, C. F. G.** "Zur Charakteristik der literarischen Verhältnisse des zweiten Jahrhunderts." In *Beiträge zur Geschichte und Erklärung des Neuen Testaments,* I. Leipzig: Elemann, 1905. 71–78 (repr. in *Pseudepigraphie in der heidnischen und jüdisch-christlichen Antike,* ed. N. Brox [Darmstadt: Wissenschaftliche Buchgesellschaft, 1977] 74–81). **Hengel, M.** "Anonymität, Pseudepigraphie und 'Literarische Fälschung' in der jüdisch-hellenistischen Literatur." In *Pseudepigrapha* 1, ed. K. von Fritz. Vandoeuvres-Geneva: Hardt, 1972. 231–308. **Hincks, E. Y.** "The Authorship of the Pastoral Epistles." *JBL* 17 (1897) 94–117. **Hitchcock, F. R. M.** "The Pastorals and a Second Trial of Paul." *ExpTim* 41 (1930) 20–23. ———. "Philo and the Pastorals." *Hermathena* 56 (1940) 113–35. ———. "Tests for the Pastorals." *JTS* o.s. 30 (1928–29) 272–79. **Hoffman, T. A.** "Inspiration, Normativeness, Canonicity, and the Unique Sacred Character of the Bible." *CBQ* 44 (1982) 447–69. **James, J. D.** *The Genuineness and Authorship of the Pastoral Epistles.* London: S.P.C.K., 1909. **Jeremias, J.** "Zur Datierung der Pastoralbriefe." *ZNW* 52 (1961) 101–4 (repr. in *Abba* [Göttingen: Vandenhoeck & Ruprecht, 1966] 314–16). **Jewett, R.** *A Chronology of Paul's Life.* Philadelphia: Fortress, 1979. **Johnson, L.** "The Pauline Letters from Caesarea." *ExpTim* 68 (1956) 24–26. **Johnson, L. T.** "II Timothy and the Polemic against False Teachers: A Re-Examination." *JRelS* 6/7 (1978–79) 1–26. ———. *The Writings of the New Testament: An Interpretation.* Philadelphia: Fortress, 1986. **Johnson, P. F.** "The Use of Statistics in the Analysis of the Characteristics of Pauline Writings." *NTS* 20 (1974) 92–100. **Kaestli, J. D.** "Luke-Acts and the Pastoral Epistles: The Thesis of a Common Authorship." In *Luke's Literary Achievement.* Sheffield: Sheffield Academic, 1995. 110–26. **Karavidopoulos, I.** "To problema tes pseudepigraphias." *Deltion Biblikon Meleton* 5 (1977–78) 178–88. **Kenny, A.** *A Stylometric Study of the New Testament.* Oxford: Oxford UP, 1986. **Koch, K.** "Pseudonymous Writing." *IDB* 5:712–14. **Koester, H.** *Introduction to the New Testament,* Vol. 2: *History and Literature of Early Christianity.* Philadelphia: Fortress, 1982. **Kohl, J.** "Verfasser und Entstehungszeit der Pastoralbriefe im Lichte der neueren Kritik." Diss., Vienna, 1962. **Kühn, K. G.** "Das Problem der Pastoralbriefe." *NKZ* 32 (1921) 163–81. **Kümmel, W. G.** *Introduction to the New Testament.* Tr. H. C. Kee. 2nd ed. Nashville: Abingdon, 1975. **Laube, F.** "Falsche Verfasserangaben in neutestamentlichen Schriften: Aspekte der gegenwärtigen Diskussion um die neutestamentliche Pseudepigraphie." *TTZ* 89 (1980) 228–42. **Lea, T. D.** "The Early Christian View of Pseudepigraphic Writings." *JETS* 27 (1984) 65–75. **Lemaire, A.** "Pastoral Epistles: Redaction and Theology." *BTB* 2 (1971) 25–42. **Libby, J. A.** "A Proposed Methodology and Preliminary Data on Statistically Elucidating the Authorship of the Pastoral Epistles." M.Div. thesis, Denver Seminary, 1987. **Lightfoot, J. B.** "The Date of the Pastoral Epistles." In *Biblical Essays.* London: Macmillan, 1893. 397–410. **Lindemann, A.** *Paulus im älten Christentum: Das Bild des Apostels und die Rezeption der paulinischen Theologie in der frühchristlichen Literatur bis Marcion.* BHT 58. Tübingen: Mohr-Siebeck, 1979. **Linnemann, E.** "Echtheitsfragen und Vokabelstatistik." *JEKT* 10 [1996] 87–109. **Macpherson, J.** "Was There a Second Imprisonment of Paul in Rome?" *AJT* 4 (1900) 23–48. **Maier, F.** *Die Hauptproblem der Pastoralbriefe Pauli.* Münster: Aschendorff, 1920. **Maloney, E. C.** "Biblical Authorship and the Pastoral Letters: Inspired and Anonymous." *TBT* 24 (1986) 119–23. **McRay, J.** "The Authorship of the Pastoral Epistles: A Consideration of Certain Adverse Arguments to Pauline Authorship." *ResQ* 7 (1963) 2–18. **Meade, D. G.** *Pseudonymity and Canon: An Investigation into the Relationship of Authorship and Authority in Jewish and Earliest Christian Tradition.* WUNT 39. Tübingen: Mohr-Siebeck, 1986; Grand Rapids, MI: Eerdmans, 1987. **Mealand, D. L.** "Computers in New Testament Research." *JSNT* 33 (1988) 97–115.

————. "The Extent of the Pauline Corpus: A Multivariate Approach." *JSNT* 59 (1995) 61–92. ————. "Positional Stylometry Reassessed: Testing a Seven-Epistle Theory of Pauline Authorship." *NTS* 35 (1989) 266–86. **Metzger, B. M.** *The Canon of the New Testament: Its Origin, Development and Significance.* Oxford: Clarendon, 1987. ————. "Literary Forgeries and Canonical Pseudepigrapha." *JBL* 91 (1972) 3–24. ————. "A Reconsideration of Certain Arguments against the Pauline Authorship of the Pastoral Epistles." *ExpTim* 70 (1958) 91–94. **Metzger, W.** *Die letzte Reise des Apostels Paulus: Beobachtungen und Erwägungen zu seinem Itinerar nach den Pastoralbriefen.* Stuttgart: Calwer, 1976. **Meyer, A.** "Besprechung von Frederik Torm: Die Psychologie der Pseudonymität im Hinblick auf die Literatur des Urchristentums (1932)." *TLZ* 58 (1933) 354–57 (reprinted in *Pseudepigraphie in der heidnischen und jüdisch-christlichen Antike,* ed. N. Brox [Darmstadt: Wissenschaftliche Buchgesellschaft, 1977] 149–53). ————. "Religiöse Pseudepigraphie als ethisch-psychologisches Problem." *ZNW* 35 (1936) 262–79 (reprinted in *Pseudepigraphie in der heidnischen und jüdisch-christlichen Antike,* ed. N. Brox [Darmstadt: Wissenschaftliche Buchgesellschaft, 1977] 90–110). **Michaelis, W.** *Pastoralbriefe und Gefangenschaftsbriefe: Zur Echtheitsfrage der Pastoralbriefe.* NTF 6. Gütersloh: Bertelsmann, 1930. ————. "Pastoralbriefe und Wortstatistik." *ZNW* 28 (1929) 69–76. **Michaelson, S.,** and **Morton, A. Q.** "Last Words: A Test of Authorship for Greek Writers.". *NTS* 18 (1972) 192–208. **Miller, J. D.** *The Pastoral Letters as Composite Documents.* SNTSMS 93. Cambridge: Cambridge UP, 1997. **Mitchell, M. M.** "New Testament Envoys in the Context of Greco-Roman Diplomatic and Epistolary Conventions: The Example of Timothy and Titus." *JBL* 111 (1992) 641–62. **Morton, A. Q.** *Christianity and the Computer.* London: Hodder & Stoughton, 1964. ————. *Literary Detection: How to Prove Authorship and Fraud in Literary Documents.* New York: Harper & Row, 1978. ———— and **McLeman, J. J.** *Paul, the Man and the Myth.* New York: Harper & Row, 1966. **Moule, C. F. D.** "The Problem of the Pastoral Epistles: A Reappraisal." *BJRL* 47 (1964–65) 430–52 (repr. in *Essays in New Testament Interpretation* [Cambridge: Cambridge UP, 1982] 113–32). **Nauck, W.** "Die Herkunft des Verfassers der Pastoralbriefe." Diss., University of Göttingen, 1950. **Neumann, K. J.** *The Authenticity of the Pauline Epistles in the Light of Stylostatistical Analysis.* SBLDS 120. Atlanta: Scholars Press, 1990. **O'Rourke, J. J.** "Some Considerations about the Statistical Analysis of the Pauline Corpus." *CBQ* 35 (1973) 483–90. **Patzia, A. G.** "The Deutero-Pauline Hypothesis: An Attempt at Clarification." *EvQ* 52 (1980) 27–42. **Penny, D. N.** "The Pseudo-Pauline Letters of the First Two Centuries." Ph.D. diss., Emory University, 1980. **Pervo, R. I.** "Romancing an Oft-Neglected Stone: The Pastoral Epistles and the Epistolary Novel." *Journal of Higher Criticism* 1 (1994) 25–47. **Pherigo, L. P.** "Paul's Life after the Close of Acts." *JBL* 70 (1951) 277–84. **Pokorny, P.** "Das theologische Problem der neutestamentliche Pseudepigraphie." *EvT* 44 (1984) 486–96. **Porter, S. E.** "Pauline Authorship and the Pastoral Epistles: Implications for Canon." *BBR* 5 (1995) 105–23. ————. "Pauline Authorship and the Pastoral Epistles: A Response to R. W. Wall's Response." *BBR* 6 (1996) 133–38. **Querdray, G.** "La doctrine des Épîtres pastorales, leur affinités avec l'oeuvre lucanienne: Remarques nouvelles." *Esprit & Vie* 88 (1978) 631–38. **Quinn, J. D.** "𝔓⁴⁶—The Pauline Canon." *CBQ* 36 (1974) 379–85. ————. "The Last Volume of Luke: The Relation of Luke-Acts to the Pastoral Epistles." In *Perspectives on Luke-Acts,* ed. C. H. Talbert. Edinburgh: T. & T. Clark, 1978. 62–75. ————. "Paul's Last Captivity." In *Studia Biblica 1978,* III. *Papers on Paul and Other New Testament Authors.* JSNTSup 3. Sheffield: JSOT, 1980. 289–99. **Ramsay, W. M.** *The Church in the Roman Empire before A.D. 170.* 5th ed. New York: Putnam, 1893. ————. *The Cities and Bishoprics of Phrygia.* 2 vols. Oxford: Clarendon, 1895–97. **Rathke, H.** *Ignatius von Antiochien und die Pastoralbriefe.* TU 99. Berlin: Akademie, 1967. **Reed, J. T.** "Cohesive Ties in 1 Timothy: In Defense of the Epistle's Unity." *Neot* 26 (1992) 131–47. **Reicke, B.** "Caesarea, Rome, and the Captivity Epistles." In *Apostolic History and the Gospel.* FS F. F. Bruce, ed. W. W. Gasque and R. P. Martin. Grand Rapids, MI: Eerdmans, 1970. 277–86. ————. "Chronologie der Pastoralbriefe." *TLZ* 101 (1976) 81–94. **Richards, E. R.** *The Secretary in the Letters of Paul.* WUNT 2/42. Tübingen: Mohr-Siebeck, 1991. **Riesner, R.**

Paul's Early Period: Chronology, Mission Strategy, Theology. Tr. D. Stott. Grand Rapids, MI: Eerdmans, 1998. **Rist, M.** "Pseudepigraphic Refutations of Marcionism." *JR* 32 (1942) 39–62. ———. "Pseudepigraphy and the Early Christians." In *Studies in New Testament and Early Christian Literature.* FS A. P. Wikgren, ed. D. E. Aune. Leiden: Brill, 1972. 75–91. **Roberts, J. W.** "The Bearing of the Use of Particles on the Authorship of the Pastoral Epistles." *ResQ* 2 (1958) 132–37. ———. "The Genuineness of the Pastorals: Some Recent Aspects of the Question." *ResQ* 8 (1965) 104–10. **Robinson, J. A. T.** *Redating the New Testament.* Philadelphia: Fortress, 1976. 67–77. **Robinson, T. A.** "Grayston and Herdan's 'C' Quantity Formula and the Authorship of the Pastoral Epistles." *NTS* 30 (1984) 282–88. **Rogers, P.** "Pastoral Authority Then and Now." *ITQ* 48 (1981) 47–59. ———. "The Pastoral Epistles as Deutero-Pauline." *ITQ* 45 (1978) 248–60. **Rohde, J.** "Pastoralbriefe und Acta Pauli." *SE* 5 (1968) 303–10. **Roller, O.** *Das Formular der paulinischen Briefe.* BWANT 4.6. Stuttgart: Kohlhammer, 1933. **Sanchez, B. J.** "L'autor de les cartes pastorals." *Revista Catalana de Teología* 12 (1987) 55–94. **Santos Otera, A. de.** "The Pseudo-Titus Epistle." In E. Hennecke, *New Testament Apocrypha,* ed. W. Schneemelcher. Vol. 2. Philadelphia: Westminster, 1965. 141–66. **Sayce, A. H.** "Were the Pastoral Epistles Written by S. Paul?" *BSac* 92 [79] (1922) 487–91. **Sedgwick, W.-B.** "The Authorship of the Pastorals." *ExpTim* 30 (1918–19) 230–39. **Shaw, R. D.** "Pseudonymity and Interpretation." In *The Pauline Epistles.* Edinburgh: T. & T. Clark, 1903. 477–86. **Simpson, E. K.** "The Authenticity and Authorship of the Pastoral Epistles." *EvQ* 12 (1940) 289–311. **Sint, J. A.** *Pseudonymität im Altertum: Ihre Formen und ihre Gründe.* Innsbruck: Universitätsverlag Wagner, 1960. **Smith, M.** "Pseudepigraphy in the Israelite Literary Tradition." In *Pseudepigrapha* 1, ed. K. von Fritz. Vandoeuvres-Geneva: Hardt, 1972. 189–215. **Soards, M. L.** "Reframing and Reevaluating the Argument of the Pastoral Epistles toward a Contemporary New Testament Theology." *Perspectives in Religious Studies* 19 (1992) 389–98. **Speyer, W.** "Fälschung, pseudepigraphische freie Erfindung und 'echte religiöse Pseudepigraphie.'" In *Pseudepigrapha* 1, ed. K. von Fritz. Vandoeuvres-Geneva: Hardt, 1972. 333–66. ———. *Die literarische Fälschung im heidnischen und christlichen Altertum: Ein Versuch ihrer Deutung.* Handbuch der Altertumswissenschaft 1/2. Munich: Beck, 1971. ———. "Religiöse Pseudepigraphie und literarische Fälschung im Altertum." *JAC* 8/9 (1965–66) 88–125 (reprinted in *Pseudepigraphie in der heidnischen und jüdisch-christlichen Antike,* ed. N. Brox [Darmstadt: Wissenschaftliche Buchgesellschaft, 1977] 195–263). **Stenger, W.** "Timotheus und Titus als literarische Gestalten: Beobachtungen zur Form und Funktion der Pastoralbriefe." *Kairos* 16 (1974) 252–67. **Stepien, J.** "Problemat autorstwa Listow Pasterskich." *Studia Theologica Varsaviensia* 6 (1968) 157–98. **Strobel, A.** "Schreiben des Lukas? Zum sprachlichen Problem der Pastoralbriefe." *NTS* 15 (1968) 191–210. **Syme, R.** "Fraud and Imposture." *Pseudepigrapha* 1, ed. K. von Fritz. Vandoeuvres-Geneva: Hardt, 1972. 1–17. **Thatcher, T.** "The Relational Matrix of the Pastoral Epistles." *JETS* 38 (1995) 41–45. **Torm, F.** *Die Psychologie der Pseudonymität im Hinblick auf die Literatur des Urchristentums.* Gütersloh: Bertelsmann, 1932 (reprinted in *Pseudepigraphie in der heidnischen und jüdisch-christlichen Antike,* ed. N. Brox [Darmstadt: Wissenschaftliche Buchgesellschaft, 1977] 111–40). ———. "Über die Sprache in den Pastoralbriefen." *ZNW* 18 (1918) 225–43. **Ullmann, W.** "Was heisst deuteropaulinisch?" *SE* 7 [= TU 126] (1982) 513–22. **Van Neste, R. F.** "The Occasion and Purpose of the Epistle to Titus." Thesis, Trinity Evangelical Divinity School, 1996. **Vögtle, A.** "Die Pseudepigraphische Briefschreibung." *BibLeb* 12 (1971) 262–64. **Wake, A. C.** "The Authenticity of the Pauline Epistles." *HibJ* 47 (1948) 50–55. ———. "Sentence-Length Distributions of Greek Authors." *Journal of the Royal Statistical Society* A120 (1957) 331–46. **Walker, W. O., Jr.** "The Timothy-Titus Problem Reconsidered." *ExpTim* 92 (1980) 231–35. **Wall, R. W.** "Pauline Authorship and the Pastoral Epistles: A Response to S. E. Porter." *BBR* 5 (1995) 125–28. **Warren, M. A. C.** "Commentaries on the Pastoral Epistles." *Theology* 63 (1960) 15–19. **Weiss, B.** "Present Status of the Inquiry concerning the Genuineness of the Pauline Epistles." *AJT* 1 (1897) 392–403. **Wilson, R. M.** *The Gnostic Problem.* 2nd ed. London: Mowbray, 1964. **Yule, G. U.** *The Statistical Study of Literary Vocabulary.*

Cambridge: Cambridge UP, 1944. **Zahn, T.** *Introduction to the New Testament.* 3 vols. Tr. from the 3rd German edition, 1909. Repr. Grand Rapids, MI: Kregel, 1953. **Ziesler, J. A.** "Which Is the Best Commentary? XII. The Pastoral Epistles." *ExpTim* 99 (1987) 264–67. **Zmijewski, J.** "Apostolische Paradosis und Pseudepigraphie im Neuen Testament." *BZ* 23 (1979) 161–71. ———. "Die Pastoralbriefe als pseudepigraphische Schriften—Beschreibung, Erklärung, Bewertung." SNTU-A 4 (1979) 97–118.

Preliminary Issues

More than perhaps for any book in the NT, exegesis of the PE is affected by one's critical assumptions. What is the relative value of external as distinct from internal evidence (e.g., witness of the early church fathers versus writing style)? How consistent can any writer be expected to be in terms of style and vocabulary? How much effect can external circumstances have on that style, such as the occasion for writing, the audience, the age of author, or theological concerns? How different does a statement have to be from expressions in the undisputed Pauline letters before it must be labeled "non-Pauline"? Does what is different or what is the same make a greater impression as the PE are compared to Paul's other writings?

These are important issues because the assumptions with which a person begins are, to a large degree, determinative of how one will interpret the PE (cf. Towner, *TynBul* 46 [1995] 287–314). If one is more impressed with the differences between the PE and Paul's other writings (and there are differences), if one sees internal evidence as more significant than external evidence, if one feels that a writer should show a significant and measurable degree of consistency across all his or her writings in terms of both writing style and theological expression, then it will be difficult to accept the self-witness of the PE that they are written by the apostle Paul to Timothy and Titus. However, if one places greater weight on external evidence (and it is considerable) and if it is felt that a writer may vary his or her writing style and theological expression to a large degree, then it is easier to interpret the PE as Pauline. The point is that the real issue is not the text. A comparison of the conclusions of scholars such as Fee and Hanson, or Jeremias and Oberlinner, reveals such a wide divergence that at times it is difficult to believe they are discussing the same text. This results not from the text but from the assumptions that are brought to the text. For example, when the text mentions "myths and genealogies" (1 Tim 1:4), are these Jewish reinterpretations of the OT or are they Gnostic teachings? When the writer says that the law is not for the just but for the unjust (1 Tim 1:9), is this Stoic or Pauline doctrine? In isolation from a context, the statements are capable of either interpretation.

When Pauline authorship is denied and the PE are placed at the end of the first century or beginning of the second, the text, identified by its own testimony as set in Paul's lifetime, is treated as a code for later events in the church, allowing for much speculation among commentators. For example, Meade interprets the rejection of Paul by the Asians (2 Tim 1:15–18) as "a rejection of the Pauline model of discipleship" (*Pseudonymity*, 125), and the mention of Onesiphorus (1:16) "is a clear illustration of the acceptance of that model" (12). The epistles are thought to be addressed to coworkers and not to churches because the interpretation of the Pauline tradition is now only "in the hands of [Paul's] legitimate representatives" (137). The "books" and "parchments" Timothy is to bring (2 Tim 4:13) become "a corpus of literature," "evidence of a canon consciousness," a reminder to "the leaders of his church of the documents which serve as the foundation of their community" (139). Paul becomes an "ideal convert and martyr" (Young, *Theology*, 22) and actually part of the tradition (cf. also Oberlinner, 56–58, 68–69; cf. Wolter, *Paulustradition*). A fragile house of cards is built on conclusions that follow from a subjective framework into which the text is placed.

The methodological assumptions must be understood in order to explain divergent interpretations that may be confusing to a new reader. (For example, to understand the discussion of 1 Tim 3:1–7, one must understand how interpreters are reconstructing early Christian ministry.) In this brief introduction it is not possible to go into great depth concerning methodological issues; rather it is feasible only to outline the position taken in this commentary and to refer to more detailed discussions elsewhere.

In fact the PE are somewhat different from Paul's other writings. The questions are, "How different?" and "Why?" Much of the discussion of the last 150 years has been an attempt to explain the differences by postulating a second-century date and an author other than Paul. If one merely provides a critique of these arguments, one has still not explained why the PE are different. Without a positive explanation for the differences, even if recent discussions are flawed, they remain the only possible explanations. I propose to begin with the starting point of the PE themselves. They claim to be written by Paul and addressed to two associates in order to answer specific questions and provide authority for Timothy's mission (1 Timothy), to provide basic catechetical instruction for a new church (Titus), and to encourage Timothy in his difficult task and to urge him to come to Paul in Rome (2 Timothy). The texts appear to be epistolary and occasional, ad hoc letters written to deal with specific historical issues in Ephesus and Crete (cf. especially Fee, *JETS* 28 [1985] 141–51). The nearly universal witness of 1800 years of church interpretation is that the self-witness of the PE is credible and true. My task will be to recreate a historical setting in Paul's lifetime in which these events may have occurred and to ask if the PE can reasonably be placed within this setting, if the picture given by the PE of the people and history is consistent with what is known, and how the differences between the PE and the other Pauline letters are to be accounted for, and in fact expected, in light of this historical situation. Especially of interest are any references to Timothy, Titus, or Ephesus in early Christian literature. Within the course of this reconstruction I will attempt to show why the differences in the text do not necessarily lead one to the conclusions that have been widely accepted in the last 150 years in scholarship.

The decisions with respect to interpretation involve not so much the details as they do the overall picture. There is no way to prove the details in any interpretation, whether "traditional" or "critical" (which, for lack of better terms, are the expressions I will use to describe the two basic sides in this debate). The question is, "Which reconstruction is generally plausible?" Is it more credible to see Paul writing the PE at the end of his life in a unique historical situation or to see an admirer of Paul, either shortly after his death or toward the end of the first century, perhaps with scraps of authentic material, writing the three letters in an attempt to make Paul's message relevant to the specific issues that arose in that generation? After recounting a historical reconstruction of the events in the PE, I will summarize the critical questions that have been raised but will not present a detailed critique of the those issues. I am not concerned to enter into detailed discussion of critical methodologies, such as statistical analysis of vocabulary or the use of external evidence, but simply wish to assess which approach is more internally coherent and possesses the least number of problems.

In my view, Gordon Fee's commentary is a trumpet call to scholarship to re-evaluate the conclusions that have been held so tightly for some time. A significant number of commentaries in English in the last twenty years hold to Pauline authorship ("authenticity"), and scholarship in general is changing in its opinions. At the 1996 national meeting of the Society of Biblical Literature, symposiums were held in which Pauline authorship was entertained as a possibility, an event that arguably would not have occurred ten years previously. Commentators such as L. T. Johnson are raising again the possibility of Pauline authorship while other specific studies are addressing questions of methodology. It is within this new atmosphere of openness that I offer this introduction to the PE.

In the following reconstruction I will accept the witness of Acts and the PE. While I understand that there are critical issues involved in this approach, my attempt is not to prove every statement in Acts but to reconstruct a general picture and ask if it is plausible. I am especially interested in finding any possible links between Acts and the PE for locations, events, and people.

To provide a framework, I will use the dates of events determined by D. Guthrie (*Introduction*, 1001–10). Again, I realize that these are debatable, but I will use them as a general framework; I am not trying to prove the dates. There are five specific historical events that help to date the events in Acts: (1) the edict of Claudius that expelled the Jews from Rome (Acts 18:2) in A.D. 49–50; (2) Gallio's term as proconsul in Corinth (Acts 18:12–17) in midsummer A.D. 52 or 53 according to an inscription at Delphi; (3) Felix's replacement by Festus as governor in Caesarea in the second half of the 50s; (4) the Feast of Unleavened Bread in A.D. 56–58 (Acts 20:6) when Paul was in Philippi, leaving for Troas and hoping to arrive in Jerusalem by Pentecost (Acts 20:16); and (5) Nero's death in A.D. 68, providing a terminus ad quem since according to one tradition Paul was executed under Nero.

The PE within the Framework of Paul's Life

HISTORICAL RECONSTRUCTION FROM ACTS

A. First Missionary Journey (Acts 13–14)

Paul and Barnabas traveled on an evangelistic mission to Lystra, Iconium, and Derbe (14:6–23), which Acts later identifies as Timothy's home (Acts 16:1) although Timothy himself is not mentioned. When Paul met Timothy on the second missionary journey, Timothy was already a disciple (Acts 16:1–3), but Paul's paternal language (1 Cor 4:15, 17; 1 Tim 1:2) suggests that Paul led Timothy to Christian faith. It is possible that Timothy was one of many converts during the first journey (so Kümmel, *Introduction*, 369), and it was not until the second journey that Timothy stood out to Paul (cf. the prophecies in 1 Tim 1:18). Timothy's mother and grandmother were also believers. Paul's comment that Timothy was acquainted with the Scriptures since childhood (2 Tim 3:15) does not mean that he knew them as a Christian but only that he was raised by a Jewish mother who maintained her ties to Judaism despite her marriage to a Gentile.

B. *Second Missionary Journey (Acts 15:36–18:22)*

Timothy is first mentioned in Acts when Paul's return to Lystra and Derbe with Silas is narrated (Acts 16:1–3).

> And he came also to Derbe and to Lystra. A disciple was there, named Timothy, the son of a Jewish woman who was a believer; but his father was a Greek. He was well spoken of by the brethren at Lystra and Iconium. Paul wanted Timothy to accompany him; and he took him and circumcised him because of the Jews that were in those places, for they all knew that his father was a Greek.

Timothy had been a believer for some time; his reputation had not only gone out through the immediate area, but even the Jews in the areas where Paul and Timothy were to go knew of Timothy, specifically that his father was a Greek. Timothy is presented to the reader of Acts as a new coworker. Paul may have wanted Timothy to accompany him because of his reputation, and prophecies about Timothy had singled him out to Paul, prophecies that he was gifted, probably as an evangelist and a teacher (1 Tim 1:18). But Paul may have been acquainted with Timothy from the first journey as well. Regardless of the amount of contact Paul and Timothy had previously had, Timothy was evidently the clear choice for ministry with Paul. This by itself calls into question the frequent stereotype of Timothy as a young, timid believer in constant need of encouragement.

Timothy accompanied Paul and Silas through Macedonia. Silas was still the major partner; it is Silas who was in prison with Paul in Philippi (Acts 16:25), and only Silas is mentioned in Thessalonica (Acts 17:4, 10). They arrived at Beroea and initially received a warm welcome, but when the Jews from Thessalonica arrived and caused dissension, Paul left for Athens. Silas and Timothy remained (Acts 17:14–15), presumably to instruct the new converts in their faith. This is a significant indication of how Paul sees Timothy's usefulness. Timothy was gifted as a teacher, and Paul had him use his skills in catechetical instruction of new converts. It is also significant that Paul was willing to leave Silas and Timothy in a hostile situation. Once again the suggestion is that Timothy was not a timid person (contra, e.g., Knight, 8).

Paul left Athens before Silas and Timothy arrived and traveled to Corinth (Acts 18:1–17), where the reader meets Aquila and Priscilla. Silas and Timothy reached Corinth (v 5), and they all remained there for over one and a half years. While in Corinth, Paul probably wrote 1 and 2 Thessalonians. Both letters were written by "Paul, Silas, and Timothy" together (1 Thess 1:1; 2 Thess 1:1). In the first epistle, Paul says that he has repeatedly tried to return to Thessalonica but has been prevented (1 Thess 2:17–20). However, while Paul was in Athens he did send Timothy to instruct them (1 Thess 3:1–3):

> Therefore, when we could bear it no longer, we were willing to be left behind at Athens alone, and we sent Timothy, our brother and God's servant in the gospel of Christ, to

establish you in your faith and to exhort you, that no one be moved by these afflictions. You yourselves know that this is to be our lot.

Timothy returned with good news (1 Thess 3:6), and Paul wrote the first epistle to the church. This is another significant statement, confirming the earlier hints about Timothy's character and usefulness. Within the context of afflictions, Paul was willing to send Timothy, this time by himself, to establish and exhort the Thessalonians. By this, Paul probably means that Timothy continued to teach them and to encourage them to live out their Christian faith, even in the face of persecution.

Paul returned to Antioch at the end of the second missionary journey (Acts 18:18–22). Acts reports his first visit to Ephesus, but it was only cursory with a commitment to return "if God wills" (Acts 18:21).

C. Third Missionary Journey (Acts 18:23–21:16)

On this third journey Paul went to Ephesus. We are told of Apollos' ministry there and of his instruction by Priscilla and Aquila. Paul stayed in Ephesus for at least two years and three months (Acts 19:8, 10; later Paul clarifies that he stayed for three years [Acts 20:31]). This is a significant stay for interpretation of the PE since 1 and 2 Timothy were written to Timothy in Ephesus. Ephesus was the main city in Asia Minor, the seat of Roman government and home to the temple of Artemis.

It was probably during this stay in Ephesus that Paul wrote his two letters to the Corinthian church and also to the Roman church. At this time Paul sent Timothy to Corinth:

> Therefore I sent to you Timothy, my beloved and faithful child in the Lord, to remind you of my ways in Christ, as I teach them everywhere in every church. (1 Cor 4:17)

Paul had once again sent Timothy into a difficult situation, to a church where sin was rampant and Paul's authority was under question, a situation similar to that which would develop in Ephesus. Paul always exerted his apostolic authority over his churches. There never was a time when the churches were allowed freely to exercise their charismatic gifts; those gifts were always controlled by the authoritative guidelines established by the apostle. The close emotional bond between Paul and Timothy and Timothy's loyalty to Paul are also evident. Timothy's job was to remind the Corinthian church, an assignment that was again most likely instructional in nature. Paul's conclusion includes these words (1 Cor 16:10–11):

> When Timothy comes, see that you put him at ease among you, for he is doing the work of the Lord, as I am. So let no one despise him. Speed him on his way in peace, that he may return to me; for I am expecting him with the brethren.

It is a somewhat enigmatic passage, but apparently Paul was concerned about how the church would treat Timothy, possibly fearing that the church's feelings toward Paul would be transferred to Timothy (cf. Fee, *1 Corinthians*, 821–23). There is no suggestion that Paul's concern was linked to Timothy's age, as it is in 1 Tim 4:12.

In Paul's second letter to the Corinthian church, he includes Timothy in the salutation (2 Cor 1:1):

Paul, an apostle of Christ Jesus by the will of God, and Timothy our brother.

He later includes Silvanus and Timothy as preachers with him (2 Cor 1:19):

For the Son of God, Jesus Christ, whom we preached among you, Silvanus and Timothy and I, was not Yes and No; but in him it is always Yes.

In his final greetings to the Roman church, Paul also includes mention of Timothy (Rom 16:21):

Timothy, my fellow worker, greets you.

Titus is not mentioned in Acts, but he does play a prominent role in 2 Corinthians. According to the traditional theory, Paul paid a "painful visit" to the Corinthian church (2 Cor 2:1) and wrote a painful letter (2 Cor 2:4), which Titus carried to the church (2 Cor 2:12–13; 7:6). Paul left Ephesus for Troas, hoping to find Titus there. When he did not, he continued on to Macedonia, where he found Titus, who brought an encouraging word about the church's repentance (2 Cor 7:13–15):

And besides our own comfort we rejoiced still more at the joy of Titus, because his mind has been set at rest by you all. For if I have expressed to him some pride in you, I was not put to shame; but just as everything we said to you was true, so our boasting before Titus has proved true. And his heart goes out all the more to you, as he remembers the obedience of you all, and the fear and trembling with which you received him.

Titus had been involved in collecting the offering for the Jerusalem church (8:6) and was to return to the Corinthians to complete the task (2 Cor 8:16–17, 23):

But thanks be to God who puts the same earnest care for you into the heart of Titus. For he not only accepted our appeal, but being himself very earnest he is going to you of his own accord. . . . As for Titus, he is my partner and fellow worker in your service.

Titus was a trusted member of Paul's inner circle. 2 Cor 12:17–18 mentions a visit by Titus to Corinth, but it is difficult to identify the precise event (cf. 2 Cor 8:6, 16–24; Martin, *2 Corinthians*, 447–48):

Did I take advantage of you through any of those whom I sent to you? I urged Titus to go, and sent the brother with him. Did Titus take advantage of you? Did we not act in the same spirit? Did we not take the same steps?

The only other references to Titus are in Paul's letter to him and in 2 Tim 4:10. Paul asks Titus to leave Crete and meet him in Nicopolis for the winter (Titus 3:12). Possibly Titus arrived and either went on to Dalmatia before winter set in or stayed for winter and spring and then went on to Dalmatia (2 Tim 4:10; see below).

We are told that Paul decided to travel to Macedonia and Achaia, to Jerusalem, and hopefully someday to Rome (Acts 19:21). In anticipation he sent Timothy and Erastus on ahead (2 Tim 4:20). Acts then records the riot with Demetrius the silversmith and Paul's trip to Macedonia (Acts 20:1). Paul spent three months in Greece (20:2–3) and left again for Macedonia. Evidently the group traveled together as far as Philippi (20:1–6), but then Timothy, Tychicus, and Trophimus (among others) went ahead to Troas. Paul and at least Luke (a "we" section of Acts) later sailed to Troas.

They eventually sailed to Miletus, the port city of Ephesus. Paul wanted to arrive in Jerusalem by Pentecost, so instead of spending time in Ephesus he called for the elders of the church (Acts 20:15–17). This is a tremendously significant passage because it describes many similarities to the Ephesian situation that are evident years later when Paul writes the PE (Acts 20:18b–35):

> "You yourselves know how I lived among you all the time from the first day that I set foot in Asia, serving the Lord with all humility and with tears and with trials which befell me through the plots of the Jews; how I did not shrink from declaring to you anything that was profitable, and teaching you in public and from house to house, testifying both to Jews and to Greeks of repentance to God and of faith in our Lord Jesus Christ. And now, behold, I am going to Jerusalem, bound in the Spirit, not knowing what shall befall me there; except that the Holy Spirit testifies to me in every city that imprisonment and afflictions await me. But I do not account my life of any value nor as precious to myself, if only I may accomplish my course and the ministry which I received from the Lord Jesus, to testify to the gospel of the grace of God. And now, behold, I know that all you among whom I have gone about preaching the kingdom will see my face no more. Therefore I testify to you this day that I am innocent of the blood of all of you, for I did not shrink from declaring to you the whole counsel of God. Take heed to yourselves and to all the flock, in which the Holy Spirit has made you guardians, to feed the church of the Lord which he obtained with his own blood. I know that after my departure fierce wolves will come in among you, not sparing the flock; and from among your own selves will arise men speaking perverse things, to draw away the disciples after them. Therefore be alert, remembering that for three years I did not cease night or day to admonish every one with tears. And now I commend you to God and to the word of his grace, which is able to build you up and to give you the inheritance among all those who are sanctified. I coveted no one's silver or gold or apparel. You yourselves know that these hands ministered to my necessities, and to those who were with me. In all things I have shown you that by so toiling one must help the weak, remembering the words of the Lord Jesus, how he said, 'It is more blessed to give than to receive.'"

There are so many hints in this passage concerning the later Ephesian situation reflected in the PE that either Paul was prophetic or the PE were written in light of Acts (or vice versa): (1) Paul's defense of his personal conduct and ministry suggests the coming attack on his authority (1 Tim 1:1, 12–17). (2) Paul's earlier trials were caused by the Jews, and the heresy mentioned in the PE is one of "Jewish myths" (Titus 1:14). (3) Paul's teaching was in public from house church to house church; Timothy's opponents worked in the privacy of homes and upset entire house churches (2 Tim 3:6). (4) Paul proclaimed the gospel to Jews and Gentiles alike, behavior expected of the apostle to the Gentiles, whom the opponents were excluding from their prayers (1 Tim 2:1–7). (5) Paul was aware that as he went to Jerusalem he would be greeted by afflictions, just as he calls Timothy to embrace suffering as a servant of Jesus Christ (2 Tim 1:8). (6) Rather than be troubled by the coming afflictions, Paul's only concern was to accomplish the task given to him by the Lord, which was to testify to the gospel of grace (1 Tim 1:12–17), and not to count his own life as precious. 2 Tim 4:6–8 contains Paul's summation that he has been faithful to this charge, and his life is now to be poured out as an offering as he waits for his crown of righteousness. (7) The overseers were to care for the "church of God," a theme throughout the PE (especially 1 Tim 1:4; 3:1–7, 15). (8) There is an emphasis on the atonement of Jesus, as opposed to the role of the law (1 Tim 2:5–6; cf. 1:8–11). (9) Paul prophesied that dissension would arise from within the church, not from outside the church (as was often the case for Paul), and that the dissenters would be partially successful. It is especially significant that this prophecy was made within the context of Paul's charge to the overseers since in the PE the problem stems from heretical teaching by some overseers and the inability of other overseers to teach truth and refute the error (see *Comment* on 1 Tim 3:2). The prophecy that they will teach "perverse" things and not just error leads into Paul's condemnation of the perversity of the Ephesian opponents in the PE and their teaching of demonic doctrines (1 Tim 4:1), which were successful in upsetting entire house churches (Titus 1:11). (10) Paul spent more time in the Ephesian church than perhaps anywhere else in his ministry. It became an established church, and many of the problems that later developed were typical not of new churches but of established churches, accounting for the unique nature of the Ephesian problem and Paul's solutions (e.g., 1 Tim 5:19–20). (11) Paul affirmed that the "word of his grace" was able to "build you up," and Paul's encouragement to Timothy is to immerse himself in the gospel, which will save both himself and his hearers (1 Tim 4:16). (12) Paul's final citation of Jesus' commendation on giving stands in contrast to the later Ephesian opponents, who teach for greed and profit (1 Tim 6:5). (13) The one statement that is somewhat problematic is that the Ephesians will not see him again (vv 25, 38), in light of Paul's later desire to visit Timothy in Ephesus (1 Tim 3:14; but see *Comment* on this verse). There is too much overlap between this passage in Acts and the situation in the PE, however, not to see some connection.

After his meeting with the Ephesian elders, Paul traveled to Tyre, Ptolemais, and Caesarea. He expressed his willingness to die (Acts 21:13; cf. 2 Tim 4:6–8), and eventually traveled to Jerusalem.

D. Imprisonment (Acts 21:17–28:31, A.D. 58–62/63)

The temple riot came about because some Jews thought Paul brought the Gentile Trophimus into the temple and defiled it. Following this came the two-year imprisonment in Caesarea and two-year open house arrest in Rome. One of the points Acts makes during this time is that Paul was innocent, leaving the reader with the expectation that Paul would be declared innocent at his trial, the gospel vindicated, and Paul released (Acts 25:20, 25, 32; 26:32). This is Paul's own attitude expressed in his epistle to the Philippians (Phil 1:19, 25–26; 2:24).

Paul also speaks highly of Timothy to the Philippians:

I hope in the Lord Jesus to send Timothy to you soon, so that I may be cheered by news of you. I have no one like him, who will be genuinely anxious for your welfare. They all look after their own interests, not those of Jesus Christ. But Timothy's worth you know, how as a son with a father he has served with me in the gospel. I hope therefore to send him just as soon as I see how it will go with me; and I trust in the Lord that shortly I myself shall come also. (Phil 2:19–24)

Timothy was not only part of Paul's inner circle, but he was unique: "I have no one like him." Timothy is also listed as a coauthor in Phil 1:1 ("Paul and Timothy, servants of Christ Jesus"), Col 1:1 ("Paul, an apostle of Christ Jesus by the will of God, and Timothy our brother"), and Phlm 1:1 ("Paul, a prisoner for Christ Jesus, and Timothy our brother").

Earlier Paul's intentions had been to travel west to Spain (Rom 15:24, 28), but evidently during his imprisonment he had decided he also (or rather) wanted to travel east (Phlm 22). Guthrie (1006) dates the imprisonments in Jerusalem in A.D. 56, and the Caesarean in A.D. 56–58.

The only other mention of Timothy in the NT outside the PE is in Heb 13:23:

You should understand that our brother Timothy has been released, with whom I shall see you if he comes soon.

This is most likely the same Timothy of the PE (cf. Bruce, *Hebrews*, 390–91). Because of the authorship and dating issues of Hebrews, and the succinctness of the comment, this imprisonment cannot be placed in a specific historical context with confidence (but cf. F. F. Bruce, *ANRW* II, 25/4 [1987] 3501 n. 43). It is interesting that there seems to be little overlap between Paul's captivity letter to the Ephesians and the situation present in the PE.

HISTORICAL RECONSTRUCTION FROM THE PE

A. *Release from Imprisonment*

Some historical sources suggest that the implication of Acts and Paul's expectation came true, that he was found innocent and released (A.D. 61–63). The ending of Acts suggests that Paul had not yet gone to trial, and many have concluded that Paul went to trial, was found innocent, and was released (see discussions in Bernard, xxi–xxxiv; Spitta, *Geschichte*, 106–7; Zahn, *Introduction* 2:4–10, 54–84; Ramsay, *St. Paul the Traveller*, 356–60; Hitchcock, *ExpTim* 41 [1930] 20–23; Pherigo, *JBL* 70 [1951] 277–84; Schlatter, *Church*, 232–39; Bruce, *New Testament History*, 361–67; Brox, 29; on the historical reconstruction, see Spicq, 1:121–46). Harnack was perhaps optimistic when he said Paul's release was "a certain fact of history" (*gesicherte Tatsache;* see *Geschichte*, "Note 46," II:1.240n), but a strong case can be made for his release (see below). There are several reasons that Paul could have been acquitted, such as the possibility that his accusers did not appear in court (cf. Cadbury, "Note XXVI: Roman Law and the Trial of Paul," in *The Beginnings of Christianity: Part 1. The Acts of the Apostles*, ed. F. J. Foakes Jackson and K. Lake [New York: Macmillan, 1933] 5:297–338; Pherigo, *JBL* 70 [1951] 271–84; Sherwin-White, *Roman Society*, 99–119; Bruce, *New Testament History*, 361–64; Marshall, *Acts*, 426). While there is no way to prove this scenario, neither can it be proven that Paul died in this one Roman imprisonment.

Clement was bishop of Rome, the traditional location of Paul's death under Nero, thirty years after Paul's death, and he shows awareness of details in Paul's life not recorded in Acts (*1 Clem.* 5:5–7 [LCL tr.]).

> Through jealousy and strife Paul showed the way to the prize of endurance; seven times he was in bonds, he was exiled, he was stoned, he was a herald both in the East and in the West [ἐν τῇ δύσει], he gained the noble fame of his faith, he taught righteousness to all the world, and when he had reached the limits of the West [καὶ ἐπὶ τὸ τέρμα τῆς δύσεως ἐλθών] he gave his testimony before the rulers, and thus passed from the world and was taken up into the Holy Place,—the greatest example of endurance.

Clement's position in Rome makes this tradition significant; his church could still have had members who witnessed Paul's final imprisonment and death. "Limits of the West" most likely is Spain (James, *Genuineness*, 32; Zahn, *Introduction* 2:68–73; J. Weiss, *History,* 390; Holtz, 18; Brox, 30). It could also be Rome from the standpoint of someone in the east (Harrison, *Problem,* 107), but this is unlikely since Clement is writing from Rome. Lightfoot argues, "It is incredible that a writer living in the metropolis and centre of power and civilization could speak of it [i.e., Rome] as 'the extreme west,' and this at a time when many eminent Latin authors and statesmen were or had been natives of Spain, and when the commercial and passenger traffic with Gades was intimate and constant" (*Apostolic Fathers,* part 1, vol. 2, p. 31; also Harnack, *Geschichte,* "Note 46," 2:240n). Ellis ("Traditions") says that, as far as he can tell, no contemporary Roman writing ever refers to Rome as "the West," citing Josephus (*Ag. Ap.* 1.67), Tacitus (*Hist.* 4.3), and Strabo (*Geog.* 1.1.8; 1.2.1; 1.4.6; 2.1.1; 2.4.4; 3.1.2). Lightfoot continues by summarizing different translations of the phrase and concludes, "Such attempts are a strong testimony to the plain inference which follows from the passage simply interpreted."

Based on the work of Lightfoot, it is generally acknowledged that the most natural meaning of τὸ τέρμα τῆς δύσεως, "the limits of the West," is as a reference to the pillars of Hercules at the Straits of Gibraltar, based on references in Strabo (2.1.4; 3.1.5) and Velleius Paterculus (1.2; citations in Lightfoot, *Apostolic Fathers,* part 1, vol. 2, p. 30; cf. also E. Dubowy, *Klemens von Rom über die Reise Pauli nach Spanien,* BibS(F) 19.3 [Freiburg im Breisgau: Herder, 1914]). But even if the reference to Spain is disputed, the tradition is a strong witness to Paul's release after the events in Acts 28.

The Muratorian Canon (c. A.D. 180) states the following:

> Luke described briefly "for" most excellent Theophilus particular [things], which happened in his presence, as he also evidently relates indirectly the death of Peter [?] and also Paul's departure from the city as he was proceeding to Spain. (Knight, 18, citing D. J. Theron, *Evidence of Tradition* [Grand Rapids, MI: Baker, 1958] 109 [§96])

The Latin is difficult in the reference to Spain, but it does attest to Paul's Roman release. As with Clement, this tradition also comes from Rome. Eusebius (fourth century) adds the following:

> Tradition has it that after defending himself the Apostle was again sent on the ministry of preaching, and coming a second time to the same city suffered martyrdom under

Nero. During this imprisonment he wrote the second Epistle to Timothy, indicating at the same time that his first defense had taken place and that his martyrdom was at hand. . . . We have said this to show that Paul's martyrdom was not accomplished during the sojourn in Rome that Luke describes. (*Hist. Eccl.* 2.22.7–8; LCL tr.)

Many writers after Eusebius show an awareness of the same tradition (Knight, 19, lists Athanasius, Epiphanius, Jerome, Theodore of Mopsuestia, Pelagius, Theodoret; cf. references in Lightfoot, "St. Paul's History," 425–26). Some argue that the tradition in the Muratorian Canon is based on the hope expressed by Paul in Rom 15:24, 28 (Harrison, *Problem*, 107–8; id., *NTS* [1956] 250–61), but the Eusebius tradition speaks only of two imprisonments, not of Spain (cf. Zahn, *Introduction* 2:74), and therefore is not open to this specific critique. It is especially significant that there is no contradictory tradition asserting that Paul died at the end of his first imprisonment (see Zahn, *Introduction* 2:74). Kümmel argues that the Muratorian Canon includes references to Peter's death as well as Paul's, which could not be inferred from Rom 15, suggesting that this is a historical tradition concerning Paul's release (*Introduction*, 377).

Zahn (*Introduction* 3:63) cites the *Acts of Peter* (A.D. 180–90) in which Paul has two imprisonments with a visit to Rome between them and which also relates the death of Peter, but there are problems with the credibility of the tradition (cf. Guthrie, *Introduction*, 624 n. 2):

And when he had fasted for three days and asked of the Lord what was right for him, Paul then saw a vision, the Lord saying to him, "Paul, arise and be a physician to those who are in Spain." So when he had related to the brethren what God had enjoined, without doubting he prepared to leave the city. (Hennecke, *New Testament Apocrypha* 2:279; Latin text in Bernard, xxx)

Arguments both for and against a release, as far as Acts is concerned, are arguments from silence. If the historical allusions in the PE contradicted the teaching of Acts, then the historical argument would be more significant. But since the historical framework of the PE does not contradict Acts, the silence in Acts is not an argument against the PE (so also Spicq, 1:170).

B. 1 Timothy

From this point on, the chronology becomes especially difficult to reconstruct. There are five major events: (1) We know that Timothy was with Paul during the Roman imprisonment. Either before the trial or after the trial, Paul sent Timothy to Ephesus to deal with the Ephesian heresy, which by now was in full force (1 Tim 1:3–7). (2) It is possible that Paul went west to Spain as he had intended according to his letter to the Romans and as is indicated in the church traditions noted above. (3) Paul and Titus took a missionary journey to Crete (Titus 1:5–16). (4) Paul also wanted to go east, especially to Ephesus to help Timothy (1 Tim 3:14–15; 4:13). (5) Timothy met Paul somewhere while Paul was on his way to Macedonia, and Timothy returned to Ephesus (1 Tim 1:3). This verse does not say that Paul was in Ephesus during this meeting, and in light of 1 Tim 3:14 it seems doubtful that he was. This may also have been the tearful parting mentioned in 2 Tim 1:4. Timothy returned to Ephesus, and the first epistle is an encouragement for him to stay and contend with the situation there.

When did Paul go to Spain (if he did), go to Crete, and travel toward Macedonia during which time he met Timothy? Did Paul write first to Titus or to Timothy? How quickly after Paul's first letter to Timothy did he write the second? There is no way to know. Paul had never preached in Crete, and yet his letter to Titus suggests a missionary journey of significant length in Crete. The church there was newly established, was quite visible, and had many locations (Titus 1:11), suggesting a large number of converts. The letter also shows that Paul was aware of the specific issues in the church. Sufficient time had passed for opponents to be somewhat successful (Titus 1:11). If Paul's desire to appoint elders (Titus 1:5) followed the pattern established on his first missionary journey (Acts 14:23), the letter was sent soon after Paul's missionary trip. Both epistles to Timothy are connected to a region east of Rome. Paul was on his way to Macedonia when he met Timothy (1 Tim 1:3), but evidently Paul was headed elsewhere and so Timothy returned alone, waiting for Paul's eventual arrival.

The following is hypothetical, but it is consistent with what little data we do have. If Paul did travel to Spain, it is possible he went there after . is release. If he went to Crete first, or to some other location that may have taken him through Macedonia where he met Timothy (1 Tim 1:3), he would have had to retrace his steps, go on to Spain, and then return to Crete and Macedonia. If he went first to Spain, the time constraints suggest he was only there for a short time. When he returned, he could have gone to Crete with Titus. He could also have gone through Macedonia, and Timothy could have left Ephesus to meet him on the way, perhaps to talk about the problems in Ephesus but especially (one would think) to see his spiritual father for the first time since Paul's release from imprisonment. If this is the tearful visit referred to in 2 Tim 1:4, it is possible that this was Timothy's first visit after Paul's release. It must have been emotionally difficult for Timothy to have been away from Paul during that time. Sometime after this visit, Paul wrote the first epistle to Timothy.

Inferences from 1 Timothy. There is much in this reconstruction that helps us understand the occasion and purpose of the first epistle to Timothy.

(1) Paul's prophecy had come true. People from within the congregation had risen up in opposition to Paul and the gospel (Acts 20:30). Their teaching was loosely based on Jewish mythical reinterpretation of the law and its genealogies, with probably a strong influence of Hellenistic thought and possibly proto-gnostic error. They had divorced doctrine from behavior, paving the way for licentiousness and greed. They had succumbed to the teaching of demons. While the teaching appears to have some similarities to what was happening in nearby Colossae, it does appear to be unusual. It is natural to assume that in this situation Paul's vocabulary, and perhaps even his method of argumentation, can be expected to be different from other situations such as those caused by Judaizers coming from outside the church as in Galatia. (See below for a detailed discussion of the heresy.)

(2) The issues were not of the type expected of a new church. Like the church in Corinth, the Ephesian church had the benefit of Paul's extended ministry and teaching. It had time to develop a structure of overseers and deacons. Yet, despite all of Paul's teaching, the overseers had not sufficiently learned the gospel

to refute the heresy. Like Timothy, they would have known Paul's theology; but more than simply knowing theology is important, and that was the focus of what Paul would tell them. It is why he told Timothy to demand that the false teachers simply stop what they were doing. By now they should have known better.

(3) Timothy was not a pastor, or elder, or bishop of the Ephesian church. He was an itinerant apostolic "delegate" (Jeremias, 1–2), doing what he had often done for Paul. He was sent into a difficult situation where true teaching and loyalty to Paul were needed (cf. Mitchell, *JBL* 111 [1992] 641–42). He stood outside the church structure described in 1 Tim 3 and 5 and had no title (cf. Brox, *BZ* 13 [1969] 87–88; Kümmel, *Introduction*, 381). Spicq (1:65–66) sees the beginning of a formal hierarchy, in which Paul's apostolic office (given by Christ) was extended as he delegated some of his authority to Timothy and Titus, who in turn delegated their authority to subordinate ministries. This seems, however, to be anachronistic. Timothy and Titus came with Paul's authority and were to appoint leaders of good moral character who would be faithful to the gospel message. These appointees did not stand above the church but were part of it.

(4) Timothy was a long-time friend and trusted coworker of Paul's. He was repeatedly sent into difficult situations, sometimes alone, to teach people and to maintain a loyalty to Paul and the gospel. This fact has significant implications. (a) Timothy knew Paul's theology and did not need to be taught. Much, if not all, of the teaching in the PE is directed toward the church. (b) Even though the bulk of 1 Timothy is intended for the Ephesian church, it is still a personal letter in style. As is expected of any personal letter, the vocabulary, style, and subject matter are different from more formal letters written to churches as a whole (so also Hort, *Christian Ecclesia*, 171–72; Lightfoot, "Additional Note," 413). Even Dibelius-Conzelmann caution against "drawing conclusions as to authenticity or imitation" because "there are no other Pauline letters addressed to a single person (in Phlm we find the plural 'to you' {ὑμῖν})" (14). This is why 1 Timothy starts on a note of authority, why there is no greeting as expected, why Paul discusses topics that may sound unusual when writing to a friend (e.g., 1 Tim 1:12–17; 2:7), and why he ends with a greeting to "you" (plural). This makes 1 Timothy essentially different from 2 Timothy and to a lesser degree from Titus.

The often-painted picture of Timothy as a weak, timid person is not supported by the evidence. He was Paul's "first lieutenant," someone Paul felt comfortable sending into difficult situations, as he did repeatedly throughout Acts (see above). Paul's exhortation is not to be seen as a castigation of Timothy for some supposed failure but as encouragement in an extremely difficult situation, and also as a statement of authority to be understood by the Ephesian church (see especially *Comment* on 2 Tim 1:6–7; also 1 Tim 1:18; 4:6, 12–16; 2 Tim 1:8; 2:1, 7).

(5) The first letter to Timothy is not a manual written to an anonymous church situation (contra the position of scholars like Kümmel, *Introduction*, 367, 384). When Paul writes about how to conduct oneself in the house of God, it is the Ephesian house of God with which he is immediately concerned. This letter is an ad hoc document addressing specific issues. If certain themes common elsewhere in Paul are absent in the PE, it means nothing more than that they were not relevant to the situations addressed. Quinn has argued that the addressees of the PE are types: "Titus and Timothy in the PE are less historical individuals than paradigmatic persons, models with which the new public is expected to identify"

(8; cf. 9, 14, 15, 19, 21). However, Quinn does not give enough attention to the frequent use of personal comments and historical references in the text, evidence that supports the conclusion that the PE are authentic, historical documents. As a hermeneutical point, however, it may be emphasized that ad hoc letters, though written to specific circumstances to deal with specific issues, can incorporate lasting principles (cf. G. W. Knight, III, "The Scriptures Were Written for Our Instruction," *JETS* 39 [1996] 3–13).

While issues of church governance do play a significant and visible role in 1 Timothy (2:11–3:13; 5:17–25), these are found in only 27 out of 113 verses. There are many other topics Paul covers that are relevant to the specific historical situation: law and grace, the scope of the offer of salvation, personal encouragement to Timothy, widows (which is not a leadership or structural issue), slaves, false teaching, and the rich. This is also true of Paul's letter to Titus. Only 5 verses (Titus 1:5–9) out of 46 deal with church leadership. In the second letter to Timothy only 2:2 deals with leadership. That means only 33 verses out of 242 in the PE deal specifically with church structure (13.6%), and almost all of them are in 1 Timothy. But even these 33 verses are ad hoc in that they are addressing specific historical issues stemming from poor leadership. As Fee says (7), the specific problems in Ephesus are both the "occasion and the purpose," not just the occasion for writing.

In the relatively few verses that speak of overseers and deacons, Paul's emphasis is not on church structure. There are not even any duties assigned (with only a few implied—teaching, oversight, service). The emphasis is on the person's character, conduct, understanding of the gospel, and ability to explain and defend the true gospel. As Fee points out, many different forms of church governance claim support from the PE: "If the Pastor intended with these letters to set the church in order, he seems not altogether to have succeeded" (21).

(6) There are therefore several reasons that Paul wrote the first epistle to Timothy: (a) to encourage Timothy to stay on at Ephesus and deal with the significant and difficult issues that had arisen; (b) to provide authoritative instruction on how the household of God was to conduct itself in case Paul delayed in coming; and (c) to combat directly the opponents and their teaching and to remind Timothy of how he was to conduct himself and what he was to teach. The underlying purpose was then to encourage Timothy in his work but also to transfer Paul's authority to Timothy in his fight against the opponents.

C. Titus

From the historical scenario painted above it can be seen generally where this letter fits in. It assumes that Titus and Paul made a missionary journey to Crete, which does not fit anywhere within the chronology of Acts. It must therefore have occurred after the events of Acts 28 and before the writing of 2 Timothy when Paul was again in prison. It seems unlikely that it took place after Paul's journey to Spain if in fact Paul went to Spain.

Paul says that he "left" Titus in Crete (Titus 1:5), suggesting that Paul had been with him. There were Cretans in Jerusalem at Pentecost (Acts 2:11), so it is possible Paul found a church in Crete when he arrived. There are several indications that the church was young: (1) Paul appointed elders but not deacons (Titus

1:5); the pattern in Acts suggests that deacons were appointed only after the church began to grow (Acts 6:1–6). (2) Titus is not told to remove offending overseers but merely to appoint them (Titus 1:5). (3) Paul does not repeat the injunction that an overseer cannot be a recent convert (cf. 1 Tim 3:6). (4) The majority of the epistle is basic catechesis appropriate for young converts, drawing out the day-to-day implications of the two salvific sayings around which the epistle is formed (Titus 2:11–14; 3:3–8). (5) The teaching of the opponents, while successful (Titus 1:11), does not play as significant a role here as it does in 1 Timothy, suggesting that the problems were not as advanced.

There are also indications that Paul's ministry in Crete was somewhat extensive: (1) There was sufficient time for the opponents to experience some success (Titus 1:11). (2) Titus was to appoint overseers in "every" city (1:5). (3) If the overseer's children must be believers (1:6), there was sufficient time to establish a pool of eligible overseers who not only would model the qualities enumerated in Titus 1:5–9 but whose children could have become believers. However, depending on what dates are accepted for Paul's first release and his second imprisonment, there is probably not enough time to postulate a missionary journey extending beyond a year.

After Titus had spent some time in Crete, during the summer months Paul sent Zenas and Apollos with the epistle to Titus. They were continuing on (home to Alexandria?), and the letter asks Titus to meet Paul (cf. 2 Tim 4:21), in this case at Nicopolis for the winter. Paul is not sure whom he will send to replace Titus, Artemas or Tychicus (Titus 3:12–13). Tychicus eventually traveled to Ephesus, possibly to replace Timothy so he could come to Rome (2 Tim 4:12); presumably Artemas replaced Titus. Paul does not identify his own location, but since he tells Titus that he has decided to winter "there" (Nicopolis, 3:12) and not "here," the suggestion is that Paul was elsewhere. If Paul wrote this letter and the first letter to Timothy at the same time, there is a chance he was somewhere in Macedonia (see below on 2 Timothy). Paul tells Timothy that Titus had gone on to Dalmatia (2 Tim 4:10), so presumably Titus made it by winter. Either he spent the winter with Paul and went on to Dalmatia the next summer, or for some reason he decided not to stay (because of Paul's second arrest?) and continued on. Traveling from Nicopolis to Dalmatia did not require sea travel, so the trip could have been made during the winter months. According to tradition, Titus eventually returned to Crete as its bishop (Eusebius *Hist. Eccl.* 3.4.6).

Inferences from Titus. There are similarities between the first epistle to Timothy and the epistle to Titus. (1) The style and vocabulary are similar. (2) Both show a concern for proper leadership, giving many of the same qualifications. But this is a relatively minor concern in Titus; although listed first, these instructions occupy only five verses out of forty-six. (3) The descriptions of the opponents in Titus 1:14 and 2:9 sound much like those in 1 Timothy (while emphasizing the Jewishness of the teaching). (4) The charge to rebuke the opponents in Titus parallels Paul's comments to Timothy. (5) Titus stands outside the formal church structure as does Timothy; he was not a Cretan pastor, overseer, or bishop. (6) Since Titus was Paul's coworker, a friend, and an individual, Paul writes to him differently from the way he would write to a church, especially a young church. (7) The letter is private in form but public in intent. (8) The letter is not a general church manual but is addressed to a specific historical situation. If Paul wrote

Titus on the heels of 1 Timothy (or vice versa), the similarity of language and thought could be explained. Speculation may also be offered on how the opponents or their teaching migrated to Crete. Since the problem in Ephesus came from within the church, it is doubtful these false teachers also traveled to Crete, about three hundred miles across the sea. The similar problems in Colossae may suggest some contact but also the general influence of Hellenistic/Jewish/protognostic thought.

On the other hand, there are significant differences between 1 Timothy and Titus, which have often been overlooked: (1) The opponents play a minor role in Titus. (2) The bulk of Titus is basic catechesis, instruction especially appropriate for new believers. The problems in Crete are those expected of a young church in a pagan environment. Paul wants their salvation from lives of sin (Titus 1:12–13; 2:12; 3:3) to show itself in good deeds (Titus 2:7, 14; 3:9, 14). (3) Elders are to be appointed, not rebuked (Titus 1:5). (4) Titus was perhaps older and less prone to discouragement than was Timothy; his personal relationship to Paul may also not have been as intimate as Timothy's (although this would be an argument from silence). (5) There is not the same sense of urgency in confronting the opponents (except 1:11). In fact, if Titus were viewed in isolation from 1 Timothy, the impression would be that the problems resulted from the conversion of Hellenistic Jews; Titus 1:10–11, 13–14, and 3:9 are the only statements that clearly connect the problem in Crete with that in Ephesus. (6) It appears that the problems arose from outside sources—aberrant Judaism, Cretan culture—and not from within as was the case in Ephesus. Kümmel is therefore wrong when he states that the PE "presuppose the same false teachers, the same organization, and entirely similar conditions in the community" (*Introduction*, 367).

There are two basic reasons for Paul's writing to Titus: (1) The first was to ask Titus to remain in Crete and care for the young church for the time being. This care included organizational issues, such as appointing qualified leadership (only five out of forty-six verses) and withstanding the opponents who are already experiencing success. Titus was also to teach the Cretan church basic catechesis, behavior and beliefs that were derived from the truth of the two core theological formulations around which the epistle is built, Titus 2:11–14 and 3:4–7. One suspects that much of the teaching was intended for the church, not Titus, who already knew it, and as validation of Titus's authority (although this is not as pronounced as in 1 Timothy). The Cretan church did not apparently have the advantage of Paul's extended teaching ministry, as did the Ephesians, and the proverbial character of the Cretans (Titus 1:12) was proving itself true; therefore, Paul had to emphasize more of the basic teaching of theology, how conversion must lead to a life of obedience. (2) The second reason for writing was to ask Titus to encourage Zenas and Apollos, the carriers of the letter, on their way and to urge Titus to winter with Paul in Nicopolis when a replacement arrived.

It is not possible to determine whether Paul wrote 1 Timothy or Titus first. Quinn points out that while the canonical ordering of Paul's letters seems to be based on length, 1 Timothy is longer than 2 Thessalonians, suggesting that the PE and Philemon form their own collection of Pauline letters addressed to individuals (*Titus*, 3, 7; "Last Volume," 63–64, 72). Quinn's argument for the priority of Titus—Titus has a lengthy prologue, appropriate for a collection of letters; themes are introduced in Titus (cf. Doty, *CBQ* 31 [1969] 192–98)—assumes his hypothesis of a collection of letters to individuals and also does not take into account the significant differences between Titus and 2 Timothy. The Muratorian Canon's order—Titus, 1 Timothy, 2 Timothy—is probably an attempt to place 2 Timothy last as Paul's last letter. I will discuss 1 Timothy first because it presents a fuller treatment of the historical issues. All that I am comfortable saying is that the similarity of language between 1 Timothy and Titus may suggest that they were written at approximately the same time.

D. 2 Timothy

Paul was back in prison in Rome (2 Tim 1:8, 17; 2:9) when he wrote his second letter to Timothy. Throughout the epistle there are comments that suggest a historical scenario, but part of the problem of reconstruction is that we do not know if the events Paul alludes to in the letter occurred before or after his arrest. Most of the historical material is in 2 Tim 1:8, 15–18, 2:9; 4:6–21.

References are made to Rome, Thessalonica, Galatia, Dalmatia, Ephesus, Troas, Corinth, and Miletus, suggesting travels in Macedonia and on the western coast of Asia Minor. The following is a possible scenario. It is possible that Paul never reached Nicopolis. He may have been arrested en route and taken to Rome. Instead of staying in Nicopolis, Titus continued on to Dalmatia. It was late summer, and Paul wanted Timothy to come quickly. If there does not seem to be sufficient time for all this to have occurred, then it is possible that Paul did reach Nicopolis for the winter, and Titus spent the winter with him, departing for Dalmatia in the spring. Paul, delayed by the winter, still desired to visit Timothy and Ephesus and got as far as Miletus before being arrested. The name Alexander is Ephesian, and he may have instigated the arrest as a personal vendetta because Paul had excommunicated him (1 Tim 1:20; 2 Tim 4:14). Trophimus became ill before or after the arrest and stayed behind at Miletus. Paul saying "I left" (2 Tim 4:20) shows that he was in Miletus with Trophimus. (Most likely not much time had elapsed between Trophimus's illness and the writing of 2 Timothy. Timothy and Trophimus were at least associates and perhaps friends, Timothy was in obvious need of support, Miletus was only thirty-five miles from Ephesus, and yet it appears from 2 Tim 4:20 that Timothy did not know of Trophimus's illness.) They would have traveled north through Troas, and there Paul left his cloak, books, and parchments. (It is possible that Paul was arrested in Troas, and a short-term arrest would explain why he left these items; but then it is difficult to place the visit to Miletus since it seems doubtful that they would have traveled from Troas south to Miletus on their way to Rome if they were traveling on foot.)

Erastus accompanied Paul as far as Corinth ("remained" [2 Tim 4:20] may suggest Paul was with him until that point), but he stayed there for some reason. Paul was taken to Rome (as would be expected of the leader of the Christian mission to the Gentiles), but this imprisonment was unlike the one recorded in Acts 28. It was much more severe. Onesiphorus had to search diligently before finding Paul (2 Tim 1:17), who was imprisoned as a serious criminal (2 Tim 2:9). His lack of shame at Paul's chains, Paul's encouragement to Timothy that he too not be ashamed, all the Asian Christians abandoning Paul, and the abandonment of Demas, one of Paul's inner circle, all suggest the seriousness of the imprisonment. The presence of Luke, a physician, and Paul's desire for a warm cloak may also point to a difficult imprisonment (although Luke was also a friend and winter was coming). Paul's eulogy and his admission of impending death (2 Tim 4:6–8, 18) show that he knew he would not be released.

Paul had already made his initial defense before the Roman court. Although he was abandoned by his friends, it appears that the court's initial ruling was positive; Paul proclaimed the gospel to all the Gentiles and was "rescued from the mouth of a lion" (2 Tim 4:17). Even though Timothy's work was not done in Ephesus, Paul saw that Timothy had time to come to Rome if he left Ephesus immediately. He was to appoint people to continue the truthful proclamation of the gospel (2:2), bring Mark (who may have been in Ephesus), stop in Troas to get the cloak, books, and parchments from Carpus, and arrive in Rome before winter, all along being wary of Alexander. While the courts had given Paul an initial reprieve, he knew that eventually they would condemn him. Paul also wanted to let Timothy know where his friends were.

We do not know if Timothy arrived in time. Church tradition reports (*1 Clem.* 5:7; Dionysius, bishop of Corinth [A.D. 170], in Eusebius *Hist. Eccl.* 2.25.8; Origen, in Eusebius *Hist. Eccl.* 2.22.2, 7; 3.1, cited above; Bruce, *New Testament History*, 367) that while in Rome Paul was executed under the Neronian persecution (which began in A.D. 65). According to tradition (Gaius of Rome, A.D. 200, in Eusebius *Hist. Eccl.* 2.25.7), Paul was beheaded (Tertullian *De praescr.* 36) at Aquae Salviae (currently named Tre Fontane) near the third milestone on the Ostian Way (Bruce, *Paul*, 450–51). Eusebius dates Paul's death in Nero's thirteenth year (A.D. 67; *Chronicle*, Year of Abraham 2083); Jerome places it one year later in his translation of Eusebius (*Chronicon Eusebii Caesariensis*). It is noteworthy that no tradition contradicts Eusebius, no other location is claimed to be the location of Paul's death (cf. Bruce, *Paul*, 451–54), and this tradition comes from Rome (Bernard, xxxiii).

Inferences from 2 Timothy. This scenario helps to understand much about the second epistle to Timothy: (1) 2 Timothy is almost totally unlike the other two letters in the corpus. While it does share a literary style, in almost every other way it is different: it is a personal letter; it is replete with encouragement and personal comments; and reference to false teachers is virtually nonexistent, except for two places (2 Tim 2:14–18; 2:23–3:9).

(2) Timothy continues to be an apostolic delegate, Paul's close personal friend, who is to find Ephesian Christians to help in the task of the gospel's proclamation (along with Tychicus) and then come to Rome so that Paul can see him one more time. Paul wants to encourage Timothy in the face of suffering and in face of his spiritual father's imminent death. Timothy knows Scripture is true and worthy of obedience.

(3) The historical situation is unique. Paul was at the end of his life and knew his work was done. Years of Roman imprisonment, interaction with his guard and people in the city, could easily have had an affect on both his thought and expression (e.g., the Latinisms in the PE; cf. Hitchcock, *ExpTim* 39 [1927–28] 347–52). Paul was writing to an individual (who was a good friend), not to teach but to encourage, recalling earlier times (2 Tim 3:10–11) and appealing for personal loyalty and loyalty to the gospel (1:6–14; 2:1–13; 3:10–4:5) in the face of suffering (1:8, 16; 2:3; 3:12; 4:5). He had spent years proclaiming the gospel and was confident that it would continue after he was gone. He was in prison and

knew he would soon die. These are all formative events that could greatly affect the way any person would think and write.

(4) Especially significant is the statement that only Luke was with Paul (2 Tim 4:11). If the "we" sections in Acts are accepted as historical (Acts 16:10–17; 20:5–15; 21:1–18; 27:1–28:6; also Col 4:14; Phlm 24), Paul had been spending more and more time with Luke, which may have affected Paul's communication style (cf. Knight, 50–51). If Paul's "thorn in the flesh" (2 Cor 12:7) was encroaching blindness, he was becoming more dependent on others, a dependency that would be heightened by a severe imprisonment. Paul had used an amanuensis for his other writings, and, given Luke's writing ability (if his authorship of the third Gospel and Acts is accepted), it is hard to imagine someone else writing for Paul. Regardless of how much freedom Paul would have given to another amanuensis, Paul's serious predicament and Luke's friendship suggest that Paul would have given Luke more freedom as an amanuensis than he would have given to others.

Paul could have used another amanuensis for 1 Timothy and Titus since the historical situation for each is different. But since Luke was with Paul during his final journey to Rome and subsequent imprisonments and the style of all three epistles is consistent, it is possible that Luke was Paul's amanuensis for all three letters and was given considerable freedom in writing to two men who, most likely, were also Luke's friends. While there are stylistic reasons that suggest that Luke was the amanuensis (discussed below), the historical scenario argues forcefully for this position.

For those not accepting Pauline authorship, dates of writing vary from shortly after Paul's death (Harrison, *Problem;* Easton; Dornier), to the 80s through the 100s (Roloff), the Domitian persecution (A.D. 100–115; Hanson [1983]), and even the time of Marcion (A.D. 135–50; Gealy).

Paul wrote his second letter to Timothy for several reasons: (1) He wanted Timothy to finish up a few details in Ephesus and come to see him in Rome before he died. (2) In light of the fierceness of the opposition in Ephesus, he encouraged Timothy to remain true to him and to the gospel message, to willingly suffer for the gospel. (3) Paul also wanted to bring Timothy up to date on the activities and whereabouts of his coworkers.

HISTORICAL RECONSTRUCTION FROM EARLY CHURCH TRADITION

The preceding picture of the historical setting for Paul's relationship with Timothy and Titus has been derived from Acts and the PE. While every element is not provable, the question being asked is whether it is consistent and plausible. Part of this picture is also corroborated by the writings of the early church. While there are inherent problems with the reliability of early traditions, their agreement (or disagreement) with the self-witness of Acts and the PE is significant. Many of the following citations and more are laid out by James, *Genuineness*, 5–19.

(1) By the end of the second century the PE were widely accepted as authoritative and Pauline (Kümmel, *Introduction*, 370; Koester, *Introduction* 2:298). (Wall's assertion that there is no "clear textual witness to them [i.e., the PE] prior to the third century" [*BBR* 5 ([1995) 125] places him in the minority among critical scholars.) Clement of Alexandria constantly connects his citations from the PE

to Paul (references in Spicq, 1:167–68). He cites 1 Tim 6:20 in his discussion of the Gnostic heretics' rejection of the letters to Timothy. Spicq argues that this is significant, for it shows that the letters were known and had been accepted into the canon by the time of Valentinus, Basilides, and Marcion (1:168). Quinn (3) notes the approximately 450 references to the PE from second-century writings listed in *Biblia Patristica* (1:507–18), which is evidence that the PE could not have been recent creations. By the second century the PE had been translated into Latin and Syriac, and included Paul's name (Lock, xxv). There are no divergent traditions and no other names suggested for authorship. This absence of alternatives argues against any view that sees the PE written to combat Gnosticism and Marcion. Bernard gives a full list of the proposed citations from and allusions to the PE in the early Fathers.

(2) The PE have not survived in the Chester Beatty Papyri, a collection of papyri that includes a codex of Paul's writings ($\mathfrak{P}^{46}$) dating from the beginning to the mid-third century. These papyri also do not include Philemon, but do include Hebrews. The last seven leaves of the codex have been lost. Thus, conclusions regarding the absence of the PE are based on assumptions concerning how many leaves the codex should have had, that the scribe could not have added extra pages, and the size of the writing on the leaves. Jeremias (4) argues that a comparison of the first and last pages reveals that the scribe's writing grew smaller toward the end of the codex, presumably because he was running out of room (cf. Finegan, *HTR* [1956] 93). Against those who question the authenticity of the PE because of their absence in the papyri, Guthrie argues, "The very fact that all that remains comprises some fragments of a codex containing the gospels and Acts, most of one containing Paul's epistles and parts of one containing Revelation, is a sufficient indication of the precariousness of this method of argument. It is not the pastorals alone that would be suspect but all the other books of the New Testament which are not represented in the papyri" (*Introduction*, 611). The absence of Philemon may suggest that the codex included only Paul's public letters, omitting letters to individuals such as Timothy, Titus, and Philemon (so Quinn, *CBQ* 36 [1974] 379–85; L. T. Johnson, 3). Thus, the omission of the PE and Philemon from $\mathfrak{P}^{46}$ may have no significance in terms of the authenticity of the PE. Kelly (4) also points out that Clement of Alexandria's familiarity with the PE is evidence that the later third-century Egyptian church knew of the PE, in spite of their absence in $\mathfrak{P}^{46}$.

(3) Bernard (xvi–xvii) cites three passages from the "Letter of the Churches of Vienne and Lyons to Their Brethren in Asia" (in Eusebius *Hist. Eccl.* 5.1) concerning the martyrdom of their bishop, Pothinus, in A.D. 177 that show a similarity of wording with 1 Timothy. Bernard notes J. A. Robinson's argument that the text of this letter "betrays a familiarity with the Latin version of the N.T., rather than the Greek original. If this could be regarded as established (and his arguments seem to me to be well founded), it would prove that by the year 180 the Pastoral Letters were so firmly received as canonical that a Latin version of them had been made and was current in Gaul" (xvii).

(4) Irenaeus, bishop of Lyons and a disciple of Polycarp (who was a disciple of the apostle John), in his *Adversus Haereses* (c. 180) cites the PE frequently and is the earliest to cite them using Paul's name (cf. Spicq, 1:167–68). Bernard lists the following citations: *Pref.* (1 Tim 1:4); 4.16.3 (1 Tim 1:9); 2.14.7 (1 Tim 6:20);

3.14.1 (2 Tim 4:9–11); 3.2.3 (2 Tim 4:21); and 1.16.3 (Titus 3:10). Concerning 1.16.3 Bernard states, "It is noteworthy that Irenaeus is appealing to the Epistle to Titus as written by St Paul, against *heretics,* who would certainly have denied the authority of the words quoted if they could have produced reasons for doing so" (xvi).

(5) The Muratorian Canon lists the PE as canonical (c. A.D. 180): *Ad Titum una et ad Timotheum duae pro affectu et dilectione, in honorem tamen ecclesiae catholicae, in ordinationem ecclesiasticae disciplinae sanctificatae sunt,* "to Titus one, and to Timothy two, (written) out of goodwill and love, are yet held sacred to the glory of the catholic Church for the ordering of ecclesiastical discipline" (in Spicq, 1:167; ET in Hennecke, *New Testament Apocrypha* 1:44).

(6) Bernard (xiii–xviii) cites quotations and allusions in (a) Theophilus, bishop of Antioch (c. A.D. 181, who cites the PE as "proceeding from 'the Divine Word'" (*Ad Autolycum* 3.14; cf. Spicq, 1:165); (b) the apocryphal *Acts of Paul and Thecla,* which attests to the existence of the PE by c. A.D. 170 through its use of names occurring in the NT only in the PE (cf. Spicq, 1:166); (c) Hegesippus (c. A.D. 170); (d) Athenagoras (c. A.D. 176; cf. Hanson, [1983] 11–12; Spicq says the similarity may be due to chance, 1:165); and (e) Heracleon (c. A.D. 165). Spicq adds the *Letter to Diognetus* (1:165).

(7) Justin Martyr (c. A.D. 155) is aware of the letters. Bernard (xiv) lists 1 Tim 4:1 and Titus 3:4 as reflected in *Dial.* 7.7; 35.3; 47.15.

(8) Marcion was a heretic from the mid-second century who was excommunicated in A.D. 144 and set up a rival church. In propounding a doctrine of love to the exclusion of the law, he rejected everything that was remotely Jewish in the NT, such as Matthew, Mark, John, and parts of Luke. His "canon" omitted the PE as well. Tertullian states:

> To this epistle alone [Philemon] did its brevity avail to protect it against the falsifying hands of Marcion. I wonder, however, when he received [into his *Apostolicon*] this letter which was written but to one man, that he rejected [*recusaverit*] the two epistles to Timothy and the one to Titus, which all treat of ecclesiastical discipline. His aim, was, I suppose, to carry out his interpolating process even to the number of [St. Paul's] epistles. (*Adv. Marc.* 5.21; ANF 3:473–74; full Latin text is in Bernard, xviii; cf. Spicq, 1:168–69).

Concerning the significance of Marcion's witness, Scott concludes, "But the fact that they were excluded, at so early a date, from the body of Paul's letters, affords grounds for suspicion. Could Marcion have passed over them if they were already accepted by the whole church as the undoubted work of Paul?" (xvi). In my opinion, if Marcion felt no compunction in dismissing Matthew, Mark, and John, why would he have felt any less restricted in ignoring the thirteen chapters of the PE?

Marcion's witness may be judged of little or no value. (a) Marcion's decisions regarding those books that should be accepted into the canon were guided by a theological position that the orthodox church ultimately rejected. (b) There are statements in the PE that Marcion would have found objectionable: "The law is good" (1 Tim 1:8); a denial of the value of asceticism (1 Tim 4:3); the high value placed on the OT (2 Tim 3:16); and the assertion that God desires to save all (1 Tim 2:4). Coincidentally, when Paul tells Timothy to avoid "the unholy chatter and contradictions [ἀντιθέσεις] of what is falsely named 'knowledge' [τῆς ψευδωνύμου γνώσεως]" (1 Tim 6:20), he uses the term ἀντιθέσεις, which is the same word Marcion used for the title of his writings on the conflict between the gospel and the law (Tertullian *Adv. Marc.* 1.19.4–5). Clement of Alexandria says that some gnostics rejected the PE because of the final phrase τῆς ψευδωνύμου γνώσεως, "what is falsely claimed knowledge" (*Strom.* 4.9). Kelly argues that Marcion's "mutilated New Testament canon" rejected the PE because of a "dislike of their anti-heretical tone." Dibelius-Conzelmann (2) note that none of Marcion's specific teachings are reflected in the Ephesian heresy that can be reconstructed from the PE. (c) While it is true that Marcion could have stripped the PE of any hint of Jewishness, as he did to other books, there is nothing in the PE that would have helped him positively in his cause. Several other Gnostics also rejected the PE. Kelly (4) notes that the *Gospel of Truth*, ascribed to Valentinus (A.D. 150), quotes from all the NT except the PE. Guthrie (*Introduction*, 610 n. 2) points out that Jerome records, in his preface to Titus, Basilides' rejection of all three of the PE (cited by James, *Genuineness*, 21) and Tatian's (died A.D. 170) rejection of 1 and 2 Timothy because of the letters' view on asceticism. Jerome comments that "these adverse judgments were not critical in any true sense, but merely arbitrary" (in White, "Pastoral Epistles," 76).

(9) In discussing Marcion's rejection of the PE, Lock points out that at this same time the PE were included in the Syriac and Latin versions, thus attesting to their canonical acceptance (xxii, xxv).

(10) The homily known as *2 Clement* was written by A.D. 140. Bernard (xviii–xix) lists three specific allusions to the PE (1 Tim 1:17 [*2 Clem.* 20]; 4:10 [*2 Clem.* 7]; 6:14, 19 [*2 Clem.* 8]) and several other passages recalling their language (cf. Spicq, 1:163).

(11) Polycarp, bishop of Smyrna and disciple of John (c. A.D. 117), cites 1 Tim 6:10 and 6:7 as authoritative without identifying their source (*Phil.* 4.1). Bernard identifies six other passages in the PE that Polycarp may cite (xiv–xv; cf. Jeremias, 4; Metzger, *Canon*, 61; Spicq finds approximately twenty, 1:163–64). However, some question the validity of seeing the PE as a source for Polycarp, arguing that the author of the PE used Polycarp (Harrison, *Polycarp's Two Epistles;* Goodspeed, *Introduction*, 344; Barnett, *Literary Influence*, 182–84) or that they both came out of the same environment (Dibelius-Conzelmann, 2). However, Guthrie argues, "There is nothing in the manner of Polycarp's citations from the Pastoral Epistles to suggest recently published works. Indeed, it is most difficult to conceive of a disciple of the apostle John (cf. Tertullian *De praescr.* 32 and Jerome *Catal. sacr. eccl.* 17) readily accepting and using Pauline epistles which were not authentic and which were not introduced until the rise of Marcionism (c. AD 140)" (*Introduction*, 610). He adds that there is no "intelligible reason why an imitator of Paul would have echoed the language of Ignatius or Polycarp" (*Introduction*, 611 n. 4). On the issue of Polycarp as a whole, see Harrison, *Problem*, 177–78; id., *Polycarp's Two Epistles to the Philippians;* Harnack, *Briefsammlung,* 72; Spicq, 1:162–63; Jeremias, 4; Dibelius-Conzelmann, 2; von Campenhausen, "Polykarp," 28–29; Brox, 26–28; Kümmel, *Introduction*, 370.

(12) Ignatius, bishop of Antioch (c. A.D. 116), has no quotations from the PE, but there are "coincidences in phraseology [that] can hardly be accidental" (so Bernard, xv, citing seven passages and also several "peculiar" words that occur in Ignatius and elsewhere only in the PE; also Kelly, 3; cf. Spicq, 1:163). Hanson

([1983] 12–13) rightly points out that the Roman persecution reflected in Ignatius' writings does not correspond to the background of the PE.

(13) Spicq (1:164–65) proposes several parallels to the *Epistle of Barnabas,* which he dates at the same time as Ignatius (*Barn.* 5:6 par. 2 Tim 1:10; 3:16; *Barn.* 1:4, 6 par. Titus 1:2; 3:7; *Barn.* 7:2 par. 2 Tim 4:1; *Barn.* 1:3 par. Titus 3:6).

(14) Clement of Rome (A.D. 96) may show an awareness of the PE (references in Bernard, xix; Spicq, 1:162–63; cf. Kelly, 10). Holtzmann thinks Clement and the PE both reflect the same "atmosphere," but Streeter (*Primitive Church,* 153) and Harrison (*Problem,* 177–78) argue that the author of the PE cites *1 Clement,* which at least shows how similar the passages in question are. The Oxford Society of Historical Theology report denies any overlap (*The New Testament in the Apostolic Fathers* [Oxford: Clarendon, 1905] 37ff.).

(15) The persecution of Domitian (A.D. 96) is not the type of suffering to which Paul is calling Timothy in the second epistle. Paul is warning Timothy that all Christians will be persecuted as they live out their commitment to Christ (especially in 2 Tim 3:12). This is decidedly different from what we would expect to be written if the government were conducting an official persecution of the church. Also, Rev 2:1–7, addressed to the Ephesian church, and Ignatius' letter to the Ephesians (c. A.D. 110; e.g., *Eph.* 9.1) show no indication of the types of problems addressed in the PE.

(16) Spicq connects the comments in 2 Pet 3:15–16 directly to 1 Tim 1:12–16, citing both verbal (ἡγεῖσθαι, "to consider," μακροθυμία, "patience") and conceptual connections (e.g., the long suffering of Christ relative to Paul; Spicq, 1:160–62). He also compares Titus 2:13 with 2 Pet 3:15, 18 because in each the author discusses mercy and salvation in the context of a believer's peace and confidence. If this connection is valid, and depending on one's dating of 2 Peter, it will have implications for the dating of the PE.

Conclusion. Kümmel is less impressed with the external attestation to the PE than I am, and yet he does admit that "from the end of the second century on . . . the Pastorals are considered without question to be letters of Paul" (*Introduction,* 370). It seems unlikely to me that writings accepted "without question" by the end of the second century would be recent creations. Bernard concludes:

> We find traces of the Pastoral Epistles in Gaul and Greece in 177, in Rome in 140 (certainly)—as far back as 95, if we accept Clement's testimony—and in Asia as early as 116. . . . And this attestation appears the more remarkable, both as to its range and its precision, if we consider the character of the letters under examination. They are not formal treatises addressed to Churches, like the epistles to the Romans and the Galatians, but semi-private letters to individuals, providing counsel and guidance which to some extent would only be applicable in special circumstances. (xx)

Bernard continues by emphasizing that these individual writers reflect not just their own "single authority" but

> the continuous tradition of their respective sees. . . . It bears witness to the belief of the primitive Christian communities at Rome, at Smyrna, at Antioch, that the Pastoral letters were, at the least, documents "profitable for teaching, for reproof, for correction, for instruction which is in righteousness." . . . We are forced to conclude, that, if not genuine relics of the Apostolic age, they must have been forged in St Paul's name and

accepted on St Paul's authority all over the Christian world, within fifty years of St Paul's death—within thirty years if we accept the testimony of Clement of Rome. (xx, xxi)

Spicq adds, "The bishops of Rome, Antioch, Smyrna, who use the [traditions] *ad verbum*, are not private naive persons editing a pious literature, but Pastors, trustees of the official doctrine and of the treasure of the Scriptures. . . . How would these eminent witnesses of orthodoxy have been able to give credence to an error when the Pauline corpus was without doubt already accepted?" (Spicq, 1:166, appealing to 2 Pet 3:16).

While some argue that the early church was not critical in its acceptance of texts into its canon, the problems of accepting John, Hebrews, 1 Peter, 2 and 3 John, Jude, and 2 Peter suggest that the early church was acutely concerned about the texts they accepted. The authenticity of the PE was not questioned until the nineteenth century. This does not make the raising of this question wrong; but it must be admitted that it is a modern concern. The external evidence for the authenticity of the PE is strong and consistent with the self-witness of the PE. This places the burden of proof on those denying authenticity. For further analysis of the external evidence for the PE, see Bernard, xi–xxi; James, *Genuineness*, 5–24; Spicq, 1:160–70; and Guthrie, *Introduction*, 608–12.

THE EPHESIAN HERESY

A. *Introduction*

The re-creation of what was being taught in Ephesus is no simple task. Paul never spells out the full nature of the heresy, and it appears to have been unlike the earlier problems in Galatia and Colossae. While we are told a few of its specific doctrines, for the most part it does not appear to have been a well-thought-out, cohesive system of belief. Exegetical discussion has centered on whether it was primarily Jewish or proto-gnostic. The primary passages are 1 Tim 1:3–7, 18–20; 4:1–5, 7a; 6:2–5, 20–21; Titus 1:10–16; 3:9–11; 2 Tim 2:14–18, 22–26; 3:6–9 (also 1 Tim 1:8–11, 12–17 and possibly 2 Tim 3:1–5 and 4:3–4; see summary in Lightfoot, "Additional Note," 411–12).

B. *Jewish Elements*

Paul explicitly calls the teaching "Jewish" (Titus 1:14) and speaks of "those of the circumcision" (Titus 1:10). The opponents want to be known as teachers of the law (1 Tim 1:7) and to apply its restrictive function to all people for both salvation and lifestyle (see *Form/Structure/Setting* on 1 Tim 1:8–11). They quarrel about the law (Titus 3:9) and may even charge Paul with being antinomian (1 Tim 1:8). This emphasis on the law is accompanied by a minimizing of faith (1 Tim 1:5; 2:1–7), grace, and mercy in God's salvific work (1 Tim 1:12–17), possibly also depreciating the role of Christ (1 Tim 1:15–17; 2 Tim 1:8–10; see below); this explains Paul's emphasis on God's salvation apart from works (Titus 3:4–7; 2 Tim 1:9–10). Paul uses the Decalogue (1 Tim 1:9–10) and the Shema (1 Tim 2:5) as part of his argument. Repeatedly Paul calls the teaching "myths" (1 Tim 1:4; 4:7; 2 Tim 4:4; Titus 1:14). "Myths and genealogies" (1 Tim 1:4; Titus 3:9) are probably haggadic midrash: allegorical reinterpretations of the OT, perhaps as fanciful interpretations of the OT genealogies (Roloff, 64), especially of the patriarchs and their families (cf. Quinn, 245–47; examples in Spicq, 1:99–104, 322), along the order of those found in *Jubilees* and Pseudo-Philo *Biblical Antiquities* (cf. *Comment* on 1 Tim 1:4). "Falsely named 'knowledge'" (1 Tim 6:20) could be a description of some form of rabbinical law (Hort, *Judaistic Christianity*, 140–43; Lock, xvii). The heresy appears to be sectarian and exclusive, or anti-Gentile (1 Tim 2:1–7), warranting Paul's emphasis on the universal offer of salvation to all people (1 Tim 2:6; 4:10; cf. 1:15), including Gentiles (1 Tim 2:7; cf. Foerster, *TDNT* 7:1016–17). The emphasis on the goodness of creation (1 Tim 4:3–5) sounds like Jesus' and Peter's teaching on the Jewish food laws (Mark 7:19; Acts 10:9–16; cf. Luke 11:40–41; 1 Cor 8–10; Rom 14) and places the asceticism in a Jewish, not a Gnostic, context. If the opponents used magic, there is a parallel with the "itinerant Jewish exorcists" (Acts 19:13) in Ephesus with whom Paul had dealt earlier. Because its basic nature is Jewish and involves asceticism, it may have some relation to the error taught in Colossae (see below).

Bernard goes one step further, suggesting "Essene Judaism" (Lightfoot's term) as the source of the heresy. He identifies five basic tenets of the Ephesian heresy: (1) speculation on the Mosaic law and Hebrew history; (2) impurity of matter leading to asceticism; (3) association with magic; (4) exclusiveness; and (5) denial of a physical resurrection. Bernard then compares all these tenets, except for the first, with Josephus's and Philo's description of the Essenes. Even if there is not a direct link between the heresy and the Essenes, the similarity strongly suggests a basically Jewish understanding of the heresy.

The heresy does not appear to be mainstream Judaism: the opponents did not know the law (1 Tim 1:7), and there is no discussion of circumcision (except perhaps Titus 1:10) and works per se, suggesting that Paul is not dealing with the type of Pharisaism taught by the Judaizers.

Those who interpret the heresy as basically Jewish include Ellicott; Hort, *Judaistic Christianity*, 132–46; Bernard; Lock; Büchsel, *TDNT* 1:663–65; Scott; Spicq, 1:91–92; Simpson; Guthrie; Kelly; Hiebert, *First Timothy;* and Fee.

C. Proto-Gnostic Elements

While there are no clear statements that the heresy is Gnostic, many of the statements in the PE can be understood within that context. Baur, for example, argues that the PE are dealing with second-century Gnosticism (*Pastoralbriefe;* cf. Moffatt, *Introduction*, 408–10). Paul's description of the heresy as "contradictions of what is falsely named 'knowledge'" (1 Tim 6:20) could even be viewed as a directly anti-Marcionite statement, using the actual title ("Contradictions" or "Antitheses") of Marcion's work. However, few, if any, follow Baur today. The use of the term *contradictions* is coincidental; the heresy reflected in the PE has little parallel with the Gnostic system of the second century, and Marcion's "literalist approach" would not have permitted "fables" (Kelly, 12), nor was he a teacher of the law as were the opponents (1 Tim 1:7). We have no example of the term *genealogy* used to describe the Gnostic aeons (Spicq, 1:322; Kelly, 44).

The evidence is better characterized as proto-gnosticism, elements that eventually formed a cohesive system of thought at a later date. Asceticism (including marriage, childbirth, and diet), licentiousness, a speculative approach to the OT, a low view of the physical world, are typical of Gnostic thought. Towner connects 1 Tim 6:20 with 2 Tim 2:15–18, concluding that the teaching on the resurrection is part of their "gnosis" (*Goal,* 29–33). Gnosticism also taught "myths" in describing the families of aeons that separated God from the physical world (Tertullian *Adv. Valent.* 3; *De praescr.* 33; Irenaeus *Adv. Haer.* praef.).

Those who interpret the heresy as basically Gnostic include Dibelius-Conzelmann; Brox (especially 31–42); Haufe, "Gnostische Irrlehre"; Schmithals, *Corpus Paulinum;* Houlden; Hanson (1983); and Oberlinner (especially 52–73).

D. Hellenistic Elements

Some of the PE reflect not so much Gnostic thought but rather Hellenistic thought in general. For example, the thought that the law is not for a just person fits well within Stoicism (1 Tim 1:9). The denial of the resurrection (2 Tim 2:18) is characteristic of both Gnostic (Brox, 36–37) and Hellenized (1 Cor 15) Christianity. Asceticism and dualism are present in Hellenistic philosophical thought (Spicq 1:494–95; Jeremias, 32) as well as Gnosticism and Judaism. Hort points out that "myths and genealogies" occur in the same context in reference to the heroes of Greek mythology (Polybius 9.2.1); perhaps these ideas were blended within the haggadic midrash in Ephesus (1 Tim 1:4). Part of Hellenistic culture was widespread superstition and magic (see *Comment* on "hope" in 1 Tim 1:1), and much of the PE is aimed at the dividing line between religion and superstition (Spicq, 1:108), which helps to explain the imprecise nature of the opponents' teaching. Acts reports that magic was a major force in Ephesus (19:19) and evidently in parts of Judaism (Acts 8:9; 19:13–14); the opponents are compared to Egyptian magicians (2 Tim 3:8), and it is possible that some of the widows were practicing magic (1 Tim 5:13; see Spicq, 1:106–10). Paul had always dealt with the dual issues of Judaism and religious syncretism. The latter provides the religious context of Paul's ministry and is addressed especially in 1 Corinthians and Colossians. Given the central role Ephesus played in Asia Minor, it is no surprise that the same forces were at work there. In all three of these locations we find issues of arrogant knowledge (Col 2:3–8), over-realized eschatology (1 Cor 15:12), asceticism (1 Cor 7:1–7 [cf. G. D. Fee, "1 Corinthians 7:1 in the NIV," *JETS* 23 (1980) 307–14]; Col 2:16–23), and OT ritual (Col 2:16, 21 [cf. O'Brien, *Colossians,* xxvii–xli, bibliography in xxxvi–xxxviii]).

For discussions of the Ephesian problem as dealing with both Jewish and Hellenistic syncretistic thought, see Lightfoot ("Additional Note," 411–18), Ellis ("Opponents," 101–15), and Fee (9–10).

E. Additional Elements

We have already seen the presence of the law-versus-grace controversy, myths and genealogies, sectarianism, and the Jewish nature of the heresy. We are also told a few of the opponents' specific teachings. (1) The heresy taught asceticism (cf. Titus 1:15), which was found in both Jewish and Gnostic settings, specifically abstention from marriage (1 Tim 4:3; cf. 5:14) and possibly child-bearing (1 Tim 2:15; cf. 5:14), the observance of dietary laws (1 Tim 4:3) that evidently did not include wine (1 Tim 3:3, 8; 5:23; Titus 1:7), and the accumulation of wealth (1 Tim 6:5; Titus 1:11; cf. 1 Tim 5:17; 3:3, 8; Titus 1:7). Paul's emphasis on the goodness of creation within the context of asceticism suggests that the opponents were teaching the evilness of creation (or at least some form of dualism). (2) The heresy taught an over-realized eschatology, that the resurrection had already occurred (2 Tim 2:18; see below). This was the same problem in Corinth, where a denial of a physical resurrection may have been based on an accomplished spiritual resurrection (1 Cor 15:12). In the PE Paul sees that he is living in the last days (1 Tim 4:1; 2 Tim 3:1). (3) The opponents may also have been teaching magic (1 Tim 5:13; 2 Tim 3:8).

(4) The emphasis on Christ throughout the PE can be seen against the backdrop of the opponents' teaching that downplayed the significance of Christ, although the heresy was not primarily christological. Salvation through Christ (1 Tim 1:12–17) is set against the opponents' misuse of the law (1 Tim 1:8–11). Christ came to save sinners (1 Tim 1:15; cf. 2 Tim 2:10; 3:15; Titus 2:13; 3:6), functioning together with God as savior (see below, *Introduction*, "Themes in the PE"). Christ (not Moses) is the unique mediator between God and people (1 Tim 2:5). Christ's life, victory, and glorification are the substance of the Christian mystery, the gospel (1 Tim 3:16) as it stands against the demonic teaching of the opponents (1 Tim 4:1–5). The opponents' teaching that the resurrection is past (2 Tim 2:18) suggests that they felt they had moved beyond Christ and the hope of his second coming. The false teaching is in contrast to healthy instruction concerning Jesus Christ (1 Tim 6:3). Timothy is to do his work without fault, waiting for the appearing of Jesus Christ (1 Tim 6:14). The object of a deacon's faith is Christ Jesus (1 Tim 3:13). As opposed to the opponents and their demonic teaching (1 Tim 4:1–5), Timothy is a good servant of Christ Jesus (1 Tim 4:6). Timothy is to follow Paul's gospel in the faith and love that are in Christ Jesus (2 Tim 1:14), a gospel rejected by Phygelus and Hermogenes (2 Tim 1:15). This faith and love stands in contrast to the opponents (1 Tim 1:5). Timothy is to do his work, strong in the grace of Christ Jesus (2 Tim 2:1) and as a soldier of Christ (2 Tim 2:3). The core of Paul's gospel is Jesus Christ (2 Tim 2:8; cf. also 1 Tim 6:13; 5:21; 2 Tim 1:9–10; 4:1). Some have detected an anti-docetic emphasis (e.g., 1 Tim 1:5; 3:16; Lütgert, *Irrlehrer*, 57, 60–61).

(5) Towner (103–4) suggests that the opponents may have been attempting "to enact the life of resurrection paradise by following the model given in Genesis 1 and 2," accounting for the prohibition on marriage and the dietary asceticism (Adam and Eve were probably regarded as vegetarians). This helps to explain the use of Gen 2 and 3 in the opponents' teaching in 1 Tim 2:13–15. It also suggests interpreting the phrase "word of God" in 1 Tim 4:5 as God's statement on the goodness of creation as well as identifying the "myths and genealogies" in 1 Tim 1:4 with the creation accounts.

(6) The PE also give a picture of the opponents. 1 Tim 6:4–5 is the most condensed expression: "foolish, understanding nothing but having a sickly craving for speculations and empty words out of which come envy, strife, slanders, evil suspicions, constant irritation among people who have been corrupted in their mind and have been robbed of the truth, thinking that godliness is a means of profit." The opponents are factious (Titus 3:10), advancing into ungodliness (2 Tim 2:16); they are rebellious, senseless babblers (Titus 1:10) and bring reproach

Introduction

on the church (1 Tim 3:2, 7, 10; Titus 1:11–14). At one time they were part of the church community but later rejected the truth of the gospel and turned away to the heresy (1 Tim 1:6, 19; 4:1; 6:10, 21; 2 Tim 4:4; Titus 1:14; cf. Gal 2:4; 2 Cor 11:4). They were not tricked by the heresy but rather made conscious decisions to turn away (1 Tim 1:19). They are deceiving the Ephesian and Cretan church (Titus 1:10); they are hypocrites, liars (1 Tim 4:2), insincere (1 Tim 4:4), and they profess to know God but deny him by their deeds (Titus 1:16). They are therefore self-condemned (Titus 3:11), and their consciences (1 Tim 4:2; 6:5; Titus 1:15; cf. 1 Tim 1:5) and minds (1 Tim 6:5; 2 Tim 3:8; Titus 1:15) are corrupted. They have a sickly craving (1 Tim 6:4) and are robbed of the truth (1 Tim 6:5). They are ignorant (1 Tim 1:7), foolish, understanding nothing (1 Tim 6:4), worthless for any good work (Titus 1:16) or for the gospel (2 Tim 3:8). The opponents are perverted (Titus 3:11), unholy (2 Tim 3:2), ungodly (2 Tim 2:16), and lacking in love (1 Tim 1:5), and their folly will eventually be evident to all (2 Tim 3:9). They are dogmatic (1 Tim 1:7) and devoted to their teachings (1 Tim 1:4; 4:1). Even their motives are corrupt, wanting prestige (1 Tim 1:7), money (1 Tim 6:5–10; Titus 1:11), sex (2 Tim 3:6), and pleasure (2 Tim 3:4). As would be expected, they do not accept Paul's or Timothy's authority (1 Tim 1:1–2; 4:12, 14; 6:12).

Spicq (1:103–9) gives an excellent summary of the opponents. He describes the opponents as dialecticians, Jewish converts who still based their teaching on the OT but did so in a way that did not respect the facts or the truth. They played mind games and became lost in endless and inextricable subtleties (1 Tim 1:4). The same apostle who told the Corinthians "not to go beyond what is written" (1 Cor 4:6) here blasts the opponents whose argumentation was more important than facts, reality, and good taste. The opponents were more rhetoricians than they were theologians (cf. Spicq, 1:157–58).

(7) It is important to consider what relation, if any, the Ephesian heresy had with the error that was taught in Colossae (cf. C. E. Arnold, *The Christian Syncretism: The Interface between Christianity and Folk Belief at Colossae* [Grand Rapids, MI: Baker, 1996]). The Colossian heresy involved magic (Arnold, *Christian Syncretism,* 239), described as "philosophy and empty deceit, according to human tradition, according to the elemental spirits of the universe" (Col 2:8), which was "not according to Christ" and downplayed the role of Christ who had "disarmed the principalities and powers" (Col 2:15). Paul's instruction about asceticism sounds as if it would have been applicable in Ephesus as well (Col 2:16–19; see lists of similarities in Bowen, *Dates,* 51–55). The error at Colossae was more clearly formulated, but it appears to have had elements in common with the Ephesian heresy as would be expected of groups in two major cities in Asia Minor sharing a syncretistic culture.

(8) Towner sees the root of the Ephesian heresy in an over-realized eschatology similar to that in Corinth (*JSNT* 31 [1987] 95–124; *Goal,* 29–33). They had misunderstood Paul's teaching that Christians had died and been raised with Christ (Rom 6:3–8; Eph 2:5; Col 2:12; *Goal,* 34–36, citing A. C. Thiselton, "Realized Eschatology at Corinth," *NTS* 24 [1978] 510–26), and had taken Paul's teaching on the present aspect of the eschatological kingdom to the extreme such that the future fulfillment was denied. Based on this error, the opponents had upset "the social equilibrium of the communities" (Towner, *Goal,* 101) since many social

structures belonged to the old age. The opponents' "gnosis" included their teaching on eschatology (connecting 1 Tim 6:20–21 with 2 Tim 2:15–18, noting that this knowledge was not the same as the Gnostics'). Their asceticism resulted from an "eschatological dualism" (Towner, *Goal,* 108) in which certain foods belonged to the old order. There was an emancipation tendency at work especially among the women. Towner's evaluation is helpful, although perhaps he gives too much credit to the opponents for having a cohesive theological basis for their teaching. In the Ephesian heresy there was also a link between realized eschatology and emphasis on the law, which does not figure in the Corinthian situation.

It appears that Paul's prophecy to the Ephesian elders in Acts 20:28–31 came true and that overseers began teaching heresy (cf. Ellis, "Opponents," 114). They still wanted to be known as teachers, but now as teachers of the law (1 Tim 1:7). This explains why there is so much emphasis in 1 Tim 3, 5 and Titus 1 on the qualities of church leaders. While the opponents had tricked a significant number of women (2 Tim 3:6; possibly 1 Tim 5:13) and some women were promulgating the heresy (1 Tim 2:12), it appears that the prominent leaders of the heresy were men. Only male leaders are named, and the discussion of church leaders in 1 Tim 3 and Titus 1 is addressed to male leaders (but cf. *Comment* on 1 Tim 2:12). The fact that the opposition came from within and not without also helps to explain the difference between the PE and the rest of Paul's writing, where the threat was external in origin.

(9) The opponents had significant success among the Ephesian women (2 Tim 3:6), and some of their ascetic teaching was directed toward them (1 Tim 4:3; possibly 1 Tim 2:15). The opponents were actively seducing the women (2 Tim 3:6), especially the young widows (1 Tim 5:11–15), which helps explain the repeated call for marital faithfulness among the church leaders (1 Tim 3:2, 12; Titus 1:6). While it appears that the prominent leaders of the opposition were men, the women were also helping to spread the heresy (1 Tim 2:12; possibly 5:13). According to one interpretation of 1 Tim 2:8–15, it is possible that the opponents were teaching the women to rebel openly against their husbands, and perhaps all male authority, and to dress seductively as an expression of that rebellion (see *Comment* on 1 Tim 2:9).

F. General Characteristics

Whatever were the specific elements of the heresy, it was a different gospel from Paul's gospel. The heresy is contrasted with Paul's gospel (1 Tim 1:3; 6:2) and experience (1 Tim 1:12–17) and is characterized as opposing the truth (2 Tim 3:8). The opponents teach human commandments (Titus 1:14) that ultimately originate from demons (1 Tim 4:1; 5:15) as a result of Satan's activity in the church (1 Tim 1:20; 3:7; 4:1, 2; 5:14–15; 2 Tim 2:26). Many of the positive qualities applied to Timothy and church officers stand in contrast to the negative qualities of the opponents (e.g., 1 Tim 1:4–5; cf. *Comment* and the table in *Form/ Structure/Setting* on 1 Tim 3:1–7). There is a sense of urgency, especially in 1 Timothy, because the opponents had achieved a considerable level of success. The mere presence of Timothy in Ephesus shows Paul's concern for the situation. There is no introductory thanksgiving section in 1 Timothy or Titus, but instead Paul launches directly into the issues. The opponents have upset entire house churches (Titus 1:11), deceiving many women (2 Tim 3:6; cf. 1 Tim 2:9–15) and, it may be assumed, also men (cf. Titus 1:11). The faith of many has been upset (1 Tim 1:19; 2 Tim 2:18), and people are straying after Satan (1 Tim 4:1; 5:15). It is a battle Timothy must fight (1 Tim 1:18).

Paul characterizes the opponents' teaching in many ways. It is unholy chatter (1 Tim 6:20; 2 Tim 2:16), endless (1 Tim 1:4), foolish (1 Tim 6:2; Titus 3:9), senseless babble (1 Tim 1:6), sickly craving for speculations and empty words (1 Tim 6:4), and utterly lacking in love (1 Tim 1:5). It promotes foolish and uneducated speculation (2 Tim 2:23; Titus 3:9; 1 Tim 6:4) rather than God's stewardship (1 Tim 1:4), fighting about empty words (1 Tim 6:4; 2 Tim 2:14), harmful and useless quarrels (Titus 3:9; 2 Tim 2:23), strife (Titus 3:9), and envy (1 Tim 6:4). It has the appearance of godliness and wisdom but has no power or wisdom (2 Tim 3:5; 1 Tim 6:20) and improperly separates theology from behavior (cf. 2 Tim 3:5; Titus 1:16). It eats away like gangrene (2 Tim 2:17). 1 Tim 6:4–5 condemns the opponents as "foolish, understanding nothing but having a sickly craving for speculations and empty words" (cf. also Titus 3:9). The teaching is at best useless, resulting in nothing beneficial, and at worst ruins those who listen (2 Tim 2:14; cf. similar description by Spicq, 1:85–88).

Paul must deal with the Ephesian opponents differently from those in Galatia who had a formulated teaching that could be described and evaluated. Paul cannot logically and theologically argue against empty chatter and quarrels about words. He must focus on the opponents' behavior, which reveals the error of their teaching. In fact, it appears that the opponents' teaching will eventually implode (2 Tim 3:9). It is thus perhaps too much to call the teaching of the opponents a "heresy" since that may incorrectly suggest a cohesiveness and clarity that was in fact missing. Lightfoot correctly describes it as "floating, speculation, vague theories, coalescing gradually to a great consistency and tendency more or less in one direction" ("Additional Note," 412).

One point is clear. The opponents' teaching was not developed Gnosticism and was much closer to the errors at Colossae and Corinth, mixed with portions of aberrant Judaism, speculative superstition, and possibly magic. The nature of the opponents' teaching does not require dating the PE later than Paul (Spicq, 1:179).

Against this literal reading of Paul's characterization of his opponents is R. J. Karris's interpretation (cf. Barrett, *NTS* 20 [1974] 240) that the author of the PE was engaging in "name-calling" (*JBL* 92 [1973] 549; cf. Scott, 158; Spicq, 1:87–88). Karris (563–64) argues that the author, using the then current method of philosophical and rhetorical polemic, was employing a schema not to describe the actual teaching of the opponents but to separate himself from them, to claim that he alone had the truth, and to "cause aversion for his opponents in the minds of his readers." Karris does not interpret literally any of the characterizations in the PE that have parallels in contemporary philosophical polemic literature: greed, deception, not practicing what they preach, quibbling, vice lists, etc. But I would argue that such parallels do not necessarily support the conclusion that the author was not describing what really was occurring in Ephesus. While the vice lists may paint a general picture—of those for whom the law was intended (1 Tim 1:9–10) and those who would be active in the last days (2 Tim 3:2–4)—there are indications that Paul was addressing a real situation, and hence the descriptions are actual. The vice list of 1 Tim 1:9–10 parallels the Decalogue, addressing the opponents' claim to be teachers of the law. As I will show throughout my detailed analysis of the text, the descriptions of the opponents parallel in reverse the positive instructions to Timothy and the Ephesian church, indicating that both the negative and positive descriptions are actual. However, the schema of the philosophers may have provided some of the specific vocabulary Paul used (cf. Spicq, 1:86 n. 1).

THE RESPONSE TO THE HERESY

How then were Timothy and Titus to respond to the issues in their churches? The PE do not give a uniform answer to this question because the situation behind each letter was unique. While there was some consistency in the opposition and hence some consistency in Paul's instructions, Timothy and Titus were different people, and they were working in different churches.

A. The Gospel

At the heart of the PE is the gospel of Jesus Christ: God has acted in grace and mercy through the death of Christ with an offer of forgiveness, to which people must respond in faith, turning from evil, receiving empowerment through God's Spirit, and looking forward to eternal life. This gospel is fully Pauline (cf. Fee, 14–16). Its essence is clearly taught (1 Tim 3:16; 4:1–5, 7–10; 2 Tim 1:9–10; 2:11–14; 3:4–7; Titus 2:11–14), and it is related to the historical context of Paul's life (e.g., 1 Tim 1:8–11, 12–17). The OT is an integral part of the gospel (2 Tim 3:14–4:2). The gospel is central to Paul and Timothy's ministry (1 Tim 4:13–16; 2 Tim 1:8–14; 3:10–4:2). It was entrusted to Paul (1 Tim 1:11; 2:7; Titus 1:3; 2 Tim 1:11) and Timothy (1 Tim 1:18; 2 Tim 1:13–14; 2:2; 3:14) and is to be passed on to the faithful (2 Tim 2:2) and valued by the church, especially the leaders (1 Tim 3:2; 5:17; Titus 1:9; cf. 2 Tim 2:24). Timothy is called to be nourished by the gospel (1 Tim 4:6,13–16) and to guard it (1 Tim 3:15; 6:20; 2 Tim 1:14), follow it (2 Tim 1:13), handle it correctly (2 Tim 2:15), and continue in it (2 Tim 3:14). The gospel is healthy (1 Tim 1:10); it is the message of love (1 Tim 1:5). It equips ministers for ministry (2 Tim 3:17). Though it includes suffering (2 Tim 1:8), it proclaims salvation (see below, *Introduction*, "Themes in the PE") and is centered on Jesus Christ (see above). In all this, the PE are fully Pauline.

What strikes some as different, in the final analysis, has more to do with form than with content. As is true throughout Paul's writings, the terminology he chooses changes depending upon the historical setting. For example, in Galatians and Romans the forensic nature of justification is pressed, owing to the historical problems in those churches. In the PE the emphasis is on doctrine as a whole, against which the teaching of the opponents is judged false (see below). Paul uses terminology such as "the faith" (1 Tim 1:19), "the truth" (1 Tim 2:4), a "deposit" (1 Tim 6:20), and that which is healthy as opposed to the sickly teaching of the opponents (1 Tim 1:10). This emphasis on the fact of doctrine, on the canon of truth that judges the opponents to be false, while intensified by the historical situations at Ephesus and Crete, in essence is no different from what is found elsewhere in Paul (see below on the development of orthodoxy under "Critical Questions, The Theological Problem, A. Doctrinal Issues"). And when it is realized that Paul is writing to two trusted friends, members of his inner circle who already know the gospel, this emphasis is not surprising.

B. *The Gospel as Right Belief*

While in the PE there is an emphasis on right behavior (see below), there is also a strong emphasis on correct doctrine, albeit doctrine applied to everyday life. This is especially evident in Titus. After dealing with the issue of leadership, Paul gives a telling description of the opponents: they claim to know God (theology), but their deeds (praxis) prove they do not (Titus 1:16). After discussing how different groups in the church must behave (Titus 2:1–10), Paul builds the rest of the letter around the two creedal statements in Titus 2:11–14 and 3:4–7. The latter emphasizes the graciousness and mercy of God's salvific work contrasted with the person's former life of sin. Titus 2:11–14 is explicit in stating that one of the very purposes for which God saved sinners is so that they would deny ungodly and worldly passions and live reverently, zealous for good works, the very thing for which the opponents are unfit (Titus 1:16). Right belief must always show itself in right behavior.

In 1 Timothy there is also doctrinal teaching, but more than in Titus it is focused on the historical situation. 1 Tim 1:8–11 and 1:12–17 open the letter by explaining theologically why the opponents' emphasis on law and corresponding lack of emphasis on faith is wrong. This provides the theological reason for the behavioral instructions elsewhere in the chapter. 1 Tim 2:1–7 is a strong theological statement that God's desire and the redeemer's work are directed toward all people, and therefore the opponents' sectarianism, revealed in their prayers, is wrong. 1 Tim 2:13–14 give Paul's theological reason for his instructions to the women in 2:9–15. The statement of the mystery of Christ in 1 Tim 3:14–16 shows why the instructions in 2:1–3:13 must be followed. 1 Tim 4:1–5 contains a theological description and refutation of the opponents' asceticism, as does 4:7–10. Chap. 6 contains theological instruction on wealth.

2 Timothy is unlike either 1 Timothy or Titus. It is an intensely personal letter written to encourage Timothy in his difficult task and to ask him to come to Rome. Since it was written to one of Paul's best friends who knew his theology, and not to a church who did not know his theology (Titus) or to a church who knew his theology but was choosing to ignore it (1 Timothy), one is not surprised if 2 Timothy does not sound like other letters. It was not intended to be a theological treatise. Yet, even within this context, Paul discusses theological issues. God gives believers a spirit of power (2 Tim 1:7). The gospel is the story of the God who saves people not because of their works but because of his purpose and grace through Christ (2 Tim 1:9–10). Paul discusses the trustworthiness and perseverance of God (2 Tim 1:12; 4:17–18), teaches a high view of Scripture (1:13–14; 2:2, 9; 3:14–4:2), the necessity of, and perseverance in, suffering (1:8; 2:3–7; 3:12; 4:5), the faithfulness of God and his call to obedience (2:11–13), the errant teaching of the opponents (2:18), the security of the believer and the necessity of obedience (2:19), prophecy of sin in the last days (3:1–5; 4:3–4), the future rewards for the believer (4:8), and God's punishment according to one's works (4:14).

Part of Paul's theological response includes what later came to be known as orthodoxy. The church was always interested in preserving the traditions of Jesus' actions and words (e.g., 1 Cor 11:23–26; 15:3). The kerygma was the essential proclamation of the early church and was in some ways solidified into a basic message. Paul was the recipient of those traditions and catechetical teachings as well as direct revelation from Jesus, beginning on the Damascus road. As the apostles and eyewitnesses grew older and died, it is natural that Paul would have viewed his teaching as in some way representing a body of doctrine that should be preserved, not by an institutional structure, such as in Ignatius, but by reliable people who would continue to teach the truth. Even as early as the epistle to the Galatians, Paul's gospel was a recognizable entity; Paul argues that if someone preached a gospel contrary to what had been received, that person was to be anathematized (Gal 1:8–9). By the time of the second epistle to the Thessalonians, Paul could characterize his teaching as "traditions" (παραδόσεις) to which they should adhere (2 Thess 2:15; 3:6). His teaching was to be passed on to other churches (Col 4:16; 1 Thess 5:27). Paul was entrusted with the gospel (1 Tim 1:11; 2:7; Titus 1:3; 2 Tim 1:11; cf. 2 Tim 2:8–9; cf. 1 Cor 9:17; 11:2; Gal 1:1; 2:7; 2 Thess 2:15; 3:16), which he entrusted to Timothy (1 Tim 1:18; 2 Tim 1:13–14; 2:2; 3:14) and which Timothy in turn was to entrust to other reliable people (2 Tim 2:2). This is not the formal transfer of power and creed that is found in the later centuries; it is an emphasis on preserving the true gospel, based on the teachings of Jesus and the apostolic interpretation of his life and death. While this emphasis is found elsewhere in Paul, it is natural and expected to find it emphasized as Paul nears the end of his life, realizing that his time of "guarding the deposit" is ending. Just as God can guard what Paul has deposited with God, so Timothy is to guard what God has deposited with him (2 Tim 1:12, 14). It is a small step to move from here to speaking of "the faith" (see below, *Introduction*, "Themes in the PE"). This is a process that could have occurred within Paul's lifetime (cf. discussions by Guthrie, 57, and Kelly, 44).

C. The Gospel as Right Behavior

Paul does not refute the theological error of the opponents' teaching in detail; his critique centers on the opponents' behavior. There are two underlying premises to this approach: (1) As discussed above, theology should affect behavior. Christ came to "redeem us from all lawlessness and cleanse for himself a special people, a zealot for good works" (Titus 2:14). The call to godly behavior is not a works righteousness; neither is it a call to be a good citizen without theological underpinning. (2) A person's belief and behavior are so closely related that behavior reflects belief; the fruit of the tree is a true representation of the roots of the tree; it is out of one's heart that one speaks (Luke 6:43–45).

Therefore, there is a significant emphasis on good works as the necessary outgrowth of salvation (see *Comment* on 1 Tim 2:10; Ellicott, 196–97). Conversely, there is an expressed desire that one's behavior not bring unnecessary reproach on the church (see *Comment* at 1 Tim 3:2; also 1 Tim 3:7; 5:7, 14; 6:1; Titus 2:5, 8, 10), a concern directed specifically at the opponents. Men and women are to stop disrupting the worship service (1 Tim 2:8–11). The leadership is charged with being above reproach, restrained, and dignified (1 Tim 3:1–13; Titus 1:5–9). People are to take care of widows in their own family (1 Tim 5:3–16). Leaders who persist in sinning must be censored (1 Tim 5:19–20). Women should learn to love their husbands (Titus 2:4–5). Slaves should treat their masters with honor (1 Tim 6:1–2) and be submissive (Titus 2:9–11). People are not to place their hope in riches but are to be generous (1 Tim 6:6–10, 17–19). Many of the types of charges found in the household codes elsewhere are repeated in the PE (e.g., Titus 2:2–6; 3:1–2). Timothy himself is to keep a close watch on his own behavior (1 Tim 4:12–16; see below).

The connection between faith and practice in the PE is established in two ways: (1) It is explicitly taught (Titus 2:11–14; 3:3–7; 2 Tim 2:19; 3:15–17). (2) The truth of the gospel is set against the falseness of the opponents' teaching (1 Tim 1:3, 5, 16; 6:3–5; Titus 3:8b–9), specifically their conduct (1 Tim 1:4, 10–11; 3:2, 9, 15; 2 Tim 2:11–14, 23–25; 3:5). God has saved believers so that they will be zealous in turning from evil to good (2 Tim 2:12–14; Titus 3:8b, 14). Consequently, the truth of a person's affirmation can be tested by that person's behavior, which either supports (1 Tim 4:12, 15; Titus 2:7–8) or contradicts (Titus 1:16) the person's claims. Positively stated, it is the call of God on a person's life that leads him or her to godly living, even a life of suffering (2 Tim 1:8–10; 3:12). The hymn in 2 Tim 2:11–13 summarizes this point: believers who endure will reign with Christ; those who deny Christ will be denied. God's character ensures his faithfulness even in the face of personal faithlessness.

The theological core of the ethics of the PE is the focus of P. H. Towner's *The Goal of Our Instruction,* building on R. Schwarz, *Bürgerliches Christentum im Neuen Testament?* Towner demonstrates that the past event of salvation creates an obligation to live out its consequences. The motive for ethical behavior is not a desire to avoid persecution and live peacefully, but it stems from the fact of salvation and a desire to proclaim the saving message. There is a strong forward look to the end of the age, the second epiphany, which will bring to completion that which was inaugurated at the first (see below, *Introduction,* "Themes in the PE"). Timothy and Titus are living in the last days, looking forward to the parousia (see the excellent summary in Fee, 19–20; Towner, *Goal,* 61–74; also Quinn, 12–13). This emphasis, Towner argues, is intended to correct the opponents' over-realized eschatology. From the historical indicative of salvation comes the ethical imperative of response.

Towner is responding to Dibelius's 1931 argument (*Die Pastoralbriefe,* 2nd ed., HNT 13 [Tübingen: Mohr-Siebeck, 1931] 24–25) that the PE present a bourgeois ethic of *christliche Bürgerlichkeit,* "Christian citizenship" (see bibliography in *Goal,* 259 n. 2; cf. Dibelius-Conzelmann, 8, 39–41; Kidd, *Wealth,* 181–85). Dibelius argues that because of the delay of the parousia, the eschatological tension of the "already but not yet" gave way to a stance in which the church was learning to settle down and live in the world, living in peaceful coexistence and adopting much of the world's ethical structure as its own. Dibelius relies heavily on verses such as 1 Tim 2:2 and its emphasis on εὐσέβεια, "godliness." The emphasis, Dibelius maintains, has shifted from a dynamic and life-changing gospel to a dogma that must be preserved (e.g., 1 Tim 6:20; 2 Tim 1:13–14; 2:2). Kümmel describes this perspective as "rationalistic ethical" (*Introduction,* 383). While Paul proclaims the coming Lord, the PE acknowledge the present Lord who rules the Christian's life (Oberlinner, 92).

Dibelius's approach is directly challenged by R. M. Kidd in *Wealth and Beneficence in the Pastoral Epistles.* He disputes Dibelius at three main points: (1) Dibelius

maintains that the church of the PE had grown beyond its beginnings as a movement among the impoverished lower class and now included a middle class, the
Christian bourgeoisie; Kidd argues that the acknowledged Paulines show that the
earliest church drew from the rich, upper class as well. (2) Dibelius also alleges
that the bourgeois church accommodated itself to the ethics of secular society.
Kidd analyzes the teaching on wealth in the PE, showing how the PE contain an
implicit critique of society's approach to wealth. For example, society taught that
wealth should be used to provide future security; people were encouraged to give
money away so others would be indebted to return the favor at a later date (reciprocity). However, the PE teach that reciprocity in the eschatological kingdom is
from God, and thus the "whole web of human reciprocity is dismantled" (*Wealth*,
157). (We may also see the error of Dibelius's approach elsewhere: the ethics of 1
Tim 2:1–7 is grounded not on society's values but on God's desire and Christ's
salvific work [see *Comment*]; the arguments of 1 Tim 2:11–15 likewise are grounded
in God's created order [vv 13–14] and not in the order of society.) (3) Dibelius
also argues that the PE show an "unheroic conservatism" by their refusal to alter
society, a refusal seen to be essential if the church is to survive. Kidd shows that
the PE teach a moral behavior motivated by future eschatological realities (citing
the work of Donelson, *Pseudepigraphy*, 148). Kidd also points out that elsewhere
in the undisputed letters of Paul there is a *bürgerlich* (i.e., "mundane") social ethic
and at the same time a strong eschatological hope (e.g., 1 Thess 4:11–12; Phil
4:8). The ethics of the PE is not determined by a dejected and disappointed church
that is coming to realize that Christ would not immediately return. The imperative of obedience is grounded in the salvific work of Christ with an expectation of
eschatological fulfillment at Christ's coming epiphany.

D. Leadership

The dual issues of doctrine and behavior are joined in the issue of leadership.
As has been shown above, much of the opposition came from church leaders
who had left the faith and were actively promoting the heresy. The requirements
of church leadership stipulate that the leaders not only know the truth of the
gospel and are able to teach it and refute the heresy, but also have personal character that controls their behavior. These are the underlying premises in 1 Tim 3;
Titus 1; and 2 Tim 2:2. Paul instructs Timothy: "what you have heard from me
through many witnesses, entrust these things to faithful men, who will also be
able to teach others" (2 Tim 2:2). The "faithful" men were those who believed
the gospel and were reliable in character. They were to take responsibility for
what God had entrusted to Paul, Paul to Timothy, and now Timothy to them.

In *Form/Structure/Setting* on 1 Tim 3:1–7, the issue of church structure is discussed in detail. The NT witnesses to Paul's desire to appoint leadership in his
churches (Acts 14:23), and such appointment occurred at the same time that the
charismatic gifts were being exercised; they were not mutually contradictory. The
Pauline churches, even the Corinthian church with its emphasis on spiritual gifts,
were always under the authority of the apostle as far as Paul was concerned. While
the historical situation of the PE led to the need for qualified people to fulfill
leadership roles, there is no suggestion in the text that these positions were new.
In the PE Paul continues the basic structure that he knew from the synagogue

and that was practiced from the earliest days of the church (Acts 6:3). As the church continued to mature and the eyewitnesses and apostles died, it would have been tremendously shortsighted (Guthrie, *Introduction*, 625) if Paul had not continued his past practices.

But how were Timothy and Titus to deal with the opponents? In Crete, where the opponents were not as entrenched (Titus 1:11), Titus was not to remove but only to appoint church leaders (Titus 1:5). Yet Paul's charge to Titus corresponds to his general charge to Timothy: "Avoid the factious person after a first and second warning" (Titus 3:10). Titus and Timothy were called to confront the opponents, to muzzle them (Titus 1:11), rebuke them (1 Tim 5:20; Titus 1:13), and command them to stop (1 Tim 1:3). Paul himself excommunicated the opponents if necessary (1 Tim 1:20). However, there may have come a time, presumably after their refusal to listen, that Timothy and Titus would simply stay away from them (Titus 3:10; 2 Tim 3:5). The same duality is in Paul's instruction concerning what the opponents were teaching. There is a point in time to argue with false teaching (2 Tim 2:25), but this false teaching was so vacuous, so void of developed content, and so destructive to a person's life that for the most part it was simply to be avoided (1 Tim 4:7; 6:11, 20; 2 Tim 2:14, 16, 22–23; Titus 3:9). Paul's language is not so harsh when directed toward the church in general (1 Tim 4:6, 11; 5:1–2; 6:2b, 17; Titus 2:2–6, 9–10; 2:15–3:2, 8).

The PE do not give institutional *authority* to the overseers and deacons. They describe the type of person who may serve the church in a certain role: one whose character is above reproach, who has illustrated management skills at home; who can teach (in the case of the overseers), etc. This person will teach what is true and will refute what is false. While some authority may be *implicit* in the title and the nature of the position, nowhere does the text *explicitly* say what is so often asserted by modern writers (e.g., Young, *Theology*, 22; cf. 120), that the author's solution to the rise of heresy was to force a structure onto the house of God (cf. *Comment* on 1 Tim 3:15) and appoint authoritative leaders who could combat the error because of their institutional position. There is no explicit institutional authority promoted in the PE.

E. Personal Advice

Paul has two basic points to make to Timothy and Titus personally: (1) They are to monitor their own behavior (1 Tim 4:12–16; 5:21; Titus 2:7, 8), including a willingness to suffer (2 Tim 1:8; 2:3–7; 3:12), and they are to monitor their teaching (1 Tim 6:20; 2 Tim 4:2; Titus 2:1, 7–8). Paul advises Timothy: "Watch yourself and the teaching; be persistent in them; for by doing this you will save both yourself and those hearing you" (1 Tim 4:16; cf. *Comment* on 2 Tim 2:15). Instead of being wrapped up in the vacuous heresy, they are to concentrate on their own work (2 Tim 4:5). Both Timothy (1 Tim 4:7, 15) and Titus (Titus 2:7) are models to their churches. (2) Paul also wants to encourage his friends, especially Timothy. The bulk of 2 Timothy is a call to loyalty and perseverance, both to the gospel and to Paul (1 Tim 1:12–17, 18; 4:6, 14; 6:11–16; 2 Tim 1:5–7, 13–14; 2:1–2, 8–13, 17–19, 25–26; 3:1–5, 9, 10–12, 14–15; 4:8, 14, 17–18). The call to faithfulness to the gospel is especially strong (1 Tim 4:13, 16; 2 Tim 1:8–14; 2:2, 8–9, 15; 3:14–4:2).

ADDITIONAL ISSUES

A. The Role of Personal Details

All three letters contain many details of the sort that would be expected in a personal letter. Paul speaks with affection (1 Tim 1:2; 2 Tim 1:3–7; 2:1; 4:9; Titus 1:4) and encouragement (2 Tim 1:8; 2:3–7) to his friends, showing concern for their well-being (1 Tim 4:6, 12–16; 5:2b, 21–23; Titus 2:7–8, 15), which assumes a personal relationship (1 Tim 1:8; 2 Tim 1:3–7). Specific historical allusions are made throughout the letters (1 Tim 1:3; 3:14; 5:20; 2 Tim 1:15–18; 4:10–13, 16–17; Titus 1:10–16; 3:12–13), including comments directed toward specific historical figures who were opposing Paul (1 Tim 1:19–20; 2 Tim 2:17) and the specific problems in Ephesus and Crete (1 Tim 1:3–7; 5:8, 11–15; 2 Tim 2:18; 4:14–15; Titus 1:10–16; 3:10). Paul writes of events (1 Tim 1:12–17; 2:7; 2 Tim 1:11; 3:10–11) and attitudes (2 Tim 1:12; 2:10; 4:6–8, 18) in his own life as well as those in Timothy's (1 Tim 1:18; 4:14; 6:11, 20; 2 Tim 1:5). Some of the details are almost casual in nature, information that might occur to a person in the course of writing (2 Tim 1:18; 3:15; 4:10–13, 19–21). Especially in the case of 2 Timothy, the emotional bond between writer and recipient is so strong and so much a part of the message that the letter's intent would be destroyed without it. These details are not literary trappings added to the letters; they are woven into the fabric of the text and are an integral part of what Paul wants to say.

B. Differences among the Three Letters

The three letters forming the PE corpus tend to be viewed as a unit, and they do contain much in common. They are written in a similar literary style purportedly by the same author to two of his inner circle who were continuing their work in two different churches as apostolic delegates and were experiencing somewhat the same opposition. This unity is reinforced by the title "Pastoral Epistles," first used in the early 1700s by D. N. Berdot and P. Anton (cited in Guthrie, 11). However, there are significant differences among the letters that should not be overlooked.

(1) In Paul's first letter to Timothy, Paul is facing a severe situation. Timothy is in an older church where the leadership has strayed from the gospel, and Paul must therefore deal with established problems and structures. He is writing to a church that knows his teaching and yet refuses to follow it. Their persecution of Timothy is severe. (2) Paul's letter to Titus begins with issues similar to those in 1 Timothy, but the Cretan church is younger. Titus is to appoint church leaders, not remove bad ones from office. While there is significant opposition, it is not as severe as in Ephesus. The bulk of Titus has to do not with church leaders but with basic catechetical instruction as would be expected in a new church. The basic thrust of this instruction is the necessity of salvation working itself out in obedience in a person's life. Salvation not only purifies sinners but prepares a people who are zealous for good deeds (Titus 2:15; 3:8). (3) In 2 Timothy, while Timothy is still confronting opposition in Ephesus, Paul writes on a much more personal level. He wants to encourage Timothy to be loyal to him and to the gospel, to suffer willingly, to rely on Scripture, and to visit him soon in Rome. It is

not primarily a public letter but a look into the apostle's heart. It does a disservice to the texts to force them into a common mold and view them homogeneously. And while it is common to view the PE as a literary unit when doing statistical analyses (see below), when the same statistical studies view the PE as independent letters, 2 Timothy is often shown to be different from 1 Timothy and Titus and fully Pauline (although there are serious questions about the reliability of these studies).

C. Why Three Letters?

If the PE were written to make Paul's message applicable to later generations, then why risk the increased possibility of exposure of pseudonymity created by three letters, especially when Titus and 2 Timothy add very little theologically to the message of 1 Timothy? The question still stands even if one believes pseudepigraphy was accepted and recognized as such by the early church. Roloff's suggestion (45) that Titus was to be a supplement to 1 Timothy falters when one realizes that Titus has very little overlap with 1 Timothy. Roloff says that 2 Timothy is simply Paul's last words.

CONCLUSION

At this point it may be asked, is the self-witness of the PE that the letters were written by the apostle Paul to Timothy and Titus consistent and historically credible? Is it consistent with what is known of Paul elsewhere? Is it supported historically by the external evidence of the early church? Although I answer these questions in the affirmative on the basis of the evidence presented above, there are a number of scholars who have concluded that the PE are in fact pseudonymous documents, and it is to their arguments that I now turn.

Critical Questions about the PE within the Framework of Paul's Life

Roloff, echoing the view of many scholars, says that today there should not even be a doubt that Paul did not write—directly or indirectly—the PE (376). Above I have painted a picture based on the self-witness of the PE; the question now becomes, is it more plausible than the picture painted by those who disagree? Does a critical reconstruction explain the specific features of the PE within a historical framework that is more plausible than the traditional one without introducing its own set of irreconcilable problems?

Much of the critical discussion involves the broader hermeneutical issue of one's view of critical methodologies. How far can a person's style be measured? How much effect do circumstances have on how a person writes (e.g., age, location, audience, content) or how a person expresses theology? I will not discuss each of the critical methodologies in depth, but I will summarize the issues as they relate to the text and point the reader to resources for further study. I am indebted to Guthrie's discussion of these issues (*Introduction*, 607–49) and recommend it for more detailed analysis.

The authenticity of the PE was not questioned until the nineteenth century. Schleiermacher (*Über den sogenannten ersten Brief des Paulus an den Timotheus* [1807]) was the first to raise the question of the authorship of 1 Timothy because of its vocabulary, and Eichhorn (*Historisch-kritische Einleitung* [1812]) extended the skepticism to 2 Timothy and Titus. Baur (*Pastoralbriefe*) and the Tübingen school dropped all three letters from the Pauline corpus for linguistic and historical reasons, postulating that only four of the canonical writings bearing Paul's name were from Paul. In the twentieth century critical scholarship began to acknowledge the personal elements and historical allusions in the PE and suggested the possibility that Pauline fragments had been included (Harrison, *Problem* [1921]; Scott, 1936; Falconer, 1937; Easton, 1948) or that the corpus was the work not of a second-century forger but of a pseudepigrapher (see below), possibly an admirer of Paul who wanted to make Paul's message relevant to the needs of a later generation. Subsequently, it has often been viewed as one of the "assured results of scholarship" that Paul could not have written the PE. For example, the NEB translates 1 Tim 1:2 "his true son," rather than "my true son" (γνησίῳ τέκνῳ), implying a distance between the writer and Paul (confirmed by personal correspondence between C. H. Dodd and R. H. Mounce, which was reported to me by the latter).

Yet there have always been defenders of Pauline authorship in continental, British, and American scholarship: Alford, *Greek New Testament* (1st ed., 1849); Ellicott (1864); Huther (ET 1885); Plummer (1st ed., 1888); F. Godet, *Studies on the Epistles* (tr. A. H. Holmden [New York; Dutton, 1889]); Lightfoot, *Biblical Essays* (1893); Bernard (1899); Zahn, *Introduction* (1st Ger. ed., 1899); B. Weiss (1902); Wohlenberg (1st ed., 1906); Hort, *Christian Ecclesia* (1914); Ramsay (1909–11); James, *Genuineness* (1909); White (1910); Parry (1920); Lock (1924); Michaelis, *Pastoralbriefe* (1930); Robertson, *Word Pictures* (1931); Thörnell, *Pastoralbrevens* (1931); Torm, *Psychologie* (1932); Roller, *Formular* (1933); Spicq (1st ed., 1948); Jeremias (1st ed., 1953); Simpson (1954); Guthrie, *Pastoral Epistles and the Mind of Paul* (1956); Hendriksen (1957); Ellis, *Paul and His Recent Interpreters* (1961); Goppelt, *Apostolic and Post-Apostolic Times* (Ger. 1962, ET 1970); E. F. Harrison, *Introduction to the New Testament* (Grand Rapids, MI: Eerdmans, 1964); Kelly (1964); Holtz (1965); Ridderbos (1967); Bürki (1974, 1975); Fee (1984); L. T. Johnson, *Writings* (1986); Knight (1992); more listed in Spicq, 1:159.

There are three basic critical issues raised by scholarship: (1) *Historical:* the PE do not fit into the historical framework of Acts. (2) *Theological:* the PE omit some themes that are central to Paul's theology and develop some in ways unlike Paul, or, it is argued, in ways that contradict Pauline thinking. (3) *Literary style:* the vocabulary and style of writing in the PE are different from the "acknowledged" Paulines.

THE HISTORICAL PROBLEM

A. The Historical Framework of Acts

It is argued that the historical events referred to the PE do not fit into the time frame of Acts and are therefore fictitious. Scott (xvi–xvii) asserts, "That Paul cannot have been the author is most clearly apparent when we examine the historical framework of the letters." However, this seems to be the least significant of the objections to Pauline authorship and is based almost entirely on an argument from silence.

This argument has significance only if Acts must tell the entire story, but, as has been shown above, this is not the case. Acts does not claim to be exhaustive (cf. the events described by Paul in Rom 15:19; 2 Cor 11:24–27), implicitly suggests that Paul was innocent and should have been released, and leaves his fate an open question. This agrees with Paul's expectations expressed elsewhere as well as with church tradition. P. N. Harrison (*Problem,* 102–15; *NTS* 2 [1956] 250–61) argues that the supposition of a release and second Roman imprisonment for Paul is only an attempt to prove the historicity of the PE, but this type of argument is not constructive since the same could be said in reverse, that a denial of the supposition is only an attempt to disprove the historicity of the PE. Similarly, Hanson ([1983] 6) observes, "It is rather an indication that those who hold to the authenticity of the Pastorals are obliged to make certain assumptions about the later course of Paul's career." But, of course, Hanson must assume that Paul died at the end of the captivity recorded in Acts and that Acts tells the entire story. In light of the frequent scholarly distrust of the reliability of Acts, it is interesting that here its reliability becomes the standard against which the PE are judged.

It seems just as unlikely that a pseudepigrapher, a person writing under Paul's name, would have created a fictitious historical setting that did not fit into Acts, especially an entire missionary journey to Crete. If his purpose in writing was to show to a later generation the relevance of Paul's teaching using Paul's name, it seems that he would have more carefully set his presentation within the historical context of Acts.

Some have attempted to place the PE within the events recorded in Acts, but they have convinced few. J. A. T. Robinson (*Redating,* 67–85) places 1 Timothy between 1 Corinthians and 2 Corinthians, Titus during Paul's third missionary journey while on his way back to Jerusalem, and 2 Timothy during the Caesarean imprisonment. Bartlet (*Exp* 8.5 [1913] 28–36, 161–67, 256–63, 325–47) puts 1 Timothy after the Ephesian ministry, Titus after the voyage by Crete on Paul's way to Rome, and 2 Timothy during the "first" Roman imprisonment (see also Bowen, *Dates;* Badcock, *Pauline Epistles,* 115–33; Binder, "Situation," 70–83; de Lestapis, *L'énigme,* 167–77; Reicke, *TLZ* 101 [1976] 81–94; van Bruggen, *JETS* 25 [1982] 381–82; Towner, 17–19). Prior places 2 Timothy during the "first" Roman imprisonment and sees 2 Tim 4:6–8 as expressing Paul's belief in his imminent release (*Letter-Writer,* 91–112).

The following are the specific issues that this reconstruction with reference to the events recorded in Acts must address (see also Lightfoot, *Biblical Essays,* 403–6, and the detailed discussion above): (1) The background for 1 Timothy is an earlier meeting of Paul and Timothy; Paul was now on his way to Macedonia, Timothy had returned to Ephesus, and Paul hoped to visit him soon (1 Tim 1:3; 3:14). The amount of time required for these events to unfold and for the Ephesian heresy to develop and become influential make it doubtful that all this could have happened during Paul's second or third missionary journey, even though he was in the general vicinity. When Paul did finally leave Ephesus (Acts 20:1), he sent Timothy on ahead; Timothy did not remain in Ephesus. There is no suggestion in Acts that Paul had to deal with this type of problem while he was in Ephesus. (2) According to Titus, Paul apparently had an extended missionary journey through Crete, requiring a longer visit than the quick visit recorded in Acts 27:7–13. Some suggest that Paul traveled to Crete during his lengthy stays in Corinth

or Ephesus, not recorded in Acts. While certainly possible, it means that Luke
omits a major missionary journey during the period of time he is recording Paul's
movements and the spread of the gospel. It can be argued that "I left" (ἀπέλιπον;
Titus 1:5) requires only that Titus, and not Paul, was in Crete (de Lestapis, *L'énigme*,
52–54; cf. Robinson, *Redating*, 67–85); but this is not the most natural reading.
(3) The suggestion of Acts (especially 26:32) and Paul's expectation (see above,
"Historical Reconstruction from Acts, D. Imprisonment"; "Historical Reconstruction from the PE, A. Release from Imprisonment") is that Paul was released. (4)
The imprisonment in 2 Timothy is much harsher than the one recorded in Acts
28. (5) The PE suggest that Paul spent time in Corinth (2 Tim 4:20), Troas, and
Miletus (2 Tim 4:13) while Timothy was in Ephesus; however, in Acts 20:4 Timothy was with Paul. The PE also suggest that Paul had been there recently, but
according to Acts, whether 2 Timothy is dated during the Caesarean or "first"
Roman imprisonment, it had been several years since his last visit to Asia Minor.
(6) Trophimus was left sick at Miletus (2 Tim 4:20), but in Acts 21:29 he accompanied Paul to Jerusalem. (7) The prophecy to the Ephesian elders in Acts 20:20
requires the heresy to have arisen after Paul's return to Jerusalem, because it
speaks of the rise of heresy in the future (Acts 20:29; cf. Lightfoot, *Biblical Essays*,
404–5). (8) 2 Tim 1:17 states that Paul is imprisoned in Rome, not Caesarea. (9)
By the time of Titus 3:13, Apollos had become a well-known traveling evangelist;
in Acts 18:24 he was not yet a believer (Kelly, 7). (10) Agabus's prophecy (Acts
21:11) only says that Paul would be imprisoned, not that he would die. (11) Clement of Rome states that Paul preached to the "boundaries" of the West (see above,
"Historical Reconstruction from the PE, A. Release from Imprisonment"; cf. J.
Weiss, *History* 1:390; Holtz, 18; Brox, 30), although it could be argued that Rome
itself was that boundary (e.g., P. N. Harrison, *Problem*, 102ff.; Dibelius-Conzelmann,
3). The force of these issues is sufficiently strong that most feel that a time period
after Acts 28 is required, or that the historical setting of the PE is fictitious.

B. Church Structure in the PE

It is also argued that the developed church structure of overseers and deacons
evident in 1 Timothy and Titus belongs to a time later than the life of Paul, closer
to the time of Ignatius (A.D. 116). Moffatt asserts, "The sub-Pauline atmosphere
is further felt unmistakably in the details of the ecclesiastical structure which is
designed to oppose these errorists" (*Introduction*, 410). The assumption is that
the church began as a charismatic, pneumatic organism and only later developed
elders, deacons, and eventually bishops in order to combat error. Timothy and
Titus are viewed by some as the leaders of the first of the "monarchical episco-
pates," bishops with institutional authority over all the churches in a given area
whose job it was to pass on tradition. Hanson ([1983] 31) observes, "One of the
distinctive features in the Pastoral Epistles, wherever they differ from all other
documents in the NT, is the attention they devote to ordained offices in the church.
This in itself marks them as belonging to a later generation than Paul's." Easton
(177) states further, "In 'Timothy' and 'Titus,' therefore, the Ignatian bishops
are actually found in everything but the title" (cf. B. H. Streeter, *The Primitive
Church* [New York: Macmillan, 1929] 118–19; Scott, 6; Gealy, 344–45; Käsemann,
Essays, 88; von Campenhausen, *Ecclesiastical Authority*, esp. 106–9).

However, every element of this approach introduces problems. (1) In *Form/Structure/Setting* on 1 Tim 3:1–7 it is argued that from the beginning Paul continued the synagogue tradition and appointed elders. Easton (226) holds that references to church offices in Acts and the PE are anachronisms, but he dismisses the evidence in order to support his conclusion. As Kelly (14) argues, "It cannot nowadays be denied that, for all the respect paid to the prophets and other Spirit-moved individuals, there were always officials of a more practical, functional kind in his churches." The emphasis on ecstatic gifts in 1 Corinthians only reflects the situation in Corinth, and even in Corinth there were spiritual gifts of "administrators" (12:28). Paul always exercised authoritative control over his churches, even over the charismatically gifted (Spicq, 1:178). The rest of the NT does not spell out the qualities of church leaders in the same detail as is done in the PE, perhaps because it was not an issue elsewhere (contra Meade, *Pseudonymity*, 119); however, there are sufficient references to indicate that the instructions in the PE should not be viewed as surprising. It can also be argued that at the end of his life, with the encroaching deaths of the eyewitnesses and apostles, Paul would be expected to place more emphasis on the structure of the church, a structure hitherto primarily supplied by the apostles and eyewitnesses.

(2) The organizational structure evident in the PE would not have taken a long time to evolve (cf. the relative quickness of the development in Acts 6), and in fact the structure in the PE is at an early stage of development. L. T. Johnson calls it "sociological fantasy" (16) not to see the need for structure for over half a century. It is to be expected that a young religious movement would have developed quickly when faced with religious, philosophical, and secular opposition (so also Lock, xxx), and this development, sociologically (L. T. Johnson, 15) and religiously (Acts 6), would require structure. Hanson ([1983] 4) overstates the evidence when he says that there was a "fixed institutional clergy" and a "regular ordained ministry," and Dibelius-Conzelmann (44) are overly cautious in thinking that Paul's requirement that an overseer not be a recent convert (1 Tim 3:6) necessitated a significantly longer period of development. The terminology of leadership is not used consistently (Titus 1:5, 7), and the duties are not defined. Paul even has to defend the right of church officers to be paid (1 Tim 5:17). There is no mention of a deacon moving up the hierarchical ladder to the office of overseer. 2 Tim 2:2 does not discuss the transfer of ecclesiastical authority (cf. Guthrie, 139). There is no concept of succession of office and no concept of an episcopate. There is only a two-tiered structure of overseers and deacons, and not the later three-tiered structure that included the monarchical bishop (Brox, xx). Paul merely wants the church leaders to be serious and dignified people who know the gospel, can refute error, and have basic managerial skills; this is not institutionalism. The instructions regarding widows in 1 Tim 5 do not show an order of widows with entrance requirements and prescribed tasks; Paul clarifies which widows should be cared for by the church and which widows should be cared for by their families. This actually is the opposite of institutionalism. There are no duties prescribed (see *Form/Structure/Setting* on 1 Tim 5:3–16). There is no theological defense or legitimation of institutionalism, and even a cursory reading of Ignatius—who goes so far as to compare the bishop to God (see *Explanation* on 1 Tim 3:1–7)—shows how different the PE are from Ignatius' age.

(3) There is no authority *explicitly* given to the church leaders, and the assumption that a church leader will by definition exercise authority over the church does

PASTORAL EPISTLES

not come from the text but from second-century authority structures such as in Ignatius or from modern presuppositions. In the PE, church leaders are to be above reproach, are to be respected (1 Tim 3:13), and are to be paid (1 Tim 5:17). The leaders are to give instructions (2 Tim 2:2), refuting those who oppose them (Titus 1:9). This is not institutionalism: no authority is expressly given; no duties are assigned apart from teaching (although some may be expected, such as hospitality); the relationship between overseer and deacon is not even spelled out.

(4) Timothy and Titus stand outside the church structure. They are not bishops or elders, and are not members of the local church. They are itinerant, apostolic delegates sent with Paul's authority to deal with local problems (see *Form/Structure/Setting* on 1 Tim 3:1–7; Lock, xix; Robinson, *Redating*, 68), just as they do in Acts. Timothy and Titus are never told to rely on their institutional position in the local church for authority; rather they rely on the authority of Paul and the gospel. If Timothy were a monarchical bishop, there would have been no reason for Paul's encouragement; Timothy could simply have relied on his ecclesiastical authority and have enforced compliance. In fact, a close reading of Ignatius shows just how different the church structure and ecclesiastical authority in the second century were from that in the PE, and this difference becomes a strong argument for the first-century date of the PE (see *Explanations* on 1 Tim 3:1–7; 3:8–13).

(5) Knight argues that Paul's instructions concerning the widows actually are a movement away from the alleged institutionalization of the church: "Essentially what Paul is doing is correcting the tendency toward institutionalization by restricting the care for widows to widows over sixty years of age, who have no family members to care for them and who are spiritually qualified for any special service the church may ask of them. This approach, which emphasizes the family and curtails institutionalization while affirming the need for the family and the church to care for the widows, is certainly moving in the opposite direction from that which developed later in the church" (31).

(6) Issues of church structure are minimal in Titus (five of forty-one verses) and are nonexistent in 2 Timothy (expect perhaps in 2 Tim 2:2). To speak of an emphasis on church structure in the Pastorals requires viewing them as a single corpus and setting aside the significant differences among the three letters.

THE THEOLOGICAL PROBLEM

A. Doctrinal Issues

It is argued that the PE lack key Pauline themes and that some of the theology in the PE is un-Pauline, either different from or contrary to the theology of the undisputed Pauline letters. For Roloff (31), this is the deciding argument. I would agree that if the theology of the Pastorals were *contradictory* to—not merely different from—what is found in Paul elsewhere, then this would be the strongest argument for inauthenticity. Related is the issue of how Paul deals with the opponents; normally he argues against their theological position, but in the PE, it is claimed, he attacks the opponents themselves and not their theology.

1. The absence of Pauline themes. It is argued that certain themes found elsewhere in Paul are altogether missing in the PE, such as the Holy Spirit, the church, the cross, flesh versus spirit, mystery, and the fatherhood (of God) (cf. Moffatt, *Introduction*, 412; Easton, 11–13). The argument from this observation is that there are some themes so central to Paul's thought that their absence calls Pauline authorship into question. For example, Hanson comments on 1 Tim 1:17 that this is the only place where mention of God's invisibility is not followed by mention of his revelation in Christ and concludes that the author "was no great theologian" ([1983] 62; cf. Easton, 203; Barrett, 6). Easton (11–12) likewise argues:

> Paul's religion is Spirit filled to the last degree; hence the merely statistical observation that he uses "Spirit" about 80 times far understates the extent of the experience of the Spirit in Paul's thought and life. But the Pastor uses "Spirit" exactly three times (2 Tim. 1.14; Tit. 3.5; 1 Tim 4.1) and exactly once in each letter—and never in a phrase written by himself! Nowhere except in 2 Tim 1.14 and Tit 3.5—and both are citations—does he remind Timothy or Titus that they and their people will have the omnipotent help of the Spirit in the arduous tasks that lie before them; there is no parallel to "if ye by the Spirit put to death the deeds of the body, ye shall live" (Rom 8.13). So little part does the Spirit play in the Pastor's own thought that in 2 Tim 1.7 his reminiscence of Rom 8.15 omits what to Paul was all-essential—and so turns triumphant ecstasy into moralistic exhortation. As a consequence, the words into which Paul pours the content of his transformed life, "it is no longer I that live but Christ lives in me" (Gal 2.20), are impossible in the Pastorals; without experience of the Spirit there can be no experience of the mystical union.

Against this type of argument, however, are the following considerations: (a) There is no legitimate reason that Paul must speak about the issues modern scholarship deems to be the core of Pauline thought every time he writes; such a requirement is artificial and overly wooden. Are we really to believe that a creative writer like Paul cannot speak of the "otherness" of God without a reference to God's revelation in Christ, as Hanson ([1983] 62) asserts? (b) The fact that the PE do not constitute a church manual but are written to specific historical circumstances makes this argument especially fallacious. Paul was writing to two members of his inner circle about the specific historical issues they faced and would not have needed to discuss basic theological topics. (c) What often skews the results of comparing themes is that the three epistles are usually viewed as a single entity. But it should be remembered that each of the PE is a relatively short, independent letter. Often the absence of a theme in 1 or 2 Thessalonians is not deemed significant because of the size and subject matter of each letter. The same consideration should be afforded to each of the PE.

(d) A quick look at the acknowledged Pauline letters shows that frequently a theme that is common in one book is of considerably less significance in another, or is totally omitted. In the first example it is apparent how skewed numbers can become when cognates are ignored (e.g., δίκαιος, "righteous," δικαιοσύνη, "righteousness," δικαιοῦν, "to reckon as righteous," δικαίωμα, "righteous deed," δικαίως, "righteously," δικαίωσις, "accounting righteous"), or when a concept rather than a word is examined.

	Rom	1 Cor	2 Cor	Gal	Eph	Phil	Col	1 Thess	2 Thess	Phlm
δικαιοῦν, "to justify, reckon as righteous;"	15	2	0	8	0	0	0	0	0	0
δικαιο-, root for "just, righteous"	63	4	7	13	4	6	1	1	0	0
δικαιοσύνη θεοῦ, "righteousness of God"	8	0	1	0	0	0	0	0	0	0
σταυρο-, root for "cross"	0	6	1	6	1	2	2	0	0	0
ἀκροβυστία, "uncircumcision"	11	2	0	3	1	0	2	0	0	0
υἱός (of Jesus), "son"	7	2	1	4	1	0	1	1	0	0
ἐλευθερία, "freedom"	1	1	1	4	0	0	0	0	0	0
σάρξ, "flesh";	26	11	11	18	9	5	9	0	0	1
σάρξ vs. πνεῦμα, "flesh vs. spirit"	13	1	1	7	0	0	1	0	0	0
νόμος, "law"	74	9	0	32	1	3	0	0	0	0

Four conclusions can be drawn from these statistics. (i) This type of statistical work confirms that the number of occurrences is directly related to the subject matter of the book and not necessarily to its length (although that should also be taken into consideration). Fee argues that "Paul employs an extensive language, with a full range of metaphors, to speak of this saving event—justification, redemption, reconciliation, ransom, cleansing, propitiation—but the essence . . . remains constant" (15). The δικαιο- word group ("just, righteous") plays a role in Romans, Galatians, and Philippians because of the opponents who are addressed. The statistics for books of approximately the same length—Romans (432 verses; 7,114 words) and 1 Corinthians (437 verses, 6,842 words), or Galatians (149 verses, 2,233 words) and the Captivity Epistles (Ephesians: 155 verses, 2,423 words; Philippians: 104 verses, 1,631 words)—demonstrate that any methodology that compares word/theme occurrences apart from historical context and theological concerns must be questioned. If the omission of themes and Pauline vocabulary in 1 and 2 Thessalonians (89 and 47 verses, 1482 and 823 words) seems insignificant, the same is true for 2 Timothy (83 verses, 1239 words) and Titus (46 verses, 659 words). Once it is admitted that themes are "clumped" in the Pauline letters, then it must be allowed that omissions are not necessarily significant. As Fee states, "One can be sure, for example, that if we did not have 1 Corinthians, one of the 'assured results' of PE scholarship would be that Paul and his churches knew nothing of the Eucharist. Indeed, but for the abuses in the church in Corinth, one can only imagine what other assured results based on silence there might be" (30 n. 25).

(ii) Is there any real difference between a theme occurring once and not occurring at all? If a theme only occurs once in a letter, it can hardly be classified as a theme in that epistle; and if it is not a theme, then it could be a passing comment, which is only slightly different from an omission. For example, is the single occurrence of δικαιοσύνη θεοῦ, "righteousness of God," in 2 Corinthians an indication of Pauline authorship? Is the omission of this phrase in all of Paul's other letters except Romans evidence of inauthenticity?

(iii) If the omission of a theme is not significant, then an *emphasis* on a theme should also not raise questions of authenticity. δικαιοσύνη θεοῦ, "righteousness of God," occurs almost exclusively in Romans, but this does not make Romans suspect, nor should themes such as εὐσέβεια, "piety, godliness," and ἐπιφάνεια, "appearance, appearing," cast doubt upon the authenticity of the PE. The problem is with any methodology that does not take the historical situation into account.

(iv) If there is a core of themes that are so central to Paul that he always must discuss them any time he writes, whether to a church or an individual, whether to people he does not know or to his inner circle, then would not a pseudepigrapher be clever enough to include those themes in his work?

According to the table presented above, if the occurrence of the thought regarding the "Spirit" in Rom 8:13 were to become the standard of authenticity as Easton's comment (above) would require, then five of Paul's letters would be of questionable authenticity. Contrary to Easton's comment, there is nothing in the PE that makes the assertion of Gal 2:20 "impossible." Paul makes it clear to Timothy that the strength to carry out his task does not come from within himself (e.g., 1 Tim 4:6). Fee's analysis of the Holy Spirit in the PE is fundamentally different from Easton's. He shows how the Holy Spirit, active in calling and empowering Timothy for ministry (1 Tim 1:18; 4:14; 2 Tim 1:6–7), is central to all the creedal statements (1 Tim 3:16; Titus 3:5–6) and is also active in prophetic utterances (1 Tim 4:1). Fee concludes, "What emerges from these final Pauline letters, therefore, is exactly what emerges elsewhere in Paul: The Spirit plays the crucial role in Christian conversion and ongoing Christian life; the Spirit is the key to Christian ministry; the Spirit is perceived in terms of power; and the Spirit is present in the church partly through gifts experienced by individuals within a community context" (*God's Empowering Presence*, 757; cf. also the "power" texts in 2 Tim 1:8; 3:5, 16; Haykin, *EvQ* 57 [1985] 291–305; Towner, *Goal*, 56–58).

Even Barrett, after listing the "missing" words in the PE, admits that they "prove little" (6; cf. summary in Knight, 33 n. 88). Spicq concludes that since the Pauline canon is not limited to the "four great letters," each new idea should not be suspect nor significance found in every omission (1:174).

2. Pauline terms used differently or in a contradictory way. It is argued that some of the terms in the PE, which also occur in the acknowledged Pauline writings, are used in ways that Paul would not use them. Either they are given a different emphasis or are used in a manner contradictory to their use in the undisputed letters of Paul. If the latter were true, this would be the strongest argument against authenticity.

For example, it is claimed that the phrase "in Christ" does not describe a mystical relationship in the PE but a "quality" available to those who are "in Christ" (Easton, 12; Allan, *NTS* 10 [1963–64] 115–21). "Faith" in the PE is not a gift from

God but "a deposit to which nothing can be added" (Dibelius-Conzelmann, 13; cf. Easton, 103; Merk, ZNW 66 [1975] 92–102; Houlden, 51; Hanson, [1983] 57). "Righteousness" is not a gift from God but a virtue to be sought (1 Tim 6:11; 2 Tim 2:22; see *Comment* on 1 Tim 1:9). Hanson comments, "It is hard to imagine a more un-Pauline phrase than 'training in righteousness'" ([1983] 152). Marshall writes of the author "think[ing] in a different kind of way," which for him is more significant than the linguistic issues ("Recent Study of the Pastoral Epistles," *Themelios* 23 [1997] 12). Allan (*NTS* 10 [1963–64] 115–21) defines the phrase "in Christ" in the PE as denoting "a profound personal identification with Christ which is the basis of salvation and new life," and adds that it includes "vivid personal emotion" and "corporate personality and the conception of Christ as inclusive representative" (115). However, he concludes that in the PE the phrase is not used that frequently and has no mystical sense: "If Paul wrote the PE his powers of varied expression must have suffered considerable atrophy" (118; cf. also Brox, 51–55; for an excellent summary and critique of Roloff's analysis of the ecclesiology and emphasis on tradition in the PE, see Towner, *TynBul* 46 [1995] 287–314).

However, the statement that Pauline themes are used differently in the PE is not necessarily significant. The assumption is that Paul's theology was so rigid that it could not allow for any significant variation. But does this square with the variations that appear elsewhere in Paul's writing? For example, "faith" is used to describe the Christian faith in 2 Cor 13:5 (cf. Martin, *2 Corinthians*, 478), Gal 1:23, Phil 1:27 (cf. Hawthorne, *Philippians*, 57), and Col 2:7 (cf. Eph 4:5; Rom 6:17; see below, *Introduction*, "Themes in the PE"). When Paul tells the Roman church that their "faith [ἡ πίστις]" is proclaimed in all the world (Rom 1:8), it is not the gift that is proclaimed but the fact that they are Christians. D. M. Hay argues that πίστις, "faith," can have a concrete meaning such as "pledge," "evidence," and "objective basis for faith" ("*PISTIS* as 'Ground for Faith' in Hellenized Judaism and Paul," *JBL* 108 [1989] 461–76). Hanson admits this ([1983] 3), but notes a shift in emphasis in the PE (41; but cannot an author emphasize different aspects at different times?). Fee comments on "righteousness," that "what began in the present as gift is to be persevered in, righteously, and thus consummated at the final glory, which is also a gift. For Paul righteousness is both *Gabe* and *Aufgabe* (gift and responsibility). Without the latter, one might surely question the reality of the former" (*1 Corinthians*, 143, on 1 Cor 3:14–15). While Hanson may argue that "love" is the chief virtue in Paul but only one among many in the PE ([1983] 3), one only need go as far as Gal 5:22 (where "love" occurs in the middle of a list) and 1 Tim 1:5 (which places it at the head) to see the error. "In Christ" is used in a fully Pauline way in 1 Tim 1:14; 2 Tim 1:9, 13, and is used in the phrase "life in Christ" both in the PE (2 Tim 1:1; 3:12) and in Paul (Rom 6:11; 8:2), and synonymously with "Christian" in Col 1:2. If the PE do not use "in Christ" with much frequency and do not emphasize the mystical sense (but cf. 2 Tim 1:9), all it means is that Paul did not feel a need in writing to Timothy in Ephesus and Titus in Crete to use the phrase this way.

The differences that are alleged between Paul and the PE often appear to be exaggerated. Some argue that the concept of the "just" person in 1 Tim 1:9 is Stoic and therefore non-Pauline, but I would maintain that the "just" person is the person saved by faith, a fully Pauline concept. Some would say that the concept of salvation in the PE is not Pauline because it teaches universalism, citing 1

Tim 2:4, yet I would argue that this passage does not teach universalism and that the salvific passages elsewhere in the PE are against universalism. While there is a strong emphasis on doing good deeds in the PE, never are they presented as a means salvation, as some allege, and Paul elsewhere strongly emphasizes the need to live out one's salvation in good deeds (cf. Acts 26:20; see above, *Introduction,* "The Response to the Heresy"). The call for believers to live "quiet and peaceful" lives in 1 Tim 2:2 is classified by some as "bourgeois" and non-Pauline (e.g., Dibelius-Conzelmann, 39–41), but it parallels Paul's charge to the Thessalonians that they "do their work in quietness and earn their own living" (2 Thess 3:12). Dibelius-Conzelmann argue that "the author of the Pastorals seeks to build the possibility of a life in this world" (39) and classify this as non-Pauline, but what else was Paul expected to maintain at a time when he realized he would soon die? Even in Romans we see Paul helping believers learn how they are to live in this age (e.g., Rom 13:1–7). Hanson argues, "Indeed, even if one only contemplated the absence of the cross and of the title 'Son' for Christ from the Pastorals, and considered no other evidence, one would be driven to the conclusion that Paul could not have written them" ([1983] 42); but words from the root σταυρ-, "cross," are absent from Romans, 1 and 2 Thessalonians, and Philemon, and υἱός, "son" (of Jesus), is absent from Philippians, 2 Thessalonians, and Philemon. Dibelius-Conzelmann say that the use of "in faith" in 1 Tim 1:2 is non-Pauline, despite the similarities in 2 Cor 13:5 and Col 2:7 (1 Cor 16:3, Gal 2:20, and 2 Thess 2:13 are alleged not to be analogous). But why could Paul not say that Timothy's sonship is "in faith," distinguishing it from the literal sense? In 2 Tim 3:11 Paul reflects on his earliest persecutions, but Hanson objects that the author "makes no reference to the many experiences which Paul must have shared with Timothy. If we want to gain an idea of how the real Paul wrote about such experiences we can read 2 C. 6:4–10; 11:22–33. It is (for me, at least) impossible to believe that the man who wrote those passages in 2 Corinthians also wrote 2 Tim. 3:10–17" ([1983] 149). As the *Comment* on this verse will show, the earliest persecutions of Paul could have been known by Timothy, even though Acts does not tell us so. But beyond this, Hanson's comment illustrates how extensive conclusions are often drawn from extremely subjective interpretations of what Paul could and could not have said and rest on a precarious exegesis of the text. Why must Paul speak only about the persecutions witnessed to in Acts? Why must he make reference only to the later persecutions? Dibelius-Conzelmann argue that "in view of Phil 3:4ff, it is inconceivable that the terms 'blasphemer' and 'evil-doer' could have been used by Paul in describing his past" (28), but Phil 3 is Paul's estimation of his pre-Christian life seen within the context of Judaism. As a Christian, looking back over his life of persecution of the church and zeal for the "traditions of [his] fathers" (Gal 1:14), why could Paul not have agreed with the voice on the Damascus road (Acts 9:5) that he had persecuted (Acts 22:5, 7–8; 26:11, 14–15; Gal 1:13) and even beaten (Acts 22:19) believers, approved of the killing of Stephen (Acts 8:1; 22:20), and tried to make believers blaspheme (Acts 26:11), and then have concluded that he was a blasphemer and evil person? It appears that many of the alleged differences between Paul and the PE are the product of exaggeration.

I would argue that flexibility and the possibility of development in a person's thought must be allowed (cf. Spicq, 1:176). The use of *savior* in the PE, which deliberately alternates between applying the title to God and applying it to Jesus, could represent such a development in Paul's thinking. Kelly comments about the use of "sound teaching" in the PE: "According to many it is a convincing token of the 'bourgeois' Christianity of the letters, and betrays a rational approach to ethics which is alien to Paul's spirit. On the other hand, an imitator is not likely to have so *repeatedly* attributed to him an idiom which is found in none of his acknowledged letters, while nothing is more common than for a man, at a certain stage of his life, suddenly to adopt a turn of phrase which strikes him as apt and then work it to death" (50, italics mine). An emphasis on what is distinctive about the PE often obscures the many points at which they are similar to Paul's other letters (cf. lists in Lock, xxvi–xxvii, and Kelly, 16–17; see also, *Introduction,* "Themes in the PE" below). While this issue of variation may be raised, it is significant to ask whether it is more likely that Paul felt free to vary his own style and expression or that a pseudepigrapher made an obvious blunder.

In response to the charge that the PE use certain Pauline themes in a contradictory manner, I would say that there is not one example where this must be true. In every case there are likely interpretations that are in line with Pauline usage elsewhere. If there are differences of emphasis, these are explained by the differing recipients and historical situations.

3. *The development of orthodoxy.* Part of the issue of the alleged theological problem of the PE is their relationship to what later became known as orthodoxy. The author of the PE appeals to "sound teaching," "the faith," and "the truth," which appear to refer to a body of doctrine. Some argue that 2 Tim 2:2 reflects the succession of office and the passing on of authoritative doctrine. The gospel tradition in the PE appears to be fixed, encapsulated in liturgical, creedal, and hymnic forms (e.g., the "faithful sayings"; 1 Tim 3:16; Titus 2:11–14), which, it is argued, was not true in Paul's day (cf. Moffatt, *Introduction,* 411–12; Easton, 202–4).

However, I maintain that there always was a desire in the church to be true to the teachings of Jesus and the apostles and that 2 Tim 2:2 merely instructs Timothy to find people of character who will continue teaching what is true. Paul was aware of the traditions of Jesus' teachings and the apostolic kerygma, which was the formalization of the basic message of salvation, repeated throughout Acts. As early as the writing of Galatians he refers to "the gospel" and says that if anyone teaches something different, he or she is to be anathematized. Paul tells the Roman church to avoid those who oppose the doctrine (τὴν διδαχήν) they have been taught (Rom 16:17). He praises the Corinthians because they "maintain the traditions [τὰς παραδόσεις] even as I have delivered [παρέδωκα] them to you" (1 Cor 11:2). Paul received (παρέλαβον) tradition and delivered (παρέδωκα) the gospel (τὸ εὐαγγέλιον) that the Corinthians received (παρελάβετε) (1 Cor 15:1–3). Paul also urges the Thessalonian church to "hold to the traditions [τὰς παραδόσεις] which you were taught by us, either by word of mouth or by letter" (2 Thess 2:15), and to stay away from any believer who is not living "in accord with the tradition [τὴν παράδοσιν] that they received [παρελάβοσαν] from us" (2 Thess 3:6). Throughout Acts, Paul's associates are charged with the responsibility of insuring a local church's loyalty to Paul's gospel (cf. above, *Introduction,* "Historical Reconstruction from Acts"). 1 Cor 4:17 shows Timothy to be a trusted associate sent to remind the Corinthians of Paul's ways and teaching. If someone argues that Paul cannot have appealed to a fixed body of tradition, these texts must be ignored.

Nowhere in the PE do we read anything like Jude 1:3 or Rev 22:18–19. The author of the PE does not say that the body of doctrine is complete, closed, and that nothing is to be added; he says that the gospel teaching is true and is to be adhered to. It is sufficiently coherent and consistent that teachings can be measured against it and shown to be true or false, as Paul also says in Gal 1:6–11.

The unusual circumstances of the PE explain why Paul's approach must have been somewhat different. He was not writing to a church that did not know the gospel. He was writing to two of his inner circle who fully understood his teaching, and in the case of the letter to Timothy, Paul was also addressing an Ephesian church that clearly knew what Paul taught. When Paul appealed to the "sound teaching," Timothy, Titus, and the Ephesian church knew what he meant.

Paul was also near the end of his life. It was only natural that Paul's teaching would have assumed a more static, concrete form, "the truth" that was to be passed on. Kümmel comments, "The presupposition of this central role of the tradition is a community which, in contrast to Paul's expectation of a near end of the age, is already making provision for the time after the death of the bearers of tradition appointed by the apostolic disciples (II Tim 2:1f.)" (382). I would assert that it is Paul who is "making provision" for the time after his own death and Timothy's departure from Ephesus. 2 Tim 2:2 does not refer to making provision for the continuance of tradition after the death of the tradition bearers; the text says that Paul wants Timothy to prepare for leaving Ephesus. Guthrie states, "It is not that orthodoxy and organization have become the absorbing passion in his last days, but rather that sagacious provisions have been made for a time when no apostolic witness will remain, and the Spirit of God will use other means to direct His people" (32). And Towner asks, "Could not the apostle himself have foreseen the implications of his passing for the church and the continuity of the gospel?" (*TynBul* 46 [1995] 307; cf. 312).

4. Traditional material in the PE. The author of the PE uses a significant amount of traditional material, both creedal and hymnic, and some object that this is unlike Paul. The uniqueness of the introductory formula "faithful is the saying" is cited as an example.

It is certainly the case that the author of the PE uses traditional material (see below, *Introduction,* "The Linguistic Problem, B. Problems with the Methodology"); however, I am not convinced that the author uses as much as is often stated, and Paul is capable of stating theological truths in hymnic form. Moreover, Paul elsewhere uses a significant amount of traditional material (cf. Rom 1:2–4; 1 Cor 11:2; 15:1–3; Phil 2:5–11; Col 1:15–20; Eph 5:14; 2 Thess 2:15; cf. Kelly, *Early Christian Creeds,* 1–29; Hunter, *Paul and His Predecessors,* 15–57; R. P. Martin, "Hymns," *DPL,* 419–23; see *Form/Structure/Setting* on 1 Tim 1:12–17), and the fact that five times he uses a new introductory formula, "faithful is the saying," is of questionable significance (compare the "God is faithful" formula in 1 Cor 1:9; 10:13; 2 Cor 1:18; cf. 1 Thess 5:24; 2 Thess 3:3). It might also be asked, why would a pseudepigrapher use a formula nowhere else attested in Paul?

5. Second-century Gnosticism. In the reconstruction of the Ephesian heresy above, I argued that it was primarily Jewish (especially Titus 1:14; 3:9) but affected by the syncretistic Hellenistic culture, possibly by a type of proto-gnosticism and perhaps

Stoicism. This is in contrast to the position of Baur and others (*Pastoralbriefe*, 228ff.;
Goodspeed, *Introduction*, 327–30; D. W. Riddle and H. H. Hutson, *New Testament
Life and Literature* [Chicago: University of Chicago Press, 1946] 205), that the PE
are a second-century refutation of Marcion's full-blown Gnosticism. But, as most
have now acknowledged, the major problem with Baur's approach is that apart
from the coincidental comment in 1 Tim 6:20 there is nothing in the PE directed
toward second-century Gnosticism (so Hort, *Judaistic Christianity*, 130–46). There
is, however, some evidence in the PE of early forms of Gnosticism (e.g., asceticism
and license; denial of Christ's physical resurrection; speculative use of the OT; need
for mediation), which existed in the first century (cf. Lightfoot, *Biblical Essays*, 413–
18, who concludes that the heresy is related to earlier forms of Gnostic thinking,
specifically that of the Ophites; Dibelius-Conzelmann, 3; Ellis, *RevExp* 56 [1959]
343–54; R. M. Wilson, *Gnostic Problem;* Yamauchi, *Pre-Christian Gnosticism*). Kümmel,
who does not accept the authenticity of the PE, argues that the teaching of the PE
on this point is understandable within Paul's historical context (*Introduction*, 379).
The Ephesian heresy has closer ties to the first-century problems in Colossae and
Corinth than it does to second-century Marcion. In fact, it can be argued that an
absence of Gnostic thought, combined with a lack of coherence in the heresy itself,
argues against a second-century setting (cf. Spicq, 1:178–79). The author of the PE
claims that the heresy is Jewish, which argues against a Marcionite context. γνῶσις,
"knowledge," is used without any Gnostic overtones. As far as we know, the term
"genealogies" is not used in Gnosticism (Spicq, 1:322–23; Kelly, 44). Baur's argument that the opponents' success among women shows that the error was Gnosticism
(cf. 2 Tim 3:6) is weak; women (as well as men) were often the prey of false teaching. Paul's use of ἀντιθέσεις, "contradictions" (1 Tim 6:20), most agree, is merely
coincidentally the title of Marcion's work. While Irenaeus (*Adv. Haer.* 1.1) and
Tertullian (*Adv. Val.* 3) use 1 Tim 1:4 against the second-century Gnostic Valentinus,
all this means is that they found it helpful in their own historical contexts; it says
nothing about the original setting of the text. Guthrie adds, "It is incredible that
both orthodox and heretical parties in the second century were so completely deceived about the origin of the epistles if they were not produced until after A.D.
140" (*Introduction*, 645). More writers are now seeing problems with the conclusion
of a second-century date for the PE and are withdrawing their support (see bibliography in Guthrie, *Introduction*, 617 n. 3).

6. *Inappropriate statements in the PE.* It is alleged that many statements in the PE
are inappropriate if addressed to Timothy and Titus, Paul's friends and confi-
dants, thus betraying their inauthenticity. Why would Paul tell Timothy that his
apostleship was according to God's "command" (1 Tim 1:1), as if Timothy were
questioning its validity? Brox argues that "there is not much historical plausibility
in Paul discussing his conversion so long ago with an old and tried colleague"
(cited in Hanson, [1983] 62). Why would Paul insist that he is called to the Gentiles (1 Tim 2:7; so Meade, *Pseudonymity*, 120)?

However, I have argued that 1 Timothy and Titus, while private in form, are
public in intention, speaking through Paul's delegates to the churches. If this is
correct, these critical objections go away. The Ephesian church was questioning
Paul's authority and was preaching a gospel for only the esoteric few, so Paul
identifies the source of his apostolic authority and his call to the Gentiles, whom
the opponents were dismissing as outside the scope of salvation. And why would

a friend not discuss his conversion with a friend, especially as it offers an example of why the Ephesian heresy is wrong (see also below)?

B. *The Issue of Paul's Approach*

Some question Paul's response to the opponents in the PE. Whereas elsewhere Paul focuses on the teaching of his opponents (e.g., against the Judaizers in Galatians), in the PE the author attacks the opponents personally, not entering into theological debate but relying on institutional offices. Houlden argues, "The right riposte to false teaching is the proper arranging of the congregation's life, in particular its worship and structure. . . . If Church life is on a sound basis, then true doctrine will win its way" (63). A. H. McNeile asserts, "A lesser mind can contradict and denounce, while it is not equal to the task of refuting" (*An Introduction to the Study of the New Testament* [Oxford, Clarendon, 1927] 181; also Brox, 39–42; Karris, *JBL* 92 [1973] 549–64, discussed above; Kümmel, *Introduction*, 380).

In response to this argument, the following points may be made. (1) This argument is based on an oversimplification of Paul's pattern of dealing with error elsewhere. When the occasion warranted, Paul did attack individuals and even anathematized them (cf. Gal 1:8–9; Rom 2:8; Phil 3:18–19; 2 Thess 3:6,14), calling them "dogs," "evil-workers," and "those who mutilate the flesh" (Phil 3:2). Paul could say "If any one has no love for the Lord, let him be accursed" (1 Cor 16:22). Paul also appealed to his teaching as a refutation without explaining it (Gal 1:8–9; Rom 16:17; 2 Thess 3:6; cf. 2:13; 3:14). (2) This argument overly simplifies Paul's dealing with the Ephesian opponents. Paul does provide both theological refutation and personal judgment. (3) This argument dismisses the uniqueness of the Ephesian situation. As was discussed above, the Ephesian error was not a well-formulated theological position that could be described and criticized. It was a loose association of ideas permeated with sinful behavior. This lack of content and coherence made it impossible for Paul to evaluate the heresy systematically, as he did in other situations. Moreover, the issue was not really theological but a matter of immorality, where conscience and sincerity were being set aside. The opponents were intentionally deceiving the Ephesian church. (4) Judging the opponents and judging their teaching are not unrelated. The roots are known by the fruit, and evaluating actions is directly related to evaluating theology (cf. above in *Introduction*, "The Response to the Heresy"). (5) This argument also misses the fact that Paul was writing to two close associates who knew his theology and were capable of evaluating the Ephesian and Cretan false teaching (so also Lightfoot, *Biblical Essays*, 413). (6) According to the words of Jesus recorded in Matthew's Gospel, there is a point at which discussion becomes fruitless and the best advise is to turn away (Matt 7:6). This is precisely what Paul is doing here (cf. Chrysostom on 1 Tim 6:7 in "Homily 17"; NPNF 13:468).

When Paul does deal with the theological error of a teaching such as in 1 Tim 1:12–17, some argue that Paul would never have said this to Timothy, who knew his theology. But when the author does not deal theologically with the error, then he is accused of being non-Pauline. A critic, however, cannot have it both ways (cf. Lightfoot, *Biblical Essays*, 413). Oberlinner is guilty of this when he criticizes the author of the PE for not appealing to Paul's authority in 1 Tim 4:1–5 (175), a passage containing a theological refutation of the heresy (see also above, *Introduction,* "Inappropriate Statements in the PE").

C. Conclusion

While there are differences between the PE and other Pauline writings, the differences are not any more significant than are found among Paul's other writings and are largely accounted for by the historical situations addressed. In the PE Paul was writing to two members of his inner circle, trusted colleagues who knew his teaching. His first letter to Timothy deals with a false teaching—although it may be overly gracious to give this loose association of ideas and sinful behavior the label of "teaching"—that was unlike anything else with which he had previously dealt. His letter to Titus is basic catechetical instruction and much less problematic than 1 Timothy. 2 Timothy is unique in its intent and situation; it should be expected to be significantly different from all of Paul's other writings. That certain themes relevant in other historical contexts are absent from the PE is irrelevant. That Paul uses some of his terms in different ways—and this is often exaggerated—is consistent with the historical situation and the ability of a creative genius like Paul who was not bound to say the same things always in the same ways. The passages in the PE that appear to be different from the other Pauline letters can be interpreted in ways consistent with Pauline usage. There may be a high use of traditional material, adaptation of local terminology, and the possible influence of a trusted amanuensis (see below), but nowhere does the author of the PE say something that is necessarily contradictory to Paul's teaching. As Paul neared the end of his life and the eyewitnesses and apostles began to die, it is of no surprise and in fact expected that Paul would place more weight on church leadership and on an orthodox presentation of the gospel, the truth, and the faith, themes found elsewhere in his writings. In all this I find nothing that parallels the developments in the second century. There is no full-blown Gnosticism apparent. There is no rigidity of ecclesiastical power such as is seen throughout Ignatius. Rather, Paul addresses two apostolic delegates dealing with the types of issues that would be expected to be found in their historical situations.

Finally, there is the issue of methodology. (1) To what extent is it possible to decide what Paul could say and what he could not say? As Fee rightly asserts, "It seems fair to observe that PE scholarship is sometimes overimpressed with its own judgments about what Paul could, or (especially) could not, have said or done" (14). (2) We must ask, What is more likely? Is it more likely that Paul felt the freedom to vary the expression of his teaching as he wrote to specific people in specific situations, or is it more likely that a pseudepigrapher introduced significant differences that seem obvious to those in the past hundred years or so to indicate that Paul could not have written the PE? Is it really likely that a pseudepigrapher would so fully reproduce Pauline themes—and they are many and significant, as Harnack admits (*Geschichte,* 480–85 n. 46)—and yet at certain key places (such as in the salutation or in his use of "in Christ") put words in Paul's mouth that Paul would never have said? It seems more likely that Paul did not feel the same wooden restrictions that some modern writers would impose on his expressions. (3) Finally, what does one do with those statements and elements of style that appear to be Pauline? Despite the differences, there is much in the PE that falls into the category of Pauline material (cf. Spicq for similarity of style [1:180, 204–8] and vocabulary [1:196–97]). Either it is evidence of Pauline authorship or the result of clever insertions by the pseudepigrapher based on his or her knowledge of Paul's writings.

THE LINGUISTIC PROBLEM

For many, the question of authenticity is most significantly raised with respect to the literary features of the PE—the vocabulary and style of writing. The high occurrence of words not found elsewhere in Paul's letters and the differences in writing style are conclusive proof to many that Paul could not have written the PE.

A notable exponent of this approach is P. N. Harrison (*Problem;* cf. critique by Gilchrist, "Authorship"). He identifies 176 *hapax legomena* (words occurring only once in the NT) in the PE as well as 130 words in the PE used elsewhere in the NT but never in Paul. These words often are Hellenistic in flavor (e.g., εὐσέβεια, "piety," ἐπιφάνεια, "appearance," σωτήρ, "savior," παιδεύειν, "to rear, teach, discipline," μεσίτης, "mediator") and often, he argues, are more characteristic of the second century (67–86). Harrison also notes the absence of particles, pronouns, and prepositions in the PE (112 "little" words in all), which are found in Paul's other writings but not in the PE, indicating a difference in style and hence non-Pauline authorship (36–37). (There are 902 different words in the PE; he does not include the 54 proper names. Harrison's word counts are confusing, subtotals often not equaling the grand total. Numbers in his text need to be compared to his appendixes.)

A. The Effect of External Influences on Writing

There is no question that there are differences among all of Paul's letters. But what do they signify? If style can be measured (i.e., if the criteria proposed are in fact valid), then all the statistics can do is suggest that these criteria indicate that certain writings are similar and certain writings are dissimilar (so Grayston and Herdan, *NTS* 6 [1960] 15)—but only at the points measured by the criteria. If Romans, 1 and 2 Corinthians, and Galatians show certain similarities, and other writings appear to be somewhat different at those points of similarity, statistics cannot show why they are different, or if the difference is of any real significance. Inauthenticity is only one explanation. Another explanation is that external influences have affected Paul's choice of vocabulary and style of writing. Some would deny this possibility. Grayston and Herdan believe it is "highly improbable that [Paul] should change his style at will, and according to circumstances" (*NTS* 6 [1960] 15). Of course, this is the main question.

1. Historical influences. The PE were written to specific historical situations that varied significantly from each other and from the historical contexts of Paul's other correspondence. The effect that this had on writing should not be underestimated. Dibelius-Conzelmann comment regarding the PE's use of "sound doctrine" that "we must assume that it is highly unlikely that in his old age Paul would have designated his gospel with other formulas—unless he had to formulate new expressions to meet new situations. But the basic terms of the Pastorals are *not* applied to an actual situation" (24). But I would argue that the PE *were* written to actual, new situations. Unless Paul already had a set terminology for precisely this type of false teaching, he would have had to use a new (at least as is recorded in the other letters, but not necessarily new in his own vocabulary) set of terms. But even so, it seems safe to assume that any writer may choose to change his or her manner of expression regardless of age.

Another example of response to the historical setting is found in 1 Tim 1:1. Hanson ([1983] 54–55) argues that Paul would never have said that his apostleship was through the "command" of God. While Paul's usual expression is to say that his apostleship is through the "will" of God, the Ephesians' attack on his authority and gospel is sufficient reason for the variation in the PE. Paul also departs from references to the "will of God" in the epistle to the Galatians, which also is sufficiently explained by the historical situation. If a variation in the greeting is evidence of inauthenticity, then the greeting in Galatians must render that epistle suspect.

Paul spent four of his later years in Roman imprisonment in both Caesarea and Rome. This may have had some impact on his vocabulary and style (e.g., Phil 4:11; cf. Fee, *Philippians,* 431–32; cf. Kelly, 25). According to Strabo, the Spaniards (specifically, the Turditanians who lived around Baetis) were so Romanized that they had actually forgotten their mother tongue and spoke mostly Latin (*Geography* 3.2.15). Paul could have learned Latin during his first imprisonment in Rome in order to extend his ministry westward. Hitchcock (*ExpTim* 39 [1928] 347–52; cf. Spicq, 1:182, 190–92 [who lists the words]; Simpson, 20–21) identifies 160 words and phrases in the PE that are "distinctly Latin" (350), mostly through comparison with Cicero. His argument is powerful; it is surprising how often he is cited, and yet his data and conclusion often seem to be passed over. Marshall writes, "The fact that the author expresses himself in a more Hellenistic and less Semitic manner might, of course, be merely the result of his rewriting his materials in better Greek, such as anybody might do in a Greek-speaking milieu, but, for what it is worth, it does seem to be indicative of a trend in his thinking to express the message in terms that were more comprehensible to his readers" (SNTU-A 13 [1988] 168). But Marshall's argument can be used to support authenticity since there is no reason why Paul himself could not have adjusted his own speech so that the hellenized Ephesian church would understand him better, a hellenization encouraged by the exposure received during his imprisonment and presumably understandable by both the Greek Timothy and the Greek Titus. Oberlinner's argument (xxxvii) that the absence of Semitic influence in the PE is a sign of inauthenticity is thus countered.

The question is, how great an influence does the historical situation play on Paul's writing? I argue that it can have a substantial influence, just as the historical situation in Corinth had a high impact on what and how Paul wrote to the believers there.

2. Theological influences. I have argued that the Ephesian heresy was unique in Paul's experience; in none of his other letters does he deal with vacuous, silly stories, squabbling about words, and teaching that has no real content or cohesiveness. It would therefore be expected that new subject matter would require new vocabulary and means of expression. Parry finds fifty cases of *hapax legomena* that result from new subject matter (cxi–cxxvi); many more can be added (see below). Spicq (1:194–95) finds the same phenomena in 1 Corinthians and Romans; of the 310 words peculiar to 1 Corinthians, 200 occur in new subject matter specific to the Corinthian situation; of the 250 in Romans, 110 are also in new material.

Related is the Hellenistic milieu of Ephesus. Repeatedly Paul uses Stoic terminology different from some of his other writings, but always reinterpreting the terminology in light of the gospel. The Stoic self-sufficiency becomes the sufficiency of Christ, and "self-discipline" is a gift from God (2 Tim 1:7; cf. Titus 2:12; Phil 4:8, 12). The emphasis on God as "savior" is in reaction to Hellenistic religion and emperor worship (see below, *Introduction*, "Themes in the PE"; Phil 3:20). Paul's use of athletic metaphors shows an acquaintance with Hellenistic culture, but the metaphors are always redefined (e.g., Pfitzner's comments on 2 Tim 4:8 [*Agon Motif*, 184–85]).

It is generally acknowledged that Paul from time to time appropriates terminology from others. His appropriation stems from two sources, society in general and the opponents' terminology (cf. Sevenster, *Paul and Seneca*, 162–64; Karris, *JBL* 92 [1973] 549–64; Pfitzner, *Agon Motif*, 157–86). Examples could be his use of athletic/military metaphors (cf. *Comment* on 2 Tim 2:4), Stoic terminology for ethical standards (cf. Phil 4:8; Lock xv–xvi; see list below), σοφία, "wisdom" (1 Cor 1–3), and possibly justification (in Galatians; so Fee, 16, and Hanson, [1983] 4; cf. 2 Tim 3:13). The problem of suggesting the appropriation of terminology is that it usually cannot be proved, and it can become a scapegoat to explain away all the unusual vocabulary. To demonstrate the use of the terminology of society and especially Stoicism, the words that are used frequently in extrabiblical literature must be found. To demonstrate the use of the opponents' terminology, there needs to be a strong suggestion in the text that the terminology is being picked up and *redefined*.

3. The use of traditional material. No one doubts that Paul uses traditional material, both in the PE and elsewhere (see above, *Introduction*, "Critical Questions, The Theological Problem, A. Doctrinal Issues"). In the PE this can be signaled by the formula "faithful is the saying" (cf. excursus in the *Form/Structure/Setting* on 1 Tim 1:12–17) and seen in the major creedal statements (1 Tim 3:16; 2 Tim 1:9–10; Titus 1:12; 2:11–14; cf. 1 Tim 2:4–6). Ellis identifies even more passages in the PE as traditional and argues that this accounts for a high percentage of the unusual vocabulary ("Traditions," 237–53). While Ellis identifies too much of the PE as traditional since much of the material addresses the specific historical situation (e.g., 1 Tim 3:1–13; 4:1–5; Titus 1:6–9) and phrases such as "knowing this" and "these things" do not necessarily indicate citations, Ellis's work does stress the importance of not considering all unusual words as indications of inauthenticity. (Ellis locates 157 of the *hapax legomena* in the PE in traditional material, which would negate Harrison's argument.) The vice list in 1 Tim 1:8–11 provides an example. The fact that Paul is paralleling the Decalogue explains some of the different vocabulary; because the Decalogue is expressed in a series of phrases and because the literary form of the vice list evidently suggests the use of single terms for each commandment, it should be no surprise that Paul chooses contemporary terminology for the list. In other words, Paul is reworking traditional material in light of contemporary literary and historical needs.

4. Personal influences. In all of Paul's other letters except Philemon, Paul is writing to a church. While there are corporate elements in the PE, especially in 1 Timothy, the PE are addressed to individuals (cf. Prior, *Paul the Letter-Writer,* 37–59). Timothy and Titus were part of Paul's inner circle; Timothy had a unique relationship with Paul as Paul tells the Philippians, "I have no one like him" (Phil 2:20). Knight asserts, "One should *expect* that the letters to apostolic assis-tants will be noticeably different in comparison with those to churches. In fact, one should think they were not genuine if they did not have these differences. . . . They may well be marks of authenticity rather than strange differences from the earlier Pauline letters" (25). And D. E. Aune observes, "The social status and relationship of sender and receiver will inevitably influence both *what* is said and *how* it is said" (*The New Testament in Its Literary Environment* [Philadel-phia: Westminster, 1987] 158). For Spicq, the best reason for the different style and vocabulary is the difference in recipients and subjects (1:193).

Paul was also old, and in 2 Timothy he knows he will soon die. He knows that the other apostles and eyewitnesses are dying. On the use of "wholesome teach-ing," Kelly comments that "an imitator is not likely to have so repeatedly attributed to him [i.e., Paul] an idiom which is found in none of his acknowledged letters, while nothing is more common than for a man, at a certain stage of his life, sud-denly to adopt a turn of phrase which strikes him as apt and then work it to the death" (50). Bernard emphasizes that in Paul's letters in general the number of unique words increases as Paul increases in age: "As a man gains experience as a writer, his command over the language becomes greater, and his vocabulary is less limited to the words in common use among his associates" (xxxvi; cf. Kelly, 25). Spicq observes the same development in the aging Plato (1:189–90, citing the work of Sedgwick [*ExpTim* 30 (1918) 230–31]), and the similar observation by Wohlenberg (55) concerning Schille and Goethe and by W. P. Workman con-cerning Shakespeare ("The Hapax Legomena of St. Paul," *ExpTim* 7 [1896] 418–19). Hanson misrepresents this position when he writes, "The Paul who wrote them was an old man, broken by labours and adversity. His very last letter, 2 Timo-thy, was written in the harsh conditions of a Roman prison. He had lost his fire, he had realised the value of some pagan philosophy, he had given up the immi-nent expectation of the parousia" ([1983] 6). Arguments referring to Paul's age do not necessarily prove this characterization. The author who wrote 1 Tim 1:12–17, 3:16, 6:14–16, Titus 2:11–14, 3:3–8, 2 Tim 1:3–14, 2:8–13, and 4:1, 6–8, 17–18 can hardly be classified as being "broken" and as having "lost his fire." Paul had always realized he might die before the parousia (2 Cor 5:1–10).

5. The use of an amanuensis. We know that Paul used amanuenses. Tertius iden-tifies himself to the Romans (Rom 16:22; cf. Eph 6:21). It is possible that Paul's reference to "large letters" (Gal 6:11; cf. Col 4:18; 2 Thess 3:17) reflects his per-sonal signature distinct from the writing style of his amanuensis, a practice possibly required by poor eyesight (2 Cor 12:7).

Bruce points out that 1 and 2 Thessalonians list Silvanus and Timothy as joint authors, and therefore "it is *prima facie* conceivable that Silvanus and Timothy played a responsible role along with Paul in the composition" (*1 and 2 Thessalonians,* xxxii). Bruce also notes that Timothy is named in 2 Corinthians, Philippians, Colossians, and Philemon and suggests that Timothy possibly was Paul's amanuensis for those letters. Moreover, Bruce suggests that the differences between 1 and 2 Thessalonians and Paul's letters to the Romans, Corinthians, and Galatians adduced by Morton can be explained by the influence of Silvanus as amanuensis (*1 and 2 Thessalonians*, xxxiv).

I will argue below, based on the historical situation and 2 Tim 4:11, that Luke most likely was Paul's amanuensis for the PE. The questions are, how much freedom would Paul give to an amanuensis, and can the use of an amanuensis partially explain the variation of vocabulary and style? O. Roller goes so far as to suggest that Paul would not have dictated his letters, but would rather have stated his basic ideas and allowed the scribe to choose the specific wording (*Formular*, 20ff.; cf. critique by Moule, *BJRL* 47 [1965] 449; Kümmel, *Introduction*, 251).

Because there is a consistency in Paul's other writings and because of the formative role his writing played in the promulgation of the gospel, it seems doubtful that Paul would give the amanuensis too much freedom under normal circumstances. But 2 Timothy was written under anything but normal circumstances—Paul was a criminal in chains, difficult to locate, and alone except for Luke—and the literary consistency of the PE suggests use of the same amanuensis for all three letters. The severity of the second imprisonment may have suggested the need for more freedom on the part of the amanuensis (so also Kelly, 26; see *Comment* on 2 Tim 4:11).

This topic will be discussed in further detail below, but suffice it to say that the use of a different amanuensis, an amanuensis who was a friend of Paul's and whom he trusted, could certainly have had a significant effect on the vocabulary and style if some freedom were allowed. I will also discuss below some of the unusual vocabulary in the PE that is found elsewhere in the NT only in the Third Gospel and Acts, both traditionally viewed as written by Luke. Kelly concludes, after emphasizing the significant linguistic differences between the PE and the other Paulines:

> Once it is conceded that the process was not one of word-by-word dictation and that the secretary enjoyed even a minimum of initiative and responsibility in drafting the letters, it becomes fruitless to engage in minutely meticulous comparisons of stylistic, or even theological, niceties. If Paul was using a new secretary when he prepared the Pastorals . . . there is ample scope for all the divergences of vocabulary, linguistic tone, style, and even doctrinal emphasis, on which critical attention has so eagerly fastened. We are even entitled to conjecture, in the light of the hints the letters themselves supply, that this new secretary may have been a Hellenistic Jewish Christian, a man skilled in rabbinical lore and at the same time a master of the higher *koine*. (27)

6. Second-century vocabulary. The weakest element of P. N. Harrison's argument (noted above) is his suggestion that much of the rare vocabulary in the PE belongs to the second century; of the 306 words in the PE that do not occur elsewhere in Paul, 211 are used in the second century. Few follow Harrison on this point today (see detailed critiques by Guthrie, *Mind of Paul*, Appendix D, 41; id., *Introduction*, 634; Knight, 43–45), and he is criticized for a skewed presentation of the evidence (e.g., citing parallels in second-century literature but keeping silent about first-century writings; cf. Spicq, 1:185; B. M. Metzger, *ExpTim* 70 [1958] 92; Hitchcock, *ExpTim* 70 [1958] 279). For Harrison's argument to be valid, he would have to prove that these words were not in use until the second century; but of the 306 words identified by Harrison, 278 occur prior to A.D. 50 (cf. Hitchcock, *JTS* o.s. 30 [1928–29] 278). 80 of the 175 *hapax legomena* are found in the LXX (listed in Hitchcock, *JTS* o.s. 30 [1928–29] 278; cf. Bernard, xxxvii; Guthrie, *Mind of Paul*, 39–40). Fewer than 20 of the 306 words in the PE that do not occur elsewhere in Paul are not attested before Paul. Even Harrison (*Paulines*, 21; cf. 135–36) admits that 165 of the "non-Pauline" words in the PE appear in Philo (30 B.C.–A.D. 45; cf. P. Treves, "Philon," *OCD*, 822).

7. *Detailed analysis of Harrison's "non-Pauline words."* Some would hold that the types of external influences noted above do not invalidate the statistical method. Kümmel asserts, "Even if these wholly questionable influences could have effected a change in his vocabulary, it would still be completely inconceivable that the relationship between the logarithms of vocabulary and of length of text should also have changed so decisively" (*Introduction*, 373). But I would maintain that the external influences do have a significant effect, invalidating much of the statistical method. Taking Harrison's 306 "non-Pauline" words, I will break them down by category to see which words can be explained historically within the setting of Paul's life. The decisions are supported in the *Comment* sections on the cited passages. Words that fit in more than one category are marked with an asterisk (*). Some cognates are listed together. (Harrison correctly does not include proper names in his list.)

a. *Historical situation.* Included here are words specifically related to the historical situation of the PE (including instructions specifically to Timothy and Titus), including terms describing the opponents as swerving from the truth, and the call to Timothy to suffer willingly, to remember Paul's teaching, and to remain loyal. There are thirty-two words and forty-seven occurrences.

προσμένειν	"to stay on"	1 Tim 1:3; 5:5
ἑτεροδιδασκαλεῖν	"to teach a different gospel"	1 Tim 1:3; 6:3
ἀστοχεῖν	"to fall short"	1 Tim 1:6; 6:21; 2 Tim 2:18
ἐκτρέπειν	"to turn aside"	1 Tim 1:6; 5:15; 6:20; 2 Tim 4:4
προάγειν*	"to make previously"	1 Tim 1:18
βραδύνειν	"to wait"	1 Tim 3:15
παρακολουθεῖν	"to follow"	1 Tim 4:6; 2 Tim 3:10
νεότης	"youth"	1 Tim 4:12
ἐπίθεσις	"laying upon"	1 Tim 4:14; 2 Tim 1:6
πρεσβυτέριον	"body of elders"	1 Tim 4:14
ὑδροποτεῖν	"to drink only water"	1 Tim 5:23
στόμαχος	"stomach"	1 Tim 5:23
ἀποπλανᾶν	"to lead astray"	1 Tim 6:10
ὑπόμνησις	"remembrance"	2 Tim 1:5
μάμμη	"grandmother"	2 Tim 1:5
δειλία	"cowardice"	2 Tim 1:7
σωφρονισμός	"self-control"	2 Tim 1:7
συγκακοπαθεῖν	"to share in suffering"	2 Tim 1:8; 2:3
κακοῦργος	"serious criminal"	2 Tim 2:9
ὑπομιμνήσκειν	"to remind"	2 Tim 2:14; Titus 3:1
ἀνατρέπειν	"to overturn"	2 Tim 2:18; Titus 1:11
βρέφος	"childhood"	2 Tim 3:15
ἀνάλυσις	"departure"	2 Tim 4:6
φαιλόνης	"cloak"	2 Tim 4:13
ἀπολείπειν	"to leave"	2 Tim 4:13, 20; Titus 1:5
μεμβράνα	"parchment"	2 Tim 4:13

χαλκεύς	"coppersmith"	2 Tim 4:14
λέων	"lion"	2 Tim 4:17
χειμών	"winter"	2 Tim 4:21
λείπειν	"to leave"	Titus 1:5; 3:13
ἐπιδιορθοῦν	"to put right"	Titus 1:5
νομικός*	"lawyer"	Titus 3:13

b. Opponents' behavior and teaching. Much of the content of the PE is directed against what the opponents were doing and teaching. Included here are words that Paul seems to be appropriating from the opponents (although some of these words are also listed in section c; cf. also Spicq, 1:195), as well as Paul's instructions on how to deal with them ("rebuke," "silence," etc.). There are forty-six words and sixty-one occurrences.

προσέχειν	"to devote"	1 Tim 1:4; 3:8; 4:1, 13; Titus 1:14
μῦθος	"myth"	1 Tim 1:4; 4:7; 2 Tim 4:4; Titus 1:14
γενεαλογία	"genealogy"	1 Tim 1:4; Titus 3:9
ἀπέραντος	"endless"	1 Tim 1:4
ἐκζήτησις	"speculation"	1 Tim 1:4
ματαιολογία	"senseless babble"	1 Tim 1:6
νομοδιδάσκαλος	"teacher of the law"	1 Tim 1:7
διαβεβαιοῦσθαι	"to assert dogmatically"	1 Tim 1:7; Titus 3:8
νομίμως*	"lawfully"	1 Tim 1:8
ψευδολόγος	"liar"	1 Tim 4:2
καυστηριάζειν	"to brand"	1 Tim 4:2
γραώδης	"silly"	1 Tim 4:7
ἐπιπλήσσειν	"to rebuke"	1 Tim 5:1
σπαταλᾶν	"to live for pleasure"	1 Tim 5:6
καταστρηνιᾶν	"to grow wanton"	1 Tim 5:11
ἀργός*	"idle"	1 Tim 5:13
περιέρχεσθαι	"to flit"	1 Tim 5:13
φλύαρος	"gossip"	1 Tim 5:13
περίεργος	"busybody"	1 Tim 5:13
ζήτησις	"speculation"	1 Tim 6:4; 2 Tim 2:23; Titus 3:9
λογομαχία	"fight about words"	1 Tim 6:4
φιλαργυρία	"love of money"	1 Tim 6:10
κενοφωνία	"chatter"	1 Tim 6:20; 2 Tim 2:16
ἀντίθεσις	"contradiction"	1 Tim 6:20
ψευδώνυμος	"falsely named"	1 Tim 6:20
λογομαχεῖν	"to fight about words"	2 Tim 2:14
καταστροφή	"ruin"	2 Tim 2:14
γάγγραινα	"gangrene"	2 Tim 2:17
νομή	"pasture (for gangrene)"	2 Tim 2:17
ἀπαίδευτος	"uneducated"	2 Tim 2:23
ἀρνεῖσθαι*	"to deny"	2 Tim 3:5; Titus 1:6
ἐνδύνειν	"to creep"	2 Tim 3:6
γυναικάριον	"weak woman"	2 Tim 3:6
ἄνοια	"folly"	2 Tim 3:9
ματαιολόγος	"senseless babbler"	Titus 1:10
φρεναπάτης	"deceiver"	Titus 1:10

ἐπιστομίζειν	"to muzzle"	Titus 1:11
Ἰουδαϊκός	"Jewish"	Titus 1:14
μιαίνειν	"to defile"	Titus 1:15 (2x)
βδελυκτός	"abominable"	Titus 1:16
ἐπιφαίνειν*	"to appear"	Titus 2:11
νομικός*	"concerning the law"	Titus 3:9, 13
ἀνωφελής	"harmful"	Titus 3:9
αἱρετικός	"factious"	Titus 3:10
ἐκστρέφειν	"to pervert"	Titus 3:11
αὐτοκατάκριτος	"self-condemned"	Titus 3:11

c. Positive teaching. Apart from criticizing the opponents, Paul does have much to say that could generally be termed positive, but it is often positive in contrast to the opponents' teaching and behavior, and some of the language may be appropriated from the opponents. There are sixty-two words and ninety-four occurrences.

ὑγιαίνειν	"to be healthy"	1 Tim 1:10; 6:3; 2 Tim 1:13; 4:3; Titus 1:9, 13; 2:1, 2
ὑγιής	"healthy"	Titus 2:8
βλάσφημος*	"blasphemer"	1 Tim 1:13
διώκτης	"persecutor"	1 Tim 1:13
ὑποτύπωσις	"illustration"	1 Tim 1:16; 2 Tim 1:13
ἤρεμος	"tranquil"	1 Tim 2:2
ἡσύχιος	"calm"	1 Tim 2:2
εὐσέβεια	"reverence"	1 Tim 2:2; 3:16; 4:7, 8; 6:3, 5, 6, 11; 2 Tim 3:5; Titus 1:1
εὐσεβῶς	"in a godly manner"	2 Tim 3:12; Titus 2:13
εὐσεβεῖν	"to show godliness"	1 Tim 5:4
σεμνότης	"godly dignity"	1 Tim 2:2; 3:4; Titus 2:7
ὅσιος*	"holy"	1 Tim 2:8
καταστολή	"attire"	1 Tim 2:9
κόσμιος*	"respectable"	1 Tim 2:9
αἰδώς	"modesty"	1 Tim 2:9
σωφροσύνη	"moderation"	1 Tim 2:9,15
σωφρόνως	"in a self-controlled manner"	Titus 2:12
κοσμεῖν	"to clothe"	1 Tim 2:9; Titus 2:10
πλέγμα	"braided hair"	1 Tim 2:9
χρυσίον	"gold"	1 Tim 2:9
μαργαρίτης	"pearl"	1 Tim 2:9
ἱματισμός	"clothing"	1 Tim 2:9
πολυτελής	"costly"	1 Tim 2:9
αὐθεντεῖν	"to be in authority"	1 Tim 2:12
τεκνογονία	"childbearing"	1 Tim 2:15
μαρτυρία	"reputation"	1 Tim 3:7; Titus 1:13
μετάλημψις	"receiving"	1 Tim 4:3
κτίσμα	"creation"	1 Tim 4:4
ἀπόβλητος	"unclean"	1 Tim 4:4
παραιτεῖσθαι	"to reject"	1 Tim 4:7; 5:11; 2 Tim 2:23; Titus 3:10
ἁγνεία	"purity"	1 Tim 4:12; 5:2
ἔκγονος	"grandchildren"	1 Tim 5:4

ἀμοιβή	"return"	1 Tim 5:4
πρόγονος*	"parent"	1 Tim 5:4
μονοῦν	"to leave alone"	1 Tim 5:5
ἀνεπίλημπτος*	"above reproach"	1 Tim 5:7; 6:14
ἀρνεῖσθαι*	"to disown"	1 Tim 5:8
καταλέγειν	"to enroll"	1 Tim 5:9
ἐλάσσων	"less than"	1 Tim 5:9
		(Rom 9:12 citation)
ἑξήκοντα	"sixty"	1 Tim 5:9
τεκνοτροφεῖν	"to raise children"	1 Tim 5:10
ξενοδοχεῖν	"to show hospitality"	1 Tim 5:10
νίπτειν	"to wash"	1 Tim 5:10
τεκνογονεῖν	"to bear children"	1 Tim 5:14
οἰκοδεσπότης	"ruler of household"	1 Tim 5:14
διατροφή	"food"	1 Tim 6:8
σκέπασμα	"clothing"	1 Tim 6:8
πραυπάθεια	"gentleness"	1 Tim 6:11
παραθήκη	"what is entrusted"	1 Tim 6:20; 2 Tim 1:12, 14
πρόγονος*	"ancestor"	2 Tim 1:3
περιιστάναι	"to shun"	2 Tim 2:16; Titus 3:9
μάχεσθαι	"to quarrel"	2 Tim 2:24
ἀνεξίκακος	"patient in midst of evil"	2 Tim 2:24
ἀποτρέπειν	"to avoid"	2 Tim 3:5
νηφάλιος*	"clearminded"	Titus 2:2
σώφρων*	"self-controlled"	Titus 2:2, 5
διάβολος*	"slanderer"	Titus 2:3
φίλανδρος	"loving one's husband"	Titus 2:4
φιλότεκνος	"loving one's children"	Titus 2:4
οἰκουργός	"working at home"	Titus 2:5
ἀφθορία	"purity"	Titus 2:7
ἄμαχος	"peaceable"	Titus 3:2; cf. 1 Tim 3:3

Under appropriation Spicq lists γυμνασία, "training," εὐσέβεια, "piety," παλιγγενεσία, "rebirth," and μέγας θεός, "great God" (1:193). Others add ἐγκράτεια, "self-control," θεοσέβεια, "religion," and αὐτάρκεια, "self-sufficency." If 1 Tim 4:8 reflects the teaching of the opponents, then the athletic imagery could also be included here.

   d. Church leadership. Some of the instruction in the PE is specifically related to issues of church leadership, describing the type of person who is to serve. Once again, it is no surprise to find words addressing this situation that do not occur elsewhere in Paul, recognizing also that these qualities also stand in contrast to the opponents (see *Form/Structure/Setting* on 1 Tim 3:1–7). There are twenty-nine words and thirty-nine occurrences.

ἐπισκοπή	"office of overseer"	1 Tim 3:1
ἀνεπίλημπτος*	"above reproach"	1 Tim 3:2
νηφάλιος*	"clear-minded"	1 Tim 3:2
σώφρων*	"self-controlled"	1 Tim 3:2; Titus 1:8
κόσμιος*	"dignified"	1 Tim 3:2, 11
φιλόξενος	"hospitable"	1 Tim 3:2; Titus 1:8
διδακτικός	"skilled in teaching"	1 Tim 3:2; 2 Tim 2:24

πάροινος	"drunkard"	1 Tim 3:3; Titus 1:7
πλήκτης	"violent"	1 Tim 3:3; Titus 1:7
ἄμαχος*	"peaceful"	1 Tim 3:3
ἀφιλάργυρος	"not a lover of money"	1 Tim 3:3
ἐπιμελεῖσθαι	"to care for"	1 Tim 3:5
νεόφυτος	"recent convert"	1 Tim 3:6
τυφοῦσθαι*	"to be conceited"	1 Tim 3:6
δίλογος	"gossip"	1 Tim 3:8
αἰσχροκερδής	"greedy for gain"	1 Tim 3:8; Titus 1:7
διάβολος*	"slanderer"	1 Tim 3:11 (Eph 4:27; 6:11; Harrison lists when it means "slanderer," not "the devil")
ἑδραίωμα	"pillar"	1 Tim 3:15
πρεσβύτερος*	"elder"	1 Tim 5:17, 19; Titus 1:5
διπλόος	"double"	1 Tim 5:17
κατηγορία	"accusation"	1 Tim 5:19; Titus 1:6
παραδέχεσθαι	"to accept"	1 Tim 5:19
πρόκριμα	"prejudging"	1 Tim 5:21
πρόσκλισις	"partiality"	1 Tim 5:21
αὐθάδης	"arrogant"	Titus 1:7
ὀργίλος	"quick tempered"	Titus 1:7
φιλάγαθος	"loving what is good"	Titus 1:8
ὅσιος*	"holy"	Titus 1:8
ἐγκρατής	"self-controlled"	Titus 1:8

e. *Vice lists.* Vice lists by their very nature can include words not normally used by the author, and their absence from the rest of Paul's writings is insignificant. There are twenty-five words and twenty-eight occurrences.

ἀνυπότακτος*	"rebellious"	1 Tim 1:9; Titus 1:10
ἀνόσιος	"unholy"	1 Tim 1:9; 2 Tim 3:2
βέβηλος*	"profane"	1 Tim 1:9
πατρολῴας	"one who beats one's father"	1 Tim 1:9
μητρολῴας	"one who beats one's mother"	1 Tim 1:9
ἀνδροφόνος	"murderer"	1 Tim 1:9
ἀνδραποδιστής	"kidnapper"	1 Tim 1:10
ἐπίορκος	"perjurer"	1 Tim 1:10
τυφοῦσθαι*	"to be conceited"	1 Tim 6:4; 2 Tim 3:4
ὑπόνοια	"suspicion"	1 Tim 6:4
διαπαρατριβή	"irritation"	1 Tim 6:5
φίλαυτος	"lover of self"	2 Tim 3:2
φιλάργυρος	"lover of money"	2 Tim 3:2
ἀχάριστος	"ungrateful"	2 Tim 3:2
ἄσπονδος	"unforgiving"	2 Tim 3:3
διάβολος*	"slanderer"	2 Tim 3:3
ἀκρατής	"uncontrolled"	2 Tim 3:3
ἀνήμερος	"untamed"	2 Tim 3:3
ἀφιλάγαθος	"not loving good"	2 Tim 3:3
προδότης	"treacherous"	2 Tim 3:4
προπετής	"reckless"	2 Tim 3:4
φιλήδονος	"loving pleasure"	2 Tim 3:4
φιλόθεος	"loving God"	2 Tim 3:4

| ἡδονή | "pleasure" | Titus 3:3 |
| στυγητός | "detestable" | Titus 3:3 |

f. Quoted and traditional material. This material, including the introductory formulae, often contains unusual vocabulary, as well as the elative vocabulary of
doxologies. Ellis identifies many more words than I have included here. There
are fourteen words and seventeen occurrences.

ἀποδοχή	"acceptance"	1 Tim 1:15; 4:9
ἀντίλυτρον	"ransom"	1 Tim 2:6
ὁμολογουμένως	"undeniably"	1 Tim 3:16
ῥητῶς	"clearly"	1 Tim 4:1
δυνάστης	"sovereign"	1 Tim 6:15
ἀπρόσιτος	"unapproachable"	1 Tim 6:16
ἀρνεῖσθαι*	"to deny"	2 Tim 2:12 (2x), 13
ἀργός*	"lazy"	Titus 1:12
ἀψευδής	"one who does not lie"	Titus 1:2
φιλανθρωπία	"philanthropy"	Titus 3:4
ἐπιφαίνειν	"to appear"	Titus 3:4
παλιγγενεσία	"regeneration"	Titus 3:5

If 1 Tim 4:8 is a faithful saying, then the athletic language should be listed here.
There are also a few words that appear to be coined, something Paul enjoyed
doing.

| θεόπνευστος. | "God-breathed" | 2 Tim 3:16 |
| καλοδιδάσκαλος | "teaching what is good" | Titus 2:3 |

While there may be a controversial decision here or there, for the most part
the words I have listed are clearly and firmly tied into a specific historical situation, a situation with many specific features Paul has not faced before that require
a new vocabulary. Even if I have not tried to explain any of the remaining *hapax
legomena,* I have explained 218. This leaves a remainder of 88 out of Harrison's
original 306. At this point, the number of *hapax legomena* is well within the biblical averages, and so the heart of Harrison's argument is removed. The unusually
high number of *hapax legomena* results from the specific details of the historical
situation and does not raise the question of authorship. But it is possible to make
the argument even stronger by establishing a few other categories.

g. Latinisms (listed by Spicq and others; 1:191–93; Simpson, 21, 40). These
include εὐσέβεια, *pietas,* χάριν ἔχειν, *gratiam habere,* ματαιολογία, *vaniloquium,*
ἑδραίωμα, *firmamentum,* δι᾽ ἢν αἰτίαν, *quamobrem,* πρόσκλισις, *inclinato,* πρόκριμα,
praeiudicium, ἀδηλότης, *incertitudo,* οἱ ἡμέτεροι, *nostri,* δίλογος, *bilinguis,* σεμνότης,
gravitas, and δεσπότης, *dominus.* Hitchcock identifies 160 "distinctively Latin" words
and phrases (*ExpTim* 39 [1928] 347–52).

h. Topical groups. Often words occur in groups and are addressing a topic or
using a metaphor. For instance, it is possible to group the words on riches and
connect them with criticism of the opponents (L. T. Johnson, 193–94). The following are words grouped as they are found in the PE: (i) γυμνάζειν, "to train," 1
Tim 4:7; σωματικός, "bodily," 1 Tim 4:8; γυμνασία, "training," 1 Tim 4:8. (ii)
εἰσφέρειν, "to bring in," 1 Tim 6:7; ἐκφέρειν, "to bring out," 1 Tim 6:7. (iii) βλαβερός,

"harmful," 1 Tim 6:9; βυθίζειν, "to sink," 1 Tim 6:9. (iv) περιπείρειν, "to impale," 1 Tim 6:10; ὑψηλοφρονεῖν, "to be proud," 1 Tim 6:17; ἀδηλότης, "uncertainty," 1 Tim 6:17; ἀπόλαυσις, "enjoyment," 1 Tim 6:17; ἀγαθοεργεῖν, "to do good," 1 Tim 6:18; εὐμετάδοτος, "generous," 1 Tim 6:18; κοινωνικός, "generous," 1 Tim 6:18; ἀποθησαυρίζειν, "to store up," 1 Tim 6:19. (v) στρατιώτης, "soldier," 2 Tim 2:3; ἐμπλέκειν, "to entangle," 2 Tim 2:4; πραγματεία, "affair," 2 Tim 2:4; στρατολογεῖν, "to enlist soldiers," 2 Tim 2:4; ἀθλεῖν, "to compete," 2 Tim 2:5 (2x); στεφανοῦν, "to crown," 2 Tim 2:5; νομίμως, "in accordance with rules," 2 Tim 2:5; γεωργός, "farmer," 2 Tim 2:6; μεταλαμβάνειν, "to receive," 2 Tim 2:6. (vi) χρύσεος, "golden," 2 Tim 2:20; ἀργύρεος, "(made of) silver," 2 Tim 2:20; ξύλινος, "wooden," 2 Tim 2:20.

i. Cognates. Statistical studies rarely take cognates into consideration. Even if Paul does not use a specific word in the PE, if he uses its cognate elsewhere, then it cannot be said that the word was unavailable for his use in the PE, and the word should not be termed un-Pauline. Words listed in other categories are marked with an asterisk (*) (cf. Spicq, 1:186–87; L. T. Johnson, 125–26).

ἀνάλυσις, "departure, " 2 Tim 4:6	ἀναλύειν, "to depart," Phil 1:23
εὐσέβεια*, "piety," 10x	ἀσέβεια, "godlessness," Rom 1:18; 11:26
	ἀσεβής, "godless," Rom 4:6; 5:6
σεμνότης*, "dignity,"1 Tim 2:2; 3:4; Titus 2:7	σεμνός, "honorable," Phil 4:8
βίος, "life," 1 Tim 2:2; 2 Tim 2:4	βιωτικός, "pertaining to life," 1 Cor 6:3
ἀπόδεκτος*, "pleasing," 1 Tim 2:3; 5:4	δεκτός, "acceptable," 2 Cor 6:2; Phil 4:8
ἡσυχία*, "quietness," 1 Tim 2:11, 12	ἡσυχάζειν, "to live quietly," 1 Thess 4:11
	ἡσύχιος, "quiet," 2 Thess 3:12
πιστοῦν*, "to be convinced," 2 Tim 3:14	πίστις, "faith," 109x
πρεσβύτιδας*, "older woman," Titus 2:3	πρεσβύτης, "old man," Phlm 9
	πρεσβεύειν, "to be an ambassador," 2 Cor 5:20; Eph 6:20
σωτήριος*, "bringing salvation," Titus 2:11	σωτήριον, "salvation," Eph 6:17
σωφρόνως*, "soberly," Titus 2:12	σωφρονεῖν, "to think soberly," Rom 12:3; 2 Cor 5:13
κῆρυξ, "herald," 1 Tim 2:7; 2 Tim 1:11	κηρύσσειν, "to proclaim," 17x

j. Remaining words not explained through historical or theological context. Some of these words may not belong in this category. For example, words like νέος, "young" (Titus 2:4), νεώτερος, "younger" (1 Tim 5:1, 2, 11, 14), νεωτερικός, "youthful" (2 Tim 2:22), and ὕστερος, "later" (1 Tim 4:1), are such common words that their inclusion may mean nothing (see Spicq, 1:187). Some are cognates with words listed above (e.g., σωφρονίζειν, "to think soberly," σωφρόνως, "soberly"); if Paul could use the cognates, it only skews the percentages to view these words as unusual terms. There are seventy-four words and ninety-seven occurrences.

ὑπερπλεονάζειν	"to be present in abundance"	1 Tim 1:14
ἔντευξις	"prayer"	1 Tim 2:1; 4:5
διάγειν	"to live"	1 Tim 2:2; Titus 3:3
ἀπόδεκτος	"pleasing"	1 Tim 2:3; 5:4
θεοσέβεια	"reverence"	1 Tim 2:10
ὀρέγεσθαι*	"to aspire to"	1 Tim 3:1, 6, 10
ἐμπίπτειν	"to fall"	1 Tim 3:6, 7; 6:9
βαθμός	"rank"	1 Tim 3:13
περιποιεῖσθαι*	"to acquire"	1 Tim 3:13
ἐντρέφειν	"to rear"	1 Tim 4:6
ὠφέλιμος	"useful"	1 Tim 4:8; 2 Tim 3:16; Titus 3:8
ἀμελεῖν	"to neglect"	1 Tim 4:14
μελετᾶν	"to practice"	1 Tim 4:15
πρεσβύτερος*	"older man"	1 Tim 5:1, 2
χείρων	"worse"	1 Tim 5:8; 2 Tim 3:13
ἐπαρκεῖν	"to help"	1 Tim 5:10, 16
ἐπακολουθεῖν	"to devote oneself to"	1 Tim 5:10, 24
λοιδορία	"abuse"	1 Tim 5:14
ἐπιτιθέναι	"to place upon"	1 Tim 5:22
πυκνός	"frequent"	1 Tim 5:23
πρόδηλος	"clear"	1 Tim 5:24, 25
προάγειν*	"to precede"	1 Tim 5:24
ἄλλως	"otherwise"	1 Tim 5:25
δεσπότης	"master"	1 Tim 6:1, 2; 2 Tim 2:21; Titus 2:9
εὐεργεσία	"doing of good"	1 Tim 6:2
ἀντιλαμβάνεσθαι	"to take part in"	1 Tim 6:2
προσέρχεσθαι	"to agree with"	1 Tim 6:3
ἐπίστασθαι	"to understand"	1 Tim 6:4
νοσεῖν	"to be sick"	1 Tim 6:4
πορισμός	"means of gain"	1 Tim 6:5, 6
ἐπιλαμβάνεσθαι	"to take hold"	1 Tim 6:12, 19
ζῳογονεῖν	"to give life"	1 Tim 6:13
ἄσπιλος	"spotless"	1 Tim 6:14
αἰτία	"reason"	2 Tim 1:6, 12; Titus 1:13
ἀναζωπυρεῖν	"to rekindle"	2 Tim 1:6
ἀναψύχειν	"to refresh"	2 Tim 1:16
βελτίων	"very well"	2 Tim 1:18
κακοπαθεῖν	"to suffer hardship"	2 Tim 2:9; 4:5
χρήσιμος	"useful"	2 Tim 2:14
ἀνεπαίσχυντος	"with no need to be ashamed"	2 Tim 2:15
ὀρθοτομεῖν	"to handle correctly"	2 Tim 2:15
μέντοι	"nevertheless"	2 Tim 2:19
στερεός	"firm"	2 Tim 2:19
ἀντιδιατιθέναι	"to oppose"	2 Tim 2:25
μήποτε	"if perhaps"	2 Tim 2:25
ἀνανήφειν	"to return to soberness"	2 Tim 2:26
ζωγρεῖν	"to capture"	2 Tim 2:26
χαλεπός	"difficult"	2 Tim 3:1
ποικίλος	"various kinds of"	2 Tim 3:6; Titus 3:3
μηδέποτε	"never"	2 Tim 3:7
καταφθείρειν	"to corrupt"	2 Tim 3:8

ἔκδηλος	"evident"	2 Tim 3:9
ἀγωγή	"conduct"	2 Tim 3:10
γόης	"imposter"	2 Tim 3:13
σοφίζειν	"to make wise"	2 Tim 3:15
ἐλεγμός	"reproof"	2 Tim 3:16
ἐπανόρθωσις	"correction"	2 Tim 3:16
ἄρτιος	"proficient"	2 Tim 3:17
ἐξαρτίζειν	"to equip"	2 Tim 3:17
εὐκαίρως	"opportune"	2 Tim 4:2
ἀκαίρως	"inopportune"	2 Tim 4:2
ἐπιτιμᾶν	"to rebuke"	2 Tim 4:2
ἐπισωρεύειν	"to accumulate"	2 Tim 4:3
κνήθειν	"to itch"	2 Tim 4:3
δρόμος	"race"	2 Tim 4:7
κριτής	"judge"	2 Tim 4:8
λίαν	"vehemently"	2 Tim 4:15
κατάστημα	"behavior"	Titus 2:3
ἱεροπρεπής	"reverent"	Titus 2:3
σωφρονίζειν	"to encourage"	Titus 2:4
ἀκατάγνωστος	"not censured"	Titus 2:8
νοσφίζειν	"to misappropriate"	Titus 2:10
πειθαρχεῖν	"to obey"	Titus 3:1
φροντίζειν	"to be careful"	Titus 3:8

The following terms may be from traditional material. There are six words and six occurrences: ἀρνεῖσθαι*, "to deny," Titus 2:12; κοσμικός, "worldly," Titus 2:12; σωφρόνως, "soberly," Titus 2:12; λυτροῦν, "to redeem," Titus 2:14; περιούσιος, "special," Titus 2:14; and περιφρονεῖν, "to look down on," Titus 2:15. Spicq says there are two hundred terms that can be found in the LXX, which would have been available to Paul (1:187).

Others propose similar lists. Lightfoot (*Biblical Essays*, 401–2) divides the words based on the divisions of new "moral and religious states" (βέβηλος, "godless," εὐσέβεια, "piety," καθαρός, "clean," καλός, "good," σεμνότης, "dignity"), "doctrine" (διδασκαλία, "teaching," ἐκζητήσεις, "speculations," ζητήσεις, "controversies," λογομαχία, -εῖν, "quarrel, to quarrel," παραθήκη, "what has been entrusted," ὑγιής, "healthy," ὑγιαίνειν, "to be healthy," νοσεῖν, "to be sick"), "certain formulae and maxims" (διαμαρτύρεσθαι ἐνώπιον, "to declare before," χάρις, "grace," ἔλεος, "mercy," εἰρήνη, "peace," πιστὸς ὁ λόγος, "the saying is faithful"), "modes of speaking of God the Father and Christ" (μακάριος θεός, "blessed is God," σωτήρ, "savior," ἐπιφάνεια, "appearing"), and other expressions (ἀρνεῖσθαι, "to deny," διάβολος, "slanderer," δεσπότης, "master," διαβεβαιοῦσθαι περί τινος, "to assert concerning something," παραιτεῖσθαι, "to reject"). Simpson (19–20) writes of Paul's fondness for compound words (αὐτοκατάκριτος, "self-condemned," διαπαρατριβαί, "constant arguings," ἑτεροδιδασκαλεῖν, "to teach a different doctrine," εὐμετάδοτος, "generous," καταστρηνιᾶν, "to become wanton against," λογομαχεῖν, "to quarrel about words," λογομαχία, "quarrel about words," ὀρθοτομεῖν, "to explain correctly," πραϋπάθεια, "gentleness," φρεναπάτης, "deceiver," θεόπνευστος, "God-breathed") and concludes that these words, while *hapax legomena* or rare, are in full accord with Paul's manner.

Even if one were to disagree with a specific decision here or there, the overall weight of the argument is impressive. Of all the "non-Pauline" words Harrison identified, only eighty-three have not been explained on the basis of these influences. Spicq says that there are only about forty words in the PE that are unusual to biblical texts. Therefore, one must wonder if any weight is to be given to stylistic arguments that do not take into consideration the expressed occasion and purpose of the PE. It seems that there is no necessary relationship between *hapax legomena* and authorship within the limited context of the biblical text (so also T. A. Robinson, *NTS* 30 [1984] 287).

B. Problems with the Methodology

Beyond the issue of external influences, there are serious problems with the methodology of statistical analysis itself. Although this is not the place to delve into a full critique of statistical analysis, a few comments are appropriate.

(1) The methodology assumes a consistency of vocabulary that does not exist among the acknowledged Pauline letters (cf. Torm, *ZNW* 18 [1918] 240–43; Dibelius-Conzelmann, 3; O'Rourke, *CBQ* 35 [1973] 483–99; E. Linnemann, *JEKT* 10 [1996] 87–90. Consider the irregularities of the following words:

	Rom	1 Cor	2 Cor	Gal	Eph	Phil	Col	1 Thess	2 Thess	Phlm
ἀποκαλύπτειν, "to reveal"	6	6	0	4	0	0	0	0	4	0
ἀπόλλυσθαι, "to destroy"	2	6	3	0	0	0	0	0	1	0
ἀνακρίνειν, "to question"	0	10	0	0	0	0	0	0	0	0
περισσεύειν, "to abound"	5	7	22	0	1	6	1	4	0	0
συνέρχεσθαι, "to assemble"	0	7	0	0	0	0	0	0	0	0
ὑπακούειν, "to obey"	11	0	3	0	2	1	2	0	0	1

Most of these words suggested in Linnemann's article occur a high number of times in Romans and Galatians but a greatly reduced number of times (or is missing) in other letters. (It is relatively easy to find words to prove any hypothesis; e.g., ἐάν occurs 47 times in 1 Corinthians and never in Philippians.) Paul does not always use words with the same frequency, and there are many reasons for the variations.

This is the thrust of a paper by E. Linnemann (*JEKT* 10 [1996] 87–109). In the thirteen Pauline epistles, she counts 49 particles, 44 pronouns, and 28 prepositions, 121 in all. In the PE she does not find 26 of these particles, 21 of these pronouns, and 6 of these prepositions, totaling 53 words. And yet, when she looks at these 53 elsewhere in Paul, she finds the following:

4 words absent from	2 Pauline letters
5 words absent from	3 Pauline letters
4 words absent from	4 Pauline letters
6 words absent from	5 Pauline letters
7 words absent from	6 Pauline letters
9 words absent from	7 Pauline letters
7 words absent from	8 Pauline letters
11 words absent from	9 Pauline letters

Her point is that there is such a wide variety in usage among Paul's writings in general that conclusions of inauthenticity based on word frequency become extremely precarious.

What is true of vocabulary is also true of style; significant variations are found throughout Paul's letters. For example, τέ, "and," occurs 18 times in Romans and not 1 time in Galatians; this is significant because both letters share much in common. Knight cites Colin Hemer's observation that τέ occurs 159 times in Acts and only 8 times in the Third Gospel—two lengthy books written by the same author (44 n. 150). Colossians and 2 Thessalonians have less than 20 of Harrison's 112 "little" words (Guthrie, *Introduction*, 635). These are significant facts since Harrison places so much weight on the little words missing in the PE, which are the connective tissue of a letter.

There may be a point at which issues of consistent vocabulary and style may raise the question of authorship (unless the amanuensis was given total freedom of expression; so Kelly, 27); most agree that Hebrews is not Pauline. But are the PE at this point?

(2) The methodology assumes a rigidity of writing style, not only for Paul but for all writers. R. C. Sproul recounts his process of learning Dutch to read Berkouwer (*Knowing Scripture*, 59–60). He started by reading *The Person of Christ* and made a vocabulary card for every new word, 6,000 for the entire book. When he read the second volume, *The Work of Christ*, which is on the same basic theme written to the same audience one year after the first volume, Sproul reports that he made 3,000 new cards. Fifty percent of the vocabulary was unique to the second volume. Does this prove that Berkouwer did not write both volumes? A comparison of C. S. Lewis's Narnia Tales with his other writings shows such a widely divergent style and vocabulary that at times it is almost impossible to believe they were all written by the same author. Bernard (xxxviii n. 1) cites W. P. Workman's observation ("The Hapax Legomena of St. Paul," *ExpTim* [1896] 418–19) that the same phenomenon occurs in Shakespeare's writing, where a word is common in one play and nonexistent in another, and that there is a wide range of unique words from one play to another. Lock (xxxviii) references A. J. Butler's similar conclusion (*Paradise of Dante Alighieri* [London: Macmillan, 1885] xi) about Dante's *Divine Comedy*. Caution is therefore urged when dealing with short and divergent letters in the Pauline corpus.

(3) Much of this statistical analysis is highly subjective, despite the appearance of mathematical objectivity. In his excellent summary and critique of statistical work, A. D. Forbes summarizes:

> Most distressingly, we have repeatedly seen investigations embarked upon with sweeping claims of assent-demanding objectivity only to witness their ultimate invalidation through special pleading and selective attention to results. One not need be a statistician to detect when an outcome has hinged on a researcher/thaumaturge and audience blinking at critical moments. (*ABD* 6:204)

Forbes criticizes Morton (*Literary Detection*) for his unscientific inclusion of 2 Corinthians and exclusion of Philippians in the data base (6:190–91, 193; also see T. A. Robinson, *NTS* 30 [1984] 172).

T. A. Robinson criticizes Grayston and Herdan for how they group the PE together and how their "C" formula produces significantly different results with different groupings of epistles (*NTS* 30 [1984] 283–84). If 1 and 2 Corinthians are grouped together, their "C" value shows them to be "markedly distinct from the other Paulines." Is it scientifically accurate to group the three PE together despite their many differences? Kenny (*Stylometric Study*, 100) and T. A. Robinson both show statistically that if 2 Timothy is viewed in isolation, it appears to be Pauline, and Prior (*Paul the Letter-Writer*) has emphasized how 2 Timothy should be viewed in isolation (also J. Murphy-O'Connor, "2 Timothy Contrasted with 1 Timothy and Titus," *RB* 98 [1991] 403–18). If the PE are viewed in isolation, does not their limited size all but prohibit statistical analysis (so Philemon)?

The subjectivity of statistical analysis is also seen in how style is measured. Criteria of measurement include sentence length, word length, use of small words (e.g., καί, "and," the article, conjunctions, prepositions), the position of small words in the sentence ("positional stylometry"; cf. Mealand, *NTS* 35 [1989] 266–86), and the last word in a sentence (Michaelson and Morton, *NTS* 18 [1972] 192–208; see critique by P. F. Johnson, *NTS* 20 [1974] 92–100). But are these true indications of style, indicators that are valid regardless of subject matter, audience, etc.?

Stylometry seems to be built on a faulty view of language. Language ebbs and flows, almost always in a state of flux and evolution (cf. Spicq, 1:184, 188, 190). Meaning is a function of larger units of thought. There is something artificial with criteria that dissect and analyze language at the level of single words.

(4) The methodology rarely, if ever, takes into consideration the external differences of audience, subject matter, and historical setting.

(5) The Cambridge statistician G. Udny Yule states that the minimum number of words required to do serious statistical work is 10,000 (*The Statistical Study of Literary Vocabulary* [Cambridge: Cambridge UP, 1944] 2, 281), the number also cited by D. Crystal (*The Cambridge Encyclopedia of Language* [Cambridge: Cambridge UP, 1987] 68, esp. "Stylistic Identity and Literature," 66–79). There are fewer than 5,800 different words in the entire Greek NT, which contains a total of 138,162 words (word counts from *Gramcord Greek New Testament* [Vancouver, WA: Gramcord Institute]). Romans is the longest letter in the NT and contains only 7,114 words, well below Yule's minimum. Even Michaelson and Morton (*NTS* 18 [1972] 192–208) state that a minimum of 100 sentences is preferable, which rules out most of Paul's letters by definition (see the similar statement by Neumann [*Authenticity*, 218]; Porter's critique of Neumann sets the sample rate at 750, even though Titus has only 659 words [*BBR* 5 (1955) 110]). The limited size of the NT brings the entire practice of statistical analysis into question. It is perhaps ironic that Yule's work was an impetus to the application of the statistical method to biblical texts (so A. D. Forbes, *ABD* 6:187), and yet his warning has not been heeded. (Mealand uses a 1,000-word sample and multiplies the word count of 2 Thessalonians [823 words] and Titus [659 words] to raise them to the minimum [1,000 words], acknowledging the problems [*JSNT* 59 (1995) 65].)

There are at least one million words in English; D. Crystal refers to the Swedish linguist A. Ellegård who used "a million-word norm" (*Cambridge Encyclopedia of Language*, 68). *Webster's New World Dictionary of the American Language: College Edition* ([New York: The World Publishing Company, 1957] vii) cites the 142,000 words that they feel are appropriate for their audience (i.e., passive vocabulary). Even if these numbers were to be cut in half (which the size of LSJ suggests is unnecessary), all the while recognizing that Paul's lifetime of training would have pushed his vocabulary far beyond the average, the total vocabulary of 2,301 words in the ten earlier Pauline letters represents only a fraction of his potential vocabulary. Certainly Paul had an active vocabulary substantially larger than 2,301 words. Out of the total vocabulary count in the ten earlier Pauline letters (2,301 words; word counts from *Gramcord Greek New Testament*), 969 words occur only once, or 42%. (In the NT there are 5,434 different words, 1,947 of which occur only once, or 36%.) If we have so little of Paul's writing that fewer than half the words occur only once, what is the possibility of doing reliable statistical work?

Spicq's straightforward conclusion seems warranted: "Good sense in exegesis must triumph over all the erudition of the world; if it is true that in his ten earlier letters, Saint Paul used 2,177 different words, one can hardly overlook why he would not have used 306 more of them in the Pastorals" (1:186). While computers have made the statistical studies more exact, they are still dealing with a limited number of words.

(6) I have shown above that the occurrence of *hapax legomena* in the PE is easily explained by the historical situation. This cuts to the heart of Harrison's argument and apparently of most modern objections to authenticity. The unique words can often be explained by the subject matter in the letter (Morton and McLeman, *Paul, the Man*, 65). T. A. Robinson's conclusion seems appropriate: "Until the time that a method is found that is much more discriminating than those before us, literary critics of the New Testament must recognize the possibility that there may exist no relationship between the percentage of hapax legomena in different works that could be used to detect a difference in authorship" (*NTS* 30 [1984] 287). Even Neumann, who concludes on the basis of statistical evaluation that the PE are non-Pauline (*Authenticity*, 213), asserts that the use of *hapax legomena* "has been shown to be among the least effective indices" (215).

(7) Those using the methodology of statistical analysis to prove inauthenticity tend to view the early church as uncritical; this is questionable. For many years Greek was the native language of much of the church, and it is fair to assume the "sense of Greek style" was better "among those who continued to be schooled in the same system of *paideia* than among those who learned their Greek in a German gymnasium or American prep school or seminary" (L. T. Johnson, 12). The church of the first few centuries was closer to the events of the NT. The difficulty of accepting 2 Peter into the canon because of stylistic differences from 1 Peter and the issue of Hebrews suggest that the church was critical in what it accepted. Yet there is no record that the church struggled with the literary features of the PE, vocabulary or style; based on the church's critical assessment, the PE were accepted as Pauline. If the Greek-speaking church showed no sign of concern about how the PE were written, one wonders why today the issue of style and vocabulary looms so large on the scholarly horizon.

(8) Numbers may not lie, but they do not always support conclusions drawn from them and in fact can be skewed. Hitchcock (*JTS* o.s. 30 [1928–29] 279) and Michaelis (*ZNW* 28 [1929] 73–74) both show that by slight alteration of the parameters (e.g., doing word counts by book and not by page, as Harrison did), the numbers provide a significantly different result; for example, the percentage of *hapax legomena* when compared to the total number of different words in Romans is about the same as it is for 2 Timothy and Titus. While Grayston and Herdan

argue that if the PE are viewed as a combined corpus, they can be shown to be non-Pauline (*NTS* 6 [1960] 9), T. A. Robinson uses their methodology to show that each individual book yields numbers supportive of its being accepted as Pauline (*NTS* 30 [1984] 286). Bird uses Grayston and Herdan's "C" formula on a passage from Romans equal in length to 1 Timothy (1,591 words, Rom 1:1–9:17) and concludes that 1 Timothy compares favorably with this passage from Romans and the other ten Paulines (*RTR* 56 [1997] 128). Carson, Moo, and Morris comment:

> On Harrison's own figures, of the 306 there are 127 that occur in 1 Timothy alone, 81 in 2 Timothy alone, and 45 in Titus alone [citing Harrison, *Problem,* 137–39]. This means that the vast majority are found in only one of the Pastorals and that the three differ from one another as much as (or more than) they differ from Paul. Are we to say that there were three pseudonymous writers? . . . We must be on our guard against taking up a position of omniscience about what went on in Paul's mind. (*Introduction,* 361)

Guthrie provides an interesting argument aimed at Harrison's 112 "little words" (*Mind of Paul,* 13, 41–44). He lists 93 "little words" separate from Harrison's 112. All but one occur in the PE (73 in 1 Timothy, 61 in 2 Timothy, 43 in Titus), and all but seven occur in Paul; apart from Philemon (32) their frequencies per book are from the mid 40s to 73. (When added to Hanson's 112, there are 205 words, 92 in the PE, 131 in Rom, 113 in 2 Cor, 86 in Phil, etc.) On this count, the PE are fully Pauline in style. I. H. Marshall identifies 55 NT words occurring only in the ten Paulines and the PE; on this count the PE also are fully Pauline (Review of *Luke and the Pastoral Epistles,* by S. G. Wilson, *JSNT* 10 [1981] 69–74). For an excellent analysis of these issues, see Prior, *Paul the Letter-Writer,* 25–35; Neumann, *Authority,* 23–114; A. D. Forbes, *ABD* 6:185–206; and Bird, *RTR* 56 (1997) 118–37.

(9) Consistent statistical studies should look at both the omission of a word, or perhaps a single occurrence, and words used with high frequency. For example, if the occurrence of δικαιοῦν, "to justify," eight times in Galatians does not raise the issue of authenticity, then the relatively high frequency of "non-Pauline" vocabulary in the PE should not call the authenticity of the PE into question.

For a defense of statistical analysis, see P. N. Harrison, *Problem;* Grayston and Herdan, *NTS* 6 (1960) 1–15; Mealand, *NTS* 18 [1972] 192–208; Morton and McLeman, *NTS* 18 (1972) 192–208; Kenny, *Stylometric Study;* and Neumann, *Authenticity.* For critiques of the methodology, see Torm, *ZNW* (1918) 225–43; Hitchcock, *ExpTim* 39 (1928) 347–52; id., *JTS* o.s. 30 (1928–29) 272–79; id., *Hermathena* 56 (1940) 113–35; Michaelis, *ZNW* 28 [1929] 69–76; Badcock, *Pauline Epistles,* 115–33; Spicq, 1:183–93; Guthrie, 212–28; id., *Mind of Paul,* 6–12; id., *Introduction,* 620 n. 2, 633 n. 3; B. M. Metzger, *ExpTim* 70 (1958) 91–94; C. Dinwoodie, "The Word, the Faith, and the Computer," *SJT* (1965) 204–18; G. B. Caird, "Do Computers Count?" *ExpTim* 65 (1965) 176; H. K. McArthur, "Computer Criticism," *ExpTim* 65 [1965] 367–70; id., "καί Frequency in Greek Letters," *NTS* 15 (1969) 339–49; O'Rourke, *CBQ* 35 (1973) 483–90; P. F. Johnson, *NTS* 20 (1974) 92–100; Clark, "Investigation"; T. A. Robinson, *NTS* 30 (1984) 282–88; Kenny, *Stylometric Study;* Knight, 40–45; cf. also Harnack, *Briefsammlung,* 74–75. Dibelius-Conzelmann agree that "the method of arguing against authenticity on the basis of statistics is inadequate" (3).

C. Conclusion

Every person's writing style and word choice are, to some degree, affected by the external influences of the particular situation of writing. While the PE do show some differences from what is found in other Pauline letters written to different historical situations and addressing different needs, the use of statistical analysis has far outreached itself. The possibility of the influence of an amanuensis and other external influences invalidates this entire approach.

B. M. Metzger concludes, "It seems, therefore, that a discreet reticence should replace the almost unbounded confidence with which many scholars have used this method in attempting to solve the problem of the authorship of the PE" (*ExpTim* 70 [1958] 94). Spicq likewise says:

> The Pastorals offer no characteristic that excludes their Pauline origin. The evolution of the style of the Apostle is perhaps due to the more sophisticated Greek and Roman culture, its vocabulary on subjects that he touches on for the first time, the tone of his. exhortations, his age and the fact that he addresses himself to some disciples. In addition there exists no canon of vocabulary, of style and of theological thought of Saint Paul to which all the other givens must be compared and reduced. To define the authentic Apostle exclusively by the language and the doctrine of the *Hauptbriefe* would be to mutilate the rich personality of the thinker, of the writer and of the man. (1:198)

PROPOSALS REGARDING AUTHORSHIP OF THE PE

There are three proposals regarding authorship of the PE, each attempting to deal with the problems outlined above. The Amanuensis Hypothesis views the letters as Pauline but allows for the influence of an amanuensis, especially in the areas of vocabulary and style. The Fragment Hypothesis proposes that after Paul's death a person collected a few genuine fragments of Paul's writing and wove them into three fabricated letters in an attempt to preserve the fragments and make Paul's message relevant to a later church. The Fiction Hypothesis sees the corpus as a total fabrication, usually placing its writing date in the second century as an attempt to make Paul's message relevant or to oppose second-century heresy.

A. Fiction Hypothesis

Proponents of this view see the PE as a total fabrication, without any element of authenticity. While the author, who is often called the "Pastor" by modern commentators, may have been an admirer of Paul, he created all three letters to address concerns of his church. The PE are usually dated at the beginning of the second century. The historical and personal allusions were included in an attempt to create an air of authenticity and credibility; the writings were intended to deceive. They have been called "spurious" and a "forgery" (cf. Holtzmann, 163), and Donelson calls them a "deception" (*Pseudepigraphy*, 24, 54–66). Proponents of this view place the text against the backdrop of second-century Gnosticism. Some see the PE as specifically anti-Marcionite (F. C. Baur, *Die sogenannten Pastoralbriefe;* Goodspeed, *Introduction;* Gealy; von Campenhausen, "Polycarp"), and some as written by Polycarp (Baur, *Pastoralbriefe;* von Campenhausen,

"Polycarp"). For defenders of this position, see Eichhorn, *Einleitung;* the Tübingen School (Baur, *Pastoralbriefe*); Holtzmann; Goodspeed, *Introduction;* Barnett, *Literary Influence;* Easton; Dibelius-Conzelmann; Gealy; Bultmann, *Primitive Christianity;* Hasler, *Studien und Texte zum Untersuchen* 28 (1958) 65–77; Barrett; von Campenhausen, "Polycarp"; Brox; Trummer, *BZ* 18 (1974) 193–207; Houlden; Hanson (1983, who originally accepted the Fragment Hypothesis in his 1966 commentary; cf. id., *BJRL* 63 [1981] 402); Cook, *JTS* n.s. 35 (1984) 120–31.

This view is not as attractive as it once was because it introduces more problems than it solves.

1. Internal problems. If the PE were a second-century corpus designed to fight the battles of that age, one would have to conclude that they failed miserably. In all aspects it can be argued that the PE are closer to Paul than to the second century. They do not combat full-blown Gnosticism, the dominant heresy of the second century, but at most deal with early forms. Kümmel says, "There is then not the slightest occasion . . . to link them with the great gnostic systems of the second century. . . . [A]ny polemic against specific Marcionite views is completely missing. The Jewish-Christian-Gnostic false teaching which is being combated in the Pastorals is therefore thoroughly comprehensible in the life span of Paul" (*Introduction,* 379; cf. Spicq, 1:lxxi). While especially 2 Timothy deals with suffering, the situation sounds nothing like the Domitian persecutions. The level of church governance and structure reflected in the PE is significantly different from that of Ignatius. Titus has little beyond basic catechetical instruction, and 2 Timothy is so personal that one has to hunt to find anything that could remotely be from the second century.

It is also difficult to accept the picture of the forger created by this position. His intent is clearly to deceive. The occurrence of personal and historical allusions, often given in an incidental manner, are woven into the very fabric of the corpus. Is it credible to have this kind of person speak so strongly against the supposed Ephesian opponents, accusing them of being deceivers, encouraging Timothy to purity and godliness? Is it plausible that the forger would create a fictitious historical framework that lies totally outside the record of Acts? There are no more eyewitnesses; there is no one that could say the added details are wrong. Why create an entire missionary journey through Crete that is nowhere else attested?

2. External problems. The Fiction Hypothesis stumbles against the external evidence as well. The canonical acceptance of the PE is extremely strong, both early and widespread. The Fiction Hypothesis requires us to dismiss in totality the witness of the early church solely on the basis of internal arguments. It is unable to provide any external evidence apart from the witness of the heretic Marcion and the incomplete $\mathfrak{P}^{46}$. This is a methodological issue, and many are willing to dismiss the external evidence. But how then is the strong external evidence to be explained? Why was a second-century forgery so significantly different from Paul's other writings—as it is claimed—accepted without any external evidence to the contrary by a church that was critical of accepting a writing into its canon, even writings purportedly from apostles and eyewitnesses (e.g., Gospel of John, James, 2 Peter)? Why are there no conflicting traditions?

3. Why three? This question is repeatedly raised by Fee (e.g., 6, 28–29 n. 14; see also his critique of Karris [*JBL* 92 (1973) 549–64]). If a forger were writing in the second century, using the name of the apostle Paul to add validity, why would this person write three forgeries, tripling the possibility of detection? Why write three documents that are significantly different in content and, in the case of Titus and 2 Timothy, add so little to the forger's argument? Titus adds virtually nothing to 1 Timothy and yet presupposes an entire missionary journey. 2 Timothy contains the most historical references and yet, because of its personal nature, has the least amount of theology that is relevant to the second century. Young says 1 Timothy taught Pauline tradition in the face of distortion, 2 Timothy guaranteed it, and Titus recapitulated it and added "theological sanctions and slogans that reinforce the message" (*Theology*, 142). But if the texts are taken at face value, they are so significantly different that, apart from a few verses on church structure and the opponents, there is little overlap of content.

B. Fragment Hypothesis

Because of the issues mentioned above, the Fiction Hypothesis has fewer supporters than in previous decades, many converting to the Fragment Hypothesis. This variation claims that while the bulk of the three letters is deutero-Pauline, there are a few authentic pieces, specifically some of the personal and historical references.

R. P. Martin (*New Testament Foundations: A Guide for Christian Students*, 2 vols. [Grand Rapids, MI: Eerdmans, 1975, 1978]), following Badcock (*Pauline Epistles*), suggests that Paul first wrote out the "headings, leading ideas, and paragraph themes."

> From what we know of Paul's letter-writing habits, his quick, staccato-like method of speaking under pressure (e.g., Phil. 1:22f.), would leave only the outline to be filled in by a trusted, sympathetic scribe, such as Tertius. . . . Suppose that Tertius kept a set of Paul's "notes" on which Romans was based; the notes would have neither particles, prepositions, or even pronouns, and be written in an abbreviated form. Let us imagine that this same procedure was followed in the case of the Pastorals. The original "notes" were destined for Timothy and Titus to aid them in their work as leaders at Ephesus and Crete, and items that were recognized as personal memoranda, travel notes, and intimate reflections formed the substance of those apostolic communications. Later the "notes" were edited by being written up and set in a form that made them more readable. To these statements of Paul's teaching were added materials such as hymns and creedal forms, based on what was common property in the Pauline churches. The completed whole, compiled by a man such as Luke who was Paul's companion in Rome (2 Tim. 4:11), were later available to be sent off to churches in Asia and Crete at a time when there was need to reinforce the Pauline emissaries who were wrestling with false teaching and also needing special reminders of what the apostle had taught. (*New Testament Foundations* 2:302–3)

Martin later adds:

> This short corpus of letters carries the *imprimatur* of Paul's authority and reveals his character as *pastor pastorum*, a leader who provides for continuing leadership in the churches. The compiler—whether Luke (as some believe) or not—had access to materials that go back to Paul's own statements of his faith and life (e.g., 1 Tim. 1:11, 12–16; 2 Tim. 1:3, 11f., 15–18; 3:10), to the apostle's prison experiences (2 Tim. 4:6–8), and to

travel-notes relating to his Asian ministry (2 Tim. 4:9–21). These he incorporated to display Paul's deep concern for the churches. (*New Testament Foundations* 2:306)

Other proponents of the Fragment Hypothesis include von Soden; Moffatt, *Introduction;* P. N. Harrison, *Problem;* Scott; Falconer; Easton; McNeile, *Introduction;* Barrett; Holtz; Hanson (originally in his commentary, 1966); Strobel, *NTS* 15 (1968) 191–210; Dornier; G. B. Wilson; and J. D. Miller, *Pastoral Letters.*

Much of the previous critique of the Fiction Hypothesis applies to the Fragment Hypothesis as well. But beyond this it brings additional problems.

(1) Martin uses the phrase "let us imagine," and the major critique of this position is that it requires too much imagination. Not one point in the hypothetical reconstruction is based on fact. There is only supposition; there are no textual indications (Spicq, 1:201–2). From the manner of writing notes and their content, to their combination with traditional material, no evidence is given that this actually ever happened. It also seems to be a jump of immense proportions to move from Paul's "staccato-like" writing style to Paul's actual manner of writing, or even to assume that this was the only way Paul would write. Is all of Paul "staccato-like"? C. F. D. Moule answers with this strong assessment:

> I must confess that it amazes me that such a solution has gained wide currency, for it presupposes (what to the best of my knowledge there is not a shred of evidence to support) that Paul wrote these little scraps on separate, detached papyri; and, even if that could be established, it requires us to believe that they were kept by the recipients—another improbable assumption; and finally, it asks us to picture an imitator going round and collecting them and copying them into the letter he had fabricated at points so captiously selected that they have puzzled commentators ever since. (*BJRL* 47 [1964–65] 448; so also Kümmel, *Introduction*, 385)

These types of issues led Hanson to change his mind and move to the Fiction Hypothesis camp ([1983] 10–11).

(2) Harrison originally found five historical fragments: Titus 3:12–15; 2 Tim 4:13–15, 20, 21a; 2 Tim 4:16–18a (18b?); 2 Tim 4:9–12, 22b; various other passages in 2 Timothy (1:16–18; 3:10–11; 4:1–2a; 4:5b–8; 4:19; 4:21b–22a; *Problem*, 115–27). He later found three fragments, joining #2 with #4, and #3 with #5 (*ExpTim* 47 [1955] 80; id., *Paulines*, 106–28). J. D. Miller (*Pastoral Letters*) suggests 1 Tim 1:1–7, 18–20; 3:14–15; 6:20–21; Titus 1:1–5; 3:9–11, 12–15a, 15c; 2 Tim 1:1–2, 3–5(?), 15–18; 4:6–8, 22a. Others offer 1 Tim 1:11, 12–16; 2 Tim 1:3, 11–12, 16–18; 3:10; 4:6–8, 9–12. However, there is no consensus. Guthrie (*Introduction*, 591 n. 1) cites ten writers, not one agreeing with another as to which fragments are authentic. If there is no consensus, perhaps the problem is the subjectivity of the methodology (Spicq, 1:201). Most of the passages are personal or historical; it can be asked why these have a greater claim to authenticity. Could not the many theological statements that sound Pauline be fragments to which fictitious personal and historical features were added to give them credence? Based on Paul's other writings, it seems that his communiqués with his associates were not "personal memoranda, travel notes, and intimate reflections" but rather theological discussions. Hanson comments on 2 Tim 4:21, "Are we to imagine the author of the Pastorals as freely inventing all these names? It does not seem likely" ([1983] 164; cf. also p. 120 on 2 Tim 1:5). But if the author felt free to create three letters

full of pronouncements supposedly from Paul, why would he hesitate to create names?

Guthrie argues that when the supposed fragments are placed in a time frame, they contradict each other (*Introduction*, 639–41). Kümmel points out the problem with the methodology, which requires a large dose of subjectivity and suffers from a lack of verifiable criteria as one attempts to reconstruct the historical setting into which these fragments can be placed: "The ordering of these fragments, which only hint at their situation, within the life of Paul as it is known to us is at best only hypothetically possible. No certainty is to be gained as to whether a section really could be a genuine fragment because it fits into a situation which we know, and there simply is no other criterion of authenticity in this case" (*Introduction*, 385).

(3) Most of the passages identified as authentic are inserted at the end of Titus and scattered throughout 2 Timothy. Why are there no fragments in 1 Timothy? It contains most of the theology that is supposedly relevant to the second century. On the other hand, 2 Timothy contains almost none of the relevant theology but the majority of the allegedly authentic historical fragments.

(4) Is the proposed motive credible? Michaelis (*Pastoralbriefe*, 134ff.) deals with this issue in detail. Does a person preserve authentic fragments by mingling them among personal writings, so hidden that they are virtually undetectable? If the fragments were known to be Pauline, would someone mix them with his own? If the fragments were not known as Pauline, why would their inclusion lend authenticity? If the compiler's goal was to preserve Pauline fragments and make Paul's instruction relevant to a later time, one is overwhelmed by his degree of failure. There is no anti-Marcionite polemic, no anti-Gnostic emphasis, no advance from Paul's day. A simple listing of the proposed third fragment raises the questions of whether it actually would have ever existed and whether it would have been used throughout the writing as it supposedly has been.

Guthrie discusses motive in light of ethical issues (*Introduction*, 643–46):

> The PE contain warnings about deceivers (1 Tim. 4:1; 2 Tim. 3:13; Titus 1:10), and in one passage the writer says that while in the past he had been led astray, that has all changed now that he has been saved (Titus 3:3). Would a person who speaks of deceit like this put the name of Paul to a letter he himself had composed? Would he say so firmly, "I am telling the truth, I am not lying" (1 Tim. 2:7)? (cf. Carson, Moo, and Morris, *Introduction*, 371)

The counterargument is that pseudepigraphy was recognized as such, and there is no conflict because there is no deception. Yet, as we have argued, especially 2 Timothy is so replete with personal allusions that either they are true or they *intend* to deceive. Kelly concludes:

> It is one thing to publish under the name of Paul or some other apostle a treatise, whether in the form of a letter or of something else, which the author sincerely believes to express the great man's teaching, or which he even believes to have been disclosed to him by the self-same Spirit which used the great man as his mouthpiece. It is quite another thing to fabricate for it a detailed framework of concrete personal allusions, reminiscences, and messages, not to mention outbursts of intensely personal feeling, which one knows to be pure fiction but which one puts together with the object of creating an air of verisimilitude. (33)

The Fragment Hypothesis is only a slightly altered form of the Fiction Hypothesis that attempts to deal with a few of the personal and historical comments. To my mind, it answers none of the problems and introduces a new set of issues. Proposing historical fragments does not explain the Pauline elements throughout the PE or the external evidence for authorship. It is highly subjective with minimal agreement in the details among interpreters, proposing a process that is highly imaginative. It does not explain why there are three letters. D. Cook concludes, "The intermediate ground occupied by the defenders of the fragment hypothesis proves to be rather a no man's land not suited for habitation" (*JTS* 35 [1984] 131).

Excursus: Pseudepigraphy

Proponents of the two preceding views often raise the issue of pseudepigraphy—the writing of a book or letter under someone else's name—claiming that it was an accepted practice. They claim that the pseudepigraphical nature of the PE would have been recognized and accepted by the church; the PE would not have been viewed as a "forgery" even though the church knew Paul was not the actual author. It is claimed that this practice does not lessen the authority of the PE; Aland argues that it even enhances their authority since the redactor felt he was sharing the same inspiration as the original author (see bibliography in Martin, *New Testament Foundations* 2:281 n. 18). Meade argues that pseudepigraphy is an "assertion of authoritative tradition, not a statement of literary origin" (*Pseudonymity*, 72; he "assume[s]" that the pseudonymity of the PE "is a foregone conclusion" [118]). It is also claimed that this practice does not raise moral issues. P. N. Harrison states that the author "was not conscious of misrepresenting the Apostle in any way; he was not consciously deceiving anybody; it is not, indeed, necessary to suppose that he did deceive anybody. It seems far more probable that those to whom, in the first instance, he showed the results of his efforts, must have been perfectly well aware of what he had done" (*Problem,* 12; cf. also Baur, *Pastoralbriefe,* 110–11; Easton, 19; Gealy, 372).

Discussions of pseudonymity have mostly concerned 2 Peter, but also Ephesians, Colossians, 2 Thessalonians, Jude, 1 Peter, and James. Kelly, who accepts Paul's authorship of the PE, uses these strong words:

> The modern reader who feels an initial shock at what he takes to be fraud should reflect that the attitude, approach, and literary standards of that age were altogether different from those accepted today. The author who attributed his own work to an apostle was probably sincerely convinced that it faithfully reproduced the great man's teaching and point of view. It is also likely that, in the first and early second century at any rate, Christians had little or no interest in the personality of the human agent who wrote their sacred books. The Spirit who had spoken through the apostles was still active in prophetic men, and when they put pen to paper it was he who was the real author of their productions. It was therefore legitimate to attribute all such writings (apart, of course, from compositions which were by their very nature personal), to one or other of the apostles, who had been the mouthpieces of the Spirit and whose disciples the actual authors, humanly speaking, were. (5–6)

But one wonders, if Kelly and others are correct, why Paul ever identified himself as an author if identity was secondary or irrelevant. Balz argues that if Aland (*JTS* n.s. 12 [1961] 39–49) is correct, then Paul's ascription of his name to his letters is somehow less than a pseudepigraphical ascription (*ZTK* 66 [1969] 419).

Space does not permit a discussion of the issue of pseudepigraphy in general, but I will address a few issues directly relevant to the PE. It is hard to get away from the impression that when the text says that Paul is writing to two friends, Timothy and Titus, either it means what it says or it is a forgery designed to deceive (cf. Candlish, *Exp* 4 [1891] 103, 262; Torm, *Psychologie*, 19; Ellis, "Pseudonymity," 220–23). The insertion of the issue of valid pseudepigraphy tries to fill in the middle ground as unsuccessfully as the Fragment Hypothesis. (Young's comparison to the use of a pen-name by modern writers is not analogous but is actually the opposite; in this situation the historical author is not attributing the work to a historically known person [*Theology*, 136].)

There is no question that pseudepigraphy existed in the ancient world (cf. Speyer, *Die literarische Fälschung*, 5–10; Ellis, "Pseudonymity," 212–13), but this is almost irrelevant to our context. The real question is whether the church *recognized* and *accepted* false *letters* that they *knew* to be pseudepigraphical. Guthrie provides a helpful and detailed discussion of epistolary pseudepigraphy (*Introduction*, 1011–28), and his discussion deserves serious attention (also Carson, Moo, and Morris, *Introduction*, 367–71). His point is that regardless of the ancient view of pseudepigraphy in general, what concerns us here is epistolary pseudepigraphy in Jewish and Christian circles (as compared to, e.g., apocalyptic). Was the forgery of epistolary correspondence identifiable and acceptable? It is one thing to write a book and claim someone wrote it (e.g., *1 Enoch*, in the name of one who had been dead for thousands of years); it is another to write a personal letter filled with personal and historical references and claim it was written by someone in the recent past (so also I. H. Marshall, "Recent Study of the Pastoral Letters," *Themelios* 23 [1997] 9). To this I would add that if it were accepted, would it help explain the internal and external evidence of the authorship of the PE, or would it introduce its own set of problems?

There are two sets of external data that help make this determination. The first is those explicit references in the early church to writings that were known to be pseudepigraphical. In every case, the external evidence shows that the church did not accept epistolary pseudepigraphy.

(1) The Muratorian Canon states about a pseudepigraphical letter, "There is current also (an epistle) to the Laodiceans, another to the Alexandrians, forged in Paul's name for the sect of Marcion, and several others, which cannot be received in the catholic Church; for it will not do to mix gall with honey" (in Hennecke, *New Testament Apocrypha* 1:44).

(2) Eusebius mentions that Serapion of Antioch (c. 190) found the *Gospel of Peter* being used in Cilicia. He wrote the following to the church at Rhossus in Cilicia: "We receive both Peter and the other apostles as Christ, but the writings which falsely bear their names we reject, as men of experience, knowing that such were not handed down to us" (*Hist. Eccl.* 6.12.2–3; LCL tr.).

(3) *3 Corinthians* was included with the *Acts of Paul*, was circulated independently in the Syrian church, and was actually accepted by some as canonical. As part of the *Acts of Paul*, it was written by a second-century bishop in Asia out of love for the apostle. When the author confessed that his work was a forgery, his actions were condemned, he was removed from office, and his forgery was not accepted. Tertullian writes, "But if the writings which wrongly go under Paul's name, claim Thecla's example as a license for women's teaching and baptizing, let them know that, in Asia, the presbyter who composed that writing, as if he were augmenting Paul's fame from his own store, after being convicted, and confessing that he had done it from love of Paul, was removed from his office" (*De Bapt.* 17; ANF 3:677). We do not know how widespread was its adoption. It was rejected by the time of the Peshitta; it is not listed in the Syriac canon from c. 400 (cf. A. Souter, *The Text and Canon of the New Testament* [New York: Scribner's, 1913] 226). There is also no evidence that it was originally known to be pseudonymous.

(4) The evidence from Paul himself shows that he did not want the church to accept a pseudepigraphical letter. He urges the Thessalonian church not to believe any false letter supposedly from him that the day of the Lord has already come (2 Thess 2:2) and goes so far as to create a mark that identifies a letter as authentic (2 Thess 3:17), a custom continued in other letters (1 Cor 16:21; Gal 6:11; Col 4:18; cf. Rom 16:22; 1 Pet 5:12). Hanson asserts, without any evidence, that "the contemporaries of the author of the Pastorals would not have condemned him for his claiming Paul's authority for his work" ([1983] 49). It appears that Paul disagrees. (On the signing of one's own name as an indication of authenticity in secular writings, cf. G. J. Bahr, "The Subscriptions in the Pauline Letters," *JBL* 87 [1968] 27–41.)

These historical facts are clear. Much of the discussion of pseudepigraphy is based on the assumption that 2 Peter is pseudepigraphical and that its inclusion in the canon indicates the church's acceptance of pseudepigraphy. But the only solid, historical facts we do possess clearly state that the church did not accept writings known to be forgeries.

Guthrie also shows in detail that there are no examples of epistolary pseudepigraphy in canonical Jewish literature, only two in noncanonical Jewish literature (and neither are actually a letter—*Letter of Jeremiah; Letter of Aristeas*), and of the approximately six in noncanonical Christian literature four are obvious forgeries and had no effect on the church, which leaves the *Acts of Paul* and the *Epistle to the Laodiceans*. Guthrie rightly argues that the near absence of pseudepigraphical letters argues that pseudepigraphy was not accepted by the church. The issue of the authorship of 2 Peter can be set aside; it is not parallel to the PE because it is not a letter. The mere presence of pseudepigraphical writings does not mean they were known to be false or that they were accepted as authoritative. There is not one example of a letter that was known to be pseudonymous that was also accepted as authoritative (cf. Balz, *ZTK* 66 [1969] 403–36; Lea, *JETS* 27 [1984] 70; Donelson, *Pseudepigraphy*, 11; Carson, Moo, and Morris, *Introduction*, 371). The examples we do have of known pseudepigraphical letters all testify to the church's refusal to accept them (see citations from the Muratorian Canon and Tertullian quoted above).

There are many other problems with postulating the acceptance of epistolary pseudepigraphy as authoritative. Perhaps the most significant is the moral issue. Despite modern objections to the contrary, is it really possible that someone would forge a personal letter of a well-known person to a well-known friend, replete with personal comments and historical asides, and at the same time emphatically condemn hypocrisy? The writer of the later *Apostolic Constitutions* seems closer to the evidence:

> We have sent all these things to you, that ye may know our opinion, what it is; and that ye may not receive those books which obtain in our name, but are written by the ungodly. . . . The same things even now have the wicked heretics done, reproaching the creation, marriage, providence, the begetting of children, the law, and the prophets; inscribing certain barbarous names, and, as they think, of angels, but, to speak the truth, of demons, which suggest things to them: whose doctrine eschew, that ye may not be partakers of the punishment due to those that write such things for the seduction and perdition of the faithful and unblameable disciples of the Lord Jesus (6.3.16; tr. ANF 7:457).

R. D. Shaw (in Simpson, 22) concludes, "A genuine Paulinist, at once so skillful and obtuse, inventing unreal situations with the utmost *sangfroid*, yet breathing an air of profoundest reverence for truth, is an absolute chimera."

But, for the sake of argument, if we accept the hypothesis that a forger could write in someone else's name and it would be known and accepted by the church, why then are the historical and personal allusions woven throughout the PE? If there is no need to make the letters sound credible, then why include these features? These details are not surface trappings; as I have argued, they are part of the very fabric of the letters, especially 2 Timothy. *I can only conclude that if the writer was a pseudepigrapher, he was attempting to deceive his audience into thinking that Paul himself actually wrote the PE. But if the author felt the need to deceive, then pseudepigraphy could not have been an acceptable practice!* (Guthrie gives an excellent discussion of the pseudepigrapher's motives, including critiques of Aland's and Meade's arguments; *Introduction*, 1018–28.) While many resist the use of the term *forgery*, Paul's condemnation of epistolary pseudepigraphy and the lack of explicit evidence to the contrary suggest that it is the only viable term (so also Fee, *God's Empowering Presence*, 784 n. 133).

Meade argues that the personal information in the PE is given because

> absolute value . . . is placed on the authority of Paul. . . . There are no other apostles even mentioned. This exclusive focus on Paul demonstrates that behind the Pastorals was a community whose identity was exclusively created and sustained by the figure of Paul. . . . Paul becomes *the* example, or outline (ὑποτύπωσις), and essential part of the tradition itself. It is this paradigmatic value of Paul's experience that leads to the use of much of the personal information in the Pastorals. (*Pseudonymity*, 123, 124)

While this might explain a few of the statements such as Paul's call for Timothy to suffer willingly, it fails to explain the more casual statements such as the whereabouts of Paul's companions. It also demonstrates how far one must go in reinterpreting straightforward statements when the stated historical context is not accepted. Why would Paul necessarily talk about other apostles in this historical situation? The conclusion does not follow from the premise, and the argument is circular. The proposal of a Pauline community in which Paul himself was encased in the tradition does not come from the text. (Meade states that his study assumes pseudonymity; it does not prove it [*Pseudonymity*, 16], although he does summarize the issues relevant to the PE [*Pseudonymity*, 118–22; cf. critique by Porter, *BBR* 5 (1995) 116–18].) Donelson argues not only that the personal details were included to authenticate the forgery, but that the presence of details was typical in forgeries and shows the pseudepigraphical character of the PE (*Pseudepigraphy*, 54–60). Of course, the presence of details in and of itself cannot prove pseudepigraphy.

Another problem is the picture that the view creates of the pseudepigrapher. On the one hand, the forger is so versed in Paul and so clever at writing that he fooled the church for 1800 years. As Fee states, he must have been a "near genius" (25, 293). Yet, on the other hand, the forger makes such obvious blunders that to modern scholarship it is inconceivable that Paul could have been the author. Is this combination of genius and foolishness possible? For example, at the very beginning the author identifies Paul's apostleship as being according to the "command" of God (1 Tim 1:1). He speaks of "grace, mercy, peace" (1 Tim 1:2) even though Paul, it is alleged, could never have said "mercy" since he does nowhere else. Houlden says that 1 Tim 2:14 is theologically shallow (72). Hanson speaks of "a truly Pauline touch" ([1983] 61) and then later comments that the author "was no great theologian" ([1983] 62), "did not know himself" what he was saying ([1983] 82), had "appalling ineptitude" ([1983] 92) and "a positive talent of concealing his precise meaning behind relatively commonplace words" ([1983] 104), was "a writer devoid of Paul's insights" ([1983] 67) with a "simple mind" ([1983] 144), created a "dismal conclusion to Paul's writings . . . pretty plain by now that they are not Pauline" ([1983] 51), and possessed an education that "probably did not extend beyond the equivalent of our modern university entrance level" ([1983] 46). Can the person described by Hanson be, at the same time, so clever? Fee comments that the pseudepigrapher's failure to imitate Paul "at easily discernible points (e.g., the greeting) . . . nearly defies reason" (25).

Related is the question of whether an admirer of Paul would create the types of statements we read, such as calling Paul a blasphemer, persecutor, and insolent person (1 Tim 1:13), and stating that Paul was abandoned by almost everyone in his hour of need (2 Tim 1:15), that one of his inner circle defected (2 Tim 4:10), and that his order of excommunication (1 Tim 1:20) was not obeyed (2 Tim 2:17). Would a forger set his fictitious writings into a historical framework that does not agree with Acts? Would a pseudepigrapher hoping to avoid detection address three letters to individuals when all but one of Paul's letters were written to churches? Is the pseudepigrapher in places "trying (not very successfully) to impart some of Paul's liveliness to his own style by using Paul's words of protest" (Hanson [1983] 70, on 1 Tim 2:7)?

The problems introduced by any theory of epistolary pseudepigraphy seem to defeat any help it may bring. The external evidence is solid; the church shows no sign of accepting known pseudepigraphical writings as authoritative. The emphasis of personal and historical details suggests that the author, if a pseudepigrapher, was intending to deceive, an unnecessary goal if epistolary pseudepigraphy were in fact accepted. It creates an implausible picture of a forger who at one time is clever and at another is a fool, blundering through obvious errors and creating information about Paul that runs counter to his admiration of the apostle. It creates a picture of a forger who castigates the Ephesian opponents for their lack of morality and conscience and for their deception of the Ephesian church and at the same time attempts to deceive his readership. To me this is not credible. The seemingly constant repetition of the claim that the church recognized and accepted pseudepigraphical letters does not prove its claim; the objective facts clearly state that the church did not accept that which they knew to be a forgery.

C. *Amanuensis Hypothesis*

The Amanuensis Hypothesis states that while Paul wrote the PE, he wrote them, as he always did, with the aid of an amanuensis. While he may have given only limited freedom to previous secretaries, in this situation he was using a different amanuensis and giving him more freedom of expression than previously allowed. This hypothesis follows the suggestion of 2 Timothy that the nature of Paul's imprisonment prohibited him from writing the letters himself (cf. Jeremias, 5–6), and the similarities among the three epistles suggest that the same freedom was granted to the same amanuensis in all three. Roller suggests that given the physical restriction of a small prison and the weight of the chains, an amanuensis was not only required but would of necessity be given significant freedom (*Formular,* 20–21). Jeremias proposes Tychicus (8). Paul's comment that only Luke was with him (2 Tim 4:11) suggests to others that Luke was the amanuensis (cf. Lock, xxix; Badcock, *Pauline Epistles,* chap. 6). As discussed above (*Introduction,* "Historical Reconstruction from the PE"), Paul and Luke had increasing contact in Paul's later years, and presumably their friendship and trust would have grown.

Strobel (*NTS* 15 [1968] 191–210) argues for Luke's role as the amanuensis for stylistic reasons, seeing Luke writing them before Paul's death. He points out that thirty-seven of the unusual words in the PE also occur in Luke-Acts, and thirty-seven other words appear in Luke-Acts, the PE, and only rarely elsewhere in the NT. Fee concludes, "The best solution is that Paul used a different amanuensis for these letters than for earlier ones (or did he actually write these himself after having used amanuenses earlier?). . . . The large number of correspondences in vocabulary with Luke-Acts makes the hypothesis of Luke as this amanuensis an attractive one" (26). (For Luke's involvement in some way, see Roller, *Formular;* Badcock, *Pastoral Epistles;* Spicq; Ellis, *EvQ* 32 [1960] 151–61; Moule, *BJRL* 47 [1964–65] 430–52; Strobel, *NTS* 15 [1968] 191–210; S. G. Wilson, *Luke;* Fee; Quinn; Knight; Towner.)

Bruce's suggestion that Timothy may have been Paul's amanuensis for 1 and 2 Thessalonians, 2 Corinthians, Philippians, Colossians, and Philemon is interesting (see above, *Introduction,* "Critical Questions, The Linguistic Problem"). Timothy is listed as a joint author of 1 Thessalonians and is mentioned in the prescript of the other letters. Since letters to Timothy would obviously require a different amanuensis, the possibility of another amanuensis for the PE is strengthened. Prior suggests that Paul's letters to churches were written with the help of an amanuensis but his letters to individuals were written by himself (*Paul the Letter Writer,* 50).

In a related vein, Quinn argues that the PE were written by Luke as a "third roll of a single work that began with Luke-Acts" ("Last Volume," 74), intended to be read as an epistolary appendix that carried the narrative up to Paul's death (also *Titus,* 19). But it seems unlikely that someone, especially Paul's personal friend, could write the corpus after Paul's death. The request that Timothy come quickly to Rome before winter is inconceivable if Paul was in fact dead. Is it plausible that Luke forged three imaginary letters from a real person (who was a friend) to two real people (who were also friends)?

For discussions and critiques of the secretary hypothesis, see Holtzmann, 92ff.; Moffatt (*Introduction,* 414); Harrison (*Problem,* 363–64); Roller (*Formular*); Badcock (*Pauline Epistles,* 115–33); Jeremias, 7–8 (summarized by Knight, 48–51); Moule (*BJRL* 47 [1965] 430–52); Strobel (*NTS* 15 [1968] 191–210, assessed by Brox, *JAC* 13 [1970] 62–77); de Lestapis (*L'énigme des Pastorales*); Quinn ("Last Volume"); S. G. Wilson (*Luke,* 3–4, who thinks Luke wrote the PE after Acts, using some "travel notes" and having read some of Paul's writings; reviewed by Quinn, *CBQ* 43 [1981] 488–90, and Larkin, *TJ* 37 [1981] 91–94); I. H. Marshall (Review of *Luke and the Pastoral Epistles,* by S. G. Wilson, *JSNT* 10 [1981] 69–74); summaries in Guthrie (*Introduction,* 647 n. 3) and Knight (48–51). On the role of an amanuensis, also see *Introduction,* "Critical Questions, The Linguistic Problem" (above), and R. N. Longenecker, "Ancient Amanuenses and the Pauline Epistles," in *New Directions in New Testament Study* (Grand Rapids, MI: Zondervan, 1974) 281–97; Ellis, *ExpTim* 104 (1992–93) 45. On issues relating to the role of an amanuensis in secular literature, see A. N. Sherwin-White (*The Letters of Pliny: A Historical and Social Commentary* [Oxford: Clarendon, 1966] 538–46) and Prior (*Letter-Writer,* 46–48), and on nonepistolary literature, see H. St. J. Thackeray (in *Josephus,* LCL [Cambridge, MA: Harvard UP, 1927, 1930] 2:xv; 4:xiv–xvii) and Richards (*Secretary*). Kümmel argues that the possibility of Luke being the amanuensis is "simply out of the question" because the theology of the PE is different from the theology of Luke-Acts (*Introduction,* 374). This is indeed a curious argument since it shows that Luke was faithful to Paul's intention.

Strobel's literary analysis (*NTS* 15 [1968] 191–210) by itself is not sufficient to prove that Luke was the amanuensis (see especially the critique by Marshall, *JSNT* 10 [1981] 69–74). Yet the literary similarities with Luke-Acts along with the historical picture in 2 Timothy are of sufficient strength to suggest that Luke is the most likely person to have written Paul's last letter to Timothy, with perhaps Paul giving him a degree of latitude in terms of vocabulary, style, and theological expression. If Luke was the amanuensis of 2 Timothy, then the consistency among the PE suggests that he was the amanuensis for all three. This best explains the external evidence, the internal issues, and why there were three letters written, and it does not introduce its own set of irreconcilable problems.

There is a position that exists in varying degrees between the Fiction and Amanuensis Hypotheses. It varies based on how much of the PE are held to be Pauline and how close in time the compilers were to Paul. Some argue that the material is Pauline but was edited by a colleague after his death (e.g., Badcock, *Pauline Epistles,* 115–33; A. C. Deane, *St. Paul and His Letters* [London: Hodder & Stoughton, 1942] 208–20). For others the scale slides to a few decades after Paul's death, with access to less Pauline material (Dornier, "Les Épîtres Pastorales"). For example, Quinn ("Last Volume") thinks that the PE began as short notes to Timothy from Paul, written with the aid of Luke. They were later modified by Luke and published as his third volume in the Luke-Acts trilogy. What seems most unlikely is any view that says that close Pauline associates immediately after Paul's death wrote 2 Tim 4:9, 21, asking Timothy to leave his work in Ephesus and come quickly to Paul's side.

D. Conclusion

The issue of authorship deals more with one's methodology than with the text itself. There are differences between the PE and the rest of Paul's writings, just as there are differences among the other Pauline writings. The questions are, how different are they and what is the significance of those differences? The Amanuensis Hypothesis best explains the internal and external evidence. It accounts for the differences between the PE and the other Pauline letters and does not introduce its own set of problems. The Fiction and Fragment Hypotheses dismiss the external evidence for authenticity and misrepresent the text in a way that creates an unnecessary division between Paul and the PE, offering a theory of composition that is implausible to me. They do not answer some of the most basic questions, such as why the pseudepigrapher wrote three letters, or why there is so little of the second century (Ignatius, Gnosticism, etc.) reflected in the corpus, or on what basis these hypotheses can pronounce judgment on what Paul could and could not have said.

As Fee concludes, "When one has as little evidence as is available from Paul—and what evidence we do have is occasional, not systematic, in nature—a much larger measure of caution than one usually finds in the literature would seem appropriate. In the final analysis the decision rests upon what impresses one more, the clearly Pauline nature of so much, or the seemingly divergent nature of much" (14). To put it another way, which view creates the most internally coherent picture, one that deals with the external evidence and does not introduce irreconcilable problems? Finally, is the critical methodology valid, or at times does it allow for conclusions to be drawn that in fact are not supported by the evidence?

Themes in the PE

Themes will normally be discussed as they appear in the text (see list below), and word studies will be done the first time the word is found; cognates will usually be discussed together. A few themes, however, are so pervasive throughout the PE that they require some initial attention here: "faith," "savior, salvation," and "good works" (see also the summary of themes in Fee, 14–20). The nature of the Ephesian heresy and the character of the opponents have been discussed above.

Reference	Section	Theme
1 Tim 1:3	Comment	Historical Situation behind 1 Timothy
1 Tim 1:8–11	Form/Structure/Setting	Vice Lists
1 Tim 1:12–17	Form/Structure/Setting	Faithful Sayings
1 Tim 1:20	Comment	Timothy's Ordination
1 Tim 2:2	Comment	Reverence (εὐσέβεια)
1 Tim 2:10	Comment	Good Works
1 Tim 3:1–7	Form/Structure/Setting	Origin of Christian Ministry
1 Tim 3:1–7	Form/Structure/Setting	Qualities of Church Leadership
1 Tim 3:1–7	Explanation	Church Leadership in the Second Century
1 Tim 3:8–13	Explanation	Deacons and Deaconesses
1 Tim 3:14–16	Comment	The Heart of the Epistle
Titus 2:1–10	Explanation	Motives of Ethical Instruction
Titus 2:11	Comment and Explanation	Necessity of Obedience
2 Tim 3:10–4:8	Comment	Role of Scripture in Ministry (also 1 Tim 4:6–16)

FAITH

In the PE πίστις, "faith," occurs thirty-three times and the adjective πιστός, "faithful," seventeen. In the NT the noun is used with five basic nuances: (1) intellectual assent (Jas 2:14–26; but cf. Jas 5:15); (2) believing Jesus could perform a miracle (Matt 9:28–29; 15:28; 17:20–21; cf. Acts 14:9; 1 Cor 12:9; 13:2); (3) trustworthy, faithful (Matt 23:23; Rom 3:3; Gal 5:22; 2 Thess 1:4); (4) a body of truth, "the faith" (Gal 1:23; 2 Cor 13:5; Jude 3, 20); and (5) trust, which is Paul's most frequent use of the term (see listing in E. D. Burton, *A Critical and Exegetical Commentary on the Epistle to the Galatians,* ICC [Edinburgh: T. & T. Clark, 1921] 481–84). In looking at the use of πίστις in the PE, it is helpful to divide the passages according to grammatical constructions: (1) articular, (2) anarthrous, and (3) the phrase ἐν πίστει, "in faith."

(1) πίστις occurs fifteen times in the PE with the article. Three of these mean "trust" (2 Tim 1:5; 2:18; 3:10 [which includes the article because it occurs in a series of articular constructions]; possibly 1 Tim 1:19b). The statement that the young widows were violating their first pledge (τὴν πρώτην πίστιν; 1 Tim 5:12) is unusual, yet somewhat related to the idea of "trustworthy." In every other use of πίστις with the article, Paul is discussing "the faith" in a creedal, objective sense

(1 Tim 1:19b; 3:9; 4:1, 6; 5:8; 6:10, 12, 21; 2 Tim 3:8; 4:7; Titus 1:13; 2:2; cf. R. Bultmann, *TDNT* 6:213–14). This objective sense is made especially clear when Paul speaks of the "counterfeit faith" (ἀδόκιμοι περὶ τὴν πίστιν; 2 Tim 3:8) and when it parallels the concepts of διδασκαλία, "doctrine" (1 Tim 4:1, 6; cf. Titus 1:13), and ἀλήθεια, "truth" (1 Tim 2:7; 2 Tim 2:18; 3:8; Titus 1:1, 13–14; see discussion of ἀλήθεια in *Comment* on 1 Tim 2:4).

(2) πίστις is used nine times in an anarthrous construction. Three times it means "with fidelity" (1 Tim 6:11; 2 Tim 2:22; Titus 2:10; see 1 Tim 5:12 above). This use of the noun parallels the use of the adjective πιστός, "faithful" (1 Tim 1:12; 3:11; 2 Tim 2:2,13; Titus 1:9), used specifically of the "faithful sayings" (1 Tim 1:15; 3:1; 4:9; 2 Tim 2:11; Titus 3:8) and as a description of believers as "the faithful ones" (1 Tim 4:3, 10, 12; 5:16; 6:2 [2x]; Titus 1:6; cf. ἄπιστος, "unbeliever," 1 Tim 5:8; Titus 1:15). In every other instance, the noun denotes the standard Pauline meaning of "trust" (1 Tim 1:5, 14; 2 Tim 3:15; Titus 1:1, 4). In two places the anarthrous πίστις is contrasted with the false teaching in Ephesus (1 Tim 1:5, 19), implying a close connection between Paul's use of πίστις in a creedal sense (i.e., articular) and his use of the word in a sense of "trust" (as is usually the case with anarthrous constructions).

(3) The third construction is the phrase ἐν πίστει, "in faith." Whereas there are some basic patterns in the articular and the anarthrous use of πίστις, when it occurs in this phrase a pattern is not easy to ascertain. This may be partly explained by the fact that articles are unnecessary with words that are the object of a preposition (Robertson, 791–92), and we therefore lose a potential exegetical aid. The phrase occurs eight times in the PE, nine if Titus 1:13 is included (ἐν τῇ πίστει). Timothy is Paul's legitimate child in faith (1 Tim 1:2). As opposed to the teaching of the opponents, divine training is in faith (1 Tim 1:4). Paul is a teacher of the Gentiles in faith and truth (1 Tim 2:7). Women will be saved if they continue in faith and love, etc. (1 Tim 2:15). Deacons have a "great confidence in the faith which is in Christ Jesus" (1 Tim 3:13 RSV). Timothy is to set an example in faith, in love, etc. (1 Tim 4:12) and "follow the pattern of the sound words which you have heard from me, in the faith [ἐν πίστει] and love which are in Christ Jesus" (2 Tim 1:13 RSV). Titus is to greet those who love Paul ἐν πίστει (2 Tim 3:15). In all these examples πίστις is anarthrous; significant then is Paul's statement that Titus should rebuke the troublemakers so that they might be sound ἐν τῇ πίστει (1 Tim 1:13), which inserts the article.

From this listing several conclusions emerge. (1) When πίστις occurs in a list such as with ἀγάπη, "love," etc., it is best to understand it in the standard Pauline sense of "trust" since this best parallels ideas such as "love" (1 Tim 2:15; 4:12; 2 Tim 1:13; cf. 1 Tim 6:11; 2 Tim 3:10; Titus 2:2). (2) Just as in the articular use of πίστις, when πίστις is paralleled with ἀλήθεια, "truth" (1 Tim 2:7), it should be understood in its creedal sense of "the faith" just as ἀλήθεια is "the truth" (see 1 Tim 2:4). In the other passages (1 Tim 1:2, 4; 3:13; Titus 3:15) the immediate context is the ultimate indicator. (3) There is some overlapping in meaning from one grammatical construction to another. For example, Paul mixes forms in 1 Tim 1:19, 3:8 and 10, and 6:11 and 12. This shows that a grammatical analysis is not sufficient in and of itself to determine the meaning of the word. (Of course, context is always the guide, but context suggests that Paul often used the article [or absence of it] to indicate the meaning of πίστις.)

A few observations are pertinent here: (1) There is no *one* single concept of πίστις in the PE. The same flexibility evident throughout the NT and Paul continues here. (2) No new use of πίστις is introduced in the PE. Although the creedal use is more evident here than in other Pauline writings, it is still present in the earliest of Paul's writings. (3) This frequency of the creedal use in the PE can be accounted for by the historical situation. The opponents were attacking the entire body of belief that comprised "the faith" (cf. *Introduction*, "The Response to the Heresy"). (4) Those who are faithful have faith in something. It is a logical progression to go from speaking about "having faith" in someone and "being faithful" to speaking about "the faith" as the embodiment of that which describes one's faith (Bernard, 36; Guthrie, *New Testament Theology*, 593–94; cf. also Quinn, *Titus*, "Excursus I," 271–76).

SAVIOR, SALVATION, AND GOOD WORKS

The word σωτήρ, "savior," and its cognates (σῴζειν, "to save," σωτηρία, "salvation," σωτήριος, "bringing salvation"; on σωτηρία in the PE, cf. Towner, *Goal*, 73–119; Quinn, *Titus*, "Excursus V," 304–15) occur some twenty times throughout the NT. The term is applied to both God and Jesus (see below). Salvation was the purpose for Jesus' coming (1 Tim 1:15) and death (1 Tim 2:6). It must be offered to all people (1 Tim 2:4; 4:10; Titus 2:11), even to a sinner like Paul (1 Tim 1:15). Though it is available to all, only those who believe (1 Tim 4:10) can call God "our" savior (1 Tim 1:1; 2:3; 2 Tim 1:10; Titus 2:10). There is no concept of universalism in the PE (see 1 Tim 2:4).

This salvation comes through Jesus Christ (Titus 3:6), not as a result of human deeds but because of God's purpose, grace (2 Tim 1:9), mercy (Titus 3:5), and through the eschatological gift of the Holy Spirit (Titus 3:5; cf. *Comment* on 1 Tim 2:10). Yet there is human responsibility in that Paul will endure his suffering so that the elect may receive their salvation (2 Tim 2:10) and Scripture can instruct Timothy "for salvation through faith" (2 Tim 3:15). Paul therefore encourages Timothy to "hold to that, for by so doing you will save both yourself and your hearers" (1 Tim 4:16 RSV). For a discussion of σῴζειν, meaning "to save" or "to keep safe," see *Comment* on 1 Tim 2:15.

In the PE, salvation is described in three tenses. It is a past event in that it was accomplished by Christ (1 Tim 1:15; Titus 3:5). It is a present reality in that death has been abolished and life and immortality have come (2 Tim 1:10). Believers are justified (Titus 3:7) and have present obligations to be holy (2 Tim 1:9; cf. Titus 2:10). Paul has the present assurance that God will protect him (2 Tim 4:18). Salvation is also future (1 Tim 2:15; 4:16) in that believers are "heirs in hope of eternal life" (Titus 3:7), will obtain "eternal glory" (2 Tim 2:10; cf. Towner, *Goal*, 61–63), and look forward as Paul does to the heavenly kingdom (2 Tim 4:18). If Towner is correct in his view that an over-realized eschatology lies behind much of what the opponents were teaching, then the emphasis on the still-future aspect of salvation and the fact of a further epiphany of the savior are corrections to the Ephesian heresy (*NTS* 32 [1986] 427–48).

One of the specific emphases in the PE is that salvation involves the commitment to obedience. Good works never merit salvation but are the necessary consequence of salvation (see especially the *Explanation* on Titus 2:11–15). God "saved us and called us to a holy calling, not because of our works but because of [his] own purpose and grace" (2 Tim 1:9). Salvation is "to" a holy life, one in which there is no place for sin (Rom 6). Paul puts these two ideas side by side several times in this corpus. While the opponents have had some success, "Nevertheless, the firm foundation of God stands firm, having this seal, 'The Lord knew those who are his,' and, 'Let everyone naming the name of [the] Lord depart from unrighteousness'" (2 Tim 2:19). The two great theological statements on which the letter to Titus is centered make the same affirmations. Both occur in the context of Paul's call to obedience.

> For the grace of God has appeared, bringing salvation for all people, teaching us that, having denied the ungodliness and the worldly passions, we should live in a self-controlled manner and justly and reverently in the present age, waiting for the blessed hope and appearing of the glory of our great God and savior Jesus Christ, who gave himself for us in order that he might redeem us from all lawlessness and cleanse for himself a special people, a zealot for good works. (Titus 2:11–14; cf. the context created in Titus 2:2–10)

> For formerly we ourselves also were foolish, disobedient, being led astray, being enslaved by desires and various pleasures, living a life of evil and envy, detestable, hating one another. But when the goodness and philanthropy of God appeared, not out of works of righteousness that we did but in accordance with his mercy he saved us, through the washing of regeneration and renewal of the Holy Spirit, whom he richly poured out for us through Jesus Christ our savior in order that having been justified by his grace, we might become heirs according to [the] hope of eternal life. (Titus 3:3–7)

Because repentance from sinful behavior and a call to holy obedience is part of the very fabric of God's salvific plans, Paul continues,

> I want you to insist emphatically on these things in order that those who have believed in God might be intent on devoting themselves to good works. These are good and profitable for people. But shun foolish speculations and genealogies and strife and quarrels about the law, for they are harmful and useless. (Titus 3:8–9)

What is significant about these verses is that they merge obedience into God's plan of salvation. While obedience does not merit salvation (2 Tim 1:9; Titus 3:5; *Comment* on 1 Tim 2:10), neither is it an ancillary or optional element in salvation; it is part of God's very intention.

While the call to obedience is made throughout Paul's writings, the nature of the Ephesian heresy and Cretan culture calls for Paul's special emphasis. All believers are to be ready for any good work (Titus 3:1, 14), including the rich, who are to be rich in good deeds (1 Tim 6:18), the "person of God" equipped by Scripture for every good work (2 Tim 3:17), Timothy as an evangelist (2 Tim 2:5), and Titus (2:7; cf. 1 Tim 4:12). A drive toward good works is to characterize the women (1 Tim 2:10; see *Comment* for the major discussion), widows (1 Tim 5:10), and church leaders (1 Tim 3:1; 5:10). This stands in contrast to the opponents, who are worthless for any good work (Titus 1:16); Alexander specifically will be punished for his bad deeds (2 Tim 4:14). The opponents are pursuing their myths and genealogies instead of God's stewardship (1 Tim 1:4), and their activity results in nothing beneficial but only the ruin of those listening to them

(2 Tim 2:14). Paul knows the Lord will rescue him from every evil work (2 Tim 4:18). Paul is arguing that the opponents have improperly separated theology from lifestyle (Titus 1:16).

The concept of salvation in the PE is therefore fully Pauline. It teaches the free offer of God's grace to sinners and the call to holiness (cf. also Marshall, SNTU-A 9 [1984] 203–18). However, there is one unusual element in the PE. Elsewhere Paul uses σωτήρ, "savior," only twice, both times in reference to Christ (Eph 5:23; Phil 3:20). Yet in the PE he uses it six times of God and four times of Jesus. Two questions arise out of this. (1) How does one account for the increase in usage? (2) How does one explain the application of the term to both Jesus and God?

The NT church (outside of Paul) spoke freely of God or Christ as "savior." σωτήρ occurs twenty-four times in the NT. Eight times God is called savior (Luke 1:47; Jude 25; cf. 1 Cor 1:21), six in the PE (1 Tim 1:1; 2:3; 4:10; Titus 1:3; 2:10; 3:4). But in 1 Cor 1:21 Paul speaks about God being pleased "to save those who believe." Sixteen times the term is applied to Jesus (Luke 2:11; John 4:42; Acts 5:31; 13:23; Eph 5:23; Phil 3:20; 2 Pet 1:1,11; 2:20; 3:2, 18; 1 John 4:14; cf. Matt 1:21), four times in the PE (2 Tim 1:10; Titus 1:4; 2:13; 3:6). Paul also feels free to speak of Christ's saving work, although he avoids using the term σωτήρ. It is common in the LXX to speak of God as savior (Deut 32:15; 1 Chr 16:35; Pss 24[23]:5; 25[24]:5; 27[26]:1, 9; 62[61]:2, 6; 65[64]:5; 79[78]:9; 95[94]:1; Isa 12:2; 17:10; 25:9; 45:15, 21; 62:11; Mic 7:7; Hab 3:18).

Paul probably avoids using the term outside the PE because of its associations in Greek thought. σωτήρ could refer to many different people, including physicians, philosophers, and statesmen, but most significantly it was used in connection with the redeemer gods and the emperor (V. Taylor, *The Names of Jesus* [London: Macmillan, 1953] 109; Kelly, 163). The emperor was considered the savior of humanity (W. Foerster, *TDNT* 7:1006–12, esp. 1012). But why is the term used so frequently in the PE? One might surmise that it was used because of its meaning in the Hellenistic culture in Ephesus. It is Jesus, not any other god or the emperor, in whom salvation resides (cf. *Introduction*, "Critical Questions, The Linguistic Problem"). S. M. Baugh documents considerable inscriptional evidence that especially in Ephesus σωτήρ was used as "a title of description of gods, emperors, provincial proconsuls, and local patrons" ("'Savior of All People': 1 Tim 4:10 in Context," *WTJ* 54 [1992] 335, citing many references). It is also possible to explain the frequency of σωτήρ in the light of the Ephesian heresy. Salvation, they claimed, was not through Christ but through adherence to their mythological reconstruction of the OT genealogies and was therefore exclusive and sectarian. Rather, Timothy is to preach that salvation is for "all" people (1 Tim 2:4) and through Jesus Christ the savior (cf. 1 Tim 1:15; *Introduction*, "The Ephesian Heresy"). Kelly (162) also points out that of the six references in the PE to God as "savior," two are in salutations and three of the remaining four occur in passages emphasizing that salvation is for all people (directly stated in 1 Tim 2:3–4; 4:10; Titus 2:10–11; indirectly in Titus 3:2, 4). For references to the Jewish background of the term, see Jeremias; V. Taylor, *The Names of Jesus,* 109. Cf. Deut 32:15; Pss 25:5; 27:1, 9; Isa 12:2; 43:3, 11; 45:15, 21; 49:26; 60:16; 63:8; Jer 14:8; Hos 13:4; Mic 7:7; Hab 3:18; Wis 16:7; Sir 51:1; Bar 4:22; 3 Macc 7:16; Philo *De Migr. Abr.* 5; *De Vit. Cont.* 11; cf. G. Fohrer, *TDNT* 7:1012–13, 1016–17; J. Schneider and C.

Brown, *NIDNTT* 3:217–19. For references to the occurrences of σωτήρ in secular literature, see Spicq, 1:315–16, but most notable are references to the redeemer gods and the emperor (MM, 621–22; W. Bousset, *Kyrios Christos* [Nashville: Abingdon, 1970] 240–46; A. Deissmann, *Light from the Ancient East*, 364; A. Richardson, *IDB* 4:176–77; W. Foerster, *TDNT* 7:1009–12, 1019–20; excursus in Dibelius-Conzelmann, 100–103; bibliographies in W. Foerster and G. Fohrer, *TDNT* 7:1003–4; J. Schneider and C. Brown, *NIDNTT* 3:221–23; BAGD, 800–801).

The second question has to do with the application of σωτήρ to both God and Christ. While some may consider its use "indiscriminate" (Hanson, [1983] 2), to me it appears deliberate. This is especially clear in the three passages that refer to both God and Christ in the same immediate context: Titus 1:3, 4; 2:10, 13; 3:4, 6. The repetition of the same significant word in the same context must be to enforce an intentional association. God and Christ are closely related in bringing salvation to people. The same is true in 2 Tim 1, in which God who "saved" us (v 9) and Christ our "savior" (v 10) are joined in the salvific process (cf. also 1 Tim 2:3, 4, 5–6). It requires little theological development to move from the OT thought of God as savior, to Jesus' salvific work, and finally to Jesus as the one who saves (Marshall, *Origins of New Testament Christology*, 168).

Outline

1 Timothy
  I. Salutation (1:1–2)
 II. The Ephesian problem (1:3–20)
     A. Problem stated (1:3–7)
     B. The true intention of the law (1:8–11)
     C. Paul's example of salvation by grace (1:12–17)
     D. Encouragement and warning for Timothy (1:18–20)
 II. Correction of improper conduct in the Ephesian church (2:1–4:5)
     A. Salvation is for all people (2:1–7)
     B. Questions of disruption and leadership (2:8–15)
     C. Overseers (3:1–7)
     D. Deacons (3:8–13)
     E. Heart of the corpus (3:14–16)
     F. The source of the heresy (4:1–5)
III. Personal notes to Timothy (4:6–16)
 IV. How Timothy is to relate to different groups in the church (5:1–6:2a)
     A. People of various ages (5:1–2)
     B. Widows (5:3–16)
     C. Payment and discipline of elders (5:17–25)
     D. Slaves (6:1–2a)
 IV. Final Instructions (6:2b–21)
     A. The final discussion of the opponents (6:2b–10)
     B. Encouragement to Timothy (6:11–16)
     C. Words to the rich (6:17–19)
     D. The final encouragement to Timothy (6:20–21)

Titus
I. Salutation (1:1–4)
II. Qualities necessary for church leadership (1:5–9)
III. Description of the problem in Crete (1:10–16)
IV. Instructions and theological basis for godly living (2:1–3:11)
   A. Instructions (2:1–10)
   B. Theological basis for godly living (2:11–15)
   C. Continued call for godly behavior (3:1–11)
V. Personal comments and final greeting (3:12–15)

2 Timothy
I. Salutation (1:1–2)
II. Thanksgiving (1:3–5)
III. Encouragement to Timothy (1:6–2:13)
   A. Call to suffer without shame (1:6–14)
   B. Examples (1:15–18)
   C. Continued appeal to Timothy (2:1–13)
IV. Instructions for Timothy and the opponents (2:14–4:8)
   A. Timothy and the opponents contrasted (2:14–26)
   B. The last word about the opponents (3:1–9)
   C. Encouragement and proclamation (3:10–4:8)
V. Final words to Timothy (4:9–22)

The flow of Paul's thought is often missed. 1 Tim 1:8–17 is frequently seen as an only somewhat relevant digression, and the line of argument in 1 Tim 2:1–7 is also often missed. Hanson goes so far as to say that the PE "have no unifying theme; there is no development of thought" ([1983] 42). At times it is difficult to imagine that we are examining the same piece of literature.

In his first epistle to Timothy, Paul greets him and moves directly to his thesis (1:3–7), gives the two basic theological reasons that the opponents' theology is wrong (1:8–17), and encourages Timothy to pursue the task (1:18–20). He next moves into discussing the problem of the Ephesian church's misconduct (2:1–3:13), pauses to put his instructions in perspective (3:14–16), and concludes this second major division by discussing the demonic source of the conflict (4:1–5). Because the epistle is written for Timothy as well as for the church, Paul turns to Timothy and encourages him specifically in his task at Ephesus (4:6–16). In the fourth section Paul addresses different groups in the Ephesian church (5:1–6:2a) and concludes with several different sets of instructions appropriate to the Ephesian church. The structure of Titus is pronounced. Paul begins by addressing specific issues in the young church—leadership, false teaching. The rest of the epistle is basic catechetical instruction centered on the two great creedal statements in 2:13–14 and 3:3–7, showing that salvation must show itself in obedience. Because of the intent of 2 Timothy, its structure is less pronounced. It is an affectionate, personal letter and is more flowing. Themes weave their way throughout: encouragement, call to loyalty, willingness to suffer. There is only slight mention of the historical problems, closing with comments expected of two friends.

1 Timothy

I. Salutation (1 Tim 1:1–2)

Bibliography

Audet, J. P. "Literary Forms and Contents of a Normal Eucharistia in the First Century." *SE* 1–3 (1961) 643–62. **Aune, D. E.** *The New Testament in Its Literary Environment.* LEC 8. Philadelphia: Westminster, 1987. **Berger, K.** "Apostelbrief und apostolische Rede: Zum Formular frühchristlicher Briefe." *ZNW* 65 (1974) 190–231. **Bornkamm, G.** "Formen und Gattungen im N.T." *RGG.* 999–1005. **Deissmann, A.** *Bible Studies.* 1–59. **Doty, W. G.** *Letters in Primitive Christianity.* Guides to Biblical Scholarship, NT Series. Philadelphia: Fortress, 1973. **Exler, F. X. J.** *The Form of the Ancient Greek Letter: A Study in Greek Epistolography.* 1923. Repr. Chicago: Ares, 1976. **Feneberg, W.** "Timotheus, mein Sohn, der Apostel zwischen Juden und Heiden." *Entschluss* 40 (1985) 27–29. **Foley, L. P.** "Fidelis, Faithful." *CBQ* 1 (1939) 163–65. **Friedrich, G.** "Lohmeyers These über 'Das paulinischen Briefpräskript' kritisch beleuchtet." *ZNW* 46 (1955) 272–74. **Funaioli, G.** *Studi in Letteratura Antica* I. Bologna: Zanichelli, 1948. 157–74. **Funk, R. W.** *Language, Hermeneutic and the Word of God.* New York: Harper & Row, 1966. 250–74. **Hatch, W. H. P.** *The Pauline Idea of Faith in Its Relation to Jewish and Hellenistic Religion.* HTS 2. Cambridge, MA: Harvard UP, 1917. **Hebert, G.** "'Faithfulness' and 'Faith.'" *Theology* 58 (1955) 373–79. **Hout, M. van den.** "Studies in Early Greek Letter-Writing." *Mnemosyne* 4th ser. 2 (1949) 19–41, 138–51. **Jewett, R.** "The Form and Function of the Homiletic Benediction." *ATR* 51 (1969) 18–34. **Käsemann, E.** "Liturgische Formeln im N.T." *RGG.* 993–96. **Kirk, J. A.** "Apostleship since Rengstorf: Towards a Synthesis." *NTS* 21 (1975) 249–64. **Koskenniemi, H.** *Studien zur Idee und Phraseologie des griechischen Briefes bis 400 n. Chr.* Helsinki: Suomalainen Tiedeakatemia, 1956. **Lieu, J.** "'Grace to You and Peace': The Apostolic Greeting." *BJRL* 68 (1985) 161–78. **Lohmeyer, E.** "Probleme paulinischer Theologie: I. Briefliche Grussüberschriften." *ZNW* 26 (1927) 158–73. **Mullins, T. Y.** "Benediction as a New Testament Form." *AUSS* 15 (1977) 59–64. **O'Brien, P. T.** *Introductory Thanksgivings in the Letters of Paul.* NovTSup 49. Leiden: Brill, 1977. **Robinson, J. M.** "Die Hodajot-Formel in Gebet und Hymnus des Frühchristentums." In *Apophoreta.* FS E. Hänchen, ed. W. Eltester and F. H. Kettler. BZNW 30. Berlin: Töpelmann, 1964. 194–235. **Roller, O.** *Das Formular der paulinischen Briefe.* **Roloff, J.** *Apostolat—Verkündigung—Kirche.* **Sanders, J. T.** "The Transition from Opening Epistolary Thanksgiving to Body in the Letter of the Pauline Corpus." *JBL* 81 (1962) 348–62. **Schenk, W.** *Der Segen in Neuen Testament: Eine begriffsanalytische Studie.* Berlin: Evangelische Verlagsanstalt, 1967. **Stowers, S.** *Letter Writing in Greco-Roman Antiquity.* LEC 5. Philadelphia: Westminster, 1986. **Thatcher, T.** "The Relational Matrix of the Pastoral Epistles." *JETS* 38 (1995) 41–45. **Torrance, T. F.** "One Aspect of the Biblical Conception of Faith." *ExpTim* 68 (1957) 111–14. **Vouga, F.** "Der Brief als Form der apostolischen Autorität." In *Studien und Texte zur Formgeschichte,* ed. K. Berger. Tübingen: Franke, 1992. 7–58. **Wendlund, P.** *Die urchristlichen Literaturformen.* HNT 1/2. Tübingen: Mohr-Siebeck, 1912. **White, J. L.** *Light from Ancient Letters.* FFNT. Philadelphia: Fortress, 1986. **Wiles, G. P.** *Paul's Intercessory Prayers: The Significance of the Intercessory Prayer Passages in the Letters of St Paul.* SNTSMS 24. Cambridge: Cambridge UP, 1974.

See also the *Bibliography* for 2 Tim 1:3–7.

Translation

[1]*Paul, an apostle of Christ Jesus because of the command* [a] *from God our savior and Christ Jesus our hope,* [2]*to Timothy, [my] true spiritual son: Grace, mercy, peace from God [the] Father* [b] *and Christ Jesus our Lord.*

Notes

א reads ἐπαγγελίαν, "promise," probably through assimilation to 2 Tim 1:1; cf. Gal 3:29. Cf. *TCGNT*[2], 571; L. T. Johnson, 110–11.

א[2] D[2] Ψ TR a vg[mss] sy sa bo[mss] insert ἡμῶν, "our," after πατρός, "Father," in imitation of ἡμῶν after κυρίου, "Lord." It is omitted by א* A D* F G I 33 81 104 365 1175 1739 1881 *pc* lat bo.

Form/Structure/Setting

The standard format in ancient letters was succinct: name of author, name of recipient, and greetings. For example: Paul, to Timothy, greetings (see examples in Exler, *Form*). Vv 1–2 follow this same pattern, yet as was typical for Paul he enlarges each element. Sometimes these enlargements are minor (2 Corinthians; Ephesians; Colossians) although with some indication of what is to follow (Philippians; cf. Hawthorne, *Philippians*, 3–4). Other times the enlargements are quite significant, laying out the basic message and flavor of the letter. For example, Rom 1:1–7 establishes the systematic, theological nature of the letter. Gal 1:1–6 and 1 Cor 1:1–3 show that Paul's authority was being questioned. It is in the salutation that the author establishes the relationship between sender and recipient (see White, *Light*, 198).

The significance of the salutation in 1 Timothy has often been overlooked. In relatively few words, a large part of the Ephesian problem is addressed, the core of Paul's solution given, and the tension between a private letter and a public message established. (1) The Ephesian problem arose because the church had turned away from Paul's authority and from the salvation through Christ that he preached. So Paul begins by asserting that his apostleship is by a command from God and Christ (cf. Spicq, 1:313); this will be placed in contrast to the opponents who merely "wish" to be teachers (v 7). (2) The solution is that the church should listen to Timothy's teaching since Timothy, and not the opponents, is Paul's spiritually legitimate son. (This is spelled out in more detail in *Form/Structure/Setting* on 1 Tim 1:3–7.) (3) The letter is private in that it is written to Timothy, but public in that Paul is writing through Timothy to the church. The epistle's conclusion (6:21) makes this dual nature obvious when it says, "Grace be with you [plural]" (cf. *Introduction*, "Historical Reconstruction from the PE").

The style of the salutation is relatively balanced and formal. ἐπιταγήν, "command," is modified by two clauses—"God our savior" and "Christ Jesus our hope"— a pattern made clear by the twice-repeated ἡμῶν, "our," at the end of each clause. The threefold blessing (v 2) also comes from both God and Christ. There is a debate regarding the origin of this greeting. It is argued that it is an adaptation from normal letter-writing style, or borrowed from Christian liturgy or a sermon, or Paul's invention, or a combination of these proposals. See summaries in Furnish (*II Corinthians*, 107) and O'Brien (*Colossians*, 4–5; this work provides an excellent bibliography).

Comment

1 Παῦλος ἀπόστολος Χριστοῦ Ἰησοῦ κατ᾽ ἐπιταγὴν θεοῦ σωτῆρος ἡμῶν καὶ Χριστοῦ Ἰησοῦ τῆς ἐλπίδος ἡμῶν, "Paul, an apostle of Christ Jesus because of the

command from God our savior and Christ Jesus our hope." There was trouble in the Ephesian church. People were turning away from Paul's gospel and were following other leaders and their heretical teaching. Therefore Paul begins on a note of authority (see *Form/Structure/Setting;* Brox, 98). Paul is in charge. He became an apostle by direct command of both God and Christ, and the Ephesians are reminded that Timothy carries Paul's authority (v 2). An apostle is someone sent as an official representative, bearing the authority of the one who sent the apostle. Whatever other nuances can be present in this term, the dominant note in this context is one of authority (cf. Spicq, 1:314; on *apostle* see Spicq, "Excursus V. Une théologie de l'apostolat," 2:595–99; Kirk, *NTS* 21 [1975] 249–64; Roloff, *Timotheus*, 55–56; id., *Apostolat*, 9–37; Burton, *Galatians*, 363–84; bibliography in Cranfield, *Romans* 1:52 n. 1). The opponents are attacking Paul's authority, but Paul is an apostle and therefore must be heeded. In all but four of Paul's letters, he introduces himself as an apostle (Romans) of Christ Jesus (1, 2 Corinthians; Galatians; Ephesians; Colossians; 1, 2 Timothy; Titus), often in apparent defense of his apostleship (especially 1 Corinthians and Galatians). He also calls himself a "servant" (Titus) of Jesus Christ (Romans; Philippians) and a "prisoner" (Philemon). In 1 and 2 Thessalonians he does not use a title, partly because he is writing with Silvanus and Timothy.

Although it is somewhat unusual—only insofar as we have a limited number of his writings for comparison—for Paul to credit his apostleship to a "command" from God, it is well suited to the context. A questioning of Paul's authority and his definition of the gospel underlies all of the PE. Instead of following Paul's gospel of grace (1 Tim 1:12–17), his opponents preached a gospel of myths and babblings about words, a message based on a misunderstanding of the law (1 Tim 1:4, 7). Lock paraphrases, "I Paul, writing with all the authority of an Apostle of Christ Jesus, and in obedience to the direct commandment of God" (4). See also B. B. Warfield's argument cited in *Form/Structure/Setting* on 1 Tim 1:3–7. Timothy is not questioning Paul's authority, but the epistle is only semiprivate, and much of it is directed toward the Ephesian church. In Titus 1:3 Paul also credits his apostleship to a command from God; in the more personal and private 2 Timothy, which does not deal with the opponents as much, Paul describes his apostleship as a result of the "will" of God (2 Tim 1:1).

1 Timothy 1:1–2

[1]Paul, an apostle of Christ Jesus because of the command from God our savior and Christ Jesus our hope, [2]to Timothy, [my] true spiritual son: Grace, mercy, peace from God [the] Father and Christ Jesus our Lord.

2 Timothy 1:1–2

[1]Paul, an apostle of Christ through [the] will of God according to [the] promise of life that [is] in Christ Jesus; [2]to Timothy [my] beloved son: Grace, mercy, peace from God [the] Father and Christ Jesus our Lord.

Titus 1:1–4

[1]Paul, a servant of God and an apostle of Jesus Christ, for [the] faith of [the] elect of God and [the] knowledge of [the] truth that produces godliness, [2]for the sake of the hope of eternal life, which the God who does not lie promised before times eternal, [3]but he revealed his word at the proper time in the proclamation, [with] which I was entrusted by the command of God our savior. [4]To Titus, a true son in a common faith. Grace and peace from God [the] Father and Christ Jesus our savior.

Since Paul's concept of his own apostolic calling came directly from the
Damascus-road experience, here he is thinking of that event (cf. Acts 9:15; 22:14–
15; 26:16–18; Gal 1:15–16; cf. S. Kim, *The Origin of Paul's Gospel* [Grand Rapids, MI:
Eerdmans, 1982]). On this use of κατά, "because," see M. J. Harris, *NIDNTT*
3:1200–1201; BAGD, 407 (II5ad).

ἐπιταγή denotes an authoritative "command" carrying associations of divine
and kingly orders. It is a forceful term, its verbal cognate, for example, being used
of Jesus' commands to demons (Mark 1:27; Luke 8:3; see G. Delling, *TDNT* 8:36–
37). In secular Greek it can refer to commands given by people and by gods (MM,
247), especially commands from oracles and the gods (LSJ, 663). Simpson refers
to inscriptional data showing that the phrase κατ' ἐπιταγήν, "because of the
command," was a standard formula equivalent to "by order of" (24). In the LXX
the verb form (ἐπιτάσσειν) occurs five times, describing a royal decree (Esth 1:8;
3:12; 8:8, 11; Dan 3:16). In Paul it denotes a command from God (Rom 16:26; 1 Cor
7:6, 25; 1 Tim 1:1; Titus 1:3), from himself (2 Cor 8:8), or the authority with which
Titus is to declare Paul's instructions (μετὰ πάσης ἐπιταγῆς, "with all authority";
Titus 2:15). The actual phrase κατ' ἐπιταγήν appears in five of these passages (Rom
16:26; 1 Cor 7:6; 2 Cor 8:8; 1 Tim 1:1; Titus 1:3). It occurs seven times in the NT,
every time used by Paul. (The verbal form ἐπιτάσσειν occurs ten times in the NT,
but only once in Paul's letters.)

Having said that his apostleship was authorized by a command, Paul identifies
the two sources of that command. It was from both "God our savior and Christ Jesus
our hope." (θεοῦ, "God," and Χριστοῦ, "Christ," both modify ἐπιταγήν, "command.") The only other Pauline salutation that says Paul's apostleship is from both
God and Christ is Gal 1:1, where Paul's authority was also under attack ("Paul an
apostle—not from men nor through man, but through Jesus Christ and God the
Father" [RSV]). In Titus Paul also credits his apostleship to a "command from God"
(1:3). As was the case in Galatia, so in Ephesus and Crete Paul's authority may have
been under attack. For a discussion of the christological implication of this, see v
2. On the concept of God as "savior" and how the use of the term in the PE is
polemical, directed toward the Ephesian worship of emperors as saviors, see
Introduction, "Themes in the PE."

Our text has the order "Christ Jesus" (reversed in the TR). This is the normal
order for Paul, although he also writes "Jesus Christ" with sufficient frequency that
the order is not necessarily significant. In 1 Timothy the UBSGNT text has "Christ
Jesus" twelve times and "Jesus Christ" twice (6:3, 14). The order "Christ Jesus"
reflects the historical sequence in which Paul came to know first the risen Christ
and then the earthly Jesus. On the other hand, the epistles by James, Peter, John,
and Jude invariably have "Jesus Christ" (thirty-three times), the writers having
known him first as the earthly Jesus (see references in Burton, *Galatians*, 393; also
Elliott, *Greek Text*, 199–201, for a list of the variants in the PE that alter the order of
the names).

Jesus is further identified as ἐλπίδος ἡμῶν, "our hope." ἐλπίς, "hope," and
ἐλπίζειν, "to hope," occur eighty-four times in the NT, fifty-five in Paul, eight in the
PE. Jesus is "not merely the object of [our hope] ... or the author of it ... but its very
substance and foundation" (Ellicott, 2). Unlike secular apathy and pessimism,
Christian hope is sure. It is never a fearful dreading of what lies ahead; rather it is an
eager and confident anticipation of what God has in store for believers. It is not so

much a subjective emotion as an objective fact. It is sure because it is centered on Christ and is a gracious gift of God (cf. Rom 5:2, 5; 8:24, 25; 15:4, 13; E. Hoffmann, *NIDNTT* 2:242–43; Spicq, 1:316). Because "our hope" is centered on Christ, it is a title for him (1 Tim 1:1; cf. Acts 28:20; Col 1:27; esp. in Ignatius [*Eph.* 21; *Magn.* 11; *Trall.* salutation, 2; *Phil.* 11]). A true widow sets her hope on God (1 Tim 5:5); the rich should do likewise and not trust in riches (1 Tim 6:17). Paul's apostleship is "to further the faith of God's elect . . . in hope of eternal life" (Titus 1:1–2), and believers await their "blessed hope, the appearing of the glory of our great God and savior Jesus Christ" (Titus 2:13). Hope is the result of regeneration (Titus 3:5, 7; cf. 1 Pet 1:3), and as a consequence it affects the believers' conduct (cf. Rom 5:2–5; Ridderbos, *Theology*, 488–89) as they look forward to God's salvation, having their "hope set on the living God, who is the savior of all people" (1 Tim 4:10). Hope describes both Jesus (1 Tim 1:1; Titus 2:13) and the believer (1 Tim 4:10; 5:5; 6:17; Titus 1:2; 3:7). The hope of the OT and Judaism has come to fruition in Jesus Christ (cf. Ps 65:5, which combines the ideas of hope and salvation). See further A. Barr, "'Hope' (ἐλπίς, ἐλπίζω) in the New Testament," *SJT* 3 (1950) 68–77; C. F. D. Moule, *The Meaning of Hope* (Philadelphia: Fortress, 1963).

The promise of hope was one of Christianity's most outstanding features in a world in which hope had little place. Popular belief was dominated by pessimism. The philosophers had dismissed the Olympian gods but had not replaced them with an alternative that provided hope for people. Most could see only the fear and senselessness of chance and the arbitrariness and finality of fate. Stoicism, perhaps the most influential philosophy among the cultured in the first century A.D., taught an apathetic determinism in which individual choice and freedom were absent; one must simply accept whatever fate decides. K. A. Kitchen cites the epitaph "I am of good courage, I who was not, and became, and now am not. I do not grieve" (*ISBE* 2:753). Magic and superstition also abounded. An example of the futility of the times is illustrated by the magical incantation to be used when approached by an unfriendly god: "Lay at once your right [fore-]finger upon your mouth and say, 'Silence! Silence! Silence!' (a symbol of the living, incorruptible god). 'Guard me, Silence!' Then whistle long, then sneeze, and say . . . and then you will see the gods looking graciously upon you" ("A Mithras Liturgy," in Barrett, *New Testament Background*, 132). Barrett omits what the person is to say, which A. Dieterich (*Eine Mithrasliturgie* [Leipzig: Teubner, 1903] 2–15) shows to be a conglomeration of sounds that appears to be gibberish. The world was without "hope and without God" (Eph 2:12; cf. 1 Thess 4:13). But "when the time had fully come, God sent forth his Son" (Gal 4:4) so that the indwelling Christ could become "the hope of glory" (Col 1:27). The world was without hope; the message that Jesus is "our hope" (1 Tim 1:1) stood out like a shining beacon in a dark world. For an excellent description of the hopelessness of the ancient world, see Angus, *Environment of Early Christianity;* see also Lohse, *New Testament Environment*, 226–32; R. Bultmann and K. H. Rengstorf, *TDNT* 2:517–33; E. Hoffmann, *NIDNTT* 2:238–44; K. A. Kitchen, *ISBE* 2:751–55.

2a Τιμοθέῳ γνησίῳ τέκνῳ ἐν πίστει, "to Timothy, [my] true spiritual son." Having identified himself, Paul turns to the second of the three parts of the standard greeting: "to Timothy." Timothy is Paul's spiritual son (cf. Phil 2:2) and therefore carries Paul's authority to the Ephesian church. This is in contrast to the opponents, who are not Paul's children and therefore should not resist Timothy's authority and teaching. Paul similarly identifies Titus as his γνησίῳ τέκνῳ κατὰ κοινὴν πίστιν, "true son in the common faith" (Titus 1:4). In 2 Timothy Paul calls Timothy his "beloved child" (1:2). (For a discussion of Timothy's identity, see *Introduction*, "Historical Reconstruction from the PE, B. 1 Timothy.")

γνήσιος, "true," conveys both intimacy and authority. It originally referred to children born in wedlock, hence "legitimate," as opposed to children born illegitimately (νόθος) or adopted (F. Büchsel, *TDNT* 1:727; Simpson, 26; MM, 128–29). It can also be used figuratively to mean "genuine," e.g., of writings, hence meaning "sincere" as in 2 Cor 8:8. In Phil 2:20 the cognate adverb γνησίως describes Timothy's sincere concern for the Philippians. Later, a Philippian is called γνήσιε σύζυγε, "true yokefellow" (Phil 4:3; cf. ἑτεροζυγοῦντες, "unequally yoked," 2 Cor 6:14). Spicq calls Timothy Paul's "legal representative" (1:317). Father-son terminology was common in the Jewish and Hellenistic world for the teacher-student relationship. Because it was so widespread, no one single example can be Paul's source (Spicq, 1:317). τέκνον, "child," was a common designation for spiritual progeny; it is possible that Timothy was converted under Paul's ministry (see *Introduction*, "Historical Reconstruction from the PE, B. 1 Timothy"; 2 Kgs 2:12; Rom 9:7; 1 Cor. 4:14, 15; Gal 3:7; 4:19; Phil 2:22; 1 Thess 2:11; Phlm 10; 1 Pet 5:13; cf. his use of τεκνίον, "little child," in his epistles; cf. Dibelius-Conzelmann, 13; Str-B 3:339–41; G. Schrenk, *TDNT* 5:953–54, 958–59, 977–78, 1005–6; A. Oepke, *TDNT* 5:638–39).

The Ephesian church must listen to Timothy because he, and he alone, is Paul's legitimate son ἐν πίστει, "in faith." There are two decisions to be made here. (1) Is ἐν instrumental ("because of faith") or locative ("within the sphere of faith")? (2) Is πίστει objective (thinking of Timothy's "faith" or "the Christian faith") or subjective ("faithfully")? To understand the phrase as "because he has been faithful" makes good sense in light of the historical situation. Timothy is Paul's true son because Timothy has been faithful to Paul's gospel, in contrast to the opponents. In this case γνήσιος, "true," is translated "legitimate" since it emphasizes Timothy's authority in contrast to the opponents' lack of authority. But this may be reading too much into the salutation, and perhaps it is best to see "in faith" as clarifying that Timothy's sonship is spiritual, not physical. Titus is called γνησίῳ τέκνῳ κατὰ κοινὴν πίστιν, "a true son in a common faith," a faith that binds together the Jewish Paul and the gentile Titus. This thought could also be present here.

2b χάρις ἔλεος εἰρήνη ἀπὸ θεοῦ πατρὸς καὶ Χριστοῦ Ἰησοῦ τοῦ κυρίου ἡμῶν, "Grace, mercy, peace from God the Father and Christ Jesus our Lord." Having identified himself and the addressee, Paul completes the third part of the salutation: the greeting. ἀπό, "from," governs both θεοῦ, "God," and Χριστοῦ, "Christ," showing that the trilogy of blessing comes from both persons of the Godhead acting in concert. This is the same grammatical and christological formulation that is in v 1 (see below).

Through subtle literary devices Paul is making a christological statement about the relationship between God and Christ. Twice Paul uses the same grammatical construction: one preposition governing two nouns. Paul is an apostle "because" of the command issued jointly by "our" God and Christ. The christologically sensitive grammatical structure is also present in Gal 1:1: Παῦλος ἀπόστολος ... διὰ Ἰησοῦ Χριστοῦ καὶ θεοῦ πατρός, "Paul an apostle ... through Jesus Christ and God the Father." Burton (*Galatians*, 5) comments that Paul does not think of God and Christ as having different relationships with himself in terms of his apostleship;

together they have only one relationship with Paul. Bruce adds that the "unselfconscious" way that Paul joins God and Christ is a witness to his Christology (*Galatians*, 73). In fact, this same construction is present in six of Paul's introductory statements, "Grace to you . . . from God . . . and Christ" (Rom 1:7; 1 Cor 1:3; 2 Cor 1:2; Eph 1:2; Phil 1:2; 2 Thess 1:2; see Cranfield, *Romans* 1:72). The grammatical structure shows that Paul sees God and Christ acting in unison. This is especially noteworthy in light of Paul's monotheistic background. I agree with Simpson that this is "no slender proof of his [Paul's] conviction of the deity of Christ" (25). Another interesting observation is made by Barrett when he says that v 2 could possibly be translated "God our Savior, *even* Christ Jesus our hope" (38). This is similar to I. H. Marshall's suggestion that 1 Tim 2:5 be translated "There is one who is God, one who is also the mediator between God and man, the man Christ Jesus" ("The Development of the Concept of Redemption in the New Testament," in *Reconciliation and Hope*, FS L. L. Morris, ed. R. Banks [Grand Rapids, MI: Eerdmans, 1974] 166). Paul, throughout his salutations, especially in the PE, joins God and Christ together.

Accompanying these two grammatical subtleties is perhaps another literary device that does not carry as much weight. In both the NT and the PE, the title σωτήρ, "savior," is applied to both God and Christ. Outside of the PE this flexibility is best explained by the words of Jude 25, "to the only God, our Savior through Jesus Christ." The Father is the source and the Son is the agent. But perhaps in the PE this fluctuation is another way in which Paul clarifies his Christology. God and Christ are so united that both perform the same task. Paul has already said as much with his grammatical construction, and he will be saying it even more clearly when he quotes the hymn, "our great God and savior Jesus Christ" (Titus 2:13). (This could be the same type of subtle literary device used by Luke when he records Jesus' words: "Return to your home, and declare how much *God* has done for you. And he went away, proclaiming throughout the whole city how much *Jesus* had done for him" [Luke 8:39; cf. the same phenomenon in Luke 17:15–16].) These observations form a substantial argument for Paul's Christology: God and Christ are so joined that they perform the same functions in unison, whether it be issuing a command, pronouncing a benediction, or acting as savior (see *Introduction,* "Themes in the PE").

This salutation is typical, although slightly different, from Paul's normal style. His usual greeting is "Grace to you and peace from God our Father and Lord Jesus Christ" (Romans; 1, 2 Corinthians; Galatians; Ephesians; Philippians; 2 Thessalonians; Philemon). Both Galatians and 2 Thessalonians have the variant πατρὸς καὶ κυρίου ἡμῶν, "Father and our Lord," as in the PE. In Colossians Paul stops the salutation at "Father" and in 1 Thessalonians at "peace." In the PE Paul says "Grace, mercy, peace from God [the] Father and Christ Jesus our Lord" (1 Tim 1:2; 2 Tim 1:2; cf. 2 John 3 and the *v.l.* in Titus 1:4) and "Grace and peace from God [the] Father and Christ Jesus our savior" (Titus 1:4; see variants). The variations are not significant and simply show that Paul, like all other writers, does not always say things in exactly the same way. Chrysostom adds that the inclusion of ἔλεος, "mercy," was appropriate for a person like Timothy—someone especially dear to Paul—and, I would add, someone in an especially difficult historical circumstance ("Homily 1"; NPNF 13:409). The normal Greek greeting was the simple verb χαίρειν, lit. "rejoice" (see Jas 1:1; Acts 15:23; 23:26; bibliography in J. H. Ropes, *A*

Critical and Exegetical Commentary on the Epistle of St. James, ICC [Edinburgh: T. & T. Clark, 1916] 127). The normal Hebrew greeting was שָׁלוֹם *šālôm,* "peace" (Tob 7:12; 2 *Apoc. Bar.* 78:2). Paul substitutes the noun χάρις, "grace," for the verb χαίρειν, and the Greek εἰρήνη, "peace," for שָׁלוֹם *šālôm.* In 1 Timothy Paul has "mercy" and not his usual "to you," again showing normal variation typical of any writer who has moved beyond a wooden style. "Grace" and "mercy" are found together in the salutation of every Pauline letter and often in their closing, although not necessarily in conjunction with each other (2 Cor 13:11, 14; Gal 6:16, 18; 2 Thess 3:16, 18; cf. Wallace, *Greek Grammar,* 51). They are closely connected in Rom 5:1–2 (cf. Rom 16:20; Eph 6:23–24). "Mercy" and "peace" occur in Gal 6:16 (with "grace" in v 18), Eph 2:4–5, and 2 *Apoc. Bar.* 78:2.

χάρις, "grace," is a one-word summary of God's saving act in Christ, stressing that salvation comes as a free gift to undeserving sinners. It is an enormously significant word in Paul's theology; of its 155 occurrences in the NT, 100 are in Paul's letters. In classical Greek it was a colorless word without religious connotations. It described something that brought pleasure or approval or something that was attractive (L. B. Smedes, *ISBE* 2:548; cf. especially the use of חֵן *ḥēn,* "to show favor, be gracious," in the OT; BDB, 336). Here too it was not especially a religious term, being used of both God and people (Burton, *Galatians,* 423). But Paul's use of the word shows a much deeper concept than "favor," being closer to חֶסֶד *ḥesed,* "steadfast kindness," "covenantal faithfulness," which, however, is translated by ἔλεος, "mercy," in the LXX (cf. Spicq, 1:317–18). This provides an excellent illustration of how the historical definition of a word, or its use in the LXX, has no necessary connection with its NT meaning. Paul chooses a neutral word devoid of any deep truth and fills it with his own understanding of God's gift of salvation. It can be defined only within the context of Paul's view of salvation (cf. use of ἀγάπη, "love," in 1 Tim 1:5).

χάρις, "grace," occurs thirteen times in the PE. Apart from salutations (1 Tim 1:2; 2 Tim 1:2; Titus 1:4), thanksgivings (1 Tim 1:12; 2 Tim 1:3), and final greetings (1 Tim 6:21; 2 Tim 4:22; Titus 3:15), grace is shown to be the basis for God saving Paul (1 Tim 1:14; cf. v 12; Rom 5:20), for God saving others (2 Tim 1:9; Titus 2:11), and for justification (Titus 3:7). Paul encourages Timothy to "be strong in the grace that is in Christ Jesus" (2 Tim 2:1). The expression of the concept is fully Pauline, especially as stated in 2 Tim 1:9 (God "saved us and called us with a holy calling, not in virtue of our works but in virtue of his own purpose and the grace which he gave us in Christ Jesus ages ago"). On χάρις, "grace," see summaries by Spicq, 1:318; Guthrie, *New Testament Theology,* 622; O'Brien, *Colossians,* 4–5; H. Conzelmann, *TDNT* 9:387–415; Trench, *Synonyms,* 225–26; W. Manson, "Grace in the New Testament," in *The Doctrine of Grace,* ed. W. T. Whitley (London: SCM Press, 1932) 33–60; J. Moffatt, *Grace in the New Testament* (New York: Long & Smith, 1932); and the bibliographies in BAGD, 878; H. Conzelmann and A. Zimmerli, *TDNT* 9:372–73 n. 115.

ἔλεος, "mercy," describes acts of pity and help that are appropriate within a relationship between two people. In classical Greek, mercy was the response when something unfortunate and undeserved happened to someone (R. Bultmann, *TDNT* 2:477). It was an emotional response to a bad situation. But in the LXX it translates חֶסֶד *ḥesed,* and this association governs its meaning in the NT. N. Glueck argues that חֶסֶד *ḥesed* indicates not so much love and faithfulness as it does the conduct proper to the covenantal relationship between God and Israel (*Hesed in the Bible* [Cincinnati: Hebrew Union College Press, 1967]; cf. N. H. Snaith, *The Distinctive Ideas of the Old Testament* [London: Epworth, 1944] 94–130; summary by R. L. Harris, *TWOT* 1:305–7). Mercy therefore primarily defines a relationship and secondarily elicits a response of pity to those within the relationship. Mercy is not a subjective emotion but an objective act appropriate for this relationship. This is why חֶסֶד *ḥesed* can also be translated by δικαιοσύνη, "righteousness," another term describing conduct appropriate to a certain relationship (cf. Ladd, *Theology*, 440; cf. Gen 19:19; 20:13; 21:23; 24:27; Prov 20:28). From this would naturally develop the association between God's mercy and his faithfulness, loyalty, and love. This also holds true when a person has mercy for another. It is not just that one should have mercy, but that one should act in a manner appropriate to the relationship and within that context have mercy (examples in E. R. Achtemeier, *IDB* 3:352–54; cf. Luke 1:58; 1 Pet 1:3). Because the biblical concept of mercy was governed by that of covenant, the concept of mercy developed the connotation of help or kindness that could be asked or requested of a superior, but never demanded (P. C. Craigie, *EDT*, 708). This accounts for the similarity between the biblical concepts of grace and mercy; both are gifts of God to an undeserving people. On the concept of mercy in the OT, see R. Bultmann, *TDNT* 2:479–81; E. R. Achtemeier, *ISBE* 3:352–53; Eichrodt, *Theology*, 232–39; H.-H. Esser, *NIDNTT* 2:594–95; Trench, *Synonyms*, 225–26.

Paul uses ἔλεος, "mercy," and ἐλεεῖν, "to be merciful," twenty-four times (Rom 12:8; 15:9; 1 Cor 7:25; 2 Cor 4:1; Gal 6:16; Eph 2:4; Phil 2:27), twelve in Rom 9–11 (Rom 9:15 [2x], 16, 18, 23; 11:30, 31 [2x], 32) and seven in the PE. Both sides of the theological coin evident in the OT are also found in Paul. On the one side, people cannot demand God's mercy (Rom 9–11); he is free to grant it as he wills. On the other, God's mercy will come to those who are in relationship with him. Thus letters can be started (1 Tim 1:2; 2 Tim 1:2; *v.l.* in Titus 1:4; cf. 1 Pet 1:3; 2 John 3; Jude 2) and ended (Gal 6:16) with a pronouncement of God's mercy. Since mercy is the appropriate conduct of God toward Christians, Paul says it is the basis of his own salvation (1 Tim 1:13, 16; cf. 1 Cor 7:25) and of others (Titus 3:5; cf. Eph 2:4; 1 Pet 1:3; especially Rom 11:32). It is both a present reality (2 Tim 1:16; cf. Phil 2:27) and a future hope (2 Tim 1:18; cf. Jas 2:13; Jude 21–23; summary in H.-H. Esser, *NIDNTT* 2:597).

εἰρήνη, "peace," likewise describes an objective relationship between God and the believer. It is not so much an emotion or feeling as it is a reality. J. Murray, commenting on Rom 5:1, says that peace "is not the composure and tranquillity of our minds and hearts; it is the status of peace flowing from the reconciliation . . . and reflects primarily upon God's alienation from us and our instatement in his favor. Peace of heart and mind proceeds from 'peace with God' and is the reflection in our consciousness of the relationship established by justification" (*The Epistle to the Romans*, NICNT [Grand Rapids, MI: Eerdmans, 1968] 159). In classical Greek, εἰρήνη meant the cessation of war and eventually included the idea of peaceful relations. In the OT, שָׁלוֹם *šālôm* describes the external absence of hostility and the ensuing general sense of well-being given by God (H. Beck and C. Brown, *NIDNTT* 2:777–79; G. Lloyd Carr, *TWOT* 2:930–32; E. M. Good, *IDB* 3:705–6). These primarily external definitions are found in the NT (H. Beck and C. Brown, *NIDNTT* 2:780), but here the word is charged with a christological significance. Peace is possessed by Christ and given to his followers (Stauffer, *New Testament Theology*, 143;

cf. John 14:27). Because believers are justified (Rom 5:1), to be at peace with God is to be in the objective position of one who has been reconciled (Gal 5:22; Phil 4:7). From this objective stance develops the subjective feeling of peace. εἰρήνη, "peace," occurs in every epistolary salutation in the NT except James and 1 John as well as in many of the closings (Rom 16:20; 2 Cor 13:11; Gal 6:16; Eph 6:23; 1 Thess 5:23; 2 Thess 3:16; cf. Phil 4:9). Its only other occurrence in the PE is in 2 Tim 2:22, where it is part of a list of goals toward which Timothy is to strive, along with righteousness, faith, and love. It is commonly found in salutations in Semitic usage (references in Str-B 3:25; see also Stauffer, *New Testament Theology,* 143–46; Ridderbos, *Theology,* 182–86; G. von Rad and W. Foerster, *TDNT* 2:400–417; bibliography in H. Beck and C. Brown, *NIDNTT* 2:783).

Explanation

Paul begins his letter to Timothy and the Ephesian church on a note of authority. His apostleship comes directly from God, and that authority now resides in Timothy, his true spiritual son. The church must therefore listen to Timothy. Two basic thoughts emerge from the salutation. Through subtle literary devices Paul is making a christological statement about the relationship between God and Christ, who work together so closely that together they issue Paul's call to apostolic ministry and give grace, mercy, and peace.

Paul's second point is that believers stand in an objective relationship with God, and as a result their hope is certain. Mercy and peace are not primarily emotions. Both are based on the fact that believers have a relationship with God, and consequently God has mercy on the believer and the believer has peace with God. God acts in accordance with the relationship as he has defined it, and that includes having mercy. Believers do not just feel peaceful; they actually are at peace with God, and the feelings of peace and security that evolve from such a relationship are more secure than mere emotions. In addition, grace, mercy, and peace are all freely given to undeserving people. If they had to be earned, they could not be, for no price would be sufficient (Ps 49:7–9, 13–15; Matt 16:26). Rather, this trilogy comes only as a gift, and this is why the Christian hope is secure. It resides not in human ability but in divine grace. Although believers can never demand it, God will shed his mercy on those who are in relationship with him. The believers do not just feel peaceful; they actually are at peace with God. Therefore, the Christian hope is sure as it looks forward to the eschatological salvation and mercy coming at the final judgment. As Spicq (1:316) comments, it is precisely because God is our savior that our salvation is secure.

II. The Ephesian Problem   (1 Tim 1:3-20)

A. The Problem Stated   (1 Tim 1:3-7)

Bibliography

Bjerkelund, C. J. *Parakalô: Form, Funkion und Sinn der Parakalô-Sätze in der Paulinischen Briefen.* Oslo: Universitetsforlaget, 1967. **Colson, F. H.** "'Myths and Genealogies'—A Note on the Polemic of the Pastoral Epistles." *JTS* o.s. 19 (1917–18) 265–71. **Harrelson, W.** "The Idea of Agape in the New Testament." *JR* 31 (1951) 169–82. **Hort, F. J. A.** *Judaistic Christianity.* 130–46. **Karris, R. J.** "The Background and Significance of the Polemic of the Pastoral Epistles." *JBL* 92 (1973) 549–64. **Kittel, G.** "Die γενεαλογίαι der Pastoralbriefe." *ZNW* 20 (1921) 49–69. **Koester, H.** "The Purpose of the Polemic of a Pauline Fragment (Philippians III)." *NTS* 8 (1962–63) 317–32. **Sandmel, S.** "Myths, Genealogies, and Jewish Myths and the Writing of the Gospels." *HUCA* 27 (1956) 201–11. **Sohn, O. E.** "Study on 1 Timothy 1, 3–11." *CTM* 21 (1950) 419–28. **Viviano, B. T.** "The Genres of Matthew 1–2: Light from 1 Timothy 1:4." *RB* 97 (1990) 31–53. **Warfield, B. B.** "Some Exegetical Notes on 1 Timothy: I. 'The Progress of Thought in 1 Timothy i. 3–20.'" *PresR* 8 (1921) 500–502.

For a bibliography on the form of ancient letter writing in general, see *Bibliography* for 1 Tim 1:1–2.

Translation

[3] *Just as I urged you to stay on in Ephesus while I was traveling to Macedonia, in order that you might command certain people not to continue teaching a different gospel* [4] *or to devote themselves to endless myths and genealogies, since they produce speculations* [a] *rather than the stewardship* [b] *from God by faith, —.* [5] *But the goal of this command is love from a clean heart and a clear conscience and a sincere faith.* [6] *Some, having fallen short of these things, have turned aside to senseless babble,* [7] *wishing to be teachers of the law even though they do not understand either what they are saying or concerning what things they are so dogmatically asserting.*

Notes

[a] The simple ζητήσεις, "speculations," is read by D F G Ψ 0285[vid] 1739 1881 TR; Ir. The compound ἐκζητήσεις, "speculations" (א A 33 81 1175 *pc*), is a rare word. It is more likely that a scribe would replace a rare word with a better-known word. Cf. *TCGNT*[2], 571.

[b] D* ([2]:-δομιαν) latt; Ir have οἰκοδομήν, "edification," instead of οἰκονομίαν, "stewardship." οἰκοδομήν was probably thought to make a better parallel to ἐκζητήσεις, "speculations." οἰκονομίαν, "stewardship," is preferred as the more difficult reading and as better related to the historical situation; i.e., the opponents were church leaders who were supposed to be good stewards of the church; see *Comment.* Cf. *TCGNT*[2], 571; Lock, xxxvi.

Form/Structure/Setting

The majority of commentators divide 1 Tim 1:3–20 into four distinct units, with vv 8–11 and vv 12–17 being digressions only somewhat related to the discussion and vv 18–20 following more naturally after v 7. However, 1:3–20 may be viewed as a unit that discusses the essentials of the Ephesian heresy and Paul's refutation. Paul uses verbal and conceptual links to tie vv 3–20 together. (1) Vv 3–7 describe the problem and what Timothy must do about it, v 3 setting the tone for the entire chapter (Spicq, 1:320). Paul must stop the opponents from teaching their myths, based on OT law, that are producing meaningless speculations. (2) In v 7 Paul says the opponents want to be teachers of the law but are ignorant of it, and in vv 8–11 he discusses the true intention of the law, not as a digression but to indicate the error of the opponents. They are using the law to govern the lives of all people, even Christians who are justified and living righteously by faith. (3) In v 11 Paul says that he was entrusted with the gospel, and in vv 12–17 he discusses his conversion (Acts 9:1–19), for it was at that time that he received his commission to preach the gospel. He identifies himself with sinners in vv 8–11 and shows how God's mercy and grace saved him so that he could be an example of the fact that salvation is not by human merit; it is not obtained by observing myths or the law but by God's mercy and grace. Vv 12–17 are a theological contrast to vv 8–11. (4) Having given his theological refutation of the Ephesian heresy, Paul reminds Timothy that God has called him to this type of work and has fully enabled him for the task. He should not be discouraged. Paul closes with a final note of urgency; the situation has become so bad that Paul has already excommunicated two of the opponents' leaders.

Warfield also sees the cohesiveness of chap. 1. Starting with 1 Tim 2:1 he shows how παρακαλῶ, "I urge," looks back to παρεκάλεσα, "I urged," in 1:3, τῆς παραγγελίας, "this command," in v 5, and ταύτην τὴν παραγγελίαν, "this command," in v 18. Then, starting with 1 Tim 1:1 and Paul's statement that he is an apostle "according to the appointment" of God, Warfield argues as follows:

As Paul writes not formally, but out of his heart, he may be thought to have held in mind at the very opening of the letter what he was about to say, and to have allowed this to color his opening expressions. Now, what these words κατ᾽ ἐπιταγὴν θεοῦ declare is that Paul is writing in fulfilment of the duty that developed on him as an apostle, appointed to that office by God. In accordance with that duty he reminds Timothy of the exhortation that he had already given him, to silence the false teachers at Ephesus (i. 3 *sq.*). These teachers, in contrast with Paul's appointment, had *taken upon themselves* (θέλοντες, verse 7) the function of teaching, and in accordance with this assumption *taught otherwise* (ἑτεροδιδασκαλεῖν, verse 3) than the Gospel that had been *intrusted to him* (verse 11). The key-words thus far are the κατ᾽ ἐπιταγήν of verse 1, the θέλοντες of verse 7, and the ἐπιστεύθην of verse 11. And the idea is that Paul had received a commission from God, these others were self-appointed; that he preached was therefore due to his obedience to the call of duty, that they preached, to their self-will; what he preached was the truth committed to him, what they preached their own crude inventions; and the result of his preaching was edification in Christian graces, while the result of their preaching was emptiness and folly. All this furnished good reason for silencing them. . . .

He goes on humbly to declare how it happens that he, of all men, was entrusted with the Gospel of the glory of the blessed God. . . . It is as much as if Paul had said, "I make no claim to be in myself superior to these teachers—it is not I, but the Gospel that I preach that is superior; and I was not entrusted with this Gospel on account of any merit in me, but only on account of God's infinite grace—a thing altogether unaccountable, since I am the chief of sinners, and yet again not unaccountable, for it is God's gracious purpose to save sinners, and in whom could be more fully shown all His long-suffering than in me, the chief?" . . .

But one thing more is needed: a justification of his selection of Timothy for this difficult and delicate task. This is what is given us in verses 18–20. "This charge," says the Apostle, "I have committed to thee, child Timothy, in accordance with ..." This is the key to these verses. The reason assigned is twofold: first, Timothy had been long ago designated by certain prophecies as a suitable soldier for such a warfare (verse 18); and secondly, he was exhibiting just the graces that proved his hold on the true Gospel of God's grace to be secure, and pointed to him as the proper person to rebuke this teaching (verse 19). These verses, of course, contain more than this. They are in their whole tone and expression an encouraging trumpet call to Timothy to play the man in this noble warfare; an expression of confidence from the Apostle; and a warning against the evils of the heresy he had to face. But their formal contents chiefly concern the designation of Timothy for this duty; and as such they visibly round out and complete the subject begun at verse 3, and leave the Apostle free to begin in the next chapter the new exhortations to convey [that for] which the letter was written. (*PresR* 8 [1921] 500–502)

Vv 3–7 break into four divisions: historical situation (v 3a), Paul's command and description of the problem (vv 3b–4), purpose for the command (v 5), and further description and historical urgency (vv 6–7). Paul is repeating a charge he has already given to Timothy to stop those in the church who are teaching error. They are teaching the law, but they are both arrogant and ignorant. Whereas the end result of their teaching is speculation, the end result of Paul's teaching is love. The keynote of this section is authority, continuing from the salutation in the use of παραγγέλλειν, "to command" (vv 3, 5). The description of the opponents is similar to the description in Titus 1. This suggests that despite the significant differences between 1 Timothy and Titus, both letters address the same heresy. The similarity also suggests that 1 Timothy and Titus were written at the same time.

1 Timothy 1	*Titus 1*
μὴ ἑτεροδιδασκαλεῖν (v 3) "not to continue teaching a different gospel"	διδάσκοντες ἃ μὴ δεῖ (v 11) "teaching what is not proper"
μηδὲ προσέχειν μύθοις (v 4) "not to devote themselves to myths"	μὴ προσέχοντες Ἰουδαϊκοῖς μύθοις (v 14) "not being devoted to Jewish myths"
καθαρᾶς καρδίας (v 5) "clean heart"	καθαρὰ τοῖς καθαροῖς (v 15) "clean to the clean"
συνειδήσεως (v 5) "conscience"	συνείδησις (v 15) "conscience"
ματαιολογίαν (v 6) "senseless babble"	ματαιολόγοι (v 10) "senseless babblers"

The urgency and seriousness of the historical situation is made clear by two facts. (1) Contrary to his usual practice, Paul gives no thanksgiving for Timothy or the Ephesian church (cf. *Form/Structure/Setting* on 2 Tim 1:3–5). The only other Pauline epistles in which this is the case are 2 Corinthians (although 2 Cor 1:3–7 may be a thanksgiving in the form of a praise), Galatians, and Titus. It is generally recognized that Paul was angry with the Galatians, prompting him to launch directly into his polemic. This is somewhat the same situation in 1 Timothy and

Titus, and to some degree in 2 Corinthians (cf. Furnish, *2 Corinthians*, 117). Although addressed to Timothy, 1 Timothy is largely public in intention, and as in Galatians one of the basic problems in Ephesus was the questioning of Paul's apostolic authority and the preaching of another gospel (cf. *Introduction*, "Reconstruction from the PE"). So dispensing with the usual niceties, Paul launches into the problem (cf. Houlden for a similar understanding). In 2 Timothy, which is a personal letter, Paul does give thanks for Timothy.

(2) The second indication that the Ephesian problem is serious is the anacoluthon in Paul's opening statement, a grammatical error that is not uncommon in Paul's writings (Rom 2:17; 5:12; 9:22; 1 Cor 1:6; Gal 3:6; Eph 1:4; Phil 1:7; 1 Thess 1:5; cf. Acts 24:2–4; 2 Pet 1:3; BDF §§465, 466–70; Robertson, *Grammar*, 435–50). Paul's intensity is likely caused in part by the attacks on his apostolic authority that Timothy was encountering. He begins with "Just as . . ." but never completes his thought. (καθώς, "just as," introduces a subordinate clause, which is a protasis without an expressed apodosis, requiring that something like οὕτω καὶ νῦν παρακαλῶ, "so also now I urge," be supplied [Ellicott, 3].) Some translations smooth out the anacoluthon here by inserting a phrase (KJV and Wey add "so do" at the end of v 4) or by altering the grammar (NEB omits "just as"; NRSV, NIV, and NASB change the infinitive *to remain* to the finite *remain*, thus changing a subordinate clause to an independent clause); the translation given here introduces a dash at the end of the sentence.

Vv 3b–4 contain three doublets: (1) two infinitives indicating what certain people are no longer to do ("to teach," "to devote themselves"); (2) two nouns describing what was absorbing the attention of these people ("myths," "genealogies"); and (3) two nouns that contrast the result of such activity ("speculations," "stewardship"). The second and third doublets are each subordinate to the one that precedes, and the second element in each is expanded by a word or phrase.

Comment

3a Καθὼς παρεκάλεσά σε προσμεῖναι ἐν Ἐφέσῳ πορευόμενος εἰς Μακεδονίαν, "Just as I urged you to stay on in Ephesus while I was traveling to Macedonia." Paul reminds Timothy of an earlier discussion in which he gave instructions on how to deal with the Ephesian heresy and encouraged Timothy to carry through with his task. Either this letter is an enlargement of that contact (which seems unlikely if their previous contact was personal and not by a letter now lost) or it is an official recapitulation for the benefit of the Ephesian church. It reinforces Timothy's authority and spells out how the Ephesian church should behave. Paul eventually wanted to come to Ephesus in order to deal with the situation personally (1 Tim 3:14–15). The opposition to Timothy was intense, fueled perhaps by a timidity of youth on Timothy's part, although this should not be overemphasized (cf. *Introduction*, "Historical Reconstruction from the PE, B. 1 Timothy"). Fee is right in stressing that this verse is key to understanding both the occasion and the purpose of the letter. The epistle is a written response to a specific historical situation, and its discussion should be interpreted in that light (cf. *Introduction*, "Historical Reconstruction from Acts"). For those rejecting the authenticity of the PE, this verse refers to a fictitious situation, and the words to Timothy are really words to postapostolic ministers (e.g., Oberlinner, 9–11).

The main point of interest here is the historical situation of this earlier encounter. There is no time period in Acts into which this verse fits (contra Roloff, 62–63, who pictures Timothy staying behind [Acts 19:21], as he often did, to help stabilize the church). In Acts 20:1 Paul is leaving Ephesus for Macedonia, but he had just spent three years in Ephesus, and it is unlikely that the theological problems recorded in the PE could have arisen during this time. On his subsequent trip back through Macedonia, Timothy went ahead to Troas (Acts 20:5) but left after seven days. There is a hint, though, that trouble would eventually come after Paul's third missionary journey; in Paul's prophecy to the Ephesian elders he says that "after my departure fierce wolves will come in among you" (Acts 20:29–30), suggesting that the problems recorded in the PE occurred after Acts. All this becomes one of the important arguments for dating the PE after Acts 28 (cf. *Introduction*, "Historical Reconstruction from Acts").

Paul says he was πορευόμενος εἰς Μακεδονίαν, "traveling to Macedonia," when he originally urged Timothy to stay on at Ephesus. Were Paul and Timothy together in Ephesus while Paul was preparing to go to Macedonia, or was Paul going to Macedonia from some other location? Dibelius-Conzelmann (15) say that "every unprejudiced reader" must think that Paul was in Ephesus (cf. also Kümmel, *Introduction*, 375), but the text does not say this. (1) Kelly argues that the epistle shows firsthand knowledge of the problem, which would necessitate Paul's having been in Ephesus. But Paul had been in Ephesus for three years (Acts 20:31). This, plus communiqués, could have kept him in touch with the church. The excommunication of the two elders (1 Tim 1:20) need not have been in person; the similar act in 1 Cor 5:5 was not in person. (2) If Paul had been in Ephesus, the emphasis on authority throughout the letter would most likely have been unnecessary. Paul would have dealt with that issue when he was present. (3) 1 Tim 3:14 shows that Paul wants to come soon, which would not make sense if he had just been there. (4) In 1 Tim 3:14 Paul says that he hopes to "come," not to "return," to Ephesus, implying that he had not been with Timothy in Ephesus during this period. It seems that the best historical reconstruction does not see the encounter occurring in Ephesus, primarily on the force of 1 Tim 3:14. Timothy had been sent to Ephesus and later traveled to meet Paul, who was on his way to Macedonia (after the Roman imprisonment and on his way to Spain or Crete?). Timothy returned to Ephesus; Paul wrote the letter in support of Timothy's task in Ephesus and planned to come himself when he could (see *Introduction*, "Historical Reconstruction from the PE"). There is no theological significance attached to this conclusion, but merely historical curiosity. If Paul were in Ephesus when he encountered Timothy, there would be a theological problem in that he earlier prophesied that the Ephesian elders would never again see him (Acts 20:25). However, this prophecy evidently did not present a problem for Paul since he was planning to see the Ephesians again (1 Tim 3:14). Perhaps Acts 20:25 refers only to the Ephesian elders at that time and not to the church as a whole.

Paul had previously "urged" (παρακαλεῖν) Timothy to keep working in Ephesus. παρακαλεῖν has a range of meanings extending from "to summon, ask" to "to comfort, encourage, request, urge" (BAGD, 617) as seen in its use in military language (Spicq, 1:321). It is frequently used in pastoral and missionary admonition (K. Grayston, "A Problem of Translation: The Meaning of *parakaleo, paraklesis* in the New Testament," *ScrB* 11 [1980] 27–31; O. Schmitz and G. Stählin, *TDNT* 5:773–99; G. Braumann, *NIDNTT* 1:569–71; MM, 484; cf. παρατίθεσθαι, "to entrust," in v 18). It does not mean

"to command" as does παραγγέλλειν in v 3b. The word occurs elsewhere in the PE
eight times. It is found in summary statements of Paul's charge, combined with
"teach" (διδάσκειν; 1 Tim 6:2) and "convict" (ἐλέγχειν; 2 Tim 4:2; Titus 2:5). Bishops
must be able to teach, urge, and convict (Titus 1:9). Paul urges Timothy to make sure
prayers are said for all people (1 Tim 2:1). Titus is to encourage younger men to
control themselves (Titus 2:6). Most significantly, Timothy is not to "rebuke"
(ἐπιπλήσσειν) the older men but to "encourage" them (παρακαλεῖν; 1 Tim 5:1).
There is a difference between how Timothy and Titus should deal with the opponents and how they should deal with others in the church. In dealing with the
opposition they are to command, to speak with the authority given by God through
Paul (1 Tim 1:1), but with the others they are to be gentle, urging and encouraging
proper belief and conduct (cf. *Introduction,* "The Response to the Heresy"). παρακαλεῖν
is repeated in 1:5 and 2:1, stylistically tying the larger unit together.

3b–4a ἵνα παραγγείλῃς τισὶν μὴ ἑτεροδιδασκαλεῖν μηδὲ προσέχειν μύθοις καὶ
γενεαλογίαις ἀπεράντοις, "in order that you might command certain people not
to continue teaching a different gospel or to devote themselves to endless myths
and genealogies." Timothy is to stop Paul's opponents from teaching their false
gospel. He is also to stop the opponents themselves from pursuing a lifestyle
devoted to these myths. In an epistle that shows a significant concern for behavior,
it is meaningful that Paul begins by stating that the opponents' teaching is wrong,
that "myths and genealogies" are opposed to the true gospel. Because the Ephesian
heresy most likely lacked a well-defined theological core, because the letter is a
repetition of what Paul and Timothy had earlier discussed, and because Timothy
already knew Paul's teaching, there is no need for Paul to go into a theological
discussion of why the opponents are wrong (see *Introduction,* "Historical Reconstruction from the PE"). For a comparison with Paul's description of the heresy in
Titus 1, see *Form/Structure/Setting.*

παραγγέλλειν, "to command," is both a military and a legal term, describing a
military command or an official summons to court (MM, 481; O. Schmitz, *TDNT*
5:762; Dittenberger, *Sylloge* 4:489). Paul directs Timothy to stand before the
Ephesian church and, as if he were a general or a judge, strictly, officially, and
authoritatively to command the false teachers to stop. Paul uses the word elsewhere
to describe his own authoritative commands (1 Cor 7:10, cf. 11:17; 1 Thess 4:10, cf.
4:2; 2 Thess 3:4, 6, 10, 12). In the PE he uses the verb five times. Twice it is addressed
to Timothy as Paul tells him to command the opponents to stop teaching heresy (1
Tim 1:3) and to keep the commandment pure (1 Tim 6:13). Three times Paul tells
Timothy to command and teach Paul's instructions to others (1 Tim 4:11),
specifically his instructions to widows (1 Tim 5:7) and the rich (1 Tim 6:17). The
cognate noun παραγγελία, "command," is a summary description of Paul's charge
to Timothy (1 Tim 1:5, 18). Rebuke is a primary theme in the PE (see *Introduction,*
"Themes in the PE").

Timothy is to command τισίν, "certain people," to stop teaching heresy; Paul
does not identify his opponents at this time (cf. 1 Tim 1:6, 19; 5:15, 24; 6:10, 21),
as is his practice elsewhere (1 Cor 4:18; 2 Cor 10:2; Gal 1:7; cf. Heb 10:25; *1 Clem.*
1:1). Lock (8) thinks this is "tactful" because most of the troublemakers had not
gone to the extreme as had Hymenaeus and Alexander (1 Tim 1:20; Paul's naming
these two indicates the severity of their opposition; cf. 2 Tim 4:10, 14–15). The
opposition appears to have been led primarily by men: (1) The named opponents

are men (1 Tim 1:20; 2 Tim 2:17; 4:14–15). (2) The opposition comes from within the leadership of the church, which was primarily male (1 Tim 3:1–7). (3) 2 Tim 3:6–7 suggests that the opponents were men who had won a following among some women.

Timothy is directed to command the opponents to stop ἑτεροδιδασκαλεῖν, "to teach another teaching." The linear aspect of the verb implies that the opponents' teaching is an ongoing process (cf. 1:20). ἑτεροδιδασκαλεῖν is a fascinating word. In this context, it means "to teach doctrine that is essentially different" from Paul's gospel. It occurs elsewhere only in 1 Tim 6:3, where the following phrase defines it as not adhering "to the healthy words of our Lord Jesus Christ and the teaching that is according to godliness." In classical Greek, ἕτερος meant "another of a different kind" (LSJ, 701), and ἄλλος meant "another of the same kind." But by the time of the NT this distinction was not always present (BAGD, 315 [1bg]; Turner, *Grammatical Insights,* 197–98; F. Selter and C. Brown, *NIDNTT* 2:739; H. W. Beyer, *TDNT* 2:702–4). However, the context of 1 Tim 1:3 shows that this old meaning is present here (cf. Mark 16:12 [TR]; Luke 9:29; Rom 7:23; 1 Cor 15:40; Jas 2:25). It is not that the teaching of the opponents was merely different; it is that their teaching was essentially different and therefore wrong. It is the same situation that Paul found himself in with the Galatians (Gal 1:6–9). They were turning to a ἕτερον εὐαγγέλιον, "different gospel," although, as Paul quickly qualifies, there is no ἄλλο, "other," gospel but only perversions. The translation "novelties" (Lock, 8; Scott, 7; Kelly 43) misses the point: it is not that the teaching is new and unusual but that this false gospel was essentially different from Paul's.

For a discussion of the heresy, see *Introduction,* "The Ephesian Heresy." It appears to have been a form of aberrant Judaism with Hellenistic/gnostic tendencies that overemphasized the law and underemphasized Christ and faith, taught dualism (asceticism, denial of a physical resurrection), was unduly interested in the minutiae of the OT, produced sinful lifestyles and irrelevant quibbling about words, and was destroying the reputation of the church in Ephesus. The opponents' teaching and behavior conflicted with what God intended, which was above all characterized by faith. The use of "different" has strong implications for the concept of orthodoxy. If this was a *different* gospel, then there must have been *the* gospel accepted as the basis of Christian truth against which this new teaching could be compared and judged "different." Kelly agrees when he comments that this "suggests that there is an accepted norm of apostolic teaching" (44). This is true even at the early time of Galatians (Gal 1:6–9).

ἑτεροδιδασκαλεῖν is a compound of two words, ἕτερος, "other," and διδασκαλεῖν, "to teach," apparently coined here by Paul. It is not found anywhere else except in 1 Tim 6:3 and later Christian literature (Ignatius *Pol.* 3.1; Eusebius *Hist. Eccl.* 3.32.8). Similar compounds are found: νομοδιδάσκαλοι, "teachers of the law" (1 Tim 1:7; Luke 5:17; Acts 5:34); καλοδιδάσκαλοι, "teaching what is good" (Titus 2:3); κακοδιδασκαλεῖν, "to teach evil" (*1 Clem.* 2:10; *2 Clem.* 10:5); κακοδιδασκαλία, "evil teaching" (Ignatius *Phil.* 2.1); ψευδοδιδάσκαλος, "false teacher" (2 Pet 2:1; Hermas *Sim.* 9.22.2; Irenaeus *Adv. Haer.* 3.4.2; cf. 1QH 4:16). The closest expression in the NT is ἕτερον εὐαγγέλιον, "different gospel" (Gal 1:6; cf. 2 Cor 11:4).

Along with stopping the heretical teaching, Timothy is to stop Paul's opponents from being "addicted to endless myths and genealogies," shifting from teaching to personal behavior. Not only are they to stop teaching others, but they themselves are no longer to devote themselves to these myths. "Endless myths and genealogies" are almost epexegetical to "another teaching," describing the content of the teaching. This is one of the few hints in the PE regarding the content of the Ephesian heresy, which presumably comprised myths based on minor people in the OT genealogies. The salvation and lifestyle the opponents preached was adherence to these mythical reconstructions.

προσέχειν has a range of meaning extending from "to pay attention to" to "to devote oneself to" and "be addicted to." (It also means "to cling to" as in the variant to 1 Tim 6:3.) It occurs twenty-four times in the NT; all five of Paul's uses are in the PE. In light of the Ephesian problem, the stronger meaning of "to devote oneself to" is probably meant. The opponents are not simply teaching error; they have adopted a lifestyle that is contradictory to Paul's gospel. Elsewhere Paul says that deacons should not be addicted to much wine (1 Tim 3:8) and that Timothy is to devote himself to the public reading of Scripture, to preaching, and to teaching (1 Tim 4:13). Paul tells Timothy that in the last days some believers will devote themselves to deceitful spirits and demonic teachings (1 Tim 4:1). Titus likewise is directed to instruct members of the Cretan church not to devote themselves to Jewish myths (Titus 1:14). προσέχειν is also used to describe the devotion of the people of Samaria to Simon (Acts 8:10, 11), another illustration of how strong the word can be.

ἀπέραντος, "endless," occurs in biblical literature elsewhere only in the LXX (Job 36:26; 3 Macc 2:9). It is a formation from πέρας, "end" or "limit," with an alpha privative, meaning "not" (cf. 1 Tim 1:9). It implies "limitlessness," possibly "interminable" or "unrestrained." One of Paul's major complaints against the heresies is not so much that they were wrong—although they were; see v 10—but that they were silly and produced only improper behavior. One can picture the teachings of the opponents, going on and on, not saying anything true or of any significance, and never coming to a conclusion, always creating more and more myths and quibbling. ἀπεράντοις, "endless," could be modifying "genealogies" or both "myths and genealogies." In either case, ἀπεράντοις would receive its gender from γενεαλογίαις, "genealogies." καί could mean either "and" or "even." This yields such possible meanings as "myths and endless genealogies," "endless myths and genealogies," or "endless myths that are derived from genealogies." Since the genealogies are probably those in the OT, it is doubtful that they would be called endless, and so the translation "endless myths and genealogies."

By calling them μῦθοι, "myths," Paul is pointing out their legendary and untrustworthy nature (Spicq, 1:93–94) and is implicitly contrasting them with the gospel that is rooted in historical events (Spicq, 1:98). Many compare the myths and genealogies to Jewish allegories of creation or interpretations of the OT patriarchs and their family trees such as are found in *Jubilees* or Pseudo-Philo *Biblical Antiquities* (Hort, *Judaistic Christianity*, 135–37; Jeremias, 14–15; Spicq, 1:94–97, 322; Towner, 45; id., *Goal*, 28; Roloff, 64; Kittel, *ZNW* 20 [1921] 49–69; Lock, xvii; see *Introduction*, "The Ephesian Heresy"). Spicq (1:97, making a comparison to the Stoic reinterpretation of Homer) and Towner (*Goal*, 28) add the possibility of speculative rabbinic exegesis. Some see a mixed background of Judaism and Gnosticism (Oberlinner, 14, although elsewhere he lessens the Jewish influence [cf. on Titus 1:14]; Quinn, 109–12, 245–47, who includes stories about Jesus, 158–65, 245). The word occurs five times in the NT, four in the PE. Elsewhere Paul calls the myths profane, silly (1 Tim 4:7), and Jewish (Titus 1:14), paralleling them with "commands of people." He says that people will wander from the truth into myths (2 Tim 4:4). The only other occurrence of the word in the NT is 2 Pet 1:16, in which the author says that those who make known the power and coming of Jesus have not followed cleverly devised myths (cf. Wis 17:4 [A]; Sir 20:19). In every occurrence the word is used in a negative sense (cf. Spicq, 1:93–98).

γενεαλογία, "genealogy," is a tracing of one's descent or family tree (cf. Colson, *JTS* 19 [1917–18] 265–71; Kittel, *ZNW* 20 [1921] 16–69; Sandmel, *HUCA* 27 [1956] 201–11; G. Stählin, *TDNT* 4:762–95). Towner sees genealogies in a broader literary category than simple lists such as are found in Matt 1:1–17. The word γενεαλογία also occurs in Titus 3:9 (cognate verb in Heb 7:6; cf. γενεά, "clan, race, tribe," in Col 1:26 and Heb 3:10). The word is found in Scripture elsewhere only in 1 Chr 5:1. *Myth* and *genealogy* are often joined in Greek literature. The scarcity of the pair in Scripture outside the PE is explained by the fact that the heresy had not arisen until the end of Paul's life. Previous to the Ephesian situation, the Judaizing influence showed itself in other ways. In *Introduction*, "The Ephesian Heresy," the background of the "myths and genealogies" is analyzed, and it is argued that they are Jewish with some Hellenistic/gnostic elements. This conclusion is largely based on this verse and other similar statements (Titus 1:14). The Jewish element accounts for the misunderstanding of the law (1:7, 8–11) and the quarrels about it (Titus 3:9).

4b αἵτινες ἐκζητήσεις παρέχουσιν μᾶλλον ἢ οἰκονομίαν θεοῦ τὴν ἐν πίστει, —. "which produce speculations rather than the stewardship from God by faith, —." Timothy must stop the opponents because their teaching leads people to mere speculation. The opponents, because they are teaching these endless myths and genealogies, are continually speculating about unimportant matters instead of administering the office of steward—an office they received from God. The proper way to administer their office is not through mythical interpretations but through faith. Paul has no objection to honest inquiry, but the opponents are anything but sincere (cf. *Introduction*, "The Ephesian Heresy").

V 4b gives both sides of the theological coin. On the negative side, it states that their teaching produces speculation. αἵτινες, "which," although normally functioning as an indefinite pronoun, can introduce a clause that gives the reason or consequence of a previous statement (Abbott-Smith, *Lexicon*, 326; cf. Titus 1:11; Gal 4:24; Phil 4:3; cf. Luke 8:3; 10:42; Acts 10:47; 11:28). The consequence of the myths is speculations. In the active voice, παρέχειν means "to present," "to grant" (1 Tim 6:17), or "to cause" (1 Tim 1:4; Gal 6:17). In the middle voice it is reflexive, meaning "to present oneself" (Titus 2:7; cf. Col 4:1). The aspect is also linear, showing that these myths were presently and constantly causing speculations.

ἐκζητήσεις, "speculations," is one of the general descriptions of the Ephesian heresy. Instead of producing godliness, the heresy resulted in futile speculation. Simpson's description (27) of the opponents as "puzzle-brains" is appropriate. ἐκζήτησις, "speculation," is an unusual word, occurring in the NT only here. In fact, this appears to be its first occurrence in Greek literature. The simple ζήτησις, "speculation," occurs in 1 Tim 6:4, 2 Tim 2:23, and Titus 3:9, where it describes the Ephesian heresy as its cognate does here (cf. variant in 1 Tim 1:4; cf. Acts 15:2, 7; 25:20; cf. John 3:25). The addition of the preposition ἐκ could make ἐκζητήσεις an intensive form, "extreme speculations." Fee argues that since the simple forms of both the verb and noun are well attested, the compound must have this intensive nuance. But since in Koine Greek distinctions between simple and perfective forms are often blurred and Paul uses both forms to describe the same phenomenon, the variation is one of style. For other examples of the perfective use of prepositions (e.g., ἀπό, διά, κατά, σύν), see Moule (*Idiom-Book*, 87–88), Robertson (*Grammar*, 563–65), BDF (§318.5), and Metzger (*Lexical Aids*, 81–84).

The other side of the theological coin contrasts "speculations" with what sound doctrine ought to produce: stewardship. οἰκονομία has a nonfigurative use, designating the office of "stewardship" (Luke 16:2–4; Col 1:25). In its figurative sense it is applied to God's "plan" of salvation. As such, it can refer to God's actual plan (Eph 1:10; 3:9) or a person's responsibility within that plan (1 Cor 9:17; Eph 3:22; Col 1:25). Related is the οἰκονόμος, who is the actual "steward" (Rom 16:23; 1 Cor 4:2; Gal 4:2). Especially important for this passage is the use of οἰκονόμος figuratively for ministers as God's stewards in Titus 1:7 (cf. 1 Cor 4:1; 1 Pet 4:10). The use of οἰκονομία in this passage is somewhat difficult as evidenced by the variant οἰκοδομήν, "edification," which forms a better parallel with ἐκζητήσεις, "speculations" (see *Note* b). Scott (9) suggests that perhaps Paul is thinking of Jesus' parable of the talents with its teaching of stewardship. A reference to the actual parable, however, is unlikely, though conceptually it makes good sense. J. Reumann suggests that both meanings are joined: God's "plan" of salvation is worked out in connection with God's "steward" ("Οἰκονομία-Terms in Paul in Comparison with Lucan *Heilsgeschichte*," *NTS* 13 [1966–67] 147–67). The troublemakers in the Ephesian church were church leaders, those who had been appointed stewards (using the language of Titus 1:7) over God's household. Instead of pursuing this office through faith, they defined salvation in terms of their mythical reinterpretations based on OT genealogies. Therefore, Paul offsets "speculations," what the opponents were producing, with "stewardship," what they should have been accomplishing. Ellicott defines οἰκονομία as "the scheme of salvation designed by God, and proclaimed by his Apostles, . . . the fables and genealogies supplied questions of a controversial nature, but not the essence and principles of the divine dispensation" (6). According to this interpretation, θεοῦ, "God," is a subjective genitive indicating the origin of the office of stewardship. By including this fact, Paul is emphasizing the severity of the heresy. These people accepted the office of steward, an office ordained by God, and yet they were abusing the office. The final phrase, ἐν πίστει, should be understood instrumentally, "by [the proper exercise of] faith." The office is accomplished by faith, not by being devoted to endless myths and genealogies. (On *faith*, see *Introduction*, "Themes in the PE.") Paul does ௱ot finish this sentence; hence the dash in the *Translation* above (see *Form/ Structure/Setting*).

5 τὸ δὲ τέλος τῆς παραγγελίας ἐστὶν ἀγάπη ἐκ καθαρᾶς καρδίας καὶ συνειδήσεως ἀγαθῆς καὶ πίστεως ἀνυποκρίτου, "But the goal of this command is love from a clean heart and a good conscience and a sincere faith." The opponents' preaching resulted in speculation. The goal of Paul's command that they stop their false preaching is love, thus repeating a basic conviction of the early church that the greatest command, in that it sums up all the other commands, is the command to love (Matt 22:34–40; Rom 13:8–10; Gal 5:14) and that love is more significant than ritual observance such as law keeping (cf. vv 8–11). Paul then gives the threefold source of this love: it comes from a clean heart, a good conscience, and a sincere faith. In Ephesus, as in Corinth, the heresy manifests itself in the absence of love, the Christian virtue fundamental to spiritual well-being. Paul may also be directing a slight warning to Timothy in this verse. His attitude must also be one of love. It will be difficult to confront and correct the opponents, and especially difficult to do so with the attitude of love, but do so he must. If this is the case, it is the first mention of an important theme in the PE: Timothy must beware of the same traps into which the opponents have fallen and must be sure always to maintain the correct attitude (cf. 1 Tim 4:16).

δέ should be given its full adversative force of "but," differentiating the results of the heresy (vv 3b–4) from the results of Paul's command (v 5). τέλος indicates the "goal" of Paul's gospel (cf. Rom 6:21–22; 10:4; cf. Matt 26:58; Heb 6:8; Jas 5:11; 1 Pet 1:9). The article τῆς, "this," is anaphoric, referring to the command (παραγγείλῃς) in v 3. The RSV translates the article with "our," joining Paul's and Timothy's ministries. παραγγελίας, "command," is the cognate noun of the verb παραγγέλλειν, "to command," in v 3, carrying the same nuance of authority. This command encompasses not only the negative aspect of prohibiting the false teaching (v 3) but also the positive aspect of true stewardship (v 4b). This idea of a command is repeated in 1:18 (cf. 2:1). Some argue that the command is the OT law, in which case Paul is saying that the OT law, properly understood and applied, results in love, not in speculation, perhaps looking forward to the discussion of law in vv 8–11; but the article τῆς, "this," appears to look back to the command in v 3. If Paul is thinking of love not just as a quality missing from the opponents but as the goal of Christianity, i.e., the greatest command, then Paul may be including the specific command in v 3 with all the commands related to being a good steward, perhaps even God's command that he be an apostle (v 1).

The concept of love runs throughout Scripture. God's love is the basis of redemption (John 3:16) and of a person's own love for both God and for others. The beauty of the word ἀγάπη, "love," has often been pointed out. As defined in Scripture, this love offers itself freely to someone who does not deserve it; this love does not seek to possess the beloved. There is little evidence for its secular use before the LXX, and whatever meaning it may have had is enhanced by Christian usage. It is a word that can be defined only within the context of biblical theology (cf. χάρις, "grace," in the *Comment* on 1 Tim 1:2). ἀγάπη stands in stark contrast to ἔρως, which designates the physical "love" that is merited and seeks to possess; it is the customary word for sexual passion (LSJ, 695). The other two words for "love" are φιλία, "friendship," and στοργή, "affection," between parents and children, the latter not occurring in the NT (cf. the negative adjective ἄστοργος, "unloving," in 2 Tim 3:3 and Rom 1:31).

In the PE, every time the word *love* occurs it is paired with *faith*, except in 2 Tim 1:7, often within a list of virtues. It characterizes Paul's life (2 Tim 3:10) as it should the lives of Timothy (1 Tim 4:12; 6:11; 2 Tim 2:22) and older men (Titus 2:2). It comes from God (2 Tim 1:7) and is the goal of Paul's gospel (1 Tim 1:5). The faith and love that are in Christ Jesus have overflowed to accomplish Paul's salvation (1 Tim 1:14), and love provides the guideline by which Timothy is to follow Paul's teaching (2 Tim 1:13). It is part of the salvation process (1 Tim 2:15). It is a key word in the PE, probably necessitated by a lack of love in the Ephesian church (cf. Gen 20:5–6; Job 11:13; Pss 24:4; 51:10; Matt 5:8; cf. cognate ἀγαπᾶν, "to love," in 2 Tim 4:8, 10; ἀγαπητός, "beloved," in 1 Tim 6:2 and 2 Tim 1:2). On love, see V. P. Furnish, *The Love Command in the New Testament* (London: SCM Press, 1973); A. Nygren, *Agape and Eros,* tr. P. S. Watson (New York: Harper and Row, 1969); J. Piper, *Love*

Your Enemies, SNTSMS 38 (Cambridge: Cambridge UP, 1979); C. Spicq, *Agape in the New Testament,* tr. M. A. McNamara and M. H. Richter (St. Louis: Herder, 1963); B. B. Warfield, "The Terminology of Love in the New Testament," *PTR* 16 (1918) 1–45, 153–203; articles and bibliography in C. Brown, W. Günther, and H.-G. Link, *NIDNTT* 2:538–51; G. Quell and E. Stauffer, *TDNT* 1:21–55.

Following ἀγάπη, "love," is a triad describing the source (ἐκ, "from") of that love. The reigning idea is sincerity. Love comes from a heart cleansed of sin, a conscience clear of guilt, and a faith devoid of hypocrisy. This trilogy is not exhaustive, nor does it claim to be. It is not an attempt to describe fully the gospel or the concept of love. It is rather three concepts particularly appropriate to the Ephesian situation since the opponents were depraved in mind (1 Tim 6:5) with seared consciences (1 Tim 4:2) and corrupt faith (2 Tim 3:8). This connection to the opponents was recognized in the last century (cf. Ellicott, 8). It is not mere "moralism taking the place of theology" (Hanson, [1983] 57) but deep truths made practical and relevant in the historical situation.

(1) Love comes from a heart cleansed of sin, the heart being the "hidden person" (1 Pet 3:4). This stands in contrast to the opponents who are liars (1 Tim 4:2), persisting in sin (1 Tim 5:20), depraved of mind (1 Tim 6:5), and bereft of the truth (1 Tim 6:5). καθαρᾶς, "clean," carries with it the OT concept of ceremonial cleansing in preparation for God's service. Paul elsewhere speaks of a cleansed heart (2 Tim 2:22), a clear conscience (1 Tim 3:9; 2 Tim 1:3), and a cleansed people (Titus 1:15). Because Israelite thought did not divide the person into material and immaterial, it associated different functions with specific bodily organs. The heart was the chief organ, the unifying organ, the source of a person's intellectual, emotional, and spiritual powers, the contact between the person and God (J. Behm, *TDNT* 3:605–14; R. C. Denton, *IDB* 2:549–50).

(2) The love produced by Paul's gospel comes from a conscience clear of guilt. (On the translation of ἀγαθός as "clear," see *Comment* on 1 Tim 2:10.) συνείδησις, "conscience," is another significant Pauline term. It is that innate and universal (Rom 2:14–15) knowledge that condemns wrong and commends right. It is the inner awareness of the moral quality of one's actions. It is a compound of σύν, "together," and εἰδέναι, "to know"; the Latin is the same construction (*con* plus *scio*) from which we get the word *conscience.* Initially it meant "to know together," corporate, universal knowledge (cf. B. F. Harris, "ΣΥΝΕΙΔΗΣΙΣ [Conscience] in the Pauline Writings," *WTJ* 24 [1962] 174–77).

The term συνείδησις, "conscience," is not found in the OT, although its function is performed by the heart (לֵב *lēb;* 2 Sam 24:10; Job 27:6; Pss 32:1–5; 51:1–9). Other than the above-mentioned references, συνείδησις is found in the NT fourteen times (Rom 13:5; 2 Cor 1:12; 4:2; 5:11; cf. Acts 23:1; 24:16 [both contained in speeches of Paul]; Heb 9:9, 14; 10:2, 22; 13:18; 1 Pet 2:19; 3:16, 21). A. M. Rehwinkel (*EDT,* 267) summarizes its threefold function in Scripture: (a) to urge right and hinder wrong; (b) to pass judgment on a decision or action; (c) to produce guilt or commendation in the heart. In the PE it occurs six times, in both positive and negative senses. An ἀγαθός, "clear," conscience is a source of love (1 Tim 1:5). Timothy is to hold on to an ἀγαθός, "clear," conscience (1 Tim 1:19) just as Paul has a καθαρός, "cleansed," conscience (2 Tim 1:3). Deacons must hold to the mystery of the faith with a καθαρός, "cleansed," conscience (1 Tim 3:9). The opponents have rejected (ἀπωθεῖν; 1 Tim 1:19), seared (καυστηριάζειν; 1 Tim 4:2a), and defiled (μιαίνειν; Titus 1:15) their own consciences. Conscience is present in Paul's life (Rom 9:1; cf. 1 Cor 4:4 [σύνοιδα]) as well as in Christians' (1 Cor 8:1–13; 10:23–11:1) and Gentiles' (Rom 2:15) lives. It is, however, not the ultimate judge of right and wrong but serves only as a guide (1 Cor 4:4) since it can be seared by sin (1 Tim 4:2; 2 Tim 3:8; Titus 1:15; Rom 14:20; 1 Cor 8:7–12). See, for example, B. J. Harris's critique (*WTJ* 24 [1962] 173–86) of H. Rashdall, who elevates conscience to the point of saying "no one really makes his submission even to the teaching of our Lord absolute and unlimited, except in so far as the ethical injunctions of that authority commend themselves to his conscience" (*Conscience and Christ* [New York: Scribner's, 1916] 33; cf. H. Osborne, "ΣΥΝΕΙΔΗΣΙΣ," *JTS* o.s. 32 [1931] 167–79). "Rejected," "seared," and "defiled," although somewhat synonymous, show a slight progression from the voluntary decision to ignore the truth ("rejected") to the consequence of that act ("seared," "defiled"). C. A. Pierce argues that conscience is not a technical Stoic term but a common word in the Koine used only to evaluate past actions (*Conscience in the New Testament* [London: SCM Press, 1955]), an interpretation corrected by M. E. Thrall to include present and future actions ("The Pauline Use of Συνείδησις," *NTS* 14 [1967–68] 118–25). For further study of conscience, see especially B. J. Harris, *WTJ* 24 (1962) 173–86; C. Maurer, *TDNT* 6:898–919; also Ladd, *Theology*, 477–78; Guthrie, *New Testament Theology*, 170–71; Ridderbos, *Theology*, 288–93; H. C. Hahn and C. Brown, *NIDNTT* 1:348–53 (see bibliography); A. M. Rehwinkel, *The Voice of Conscience* (St. Louis: Concordia, 1956); id., *EDT*, 267–68; O. Hallesby, *Conscience* (London: Inter-Varsity Press, 1950); C. Spicq, "La conscience dans le Nouveau Testament," *RB* 47 (1938) 50–80; bibliography in *TLNT* 3:335–36; J. Stelzenberger, *Syneidēsis im Neuen Testament* (Paderborn: Schöningh, 1961).

(3) In the third part of the triad Paul tells Timothy that love should issue from a sincere, genuine, unhypocritical faith. The opponents have destroyed their consciences and are so hypocritical that they teach for the insincere motive of making money (1 Tim 6:5, 10). This helps us see that the opponents were not sincere but were knowingly and purposefully deceiving the church. ἀνυποκρίτου, "sincere," is a compound of an alpha privative, meaning "not" (cf. 1 Tim 1:9), and ὑπόκρισις, "hypocrisy," hence "without hypocrisy." Elsewhere it is connected with faith (2 Tim 1:5) and love (Rom 12:9; 2 Cor 6:6; cf. 1 Pet 1:22; it modifies *wisdom* in Jas 3:17). πίστεως, "faith," here is the usual Pauline use, meaning "trust" (cf. *Introduction*, "Themes in the PE"). Love proceeds from a trusting faith that is sincere. Some writers object that this could hardly be Pauline since an insincere faith is no faith at all (see similar discussion in *Comment* on 2 Tim 1:5). The same objection, however, could be raised with the phrases "sincere love" (Rom 12:9; 2 Cor 6:6), "counterfeit faith" (2 Tim 3:8), or "a different gospel" (Gal 1:6). ἀνυποκρίτου, "sincere," highlights a characteristic already present in faith. Deception of oneself and others is always possible (Kelly, 46; Fee, 8). By saying "sincere faith" Paul is contrasting himself with the opponents who have seared their consciences and are deceiving themselves and others.

6 ὧν τινες ἀστοχήσαντες ἐξετράπησαν εἰς ματαιολογίαν, "Some, having fallen short of these things, have turned aside to senseless babble." Instead of pursuing love coming from a clean heart, a clear conscience, and a sincere faith, the opponents had digressed into senseless babble. They wanted to teach the law, but they did not even know what they were talking about. These two verses emphasize the urgency of the problem, as do vv 19–20. They hint at the content of the heresy and the attitude of the opponents, and also introduce an important theme in the PE. The opponents did not choose to follow the heresy because it was intellectually more acceptable; they chose to abandon love. In other words, the root of the heresy was not an intellectual but a moral problem (cf. 1:19; Spicq, 1:329).

ἀστοχεῖν is a compound of an alpha privative, meaning "not," and στόχος, "mark." The original idea was "to miss the mark" (LSJ, 262); other suggestions are "to not aim at" (Lock, 10–11) and "to fall short of" (Barrett, 42). It occurs elsewhere in the NT in 1 Tim 6:21 and 2 Tim 2:18, both in connection with the false teachers (cf. Sir 7:19; 8:9). ὧν, "of which" (genitive of separation; Moule, *Idiom-Book*, 41), is the object of ἀστοχήσαντες, "having fallen short," referring back to the three sources of love in v 5. Paul continues his practice of not specifically identifying the opponents; he refers to them as τινές, "some" (cf. 1 Tim 1:3). ἐκτρέπειν means "to turn aside." Of its five occurrences in the NT, four are in the PE, and each time it is used figuratively (cf. Amos 5:8 and Heb 12:13 for the literal use; Spicq, 1:329). The opponents had turned aside to senseless babble (1 Tim 1:6), the people were wandering off into myths (2 Tim 4:14), and some young widows had strayed after Satan (1 Tim 5:15). Timothy also must avoid godless chatter (1 Tim 6:20). There is an entire collection of words in the PE that continues this theme, words such as ἀπωθεῖν, "to repudiate" (1 Tim 1:19), ἀφιστάναι, "to depart" (1 Tim 4:1; cf. 2 Tim 2:19; cf. Luke 8:13), ἀποπλανᾶν, "to wander away" (1 Tim 6:10), and ἀποστρέφειν, "turn away" (2 Tim 4:4; cf. 2 Tim 1:15; Titus 1:14). This gives weight to the argument that the trouble arose from within the Ephesian church; the leaders themselves, who had once been going down the right path, had wandered off into another direction. Spicq refers to the path of these false teachers as "progressive deviation" (1:329).

Instead of pursuing love, they turned aside into ματαιολογία, "senseless babble." The basic meaning of the word group μαται- is the difference between what appears to be and what actually is, hence "senseless," "vain," "nothing" (O. Bauernfeind, *TDNT* 4:519). The heresy discusses what on the surface appears to have substance, but in reality does not even exist. It is senseless babble, what is falsely called knowledge (1 Tim 6:20) but really is a morbid (1 Tim 6:4), stupid (Titus 3:9), and senseless (2 Tim 2:23) controversy that is unprofitable and futile (Titus 3:9). ματαιολογία occurs only here in the NT. ματαιολόγος, "senseless babbler," occurs only in Titus 1:10. The adjective μάταιος, "senseless," occurs six times: the Ephesian heresy was unprofitable and senseless (Titus 3:9); if Christ has not been raised, then the believer's faith is senseless (1 Cor 15:17); compared to the Lord, the thoughts of the wise are senseless (1 Cor 3:20); the ways of non-Christians are senseless (Acts 14:15; 1 Pet 1:18; cf. Jer 2:5; 4 Kgdms 17:15); one's religion is senseless if the tongue is not controlled (Jas 1:26). The cognate ματαιότης, "vanity," occurs some forty times in Ecclesiastes in the phrase "Vanity of vanities; all is vanity" (cf. Rom 8:20; Eph 4:17; 2 Pet 2:18). When the OT wants to ridicule idols, it can call them שָׁוְא šāwĕʾ ("vain," "non-existent"; Jer 18:15; Pss 24:4; 31:7; *NIDOTTE* 4:54–55).

From these examples it is clear that the Ephesian elders had wandered off into that which was completely and totally worthless, vain, ineffectual. This is one of Paul's most frequent charges: they do nothing but engage in senseless arguments about insignificant words. O. Bauernfeind calls it "empty prattle" (*TDNT* 4:524). Simpson says that "these whipper-snappers have an exchequer of words, but no fund of insight," and adds that this is what Philo calls "syllable squabblers" (29). By contrast, Spicq says that "the gospel message is not a rational philosophy, but an immutable divine revelation" (1:329). What a difference between the false teaching and love coming from a clean heart, clear conscience, and a sincere faith!

7 θέλοντες εἶναι νομοδιδάσκαλοι, μὴ νοοῦντες μήτε ἃ λέγουσιν μήτε περὶ τίνων διαβεβαιοῦνται, "Wishing to be teachers of the law, even though they do not understand either what they are saying or concerning what things they are so dogmatically asserting." Their senseless babble results from a desire to teach the law even though they are ignorant of it. Their desire is exceeded only by their ignorance, and this theme of their ignorance continues throughout the PE (cf. 1 Tim 6:4). Along with the overt references to the Ephesian heresy being Jewish, this verse shows that the heresy involved the OT. However, this verse also shows that the opponents were not part of Judaism proper, which could not be described as being ignorant of the law. The opponents were at best a splinter group of Judaism, and calling them a group may suggest more organization and coherence than the opponents exhibited.

The opponents' motive was a desire to teach the law or, perhaps in a less noble vein, a desire to be known as teachers of the law and to receive the admiration associated with such a position (cf. the Jewish scribes castigated by Jesus). Phillips translates, "They want a reputation as teachers of the law." In light of the tenor of v 7b, "teachers of the law" can be sarcastic, impugning their motives (although the word itself is not derogatory; Oberlinner, 19). This accords with Paul's comments elsewhere that they were teaching for the sake of money, an impure motive (1 Tim 6:5, 10; cf. 1 Tim 3:3, 8; 6:17–18; Titus 1:7; *Introduction,* "The Ephesian Heresy"). Chrysostom speaks of their love of power and preeminence ("Homily 1"; NPNF 13:413). In chap. 3 Paul will give his response to the problem: Timothy must be sure that an overseer is a skilled teacher who is able to confront and rebuke the opponents (see *Comment* on 1 Tim 3:2).

νομοδιδάσκαλοι, "teachers of the law," is a compound of νόμος, "law," and διδάσκαλος, "teacher" (for similar constructions, see ἑτεροδιδασκαλεῖν, "to teach a different gospel," in 1 Tim 1:3, and especially καλοδιδάσκαλος, "teaching what is good," in Titus 2:3). Paul does not actually specify what law they were teaching, but 1 Tim 1:8–11 suggests that it was the Mosaic law. The heresy was primarily Jewish (cf. *Introduction,* "The Ephesian Heresy"), and the two other occurrences of the word νομοδιδάσκαλος are used of Gamaliel (Acts 5:34) and the scribes (Luke 5:17), also suggesting a Jewish background (cf. K. H. Rengstorf, *TDNT* 2:159, who says the word was a Christian term that differentiated Christianity from Judaism on the essential point of the law). Another question concerns what part of the OT law they were teaching: ceremonial, moral (NEB translates "teachers of the moral law"), or all of it? Vv 8–11 deal with the moral law, but genealogies (1 Tim 1:3) are in the narrative portion of the Torah. Therefore "law" should be understood as the Mosaic law (cf. discussion of law in *Comment* on 1 Tim 1:8–11).

νοεῖν does not mean simply "to know" but rather "to understand," "to comprehend." A look at its use elsewhere in the NT implies that there is an element of contemplation as well (Matt 16:9, 11; John 12:4; Rom 1:20; Eph 3:4; Heb 11:3; cf. J. Behm, *TDNT* 4:950–51). For example, Timothy is instructed to "contemplate [νόει] on what I [Paul] say, for the Lord will give you understanding [σύνεσιν] in all things" (2 Tim 2:7; cf. 1 Cor 1:19; Eph 3:4; Col 1:9;). μὴ νοοῦντες, "not understanding," is used here as a concessive participle ("even though").

The opponents do not know ἅ λέγουσιν, "what they are saying," or περὶ τίνων διαβεβαιοῦνται, "concerning what things they are so dogmatically asserting." The two phrases are basically synonymous, their plurality emphasizing the ignorance of these so-called teachers. The shift from ἅ, "which," to τίνων, "what," need only be stylistic (but see below) since τίς, "what," was becoming a substitute for the relative pronoun (Lock, 11; Robertson, *Grammar,* 737). διαβεβαιοῦνται, "dogmatically asserting," however, is a little different from λέγουσιν, "are saying." It is a compound verb of βεβαιοῦν, meaning "to confirm," "to guarantee," with the preposition διά in its perfective use (cf. ἐκζητήσεις; 1 Tim 1:4). This gives the meaning of "to assert dogmatically," which fits this context (cf. LSJ, 390, for examples, especially the meaning "to be positive"). They are proclaiming their gospel with complete and total confidence, and with complete and total ignorance. They are devoted to their gospel (προσέχειν; v 4), preaching with dogmatic authority, and are wrong. It is no wonder that Paul begins his epistle on a note of authority. διαβεβαιοῦν, "to assert dogmatically," occurs elsewhere in the NT only in Titus 3:8 where Paul tells Titus to assert dogmatically and confidently the instructions Paul had given him.

Lock (11) mentions Hort's argument that διαβεβαιοῦνται may be a subjunctive (citing forms in 1 Cor 4:6; Gal 4:17), which would be translated "or on what points they ought to insist." Paul criticizes them not for being dogmatic but for being dogmatic about the wrong issues. This is an interesting distinction, but in light of the severity of the problem it is doubtful that Paul would want the opponents to be dogmatic about anything. Another interesting variation is Barrett's suggestion (42) that τίνων is masculine, indicating that these so-called teachers of the law did not understand the law (ἅ, neuter "which") and did not apply the law to the right people (τίνων, masculine "whom"). This interpretation would provide a link to vv 8–11, which discuss for whom the law was intended. But to differentiate the two words is perhaps too fine. If something that specific had been intended, we should expect some sort of grammatical or lexical indication. ἅ and τίνων are general terms. (Moffatt translates ἅ as "words" and τίνων as "themes.")

Explanation

At some time before the writing of this letter, Timothy had gone to Ephesus to deal with false teaching in the church. He had wanted eventually to leave Ephesus, but Paul, while on his way to Macedonia, met with Timothy and urged him to stay. Paul was now writing as a follow-up to that conversation. The situation in Ephesus was serious. Some of the people had already gone astray, and what they were teaching was foolishness. Paul launched into the matter at hand in much the same way as he did in the letter to the Galatians, not following his usual practice of expressing thanks for the people to whom he was writing. This might seem unusual in writing to a friend, but quite natural when it is realized that he was writing through Timothy to the Ephesian church. This also explains the note of authority running throughout this section. The language is strong; Timothy was to command the opponents to stop their senseless babble.

Vv 3–7 set the historical stage for the epistle. Certain people were teaching a gospel that was essentially different from Paul's. Leaders in the church were teaching myths they had created based on OT genealogies. Not only were they in error theologically, but their lifestyle was also wrong. Rather than exercising their responsibilities in the church as good stewards of God through faith, they were producing nothing except mere speculation. The goal of Timothy's command—that the false teachers stop teaching—was love. Not only was love absent in the opponents' lives, but Timothy needed to maintain love as the goal of his teaching and behavior as well. Paul's opponents had made a moral choice to set aside cleansed hearts, clear consciences, and a sincere faith. Their problem was not intellectual but moral, and their behavior was a direct result and a clear indicator of their immorality. But Paul's emphasis on their behavior did not mean that their theology was acceptable. Along with being immoral, they were charged with being ignorant of what they were dogmatically teaching.

B. The True Intention of the Law (1 Tim 1:8–11)

Bibliography

Dodd, C. H. *The Bible and the Greeks*. 1935. London: Hodder & Stoughton, 1964. **Easton, B. S.** "New Testament Ethical Lists." *JBL* 51 (1932) 1–12. **Ide, A. F.** *Battling with Beasts: Sex in the Life and Letters of St. Paul: The Issue of Homosexuality, Heterosexuality and Bisexuality*. Garland, TX: Tangelwuld, 1991. **Kamlah, E.** *Die Form der katalogischen Paränese im Neuen Testament*. Tübingen: Mohr-Siebeck, 1964. **Lagrange, M. J.** "Le catalogue de vices dans l'épître aux Romains, 1.28–31," *RB* n.s. 8 (1911) 534–49. **Malherbe, A. J.** "Medical Imagery in the Pastoral Epistles." In *Texts and Testaments: Critical Essays on the Bible and Early Christian Fathers*, ed. W. E. March. San Antonio, TX: Trinity UP, 1980. 19–35 (reprinted in A. J. Malherbe, *Paul and the Popular Philosophers* [Minneapolis: Fortress, 1989] 121–36). ———. *Moral Exhortation: A Greco-Roman Sourcebook*. Philadelphia: Westminster, 1986. **McEleney, N. J.** "The Vice Lists of the Pastoral Epistles." *CBQ* 36 (1974) 203–19. **Sabugal, S.** "El autotestimonio sobre la conversión de San Pablo en 2 Cor 4,6 y 1 Tim 1,11–14." *Revista Agustiniana de Espiritualidad* 16 (1975) 355–62. **Vögtle, A.** *Die Tugend- und Lasterkataloge: Exegetisch, religions- und formgeschichtlich untersucht*. NTAbh 16.4–5. Münster: Aschendorff, 1936. **Westerholm, S.** "The Law and the 'Just Man' (1 Tim 1:3–11)." *ST* 36 (1982) 79–95. **Wibbing, S.** *Die Tugend- und Lasterkataloge im Neuen Testament und ihr Traditionsgeschichte unter besonderer Berücksichtigung der Qumran-Texte*. BZNW 25. Berlin: Töpelmann, 1959.

Translation

[8] *But we know that the law is good if someone uses* [a] *it lawfully,* [9] *knowing this, that law is not valid for a righteous person but for [the] lawless and rebellious, irreligious and sinners, unholy and profane, those who beat their fathers and mothers, murderers,* [10] *fornicators, homosexuals, kidnappers, liars, perjurers, and everything else that is contrary to healthy teaching,* [11] *which is in conformity to the gospel of the glory of the blessed God with which I was entrusted.*

Notes

[a] The present is replaced with the aorist χρήσηται, "used," by A P; Cl.

Form/Structure/Setting

Vv 8–11 constitute the second of four subsections in vv 3–20. On the surface they may appear to be a digression. Paul used the sarcastic title "teachers of the law" in v 7, and it is possible that vv 8–11 are a correction of any possible misconception that he has a low view of the law. But vv 8–11 are more than that. Vv 3–20 set the stage for the rest of the epistle. The heresy as described in vv 3–7 has two flaws: (1) a misuse of the law (1 Tim 1:8–11) and (2) a corresponding misunderstanding of the role of God's grace and mercy in salvation (1 Tim 1:12–17). The paragraph forms an integral part of the response of the epistle to the Ephesian situation, acting as a corrective to the opponents (cf. Spicq, 1:330, 332–33; *Form/Structure/Setting* on 1 Tim 1:3–7).

The opponents have misunderstood the law. They are probably saying that Paul did not think the law was good. Vv 8–10 assert that the law is good but it must be used as it was intended. It does not apply to everyone but only to those living unrighteously. Those who are righteous in Christ live according to a principle entirely different from the Mosaic law. Their righteous conduct is the outward expression of an inner transformation brought about by the indwelling presence of God. The opponents' misunderstanding of the law's function has led to spiritual sickness. Paul's gospel, on the other hand, brings spiritual health, revealing God's wondrous glory. This gospel was entrusted to Paul by the blessed God, and the church must therefore listen to what Paul says.

Vv 8–11 do not provide a complete presentation of Paul's view of the law. Even the discussions in Romans and Galatians are limited. The PE present only Paul's view of the law that is relevant to the historical situation. The literature on Paul and the law has mushroomed since Sanders's work, *Paul and Palestinian Judaism: A Comparison of Patterns of Religion* (Philadelphia: Fortress, 1977). For a summary see T. Schreiner, *Paul and the Law* (Grand Rapids, MI: Baker, 1994), and his bibliography.

The list of fourteen vices in vv 9–10 describes the kinds of people for whom the law was laid down and contrasts them with the one kind of person—the "just"—for whom the law was not intended. The list follows distinctive, yet inconsistent, literary patterns. Paul pairs twelve terms into eight groups. He also employs alliteration with an initial alpha, most of the words being formed with an alpha privative much like the English *un-*. The salient feature of the vice list is its resemblance to the Decalogue, upon which it is based. The first three couplets are offenses against God, corresponding to the first four commandments in the Decalogue. The remaining vices, offenses against people, correspond to the next five commandments:

those who beat their fathers and mothers	Honor your father and mother (Exod 20:12; Deut 5:16).
murderers	You shall not kill (Exod 20:13; Deut 5:17).
fornicators, homosexuals	You shall not commit adultery (Exod 20:14; Deut 5:18).
kidnappers	You shall not steal (Exod 20:15; Deut 5:19).
liars, perjurers	You shall not bear false witness (Exod 20:16; Deut 5:20).

Paul rounds off the list by adding "and everything else that is contrary to healthy teaching." The language Paul uses is somewhat rare in comparison to the LXX, but it is not surprising that Paul uses contemporary terms since only three of the commandments are single words (plus the negation) and the nature of the vice list requires single words (so Knight, 87–88).

Vice lists are common in Paul (Rom 1:29–31; 6:9–10; 13:13; 1 Cor 5:10–11; 2 Cor 6:9–10; 12:20; Gal 5:19–21; Eph 4:31; 5:3–5; Col 3:5, 8; 1 Tim 6:4–5; Titus 3:3; 2 Tim 3:2–5; cf. 1 Pet 4:3; Wis 14:25–26; *3 Apoc. Bar.* 4:17; 8:5; 13:4; *T. Reub.* 3:3–6; *T. Jud.* 16:1; *2 Enoch* 10:4–5) and in the Hellenistic world (cf. Malherbe, *Moral Exhortation*, 138–41). They are not found in rabbinic Judaism, but Qumran produced a double list of good and evil qualities (1QS 4:2–6, 9–11). Vögtle sees the origin of the NT vice lists in Hellenistic philosophy and Wibbing in Judaism, but McEleney stresses that there was not one source from which Paul drew. He was influenced by the OT, by the historical Jewish polemic against idol worship, and by Hellenism. Although some vices appear in more than one Pauline list, no one vice appears in all the lists. It is not clear whether this list in the PE describes the actual sins of the opponents or it is a list of general sins unrelated to any specific historical situation. The first six vices have parallels in the Ephesian situation (see *Comment*) and are most likely addressed to the opponents. But the vices that more closely follow the Decalogue have such significant social repercussions—beating parents, murder, adultery, sexual perversion, kidnapping, lying, perjury—that we would expect a more specific condemnation from Paul if in fact the opponents were guilty of these specific sins. While Paul's condemnation can be strong (1 Tim 1:7, 20; 4:1–3; 6:3–6; Titus 1:12–13; 2 Tim 3:3–8), he focuses on the opponents' ignorance, immorality, and irrelevance (see *Introduction*, "The Ephesian Heresy").

Vice lists tend to be general (Dibelius-Conzelmann, 22–23, liken them to the effects of public posters) and to include especially heinous sins. The suggestion is that Paul is not describing the specific sins of the opponents but rather is describing in general the type of person for whom the law is still applicable. In other words, Paul is not accusing the opponents of murder, etc. It would be wrong, however, to divorce the vice list totally from the opponents since elsewhere some of these descriptions are applied to the opponents and since Paul ties his pre-Christian life to these sins (1:13). For further study, see McEleney, *CBQ* 36 (1974) 203–19; Vögtle, *Tugend- und Lasterkataloge;* Wibbing, *Tugend- und Lasterkataloge;* Easton, *JBL* 51 (1932) 1–12; Kamlah, *Form;* Lagrange, *RB* n.s. 8 (1911) 523–49; and O. J. F. Seitz, *IDB* 3:137–39.

Comment

8 Οἴδαμεν δὲ ὅτι καλὸς ὁ νόμος ἐάν τις αὐτῷ νομίμως χρῆται, "But we know that the law is good if someone uses it lawfully." δέ, "but," carries its full adversative force with the accent of the sentence on "we" and "if." Just because the law is good does not mean that the opponents are justified in basing their myths on it. The law has specific functions and limitations, and these must be respected (cf. Spicq, 1:330). It is when this is recognized that the law is used νομίμως, "lawfully." In vv 9–10 Paul will spell out what he means by "lawfully." If we read between the lines, we can see the charge by his opponents that Paul is antinomian. Paul's theology, they allege, does away with the law, and they are restoring it to its proper place. Paul begins by pointing out that they have misunderstood his position and that both he and the opponents do agree on one essential point: the law is good (so Bernard, 26; Ellicott, 27). But, Paul adds, the law must be used as it was intended, lawfully. Elsewhere in his writings Paul identifies other limitations regarding the use of the law. For example, in Gal 3:24–25 Paul asserts that the law was intended to lead people to Christ (justification by faith) and that after Christ they are "no longer under a custodian." In Rom 3:20 Paul speaks about the law bringing knowledge of sin, making it impossible for someone to be justified by works of the law. Chrysostom says that Paul censures the opponents "because they know not the end and the aim of the law, nor the period for which it was to have authority" ("Homily 2"; NPNF 13:413). He continues by discussing practical ways the law is used lawfully and concludes that the righteous person (i.e., the Christian) keeps the law through desire, not fear of punishment, led by "the grace of the Spirit" (NPNF 13:413–14).

Paul does not specify what he means by ὁ νόμος, "the law" (see below on the "just" person). In this verse it seems clear, however, that Paul is speaking of the Jewish law, the OT (or just the Mosaic law), as opposed to a general moral law and order of life (*Lebensordnung;* Oberlinner, 24). (1) It can be generally assumed that when Paul refers to law, he is thinking of the Mosaic law unless context requires otherwise. (2) Paul is contrasting his view of the law with that of the opponents (v 7), who are devoted to the Jewish law (Titus 1:10, 14). (3) Paul goes on to discuss the Decalogue. (4) The presence of the article suggests Paul refers to the specific (i.e., Jewish) law and not law in general. But is Paul speaking of the OT as a whole, the Torah in particular, or the moral law within the Torah? He refers in the context to genealogies (v 4), which occur in the narrative material of the Pentateuch, and to elements of the Decalogue (vv 9–10), which suggest that he is thinking at least of the Mosaic law. It does not appear, however, that the opponents have an articulated, well-defined belief structure based on the OT that can be analyzed.

οἴδαμεν δέ, "but we know," is typical for Paul (Rom 2:2; 3:19; 8:28; 1 Cor 8:1, 4; 2 Cor 5:1; Spicq, 1:330). οἶδα originally meant "to perceive," "to realize," "to know" in the absolute sense; γινώσκειν meant "to come to know," emphasizing the process or the end of the process. At times this distinction can still be felt in Hellenistic literature (cf. Lightfoot, *Galatians,* 171) although the two terms can be used synonymously (MM, 439–40; H. Seesemann, *TDNT* 2:116). οἶδα here, however, is closer to the older meaning of γινώσκειν. The plural "we" includes Timothy and perhaps other like-minded people who disagree with the opponents.

The statement that the law is καλός, "good," is also typical for Paul (Rom 7:14, 16; cf. 2 Tim 3:15–17; Brox, 105). The law is good because it accurately reflects the will of God and is beneficial to people (Cranfield, *Romans* 1:354). Originally καλός meant aesthetically "good, beautiful"; ἀγαθός denoted a moral, ethical, spiritual "good" (Quinn, 175; W. Grundmann, *TDNT* 1:10; 2:98). This difference can still be seen in the Koine (Lock, 22–23), although not in the PE where the terms are used synonymously as in 1 Tim 5:10. The PE also fluctuate between καλός and ἀγαθός in the phrase "good work(s)" (see *Comment* on 1 Tim 2:10; καλός: 1 Tim 3:1; 5:10, 25; 6:18; Titus 2:7, 14; 3:8, 14; ἀγαθός: 1 Tim 2:10; 5:10; 2 Tim 2:21; 3:17; Titus 1:16; 3:1).

Good is a major theme in the PE. καλός is used twenty-four times and ἀγαθός ten (see *Comment* on 1 Tim 2:10). Seven times καλός describes "good" or "proper" conduct (1 Tim 1:18; 2:3; 3:7; Titus 3:8), especially in connection with the imagery of warfare (1 Tim 6:12; 2 Tim 4:7 ["good fight"]; 2 Tim 2:3 ["good soldier"]; cf. καλῶς used in connection with managing a family "well" [1 Tim 3:4, 12] and church leaders ruling "well" [1 Tim 3:13; 5:17]). Seventeen times καλός describes the quality of something as "good": law (1 Tim 1:8); standing of the deacons (3:13); God's creation (4:4); Timothy as a good minister (4:6); doctrine (4:6); confessions of Timothy and Christ (6:12, 13); foundation in heaven (6:19); covenant (2 Tim 1:14; see summaries by Quinn, 175; W. Grundmann, *TDNT* 3:549–50; R. C. Togtman, *ISBE* 2:525–26; Lock, 22–23; Spicq, "Excurses VIII. Vie Chrétienne et Beauté," 2:676–84). Paul is concerned not only that Christians believe the correct things but also that they behave properly.

ἐάν τις, "if someone," introduces a present general conditional sentence (Burton, *Syntax* §260). τὶς, "someone," is not a reference to the opponents (cf. v 3) but an indefinite reference appropriate to an axiomatic truth (which includes the opponents). νομίμως, "lawfully," is a wordplay (paronomasia): the law must be used lawfully, as it was intended, i.e., "appropriately" (cf. Plato *Symposium* 182A). Paul spells this out in the following verse. νομίμως occurs elsewhere in the NT only in 2 Tim 2:5, which says that an athlete must compete lawfully, according to the rules (cf. W. Gutbrod, *TDNT* 4:1088–89). Spicq argues that the word was used in Jewish-Hellenistic circles for conformity to the law (1:331; cf. Josephus *Ag. Ap.* 2.152, 218; 4 Macc 6:18).

9–10 εἰδὼς τοῦτο, ὅτι δικαίῳ νόμος οὐ κεῖται, ἀνόμοις δὲ καὶ ἀνυποτάκτοις, ἀσεβέσι καὶ ἁμαρτωλοῖς, ἀνοσίοις καὶ βεβήλοις, πατρολῴαις καὶ μητρολῴαις, ἀνδροφόνοις, πόρνοις, ἀρσενοκοίταις, ἀνδραποδισταῖς, ψεύσταις, ἐπιόρκοις, καὶ εἴ τι ἕτερον τῇ ὑγιαινούσῃ διδασκαλίᾳ ἀντίκειται, "knowing this, that law is not valid for a righteous person but for [the] lawless and rebellious, irreligious and sinners, unholy and profane, those who beat their fathers and mothers, murderers, fornicators, homosexuals, kidnappers, liars, perjurers, and everything else that is contrary to healthy teaching." Paul explains more precisely how the law is to be used lawfully. It is not to be applied to everyone, for some are living righteously. Rather, the law is for those living sinful lives. Spicq (1:331) compares Rom 3:19: "Now we know that whatever the law says it speaks to those who are under the law." Paul lists eight types of people and then sums up all other examples in the phrase "everything else that is contrary to healthy teaching." Chrysostom is too restrictive in applying these verses only to the Jews ("Homily 2"; NPNF 13:414); the function of the law is for all.

The identity of νόμος, "law," is tied up with the identity of the δικαίῳ, "righteous person," and the two must be discussed together. The task of interpretation is hampered by the fact that Paul does not launch into a full discussion of the topic, which would have been inappropriate since he is writing to Timothy, who already understood his theology. Paul is emphasizing only one aspect of the law relevant to the Ephesian situation, of which we have only glimpses. Paul also does not tell us to whom the law does not apply; he only tells us that the opponents have misunderstood the law and are improperly basing their myths on its genealogies and in some way improperly applying the law to all people (cf. S. Westerholm, *ST* 36 [1982] 83).

One approach interprets νόμος, "law," here as law in general, rules to govern people and nations. The δικαίῳ, "righteous person," thus is a "decent citizen" (Easton, 110). The passage then reflects a common thought in Hellenism that some people are self-regulated and do not need law while others require external regulation (references in S. Westerholm, *ST* 36 [1982] 88–89). Dibelius-Conzelmann refer to the golden age of Stoicism when no law will be required (22; cf. references in Lock, 11–12; Quinn, 14). Others follow this understanding of the "just" person but say that the "law" is the Mosaic law. On this interpretation the passage is often judged to be non-Pauline (a "positive travesty of [Paul's] teaching" [Houlden, 53]; "nothing could be further from Paul's teaching" [Hanson, (1983) 25]). But there are factors that weigh against this interpretation: (1) The listed sins are contrasted with both the "just person" and the "healthy teaching, which is in conformity with the gospel" (vv 10b–11a), thus aligning the "just person" with the gospel and suggesting that Paul is thinking of the Christian. (2) The author of the PE sees conversion as a necessity. Having identified Paul with sinners in vv 8–11, the author declares that Paul was saved from his sin as an example of salvation by faith (vv 12–17), which is in line with Christ's basic desire to save sinners (v 15; cf. 2:4). God has saved people out of their sin, justifying them by his grace (Titus 3:3–7; cf. 2:11–12). If "law" is the Mosaic law, that which leads one to Christ (Gal 3:24), the author would not say conversion and the law are unnecessary for a decent person. (3) The PE show little concern for people outside the church, except that the Ephesian Christians should not behave so badly that outsiders will look with disgust on the church. V 9 would be out of context if it referred to a non-Christian. (4) It seems likely that Paul is speaking not of law in general but of the Mosaic law. Although "law" here is anarthrous, it is articular in the preceding verse, and the following verses deal with the Decalogue. The anarthrous "law" also can designate the Mosaic law in Paul (cf. Rom 2:25; 3:20; Gal 2:19; 6:13; W. Gutbrod, *TDNT* 4:1070). It therefore seems doubtful that Paul is speaking of a "decent citizen" who does not need secular law or the Mosaic law.

A second approach sees the "righteous person" as one who is justified by Christ's work and lives by faith, not by the law (Spicq, 1:332; cf. Rom 1:17; 5:19; Gal 3:11; Heb 12:23), and "law" as the Mosaic law. In line with Pauline thought elsewhere, but not expressed here, the law functions to reveal sin (Rom 3:20; 5:13; 7:7–12; 1 Cor 15:56; Gal 3:19). The law is good (Rom 7:7, 12, 14; 3:31), but human sin has made it ineffectual (Rom 7:13–25; 8:3) because it could not empower a person to follow the law. The righteous have outgrown the law (Rom 7:1–4; Gal 3:19, 23–4:7), have died to it (Rom 7:6; Gal 2:19), and are now captive to the law of Christ (Rom 7:4–6, 22, 25; 8:2, 7), slaves of righteousness (Rom 6:18) and of God (Rom 6:22; Gal 2:19), not under the law but under grace (Rom 6:14). This does not mean that the Christian and the law have nothing in common. It means that the Mosaic law is not the key to righteous living, and the commandments are summed up in the command to love God and one's neighbor: "Love does no wrong to a neighbor; therefore love is the fulfilling of the law" (Rom 13:9–10; cf. Gal 5:14). While δίκαιος, "righteous," can describe a person who is moral and ethical, it can also describe someone who in the fullest Christian sense has been made righteous, justified through faith in Christ (cf. Jeremias, Roloff, Spicq, Oberlinner, Guthrie, Kelly, L. T. Johnson, Towner), and is living a righteous life.

There remains one matter to decide. Is Paul thinking of δίκαιος, "righteous," in the sense of one's standing before God or one's righteous behavior? Because of the need for conversion expressed throughout the PE, the second option would assume the first: the only person who lives righteously is the one who has been made righteous. This question is tied into a much larger issue: what are the opponents teaching about the law? Are they teaching a law-based works righteousness, or are they accepting salvation by faith but asserting that the Christian lifestyle is governed by their reinterpretation of the Mosaic law? In other words, do the myths (v 4) deal with salvation, or sanctification, or both? (1) There are indications that the opponents are primarily concerned with lifestyle: (a) They are teaching asceticism (no marriage, abstinence from certain foods [1 Tim 4:3], possibly downplaying childbearing [1 Tim 2:15]), and a spiritualized resurrection typical of Greek dualism. (b) The vice list can be understood to speak of lifestyles. (c) δικαιοσύνη, "righteousness," in the PE is primarily a virtue to be pursued (see below). (d) The primary critique of the opponents is in reference to their behavior. (e) If the opponents were teaching works righteousness, we would expect Paul or even a pseudepigrapher imitating him to answer more in line with Galatians. (2) But there are also indications that the opponents are using the law and their myths to teach their own form of salvation: (a) V 4 and vv 12–17 suggest that the opponents adhere to the law to the exclusion of faith, a factor more relevant to salvation. (b) The theme of 1:15, which occurs in a paragraph specifically intended to counter the opponents' use of the law, is salvation for all (cf. also 1 Tim 2:4, 5–6). (c) Since the opponents are Jewish (cf. Titus 1:10, 14), it is difficult to envision them not using the law in relation to salvation. (d) While Paul does not deal with the debate as he does in Galatians, this may be explained by the historical context. Unlike the Galatian church, Timothy knows and accepts Paul's teaching on justification by faith. Also, the heresy is most likely not a cohesive, well-thought-out system of beliefs. As Westerholm suggests, "Their interest in the law was a selective one indeed, the uses they made of it being determined less by the structure and content of the Pentateuch itself than by patterns of thought and behavior which they brought to the text and attempted to foist on it" (*ST* 36 [1982] 80). Issues such as circumcision may not have played a role as might be expected in a Hellenistic milieu (*Introduction*, "The Ephesian Heresy"). Although δίκαιος is used in the PE primarily of sanctification, it is also used of salvation (Titus 3:7). Of course, both these options can work together, and Paul is stressing that the opponents' application of the law to all people is wrong; it does not apply to the Christian who is made righteous through faith and who lives righteously. Because of the lack of clarity, perhaps it is best not to try to be more precise; perhaps the opponents were not any more precise in their empty prattle.

εἰδὼς τοῦτο, "because we know this," is a causal participle giving the reason that the statement in v 8 is true (the ὅτι, "that," clause). The subsequent ὅτι clause is in apposition to τοῦτο, "this" (Wallace, *Greek Grammar*, 459). It modifies οἴδαμεν, "we know" (v 8), and perhaps includes anyone else who understands how the law is to be used lawfully. κεῖται, "is . . . valid," can be a technical term for legal matters (BAGD, 426 [2b]; Spicq, 1:331).

Righteousness is a significant theme in Paul's theology. It is forensic in that the righteous person is declared not guilty and eschatological in that the person will ultimately be declared righteous at the final judgment. It is not only a gift appropriated by faith but also a virtue to be sought. Since the work of E. Käsemann and others, the transforming nature of righteousness has been correctly emphasized. Righteousness is not just a gift to be given but a virtue to be pursued (Rom 6:13; 14:17; 2 Cor 6:14; 11:15; Eph 5:9; Phil 1:11 [Hawthorne, *Philippians*, 29]; cf. Acts 10:35; 13:10; 24:25; cf. E. Käsemann, "The Righteousness of God in Paul," in *New Testament Questions of Today* [Philadelphia: Fortress, 1969] 168–82; P. Stuhlmacher, *Gerechtigkeit Gottes bei Paulus*, FRLANT 87 [Göttingen: Vandenhoeck & Ruprecht, 1966]; id., "The Apostle Paul's View of Righteousness," in *Reconciliation, Law, and Righteousness: Essays in Biblical Theology* [Philadelphia: Fortress, 1986] 68–93; J. Reumann, *Righteousness in the New Testament* [Philadelphia: Fortress, 1982]; R. P. Martin, *Reconciliation: A Study in Paul's Theology* [Atlanta: John Knox, 1981] 32–37). Fee comments on 1 Cor 3:14–15, "What began in the present as gift is to be persevered in, righteously, and thus consummated at the final glory, which is also a gift. For Paul righteousness is both *Gabe* and *Aufgabe* (gift and responsibility). Without the latter, one might surely question the reality of the former" (*Corinthians*, 143; citing further, K. P. Donfried, "Justification and Last Judgment in Paul," *Int* 30 [1976] 140–52).

This double aspect, gift and transformation, is present in the PE in the use of δίκαιος, "righteous," and cognates, which appear ten times. The Lord is a righteous judge (2 Tim 4:8). A crown of righteousness awaits Paul (2 Tim 4:8). God poured out the Holy Spirit in order that believers might be justified (Titus 3:7). Salvation does not come because of works done in righteousness (Titus 3:5). Righteousness is to be a quality of those who call upon the Lord (2 Tim 2:22), for God's grace came so that believers might live sober, righteous, and truly religious lives (Titus 2:12). With a somewhat different meaning, a hymn says that Jesus was "justified in spirit" (1 Tim 3:16). For summaries of Paul's use of δίκαιος, "righteous," see references cited above and bibliography in T. Schreiner, *Interpreting the Pauline Epistles* (Grand Rapids, MI: Baker, 1990) 133 n. 7; P. Stuhlmacher, "The Apostle Paul's View of Righteousness," in *Reconciliation, Law, and Righteousness: Essays in Biblical Theology* (Philadelphia: Fortress, 1986) 68–93; Ladd, *Theology*, 437–49 (bibliography on p. 437); Guthrie, *New Testament Theology*, 492–504; O. Schrenk and G. Quell, *TDNT* 2:174–225; H. Seebass and C. Brown, *NIDNTT* 3:352–77 (bibliography on pp. 374–77).

Paul now begins his list of those for whom the law is still in effect. (1) ἀνόμοις δὲ καὶ ἀνυποτάκτοις, "lawless and rebellious." δέ, "but," firmly separates the just (v 9a) from the unjust (vv 9b–10). The adjectives describe people who oppose the law. To use the law lawfully is to apply it to those who oppose it. Ellicott suggests that ἀνόμοις may refer to a "passive regard" while ἀνυποτάκτοις may refer to "a more active violation of it arising from a refractory will" (11). The phrase "lawless and rebellious" is probably introductory since both words describe antilaw attitudes and contrast most clearly with the preceding (cf. Knight, 85). The law is not for the just but rather for those who oppose the law; the fact that δέ, "but," is not repeated with the other vices may suggest that these two adjectives are more closely associated with the law. ἄνομος is a compound of an alpha privative, "not," and νόμος, "law." It describes someone who follows no law, or someone who fights against the law. Here it would be the latter since the opponents followed their understanding of the law but were so wrong that they were actually fighting its true intention. ἄνομος, "lawless," does not occur again in the PE (cf. 1 Cor 9:21; 2

Thess 2:8; cf. Luke 22:37; Acts 2:23; 2 Pet 2:8), although the noun ἀνομία, "lawlessness," is used to say that Christ redeemed believers from lawlessness (Titus 2:14; cf. Rom 4:7; 6:19; 2 Cor 6:14; 2 Thess 2:3, 7; cf. Matt 7:23; 13:41; 23:28; 24:12; Heb 1:9; 10:17; 1 John 3:4; W. Gutbrod, *TDNT* 4:1085–86). ἀνυπότακτος, "rebellious," is a compound of an alpha privative, "not," and ὑπότακτος, "submissive" (cf. ὑποταγή, "submission"; 1 Tim 3:4, 11). Here it is synonymous with ἄνομις, "lawless," describing someone who is not under subjection to the true intention of the law. The word occurs elsewhere in the NT only in Titus 1:6 (of rebellious children) and 1:10 (of the rebellious opponents). ὑπότακτος, "submissive," and the cognate verb (ὑποτάσσειν) occur with more frequency than does ἀνυπότακτος, "rebellious" (cf. G. Delling, *TDNT* 8:47; the concept of submission is discussed in the *Comment* on 1 Tim 2:11).

(2) ἀσεβέσι καὶ ἁμαρτωλοῖς, "irreligious and sinners." ἀσεβής, "irreligious," is a compound of an alpha privative, "not," and the root σεβ-, "worship." It is the opposite of εὐσέβεια, "reverence," which is a major emphasis in the PE, describing a truly religious person (cf. 1 Tim 2:2). Fee (10) and Bernard (27) say that ἀσεβής, "irreligious," corresponds to inward irreverence and ἁμαρτωλός, "sinner," to outward disobedience. ἀσεβής, "irreligious," does not occur again in the PE (cf. Rom 4:5; 5:6; 1 Pet 4:18; 2 Pet 2:5, 6; 3:7; Jude 4, 15), although its cognate noun ἀσέβεια, "irreverence," does (2 Tim 2:16; Titus 2:12). ἁμαρτωλοῖς, "sinners," breaks the pattern of words formed with the alpha privative, although it does continue the alliteration of the passage. The term occurs elsewhere in 1 Tim 1:15, which says that sinners are the object of God's salvation (cognate in 1 Tim 5:20–22). Both words are paired in 1 Pet 4:18 and Jude 15.

(3) ἀνοσίοις καὶ βεβήλοις, "unholy and profane." Again, both words are basically synonymous, denoting conduct that is directly opposed to God. ἀνόσιος, "unholy," continues the pattern of compound words formed with the alpha privative, "not" (ἀν- when the following word begins with a vowel), and in this case ὅσιος, "holy." The basic idea of ὅσιος, "holy," is the sphere in which God is encountered as opposed to the "profane," which is everything else. ἀνόσιος, "unholy," conduct is behavior inappropriate within the sphere of the divine. ἀνόσιος occurs elsewhere in the NT only in 2 Tim 3:2, where it describes the unholy people who will come in the last days. The adverb ὁσίως, "in a holy manner," occurs in the NT only in 1 Thess 2:10, describing Paul's earlier conduct in Thessalonica. ὅσιος, "holy," appears in the NT eight times, including 1 Tim 2:8 (men should lift up holy hands in prayer) and Titus 1:8 (holiness is to be a quality of elders). In the LXX, ὅσιος translates the Hebrew חסיד *ḥāsîd*, "the man who readily accepts the obligations which arise from the people's relationship to God" (H. Seebass, *NIDNTT* 2:237), and is connected with the concept of the covenant through the term חסד *ḥesed*, "covenantal faithfulness." The parallel term ἅγιος, "holy," and cognates occur six times in the PE. They describe the Holy Spirit (2 Tim 1:14; Titus 3:5), God's holy calling (2 Tim 1:9), the saints (1 Tim 5:10), food made holy by the word of God and prayer (1 Tim 4:5), and purified (ἡγιασμένον) vessels of noble use (2 Tim 2:21; cf. MM, 460; Cremer, *Lexicon*, 462–64; F. Hauck, *TDNT* 5:489–92). Elsewhere in the NT ὅσιος is applied to Christ as the Messiah in OT quotations (Acts 2:27; 13:34, 35) and as the high priest (Heb 7:26), as well as to God the Father (Rev 15:4; 16:5). ἁγιασμός, "holiness," occurs in the PE only in 1 Tim 2:15, describing a quality necessary for salvation.

βέβηλος, "profane," breaks the alliteration of the passage but continues the pattern of pairing synonymous terms. The term designates a place that is accessible to anyone (F. Hauck, *TDNT* 1:604). In the LXX it translates 'חל *ḥēl*, that which can be approached or used without ceremony. For example, Ahimelech told David that he had no "ordinary" bread in the temple (1 Sam 21:4 [MT 5]). In the PE it commonly describes the opponents (1 Tim 1:9; cf. Heb 12:16) and their heresy (1 Tim 4:7; 6:20; 2 Tim 2:16), showing that Paul intended the vice list to be understood within the Ephesian context. It is found throughout the OT and NT, and therefore does not necessarily refer to Gnostic myths (contra F. Hauck, *TDNT* 1:605). Its verbal cognate βεβηλοῦν, "to desecrate," describes the desecration of the Sabbath (Matt 12:5) and the temple (Acts 24:6), examples showing its cultic usage.

(4) πατρολῴαις καὶ μητρολῴαις, "those who beat their fathers and mothers." Paul now begins to follow the second half of the Decalogue, which concerns conduct toward a neighbor (see *Form/Structure/Setting*). The fifth commandment is "Honor your father and your mother" (Exod 20:12; Deut 5:16). Both Pauline words are compounds of πατήρ/μήτηρ, "father/mother," and ἀλοᾶν, "to hit, crush, destroy" (LSJ, 72). These compounds could mean either "smiters" (classical references in Ellicott, 11) or "murderers" of parents (parricide, the only option in BAGD). Since Paul's next description is "murderer," here he is probably thinking of those striking their parents; otherwise both vices would refer to the same activity, and Paul would be unnecessarily repetitious. Also, since beating would be more common than killing one's parents, the former would be more appropriate in a vice list (Ellicott, 11). The fifth commandment was so important that if a son proved to be stubborn and rebellious, let alone strike a parent (Exod 21:15; cf. Lev 20:9), he was to be stoned (Deut 21:18–21). This is the only place in the NT where these two words occur; they do not occur in the LXX. The OT does not appear to have a technical term for parricide.

(5) ἀνδροφόνοις, "murderers." The sixth commandment is "You shall not kill" (Exod 20:13). The alliterative pattern is repeated with another compound word beginning with alpha: ἀνήρ, "man," plus φόνος, "murder." The simple φονεύς, "murderer," is more common (seven times in the NT) than the compound ἀνδροφόνος (only here in the NT; cf. 2 Macc 9:28; Acts 3:14 has ἄνδρα φονέα, "a man, a murderer"). The compound is probably chosen for stylistic reasons since the vice list contains many compound words. Murder was a capital offense in the OT.

(6) πόρνοις ἀρσενοκοίταις, "fornicators, homosexuals." The seventh commandment is "You shall not commit adultery" (Exod 20:14; Deut 5:18). In our list, the two words describe two different ways in which that commandment can be broken; Paul is interpreting the commandment in a wider sense than adultery (see "liars" below). The first word refers to male fornicators, and the second to sexual relations with the same sex. πόρνος, "fornicator," can be a male prostitute or, less specifically, someone practicing illicit sexual relations (perhaps more broadly, "immoral person"; 1 Cor 5:9–11; 6:9; Eph 5:5; Heb 12:16; 13:14; Rev 21:8; 22:15; cf. Matt 5:32, where πορνεία, "fornication," and μοιχεύειν, "to commit adultery," are juxtaposed; F. Hauck and S. Schulz, *TDNT* 6:579–95; H. Reisser, *NIDNTT* 1:497–501). Neither πόρνος, "fornicator," nor its cognates occur elsewhere in the PE.

ἀρσενοκοίτης is a compound of ἄρσην, "male" (continuing the alliteration of the list), and κοίτη, "bed" (cf. Luke 11:7, especially the marriage bed [Heb 13:4]). Its meaning has come under detailed discussion with philology (whether it refers to the *act* of a male sleeping with a male, or the *attitude/condition* of a same-sex orientation) and the appropriateness of the translation "homosexual" in light of its meaning today. The task is made difficult by the fact that ἀρσενοκοίτης is rare and does not appear to have existed before the time of Paul. D. S. Bailey argues that it refers just to the sex act with someone of the same sex (*Homosexuality and the Western Christian Tradition* [London: Longmans, Green, 1975]). J. Boswell says that it refers to "active male prostitutes," arguing that the first half of the word ("male") refers not to the object of the second half ("to sleep", i.e., to sleep with males) but to the subject (i.e., a male who sleeps; *Christianity, Social Tolerance and Homosexuality* [Chicago: Chicago UP, 1980]). R. Scroggs says it refers to a male who uses an "effeminate call-boy" (*The New Testament and Homosexuality* [Philadelphia: Fortress, 1983] 108; cf. also W. L. Petersen, "Can ΑΡΣΕΝΟΚΟΙΤΑΙ Be Translated by 'Homosexual'? [1 Cor 6.9; 1 Tim 1.10]," *VC* 40 [1986] 187–91). These positions are summarized and evaluated by D. F. Wright ("Homosexuals or Prostitutes? The Meaning of ΑΡΣΕΝΟΚΟΙΤΑΙ [1 Cor. 6:9, 1 Tim. 1:10]," *VC* 38 [1984] 125–53), J. B. de Young ("The Source and NT Meaning of *ARSENOKOITAI*, with Implications for Christian Ethics and Ministry," *Masters Seminary Journal* 3.2 [1992] 191–215, who argues that Paul coined the word based on Lev 20:13 [ὃς ἂν κοιμηθῇ μετὰ ἄρσενος κοίτην γυναικός, "whoever sleeps with a man as in the bed of a woman"]), and R. B. Hays ("Relations Natural and Unnatural: A Response to John Boswell's Exegesis of Romans 1," *JRE* 14.1 [1986] 184–215). Wright especially argues that the evidence does not support Boswell's conclusion, that Paul's argument is based on the OT prohibition in Lev 18:22 and 20:13, and that the term should be understood generally to mean "homosexual," including but not limited to the most common form in Greek culture, i.e., an adult male with a male teenager (παιδοφθορία, "pederasty"). BAGD defines ἀρσενοκοίτης as a "male homosexual" (109; cf. NASB; cf. Rom 1:27), or a man who has sexual relations with a young boy (pederast) or with animals (one who engages in bestiality). It occurs elsewhere in the NT only in 1 Cor 6:9–10 in a similar list of vices that includes πόρνος, "fornicator": "Do you not know that the wicked [ἄδικοι] will not inherit the kingdom of God? Do not be deceived: Neither the sexually immoral [πόρνοι] nor idolaters nor adulterers [μοιχοί] nor male prostitutes [μαλακοί] nor homosexual offenders [ἀρσενοκοῖται] nor thieves nor the greedy nor drunkards nor slanderers nor swindlers will inherit the kingdom of God" (NIV; the NRSV translates "male prostitutes, sodomites"; the RSV combines the last two in v 9 as "sexual perverts"). Whatever the specific meaning of ἀρσενοκοίτης in 1 Tim 1:10, it denotes a type of illicit sexual activity that breaks the seventh commandment. Fornication (H. Reisser, *NIDNTT* 1:498–99), homosexuality (Lev 18:22; 20:13; Rom 1:27; 1 Cor 6:9; cf. Wis 14:26), and bestiality (Exod 22:19; Lev 18:23; 20:15; Deut 23:18; 27:21; bibliography in B. L. Eichler, *IDB* 5:97) are prohibited in the OT and NT, the latter two punishable by death in the OT. Hanson ([1983] 59) says there is evidence that homosexuality was especially common in Ephesus. For further study, see T. Schmidt, *Straight and Narrow? Compassion and Clarity in the Homosexual Debate* (Downers Grove, IL: InterVarsity Press, 1995); bibliography in Oberlinner.

(7) ἀνδραποδισταῖς, "kidnappers." The eighth commandment is "You shall not steal" (Exod 20:15; Deut 5:19). ἀνδραποδιστής, "kidnapper," is another compound

word beginning with alpha and means either a slave trader or a kidnapper. Slavery and kidnapping were considered theft where the booty was human (cf. Str-B 1:810–13; Philo *Spec. Leg.* 4.4). McEleney (*CBQ* 36 [1974] 209) refers to A. Alt's argument that the eighth commandment originally prohibited kidnapping a free Israelite man. The penalty for kidnapping in the OT was death (Exod 21:16; Deut 24:7). Because of the crassness of the term, it was not used as often as δοῦλος, "slave" (MM, 40). This is the only occurrence of the word in the Greek Bible (cf. C. Spicq, "Vocabulaire de l'esclavage dans le Nouveau Testament," *RB* 85 [1978] 201–6).

(8) ψεύσταις ἐπιόρκοις, "liars, perjurers." The ninth commandment is "You shall not bear false witness against your neighbor" (Exod 20:16; Deut 5:20). A "liar" is someone who swears what is untrue, or someone who breaks an oath. By including "liar," Paul is interpreting the ninth commandment in a larger context than courtroom perjury, as he does with "fornicators, homosexuals." ψεύστης, "liar," occurs in the PE elsewhere only in Titus 1:12 as a description of the Cretans (cf. variant at Titus 1:9). ψευδο-, "false," is found in 1 Tim 2:7 (Paul says that he is not lying [ψεύδεσθαι]), 1 Tim 4:2 (liars [ψευδολόγοι] will come in the end times), and 1 Tim 6:20 (the Ephesian heresy is falsely called [ψευδώνυμος] knowledge). ἐπίορκος, "perjurer," occurs in the NT only here (cf. Zech 5:3). Its verbal cognate ἐπιορκεῖν, "to perjure," occurs once, at Matt 5:33, which speaks of swearing falsely.

(9) Instead of including a parallel to the tenth commandment ("You shall not covet"; Exod 20:17; Deut 5:21), Paul summarizes all that he has been saying, as he does with similar vice lists elsewhere (cf. Rom 13:9 [which also parallels the Decalogue]; Gal 5:21, 23; cf. 1 Pet 5:5; 1 Tim 5:10, although this does not occur in a list; Hanson calls it "a rather lame ending" [(1983) 59]). The law is intended for καὶ εἴ τι ἕτερον τῇ ὑγιαινούσῃ διδασκαλίᾳ ἀντίκειται, "everything else that is contrary to healthy teaching," i.e., Paul's gospel. Elsewhere, Paul describes his opponents as having "a morbid craving for controversy" (1 Tim 6:4), being "depraved in mind" (1 Tim 6:5), and their talk as eating "its way like gangrene" (2 Tim 2:17). Both the opponents and their teaching are spiritually sick. In contrast, Paul's gospel is spiritually healthy. It may not be helpful to speculate why Paul did not include a parallel to the tenth commandment (see Knight, 87). Perhaps the tenth commandment lay beyond the emphasis of the list, or the needs of the historical situation required discussion of visible sins (although the first six vices are more attitudes than visible traits).

ἀντίκεισθαι, "to be opposed to," occurs in the PE elsewhere only in 1 Tim 5:14, where Paul's instructions to widows are given so that Satan (τῷ ἀντικειμένῳ, "the adversary") has no reason to revile them. The term describes strong opposition (cf. Luke 13:17 [Jesus' description of the ruler of the synagogue and those with him]; Luke 21:15 [opponents of the disciples as they bear witness to Jesus in the courts]; *1 Clem.* 51:1 [of the devil]). Elsewhere Paul uses it to describe his opponents in Corinth (1 Cor 6:9), the Philippians' opponents (Phil 1:28), and the antichrist (2 Thess 2:4). It describes the conflict between flesh and spirit (Gal 5:17). Here it provides a wordplay with the previous κεῖται, "is valid" (v 9).

Dibelius-Conzelmann define ὑγιαίνειν, "to be healthy," in terms of Greek philosophy as designating "rational speech and opinions," concluding that it is wholly unlike Paul, who they claim is "pneumatic throughout" (24–25). Regarding Paul's use of terminology, they comment, "We must assume that it is highly unlikely that in his old age Paul would have designated his gospel with other formulas—unless he had to formulate new expressions to meet new situations. But the basic terms of the Pastorals are *not* applied to an actual situation" (24). While I disagree that the NT is purely pneumatic and I would not limit a creative genius like Paul in his later years, the basic argument here is that the PE should be understood as ad hoc writings dealing with a specific historical situation, and it is precisely this situation that has caused Paul to be creative in his terminology. While the Ephesian heresy appears to have had some similarity to the problem in Colossae, it was unique. Sometimes ὑγιαίνειν is used to emphasize the fact that the gospel is correct and true (Titus 2:1, 2; 2 Tim 1:13), in which case there is a rational component. But as Malherbe states, "While it is affirmed that the orthodox do have understanding, it was not the rationality of the sound teaching that made them so, but rather the apostolic tradition" ("Medical Imagery," 136). Other times in the PE the healthy (ὑγιαίνειν as "to be healthy") gospel stands in contrast to sin and the sick and morbid cravings of the Ephesian heresy (1 Tim 6:4) that was spreading like gangrene (2 Tim 2:17; cf. 1 Tim 1:10; 6:3; Titus 1:9, 13; 2 Tim 4:3; cf. ὑγιής, "healthy," Titus 2:8). Malherbe's argument is that medical language was very common in the philosophical rhetoric of the moral philosophers and Cynics (cf. Spicq, 1:115–17), in which opposing philosophical positions were characterized as "sick" and "diseased," and his documentation is convincing. He agrees with Michaelis (79–85), against Dibelius-Conzelmann, that "the terms should not be understood in a philosophical sense but in a context of a polemic against heresy" (122; cf. Roloff, 78, who sees "healthy" as the standard against which the error is compared, but without the medical imagery). Malherbe identifies the extremely polemical "severe Cynics" as part of the background of the PE, which Michaelis also suggests (see *Introduction,* "The Ephesian Heresy"). Paul says that in contrast to the wrong and sickly heresy being taught by the false teachers, the gospel is correct and is spiritually healthy, perhaps recalling the spiritual goal in v 5. The term is not found elsewhere in biblical expression with reference to spiritual health although this use of a metaphor regarding health is consistent with Paul's metaphor of the church as the body of Christ. Malherbe also suggests that the description of the opponents as being "conceited" (τετύφωται; 1 Tim 6:4) can be understood as mental illness (124 n. 7), and "constant irritation" (διαπαρατριβαί; 1 Tim 6:5) as infectious abrasions— additional medical imagery.

ὑγιαίνειν, "to be healthy," occurs twelve times in the NT, all but four in the PE (Luke 5:31; 7:10; 15:27; 3 John 2, all denoting physical health). Four times it modifies διδασκαλία, "teaching" (1 Tim 1:10; 2 Tim 4:3; Titus 1:9; 2:1; cf. 1 Tim 6:3). Paul speaks of "the sound words [λόγοις] of our Lord Jesus Christ and the teaching [διδασκαλία] that accords with godliness" (1 Tim 6:3), and of the "pattern of sound words [ὑγιαινόντων λόγων]" Timothy is to follow (2 Tim 1:13). Titus is to rebuke the opponents so that they will be ὑγιαίνωσιν ἐν τῇ πίστει, "sound in the faith" (Titus 1:13), to encourage older men to be ὑγιαίνοντας τῇ πίστει, "sound in faith," in love, etc. (Titus 2:2), and to be a model of λόγον ὑγιῆ, "sound speech," that cannot be censored (Titus 2:8). ὑγιής, "healthy," occurs eleven times in the NT, but only once in the PE (Titus 2:8). It is often suggested that Luke, acting as Paul's amanuensis, may have introduced the medical imagery (see *Introduction,* "Historical Reconstruction from the PE").

διδασκαλία, "teaching," occurs twenty-one times in the NT, fifteen in the PE.

One of the predominant emphases of this word is authority (K. H. Rengstorf, *TDNT* 2:160–63). The teaching carries the authority of the teacher, who is God speaking through Paul (1 Tim 1:1). This is particularly appropriate for an epistle in which authority is one of the underlying issues. Rather than describing the basic message of the gospel, διδασκαλία describes the doctrinal formulations of the gospel (cf. 1 Tim 4:6). Every time διδασκαλία occurs in the PE it is singular (except 1 Tim 4:1, which speaks of the "teachings" of the demons). Christian truth is not a collection of multiple ideas; it is a body of truth against which the error of the opponents can be measured and declared wrong.

Six times διδασκαλία denotes the act of teaching: Timothy is to teach (1 Tim 4:13, 16) as are the elders (1 Tim 5:17; cf. Titus 1:9); Titus is to show integrity in his teaching (Titus 2:7); Paul's teaching is a model for Timothy (2 Tim 3:10); Scripture is the basis of Christian teaching (2 Tim 3:16). The other nine times διδασκαλία denotes that which is taught: healthy teaching (1 Tim 1:10; 2 Tim 4:3; Titus 1:9; cf. 1 Tim 6:3; 2 Tim 1:13) as opposed to the demonic teaching (1 Tim 4:1); it is a source of spiritual training (1 Tim 4:6) and accords with godliness (1 Tim 6:3); an elder must be able to teach healthy teaching (Titus 1:9; cf. 1 Tim 5:17); believers' conduct should be in conformity to this teaching (1 Tim 6:1; Titus 2:1, 10). The cognate διδαχή, "teaching," is used twice: Timothy is to be unfailing in patience and teaching (2 Tim 4:2); an elder must ἀντεχόμενον τοῦ κατὰ τὴν διδαχὴν πιστοῦ λόγου, "hold firmly to the faithful word that is in accordance with the teaching" (Titus 1:9). On the cognates διδάσκαλος, "teacher," and διδάσκειν, "to teach," see *Comments* on 1 Tim 2:7 and 1 Tim 2:12, respectively; both words are also used throughout the NT to describe the act of teaching and the content of that teaching (cf. BAGD, 191–92). On the relationship between διδασκαλία and the gospel (λόγος), see the *Comment* on 1 Tim 4:6.

11   κατὰ τὸ εὐαγγέλιον τῆς δόξης τοῦ μακαρίου θεοῦ ὃ ἐπιστεύθην ἐγώ, "which is in conformity to the gospel of the glory of the blessed God with which I was entrusted." κατά, "which is in conformity to," designates the standard against which something is judged (BAGD, 407; M. J. Harris, *NIDNTT* 3:1200–1201; Moule, *Idiom-Book,* 59). There is a question of what is modified in the prepositional phrase. Most see it connected generally to v 8 or vv 8–10: the proper use of the law is in accordance with the gospel message. Some see κατά more specifically linked to ἀντίκειται, "is contrary," εἰδώς, "knowing," or τῇ ὑγιαινούσῃ διδασκαλίᾳ, "healthy teaching," of which the latter is the most natural of the three since it is the closest in context and makes good sense (cf. Knight, 90). Paul's teaching, which recognizes the limitations of the law and produces spiritual health, is in conformity with the gospel. The message of the opponents does not recognize the limitations and is not consistent with the gospel.

εὐαγγέλιον, "gospel," is a favorite word for Paul, occurring sixty times throughout his writings (cognates twenty-three times). It describes the good news that God was and is at work in Jesus Christ. It is good news especially in contrast to the gross sins of humanity (vv 9–10). The word occurs elsewhere in the PE in 2 Tim 1:8, 10 and 2:8 (cf. εὐαγγελιστής, "preacher," in 2 Tim 4:5). In secular Greek it meant merely a good message, but because of its use to describe the message of Jesus, it eventually became a technical term in Christian teaching for the good news of Christ (cf. G. Friedrich, *TDNT* 2:707–37). On the role of the gospel in the PE, see *Introduction,* "The Response to the Heresy."

Two phrases modify the word εὐαγγέλιον, "gospel." First, the gospel reveals τῆς δόξης τοῦ μακαρίου θεοῦ, "of the glory of the blessed God." Most agree that the genitive τῆς δόξης, "of the glory," does not modify εὐαγγέλιον (as a descriptive genitive; contra ĸjv, ʀsv; "according to the glorious gospel"). Rather, τῆς δόξης is the actual content of that gospel, i.e., "the gospel which tells of the glory of God" (ɴᴇʙ; cf. 2 Cor 4:4–6). Glory is more than a visible manifestation; it is an indication of the essence of God; he is glory. E. F. Harrison states, "God's glory is not confined to some outward sign which appeals to the senses, but is that which expresses his inherent majesty, which may or may not have some visible token" (*EDT*, 443; cf. Exod 33:18; Isa 6; Rom 1:23; 3:23). The law reveals sin and is for sinners (vv 9–10). The gospel is provided for the righteous person (v 8) and reveals the glory of God. δόξα, "glory," appears six times in the PE, once directed toward believers (2 Tim 2:10) and elsewhere of God (1 Tim 1:11; especially in doxologies, 1 Tim 1:17; 2 Tim 4:18; cf. Rom 11:36) or of Christ (1 Tim 3:16; Titus 2:13; cf. 2 Cor 4:4). In secular Greek δόξα meant "opinion" or "reputation." However, in the LXX it translates כבוד *kābôd*, meaning "heavy," "important." It came to be the primary description of God's radiance and power, especially as seen in creation and salvation history. There was therefore a shift in the word's meaning from subjective "opinion" to objective "glory" possessed by God (cf. G. Kittel and G. von Rad, *TDNT* 2:232–55; S. Aalen, *NIDNTT* 2:44–48 [bibliography on pp. 51–52]; E. C. E. Owen, "*Doxa* and Cognate Words," *JTS* n.s. 33 [1982] 132–50, 265–79).

The gospel reveals the glory of the blessed God. Here and in 1 Tim 6:15 are the only times in the OT or NT that μακάριος, "blessed," describes God. (It appears elsewhere in the PE only in Titus 2:13, which describes the believers' expectation of Christ's return.) The word is often found in the formula "blessed is" in both the NT and secular Greek (e.g., the beatitudes in Matt 5:4–11; F. Hauck, *TDNT* 4:362–64). It was also typical of Homer and others (Josephus *Ag. Ap.* 2.22 §190; *Ant.* 10.11.7 §278), especially Philo (*De Mig. Abr.* 202; *Spec. Leg.* 1.209; 2.53), who applied the word to the gods (Dibelius-Conzelmann, 26–27; Spicq, 1:337–8; cf. references in the *Comment* on 1 Tim 6:15). Normally εὐλογητός, "blessed," is used to acknowledge the blessedness of God (Mark 14:61; Luke 1:68; Rom 1:25; 9:5; 2 Cor 1:3; 11:31; Eph 1:3; 1 Pet 1:3). While μακάριος may point to a Hellenistic milieu, its frequent use in the NT (thirteen times in Matt; seven times in Revelation) shows that the word was part of the Jewish world as well.

This gospel that shows the glory of God was entrusted to Paul (ὃ ἐπιστεύθην ἐγώ, "with which I was entrusted"). This provides an important link between vv 8–11 and vv 12–17. Paul ends the discussion of the first part of the Ephesian problem, a misunderstanding of the law, by leading into the second part, a failure to understand that salvation is obtained through God's mercy and grace, not through the law. Throughout the PE Paul shows an acute awareness that he has been entrusted with the gospel (see *Comment* on 1 Tim 1:13; this entrusting is also part of the argument of 1 Tim 2:1–7 [see v 7]). The gospel has also been entrusted to Timothy (1 Tim 1:13–14), and as Timothy prepares to come to Rome, he must find reliable men to whom he can entrust the gospel (2 Tim 2:2). Sabugal (*Revista Agustiniana de Espiritualidad* 16 [1975] 355–62) emphasizes that ἐπιστεύθην, "was entrusted," is a divine passive and points out the similarity between this passage and Gal 1:15–16. Both passages refer to Paul's conversion, speaking of a divine revelation and Paul's call to the Gentile mission. πιστεύειν, "to believe," occurs six times in the PE. Four times it denotes the act of believing in Christ (1 Tim 1:16; 3:16; 2 Tim 1:12; Titus 3:8); twice it means "to entrust" (1 Tim 1:11; Titus 1:3; cf. Rom 3:2). On *faith,* see *Introduction,* "Themes in the PE."

Explanation

Paul launches into the theological problems of the heresy. In this paragraph he discusses the law and how the opponents were misusing it. That Paul is dealing theologically with the heresy may not be apparent at first. He is writing to a close friend who knows this theology well. Paul's opponents pride themselves on being teachers of the law, even though they are ignorant of its proper function (v 7). While Paul agrees that the law is good, its essential goodness does not negate the fact that it must be used only as it was intended. The restrictive function of the Mosaic law does not apply to those who have been justified by faith in Christ and are living righteous lives. The opponents were apparently applying the restrictive function of law—interpreted by them to include, e.g., marriage and certain foods (1 Tim 4:3)—to all people. But, Paul says, the restrictive function of the law is not for everyone. Then following the Decalogue, Paul lists the types of people for whom the law was intended. To use the law lawfully is to recognize its necessary limitations. The law is only for sins and sinners who stand opposed to the healthy teaching of the gospel that reveals the glory of God, the gospel that God gave Paul to proclaim.

C. Paul's Example of Salvation by Grace (1 Tim 1:12–17)

Bibliography

Allan, J. A. "The 'in Christ' Formula in the Pastoral Epistles." *NTS* 10 (1963/64) 115–21. **Botha, F. J.** "The Word Is Trustworthy." *Theologia Evangelica* 1 (1968) 78–84. **Bruggen, J. van.** "Vaste grund onder de voeten: De formule pistos ho logos in de Pastorale Brieven." In *Bezield Verband,* ed. M. Arntzen et al. Kampen: Van den Berg, 1984. 38–45. **Champion, L. G.** *Benedictions and Doxologies in the Epistles of Paul.* Oxford: Kemp Hall Press, 1935. **Deichgräber, R.** *Gotteshymnus und Christushymnus in der frühen Christenheit.* SUNT 5. Göttingen: Vandenhoeck & Ruprecht, 1967. **Delling, G.** "ΜΟΝΟΣ ΘΕΟΣ." *TLZ* 77 (1952) 469–76. **Duncan, J. G.** "Πιστὸς ὁ λόγος." *ExpTim* 35 (1922) 141. **Dvorácek, J. A.** "Prisel (1 Tim 1:15)." *KR* 33 (1966) 219–21. **Hunter, A. M.** "The Sure Sayings." In *Probing the New Testament.* Richmond, VA: John Knox, 1972. 126–29. **Knight, G. W.** "1 Timothy 1:15 and Its Saying." In *The Faithful Sayings in the Pastoral Letters.* Kampen: Kok, 1968. Repr. Grand Rapids, MI: Baker, 1979. 4–49. **Noack, B.** "Pastoralbrevens 'trovaerdige tale.'" *DTT* 32 (1969) 1–22. **Oke, C. C.** "A Doxology not to God, but Christ." *ExpTim* 67 (1955) 367–68. **Oldfather, W. A.,** and **Daly, L. W.** "A Quotation from Menander [Adelphi 995] in the Pastoral Epistles [1 Tim 1:15; 4:9]." *CP* 38 (1943) 202–4. **Robertson, A. T.** "The Greek Article and the Deity of Christ." *Exp* 8 (1921) 182–88. **Standaert, B. H. M. G. M.** "Paul, exemple vivant de l'Évangile de grâce: 1 Tim 1:12–17."

As Seign 55 (1974) 62–69. **Swete, H. B.** "The Faithful Sayings." *JTS* o.s. 18 (1917) 1–7. **Wagner, W.** "Über σώζειν und seine Derivata im Neuen Testament." *ZNW* 6 (1905) 205–35. **Walder, E.** "The Logos of the Pastoral Epistles." *JTS* o.s. 24 (1923) 310–15. **Warfield, B. B.** "The Saving Christ." In *The Person and Work of Christ.* Ed. S. G. Craig. Philadelphia: Presbyterian & Reformed, 1950. 549–60. **Wolter, M.** "Paulus, der bekehrte Gottesfeind: Zum Verständnis von 1 Tim 1,13." *NovT* 31 (1989) 48–66.

On benedictions and doxologies, see *Bibliography* for Titus 3:12–15.

Translation

[12]*I*[a] *continually thank him who strengthened*[b] *me, Christ Jesus our Lord, since he considered [that even] I [would be] faithful, [as evidenced by his] appointing me to service,* [13]*even though formerly*[c] *I*[d] *was a blasphemer, persecutor, and an insolent person. But I was shown mercy since, being ignorant, I had acted in unbelief;* [14]*and the grace of our Lord completely overflowed with faith and love that are in Christ Jesus.* [15]*Trustworthy*[e] *is the saying and worthy of complete acceptance: "Christ Jesus came into the world in order to save sinners,"* *of whom I am the foremost.* [16]*But for this reason I was shown mercy: so that in me as foremost Christ Jesus*[f] *might display his complete patience as an illustration for those who would believe in him for eternal life.* [17]*Now to the king eternal, incorruptible,*[g] *invisible, the only God,*[h] *be honor and glory forever. Amen.*

Notes

[a]καί, "and," is inserted before χάριν, "thanks," by D TR a b f* sy; Lcf Ambst. It emphasizes the connection between the two paragraphs but does not recognize that the connection is one of contrast. It is the weaker reading; our text is read by א A F G H I P Ψ 6 33 81 104 365 1175 1739 1881 *pc* m vg co; Epiph.

[b]The present ἐνδυναμοῦντι, "strengthens" (א* 33 *pc* sa), is an assimilation to the more usual idea of continual empowering (see *Comment*). The aorist ἐνδυναμώσαντι, "strengthened," is the stronger reading (א[c] A D G H I K L P Ψ et al.), is the more difficult reading (resisting assimilation), and makes better sense in the paragraph that is referring to Paul's conversion (see *Comment*). Cf. *TCGNT*[1], 639; L. T. Johnson, 118.

[c]Τόν is read by D² Hᶜ TR (a r vg^ms). τό is read by א A D* F G H* I P Ψ 6 33 81 365 630 1175 1505 1739 1881 *pc.*

[d]A Ψ 81 *pc* add με, "I," after ὄντα, "was," making the "subject" explicit.

[e]Both here and in 1 Tim 3:1 several Latin witnesses (b m r vg^ms; Ambst) have *humanus* (ἀνθρώπινος), meaning "commonly accepted," rather than πιστός, "trustworthy." See *Comment* on 1 Tim 3:1. Cf. *TCGNT*[2], 571; L. T. Johnson, 118.

[f]The order is reversed in א D² TR a vg^ms sy. Our text follows A D* H Ψ 0262^vid 33 104 326 365 629 1175 *pc* lat. Only Ἰησοῦς is in F G 1739 1881 *pc;* Ἰησοῦς ὁ Χριστός, "Jesus, the Christ," in 614 *pc.*

[g]The rare ἀφθάρτῳ, "incorruptible," is replaced by the better known ἀθανάτῳ, "immortal," in D*·ᶜ latt sy^hmg; Tert. Cf. *TCGNT*[2], 571. ἀθανάτῳ is inserted after ἀοράτῳ, "invisible," in F G (a m r).

[h]Some MSS add σοφῷ, "wise," after μόνῳ, "only," in possible imitation of the phrase in Rom 16:27 (א² D¹ Hᶜ Ψ 1881 TR sy^h; Epiph). The shorter reading is much stronger (א* A D* F G H* 33. 1739 *pc* lat sy^p co). Cf. *TCGNT*[2], 572.

Form/Structure/Setting

Most commentators view these verses as a digression. Some see them as only partly relevant (Fee, 15; Guthrie, 63). They feel that just as the mention of law in v 7 leads into a tangent discussion of the law in vv 8–11, so here the personal reference in v 11 leads into a tangent discussion of Paul's own conversion in vv 12–

17. However, just as we saw that vv 8–11 are not a digression, so also vv 12–17 form an integral part of Paul's response to the Ephesian situation.

Vv 12–17 constitute the third subsection of vv 3–20 (see *Form/Structure/Setting* on 1 Tim 1:3–7). In the first subsection, Paul presents the basic facts of the problem and instructs Timothy to stop the heresy (vv 3–7). He then discusses the actual problem in vv 8–11: his Ephesian opponents are misusing the law, apparently applying it to everyone and seeing it as the way to salvation and a virtuous life. In contrast, Paul uses his personal testimony in vv 12–17 to argue that salvation is through mercy and grace, and not (implied) through adherence to Jewish myths based on the law. Paul, as the ultimate example (v 16), stands in contrast to the false teachers in vv 8–11. L. T. Johnson comments, "It is precisely Paul's point in this passage that being a sinner is not mitigated by allegiance to law but only by personal transformation" (122). These verses are an intimate look at Paul as he holds up his personal testimony as an example of God's mercy and grace. They are not a digression but are the heart of the argument. (Another argument that vv 12–18 are not a digression is that vv 18–20 follow more naturally after vv 12–17 than after vv 3–7. See *Form/Structure/Setting* on 1 Tim 1:18–20.)

The structure of the paragraph is somewhat difficult to determine, especially in the minor points. It appears to break into three divisions: Paul's thankfulness for what God has done (vv 12–14); God's purpose in saving Paul (vv 15–16); and a doxology in praise of God's acts (v 17). Vv 12–14 discuss Paul's previous state and what God did for him. The structure is difficult to identify because the breaks in thought do not follow the grammatical clues. There are three subdivisions: the statement of blessing (v 12a); Paul's former condition (vv 12b–13a); and God's act of mercy (vv 13b–14).

There are three themes in this paragraph: (1) the true nature of the gospel; (2) encouragement to Timothy; and (3) Paul's authority.

(1) The primary theme of this paragraph is the true nature of the gospel as seen in Paul's conversion. Because the discussion is couched in terms of personal experience, this may not be clear at first. Some of Paul's better-known doctrines such as justification are absent (but see v 8), but one assumes that Paul includes the themes that he feels are necessary for the Ephesian situation. Paul defines the gospel by contrasting the role of the law with his personal salvation that was obtained by God's grace. On the one hand, we have the bleak picture of sin in vv 8–11, and it is this picture with which Paul identifies himself when he says that he was a blasphemer, a persecutor, an insolent person, ignorant (v 13), and the worst of sinners (v 15). On the other hand, we have Paul's salvation by God's mercy (mentioned twice), grace, faith, and love (recalling v 5), a salvation so marvelous that Paul breaks into praise, calling for honor and glory to be bestowed upon God for what he has done. This is the gospel. It is not something tied up in endless myths based on OT genealogies and the law. It is the gracious and merciful act of God in saving sinners, facts clearly seen in the salvation of the worst of sinners.

(2) The second theme is that of encouragement to Timothy, who should be strengthened when he realizes that the God who strengthened Paul (v 12) is the same God who appointed Timothy to ministry (v 18). Just as Paul was adequately strengthened, so also Timothy's gifts are sufficient to the task. As Easton says, "If Christ could change Paul, the greatest of sinners, into an Apostle, there is no limit to His transforming power. So let no man say that his duties as a Christian are

beyond his abilities" (114). It may also be possible that this theme has another nuance: if God's graciousness can save even a person like Paul, then it can also extend to the opponents in Ephesus.

(3) Paul's defense of his authority may be a third theme. The issue of authority has been established in v 1 when Paul announces that his apostleship is by command of both God and Christ. Perhaps his Ephesian opponents were attacking his past, but Paul turns it around by showing that his past sins are an ever-present paradigm of God's mercy (v 16). Or perhaps, more likely, it is not so much the example of the redemption from his sinful past as it is his having been chosen by God that places him in the prime position of authority. Fee comments that "Paul's 'authority' finally lies in the 'authentic' nature of his gospel, as he both preached and experienced it" (15).

The literary techniques employed in the paragraph are complex. (1) Paul uses inclusio, beginning and ending on similar notes. He starts with a statement of thanksgiving for what God has done and ends with a doxology for who God is. (2) The repetition of the phrase "but I was shown mercy" highlights the central purpose of the unit. (3) Paul says "I" eight times, showing the personal nature of his argument. (4) There is a wordplay built upon the πίστις, "faith," word group. The gospel was ἐπιστεύθην, "entrusted," to Paul (v 11). God considered Paul πιστόν, "trustworthy" (v 12). Paul was shown mercy because he had acted in ἀπιστία, "unbelief" (v 13), but God's grace overflowed with πίστεως, "faith" (v 14). Consequently Paul becomes an example for those who will πιστεύειν, "believe" (v 16). One might also add "faithful [πιστός] is the saying" (v 15). This wordplay is also continued into vv 18–20. (Cf. the similar wordplay on πλούσιος, "rich," in 1 Tim 6:17–19.) This contrasts with the opponents' adherence to the law. (5) Other verbal links with earlier verses are present with χάρις, "grace" (vv 2, 11, 12, 14), δόξα, "glory" (vv 11, 17), and possibly Χριστὸς Ἰησοῦς, "Christ Jesus" (vv 1 [2x], 2, 12, 14, 15, 16). The prevalence of the latter may be significant, especially in light of Christ's central role in the faithful saying (v 15). If the opponents were preaching a form of OT law righteousness, then Christ and his salvific function would be downplayed. There is also a conceptual link between the sins of vv 9–10 and Paul's previous life of sin (vv 13, 15). (6) Paul characteristically pairs terms like "faith and love" (v 14), "faithful and worthy" (v 15), and "honor and glory" (v 17). Likewise, he uses triads. Paul had been a blasphemer, persecutor, and insolent person (v 13), but these character traits were fully overcome by God's grace and the ensuing faith and love (v 14), the latter recalling the triad of heart, conscience, and faith (v 5). The doxology describes the eternal God as incorruptible, invisible, the only God (v 17). (7) Finally, Paul uses a threefold alliteration of words beginning with alpha in the doxology (v 17).

Along with the faithful saying (see below), there is another literary form worthy of note in vv 12–17—the doxology (v 17). Hanson ([1983] 62) says that "all editors agree that this is a liturgical fragment." Kelly (55) says it may have come from the Hellenistic synagogue, and Houlden (61) says the parallel phrase "King of Ages" in Tob 13:7, 11 confirms its Jewish origin, an assertion weakened by a textual problem with the phrase in Tobit. The parallel in Tobit, however, is not sufficient evidence for the source of Paul's doxology. The words ἀφθάρτῳ, "incorruptible," and ἀοράτῳ, "invisible," are Hellenistic, although the concepts they describe are fully Jewish, so it is difficult to decide what they actually indicate in terms of source.

It seems that caution is necessary when attributing any formalized speech to the realm of a liturgical fragment. It is possible that a creative genius like Paul could couch his thought in exalted poetic terminology.

Doxologies occur two other times in the PE (1 Tim 6:16; 2 Tim 4:18) and throughout the Pauline literature, sometimes in the opening of a letter (Gal 1:5; cf. Rev 1:6), or the closing (1 Tim 6:16; cf. Phil 4:20; cf. 1 Pet 4:11; 5:11; 2 Pet 3:18; Heb 13:20–21; Jude 24–25), or the middle (Rom 9:5; 11:36; 16:27; Eph 3:20–21; cf. Rev 5:13). One often finds αἰών, "age" (1 Tim 1:17; Gal 1:5; Phil 4:20; cf. Eph 3:21), and δόξα, "glory" (1 Tim 1:17; cf. Rom 11:36; 16:27; Gal 1:5; Eph 3:21; Phil 4:20), in doxologies. On doxologies, see A. C. Meyers, "Doxology," *ISBE* 2:989–90; Bauckham, *Jude, 2 Peter*, 119–21; B. F. Westcott, *The Epistle to the Hebrews*, 3rd ed. [London: Macmillan, 1909] 466–67; Champion, *Benedictions;* G. F. Moore, *DACL* 4:1525–36; A. Stuiber, *RAC* 4:210–26; E. Käsemann, *RGG*, 993–96; Deichgräber, *Gotteshymnus*, 25–40, 99–101.

Excursus: "Faithful Is the Saying"

Five times in the PE Paul uses a formula to introduce an important saying. The statement that it introduces is called a faithful saying, and the introductory formula is πιστὸς ὁ λόγος, "trustworthy [faithful] is the saying" (1 Tim 3:1; 2 Tim 2:11; Titus 3:8). Twice Paul adds καὶ πάσης ἀποδοχῆς ἄξιος, "and worthy of complete acceptance" (1 Tim 1:15; 4:9). This formula occurs nowhere else in the Greek Bible or Jewish literature. Several basic questions arise concerning this formula.

(1) What is a faithful saying? Hanson ([1983] 63–64) shows how difficult it is to reduce the faithful sayings to one basic category such as "salvation" or "statements of faith." Some of the sayings seem to be maxims currently known and possibly accepted by the Ephesian church. Difficult to categorize is 1 Tim 3:1, where Paul may use the formula merely to add emphasis to what he is saying. The same may also be true of Titus 3:5–7, which is so full of Pauline language that it does not seem to be traditional material, and the formula, as in 1 Tim 3:1, may simply be adding emphasis. Oberlinner calls the faithful saying a "confirmation-formula" (*Bekräftigungsformel;* 113), with which Paul introduces sayings as supporting evidence for his argument. For example, in 1 Tim 1:15b–16 Paul argues that God saved him, the worst of sinners, as an example of the nature of salvation; to buttress his argument, he cites the faithful saying that Christ came to save sinners (v 15a). Presumably the Ephesian church had already accepted the truth of the faithful sayings that were traditional material.

(2) How can the faithful sayings be delimited? In several cases it is easy to delimit the faithful saying, which can come before or after the introductory formula. The basic criterion is: What appears to be a traditional saying that would have been passed down through the church, both in terms of its poetic form and its content? This is a subjective criterion since what appears to be a doctrinal statement to some may not so appear to others. There are five sayings that may cautiously be offered as faithful sayings. (See *Comment* on specific verses. Titus 3:5–8a is the most difficult saying to isolate from its context.)

Trustworthy is the saying and worthy of complete acceptance: "Christ Jesus came into the world in order to save sinners." (1 Tim 1:15)

Trustworthy is the saying: "If anyone aspires to the office of overseer, he is desiring a good work." (1 Tim 3:1)

Trustworthy is the saying and worthy of complete acceptance, [and] for this reason we are toiling and struggling, since: "We have placed [our] hope in the living God, who is the savior of all people, particularly of those who believe." (1 Tim 4:9–10)

Trustworthy is the saying: "For, if we died together, we will also live together. If we endure, we will also reign together. If we will deny [Christ], he will also deny us. If we are faithless, he remains faithful, for he is unable to deny himself." (2 Tim 2:11–13)

"He saved us, through the washing of regeneration and renewal of the Holy Spirit, who was richly poured out for us through Jesus Christ our savior, in order that having been justified by his grace we might become heirs according to hope of eternal life." Trustworthy is the saying. (Titus 3:5–8a)

The topic of four out of the five faithful sayings is salvation. Christ came to save sinners (1 Tim 1:15). God is the savior of all people (1 Tim 4:9–10). Believers were saved by God's mercy (Titus 3:5–8). Salvation requires perseverance but allows for temporary unfaithfulness (2 Tim 2:11–13). 1 Tim 3:1 could refer back to 2:15, which speaks of women being saved through childbirth, in which case all the faithful sayings would speak of salvation. A. M. Hunter offers the following summary: "the worth of religion for life, the Saviourhood of Christ, the call to Christian fidelity and fortitude, the good news of God's grace to sinners in Christ and the blessed hope of eternal life. For the early Christians these were among 'the things most surely believed'" ("Sure Sayings," 128).

(3) What does the introductory formula mean? The emphatic position of πιστός, "faithful," emphasizes above all else that the saying is trustworthy, reliable, believable, and correct (cf. use of πιστός in 1 Cor. 4:2 and 7:25). "Worthy of all [πάσης] acceptance" could mean that the saying should be accepted by everyone, especially the Ephesian church; this would be appropriate in the historical situation. It could also mean that the saying should be totally and unreservedly received. This is how a similar phrase is used in 1 Tim 6:1, which says that slaves should regard their masters as being worthy of all honor. The phrase "worthy of complete acceptance" occurs in two faithful sayings and nowhere else in the PE, but it was common in secular Greek (references in Lock, 15). For further study on this introductory formula, see the *Bibliography*, especially van Bruggen, "Vaste grund onder de voete"; Duncan, *ExpTim* 35 (1922) 141; P. Ellingworth, "The 'true saying' in 1 Timothy 3.1," *BT* 31 (1980) 443–45; Hunter, "Sure Sayings," 126–29; Knight, *Faithful Sayings*, 4–49; Swete, *JTS* o.s. 18 (1917) 1–7; Walder, *JTS* o.s. 21 (1923) 310–15.

Comment

12a Χάριν ἔχω τῷ ἐνδυναμώσαντί με Χριστῷ Ἰησοῦ τῷ κυρίῳ ἡμῶν, "I continually thank him who strengthened me, Christ Jesus our Lord." Paul begins by thanking Christ for strengthening him. This strengthening is not a daily empowering but refers to his initial call to the ministry and the gifts he received that enabled him to perform his apostolic tasks. Paul then identifies Christ as the one who empowered him, and in calling him "our" Lord includes Timothy with himself as he does in v 16. Underlying vv 12–17, and explicitly stated in vv 18–20, is Timothy's own call to ministry and his gifts. Paul is implicitly arguing that just as his own calling was sufficient for his task, so also Timothy's is equal for his task.

This is the first of eight uses of "I," in this paragraph, showing the personal nature of the discussion. It is common for Paul to thank God for what he has done for Paul and for others, and often his thanksgiving expands into a personal note giving the reason for the thanksgiving (Rom 6:17; 7:25; 1 Cor 15:57; 2 Cor 2:14–17;

8:16; 9:15). The phrase χάριν ἔχω, "I continually thank him," is in a linear aspect, emphasizing that this is Paul's continual practice. It is an idiomatic and regular construction (2 Tim 1:3; cf. Luke 17:9; Acts 2:47; 2 Cor 1:15; Heb 12:28), although Paul normally uses a form of εὐχαριστεῖν, "to thank" (Rom 1:8; 1 Cor 1:4; Eph 1:16; Phil 1:3; Col 1:3; 1 Thess 1:2; 2 Thess 1:3; Phlm 4). This may be one piece of evidence for Hitchcock's thesis (*ExpTim* 39 [1927/28] 347–52) that because Paul wanted to work in the West, he immersed himself in Latin culture (the Latin construction is *gratiam habeo;* see Kelly, 52; Spicq, 1:340–41). He may also have wanted to use this idiom because χάρις, "grace," is one of the primary themes of the paragraph. On χάρις, "grace," see *Comment* on 1 Tim 1:2b.

ἐνδυναμοῦν, "to strengthen," is used seven times in the NT, all by Paul. Three times Paul says his audience should be continually strengthened (2 Tim 2:1; Eph 6:10; Phil 4:13; cf. Acts 9:22; variant ἐνδυναμοῦντι, "strengthens," in 1 Tim 1:12; see *Note* b). But the verb here is aorist (cf. 2 Tim 4:17, where Paul says he was strengthened [ἐνεδυνάμωσεν] at his first defense; cf. Rom 4:20). It is possible that the aorist is looking back at his life of ministry as a whole, but throughout this passage Paul's use of the aorist suggests he is thinking of one specific event in the past: ἡγήσατο, "considered"; θέμενος, "appointing"; ἠλεήθην, "shown mercy"; ὑπερπλεόνασεν, "overflowed." Paul is thinking back to the Damascus-road experience when he received his commission to carry out his task (Acts 9:5). This provides a parallel to vv 18–20, where Paul refers both to Timothy's call into the ministry and to his gifts. In both of their calls, it is God who empowers them for their tasks. Some point out that Paul usually thanks God and not Christ; but since he is thinking of the Damascus-road experience, and since it was Christ who appeared to him there ("Who are you Lord? . . . I am Jesus," Acts 9:5), this slight variation poses no problem. The clear identification of Jesus as "Lord" here is a strong argument that in v 14 "Lord" again refers to Jesus (as is generally true throughout the PE; cf. 1 Tim 1:2). Since Jesus appears to be the only divine actor in vv 12–16, this also suggests that the doxology ("to the king eternal") is also addressed to Jesus. Jesus is called "Lord" in 1 Tim 6:3, 14 (cf. "The grace of [our] Lord," Rom 16:20, 24; 1 Cor 16:23; 2 Cor 8:9; 13:13; Gal 6:18; Phil 4:23; 1 Thess 5:28; 2 Thess 1:12; 3:18; Phlm 25).

12b–13a ὅτι πιστόν με ἡγήσατο θέμενος εἰς διακονίαν τὸ πρότερον ὄντα βλάσφημον καὶ διώκτην καὶ ὑβριστήν, "since he considered [that even] I [would be] faithful, [as evidenced by his] appointing me to service, even though formerly I was a blasphemer, persecutor, and an insolent person." Paul now tells Timothy why he thanked the empowering Christ. His reasoning is somewhat difficult to follow because the structure of his thought does not follow the grammatical structure of the sentence, and the versification also hides the structure. It divides into three thoughts: (1) God strengthened Paul because he considered Paul faithful; (2) this was evidenced by Paul's appointment to ministry; (3) this appointment was especially gracious since Paul had been a persecutor of the Church.

(1) God strengthened Paul because he considered Paul faithful. Paul is picking up πιστεύειν, "to entrust," from v 11 (see *Form/Structure/Setting*) and making a wordplay: Paul was ἐπιστεύθην, "entrusted," with the gospel because God reckoned him πιστόν, "trustworthy." Being πιστός, "trustworthy," is required of all Christian stewards (1 Cor 4:2). The emphasis here is on the με, "I"; Paul continues in amazement that even he, a blasphemer, persecutor, and insolent person, was chosen by God. But what does it mean to be πιστὸν . . . ἡγήσατο, "considered

faithful"? (a) It seems doubtful that Paul is saying God knew he was a trustworthy person and therefore appointed him to ministry. The thrust of this paragraph is that Paul's salvation, and ultimately everyone's salvation, is not merited but is the result of God's mercy and grace (in contrast to salvation through the law [vv 8–11]). Spicq quotes Augustine as saying, "God does not choose anyone who is worthy, but in choosing him renders him worthy" (1:341). Fee and Knight interpret πιστός, "faithful," as God's trust, emphasizing Paul's amazement that God would consider him worthy of divine trust. (b) Paul is probably saying that God knew that he would be trustworthy in the future and therefore appointed him to service in the present. Paul's faithfulness was a potential yet to be realized. Chrysostom adds that Paul's subsequent faithfulness was only possible because of God's empowerment, citing 1 Cor 15:10 and Phil 2:13 ("Homily 2"; NPNF 13:417). ἡγήσατο, "considered," here takes a double accusative; see similar constructions in Acts 26:2; Phil 2:3, 6; 3:7, 8; 2 Thess 3:15; 1 Tim 6:1; Heb 10:29; 11:11, 26; 2 Pet 2:13; 3:15. On πιστός, "faithful," see *Introduction*, "Themes in the PE."

(2) The fact that God considered Paul to be faithful was evidenced by his appointment of Paul to ministry (θέμενος εἰς διακονίαν, "appointing to service"). θέμενος, "appointing," is a participle of attendant circumstance, giving the evidence for Paul's previous statement. τιθέναι, "to appoint," is often used of God's actions (Jer 1:5; Acts 13:47 [Isa 49:6]; Rom 4:17; 1 Cor 12:18, 28; 15:25; 2 Cor 5:19; 1 Thess 5:9; 1 Pet 2:8), and the three times it occurs in the PE all refer to Paul's call to ministry (1 Tim 1:12; 2:7; 2 Tim 1:11). It is significant that Paul chooses the word διακονία, "service," and not ἀποστολή, "apostleship," which he uses elsewhere (cf. 1 Tim 2:7). The primary theme of the paragraph is that salvation is the result of God's mercy and grace, not the result of a person's ability to keep the law. So within this context of humility and awe Paul labels himself a server. Barrett says that this "calls to mind the truth that there is no office in the Church, even the most exalted, that does not consist in serving rather than in being served" (44). A claim to apostleship would be out of tenor with the paragraph (contra Dibelius-Conzelmann, 26). On διακονία, "service," and διάκονος, "deacon," see *Comment* on 1 Tim 3:8.

(3) Paul's appointment to ministry was especially gracious since he τὸ πρότερον ὄντα βλάσφημον καὶ διώκτην καὶ ὑβριστήν, "formerly . . . was a blasphemer, persecutor, and an insolent person" (v 13). In order to emphasize the graciousness and mercifulness of God's salvation, Paul expresses his awe that even a sinner such as himself was shown mercy. He is associating himself with the sinners in vv 8–11, saying that what the law could not do, God's graciousness could. He is also providing a contrast between what he was and what God did for him (vv 13b–14). All this serves to highlight the general purpose of vv 8–17: to contrast the law with God's merciful and gracious salvation. The triad of descriptions—blasphemer, persecutor, insolent—intensifies from bad to worse: he spoke offensively against the Jesus and the Way, he put these words into actions by persecuting the church, and he was a completely insolent person. This is not Saul the rabbi speaking (Phil 3:4–6) but Paul the repentant sinner (1 Tim 1:15). His offenses were especially horrendous because in persecuting the church he was persecuting Christ himself as the voice on the Damascus road makes clear (Acts 9:5; 22:8; 26:15; cf. Luke 10:16; 1 Cor 8:12). It is possible to compare the language here to that in Rom 1:18–32. If we understand the language there as a human evaluation of society in Paul's day, then surely it was the darkest blot in the history of the world. But as Cranfield

(*Romans* 1:104) argues, those verses show not a human evaluation but the gospel's judgment on all people. Likewise, in our passage we read not a human evaluation of Saul but the gospel's judgment seen through the eyes of the repentant Paul.

ὄντα is a concessive participle ("even though . . . I was"). βλάσφημον, "blasphemer," is an adjective used substantivally, and the following two descriptive terms are nouns; the rsv translates them as verbs, supplying "him" at the end: "though I formerly blasphemed and persecuted and insulted him." These three terms are strong, emphasizing by contrast the magnitude of God's grace. βλάσφημος, "blasphemer," is someone who is abusive in speech, a slanderer. The word group occurs thirteen times in Paul, seven in the PE. It is a major theme in the PE in that Christians must conduct themselves so that the church is not blasphemed (1 Tim 6:1; Titus 2:5; cf. ἀνεπίλημπτος, "above reproach," in 1 Tim 3:2). Believers are not to blaspheme others (Titus 3:2). Paul had been a blasphemer (1 Tim 1:13), and he tells Timothy that blasphemy will be characteristic of the people living in the last days (2 Tim 3:2) and was already being produced by the morbid controversies of the Ephesian opponents (1 Tim 6:4). Hymenaeus and Alexander had been excommunicated so they would learn not to blaspheme (1 Tim 1:20). In recounting in Acts 26:9–11 his previous activity of persecuting the church, Paul uses the word βλασφημεῖν, "to blaspheme": "I myself was convinced that I ought to do many things in opposing the name of Jesus of Nazareth. . . . And I punished them often in all the synagogues and tried to make them blaspheme." Almost one hundred years later βλασφημεῖν played a central role in Polycarp's famous refusal to deny Christ ("Away with the Atheists") when he replied to the proconsul, "For eighty and six years have I been his servant, and he has done me no harm, and how can I blaspheme my King [πῶς δύναμαι βλασφημῆσαι τὸν βασιλέα μου] who saved me?" (*Mart. Pol.* 9:3, LCL tr.).

διώκτης, "persecutor," occurs nowhere in the Greek Bible or in pre-Christian literature (cf. *Did.* 5:2; *Barn.* 20:2), although the verbal cognate διώκειν, "to persecute," occurs twenty-one times in Paul (cf. 1 Tim 6:11). ὑβριστής, "insolent person," is the strongest of these three terms, climaxing the triad with the meaning "a thoroughly objectionable character" (Guthrie, 64). G. Bertram compares it to ἀδικία, "wickedness," by saying that wickedness becomes insolence when it is done "out of overweening pride or arrogance. Thus the motive makes simple ἀδικία into an act of ὕβρις" (*TDNT* 8:296 n. 7). The word occurs in the NT elsewhere in Rom 1:30 in a vice list that also contains κατάλαλοι, "slanderers," a term similar to βλάσφημοι, "blasphemers." Cognate forms occur seventeen times in the NT and once in the PE as a variant in Titus 1:11 (cf. Trench, *Synonyms*, 137–44).

13b–14 ἀλλὰ ἠλεήθην, ὅτι ἀγνοῶν ἐποίησα ἐν ἀπιστίᾳ· ὑπερεπλεόνασεν δὲ ἡ χάρις τοῦ κυρίου ἡμῶν μετὰ πίστεως καὶ ἀγάπης τῆς ἐν Χριστῷ Ἰησοῦ, "But I was shown mercy since, being ignorant, I had acted in unbelief; and the grace of our Lord completely overflowed with faith and love that are in Christ Jesus." As Paul continues to think back to his time of ἐνδυναμοῦν, "strengthening," on the Damascus road as it contrasted with the sinful person he had been, he now says that God's mercy and grace were all-sufficient for his salvation. With two similar statements, both contrasting what he was with what God had done, Paul says that God showed him mercy because he had been ignorant and that God's grace overflowed with faith and love. The triad of blasphemer, persecutor, and insolent person was obliterated by the triad of mercy, faith, and love that Paul now possesses through his relationship with Christ. Both v 13b and v 14 emphasize that Paul's salvation was not merited but was given because of God's mercy and grace, and stands in contrast to the opponents' devotion to the law.

When Paul says he was shown mercy "since being ignorant I acted in unbelief" (v 13b), he cannot be saying that he deserved God's mercy. The primary purpose of the paragraph is to show that salvation is not deserved but is a merciful and gracious act by God. To say that he deserved mercy is a contradiction in terms. Paul is making use of the common Jewish distinction between purposeful and accidental sins (Lev 4:1–35; 22:14; Num 15:22–31; Str-B 2:264; Josephus *Ant.* 3.9.3 §§230–32; *T. Jud.* 19:3; Luke 23:34; Acts 3:17; there is no need to consider Greek thought, contra Dibelius-Conzelmann, 27). Purposeful sins are severely condemned: "But the person who does anything with a high hand [as opposed to sinning 'unwittingly'] ... reviles the LORD, and that person shall be cut off from among his people" (Num 15:30). Paul's sins, however, were not done in defiance of what he knew to be right, as were the sins of his insincere Ephesian opponents (see 1 Tim 1:5); his unbelief was fueled by his ignorance. Consequently, God in his mercy and grace chose to save Paul and not punish him. As Ellicott explains, "His ignorance did not give him any claim on God's ἔλεος [mercy], but merely put him within the pale of its operation" (15; cf. *Explanation* below). V 16 says that Paul was shown mercy because (ἵνα) he was to be an example.

ἀλλά, "but," has its full force, separating Paul's sinful condition from God's grace and mercy. ἠλεήθην, "shown mercy," is passive, emphasizing that it was totally an act of God (cf. Rom 11:30–31; 1 Cor 7:25; 2 Cor 4:1; cf. Matt 5:7; 1 Pet 2:10; see 1 Tim 1:2). The following verses spell out what this mercy-giving entails. ὅτι is translated "since" and not with the stronger "because" (cf. ἵνα, v 16); it is giving not the reason for God's mercy but a consideration leading to God's mercy. ἀγνοῶν, "being ignorant," is a Pauline term, occurring fifteen times, only once in the PE. One assumes that Paul was ignorant at least of the true intention of the law, and possibly more generally of God's ways in general. Like his fellow countrymen, Paul had been zealous but without knowledge (Rom 10:2). ἐποίησα, "acted," looks back at his blasphemy, persecution, and insolence. ἀπιστία, "unbelief" (see *Introduction*, "Themes in the PE"; cf. Rom 3:3; 11:20, 23), is used in reference to the gospel proclaimed by the early Christians whom Paul persecuted. ἀπιστία picks up the wordplay going on throughout this paragraph (see *Form/Structure/Setting*).

In v 14 Paul adds a second thought that ὑπερεπλεόνασεν δὲ ἡ χάρις τοῦ κυρίου ἡμῶν μετὰ πίστεως καὶ ἀγάπης τῆς ἐν Χριστῷ Ἰησοῦ, "the grace of our Lord completely overflowed with faith and love that are in Christ Jesus." V 13b and v 14 are parallel. Although they have somewhat different messages, they both contrast who Paul was with what God did for him. Spicq calls this an "axiom of Pauline theology," citing Rom 5:20 (1:342). δέ, "and," carries none of its adversative force against v 13b, although perhaps some against v 13a. χάρις, "grace," parallels ἠλεήθην, "shown mercy" (v 13b), emphasizing the true nature of God's salvation. The triad of grace, faith, and love offsets the triad of sins in v 13a and is reminiscent of the triad in 1:5. It also counters any possible misconception arising from v 13a that Paul thought he deserved salvation. On χάρις see *Comment* on 1 Tim 1:2. Once again Paul includes Timothy with himself as he uses the plural ἡμῶν, "our," Lord, continuing the implicit argument that Paul and Timothy are joined in their gifts and ministry (cf. v 12). τοῦ κυρίου ἡμῶν, "our Lord," is Jesus; see v 12.

ὑπερπλεόνασεν, "completely overflowed," is the first word in the verse, its position emphasizing that God's grace was totally sufficient for Paul. It is the same type of word as in Rom 5:20, where Paul says "where sin increased [ἐπλεόνασεν], grace abounded [ὑπερπερίσσευσεν] all the more." It is a rare word, not occurring elsewhere in the Greek Bible and rarely in secular literature; LSJ cites only two references. It is likely that Paul coined the word here, the compound use of ὑπέρ, "more than," emphasizing the superabundance of God's grace. This type of compound construction is a favorite with Paul. (BAGD lists ten compounds with ὑπέρ used by Paul.) This particular word was the source of the title for John Bunyan's autobiography, *Grace Abounding to the Chief of Sinners* (1666).

Along with God's grace came πίστεως καὶ ἀγάπης τῆς ἐν Χριστῷ Ἰησοῦ, "faith and love that are in Christ Jesus." Faith and love complete the triad begun by grace and continue the wordplay on πίστις, "faith" (see *Form/Structure/Setting*). On πίστις see *Introduction*, "Themes in the PE." On ἀγάπη, "love," see *Comment* on 1 Tim 1:5. There are two questions raised by this phrase: (1) Whose faith and love are they, God's or Paul's? (2) Why is grace mentioned separately from faith and love?

(1) Paul could be saying that God's faithfulness (cf. Rom 3:3) and love, along with his grace, motivated him to extend mercy to Paul. However, the flow of the passage suggests that faith and love were gifts given to Paul by a gracious God. Formerly, Paul had been a blasphemer, persecutor, and insolent because he acted in ἀπιστίᾳ, "unbelief" (v 13). This triad is countered by the triad of grace, faith (πίστεως), and love. While grace is God's grace, faith is a gift given by God to counter Paul's lack of faith (cf. Calvin, Kelly, Knight). Love would then also be God's gift so Paul could love those he formerly persecuted, Christ and Christians, a trait presumably lacking from someone described as a blasphemer, a persecutor, and an insolent person. Knight points out that when Paul elsewhere speaks of faith and love, and gives thanks to Christ for what he has done, "it is believing faith and love in Christ that are in view (1 Cor. 13:13; Eph. 1:15; 1 Thes. 1:3; 3:6; 2 Thes. 1:3)" (98). This seems to be how the same phrase in 2 Tim 1:13 is understood (cf. Gal 5:22). Faith and love are often paired in Paul (2 Tim 1:13; Gal 5:6; Eph 1:15; 3:17; 6:23; 1 Thess 1:3; 5:8; Phlm 5).

(2) Some object that Paul would never separate grace from faith and love. Scott (13) calls the latter two mere moral qualities separate from grace. Gealy (390) and Easton (11) say that here they are the results of justification and not its condition. Oberlinner (42) says that they have become Christian qualities (although their christological character is emphasized). Hanson ([1983] 60) says the author himself did not understand what he meant by all this. But the thrust of this paragraph is that salvation is not through merit but through God's mercy and grace. Paul isolates grace to emphasize this fact; by contrast, faith and love are not qualities leading to salvation but gifts to Paul countering his previous unbelief and unloving persecution. μετά, "with," describes the closest connection possible between these three (Kelly, 54; contra Dibelius-Conzelmann, 28). Guthrie argues that grace is visible only when seen in the qualities of faith and love, and without grace, faith and love do not exist (64–65). As happens so often, interpretation of the text varies widely if the ad hoc nature of the PE is not considered significant. Fee comments, "For Paul, God's is always the prior action. Faith is a response to grace (Rom. 3:23–25; Eph. 2:18), and faith acts in love (Gal. 5:6; cf. 1:5)," and concludes, "the theology of this passage is thoroughly Pauline" (52).

This is the first of nine uses of the phrase ἐν Χριστῷ, "in Christ," in the PE. It describes "a profound personal identification with Christ which is the basis of salvation and new life" (Allan, *NTS* 10 [1963–64] 115), which may include the idea of mystical union (cf. Rom 6:11; 8:1) and incorporation into Christ as the new Adam. Although most usages in Paul have a mystical component, there is flexibility of usage in the acknowledged Pauline letters where "in Christ" can point "to Christ as the channel or medium of redemption and love" (Allan, *NTS* 10 [1963–64] 117; cf. Rom 3:24: "through the redemption which is in Christ Jesus"; Rom 8:39: "love of God in Christ Jesus") and can be synonymous with "Christian" (1 Cor 4:17: "my ways in Christ"; Gal 1:22: ταῖς ἐκκλησίαις ... ταῖς ἐν Χριστῷ, "the church of Christ"; Col 1:2: "saints and faithful brethren in Christ"). Paul usually uses the phrase in connection with people, saying they are "in Christ"; significant then is the use of "in Christ" with the gift of grace in 1 Cor 1:4: "I give thanks to God always for you because of the grace of God which was given you in Christ Jesus." This same flexibility of usage is present in the PE, although nowhere in the PE does Paul speak of a person being "in Christ" (see *Introduction,* "The Theological Problem"). Paul speaks of the gifts of "faith and love" (1 Tim 1:14), "life" (2 Tim 1:1), "salvation" (2 Tim 2:10; although this may be traditional material Paul is quoting and not his own construction), and "grace" (2 Tim 1:9) as being available "in Christ."

While some interpreters speak of faith, love, etc. in the PE as virtues, this is not helpful. Paul is not saying that Timothy should strive to achieve faith. Rather, he is saying that God has made these gifts available to those who are "in Christ," and Timothy should make use of the "faith and love" (2 Tim 1:13) and "grace" (2 Tim 2:1) that are his in Christ, and empowered by them he should perform his ministry. The mystical sense is seen in 2 Tim 3:12 when Paul says "All wishing to live godly lives in Christ Jesus will be persecuted" (here "in Christ" denotes the sphere in which Christians exist). It is possible that 1 Tim 3:13 ("faith which is in Christ Jesus") and 2 Tim 3:15 ("the holy writings, which are able to make you wise for salvation through faith that is in Christ Jesus") stand outside the scope of this discussion because the phrase may simply identify the object of Timothy's faith. Yet these too could be speaking of the faith available for those "in Christ." While somewhat different in expression (albeit with Pauline parallels), there is little difference between these uses of "in Christ" and Paul's description elsewhere of a person being "in Christ." It is only the person "in Christ" who is able to receive the gifts that are "in Christ." As Kelly states, "Faith and love are not qualities hanging in the air but always belong to persons; even if he remains unmentioned, their personal possessor is always implied" (53).

Within the Ephesian situation the opponents are teaching adherence to their mythical reinterpretations of Jewish law that downplay the role of Christ (cf. *Introduction,* "The Ephesian Heresy"). Here Paul stresses that the gifts of God are only available for those who are ἐν Χριστῷ, "in Christ," and this should be an encouragement to Timothy as he faces severe opposition, knowing that these gifts are his. Seven of the nine occurrences of ἐν Χριστῷ in the PE are found in 2 Timothy, which of all the letters in the PE offers the most encouragement.

15 In vv 12–14 Paul contrasted what he was with what God had done for him. His personal testimony was the basis of his argument that God saves sinners through his mercy and grace. In v 15 he now backs up his argument by quoting a general principle concerning the purpose for Christ's coming and appends a personal note that ties the general principle back to his personal testimony. The Ephesians should not be pursuing the law; they should be pursuing Christ, who came to save sinners, which is clearly seen in his saving of Paul, the worst of sinners.

πιστὸς ὁ λόγος καὶ πάσης ἀποδοχῆς ἄξιος, ὅτι Χριστὸς Ἰησοῦς ἦλθεν εἰς τὸν κόσμον ἁμαρτωλοὺς σῶσαι, ὧν πρῶτός εἰμι ἐγώ, "Trustworthy is the saying and worthy of complete acceptance: 'Christ Jesus came into the world in order to save sinners,' of whom I am the foremost." This is the first of the faithful sayings in the PE; see *Form/Structure/Setting*. In this case, the saying is "Christ Jesus came into the world in order to save sinners," and to this Paul appends a personal note, "of whom I am the foremost." Thus Paul presents the same dichotomy that was observed in vv 12–14. The belief that Jesus came to save people from their sin is part of the very fabric of Pauline and NT proclamation (1 Cor 15:3; cf. Mark 2:17; 10:45). Theological issues relating to universalism and particular atonement, which some find in this text (e.g., Oberlinner, 43), are not actually developed until 1 Tim 2:4.

The final phrase, ὧν πρῶτός εἰμι ἐγώ, "of whom I am the foremost," is of primary importance because it ties the faithful saying into Paul's argument. The emphatic position of πρῶτος, "foremost," and the emphatic use of the pronoun ἐγώ, "I," drive the point home. A number of interpretations of the phrase have been offered. (1) We can dismiss any notion that Paul is being hyperbolic. If God's mercy and grace have shone forth most clearly in Paul's conversion (vv 12–14) as an illustration for all future believers (v 16), then Paul's sin must have been real. (2) Paul could be understood to be saying not that he was the vilest person who ever lived but that he had done the vilest of all things: He had persecuted the church and Christ (Gal 1:13). As he says elsewhere, "I am the least of the apostles, who am not worthy to be called an apostle since I persecuted the church of God" (1 Cor 15:9; cf. Eph 3:8). Paul is judging himself not by the world's standards (cf. 2 Cor 11:5; 12:11; Phil 3:4–6) but from God's point of view. The problem with this interpretation is that Paul says εἰμί, "I am," not ἦν, "I was." (3) πρῶτος could indicate degree, hence "most significant," "most visible" (BAGD, 1c). It is not that Paul was the worst sinner but that he was the most prominent sinner. This would fit with v 16, which says that God held Paul up as an example of salvation by grace. When people see that even a sinner like Paul can be saved, they will know that salvation is by God's mercy and not by works (cf. Acts 9:21). In Paul's lifetime there was no other individual whose persecution of the church was as well known as his. (4) πρῶτος could also be understood as the "worst" in the sense that Paul had an abiding sense of being a forgiven sinner (cf. Spicq 1:344). Certainly Paul must have shuddered whenever he remembered his previous acts of persecution, and certainly this would have produced a continual amazement at the incomprehensible gifts of God's mercy and grace that had been so undeservedly bestowed upon him in superabundant measure. The context favors this latter interpretation since the purpose of this paragraph is to stress God's mercy in salvation. Bunyan, having drawn the title of his autobiographical *Grace Abounding to the Chief of Sinners* from vv 14–15, apparently understood the present verb this way. See comment by Stott (53) and his reference to the gospel account of the Pharisee and tax collector: "God have mercy on me, *the* sinner" (the use of the article "Par Excellence"; Wallace, *Greek Grammar*, 223).

That Paul would have made such a statement has been denied by some. Easton (117) calls it a mere "formality," and Scott says that "we cannot but feel that the self-abasement is morbid and unreal; it suggests a type of piety which is out of keeping with the manly sincerity of Paul" (14). Yet it is anything but formal, morbid, theatrical, and unreal. It is historically accurate as far as we know. It is a humble recognition of the grossness of sin and of the awesomeness that God's mercy and grace would extend to someone like him. It is similar in spirit to Paul's admission in Rom 7:13–25 (if in fact Rom 7 refers to his current life). Paul carried with himself not only the victory of one justified but also the constant awareness that he was a sinner saved by grace.

The faithful saying is an excellent example of theological teaching (see Barrett, 45). The major part of the PE deals with practical issues, but behind them lies a theological base, most clearly defined in 1 Tim 3:15. Throughout 1 Timothy are thus found a smattering of theological truths. ἦλθεν εἰς τὸν κόσμον, "came into the world," is language reminiscent of the Fourth Gospel (cf. John 1:9; 3:19; 6:14; 9:39; 11:27; 12:46; 16:28; 18:37) as it joins the incarnation and redemption. Most agree that the primary purpose of the faithful saying is not to teach preexistence, as does similar language in John (e.g., John 6:41, 51, 58; 8:42; 16:27–30, 38, 42; 7:28; 13:3); yet the saying is compatible with such a doctrine. This saying could be an adaptation of a tradition coming from Jesus (Luke 5:32; 19:10; see Knight, 101–2). On σῶσαι, "to save," see *Introduction,* "Themes in the PE." Here the past aspect of salvation is emphasized. While it is an overstatement to speak here of the "universal saving intention of God" (contra Hanson, [1983] 61), the verse does prepare the way for the emphasis in 1 Tim 2:1–7 that salvation should be offered to all and not just to the elect few.

16 ἀλλὰ διὰ τοῦτο ἠλεήθην, ἵνα ἐν ἐμοὶ πρώτῳ ἐνδείξηται Χριστὸς Ἰησοῦς τὴν ἅπασαν μακροθυμίαν πρὸς ὑποτύπωσιν τῶν μελλόντων πιστεύειν ἐπ' αὐτῷ εἰς ζωὴν αἰώνιον, "But for this reason I was shown mercy: so that in me as foremost Christ Jesus might display his complete patience as an illustration for those who would believe in him for eternal life." Previously Paul said that he was shown mercy since he had been ignorant (v 13). This was the condition that allowed God to overlook his sins. Now in v 16 Paul gives the reason for God's mercy: Paul was to be an illustration of God's grace and mercy in salvation for all who would believe. In vv 13–15 Paul is acting out his role as a living example of God's patience and mercy, a role assigned to him at his conversion as v 16 says. It is the Jewish rabbinic argument of the harder to the easier (*qal wāḥômer*): if God's mercy can extend to someone as sinful as Paul, surely it can reach anyone. This also shows that Paul is recounting his conversion experience not merely for informational purposes but for the Ephesian church; Timothy already knows it.

ἀλλά, "but," carries its full adversative force, contrasting Paul's state of sin with God's mercy. διὰ τοῦτο, "for this reason" (cf. 2 Tim 2:10), looks forward to the following clause for the reason that God showed Paul mercy. ἀλλα . . . ἠλεήθην, "but . . . I was shown mercy," repeats the same phrase from v 13. This repetition serves to emphasize the point of the paragraph—God's mercy. Moule (*Idiom-Book,* 77) classifies the prepositional phrase ἐν ἐμοί, "in me," as a subcategory of the instrumental use called exemplary (1 Cor 4:6; 9:15): "in my case, as the foremost example." πρῶτος, "foremost," repeats the same word from v 15, where it describes Paul as the foremost of sinners. Either it contains the same meaning as in v 15, its repetition here being a reminder of what was just said, or it has shifted its meaning: as the worst of sinners Paul serves as the primary example.

ἐνδεικνύναι, "to demonstrate," is an important word for Paul. He uses it eight times and its two cognates four times (ἔνδειξις, "evidence": Phil 1:28; Rom 3:25, where Christ's death is evidence of God's righteousness; 2 Cor 8:24; ἔνδειγμα, "evidence": 2 Thess 1:5). It is used with both God and people as the subject. Slaves are to show entire and true fidelity (Titus 2:10). All believers are to show courtesy to all people (Titus 3:2). Alexander showed great harm to Paul (2 Tim 4:14). Outside the PE Paul says that God demonstrates his power (Rom 9:17), wrath (Rom 9:22), and riches (Eph 2:7). Gentiles who do what the law requires show that these requirements are written on their hearts (Rom 2:15). The Corinthian church is to give proof of its love (2 Cor 8:24; cf. Heb 6:10).

μακροθυμία, "patience," is usually understood as God's patience with the response he receives from people, a patience exhibited by his refusal to punish them. Although this is typical in the OT (Exod 34:6; Num 14:18) and Paul (see below), this is not its meaning here. Christ's patience was demonstrated in Paul, and Paul is the illustration for future believers. Therefore, the patience that Christ exhibited is his patience with Paul in particular. The OT frequently pictures God as being patient with the world, slow to anger and abounding in love (Exod 34:6 [Hanson ([1983] 62) thinks 1 Tim 1:14–17 is a midrash on Exod 34:6]; Num 14:18; Pss 86:15; 103:8; Joel 2:13; Jonah 4:2; cf. Rom 2:4; 9:22; 1 Pet 3:20).

μακροθυμία and its verbal cognate μακροθυμεῖν, "to be patient," occur eleven times in Paul. With much the same thought as in 1 Tim 1:16, Paul elsewhere says that the purpose of God's patience and ἀνοχή, "forbearance," is to lead sinners to repentance (Rom 2:4; cf. Rom 3:25, where Christ's death is a demonstration [ἔνδειξις] of God's righteousness because in his forbearance [ἀνοχή] he had passed over previous sins). Paul also says that God, wishing to demonstrate (ἐνδείκνυναι) his wrath, endured with all patience (μακροθυμία) the vessels of wrath (Rom 9:22). Patience is a fruit of the Spirit (Gal 5:22), a characteristic of love (1 Cor 13:4), and a quality that should be possessed by all believers (Eph 4:2; Col 1:11; 3:12; 1 Thess 5:14). Paul says he was patient (2 Tim 3:10), especially with the Corinthian church (2 Cor 6:6), and so Timothy should be patient (2 Tim 4:2; cf. W. Meikle, "The Vocabulary of 'Patience' in the New Testament," *Exp* 19 [1920] 304–13).

ἅπας, "complete" (cf. Moule, *Idiom-Book*, 93–94), occurs elsewhere in the Pauline corpus only in Eph 4:13. Bernard (33) says it is a strengthened form of πᾶς, "all" (cf. LSJ, 181). The Attic distinction was to use πᾶς when the preceding letter was a vowel and ἅπας when it was a consonant, although this was not followed in the Koine (Robertson, *Grammar*, 771). In the NT ἅπας is used most often by Luke (twenty-one of the thirty occurrences in the NT).

God was patient with Paul so that he would be πρὸς ὑποτύπωσιν, "as an illustration." πρός here indicates the "goal aimed at or striven toward" (BAGD, 710 [III 3]). ὑποτύπωσις, "illustration," occurs in the NT only here and in 2 Tim 1:13, where Paul tells Timothy to hold on to the "pattern" of healthy words that he has heard from Paul. It can mean "model" or "sketch" (L. Goppelt, *TDNT* 8:248). Thus in the NT it has the same basic meaning as τύπος, "type, example" (cf. discussion in *Comment* on 1 Tim 4:12). Helpful then are Paul's statements that he is an example to the church (Phil 3:17; 2 Thess 3:9) and that the Thessalonian church is to be an example for the believers in Macedonia and Achaia (1 Thess 1:7; cf. 1 Tim 4:12 for Timothy's role as an example). Some liken ὑποτύπωσις to the initial sketch drawn by the artist (Guthrie, 66; references in Lock, 16–17).

Paul is an example τῶν μελλόντων πιστεύειν ἐπ' αὐτῷ εἰς ζωὴν αἰώνιον, "for those who would believe in him for eternal life." The phrase has a somewhat universal feel to it. This may be in anticipation of the theme of 2:1–7, that salvation should be offered to all people. πιστεύειν, "to believe," is normally used with the simple dative or εἰς, "in, into," but it does occur several times with ἐπί, "in," and the dative (BAGD, 661 [2αγ]) or accusative. It is difficult to know what nuance, if any, is present in this particular construction. Robertson (*Grammar,* 601) says "the accusative suggests more the initial act of faith (in trust) while the locative [dative] implies that of state (trust)" (πιστεύειν ἐπί occurs usually with a personal object [Rom 9:33; 1 Pet 2:6; Rom 10:11], only once with an impersonal one [Luke 24:25; Moule, *Idiom-Book,* 50].) The NT, however, does not seem to make a distinction in meaning between the two constructions (Rom 9:33 [Isa 28:16]; 10:11; cf. Acts 11:17; Matt 27:42; 1 Pet 2:6 [Isa 28:16]; variant in John 3:15). Kelly (55) thinks that Isa 28:16 may have been in Paul's mind, and this would account for the construction.

ζωή, "life," in the PE is more than physical existence. In John's terminology (cf. 10:10), it is an abundant life lived as God intended and is possible only through the work of Christ. Paul tells the rich that they should not set their hope on riches but should be rich in good deeds. By doing this they will create a good foundation for the future and take hold of τῆς ὄντως ζωῆς, "the true life," life in the fullest sense of the word (1 Tim 6:17–19). The ἐπαγγελίαν ζωῆς, "promise of life," is for a quality of life that is available only through a relationship τῆς ἐν Χριστῷ Ἰησοῦ, "in Christ" (2 Tim 1:1), and the work of God's Spirit (Titus 3:7; cf. 1 Tim 1:16), and therefore is the sure hope (cf. 1 Tim 1:1) of believers (Titus 1:2) who pursue godliness (1 Tim 4:8). It is eternal life (1 Tim 1:16; 6:12; Titus 1:2; 3:7; cf. Rom 2:7; 5:21; 6:22, 23; Gal 6:8), the opposite of death and synonymous with immortality (2 Tim 1:10; cf. Trench, *Synonyms,* 128–33). These references confirm that the concept of ζωή, "life," in the PE is much more than simple existence; it is a sharing of the eschatological age here and now in anticipation of life in the eschaton, a totally different kind of life. αἰώνιος, "eternal," in the PE also modifies God as the "king eternal" (1 Tim 1:17), who has eternal dominion (1 Tim 6:16), and salvation as "eternal glory" (2 Tim 2:10). αἰώνιος also contains the idea of "without beginning," πρὸ χρόνων αἰωνίων, "before time" (2 Tim 1:9; Titus 1:2b; cf. Rom 16:25).

17 τῷ δὲ βασιλεῖ τῶν αἰώνων, ἀφθάρτῳ ἀοράτῳ μόνῳ θεῷ, τιμὴ καὶ δόξα εἰς τοὺς αἰῶνας τῶν αἰώνων, ἀμήν, "Now to the king eternal, incorruptible, invisible, the only God, be honor and glory forever. Amen." It is fitting and usual for Paul, having reflected upon God's grace and mercy and what he has done for him, to burst into a doxology of praise. While this doxology stresses the transcendent nature of God, this only serves to heighten Paul's amazement that God would, in his mercy and grace, stoop to save a sinner such as Paul. See discussion of doxologies in *Form/ Structure/Setting.*

The literary style of the doxology is well thought out. The cognate of αἰώνιος, "eternal" (life), in v 16 is found in the phrase βασιλεῖ τῶν αἰώνων, "king eternal," in v 17. Modifying βασιλεῖ, "king," are three words beginning with alpha (αἰώνων, "eternal," ἀφθάρτῳ, "incorruptible," and ἀοράτῳ, "invisible") and the phrase μόνῳ θεῷ, "only God." What began with a statement of blessing (v 12) ends on a similar note of honor and glory. Paul closes on a note of δόξα, "glory," in much the same way that vv 8–11 closed with mention of the gospel revealing the glory of God. Then Paul invites Timothy and the readers to join with him in the ἀμήν, "amen." We therefore reach the end of Paul's initial argument against his Ephesian opponents: the law regulates the lives of the unrighteous; God's salvation, as seen in Paul, is through mercy and grace; praise God. While some of the terminology is rare in the Greek Bible and common in Hellenism (cf. Dibelius-Conzelmann, 30 n. 22), the concepts are fully Jewish Christian.

Is the βασιλεύς, "king," God the Father or Christ? βασιλεύς occurs in the PE elsewhere in 1 Tim 2:2, describing earthly kings, and in the doxology in 1 Tim 6:15, where it is addressed to God the Father. The only other doxology in the PE is in 2 Tim 4:18, where the subject, ὁ κύριος, "the Lord," is Jesus. βασιλεία, "kingdom," is used twice, both times referring to Christ (2 Tim 4:1,18), the latter occurring immediately before a doxology. The only divine actor in 1:12–17 seems to be Christ (unless τοῦ κυρίου, "Lord," in v 14 is God the Father), who is specifically addressed in vv 12, 14, 16. However, doxologies tend to be addressed to God and not to Christ, as in 1 Tim 6:15 (see references in *Form/Structure/Setting*). The theological question is whether Paul can describe Christ as "incorruptible, invisible, the only God." Perhaps this is another indication of the Christology of the PE, which joins God and Christ in such close union that at times it is difficult to distinguish them (see *Explanation* on 1 Tim 1:2). If the doxology is addressed to Christ, declaring him to be the "only God," it is theologically significant (cf. *Comment* on Titus 2:13). Oke's translation "alone divine" (*ExpTim* 67 [1955] 368), based on the anarthrous construction emphasizing quality rather than identity, seems doubtful. τῷ . . . βασιλεῖ, "to the king," is articular according to Apollonius's Canon (a noun modified by an articular genitive is normally articular; cf. Wallace, *Greek Grammar*, 239–40), and no article is required of the modifying adjective because the referent is already unique. The author could have made this clear by using θεῖος, "divine." The idea of God as king is commonly found throughout the OT, NT, and rabbinic literature (see G. von Rad, K. G. Kuhn, and K. L. Schmidt, *TDNT* 1:564–93).

The king is described with four qualities. (1) αἰών, "eternity," is a cognate of αἰώνιος, "eternal," in the previous verse. αἰών can mean "age," as seen in the phrase τὸν νῦν αἰῶνα, "the present age" (1 Tim 6:17; 2 Tim 4:10; Titus 2:12). Because of the Jewish concept of time, it can also refer to the age to come, consequently "eternity." It is found in the common Semitic idiom εἰς τοὺς αἰῶνας τῶν αἰώνων, "into the ages of ages," meaning "forever" (cf. Wallace, *Greek Grammar*, 88, 103–4) later in the same verse and in 2 Tim 4:18. On the one hand, because αἰών (v 17) is not the same word as αἰώνιος (v 16), the translation should reflect the shift. On the other hand, αἰών is used later in the same verse in the idiom meaning "forever." Since English does not have similar synonyms, it is best to preserve the wordplay and translate as "king eternal." On αἰών and αἰώνιος, see Burton, *Galatians*, 426–32. The actual phrase ὁ βασιλεὺς τῶν αἰώνων, "king of ages," is found in the Greek Bible elsewhere only in Rev 15:3 (*v.l.*) and Tob 13:7, 11 (cf. Exod 15:18; Ps 145:13; Sir 36:17), but the idea of God being eternal is a mainstay of OT thought (Gen 21:33; Pss 10:16; 74:12; 90:2; Isa 6:5; 9:5; 26:4; Hab 1:12; cf. Jer 10:10; Spicq, 1:347), and "eternal" is often applied to his attributes or activities (1 Kgs 10:9; Pss 16:11; 21:6; 33:11; 110:10; 119:89, 160; 136; Dan 4:3, 43; Hab 3:6; cf. H. Sasse, *TDNT* 1:197–209; J. Guhrt, *NIDNTT* 3:826–33; Str-B 3:643). It should not, therefore, be assumed that this appellation is only Hellenistic.

(2) God is ἄφθαρτος, "incorruptible," "unchangeable." This term is applied to

God in the NT elsewhere only in Rom 1:23 to distinguish him from mortal creatures. It is also used in reference to the Christian's resurrected body (1 Cor 15:52) and crown (1 Cor 9:25; 1 Peter uses it to describe the believer's inheritance [1:4] and a woman's spirit [3:5]). The cognate noun ἀφθαρσία describes the "incorruptibility" brought by Christ (2 Tim 1:10; Rom 2:7) and the nature of the resurrected body (1 Cor 15:42). In Eph 6:4 it qualifies love as being either an "undying love" or something Paul wishes for the readers along with grace (Bruce, *Colossians*, 416). Somewhat the same idea is conveyed by ἀθανασία, "immortality," in 1 Tim 6:16 (ὁ μόνος ἔχων ἀθανασίαν, "the only one having immortality"; cf. *v.l.* in 1 Tim 1:17 in *Note* g; R. Bultmann, *TDNT* 3:22–25). The idea that God does not change is fully biblical, even if the actual words are not widely used (Ps 102:26–27; Isa 41:4; 48:12; Mal 3:6; Rom 1:23; Heb 1:11–12 [Ps 102:26–27]; Jas 1:17). ἄφθαρτος and ἀθάνατος, "immortal," appear frequently in Greek literature and especially in Philo (BAGD, 20, 125; cf. G. Harder, *TDNT* 9:93–106).

(3) God is ἀόρατος, "invisible." The same thought occurs in the doxology in 1 Tim 6:16: "the only one having immortality, the one dwelling in unapproachable light, whom no human has seen or is able to see." The OT never describes God as invisible (ἀόρατος occurs only in Gen 1:2, Isa 4:5, and 2 Macc 9:5). Yet the idea that God cannot be seen (Exod 33:18), even though his actions manifest him, permeates the entire corpus. This is why the Fourth Gospel can say that no one has ever seen God (John 1:18; 5:37) except the Son who makes him known (John 6:46; 12:45; 14:9). On the other hand, the Greek world used the term with great frequency, often in connection with the Platonic view of sense perception and ideas—the unseen. Philo uses ἀόρατος over one hundred times and ὁρατός, "visible," often with a negation, over seventy times, usually in describing God or his powers (cf. W. Michaelis, *TDNT* 5:320–27, 331–38, 368–70). ἀόρατος occurs in the NT elsewhere in describing God's nature (Rom 1:20; Col 1:15; Heb 11:27) and the spirit world (Col 1:16). Hanson ([1983] 62) says that this is the only place where God's invisibility is mentioned in the NT without its being followed by mention of his revelation in Christ (as in 1 Tim 6:16; cf. Rom 1:20; Col 1:15; cf. John 1:15; 6:46) and concludes that this was an oversight and the author "was no great theologian." But only a wooden appeal to formality would insist that every mention of God's invisibility be necessarily followed by mention of Christ's revelation.

(4) God is μόνῳ θεῷ, "the only God." This is the central affirmation of Judaism as the Shema so eloquently states: "Hear, O Israel: the LORD our God is one LORD" (Deut 6:4; cf. Mark 12:29, 32; cf. 1 Tim 2:5; 6:15–16; cf. John 5:44; 17:3; Rom 3:30; 1 Cor 8:4–6; Eph 4:6; Jude 25). The Shema was repeated every day at the synagogue and is still part of the daily prayer life of the pious Jew. It was perhaps this confession more than any other that made the Judeo-Christian outlook unique in the ancient world.

Paul began this paragraph by thanking Christ. He closes it by ascribing to God honor and glory, saying that God should be treated with the respect and the esteem he rightly deserves (cf. Lev 10:3; 1 Chr 29:12; Prov 3:9; 14:31; Dan 4:37; John 5:23; Phil 1:20; Rev 4:11). This idea is found in several NT doxologies (1 Tim 6:16; Rev 5:12; 7:12; cf. 4:9, 11; see summary in W. D. Mounce, *EDT*, 531). Glory in this case describes not the nature of God (cf. v 11) but the proper response of people toward God (e.g., Isa 66:5; Dan 4:34; Pss 34:3; 63:3; 69:30; 86:12). Honor and glory are closely related ideas, as demonstrated by their frequent association (Rom 2:7, 10;

Rev 4:9, 11; 5:12, 13; 7:12; cf. Exod 28:2; Job 37:22; 40:10; Pss 8:5; 28:1; 95:7; Dan 2:37; 4:27; Sir 3:11; 1 Macc 14:21; 2 Macc 5:16) and by the fact that τιμή, "honor," and δόξα, "glory," are both used to translate כבוד *kābôd*, "glory," in the LXX. See further references in *Comment* on 1 Tim 1:11; Delling, *TLZ* 77 (1952) 469–76; Robertson, *Exp* 8 (1921) 182–88; Owen, *JTS* n.s. 33 (1982) 132–50, 265–79.

On the idiom "forever," see αἰών above. Paul concludes the doxology with ἀμήν, "amen," inviting congregational assent with the meaning "So be it!" This was a common practice in the OT and synagogue, which passed over into the NT (Deut 27:15–26; Rom 15:33; 1 Cor 14:16; 2 Cor 1:20; Rev 1:7; 22:20). It is commonly used to conclude an epistle (1 Cor 6:24; Gal 6:18; Heb 13:25) or a doxology (Pss 41:13; 72:19; 89:52; 106:48; Rom 1:25; 9:5; 11:36; 16:27; Gal 1:5; Eph 3:21; Phil 4:20; Heb 13:21; 1 Pet 4:11; 5:11; 2 Pet 3:18; Jude 25; Rev 1:6; 7:12; cf. *v.l.* in Matt 6:13). It occurs elsewhere in the PE in 1 Tim 6:16 and 2 Tim 4:18, both in doxologies. On ἀμήν, "amen," see H. Schlier, *TDNT* 1:355–38; A. Stuiber, "Amen," *JAC* 1 (1958) 210–16; H. Bietenhard, *NIDNTT* 1:97–99; Burton, *Galatians*, 16–18.

Explanation

1 Tim 1 reveals that Paul's opponents have created myths based on the OT law and are teaching that these are the means of salvation and the regulations for daily life. Paul's argument against them falls into two parts. In vv 8–11 he argues that the law does not apply to those who live righteous lives but only to those sinning. He ends on a personal note that leads into the second half of his argument (vv 12–17): salvation is not achieved by any individual through works righteousness but by God's mercy and grace alone. This is shown by Paul's conversion experience, to which he refers.

Paul begins by thanking Christ for what he has done (vv 12–14): Christ strengthened Paul by giving him the gifts necessary for his task. His appointment to ministry is evidence that God knew he would be trustworthy. What is amazing is that God did this even though Paul had been a sinner. Yet his sins were not "sins of the high hand" but sins of ignorance, and so God chose to show him mercy and grace, free gifts, totally absolving Paul of his former sins. Paul next gives two reasons why God showed him mercy (vv 15–16). Citing a known saying, Paul argues that Christ's primary purpose in coming was to save sinners. Particularly in Paul's case, God saved him so that he could be held up to everyone as an example of God's mercy and patience with sinners. These two verses give us one of the clearest insights into Paul's heart. Speaking as a Christian, he now sees that his violent persecution of the church and of Christ made him the worst of sinners, not in any morbid sense but with a continuing remembrance of being a sinner redeemed by the mercy of God. Paul closes with a doxology to God (v 17). As is often the case, reflection upon what God has done causes Paul to burst into praise of the only true God, who is deserving of honor and glory forever. Throughout this paragraph Paul is establishing at least two basic points: (1) Salvation is not something done by observance of law. It is a free gift of God's mercy and grace. With Paul as an example, this should be clear. (2) Timothy should be encouraged because God's grace is sufficient. It strengthened Paul for his task, and it will do the same for him (v 18).

Several questions come to mind after Paul's statement that his previous unbelief was prompted by ignorance. (1) Did Paul deserve mercy since he was ignorant? No.

Paul never says he deserved anything, and in fact the whole paragraph is an argument against this very position. Unbelief caused by ignorance provides no grounds for demanding God's mercy, but Paul understands it to be the reason God chose to show him mercy instead of the condemnation that his actions justifiably deserved. (2) Was Paul not guilty because he was ignorant? No. Ignorance is never an excuse for sin, but yet some sins are more easily pardoned than others (Luke 23:34). (3) Would Paul have been shown mercy if he had not been ignorant? It is rarely profitable to ask "What if?" questions, but in this context Paul seems to be implying that he would not have received mercy if he had known what he was doing. (4) Is Paul a paradigm of how God will deal with all ignorant sinners? Rom 2 answers this in the negative. 1 Tim 1:13 does not present a complete doctrine of how God deals with sin; it is Paul's personal testimony of how God dealt with him. The passage should not be pushed beyond its intention.

D. Encouragement and Warning for Timothy (1 Tim 1:18–20)

Bibliography

Beasley-Murray, P. "Ordination in the New Testament." In *Anyone for Ordination? A Contribution to the Debate on Ordination,* ed. P. Beasley-Murray. Tunbridge Wells: MARC, 1993. 1–13. **Browne, F. Z.** "What Was the Sin of Hymenaeus and Philetus?" *BSac* 102 (1945) 233–39. **Brox, N.** "Προφητεία im ersten Timotheusbrief." *BZ* 20 (1976) 229–32. **Bruggen, J. van.** *Die geschichtliche Einordnung der Pastoralbriefe.* **Fee, G. D.** *God's Empowering Presence.* 758–61. **Hort, F. J. A.** "Lecture XI: Titus and Timothy in the Pastoral Epistles." In *The Christian Ecclesia.* London: Macmillan, 1914. 177–88. **Käsemann, E.** "Das Formular einer neutestamentlichen Ordinationsparänese." In *Neutestamentliche Studien für Rudolf Bultmann,* ed. W. Eltester. BZNW 21. Berlin: Töpelmann, 1957. 261–68. **Lackmann, M.** "Paulus ordiniert Timotheus: Wie das katholische Bischofs- und Priesteramt entsteht." *Bausteine* 3.12 (1963) 1–4; 4.13 (1964) 1–6; 4.14 (1964) 1–4; 5.17 (1965) 1–4; 5.18 (1965) 1–5. **Lohse, E.** *Die Ordination im Spätjudentum und im Neuen Testament.* Berlin: Evangelische Verlagsanstalt, 1951. 501–23. **Pfitzner, V. C.** *Paul and the Agon Motif.* 165–86. **Ranft, J.** "Depositum." *RAC* 3:778–84. **Roloff, J.** "Der Kampf gegen die Irrlehrer: Wie geht man miteinander um?" *BK* 46 (1991) 114–20. **Sevenster, J. N.** *Paul and Seneca.* 162–64. **Thornton, T. C. G.** "Satan—God's Agent for Punishing." *ExpTim* 83 (1972) 151–52. **Warkentin, M.** *Ordination: A Biblical-Historical View.* Grand Rapids, MI: Eerdmans, 1982. 136–52.

Translation

[18]*This command I am entrusting to you, child Timothy, in accordance with the prophecies previously made about you, in order that by them you might fight* [a] *the good fight,* [19]*holding on to faith and a good conscience. By rejecting [their faith and good conscience], some have shipwrecked the faith,* [20]*among whom are Hymenaeus and Alexander, whom I have delivered over to Satan in order that they might be taught through punishment not to blaspheme.*

Notes

ᵃOur text has the present-tense στρατεύῃ (ℵ² A D² F G H 33 1739 1881ᵛⁱᵈ TR). Some alter to the aorist στρατεύσῃ (ℵ* D* Ψ 1175 *pc;* Cl).

Form/Structure/Setting

Paul now brings his argument of the chapter to a close. There are several verbal and conceptual links with vv 3–7 that have led many to connect vv 18–20 more closely with them than with vv 8–17. παραγγελία, "command," in v 18 repeats the same noun and its verbal cognate in v 3 and v 5. πίστις, "faith," and ἀγαθὴ συνείδησις, "good conscience," are paired in both paragraphs (vv 5, 19). Paul repeats the connection between deliberately choosing to abandon moral and spiritual virtues and the resulting improper behavior of his opponents (vv 6, 19). The opponents are again in the forefront with two leaders singled out for special attention. Paul's command to stop the opponents comes not only from himself (v 3) but is also in accordance with the prophecies about Timothy (v 18).

But there are also considerable links between vv 8–17 and vv 18–20. βλασφημεῖν, "to blaspheme" (v 20), looks back to Paul's earlier blasphemy (v 13) and back even further to those for whom the law was intended (vv 9–10). Just as God entrusted Paul with the gospel (v 11), so also Paul is entrusting Timothy with this request to guard the gospel (v 18). Just as Paul was adequately strengthened by God (v 12), so also Timothy's gifts, which were given through prophecy, are more than adequate weapons for his Ephesian warfare (v 18). Note also that vv 18–20 do not repeat the command of v 3. Vv 18–20 build upon the teaching given in vv 8–17, provide the incentive for accomplishing Timothy's task, and act as an inclusio by repeating words and ideas from the first paragraph.

There are several significant themes in vv 18–20 that are intertwined. (1) The passage gives divine validation for what Paul has been saying: it is in accordance with divine prophecy. (2) Encouragement is provided for a possibly discouraged Timothy with a reminder of the prophecies and the fact that the God who strengthened Paul will do the same for him. (3) Timothy is cautioned not only to take the problem seriously but to be careful that he himself not fall prey to the same errors. (4) Notes of seriousness and urgency are added to the problem. A παραγγελία, "command," is given in accordance with divine prophecy, and the situation is so advanced that excommunication has already proven necessary. (5) There also is a note of warning to the Ephesians. Paul will take, and in fact already has taken, necessary steps to protect the truth of the gospel. If Paul can discipline two of the opposition's leaders, then no one else is exempt from what Timothy must do. This in turn should encourage Timothy.

Vv 18–20 are one sentence linked by a preposition (κατά, "in accordance with"), conjunction (ἵνα, "in order that"), participle (ἔχων, "holding on to"), and three relative pronouns (ἥν, ὧν, οὕς): "This command I am entrusting . . . *in accordance with* the prophecies . . . *in order that* . . . you might fight . . . *holding on to* faith . . . *which* some have rejected . . . among *whom* are Hymenaeus . . . *whom* I have delivered over to Satan." The passage divides in half: Paul encourages Timothy by reminding him of the prophecies (vv 18–19a) and then contrasts Timothy with the opponents (vv 19b–20). The translation offers two sentences to clarify this division.

Comment

18–19a Ταύτην τὴν παραγγελίαν παρατίθεμαί σοι, τέκνον Τιμόθεε, κατὰ τὰς προαγούσας ἐπὶ σὲ προφητείας, ἵνα στρατεύῃ ἐν αὐταῖς τὴν καλὴν στρατείαν ἔχων πίστιν καὶ ἀγαθὴν συνείδησιν, "This command I am entrusting to you, child Timothy, in accordance with the prophecies previously made about you, in order that by them you might fight the good fight, holding on to faith and a good conscience." Paul had urged Timothy to command his Ephesian opponents to stop teaching (v 3), a command that had love as its goal (v 5). He had also given Timothy the theological reason that the opponents' theology was wrong (vv 8–17), and in so doing had said that God had adequately strengthened him for the task. Now Paul stresses that this command is not merely his own idea but is in accordance with prophecies made about Timothy at an earlier time. In other words, this charge is coming not only from Paul but also from God. Timothy should also be encouraged when he reads that just as God strengthened Paul for his task (cf. 2 Tim 1:5–6; 2:1; 1 Tim 1:12), so also the spiritual gifts witnessed to by the prophecies are sufficient for Timothy's task. But as Timothy fights the spiritual war, he must be cautious to preserve his faith and his good conscience, not compromising himself as others have done (i.e., Hymeneaus and Alexander). For a discussion of the prophecies about Timothy, see the excursus following v 20.

παραγγελία, "command," repeats the same word as in v 5 and its verbal cognate in v 3, so the primary reference in v 18 appears to be Paul's charge to Timothy that he stop the false teachers. However, v 3 and v 5 refer to an accomplished past event while παρατίθεμαι, "I am entrusting," is present tense. Some (Chrysostom, Fee) think it looks forward to v 18b: "in order that [ἵνα] by them you might fight the good fight." However, the ἵνα clause provides not the content of the command but the desired result (i.e., the command is not to fight), and hence the command is not identified. The verbal link with vv 3, 5 seems very strong. Paul may be thinking of the command as it is expounded in vv 4–17, and thus v 18 acts as a summary of vv 13–17, adding that Timothy's ministry in Ephesus is aided by the knowledge gained through the prophecies, which will become weapons of his good spiritual warfare. παρατιθέναι, "to entrust," picks up the thought of Paul being entrusted with the gospel (πιστεύειν, v 11), and is continued in 2 Tim 2:2 where Paul tells Timothy to entrust (παρατιθέναι) what he has learned to faithful men who in turn will teach others (cf. *Comment* on 2 Tim 1:12). This concept of entrusting the gospel message to others is a significant theme in the PE (cf. 2 Tim 1:13), but it is nothing new. It is found in Judaism in the transmission of the oral tradition and in the oral period of gospel transmission. It is what Paul has always said about himself, that the gospel was entrusted to him (v 11; cf. παραδιδόναι, "to hand on," 1 Cor 15:3; BAGD, 3). Now, especially as Paul and the other leaders of the early church are aging or dying, the emphasis continues to be on the necessity of properly transmitting the authoritative gospel message. Orthodoxy was not a second-century phenomenon alone; there always was a kerygma and the need to pass it on faithfully (see *Introduction,* "The Response to the Heresy").

The cognate noun παραθήκη, "what has been entrusted," is used in the NT only in the PE and always in an injunction φυλάσσειν, "to guard," what was entrusted (1 Tim 6:20; 2 Tim 1:12, 14). παρατιθέναι, "to entrust," is a legal term indicating something left in another's care for whose safety that person is responsible (C. Maurer, *TDNT* 8:162; bibliography in n. 2; cf. 1 Tim 1:11). Spicq ("S. Paul et la loi des dépôts," *RB* 40 [1931] 481–502) identifies its background in legal Roman thought. Ranft (*RAC* 3:781) prefers a rabbinic background with a Hellenistic-Roman flavor. See the excursus "Prophecies about Timothy" below.

On Paul's use of τέκνον, "child," see *Comment* on v 2. στρατεύῃ . . . τὴν καλην στρατείαν, "you might fight the good fight," is a wordplay similar to that in 2 Cor 10:3–4, which says believers do not fight a worldly war, for their weapons are divine. The terminology is military, describing a soldier at war, and is typically Pauline. Elsewhere Paul tells Timothy to suffer as a good soldier of Christ Jesus, being concerned to please God alone (2 Tim 2:3–4; cf. Rom 6:13; 7:23; 13:13; 1 Cor 9:7; 2 Cor 6:7; 10:3–5; Eph 6:10–17; Phil 2:25; 1 Thess 5:8; Phlm 2; 1 Pet 2:11; Jas 4:1; cf. Wis 5:17–20; O. Bauernfeind, *TDNT* 7:701–13; bibliography in BAGD, 608, on πανοπλία, "full armor"). Paul also uses the similar metaphor of the athletic struggle frequently (cf. 1 Tim 6:12; Pfitzner, *Agon Motif*). On καλός, "good," see *Comment* on 1 Tim 1:8.

What is the relationship between Timothy's spiritual fight and the phrase ἔχων. πίστιν καὶ ἀγαθὴν συνείδησιν, "holding on to faith and a good conscience"? πίστις, "faith," and ἀγαθὴ συνείδησις, "good conscience," could be the weapons of Timothy's warfare along with his spiritual gift (cf. Eph 6:16). But in the next verse Paul refers to Hymenaeus and Alexander, who have shipwrecked the faith (v 19b), which reminds Timothy of his opponents in general, who have seared their consciences (4:2). This suggests that Paul is contrasting Timothy's faith and good conscience with the opponents' lack of the same and urging Timothy to watch himself closely, lest he fall into the same trap ("holding on to [ἔχων] *your own* faith and good conscience"). Throughout the PE Paul cautions Timothy to watch himself carefully (cf. 1 Tim 4:16). This is the first mention of an important theme in the PE: personal integrity. That Timothy is Paul's lieutenant in a position of authority does not make him exempt from the same temptations that led Paul's opponents to defile their integrity. Therefore Paul urges Timothy to watch both himself and his teaching. Paul also stresses the idea, found throughout the PE, that a leader must possess the qualities he is trying to enforce in others (see *Comment* on 1 Tim 4:16). On πίστις, "faith," see *Introduction*, "Themes of the PE." πίστις and ἀγαθὴ συνείδησις, "good conscience," are paired three times in the PE (1 Tim 1:5, 19; 3:9). For Paul, what a person believes (faith) and how that person behaves (conscience) are inseparable. This is a major theme in the PE and explains why Paul attacks the behavior of his opponents; their illicit behavior is a clear indication of the falseness of their teaching. For further discussion, see *Introduction*, "The Response to the Heresy."

19b–20 ἥν τινες ἀπωσάμενοι περὶ τὴν πίστιν ἐναυάγησαν, ὧν ἐστιν Ὑμέναιος καὶ Ἀλέξανδρος, οὓς παρέδωκα τῷ σατανᾷ, ἵνα παιδευθῶσιν μὴ βλασφημεῖν, "By rejecting [their faith and good conscience], some have shipwrecked the faith, among whom are Hymenaeus and Alexander, whom I have delivered over to Satan in order that they might be taught through punishment not to blaspheme." The reason it is so important that Timothy maintain his own faith and good conscience is that Paul's opponents have already chosen to abandon theirs and consequently have shipwrecked the Christian faith by bringing it into reproach. This adds notes of urgency and seriousness; the destructiveness of the opponents' teaching has already had devastating results, and Timothy must quickly command them to stop teaching.

ἀπωσάμενοι, "rejecting," indicates a conscious, deliberate rejection, an "active spurning" (Kelly, 57) and not a passive, careless slipping away from faith (cf. Acts 7:27, 39; Rom 11:1, 2). Paul's opponents made a deliberate decision to abandon their faith and to sear their consciences. (ἥν, "which," is the direct object of the participle ἀπωσάμενοι, "rejecting," and refers to both πίστιν, "faith," and ἀγαθὴν συνείδησιν, "good conscience.") Three issues arise in the passage: (1) What are the meanings of the two occurrences of πίστις, "faith"? (2) Why did the opponents make the decisions they made? (3) What does it mean to παραδιδόναι, "deliver," someone over to Satan?

(1) Did Paul's opponents abandon their personal trust in God or in the Christian faith, and did they shipwreck their personal faith or the Christian faith? To reject personal faith is the same as shipwrecking one's personal faith, so that combination seems unlikely. It is also doubtful Paul would say that they rejected the Christian faith and as a result shipwrecked their personal faith; one would expect rejection of personal faith to precede the consequences to the Christian faith. Within the overall context of the PE (see [2] below) it seems that Paul is saying that the opponents rejected their personal faith and as a result have brought the Christian faith into reproach, interpreting ναυαγεῖν, "to shipwreck," in the sense of bringing the church under reproach. See the similar construction of πίστις, "faith," with a preposition in 1 Tim 6:10, 21 and 2 Tim 2:18; 3:8, where πίστις is the Christian faith. The metaphor is not used elsewhere in the NT (cf. 2 Cor 11:25 for its literal use) but was common in secular Greek (Dibelius-Conzelmann, 33; Simpson, 38). This is an interesting mixing of metaphors with that of a good soldier in v 18. As Lock says, "The Christian teacher must be [a] good soldier and [a] good sailor too" (19). Does περὶ τὴν πίστιν, "concerning the faith," modify ἀπωσάμενοι, "rejecting [the faith]," or ἐναυάγησαν, "shipwrecked [the faith]"? The same expression occurs in 1 Tim 6:21 (περὶ τὴν πίστιν ἠστόχησαν, "departed from the faith") and 2 Tim 3:8 (ἀδόκιμοι περὶ τὴν πίστιν, "worthless concerning the faith"), with a similar expression in 2 Tim 2:18 (περὶ τὴν ἀλήθειαν ἠστόχησαν, "fallen short concerning the truth"; cf. 1 Tim 6:4; Titus 2:7). These parallels support the translation "shipwrecked the faith" here.

(2) We have here the same two thoughts as in 1:6. (a) Paul's opponents were neither coerced nor tricked into the heresy. They made a conscious, deliberate choice to reject the truth and as a result have brought the church into reproach. (b) Their choice was not built upon an intellectual problem or a sincere theological decision; it was a moral issue because it was based on a rejection of faith and conscience. As Scott asserts, "More often than we know, religious error has its roots in moral rather than in intellectual causes" (17).

(3) The Ephesian situation had become serious. Paul had delivered two of his opponents over to Satan so that they would learn not to blaspheme. In contrast to his usual practice of not naming his opponents (cf. 1 Tim 1:3), Paul mentions two by name, Hymenaeus and Alexander, who presumably were leaders in the opposition (ὧν, "among whom," is a partitive genitive; cf. Moule, *Idiom-Book*, 43). Hymenaeus is paired with Philetus as teaching that the resurrection is past (2 Tim 2:17), but he is not mentioned elsewhere, even in the noncanonical literature. An Alexander is mentioned four other times in the NT: (a) a member of the Jewish high priestly family (Acts 4:6); (b) the son of Simon (who carried Jesus' cross) and the brother of Rufus (Mark 15:21); (c) the Jewish Alexander who was shouted down

when he tried to speak to the rioting Ephesians (Acts 19:33; this Alexander probably would have argued that Christianity was different from Judaism and as such would have been an opponent of Paul [Marshall, *Acts*, 319]); and (d) a metal worker in Ephesus who did Paul great harm (2 Tim 4:14). The name Alexander was common, and therefore it is impossible to know for sure if one of these four could be the Alexander mentioned in 1 Tim 1:20. If the Alexander in 1 Tim 1:20 is the same as the fourth option, then Paul's excommunication must not have been effective. Hanson ([1983] 65) admits that Hymenaeus and Alexander were "known opponents of Paul," and criticizes Dibelius-Conzelmann's assertion that Hymenaeus and Alexander were contemporaries of the post-Pauline author, which incorrectly assumes that the author's readers were "so simple minded as to believe that persons living in their own day could have been alive and active forty years previously when Paul was still living" ([1983] 65).

The phrase παρέδωκα τῷ σατανᾷ ἵνα παιδευθῶσιν μὴ βλασφημεῖν, "I have delivered over to Satan in order that they might be taught through punishment not to blaspheme," is one of the more difficult statements in the PE to interpret. βλασφημεῖν, "to blaspheme," repeats the earlier reference in 1:13: just as Paul identified his pre-Christian life with sinners (vv 8–11) by calling himself a blasphemer (v 13), so also these two opponents are blaspheming and must learn to stop. They, like Saul of Tarsus, are persecuting the true church and therefore are persecuting Christ (see 1:13). βλασφημεῖν in the present tense indicates that blasphemy is part of their lifestyle, a continual practice (in 1 Tim 6:1 Paul speaks of blaspheming both God and the gospel message).

Despite all the trouble Hymenaeus and Alexander have caused, the purpose of Paul's delivering them to Satan is not merely punishment but remedial, looking forward to the day when they might learn not to blaspheme. παιδεύειν, "to instruct," means not only to educate but more significantly "to practice discipline," "to discipline with punishment" (BAGD, 603–4). Timothy and the Ephesian church must discipline to the extent of punishment, but they must do it with the goal of redemption. (Tertullian thought that both men were eternally lost [*Pud.* 13.19ff.].) The word is used of divine discipline (1 Cor 11:32 [where it is remedial]; 2 Cor 6:9; cf. Heb 12:6,10; Rev 3:19 [where it is also remedial]) as well as human discipline (Luke 23:16, 22; cf. discussion of its meaning "to instruct" in *Comment* on Titus 2:12). This difficult balance of firm yet not vindictive discipline is admirably represented by the only other occurrence of the word in the PE. Paul tells Timothy that he must discipline his opponents with gentleness, hoping that God will grant that they repent, come to know the truth, and escape the snare of the devil (2 Tim 2:25–26). Throughout the PE we see that Paul desires not only that the opponents be silenced but that they turn from their evil ways (cf. Titus 1:13).

παρέδωκα τῷ σατανᾷ, "I have delivered over to Satan," could include the idea of physical pain and death as punishment for sin. Parallel then would be the deaths of Ananias and Sapphira (Acts 5:1–11, where Satan filled Ananias's heart to lie, although Satan did not kill them), the blindness of Elymas the magician (Acts 13:11), and the sickness and death of some Corinthians who were partaking of the Lord's Supper improperly (1 Cor 11:30). Chrysostom includes the example of Job, but in his case punishment was not the issue, although he did suffer physical pain ("Homily 5"; NPNF 13:424). This parallel would introduce the concept of Satan being an agent of God. T. C. G. Thornton (*ExpTim* 83 [1971–2] 151–52) includes

Paul's thorn in the flesh (2 Cor 12:7), "a messenger of Satan," as another parallel. He argues from rabbinical statements that this view of Satan was current in Judaism, along with the view of Satan being God's chief adversary, which he labels an "inconsistency." Parallel also could be the passage in 1 Cor 5 (see below) where Satan seems to be acting as an agent of God in punishing sinners. The history of Israel shows that God used the enemy to deal with his chosen people (cf. 1 Kgs 11:14; Isa 45:1–13; Rom 9:15–18; possibly Job 1:12; 2:6), and the NT teaches that there are beneficial aspects to temptation and suffering (1 Cor 10:13–14; 12:7–10; Jas 1:12; 1 Pet 1:6–7). Chrysostom comments, "As executioners, though themselves laden with numerous crimes, are made the correctors of others; so it is here with the evil spirit" ("Homily 5"; NPNF 13:424).

Yet every other reference to Satan (σατανᾶς, διάβολος) in the PE pictures him as an enemy of the church. An elder must have a good reputation outside the church or he may fall into the snare set by Satan (1 Tim 3:7). Paul's hope is that the opponents will escape the snare of the devil, having been captured by him in order to do his will (2 Tim 2:26). Some of the women in Ephesus have already strayed after Satan (1 Tim 5:15). The only other reference to Satan in the PE is in 1 Tim 3:6 where Paul says new converts cannot be elders lest they become conceited and fall into the same condemnation as did Satan. Related is Paul's comment that ultimately the teaching of the Ephesian opponents is demonic (διδασκαλίαις δαιμονίων, "teachings of demons") in origin (1 Tim 4:1). (Paul uses διάβολος, "slanderous," to characterize slanderers in 1 Tim 3:11, 2 Tim 3:3, and Titus 2:3.) It may be easier to accept the idea of Satan being an agent of God if his punishment of sinners is seen not so much as voluntary obedience to the wishes of God as it is the natural consequences of a sinner being thrust into the Satanic sphere without divine protection. Paul and the rest of the NT are conscious of Satan's fight against believers (Luke 22:3, 31; John 13:27; Acts 5:3; 2 Cor 2:11; 4:4; Eph 2:2; 1 Thess 2:18; in general see Mark 4:15; Luke 13:16; 1 Cor 5:5; 7:5; 2 Cor 11:14; 1 Pet 5:8; Rev 2:9; 3:9).

Most commentators see the phrase παρέδωκα τῷ σατανᾷ, "I have delivered to Satan," as excommunication (not using the term as an anachronism). The world outside the church is Satan's realm. By being removed from Christian fellowship, Hymenaeus and Alexander are separated from the spiritual protection of the church and fully exposed to the power of Satan. The lesson they must learn is best taught by personal exposure to the malice of those who like themselves are fighting the truth. This does not exclude any idea of possible physical punishment, but that is not its primary purpose here. Kelly (38) and Lock (19) point to the similar language in Job 2:6 LXX: "And the Lord said to the devil, 'Behold, I deliver him to you'" (εἶπεν δὲ ὁ κύριος τῷ διαβόλῳ, Ἰδοὺ παραδίδωμί σοι αὐτόν). Social ostracism as a form of discipline is proposed in Titus 3:10 and was present in Judaism (John 9:22, 34; 12:42).

The text does not say when this excommunication occurred. A decision would be based to some degree on whether 1 Tim 1:3 implies that Paul was or was not at Ephesus when he originally asked Timothy to deal with the problem. The excommunication could have been done at a previous visit, through a letter, or by Paul in his apostolic authority and announced through this letter to Timothy. In 1 Cor 5:1–5, a similar passage (see below), Paul says that even though he is not present in Corinth he is present in spirit and has already pronounced judgment on the sinner; therefore the church is to deliver him over to Satan. The similarity of the language allows, and perhaps implies, that he was not present at Ephesus at the time of the excommunication in 1 Tim 1:20.

The only other time the phrase παραδιδόναι τῷ σατανᾷ, "to deliver to Satan," occurs in the NT is in 1 Cor 5:5. Instead of boasting over the immorality present among them and their tolerance of it, the church was παραδοῦναι τὸν τοιοῦτον τῷ σατανᾷ εἰς ὄλεθρον τῆς σαρκός, ἵνα τὸ πνεῦμα σωθῇ ἐν τῇ ἡμέρᾳ τοῦ κυρίου, "to deliver this man to Satan for the destruction of the flesh, that his spirit may be saved in the day of the Lord Jesus." Paul seems to be suggesting that physical punishment is remedial. Satan can punish the body but not the spirit, and all for the purpose of the person's eventual redemption. This is the same idea as in 1 Tim 1:20. Excommunication, as the final means of discipline, is a thoroughly biblical principle and is a Pauline demand laid on all churches (cf. Matt 18:15–20; Quinn, 250–53). Because of the similarity of the two passages, there is no reason to assume that the author of the PE thinks Paul has magical power (contra Dibelius-Conzelmann, 34). In 1 Cor 5 Paul is speaking as the authoritative apostle responsible for the Corinthian church, and in 1 Tim 1 for the Ephesian church.

Excursus: Prophecies about Timothy

The prophecies of 1 Tim 1:18 are mentioned in two other places. In 1 Tim 4:14 Paul urges Timothy not to "neglect the gift [χάρισμα] that is in you, which was given to you through a prophecy accompanied by the laying on of hands of the council of elders." In 2 Tim 1:6 Paul reminds Timothy to "rekindle the gift from God that is in you through the laying on of my hands." 2 Tim 1:5–7 is an encouragement to Timothy to continue firmly with his task; this note of encouragement is also found in the present passage. The mention of confessing "the good confession before many witnesses" (1 Tim 6:12) may also refer to this event. Five issues are raised concerning these passages. (See *Comment* on 1 Tim 4:14 for a discussion of the issues specifically related to that passage.)

(1) The three passages seem to refer to the same event. Twice Paul refers to the χάρισμα, "gift," Timothy received, presumably the gift of evangelism/teaching necessary for his ministry (see 1 Tim 4:14). Twice Paul mentions that the prophecy was accompanied by the laying on of hands. There are some differences, however. In 1 Tim 4:14 Paul refers to προφητεία, "prophecy" (singular), and in 1 Tim 1:18 to προφητεῖαι, "prophecies" (plural). In 1 Tim 4:14 it was the council of elders that laid on hands, while in 2 Tim 1:6 it was Paul himself. But these differences are not insurmountable. (a) Several elders could have prophesied the same message; while they were different utterances, they were the same prophecy. (b) Paul could have been part of the council of elders (1 Tim 4:14 refers to the group), and 2 Tim 1:6 could refer only to Paul's personal role. 2 Tim 1:3–7 is a personal paragraph, and it would be natural for Paul to think of his own role in Timothy's commission (cf. G. Bornkamm, *TDNT* 6:666 n. 92). Even if these prophecies were made at different times, they could carry the same message. (c) Zahn argues that "where Timothy is thought of as overseer and director of the life of the church," it is natural to think of the corporate call to ministry, but "where he is thought of as an evangelist," the emphasis is on Paul's individual role (*Introduction* 2:98).

(2) The precise meaning of προαγούσας, "previously made" (1 Tim 1:18), is questioned. The verb can mean either "to lead, precede" (of place) or "to come before" (of time). It can therefore be translated "prophecies that led (me) to you," or "prophecies previously made concerning you." The only other occurrence of the verb in Paul is in 1 Tim 5:24 where it is used locatively. The preposition ἐπί, "about," is not decisive because it can designate motion toward a goal (BAGD, 288 [III 1a]) or introduce the person upon

whom something happens (BAGD, 289 [III 1bζ]). Context requires that the prophecies concerned Timothy's call to ministry because Paul is using them as divine validation that Timothy should stay in Ephesus. The only other indications are the two other references to this event, and they only say that Timothy was given a gift at that time. A decision is difficult to make, but the translation "prophecies previously made about you" is to be preferred because of the flow of the argument. The gifts Timothy received probably included the gift of teaching (see 1 Tim 4:14), and Paul is arguing that just as his own gifts were sufficient for his ministry (v 12) so also Timothy's gifts, made known through the prophecies, are sufficient for his task. However, Hort makes a powerful argument for "prophecies which led [me] to you." His thesis is that when Barnabas and Paul separated (Acts 15:36–41), Paul chose Silas (although v 41 says that only "he," i.e., Paul, traveled through Syria and Cilicia), but wanted to "find a Divinely provided successor to Barnabas" through a vision like those given to Ananias (Acts 9:10–11, 17) and Cornelius (Acts 10:5–6). When Paul arrived at Ephesus (Acts 16), prophecies pointed him to Timothy as that divinely appointed successor ("Lecture XI," 177–84).

(3) The basic content of the prophecies is the same regardless of one's decision above. If the prophecies were "previously made," then they pointed to Timothy's spiritual gift of evangelism (2 Tim 4:5), although Hort emphasizes that as Paul's associate Timothy's giftedness would have been unique ("Lecture XI," 185), and perhaps an indication of "his future zeal and success in the promulgation of the Gospel" (Ellicott, 21). If the prophecies pointed Paul to Timothy, one would expect them not only to single Timothy out but to tell Paul why Timothy was qualified for the task.

(4) When did this occur? The other two references associate it with the laying on of hands. (See discussion of the laying on of hands in *Comment* on 1 Tim 4:14.) If we are correct in assuming that this is somewhat parallel with the commission of Barnabas and Saul (Acts 13:1–3; cf. 1 Tim 4:14), then the prophecies were made either at Timothy's ordination into service in general (assuming such was the practice of the early church) or at a commission for a special task such as his ministry to Ephesus. We know nothing about how Timothy initially came to Ephesus; in 1 Tim 1:3 he is already there and Paul is urging him to stay; therefore any decision is tentative. However, Hort's judgment is convincing:

> If St Paul received Timothy as Divinely made the partner of his work in place of Barnabas, it would be at least not unnatural that there should be some repetition of the solemn acts by which human expression had been given to the Divine mission in the first instance. If this explanation of "the prophecies" is right, they must on the one hand have in substance included some such message as "Separate for me Timothy for the work whereunto I have called him"; and on the other hand that separation or consecration would naturally take outward form in fasting and prayer and laying on of hands by the representatives of the Lycaonian Ecclesiae, in repetition of what had been done at Antioch (xiii. 3). In this case however one additional element would be present, viz. the special relation in which St Paul stood to Timothy: he was Timothy's father in the faith, and his subsequent language shews that this essential fact was to be of permanent significance. It would be natural therefore that as Jewish Rabbis laid hands on their disciples, after the example of Moses and Joshua, so not only the representatives of the Lycaonian Ecclesiae but also St Paul himself should lay hands on the disciple and spiritual son now admitted to share his peculiar commission. ("Lecture XI," 183–84)

For many who deny authenticity, this event is fictitious (Oberlinner, 52–53).

(5) What is of prime significance is the role these prophecies are to have in relation to the spiritual war Timothy is to wage. Along with encouraging Timothy, Paul mentions these prophecies because ἐν αὐταῖς, "by them" (instrumental use of ἐν), Timothy is to fight the good fight. Either Timothy will be inspired by them, or the spiritual gift to which

these prophecies bore witness is his weapon of warfare. The former agrees well with the note of encouragement running throughout this chapter. The latter accords well with the emphasis, especially in 2 Timothy, that Paul places on Timothy's role as a teacher of the word.

There is nothing in the context of these three passages to suggest that we have here a sacramental act whereby "the grace of the office is transferred" (contra Dibelius-Conzelmann, 70). The Spirit showed that Timothy was equipped for ministry, and in accordance with custom this fact was publicly recognized by the leadership of the community. The predominant note is not one of authority transferred or of the importation of an official status but of blessing given. There is also nothing to suggest that Timothy was commissioned as the bishop over the church in Ephesus and the first in a line of unbroken apostolic succession (contra Lackmann, "Paulus ordiniert Timotheus"). The references to this event are sufficiently general that they need only refer to Timothy's general call to ministry. If the self-witness of the text is accepted, Timothy was in Ephesus because Paul sent him, not because the church commissioned him (cf. *Introduction,* "Historical Reconstruction from the PE"). We will therefore avoid speaking of this event as an "ordination," lest we anachronistically read in later church development (cf. *Explanation* on 1 Tim 3:1–7 and H. E. Dosker, *ISBE* 1:516). Warkentin sees the laying on of hands as indicating that Paul views Timothy as his successor "analogous to that of Moses and Joshua" (*Ordination,* 137) and interprets much of the PE within that Jewish/rabbinic context. On ordination in general, see the excursus in Roloff, 263–81.

Explanation

Paul has given Timothy a charge to stop the Ephesian opponents from teaching. Having discussed the theological problems of the heresy, he now returns to that charge and reminds Timothy that it is in accordance with the prophecies originally identifying Timothy as having the spiritual gifts necessary to do the task. Just as God entrusted Paul with the gospel, so now Paul entrusts this charge to Timothy. The note of authority is strong: Paul is God's apostle; the gospel he preaches is true; Timothy's function is divinely validated through prophecy. Timothy should be encouraged because the same God who adequately strengthened Paul also has provided the proper gifts for Timothy to use in fighting the spiritual war. He should also be careful. The same traps that ensnared the opponents are also present for him, and he is therefore to concentrate on remaining faithful and keeping his conscience clear. He must maintain his spiritual integrity.

Paul then emphasizes the seriousness and urgency of the situation. Some have not kept their faith and conscience but have chosen to abandon them, and consequently the faith has been shipwrecked, bringing reproach upon the church. Paul also indicates that moral delinquency, not intellectual problems, is the root of the heresy. Morality and lifestyle, or perhaps faith and lifestyle, cannot be separated.

The problem in Ephesus is so advanced that Paul has excommunicated two of the opposition's leaders, not so much as an act of punishment (although that is included) but as an impetus toward redemption. It is difficult to maintain the balance between firmness and proper motivation in discipline, but a balance Timothy must keep. The appropriate remedial measure for those who live within believing fellowship but conduct themselves as outsiders is to return them to Satan's realm. There Satan will deal with them as recaptured deserters, sinners experiencing the natural consequence of their sin. In Satan's realm they will learn (in the full experiential sense of the word) not to speak evil of God by distorting his message for ulterior reasons and personal gain. The Ephesian church must realize that Timothy has full authority, and they must submit to him or suffer the consequences.

III. Correction of Improper Conduct in the Ephesian Church (1 Tim 2:1–4:5)

A. Salvation Is for All People (1 Tim 2:1–7)

Bibliography

Alonso, D. J. "La salvacion universal a partir de la exégesis de 1 Tim 2:4." *CB* 28 (1971) 350–61. **Baugh, S. M.** "'Savior of all people': 1 Tim 4:10 in Context." *WTJ* 54 (1992) 331–40. **Biagi, R.** "Cristo mediatore." *SacD* 27 (1982) 488–511. **Blanco, S.** "Un Dios y un mediator: Nota exégetica a 1 Tim 2,5." *EM* 39 (1989) 287–92. **Cavalcoli, G.** "La 'rivelazione originaria' di Karl Rahner." *SacD* 30 (1985) 537–59. **Davies, R. E.** "Christ in Our Place: The Contribution of the Prepositions." *TBT* 21 (1970) 71–91. **Denk, F.** "Die Geschichte der Deutung von 1. Tim. 2,5: 'Unus et mediator Dei et hominum homo Christus Jesus.'" Diss., University of Vienna, 1954. **Dibelius, M.** "Ἐπίγνωσις ἀληθείας." In *Botschaft und Geschichte: Gesammelte Aufsätze*, ed. H. Kraft and G. Bornkamm. Tübingen: Mohr-Siebeck, 1956. 2:1–13. **Doucet, L.** "L'exégèse Augustinienne de 1 Tim 2:4: 'Dieu veut que tous les hommes soient sauvés.'" *BFCL* 73 (1984) 43–61. **Foerster, W.** "εὐσέβεια, ἀσέβεια, σεμνότης." *TDNT* 7:175–96. ———. "ΕΥΣΕΒΕΙΑ in den Pastoralbriefen." *NTS* 5 (1958–59) 213–18. **Gaide, G.** "L'Épître (de la messe 'Propag. de la foi') 1 Tim 2:1–7: La prière missionnaire." *AsSeign* 98 (1967) 15–24. **Grossi, V.** "Il porsi della questione della 'voluntas salvifica' negli ultimi scritti di Agostino." *Collectanea* (1986) 315–28. **Hanson, A. T.** "The Mediator: I Timothy 2.5–6." In *Studies in the Pastoral Epistles*. 56–64. **Le Fort, P.** "La responsabilité politique de l'Église d'après les épîtres pastorales." *ETR* 49 (1974) 1–14. **Lemaire, A.** "Conseils pour une liturgie authentique: 1 Tim 2,1–8." *AsSeign* 56 (1974) 62–66. **Lipinski, E.** "Bog pragnie zbawienia wszystkch [Polish]" ("Deus vult omnes homines salvos fieri"). *Ruch Biblijny i Liturgiczny* 9 (1958) 134–40. **Marshall, I. H.** "The Development of the Concept of Redemption in the New Testament." In *Reconciliation and Hope*. FS L. L. Morris, ed. R. Banks. Grand Rapids, MI: Eerdmans, 1974. 153–69. ———. "Universal Grace and Atonement in the Pastoral Epistles." In *The Grace of God, the Will of Man*, ed. C. Pinnock. Grand Rapids, MI: Zondervan, 1989. 51–69. **Murphy-O'Connor, J.** "Community and Apostolate [Reflections on 1 Timothy 2:1–7]." *TBT* 67 (1973) 1260–66. **Oberlinner, L.** "'Ein ruhiges und ungestörtes Leben führen': Ein Ideal für christliche Gemeinden?" *BK* 43 (1991) 98–106. **Quinn, J. D.** "Jesus as Savior and Only Mediator (1 Tim 2:3–6): Linguistic Paradigms of Acculturation." In *Fede e cultura /Foi et culture*, ed. J.-D. Barthélemy. Torino: Elle di Ci, 1981. 249–60. **Reumann, J.** "How Do We Interpret 1 Timothy 2:1–5 (and Related Passages)?" In *The One Mediator, the Saints, and Mary*, ed. H. G. Anderson. Lutherans and Catholics in Dialogue 8. Minneapolis: Augsburg, 1992. 149–57. **Romaniuk, K.** "L'origine des formules pauliniennes 'Le Christ s'est livré pour nous': 'Le Christ nous a aimés et s'est livré pour nous.'" *NovT* 5 (1962) 55–76. **Rosiak, J.** "Homo Jesus Christus." *Homo Dei* 28 (1959) 38–45. **Schweizer, E.** "The Lord of the Nations." *SEAJT* 13 (1972) 13–21. **Spicq, C.** "Excursus IV—La 'Piété' dans les Épîtres Pastorales." In *Saint Paul: Le Épîtres Pastorales*. 1:482–92. **Stolle, V.** "Gottes Hilfe für alle Menschen: 1 Tim 2:4 bei Luther, Calvin." In *Unter einem Christus sein und streiten*. FS F. Hopf, ed. J. Schone and V. Stolle. Erlangen: Verlag der Ev.-Luth. Mission, 1980. 26–36. **Turmel, J.** "Historie de l'interpretation de 1 Tim II,4." *RHPR* 5 (1900) 385–415. **Usey, M. S.** "Christology in Service of Paraenesis: The Command in 1 Tim 2:1–7 to Pray for Kings and Those in Authority." Paper presented at the annual meeting of the Society of Biblical Literature, Washington, DC, November 22, 1993.

Translation

[1] *Therefore, above everything else, I urge* [a] *[you] to make requests, prayers, petitions, [and expressions of] thanksgiving on behalf of all people,* [2]*—on behalf of kings and all who are in positions of authority—in order that we might live out our lives in tranquility and calmness with complete reverence and godly dignity.* [3] *This* [b] *is good and pleasing before God our savior,* [4]*who wishes all people to be saved and to come into a knowledge of [the] truth.* [5]*For,*

> *there is one God,*
> *and one mediator between God and people;* [c]
> *a person, Christ Jesus,*
> [6]*who gave himself as a ransom for all,*

the witness at the proper time. [d] [7] *[It is] with reference to this [witness that] I was appointed* [e] *a herald and apostle—I am speaking the truth;* [f] *I am not lying—a teacher of the Gentiles in faith* [g] *and truth.*

Notes

[a]Metzger notes: "In place of παρακαλῶ, several witnesses (D* F G b vg^ms; Ambst) have the imperative παρακάλει, a scribal modification intended to give the sentence the form of a specific command to Timothy" (*TCGNT* [2], 572; cf. Lock, xxxvi).

[b]℘[2] D F G H Ψ TR latt sy insert γάρ, "for," after τοῦτο, "this," thus strengthening the link between v 2 and v 3, a later clarification that is in error. See *Comment* and a similar insertion in Gal 1:10. Our text is supported by ℘* A 6 33 81 1739 1881 *pc* co.

[c]The two persons between whom the μεσίτης, "mediator," is mediating will be in the genitive (BAGD, 506–7).

[d]The terseness and confusing nature of τὸ μαρτύριον καιροῖς ἰδίοις, "the witness at the proper time," are illustrated by the variants. Some MSS insert οὗ, "whose," before τὸ μαρτύριον, "the witness" (D* F G 104 *pc* a [m] vg^a; Ambst *et*), as well as ἐδόθη, "was given," after ἰδίοις, "proper" (D* F G it vg^mss; Ambst). ℘* reads καὶ μαρτύριον, "and witness," and A omits τὸ μαρτύριον, "the witness." The plural is probably idiomatic. Lock cites Luke 20:9 and 23:8 as syntactical parallels (also Jer 50 [LXX 27]:26; 50:31; Luke 12:36); cf. L. T. Johnson, 124.

[e]εἰς ὃ ἐτέθην, "to which I was appointed," is replaced by ὃ ἐπιστεύθην, "with which I was entrusted," by A, probably in an attempt to smooth out the text in imitation of Titus 1:3.

[f]A *v.l.* inserts ἐν Χριστῷ, "in Christ," after λέγω, "I am speaking," making the interjection even stronger (℘* D[2] H 33^vid TR a vg^mss). It is an addition, possibly by analogy to Rom 9:1. Our text is supported by ℘[2] A D* F G P Ψ 6 81 104 629 1175 1505 1739 1881 *pc* lat sy co. See *TCGNT* [2], 572.

[g]πίστει, "in faith" (D F G H Ψ 33 1739 1881 TR latt sy co; Tert), is replaced with γνώσει, "in knowledge" (℘ *pc*), and πνεύματι, "in spirit" (A).

Form/Structure/Setting

It has been common to view chaps. 2 and 3 as a manual of church organization, independent of the Ephesian context and the problems of the false teachers, laying down guidelines for prayer, the role of women in public worship, and the appointment of church leaders. But the self-witness of the letter presents these guidelines within a specific historical situation in Paul's lifetime. The opponents are teaching exclusivism, limiting salvation to only a select few. Many of the women, much as was the case in Corinth, are exercising their newly found freedom in Christ to excess. Some of the Ephesian elders are teaching error, and their conduct shows that they are not suitable for church leadership. All of this has produced an intolerable situation, and therefore Paul sends Timothy (1:3) and this letter to deal with the situation. Although these instructions have implications for the church universal, as do most of the biblical instructions that are given in response to a specific historical situation, nevertheless these chapters should first be interpreted in light of the Ephesian situation (see *Introduction*, "The Ephesian Heresy").

At first glance, the topic of vv 1–7 appears to be prayer because it begins by talking about prayer for all people and v 8 discusses men praying. However, v 8 belongs with vv 9–15 (see *Form/Structure/Setting* on 1 Tim 2:8–15), and prayer is never mentioned in vv 2–7. Salvation, on the other hand, one of the dominant themes in chap. 1, is repeated again in 2:4, tying 2:1–7 into the flow of the discussion. Already Paul has shown that salvation is the result of God's mercy and grace, a gift illustrated most clearly in Paul's conversion (1:12–17). Paul has cited the faithful saying that "Christ Jesus came into the world to save sinners" (1:15), and now he offers a confession that Christ Jesus gave himself as a ransom for all (2:6) in accordance with God's desire that all people be saved (2:4). Prayer, therefore, is not the topic of this paragraph but rather the stage upon which Paul bases his teaching on the topic of salvation. Prayer is the context, salvation the content.

More specifically, the emphasis appears to be on the universal offer of salvation to all people. (1) Four times Paul uses "all," and this sets the tone for the paragraph: "prayers . . . be made for all people" (v 1); "for kings and all who are in high positions" (v 2); "who desires all people to be saved" (v 4); "a ransom for all" (v 6; cf. "complete [πάσῃ] reverence" in v 2). This theme of salvation for all comes out of the universal implication of 1:15 and is continued later in 1 Tim 4:10 ("savior of all people") and Titus 2:11 ("salvation of all people"; cf. 2 Tim 4:17; 1 Tim 4:15; Stott, 60). (2) Paul cites a creed perhaps solely because it asserts that Christ is a "ransom for all." Yet the creed implies in another way that the Ephesian church should pray for all people: there is (only) one God and (only) one mediator. If people are not offered Christian salvation, then there is no other God and no other mediator to save them, and all people are the proper objects of prayer. (3) If the heresy is a form of Jewish legalism, it would be natural for the opponents to exclude Gentiles. Thus, Paul strongly emphasizes ("I am telling the truth; I am not lying"; v 7) that his call to apostolic ministry is specifically for the Gentiles, and hence his call is proof that the offer of salvation is to be extended to all, Jews and Gentiles alike. It would appear that Paul's opponents are teaching an exclusive gospel that offers salvation only to a select few, and this exclusivism is made clear by their practice of praying for only certain people. This would be expected from an overemphasis on the law (cf 1:7). As Spicq notes, the "fundamental intention [of vv 1–7] is the universality of salvation—perhaps in opposition to Jewish particularism" (1:356). Lock paraphrases, "I want to urge first of all that Christians should realize the universality of the message of the gospel" (23).

V 1 connects 2:1–7 with chap. 1 using an initial οὖν, "therefore," along with the repeated use of παρακαλεῖν, "to urge," in 1:3 and 2:1 (notice the third repetition in 2:8) and the repetition of ideas from 1:15. Paul has urged Timothy to stay in Ephesus and rebuke the false teachers (see *Form/Structure/Setting* on 1 Tim 1:3–7). It is important for the church to know that Christ came in order to save sinners, even someone like Paul (1:15). He reminds his younger colleague of his gifts that will enable him to carry out this mission (1:18), and then adds a note of urgency by pointing out that the opposition is so strong that Paul has excommunicated two of their leaders (1:19–20). οὖν, "therefore," Timothy must insist that correct doctrine be taught, beginning with the proper concept of salvation (2:1–7); all people must be the subject of prayers. See Lock, Fee, Guthrie, Spicq, and Usey, "Christology." Ellicott (24) ties "therefore" directly to 1:18; in 1:18 Paul gives the *general* commission and then beginning in 2:1 he gives the *particulars* of how this is to be done.

1 Tim 2:1–7 divides into two parts. (1) Paul urges Timothy and the Ephesian church not to exclude some people from church prayers and consequently the offer of salvation (v 1). He parenthetically specifies one group of people who especially should not be excluded: (secular) leaders (v 2). (2) Paul follows with three reasons why the Ephesian church should include all people in their prayers and the scope of salvation: (a) in general this is pleasing to God, who wishes all people to be saved (vv 3–4); (b) it is in line with the mediator's work, which provided a ransom for all people (vv 5–6); and (c) excluding the Gentiles from the scope of salvation runs counter to Paul's divinely appointed ministry (v 7).

Most (contra Scott, 21–22) think that vv 5–6 are a citation of a creedal fragment known to Timothy and the Ephesian church (cf. R. P. Martin, "Hymns," *DPL*, 419–23), but this question does not greatly affect interpretation. The theology of the verses is fully compatible with Paul's teaching, and throughout the PE Paul cites traditional material (*Introduction*, "The Linguistic Problem"). It is possible, however, that vv 5–6 are Paul's own construction. μεσίτης, "mediator," is an unusual word for Paul, but he may be setting his gospel up against a false teaching that sees Moses as the mediator between people and God, and this may explain his word choice.

The creed has two stanzas. The first stanza asserts the uniqueness of God and the uniqueness of the mediator (v 5ab); the second stanza (vv 5c–6a) emphasizes the nature of the mediator (i.e., that he was human, a person) and the nature of his mediatorial work (i.e., that it was in place of and on behalf of all people). The creed begins at v 5, but whether v 6b is part of the creed or Paul's comment on the creed is difficult to decide. Among others, Jeremias (19) thinks that v 6b is part of the creed and arranges it as such (although Jeremias translates "the Man," not "a Man"):

> There is one God,
> also one mediator between God and men,
>> a Man, Christ Jesus,
>> who gave himself as a ransom for all men,
>> the witness at the proper time.

It seems more likely, however, that v 6b is Paul's comment on the creed (so Kelly et al.). (1) Its meaning is not clear if it is part of the creed, but it is clear if with it Paul is stating that the creed is relevant to the Ephesian situation. (2) The parallelism is better with v 6b omitted. (3) The expression in v 6b καιροῖς ἰδίοις, "at the proper time," is peculiar to the PE (cf. Titus 1:3; 1 Tim 6:15; see *Comment*). Thus the translation here is as follows:

> There is one God,
>> and one mediator between God and people,
> a person, Christ Jesus,
>> who gave himself as a ransom for all,
> the witness at the proper time.

Comment

1 Παρακαλῶ οὖν πρῶτον πάντων ποιεῖσθαι δεήσεις προσευχὰς ἐντεύξεις εὐχαριστίας ὑπὲρ πάντων ἀνθρώπων, "Therefore, above everything else, I urge [you] to make requests, prayers, petitions, [and expressions of] thanksgiving on behalf of all people." We have already seen that this paragraph is not primarily concerned with prayer; rather it stresses the universal offer of salvation (see *Form/Structure/Setting*). The Ephesian church's habit of not praying for all people was symptomatic of the more significant issue of the leaders' selective theology. There are three words/phrases that alert us to the paragraph's true intention. (1) οὖν, "therefore," tells us that 2:1-7 is closely related to chap. 1 and in some way issues from it (see *Form/Structure/Setting*). (2) πρῶτον πάντων, "above everything else," tells us that the instruction in 2:1-7 is the single most significant change Timothy can effect; a general discussion on prayer, as significant as prayer is, would not in and of itself address the Ephesian situation. (3) ὑπὲρ πάντων ἀνθρώπων, "on behalf of all people," is the first mention of the dominant theme in 2:1-7, the universality of salvation (i.e., offered to all people). Therefore, the primary emphasis of v 1 lies on the statement "on behalf of all people" and not on prayer in general. Any theology that limits the scope of prayers for salvation is deficient. This theme is repeated in vv 2, 4, and 6, where the statement ἀντίλυτρον ὑπὲρ πάντων, "ransom for all people," looks back to πάντων ἀνθρώπων, "all people," in v 1. Chrysostom comments, apparently sarcastically, "Was Christ then a ransom for the Heathen? Undoubtedly Christ died even for Heathen; and you cannot bear to pray for them" ("Homily 7"; NPNF 13:431).

The use of ἄνθρωπος, "person," ties the passage together. When Paul makes the theological pronouncement in vv 4-5, the use of both πᾶς, "all," and ἄνθρωπος, "person," reminds the reader of the foremost request to pray for πάντων ἀνθρώπων, "all people," in v 1. The translation "man/men" would most clearly show the flow of thought from "praying for all men," to God's wish to save "all men," to the role of the mediator between God and "men," a mediator who himself is a "man," a human, as long as the use of "man" would not appear to exclude women in the first three cases or emphasize Jesus' maleness in the fourth. The use of the inclusive "people/person," however, hopefully accomplishes this same purpose.

The universal scope here is implicit in the arguments of v 5 and v 7 as well as in the faithful saying in 1:15. παρακαλῶ retains the force of "I urge" from 1:3 rather than the meaning "I ask." It is a common word for Paul, often being combined with οὖν, "therefore" (Rom 12:1; 1 Cor 4:16; Eph 4:1; cf. 2 Cor 9:5), and δέ, "but" (Rom 15:30; 16:17; 1 Cor 1:10; 16:15; 1 Thess 4:10; 5:14; cf. 2 Cor 2:8). πρῶτον πάντων, "above everything else" (lit. "first of all things"), should be understood as first in importance and not as first in time (Roloff, 113). (πρῶτον πάντων, "above everything else," probably modifies παρακαλῶ, "I urge," not ποιεῖσθαι, "to make." On the anarthrous use of πᾶς, "all," see B. Reicke, *TDNT* 5:889.) It is not so much that prayer for all people is the first on the list (contra Chrysostom, L. T. Johnson) but that it is the most important on the list (Bernard, Spicq, Guthrie, Fee). The early church certainly valued the power of prayer, and it was the "fundamental activity in the life of the church" (Spicq, 1:357). Most of the commentators follow this line of reasoning, but the emphasis is not so much on prayer in general as on prayer for the salvation of all people, not just the select few who followed the opponents' teaching.

To emphasize that prayers should be made for all people, Paul adds four types of prayers one after another. It is a Semitic literary device that groups synonyms to add luster to the basic concept (see the description of wisdom in Prov 1:1–6). Although each of these words can describe slightly different types of prayers (see below), that is not the point here (contra Origen, Augustine [both cited by Bernard], Hendriksen). The point is that all prayers, of all types, should be for all people. δέησις, "request," προσευχή, "prayer," and εὐχαριστία, "thanksgiving," are repeated together in Phil 4:6, the first two are paired in Eph 6:18 and 1 Tim 5:5, and προσευχή, "prayer," and εὐχαριστία, "thanksgiving," are found in Col 4:2–3. It is possible that only the first three in 1 Tim 2:1 designate different types of prayers, and that all three are to be offered μετὰ εὐχαριστίας, "with thanksgiving" (cf. Phil 4:6; Col 4:2; Justin *Apol.* 1.13.67; Towner, 62 n.). However, the structure of four consecutive accusative plurals suggests that they are four types of prayers.

δέησις, "request," is a common Pauline term. He uses it twelve times, including once in 1 Tim 5:5 (where it is joined with προσευχή, "prayer") and once in 2 Tim 1:3. (Its cognate δεῖσθαι, "to request," occurs six times in Paul.) It has two characteristics. (1) It is a request, a statement of a need (a development from the classical meaning "to lack"; H. Greeven, *TDNT* 2:807). It means "supplication," "cry of lamentation," and "cry for help" in the LXX (H. Schönweiss, *NIDNTT* 2:860). Spicq says that it involves a "pressing necessity" (1:357). (2) It also describes an actual instance of prayer and not prayer in general (see Rom 10:1; 2 Cor 9:14; Eph 6:18; Phil 1:19; cf. the use of δεῖσθαι in the NT). In the NT it is used only with God as its object (although the verb can be addressed to others; cf. Luke 5:12; 8:28; 9:38; Acts 8:34; 21:39; Gal 4:12; 2 Cor 5:20; 10:2). Some think that it is a "request" for oneself while ἔντευξις is a "petition" for another (see below). It is difficult to be precise about the meaning of this word since it is interchanged with other words for prayer. In Phil 1:4 Paul says, "I thank [εὐχαριστῶ] my God . . . in every prayer [δεήσει] of mine . . . making my prayer [δέησιν] with joy [χαρᾶς]." It is similarly joined with the εὐχαριστ-, "thanks," word group in 2 Cor 1:11 and Phil 4:6 (cf. 1 Tim 1:3; 2 Cor 9:12, 14), with ἔντευξις, "petition" (1 Tim 4:4–5; a word similar in meaning to δέησις), and with προσευχή, "prayer" (1 Tim 5:5; Eph 6:18). One might surmise that the meaning of δέησις had run over into εὐχαριστία, "[expression of] thanksgiving," but the association here may be more theological than etymological: one should always accompany requests with thanksgiving.

προσευχή, "prayer," is the general term for prayer and can even be used to describe a place of prayer (cf. Acts 16:13, 16; Schürer, *History* 2:439 n. 61). The noun and verb occur 122 times in the NT, 33 times in Paul (including 1 Tim 5:5, where it is paired with δεήσεις, "requests"). It is used in the NT only of prayers to God.

ἔντευξις, "petition," is an unusual word, occurring here, in 1 Tim 4:5, and elsewhere in biblical literature only in 2 Macc 4:8, which says that Jason bribed Antiochus "by means of a petition [δι' ἐντεύξεως]." O. Bauerfeind cites in the secular literature a range of meaning including "encounter, conversation, address, conduct, and petition" (*TDNT* 8:244). ἔντευξις was also used to describe an official petition to a superior, often the king (see in Spicq, 1:357, and Deissmann, *Biblical Studies*, 121, 146); the same was true of δέησις, "request" (see MM). Paul uses its cognate verb ἐντυγχάνειν, "to intercede," to speak of the Holy Spirit's intercession (Rom 8:27), of Christ's intercession for the saints (Rom 8:34; cf. Heb 7:25), and of Elijah's accusation to God against a sinful Israel (Rom 11:2; cf. Acts 25:24; for Jewish examples of intercession, see Stauffer, *New Testament Theology*, 304 n. 597). Bernard (38) says that the leading idea of the verb is "boldness of access, of confidence" (so also Trench, *Synonyms*, 178). The pairing of ἐντεύξεις, "petitions," and εὐχαριστίας, "thanksgivings," in 1 Tim 2:1 is similar to that in 1 Tim 4:3–5, which discusses eating food μετὰ εὐχαριστίας, "with thanksgiving," since it has been consecrated by the word of God and ἐντεύξεως, "prayer." In 2:1, although context does not allow us to decide with much precision, ἐντεύξεις probably denotes prayers that make requests for others and are addressed to a superior, possibly carrying the nuance of an intercession made to the divine king (cf. 1:17). Some argue that the word contains no idea of intercession for others; it simply means "intercession," and the context determines its scope (so Bernard; Plummer; Kent, *Pastoral Epistles;* Ellicott, who says it is "prayer in its most individual and urgent form" [24]; contra Barclay; Houlden). Here the context shows that the ἐντεύξεις are for others.

εὐχαριστία, "thanksgiving," occurs twelve times in Paul (including 1 Tim 4:3–4). It is common for Paul to express thanksgiving to God for a church in the opening of his letter to that church (Phil 1:3; Col 1:3; 1 Thess 1:2; 2 Thess 1:3 [cf. 2:13]; Phlm 4), and the Jewish practice of giving thanks before meals is reflected in 1 Tim 4:5 (cf. Matt 15:36; Mark 8:6; John 6:11, 23; Acts 27:35). Here εὐχαριστία is a prayer of thanksgiving. There is no need to see a developed sense of the word denoting the Eucharist (contra Augustine; Kelly; and the scribe of MS 665 who wrote εὐχαριστίαν, evidently thinking of the [singular] Eucharist; see Elliott, *Greek Text*, 34) since 4:5 shows a primitive understanding of the word (cf. 1 Cor 14:16; Phil 4:6; cf. Spicq; Bernard; Lock; Swete, *JTS* 3 [1902] 161). In the NT, εὐχαριστία, "thanksgiving," and εὐχαριστεῖν, "to give thanks," are offered only to God, except in Luke 17:16, Acts 24:3, and Rom 16:4 (see H.-H. Esser, *NIDNTT* 3:818).

Bernard agrees that the different meanings of these four words for prayer should not be overemphasized, but he does offer an interesting arrangement of the four: "we may more simply take the words in two contrasted pairs, δέησις being related to προσευχή as the particular to the general (see Eph. vi 18), and ἔντευξις to εὐχαριστία as petition to thanksgiving" (38–39). Ellicott says, "the first term marks the idea of our insufficiency, . . . the second that of devotion, the third that of childlike confidence" (25).

2   ὑπὲρ βασιλέων καὶ πάντων τῶν ἐν ὑπεροχῇ ὄντων, ἵνα ἤρεμον καὶ ἡσύχιον βίον διάγωμεν ἐν πάσῃ εὐσεβείᾳ καὶ σεμνότητι, "—on behalf of kings and all who are in positions of authority—in order that we might live out our lives in tranquility and calmness with complete reverence and godly dignity." There are two ways to view v 2. (1) Prayers should be made for all people, especially for secular authorities, and as a result of praying for these authorities the Christian will have a calm life. V 2a receives the primary emphasis, and ἵνα, "in order that," gives the result of praying, especially praying for secular rulers (i.e., all of v 2 is parenthetical). (2) Prayers should be made for all people (including authorities), and as a result of praying for all people the Christian will have a calm life. In this case v 2a is a parenthesis and ἵνα, "in order that," follows upon v 1.

(1) The primary emphasis could be on v 2a. Prayers for the prosperity of secular leaders were common in Judaism (Ezra 6:9–10; Bar 1:11; 1 Macc 7:33; *Ep. Arist.* 44–45; *m. Abot* 3.2 (cf. Jer 29:7); Philo *Flacc.* 524; *Leg.* 157, 317; Josephus *J.W.* 2.17.1 §§405–7; Str-B 3:643; cf. references in C. S. Keener, *Paul, Women and Wives* [Peabody, MA: Hendricksen, 1992] 121 n. 7) and were encouraged by Paul (Titus

3:1; Rom 13:1) and others (1 Pet 2:14, 17). This practice becomes even more significant when it is remembered that Nero (A.D. 54–68) was emperor (assuming Pauline authorship). Le Fort (*ETR* 49 [1974] 1–14) notes that this statement is made against the backdrop of the *pax romana*, the "Roman peace," and suggests that Paul may not have intended it to be valid everywhere and for all times; the goal of living peaceful lives may suggest that other considerations could come into play in other situations. It was emphasized by the early apologists that the church's prayers for the state were a sign of their loyalty (Tertullian *Apol.* 30–32, 39; Justin *Apol.* 1.17.3; cf. *Apostolic Constitutions* 7.1; *1 Clem.* 60–61; Athenagoras *A Plea regarding Christians* 37 [in ANF 2:148]). Ellicott (25) refers to Josephus's comment (*J.W.* 2.17.2 §§408–10) that the Jewish neglect of this duty led to the war with the Romans. Paul says that political power is given by God and that the church is to recognize the rightful role of government (Rom 13:1–7; see excursus in Dibelius-Conzelmann, 37–39; Stauffer, *New Testament Theology,* 196–99; Ridderbos, *Paul,* 320–26). However, there are two serious problems with seeing v 2a as primary and not parenthetical. (a) The topic of the paragraph is the necessity of offering salvation to all, and this emphasis would detract from it. (b) Throughout the PE, Paul is concerned with secular rulers and non-Christians, but it is not a concern for peace or a desire for the rulers to allow the church to grow unimpeded. Rather, Paul is anxious that the church provide a good witness to nonbelievers.

(2) If v 2a is parenthetical, then Paul wants the Ephesian church to pray for all people (including the secular rulers). If members of the Ephesian community do pray for all people, including those within the scope of salvation, and do not become sectarian in their approach, then they will not alienate those outside the church and will not bring the church into disrepute. Rather they will be able to follow lifestyles characterized by peace and tranquility. βασιλέων καὶ πάντων τῶν ἐν ὑπεροχῇ ὄντων, "kings and all who are in positions of authority," constitute a subgroup of the πάντων ἀνθρώπων, "all people," in v 1. Easton says that the "wording [of v 2a] is that of an actual prayer and is almost certainly cited from a form familiar in Christian worship" (121). Consequently he is unwilling to draw a close connection between v 1 and v 2. There is no question that in the PE Paul uses traditional material, but there is nothing especially liturgical about v 2, and it flows logically from v 1. In contrast to examples of secular prayers, Christians' prayers are ὑπέρ, "on behalf of," and not πρός, "to," the rulers.

ἐν ὑπεροχῇ ὄντων, "being in authority," according to Dibelius-Conzelmann, "designates a distinguished position" (36). βασιλεύς, "king," can refer to the emperor (BAGD, 136; Dibelius-Conzelmann, 36 n. 10; Spicq, 1:359–60). Because βασιλέων, "kings," is plural, Baur (*Pastoralbriefe*, 126–27) argued that this points to a date in the A.D. 130s after Hadrian's death during the dual emperorship of the Antonines. Hadrian died in A.D. 138, and Antoninus Pius ruled from A.D. 138 to 161, in A.D. 139 conferring the title "Caesar" upon Marcus Aurelius. Upon Antoninus's death, Aurelius (A.D. 161–80) chose Lucius Verus (A.D. 161–69), his adopted brother, to be co-ruler. Almost no one follows Baur in his argument now, however, since the plural βασιλέων, "kings," is anarthrous, designating not "the" kings (τῶν βασιλέων) but kings in general. βασιλεύς can refer to rulers other than the Roman emperor, such as Pharaoh (Acts 7:10), Herod the Great (Matt 2:1, 3; Luke 1:5), Herod Antipas, who was not really a king (Matt 14:9; Mark 6:14), Aretas (2 Cor 11:32), Melchizedek (Heb 7:1), David (Matt 1:6; Acts 13:22), the messianic king, and God (references for the latter two in BAGD, 136). It is also used in the plural of several kings (Matt 10:18; 17:25; Mark 13:9; Luke 10:24; 21:12; 22:25; Acts 4:26; 9:15; Rev [15x]; see K. L. Schmidt, *TDNT* 1:577). Paul will ask Titus to remind the Cretans to be subject to ἀρχαῖς ἐξουσίας, "rulers, authorities" (Titus 3:1).

Having specified that secular rulers are included in the πάντων ἀνθρώπων, "all people," of v 1, Paul gives not the content of those prayers but their purpose (ἵνα): that Christians might "live out their lives in tranquility and calmness with complete reverence and godly dignity." In contrast to the opponents who are bringing disrepute on the church, the church is to pursue a lifestyle characterized by tranquility, calmness, reverence, and dignity. Dibelius-Conzelmann write, "In no small degree the significance of the Pastoral Epistles rests on the fact that they are the only documents in the canon which enjoin such a structuring of life under the ideal of good Christian citizenship" (40). Yet, as they earlier pointed out (37 n. 19), the NT does speak of submission to the governing authorities and paying taxes. As early as his first letter to the Thessalonian church, Paul saw the value of Christians living quietly and minding their own affairs (1 Thess 4:11–12; cf. 1 Cor 14:23; Col 4:5–6; 2 Thess 3:12). διάγειν is not "to live" in terms of living a single day; it describes life as an ongoing process, a lifestyle. According to Spicq, it "expresses the manner of conducting oneself, of leading this kind of existence" (1:360; see Titus 3:3 and the *v.l.* in Luke 7:25). This is not a wish that Christians live conflict-free lives (see 2 Cor 11:23–33; 2 Tim 1:8; 3:12; and below), but within the context of chap. 2 it is a wish that their conduct not bring unnecessary disrepute, thereby facilitating the spread of the gospel (Oberlinner, 68). On the differences between βίος, "manner of life" (cf. 2 Tim 2:3), and ζωή, "life," see *Comment* on 1 Tim 1:16 (cf. Rom 12:18).

ἤρεμος, "tranquil," does not occur elsewhere in the NT. LSJ (778) lists only one reference before the NT era (Theophrastus *De Lapidibus* 6.2 [fourth/third century B.C.]). It is a later form of ἠρεμαῖος, "quiet," which was in use beginning in the fifth century B.C. (LSJ, 777). ἡσύχιος, "calmness," is a virtual synonym (see extrabiblical references in Spicq, 1:361–62). ἡσύχιος occurs elsewhere in the NT only in 1 Pet 3:4, which speaks of a "gentle [πραέως] and quiet [ἡσυχίου] spirit" that Christian women should possess. The related form ἡσυχία, "quietness," occurs in 1 Tim 2:11–12, describing how a woman should learn, and in Acts 22:2, which says that the crowd became silent (παρέσχον ἡσυχίαν) in order to hear Paul's defense. (BAGD, 349, lists extrabiblical examples meaning "inner peace" and "peace and harmony among citizens"; see also LSJ, 779.) The desire for peace is contrasted to the uproar caused by the opponents (e.g., Titus 1:11). ἡσυχάζειν similarly can mean "to cease speaking" (Luke 14:4; Acts 11:18; 21:14; *v.l.* in Acts 22:2) and "to cease working" (Luke 23:56). The meaning "cease speaking" does not fit the context in 1 Tim 2:2 or in 1 Tim 2:11–12, where it means "quiet demeanor." The association of ἡσύχιος with πραΰς, "gentle," in 1 Pet 3:4 and with a woman's demeanor in 1 Tim 2:11–12 argues for understanding ἤρεμος and ἡσύχιος as denoting not silence of speech but quietness, calmness of demeanor, serenity. This is confirmed by Paul's command to the Thessalonian church to "aspire to live quietly [ἡσυχάζειν], [and] to mind your own affairs, . . . so that you may command the respect of outsiders" (1 Thess 4:11). In both 1 Timothy and 1 Thessalonians Paul has the same consideration in mind: a good reputation outside the church. This also accords with Paul's concern throughout the PE that the church not suffer unnecessary reproach. A Christian's life is not to be quiet of speech, but it should be quiet in nature, a tranquility stemming from a godly and reverent life. Among others, Ellicott (26) defines ἤρεμος as a quietness rising from the absence of outward disturbance and ἡσύχιος as a tranquility arising from within (contra Bernard).

After the two qualities of tranquility and calmness, Paul adds the prepositional phrase ἐν πάσῃ εὐσεβείᾳ καὶ σεμνότητι, "with complete reverence and godly dignity." It could modify διάγωμεν, "might live," in which case εὐσέβεια, "reverence," and σεμνότης, "dignity," are third and fourth characteristics of a Christian's life. The phrase could also modify ἤρεμον καὶ ἡσύχιον, "tranquility and calmness," in which case reverence and dignity qualify the Christian's tranquility and calmness. In either case, there are two pairs of characteristics of a Christian's life. The lifestyle is to be tranquil and calm; attitude and behavior toward God are to be fully reverent and dignified. πάσῃ, "complete," describes both εὐσεβείᾳ and σεμνότητι.

εὐσέβεια, "reverence," is almost a technical term in the PE. Spicq defines it as being "totally consecrated to God, to his worship, and to the fulfillment of his will . . . and it places emphasis on the outward appearances of worship and piety in honor of God . . . [and denotes] an extreme devotion to accomplish the divine will" (1:362; cf. "Excursus IV—La 'Piété' dans les Épîtres Pastorales," 1:482–92). 2 Tim 3:12 illustrates this: everyone desiring to live a religious life will be persecuted because their total consecration to God and outward piety will conflict with this sinful age. Dibelius-Conzelmann, relying heavily on its occurrence in v 2, argue that the thrust of εὐσέβεια is directed toward behavior (39–40). Foerster defines it as a lifestyle that stems from faith (*NTS* 5 [1958–59] 217–18). Towner emphasizes this connection between the Christ-event and ethics (*Goal*, 147–52; esp. 1 Tim 3:16; Titus 1:16; 2:12), and also argues that εὐσέβεια was the opponents' term, a knowledge of God that allowed them to drive a wedge between faith and praxis (*Goal*, 152; cf. 1 Tim 6:5; 2 Tim 3:5). Towner concludes, "The horizontal dimension is an irreducible element of genuine Christian experience" (*Goal*, 154). εὐσέβεια is roughly equivalent to the "fear of God" in the OT (cf. Ps 111:10; Prov 1:7; Isa 11:2); it therefore describes a fully reverential attitude and behavior stemming from a true knowledge of God; thus it includes both belief and behavior (cf. Roloff, 117–19; Brox, 172–77; Dibelius-Conzelmann, 39; Falconer, 30–39; W. Foerster, *TDNT* 7:182–84; id., *NTS* 5 [1958] 213–18; Knight, *Faithful Sayings*, 68–73).

While εὐσέβεια is one of several goals Paul maintains, it is done with the recognition that everyone seeking to live a godly (εὐσεβῶς) life will be persecuted (2 Tim 3:12), a truth borne out in Paul's own life (2 Tim 3:11). This is the same tension felt in 2 Cor 6:3–10, where Paul recounts his endurance of persecution in order that he might put "no obstacle in any one's way" (v 3) and "commend himself in every way" (v 4). Paul's message itself is offensive (Barrett), as opposed to the offense caused by the false teachers that is unnecessary and a poor witness.

The εὐσεβ- word group (εὐσέβεια, εὐσεβεῖν, εὐσεβής, εὐσεβῶς) was common in Hellenistic Greek; it is found in Acts, the PE, 2 Peter/Jude, and 4 Maccabees (forty-seven times out of the fifty-three times in the LXX). Although εὐσέβεια is not a frequent term with Paul (he does use ἀσέβεια, "godlessness," and ἀσεβής, "godless," in Rom 1:18; 4:5; 5:6; 11:26), it was common in his world and available for his use (Foerster, *NTS* 5 (1959) 214–15; Dibelius-Conzelmann, 39; Spicq, 1:362; MM, 265–66; LSJ, 731; S. C. Mott, "Greek Ethics and Christian Conversion: The Philonic Background of Titus II 10–14 and III 3–7," *NovT* 20 [1978] 23–26; Quinn, "Excursus III," 282–91). In the PE it is the goal of every true believer (1 Tim 2:2;

6:11; 2 Tim 3:12; Titus 2:12) as opposed to the result of the opponents' teaching (2 Tim 2:16). It is of great worth (1 Tim 4:7, 8; 6:6), even to the point of it being mistaken as a means to unjust gain (1 Tim 6:5). It has a cognitive element so that it is a set of beliefs (1 Tim 3:16) equivalent to "sound teaching" (1 Tim 6:3; cf. 1:10) and is in accordance with the truth (Titus 1:1; cf. 1 Tim 1:9; 2:4). It also has an observable behavioral element so that it becomes a description of proper conduct (1 Tim 5:4), so much so that someone can appear to be εὐσέβεια but deny its true power (2 Tim 3:5). Simpson says that "perhaps St. Paul's resort to it in his latest writings may be traced to the Roman circles in which he has been moving, where the Latin *pietas* was so perpetually harped upon" (40). θεοσέβεια, "godliness" (1 Tim 2:10), is somewhat synonymous, although εὐσέβεια can be directed to objects other than God (though not in the NT; cf. Bernard). It has also been argued that εὐσέβεια had special significance in Ephesus in connection with Artemis and that its frequent use in the PE may be an answer to the pagan claims (cf. Knight, *Faithful Sayings*, 78). Since Paul does not use the term outside the PE, and because of its occurrence in 1 Tim 3:16 where it stands in contrast to the opponents' teaching (4:1–5), it is possible that εὐσέβεια is a term of the opponents (Towner, 64 n.); it is a proper goal, but one so totally misunderstood by the opponents that they have the form of εὐσέβεια but deny its essence (2 Tim 3:5; cf. 2 Tim 2:16).

σεμνότης, "dignity," occurs in the NT only in the PE (1 Tim 2:2; 3:4 [describing overseers]; Titus 2:7 [describing Timothy]). The cognate adjective σεμνός, "dignified," also appears in 1 Tim 3:8 (of a deacon), 3:11 (of deacons' wives or deaconesses), Titus 2:2 (of older men), and Phil 4:8 (in which Paul admonishes the Philippians to set their minds on whatever is σεμνός). σεμνότης denotes a solemn, serious, dignified attitude and behavior, "the attitude (interior and exterior) of respect with regard to the sacred realities, such as decency, seriousness, gravity" (Spicq, 1:406–9). It is the "moral earnestness" that affects "outward demeanor as well as interior intention" (Kelly, 61). Spicq adds, "It refers especially to honorable conduct, a dignified and level-headed existence, and a high standard or morality" (*TLNT* 3:244–45). Because of its association with the divine, it also carries the connotation of the majestic, that which is above the profane and within the context of the holy (see *Comment* on 1 Tim 3:8). We have, therefore, one of the major themes in the PE summed up in two pairs of complementary terms. A Christian's life should be characterized by peace and tranquility, reverence and godly dignity. Lock (26–27) and Kelly (61) comment that this is the Hellenistic counterpart to the Hebraic ἐν ὁσιότητι καὶ δικαιοσύνῃ, "in holiness and righteousness," in Luke 1:75.

3–4a τοῦτο καλὸν καὶ ἀπόδεκτον ἐνώπιον τοῦ σωτῆρος ἡμῶν θεοῦ, ὃς πάντας ἀνθρώπους θέλει σωθῆναι, "This is good and pleasing before God our savior, who wishes all people to be saved." Vv 3–4 contain the first of three reasons that the Ephesian church should pray for the salvation of all people and not just for a select few; it is pleasing to God because it is in line with his basic desire that all people be saved. Although God is the Christians' (ἡμῶν, "our") savior (see 1:1), he wishes that the benefits of his salvific work be enjoyed by all (πάντας), even by the "worst of sinners" (1:15). This thought is repeated later when Paul says "... God, who is savior of all people, especially of those who believe" (4:10) and in Titus 2:11, "for the grace of God has appeared bringing salvation for all people."

This universal thrust is typical of the PE (cf. especially Marshall, "Universal Grace"). God's will is the basis of salvation and that which enables salvation (so

Oberlinner, 72), but the text does not move into universalism. In the PE, salvation is by grace only for those who believe (cf. *Introduction,* "Themes in the PE"). Roloff stresses that the universal emphasis relates only to the scope of God's plan; salvation is only for those who have come to the knowledge of truth, heard the gospel, and received it (119–20). Some interpret Paul to mean that the offer of salvation is to be made to all people (cf. Grudem, *Systematic Theology,* 594–603). Others (e.g., Calvin, Knight) claim that Paul means all groups or all kinds, including rulers and authorities (1 Tim 2:1) and Gentiles (1 Tim 2:7), although textually (i.e., not theologically) it is extremely difficult to read "all groups" into 1 Tim 4:11 and Titus 2:11. The force of the statement is directed toward the opponents' sectarian theology. As Jeremias (20) points out, this statement stands in firm opposition to the synagogue's belief that God hates the sinner and wishes to save only the righteous and to the gnostic belief that salvation is only for those "in the know" (*Wissenden*). See *Explanation* for further discussion.

Ellicott says, "To please God is the highest motive that can influence a Christian" (26). Barrett thinks that vv 4–7 are a digression from Paul's argument, but v 4 gives the reason for his statement in v 3, and vv 5–7 give two more reasons for his statement in v 1. V 4 says the opponents are wrong in their salvific exclusivism; the Savior wants salvation offered to all, Jew and Gentile alike.

τοῦτο, "this," could refer to v 2a, saying that prayers for kings are pleasing to God, or it could refer to v 2b, thereby explaining that reverent lives are pleasing to God (see *Note* b on the variant γάρ inserted after τοῦτο). It is best to see τοῦτο as referring to v 1 (Bernard, Jeremias, Guthrie, Fee) for several reasons. (1) V 4 continues the theme of the universality of Christian salvation from v 1, and probably so does v 2b. (2) The main point of the passage is that salvation is for all, and praying for all is good and pleasing to God. (3) V 2a is parenthetical, so it is unlikely that Paul would be building upon it. ἐνώπιον, "before," could modify both καλόν, "good," and ἀπόδεκτον, "pleasing," in which case Paul is saying that God finds this type of prayer both good and pleasing, or it could be modifying just the latter; both are possible (see the construction in 2 Cor 8:21). If it modifies only ἀπόδεκτον (Bernard; Spicq, 1:363–64), then καλόν could refer to people (Lock, 27) in that they think this is good behavior, or to God in that God thinks it is good. Ellicott separates the two by saying it is "good (per se) and acceptable before God" (27), which perhaps properly avoids any possible redundancy. ἀπόδεκτος, "pleasing," occurs in the NT only here and in 1 Tim 5:4 (cf. Rom 15:16), which says that the religious (εὐσεβεῖν) duty of children is to take care of the widows in their family because this is ἀπόδεκτον ἐνώπιον τοῦ θεοῦ, "pleasing before God" (see v 3b below, almost verbatim the same statement). For the distinction between καλός, meaning "beautiful," and ἀγαθός, meaning "morally good," see Lock, 22–23. On the translation "people," see the *Comment* on v 6. Simpson (41–42) says that σωθῆναι, "to be saved," here means to preserve or protect (citing Matt 19:30; John 11:12; 12:27; Acts 27 passim; and the use of σωτήρ, "savior," in the LXX of Judg 3:9 and Neh 9:27): a Christian's prayer should be that "all men should be preserved from lawless misrule," and thereby the following phrase denotes a peace suitable "for the propagation of the gospel." But this makes v 2 the theme of the passage, which it is not, and it misses the statement that God wants everyone to know the truth, a decidedly theological understanding of σώζειν, "to save" (Guthrie, 81).

The theological debate over issues concerning the Christian doctrine of election arising from v 4 was not the focus of the text in its historical situation (see J.

Turmel, *RHPR* 5 [1900] 385–415). Within the context of the false teachers in Ephesus, Paul was saying that the church was not to exclude anyone, not even the governing authorities (v 2), from the proclamation of the gospel since God's desire was to save all people (possibly from all classes/groups of humanity; see *Comment* on 1 Tim 4:10; summary in Baugh, *WTJ* 54 [1992] 338–40; Marshall, "Universal Grace"). The supposed universalism of v 4, however, has led to much theological reflection throughout the history of the church. Some have tried to distinguish θέλειν, "to wish," in v 4 (as an "instructive desire") from βούλεσθαι, "to intend" (a mental decision; D. Müller, *NIDNTT* 3:1015) and on the basis of this argue that v 4 does not designate an absolute divine will (Bernard; E. Lipinski, *Ruch Biblijny i Liturgiczny* 11 [1958] 135–40; Spicq, 1:364–65; Kent, *Pastoral Epistles*). Although there are some examples where these original meanings are still present, and while there is much to be said for distinguishing between God's preference and what he wills to accomplish, it is the context that determines meaning and not the choice of words (G. Schrenk, *TDNT* 1:629–32; Marshall, "Universal Grace," 55–57). In 2 Pet 3:9 the author uses βούλεσθαι to say that God does "not wish that any should perish." The theological issue must thus be resolved by reflection on the nature of God and the context of the passage (see further G. Schrenk, *TDNT* 3:44–62).

Usey ("Christology") rightly emphasizes that the "Christology is in service of paraenesis" (12). The passage teaches that the church should pray for everyone, including secular rulers and Gentiles in general, since Christ died for them in line with God's salvific design. This joining of exhortation and theology, of Christology supporting paraenesis, is also illustrated in Phil 2:1–11 where Paul calls the Philippians to practice humility (2:1–4) by having the same mind as did Christ who, being in the form of God, "did not count equality with God a thing to be grasped, but emptied himself" (2:5–11).

4b καὶ εἰς ἐπίγνωσιν ἀληθείας ἐλθεῖν, "and to come into a knowledge of [the] truth." While σωθῆναι, "to be saved," is "the *ultimate* goal, this phrase gives the more *immediate* end leading naturally and directly to the former" (Ellicott, 28). Paul uses the phrase "come into the knowledge of the truth" only in the PE (1 Tim 4:3; 2 Tim 2:25; 3:7; Titus 1:1; see Heb 10:26), although the themes of knowledge and truth are found throughout his writings (below). Knowing the truth is equivalent to accepting the gospel message and emphasizes the cognitive element in the acceptance. Much of the teaching in the PE is directed not against the truth or falseness of the teaching of the opponents but against their improper conduct and the ungodly results of their teaching. This phrase rounds out Paul's critique by showing that their teaching, as well as their behavior, is untruthful.

ἐπίγνωσις, "knowledge," denotes more than knowing something. It is "active apprehension, not mere acquiring of information" (Houlden, 67). It is "not as much intellectual comprehension as it is discernment and appropriation by faith" (Spicq, 1:365). Paul uses the noun fifteen times (including 1 Tim 2:4; 2 Tim 2:25; 3:7; Titus 1:1) and the verb (ἐπιγινώσκειν, "to know") eleven times (including 1 Tim 4:3). Every occurrence of the idea in the PE has to do with knowing the truth, although the theme of knowledge is common in Paul (cf. Rom 1:28; 3:20; 10:2; Eph 1:17; 4:13; Phil 1:9; Col 1:9, 10; 2:2; 3:10; Phlm 6; J. A. Robinson, *St Paul's Epistle to the Ephesians* [London: Macmillan, 1903] 248–54; Dibelius-Conzelmann, 41 n. 34; R. Bultmann, *TDNT* 1:244).

ἀλήθεια, "truth," is used in the PE as a technical term for the gospel message— the truth. It is the "whole revelation of God in Christ" (Kelly, 62). It occurs fourteen times in the PE. Once it describes what is true (1 Tim 2:7a; cf. use of ἀληθής, "true," in Titus 1:13). In every other instance it is used objectively as the embodiment of the truth—Paul's gospel (1 Tim 2:7b). To know the truth is to be a Christian (1 Tim 2:4; 2 Tim 2:25), which among other things means that one can eat all foods (1 Tim 4:3). The truth is to be protected by the church (1 Tim 3:15) and understood by believers (2 Tim 2:15). It is what separates Paul from the opponents (1 Tim 6:5; 2 Tim 2:18; 3:7, 8; cf. 2 Tim 2:25) and stands opposed to the false myths (2 Tim 4:4; Titus 1:14). Similar phrases are found throughout the NT, phrases such as ἡ ἀλήθεια τοῦ εὐαγγελίου, "the truth of the gospel" (Gal 2:5, 14), ἡ ἀλήθεια, "the truth" (Rom 2:8; Gal 5:7; Jas 5:19), and ἐν λόγῳ ἀληθείας, "the message of truth" (2 Cor 6:7; cf. Rom 2:8; Gal 5:7; 2 Thess 2:10, 12, 13; cf. John 8:32; 17:17; 14:6; 1 John 5:20; 2 Pet 1:2; Spicq, 1:364). It is therefore unnecessary to equate the word ἀλήθεια, "truth," with the second-century sense of orthodoxy. On the lack of the article, cf. Moule, *Idiom-Book*, 111–12.

5–6 εἷς γὰρ θεός, εἷς καὶ μεσίτης θεοῦ καὶ ἀνθρώπων, ἄνθρωπος Χριστὸς Ἰησοῦς, ὁ δοὺς ἑαυτὸν ἀντίλυτρον ὑπὲρ πάντων, "For, 'there is one God, and one mediator between God and people, a person, Christ Jesus, who gave himself as a ransom for all.'" Vv 5–6 may have been a creed, or part of a creed, known by Timothy and the Ephesian church, which Paul quotes in order to strengthen his argument (see *Form/Structure/Setting*). γάρ, "for," connects the theology of the creed with the theme of the paragraph. The statement in v 6a about Christ's ransom being ὑπὲρ πάντων, "for all," is the focal point of the creed as far as this context is concerned: the second reason that the Ephesian church should pray for the salvation of all people is that it is in line with the purpose of Christ's death.

V 5 possibly adds another argument to 1 Tim 2:1–7. Since there is only one God and only one mediator between God and people, all people are united under that oneness and all people should be offered the benefit of Christ's ransom. If someone is excluded from salvation in Christ, there is no other salvation available. Houlden misses the creed's significance when he says that it is not "integral to the argument of the passage" (67). The creed has two stanzas: the first asserts the uniqueness of the one God and the one mediator; the second asserts the nature of the mediator (i.e., his humanity) and the nature of his work (i.e., that it is for all; see *Form/Structure/Setting*). V 6b is Paul's commentary on the appropriateness of the creed to the Ephesian situation.

εἷς γὰρ θεός, "For 'there is only one God,'" rephrases the Shema, the central affirmation of Judaism: "Hear, O Israel: the LORD our God is one LORD" (Deut 6:4; cf. discussion in *Comments* on 1:17 and 2 Tim 3:4, φιλόθεοι, "lovers of God"). In Paul's day, sectarian Judaism emphasized "our" in an exclusive sense, and the opponents in the PE were making the same mistake. As a corrective, Paul's usage goes back to the original emphasis of the Shema on "one" God as opposed to "many" gods. God is not the God of the opponents alone but is the only God and consequently the God of all. (On this note of inclusivism, see Ridderbos, *Paul*, 338–41.) In Rom 3:29–30 (cf. 10:12) Paul argues that because there is only one God, all people will be justified in relation to their faith. Likewise here Paul argues that because there is only one God, all people must be the object of prayer since all can be saved only through the one God and the one mediator. This verse provides one of the strongest arguments that the Ephesian heresy was primarily Jewish (see *Introduction*, "The Ephesian Heresy").

Paul has been juxtaposing God and the people in a poetic way: "our savior . . .
all people . . . one God . . . one mediator . . . all people" (cf. 1 Cor 8:6; 12:13; Eph
4:5–6 for similar patterns). εἷς καὶ μεσίτης θεοῦ καὶ ἀνθρώπων, "and one mediator
between God and people," adds the Christian aspect of the creed: there is only one
mediator between God and people (cf. John 14:6). Originally μεσίτης, "mediator,"
was a business term, but its use broadened to denote a mediator of any sort. The
concept of a mediator between God and humanity was common in Hellenism and
Judaism (BAGD, 506–7; A. Oepke, *TDNT* 4:598–620; Str-B 3:644). It is found in
Gnosticism (K. Rudolph, *Gnosis,* 92–94, 113–48) and in the mystery cult of Mithras
(Plutarch, *Isis and Osiris,* 46). Philo uses the concept to describe Moses (*Mos.* 2.166;
3.19), angels (*Somn.* 1.142), and the word of God (*Her.* 42). Judaism spoke of angels
as mediators (*T. Dan* 6:21; cf. Acts 7:53; Heb 2:5–9, 16). Hebrews also contrasts the
role of the Jewish high priest and the work of Christ (Heb 8:6), who is elsewhere
called the mediator of the new covenant (Heb 9:15; 12:24; cf. 6:17).

The only other place Paul speaks about a mediator is in Gal 3:19, where he
identifies Moses as the mediator of the OT law (cf. *As. Mos.* 1:14; 3:12, and Philo
above; Col 2:18 may perhaps be understood as a worship of angels in a mediatorial
role). In our context the text does not suggest that the mediator is inferior (contra
Hanson, "Mediator," 57); the verse merely describes a specific function. It is
possible that here Paul is citing a creed and therefore unusual concepts are
expected, although the creed's use of μεσίτης is a fine parallel to Paul's "Second
Man" concept (Jeremias, Kelly). It is also possible that here Paul is contrasting
Christ's mediatorial work for all people with the Jewish concept of Moses as
mediator for Jews alone (cf. passages cited above and the emphasis on Christ's role
in 2 Tim 1:9–10; cf. Bernard; Trummer, *Paulustradition,* 196; Wengst sets it in
contrast to the gnostic doctrine of multiple aeons [*Formeln,* 72]). The opponents
are teaching a veneration of certain aspects of the law and relegating the gospel to
second place. As in Hebrews, Christianity is shown to be superior because Christ is
superior to Moses (see Houlden, 68; Richardson, *Theology,* 229). Hanson ([1983]
68–69; id., "Mediator," 56–62) and Usey see the use of μεσίτης as a reference to
Job's complaint to God: "For you are not a man in relation to me, against whom I
contend, that we should come together to trial. O that there were our mediator [ὁ
μεσίτης] and accuser and one to hear midway between both of us" (Job 9:32–33
LXX). They see the creed as an answer to "Job's pathetic cry for an *internuntius*" by
God who has "'extended a fraternal hand to man' (Calvin)" (Simpson, 42). μεσίτης
requires the following noun to be genitive (Wallace, *Greek Grammar,* 135).

ἄνθρωπος Χριστὸς Ἰησοῦς, "a person, Christ Jesus," begins the second stanza,
ἄνθρωπος, "person," being repeated from the previous line. Christ was able to
mediate between God and people because he was a human being and also anointed
(Χριστός) by God. ἄνθρωπος is anarthrous, emphasizing the quality of being human;
i.e., it was as a human being that Christ gave himself for all humanity (cf. Marshall,
SNTU-A 13 [1988] 173). This is not a denial of Christ's divinity (contra Windisch
[*ZNW* 34 [1935] 213–38], who says the PE teach that Jesus is exalted but subordinate
to God and not divine) but an emphatic assertion of the incarnation. Marshall
suggests that perhaps the phrase expresses "the divinity and humanity of Christ" and
translates "There is one who is God, one who is also (καί) the mediator between God
and man, the man Christ Jesus" ("Redemption," 166 n. 3). Titus 2:13, which is
followed by a mention of redemption (v 14) as is the case here, also calls Jesus τοῦ

μεγάλου θεοῦ καὶ σωτῆρος ἡμῶν Ἰησοῦ Χριστοῦ, "our great God and savior Jesus Christ." If this is the proper translation of Titus 2:13, then Marshall's understanding of 1 Tim 2:5 is certainly possible and consistent with the Christology of the PE. Jeremias (20) translates "*the* Man" (italics his), equating ἄνθρωπος, "a man," with "the Son of man" (cf. Mark 8:27–9:1). But ἄνθρωπος is anarthrous, designating not identity ("the Son of man") but quality (i.e., that which makes a person human). The verse could also be distinguishing the Godhead, God the Father, and Christ Jesus the Mediator (cf. 1 Cor 8:6; Eph 4:4–6). There is no concept of the subordination of the Son here but only a differentiation of task (or perhaps a subordination in reference to the office alone; cf. Grudem, *Systematic Theology,* 245).

It is difficult, but acceptable, to translate ἄνθρωπος in v 5c generically as "person" as is often the case with this term (cf. 1 Tim 4:10; 2 Tim 3:2). Paul uses ἄνθρωπος throughout the paragraph to tie his argument together, specifically tying v 1 with vv 4–5: pray for all ἀνθρώπων (v 1) because God wants all ἀνθρώπους to be saved (v 4) through the mediator between God and ἀνθρώπων (v 5b), an ἄνθρωπος, Christ Jesus (v 5c; cf. the unspecified πάντων, "all," in v 6a, retained in the translation of the RSV). The NRSV loses the connection when it translates "everyone . . . everyone . . . humankind . . . humankind," as does the NIV, which translates "everyone" in v 1 and unnecessarily adds "men" in v 6.

6a ὁ δοὺς ἑαυτὸν ἀντίλυτρον ὑπὲρ πάντων, "who gave himself as a ransom for all." Paul now arrives at the focal point of the creed and the second reason for his command in v 1. Building on his earlier statement that "Christ Jesus came into the world to save sinners" (1:15), he now says that Christ died for everyone in keeping with God's desire that all people be saved, the accent being on the word *all* (Jeremias, 20). Therefore, not to pray for everyone is to treat the death of Christ with contempt. Paul repeats the same idea in Titus 2:14, where he says that Christ ἔδωκεν ἑαυτὸν ὑπὲρ ἡμῶν, ἵνα λυτρώσηται ἡμᾶς, "gave himself for us to redeem us." On the connection between this thought and the love of God, see K. Romaniuk, *L'amour du Père et du Fils dans la Sotériologie de Saint Paul* [Rome: Pontificio Istituto Biblico, 1961] 58–63; also F. Denk, *Geschichte;* Rosiak, *Homo Dei* 28 (1959) 38–45.

This is the only NT use of ἀντίλυτρον, "ransom" (Lock cites a *v.l.* in Ps 48:9 LXX [ET 49:8]). Most commentators, using terms such as "echo" (Spicq, 1:367; Guthrie, 67), "free version" (Kelly, 63), and "reminiscence" (Lock, 28), agree that this idea in some way goes back to the thought of Mark 10:45. The idea of δοὺς ἑαυτόν, "gave himself," is typical for Paul (cf. Rom 8:32, ὑπὲρ ἡμῶν πάντων παρέδωκεν αὐτόν, "gave him up for us all"]; Gal 1:4; 2:20; Eph 5:2; cf. N. Perrin, "The Use of (παρα)διδόναι in Connection with the Passion of Jesus in the New Testament," in *A Modern Pilgrimage in New Testament Christology* [Philadelphia: Fortress, 1974] 94–103). Kelly comments, "Since Paul is not setting out a theory of the Atonement of his own but citing what has become a theological cliché, it is fruitless to speculate about the complex of ideas lying behind it. The important words for him are 'for all'" (63–64). But the idea of ransom does appear in Titus 2:14, so the concept is worthy of some discussion.

There are two issues. (1) What is the meaning of the prepositions ἀντί and ὑπέρ? (2) Does ἀντίλυτρον, "ransom," designate price paid or freedom gained? (1) There is an important wordplay occurring with the two prepositions: Christ is an ἀντίλυτρον made ὑπέρ, "for," all people. If the prepositions carry their classical meanings, then the phrase is saying that Christ's ransom was ἀντί, "in place of," and ὑπέρ, "on behalf of," all people (notice use of ὑπέρ in vv 1–2; cf. Wallace, *Greek Grammar*, 366, 388). At a minimum, there is here the idea of substitution (Ridderbos, *Paul*, 196; ὑπέρ modifies ἀντίλυτρον, not ὁ δούς, "who gave"). By the Koine period ὑπέρ had started to share the meaning of ἀντί, so the phrase could be emphasizing almost exclusively the idea of substitution (Moule, *Idiom-Book*, 64, citing references; Robertson, *Grammar*, 630–32; Ladd, *Theology*, 428, citing L. Radermacher, *Neutestamentliche Grammatik*, 2nd ed. [Tübingen: Mohr-Siebeck, 1925] 139; see Simpson, 110–12, for references to ὑπέρ denoting substitution). Spicq (1:367) argues that ἀντίλυτρον and λύτρον have basically the same meaning, citing the parallels in Eph 1:7, Col 1:14, Heb 9:15, and 1 Pet 1:18. Titus 2:14 has ἵνα λυτρώσηται, "in order that he might redeem," with no ἀντί. Guthrie says that ἀντίλυτρον is a strengthened form of λύτρον "drawing special attention to its substitutionary character" (*New Testament Theology*, 478). On the prepositions, see R. E. Davies, *TBT* 21 (1970) 71–91; Guthrie, *New Testament Theology*, 441, 467; H. Riesenfeld, *TDNT* 8:507–16; Robertson, *Grammar*, 630–32; Moule, *Idiom-Book*, 64; M. J. Harris, *NIDNTT* 3:1179–80, 1196–97.

(2) ἀντίλυτρον, "ransom," can carry the idea of payment and of freedom, and freedom can have a variety of backgrounds, such as freedom from slavery or the OT idea of a forfeited life. In both 1 Tim 2:6 and Titus 2:14 the price of the ransom is emphasized: Christ gave himself. This complements the essential message of the paragraph: because Christ's death for all people was so costly, to exclude people from the offer of salvation is especially horrendous. But the idea of ransom must include both payment and freedom, because freedom can only be gained by a price (e.g., 1 Cor 6:19–20; 7:22–23), and the result of paying the price is freedom (e.g., Gal 4:3–5). F. Büchsel warns against trying to be too exact in defining this concept. Commenting on Mark 10:45, he says, "By intention, the saying of Jesus is only allusive. It gives an insight into the mystery of God which is to be humbly venerated and yet also protected against over-subtle curiosity; hence its figurative form. It is to be understood in terms of the history narrated in the Gospels. . . . It is part of the history of the death of Jesus . . . [and] only those who see it from this standpoint can fully understand it" (*TDNT* 4:343). On the idea of ransom/redemption, see Ladd, *Theology*, 433–34; L. Morris, *Apostolic Preaching*, 9–59; Marshall, "Redemption," 153–69; F. Büchsel, *TDNT* 4:340–56; Jeremias, *New Testament Theology*, 292–94.

6b τὸ μαρτύριον καιροῖς ἰδίοις, "the witness at the proper time." This is a compact and difficult phrase to understand (see *Note* d for the variants). Because it disrupts the structure of the creed and because its language is peculiar to the PE, it should be interpreted as Paul's comment on the creed (see *Form/Structure/ Setting*). The phrase καιροῖς ἰδίοις, "at the proper time," occurs elsewhere in 1 Tim 6:15, which says that Christ's second coming will be made manifest at the proper time, and in Titus 1:3, which says that God at the proper time manifested eternal life through his word. There are four questions to be answered. To a large extent, the answer to the first determines the answer to the rest.

(1) To whom, or to what, is the witness directed? Hanson says that Christ's death was "a fulfillment of God's promises in God's good time" ([1983] 34–35) and that therefore his death is a witness to salvation history (see Dibelius-Conzelmann, Kelly, Houlden). Oberlinner says that God's design to save is witnessed to— historically revealed—in Christ's death, but also includes the apostolic and postapostolic proclamation of the event (76). Towner concludes that the testimony

is "God's message to the world through the medium of his Son's redemptive death" (*Goal*, 83). In the historical context of Paul's life it is a witness to the Ephesian church that they should pray for all people.

(2) Who, or what, is the witness? Most see μαρτύριον, "witness," in apposition to the whole of vv 5–6a; therefore, both the nature of God and the mediator and the work of the mediator are the witness at the proper time. But since the phrase ὑπὲρ πάντων, "for all," is the crux of the passage, it is best to see this phrase as the witness: Christ's ransom for all people is the appropriate witness to the Ephesian church that they are not to exclude anyone from the offer of salvation (see Scott, 22–23; Kelly, 64).

(3) When was the witness given? It is possible that the time reference is future as it is in 1 Tim 6:15 (cf. 2 Thess 2:6, ἐν τῷ ἑαυτοῦ καιρῷ, "in his own time"). But the context needs a present witness since Paul is directing his exhortation to the Ephesian church. This is confirmed by Titus 1:3, in which καιροῖς ἰδίοις designates the present witness of God in the preaching of the gospel. The thought is similar to that in Gal 4:4, which says that in τὸ πλήρωμα τοῦ χρόνου, "the fullness of time," God sent his son, and in Rom 5:6, which says that "while we were still weak, at the right time [κατὰ καιρόν] Christ died for the ungodly" (cf. Eph 1:10, and Lock on Titus 1:3). The classical distinction is that καιρός indicates a "suitable opportunity" while χρόνος is "used for duration or succession of time" (Guthrie, 180; cf. 1 Tim 4:1; 6:15; 2 Tim 3:1; 4:3, 6; Titus 1:3). This distinction could be present here. The plural is probably idiomatic, referring to a single time or period of time (Knight, 124). It is plural in 1 Tim 6:15 and Titus 1:3, both referring to a single time period (parousia and apostolic proclamation, respectively), but singular the only other time the two words occur together in the NT (Gal 6:9).

(4) Whose time frame defines the appointed time? The subject of the action in 1 Tim 2:6 is *God*, as it is in 1 Tim 6:15 and Titus 1:3. God is the savior, and therefore salvation happens according to his time schedule (contra Bernard who says that the phrase simply means "in due season"). The variant reading that inserts οὗ, "whose," before τὸ μαρτύριον, "the witness" (see *Note* d), would make Jesus the subject of the witness. μαρτύριον, "witness," occurs elsewhere in the PE only in 2 Tim 1:8, where Timothy is encouraged not to be ashamed of God or Paul. The cognate μαρτυρία, "witness," occurs twice, referring to the reliability of a popular saying (Titus 1:13) and the good reputation that an overseer should possess with those outside the church (1 Tim 3:7). The verb μαρτυρεῖν, "to bear witness," is used to say that a widow must be well attested for her good deeds (1 Tim 5:10) and to refer to the witness that Jesus had before Pilate (1 Tim 6:13).

7 εἰς ὃ ἐτέθην ἐγὼ κῆρυξ καὶ ἀπόστολος, ἀλήθειαν λέγω οὐ ψεύδομαι, διδάσκαλος ἐθνῶν ἐν πίστει καὶ ἀληθείᾳ, "[It is] with reference to this [witness that] I was appointed a herald and apostle—I am speaking the truth; I am not lying—a teacher of the Gentiles in faith and truth." This is Paul's third and final argument exhorting the Ephesian church to pray for all people. The universal gospel, as described in vv 5–6a, is a witness to the Ephesian church (v 6b) that the message of salvation should be proclaimed to all people. It is with reference to this gospel that Paul was appointed (cf. discussion at 1:11) a herald and an apostle, even a teacher to the Gentiles. ἐτέθην, "was appointed," is passive, emphasizing that God was the author of his appointment. The force of the disclaimer "I am speaking the truth; I am not lying" is directed toward his claim to being a teacher of the Gentiles, unlike other historical contexts in which his apostolic office was questioned. From this we can assume that his opponents were excluding Gentiles from their offer of salvation; yet these are the very people to whom God sent Paul. Consequently, the Ephesian church must pray for all people, even Gentiles (v 1). Chrysostom paraphrases Paul's message thus: "Since therefore Christ suffered for the Gentiles, and I was separated to be a 'teacher of the Gentiles,' why dost thou refuse to pray for them?" ("Homily 7"; NPNF 13:431).

The antecedent of ὅ, "which," could be either μαρτύριον, "witness," or the gospel as proclaimed in vv 5–6a. There would be no substantial difference in meaning. On this use of τιθέναι, "to appoint," see BAGD, 816 (I2aα). The strong language is not directed to Timothy who, as a close friend and coworker with Paul, would not question Paul's call, but to the Ephesian church, showing again the semiprivate nature of the epistle (see *Introduction*, "Historical Reconstruction from the PE"). As Guthrie says, "No less an issue was at stake than the veracity of the Gentile mission" (83), and consequently such a strong interjection is appropriate. In contrast to the opponents, Paul emphasizes that God appointed him (notice the emphatic use of ἐγώ, "I," possibly reminiscent of his expression of humility in 1:12–17) as a teacher, and a teacher to the very people whom the opponents were excluding from salvation. Not only was their salvific exclusiveness running counter to the savior's desires (v 4) and the mediator's death (v 6), but it also contradicted the core of Paul's divinely appointed ministry.

κῆρυξ, "herald," appears elsewhere only in 2 Tim 1:11 ("For this gospel I was appointed a preacher [κῆρυξ] and apostle and teacher") and 2 Pet 2:5 (which calls Noah a "herald of righteousness"). But its verbal cognate κηρύσσειν, "to proclaim," is common, occurring nineteen times in Paul, including 1 Tim 3:16 ("he was . . . proclaimed among the nations") and 2 Tim 4:2 ("preach the word!"). In secular society, the herald made public announcements (for references see Spicq, 1:368–69, and Dibelius-Conzelmann, 43 n. 54, 55). A herald was the crier of public sales and of official actions such as taxes; he announced the freedom of slaves and was active in the law courts. A herald announced the beginning of the public games, the name of each participant, and the name of the winner's father. He announced the orders of the king and the king's arrival. A herald was also involved in religious ceremonies. Spicq draws a parallel with the Qumran Teacher of Righteousness (1:369–70; cf. 1QH 2:13–14, 18; 4:27; 8:21). The two main requirements of a herald were that he have a loud voice and that he be able to repeat strictly what he had been told (see J. Roloff, *Apostolat—Verkündigung—Kirche*, 239–44). Chrysostom comments, "for the excellence of a herald consists in proclaiming to all what has really happened, not in adding or taking away anything" ("Homily 1" on Titus 1:3; NPNF 13:521). Because in the NT what is being proclaimed is usually the gospel, κηρύσσειν is practically synonymous with εὐαγγελίζεσθαι, "to preach the gospel" (e.g., Matt 4:23; 9:35; 24:14; 26:13; Mark 14:9; Rom 10:15; Gal 2:2; 1 Thess 2:9). Yet its basic meaning is not so much "to preach the gospel" as "to make public" (cf. Mark 1:45; 5:20; 7:36; Luke 8:39). On ἀπόστολος, "apostle," see *Comment* on 1 Tim 1:1.

Paul includes two statements that emphasize that God sent him as a teacher to the Gentiles. (1) He inserts the emotional appeal "I am speaking the truth; I am not lying" (the word order being emphatic: ἀλήθειαν λέγω οὐ ψεύδομαι, "the truth I am speaking; not I am lying"). This type of appeal is common for Paul (Rom 9:1; 2 Cor 11:31; cf. the force of the [divine] passive ἐτέθην, "I was appointed"; cf. 1 Tim 1:12;

Acts 13:47; Spicq, 1:369–70; and C. Maurer, *TDNT* 8:156–57, on the theological use of τιθέναι, "to appoint"). (2) Paul also insists that he is a teacher ἐν πίστει καὶ ἀληθείᾳ, "in faith and truth." Contrary to the false teachers who are teaching what is opposed to proper doctrine and what is false, Paul is teaching the Gentiles the true Christian faith. These two words can be understood (a) subjectively to mean "with fidelity and truthfulness" (Scott, Simpson, Hanson [1983]), or (b) objectively as the content of Paul's teaching, i.e., that which is the faith and the truth (Bernard, Lock, Spicq, Guthrie). (c) Barrett (53) suggests that the two words are a hendiadys, combining to mean "the true faith" (cf. Fee [67]; NEB; NIV). Throughout the PE, πίστις, "faith," and ἀλήθεια, "truth," are often used objectively as descriptions of the gospel (see 1 Tim 1:2 and 2:4), and therefore interpretation (b) is to be preferred. On the idea of being entrusted with the gospel, see *Comment* on 1 Tim 1:11. On πίστις, "faith," see *Introduction*, "Themes in the PE." On ἀλήθεια, "truth," see *Comment* on 1 Tim 2:4.

Explanation

There was trouble in the Ephesian church. Some of its leaders were teaching a doctrine of salvation and regulations of life based on myths they had created from OT genealogies. Out of this flowed naturally a salvific exclusivism similar to that in sectarian Judaism. Also, the conduct of the elders was unacceptable. They were leading many astray, and the witness of the church was being damaged.

Paul responds in two ways: (1) he excommunicates two of the ringleaders (1:19–20), and (2) he gives Timothy a series of instructions on how the church should conduct itself (2:1–3:16). At the head of the list Paul goes to the root of the Ephesian problem: a deficient understanding of salvation. This deficiency showed itself in the Ephesian practice of praying only for the select group of people who adhered to their mythological teaching, excluding among others the secular rulers and all Gentiles. Therefore, Paul says that all types of prayers, especially requests for salvation, should be made on behalf of all people, even the rulers. If this is done, the church can continue to live in peace and tranquility, with reverence and godly dignity, not for the sake of avoiding necessary conflict but in order to have a good witness to non-Christians.

Paul follows with several reasons that the church should include all people in their prayers. (1) This type of prayer is good and pleasing to God. (2) It is in line with the savior's wishes that all people be saved. Understood within its Ephesian historical context, this is not a statement of universalism, election, adoption, or any such developed theological concern. It is rather a reason that the Ephesian church should include everyone. (3) It is also in line with the work of Christ, himself human, because he provided the ransom for all people. To say this, Paul cites what may have been a creed already known to Timothy and the Ephesian church. Its first line, "There is only one God," is a restatement of the Shema, the basic tenet of Judaism: "Hear, O Israel: the LORD our God is one LORD." But whereas sectarian Judaism and the Ephesian opponents were emphasizing that God was "our" God and were therefore not interested in those outside their circle, Paul emphasizes that God is one. The second line, "and there is one mediator between God and people," is the Christian expansion of the Shema, asserting that Jesus (perhaps in contrast to Moses) is the only mediator. If Christian salvation is not offered to all, then there is no other salvation possible. Most of the emphasis of the creed lies on the final statement, "who gave himself as a ransom for all people," Jew and Gentile (v 7). Not to pray for all people is to run counter to the purpose for which Christ died. This is the appropriate witness to the Ephesian church that they should pray for all people. (4) Finally, Paul emphasizes that God sent him as an apostle, a herald, and especially as a teacher for the Gentiles, people whom the opponents were excluding. Contrary to what had been taught in the Ephesian church, Paul insists that not the myths but his gospel, which included the Gentiles, is the faith and the truth.

The call to pray for all people is reflected in early Christian worship:

> Thou, Master, hast given the power of sovereignty to them through thy excellent and inexpressible might, that we may know the glory and honour given to them by thee, and be subject to them, in nothing resisting thy will. And to them, Lord, grant health, peace, concord, firmness that they may administer the government, which thou hast given them without offence. For thou, heavenly Master, king of eternity, hast given to the sons of men glory and honour and power over the things which are on the earth; do thou, O Lord, direct their counsels according to that which is "good and pleasing" before thee, that they may administer with piety in peace and gentleness the power given to them by thee, and may find mercy in thine eyes. (*1 Clem.* 61:1–2, LCL tr.)

> "Pray for all the saints. Pray also for the Emperors," and for potentates, and princes, and for "those who persecute you and hate you," and for "the enemies of the Cross" that "your fruit may be manifest among all men, that you may be perfected" in him. (Polycarp *Phil.* 12.3, LCL tr.)

B. Questions of Disruption and Leadership (1 Tim 2:8–15)

Bibliography

Adeney, W. F. *Women of the New Testament.* London: Service & Patton, 1899. **Adinolfi, M.** "Il velo della donna e la rilettura paolina di I Cor. II, 2–16." *RB* 23 (1975) 147–73. **Aldunate, J. B.** "Three Submissions and Continual Renewal." *Concilium* 39 (1968) 45–68. **Allmen, J. J. von.** *Pauline Teaching on Marriage.* London: Faith, 1963. **Archer, G. L.** "Does 1 Timothy 2:12 Forbid the Ordination of Women?" In *Encyclopedia of Bible Difficulties.* Grand Rapids, MI: Zondervan, 1982. 411–15. **Arnold, F. X.** *Woman and Man: Their Nature and Mission.* New York: Herder, 1963. **Babbage, S. B.** *Christianity and Sex.* Downers Grove, IL: InterVarsity Press, 1963. **Bailey, D. S.** *Sexual Relation in Christian Thought.* New York: Harper & Row, 1959. **Bainette, H.** "Coarchy: Partnership and Equality in Man-Woman Relationship." *RevExp* 75 (1978) 19–24. **Balch, D. L.** *Let Wives Be Submissive: The Domestic Code in 1 Peter.* SBLMS 26. Chico, CA: Scholars Press, 1981. **Baldwin, H. S.** "Appendix 2: αὐθεντέω in Ancient Greek Literature." In *Women in the Church*, ed. A. J. Köstenberger, T. R. Schreiner, and H. S. Baldwin. Grand Rapids, MI: Baker, 1995. 271–307. ———. "A Difficult Word: αὐθεντέω in 1 Timothy 2:12." In *Women in the Church*, ed. A. J. Köstenberger, T. R. Schreiner, and H. S.

Baldwin. Grand Rapids, MI: Baker, 1995. 65–80. **Baldwin, J. G.** "A Response to G. Wenham." *Churchman* 93 (1979) 54. ———. *Women Likewise.* London: Falcon, 1973. **Balsdon, J. P. V. D.** *Roman Women: Their History and Habits.* London: Bodley Head, 1962. **Bangerter, O.** "Les veuves dans les épîtres pastorales, modèle d'un ministère féminin dans l'église ancienne." *FV* 83 (1984) 27–45. **Banks, R.** "The Contribution of Women in Church." In *Paul's Idea of Community.* 122–30. **Barnett, P. W.** "Wives and Women's Ministry (1 Timothy 2:11–15)." *EvQ* 61 (1989) 225–38. **Barrois, G.** "Women and the Priestly Office according to the Scriptures." *St. Vladimir's Theological Quarterly* 19 (1975) 174–92. **Barron, B.** "Putting Women in Their Place: 1 Timothy 2 and Evangelical Views of Women in Church Leadership." *JETS* 33 (1990) 451–59. **Bartchy, S. S.** "Power, Submission, and Sexual Identity among the Early Christians." In *Essays in New Testament Christianity,* ed. C. R. Wetzel. Cincinnati: Standard, 1978. 50–80. **Bartlet, P. W.** "Women and Judaism." In *God, Sex and the Social Project,* ed. J. H. Grace. Lewiston, NY: Mellen, 1978. 53–92. **Bassler, J. M.** "Adam, Eve, and the Pastor: The Use of Genesis 2–3 in the Pastoral Epistles." In *Genesis 1–3 in the History of Exegesis.* Lewiston, NY: Mellen, 1988. 43–65. **Baugh, S. M.** "The Apostle among the Amazons." *WTJ* 56 (1994) 153–71. ———. "A Foreign World: Ephesus in the First Century." In *Women in the Church,* ed. A. J. Köstenberger, T. R. Schreiner, and H. S. Baldwin. Grand Rapids, MI: Baker, 1995. 13–52. **Baumert, N.** *Antifeminismus bei Paulus? Einzelstudien.* FB 68. Würzburg: Echter, 1992. 282–300. **Bellis, M.** "Lavantes puras manus (1 Tim 2:8)." Diss., University of Torino, 1948. **Bilezikian, G.** *Beyond Sex Roles.* Grand Rapids, MI: Baker, 1985. **Bliss, K.** *The Service and Status of Women in the Church.* London: SCM Press, 1952. **Bloesch, D. G.** *Is the Bible Sexist? Beyond Feminism and Patriarchalism.* Westchester: Crossway, 1982. **Blomberg, C. L.** "Not beyond What Is Written: A Review of Aída Spencer's *Beyond the Curse.*" *CTR* 2 (1988) 403–22. **Blum, G. G.** "The Office of Woman in the New Testament." *Churchman* 85 (1971) 175–89. **Boer, P. A. H. de.** *Fatherhood and Motherhood in Israelite and Judean Piety.* Leiden: Brill, 1974. **Boldrey, R.** *Chauvinist or Feminist? Paul's View of Women.* Grand Rapids, MI: Baker, 1976. **Boomsma, C.** *Male and Female, One in Christ: New Testament Teaching on Women in Office.* Grand Rapids, MI: Baker, 1993. **Boucher, M.** "Some Unexplored Parallels to 1 Cor. 11.11–12 and Gal. 3.28: The New Testament on the Role of Women." *CBQ* 31 (1969) 50–58. **Bowman, A. L.** "Women in Ministry: An Exegetical Study of 1 Timothy 2:11–15." *BSac* 149 (1992) 193–213. **Brauch, M. T.** *Hard Sayings of the Bible.* Downers Grove, IL: InterVarsity Press, 1996. 665–71. **Bristow, J. T.** *What Paul Really Said about Women.* San Francisco: Harper & Row, 1988. **Brooten, B. J.** *Women Leaders in the Ancient Synagogue: Inscriptional Evidence and Background Issues.* BJS 36. Chico, CA: Scholars Press, 1983. **Bruce, F. F.** *All Things to All Men: Unity and Diversity in New Testament Theology.* Grand Rapids, MI: Eerdmans, 1978. ———. "Women in the Church: A Biblical Survey." *Christian Brethren Review* 33 (1982) 7–14. **Bruce, M.,** and **Duffield, G. E.** *Why Not? Priesthood and the Ministry of Women.* Appleford, Berkshire: Marcham Books, 1976. **Brunner, P.** *The Ministry and the Ministry of Women.* St. Louis: Concordia, 1971. **Caird, G. B.** "Paul and Women's Liberty." *BJRL* 54 (1972) 268–81. **Cameron, A.** "Neither Male nor Female." *Greece and Rome* 27 (1980) 60–68. **Carle, P.-L.** "La femme et les ministères pastoraux d'après la tradition." *Nova et Vetera* 47 (1972) 263–90. ———. "La femme et les ministères pastoraux: Etude theologique." *Nova et Vetera* 48 (1973) 17–36. ———. "La femme et les ministères pastoraux selon l'Ecriture." *Nova et Vetera* 47 (1972) 161–87. **Catholic Biblical Association of America's Task Force on the Role of Women in Early Christianity.** "Women in Priestly Ministry: The New Testament Evidence." *CBQ* 41 (1979) 603–13. **Cerling, C. E., Jr.** "An Annotated Bibliography of the New Testament Teaching about Women." *JETS* (1973) 47–53. ———. "Women Ministers in the New Testament Church." *JETS* 19 (1976) 210–15. **Chilton, B. D.** "Opening the Book: Biblical Warrants for the Ordination of Women." *Modern Churchman* 20 (1977) 32–35. **Christenson, L.** *The Christian Family.* Esher, Surrey: Fountain Trust, 1971. **Clark, E. A.** *Women in the Early Church: Message of the Fathers of the Church.* Wilmington, DE: Glazier, 1983. **Clark, G.** "The Ordination of Women." *The Trinity Review* 17 (1981) 1–6. **Clark, S. B.** *Man and Woman in Christ: An*

Examination of the Roles of Men and Women in Light of Scripture and the Social Sciences. Ann Arbor, MI: Servant, 1980. **Clouse, B.,** and **Clouse, R. G.,** eds. *Women in Ministry: Four Views.* Downers Grove, IL: InterVarsity Press, 1989. **Collins, R. F.** "The Bible and Sexuality." *BTB* 11.7 (1977) 149–67; 11.8 (1978) 318. **Coyle, J. C.** "The Fathers on Women and Women's Ordination." *Église et Théologie* 9 (1978) 50–101. **Culver, R. D.** "A Traditional View: Let Your Women Keep Silence." In *Women in Ministry: Four Views,* ed. B. Clouse and R. G. Clouse. Downers Grove, IL: InterVarsity Press, 1989. 25–52. **Danet, A.** "1 Timothée 2,8–15 et le ministère pastoral féminin." *Hokhma* 44 (1990) 23–44. **Daniélou, J.** *The Ministry of Women in the Early Church.* London: Faith, 1961. **Daube, D.** "Concessions to Sinfulness in Jewish Law." *JJS* 10 (1959) 121. **Davis, J. J.** "Some Reflections on Gal. 3:28, Sexual Roles, and Biblical Hermeneutics." *JETS* 19 (1976) 201–8. **Dayton, D. W.,** and **Lucille, S.** "Women as Preachers: Evangelical Precedents." *Christianity Today* 19 no. 17 (1975) 4–7. **Diaz, J. A.** "Restricción en algunos textos paulinos de las reivindicaciones de la mujer en la Iglesia." *Estudios Eclesiásticos* 50 (1975) 77–93. **Dockery, D. S.** "The Role of Women in Worship and Ministry: Some Hermeneutical Questions." *CTR* 1 (1987) 363–86. **Dodd, C. H.** "New Testament Translation Problems II." *BT* 28 (1977) 112–16. **Donaldson, J.** *Woman: Her Position and Influence in Ancient Greece and Rome and in the Early Church.* New York: Gordon, 1973. **Doriani, D.** "Appendix 2: History of the Interpretation of 1 Timothy 2." In *Women in the Church,* ed. A. J. Köstenberger, T. R. Schreiner, and H. S. Baldwin. Grand Rapids, MI: Baker, 1995. 215–69. **Doughty, D. J.** "Women and Liberation in the Churches of Paul and the Pauline Tradition." *Drew Gateway* 50 (1979) 1–21. **Dumais, M.** "Couple et sexualité selon le Nouveau Testament." *Église et Théologie* 8 (1977) 42–72. **Edwards, R. B.** *The Case for Women's Ministry.* London: S.P.C.K., 1989. **Elliot, E.** *Let Me Be a Woman.* Wheaton, IL: Tyndale House, 1976. ———. "Why I Oppose the Ordination of Women." *Christianity Today* 19 no. 18 (1975) 12–16. **Ellis, E. E.** *Paul's Use of the Old Testament.* **Epstein, L. M.** *Sex Laws and Customs in Judaism.* New York: Bloch, 1948. **Evans, M. J.** *Woman in the Bible.* Downers Grove, IL: InterVarsity Press, 1983. **Falconer R.** "1 Timothy 2:14–15: Interpretative Notes." *JBL* 60 (1941) 375–79. **Fee, G. D.** "Issues in Evangelical Hermeneutics: Part III. The Great Watershed, Intentionality and Particularity/ Eternality: 1 Timothy 2:8–15 as a Test Case." *Crux* 26 (1990) 31–37 (repr. in *Gospel and Spirit* [Peabody, MA: Hendrickson, 1991] 52–65). ———. "Reflections on Church Order in the Pastoral Epistles, with Further Reflections on the Hermeneutics of ad hoc Documents." *JETS* 28 (1985) 141–51. ———. "Women in Ministry: The Meaning of 1 Timothy 2:8–15 in Light of the Purpose of 1 Timothy." *Journal of the Christian Brethren Research Fellowship* 122 (1990) 11–18. ———, and **Stuart, D.** *How to Read the Bible for All It's Worth.* 2nd ed. Grand Rapids, MI: Zondervan, 1993. 57–71. **Ferguson, E.** *Backgrounds of Early Christianity.* Grand Rapids, MI: Eerdmans, 1987. ———. "Τόπος in 1 Timothy 2:8." *ResQ* 33 (1991) 65–73. **Feuillet, A.** "La dignité et le role de la femme d'après quelques textes pauliniennes: Comparaison avec l'Ancien Testament." *NTS* 21 (1975) 157–91. ———. "L'homme 'gloire de Dieu' et la femme 'gloire de l'homme' (1 Cor. XI, 7b)." *RB* 81 (1974) 161–82. ———. "Le signe de puissance sur la tête de la femme: I Cor. 11, 10." *NRT* 95 (1973) 945–54. **Foh, S. T.** "A Male Leadership View: The Head of the Woman Is the Man." In *Women in Ministry: Four Views,* ed. B. Clouse and R. G. Clouse. Downers Grove, IL: InterVarsity Press, 1989. 69–105. ———. "What Is Woman's Desire?" *WTJ* 37 (1975) 367–93. ———. *Women and the Word of God.* Philadelphia: Presbyterian & Reformed, 1980. **Ford, J. M.** "Biblical Material Relevant to the Ordination of Women." *JES* 10 (1973) 669–94. **Ford, P. J.** "Paul the Apostle: Male Chauvinist?" *BTB* 5 (1975) 302–11. **Forster, W.** *Palestinian Judaism in New Testament Times.* London: Oliver and Boyd, 1964. **Foster, J.** "St. Paul and Women." *ExpTim* 63 (1951) 376. **Fraine, J. de.** *Women in the Old Testament.* De Pere, WI: St. Norbert's Abbey Press, 1968. **Fraser, D.,** and **Fraser, E.** "A Biblical View of Women: Demythologizing Sexogesis." *Theology, News and Notes (Fuller Theological Seminary)* 21 (1975). **Fung, R. Y. K.** "Ministry in the New Testament." In *The Church in the Bible and the World,* ed. D. A. Carson. Grand Rapids, MI: Baker, 1987. **Gärtner, B.** "*Didaskalos:* The Office, Man and Woman in the New Testament."

Tr. J. E. Harborg. *Concordia Journal* 8 (1982) 52–60. **Gasque, W. W.** "The Role of Women in the Church, in Society, and in the Home." *Crux* 19.3 (1983) 3–9. **Gerstenberger, E. S.,** and **Schrage, W.** *Woman and Man.* Tr. D. Stott. Nashville: Abingdon, 1981. **Giles, K.** "The Order of Creation and the Subordination of Women." *Interchange* 23 (1978) 175–89. ———. *Women and Their Ministry.* East Malvern: Dove, 1977. **Goodwater, L.** *Women in Antiquity: An Annotated Bibliography.* Metuchen, NJ: Scarecrow, 1975. **Graham, R. W.** "Women in the Pauline Churches: A Review Article." *Lexington Theological Quarterly* 11 (1976) 25–34. **Greer, T. C.** "Admonitions to Women in 1 Tim 2:8–15." In *Essays on Women in Early Christianity,* ed. C. D. Osburn. Joplin, MO: College Press, 1995. 1:281–302. **Grenz, S. J.,** and **Kjesbo, D. M.** *Women in the Church: A Biblical Theology of Women in Ministry.* Downers Grove, IL: InterVarsity Press, 1995. **Grey, M.** "'Yet Woman Will Be Saved through Bearing Children' (1 Tim 2.16): Motherhood and the Possibility of a Contemporary Discourse for Women." *Bijdragen* 52 (1991) 58–69. **Gritz, S. H.** *Paul, Women Teachers, and the Mother Goddess at Ephesus: A Study of 1 Timothy 2:9–15 in Light of the Religious and Cultural Milieu of the First Century.* Lanham, MD: University Press of America, 1991. ———. "The Role of Women in the Church." In *The People of God: Essays on the Believers' Church,* ed. P. Basden and D. S. Dockery. Nashville: Broadman, 1991. 299–314. **Groothuis, R. M.** *Good News for Women: A Biblical Picture of Gender Equality.* Grand Rapids, MI: Baker, 1997. **Grudem, W.** "Prophecy—Yes, But Preaching—No: Paul's Consistent Advocacy of Women's Participation without Governing Authority." *JETS* 30 (1987) 11–23. **Gryson, R.** *The Ministry of Women in the Early Church.* Collegeville, MN: Liturgical, 1976. **Gundry, P.** *Women Be Free!* Grand Rapids, MI: Zondervan, 1977. **Hall, B.** "Paul and Women." *TToday* 31 (1974) 50–55. **Hamann, H. P.** "The New Testament and the Ordination of Women." *Lutheran Theological Journal* 9 (1975) 100–108. **Hanson, A. T.** "Eve's Transgression: I Timothy 2.13–15." In *Studies in the Pastoral Epistles.* London: S.P.C.K., 1968. 65–77. **Harper, J.** *Women and the Gospel.* Pinner, Middlesex: Christian Brethren Research Fellowship, 1974. **Harper, M.** *Equal and Different: Male and Female in Church and Family.* London: Hodder & Stoughton, 1994. **Harris, R. J.** "The Background and Significance of the Polemic of the Pastoral Epistles." *JBL* 92 (1973) 549–64. **Harris, T. J.** "Why Did Paul Mention Eve's Deception? A Critique of P. W. Barnett's Interpretation of 1 Timothy 2." *EvQ* 62 (1990) 335–52. **Haubert, K. M.** *Women as Leaders: Accepting the Challenge of Scripture.* Monrovia, CA: MARC, 1993. **Hayter, M.** *The New Eve in Christ: The Use and Abuse of the Bible in the Debate about Women in the Church.* London: S.P.C.K., 1987. **Hestenes, R.,** and **Curley, L.,** eds. *Women and the Ministries of the Church.* Pasadena, CA: Fuller Theological Seminary, 1979. **Holsey, N. W.** "Response to Scholer and Kroeger." In *Women, Authority and the Bible,* ed. A. Mickelsen. Downers Grove, IL: InterVarsity Press, 1986. 248–53. **Hommes, N. J.** "Let Women Be Silent in the Church: A Message concerning the Worship Service and the Decorum to Be Observed by Women." *CTJ* 4 (1969) 5–22. **Hooker, M. D.** "Authority on Her Head: An Examination of 1 Cor 11:10." *NTS* 10 (1964) 410–16. **Hoover, K. W.** "Creative Tension in 1 Timothy 2:11–15." *Brethren Life and Thought* 22 (1977) 163–66. **House, H. W.** "The Ministry of Women in the Apostolic and Postapostolic Periods." *BSac* 145 (1988) 387–99. **Howard, J. K.** "Neither Male nor Female: An Examination of the Status of Women in the New Testament." *EvQ* 55 (1983) 31–42. **Howe, E. M.** "The Positive Case for the Ordination of Women." In *Perspectives on Evangelical Theology: Papers from the Thirtieth Annual Meeting of the Evangelical Theological Society,* ed. K. Kantzer and S. Gundry. Grand Rapids, MI: Baker, 1979. 267–76. ———. *Women and Church Leadership.* Grand Rapids, MI: Zondervan, 1982. **Hugenberger, G. P.** "Women in Church Office: Hermeneutics or Exegesis? A Survey of Approaches to 1 Tim 2:8–15." *JETS* 35 (1992) 341–60. **Huizenga, H.** "Women, Salvation and the Birth of Christ: A Reexamination of 1 Timothy 2:15." *Studia Biblica et Theologica* 12 (1982) 17–26. **Hull, G. G.** *Equal to Serve.* Old Tappan, NJ: Revell, 1987. **Hull, W. E.** "Woman in Her Place: Biblical Perspectives." *RevExp* 72 (1975) 5–17. **Hunt, G.** *Ms. Means Myself.* Grand Rapids, MI: Zondervan, 1972. **Hurley, J. B.** "Did Paul Require Veils or the Silence of Women? A Consideration of 1 Cor. 11:2–16 and 1 Cor. 14:33b–36." *WTJ* 35 (1973) 190–220. ———. "Man and Woman in 1

Corinthians." Ph.D. Diss., Cambridge University, 1973. ———. *Man and Woman in Biblical Perspective.* Grand Rapids, MI: Zondervan, 1981. **Ilan, T.** *Jewish Women in Greco-Roman Palestine: An Inquiry into Image and Status.* TSAJ 44. Tübingen: Mohr-Siebeck, 1995. Repr. Peabody, MA: Hendrickson, 1996. **Irwin D.** "The Ministry of Women in the Early Church: The Archaeological Evidence." *Duke Divinity Review* 45 (1980) 76–86. **Isaksson, A.** *Marriage and Ministry in the New Temple: A Study with Special Reference to Mt. 19:3–12 and 1 Cor. 11:3–16.* Lund: Gleerup, 1965. **Jagt, K. A. van der.** "Women Are Saved through Bearing Children (1 Timothy 2.11–15)." *BT* 39 (1988) 201–8 (repr. in *Issues in Bible Translation,* ed. P. C. Stine, UBSMS 3 [London: United Bible Societies, 1988] 287–95). **Jaubert, A.** "Le voile des femmes (1 Cor. 11:2–16)." *NTS* 18 (1972) 419–30. **Jebb, S.** "A Suggested Interpretation of 1 Tim 2:15." *ExpTim* 81 (1969) 221–22. **Jewett, P. K.** *Man as Male and Female.* Grand Rapids, MI: Eerdmans, 1975. ———. "Why I Favor the Ordination of Women." *Christianity Today* 19 no. 18 (1975) 7–12. **Johnston, R. K.** "The Role of Women in the Church and Family: The Issues of Biblical Hermeneutics." In *Evangelicals at an Impasse: Biblical Authority in Practice.* Atlanta: John Knox, 1979. 48–76. **Kahler, E.** *Die Frau in den paulinischen Briefen.* Zürich: Gotthelf, 1960. **Kaiser, W. C., Jr.** "Paul, Women and the Church." *Worldwide Challenge* (September 1976) 9–12. **Kamlah, E.** "ΥΠΟΤΑΣΣΕΣΘΑΙ in den neuestestamentlichen 'Haustafeln.'" In *Verborum Veritas.* FS G. Stahlin, ed. O. Bocher and K. Haacker. Wuppertal: Theologischer Verlag Brockhaus, 1970. 237–43. **Kassing, A.** "Das Heil der Mutterschaft: 1 Tim 2:15 in biblischen Zusammenhangen." *Liturgie und Mönchtum* 23 (1958) 39–63. **Keener, C. S.** *Paul, Women, and Wives: Marriage and Ministry in the Letters of Paul.* Peabody, MA: Hendrickson, 1992. **Kimberley, D. R.** "1 Tim 2:15: A Possible Understanding of a Difficult Text." *JETS* 35 (1992) 481–86. **Kleinig, J. W.** "Scripture and the Exclusion of Women from the Pastorate." *Lutheran Theological Journal* 29 (1995) 74–81, 123–29. **Knight, G. W.** "ΑΥΘΕΝΤΕΩ in Reference to Women in 1 Timothy 2:12." *NTS* 30 (1984) 143–57. ———. *The Role Relationship of Men and Women.* Rev. ed. Chicago: Moody, 1985. **Kosnik, A.** *Human Sexuality: New Directions in American Catholic Thought.* New York: Paulist, 1977. **Köstenberger, A. J.** "A Complex Sentence Structure in 1 Timothy 2:12." In *Women in the Church,* ed. A. J. Köstenberger, T. R. Schreiner, and H. S. Baldwin. Grand Rapids, MI: Baker, 1995. 81–103. ———, **Schreiner, T. R.,** and **Baldwin, H. S.,** eds. *Women in the Church.* Grand Rapids, MI: Baker Book House, 1995. **Kraemer, R. S.** "Women in the Religions of the Greco-Roman World." *RelSRev* 9 (1983) 127–39. **Kroeger, C. C.** "1 Timothy 2:12—A Classicist's View." In *Women, Authority and the Bible,* ed. A. Mickelsen. Downers Grove, IL: InterVarsity Press, 1986. 225–44. ———. "Ancient Heresies and a Strange Greek Verb." *Reformed Journal* 29 (1979) 12–15. ———. "The Apostle Paul and the Greco-Roman Cults of Women." *JETS* 30 (1987) 25–38. **Kroeger, R. C.,** and **Kroeger, C. C.** *I Suffer Not a Woman: Rethinking I Timothy 2:11–15 in Light of Ancient Evidence.* Grand Rapids, MI: Baker, 1992. ———. "May Women Teach? Heresy in the Pastoral Epistles." *Reformed Journal* 30.10 (1980) 14–18. **Kubo, S.** "An Exegesis of 1 Timothy 2:11–15 and Its Implications." In *Symposium on the Role of Women in the Church,* ed. J. Neuffer. Biblical Research Institute Committee, General Conference of Seventh-Day Adventists, 1984. **Kuchler, M.** *Schweigen, Schmuck und Schleier: Drei neutestamentliche Vorschriften [1 Tim 2:8–15; 1 Cor 14:33–36; 11:3–16; 1 Pt 3:1–6] zur Verdrängung der Frauen auf dem Hintergrund einer frauenfeindlichen Exegese des AT im antiken Judentum.* NTOA 1. Göttingen: Vandenhoeck & Ruprecht, 1986. **Kuhns, D. R.** *Women in the Church.* Focal Pamphlets 28. Scottdale, PA: Herald, 1978. 48–52. **Kuske, D. P.** "An Exegetical Brief on 1 Timothy 2:12 (οὐδὲ αὐθεντεῖν ἀνδρός)." *Wisconsin Lutheran Quarterly* 88 (1991) 64–67. **Lampe, G. W. H.** "Church Tradition and the Ordination of Women." *ExpTim* 76 (1965) 123–25. **Langley, M.** *Equal Women: A Christian Feminist Perspective.* Basingstoke: Marshall Morgan & Scott, 1983. **La Port, J.** *The Role of Women in Early Christianity.* Lewiston, NY: Mellen, 1982. **Lazenby, H. F.** "The Image of God: Masculine, Feminine, or Neuter?" *JETS* 30 (1987) 63–70. **Lees, S.,** ed. *The Role of Women.* Leicester: Inter-Varsity Press, 1984. **Legrand, L.** "Women's Ministries in the New Testament." *Biblebhashyam* 2 (1976) 286–99. **Leonard, E. A.** "St. Paul on the Status of Women."

CBQ 12 (1950) 311–20. **Liefeld, W. L.** "A Plural Ministry View: Your Sons and Your Daughters Shall Prophesy." In *Women in Ministry: Four Views,* ed. B. Clouse and R. G. Clouse. Downers Grove, IL: InterVarsity Press, 1989. 127–53. ———. "Response to '1 Timothy 2:12—A Classicists's View,' by C. C. Kroeger." In *Women, Authority and the Bible,* ed. A. Mickelsen. Downers Grove, IL: InterVarsity Press, 1986. 244–48. ———. "Women and the Nature of Ministry." *JETS* 30 (1987) 49–61. **Lightfoot, N. R.** "The Role of Women in Religious Services." *ResQ* 19 (1976) 129–36. ———. *The Role of Women: New Testament Perspectives.* Memphis: Student Association Press, 1978. **Lindsell, H.** "Egalitarianism and Biblical Infallibility." *Christianity Today* 26 (1976) 45–46. **Litfin, A. D.** "Evangelical Feminism: Why Traditionalists Reject It." *BSac* 146 (1979) 258–90. **Loewe, R.** *The Position of Women in Judaism.* London: S.P.C.K., 1966. **Loewen, H.** "The Pauline View of Women." *Direction* 6 (1977) 3–20. **Longenecker, R.** *New Testament Social Ethics for Today.* Grand Rapids, MI: Eerdmans, 1984. **Longstaff, T. R. W.** "The Ordination of Women: A Biblical Perspective." *ATR* 57 (1975) 322–27. **Love, S. L.** "Women's Roles in Certain Second Testament Passages: A Macrosociological View." *BTB* 12 (1987) 50–59. **Low, M.** "Can Women Teach? A Consideration of Arguments from 1 Tim. 2:11–15." *Trinity Journal* 3 (1994) 99–123. **Lowe, S. D.** "Rethinking the Female Status/Function Question: The Jew/Gentile Relationship as Paradigm." *JETS* 34 (1991) 59–75. **Mack, W.** *The Role of Women in the Church.* Easton, PA: Mack, 1972. **Maertens, T.** *The Advancing Dignity of Woman in the Bible.* De Pere, WI: St. Norbert's Abbey Press, 1969. **Malingrey, A. M.** "Note sur l'exégèse de 1 Tim 2,15." In *International Conference on Patristic Studies 6,* ed. E. A. Livingstone. Berlin: Akademie, 1975–76. 334–39. **Martin, F. B.** *Call Me Blessed.* Grand Rapids, MI: Eerdmans, 1988. **Marucci, C.** "La donna e i ministeri nella Bibbia e nella tradizione." *Rassegna di Teologia* 17 (1976) 273–96. **McDermond, J. E.** "Modesty: The Pauline Tradition and Change in East Africa." *African Christian Studies* 9 (1993) 30–47. **McKeating, H.** "Jesus ben Sira's Attitude to Women." *ExpTim* 85 (1973) 85–87. **Meeks, W. A.** *The First Urban Christians: The Social World of the Apostle Paul.* New Haven, CT: Yale UP, 1983. **Menoud, P. H.** "Saint Paul et la femme." *RTP* 19 (1969) 318–30. **Merode, M. de.** "Une théologie primitive de la femme?" *RTL* 9 (1978) 176–89. **Mettinger, T. N. D.** "Eva och revbenet—Manligt och kvinligt i exegetisk belysnillg." *STK* 54 (1978) 55–64. **Meyer, C. R.** "Ordained Women in the Early Church." *JETS* 20 (1977) 337–52. **Mickelsen, A.** "An Egalitarian View: There is Neither Male nor Female in Christ." In *Women in Ministry: Four Views,* ed. B. Clouse and R. G. Clouse. Downers Grove, IL: InterVarsity Press, 1989. 173–206. ———, ed. *Women, Authority and the Bible.* Downers Grove, IL: InterVarsity Press, 1986. **Mollenkott, V.** "Foreword." In P. K. Jewett, *Man as Male and Female.* Grand Rapids, MI: Eerdmans, 1975. 7–12. ———. *Women, Men and the Bible.* Nashville: Abingdon, 1977. **Moo, D. J.** "1 Timothy 2:11–15: Meaning and Significance." *Trinity Journal* 1 (1980) 62–83. ———. "The Interpretation of 1 Timothy 2:11–15: A Rejoinder." *Trinity Journal* 2 (1981) 198–222. ———. "What Does It Mean Not to Teach or to Have Authority over Men? (1 Timothy 2:11–15)." In *Recovering Biblical Manhood and Womanhood,* ed. J. Piper and W. Grudem. Wheaton, IL: Crossway, 1991. 179–93. **Moody, D.** "Charismatic and Official Ministries: A Study of the New Testament Concept." *Int* 19 (1965) 168–81. **Moore, P.,** ed. *Man, Woman and Priesthood.* London: S.P.C.K., 1978. **Morris, L.** "The Ministry of Women." In *Women and the Ministries of the Church,* ed. R. Hestenes and L. Curley. Pasadena, CA: Fuller Theological Seminary, 1979. 14–25. **Motyer, S.** "Expounding 1 Timothy 2:8–15." *Vox Evangelica* 24 (1994) 95–96. **Murphy-O'Connor, J.** "St. Paul: Promoter of the Ministry of Women." *Priests & People* 6 (1992) 307–11. **Neuer, W.** *Man and Woman in Christian Perspective.* Tr. G. J. Wenham. London: Hodder & Stoughton, 1990. **Nürnberg, R.** "Non decent neque necessarium est, ut mulieres doceant: Überlegungen zum altkirchlichen Lehrverbot für Frauen." *JAC* 31 (1988) 57–73. **O'Donovan, O. M. T.** "Towards an Interpretation of Biblical Ethics." *TynBul* 27 (1976) 54–78. **Omansen, R. L.** "The Role of Women in the New Testament Church." *RevExp* 83 (1986) 15–25. **Osborne, G. R.** "Hermeneutics and Women in the Church." *JETS* 20 (1977) 337–52. **Osburn, C. D.** "ΑΥΘΕΝΤΕΩ (1 Timothy 2:12)." *ResQ* 25 (1982) 1–12. **Osiek, C.** "Women's

Role in the Pastorals." *TBT* 23 (1985) 246–47. **Padgett, A.** "The Pauline Rationale for Submission: Biblical Feminism and the *hina* Clauses of Titus 2:1–10." *EvQ* 59 (1987) 39–52. ————. "Wealthy Women at Ephesus: 1 Timothy 2:8–15 in Social Context." *Int* 41 (1987) 19–31. **Pagels, E. H.** "Paul and Women: A Response to Recent Discussions." *JAAR* 42 (1974) 538–49. **Panning, A. J.** "AUTHENTEIN—A Word Study." *Wisconsin Lutheran Quarterly* 78 (1981) 185–91. **Pape, D. R.** *In Search of God's Ideal Woman: A Personal Examination of the New Testament.* Downers Grove, IL: InterVarsity Press, 1976. **Patterson, L. G.** "Women in the Early Church: A Problem of Perspective." In *Toward a New Theology of Ordination: Essays on the Ordination of Women*, ed. M. H. Micks and C. P. Price. Alexandria: Virginia Theological Seminary, 1976. **Payne, P. B.** "The Interpretation of 1 Timothy 2:11–15: A Surrejoinder." In W. L. Liefield, D. Moo, and P. B. Payne, *What Does Scripture Teach about the Ordination of Women?* Minneapolis: Evangelical Free Church of America, 1986. 96–115. ————. "Libertarian Women in Ephesus: A Response to Douglas J. Moo's Article '1 Timothy 2:11–15: Meaning and Significance.'" *Trinity Journal* 2 (1981) 169–97. ————. "Οὐδέ in 1 Timothy 2:12." Paper presented at the annual meeting of the Evangelical Theological Society, Atlanta, November 1986. **Perriman, A. C.** "What Eve Did, What Women Shouldn't Do: The Meaning of ΑΥΘΕΝΤΕΩ in 1 Timothy 2:12." *TynBul* 44 (1993) 129–42. **Pierce, R. W.** "Evangelicals and Gender Roles in the 1990s: 1 Tim 2:8–15: A Test Case." *JETS* 36 (1993) 343–55. **Piper, J.,** and **Grudem, W.,** eds. *Recovering Biblical Manhood and Womanhood.* Wheaton, IL: Crossway, 1991. **Pomeroy, S. B.** *Goddesses, Whores, Wives, and Slaves: Women in Classical Antiquity.* New York: Schocken, 1975. **Porter, S. E.** "What Does It Mean to Be 'Saved by Childbirth' (1 Timothy 2.15)?" *JSNT* 49 (1993) 87–102. **Pousset, E.** "L'homme et la femme de la creation a la réconciliation." *Lumiere et Vie* 21 (1972) 60–74. **Powers, B. W.** "The Ethical Teaching of the New Testament and Its Bases in Relation to the Spheres of Sex and Marriage and Family Relationships." Diss., University of London, 1972. ————. "Women in the Church: The Application of 1 Timothy 2:8–15." *Interchange* 17 (1975) 55–59. **Pretlove, J.** "Paul and the Ordination of Women." *ExpTim* 76 (1965) 294. **Prohl, R. C.** *Women in the Church.* Grand Rapids, MI: Eerdmans, 1957. **Redekop, G. N.** "Let the Women Learn: 1 Timothy 2:8–15 Reconsidered." *SR* 19 (1990) 235–45. **Reumann, J.** "What in Scripture Speaks to the Ordination of Women?" *CurTM* 44 (1973) 5–30. **Rihbany, A. M.** "Paul and Women." In *The Syrian Christ.* New York: Houghton Mifflin, 1916. 325–39. ————. "Women East and West." In *The Syrian Christ.* New York: Houghton Mifflin, 1916. 313–24. **Roberts, M. D.** "'Woman Shall Be Saved'—A Closer Look at 1 Timothy 2:15." *Reformed Journal* 33 (1983) 18–20. **Rowe, A.** "Hermeneutics and 'Hard Passages' in the New Testament on the Role of Women in the Church." *Epworth Review* 18 (1991) 82–88. **Ruether, R. R.** "Frau und kirchliches Amt in historischer und gesellschaftlicher Sicht." *Concilium* (Einsiedeln) 12 (1976) 17–23. **Ryrie, C. C.** *The Place of Women in the Bible.* Chicago: Moody Press, 1968. **Sakenfeld, K. D.** "The Bible and Women: Bane or Blessing?" *TToday* 32 (1975) 222–33. **Sandnes, K. O.** "Shame and Honour in 1 Tim 2:11–15." *TTKi* 59 (1988) 97–108. **Sapp, S.** "Biblical Perspectives on Human Sexuality." *Duke Divinity Review* 41 (1976) 105–22. ————. *Sexuality, the Bible and Science.* Philadelphia: Fortress, 1977. **Saucy, R. L.** "The Negative Case against the Ordination of Women." In *Perspectives on Evangelical Theology: Papers from the Thirtieth Annual Meeting of the Evangelical Theological Society*, ed. K. Kantzer and S. Gundry. Grand Rapids, MI: Baker, 1979. 277–86. ————. "Women's Prohibition to Teach Men: An Investigation into Its Meaning and Contemporary Application." *JETS* 37 (1994) 79–97. **Scaer, D. P.** "The Office of the Pastor and the Problem of Ordination of Women Pastors." *Springfielder* 38 (1974) 127–33. **Scanzoni, L.,** and **Hardesty, N.** *All We're Meant to Be: A Biblical Approach to Women's Liberation.* Waco, TX: Word, 1974. **Schneiders, S. M.** "Women in the Fourth Gospel and the Role of Women in the Contemporary Church." *BTB* 12 (1982) 35–45. **Schoeps, H. J.** *Paul: The Theology of the Apostle in the Light of Jewish Religious History.* Philadelphia: Westminster, 1961. **Scholer, D. M.** "1 Timothy 2:9–15 and the Place of Women in the Church's Ministry." In *Women, Authority and the Bible*, ed. A. Mickelsen. Downers Grove, IL: InterVarsity Press,

1986. 193–224. ———. "Exegesis: 1 Timothy 2:8–15." *Daughters of Sarah* 1 (1975) 7–8 (repr. in *Women and the Ministries of the Church*, ed. R. Hestenes and L. Curley [Pasadena, CA: Fuller Theological Seminary, 1979] 74). ———. "Feminist Hermeneutics and Evangelical Biblical Interpretation." *JETS* 30 (1987) 407–20. ____. "Hermeneutical Gerrymandering: Hurley on Women and Authority." *Theological Students' Fellowship Bulletin* (1983) 11–13. ———. "Women in Ministry, Session Seven: 1 Timothy 2:8–15." *Covenant Companion* 73 (1984) 14–15. ———. "Women in the Church's Ministry: Does 1 Timothy 2:9–15 Help or Hinder?" *Daughters of Sarah* 16 (1990) 7–12. ———. "Women's Adornment: Some Historical and Hermeneutical Observations on the New Testament Passages." *Daughters of Sarah* 6 (1980) 3–6. **Schottroff, L.** *Lydia's Impatient Sisters: A Feminist Social History of Early Christianity.* Tr. B. Rumscheidt and M. Rumscheidt. Louisville: Westminster John Knox, 1995. **Schreiner T. R.** "An Interpretation of 1 Timothy 2:9–15: A Dialogue with Scholarship." In *Women in the Church*, ed. A. J. Köstenberger, T. R. Schreiner, and H. S. Baldwin. Grand Rapids, MI: Baker, 1995. 105–54. ———. *Interpreting the Pauline Epistles.* Grand Rapids, MI: Baker, 1990. **Schüssler Fiorenza, E.** *In Memory of Her.* ———. "Die Rolle der Frau in der urchristlichen Bewegung." *Concilium* (Einsiedeln) 12 (1976) 3–9. ———. "Women in Pre-Pauline and Pauline Churches." *USQR* 33 (1978) 153–66. **Scroggs, R.** "Paul and the Eschatological Woman." *JAAR* 40 (1972) 283–303. ———. "Paul: Chauvinist or Liberationist?" *The Christian Century* 15 (1972) 307. **Siddons, P.** ———. *Speaking Out for Women—A Biblical View.* Valley Forge, PA: Judson, 1980. 82–85. **Sigountos, J. G.**, and **Shank, M.** "Public Roles for Women in the Pauline Church: A Reappraisal of the Evidence." *JETS* 25 (1983) 283–95. **Snodgrass, K.** "Paul and Women." *Covenant Quarterly* 34 (1976) 3–19. **Spencer, A. B.** *Beyond the Curse: Women Called to Ministry.* Nashville: Nelson, 1985. ———. "Eve at Ephesus: Should Women Be Ordained as Pastors according to the First Letter to Timothy, 2:11–15?" *JETS* 17 (1974) 215–22. ———. "God's Order Is Truth (1 Timothy 2:11–15)." *Brethren in Christ, History and Life* 13 (April 1990) 51–63. **Stagg, E.**, and **Stagg, F.** *Women in the World of Jesus.* Philadelphia: Westminster, 1978. **Stein, D.** "Le statut des femmes dans les lettres de Paul." *Lumière et Vie* 27 (1978) 63–85. **Stendahl, K.** *The Bible and the Role of Women: A Case Study in Hermeneutics.* Tr. E. T. Sander. Philadelphia: Fortress, 1966. **Stephens, S.** *A New Testament View of Women.* Nashville: Broadman, 1980. **Stitzinger, M. F.** "Cultural Confusion and the Role of Women in the Church: A Study of 1 Timothy 2." *Calvary Bulletin* 4 (1988) 24–42. **Swidler, L.** *Women in Judaism: The Status of Women in Formative Judaism.* Metuchen, NJ: Scarecrow, 1976. **Talbert, C. H.** "Biblical Criticism's Role: The Pauline View of Women as a Case in Point." In *The Unfettered Word*, ed. R. B. James. Waco, TX: Word, 1987. 62–71. **Tertullian.** "On the Apparel of Women." ANF 4:14–25. **Thrall, M. E.** *The Ordination of Women to the Priesthood.* London: SCM Press, 1958. **Tidball, D.** *The Social Context of the New Testament.* Grand Rapids, MI: Zondervan, 1984. **Tiemeyer, R.** *The Ordination of Women.* Minneapolis: Augsburg, 1970. **Toews, J.** "Women in Church Leadership." In *The Bible and the Church.* FS D. Ewert, ed. A. J. Dueck et al. Hillsboro, KS: Kindred, 1988. **Topping, E. C.** "Patriarchal Prejudice and Pride in Greek Christianity: Some Notes on Origen." *Journal of Modern Greek Studies* 1 (1983) 7–17. **Towner, P. H.** "Gnosis and Realized Eschatology in Ephesus (of the Pastoral Epistles) and the Corinthian Enthusiasm." *JSNT* 31 (1987) 95–124. **Trible, P.** "Eve and Adam: Genesis 2–3 Reread." *Andover Newton Quarterly* 13 (1973) 251–58. ———. *God and the Rhetoric of Sexuality.* Overtures to Biblical Theology. Philadelphia: Fortress, 1978. **Tucker, R. A.**, and **Liefeld, W. L.** *Daughters of the Church.* Grand Rapids, MI: Zondervan, 1987. **Tucker, T. G.** *Life in the Roman World of Nero and St. Paul.* New York: Macmillan, 1910. **Ulrichsen, J. H.** "Heil durch Kindergebären: Zu 1 Tim 2,15 und seiner syrischen Version." *SEÅ* 58 (1993) 99–104. ———. "Noen Bemerkninger til 1 Tim 2:15." *NorTT* 84 (1983) 19–25. **Unnik, W. C. van.** "Les cheveux defaits des femmes baptisées." *VC* 1 (1947) 77–100. **Vaux, R. de.** "Sur le voile des femmes dans l'Orient ancien." *RB* 44 (1935) 397–412. **Walker, W. O., Jr.** "1 Corinthians 11:2–16 and Paul's Views Regarding Women." *JBL* 94 (1975) 94–110. ———. "The 'Theology of Women's Place' and the 'Paulinist' Tradition." *Semeia* 28 (1983) 101–12. **Waltke, B. K.** "1

Timothy 2:8–15: Unique or Normative?" *Crux* 28 (1992) 22–23, 26–27. **Warfield, B. B.** "VIII. Critical Note: Some Exegetical Notes on 1 Timothy: II. Connection and Meaning of I Timothy II. 8–15." *PresR* 8 (1921) 502–4. **Weeks, N.** "Of Silence and Head Covering." *WTJ* 35 (1972–73) 21–27. **Wenham, G. J.** "The Ordination of Women: Why Is It So Divisive?" *Churchman* 92 (1978) 310–19. **Wiebe, B.** "Two Texts on Women (1 Tim 2:11–15; Gal 3:26–29): A Test of Interpretation." *HBT* 16 (1994) 54–85. **Wijngaard, J. N. M.** *Did Christ Rule Out Women Priests?* Great Wakering, Essex: McCrimmon's, 1977. **Williams, D.** *The Apostle Paul and Women in the Church.* Ventura, CA: Gospel Light Publications, 1977. **Williams, M. J.** "The Man/Woman Relationship in the New Testament." *Churchman* 91 (1977) 33–46. **Williams, N. P.** *The Ideas of the Fall and of Original Sin.* London: Longmans, 1927. **Wilshire, L. E.** "1 Timothy 2:12 Revisited: A Reply to Paul W. Barnett and Timothy J. Harris." *EvQ* 65 (1993) 43–55. ———. "The TLG Computer and Further Reference to ΑΥΘΕΝΤΕΩ in 1 Timothy 2:12." *NTS* 34 (1988) 120–34. **Witherington, B.** "Rite and Rights for Women—Galatians 3.28." *NTS* 27 (1981) 593–604. ———. *Women and the Genesis of Christianity.* Cambridge: Cambridge UP, 1990. ———. *Women in the Earliest Churches.* SNTSMS 59. Cambridge: Cambridge UP, 1988. ———. *Women in the Ministry of Jesus.* SNTSMS 51. Cambridge: Cambridge UP, 1984. **Wolters, A.** Review of *I Suffer Not a Woman,* by R. C. Kroeger and C. C. Kroeger. *CTJ* 28 (1993) 208–13. **Yamauchi, E. M.** "Cultural Aspects of Marriage in the Ancient World." *BSac* 135 (1978) 241–52. **Yarbrough, R. W.** "The Hermeneutics of 1 Timothy 2:9–15." In *Women in the Church,* ed. A. J. Köstenberger, T. R. Schreiner, and H. S. Baldwin. Grand Rapids, MI: Baker, 1995. 155–96. ———. "I Suffer Not a Woman: A Review Essay." *Presbyterian* 18 (1992) 25–33. **Zerbst, F.** *The Office of Woman in the Church.* St. Louis: Concordia, 1955.

Translation

[8]*Therefore, I desire [that] the men should pray in every place by lifting up holy hands, without anger and arguing.*[a] [9]*Likewise,*[b] *[I] also [desire that the] women should adorn themselves in respectable*[c] *attire, with modesty and moderation, not with braided hair and*[d] *gold*[e] *or pearls or costly clothing,* [10]*but what is appropriate for women who are committed to godliness, [namely,] in good deeds.*

[11]*A woman should learn in quietness, in all submissiveness;* [12]*but I do not permit a women to teach or to exercise authority over a man, but [she is] to be in quietness.* [13]*For Adam was created first, then Eve.* [14]*And Adam was not deceived, but the woman, having been deceived,*[f] *has come into transgression;* [15]*but she will be saved through childbearing, if they remain in faith and love and holiness, with modesty.*

Notes

L. T. Johnson notes that "for a passage with such potential for misunderstanding, the text is remarkably stable, with no critically significant variants" (132). Apparently the ancients did not have the same exegetical problems with the passage as do moderns.

[a]Our text has the singular διαλογισμοῦ, "arguing" (ℵ* A D Ψ TR lat), while others have the plural διαλογισμῶν, "arguings" (ℵ² F G H 33 81 104 365 630 1505 1739 1881 *al* sy).

[b]ὡσαύτως καὶ τὰς γυναῖκας, "likewise also the women," is read by D¹ Ψ 1881 TR. Both καί, "also," and τάς, "the," are omitted by ℵ* A H P 33 81 1775 *pc* sa^{ms} bo^{ms}. καί is included and τάς omitted by ℵ² D* F G 6 365 1739 *pc;* Ambst Spec.

[c]κοσμίῳ, "respectable," is read by ℵ* A D² Ψ TR latt sy; Cl. The adverb κοσμίως, "respectably," is read by ℵ² D* F G H 33 365 1739 1881 *pc.*

[d]καί, "and," is read by ℵ A D*ᶜ F G 1175 1739 1881 *pc* sy^p co. It is replaced with ἤ, "or," in D² H Ψ TR lat sy^h; Cl. Neither occur in P 33 *pc.*

[e]χρυσίῳ, "gold" (from χρυσίον), is read by A F(*) G H I P 33 81 104 1175 1505 1739 1881 *pc.* χρυσῷ (from χρυσός) is found in ℵ D Ψ TR; Cl.

ᶠThe simple ἀπατηθεῖσα, "having been deceived" (ℵ² D² TR), replaces the compound ἐξαπατηθεῖσα, "having been deceived." The compound is supported by ℵ* A D* F G P Ψ 33 81 104 365 630 1175 1739 1881 *al.* See *Comment.*

Form/Structure/Setting

This is the most discussed passage in the PE today. Interpretations range from seeing Paul as a liberator and champion of women's rights to dismissing Paul as wrong and irrelevant in today's culture. George Bernard Shaw called Paul the "eternal enemy of women" (cited by Pagels, *JAAR* 42 [1974] 538). The literature is voluminous, and within the scope of this commentary it is not possible to enter into the whole of the discussion. The differing interpretations, however, will be reviewed as they relate directly to the historical meaning of this text; to do more than this would place too great an emphasis on this one passage and detract from the PE corpus as a whole. For the best presentations of the complementarian interpretation of the text, see Köstenberger et al., eds., *Women in the Church* (hereafter referred to by the authors of individual articles), and the works by Piper and Grudem, Moo, Fung, Hurley, and Foh. For the egalitarian interpretation, see Gritz, *Paul, Women Teachers, and the Mother Goddess at Ephesus,* and the works by Fee, Groothuis, Scholer (especially "1 Timothy 2:9–15 and the Place of Women in the Church's Ministry"), Perriman, and Spencer. The interchange between Moo and Payne is especially helpful.

I will try to stay away from antagonistic terms such as "clearly," "obviously," and "ignores," and avoid accusing the other position of having an agenda (what position does not?), or any other tactic that might deteriorate into labeling and name calling. I will not call someone's conclusion his or her assumption.

If one position were truly clear or obvious, then there would not be significantly divergent positions held by respectable scholars. As Scholer comments, "The concept of genuinely objective biblical interpretation is a myth. All interpretation is socially located, individually skewed, and ecclesiastically and theologically conditioned. . . . All biblical interpreters, regardless of where they now stand on the issue of women in ministry, have been deeply influenced by both the sexism and misogyny of our culture and also the currents of nineteenth-century women's rights and twentieth-century feminist movements" ("1 Timothy 2:9–15," 213–14). No labels can escape offending someone, and yet since labels are necessary "complementarian" will be used for the position that believes Paul sees some restrictions on women's ministry, and "egalitarian" for the position that sees none.

The structure of this passage highlights its two basic themes. It is usual to divide vv 8–15 between v 8 and v 9, the first dealing with men and the latter with women. Yet there is a more significant shift between v 10 and v 11. The problem being discussed in vv 8–10 is disruption in the church. The men are acting in anger, even during times of prayer; the women are dressing immodestly and putting too much emphasis on external appearances while neglecting the more significant aspects of Christian life such as godly behavior. Paul begins by addressing these concerns. When the men pray, they are to be sure that their anger has ceased. Likewise, the women are to put a priority on what is godly, making sure that their dress is appropriate for who they are. Grammatically, v 9 is dependent on v 8 since it does not contain a finite verbal form, and v 10 must be read with the preceding; so the break at v 11 is more substantial, grammatically and contextually. (But see *Comment* on scope in v 9 and Scholer's connection between vv 9–10 and vv 11–12 below.)

In vv 11–15 the topic changes. While Paul is still dealing with the Ephesian women, he is addressing not the topic of disruption but the topic of leadership, albeit the two are related. The women's attempts to gain positions of leadership are causing disruption; hence the connection with the preceding verses. But now the disruption is not caused by seductive and extravagant dress but rather by the issue of gender roles. Vv 11–15 also have strong connections with chap. 3, which goes into detail describing the leadership qualities expected of overseers and deacons, specifically the ability to teach.

Scholer sees a tighter connection between vv 9–10 and vv 11–12:

> In virtually all the Jewish and pagan texts, the rejection of external adornment was part of a woman's submission to her husband and a recognition of her place among men in general. The use of external adornments such as pearls, gold jewelry, hair styling and expensive, provocative clothing indicated two undesirable characteristics—material extravagance and sexual infidelity. Thus, the progression of thought in 1 Timothy 2:9–15 moves from concern for women's adornment (vv. 9–10) to concern for women's submission and silence in public worship (vv. 11–12). These are two sides of the same coin in the cultural settings of the first century A.D. ("1 Timothy 2:9–15," 201–2)

While it is true that vv 11–15 are dealing with roles, they are also dealing with attitudes. Paul says women are to learn in quietness and submission and are to continue in faith, love, holiness, and modesty. Vv 9–10 add that they are to place a priority on good deeds, and their dress should show that they are godly women, with modesty and sensibility. In fact, the discussion begins and ends on the same note: modesty. While Paul is concerned to determine appropriate behavior, he is also concerned to request appropriate attitudes.

Because both v 1 and v 8 discuss prayer, it is possible to see v 8 as the conclusion to vv 1–7 and begin this paragraph at v 9. There are, however, good reasons to include v 8 with the following and not the preceding. (1) Prayer is not the main concern of either vv 1–7 or v 8, and therefore the connection is secondary. Vv 1–7 are dealing with the universality of the offer of salvation, and v 8 requests that the Ephesian men stop arguing, especially while they are praying. In both cases prayer is only the stage upon which Paul is making his point. (2) V 8 begins with the words βούλομαι οὖν, "therefore I desire," which parallels the beginning of v 1, παρακαλῶ οὖν, "therefore I urge." The repetition has the effect of initiating a new discussion. (3) The strongest argument for including v 8 with vv 9–15 is that it shares a basic theme with vv 9–10, namely, that those causing disruption in the church must cease.

There is also the question of whether the phrase πιστὸς ὁ λόγος, "the saying is trustworthy," in 3:1a points back to 2:15 or forward to 3:1b, an issue that will be discussed more fully in *Form/Structure/Setting* on 1 Tim 3:1–7. If 2:15 replicates the language of the opponents, then 2:15 is the faithful saying. Paul uses the opponents' language, redefines it, and then adds the final "now *this* saying is faithful" for emphasis. All the faithful sayings then deal with the topic of salvation, and the formula is used more for emphasis than to introduce a citation. For a general discussion of the faithful sayings, see *Form/Structure/Setting* on 1 Tim 1:12–17.

Vv 8–15 fit nicely into Paul's flow of thought in chaps. 2 and 3. First and foremost, he wants the Ephesian church to pray for the salvation of all people. While they are praying, they must do it properly, not colored by anger or disputing, but characterized by holiness. Likewise, the women are to cease disrupting the church by their improper dress and emphasis on externals. In speaking about women and the disruption in the church, Paul adds that they are not to seek roles that would place them in positions of authority over men. Enlarging upon that point, he spells out the type of person who is to be in leadership. As is his style throughout the PE, Paul's train of thought flows smoothly from one topic to the next.

This passage, among many, is a witness to part of Oberlinner's basic approach to the PE (84): he sees various strands of teaching present in the author's postapostolic church, and part of the author's method is to restrict previous freedoms. So, for example, the proposed limitation on wearing jewelry in church is extended by the author to all spheres of life. Likewise, originally women had no restrictions, but because of the rising threat of Gnosticism the role of women was restricted from the preaching office and eventually from all spheres of life (84, 89, 92–93; following Bartsch, *Anfänge*, 63; often citing L. Schottroff [e.g., 142 n. 34, 149 n. 53] and E. Schüssler Fiorenza).

Comment

8 Βούλομαι οὖν προσεύχεσθαι τοὺς ἄνδρας ἐν παντὶ τόπῳ ἐπαίροντας ὁσίους χεῖρας χωρὶς ὀργῆς καὶ διαλογισμοῦ, "Therefore, I desire [that] the men should pray in every place by lifting up holy hands, without anger and arguing." In vv 8–10 Paul addresses the problem of disruption during the church service, beginning with the men. Paul's desire is that they cease from their anger (cf. Str-B 3:645), an anger manifested even during times of prayer. It is generally agreed that this verse is not a demand that only men pray (in 1 Cor 11:5 women are allowed to pray; contra R. D. Culver, "Traditional View," 35), nor is it an injunction that they must pray with their hands lifted up. Rather its emphasis is upon the necessity that they not be angry during their times of prayer. While διαλογισμός, "arguing," does not occur elsewhere in the PE, it is reminiscent of other descriptions of the Ephesian heresy, such as "myths . . . produce speculations" (1 Tim 1:4) or "speculations and empty words" (1 Tim 6:4). If Paul is thinking about anger caused by debates over the opponents' teaching (so L. T. Johnson, 134–35; Towner, 70), then this becomes an indication at the beginning of the paragraph that Paul is thinking specifically of problems in Ephesus (see discussion of the scope of the teaching in *Comment* on v 9).

This idea of the absence of anger can be understood two ways. (1) It could mean that during times of prayer the men should set aside their anger and pray as brothers. The problem is that this sounds superficial. Would Paul merely request that they repress their anger temporarily, or would he request that it be dealt with properly? (2) It could also parallel Eph 4:26, "Do not let the sun go down on your anger." Paul could be saying that the men in the Ephesian church should learn to deal with their anger properly by not letting it continue from week to week. Hanson is wrong, however, when he says, "The author [of the PE] dislikes arguing about anything, unlike Paul" ([1983] 71). The arguing here is nonproductive speculation producing ungodly behavior; it is not a helpful, constructive interchange. Paul also says to the Thessalonian church that they should "live quietly" (1 Thess 4:11) and do their work "in quietness" (2 Thess 3:12).

βούλομαι οὖν, "therefore I desire," parallels παρακαλῶ οὖν, "therefore I urge," in v 1 and has the force of beginning a new, but related, topic (cf. v 9). Having defined the proper scope of prayer (2:1–7), Paul moves to the conduct appropriate for prayer (2:8): men are to pray for all people without anger. His use of βούλομαι, "I desire," does not diminish the authority of the exhortation. It is not a request that may or may not be followed, for it comes from the authoritative apostle Paul who has just finished asserting his authority in v 7 (cf. 1 Tim 1:1; 1:3 [παρεκάλεσα, "I urged"]; Warfield, PresR 8 [1921] 502; Schrenk, TDNT 1:632; Spicq, 1:371–72; Roloff, 130). βούλεσθαι, "to desire," is used in "legislative regulation" (Dibelius-Conzelmann, 75; citing PLond 3.904.30; Josephus Ant. 12.3.4 §150). The precise meaning of βούλεσθαι is debated, and the question is further complicated by its relationship with the parallel term θέλειν, "to wish," and the history of the terms' uses. Its primary meaning in the NT indicates a simple wish, a desire, but in the PE it occurs three times carrying an authoritative note established by the context (1 Tim 2:8; 5:14; Titus 3:8). Similar is its use to describe the will of God (Matt 11:27 [Luke 10:22]; Luke 22:42; 1 Cor 12:11; Heb 6:17; Jas 1:18; 2 Pet 3:9; cf. similar use of the noun βουλή, "will"; G. Schrenk, TDNT 1:629–37). The parallel term θέλειν is used in the PE to denote both divine intention (1 Tim 2:4) and human desire (1 Tim 1:7; 5:11; 2 Tim 3:12). Evidently Paul is using the terms interchangeably, and ultimately the context must determine whether the word carries a note of authority, as it does here. L. T. Johnson ties both v 8 and vv 9–10 back to v 2 (319); the goal of both requests is the desire to live peaceful lives.

Paul says that the men should pray with holy hands. Because Paul encourages women to pray in public worship (1 Cor 11:5) and because the emphasis of v 8 is on men's holy *attitude,* Paul is not saying here that only men should pray. Why he specifies only men is not stated. It is possible that, because of the church's roots in the synagague, where only men could pray, most of the public prayer in the church was done by men. It also is possible that anger was more visible in men's prayers than in women's. Padgett suggests that the men's anger was caused by the women addressed in vv 9–10, specifically the women who were deceived by the false teachers (Int 41 [1987] 22, 30). This ties v 8, along with vv 9–10 and vv 11–15, into the heresy (cf. Comment on v 9 regarding scope), the setting already established in vv 1–7. The problem, and it is not insurmountable, is that the verse does not make the connection explicitly, and anger is not the most expected response to indecent dress. The imagery of ὁσίους χεῖρας, "holy hands," comes from the OT (Exod 30:19–21; Ps 24:4; Isa 1:15; 59:3), which requires that hands be ritually clean before approaching God; the cleansing later became moral (cf. Jas 4:8; 1 Pet 3:7). Jesus himself insisted that "reconciliation must precede worship" (Stott, 82; cf. Matt 5:23–24; 6:12, 14–15; Mark 11:25). The topic of prayer does not arise again in this passage, showing that prayer is not the main concern. In 1 Tim 5:5 Paul requires a widow to have shown herself to be a woman of prayer before the church supports her. On whether ἄνδρας should be translated "men" or "husbands," see discussion of γυναῖκας, "women," in Comment on v 9.

ἐν παντὶ τόπῳ, "in every place," brings to focus a central issue in vv 8–15—the issue of scope. There are two related questions. Is παντὶ τόπῳ, "every place," in

Ephesus or more generally in the world? Does it refer to only public worship or also to conduct in the outside world? The answers here may also affect conclusions regarding the object of the woman's submission (v 11), where she may not teach (v 12a), and the identity of the man over whom she may not exercise authority (v 12b). There are indications in the context that the phrase refers to the setting of the church universal gathered for worship.

(1) 1 Tim 3:15 states that these instructions govern how one is to act in the "house of God, . . . the church of the living God." While there is nothing in the actual phraseology of v 15 or Paul's doctrine of the church that limits the scope of "house of God" to any one time or place (contra Scholer, "1 Timothy 2:9–15," 200), the topics in chaps. 2 and 3 suggest that Paul is thinking of the church gathered for public worship. For example, while prayer can be a private issue, speaking of ἄνδρας, "men" (plural), not just praying but praying without anger suggests public interaction. Paul is not discussing conduct in other settings outside the scope of the church, such as secular work. However, there is nothing in the phrase "house of God" that limits these instructions to Ephesus. Authoritative instruction in the gospel and official refutation of error would govern not only the public worship in Ephesus but worship wherever overseers conflicted with false teachers. Because 1 Tim 3:14–16 is the heart of the epistle, v 15 is normative in determining the scope of the teaching.

(2) Paul is thinking of specific, historical issues in chaps. 2 and 3: the Ephesians' refusal to pray for all people, the mixing of anger and prayer by the Ephesian men, the seductive and extravagant dress of the Ephesian women, the problem of church leadership in Ephesus, etc. Fee says that "to universalize the prepositional phrase ['in every place'] when the rest of the sentence so clearly fits the specific situation in Ephesus makes little sense" (*JETS* 28 [1985] 145 n. 12). And yet, while addressing specific situations, Paul's answer gives no *explicit* indication that his solutions apply only to the Ephesians. One would expect that men everywhere are not to be angry when they pray. Women everywhere are to place an emphasis not on external beauty but on deeds of godliness. All church leaders are to be above reproach. In fact, the appeal to creation in v 13 *explicitly* universalizes at least that specific instruction. 1 Tim 2:1–7 is also closely tied to the following verses with the οὖν, "therefore," in v 8, suggesting that there has not been a change of audience. The universality of the instructions in 2:1–7 thus suggests that the subsequent instructions are also universal. This is one of the key—and controversial—points of the hermeneutical questions surrounding this passage. As will be argued throughout this discussion, merely because a statement is addressed to a specific locality does not mean its teaching is necessarily limited to that historical setting (cf., e.g., the epistle to the Galatians). Roloff ties ἐν παντὶ τόπῳ to the repeated use of πᾶς, "all," throughout the previous paragraph: that believers everywhere are to gather together is the visible consequence of Christ's being given for all (130).

With this as background, it is easier to interpret ἐν παντὶ τόπῳ. It could refer to every house church in Ephesus and as such refer to the public worship meetings; it could also refer to everywhere that there are Christians (cf. Mal 1:11; 2 Cor 2:14; 1 Thess 1:8; cf. Lock; Towner, *Goal*, 205–6; Keener, *Paul, Women, and Wives*, 123 n. 19). The context suggests that Paul is thinking of every place in the world where Christians worship. Some see ἐν παντὶ τόπῳ as a quotation of Mal 1:11 (LXX) that some in the early church claimed was a prophecy of the Eucharist (Dibelius-Conzelmann; Brox;

Houlden; Hanson [1983]; Oberlinner; cf. Justin *Dial.* 41, 117; Irenaeus *Adv. Haer.*
4.17.5; *Did.* 14): "For from the rising of the sun to its setting my name is glorified
among the nations, and in every place [ἐν παντὶ τόπῳ] incense is offered to my name,
and a pure offering; for my name is great among the nations, says the Lord Almighty."
Did. 14 connects the Eucharist and this citation. The suggestion that Malachi is
behind 1 Tim 3:8, however, seems implausible because the scope envisaged here is
greater than eucharistic prayers and extends to all prayers (cf. especially 2:1). The
parallel is nothing more than a coincidence, as the occurrences of the same phrase
elsewhere in Paul illustrate (1 Cor 1:2; 2 Cor 2:14; 1 Thess 1:8).

The standard posture of prayer in Judaism is standing (Matt 6:5; Mark 11:25;
Luke 18:11), arms raised, with palms turned upward (1 Kgs 8:22, 54; Ezra 9:5; Pss
28:2; 63:4; 134:2; 141:2; Lam 2:19; 3:41; Isa 1:15; 2 Macc 3:20; *1 Clem.* 29; cf. Str-B
2:261; 4:645; references in Keener, *Paul, Women, and Wives,* 123 nn. 16, 17). Other
positions, such as kneeling and lying prostrate, are also described in Scripture (1
Kgs 8:54; Ps 95:6; Dan 6:10; Matt 26:39; Luke 22:41; Acts 9:40; Rev 11:16; cf. C. W.
F. Smith, *IDB* 3:866). But the emphasis here is not on the posture of prayer but on
the hands being ὅσιος, "holy," meaning that the conduct of the person praying
should be acceptable and appropriate to God (cf. Ps 24:3–5; cf. Stott, 82). This is
confirmed by the final phrase, "without anger and dissension," which makes best
sense if Paul's emphasis is upon holiness and not the mode of praying (i.e., with
lifted hands). (This same combination of custom and moral exhortation is also
present when Paul says "Greet one another with a holy kiss" [Rom 16:16].) ὅσιος
is used again in the PE only in Titus 1:8 as a qualification for an elder. It refers to
conduct that is appropriate within a certain relationship. (See *Comment* on 1 Tim
1:9 for a discussion of holiness.) In the NT it is used of God and Christ (Acts 2:27;
13:35; Heb 7:26; Rev 15:4; 16:5).

χωρὶς ὀργῆς καὶ διαλογισμοῦ, "without anger and arguing," is the only mention
of the words ὀργή, "anger," and διαλογισμός, "arguing," in the PE although both
words occur in Paul in references to the "wrath of God" (Rom 1:18; Eph 5:6; Col
3:16; cf. Rom 2:5, 8; 3:5; 4:15; 5:9; 9:22; 12:19; 13:4, 5; 1 Thess 2:16; 5:9) and the final
"day of wrath" (Rom 2:5; cf. 1 Thess 1:10). But twice Paul addresses the issue of
wrath among believers, as he does here, and admonishes them to put it away (Eph
4:31; Col 3:8; cf. Rom 9:22; Eph 2:3). διαλογισμός is used two different ways in the
NT. It can describe a person's thinking or opinion, often in a negative sense of an
opinion that is not good (cf. Matt 15:19 [Mark 7:21]; Luke 5:22; 6:8; 9:47; 24:38;
Rom 1:21; 1 Cor 3:20). It can also describe an argument (Luke 9:46). Phil 2:14 is
parallel to the thought here: "Do all things without grumbling or questioning
[διαλογισμῶν]."

9a Ὡσαύτως [καὶ] γυναῖκας ἐν καταστολῇ κοσμίῳ μετὰ αἰδοῦς καὶ σωφροσύνης
κοσμεῖν ἑαυτάς, "Likewise, [I] also [desire that the] women should adorn themselves in respectable attire, with modesty and moderation." Having dealt with the
disruptive men, Paul turns to the disruptive women; just as the men are to stop
fighting, the women are to dress appropriately. For a discussion of the shifts
between the plural γυναῖκες, "women" (vv 9–10, 15), and singular γυνή, "woman,"
(vv 11–14), see *Comment* on v 15. While the immediate context remains that of
public worship (v 8; cf. below on γυνή), the shift to good deeds suggests that Paul
sees the teaching as having ramifications in other contexts; good deeds cannot be
relegated only to the context of worship. For a discussion on women throughout

the PE, see Spicq, "Excursus I.—La femme chrétienne et ses vertus," 1:385–425. While these ideals are often found in secular thought (see below), it does not mean that Paul is simply borrowing Hellenistic ideals, and the ultimate ideal—conduct appropriate to godly women—is thoroughly Christian.

There are three keys to interpreting this verse. (1) αἰδοῦς, "modesty," and σωφροσύνης, "moderation," both carry sexual connotations. (2) Paul shifts from speaking about actual clothing to emphasizing the true priority of good deeds (v 10). (3) κοσμεῖν, "to adorn," and καταστολή, "attire," have a dual meaning: clothing and a person's general deportment. Paul's central concern moves beyond appearances to behavior. It would appear that the women were dressing immodestly to the point that it was causing disruption; they were becoming preoccupied with the externals of beauty (the clothing being condemned is opulent, the jewelry excessive) and neglecting things that were truly important such as doing good deeds. Therefore, Paul says that they are to dress in a way that is in keeping with their Christian character and to concentrate on what is most important. While their dress is an issue, their attitude is Paul's true concern. As Prov 31:25 says, "strength and dignity are her clothing."

Three significant exegetical issues are encountered here that continue to surface throughout this paragraph. (1) What is principle and what is cultural application in this verse? (2) How closely connected to the Ephesian heresy are these verses. (3) Does γυνή mean "woman" or "wife"?

(1) Fee has a helpful discussion of the hermeneutical issue of cultural relativity and authorial intent, pointing out that while Paul's request that Timothy bring his cloak (2 Tim 4:13) has no application except to Timothy, his exhortation that Timothy share in suffering (2 Tim 2:3) is generally recognized "as moving beyond that historical particular to all who would be disciples of Christ" ("Issues in Evangelical Hermeneutics," 60). In reference to 1 Tim 2:9–10 and 2:15, he comments, "We relegate those texts to cultural change, and rightly so. We still need to hear the word about modesty and appropriateness of dress, but on the specifics most evangelicals have long ago yielded to cultural change" ("Issues in Evangelical Hermeneutics," 61). In other words, evangelicals recognize modesty and appropriateness of dress as a Pauline principle but hair braided with gold or pearls as a cultural expression of that principle. This hermeneutical distinction applies also to vv 11–12, where the statement of a principle is the basis for a specific application. In both cases the principle could have given rise to many applications, and Paul chooses applications relevant to his specific historical setting.

(2) How closely connected to the Ephesian culture and the opponents' teaching are vv 9–10? (a) Seductive dress and excessive ornamentation with an accompanying lack of emphasis on character and doing good deeds find expression almost everywhere, both in Paul's culture and throughout the centuries. Many have pointed out that vv 9–10 parallel much of ancient society's teaching about women's clothing and the primacy of character over dress (Scholer, *Daughters of Sarah* 6 [1980] 3–6; Keener, *Paul, Women, and Wives,* 103–5). We even read of the connection between seductive dress and its suggestion of marital infidelity. It is not necessary, therefore, to see vv 9–10 as countering a specific false teaching in Ephesus any more than v 8 and its injunctions for men to refrain from anger prove that the false teachers are teaching men to be angry. (For an argument that society should never be seen as the basis of Paul's beliefs, see *Explanation* on Titus 2:1–10.)

(b) Some interpreters, however, see a necessary link between the teaching in vv 9–10 and the Ephesian heresy: the opponents are encouraging seductive and extravagant dress, and vv 9–10 are Paul's rebuttal of their instruction. The following table shows the differences of interpretation.

Verse	Reference	(a) Not Directed toward the Heresy	(b) Directed toward the Heresy
8	"in every place"	Where Christians meet	Ephesian house churches
	"anger"	General	At heresy or at women
	"arguing"	General	About the heresy
9–10	Clothing; demeanor	Excesses resulting from sin	Opponents' teaching to resist gender roles and dress in opposition to the church's teaching
11	"learn"	About gospel	About gospel vs. Ephesian heresy
12	"I do not permit"	Paul's principle	Temporary, resulting from Ephesian heresy ("I am not permitting")
	"women"	All women	Women deceived by opponents
	"teach"	Scripture	Heresy's interpretation of Scripture
	"exercise authority"	Paul's principle	Domineer, or teach Gnostic doctrine
	"man"	Overseers	Overseers, or object of myths (Kroeger)
13–14	"Adam" and "Eve"	Paul's reasons for vv 11–12	Counter to false doctrine
15	"saved through childbearing"	Continued reflection on the curse	Counter false teaching on childbearing
	"modesty"	Modesty	Modesty instead of Gnostic rejection

Moo suggests that the false teachers were encouraging the women to discard "traditional female roles in favor of a more egalitarian approach" ("What Does It Mean?" 181). The opponents taught asceticism, including abstinence from food and marriage (1 Tim 4:3), and Paul's desire for young widows to remarry and have children (1 Tim 5:14; cf. 1 Tim 2:15) suggests that family roles were being devalued. There is also a significant similarity between the errors in Ephesus and Corinth (resurrection, 2 Tim 2:18, 1 Cor 15; marriage, 1 Tim 4:3, 1 Cor 7; food, 1 Tim 4:3, 1 Cor 8:1–13; cf. Towner, *JSNT* 31 [1987] 95–124), which included erroneous teaching on the wives' relationships with their husbands (1 Tim 5:13–14; 1 Cor 11:2–18; 14:33b–36). Following the work of Towner (*JSNT* 31 [1987] 95–124), Moo concludes,

> While we cannot be sure about this, there is good reason to think that the problem in both situations was rooted in a false belief that Christians were already in the full form of God's kingdom and that they had accordingly been spiritually taken 'out of' the world so that aspects of this creation, like sex, food, and male/female distinctions, were no longer relevant to them. It may well be that these beliefs arose from an unbalanced emphasis on Paul's own teaching that Christians were "raised with Christ" (Ephesians 2:6; Colossians 2:12; 3:1) and that in Christ there is neither "male nor female" (Galatians 3:28). What Paul would be doing in both 1 Corinthians and the pastoral epistles is seeking to right the balance by reasserting the importance of the created order and the ongoing significance of those role distinctions between men and women that he saw rooted in creation.... The similarity between the battery of problems in the two situations strongly suggests that in Ephesus, as in Corinth, a tendency to remove role distinctions between men and women was part of the false teaching. (181–82, citing Scholer, "1 Timothy 2:9–15," 198)

Fee provides an especially helpful discussion of the significant similarities between 1 Tim 2:9–15 and the problem of widows in 5:11–15 ("Issues in Evangelical Hermeneutics," 57–59), suggesting that vv 9–15 are closely tied to the specific Ephesian problem. He concludes, "This, then, is the point of the whole—to rescue these women and the church from the clutches of the false teachers. Their rescue includes proper demeanor in dress, proper demeanor in the assembly (including learning in all quietness), and getting married and bearing children (one of the good works urged in v. 10, seen in light of 5:9–10)" ("Issues in Evangelical Hermeneutics," 59). Padgett points out that the mention of expensive dress and jewelry suggests that these women were very wealthy and concludes, "the wealthy women were prime targets for the 'greedy' false teachers (II Tim. 3:1–7), and we should probably identify these particular women as followers of the false teachers. What is more, as rich women they would likely have churches meet in their homes. Such women would naturally aspire to leadership in the churches at Ephesus and thus they would need training in the Christian faith and the interpretation of Scripture" (*Int* 41 [1987] 23). Many interpreters allude to the influence of false teachers on the Ephesian women (Scanzoni and Hardesty, *All We're Meant to Be*, 37, 70–71; Spencer, *JETS* 17 [1974] 216–22 [who does not see the topic of the heresy introduced until v 11]; id., *Beyond the Curse*, 84–91; Payne, *Trinity Journal* 2 [1981] 185–97; Scholer, "1 Timothy 2:9–15," 211; Evans, *Woman*, 104–6; Padgett, *Int* 41 [1987] 25–27; Bilezikian, *Beyond Sex Roles*, 179–81).

It is argued throughout this study that 1 Timothy especially is primarily an ad hoc document addressing specific issues in Ephesus. The same holds true here, and yet there is no textual evidence—apart from the possible implications of these two verses and 1 Tim 5:11–15—that the opponents were teaching about dress. The strong grammatical and contextual connection with v 8, which offers a universal exhortation about male anger, cautions against seeing the former as necessarily correct. (While the opponents may have been teaching women to dress rebelliously, it seems doubtful that they would teach men to be angry.) But even if Paul were addressing specific false teachers, it does not follow that in addressing a cultural issue the principle behind the application somehow becomes culturally encumbered outside that culture; the principle of modesty would remain a principle even when applied to a culture of braided and jewelry-adorned hair.

(3) The third exegetical question is whether γυνή is to be translated "woman" or "wife." In favor of the translation "wife" are the following arguments (cf. Prohl, *Women*, 31–32; Barrett, 55–56; Hommes, *CTJ* 4 [1969] 13; Powers, *Interchange* 17 [1975] 55–59; Hanson, [1983] 72; Gritz, *Paul, Women Teachers, and the Mother Goddess*, 125, 131–36; Hugenberger, *JETS* 35 [1992] 341–60, who cites others). (a) The woman in v 15 is married since she has children. (b) This is the more natural reading since most women were married. (c) Hugenberger sees a strong parallel with 1 Pet 3:1–7 (which discusses husbands and wives) and argues that the topics of prayer (v 8), clothing (v 9), good works (v 10), and child rearing (v 15) should not be restricted to public worship. "In every place" can be more universal than church meetings (cf. 1 Cor 1:2; 1 Thess 1:8), and in Paul γυνή and ἀνήρ usually refer to wives and husbands. Concerning v 12 he concludes, "Paul's concern is to prohibit only the sort of teaching that would constitute a failure of the requisite wifely 'submission' to her husband" (*JETS* 35 [1992] 358).

Most favor the translation "woman." (a) A large part of the problem in Ephesus has to do with widows (1 Tim 5:3–16; 2 Tim 3:6–7). If Paul is thinking of wives, then this large group would be omitted, perhaps the very group to whom he is speaking (cf. especially the description of the younger widows [1 Tim 5:3–16] and how they fit into the picture painted by v 9). (b) Would Paul be saying that wives must dress modestly, but exclude single women from this same injunction? This argument gains strength as the rest of the paragraph is considered. Is Paul saying that married women cannot teach, but by implication single women can? (c) If γυνή is translated "wife" here, then in order to be consistent ἀνήρ in v 8 should be translated as "husband" and not "man." But then there is the same problem as above. Should only the married men, but not the single ones, cease from their anger before they pray? (d) Schreiner criticizes Hugenberger's argument ("Interpretation of 1 Timothy 2:9–15," 115–17), pointing out that elsewhere when Paul uses γυνή and ἀνήρ there are indications in the context if he is speaking of husbands and wives (e.g., "married," in Rom 7:2; "own," in 1 Cor 7:2), but here (and in 1 Cor 11:2–16) there are no such qualifications, suggesting that Paul's instructions are general, directed to women and men. Schreiner also considers it unlikely that "Paul would insert a teaching on husbands and wives at home in the midst of his polemic against false teachers" (117). Rather, it is more likely within the context of instruction on public worship that Paul would discuss prayer *and teaching* (v 12), and Paul then discusses marriage relationships in 1 Tim 6:1–2 (cf. Eph 5:22–6:9; Col 3:8–4:1). There is also validity in Roloff's argument that the church is seen as an expansion of the Christian house where the same rules apply (138); husband-wife relationships are also to be maintained in public worship.

ὡσαύτως, "likewise," emphasizes that women, like men, have to do their part in stopping the disruption in the church. (1) Some see v 9 as being close in thought to v 8—"I want men to pray without anger and [I want] women [to pray] with respectable clothing"—reasserting women's vocal role in public worship as guaranteed by 1 Cor 11:5 (Warfield, *PresR* 8 [1921] 503; Holtz, 65–66; Barrett, 55; Spencer, *Beyond the Curse*, 73; Scholer, "1 Timothy 2:9–15," 200–201; Gritz, *Paul, Women Teachers, and the Mother Goddess*, 126; Keener, *Paul, Women, and Wives*, 102; Towner, 70). However, if προσεύχεσθαι, "to pray," is assumed with γυναῖκας, "women," the following κοσμεῖν, "to adorn," is awkward. More significantly, the full thought of the verse is that women are to concentrate on doing good deeds, dressed modestly; the issue is not women praying. (2) Others see κοσμεῖν as parallel to προσεύχεσθαι and complementary to βούλομαι, "I desire": "I desire men to pray . . . women to adorn" (Brox, 132; Foh, *Women,* 122; Roloff, 126; Towner, *Goal,* 207). ὡσαύτως does not require the same topic to be discussed (cf. 1 Tim 3:8, 11; 5:25; Titus 2:3, 6).

κοσμεῖν, "to adorn," can mean "to dress," but its scope of meaning is larger, including the ideas of slaves adorning the doctrine of God by being submissive to their masters (Titus 2:10), of the temple being adorned with "noble stones and offerings" (Luke 21:5), and of the scribes and Pharisees adorning the graves of righteous people (Matt 23:29; see BAGD, 445, for further examples). This breadth of meaning is significant in that the primary focus of this verse is not so much on what the women wear (although this is included) but on their priorities; Paul wants them to be adorned not with beautiful clothing but with good deeds. The flexibility of κοσμεῖν opens the door to the shift in emphasis that becomes explicit in v 10.

καταστολή, "attire," is more than outward dress but includes the idea of the inner person, hence "deportment" (BAGD, 419) or "demeanor." MM give illustrations where the meaning is "restraint" (333). κοσμίῳ, "respectable," attire is clothing that is honorable or appropriate. The wide scope of meaning for κοσμεῖν and καταστολή continues to open the way for the true emphasis of vv 9–10, that a woman conduct herself in a way that is appropriate to her Christian calling, a conduct that includes but is not limited to her clothing. Paul is focusing on the character of the person (Warfield, *PresR*8 [1921] 503). καταστολή is not used again in the NT (cf. Isa 61:3). κόσμιος is used elsewhere in the NT only in 1 Tim 3:2, where Paul says that the elders are to be "honorable" (cf. H. Sasse, *TDNT* 3:896).

Having urged the women to dress respectably, Paul adds three phrases to clarify what he means. The first is that they are to clothe themselves, μετὰ αἰδοῦς καὶ σωφροσύνης, "with modesty and moderation." αἰδώς, "modesty," "a sense of shame" (Abbott-Smith, *Lexicon,* 12), occurs in the NT elsewhere only as a *v.l.* in Heb 12:28 describing what is acceptable worship of God. R. Bultmann gives references where the term denotes reverence toward God, a priest, an oath, a king, singers, orators, parents, elders, the law of hospitality, the home, marriage, and the city (*TDNT* 1:169; cf. Trench, *Synonyms,* 98–101). It seems to indicate a reverence that is appropriate for a specific person or situation, a nuance that fits our context. Many say it has sexual overtones (Kelly, 66; Scholer, "1 Timothy 2:9–15," 201–2; Keener, *Paul, Women, and Wives,* 103–6) and as such helps explain the disruption in the Ephesian worship. Its only other use in the Greek Bible is in 3 Maccabees. When Ptolemy IV tried to enter the Holy of Holies, all the people prostrated themselves with cries of opposition. Even the "women who had recently been arrayed for marriage abandoned the bridal chambers prepared for wedded union, and, neglecting proper modesty [αἰδὼ παραλείπουσαι], in a disorderly rush flocked together in the city" (3 Macc 1:19). Later, when Ptolemy had arrested all the Jews, the author says that even the old men were "forced to march at a swift pace by the violence with which they were driven in such a shameful manner [αἰδοῦς ἄνευ]" (3 Macc 4:5). R. Bultmann says it is the opposite of ὕβρις, "insolence, lewdness" (see *Comment* on 1 Tim 1:13 for ὑβριστής, "insolent person") and synonymous with εὐσέβεια, "reverence" (1 Tim 2:2; *TDNT* 1:169).

σωφροσύνη, "moderation," has a basic meaning of "restraint," "self-control," the mean between two extremes, and it can mean "chastity" (Plutarch *Amat.* 21 [*Mor.* 2:767e]; Diodorus Siculus 3.57.3; Phalaris *Ep.* 78.1; Philo *Spec. Leg.* 3.51; Josephus *Ant.* 18.3.4 §73; cf. U. Luck, *TDNT* 7:1100). It is a Hellenistic word, frequent in Philo and Stoicism, and it is one of Plato's four cardinal virtues (cf. excursus in Lock, 148–50; BAGD, 802; MM, 622; Trench, *Synonyms*, 102–3). The word group occurs ten times in the PE (and six more times in the NT). It is a requirement for elders (1 Tim 3:2; Titus 1:8), older men (Titus 2:2), younger men (Titus 2:6), younger women (Titus 2:5; cf. 1 Pet 4:7), and all women (1 Tim 2:9, 15). The older women are to train the younger women to be moderate (Titus 2:4), God's gracious gift of salvation teaches believers to live self-controlled lives in this wicked world (Titus 2:12), and Paul reminds Timothy that God gave him not a spirit of cowardice but a spirit of power and love and self-control (2 Tim 1:7; cf. 2 Cor 5:13; Rom 12:3). A lack of moderation and self-control is evidently a visible part of the Ephesian heresy. In contrast to Hellenistic thought, Paul affirms that σωφροσύνη is possible only because of what Christ had done (Titus 2:12); it is not achieved through human effort (Towner, *Goal,* 161–62).

9b μὴ ἐν πλέγμασιν καὶ χρυσίῳ ἢ μαργαρίταις ἢ ἱματισμῷ πολυτελεῖ, "not with braided hair and gold or pearls or costly clothing." This is the second qualifier of what Paul means by καταστολῇ κοσμίῳ, "respectable clothing." This verse must be read in light of the overall context of the passage. The preceding phrases suggest that the problem is one of disruption caused by immodest and extravagant clothing. V 10 will fill out the picture by showing that what Paul wants is a priority placed on what really matters: doing good deeds. Therefore, here Paul is not requesting the total absence of external beauty but a priority placed on the internal. Actually, this phrase reads as a cultural expression of the timeless Christian principles of respectability, modesty, and moderation just expounded (cf. Hurley, *Biblical Perspective*, 198–99), recognizing that in many cultures extravagant and seductive dress often involve an excessive emphasis on hairstyles and jewelry. This is why Mickelsen is wrong in making an application of this passage for Christians when she states, "if this passage [v 12] is universal for all Christian women of all time, then no woman should ever wear pearls or gold" ("Egalitarian View," 201). Kelly cites church fathers who interpreted this injunction literally, but whose intentions ultimately were "to inculcate a proper sense of values" (*Commentary on the Epistles of Peter and Jude*, 129; Clement of Alexandria *Paed.* 3.2.66; Tertullian *De orat.* 20; *De cultu fem.* 1.6; 2.7–13; Cyprian *De hab. virg.* 8). This is parallel to the thought of 1 Pet 3:3–4: "Let not yours be the outward adorning [κόσμος] with braiding of hair, decoration of gold [χρυσίων], and wearing of fine clothing, but let it be the hidden person of the heart with the imperishable jewel of a gentle and quiet [ἡσυχίου] spirit, which in God's sight is very precious."

Paul may be specifying three negative (μή) characteristics set apart with the twice-repeated ἤ, "or": braided hair and gold, pearls, and costly clothing. It is also possible that he is specifying two negative characteristics: costly clothing and braided hair adorned with gold or pearls. In either case, Paul is not speaking simply of braided hair, but of braided hair adorned with indications of wealth. Braided hair was a common style, and alone would not raise the issue of impropriety.

πολυτελής, "expensive," carries the connotation of being extremely costly. This word is used to describe the ointment costing a year's wages that was poured on Jesus' head (Mark 14:3–5). Its cognate adjective πολύτιμος, "expensive," describes the pearl of great worth for which the merchant sold everything he owned (Matt 13:46). The clothing Paul is considering is not slightly expensive but extravagantly expensive as suggested by the use of gold jewelry. A. H. M. Jones says clothing could cost as much as 7000 denarii, which equaled more than nineteen years' wages for an average day laborer (*The Roman Economy: Studies in Ancient Economy and Administrative History*, ed. P. A. Brunt [Oxford: Blackwell, 1974] 350–64).

Baugh describes the ancient hairstyles:

> Greek hairstyles for women during this period were for the most part simple affairs: hair was parted in the middle, pinned simply in the back or held in place with a scarf or headband. Roman coiffures were similar until the principate. The women of the imperial household originated new styles; by the Trajanic period they had developed into elaborate curls, braids, high wigs, pins, and hair ornaments that were quickly copied by the well-to-do throughout the empire: "See the tall edifice rise up on her head in serried tiers and storeys! (Juvenal *Satire* 6)." ("Foreign World," 47–48)

See further descriptions in Philo *Sacrif.* 21; BAGD, 256, 667; Str-B 3:428–34, 645; W. Smith, *A Dictionary of Greek and Latin Roman Antiquities* (London: Murray, 1872) 328–30; Hurley, *Biblical Perspective*, 198–99, additional references in n. 3; Keener, *Paul, Women, and Wives*, 103–4, who lists extensive extrabiblical references. This same basic imagery is repeated in Revelation where the great harlot (Rev 17:4) and the great city (Rev 18:16) are described decked out in gold, jewels, and pearls. The theme can also be found in the OT (cf. Isa 3:18–24) and is common in Greek culture (Plutarch *Conj. praec.* 28–29 [*Mor.* 142AB]). Perhaps most instructive are those parallels that equate this sort of extravagant dress with marital infidelity (*Sentences of Sextus*, "A woman who likes adornment is not faithful" [cited by Fee, 76, who also cites *1 Enoch* 8:11–12; *T. Reub.* 5:1–5; Ps.-Phintys 84–86; Perictione 135; Seneca *Helvia* 16:3–4; Plutarch *Conj. praec.* 26, 30–32 [*Mor* 141DE, 142CD]). The issue is not clothing or braided hair, but excess, possibly appearing to be immoral (so Keener, *Paul, Women, and Wives*, 105). Christian women are to present themselves faithful and godly. While certain aspects of this are somewhat culturally bound (e.g., braided hair with gold), the basic principles are timeless; priorities should not be based on the external, and the external must be an accurate representation of the internal.

10 ἀλλ' ὃ πρέπει γυναιξὶν ἐπαγγελλομέναις θεοσέβειαν, δι' ἔργων ἀγαθῶν, "but what is appropriate for women who are committed to godliness, [namely,] in good deeds." This is the third qualifying phrase of ἐν καταστολῇ κοσμίῳ ... κοσμεῖν ἑαυτάς, "to adorn themselves in respectable attire." The words in v 9b can refer to clothing but are also capable of a wider sphere of meaning including the idea of inner adornment, demeanor, and now what has been only implicit is made explicit. What Paul wants the Ephesian women to do is to place a priority on what really matters, i.e., behavior appropriate to a person who has made a commitment to godliness. Chrysostom gives an impassioned plea for women to dress in accordance with their character and the activity of the church, ridiculing the thought of pleading for forgiveness of sins in clothing more appropriate for a dance or marriage (NPNF 13:433).

Doing good deeds is a primary concept in the PE in accordance with the preeminently practical nature of their instructions. Paul says that Jesus gave himself to prepare a people zealous to do good deeds (Titus 2:14), and therefore believers should pursue them (2 Tim 2:21; Titus 3:1, 8, 14), equipped by Scripture (2 Tim 3:17). Christ's coming is not only for the salvation of believers but also to instill the desire to live out one's faith. Good deeds are conspicuous, either immediately or eventually (1 Tim 5:25). Titus is to be a role model of good deeds (Titus 2:7). Paul also spells out what constitutes a good work: a widow supported by the church must be widely recognized for her good deeds such as raising children, showing hospitality, washing the feet of saints, helping the afflicted, and "devoting herself to doing good in every way" (1 Tim 5:10–11). The rich are to be liberal and generous (1 Tim 6:18). Desiring to be an elder is a good work (1 Tim 3:1). Women in general should place a priority on pursuing good deeds (1 Tim 2:10), which might include bearing children (1 Tim 2:15) in contrast to the ban Paul's opponents placed on marriage (1 Tim 4:3). It is also possible that Timothy's work as an evangelist is seen as a good work (2 Tim 4:5). Because of their evil behavior (τοῖς δὲ ἔργοις ἀρνοῦνται, "they deny [him] by their deeds"), Paul's opponents are unfit for any good work (Titus 1:16). Alexander will be punished for his evil deeds (κατὰ τὰ ἔργα αὐτοῦ, "on account of his deeds"; 2 Tim 4:14), and Paul is sure that God will rescue him ἀπὸ παντὸς ἔργου πονηροῦ, "from every evil work" (2 Tim 4:18).

This emphasis on good deeds is not salvation by works. In the PE, God's salvation does not come because of anyone's works (οὐ κατὰ τὰ ἔργα ἡμῶν, "not according to our works"; 2 Tim 1:9) done ἐν δικαιοσύνῃ, "in righteousness" (Titus 3:5), but only because of God's grace, mercy, love, purpose, and goodness (1 Tim 1:12–17). Good works are the necessary response by the believer to God's grace and mercy and are one of the purposes for which Christ came. Any theology that sees Christ's work merely as a means to salvation, divorcing it from any notion of obedience and behavior, falls short of the theology of the PE (cf. *Explanation* on Titus 2:11–15). This idea of Christ coming not only to save but to change lives is found throughout Paul (Eph 2:10) and the NT (see Marshall, SNTU-A 9 [1984] 203–18).

The phrase ἔργα ἀγαθά, "good works," does occur in Paul (Rom 2:7; 13:3; 2 Cor 9:8; Eph 2:10; Phil 1:6; Col 1:10; 2 Thess 2:17; for a discussion of the use of ἀγαθός, "good," in the PE see *Comment* on 1 Tim 1:8), and throughout Paul there is an emphasis on the necessity of one's conversion leading necessarily to a life of obedience (e.g., Rom 2:7; 6:1–23; 7:4 ["bear fruit"]; 2 Cor 9:8; Eph 2:10; Col 1:10). Because of the historical needs of the Ephesian and Cretan churches, good works receive special emphasis in the PE. The opponents' teaching leads to immorality; Christians must live out the commitment to God in holiness, being above reproach (see *Introduction,* "The Ephesian Heresy").

ὅ, "what," continues the thought from κοσμεῖν ἑαυτάς, "to adorn themselves," adding the contrast of what is appropriate. πρέπει, "is appropriate," is used in the PE elsewhere only in Titus 2:1, where Titus is told to teach what is appropriate for sound teaching. ἐπαγγελλομέναις, "who are committed to," is a periphrastic translation. The basic idea of the verb is that a promise is made. In the NT it is most often used of promises made by God (BAGD, 281), which may add a note of solemnity to the women's confession: a solemn promise, a commitment, to godliness. The linear aspect of the participle emphasizes that this is a daily commitment. This same verb describes the opponents' adherence to their heresy and subsequent missing of the mark (1 Tim 6:21). Elsewhere Paul says that long ago God promised eternal life, which has now been manifested through the preaching of the gospel (Titus 1:2). The cognate noun ἐπαγγελία, "promise," occurs twice in the PE. Godliness has value in every way since it holds out a promise for the present life and for the life to come (1 Tim 4:8). Paul's apostleship is "according to the promise of life that is in Christ Jesus" (2 Tim 1:1). θεοσέβεια, "godliness," occurs only here in the NT (cf. Gen 20:11; Job 28:28; Sir 1:25; Bar 5:4). It is a virtual synonym of εὐσέβεια, "reverence" (cf. 1 Tim 2:2; MM, 288). διά, "in," indicates the means by which a woman may adorn herself properly (M. J. Harris, *NIDNTT* 3:1183). Moule labels it "environment, attendant circumstances" (*Idiom-Book*, 57).

11 Γυνὴ ἐν ἡσυχίᾳ μανθανέτω ἐν πάσῃ ὑποταγῇ, "A woman should learn in quietness, in all submissiveness." The topic now changes: Paul shifts from the disruption caused by women's clothing (vv 9–10) to the larger question of leadership. The issue of leadership is a central concern in the PE since the opposition to Timothy is coming from the Ephesian leaders. The topic continues into chap. 3, where Paul establishes the basic leadership qualities that elders and deacons must have, with a pause to put these stipulations into perspective (3:14–16). Paul closes by pointing out that the opposition is in fulfillment of prophecy (4:1–5), proving that the Ephesians are living in the last days. (See *Form/Structure/ Setting* for the view that vv 11–12 are a restatement of vv 9–10.)

Vv 11–12 comprise several phrases:

v 11a	A woman should *learn* in *quietness,*		
v 11b		in all submissiveness;	
v 12a	but I do not permit a woman		to *teach,*
		or	
v 12b			to exercise authority over a man,
v 12c	but [she is] to be in *quietness.*		

V 11a is the main point and is repeated in v 12c for emphasis (inclusio). ἐν πάσῃ ὑποταγῇ, "in all submissiveness" (v 11b), defines ἡσυχίᾳ, "quietness." V 12ab further defines in practical terms what learning in quietness/submissiveness means. διδάσκειν, "to teach" (v 12a), contrasts specifically with μανθανέτω, "should learn" (v 11a); the woman is to learn, not to teach. If Paul intends the two parts of v 11 to parallel the two parts of v 12ab, then ἐν ἡσυχίᾳ μανθανέτω, "should learn in quietness," parallels διδάσκειν . . . γυναικὶ οὐκ ἐπιτρέπω, "I do not permit a woman to teach," and ἐν πάσῃ ὑποταγῇ, "in all submissiveness," parallels αὐθεντεῖν ἀνδρός, "to exercise authority over a man." If the parallelism is not intended, then all of v 12ab defines what it means to learn in quiet submissiveness. The relationship of v 12a to v 12b is debated, but it will be argued here that v 12b is a general principle and v 12a is a specific application of that principle.

Although there are other passages in the PE more difficult to interpret, in recent years more has been written on vv 11–12 than on any other passage in the PE. Interpretations are so varied that one wonders how much of the exegesis is based on the text and how much on presuppositions and varying methodologies. The most that I can do is deal with the text, and leave the ramifications to other studies. The historical reading of the text sees Paul limiting the scope of women's ministry and grounding that prohibition in the creation of Adam and Eve before the curse of the Fall. If it could be proven that elsewhere Paul allows women to teach overseers (i.e., men) authoritatively within the context of the household of God (1 Tim 3:15), then it would have to be concluded that Paul is inconsistent or that vv 11–14 have been misunderstood.

The anarthrous γυνή, "woman," functions as a generic noun here as in v 9 and v 12 (Wallace, *Greek Grammar*, 253–54), appropriate in the statement of a general truth. The text does not say that women should learn *so that they can teach* (contra Spencer, *JETS* 17 [1974] 21; id., *Beyond the Curse*, 74–80; and many others). Spencer asserts, "If anyone is taught, eventually they will teach" (*Beyond the Curse*, 85), but this contradicts chap. 3, which sees authoritative instruction (which, it will be argued, is the context here) as the prerogative of the overseers (1 Tim 3:2; 5:17). There are many reasons to learn, and teaching is only one of them. As Moo comments, "All Jewish men were encouraged to study the law; did they all become rabbis?" ("What Does It Mean?" 184). Deut 31:12 says, "Assemble the people, men, women, little ones . . . that they may hear [the law] and *learn to fear* the LORD your God, and *be careful to do* all the words of this law." Keener points out that in Judaism one was to learn in order *to be obedient* (*Paul, Women, and Wives*, 128 n. 94; cf. *m. Abot* 6.6). The authoritative act of teaching, the proclamation of the gospel truth and the refutation of error, is the responsibility not of any person who has learned but of the leadership (1 Tim 3:2; 2 Tim 2:2).

Whatever ἡσυχία, "quietness," means, it must be understood against the back-drop of the situation of the Ephesian women (cf. discussion of the scope of the teaching in *Comment* on v 9). Some of the women are characterized as learning to be idlers, gadding about from house to house, gossiping (or talking foolishly), and in general being busybodies (1 Tim 5:13). They were anything but quiet. Evidently the lack of constraint, also characteristic of the Corinthian church, was a problem at Ephesus. Foh is right that "quietness and submission are not negative qualities with reference to learning; they are the way to learn (see Eccles 9:17)" ("Male Leadership View," 80). While this way of learning may not characterize much of current American education, it has done so in the past and was characteristic of ancient rabbinic instruction (Keener, *Paul, Women, and Wives*, 107–8).

The noun ἡσυχία occurs only four times in the NT. The cognate adjective ἡσύχιος, "quiet," occurs twice and the verb ἡσυχάζειν, "to be quiet," four times. It appears that the ἡσυχ- word group maintained the same basic meaning among the cognates. Four times in the NT the word group means "silence": the Pharisees are silent when Jesus asks them if he can heal on the Sabbath (Luke 14:4); the Judaizers are silenced when Peter tells them that the Spirit has come upon the Gentiles (Acts 11:18); the Ephesians cease arguing when they realize Paul is determined to go to Jerusalem (Acts 21:14); and the temple rioters become silent when they hear Paul speaking in Aramaic (Acts 22:2). Four times the word group means a "quiet demeanor": Paul tells the Thessalonians to live quietly (ἡσυχάζειν), mind their own affairs, and work with their hands (1 Thess 4:11); he later tells them to do their own work in quietness (μετὰ ἡσυχίας) and to earn their own living (2 Thess 3:12); Peter says that women should have a quiet spirit (1 Pet 3:4).

Several considerations favor the translation "quiet demeanor," "quietness," in v 11 (Clark, *Man and Woman*, 195; Fee, 84; Spencer, *Beyond the Curse*, 75–77, with Jewish parallels, 77–80; Keener, *Paul, Women, and Wives*, 108). (1) 1 Cor 11:5 secures a vocal role for women in the public worship service. (1 Cor 14:34–35 prohibits a certain type of speech, perhaps the authoritative evaluation of a prophet's message; cf. Hurley, *Biblical Perspective*, 185–94. Otherwise Paul would contradict himself within the space of four chapters. In 1 Corinthians, Paul also uses σιγᾶν, "to be silent," and λαλεῖν, "to speak," not ἡσυχάζειν.) (2) The cognate adjective ἡσύχιος is used nine verses earlier to denote a quiet demeanor (1 Tim 2:2). (3) In Paul's two other uses it means "quietness" (1 Thess 4:11; 2 Thess 3:12; cf. Payne, *Trinity Journal* 2 [1981] 169). (4) Total silence is not required either by the context or by the parallel with ὑποταγῇ, "submissiveness," or διδάσκειν, "to teach" (contra Schreiner, "Interpretation of 1 Timothy 2:9–15," 123); "a quiet demeanor" provides sufficient contrast with "to teach." If the translation "silence" is adopted, then the context limits this silence to the times of teaching. Neither the meaning of this word nor vv 11–12 hold up the ideal woman as one who is totally passive (contra Oberlinner, 91).

It has been correctly pointed out that Paul here, in contrast to segments of Judaism that prohibited women from learning, asserts the ability and value of women's education (e.g., contrast *y. Sot.* 3.19a, 3: "Better to burn the Torah than to teach it to a woman"; cf. *m. Sot.* 3.4; *b. Qid.* 29b, 34a; *b. Sanh.* 94b). While this is true, the emphasis of the verse is not that women *should* learn but *how* they should learn. The Greek word order and use of inclusio show that the emphasis is on the manner ("in quietness"). Mickelsen's reconstruction of v 12b (but [I am commanding her] to be [learning] in quietness" ["Egalitarian View," 201]) misses the point. Her move from πρέπει, "permit," to "command" is textually unwarranted. The shift from the plural γυναῖκας, γυναιξίν, "women," to the generic singular γυνή, γυναικί, "woman," here occurs because Paul is stating a principle (see *Comment* on v 15). Paul is attempting to correct the Ephesian situation in which the women are characterized as ἀργαὶ μανθάνουσιν, "learning to be idlers" (1 Tim 5:13), who are πάντοτε μανθάνοντα, "always learning"(2 Tim 3:7), but never coming to a knowledge of the truth. Because the discussion in chap. 2 is within the context of the house of God (see on v 9) and because the teaching is probably the teaching of Scripture (see on v 12), the content of the learning is general instruction within the church, specifically the teaching of Scripture. The topic of learning does not occur again in the PE in direct relation to women. Children are to learn their religious duty and take care of their parents/grandparents (1 Tim 5:4); Timothy is to continue in what he has learned (2 Tim 3:14); and believers should learn to apply themselves to good deeds (Titus 3:14; cf. K. H. Rengstorf, *TDNT* 4:410).

ἐν πάσῃ ὑποταγῇ, "in all submission," is the first of two qualifications of what Paul means by quietness: to learn in quietness means to learn in a submissive manner. The noun ὑποταγή, "submission," and its cognate verb ὑποτάσσειν, "to submit," are used throughout the NT. They describe the relationship of people to authorities (Titus 3:1; cf. Mark 12:17; Rom 13:1–7; 1 Pet 2:13–14), wives to husbands (Titus 2:5; cf. Col 3:18; Eph 5:22; 1 Pet 3:1), children to parents (1 Tim 3:4; cf. Luke 2:51), slaves to masters (1 Tim 6:1–2; Titus 2:9; cf. Phlm 16; 1 Pet 2:18), and the younger to the older (1 Pet 5:5). In the active voice the verb is used to describe the submission of creation to futility and of all things to Christ (cf. G. Delling, *TDNT* 8:41–45, 46; Spicq, 1:379). Depending upon the context of the passage, a particular occurrence may refer to submission to an authority or to voluntary submission. For example, Luke uses the verb to describe the involuntary submission of demons to the disciples (Luke 10:17, 20). The noun form (as in 1 Tim 2:11) is used by Paul to describe the voluntary submission of the Gentile church in giving an offering to the Jerusalem church (2 Cor 9:13), Paul's refusal to submit to the Judaizers (Gal 2:5), and the necessary submission of children to their parents (1 Tim 3:4; cf. ἀνυπότακτος, "rebellious," in 1 Tim 1:9).

There remains the question of submission to whom and in what context? Suggested objects include men, the teachers (overseers), the sound teaching, the congregation, and the current social condition. Caution warns that since the object of submission is not specified, this may not be the right question; the emphasis is on the woman's attitude. (1) The general nature of the statement and the use of ἀνδρός, "man," in the next verse may suggest that Paul is speaking of submissiveness to all men. Yet elsewhere Paul never requires submission of all women to all men (cf. Titus 2:5; cf. also 1 Pet 3:5). (2) Because the context is about learning, the object more likely is the person teaching. Since 2:11–15 is as tightly connected to 3:1–7 as it is to 2:8–9 (see *Form/Structure/Setting*) and since chap. 3 discusses overseers who teach, the context limits the women's submission to the teaching overseers, those who are responsible for teaching the true gospel and refuting error. As Schreiner points out, not all men taught or had authority when the church gathered, and so the submission would have been to the teaching leaders and their teaching ("Interpretation of 1 Timothy 2:9–15," 124; cf. Dibelius-Conzelmann, 47; Moo, *Trinity Journal* 1 [1980] 64; id., "What Does It Mean?" 183; Padgett, *Int* 41 [1987] 24; Roloff, 137; Barnett, *EvQ* 61 [1989] 230; Knight, 139). This places v 11 in line with other scriptural calls for men and women alike to be subject to the ruling authorities, be they secular (Titus 3:1; Rom 13:1) or spiritual (Heb 13:17; cf. 1 Pet 5:5; Jas 4:7; see *Comment* on ἀνδρός, "man," in v 12). If the submission is to the teachers, then the context is the public times during which the overseers teach (cf. Foh, *Women*, 125, 182–97).

12 διδάσκειν δὲ γυναικὶ οὐκ ἐπιτρέπω οὐδὲ αὐθεντεῖν ἀνδρός, ἀλλ' εἶναι ἐν ἡσυχίᾳ, "but I do not permit a woman to teach or to exercise authority over a man, but [she is] to be in quietness." This is the second qualifying clause Paul uses to explain what he means by ἐν ἡσυχίᾳ, "in quietness." Paul means that a woman (cf. v 11) may not exercise authority in the church (cf. 1 Tim 3:15) over men (possibly the male overseers; general principle), and this includes teaching (specific application). While the text never says women are teaching the heresy, names only men as teachers (1 Tim 1:20; 2 Tim 2:17; 3:6), and explicitly pictures only women as being influenced by the heresy (2 Tim 3:6–7; possibly 1 Tim 5:11–13, 15), the charge here suggests that women, at least in some way, are promulgating the heresy even if they are not leaders of the opposition. The repetition of the initial phrase ἐν ἡσυχίᾳ here and in v 11 serves to highlight quietness as Paul's basic concern. γυνή, "woman," and ἀνδρός, "man," are both generic singulars, appropriate for the statement of a general rule (see *Comment* on v 15).

Three specific issues have been raised concerning the phrase οὐκ ἐπιτρέπω, "I do not permit," each of which would limit the applicability of Paul's instruction. To be consistent, if v 12 is temporally and geographically limited to ancient Ephesus, then other statements made in the immediate context should be so limited, statements such as Paul's admonition for women to learn (v 11). (1) Some feel that Paul's use of "I" represents his personal opinion and not his binding judgment. Comparison is often made to 1 Cor 7 where Paul differentiates between a charge coming from himself and a charge coming from the Lord (vv 10, 12). His language is even less authoritative when he encourages single people not to get married: "I have no command of the Lord, but I give my opinion as one who by the Lord's mercy is trustworthy. I think that . . ." (1 Cor 7:25–26). However, Paul is discussing two different (but related) items: divorce and marriage/remarriage. On his comments about divorce (1 Cor 7:10–16), it is generally agreed that Paul is not distinguishing between command and opinion but between traditions coming from the earthly Jesus through the church and what he, as an apostle of Jesus, knows to be true. This does not lessen the authority of his pronouncements but rather identifies their authoritative source as Jesus (cf. Barrett, *First Epistle to the Corinthians*, 163). In fact, Paul equates, in terms of authority, the Jesus traditions and his own judgments. In v 10 he says, "To the married I give charge," and to make sure they realize that his charge carries full authority, he identifies the ultimate source of authority by adding "not I but the Lord," making reference to the tradition as recorded in Mark 10:11–12 (cf. 1 Cor 9:8; 14:37). In other words, Paul can say "I command" or "the Lord commands," and to him they are both fully authoritative. However, when Paul discusses marriage/remarriage, he is not making an authoritative judgment, and in fact does not require the Corinthians to follow his advice (1 Cor 7:38). But in 1 Corinthians, it is the context—specifically his qualifying statements, his vocabulary, and his reasons (1 Cor 7:32, 35, 40)—that show he is giving his opinion, not that he says "I."

Paul uses "I" throughout his writings, often speaking with absolute authority (e.g., Rom 8:38; 12:1; 14:14; 1 Cor 5:3; 10:20–21; 13:1; Gal 5:16; also Rom 15:8, 30; 16:17; 1 Cor 1:10; 4:16; 7:10; 11:3; 12:3; 14:5; 15:50, 51; 16:1; 2 Cor 10:1; 12:11; Gal 4:1; 5:3; Eph 4:1,17; Phil 4:2; 1 Thess 4:1, 10; 5:14; 2 Thess 3:6, 12). This same pattern continues throughout the PE (1 Tim 1:20; 2:8; 5:21; 6:13–14; cf. 1 Tim 1:11; 2:1; 5:11; 2 Tim 1:6; 2:7; Titus 1:5; 3:8). Only someone who considers his personal judgment to be absolutely binding could say "Follow the pattern of the sound words that you have heard from me" (2 Tim 1:13). It does not matter whether Paul says "I do not want the rich of this world to be haughty" or "As for the rich in this world, charge them not to be haughty!" (1 Tim 6:17). Paul can mix the indicative and imperative, and both forms carry his full authority (cf. 2 Tim 4:1–2; 1 Cor 11:34).

(2) The second concern has to do with the word ἐπιτρέπω, "I permit." To some this suggests that this is not a command but an opinion that may or may not be followed (e.g., J. M. Ford, *JES* 10 [1973] 682; Kaiser, *Worldwide Challenge* [September 1976] 10; G. R. Osborne, *JETS* 20 [1977] 347; Payne, *Trinity Journal* 2 [1981] 170–73; G. Redekop, *SR* 19 [1990] 235–45). Much of what has been said regarding Paul's use of "I" also argues against this interpretation. But there are additional considerations. Perriman argues that v 12 is parenthetical as evidenced by the shift from the imperative to the indicative (*TynBul* 44 [1993] 129–30, 139–40); but the indicative can carry the force of the imperative contextually, and v 12 is an explanation of v 11 and should not be separated from it. The word ἐπιτρέπειν, "to permit," can be a strong term (MM, 249, cite its use in a legal context). It occurs elsewhere in Paul in 1 Cor 14:34 (women are not permitted to speak in church) and 16:7 (Paul wishes to spend time with the Corinthians if the Lord permits; cf. Heb 6:3). Elsewhere in the NT it describes the permitting of divorce by Moses (Matt 19:8; Mark 10:4), of the demons to go into the pigs (Mark 5:13; Luke 8:32), of the burial of one's father (Matt 8:21; Luke 9:59), of saying farewell prior to discipleship (Luke 9:61), and of the removal of Jesus' body by Joseph of Arimathea (John 19:38). The word is also used in Paul's request of permission from the tribune (Acts 21:39, 40), from Agrippa (Acts 26:1), from a centurion (Acts 27:3), and from the Roman authorities (Acts 28:16). ἐπιτρέπειν can be an authoritative demand bordering on the legal (cf. also 1 Cor 7:17; 11:16; Phil 3:15). Spicq says it is a rabbinic formula for prohibition (1:379). While at times it does refer to a specific situation (Matt 8:21; Mark 5:13; John 19:38; Acts 21:39, 40), it is the context that

limits its scope and not the intrinsic meaning of the word (so Moo, *Trinity Journal* 2 [1981] 199–200; contra Payne, *Trinity Journal* 2 [1981] 172; cf. 1 Cor 14:34; Heb 6:3; Ignatius *Eph.* 10.3). The point is that if the semantic force of the word is authoritative, the use of the indicative does not lessen its force. The imperative in v 11 has already established the tone of the passage. It can also be argued that the shift from βούλομαι, "I desire" (v 8; itself a strong term), to the stronger ἐπιτρέπω, "I permit," signals an increasing sense of authority.

(3) The third issue raised concerning the phrase οὐκ ἐπιτρέπω, "I do not permit," has to do with the present tense of the verb. It is argued that because the present tense is used, it should be translated "I am not presently allowing a woman to teach" (Spencer, *Beyond the Curse,* 85) or "I am not permitting" (Payne, *Trinity Journal* 2 [1981] 172). Spencer comments, "Yet at this time Paul wanted to restrain the women at Ephesus from teaching the men until they themselves were well instructed" (*JETS* 17 [1974] 219). If Paul had intended the instruction to be for all time, it is argued, Paul would have used another form such as the imperative or future indicative or aorist subjunctive, or otherwise specifically indicated such (Payne, *Trinity Journal* 2 [1981] 171; Fee, 72; Bilezikian, *Beyond Sex Roles,* 180; Padgett, *Int* 41 [1987] 25; Witherington, *Women in the Earliest Churches,* 120–21; Kroeger and Kroeger, *I Suffer Not a Woman,* 83). This is the least convincing of the three attempts to weaken Paul's language. (a) Wallace points out that the generic γυνή, "woman," indicates that ἐπιτρέπω, "I permit," is gnomic and concludes that "the normal use of the present tense in didactic literature, especially when introducing an exhortation, is not descriptive, but a general precept that has gnomic implications" (*Greek Grammar,* 525, citing forty-one passages). To argue that Paul would have had to use a different verbal form if he were to indicate a timeless truth is simply not correct; this is the force of the gnomic use—to describe an action that always occurs (cf. Fanning, *Verbal Aspect,* 208–17). (b) If use of the present tense automatically necessitated that the statement be relegated to the author's present, then this would raise serious problems with much of Paul's writing. In his thirteen epistles, Paul uses 1,429 present-tense active indicative verbs (out of a total of 2,835 indicative verbs). If this objection is true, then almost nothing Paul says can have any significance beyond the narrow confines of its immediate context. To be sure, many of these present-tense verbs refer to a specific historical situation (e.g., 1 Cor 8:13); but the reference is indicated not by the tense of the verb but by the context of the verse (cf. Wallace's comments on Eph 5:18; *Greek Grammar,* 525). (c) When one looks at the use of the present tense in the PE, the general, universal scope of the tense is continually illustrated. In the PE there are 111 present-tense indicative verbs. If all of these were relegated also to the author's present situation, then the PE would no longer teach that the law is not for the just (1 Tim 1:9), that God wishes that all could be saved (1 Tim 2:4; 4:10), that it is a good thing to pursue the office of elder (1 Tim 3:1), that the mystery of the Christian religion is great (1 Tim 3:16), that physical exercise is of some value but godliness is infinitely more valuable (1 Tim 4:8), that children should take care of their parents and grandparents (1 Tim 5:4), that there is great gain in godliness (1 Tim 6:6), that those desiring to be rich fall into temptation (1 Tim 6:9), that the love of money is a root of all evils (1 Tim 6:10); and the list goes on (cf., e.g., 1 Tim 3:2–13; 4:5; 5:4–18; 24–25; 6:7). While the use of the present tense does not require that a statement be true in the future, neither is there anything in the tense that

requires it to be true only in the present but not later. Spencer's translation, "I am not presently allowing a woman to teach" (*Beyond the Curse*, 85), implies to many ears that the statement would not be true later, something the present tense cannot by itself connote. (d) The previous counterargument also holds for first-person (see above) present-tense verbs. Moo finds twelve uses of the first-person-singular indicative in Paul that make a universal statement (Rom 12:1, 3; 1 Cor 4:16; 2 Cor 5:20; Gal 5:2, 3; Eph 4:1; 1 Thess 4:1; 5:14; 2 Thess 3:6), two of which (1 Tim 2:1, 8) specifically indicate that the statement is universal, which would imply by default that Paul uses the construction to make a universal statement (*Trinity Journal* 2 [1981] 200). Wallace argues that there is no instance in Paul that the combination "first person singular present tense with an infinitive ever means 'right now, but not later'" (*Greek Grammar*, 526 n. 30; see *Comment* on 1 Tim 2:1 regarding the same construction). The present tense views an action from inside the action "without beginning or end in view" (Fanning, *Verbal Aspect*, 103). It says nothing about the completion of the event but only that from the speaker's point of view it is an ongoing process. οὐκ ἐπιτρέπω, "I do not permit," therefore, represents the apostle's binding command for all churches.

Paul specifies that he does not permit γυναικί, "a woman," to teach. Padgett and others suggest that Paul is thinking only of the women deceived by the heresy (*Int* 41 [1987] 25). However, if Paul had meant "deceived women," he could have said so. A decision here is usually made by one's general approach to the passage and by how tightly one sees vv 8–15 tied to the specific teachings of the opponents, but the text makes the statement general. Grammatically, the anarthrous noun functions generically (cf. on v 11); Padgett's view requires the article.

Paul continues by saying, "I do not permit a woman to teach [διδάσκειν]." Actually, the verb διδάσκειν, "to teach," is the first word in the sentence and as such stands as the most important and contrasts with the previous μανθανέτω, "should learn." Much of the problem in Ephesus came from incorrect teaching, and Paul is saying that the Ephesian women may not be involved in this teaching process. Beyond this, there are questions regarding exactly what he means.

(1) There is no supplied object for διδάσκειν. (a) The statement cannot be a blanket prohibition of women teaching anyone. Older women are told to teach what is good (καλοδιδασκάλους) and so train (σωφρονίζωσιν) younger women (Titus 2:3–4). Timothy has the same faith as did his mother and grandmother (2 Tim 1:5; 3:15; Paul never says they taught Timothy, but it is the apparent meaning of the text). Priscilla, along with her husband, Aquila, taught Apollos (Acts 18:26). Believers are to teach each other (Col 3:16; even in Judaism women could teach little children; Str-B 3:467). The context thus limits the universal application to some extent.

(b) Context and grammar allow ἀνδρός, "man," to be the object of both διδάσκειν, "to teach," and αὐθεντεῖν, "to exercise authority." Moo notes, "In Greek, objects and qualifiers of words which occur only with the second in a series must often be taken with the first also (cf. Acts 8:21)" (*Trinity Journal* 2 [1981] 202). In this verse, the case of the object (ἀνδρός in the genitive) is determined by the closer verb (αὐθεντεῖν, not διδάσκειν; cf. Smyth, *Greek Grammar* §1634). ἀνδρός is not too far removed from διδάσκειν for it to function as its object (contra Payne, *Trinity Journal* 2 [1981] 175; Fung, "Ministry," 198–99). διδάσκειν is moved forward in word order for emphasis, separating it from ἀνδρός further than perhaps expected. If v 12b is a general principle and v 12a a specific application (see below), the meaning remains the same.

(c) But which men must not be taught? All men? Because there are no limiters in v 12 and because vv 13–14 are general in scope, it would appear that Paul is saying that women may teach no men, understanding ἀνδρός as older males as suggested by the historical situation. But there may be contextual hints that the scope of ἀνδρός should be more limited. (i) The scope of ἀνδρός here could be the same as the object of women's submission (v 11) since v 12 is defining ὑποταγῇ, "submissiveness." Because the idea of a woman being submissive to all men is foreign to Paul's teaching, it is more likely that he means that they are to be submissive to a certain group of men. It fits within Pauline theology for women to be submissive to their husbands and for all believers, men and women, to submit to the leadership of the overseers (see *Comment* above). (ii) Saying that women cannot teach men may come within a contextual limitation since women are allowed to teach in other circumstances. This suggests that ἀνδρός does not refer to all men. (iii) 1 Tim 2:9–15 is closely related to the subsequent discussion of overseers (see *Form/Structure/Setting*), and there Paul states that overseers must be able to teach (3:2; also 2 Tim 2:2). The church is led by its overseers, and they lead by teaching truth and refuting error (see *Form/Structure/Setting* on 1 Tim 3:1–7). Since this is the context within which Paul says women may not exercise teaching authority over a man, it is possible that the ἀνδρός a woman is not to teach is an overseer. (iv) The limitation of ἀνδρός to overseer accords well with the Ephesian situation. The opponents are teaching error, and the women are being deceived, perhaps also promoting the heresy (although the text never says the latter). Part of Paul's overall response is to ensure that the overseers are able teachers, able to teach truth and refute error. Women may not, therefore, authoritatively teach the men in authority. For the same general conclusion, see Lenski, 564; Spencer, *JETS* 17 (1974) 220; Moo, *Trinity Journal* 1 (1980) 65–66; id., "What Does It Mean?" 183; Clark, *Man and Woman*, 199; Foh, *Women*, 125–26; Hurley, *Biblical Perspective*, 201; Howard, *EvQ* 55 (1983) 31–42; Dockery, *CTR* 1 (1987) 363–86; Blomberg, *CTR* 2 (1988) 413.

The criticisms of this interpretation, however, are several. (a) The text does not say ἐπίσκοπος, "overseer"; it says ἀνδρός, "man" (generic). (b) The object of submission (v 11) does not necessarily have to be the same as ἀνδρός (v 12). (c) Vv 13–14 deal with the man-woman relationship, not leader-woman. Why would Paul appeal to Adam's priority in creation and his not having been deceived if Paul is not concerned with the man-woman relationship? (d) The examples of women teaching seen in the PE do not involve the authoritative transmission of the gospel, and the text does not say that the women taught men (1 Tim 5:10, 14; Titus 2:2–3). (e) This interpretation would make application difficult, to the point that one wonders if Paul could have meant this (e.g., a woman could teach men authoritative doctrine only if any overseers present first excused themselves).

(2) Paul does not identify *what* it is that women may not teach. (a) Many argue that Paul's prohibition is that the Ephesian women not teach error. Kroeger and Kroeger state that "the verb here [i.e., διδάσκειν in 1 Tim 2:12] forbids women to teach a wrong doctrine, just as 1 Tim 1:3–4 and Titus 1:9–14 also forbid false teaching" (*I Suffer Not a Woman*, 81). There are several problems with this argument, however. (i) The text does not specify wrong doctrine when it easily could have. (ii) In 1 Tim 1:3–4 the verb is not διδάσκειν but ἑτεροδιδασκαλεῖν, which explicitly states that what is being taught is ἑτερο-, "other," and context makes it clear in Titus 1:9–14 that the heresy is being discussed (cf. Liefeld,

"Response," 245; Wolters, *CTJ* 28 [1993] 210). (iii) διδάσκειν is used almost always in a positive sense in the PE, i.e., to teach truth (see below). (iv) While the cognate διδαχή, "teaching," can refer to the content of what is taught (Titus 1:9; 2 Tim 4:2), the verb διδάσκειν refers exclusively in the PE to the act of teaching as would be expected of a verb. Twice it occurs in summary admonitions (1 Tim 4:11; 6:2), each time with the object specified (ταῦτα, "these things"). In 2 Tim 2:2, Timothy is to entrust the gospel to faithful men/people who will teach others (ἑτέρους). In Titus 1:11 the opponents are teaching ἃ μὴ δεῖ, "what is not proper." But here in v 12 Paul supplies no object, and the verb refers to the act of teaching (cf. Liefeld, "Response," 245). (v) It seems a strange twist of logic to say that women may not teach error while implicitly allowing men to teach error. If all the women, and only the women, are deceived, then this interpretation would be more feasible. Yet it seems unlikely that Priscilla would have been tricked (2 Tim 4:19; Acts 18:24–28). (vi) An appeal to v 14 does not help because it too does not say that women may not teach men error, nor does its OT background in Gen 3:13, which never says that Eve taught Adam (cf. *Comment* on v 14). Rather, the implication of the Genesis account is that Adam was present, watched his wife being deceived, was not deceived himself (1 Tim 2:14a), and yet said nothing. Paul says, "Let a woman learn"; he does not say, "Let the women convinced by the opponents learn." This suggests that Paul is thinking of all the women in the church and argues against limiting the command elsewhere to women teaching error. (vii) 1 Tim 5:13 is not necessarily parallel (contra Keener, *Paul, Women, and Wives,* 108). There the women are "talking" (λαλεῖν), not "teaching" (διδάσκειν, but cf. Fee's comments), and the opponents who are identified are all male (1 Tim 1:20; 2 Tim 2:17–18; cf. 2 Tim 4:14). The picture in the text is of the women being influenced by the opponents (1 Tim 5:11–15; 2 Tim 3:5–9). In fact, 2 Tim 3:7 describes some women as always listening but never being *able* to arrive at the truth. But the women in 2:11 can learn (cf. Foh, *Women,* 122). (viii) If Paul is prohibiting women from teaching error, v 13 seems irrelevant, even if the γάρ, "for," is illustrative. (ix) Liefeld points out that the Greek word order places emphasis on διδάσκειν and γυναικί, whereas Kroeger proposes to demonstrate that the emphasis of the text is on the implied object, *error* ("Response," 245).

(b) Rather, διδάσκειν in the PE is used in a positive sense of teaching the truth of the gospel (1 Tim 4:11; 6:2; 2 Tim 2:2; cf. *Comment* on 1 Tim 1:10 and discussion of the noun cognate in *Comments* on 2 Tim 4:2 and Titus 1:9), except in Titus 1:11, where the context shows that it is false teaching (but still authoritative instruction). (In 1 Tim 1:3 and 6:3, which speak of teaching false doctrine, the verb is ἑτεροδιδασκαλεῖν, "to teach another doctrine.") The cognate noun διδαχή, "teaching," occurs twice in the PE, both times describing the gospel message. The cognate διδασκαλία, "teaching," occurs fifteen times in the PE, and every time except once (1 Tim 4:1, referring to doctrines of demons) it refers to the gospel (1 Tim 1:10; 4:6, 13, 16; 5:17; 6:1, 3; 2 Tim 3:10, 16; 4:3; Titus 1:9; 2:1, 7, 10). While elsewhere Paul speaks of teaching in more general terms (1 Cor 14:26; Eph 4:11–12; Col 3:16), the overwhelming use of the word group in the PE is to describe the positive teaching of the gospel, often (as the context shows) by a person in authority (especially 2 Tim 2:2; 1 Tim 5:17; Titus 1:9; cf. 1 Tim 3:2). Elsewhere in the PE Paul specifies the content (1 Tim 4:11; 6:2) or object (2 Tim 2:2; Titus 1:11) of teaching. That διδάσκειν here has no object or any term indicating false teaching proves that the verse is a positive command not to teach "the authoritative and public transmission of tradition about Christ and the Scriptures (1 Cor. 12:28–29; Eph. 4:11; 1 Tim. 2:7; 2 Tim. 3:16; James 3:1)" (so Schreiner, "Interpretion of 1 Timothy 2:9–15," 127, citing Fung, "Ministry," 198; cf. Clark, *Man and Woman,* 196; Moo, *Trinity Journal* 1 [1980] 65–66; id., "What Does It Mean?" 185–86; Towner, *Goal,* 215). Saucy (*JETS* 37 [1994] 81–91) develops the thesis that the concept of teaching in the PE, while capable of a wider range of meaning in Paul and in general usage (cf. also Payne, *Trinity Journal* 2 [1981] 173–75), carries the meaning of authoritative instruction, "the preservation and transmission of the Christian tradition" (87), hence the teaching appropriate to an overseer. On the view that Paul is telling women that they can teach after they learn, see on μανθανέτω, "should learn" (v 11), above.

(3) Paul does not specifically identify *where* women may not teach men. ἐν παντὶ τόπῳ, "in every place" (v 8), and the general nature of v 12 may suggest that this applies everywhere one finds the house of God. We do know that Priscilla and Aquila "expounded" (ἐξέθεντο) the way of God to Apollos (Acts 18:26), but this reference can hardly bear the weight often placed on it. ἐν παντὶ τόπῳ can also mean "in all the churches" (cf. *Comment* on 1 Tim 2:8), and 1 Tim 3:15 defines the scope of this passage as how one ought to act in the household of God (cf. *Comment* on v 9). How one defines the scope of "household of God" (e.g., wherever believers are gathered; public worship) is problematic, but in the *Comment* on 1 Tim 3:15 it is defined as primarily public worship. The conclusion suggested here is that Paul says women may not authoritatively teach the gospel to men (possibly overseers) in the public assembly of the church.

Paul joins the prohibition of teaching with another: "I do not permit a woman . . . to exercise authority over a man [οὐδὲ αὐθεντεῖν ἀνδρός]." The translation of αὐθεντεῖν, "to exercise authority," has become the crux of the passage.

αὐθεντεῖν is a difficult word to define. It occurs nowhere else in the NT and rarely in secular Greek. Most agree that its basic meaning is either the neutral "to exercise authority" or the negative "to domineer" in the sense of exerting authority in a coercive manner. Either definition provides an adequate parallel to ὑποταγῇ, "submission," in v 11. For the translation "to exercise authority," see Lock, 32; Guthrie, 76–77; Kelly, 68; Moo, *Trinity Journal* 1 (1980) 66–76; Hurley, *Biblical Perspective,* 202; Panning, *WLQ* 78 (1981) 185–91; Knight, 141–42; id., *NTS* 30 (1984) 143–57; Fung, "Ministry," 198; Padgett, *Int* 41 (1987) 25 n. 27; Wilshire, *NTS* 34 (1988) 120–34; Barnett, *EvQ* 61 (1989) 231–32; Gritz, *Paul, Women Teachers, and the Mother Goddess,* 134–35; Baldwin, "Difficult Word," 65–80; Schreiner, "Interpretation of 1 Timothy 2:9–15," 130–33. For the translation "to domineer" (in a coercive manner), see Simpson, 47; Dibelius-Conzelmann, 47; Barrett, 55; Payne, *Trinity Journal* 2 (1981) 175; Osburn, *ResQ* 25 (1982) 1–12; Fee, 73; Spencer, *Beyond the Curse,* 86–87; Scholer, "1 Timothy 2:9–15," 204–5; Witherington, *Earliest Churches,* 121–22; Towner, 77; id., *Goal,* 215–16; Harris, *EvQ* 62 (1990) 335–52; Keener, *Paul, Women, and Wives,* 108–9 (who says that the evidence is not entirely clear); Boomsma, *Male and Female,* 71–72; Kroeger and Kroeger, *I Suffer Not a Woman,* 84–104; Motyer, *Vox Evangelica* 24 (1994) 95–96; Groothuis, *Good News,* 215–16. Oberlinner does not commit himself to a position (96).

H. S. Baldwin gives an excellent summary of research on the meaning of αὐθεντεῖν ("Difficult Word," 66–69). (1) Historically the word in this context was understood to mean "to have authority" (but cf. the kjv's "to usurp authority"). (2)

C. C. Kroeger originally argued that it was an erotic term meaning "to thrust oneself" and was used in connection with fertility practices (*Reformed Journal* 29 [1979] 12–15). (3) Osburn faults Kroeger's argument, showing that she had misread the supposed parallels (see also Gritz, *Paul, Women Teachers, and the Mother Goddess,* 134) and concludes that αὐθεντεῖν means "to dominate or domineer" (*ResQ* 25 [1982] 1–12; see also Panning, *Wisconsin Lutheran Quarterly* 78 [1981] 185–91). (4) Knight argues against the translation "to usurp authority" and also advocates "to have authority" (*NTS* 30 [1984] 143–57). (5) Wilshire finds 314 occurrences of αὐθεντεῖν and cognates used in the *Thesaurus Linguae Graecae* database and translates "instigating violence," stating that the issue in 1 Tim 2:12 is one of authority (*NTS* 34 [1988] 120–23). He has since raised the issue of whether he has been correctly understood (*EvQ* 65 [1993] 43–55; see summary in Schreiner, "Interpretation of 1 Timothy 2:9–15," 130–31). (6) R. C. and C. C. Kroeger have returned to the discussion with a presentation of four possible meanings: "(a) to begin something, to be responsible for a condition or action, (b) to rule, to dominate, (c) to usurp power or rights from another, (d) to claim ownership, sovereignty, or authorship." In 1 Tim 2:12 they translate αὐθεντεῖν as "proclaim herself author of man," relying heavily on a reconstruction of Ephesian culture (*I Suffer Not a Woman,* 84–104, 185–88; see critiques by Perriman, *TB* 44 [1993] 132–34; Wilshire, *EvQ* 65 [1993] 54; Wolters, *CTJ* 28 [1993] 210–11; and responses to C. C. Kroeger's "1 Timothy 2:12" article by Liefeld, 244–48, and Holsey, 248–53; see *Comment* on v 13 for further discussion).

(7) H. S. Baldwin himself argues that αὐθεντεῖν and its cognate noun αὐθέντης do not have the same range of meaning and therefore concentrates on the eighty-two occurrences of the verb (searching for the forms αὐθεντ- and ηὐθεντ- in the *Greek Documentary CD-ROM [#6]* and *Thesaurus Linguae Graecae CD-ROM #D*), not including the more than twenty direct references to 1 Tim 2:12 in the church fathers and the ten occurrences in *Alexander Romance* (because of dating problems). He gives a helpful listing of all these occurrences, Greek with English translation, in his "Appendix 2: αὐθεντέω in Ancient Greek Literature," as well as a summary of all usages. He settles on five possible meanings of αὐθεντεῖν, and "the one unifying concept is that of *authority*" (73). (a) "To rule, to reign sovereignly: unhindered authority to act based on inherent or divine right." (b) "To control, to dominate: reflecting authority from the standpoint of actually having control or ability to dominate an object" (which he firmly separates from "to domineer, tyrannize, coerce," which results from improper domination). He cites Chrysostom's statement that Eve "exercised authority once *wrongly* [ηὐθέντησεν ἅπαξ κακῶς]," the significance being that αὐθεντεῖν does not contain an inherently negative meaning as evidenced by the necessary addition of κακῶς, "wrongly." He finds only one unambiguous instance where αὐθεντεῖν "is plainly intended to convey the negative meaning 'tyrannize.'" (See also his comments on the appearance of "domineer" in BAGD, which is not necessarily a translation of the German *herrschen über jemand* [67j].) (c) "To act independently: being one's own authority" is a meaning that occurs eight times and, he argues, is not inherently negative (but see his qualifications on the subcategory "to exercise one's own jurisdiction"). (d) "To be primarily responsible for or to instigate something." Baldwin claims that Kroeger and Kroeger have mistakenly taken this usage "to mean 'to be the organic origin of something' with a sense analogous to γεννάω or τίκτω"; rather, the five

uses of αὐθεντεῖν with this meaning are closer to Lampe's definition "to instigate," showing that two of these five uses are directly paralleled by προϊστάναι, "to be the leader, to direct, to be the ringleader." (e) "To commit murder." Baldwin shows that while the cognate noun does have this meaning centuries earlier, the earliest use of the verb with this meaning is in the tenth century A.D. Baldwin also discusses the issue of whether the noun is the root of the verbal form and what, if any, are the implications. Of the several subdivisions of Baldwin's five categories, he suggests four as possible in 1 Tim 2:12: "To control, to dominate; To compel, to influence; To assume authority over; To flout the authority of" (78–79).

The question of the meaning of αὐθεντεῖν is not insignificant. If it means "to exercise authority," then Paul is prohibiting any type of authoritative teaching (see the next phrase) that places a woman over a man (cf. 1 Cor 11:2–12; Eph 5:22–33; 1 Pet 3:1–7). If it means "to domineer" in a negative sense, then it is prohibiting a certain type of authoritative teaching, one that is administered in a negative, domineering, coercive way, thus leaving the door open for women to exercise teaching authority in a proper way over men. While word studies have their limitations, as Baldwin points out, he has proven his point. His definition of αὐθεντεῖν is also supported by the context in 1 Timothy. The parallel of αὐθεντεῖν with διδάσκειν, "teaching," suggests that it is a positive term (see below). Especially Kroeger and Kroeger's translation raises serious contextual problems. It seems doubtful that Paul would prohibit only women (and not men) from teaching in a coercive way, especially since the text only names male opponents (1 Tim 1:20; 2 Tim 2:17–18; 4:14). This same argument applies to the suggestion that Paul is saying the women may not teach error (see above); in the PE neither women nor men are allowed to teach error.

A crucial question concerns the relationship between the two prohibitions, i.e., the significance of οὐδέ, which is translated here as "or." (1) Some argue that the two prohibitions are a hendiadys, the use of two different terms to denote one concept. Paul would then be prohibiting women from authoritative teaching (or domineering teaching, depending upon the translation of αὐθεντεῖν; cf. Hurley, *Biblical Perspective*, 201; Payne, "οὐδέ"; Motyer, *Vox Evangelica* 24 [1994] 96; Saucy, *JETS* 37 [1994] 90; Boomsma, *Male and Female*, 72–73 [although Hurley's and Saucy's understandings of the meaning of the text differ significantly from the others]). The problem with this is that διδάσκειν and αὐθεντεῖν are separated by five words; words forming a hendiadys are usually side by side since the construction is used "to avoid a series of dependent genitives" (BDF §442[16]). Payne argues that the conjunction οὐδέ links not two unrelated terms but two related concepts in order to convey a "single coherent idea" ("οὐδέ," 1). He likens it to the slang connective "'n" as in the phrase "hit 'n run" where the two different verbs, "hit" and "run," describe one event. His translation is built on his conclusion that αὐθεντεῖν means "to domineer." Payne concludes, "[οὐδέ] joins together two elements in order to convey a single coherent idea, or if it conveys two ideas these should be very closely interrelated. Since the two elements joined by οὐδέ in 1 Tim 2:12 are not nearly as closely interrelated as any of the other such pairs of separate ideas in the Pauline corpus, they should be translated as a single coherent idea" ("οὐδέ," 4).

However, an examination of Payne's examples shows that they do not prove his conclusion (cf. Moo, "What Does It Mean?" 187). For example, Gal 3:28 speaks of Jew and Gentile, slave and free. While they are related concepts and are expressing a coherent idea (i.e., all people), one does not define the other; in fact they are opposites (cf. Rom 11:21). If 1 Tim 2:12b is a principle and 2:12a a specific application, then they are very closely interrelated and even by Payne's approach do not support his conclusion. He also appears to equate a single coherent idea with very closely related events; these are not the same. 1 Tim 6:16 is helpful. Speaking of God, Paul says, "whom no human has seen or [οὐδέ] is able to see." The latter is a general principle out of which the former specific historical assertion comes. A. J. Köstenberger provides a detailed critique of Payne's work ("Complex Sentence Structure," 82–84):

> Since Payne presupposes that αὐθεντεῖν means "domineer," he concludes that "teach" and "domineer" by themselves are conceptually too far apart to be joined by οὐδέ (which usually joins closely related terms) in a coordinating manner. Thus, Payne views the second term joined by οὐδέ in 1 Timothy 2:12, αὐθεντεῖν, as subordinate to the first, διδάσκειν. But if αὐθεντεῖν were to mean "to have authority" rather than "to domineer," it would be quite closely related to διδάσκειν, "to teach." In that case, consistent with Payne's own observation on how οὐδέ generally functions, οὐδέ could well link the two closely related terms, "to teach" and "to have authority," in a coordinating fashion. ("Complex Sentence Structure," 83)

Cf. also Payne's shift in definition for the third category from "those which specify with greater clarity the meaning of one word or phrase by conjoining it with another word or phrase" ("οὐδέ," 1) to "[οὐδέ joins] together two elements in order to convey a single coherent idea" ("οὐδέ," 4).

Kroeger and Kroeger's position is especially tenuous when they translate "I do not allow a woman to teach nor to proclaim herself author of man" (*I Suffer Not a Woman,* 103). οὐδέ is a negative conjunction (BAGD, 591) and yet, in Liefeld's words, "[C. C. Kroeger] seems to assume that the *authenteo* phrase expresses the *object* of the teaching" ("Response," 246). Köstenberger asserts, "The effort to make αὐθεντεῖν subordinate to διδάσκειν so that it in effect functions as an adverb and to give it a negative connotation, as in 'to teach in a domineering way,' is contradicted by the fact that οὐδέ does not function as a subordinating but as a coordinating conjunction" ("Complex Sentence Structure," 90).

(2) The second possibility is that διδάσκειν and αὐθεντεῖν are distinct yet related concepts, both of which are prohibited to women by Paul or the author of the PE (most commentaries; Moo, *Trinity Journal* 1 [1980] 68; Fung, "Ministry," 199; Schreiner, "Interpretation of 1 Timothy 2:9–15," 133–34). Köstenberger provides a detailed analysis of this construction: "infinitive + negated finite verb + οὐδέ + infinitive" ("Complex Sentence Structure," 84–103, noting that there does not seem to be any significance syntactically that the first infinitive precedes the negated finite verb). While Payne limits his study to the Pauline literature and includes constructions with nouns, Köstenberger limits his searches to verbal parallels, not only in the NT but also in the extrabiblical literature. There is only one close syntactical parallel in the NT (Acts 16:21). If verbal forms of any kind are allowed, there are fifty-two. In the NT he finds two distinct patterns: "Two activities or concepts are viewed positively in and of themselves, but their exercise is prohibited or their existence denied due to circumstances or conditions adduced in the context; two activities or concepts are viewed negatively and consequently their exercise is prohibited or their existence denied or to be avoided" (85). The most significant point is that both verbal forms

must be positive or they both must be negative. After giving a complete listing of parallels he concludes, "There are only two acceptable ways of rendering that passage: (1) 'I do not permit a woman to teach [error] or to domineer over a man,' or (2) 'I do not permit a woman to teach or to exercise authority over a man" (89). Later he adds, "Since, therefore, the term διδάσκειν is viewed absolutely in the New Testament for an activity that is viewed positively in and of itself, and since οὐδέ coordinates terms that are either both viewed positively or negatively, αὐθεντεῖν should be seen as denoting an activity that is viewed positively in and of itself as well" (91; it might be better to look at διδάσκειν in the PE and not in the NT as a whole). Köstenberger then turns to the IBYCUS computer system and finds forty-eight syntactical parallels to 1 Tim 2:12 (he lists the results), discovering that the two patterns exist there as well. In a final note he categorizes the NT passages based on the nature of the relationships of the two verbal forms: synonymous, conceptually parallel, complementary, sequential, ascensive, general to specific, and specific to general, which is where he places 1 Tim 2:12 (103 n. 15). αὐθεντεῖν is not adverbial, modifying διδάσκειν, "to teach in a domineering way": "Neither the syntactical parallels in the New Testament nor the extrabiblical parallels lend support to the contention that the second term linked by οὐδέ modifies the first term adverbially" (Köstenberger, "Complex Sentence Structure," 90–91).

It seems therefore that Paul is prohibiting two separate events: teaching and acting in authority. The relationship that exists between the two is that of a principle and a specific application of that principle (cf. Spicq, 1:379–80; Moo, *Trinity Journal* 1 [1980] 67–68; Saucy, "Negative Case," 278). In conclusion: Paul does not want women to be in positions of authority in the church; teaching is one way in which authority is exercised in the church. This agrees with the same pattern noted in vv 9–10; the principles of modesty and dress appropriate to one's character find specific application in the proper adornment of hair. It may be added as a hermeneutical observation that the specificity of the application does not relegate the principle to the halls of cultural relativity.

13 Ἀδὰμ γὰρ πρῶτος ἐπλάσθη, εἶτα Εὕα, "For Adam was created first, then Eve." Having stated his rule for the participation of women in church leadership, Paul now gives a reason, possibly two, why his rule is valid: Gen 2 states that Adam was created first, and then Eve. For Paul, this indicates that God intended male authority. The specific application of this principle is that the Ephesian women should not try to reverse the created order by being in authority over men. The emphasis on temporal priority is brought out by the πρῶτος ... εἶτα, "first ... then," combination. This is somewhat the same argument as in 1 Cor 11:8–9 where Paul says "for man was not made from woman, but woman from man. Neither was man created for woman, but woman for man" (although Paul clarifies himself later by stating that men are not independent of women [vv 11–12]).

Paul's emphasis is built on his understanding of the Gen 2 account, that God created Eve from Adam's rib (vv 21–23) to be his "helper" (vv 18, 20; RSV), uniquely different from the rest of creation and named by Adam (vv 19–20, 23). Paul is not stating a general principal concerning the order of creation; he is explaining his understanding of the relationship between Adam and Eve as expressed in Gen 2. Some speak of this verse in terms of primogeniture, the firstborn (in this case, first-formed) receiving the responsibility of leadership in the family (Hurley, *Biblical Perspective*, 207; Stott, 79–80; cf. doctrine applied to Christ in Col 1:15–18).

That Gen 2 provides the historical and theological backdrop of v 13 explains Paul's use of πλάσσειν, which means "to form, mold" (BAGD, 666). While it has a wider semantic range than κτίζειν, "to create, make," it has sufficient overlap in describing the creative work of God, specifically in Gen 2:7, 8, 15, 19, and is used in other writings that speak of God's creative works (references in BAGD, 666). (Gen 1:26–27 uses ποιεῖν, "to do, make," not κτίζειν.) While πλάσσειν can be used in a wide variety of contexts such as education (Plato *Rep.* 377c; *Laws* 671c) or the manufacture of objects (e.g., Rom 9:20), the vast majority of uses in the LXX are of God's creative works (H. Braun, *TDNT* 6:256–58), utilizing the imagery of a potter (יֹצֵר *yōṣēr*, BDB, 427–28). That Paul uses πλάσσειν elsewhere only in Rom 9:20, where he is quoting Isa 29:16, shows that πλάσσειν is not a usual word for him (he uses κτίζειν ten times), and its use here signals dependence on Gen 2.

Paul does not say Adam was without guilt; he says he was not deceived. Gen 3 pictures Adam standing by and watching Eve being deceived, and then following in sin.

Unfortunately, much of the interpretation of v 14 has influenced the reading of v 13. While the issue of the curse is raised in v 14, v 13 refers to the period before the curse and indicates God's original intention. It is this "good" (Gen 1:4, 10, 12, 18, 21, 25), "very good" (Gen 1:31) creation to which Paul appeals (Jeremias, 19; Clark, *Man and Woman*, 191; Foh, *Women*, 127; Moo, *Trinity Journal* 1 [1980] 68; Hurley, *Biblical Perspective*, 205; Fung, "Ministry," 201; Roloff, 138; Knight, 142–43). While some find v 13 offensive or claim its meaning is unclear or illogical (Hanson, [1983] 72; Scholer, "1 Timothy 2:9–15," 208–13; Keener, *Paul, Women, and Wives*, 116), the history of the church suggests that its meaning is relatively straightforward. Even many of the more critical interpreters agree on its clarity (cf. Oberlinner), even though they disagree with Paul's logic and conclusions (e.g., Jewett, *Man as Male and Female*, 116, 126).

One question concerns the specific meaning of the conjunction γάρ, "for." There is a rather infrequent use of this word in which the clause introduced by γάρ gives not a reason for the preceding statement (illative use) but an illustration or example. If this is the use of γάρ here, then Paul has not grounded his demand in the order of creation but has appealed to Gen 2 as an illustration of what happens when women teach men (Payne, *Trinity Journal* 2 [1981] 176; Scholer, "1 Timothy 2:9–15," 208; Padgett, *Int* 41 [1987] 25; Witherington, *Earliest Churches*, 122; Gritz, *Paul, Women Teachers, and the Mother Goddess*, 136). Mickelsen comments, "The meaning here would simply mean that Eve was being used as an illustration of a woman who was deceived by Satan—as other women at Ephesus were being deceived by Satan" ("Egalitarian View," 203).

The most frequent use of γάρ is to express cause or reason (cf. Zerwick, §§472–77; BAGD, 151–52). It occurs thirty-three times in the PE; and of those, thirty express cause (1 Tim 2:5; 4:5, 8, 10 [which looks forward to the following clause], 16; 5:4, 11, 15; 6:7 [which looks back not to v 6 but to the previous description of the opponents, giving the reason that their thirst for money is wrong], 10; 2 Tim 1:7, 12; 2:7 [in which the γάρ clause gives both the reason that Timothy should reflect on what Paul is saying and the promised results of that reflection], 13, 16; 3:2 [in which the γάρ clause does not merely spell out the specifics of the claim in v 1, which is the title for that particular discussion, but validates its claim by giving the reasons that the last days will be a time of stress], 6, 9; 4:3, 6, 10, 11, 15; Titus 1:7 [where the γάρ clause gives the reason that a bishop must have certain personal qualities], 10; 2:11; 3:3, 9, 12; cf. Moo, *Trinity Journal* 2 [1981] 202–3). Apart from our present passage, only two of the passages in the PE appear to illustrate a weakened use of γάρ, expressing not cause but continuation or result (cf. the force of δέ, "and, but," and the variant readings in Rom 14:5; Gal 1:11; etc.; BAGD, 152). 1 Tim 3:13 gives the result of deacons serving well (although it can be seen as a reason). 2 Tim 2:11 connects the formula "this is a faithful saying" to the saying itself.

BAGD (152) lists the fourteen references in Paul in which γάρ is not used to describe cause or reason (Rom 1:18; 2:25; 4:3; 9:5, 7; 12:3; 14:5; 1 Cor 10:1; 2 Cor 1:12; 10:12; 11:5; Gal 1:11; 5:13; 1 Tim 2:5), but this interpretation is debatable in seven of these verses. Rom 1:18 gives the reason that righteousness is through faith (cf. Cranfield, *Romans* 1:106–8). Rom 4:3 gives the reason that Abraham could not boast before God. 1 Cor 10:1 gives the reason that Paul does not relax in his Christian perseverance (cf. Morris, *First Epistle of Paul to the Corinthians*, 140). 2 Cor 11:5 links this paragraph with the preceding (Martin, *2 Corinthians*, 342), giving the reason that Paul is skilled in knowledge (v 6) and therefore why the Corinthians should not listen to other gospels which, presumably, are being taught by other self-styled apostles or by those appealing to the apostles in Jerusalem. If γάρ is the preferred reading in Gal 1:11, then γάρ links vv 11–12 with vv 6–9 as a justification of Paul's previous claims (Burton, *Galatians*, 35). Gal 5:13 is a transitional verse, giving a reason that Paul wishes the Judaizers would mutilate themselves (5:12; Burton, *Galatians*, 291). 1 Tim 2:5 gives one of three reasons that the Ephesian church should pray for all people. While there perhaps are other examples in Paul of γάρ used in a weakened sense, it is interesting that out of the 454 uses of γάρ by Paul, BAGD lists only 7 that actually illustrate the weakened sense, and in each case the context gives a clue that the use is not fully illative. The illustrative use of γάρ in 1 Tim 2:13 is certainly possible, but it would be another rare case. Robertson (*Grammar*, 1190–91) is apparently the only major grammarian that does not see the illative use as primary for γάρ (so Moo, *Trinity Journal* 2 [1981] 203). Although οὐκ ἐπιτρέπω, "I do not permit," in 2:12 is indicative, it carries the force of an imperative. In Paul an imperative followed by γάρ in the same sentence is found nine times (Rom 12:19; 14:3; 1 Cor 7:9; 15:34; Eph 5:8–9; Col 3:20; 2 Tim 4:11, 15; Titus 3:12). In every other case, the clause introduced by γάρ gives the reason for the imperative. Moo comments, "In the Pastorals alone, for instance, an imperative or imperatival idea is followed 21 times by a clause introduced with γάρ— and in each case the causal idea appears to be required" (*Trinity Journal* 2 [1981] 203, citing 1 Tim 3:13 [?]; 4:5, 8, 16; 5:4, 11, 15; 2 Tim 1:7; 2:7, 16; 3:6; 4:3, 6, 10, 11, 15; Titus 1:10; 2:11 [?]; 3:3, 9, 12).

All of this evidence is overwhelming in support of reading the γάρ of 1 Tim 2:13 as introducing a reason for Paul's previous statement. In Paul's general usage, this is his primary definition; in the other passages that use the illustrative meaning, there is clear contextual evidence that γάρ is not illative. In the PE themselves, out of the thirty-three occurrences of γάρ only two are weakened to the equivalent of δέ, "and, but," and one of those (2 Tim 2:11) introduces a saying. In 1 Tim 2:13 there is no contextual evidence that Paul intends the unusual weakened force of γάρ. The most natural reading and the most lexically supported conclusion is that here γάρ is not illustrative but gives a reason (illative) that v 12 is true. (If v 14 is also a reason that v 12 is true, then this as well would suggest that v 13 is a reason and not an illustration; see below.)

But if for the sake of argument one were to concede the illustrative use of γάρ, it remains to be seen how v 13 provides an illustration (e.g., see Padgett's attempt to create a typology of Adam and the teachers as spiritually older and hence formed first [*Int* 41 (1987) 26–27]). How does Adam's prior creation illustrate that women may not teach? While it is somewhat easier to see v 14b as providing an illustration, it is especially difficult to see v 14a in this way. It is perhaps instructive that Payne argues that γάρ is explanatory, and yet in his ensuing discussion he omits mention of v 13 and v 14a (*Trinity Journal* 2 [1981] 176–77). This omission is the Achilles' heel of this position. The assumption of the flow of the text is that v 13 supports Paul's previous statement (cf. Moo, *Trinity Journal* 2 [1982] 203).

Jewett argues that since the animals were created before Adam, then by Paul's logic (or lack of it) only the animals should teach (*Man as Male and Female*, 119–27; cf. L. T. Johnson, 141). Jewett concludes that Paul is simply wrong; he says that Gen 1 asserts the full equality of men and women, but Paul interpreted Gen 2 in isolation from Gen 1, accepting "the traditional rabbinic understanding of that narrative whereby the order of their creation is made to yield the primacy of man. Is this rabbinic understanding of Genesis 2:18f. correct? We do not think that it is" (*Man as Male and Female*, 119; similar statements in H. Braun, *TDNT* 6:261; cf. L. T. Johnson, 135–36, 141, who says that "like most men in similar situations, Paul moves to defend male prerogatives" [140]; cf. also Hoover, *Brethren Life and Thought* 22 [1977] 163–65; Catholic Biblical Association of America, *CBQ* 41 [1979] 612; H. van der Meer, *Women Priests in the Catholic Church? A Theological-Historical Investigation* [Philadelphia: Temple UP, 1973] 29). In arguing that "derivation does not entail subordination," Jewett discusses man's creation from the ground:

> Who would argue that the man is subordinate to the ground because taken from it? . . . So far as temporal priority is concerned, according to the first creation narrative animals were created before Man, yet this does not imply their superior worth over Man. Quite the reverse: Man, who is last, is the crown of creation and has dominion over the creatures. If one were to infer anything from the fact that the woman was created after the man, it should be, in the light of the first creation narrative, that the woman is superior to the man. (126–27)

But the text never claims that Paul is stating an axiomatic truth that applies to the sequence of creation (e.g., the relationship of people to animals or of animals to the ground). Paul says Adam was created before Eve; he is retelling the Gen 2 account, and he sees significance in the fact that Adam was created before Eve and presumably in the rest of the details of the account. If Paul was thinking of primogeniture, then it is easy to point out, as Hurley does, that "the laws of primogeniture apply to humans born in a home. They do not apply in such a way as to confuse the first animal with the first son!" (*Biblical Perspective*, 208). Jewett rightly sees that Paul's comments here are based on Gen 2, not Gen 1, where God says "It is not good that the man should be alone; I will make a helper fit for him" (Gen 2:18); cf. Gen 2:20: "For the man there was not found a helper fit for him" (also vv 22–23). Only Gen 2 speaks of Adam being created first (2:7, 18–25). As in 1 Tim 2:13, Gen 2 uses πλάσσειν, "to form, mold" (vv 7, 8, 15, 19), and not ποιεῖν, "to do, make," as in Gen 1:26–27.

Many who do not see vv 13–14 as reasons for vv 11–12 have offered other possible interpretations (of necessity they view γάρ and vv 13–14 as illustrative). A general criticism of all of these interpretations is that they do not find support in the text.

(1) Some argue that Paul placed limitations on women because the women lacked education, specifically theological training (Spencer, *JETS* 17 [1974] 218–19; Bilezikian, *Beyond Sex Roles*, 179; Padgett, *Int* 41 [1987] 24; Keener, *Paul, Women, and Wives*, 107–8, 111–12), and suggest that once the women had had opportunity to be educated Paul would have allowed them to teach men (cf. *Comment* on v 12 regarding μανθανέτω, "should learn"). But the text does not say this, and it would have been relatively easy for Paul to have said so if this had been his intent. If Paul's concern were education, one would expect him to forbid all uneducated people to teach, men and women. As Schreiner observes, "The serpent deceived Eve by promising her that she could function as a god, independent of the one true God (Gen. 3:4–6). Eve was deceived not because she had an intellectual deficiency, but because of a moral failing" ("Interpretation of 1 Timothy 2:9–15," 143).

Keener comments, "Given the pressures the church was facing at this point, women who tried to hold a teaching office could thus contribute to outsiders gaining a negative impression of Christianity" (*Paul, Women, and Wives*, 111). But if this was really Paul's motivation, then to be consistent with this principle, any teaching that could cause offense to the secular world would have to be removed from Paul's teaching, including central doctrines such as the offense of the cross, teaching that Keener would never agree to removing (cf. the discussion of Padgett's similar position in the *Explanation* on Titus 2:1–10).

Some who hold to this position argue that the issue in the Garden was also one of education: Eve had not been taught God's command, and her deception illustrates the danger of untrained people taking a leadership role. Yet when Eve entered into discussion with the serpent, she did know the rule even if she (or Adam?) enlarged it. 1 Tim 2:14 also says that she was deceived, not that she acted in ignorance. Schreiner emphasizes that this argument comes back on its head: if the point of the Garden story is that Eve was not properly taught by Adam, then why would Paul cite it in the first place? If Paul was trying to teach that the untrained women in Ephesus should not teach until they learn, then why would he cite a passage showing that Adam (corresponding to the Ephesian men who teach) was unable to teach? Schreiner concludes, "It does not make sense to say that women were deceived because they lacked knowledge. Such a view would pin the blame on Adam as a teacher, not Eve. If such were Paul's understanding of the events associated with the fall, his admonition that men should teach women (even temporarily) on the basis of the Genesis narrative would be incoherent" ("Interpretation of 1 Timothy 2:9–15," 142).

(2) Others argue that Paul is prohibiting women from teaching error. This interpretation has already been discussed above (see *Comment* on v 12). Unless all women, and only women, were deceived, this view is not persuasive.

(3) Some propose an underlying principle other than male leadership as a background for the text. Spencer suggests that "the norm which Paul wished to foster was liberation" (*JETS* 17 [1974] 220), but this cannot come from a text dominated by the command "I do not *permit*" (v 12). Doriani shows how modern is the cry for liberation in contrast to the older cry for order, duties, and responsibilities ("History of the Interpretation of 1 Timothy 2," 218–20). Padgett (*Int* 41 [1987] 24) says the principle is the desire for the church to be at peace, citing

v 2 (which is connected to our passage through the common use of the cognate for ἡσυχία, "quietness"). Padgett and others also connect the learning in v 11 with v 4 ("to come into a knowledge of [the] truth") as a principle at work in Paul's mind.

(4) Others such as Kroeger and Kroeger and Gritz argue that Ephesus was home to an ancient feminism that taught the priority of Eve, specifically that Eve taught Adam, and this provides the backdrop for Paul's limiting instructions. Many writers are confident that they can reconstruct a detailed description of the Ephesian heresy based on hints in the text and secular descriptions of Ephesus. Kroeger and Kroeger see a Jewish-Gnostic belief combined with a devotion to Artemis, the patron goddess of Ephesus, as the source of the heresy (*I Suffer Not a Woman,* esp. 42–43, 50–52, 59–66, 70–74, 93, 105–13). From this reconstruction it is argued that Ephesus was distinctive in the ancient world for being "a bastion and bulwark of women's rights" (so Barth, *Ephesians* 2:661). As this attitude infiltrated the Ephesian church, women were actively teaching this heresy. Gritz comments, "In a religious environment saturated with the 'feminist principle' due to the Artemis cult, attitudes of female exaltation or superiority existed. Verse 13 attempts to correct such an emphasis" (*Paul, Women Teachers, and the Mother Goddess,* 308). If this was the case, then Paul's instructions in vv 11–15 were directed toward this specific Ephesian problem with no implication outside of Ephesus. The work of Kroeger and Kroeger has been extensively criticized (Yarbrough, *Presbyterion* 18 (1992) 25–33; Wolters, *CTJ* 28 (1993) 208–13; Baugh, *WTJ* 56 (1994) 153–71). Baugh especially has shown that the Kroeger and Kroeger reconstruction of Ephesus is significantly flawed and that Ephesus was a somewhat normal ancient city, even with the great temple of Artemis ("Foreign World," esp. 49–50). It was thoroughly Greek, yet with a strong Roman influence. The secular culture praised feminine modesty and faithfulness. Ephesus was not a unique, feminist society. Oberlinner likewise denies the influence of the Artemis cult, but for the reason that he sees the historical setting of the PE as totally fictitious (100). While there are some clear statements and hints throughout the PE regarding the precise nature of the Ephesian heresy, the overall picture is foggy in many places (cf. *Introduction,* "The Ephesian Heresy"; Harris, *JBL* 92 [1973] 550), and caution is appropriate in being too specific in one's reconstruction of the heresy.

These criticisms of alternative interpretations reinforce the view that v 13 reads most naturally as Paul's reason for believing that vv 11–12 are true.

14 καὶ Ἀδὰμ οὐκ ἠπατήθη, ἡ δὲ γυνὴ ἐξαπατηθεῖσα ἐν παραβάσει γέγονεν, "And Adam was not deceived, but the woman, having been deceived, has come into transgression." While v 14 may be difficult to interpret, a few major points are clear. (1) The emphasis of the verse is on deception: Adam was not deceived; Eve was deceived (Gen 3:1–7, 12; cf. Str-B 3:646). Whatever specific interpretation is adopted, this point should come through clearly. (2) V 14 is parallel to v 13. In both, Adam is the subject of the verb and is emphatically listed at the beginning of the sentence. In both, Adam plays the dominant role: he was created first; he was not deceived (contra Oberlinner, 99, who says the only interest of v 14 is in Eve's seduction). (3) In some way, Adam and Eve are parallel to the Ephesian men and women; otherwise vv 13–15 would be irrelevant and it would be difficult to explain the shift in v 15 from the sin of the singular Εὕα, "Eve," in the Garden to the salvation of the plural women (ἐὰν μείνωσιν, "if they remain") in Ephesus. Adam and Eve's behavior demonstrates for Paul something about the respective roles for the

Ephesian men and women. (4) Gen 3 provides the background for Paul's instructions and imagery in v 14, just as Gen 2 provides the backdrop for v 13. In saying Eve was deceived, Paul is repeating Eve's own confession in Gen 3:13. While many feel Paul is being unfair to Eve, it is helpful to remember that what he says is almost inconsequential compared to how she was treated in rabbinic circles (cf. Keener, *Paul, Women, and Wives*, 114–15).

Historically, v 14 has been viewed as the second reason that vv 11–12 are true. Not only was Eve created second (v 13), but she was deceived (v 14). This is the most natural reading of the verse, primarily because its syntax so closely parallels that of v 13: "Adam was created first, and then Eve; and Adam was not deceived, but the woman was." While καί, "and," can have a variety of meanings, the parallel structure of the verses suggests that it is connecting a second idea that functions similarly to the first idea. The major argument of many against this interpretation is that v 14 does not seem to make sense as a reason. There are three basic interpretations with a variety of opinions within each.

(1) Historically, v 14 has been understood as teaching something about the nature of women in general (cf. Doriani, "History of the Interpretation of 1 Timothy 2," 215–69), as making an ontological distinction. V 14 is held to assert that men and women are equal before God, but God intended different roles for each. Just as Eve was deceived and Adam was not, so also the Ephesian women were more open to deception than the Ephesian men; therefore, the authority in the Ephesian church rested on the male leaders. To that extent there is a typological relationship between Eve and the Ephesian women (cf. Paul's use of Abraham, Hagar, and Sarah [Gal 4:21–31], Israel [1 Cor 10:1–13], Adam [1 Cor 15:22; Rom 5:12–14], and Eve [2 Cor 11:3]). This gives full force to the perfect-tense ἐν παραβάσει γέγονεν, "has come into transgression," which looks at the present consequences of a past action. It also explains the shift between the singular Eve sinning in the past (v 14) and the plural Ephesian women being saved in the present (v 15). Oberlinner (99) goes so far as to suggest that the theology of Sir 25:24 had become established by this time (i.e., that sin originated with Eve, not Adam), and that the author of the PE is in agreement.

Those who intrepret the text in this way differ on what is meant by women being more open to deception. Doriani subdivides the historic position into the Scotist view (God decreed male headship even though men are not better suited for leadership), the Thomist view (women are weaker and less rational than men [Doriani's wording]), and the Congruent Creation view, which teaches that God "sovereignly chose to order [creation] through male headship, a headship given to them without a view to any merit on their part. Yet God established a coherence or congruence between his decree and his creation. Congruence thinkers affirm that God shaped the minds, proclivities and perhaps even the bodies of humans to reflect his decree. . . . Women are as capable as men, but have other interests, and have developed their capacities in different directions" ("History of the Interpretation of 1 Timothy 2," 265, cf. 264–69). Doriani asserts, "Throughout the ages the church has preferred to affirm that God has engraved reflections of his sovereign decree into human nature. This has had an ugly side, in denigrations of woman's mind and character. But we can also recognize variety in human nature, without labeling anything inferior or superior" ("History of the Interpretation of 1 Timothy 2," 267).

Unfortunately, many have held that this means women are intellectually inferior to men. This cannot be or Paul would never have encouraged women to teach children (2 Tim 3:15) and younger women (Titus 2:3–4). Doriani prefers to speak of men and women having different interests ("History of the Interpretation of 1 Timothy 2," 264–69). Schreiner also talks about "different inclinations" ("Interpretation of 1 Timothy 2:9–15," 145), allowing for the dangers of stereotyping and "misogynistic implications." He says that what concerns Paul "are the consequences of allowing women in the authoritative teaching office, for their gentler and kinder nature inhibits them from excluding people from doctrinal error" (145). Later he says, "Women are less likely to perceive the need to take a stand on doctrinal non-negotiables since they prize harmonious relationships more than men do" (153), and then once again qualifies himself because of the abuse that tends to be associated with his understanding of Paul: "It must be said again that this does not mean that women are inferior to men. Men and women have *different* weaknesses, and that is why there are different roles. Men who value accuracy and objectivity can easily fall into the error of creating divisions where none should exist and become hypercritical. They should learn from the women in the church in this regard!" (153 n. 227).

Today there is, of course, strong opposition to seeing Paul making an ontological statement about the essential nature of women. (a) Many claim that the statement simply is not true: "The implications are disturbing and contradict the reality of the whole of biblical teaching, church history and human experience" (Scholer, "1 Timothy 2:9–15," 212). (b) They argue that if women are inherently more gullible, then they should not be allowed to teach anyone, especially children, who are the most gullible (cf. Titus 2:3; 2 Tim 1:5; 3:15). (c) Paul's acceptance of Priscilla and her husband may suggest she was a capable teacher, thus providing an example that breaks the rule. (d) If v 14 is teaching something about the nature of Eve that corresponds to the nature of the Ephesian women, then by implication it is teaching something about the nature of Adam that corresponds to the nature of the Ephesian men. If Ephesian women may not teach because Eve was deceived, would it not follow that the Ephesian men may not teach because Adam sinned knowingly, without the excuse of deception (Gen 3:12, 17)? Since this is senseless, either v 14 is not making an ontological statement, or there is not an ontological connection between Adam and Eve and their Ephesian counterparts (cf. Schreiner's discussion, "Interpretation of 1 Timothy 2," 142–43).

(2) The second interpretation says that v 14 makes no ontological statement about women and yet does support vv 11–12. Most in this camp see v 14 as making a statement about what happens when roles are interchanged and women take leadership. (a) Barnett (*EvQ* 61 [1989] 234) notes that Paul has just finished saying that Adam was created first and then Eve. In a sentence whose structure closely parallels the preceding (see above), Paul carries over the idea of "first" and says that Adam was not deceived (first) but Eve was. The logical question to ask then is, why did Adam receive the blame? Why did God seek him out first (Gen 3:9)? Why did Paul lay the blame at Adam's feet (Rom 5:12–21) and not at Eve's (cf. Sir 25:24)? One answer is male headship. Paul would be arguing that even though Adam did not sin first, he was still held responsible for the entrance of sin into the world. This would be convincing proof for Paul that God intended male headship. The weakness in this argument is that v 14 does not say "first" (so Harris, *EvQ* 62 [1990] 346). Yet vv 13–14 are parallel structurally, and some may be willing to make this assumption. It explains why Paul says Adam was not deceived when deception

seems to be part of all sin (although the emphasis here is on the primary reasons for the Garden sins—Adam knew what he was doing—and not a theological discussion of the nature of sin). It does not necessitate that Timothy knew Paul's teaching on the subject of original sin because v 14 is built on Gen 3.

(b) Paul's reflection on Gen 3 teaches that God intended male leadership in the church, and just as the serpent and Eve usurped that order so also the Ephesian women were trying to change their roles. V 14 sees the Garden sin as an example of what happens when roles are changed. Moo comments,

> Verse 14, in conjunction with verse 13, is intended to remind the women at Ephesus that Eve was deceived by the serpent in the Garden (Genesis 3:13) precisely in taking the initiative over the man whom God had given to be with her and to care for her. In the same way, if the women at the church at Ephesus proclaim their independence from the men of the church, refusing to learn "in quietness and full submission" (verse 11), seeking roles that have been given to men in the church (verse 12), they will make the same mistake Eve made and bring similar disaster on themselves and the church. ("What Does It Mean?" 190; cf. Stott, 80–81; Towner, 72–73)

Schreiner suggests this as a possibility (although he settles on the first position):

> In approaching Eve, then, the serpent subverted the pattern of male leadership and interacted only with Eve during the temptation. Adam was present throughout and did not intervene. The Genesis temptation, therefore, is a parable of what happens when male leadership is abrogated [citing similar suggestions by Fung, "Ministry," 202]. Eve took the initiative in responding to the serpent, and Adam let her do so. Thus the appeal to Genesis 3 serves as a reminder of what happens when God's ordained pattern is undermined. ("Interpretation of 1 Timothy 2:9–15," 145)

The analogy is that just as Eve listened to the snake and was deceived, so also the Ephesian women are listening to demonic teaching (1 Tim 4:1) and are deceived.

(c) Hurley looks more to the issue of preparation:

> Could it be that his point in verse 14 is that Adam was the one appointed by God to exercise religious headship, and that he was the one prepared by God to do so? On this basis there is no need to generalize to the preparation of other women to make religious decisions, as the divine assignment of headship in religious affairs to the husband is the point in view. Paul's point might then be paraphrased, "The man, upon whom lay responsibility for leadership in the home and in religious matters, was prepared by God to discern the serpent's lies. The woman was not appointed religious leader and was not prepared to discern them. She was taken in. Christian worship involves re-establishing the creational pattern with men faithfully teaching God's truth and women receptively listening." (*Biblical Perspective*, 216)

Moo, in his interaction with Payne in 1981 (prior to his view as quoted above), states, "The difficulties with viewing v 14 as a statement about the nature of women are real. I am now inclined to see the reference as a means of suggesting the *difference* between Adam and Eve in the fall—he sinned openly; she was deceived. With this in mind, Paul may be seeking to suggest the need to restore the pre-fall situation in which the man bears responsibility for religious teaching" (*Trinity Journal* 2 [1981] 204, citing Hurley).

There are several perceived advantages to this approach. (a) For those struggling with viewing v 14 as making an ontological statement, it allows v 13 to stand as a reason. (b) It does not read into the text issues that are not explicitly there, such as the false teachers teaching error, etc. (see the third interpretation below). All these variations allow for an ontological equality but an "economic or functional subordination" (Foh, *Women*, 260). However, this position can be criticized. (a) It removes the parallel structure with v 13. (b) It misses the emphasis of the verse: Adam was not deceived. If the verse only said that Eve was deceived (v 14b), then this understanding would have more weight; but the verse's thrust is on the fact that Adam was not deceived, but Eve was. (c) Doriani adds: "Why do traditionalists expect 'similar disasters' [citing Moo] to occur if Eve in no way typifies women? If women have no more propensity toward doctrinal error than men, why should the church expect disaster if roles reverse?" ("History of the Interpretation of 1 Timothy 2," 261). He continues: "Does disaster occur purely because the wrong person leads? Surely that leader has to make an erroneous decision! Do Scotists believe women possess sound judgment until they usurp leadership, when it suddenly flees?" ("History of the Interpretation of 1 Timothy 2," 266–67).

(3) The third basic interpretation of v 14 sees no ontological statement about women being made, nor does it see a suggestion that there are different roles for men and women (cf. the works by Payne, Fee, Scholer, Keener, and Kroeger and Kroeger).

(a) Keener comments, "Paul intends to connect Eve's later creation to why she was deceived: she was not present when God gave the commandment, and thus was dependent on Adam for the teaching [citing Kaiser, *Exegetical Theology*, 120; Spencer, *Beyond the Curse*, 88–98]. In other words, she was inadequately educated— like the women in the Ephesian church" (*Paul, Women, and Wives*, 116). Scholer adds,

> 1 Timothy 2:13–14 should be understood as an explanatory rationale for verses 11–12 that uses the data from Genesis 2–3 selectively to suit the needs of the argument at hand. The women who were falling prey to the false teachers in Ephesus were being deceived and were transgressing as Eve did. The rationale using Eve's deception in verse 14 is, therefore, ad hoc and occasional and is no more a 'timeless' comment about women than the use of the same point in 2 Corinthians 11:3. In both cases, Paul was warning against false teachers and false teaching. ("1 Timothy 2:9–15," 211)

If vv 13–14 read "for Adam was created first, then Eve, *and then* Eve was deceived," Keener's position would be stronger. But of necessity he must make v 14a ("Adam was not deceived") parenthetically irrelevant and insert a connective implying consequence ("then"). (But even if this were the case, the text still says nothing about teaching or education.) V 14a, by way of its emphatic position and parallel with v 13, cannot be dismissed without altering what Paul says. Keener's reconstruction is also based on his oft repeated—but unsubstantiated, except from his general understanding of the culture—conclusion that the issue in Ephesus is the women's lack of education in the gospel: "If Paul does not want the women to teach in some sense, it is not because they are women, but because they are unlearned" (*Paul, Women, and Wives*, 120). However, as far as Gen 3:2–3 is concerned, Eve claims to have received sufficient instruction (ultimately) from God ("but God said" [Gen

3:3]; even the snake knew God's instructions [Gen 3:1]) to avoid deception and sin. The serpent did not question Eve's understanding of God's command; it questioned the goodness of God by calling him a liar. Scholer's contention that Paul uses the OT selectively appears especially specious; the OT is always used selectively in the NT (cf. Moo, "What Does It Mean?" 498 n. 32).

(b) Spencer states:

> The women of Ephesus were reminiscent of the woman (Eve) in Eden. The Ephesian women were learning and teaching a body of heretical beliefs to others in an authoritative manner, while submitting themselves to unorthodox teachers. Eve too had in her time been deceived into believing certain false teachings: "If she touched the fruit of the tree of knowledge of good and evil, she would become like God yet she would not die" (Gen. 3:3–4). God never had forbidden touching the fruit, only eating it. Moreover, Eve did die. Eve authoritatively taught these teachings to Adam. (*Beyond the Curse*, 91; cf. Payne, *Trinity Journal* 2 [1981] 177)

She concludes, "When women anywhere, including Ephesus, grow beyond a resemblance to Eve in this respect, then the analogy is no longer valid" (*Beyond the Curse*, 94). Spencer's position is open to some of the same criticism as is Keener's. The parallel structure between v 13 and v 14 as well as the emphatic teaching of Adam's prior creation and lack of deception is not accounted for (see the previous critique of Payne's omission on vv 13–14a). The PE name only male teachers, not the single female teacher as Spencer repeatedly suggests. And the expansion of the original command, from not eating to not touching, is not stated by the serpent; it is not part of the lie he is telling Eve.

(c) Kroeger and Kroeger paint a picture of the influence of "male-rejecting Amazons," the cult of Artemis, Gnostic myths that teach that women are the originators of man (cf. C. C. Kroeger, "1 Timothy 2:12," 234; R. C. and C. C. Kroeger, *I Suffer Not a Woman*, 105–13) and the universe, and the role of the serpent in Ophitism. From this C. C. Kroeger concludes that αὐθεντεῖν in v 12 means "'I do not allow a woman to teach nor to represent herself as the originator or source of man.' This then might be a prohibition against a woman teaching a mythology similar to that of the Gnostics in which Eve predated Adam and was his creator. Certain Gnostic myths also included the notion that Adam, who had been deluded, was liberated by the Gnosis of his more enlightened spouse" (C. C. Kroeger, "1 Timothy 2:12," 232). Vv 13–14 then become a specific theological refutation of what Kroeger proposes was being taught by the Artemis-influenced women. Adam was created first, not Eve; Eve did not teach Adam but was deceived and was disobedient to God (237; also Kroeger and Kroeger, *I Suffer Not a Woman*, 117–25; Barron, *JETS* 33 [1990] 454–55).

C. C. Kroeger's position relies heavily on late parallels that often cannot be shown to predate the Ephesian situation. In his critique, Liefeld says,

> Kroeger proposes a theory that involves a projection backward from the fourth-century Nag Hammadi materials. Kroeger recognizes the problem and seeks to be cautious. Nevertheless, the vivid descriptions can easily captivate the nonspecialist who does not realize how tenuous their relationship to the church at Ephesus is. . . . The serpent motif was so common that we must not read too much into its appearance. Its presence in the Timothy passage is only an inference. Kroeger develops a network of phenomena without

carefully explaining how closely these items truly are to each other and to the text in 1 Timothy. ("Response," 247)

Keener also criticizes Kroeger's use of later Gnostic texts to define her proposed nascent gnosticism in the first century (*Paul, Women, and Wives,* 128 n. 98). As has been stated throughout this discussion, that some ancient sources appear to parallel Paul's discussion does not necessarily mean that Paul is addressing those parallels. Paul specifically states that the Ephesian myths are Jewish (Titus 1:14), which, allowing for gnostic influences in Hellenistic Judaism, speaks against a purely Gnostic heresy.

The Genesis account does not say that Eve *taught* anything. Even Chrysostom reads the idea of Eve teaching Adam into the text: "The woman taught once, and ruined all" ("Homily 9"; NPNF 13:436; cf. Spencer's statement above). However, once again it must be emphasized that this is not what the Genesis text says. It does not say Eve taught anything to Adam, or that she taught something that was false; it says that Eve was deceived and that she "gave." She did not have to teach him anything; he was standing there (see Liefeld's criticism in his response to Mickelsen ["Egalitarian," 220] and to Kroeger ["Response," 245]). In fact, if Eve was deceived, taught Adam, and he sinned, one would have to conclude that Adam was in fact deceived (by Eve's false teaching), which contradicts v 14a (so Hugenberger, *JETS* 35 [1992] 349–50).

(d) Fee compares vv 10–15 with Paul's discussion of widows in 5:11–15 and concludes:

> The point of vv. 13–14, therefore, is not primarily with the illustration from Genesis 2, about Adam's having been formed first—although that is clearly there and is not to be dismissed. What needs to be noted is that Paul does not elaborate that first point. He merely states it; its application can only be inferred. The second point, however, from Genesis 3, seems to be his real concern, since it receives an elaboration and leads directly to the conclusion in v. 15. Based on words of Eve in Genesis 3:13 ("the serpent *deceived* me, and I ate"), Paul states that Adam was *not* deceived (by the snake, that is), but rather it was the woman (note the change from Eve to "the woman"), who, having been deceived (by Satan is implied) fell into transgression. That is exactly the point of 5:15—such deception of woman by "Satan" has already been repeated in the church in Ephesus. *But,* Paul says in v. 15, there is still hope. She can be saved (eschatological salvation is ultimately in view, but in the context she shall be saved from her deception with its ultimate transgressions), provided she is first of all a woman of faith, love, and holiness. This, then, is the point of the whole—to rescue these women and the church from the clutches of the false teachers. Their rescue includes proper demeanor in dress, proper demeanor in the assembly (including learning in all quietness), and getting married and bearing children (one of the good works urged in v. 10, seen in light of 5:9–10). ("Issues in Evangelical Hermeneutics," 58–59)

Fee concludes, "All these instructions, including 2:11–12, were ad hoc responses to the waywardness of the young widows in Ephesus who had gone astray after Satan and were disrupting the church" ("Issues in Evangelical Hermeneutics," 61).

The weakness of Fee's position is that, despite his own caution, he does appear to dismiss the emphatic reference to Adam's lack of deception in v 14a, which parallels the emphatic reference to Adam's prior creation in v 13. Lack of elaboration may only mean that Paul thought that its meaning was clear (as is suggested by the church's history of consistent interpretation), and v 15 is usually read as a parenthetical correction of a possible misconception, not the conclusion. Fee does differ significantly from Kroeger in that he concludes "It is hard to deny that *this* text prohibits women teaching men in the Ephesian church." But he does continue, "But it is the unique text in the New Testament, and as we have seen, its reason for being is *not* to correct the rest of the New Testament, but to correct a very ad hoc problem in Ephesus" ("Issues in Evangelical Hermeneutics," 63–64). Of course, the same hermeneutical evaluation could be made of Gal 3:28.

(e) Others see v 14 more closely connected with v 15 than with v 13. Blomberg (*CTR* 2 [1988] 414) says that Paul has made what could be understood as two limiting statements: women may not teach authoritatively; Eve was created second, chronologically. Lest Paul be misunderstood, or perhaps through a desire to give back something to Eve and the Ephesian women, he wants to assert the relevance of Gen 3:15 and the inclusion of women in God's salvific plans. He therefore in v 14 continues to reflect on the imagery of Gen 2 begun in 1 Tim 2:13 and states that after her creation and despite her fall into sin, the woman will still be saved. This makes v 15 primary, and v 14 builds toward its assertion that "she will be saved." While this interpretation has some attractive elements, it does have some hurdles to clear. (i) Would vv 12–13 raise the concern for Eve's salvation in Paul's mind? (ii) Because this interpretation sees v 14 more closely connected with v 15 than with v 13, it misses the structural similarities between v 13 and v 14. (iii) It is not clear why v 14 starts with an emphatic negation of Adam's deception if the issue is the salvation of women.

A few final points may be made. V 14 does not say that Adam was sinless. Paul lays the transmission of sin at Adam's feet (cf. Rom 5:12–21) and not at Eve's even though she was the first to sin (in the stated chronology of Gen 3; yet if Adam was present, as the text probably implies, and said nothing, his sin of omission occurred at the same time as Eve's sin of commission). Eve was tricked. This does not mean that she was not responsible for her actions; she received the curse of increased pain in childbirth (Gen 3:16). It does mean, however, that the avenue through which sin worked in her was that of deception. ἀπατᾶν, "to deceive," occurs in the NT two other places (Eph 5:6; Jas 1:26). Its primary sense in the NT is to deceive into sin (A. Oepke, *TDNT* 1:384–85). BAGD (82) say that ἀπατᾶν can have sexual overtones in light of later Jewish speculation that sometimes saw the snake's seduction as sexual (cf. Dibelius-Conzelmann, 48; Holtz, 70; Houlden, 71–72; Hanson, [1983] 73; Roloff, 139). But it cannot be proven that Paul was thinking of this particular nuance since there is no indication in the context and the Jewish parallels postdate the NT (cf. Witherington, *Earliest Churches*, 123; Towner, *Goal*, 313–14 n. 78; Gritz, *Paul, Women Teachers, and the Mother Goddess*, 139). The second verb referring to deception is the intensified compound ἐξαπατᾶν, "to deceive," which occurs elsewhere in the NT four times (Rom 7:11; 16:18; 2 Cor 11:3 [in which Paul speaks of the serpent's deception of Eve]; 2 Thess 2:3) and does not mean "sexual seduction" (especially 2 Cor 11:3). The shift from the simple to compound form may be nothing more than a stylistic variation, and yet a slight emphasis does fit the context: Adam was not deceived, but Eve completely fell prey to the deceiving snake. The perfect-tense γέγονεν, "has come," makes the connection between the historical example and the consequence that will follow in v 15. Even though Eve was deceived and sinned, at the time Paul is writing there is a means of salvation (v 15). παραβάσει, "transgression," is an important word as it defines the context of v 15 and Paul's comment about women's salvation.

15 σωθήσεται δὲ διὰ τῆς τεκνογονίας, ἐὰν μείνωσιν ἐν πίστει καὶ ἀγάπῃ καὶ ἁγιασμῷ μετὰ σωφροσύνης, "But she will be saved through childbearing, if they remain in faith and love and holiness, with modesty." Paul has finished saying that Eve was deceived and γέγονεν, "has come," into transgression, the verb tense (γέγονεν—perfect) emphasizing the continuing effect of her past act. Because Paul is creating an analogy/typology between Eve and the women in Ephesus, it is evidently important that he not leave the discussion on this note. Therefore v 15 shows that what Eve did, although it had consequences, has been dealt with, and both Eve and all women can be saved. As such v 15 is a qualification of v 14 (so most; cf. Clark, *Man and Woman*, 207; Gritz, *Paul, Women Teachers, and the Mother Goddess*, 141; Porter, *JSNT* 4 [1993] 93); it is *not* "clearly the climactic resolution of the whole unit" (contra Scholer, "1 Timothy 2:9–15," 196). Yet it is tempting to tie v 15 to vv 1–7, whose primary purpose is to assert the universal offer of salvation to all, contrary to what is being taught by the law-oriented exclusive opponents (1:8–11); so perhaps v 15 is more than a qualification. Were the opponents teaching that unless the Ephesian women gave up conventional female roles they could not be saved? L. T. Johnson (133) suggests that here Paul may be recasting the opponents' thought; this may account for its unusualness (cf. also Towner, 80). Paul closes with mention of the same topic with which he began—modesty (vv 9, 15). V 15 is certainly one of the strangest verses in the NT. Comments like Mickelsen's, "the advocates of male dominance generally *ignore* verse 15" ("Egalitarian View," 204; italics mine), are unhelpful (cf. her comments about "ignoring" in the *Comment* on v 9, "Egalitarian View," 203, and Culver's critique, "Traditional View," 209).

Throughout the paragraph Paul has been shifting back and forth between the Ephesian women and Eve in the Garden, between the plural and the singular, and between present, past, and future tenses. Although this is confusing at first, once the logic of Paul's argument is seen, the shifts make good sense. He begins by addressing the men and women (plural; present tense) in Ephesus and how they are to pray (v 8) and dress (vv 9–10). He then states a general principle, shifting into the singular for woman and man (vv 11–12). In order to give this principle scriptural backing, Paul shifts to talking about the singular Adam and Eve (vv 13–14; aorist tense). Finally, in order that his last statement not be misunderstood, he shifts back to the present tense in making the necessary qualification (v 15). But this final shift takes place in two steps. In the first half of the verse Paul is discussing the singular Eve (σωθήσεται, "she will be saved"; future tense, from the time perspective of Eve). However, he is discussing Eve not in isolation but as the representative of the Ephesian women. Therefore, Paul shifts to the plural (present tense) in the following clause, ἐὰν μείνωσιν, "if they remain," in order to make this clear. Paul is also moving through the story in Genesis, from human creation (2:4–25) to Eve's and Adam's sin (3:1–7) and then to their promised salvation (3:15). Because the analogy between Eve and the Ephesian women is complex, the grammar of the argument becomes complex; but Paul is saying that there is an analogy or typological connection between Eve and the Ephesian women.

The difficult term in this verse is σωθήσεται, "she will be saved." It is qualified by the subsequent ἐὰν μείνωσιν, "if they remain," clause (see the end of this discussion). Whatever it means to be "saved through childbearing," this salvation must be accompanied by faith, love, holiness, and modesty. The doctrine of salvation in the PE is fully Pauline. Salvation is through God's grace and mercy, appropriated by believers through faith (cf. *Introduction*, "Themes in the PE"); it is not salvation by works, much less salvation by procreation. Interpretations of v 15 fall into two camps: physical safety and spiritual salvation.

σῴζειν can be translated "to keep safe" in the sense of physical safety (cf. possible use of σῴζειν in 1 Tim 4:16 and 2 Tim 4:18). (1) Some view the verse as saying that women will be kept safe through childbirth if they continue in faith (NIV [1978]; NASB; Moffatt tr. ["get safely through childbirth"]; Simpson; Moule, *Idiom-Book*, 56; Barrett; Jewett, *Man as Male and Female*, 60; Barron, *JETS* 33 [1990] 457; Keener, *Paul, Women, and Wives*, 118–19, who relies heavily on extrabiblical sources). Barrett interprets, "In consequence of her place in creation, and of Eve's fall, woman is involved in distress and danger (Gen. 3:16); nevertheless, she will be preserved through these, if they . . . continue as devout Christians" (56–57). However, this does not accord with experience. Godly women die in childbirth and ungodly women pass through safely. While the curse in Gen 3:16 is part of the backdrop of our passage, the curse is not that women bear children but that there be pain. (2) Others see this verse as a promise that the Ephesian women will be kept safe from the errors being taught in Ephesus (Jebb, *ExpTim* 81 [1970] 221–22), either in general or from the opponents' specific teaching on role reversals. Hurley suggests, "Eve and women in general will be saved or kept safe from wrongly seizing men's roles by embracing a woman's role" (*Biblical Perspective*, 222). However, the text does not say this (cf. Hanson, [1983] 74; Fee, 75; Roloff, 141; Porter, *JSNT* 49 [1993] 95). (3) Others interpret "saved" with a psychological sense—salvation of the sense of worth and well-being. Foh comments, "Undoubtedly, Paul means to encourage the woman after he has limited some of her activities. He may be suggesting that bearing and raising children is not demeaning to a woman, that motherhood is an honorable and significant profession if she continues in her faith in Christ. Paul is in favor of motherhood" (*Women*, 128). Blomberg's comments about v 14 building toward v 15 as an attempt to give something back to the Ephesian women have already been mentioned.

The main problem with these interpretations is that the context of 1 Timothy suggests that σῴζειν be understood as spiritual salvation. (1) The preceding verse has established salvation as the context of the discussion. ἀπατᾶν, ἐξαπατᾶν, "to deceive," means to entice into sinning. Eve fell into transgression and sin, and v 15 is a qualification that this fall was not irremediable but that salvation was still possible. The two words, παραβάσει, "transgression," and σωθήσεται, "she will be saved," have only one word in between them; one term defines the other. (2) The verb σῴζειν occurs seven times in the PE. Four times it refers to salvation from sin (1 Tim 1:15; 2:4; 2 Tim 1:9; Titus 3:5). While it is possible that the other two might refer to preservation, these also may refer to salvation. The Pauline doctrine of preservation is reflected in 1 Tim 4:16 where Timothy is told to hold to his teaching, "for by so doing you will save both yourself and your hearers." Later Paul expresses his assuredness that his salvation is safe with the Lord (2 Tim 4:18). If Pauline authorship is accepted, then Paul's usage elsewhere would confirm this conclusion, for nowhere does Paul use σῴζειν to refer to salvation from anything other than sin (Foerster, *TDNT* 7:992–5; BAGD, 798; cf. Lock, 31; Houlden, 72; Moo, *Trinity Journal* 1 [1980] 71; Payne, *Trinity Journal* 2 [1981] 178; Fung, "Ministry," 203; van der Jagt, *BT* 39

[1988] 293; Gritz, *Paul, Women Teachers, and the Mother Goddess*, 141; Kimberly, *JETS* 35 [1992] 481–82; Porter, *JSNT* 49 [1993] 93–94). Instead, Paul uses ῥύεσθαι, "to deliver," to say that God will preserve believers from evil people, persecutions, etc. (cf. Rom 7:24; 11:26; 15:31; 2 Cor 1:10; Col 1:13; 1 Thess 1:10; 2 Thess 3:2; 2 Tim 3:11; 4:17, 18; see *Comment* on 2 Tim 3:11). Especially instructive is 2 Tim 4:18 where Paul says that the Lord will rescue (ῥύσεται) him from every evil and will save (σώσει) him for the heavenly kingdom. This shows a firm distinction between being kept safe from evil and being saved from sin (in this case seen as perseverance). Both the context and the use of the verb, in both the PE and in Paul, confirm that v 15 is speaking about salvation from sin. While the psychological approach makes statements that appear to be true, that does not mean this is Paul's central intent, and it views σώζειν in a particularly difficult way.

If σώζειν describes spiritual salvation, how will women be saved from their sins? (1) V 15 cannot be teaching salvation by works, specifically by procreation. As stated above, this would run counter to the theology of the PE (that salvation is by God's mercy and grace), and it would be absurd to imagine that the work would be child bearing.

(2) A more serious suggestion is that τεκνογονίας be translated not as "child-bearing" but as "the childbirth," namely the birth of Jesus (Ellicott, 37; Warfield, *PresR* 8 [1921] 504; Lock, 32–33; Spencer, *JETS* 17 [1974] 220; id., *Beyond the Curse*, 92–94; Jewett, *Man as Male and Female*, 60; D. Williams, *Apostle Paul and Women*, 113; Payne, *Trinity Journal* 2 [1981] 177–78, 180–81; Huizenga, *Studia Biblica et Theologica* 12 [1982] 17–26; Roberts, *Reformed Journal* 33 [1983] 6–7; Padgett, *Int* 41 [1987] 29; Oden, 101–2; Knight, 146–47; references to the early church fathers in Stott, 87; Porter, *JSNT* 49 [1993] 90 n. 8). This would recognize the presence of the definite article τῆς, "the," before τεκνογονίας. It also builds on the context of Gen 3: Eve's deception (1 Tim 2:14; Gen 3:1–7, 16) will be overcome by the deliverance prophesied in Gen 3:15, which foretells that Eve's seed (descendant) will bruise the serpent's head, i.e., "salvation is announced in terms of a child to be borne by the woman" (Knight, 146). Although Eve fell into transgression and this has had its effects on women throughout the centuries, women will still be saved through the birth of Jesus and the salvation that he will bring. Knight comments, "By fulfilling her role, difficult as it may be as a result of sin (Gen. 3:16), she gives birth to the Messiah and thereby 'she' (ἡ γυνή, fulfilled, of course, in Mary; cf. Gal 4:4) brings salvation into the world" (Knight, 146). This interpretation assigns διά, "through," its normal meaning.

τεκνογονία is a difficult term to define. It occurs only here in the NT and rarely elsewhere (BAGD, 808; MM, 628). Its only biblical cognate is the verbal form τεκνογονεῖν, "to bear children," which occurs once in the NT where Paul says that he wishes the younger widows would marry and have children (1 Tim 5:14). The verbal cognate emphasizes the act of bearing, not the children who are borne, suggesting that τεκνογονία in 1 Tim 2:15 refers to Mary's act of giving birth, not the birth itself (which the interpretation above requires). But Paul never says that salvation is by the Incarnation or by Mary, and to see Mary as the agent of the salvation of women unnecessarily complicates an already confusing passage by introducing a new player into the drama. There is also the question of whether the lexical data for τεκνογονία itself allow for this meaning (cf. Spicq, 1:382–83). If this is what Paul meant, he chose an extremely obscure way of saying it (cf. Bernard, 49).

Chrysostom and Houlden translate the noun as "child rearing," understanding μείνωσιν, "they continue," to refer to the children, but there is no evidence that this is a possible meaning of the word (so Spicq, 1:383–84; Jeremias, 19; Hanson, [1983] 74; Moo, *Trinity Journal* 1 [1980] 71–72; Oberlinner expands it to the entire sphere of marriage [103]). See below for a discussion of the plural μείνωσιν, "they continue." Most argue that τεκνογονία means "childbirth." Either the article is generic (Moo, *Trinity Journal* 2 [1981] 206; Porter, *JSNT* 49 [1993] 92; Schreiner, "Interpretation of 1 Timothy 2:9–15," 149), or it identifies the specific good work of childbirth as opposed to other possible ways of working out salvation.

(3) In a somewhat awkward manner, Paul is saying that a woman's salvation and the practical outworking of that salvation (cf. Phil 2:12) do not consist in altering her role in the church. Rather, she is to accept her God-given role, one of the specific functions being the bearing of children (synecdoche). Of course, her salvation—and man's—ultimately is predicated upon perseverance; she must live out her salvation in all faith and love and holiness, with modesty. This is the standard Pauline thought that salvation requires continual perseverance (cf. 1 Tim 4:16), and good works, far from meriting salvation (cf. 1 Tim 1:12–17), are evidence of that salvation (cf. Rom 2:6–10, 26–29; 1 Cor 6:9–11; Gal 5:21; cf. T. R. Schreiner, "Did Paul Believe in Justification by Works? Another Look at Romans 2," *BBR* 3 [1993] 131–58). This somewhat parallels Paul's instruction to the widows in 1 Tim 5: they were living recklessly and reproachfully (cf. 2:9–10); they should remarry, bear children, and like the godly widows they should pursue good deeds. However, it does sound awkward to speak of being saved through adopting a role.

The example of bearing children is probably chosen because the false teachers are downplaying the importance of marriage (cf. 1 Tim 3:4, 12; 4:3) and therefore probably also of childbirth (Jeremias, 19; Kelly, 70; Fee, 74–75; Scholer, "1 Timothy 2:9–15," 197–98; Padgett, *Int* 41 [1987] 28; Gritz, *Paul, Women Teachers, and the Mother Goddess*, 143; Moo, "What Does It Mean?" 192; Kroeger and Kroeger, *I Suffer Not a Woman*, 171–77; Schreiner, "Interpretation of 1 Timothy 2:9–15," 150). Kimberley emphasizes that some forms of Gnosticism also deprecated male/female distinctions, and this too may have been a part of the Ephesian heresy (*JETS* 35 [1992] 484–86; also Barron, *JETS* 33 [1990] 456–57). C. C. Kroeger notes, "Childbearing and marriage were forbidden by certain Gnostic groups because they pulled the soul-atoms back into material bodies instead of liberating them to ascend to their ultimate source" ("1 Timothy 2:12," 243). Yet these data come from later sources. The downplaying of sexual relationships was also evident elsewhere in the early church (cf. 1 Cor 7:1–5, 36) in a context in which Paul chooses to advocate celibacy (1 Cor 7:25–40). While childbearing is not a woman's only role, it is a significant one (as is being increasingly understood today in disciplines such as psychology, sociology, and anthropology; cf. Clark, *Man and Woman*, 369–570). If v 15 is tied to the call for the offer of salvation to all in vv 1–7, then σῴζειν must refer to spiritual salvation and most likely is proclaiming the possibility of salvation for women who do not follow the opponents' teaching and decide to accept domestic values such as having children.

Schreiner suggests that the choice of this particular good work has more to do with the role distinction discussed in vv 13–14:

This does not mean that all women must have children in order to be saved. Paul is hardly attempting to be comprehensive here. He has elsewhere commended the single state (1

Cor. 7). He selects childbearing because it is the most notable example of the divinely intended difference in role between men and women, and most women throughout history have had children. . . . To select childbearing is another indication that the argument is transcultural, for childbearing is not limited to a particular culture, but is a permanent and ongoing difference between men and women. The fact that God has ordained that women and only women bear children indicates that the differences in role between men and women are rooted in the created order. ("Interpretation of 1 Timothy 2:9–15," 151)

If v 15 contrasts with vv 11–12, then childbearing contrasts specifically with teaching. If v 15 is more closely connected with vv 13–14, then it is meant to encourage women "in light of their position resulting from the fall" (Foh, "Male Leadership View," 82). These two interpretations are not mutually exclusive.

There is a question as to the precise meaning of διά, "through." (1) Scott translates it as "even though she must bear children [i.e., bear the curse], she can still be saved" (28). But not only does διά not carry this meaning, but the curse on Eve was not the bearing of children but the accompanying pain (cf. Moo, *Trinity Journal* 1 [1980] 71; Porter, *JSNT* 49 [1993] 96–97). (2) Some suggest that διά denotes attendant circumstances, women being saved in the experience of childbirth (Falconer, 376; Roloff, 141–42; analyzed by Porter, *JSNT* 49 [1993] 97). (3) Most view διά as having its normal instrumental use. Knight (147) points out that σώζειν, "to save," occurs with διά six other times in the NT (Acts 15:11; Rom 5:9; 1 Cor 1:21; 15:2), and in all but two (1 Cor 3:15; 1 Pet 3:20) διά indicates the means of salvation (Moule, *Idiom-Book*, 56). Context shows that διά indicates the efficient, not the ultimate, means, albeit a rare use of the preposition (cf. Gal 5:6; M. J. Harris, *NIDNTT* 3:1182).

On the conditional clause ἐὰν μείνωσιν, "if they continue," see Porter, *JSNT* 49 (1993) 99–101. The plural does not indicate both wife and husband (contra Brox, 137) since the husband has no necessary connection with his wife's salvation and because the previous σωθήσεται, "she will be saved," is singular. The plural also is not a reference to children (contra Jeremias, 22; Houlden, 72–73; L. T. Johnson, 133) since they are not an issue here and have no necessary effect on their mother's salvation. A switch of subject to either of these would also be disruptive of the flow of thought. In this context πίστει, "faith," is the woman's continuing trust in Christ's work on the cross (cf. *Introduction*, "Themes in the PE"). On ἀγάπη, "love," see *Comment* on 1 Tim 1:5. On ἁγιασμός, "holiness," see *Comment* on 1 Tim 1:9. This is the only occurrence of the form ἁγιασμός in the PE. Paul ends on the same note with which he began: he wants the women to dress modestly (v 9) since this is appropriate for their salvation (v 15).

Kroeger and Kroeger (*I Suffer Not a Woman*, 161–70) and others place heavy emphasis on the serpent in Gen 3 and its proposed relationship to the false teachers in Ephesus. Padgett comments, "Eve was saved from the snake, that is, from Satan. Of course, this would include salvation from sin and from the wrath of God upon the followers of Satan. But the emphasis of 'she will be saved' in the light of Genesis would mean that woman was saved from Satan by bearing the seed" (*Int* 41 [1987] 28). The problem with placing too much emphasis on the serpent, however, is that Paul never mentions it here; it must be surmised from the analogy to Gen 3. And Eve was not saved from the serpent; she and the Ephesian women will be saved from sin (see also Liefeld's critique about the snake in the *Comment* on v 14).

Explanation

Having asserted that the Ephesian church is to pray for all people, kings and Gentiles (vv 1–7), Paul moves into the issue of disruption in the Ephesian church. When men everywhere pray for all people, they are to do so without anger, settling any issues before prayer time. Likewise, women are to avoid disruption by dressing in accordance with who they are, women who have made a commitment to godliness. On the one hand, this means that they are not to place an emphasis on external beauty that is luxurious and seductive. Rather, they are to concentrate on moderation and doing good deeds. Paul then moves to the issue of leadership, a topic that he will discuss throughout chap. 3. Women are not to take the reins of the church, exercising authority over the men and teaching them; rather they are to learn in quietness, in submissiveness. Paul sees the prior creation of Adam (Gen 2) as justification for male leadership in the church. He also sees Eve's deception in Gen 3 as a reason for women not to exercise authority. But lest he be misunderstood, Paul moves from Eve's sin in the Garden and her punishment to the Ephesian women and the fulfillment of the promise of Gen 3:15 that salvation extends to them. But they are to work out their salvation by accepting their role, one example being that of bearing children. On the history of interpretation of this passage, see Doriani, "History of the Interpretation of 1 Timothy 2."

One of the foundational issues underlying most of the discussion of the role of women in the church today is the question of whether worth is determined by role? Can essential equality and functional differentiation exist side by side? Underlying much of the discussion lies an implicit assumption that a limited role necessitates a diminished personal worth. It is no wonder that the discussion of women in ministry can become so heated. Yet the equating of worth and role is a nonbiblical, secular view of reality. Nowhere in Scripture are role and ultimate worth ever equated. In fact, we constantly find the opposite. The last will be first (Matt 19:30; John 13:16; cf. 1 Pet 3:1–7; Luke 7:28). The Suffering Servant himself is not worth less than those he served. Paul's analogy of the church as Christ's body teaches that role and worth are unrelated: "The body is a unit, though it is made up of many parts; and though all its parts are many, they form one body" (1 Cor 12:12). This was done "so that there should be no division in the body, but that its parts should have equal concern for each other" (1 Cor 12:25; cf. Rom 12:4–5). Even in the Godhead there is an eternal division of roles, but the three members of the Godhead are coequal, of equal essence. After the final judgment "the Son himself will be made subject to him [God the Father] who put everything under him, so that God may be all in all" (1 Cor 15:28). If role and worth are equated, then one must necessarily conclude that God the Son is of less worth than God the Father because he performs a different, subservient role. The good news of God's kingdom is that it does not matter what function a person performs. What matters is repentance from sins, entrance into the kingdom, and the living out of one's salvation as a regenerated human being of equal worth with all members of the same body, regardless of role. With this all biblical egalitarians and biblical complementarians can agree.

This is a considerably different position than is held by some. For example, Frances Young apparently writes against any form of hierarchy and equates any form of subordination with worth:

As scripture, the Pastorals have shaped a world in which women and others have been subordinated and devalued. . . . Such texts contained in a sacred authoritative canon cannot but become "texts of terror" [Phyllis Trible's phrase] in a democratic society which views the position of women, lay people, servants, slaves, etc. in a totally different light. . . . The very nature and being of God is conceived as the great imperial power, benevolent rather than tyrannical, it is true, effecting salvation rather than oppression, and yet without question at the apex of a hierarchy, demanding obedience from his subjects, a majestic, male superpower, access to whom comes through his servants and officials. Everything comes from the top down. . . . The theology of the Pastorals presents us with a whole culture of subordination. . . . a view of "teaching" . . . with no sense of training a person to be free and independent, creative, or autonomous in taking responsibility for his or her own actions. . . . How can we be true to ourselves, to our deepest social and moral commitments, while remaining true to the Christian tradition? (*Theology of the Pastoral Letters*, 146–47)

As will be seen, especially in the exposition of 1 Tim 3, Young has misunderstood the role of leadership in the church and the role of authority in Paul's theology. But she is correct in finding that the PE (and, it might be added, all of Scripture) see God at the apex of an authoritative hierarchy, a God who demands obedience from his creation. The call to obedience is a necessary corollary of salvation.

C. Overseers (1 Tim 3:1–7)

Bibliography

Adam, A. "Die Entstehung des Bischofsamtes." *WD* 5 (1957) 104–13. **Baltensweiler, H.** *Die Ehe im Neuen Testament.* ATANT 52. Zürich: Zwingli, 1967. **Beare, F. W.** "The Ministry in the New Testament Church: Practice and Theory." *ATR* 37 (1955) 3–18. **Benoit, P.** "Les origines de l'épiscopat dans le Nouveau Testament." In *Exégèse et Théologie II.* Paris: Cerf, 1961. 232–46. **Beyer, H. W.** "ἐπίσκοπος." *TDNT* 2:608–20. **Botha, F. J.** "The Word Is Trustworthy." *Theologia Evangelica* 1 (1968) 78–84. **Bover, J. M.** "*Fidelis sermo.*" *Bib* 19 (1938) 74–79. **Brandt, W.** *Dienst und Dienen im Neuen Testament.* Gütersloh: Bertelsmann, 1931. **Braun, F.-M.** *Neues Licht auf die Kirche.* Einsiedeln: Benziger, 1946. **Brown, R. E.** *The Critical Meaning of the Bible.* New York: Paulist, 1981. ———. "*Episkopê* and *Episkopos:* The New Testament Evidence." *Theological Studies* 41 (1980) 322–38. **Caddeo, S.** "La figura degli anziani sorveglianti." In *Aux origines de l'Église,* ed. J. Giblet et al. RechBib 7. Paris: Desclée de Brouwer, 1972. 165–92. **Campenhausen, H. F. von.** *Ecclesiastical Authority and Spiritual Power in the Church.* **Cerling, E.** "Women Ministers in the New Testament Church?" *JETS* 19 (1976) 209–15. **Colson, J.** "Der Diakonat im Neuen Testament." In *Diakonia in Christo: Über die Erneuerung des Diakonates,* ed. K. Rahner and H. Vorgrimler. Freiburg: Herder, 1962. 3–22. **Condon, K.** "Church Offices by the Time of the Pastoral Epistles." In *Church Ministry.* Dublin: Dominican, 1977. 74–94. **Cousineau, A.** "Les sens de *presbuteros* dans les Pastorales." *ScEs* 28 (1976) 147–62. **Daniélou, J.** "La communauté de Qumrân et l'organization de l'Église ancienne." *RHPR* 35 (1955) 104–15. **Dautzenberg, G.** *Urchristliche Prophetie: Ihre Erforschung, ihre Voraussetzungen im Judentum und ihre Struktur im ersten Korintherbrief.* BWANT 104. Stuttgart: Kohlhammer, 1975. 257–98. **Davies, W. D.** "A Normative Pattern of Church Life in the New Testament?" 1950. Repr. in *Christian Origins and Judaism.* Philadelphia: Westminster, 1962. 199–229. **Delling, G.** *Paulus Stellung zu Frau und Ehe.* BWANT

4.5. Stuttgart: Kohlhammer, 1931. **Dibelius, M.,** and **Conzelmann, H.** "The Position of the Bishop in the Pastoral Epistles." In *The Pastoral Epistles.* 54–57. **Dibout, C.,** and **Faivre, A.** "Les chrétiennes, entre leurs devoirs familiaux et le prestige de l'épiskopè: Un dilemme aux sources de la documentation canonico-liturgique." *LTP* 49 (1993) 69–92. **Dodd, C. H.** "New Testament Translation Problems II." *BT* 28 [1977] 112–16. **Duncan, J. G.** "Πιστὸς ὁ λόγος." *ExpTim* 35 (1922) 141. **Ehrhardt, A.** *The Apostolic Succession in the First Two Centuries of the Church.* London: Lutterworth, 1953. **Ellingworth, P.** "The 'True Saying' in 1 Timothy 3:1." *BT* 31 (1980) 443–45. **Elliott, J. H.** "Ministry and Church Order in the New Testament: A Traditio-Historical Analysis." *CBQ* 32 (1970) 367–91. **Fee, G. D.** "*Laos* and Leadership under the New Covenant: Some Exegetical and Hermeneutical Observations on Church Order." In *Gospel and Spirit.* 120–43. ———. "Reflections on Church Order in the Pastoral Epistles: With Further Reflections on the Hermeneutics of Ad Hoc Documents." *JETS* 28 (1985) 141–51. **Floor, L.** "Church Order in the Pastoral Epistles." *Neot* 10 (1976) 81–91. **Frey, J. B.** "La signification des termes μόνανδρος et univira." *RSR* 20 (1930) 48–60. **Fronhofen, H.** "Weibliche Diakone in der frühen Kirche." *Stimmen der Zeit* 204 (1986) 269–78. **Ghidelli, C.** "Una comunità che si organizza e si consolida." *Rivista del Clero Italiano* 59 (1978) 756–65. **Giesen, H.** "Im Dienst der Einheit: Die Function der Dienstämter im Zeugnis neutestamentlichen Schriften." SNTU-A 15 (1990) 5–40. **Glasscock, E.** "The Husband of One Wife Requirement in 1 Timothy 3:2." *BSac* 140 (1983) 244–58. **Goerl, G.** "As Qualidades de Bispos, Presbiteros e Diaconos Segundo 1 Tim 3 e Tito 1." *Igreja Luterana* 19 (1958) 245–55. **Greeven, H.** "προΐστημι." *ZNW* 44 (1952) 31–41. **Hainz, J.** "Die Anfänge des Bischofs- und Diakonenamtes." In *Kirche im Werden: Studien zum Thema Amt und Gemeinde im Neuen Testament,* ed. J. Heinz. Vienna: Schöningh, 1976. 91–107. **Harnack, A. von.** *The Constitution and Law of the Church in the First Two Centuries.* Tr. F. L. Pogson, ed. H. D. A. Major. New York: Putnam, 1910. ———. *The Mission and Expansion of Christianity in the First Three Centuries.* Tr. J. Moffatt. New York: Harper & Row, 1968. **Harvey, A. E.** "Elders." *JTS* n.s. 25 (1974) 318–32. **Hatch, E.,** ed. *The Organization of the Early Christian Churches.* New York: Longmans, Green, 1892. **Headlam, A. C.,** and **Gerke, F.** "The Origin of the Christian Ministry." In *The Ministry and the Sacraments,* ed. R. Dunkerley. New York: Macmillan, 1937. 326–87. **Hillman, E.** *Polygamy Reconsidered: African Plural Marriage and the Christian Churches.* New York: Orbis, 1975. **Holl, K.** "Der Kirchenbegriff des Paulus in seinem Verhältnis zu dem der Urgemeinde." 1921 (repr. in *Gesammelte Aufsätze zur Kirchengeschichte* [Tübingen: Mohr-Siebeck, 1928] 2:44–67). **Holtz, T.** "Christus Diakonos: Zur christologischen Begründung der Diakonia in der nachösterlichen Gemeinde." In *Diakonie—Biblische Grundlagen und Orientierungen,* ed. G. K. Schäfer and T. Strohm. Heidelberg: Heidelberger Verlagsanstalt, 1990. 127–43 (repr. in *Geschichte und Theologie des Urchristentums: Gesammelte Aufsätze,* WUNT 57 [Tübingen: Mohr-Siebeck, 1991] 399–416). **Holzmeister, U.** "Si quis episcopatum desiderat, bonum opus desiderat." *Bib* 12 (1931) 41–69. **Hort, F. J. A.** *The Christian Ecclesia.* **Jeremias, J.** "ΠΡΕΣΒΥΤΕΡΙΟΝ ausserchristlich bezeugt." *ZNW* 48 (1957) 127–32. **Keener, C. S.** . . . *And Marries Another: Divorce and Remarriage in the Teaching of the New Testament.* Peabody, MA: Hendricksen, 1991. 83–103. **Kirk, K. E.,** ed. *The Apostolic Ministry: Essays on the History and the Doctrine of Episcopacy.* London: Hodder & Stoughton, 1946. **Knight, G. W., III.** "1 Timothy 3:1 and Its Saying." In *The Faithful Sayings in the Pastoral Epistles.* 1968. Repr. Grand Rapids, MI: Baker, 1979. 50–61. **Knox, J.** *The Early Church and the Coming Great Church.* New York: Abingdon, 1955. 101–29. **Kühl, E.** *Die Gemeindeordnung in den Pastoralbriefen.* Berlin: Besser'sche Buchhandlung, 1885. **Lampe, G. W. H.** *Some Aspects of the New Testament Ministry.* London: S.P.C.K., 1949. **Lassman, E.** "1 Timothy 3:1–7 and Titus 1:5–9 and the Ordination of Women." *CTQ* 56 (1994) 291–95. **Lattey, C.** "Unius uxoris vir (Tit 1:6)." *VD* 28 (1950) 288. **Lewis, R. M.** "The 'Women' of 1 Tim 3,11." *BSac* 136 (1979) 167–75. **Lietzmann, H.** "Zur altchristlichen Verfassungsgeschichte." *ZWT* 55 (1913) 97–153. **Lightfoot, J. B.** "The Christian Ministry." In *St. Paul's Epistle to the Philippians.* 181–269. **Lindsay, T. M.** *The Church and the Ministry in the Early Centuries.* 2nd ed. New York: Hodder & Stoughton, 1903. **Linton, O.** *Das Problem der Urkirche in der neueren Forschung.* Uppsala: Lundequist, 1932. **Loewe, R. L.** *Ordnung in der Kirche im Lichte* *des Titus.* Gütersloh: Der Rufer, 1947. **Lohfink, G.** "Weibliche Diakone im Neuen Testament." In *Die Frau im Urchristentum,* ed. G. Dautzenberg et al. 2nd ed. QD 95. Freiburg im Breisgau: Herder, 1986. 320–38. **Lohse, E.** "Die Entstehung des Bischofamtes in der frühen Christenheit." *ZNW* 71 (1980) 58–73. ———. "Episkopos in den Pastoralbriefen." In *Kirche und Bibel.* FS E. Schick. Vienna: Schöningh, 1979. 225–31. ———. *Die Ordination im Spätjudentum und im Neuen Testament.* Berlin: Kertelge, 1951. **Lowrie, W.** *The Church and Its Organization in Primitive and Catholic Times: An Interpretation of Rudolph Sohm's Kirchenrecht.* New York: Longmans, Green, 1904. 331–71. **Lyonnet, S.** "Unius uxoris vir (1 Tim 3:2, 12; Tit 1:6)." *VD* 45 (1967) 3–10. **MacDonald, M. Y.** *The Pauline Churches.* **Manson, T. W.** *The Church's Ministry.* London: Hodder & Stoughton, 1948. **Martimort, A.-G.** *Deaconesses: An Historical Study.* Tr. K. D. Whitehead. San Francisco: Ignatius, 1986. **McEleney, N. J.** "The Vice Lists of the Pastoral Epistles." *CBQ* 36 (1974) 203–19. **Meier, J. P.** "Presbyteros in the Pastoral Epistles." *CBQ* 35 (1973) 323–45. **Molland, E.** "Le dévelopment de l'idée de succession apostolique." *RHPR* 34 (1954) 1–29. **Müller-Bardorff, J.** "Zur Exegese von 1 Tim 5:3–16." In *Gott und die Götter.* FS E. Fascher, ed. H. Bardtke. Berlin: Evangelische Verlagsanstalt, 1958. 113–33. **Nagy, S.** "Hierarchia koscielna w ostatnim okresie zvycia svw: Pawla (La hiérarchie ecclésiastique dans la dernière période de la vie de St. Paul)." *RTK* 13 (1966) 23–44. **Noack, B.** "Pastoralbrevenes 'trovaerdige tale.'" *DTT* 32 (1969) 1–22. **North, J. L.** "'Human Speech' in Paul and the Paulines: The Investigation and Meaning of ἀνθρώπινος ὁ λόγος (1 Tim. 3:1)." *NovT* 37 (1995) 50–67. **Nötscher, F.** "Vorchristliche Typen urchristlichen Ämter? Episcopos und Mebaqqer." In *Vom Alten zum Neuen Testament: Gesammelte Aufsätze.* BBB 17. Bonn: Hanstein, 1962. 188–220. **Oates, W. E.** "Conception of Ministry in the Pastoral Epistles." *RevExp* 56 (1959) 91–94. **Page, S.** "Marital Expectations of Church Leaders in the Pastoral Epistles." *JSNT* 50 (1993) 105–20. **Porter, L.** "The Word ἐπίσκοπος in Pre-Christian Usage." *ATR* 21 (1939) 103–12. **Potterie, I. de la.** "Mari d'une seule femme: Le sens théologique d'une formule paulinienne." In *Paul de Tarse, Apôtre de notre temps,* ed. L. de Lorenzi. Rome: Abbaye de S. Paul, 1979. 619–38. **Preisker, H.** *Christentum und Ehe in den ersten Jahrhunderten.* 1927. Repr. Aalen: Scientia, 1979. **Reicke, B.** "The Constitution of the Church in the Light of Jewish Documents." In *The Scrolls and the New Testament,* ed. K. Stendahl. London: SCM Press, 1958. 143–56. **Ridderbos, H. N.** "Kerkelijke orde en kerkelijk recht in de brieven van Paulus." In *Ex auditu verbi.* FS G. C. Berkouwer. Kampen: Kok, 1965. 194–215. ———. *Paul: An Outline of His Theology.* 438–46, 456–63. **Riddle, D. W.** "Early Christian Hospitality: A Factor in the Gospel Transmission." *JBL* 57 (1938) 141–54. **Roberts, C. H.** "Elders: A Note." *JTS* n.s. 26 (1975) 403–5. **Romaniuk, K.** "Was Phoebe in Romans 16,1 a Deaconess?" *ZNW* 81 (1990) 132–34. **Saucy, R. L.** "The Husband of One Wife." *BSac* 131 (1974) 229–40. **Schäfer, G. K.,** and **Strohm, T.,** eds. *Diakonie—Biblische Grundlagen und Orientierungen: Ein Arbeitsbuch zur theologischen Verständigung über den diakonischen Auftrag.* Heidelberg: Heidelberger Verlagsanstalt, 1990. **Schlier, H.** "Die Ordnung der Kirche nach den Pastoralbriefen." In *Das kirchliche Amt im Neuen Testament,* ed. K. Kertelge. Wege der Forschung 439. Darmstadt: Wissenschaftliche Buchgesellschaft, 1977. 475–500. **Schmidt, K. L.** "Le ministère et les ministères dans l'Église du Nouveau Testament." *RHPR* 17 (1937) 313–36. **Schnackenburg, R.** "Episkopos und Hirtenamt." In *Schriften zum Neuen Testament.* Munich: Kösel, 1971. 247–67. **Schöllgen, G.** "Monepiskopat und monarchischer Episkopat: Eine Bemerkung zur Terminologie." *ZNW* 77 (1986) 146–51. **Schottroff, L.** "Diener innen der Heiligen: Der Diakonat der Frauen im Neuen Testament." In *Diakonie—Biblische Grundlagen und Orientierungen,* ed. G. K. Schäfer and T. Strohm. Heidelberg: Heidelberger Verlagsanstalt, 1990. 222–42. **Schulze, W. A.** "'Ein Bischof sei eines Weibes Mann . . .' Zur Exegese von 1. Tim. 3,2 und Tit. 1,6." *KD* 4 (1958) 287–300. **Schweizer, E.** *Church Order in the New Testament.* SBT 32. London: SCM Press, 1961. ———. "Die diakonische Struktur der neutestamentlichen Gemeinde." In *Diakonie—Biblische Grundlagen und Orientierungen,* ed. G. K. Schäfer and T. Strohm. Heidelberg: Heidelberger Verlagsanstalt, 1990. 159–85. **Shepherd, M. H.** "The Development of the Early Ministry." *ATR* 26 (1944) 135–50. ———. "Ministry, Christian." *IDB* 3:386–92. **Sohm, R.** *Kirchenrecht.* 2 vols. Leipzig: Duncker & Humblot, 1892, 1923. ———.

Wesen und Ursprung des Katholizismus: Durch ein Vorwort vermehrter zweiter Abdruck. 2nd ed. Leipzig; Berlin: Teubner, 1912. **Spicq, C.** "Excursus II.—Épiscope et épiscopat d'après les Épîtres pastorales." In *Saint Paul: Les Épîtres pastorales.* 1:439–54. ———. "᾽Επιποθεῖν, Désire ou Chérir?" *RB* 64 (1957) 184–95. ———. "Si quis episcopatum desiderat." *RSPT* 29 (1940) 316–25. **Stalder, K.** "ΕΠΙΣΚΟΠΟΣ." *IKaZ* 61 (1971) 200–232. **Streeter, B. H.** *The Primitive Church: Studied with Special Reference to the Origin of the Christian Ministry.* New York: Macmillan, 1929. **Swete, H. B.,** ed. *Essays on the Early History of the Church and the Ministry.* 2nd ed. London: Macmillan, 1921. **Tauzin, E.** "Note sur un texte de S. Paul." *Revue Apologetique* 20[39] (1924–25) 274–88. **Trummer, P.** "Einehe nach den Pastoralbriefen: Zum Verständnis der Termini μιᾶς γυναικὸς ἀνήρ und ἑνὸς ἀνδρὸς γυνή." *Bib* 51 (1970) 471–84. **Verner, D. C.** *The Household of God: The Social World of the Pastoral Epistles.* Chico, CA: Scholars Press, 1983. 127–80.

Translation

[1] *Trustworthy is the saying.*[a] *If anyone aspires to the office of overseer, he is desiring a good work.* [2] *Therefore, it is necessary for an overseer to be above reproach: a "one-woman" man, clear-minded, self-controlled, dignified, hospitable, skilled in teaching,* [3] *not a drunkard, not violent* [b] *but gracious, not quarrelsome, not a lover of money,* [4] *managing his own household well, having submissive children with all dignity* [5] *(for if someone does not know [how] to manage his own household, how will he care for [the] church of God?),* [6] *not a recent convert, lest having become conceited, he fall into [the] judgment of the devil.* [7] *And* [c] *it is also necessary [for an overseer] to have a good reputation with those outside, lest he fall into reproach, which is [the] snare of the devil.*

Notes

[a] The variant ἀνθρώπινος, replacing πιστός, "trustworthy," occurs in D* b g m; Ambst Spec; and is accepted by NEB, Moffatt tr., Wohlenberg, Easton, Barrett, and apparently Houlden. Here it would mean "popular" or "common." A scribe probably substituted the word thinking that 3:1b was not deserving of the formula "it is a trustworthy saying," which elsewhere in the PE deals with statements of salvation, and lacked real spiritual insight. Our reading is much stronger (cf. *TCGNT*[2], 572; Elliott, *Greek Text,* 27–28; Knight, *Faithful Sayings,* 50–52).

[b] μὴ αἰσχροκερδῆ, "not greedy for gain," is inserted after πλήκτην, "violent," by 326 365 614 630 *pm.* Nestle-Aland[27] suggests it is in imitation of Titus 1:7. See *TCGNT*[2], 573.

[c] D 1739[ms] TR insert αὐτόν, "him," after δέ, "and." The omission is supported by ℵ A F G[c] H I Ψ 33 81 326 1739* 1881 *pc.*

Form/Structure/Setting

Chap. 3 is a continuation of the preceding discussion. In 1 Tim 2:11–15 Paul discussed women and leadership. He now turns to men and leadership, spelling out the personal qualities necessary for effective church leaders (1 Tim 3:1–7; ἐπίσκοποι, "overseers") and workers (3:8–13; διάκονοι, "deacons"). He pauses to put all these instructions into perspective (3:14–16) and concludes by pointing out that the problems in the Ephesian church are the fulfillment of prophecy and stem ultimately from Satan (4:1–5).

This paragraph (1 Tim 3:1–7) divides into three parts. (1) Paul commends the office of overseer (v 1). (2) He lists eleven qualities that should be possessed by an overseer (vv 2–3). The first stands as the title over all these qualities: an overseer must be above reproach; all that follows spells out what this entails. (3) Paul then speaks to three specific situations: an overseer must manage his household well (v 4–5); he should not be a recent convert (v 6); he must be well thought of by non-Christians (v 7). Paul joins each of these three situations with a reason: if an overseer cannot manage his family, he cannot manage God's household; if he is a recent convert, he may become conceited and fall into the same trap as did Satan; he must have a good reputation or else he may be caught in Satan's snare. It is significant that Paul both begins and ends on the same note: a church leader should be above reproach; he should have a good reputation. This is one of the overriding concerns in the PE. The church has not guarded its reputation, and the misconduct of the false teachers is bringing it into more and more disrepute. Therefore, Timothy must be sure that its leaders are above reproach. The grammar of the paragraph serves to heighten this: 1 Tim 3:2–6 constitutes one sentence with a parenthetical comment (v 5). 1 Tim 3:7 begins a new sentence and repeats the initial and primary concern.

Chap. 3, perhaps more than any other chapter in the PE, has been interpreted as a church manual written apart from a specific historical situation. Dibelius-Conzelmann (50–51), assuming the historical setting is fictitious, argue that the real interest of the author is not to instruct Timothy but to instruct the bishops. However, the message of the chapter is missed if the reader does not interpret it in light of the Ephesian situation. Almost every quality Paul specifies here has its negative counterpart in the Ephesian opponents. They are bringing the church into disrepute, so at the head of the list Paul says that a church leader must be above reproach. They are teaching only for financial gain; Paul says that an overseer must not be greedy or a lover of money. They are promiscuous; Paul says the overseer must be a "one-woman" man (see table below). Once a full picture of the opponents is developed, chap. 3 becomes one of the strongest arguments that the PE are directed toward a specific historical problem and should be understood in light of that situation.

THE DEVELOPMENT OF CHRISTIAN MINISTRY

While a discussion of the development of Christian ministry lies outside the scope of this commentary, at times this issue forces itself into the exegesis of the PE. A summary, therefore, will help to provide the necessary background to the specific points made below and in the *Comment*. There are at least three basic questions related to the nature of the church. (1) Was the church a fully eschatological entity, or did it have a formalized structure to help it function until Christ's return? Are these two mutually exclusive, or did they function in tandem? (2) Was the church fully pneumatic, exercising the gifts of the Spirit (*charismata*), or did it have a formalized structure of offices? Did these coexist, or did the latter develop out of and become incompatible with the former? (3) Is the type of church we see in Ignatius in the first part of the second century parallel to what we see in the PE, or was it a later development out of the Pauline churches (including the PE)? How consistent was the formal structure of the church outside of Ignatius' influence? To put it another way, where on the spectrum of development from Paul to Ignatius do we place the PE?

In 1892 R. Sohm published the first volume of his *Kirchenrecht*, in which he argued that any form of polity or structure was directly opposed to the essence of the church, which to his mind should be thoroughly pneumatic and Spirit-based. There were no formal structures in the early church, but people were led by the Spirit. Sohm's thesis was revised by, among others, A. von Harnack in *The Constitution and Laws of the Church in the First Two Centuries* (ET 1910), who acknowledged some organizational structure and yet maintained that it was foreign to the heart of the church (cf. also Hatch, *The Organization of the Early Christian Church*, 1892). He distinguished between the charismatic ministries given by the Spirit and the administrative ministries to which people were appointed and which were localized to specific churches (so von Campenhausen, *Ecclesiastical Authority* [ET 1969]). As debate on these points continues, the proposed rift between *charisma* and office has been lessened in the eyes of many (e.g., Ridderbos is able to say that the office is the *charisma* [*Paul*, 444–45, 458–59], citing Rom 12:6–8, 1 Cor 12:28, and R. Bultmann [*Theology* 2:104]), but others still feel that the PE represent a development beyond Paul's day, perhaps standing closer to Ignatius than to Paul, and that charismatic leadership is incongruous with church structure. In Ignatius there is a three-tiered structure. The monarchical ἐπίσκοπος, "bishop," rules as the single leader over the Christian community in the city/province. Under him are the college of presbyters (πρεσβύτεροι, "elders") and the deacons (διάκονοι), both of whom serve the bishop as well as the church. However, there are historical questions regarding how entrenched this three-tiered structure really was at this time (see *Explanation*) and how widespread it was throughout the early church. For summaries of the debate, see O. Linton, *Problem der Urkirche;* F.-M. Braun, *Neues Licht auf die Kirche,* 29ff.; M. H. Shepherd, *IDB* 3:386–92; Ridderbos, *Paul,* 438–46, 467–80.

This brief history of interpretation provides background for understanding positions taken in commentaries regarding the references to church offices in the PE. According to Sohm's view, any discussion of church offices in the NT must reflect later developments in the early church, so, for example, the references in Acts to elders should be interpreted as anachronistic insertions into the history of the early church. But if the texts of the NT and particularly the PE are allowed to stand apart from Sohm's interpretive framework, then the PE do not appear to involve any significant development and in fact are closer to Paul's other writings than to Ignatius. The silence of the NT elsewhere on the structure of the church may simply be due to the ad hoc nature of the NT literature. With respect to this matter Ridderbos cautions, "we shall have to be very careful indeed with the argument from silence, especially when this is pressed into the service of certain preconceived opinions with respect to the manner in which the Spirit works and equips the church" (*Paul,* 446). The difference between Paul and the PE and the similarity between the PE and Ignatius can thus be exaggerated beyond the evidence. Shepherd comments that the PE "provide the clearest testimony in the NT to the developed norm of a threefold hierarchy" (*IDB* 3:390) and that the idea of "ministerial succession" is "implicit in the Pastoral letters, with their emphasis upon a regular appointment of ministers who will teach sound doctrine and manifest exemplary character" (3:391). He uses Paul's reference to Timothy's commissioning (1 Tim 4:14) as descriptive of the bishop's ordination (3:390). But a reading of the PE independent of a preconceived theory gives a considerably different picture. An ability to teach and an exemplary character do not point to developments beyond the Pauline churches. The PE only show two offices in an undeveloped form (overseer and deacon): the overseer is not over the deacon, nor does the deacon advance to the role of overseer. Nowhere is Timothy included within the structure of the Ephesian church, and therefore he should not be viewed as a bishop over the church. That Paul is more concerned with character than with duties should in and of itself warn us against associating the PE too closely with the age of Ignatius. 2 Tim 2:2 is a helpful test case. Is Paul teaching the succession/ordination of ministerial office and power, or is he asking Timothy to get his affairs in order so that he can come quickly to Rome before Paul dies? The text indicates the latter. Timothy is a temporary apostolic delegate sent to deal with a specific problem; he is not the bishop of Ephesus. (For a discussion of the development of the monarchical episcopate and Ignatius' church see the excursus following the *Explanation*.)

LISTS OF QUALITIES FOR CHURCH LEADERSHIP
(1 TIM 3:1–7 [5:17–23], 8–13; TITUS 1:5–9)

The similarities among the three lists of qualities for church leadership in the PE are remarkable. The overall concern is that church leaders be above reproach in their daily lives. There are several qualities repeated in all three lists: above reproach, "one-woman" man, dignified (using different words), not addicted to wine, not greedy for money, and good manager of family. These positive qualities contrast with their negative counterparts, which characterize the opponents. Often there is a word-for-word equivalence in the lists, other times there are conceptual parallels, and other times the parallels are broader but still related (e.g., a requirement to be clear-minded would rule out someone who is quick tempered). The table below follows the order of requirements in 1 Tim 3:1–7, and the discussion of elders in 1 Tim 5:17–23 is included with the overseers (see *Form/ Structure/Setting* on 1 Tim 5:17–23 for justification). The clearest descriptions of the opponents are found in 1 Tim 1:3–7; 4:1–5; 6:3–5; 2 Tim 2:14, 16–18, 23; 3:1–9 (which may include a general description of evil in the last days); 4:3–4; and Titus 1:10–16; 3:9–10. There are other passages that may reflect the opponents (e.g., 1 Tim 1:8–11; 2:1–7, 9–15; 2 Tim 3:24–26), but the table is drawn only from the clearest examples. There may be some overlap between the discussion of widows (1 Tim 5:3–16) and the discussion of the opponents since the opponents seem to have been successful among them. Similar lists of good qualities are found for those in the church (1 Tim 5:3–16; Titus 2:1–10; 3:1–2) and for Timothy (1 Tim 1:19; 4:6–16; 6:11; 2 Tim 2:15, 22–24; Titus 2:7–8).

If 1 Tim 3:11 refers to deaconesses, then four qualifications could be added: σεμνάς, "dignified" (#6), μὴ διαβόλους, "not slanderers" (#19), νηφαλίους, "clear-minded" (#4), and πιστὰς ἐν πᾶσιν, "faithful in all things." When Paul's description of the results of the opponents' teaching is compared with the list of qualifications in general, it is clear that the opponents would not qualify for church leadership, for their teaching resulted in speculations (1 Tim 1:4; 6:4; 2 Tim 2:23), senseless babble (1 Tim 1:6; Titus 1:10), foolishness, strife, quarrels (Titus 3:9), ungodliness (2 Tim 2:16), envy, strife, slander, evil suspicions, constant irritation (1 Tim 6:4–5; cf. 2 Tim 3:1–9), fighting about words resulting in ruin (2 Tim 2:14), and that which is harmful and useless (Titus 3:9). The requirements that an overseer not be a recent convert and that an elder go through a testing period (#14 in the table) are not repeated for Titus, suggesting that the Cretan church was younger than the one at Ephesus (see *Comment*).

	Overseer (1 Tim 3:1–7; 5:17–23)	Deacon (1 Tim 3:8–13)	Elder (Titus 1:5–9)	Opponents
1.	Desiring to be an overseer is a καλὸν ἔργον, "good work" (cf. 2 Tim 2:15).	Cf. #20 below.		Cf. worthless for any ἔργον ἀγαθόν, "good work" (Titus 1:16).
2.	ἀνεπίλημπτος, "above reproach"; μαρτυρία καλή, "good reputation," with outsiders	ἀνέγκλητος, "above reproach"	ἀνέγκλητος, "above reproach"	Have brought reproach on the church (esp. Titus 1:11–14); also the overall picture of their activities
3.	μιᾶς γυναικὸς ἀνήρ, "'one-woman' man" (cf. 1 Tim 5:9)	μιᾶς γυναικὸς ἀνήρ, "'one-woman' man"	μιᾶς γυναικὸς ἀνήρ, "'one-woman' man"	Forbid marriage (1 Tim 4:3), possibly child-bearing (1 Tim 2:15), and seduce women (2 Tim 3:6)
4.	νηφάλιον, "clear-minded"		ἐγκρατής, "disciplined"	
5.	σώφρων, "self-controlled"		σώφρων, "self-controlled"	ἀκρατής, "uncontrolled" (2 Tim 3:3)
6.	κόσμιος, "dignified"	σεμνός, "dignified" (also his wife, or deaconess, v 11)		
7.	φιλόξενος, "hospitable"	See *Comment* on 1 Tim 3:11.	φιλόξενος, "hospitable"	Upset house churches (Titus 1:11); worm their way into women's houses (2 Tim 3:6)
8.	διδακτικός, "skilled in teaching" (cf. 1 Tim 5:24–25)		δυνατὸς ... καὶ παρακαλεῖν ἐν τῇ διδασκαλίᾳ τῇ ὑγιαινούσῃ καὶ ... ἐλέγχειν, "able to exhort with sound teaching and rebuke"	ἑτεροδιδασκαλεῖν, "teaching a different gospel" (1 Tim 1:3; cf. 4:7; 5:3; 6:4, 20; 2 Tim 4:3–4); want to be νομοδιδάσκαλοι, "teachers of the law," but are ignorant and dogmatic (1 Tim 1:7); heaping up false διδασκάλους, "teachers" (2 Tim 4:3); devoted to the διδασκαλίαις, "teachings," of demons (1 Tim 4:1; cf. *Introduction*, "The Ephesian Heresy")
9.	μὴ πάροινος, "not a drunkard"	μὴ οἴνῳ πολλῷ, "not addicted to wine"	μὴ πάροινος, "not a drunkard"	

10.	μὴ πλήκτης, "not violent"		μὴ πλήκτης, "not violent"	
11.	ἐπιεικής, "gracious" (cf. 2 Tim 2:24)		μὴ αὐθάδης, "not arrogant"	Lack love (1 Tim 1:5–6)
12.	μὴ . . . ἄμαχος, "not quarrelsome"		μὴ ὀργιλος, "not quick tempered"	Teaching results in μάχας, "quarrels" (2 Tim 2:23; Titus 3:9)
13.	μὴ . . . ἀφιλάργυρος, "not a lover of money"	μὴ αἰσχροκερδεῖς, "not greedy for gain"	μὴ αἰσχροκερδής, "not greedy for gain"	Think godliness is a πορισμόν, "means of profit" (1 Tim 6:5); wish πλουτεῖν, "to be rich" (1 Tim 6:9–10); φιλάργυροι, "lovers of money" (2 Tim 3:2); teach for αἰσχροῦ κέρδους, "shameful gain" (Titus 1:11)
14.	τοῦ ἰδίου οἴκου καλῶς προϊστάμενον, τέκνα ἔχοντα ἐν ὑποταγῇ, "managing his own household well, having submissive children"	τεκνῶν καλῶς προϊστάμενοι καὶ τῶν ἰδίων οἴκων, "managing their children and their own household well"	τέκνα ἔχων πιστά, μὴ ἐν κατηγορίᾳ ἀσωτίας ἢ ἀνυπότακτα, "having faithful children, not with accusation of debauchery or rebellious"	γονεῦσιν ἀπειθεῖς, "disobedient to parents" (2 Tim 3:2); ἀνυπότακτοι, "rebellious" (Titus 1:10)
15.	μὴ νεόφοτος, "not a recent convert"	Test first to see if δόκιμος, "approved" (cf. 2 Tim 2:15; 1 Tim 5:22)		Do not appoint elders too quickly (1 Tim 5:22, 24–25), who are ἀδόκιμος, "not approved" (Titus 1:16)
16.	So they do not fall into the devil's (διάβολος) snare; not fall into the devil's judgment (cf. 2 Tim 2:26)			Turned two leaders over to Satan (σατανᾶς; 1 Tim 1:20); follow teachings of demons (δαιμόνια; 1 Tim 4:1); some widows stray after Satan (σατανᾶς; 1 Tim 5:15; cf. v 14); devil has taken them captive (διάβολος; 2 Tim 2:26)
17.		ἔχοντας τὸ μυστήριον τῆς πίστεως, "possessing the mystery of the faith"	ἀντεχόμενον τοῦ . . . πιστοῦ λόγου, "holding firmly to the faithful word"	Teach a different gospel that downplays πίστις, "faith" (1 Tim 1:4, 5, 12–17, 19)
18.		ἐν καθαρᾷ συνειδήσει, "with a clear conscience" (cf. 2 Tim 2:22)		συνείδησις, "conscience," is seared/branded (1 Tim 4:2; cf. 1 Tim

					1:5), defiled (Titus 1:15); καρδία, "heart," is not pure (1 Tim 1:5); πίστις, "faith," is insincere (1 Tim 1:5); ἐν ὑποκρίσει, "in hypocrisy" (1 Tim 4:2); corrupt νοῦν, "mind" (1 Tim 6:5; 2 Tim 3:8); πλανῶντες καὶ πλανώμενοι, "deceiving and deceived" (2 Tim 3:13; cf. Titus 1:10)
19.			μὴ διλόγους, "not gossips" (cf. 1 Tim 3:11)		Cf. gossiping widows (φλύαροι)who may be following the false teaching (1 Tim 5:13)
20.			βαθμὸν . . . καλὸν περιποιοῦνται και πολλὴν παρρησίαν ἐν πίστει, "acquire a good standing . . . and confidence in the faith"		περὶ τὴν πίστιν ἐναυάγησαν, "shipwrecking the faith" (1 Tim 1:19), and ἀνατρέπουσιν τὴν . . . πίστιν, "destroying the faith" (2 Tim 2:18)
21.				φιλάγαθον, "love what is good"	ἀφιλάγαθοι, "not love the good" (2 Tim 3:3); φιλήδονοι μᾶλλον ἢ φιλόθεοι, "lovers of pleasure rather than God" (2 Tim 3:4)
22.				θεοῦ οἰκονόμος, "steward of God"	Not pursue οἰκονομίαν θεοῦ τὴν ἐν πίστει, "stewardship of God by faith" (1 Tim 1:4)
23.				δίκαιος, "just"	
24.				ὅσιος, "holy"	ἀνόσιοι, "unholy" (2 Tim 3:2); ἀσεβείας, "un-godly" (2 Tim 2:16)

Several conclusions can be drawn from this list. (1) The first is its ad hoc nature. While the qualities enumerated are significant in and of themselves, they gain added significance when seen in light of the opponents' behavior. For example, an overseer must be able to teach, especially since heresy is being taught in Ephesus. While the passage has been rightly used throughout church history as a guide for church leadership, it first should be interpreted in light of its historical situation.

(2) The ad hoc nature of the list indicates how Timothy is to apply the qualifications. They are official in that they govern the selection of overseers; if someone is not able to manage his household, he has shown himself unqualified to manage the church. But the list is not a checklist requiring, for example, that all church leaders be married and have more than one child. Paul and Timothy were

not married, nor did they have families (as far as we know), so neither of them could be a "one-woman" man or manage his household well. It seems doubtful that Paul would be telling Timothy that both of them were unqualified for church leadership (even though Timothy was not an overseer; see below). Such a rigid application of the list would also contradict Paul's preference for celibacy (1 Cor 7:7, 26–38). The ad hoc nature of the list, rather, suggests that Paul is thinking that these are the *types* of qualities an overseer should have. Some of the qualities would by definition apply to all candidates: above reproach, hospitable, skilled teacher, etc. Other qualities would depend on their life situations. If an overseer was married, he would have to be a "one-woman" man. If he had a family, he would have to manage the family well. The requirement that an overseer or a deacon be a "one-woman" man suggests that the overseers and elders were men (the NRSV translates the passage with masculine pronouns).

(3) A third conclusion is that these lists are not primarily vocational qualifications and duties. First and foremost—and this is understood in light of the Ephesian situation—Paul is concerned that the right *type* of person be appointed to leadership, a person whose personal qualities set him apart. Jeremias comments that Paul is concerned not with organizational or rhetorical ability but rather with readiness to be obedient to God (25; cf. Spicq, 1:425–26). What the responsibilities of office may have been, however, may be surmised (cf. Spicq, 1:442–50). (a) The words used suggest that the ἐπίσκοποι, "overseers," were responsible for general oversight and the διάκονοι, "deacons," dealt with the day-to-day needs of serving the church. This would explain why it was important to confirm management abilities as seen in their families before appointing them to church leadership. 1 Tim 3:5 speaks of "caring" (ἐπιμελεῖσθαι) for the church of God. Paul also talks about "ruling" (προϊστάναι; cf. v 4); this would include the power of authority sufficient to rebuke the false teachers (Titus 1:13). There were therefore two basic categories: the ministry of oversight and the ministry of daily service. This follows the pattern set in Acts 6 of one group of leaders dedicated to the preaching of the word of God and prayer and a second group of leaders dedicated to daily service (e.g., caring for widows; serving tables). (b) Because Paul says that the overseer must be a skilled teacher and since the same ability is not required of deacons, most agree that this was the primary difference between the two (but see *Comment* on 1 Tim 5:17): overseers taught and deacons did not. Dibelius-Conzelmann argue that since teaching is a charismatic gift (citing 2 Tim 2:2), "teaching cannot be presupposed as a *special* function of the bishop" (55, citing von Campenhausen, *Ecclesiastical Authority,* 109–10). Yet this reasoning is based on a false a priori assumption that office should be separated from charisma (see above). Those skilled in teaching, however, were those gifted in teaching. Dibelius-Conzelmann's argument also fails to explain why the requirement regarding teaching was given and the nature of its relationship to the Ephesian problem of false teachers. (c) The requirement that both overseers and deacons not be greedy for gain, in contrast to the opponents' desire to get rich, may suggest that they were responsible for church finance, but it also may only refer to their motivation to serve and their payment for preaching and not to general financial issues. (d) Paul sees the responsibility of hospitality falling on the overseers (not repeated for the deacons), suggesting that the overseers provided housing for visiting Christians. (e) 1 Tim 5:17–25 may suggest that the overseers/elders (along with Timothy initially) were responsible for

church discipline. (f) Dibelius-Conzelmann add that the overseer was the "representative of the congregation, even to the outside world" (55), citing 1 Tim 3:7. But the call for a good reputation can be explained as a response to the misconduct of the opponents; that the same requirement occurs for deacons shows that it was not an issue for one office. It would be natural, nevertheless, for the leadership within the church to be the point of contact with those outside.

CRITICAL ISSUES

Several questions have been raised concerning Paul's instructions. (1) There is nothing necessarily Christian about these qualities, and they are often termed bourgeois. (a) But Paul was addressing a specific historical problem in which the opponents had gone far beyond Christian standards. In fact, they were not even meeting pagan standards. Therefore, Paul exhorted the church leaders to conduct themselves at a minimum in such a way that secular society would admire their ethics and behavior. This is not to say that a church leader only had to be a good pagan, or that the author drew his ethics from secular thought (contra Oberlinner, 119; see *Introduction*, "The Response to the Heresy"), but in the Ephesian situation it was necessary to emphasize this rudimentary level of standards. Paul's answer was intended not to be all inclusive but to emphasize what was appropriate to Ephesus. (b) It might also be that the Christian virtues were assumed by Paul and did not need to be stated (cf. Fee, 42). (c) These qualities are also Christian. For example, Paul says that "the fruit of the Spirit is love, joy, peace, patience, kindness, goodness, faithfulness, gentleness, self-control" (Gal 5:22–23a). The fact that the non-Christian world also sees these qualities as laudable does not prevent them from being Christian. In fact it can be argued that these qualities are not fully attainable apart from the working of God, which is the ethical structure of the PE, ethics coming from soteriology (cf. *Introduction*, "The Response to the Heresy"). Paul was a blasphemer, persecutor, and insolent person (1 Tim 1:13); it was only by God's grace and mercy that these sins were overcome. (d) Moreover, some of the qualities in the list are distinctly Christian: a leader must be a good teacher of Scripture (cf. *Comment*); he cannot be a recent convert; he must have a good reputation with those outside the church. (e) While these qualities may have been respected in the secular society of that day, it is questionable to what degree they were attained by the general populace (so Kelly, 74). Paul was not so much saying that the church leader must be as good as non-Christians as he was saying that they must be as good as the goals set by non-Christians. (f) Kelly (75) suggests that Paul was being a realist. Because the actual standards of behavior were so low (cf. Guthrie, 80), it might have been too much to insist that the Ephesian Christians attain the same level of spiritual maturity as perhaps Jewish converts. Rather, they were to concentrate on the basics of observable behavior; they must learn to crawl before they attempt to walk (cf. Scott, 32). L. T. Johnson adds, "'It is required of stewards that they be found trustworthy' (1 Cor 4:2). Fidelity to one spouse, sobriety, and hospitality may seem trivial virtues to those who identify authentic faith with momentary conversion or a single spasm of heroism. But to those who have lived longer and who recognize how the administration of a community can erode even the strongest of characters and the best of intentions, finding a leader who truly is a lover of peace and not a lover of money can be downright exciting" (148–49).

(2) Why does Paul list only observable qualities and not inner qualities essential for Christian leadership? Much of what was said above deals also with this question. (a) The problem in Ephesus was one of improper behavior, and Paul's instructions address that specific issue. These are the qualities that were essential for the Ephesian leaders to adopt in contrast to the Ephesian opponents. (b) There was the practical problem. Paul's letter was to help Timothy confront the current church leadership and put guidelines in place to keep the problem from recurring. While it would have been impossible to know if a person's heart was pure, it was possible to ask if a person's behavior showed a pure heart. The historical setting required an emphasis on observable traits.

(3) Who were the overseers, and what was their relationship to the deacons of 1 Tim 3:8–13 and the other church workers mentioned elsewhere in the NT? To answer this question, it is helpful to summarize the different groupings of church workers. (a) ἐπίσκοπος, "overseer" (often translated "bishop"), in 1 Tim 3:1–7 describes a leader who has the ability to manage (προϊστάναι) a household and the church. A similar discussion concerning overseers is found in Titus 1:5–9 where Paul calls the same group both elders (πρεσβύτεροι) and overseers. Paul greets the overseers and deacons (διάκονοι) in Philippi (Phil 1:1) and speaks to the Ephesian elders at the end of his third missionary journey (Acts 20:17), encouraging them to shepherd (ποιμαίνειν) their flock as overseers (Acts 20:28). Peter calls Jesus the "overseer of your souls" (1 Pet 2:25). ἐπισκοπή, "office of overseer," occurs in 1 Tim 3:1 and in reference to Judas's office (Acts 1:20). In addressing the elders, Peter admonishes them to tend (ἐπισκοπεῖν) God's flock properly (1 Pet 5:2). The verb is also used in Heb 12:15 but with no relation to the function of overseer. For a discussion of the pre-Christian usage of ἐπίσκοπος, see L. Porter, *ATR* 21 (1939) 103–12.

(b) διάκονος, "deacon," is a more common term because of its nontechnical use to describe anyone who serves. It is used of an official of the church in 1 Tim 3:8, 12 and Phil 1:1. See *Comment* on 1 Tim 3:8 for a more detailed discussion. In both the PE and Phil 1:1 ἐπίσκοπος and διάκονος are used side by side. In the young churches (Acts 14:23; Titus 1:5) Paul appointed only elders (πρεσβύτεροι); perhaps the assumption was that as the churches grew and the work load increased, deacons would be appointed to help, a process paralleling the growth of the Jerusalem church (Acts 6; cf. Knight, 175).

(c) πρεσβύτερος, "elder," is the third major title. Paul gives Timothy a list of rules governing elders in the Ephesian church in 1 Tim 5:17–25, where he also speaks of them as ruling (προϊστάναι). (Paul left Titus in Crete in order to appoint elders [Titus 1:5].) He then gives a list of personal characteristics that closely parallel those of overseers in 1 Tim 3:1–7 and even uses the term ἐπίσκοπος, "overseer" (Titus 1:7). Paul uses the cognate πρεσβυτέριον, "body of elders," of the ones who participated in Timothy's commissioning, a word also used of the Sanhedrin (Luke 22:66; Acts 22:5). Luke says that when Paul arrived at Miletus, he summoned the elders (πρεβύτεροι) of the Ephesian church (Acts 20:17). In his address, Paul also calls them overseers (ἐπίσκοποι; Acts 20:28). This suggests that ἐπίσκοπος, "overseer," and πρεσβύτερος, "elder," were synonymous terms. Meier argues that the ἐπίσκοπος was a "specialized presbyter" assigned the particular duties of preaching and teaching (*CBQ* 35 [1973] 345; but see *Comment* on 1 Tim 5:13). More likely πρεσβύτερος was either a general term for church leaders, including overseers (who teach) and deacons (who do not teach), or 1 Tim 5:17 is speaking of elders, namely, overseers who teach (cf. *Form/Structure/Setting* on 1 Tim 5:17–25). In the NT πρεσβύτερος can describe an elderly person (1 Tim 5:1; Luke 15:25; John 8:9; Acts 2:17), but usually it describes a person holding an official position in the Jewish hierarchy (e.g., Matt 16:21; 21:23; 26:3, 47, 57; 27:1, 3, 12, 20, 41) and the church (e.g., Acts 11:30; 14:23; 15:2, 4, 6, 22, 23; 16:4; 20:17; 21:18; Jas 5:14; 1 Pet 5:1, 5; cf. Rev 4:4). Luke uses the title πρεσβύτερος more than any other NT writer. Seven times it is used of the Jewish rulers (Acts 4:5, 8, 23; 6:12; 23:14; 24:1; 25:15) and ten times of elders in the church. The Antioch church sent a gift to the elders in Jerusalem (Acts 11:30). At the end of his first missionary journey, Paul appointed elders in all the churches (Acts 14:23). In the account of the Jerusalem Council apostles and elders are paired as the authoritative body six times (Acts 15:2, 4, 6, 22, 23; 16:4). At the end of his third journey Paul called the Ephesian elders to a meeting in Miletus (Acts 20:17), and when he arrived in Jerusalem he visited James and some of the elders (Acts 21:18). Only once does Luke use the word to refer to elderly people, and that is in a quotation from Joel (Acts 2:17). Elders are also referred to in Jas 5:14; 1 Pet 5:1, 5; 2 John 1; 3 John 1, and twelve times in Revelation (4:4, 10; 5:5, 6, 8, 11, 14; 7:11, 13; 11:16; 14:3; 19:4).

(d) Several times Paul refers to people in positions of authority in the church using other designations. Paul exhorts the Thessalonian church "to respect those who labor among you and are over you [προϊσταμένους] in the Lord and admonish you, and to esteem them very highly in love because of their work" (1 Thess 5:12–13). This same verb is used of the work of overseers (1 Tim 3:4–5), deacons (1 Tim 3:12), and elders (1 Tim 5:17). In discussing spiritual gifts, Paul says that those who rule should do so with zeal (ὁ πρὸϊστάμενος ἐν σπουδῇ; Rom 12:8), although it is possible to translate "He who gives aid, with zeal" (cf. Titus 3:8, 14). In the Corinthian church, along with the more ecstatic gifts are the gifts of being helpers (ἀντιλήμψεις) and administrators (κυβερνήσεις; 1 Cor 12:28). Paul also cites the spiritual gifts of being an evangelist, pastor, and teacher (Eph 4:11).

From this quick listing, several conclusions can be drawn relating to the general issues discussed above (in "The Development of Christian Ministry"). (a) Nowhere are any of these titles applied to Timothy. Paul's admonition to Timothy as the "Lord's servant" (2 Tim 2:24–25) lists qualities that are similar to those listed for overseers and deacons, but it says nothing about Timothy being an overseer. He stands outside the local church structure as Paul's delegate with the authority to enforce Paul's decisions. This is significant when considering arguments both for and against the proposition that Timothy was a monarchical bishop, or at least at the beginning of the development of the chief bishop. (Cf. Easton's assertion: "In 'Timothy' and 'Titus,' therefore, the Ignatian bishops are actually found in everything but the title" [177].) Such theories are not based on the text (cf. Meier, *CBQ* 35 [1973] 323–45).

(b) The titles of overseer and elder are used interchangeably. Paul instructs Titus concerning elders (Titus 1:5) and then in the next breath calls them overseers (Titus 1:7) with no indication that the audience has changed. That the list of qualities in Titus 1 so closely parallels that of the overseers in 1 Tim 3:1–7 suggests that the two terms refer to the same office. This same interchangability is found in Acts 20 where Paul calls the Ephesian elders (v 17) and tells them that as overseers (v 28) they should take care of the church. προϊστάναι, "to rule," can also be used with both titles; this is especially significant if ὁ προϊστάμενος, "leader," in Rom 12:8

is a title. Perhaps πρεσβύτερος reflected more the patriarchal background in Judaism while ἐπίσκοπος was sometimes used when the emphasis was more on the function of providing oversight. Fee comments, "It seems very likely on sociological grounds that the head of the household, the *paterfamilias*, functioned in a similar role of leadership in the house church that met in his or her household as he or she did in the household itself" (*Philippians*, 67 n. 46).

(c) The use of the singular ἐπισκοπῆς, "office of overseer" (1 Tim 3:1), and the singular forms that follow (3:2–7) suggest to some the beginning of the monarchical episcopate: one bishop over a city with many church leaders under him (von Campenhausen, *Ecclesiastical Authority*, 107–8; cf. *Introduction*, "The Historical Problem"). Others suggest that a single overseer was appointed from within the group of elders, or a smaller group (von Lips, *Glaube—Gemeinde—Amt*, 113–14; Dibelius-Conzelmann, 56; Kertelge, *Gemeinde und Amt*, 147). However, elsewhere in Paul we see a plurality of church leaders functioning on an equal par. In his salutation to the Philippian church, Paul addresses the ἐπισκόποις, "overseers," plural (Phil 1:1). In 1 Tim 5:17 Paul gives rules for πρεσβύτεροι, "elders," plural. He tells Titus what type of people should be elders (plural; Titus 1:5), and then two verses later says that an overseer (singular; Titus 1:7) should have certain qualities. In 1 Timothy it appears that since there is only one office of overseer (with many fulfilling the role), Paul begins 3:1–7 with the generic singular (Kelly, 13, 73–74; Michaelis, *Ältestenamt*, 52–53) and to stay consistent continues with singular forms (see a similar shift from plural to singular in 1 Tim 2:11). Fee also points out that "the 'if anyone' clause in v. 1, which has led to the singular in this verse, is a non-limiting, or generalizing, conditional sentence. It recurs in 1 Tim 5:8 and 6:3, and in both cases—esp. 6:3—refers to a group of more than one" (84). If the elders in Titus 1:5 (also called overseers; v 7) are the same as the overseers in 1 Tim 3:1–7, then Paul's instruction that Titus appoint κατὰ πόλιν πρεσβυτέρους, "elders in every city," attests to plural leadership of overseers in every city. Throughout the NT the terms for leadership are usually plural (1 Cor 12:28; Eph 4:11; 1 Thess 5:12, 13; Heb 13:7, 17; Jas 5:14; cf. Lightfoot, *Philippians*, 194). This is to be expected, given the nature of the early church, which was not centralized in large meeting halls but distributed throughout a city in homes (cf. Titus 1:11). There is also nothing in the list that requires a singular overseer over an entire city, which was the case by the second century as seen in Ignatius (see *Explanation*). While overseers are over the church and deacons serve, nowhere in the PE does Paul teach a two-tiered structure of church authority, much less the three-tiered one found in Ignatius. As Fee asserts, "No evidence exists for a single leader as the 'head' of the local assembly in the Pauline churches" (*Philippians*, 67).

(d) From the data in the NT it is possible to deduce a two-step growth process analogous to the pattern of the early church in Jerusalem. At first the apostles led the church in Jerusalem, but as it grew in size they needed help, and so seven men were appointed to serve (Acts 6:1–6), although they were not called deacons. At the end of his first missionary journey (Acts 14:23) and his preaching in Crete (Titus 1:5–9) when the churches were young, Paul appointed overseers, not deacons. But in the more established churches of Philippi (Phil 1:1) and Ephesus (1 Tim 3:8–13) there were both overseers and deacons. Perhaps the latter office developed on a church-by-church basis as the size and needs of the church increased.

(4) The fourth major question asks when the church started institutionalizing leadership. As has been noted above (see "The Development of Christian Ministry"), many scholars have assumed that institutionalism was a later development out of the more primitive charismatic leadership. Since the PE discuss different offices/functions, it is argued that they must belong to a later period of the church's development. Yet others argue that there always were leadership groups in the church along with the exercise of charismatic gifts, despite the expectation of the imminent return of Christ.

Acts 6:1–6 speaks of the division of labor between the apostles and the seven who were "of good repute, full of the Spirit and of wisdom" (which is the basic thrust of the lists in the PE). Acts 14:21 tells of the appointment of elders at the end of Paul's first missionary journey, and elders are present at the end of his third missionary journey as well (Acts 20:17). Acts 15 deals with the meeting of an authoritative body and its binding decree. As early as 1 Thessalonians there are church rulers (5:12). Even in the Corinthian church, where the ecstatic gifts played such a large role, there are gifts of oversight (teachers, administrators) and service (helpers; 1 Cor 12:28), gifts suited to the running and oversight of the church (cf. possibly the implication of judgments by the leadership in 1 Cor 6:1–8). 1 Cor 16:15–16 shows Paul's desire that the church "be subject to" (ὑποτάσσησθε) those who have priority as "first-fruits" such as the household of Stephanus. In Rom 12:6–8 Paul speaks of serving and teaching (cf. the PE, which assign teaching to the overseers). By the time of Paul's imprisonment, the offices of overseer and deacon were well established, at least in the Philippian church (1:1). Jas 5:14 speaks of calling the elders to pray over a sick person. Heb 13:17 exhorts the community to "obey your leaders [ἡγουμένοις] and submit to them; for they are keeping watch [ἀγρυπνοῦσιν] over your souls, as men who will have to give account. Let them do this joyfully, and not sadly, for that would be of no advantage to you." Peter also exhorts the elders to "tend [ποιμάνατε] the flock of God that is your charge, not by constraint but willingly, not for shameful gain but eagerly, not as domineering over those in your charge but being examples to the flock. . . . Likewise you that are younger be subject to the elders" (1 Pet 5:2–3, 5).

Although the actual functions of overseers/elders and deacons are rarely discussed in the NT, the evidence for the existence of church leadership is found so widely in the NT that more than a questioning of the historicity of Acts is required to argue that the church had no interest in formal leadership. As Fee contends, "That there is little or no evidence for a *hierarchy* in the Pauline churches does not mean that *leadership* did not exist; it undoubtedly did, and there is no good reason to think that the title given here [in Phil 1:1], and found again in 1 Timothy and Titus, did not exist from the beginning" (*Philippians*, 67). The flexibility of the NT terms (seen above) betrays an early date, for by the turn of the century the titles had become assigned to specific responsibilities with the three-tiered hierarchy of bishop, elder/presbyter, and deacon. The fact that Paul's emphasis is not on duties but on character suggests that the hierarchical structure of the church was not firmly established. There was as yet no technical term for deaconess (if 1 Tim 3:11 refers to such a position; cf. Rom 16:1). That Paul has to tell the church that leaders should be paid (1 Tim 4:17) also indicates an early date. A number of passages in early, middle, and late NT writings from Palestine, Asia Minor, and Greece attest to the presence of formal leadership.

It seems only natural that Paul would have established positions of formal leadership within the church. He grew up within the synagogue, which both inside and outside of Israel was governed by a board of elders who were responsible for the community's affairs. Society had ἐπίσκοποι in secular and religious settings (Vincent, *Word Studies* 4:227; Deissmann, *Bible Studies*, 230–31; H. W. Beyer, *TDNT* 2:608–15). Jesus appointed twelve leaders. Kelly points out that a close parallel to the office of overseer in the PE is seen in Qumran, where the overseer (*mĕbaqqēr*) was responsible for "commanding, examining, instructing, receiving alms or accusations dealing with the peoples' sins, and generally shepherding them" (74; cf. 1QS 6:10–20, 9:19–22; CD 13:7–16; 14:8–12). It would have been a natural transition for Paul to adapt the organizational structure of the synagogue to the church. When the needs of the early church outgrew the ability of the apostles to manage, they "restructured." This is not an anachronistic creation of the deaconry, but it does show that organizational structures were natural for them.

Any silence in the NT concerning elders is precisely that. The NT's lack of explanation of leadership positions may suggest that they were natural adaptations from what the early church already knew and accepted. It was not until the Ephesian heresy that the leadership not only failed but became instrumental in the promulgation of the heresy, and therefore in the PE the positions of leadership required discussion. Since Paul's Gentile churches were familiar with governance by a senate, what may have originated in Judaism as rule by elders would have seemed natural to the Gentile converts as well (Kelly, 123–24). Luke's witness to Paul's early practice of appointing elders thus seems credible (Acts 14:23).

Fee is also correct in his emphasis on the eschatological nature of the early church and its impact on church leadership ("*Laos* and Leadership," especially 121–24, 130–34, 139–43). Those with leadership gifts "are not 'set apart' by 'ordination'; rather, their gifts are part of the Spirit's work among the whole people" (131). The leadership was part of the body and labored among the body; it was not separate from and over the laity (contra Spicq, 1:65–66).

While there are many parts of this discussion that lie outside matters touched by the PE, it seems plausible that the PE provide evidence of the earliest forms of church organization based to some degree on the Jewish background of the church but also on the fundamental needs of leadership felt by any group: having gifted and qualified people care for general oversight and for the daily needs of the people. Once the ad hoc nature of the PE and the rest of the NT epistles is recognized, the lack of discussion of the structure of the church elsewhere in the NT is understandable and the appearance of formal church structure in the PE is consistent with the few existing references.

Many argue that the author of the PE sees institutionalism as the key to controlling the growing threat of false teaching (cf., e.g., M. Y. MacDonald, *The Pauline Churches*). But the emphasis on leadership in the PE is not on the office but on the personal character of the leader. This indicates that the author is not instituting a structure to deal with a problem (cf. *Introduction*, "The Response to the Heresy").

(5) The issue of the origin of the title ἐπίσκοπος, "overseer," is shrouded in mystery. While there are some counterparts in non-Christian thought (Lietzmann, *ZWT* 55 [1914] 97–153; Dibelius, *Thessalonicher; Philipper*, excursus on Phil 1:1; Spicq, 1:440–42), none provides an exact parallel. In pre-Christian literature it is

not an especially religious term although it is used of the gods. There are sufficient references to ἐπίσκοπος in both secular (MM, 244–5) and Jewish (H. W. Beyer, *TDNT* 2:614–15) texts to show that it was a common title and function. But the word group has no distinctively theological significance, and there is no specific office of episcopate that could be the source of the Christian use of the word. Harnack (*Constitution and Law*) and Hatch (*Organization*) viewed Hellenism as the source of both the title and the function of the overseer and deacon. Harvey, following Lietzmann's judgment (*ZWT* 55 [1913] 111), says, "The small amount of evidence at our disposal does not lead to any positive conclusion about the origin of ἐπίσκοποι. To derive the term from official and private supervisory commissions, such as are known to us from coins and inscriptions, is as capricious as to derive it from the occasional appearance of an 'overseer' in a religious association. The same is true to a still greater degree of διάκονοι" (*JTS* n.s. 25 [1974] 318). Some have looked to the ruler of the synagogue (ἀρχισυνάγωγος) who had helpers (ὑπηρέται, deacons?), although in the PE deacons serve the church, not the overseers. Others suggest the *mĕbaqqēr* in Qumran (1QS 6:10–20; 9:19–22; CD 13:7–16; 19:8–12; Josephus *J.W.* 2.8.3 §§122–23) as a possible source (Spicq 1:72–73, 448–50; contra K. G. Goetz, *ZNW* 30 [1931] 89ff.; Jeremias, 23; id., *Jerusalem in the Time of Jesus,* tr. F. H. and E. C. H. Cave [Philadelphia: Fortress, 1969] 261–62; Kelly). One would suspect that Judaism and its reverence for age would have exerted some influence, especially in the use of πρεσβύτερος, "elder." Harvey argues that the leadership in the early church lay predominantly with the older members (*JTS* n.s. 25 [1974] 318–32; see critique by Roberts, *JTS* n.s. 26 [1975] 403–5), a point emphasized by Spicq, who documents the reverence for age and wisdom (1:66–69). Regardless of the linguistic background to the term, the function is defined within the context of Christian ministry, and parallels with non-Christian usage can be explained as common traits required in leadership.

THE SOURCE OF THE LISTS

Virtue lists were very common in secular society and are found throughout the NT (cf. CD 4; Col 3:12–17; Polycarp *Phil.* 5ff.; cf. Vögtle, *Tugend- und Lasterkataloge,* for vice lists; cf. *Form/Structure/Setting* on 1 Tim 1:8–11). Dibelius-Conzelmann (158–60) refer to the list of virtues by Onosander (*De imperitoris officio* 1) that shares similarities with the list in 1 Tim 3:1–7 (two words are identical; three are similar) and suggest that the author of the PE adopted Onosander's list even though it does not discuss church leadership. It is characteristic of these lists to be somewhat general (Kelly, 74), although this should not be overemphasized insofar as the list in 1 Timothy is dealing with specific problems. The similarity between the list in 1 Timothy and Onosander is explained by noting the function of the list in the PE: Paul wants the church leaders to possess at a minimum those basic, observable traits that were highly regarded in pagan society. One would be surprised if Paul did not choose some of those qualities that were the common stock of the society to which he was appealing (cf. Fee, 47). Instructive here is Bernard's (57; cf. Lock, 36) detailed comparison of the requirements of an overseer and Diogenes Laertius's (7:116ff.) description of the Stoic σοφός, "wise man." There are quite a few similarities, and Bernard thinks that it is possible that Paul knew this description. Although it is difficult to date Diogenes Laertius, H. S. Long places him in the "first

half of the third century A.D." (*OCD*², 348), which means that Paul could not have
known it. But what is instructive is how these two lists could be so similar and yet
have no connection (unless Diogenes Laertius copied Paul). Fee says the similarity
with Onosander is merely coincidental, citing "the equally striking correspondence between 1 Thess. 2:1–10 and Dio Chrysostom's *Oration* 32. The *language*
belongs to the milieu; the presence of the false teachers explains the specifics" (84).
The qualities are those that all people, Christians and non-Christians, hold as
laudable. That is the common denominator among the lists, and searching for a
common source is at best tentative and not helpful in determining meaning.

Comment

1a Πιστὸς ὁ λόγος, "Trustworthy is the saying." This is the second faithful
saying in the PE (see *Comment* on 1 Tim 1:15 for a general discussion). Some think
it refers back to 1 Tim 2:15 (Nestle-Aland²⁷; NEB; Chrysostom; White; Parry; Duncan,
ExpTim 35 [1922] 141; Lock; Robertson, *Word Pictures* 4:572; Falconer; Bover, *Bib*
19 [1938] 74–79; Nauck,"Herkunft"; Dibelius-Conzelmann; Barrett; B. Noack,
DTT 32 [1969] 1–22; L. T. Johnson). This would mean that all the faithful sayings
deal with the issue of salvation, and the consistency of theme makes this interpretation attractive. If 1 Tim 2:15 reflects the opponents' language, then this interpretation seems the better choice. The formula then calls attention to the significance
of 2:15 and does not introduce a citation. But most believe that the formula points
forward to 3:1b (cf. Knight, *Faithful Sayings*, 52–55; Ellingworth, *BT* 31 [1980] 443–
45). They argue that even though 3:1b does not sound like a saying that would be
passed down through church tradition, 2:15 sounds even less like one. Hanson
([1983] 74–75) contends that the primary function of the formula "the saying is
trustworthy" is to add solemnity to the saying, and it is not intended to indicate that
the saying is traditional material. Fee (42) calls it a "reinforcement formula." While
the other faithful sayings appear to be traditional material, this one does not, and
Hanson's argument regarding the function of the formula is strongest here. The
formula does not have to have the same significance in every case.

1b Εἴ τις ἐπισκοπῆς ὀρέγεται, καλοῦ ἔργου ἐπιθυμεῖ, "If anyone aspires to the
office of overseer, he is desiring a good work." Rather than downplaying the
position of church leader, Paul elevates it by saying that it is a good work. Why does
this statement warrant the solemn introduction of a faithful saying? Most answer
that the church placed its greatest esteem on the more visible, ecstatic gifts, and the
Ephesians needed to be reminded that the more practical functions such as
overseer were also significant and worthy of honor. However, while the exercise of
the gift of teaching may not visibly involve the work of the Spirit, it seems safe to
assume that being a teacher and leader would have been held in high regard. It
seems, rather, that any hesitancy to accept positions of leadership by members of
the Ephesian church was the result of the excess of the opponents. They were
bringing reproach not only upon the church itself but also upon anyone in
leadership. Perhaps as well people were hesitant to accept positions that would
bring them in direct confrontation with the opponents. Thus, when Paul says that
rulers who rule well are worthy of double honor (1 Tim 5:17), the emphasis is on
the "well" (καλῶς); the church needed leaders who would do their job well, and it
was therefore a good thing to aspire to the office of overseer. (Hanson [(1983) 75]

says that "there is evidence in the *Didache* that in the first or early second century the charismatic officers, such as the prophet, exercised more attraction." Unfortunately he gives no references. *Did.* 15 is the closest parallel to our passage, but it offers nothing to support Hanson's statement.)

The use of the singular indefinite τὶς, "anyone," signals that Paul is stating a general truth (see on 2:11). The masculine pronoun (used also in the NRSV) is appropriate since Paul envisions an Ephesian overseer to be a "one-woman" man (1 Tim 3:2). ὀρέγεται, "aspires," elsewhere describes an improper craving for money (1 Tim 6:10), the sexual impulse that has been perverted by sin (Rom 1:27; the cognate noun ὄρεξις, "lustful passion"), and a desiring for a heavenly homeland (Heb 11:16). The word describes an "ambitious seeking" (MM, 456); whether the aspiration is good or bad is determined by context. In our text it must be good since Paul is recommending it (contra Scott [30] who says, "It is a noble glutton that is greedy for church office"). It describes not only a desire (cf. ἐπιθυμεῖν, "to desire," below) but an actual seeking after (Vincent, *Word Studies* 4:227). The picture we have of the early church suggests that elders were appointed (cf. Acts 14:23); aspiration would motivate them to make their desires known. (A possible parallel may be Paul's comment that the Corinthians should "earnestly desire the higher gifts" [1 Cor 12:31].)

ἐπισκοπή, "office of overseer," occurs four other places in the NT. It can mean "visit" (Luke 19:44; 1 Pet 2:12) or "office" (Acts 1:20, a modified citation of Ps 108:8 LXX [MT 109:8]; cf. Num 4:16). While ἐπίσκοπος, "overseer" (v 2), can refer to the office as well as the person holding the office (H. W. Beyer, *TDNT* 2:608), the use of the different form ἐπισκοπή suggests that Paul is differentiating the two and in v 1 is thinking specifically of the office. This would help explain the use of the singular form when elsewhere church leadership is spoken of in the plural (see *Form/Structure/Setting*). There is one office held by many people. The occurrences of "overseer" have already been summarized in *Form/Structure/Setting*. The basic meaning of the word group is "oversight": the idea of watching over someone or something. The TEV translates ἐπίσκοπος as "church leader" and διάκονος (v 8) as "church helper." This clearly differentiates the two offices and avoids any possible anachronism of the translation "bishop." The translation here uses "overseer" because it too avoids anachronism and emphasizes that the primary function of this office was general oversight.

ἐπιθυμεῖν, "to desire" (followed by a genitive; cf. Wallace, *Greek Grammar*, 132), occurs only here in the PE, but the cognate noun ἐπιθυμία, "desire," occurs six other times. It describes a strong desire; Kelly (72) translates "sets his heart on a worthwhile job." Although the word group can designate desires that are good and proper, as in this case (cf. Luke 22:15; Phil 1:23; 1 Thess 2:17), in most cases in the NT the desires are evil and wicked. Every occurrence of the noun in the PE denotes bad desires. People who desire to be rich fall into hurtful desires (1 Tim 6:9). Timothy is to flee youthful passions (2 Tim 2:22). The opponents are taking advantage of the impulses of the weak women (2 Tim 3:6), and the time is coming when people will gather around themselves teachers who teach what they desire to hear (2 Tim 4:3). Even though believers have been slaves to passions (Titus 3:3), the grace of God has appeared to teach believers to renounce worldly desires (Titus 2:12). This usage in the PE accords with Paul's general use throughout the corpus and with the Stoics who list ἐπιθυμία as one of the four great passions (cf. F. Büchsel,

TDNT 3:167–72), although for the Stoic ἐπιθυμία arose from irrationality and for Paul it was the result of sin (cf. Spicq, *RB* 64 [1957] 184–95).

On καλός, "good," see the *Comment* on 1 Tim 1:8. On the concept of καλὸν ἔργον, "good work," see the *Comment* on 1 Tim 2:10. In light of 1 Tim 3:14–16, aspiring to the office of overseer is a good work because the overseer is instrumental in helping the church protect the truth of the gospel. Chrysostom calls it "a work of protection" ("Homily 10"; NPNF 13:437). Knight (154–55) emphasizes that the phrase can mean "good task" or in a weakened sense "good thing." The former fits the context better and is analogous to Acts 13:2 ("the work to which I called them") and 2 Tim 4:5 ("the work of an evangelist"; cf. Acts 14:26; 15:38; 1 Thess 5:12, 13; Eph 4:12). Chrysostom adds that it is a good work if the person's desire is to protect the church, but not if the person is coveting "the dominion and authority" ("Homily 10"; NPNF 13:437). This emphasis is felt later when Paul says an overseer should care for his family (not rule as a dictator; vv 4–5) and that he should *have*, not *make*, his children in submission (cf. *Comment* on vv 4–5). It is also similar to Peter's charge to "tend the flock of God that is your charge, not by constraint but willingly, not for shameful gain but eagerly, not as domineering over those in your charge but being examples to the flock" (1 Pet 5:2–3).

2a δεῖ οὖν τὸν ἐπίσκοπον ἀνεπίλημπτον εἶναι, "Therefore, it is necessary for an overseer to be above reproach." Because the office of overseer is such an important position, those who fulfill that role must be of a certain character—above reproach. The opponents were leaders in the church whose character and behavior had been so horrendous that they were dragging the church down into disrepute; a true overseer must be the type of person whose personal behavior will counter that of the opponents and help the church regain its credibility. ἀνεπίλημπτον, "above reproach," acts as the title (Chrysostom says, "every virtue is implied in this word" ["Homily 10"; NPNF 13:438]); what it entails is spelled out in the following eleven attributes and three specific concerns. It is reinforced by the threefold repetition of καλός, "good" (3:1, 4, 7; cf. 3:12, 13).

οὖν, "therefore," emphasizes the connection between the list and the office (v 1). Because the office is significant, a certain type of person must hold it. δεῖ, "it is necessary," denotes necessity due to fate (in secular thought), duty, law, and inner necessity in order to achieve a certain result (BAGD, 172). In the PE δεῖ occurs nine times. Twice it denotes a necessity that is not always observed: widows are saying what is not necessary (1 Tim 5:13); the farmer ought to receive the first fruits (2 Tim 2:6). Four times it refers to the necessity that a church leader be a certain type of person (1 Tim 3:2, 7; 2 Tim 2:24; Titus 1:7). Twice it is related to the opponents, saying that it is necessary that they be silenced because they are teaching what they of necessity must not teach (Titus 1:11 [2x]). Its final occurrence in 1 Tim 3:15 is the most significant: Paul is instructing Timothy so that he can know how it is necessary to behave in the household of God. This is important because the church is a pillar and protector of the truth, and it is essential that church leaders be a certain type of person because the clear presentation of the gospel is at stake. In light of this, Paul's admonition in 1 Tim 3:2 is clear. Paul uses δεῖ twenty-five other times. Some of these refer to a necessity that is not absolute (Rom 8:26; 12:3; 1 Cor 8:2; 11:19; 2 Cor 2:3; 11:30; 12:1; Eph 6:20; Col 4:4, 6; 1 Thess 4:1; 2 Thess 3:7). But several times what is necessary is mandate: homosexuals must receive the penalty for their perversion (Rom 1:27); Christ must reign until all his enemies are under his feet (1 Cor 15:25); at death the perishable and mortal must be replaced by the imperishable and immortal (1 Cor 15:53); all people must appear before the judgment seat of Christ (2 Cor 5:10).

The article identifies τὸν ἐπίσκοπον, "the overseer," as a special class appropriate for a general statement; the context indicates that it is not monadic (cf. Wallace, *Greek Grammar*, 229). On ἐπίσκοπος, "overseer," see *Comment* on v 1 and *Form/Structure/Setting.* ἀνεπίλημπτος, "above reproach," is the key term in the list. It stands as the leading concern, and all that follows spells out in more detail what it means. (It is the only requirement in the list that needs further explanation [Towner, 84].) The basic idea will be repeated at the end of this list (v 7). A similar command also stands at the head of the list for elders (Titus 1:6); the principal requirement for deacon is σεμνός, "dignified" (1 Tim 3:8). This concern for a Christian's reputation runs throughout the PE and is frequent in Paul (cf. Titus 2:5; also 1 Cor 10:32; Phil 2:15; Col 4:5; 1 Thess 4:1; cf. Acts 6:3). The opponents are not only hurting themselves and other believers; they are damaging the church's reputation.

ἀνεπίλημπτος, "above reproach," occurs in the NT elsewhere only in a similar command for widows (1 Tim 5:7) and for Timothy with reference to keeping the commandments (1 Tim 6:14). A synonymous term, ἀνέγκλητος, "beyond reproach," is used later in v 10 of deacons. ἀνεπίλημπτος is a compound formed with an alpha privative (like the English *un-*) and ἐπίλη[μ]πτος, "caught, culpable" (cf. 1 Tim 6:12). Bernard (52) and Kelly (80) point out that it means not only that the person is without reproach but that the person truly deserves to be viewed as irreproachable (on the similar use of ὀνειδισμός, "reproach," see *Comment* on 1 Tim 3:7). It cannot mean that an overseer must be free from any sin, internal or visible, but the emphasis here is on the type of external personal reputation that would be a credit to the church (cf. similar statement that a steward [οἰκονόμος] must be found to be faithful [πιστός; 1 Cor 4:2]).

2b μιᾶς γυναικὸς ἄνδρα, νηφάλιον σώφρονα κόσμιον φιλόξενον διδακτικόν, "a 'one-woman' man, clear-minded, self-controlled, dignified, hospitable, skilled in teaching." Paul spells out what he means by ἀνεπίλημπτον, "above reproach." The eleven characteristics in vv 2b–3 are grammatically dependent upon the δεῖ, "it is necessary," of v 2. The first is that an overseer must be μιᾶς γυναικὸς ἄνδρα, the "husband of one wife" or "a 'one-woman' man." The historical assumption, continued from 2:12, is that the overseers are male. This phrase is one of the most difficult phrases in the PE, and yet it is one of the most significant because the opponents have forbidden marriage (1 Tim 4:3; cf. 2:15) and sexual promiscuity is a serious problem (see on 2 Tim 3:6). That it is first on the list after ἀνεπίλημπτον, as it is in Titus 1:6 (after ἀνέγκλητος, "beyond reproach"), suggests that marital faithfulness is a serious problem in the Ephesian church. Paul repeats this same qualification in Titus 1:6 and in 1 Tim 3:12 (to deacons). The emphasis is on the word μία, "one." There are four basic interpretations. Proponents of each interpretation often claim that their reading of the text relates specifically to the Ephesian heresy. But since this argument can be applied to three of the four interpretations (i.e., not the first), it carries no weight. It is also often said that the awkwardness of the expression argues against a specific interpretation, but that argument can be applied to all interpretations. Paul could have said clearly (1) "Must be married," (2) "Not polygamous," (3) "Faithful to his wife," or (4) "Not remarried/divorced."

(1) The interpretation that the phrase means that an overseer must be married

should be rejected (contra the Eastern Orthodox practice). This sees ἀνήρ and γυνή as "husband" and "wife," not "man" and "woman." The counterarguments are as follows: (a) the emphasis of the phrase is on the word μία, "one," and not on the marital state; (b) Paul and Timothy would not be eligible to be overseers; (c) it runs counter to Paul's teaching that being single is a better state for church workers (if they have the gift; 1 Cor 7:17, 25–38); (d) this line of reasoning, to be consistent, would have to argue that the overseer is required to have more than one child since τέκνα, "children" (v 4) is plural; and (e) most adult men were married so it would have been a moot point.

(2) The interpretation that this verse forbids polygamy and keeping concubines is stronger than might be expected from its nearly universal rejection (but held by Justin Martyr *Dial.* 100.134; cf. Lock, 36–37; Robertson, *Word Pictures* 4:572; Easton; Simpson; Dibelius-Conzelmann, 52 [possibly]; Hiebert; Roloff, 156, who views successive divorce and remarriage as polygamy; Grudem, *Systematic Theology,* 916–17; but see Schulze, *KD* 4 [1958] 287–300; Caddeo, "La figura degli," 165–92). (a) This is the most natural undertanding of μιᾶς γυναικός, "one-woman." (b) Polygamy did exist in Judaism (Josephus *Ant.* 17.1.2 §14; Justin Martyr *Trypho* 134; cf. Str-B 3:647–50; Moore, *Judaism* 1:201–2), even to the point that the rabbinic laws regulated it (*m. Yeb.* 4.11; *m. Ket.* 10.1, 4, 5; *m. Sanh.* 2.4; *m. Ker.* 3.7; *m. Qid.* 2.7; *m. Bek.* 8.4; cf. Justin Martyr *Dial.* 134). Knight (158) cites the *lex Antoniana de civitate* that made monogamy the Roman law but allowed an exception for Judaism, and Theodosius' enforcement of monogamy on the Jews (A.D. 393) since they persisted in polygamy. Most feel polygamy was rare and therefore would not have warranted being singled out in all three lists. In reference to Palestinian Judaism, Moore says that the writings "suppose a practically monogamous society" (*Judaism* 2:122). However, marital infidelity was common in Greco-Roman culture. As an example, Fee (84) cites Demosthenes: "Mistresses we keep for the sake of pleasure, concubines for the daily care of the body, but wives to bear us legitimate children" (*Oration* 59.122). Dibelius-Conzelmann argue that this list was brought over from a secular source, and in its original context it was addressing the problem of polygamy. But not only is this source theory unlikely (see above), but it is even more unlikely that a list would be brought over without any modification to make it relevant to the Ephesian situation. (c) Since the phrase is somewhat unusual, it is safe to insist that it had the same meaning in reverse when applied to widows (1 Tim 5:9), and there is no evidence of polyandry. (It is often argued that polygamy would have been forbidden to all Christians, and it would make no sense to specify this in reference to overseers. But many of the qualities required of an overseer are also required of all believers, and so this argument carries little weight; cf. Lyonnet, *VD* 45 [1967] 3–10.) (d) Even if polygamy existed among the Jews, evidence is lacking that it was practiced by Christians, and therefore "Christian polygamy" most likely is not in view. The following two interpretations in any case would include a prohibition against polygamy even if polygamy were not explicitly in Paul's mind.

(3) Others argue that the phrase means an overseer must be faithful to his wife (NEB; Lyonnett, *VD* 45 [1967] 3–10; Trummer, *Bib* 51 [1970] 471–84; Houlden; Dodd, *BT* 28 [1977] 112–16; Fee; Keener, . . . *And Marries Another,* 83–103; Page, *JSNT* 50 [1993] 105–20; Towner; L. T. Johnson), even if he was previously divorced (Saucy, *BSac* 131 [1974] 229–40). Scott paraphrases, "A bishop must be an example of strict morality" (31). Oberlinner goes a little further by defining it as a "good

marriage" that will serve as an example (121). This would allow for the possibility of an overseer being remarried after a death, divorce, or possibly adultery in the distant past but would disallow polygamy and sexual immorality (even if the overseer were not married, since the guidelines would be no less stringent for the unmarried than the married). Marital faithfulness also has the advantage of being a positive way of stating the requirement (as opposed to the negative, not divorced/ remarried) that parallels the rest of the positive statements in the verse. The real question is if the Greek can possibly give this meaning. Kelly says that it "squeezes more out of the Greek than it will bear" (75; cf. Bernard, 53). However, the phrase is unusual, and the Greek has to be "squeezed" to illicit any meaning. Fee interprets the phrase in terms of fidelity, but when the same phrase (in reverse) is applied to widows (1 Tim 5:9) he thinks that it means not only fidelity but also excludes a second marriage (80). Saucy (*BSac* 131 [1974] 229–40) and Knight (159) refine this interpretation by saying that it refers to fidelity since the time of conversion.

(4) The final interpretation, which does give full emphasis to the word μία, "one," is that an overseer can only have been married once. This was the position of the early church (see discussion in Dodd, *BT* 28 [1977] 112–16). (a) Although there are clearer ways to specify a single marriage, this is the easiest reading. (b) There is ample evidence that both society and the early church viewed celibacy after the death of a spouse to be a meritorious choice (Clement of Alexandria *Strom.* 3.1ff.; cf. Ellicott, 40; Kelly, 75, 116; Hanson, [1983] 77). In the second century, parts of the church went beyond the biblical mandate. The Montanists made the forbidding of a second marriage an article of faith, while Athenagoras (died c. 177) called a second marriage "a specious adultery" (Vincent, *Word Studies* 4:229). Tertullian (who became a Montanist) said, "If it be granted that second marriage is lawful, yet all things lawful are not expedient" (*De pud.* 8). The *Shepherd of Hermas* (*Mand.* 4.1) says that if a man, having divorced his unfaithful wife, marries again, he is committing apostasy. If one's spouse dies, the remaining partner may remarry, but if he or she remain single, "he investeth himself with more exceeding honour" (*Mand.* 4.4; cf. the extended set of rules in *Apostolic Constitutions* 6.3.17 [ANF 7:457] cited in the *Explanation*). But none of these citations proves Paul is forbidding a second marriage in 1 Tim 3:2, and it is possible that they are a development influenced by Hellenistic asceticism and in some cases Montanism. (c) This interpretation is in accord with Paul's instructions about the married and the single (1 Cor 7:9, 39), which allows remarriage but prefers celibacy. (d) It may be that Paul distinguishes between the leaders in the church and the laity, assigning a stricter code to the former (cf. Jas 3:1; cf. Bernard, 52). The leader must be completely and totally above reproach (as long as this does not imply that remarriage has any necessary reproach since Paul elsewhere recommends it [1 Tim 5:14; cf. Rom 7:2–3; 1 Cor 7:8–9]).

This interpretation can be subdivided into two views. Some argue that the phrase prohibits a second marriage for an overseer under any condition, whether the first marriage ended by death or divorce (Ellicott; Fairbairn [Appendix B]; Bernard; Preisker, *Christentum und Ehe*, 148; Delling, *Paulus Stellung zu Frau*, 136ff.; A. Oepke, *TDNT* 1:788; Spicq; Kelly; Baltensweiler, *Ehe*, 240; Brox; Dornier; Hasler). Others argue that it prohibits a second marriage only if the first ended in divorce (Lock [see references to Christian literature]; Jeremias [as long as the wife is still living]; Schulze, *KD* 4 [1958] 300; Bartsch, *Anfänge*, 130; Hanson [1983]; Roloff [see above on "polygamy"]). The interpretation here appears to be governed by the exegete's overall view of the early Christian teaching on remarriage (cf. Matt 19:9; Rom 7:1–3; 1 Cor 7:15, 39); there is nothing in our passage that suggests or supports either position. Quinn relies heavily on the Qumran practice of five-year marriages and then a forced separation, and says that the passage speaks of the person "now separated from his spouse, who has not remarried" (86). He follows de la Potterie ("Mari d'une seule femme," 620–23) in asserting that the marriage "is a visible expression of the relation of Christ to his church" (87) and therefore a candidate for church leadership could not break the imagery by remarrying. For further discussion on this passage, see Saucy (*BSac* 131 [1974] 229–40).

The major problem with this interpretation is that elsewhere Paul allows (1 Cor 7) and even encourages (1 Tim 5:14) remarriage. The latter reference (applied to "younger widows") is in the context of Paul's instructions to widows where earlier Paul says that a widow may be enrolled if she has been a ἑνὸς ἀνδρὸς γυνή, "'one-man' woman" (1 Tim 5:9), the exact phrase applied to overseers and deacons but reversed in gender. Because the phrases are so unusual, we expect them to have the same meaning. It seems doubtful that Paul would encourage the remarriage of "younger widows" if this meant that they could never later be enrolled if they were again widowed. For such widows, it could be presumed that remarriage would not be inconsistent with being a "one-man" woman, and hence the phrase in 1 Tim 5:9 would not be a call for a single marriage. The other interpretive key seems to be the unusualness of the phrase. The translation "one-woman man" maintains the emphasis on "one" and carries over what seems to be Paul's emphasis on faithfulness. The quotation marks highlight the unusualness of the phrase, but the expression is not to be understood as a twentieth-century idiom.

νηφάλιος, "clear-minded," occurs elsewhere in the description of deacons' wives (or deaconesses; 1 Tim 3:11) and older men (Titus 2:2). It has a cultic meaning of "holding no wine," including objects made from the wood of the vine (O. Bauernfeind, *TDNT* 4:942–45). In the NT it describes a sobriety of judgment, clear-mindedness, with the nuance of self-control (BAGD, 538). It carries the meaning of abstention from wine as does the English "sober," which will be made explicit below. Paul uses the cognate verb νήφειν, "to be sober," in a personal admonition to Timothy (2 Tim 4:5; cf. 1 Thess 5:6, 8; 1 Pet 1:13; 4:7; 5:8; and the verb ἐκνήφειν, "to be sober," in 1 Cor 15:34; cf. ἀσωτία, "debauchery," in Titus 1:6).

σώφρων, "self-controlled," occurs in the list of qualities for an elder (Titus 1:8) and for older men (Titus 2:2). It can carry the nuance of (sexual) decency as perhaps it does in Titus 2:5 (cf. *Comment* on 1 Tim 2:9 for a discussion of the word group). In society it is upheld "as an ideal for womanhood" (MM, 622–23).

κόσμιος, "decent" or "dignified," refers to a person's outward deportment or outward appearance. It balances the more inward quality of self-control. It occurs elsewhere in the NT only in the description of women's clothing (1 Tim 2:9; see there for discussion; it is paired with the verb σωφρονεῖν, "to be sensible," in 1 Pet 4:7).

φιλόξενος, "hospitable," is also a requirement of overseers (Titus 1:8) and widows who are to be cared for by the church (1 Tim 5:10; ξενοδοχεῖν, "to show hospitality"). It is a trait highly esteemed by both the early church (Rom 12:13; Heb 13:2; 1 Pet 4:9 [same word]; 3 John 5–10; *1 Clem.* 1:2; *Did.* 11–12) and ancient society (Riddle, *JBL* 57 [1938] 141–54). Hospitality was essential in Jesus' ministry and later in taking care of itinerant preachers (Matt 10:11–14; Acts 10:6, 18, 32; Phlm 22; 3 John 8). This concern developed into the creation of hospices and hospitals (G.

Stählin, *TDNT* 5:31-32). The *Shepherd of Hermas* says that "the episkopos must be hospitable, a man who gladly and at all times welcomes into his house the servants of God" (*Sim.* 9.27.2; tr. Lightfoot, *Apostolic Fathers,* 477). It is also possible that providing shelter for church delegates and needy Christians is an official responsibility of an overseer (so Kelly, 76), but most of the qualities that Paul is listing here are not duties but personal characteristics, and hospitality is required of all believers (Rom 12:13; 16:23; cf. Acts 28:7; 1 Pet 4:9). Overseers must be the type of people who will gladly welcome people into their homes. As Knight asserts, "He who must teach others and take care of and exercise oversight over them must be open and loving to them" (159). This requirement is not repeated for the deacons as might be expected (but see *Comment* on v 11). For further study on the issue of Christian hospitality as it relates to the spread of the gospel in the early church, see Riddle, *JBL* 57 (1938) 141-54.

διδακτικός, "skilled in teaching" (BAGD, 191), occurs elsewhere in the NT only in a similar list of requirements for the Lord's servant, who must be "skilled in teaching . . . instructing those who oppose" (2 Tim 2:24). Elsewhere, Paul tells Titus that church elders must hold firmly to what they were taught, able to instruct and refute those who are teaching error (Titus 1:9). διδακτικός may be translated "able to teach" (NIV), possibly suggesting that the overseer be able but not necessarily actively engaged in teaching. Yet the problem in Ephesus was false teaching, and it is difficult to see Paul allowing for only the passive possession of the gift and not active participation. The two citations above confirm that those who could teach did teach (cf. Ellicott, 40). This is one of the more significant requirements of an overseer (cf. Roloff, 157-58; contra Oberlinner who says it is in the list simply to add prestige to the position [117]) and sets him apart from the deacons. The elders are the teachers; the deacons are more involved in the day-to-day serving. Because of the historical needs of the Ephesian church, the assumption is that the overseers taught Scripture. The opponents taught a different gospel (1 Tim 1:4); Timothy (1 Tim 4:13) and others (2 Tim 2:2) are to teach the true gospel. This quality also illustrates the ad hoc nature of the PE. While it is true that any overseer of any time should be able to teach, it is the Ephesian situation that brings this particular ability to a place of prominence. It is possible that 1 Tim 5:17 speaks of teaching and nonteaching elders (πρεσβύτεροι), and if elders and overseers were the same group, the suggestion could be that there were nonteaching overseers. But (1) elders could be a general term for overseers and deacons (who did not teach). (2) 1 Tim 5:17 could be referring to elders, *namely,* overseers who teach. (3) 1 Tim 5:17 could also reflect the practical concern that even a gifted overseer may not always have opportunity to teach; but all overseers must be *able* to teach (cf. *Comment* on 1 Tim 5:17).

Bernard suggests that teaching ability was "perhaps, not part of the formal duty of the ἐπίσκοπος; it was a desirable qualification in view of the special circumstances of Ephesus and Crete" (54). As evidence he cites the fact that the teaching responsibilities were assumed by the elders in the early church and that according to 1 Tim 5:17 all the elders did not teach (lxxii). But Bernard's argument is built on the faulty equation of what was originally intended for the overseer and what some overseers actually did in the developing church. A straightforward reading of the text would infer that all overseers were supposed to be skilled teachers.

3 μὴ πάροινον μὴ πλήκτην, ἀλλὰ ἐπιεικῆ ἄμαχον ἀφιλάργυρον, "not a drunkard, not violent but gracious, not quarrelsome, not a lover of money." V 2 lists a series of positive qualities that an overseer should have; v 3 begins a series of negative qualities to avoid. μὴ πάροινον, "not a drunkard," occurs elsewhere in the NT only in Titus 1:7 as a requirement for elders. The same idea is repeated for deacons (v 8); they are not to be addicted to much wine (μὴ οἴνῳ πολλῷ προσέχοντας). The fact that the same injunction is repeated in all three lists suggests that this was a serious problem in the Ephesian church; evidently the opponents were well known for their drunkenness even though they were ascetics with respect to their food (1 Tim 4:3). Drinking is mentioned two other times in the PE: Timothy is to use a little wine for medicinal purposes (1 Tim 5:23), and the older women are not to be enslaved to drink (Titus 2:2). It is possible that Timothy himself was totally abstaining from alcohol because of its overuse in the Ephesian church (see *Comment* on 1 Tim 5:23). If this is the case, then he becomes an example of Paul's admonition to be willing not to exercise one's Christian liberty (Rom 14:15, 21; 1 Cor 8:13). It is difficult to see differences in meaning among the different terms for drunkenness: μέθη, "drunkenness," and cognates are the usual terms, joined by οἰνοπότης, "drunkard," οἰνοφλυγία, "drunkenness," and πάροινος (the term here). Bernard (54) says that the latter is a stronger term than φίλοινος, "fond of wine," or the phrase in 3:8; it denotes a person "given over to wine." Kelly (77) translates as "a slave to drink." The word is a compound of παρά, "alongside of," and οἶνος, "wine." The picture is of a person who spends too much time sitting with their wine. The verb παροινεῖν also has a wider meaning of "to assault with drunken violence" (MM, 496).

In several places in the OT drinking wine is pictured as something good (e.g., Prov 31:4–7), although it is also viewed as an evil (Prov 20:1; 21:17; Isa 5:12; Amos 2:8; 4:1). Drunkenness, however, is always an evil (Deut 21:20; Prov 23:20–21, 29–35; Isa 5:11–12; 19:14; 28:7–8; 56:12; Jer 13:13; 25:17; Ezek 23:33; Hos 4:11, 18; Amos 6:6). Isaiah ridicules people whose pride lies in their ability to drink: "Woe to those who are heroes at drinking wine, and valiant men in mixing strong drink" (5:22; cf. Sir 31:25). In the NT, drunkenness is always pictured as an evil (Matt 11:19 [= Luke 7:34]; 24:49 [= Luke 12:45]; Acts 2:15; 1 Cor 11:21; Eph 5:18; 1 Thess 5:7), where it appears in lists of sins (Luke 21:34; Rom 13:13; 1 Cor 6:10; Gal 5:21; 1 Pet 4:3), including the admonition that a Christian is not to associate with someone who claims to be a Christian but is a drunkard (1 Cor 5:11). The most graphic use of the imagery appears in Revelation with its description of the great harlot and the people on earth, drunk with the blood of the saints (Rev 17:2, 6; cf. 14:8, 10; 16:19; 17:2; 18:3, 13; cf. also the absurd picture of a drunkard in Prov 23:29–35; other examples in D. M. Edwards and C. E. Armerding, "Drunkenness," *ISBE* 1:994–95). Whereas in the OT drinking wine is sometimes pictured as a good thing, in the NT wine is not pictured in a positive light (except for medicinal use). Its neutral use in, for example, the wedding at Cana (John 2:1–11), the parable of the wineskins (Mark 2:22), the Last Supper (Mark 14:23–25), and the messianic banquet (Luke 22:29–30), is precisely that; drinking for enjoyment is never recommended. This is an interesting shift from the OT. Most commentators point out that total abstinence is not required by Scripture, as the example of Paul encouraging Timothy to drink a little wine shows (1 Tim 5:3). While it is true that wine is not forbidden, Timothy cannot be held up as an example of moderate drinking. The recommended wine is medicinal and has no necessary connection to his daily practice, as is argued in the *Comment* on 1 Tim 5:3. Timothy was probably abstaining because of the excesses of alcohol around him.

μὴ πλήκτην, "not violent," occurs in the NT only here and in the list of the qualifications for an elder (Titus 1:7) where it also follows an identical injunction against drunkenness. It describes a violent person, one who is a brawler (LSJ, 1418), a bully (BAGD, 669; cf. ἀνήμεροι, "untamed," in 2 Tim 3:3). Its cognates continue the imagery of one who strikes and beats. Its precise meaning here depends upon whether it is to be paired with the preceding μὴ πάροινον, "not a drunkard," or the following ἐπιεικῆ, "gracious." If it parallels the preceding term, then it probably describes someone who, in a drunken stupor, beats people. If it goes with the following term as suggested by ἀλλά, "but," it would be more general, describing the opposite of gentle.

ἀλλὰ ἐπιεικῆ, "but gracious," is also a requirement of all people (Titus 3:2). Hawthorne (*Philippians*, 182) says it is "one of the truly great Greek words that is almost untranslatable" and suggests "magnanimity, sweet reasonableness." In Greek literature it is often associated with rulers (cf. Acts 24:4). In Plato and Plutarch it is a legal term denoting clemency or leniency, the personal quality of not insisting on the precise letter of the law (H. Preisker, *TDNT* 2:588–90). Hawthorne points out that "Aristotle contrasted it with ἀκριβοδίκαιος ('strict justice') meaning a generous treatment of others which, while demanding equity, does not insist on the letter of the law" (*Philippians*, 182; citing Aristotle *Eth. Nic.* 5.10; cf. Bernard, 54). An overseer who is gracious does not insist on his full rights but rather is willing to rise above injury and injustice (cf. Wuest, *Wuest's Word Studies* 4:230). The ἀλλά, "but," may separate the following positive requirements from the preceding negative ones, but the final two qualities of v 3 are negative so it is better to see ἀλλὰ ἐπιεικῆ as the opposite of μὴ πλήκτην.

ἐπιεικής, "gracious," is paired with ἄμαχος, "not quarrelsome," as here, in Titus 3:2 (cf. Spicq, 1:263–67). It occurs in the NT in Paul's statement to the Philippians that all people should know of their graciousness because the Lord is at hand (Phil 4:5). James says that the wisdom from above is gracious as well as pure, peaceable, open to reason, full of mercy and good fruits, without uncertainty or insincerity (Jas 3:17). Servants are to be submissive, not only to kind and gracious masters but also to the harsh (σκολιός; 1 Pet 2:18). The cognate ἐπιείκεια, "graciousness," occurs in 2 Cor 10:1 where Paul is entreating the Corinthians "by the meekness and gentleness of Christ" (cf. C. Spicq, "Bénignité, mansuétude, douceur, clémence," *RB* 54 [1947] 333–39). A reading of Paul's descriptions of the opponents (cf. *Form/ Structure/Setting*) shows them to be anything but gracious.

ἄμαχος, "not quarrelsome, peaceable," occurs elsewhere in the NT only in Titus 3:2 where Paul is telling Timothy to encourage all people not to be quarrelsome but gracious. It is a strong term describing active and serious bickering; it even can refer to physical combat (O. Bauernfeind, *TDNT* 4:527–28; cf. Acts 7:26; and Paul's mention of ἔξωθεν μάχαι, "fighting without," in reference to his tribulations in Macedonia [2 Cor 7:5; cf. 1 Cor 15:30–32; 16:9]). It is used elsewhere in the NT to describe the internal fighting that is caused by a person's passions (Jas 4:1–2) and the war of words caused by Jesus' teaching on the bread of life (John 6:52). This quality stands in direct opposition to the opponents, whose lives were characterized by their quarrelsome attitudes (see *Form/Structure/Setting*). Elsewhere Titus and Timothy are warned to stay away from quarrels over the law (μάχας νομικάς; Titus 3:9) and away from stupid and senseless controversies that only breed quarrels (ὅτι γεννῶσιν μάχας; 2 Tim 2:23). Ellicott comments, "the ἄμαχος is the man who is not aggressive . . . or pugnacious, who does not contend; the ἐπιεικής goes further, and is not only passively non-contentious, but actively considerate and forbearing, waving even just legal redress" (41).

ἀφιλάργυρον, "not a lover of money," is another significant indication of the nature of the Ephesian heresy. The same prohibition is repeated for deacons (μὴ αἰσχροκερδεῖς, "not greedy for gain"; 3:8) and elders (μὴ αἰσχροκερδῆ, "not greedy for gain"; Titus 1:7). This is the first hint of what Paul will later spell out with absolute clarity. The opponents were teaching not for the sake of the gospel but in order to make money. Not only were they liars, but they were also hypocrites (cf. *Comment* on 1 Tim 6:5). The overseers may have controlled the church's finances, so it was especially important that they be above reproach in this area. The word occurs in the NT elsewhere in a similar admonition to "keep your life free from the love of money, and be content with what you have" (Heb 13:5). The same word without an alpha privative is used to describe people in the last days as φιλάργυροι, "lovers of money" (2 Tim 3:2; cf. Luke 16:14). φιλάργυρος, "lover of money," is a literal translation of the compound φίλος, "lover," and ἄργυρος, "money." The cognate φιλαργυρία occurs in the proverbial statement "a root of all kinds of evils is the love of money" (1 Tim 6:10). The *Didache* has instructions for dealing with apostles, prophets, and money: "If he asks money, he is a false prophet" (11); "Appoint for yourselves therefore bishops and deacons worthy of the Lord, men who are meek and not lovers of money" (15; tr. Lightfoot, *Apostolic Fathers*, 233–34).

4 τοῦ ἰδίου οἴκου καλῶς προϊστάμενον, τέκνα ἔχοντα ἐν ὑποταγῇ, μετὰ πάσης σεμνότητος, "managing his own household well, having submissive children, with all dignity." Having listed eleven qualities that are to characterize an overseer as ἀνεπίλημπτον, "above reproach," Paul now centers on three (vv 4–7): an overseer must be able to manage his own household as a prerequisite to managing the household of God; because of the temptations involved in the position, he must not be a new convert; he must have an excellent reputation with those outside the church, because Satan has set a snare for him. The emphasis these three receive shows that they are especially important in the Ephesian situation.

An overseer must be a good manager at home; specifically, this means that his children are submissive and that he maintains his personal dignity in the process. This same qualification is repeated for deacons (1 Tim 3:12) and again for elders where Paul further defines what he means by managing well. The children must be faithful (or believers) and should not be known as incorrigible or insubordinate (Titus 1:6). In 1 Tim 5:4 caring for one's parents is another way Christian maturity shows itself. Paul's reason for saying this, a reason that will be made explicit in the next verse, is that what holds true in the home also holds true outside the home. A person's ability to manage the church, which is God's household, will be evident in the managing of his own household. This verse also assumes that an overseer would be married and have children. Given the nature of the list (see *Form/Structure/Setting*), this is not a demand that an overseer be married or have more than one child; it is saying that a person who is married and has children must exhibit the proper leadership in his own household before attempting to do the same in God's household. The requirement of a celibate clergy, while not totally absent in the NT (cf. 1 Cor 7), was never mandated or assumed by the primitive church. In the history of the Western church, Paul's preference for celibacy gained predominance over marriage, but the Eastern Orthodox church allowed marriage for bishops. It is helpful to compare this verse to 1 Tim 5:14, which calls for the young widows to remarry and "rule their households." Evidently Paul is not here calling for the man's one-sided control of the family but sees some form of joint responsibility.

προϊστάμενον, "managing," one's own household is also a requirement of deacons (1 Tim 3:5, 12). The ability to manage in general is required of elders (1 Tim 5:17); management is to be done with zeal (ἐν σπουδῇ; Rom 12:8), and it is an ability worthy of the church's respect (1 Thess 5:12–13). The verb is used with the laity as the subject, saying that they should apply themselves to doing good deeds (Titus 3:8, 14).

προϊστάναι is an interesting word (cf. B. Reicke, TDNT 6:700–703, for what follows). Its primary meaning is "to lead, govern." The idea of "going before" evolved into the notion of "to protect, care." This second nuance is especially prevalent in the cognates προστάτις, which means "protectress, patroness," and προστάτης, meaning "protector." It provides a commentary on the nature of a Christian father's role within his family: his leadership should be not dictatorial but caring and protecting (cf. Fee, 45). This double nuance of leadership and caring is visible when Paul asks how someone who cannot manage his own household can be expected ἐπιμελεῖσθαι, "to care for," God's household (1 Tim 3:5). Leaders are not to be autocrats; they are servant leaders, following the model of Christ as a leader (ὁ ἡγούμενος) who serves (ὁ διακονῶν; Luke 22:26; cf. καλοῦ ἔργου, "good work," in v 1). Whether or not προϊστάναι describes an office in Rom 12:8, the context of this passage, 1 Thess 5:12, and the PE confirm that those who would lead in the church must do so by caring and serving. This is not to deny the authority of the office; it is to define the nature of that office.

Paul uses καλῶς four times in the PE to describe a job being done "well," three of the occurrences being in conjunction with προϊστάναι, "to serve, manage." In 1 Tim 3:4 he further defines τοῦ ἰδίου οἴκου καλῶς προϊστάμενον, "managing his own household well," as τέκνα ἔχοντα ἐν ὑποταγῇ μετὰ πάσης σεμνότητος, "having submissive children with all dignity." In 1 Tim 3:12 he discusses the need for a deacon τέκνων καλῶς προϊστάμενοι καὶ τῶν ἰδίων οἴκων, "managing his children well and his household." In 1 Tim 5:17 Paul says that οἱ καλῶς προεστῶτες πρεσβύτεροι, "the elders who rule well," are worthy of double honor. But what does it actually mean to do something καλῶς? Included in the word is the idea of doing a task in a satisfactory manner, of achieving the desired results. But in addition BAGD (401) defines καλῶς as "fitly, appropriately, in the right way, commendably, rightly, correctly." The emphasis is not so much on the quality of the performance (although that is certainly part of it) as it is on doing something in the correct way. In light of the Ephesian situation, to perform the task of a deacon (1 Tim 3:13) or elder (1 Tim 5:17) well, to do it in the right way, is to follow Paul's teaching and not the teaching of the opponents. A μαρτυρία καλή, "good reputation" (1 Tim 3:7), and διπλῆ τιμή, "double honor" (1 Tim 5:17), are earned not so much by efficient operation as by doing what is right.

οἶκος, "household," is a significant metaphor in this chapter and ties the argument together. The church is the household of God, and the church must protect the truth of the gospel (1 Tim 3:15). Yet the opponents were leading whole households away from the truth (Titus 1:11). οἶκος can mean both the building and what it houses, the household (2 Tim 4:19; Titus 1:11; cf. 1 Cor 1:16; cf. Acts 10:2; 11:14; 16:15, 31; 18:8; Heb 11:7). In the OT the temple is the house of God (O. Michel, TDNT 5:120–21), and this use has come into the NT (Matt 12:4 [= Mark

2:26; Luke 6:4]; cf. Matt 21:13 [= Mark 11:17; Luke 19:46; John 2:16–17]). The metaphor is commonly associated with the church (1 Tim 3:15; cf. 1 Cor 3:16; 6:19; Gal 6:10; Eph 2:19 [cf. use of οἰκοδομή, "building," in Eph 2:21; 4:12]; Heb 3:1–6; 10:21; 1 Pet 4:17 [cf. 1 Pet 2:4–10; Selwyn, *First Epistle of St. Peter*, 285–91]). Paul expands this basic idea when he tells Timothy to treat older men as fathers, younger men as brothers, older women as mothers, and younger women as sisters (1 Tim 5:1–2).

τέκνα ἔχοντα ἐν ὑποταγῇ, "having submissive children," is the first of two statements that define what Paul means by managing well. An indication of a person's managerial ability is the general posture of his children. If they are rebellious and troublesome, if they are not submissive but out of control, the father should not be allowed to manage the church. The similar requirement of elders refines what Paul means by submissive: faithful (or believers), not incorrigible or insubordinate (Titus 1:6). The phrase ἔχοντα ἐν, "having in," occurs elsewhere in Paul only in Rom 15:23 (cf. Rom 2:20; 1 Cor 8:10; Eph 2:12; Phil 3:4; Col 2:23). Similar is Paul's charge that a deacon must hold the mystery of faith with a clear conscience (ἔχοντας τὸ μυστήριον τῆς πίστεως ἐν καθαρᾷ συνειδήσει; 1 Tim 3:9) and that an elder have faithful (or believing) children (τέκνα ἔχων πιστά; Titus 1:6). The phrase in 1 Tim 3:4 means that an overseer's children must be characterized by submissiveness to their father. Fee emphasizes the difference between having children who are submissive and making children submissive, concluding that there is a "fine line between demanding obedience and gaining it" (45). This can be inferred from the meaning of ἐπιμελεῖσθαι, "to manage (with care)," in v 5 (cf. *Comment* on "good work" in v 1). In Roman law the father had the right and responsibility of discipline, extending even to the determination of life and death with authorization from the family council (*ius vitae necisque;* Lyall, *Slaves, Citizens, Sons*, 126–27).

ἔχειν, "to have," can "denote the possession of persons to whom one has close relations," specifically relatives (BAGD, 332). ἐν, "in," denotes "a state of being" (BAGD, 259). Paul talks about ἐν ἑτοίμῳ ἔχοντες, "being in readiness," to punish (2 Cor 10:6) and about not walking ἐν πανουργίᾳ, "in cunning" (2 Cor 4:2). A woman is to remain ἐν πίστει, "in faith" (1 Tim 2:15), and nonbelievers pass their days ἐν κακίᾳ καὶ φθόνῳ, "in malice and envy" (Titus 3:3).

μετὰ πάσης σεμνότητος, "with all dignity," can refer to either the children or the father (on σεμνότης, "dignity," see *Comment* on 1 Tim 2:2). The word order argues for the former: an overseer's children should be known to be respectful, dignified. This would parallel the similar statement about elders in which the elders' children are not to be incorrigible or insubordinate. However, the cognate adjective σεμνός, "dignified," is used later to describe deacons (1 Tim 3:8), their wives (or deaconesses; 1 Tim 3:11), and older men (Titus 2:2), and the noun is used to describe believers in general (1 Tim 2:2; cf. the adjective in Phil 4:8) and Titus in particular (Titus 2:7). Kelly therefore is correct that this term is more appropriate for the father than the children: an overseer should be able to manage his own family "with unruffled dignity" (78). As Knight comments, "The subjection shown by the children must reflect the character of their father's leadership" (161).

5 εἰ δέ τις τοῦ ἰδίου οἴκου προστῆναι οὐκ οἶδεν, πῶς ἐκκλησίας θεοῦ ἐπιμελήσεται, "for if someone does not know [how] to manage his own household, how will he care for [the] church of God?" With this rhetorical question Paul makes explicit what is implicit in v 4: there is a direct connection between a person's ability to manage his family and his ability to manage the church. It was a well-known maxim that whoever could manage his own household could manage the state (Hanson, [1983] 76). However, this does not mean that this Christian virtue is "rooted in natural virtue" (contra Brox, 144–45). Jesus endorsed a similar principle in the parable of the talents: he who is faithful over a little will be faithful over much (Matt 25:14–30).

For Paul's use of rhetorical questions, cf. 1 Cor 14:7, 9, 16. The translation "for" reflects the function of δέ as a transitional particle introducing an explanation (cf. Rom 3:22; 9:30; 1 Cor 10:11; 15:56; Eph 5:32; Phil 2:8; cf. Acts 12:3; BAGD, 171). ἐπιμελεῖσθαι, "to care for," occurs in the NT elsewhere only in the description of the Good Samaritan's care of the injured man (Luke 10:34–35; cf. cognates in Luke 15:8 and Acts 27:3). MM (241–42; cf. Malherbe, "Medical Imagery") refer to evidence that the term was frequent in medical terminology describing care of the sick. Its use in this verse clarifies what Paul expects of an overseer: he is to manage his own family and the church by taking care of it, perhaps as someone would take care of a sick friend. As is the case with προϊστάναι, "to manage" (cf. above), the overseer's managing is to be characterized by a sensitive caring, not a dictatorial exercise of authority and power.

ἐκκλησία, "church," had the basic meaning of "assembly" in Greek literature. In the LXX it acquired the specific meaning of ἐκκλησία κυρίου, "the assembly of the LORD" (for קְהַל יהוה qěhal YHWH; cf. Deut 23:2, 3; 1 Chr 28:8; Neh 13:1; Mic 2:5), meaning Israel. This is the background to Paul's frequent use of the phrase ἡ ἐκκλησία τοῦ θεοῦ, "the church of God," to denote the Christian community (1 Cor 1:2; 10:32; 11:16, 22; 15:9; 2 Cor 1:1; Gal 1:13; 1 Thess 2:14; 2 Thess 1:4; 1 Tim 3:5, 15 [cf. 5:16 for the only other use of ἐκκλησία in the PE]; cf. similar expression in Rom 16:4, 16; 1 Cor 14:33; Trench, Synonyms, 17–23). In light of this, Hanson's comment ([1983] 76) that the phrase ἐκκλησία θεοῦ, "God's church," is the coinage of the author of the PE seems unnecessary. The parallelism in this verse between the overseer's household and the church as God's household is made explicit in 1 Tim 3:15 where Paul says that he provides these instructions so that Timothy will know how people should behave in the household of God. The anarthrous ἐκκλησία, "church," shows that Paul is speaking in general terms and not of one local assembly. For a discussion of the NT concept of the church, cf. Ladd (Theology, 531–49) and the bibliographies in BAGD (241) and K. L. Schmidt (TDNT 3:501 n. 3); cf. also Roloff, "Exkursus: Das Kirchenverständnis der Pastoralbriefe," in Timotheus, 211–17.

6 μὴ νεόφυτον, ἵνα μὴ τυφωθεὶς εἰς κρίμα ἐμπέσῃ τοῦ διαβόλου, "not a recent convert, lest having become conceited, he fall into [the] judgment of the devil." Paul's second specific area of concern is the spiritual maturity of those being appointed to the office of overseer. Because new converts are not spiritually mature, it is dangerous to place them in leadership positions. If they become proud because of their quick advancement, it is likely that they will fall into the same trap of pride as did the devil. This same imagery of τυφοῦσθαι, "to be conceited," is repeated two other times in descriptions of the opponents (1 Tim 6:4; 2 Tim 3:4), showing that this was a problem in the Ephesian church. Whereas some of the preceding requirements are somewhat general, this one is very specifically applicable to the position of overseer. The desire to appoint rich and well-known people into leadership positions, often for the wrong reasons, was as much a problem then as it is today. On whether this qualification included a period of testing before appointment to office, see *Comment* on 1 Tim 3:10.

νεόφυτος, "recent convert," occurs only here in the NT. Its nonmetaphorical sense is "newly planted" (BAGD, 536), and this basic imagery occurs elsewhere in Paul's description of his work in the Corinthian church (1 Cor 3:6–8; cf. Ps 144:12). It cannot refer simply to a young person; otherwise Timothy would be disqualified (1 Tim 4:12, although Timothy is not an overseer). The application of this rule would depend upon the relative age of the local church, its speed of growth, and many other factors that would vary from place to place and from time to time. A similar injunction does not occur in the list of qualifications for elders in Titus 1. The Ephesian church had been established at least ten years earlier and sufficient time had passed for the heresy to form after Paul's final missionary journey, but in Crete Titus was to appoint (not discipline) elders, which implies that the Cretan church was newly formed (assuming Pauline authorship). Hanson ([1983] 76) says that this rule was not strictly followed, citing Cyprian's appointment as bishop at Carthage two years after his conversion. The NEB implies too much with "a convert newly baptized."

τυφοῦσθαι, "to be conceited," is a difficult term to translate. According to BAGD (831) it can mean either "to be puffed up, conceited" or "to be blinded, become foolish." Spicq (1:437) says that the former is not a possibility. BAGD defines the cognate noun τῦφος as "delusion, conceit, arrogance." Abbott-Smith, *Lexicon,* says τυφοῦν properly means "to wrap in smoke" (453). Vincent defines τυφοῦν as "to blind with pride or conceit . . . a beclouded and stupid state of mind as the result of pride" (*Word Studies* 4:232). The word occurs in the NT only two other places, both in the PE. (a) Anyone who disagrees with Paul τετύφωται, μηδὲν ἐπιστάμενος, "is foolish, knowing nothing" (1 Tim 6:4). Here τετύφωται is parallel with μηδὲν ἐπιστάμενος, "knowing nothing," suggesting the meaning "is foolish." (b) In the last days people will be "treacherous, reckless, conceited [τετυφωμένοι], lovers of pleasure" (2 Tim 3:4). Whatever may be the specific nuance of τυφοῦσθαι in 1 Tim 3:6, the basic picture it paints is clear: a new convert does not belong in a position of authority because the temptations and punishments are great. If the following phrase, εἰς κρίμα . . . τοῦ διαβόλου, "into judgment of the devil," refers to the judgment Satan incurred because of his pride, then most likely τυφοῦσθαι should be translated "conceited" because of the comparison being made between the neophyte and Satan.

The phrase κρίμα . . . τοῦ διαβόλου, "[the] judgment of the devil," raises two questions. (1) Bernard argues that διάβολος is not the devil but refers to gossiping members of the non-Christian Ephesian society: "The *accuser* or *slanderer* is one of these people, to be found in every community, whose delight is to find fault with the demeanour and conduct of anyone professing a strict rule of life" (56). διάβολος occurs six times in the PE. Three times it is anarthrous and plural (1 Tim 3:11; Titus 2:3; 2 Tim 3:3), and in each of these cases it means "slanderous." However, in the first two it describes a quality that should not characterize a church member; the third reference describes what people will be like in the last days. In none of these does the term describe an outsider who is slandering the church. In the other three occurrences of διάβολος in the PE, it is preceded by the definite article and is singular (1 Tim 3:6, 7; 2 Tim 2:26) as it is here. That it is used in the next verse (3:7) to mean the devil as it also does in 2 Tim 2:26 argues for the interpretation "the devil" in 3:6. Also, with one exception, every other occurrence of the term διάβολος in the NT (twenty-nine times) is articular, singular, and always means the devil (in the exception it is anarthrous but still means the devil [John 6:70; cf. Barrett, *John*, 307–8]). The judgment into which the neophyte might fall then is Satan's judgment.

(2) The second question raised by this phrase is that of the relationship between κρίμα, "judgment," and διαβόλου, "devil." (a) If διαβόλου is a subjective genitive, then the devil is actively involved in the judgment of young overseers. This could mean that Satan set up the judgment or that he is God's agent in punishing sin (cf. 1 Tim 1:20). (b) If διαβόλου is an objective genitive, then Paul is saying that the spiritually immature overseer is more liable to fall prey to judgment for that pride, the same judgment that befell Satan. A decision on this point is not easy to make. A similar phrase, παγίδα τοῦ διαβόλου, "snare of the devil," occurs in the next verse, where the devil is probably the subject of the action; Satan sets the snare. But parallel structure is not necessarily a valid argument in this case, and in fact might work against this interpretation since it makes v 8 redundant. If τυφωθείς means "conceited," then most likely the judgment is the same judgment into which the devil fell. This would make good sense of the flow of the verse, comparing the conceit of a too quickly advanced overseer and the possible dangers that lie ahead for him to the conceit of the devil and the obvious dangers of his fall. Ellicott remarks on the similarity: "The devil was once a ministering spirit of God, but by insensate pride fell from his hierarchy" (43). Fee (46) emphasizes that the judgment of Satan is a common theme in Christ's ministry. Especially in Christ's death and resurrection, Satan is dealt his decisive defeat to be realized fully at the end (cf. Rev 12:7–17; 20:7–10). Demonic forces are mentioned three other times in the PE: Paul tells Timothy that the ultimate source of the opponents' teaching is the demons (1 Tim 4:1); he turns two of the opponents over to Satan (1 Tim 1:20); and some of the young widows have already strayed after Satan (1 Tim 5:15).

7 δεῖ δὲ καὶ μαρτυρίαν καλὴν ἔχειν ἀπὸ τῶν ἔξωθεν, ἵνα μὴ εἰς ὀνειδισμὸν ἐμπέσῃ καὶ παγίδα τοῦ διαβόλου, "And it is also necessary [for an overseer] to have a good reputation with those outside, lest he fall into reproach, which is [the] snare of the devil." This is Paul's third specific concern for overseers: it is essential that church leaders have a good reputation among those outside the church; if not, they will bring reproach and disgrace not only upon themselves but also upon the church and therefore will have fallen prey to Satan's snare. In the words of 1 Pet 5:8, Satan is a roaring lion, looking for church leaders to devour. Rather than being an unknown neophyte, the overseer should be one whose reputation is tried and known. This same concern can be found throughout Paul's epistles (cf. 1 Cor 10:32–33; Col 4:5; 1 Thess 4:12; cf. 1 Pet 2:12, 15). There are three indications that this concern for one's reputation is central to Paul. (1) He began this paragraph on the same note: "Therefore, it is necessary for an overseer to be above reproach" (3:2). Throughout the paragraph Paul has been spelling out exactly what this entails, and he now closes the discussion by repeating his main point. (2) Vv 2–6 constitute one sentence but in v 7 Paul pauses, begins a new sentence, and thus draws special attention to his theme (see *Form/Structure/Setting*). (3) It is clear from Paul's descriptions of the opponents that they were bringing society's disrepute upon themselves and the church (cf. 1 Tim 6:1; Titus 2:5).

Another way to recognize the significance of this verse is to see its relationship to the rules in chaps. 2 and 3. There are two reasons given in the PE to explain why these rules are necessary. (1) The more theological reason is 1 Tim 3:15; the rules show how it is necessary to behave in God's church because the church is a protector of the truth, which is the gospel. (2) A second, more practically oriented, reason is 1 Tim 3:7; all these rules spell out what it means to have a good reputation, to be above reproach. This was an immediate, practical need of the Ephesian church. 1 Tim 3:7 puts all this in perspective by emphasizing Paul's basic concern: the leadership of the church should bring no unnecessary disrepute upon the church through improper and immoral actions. This means that the rulers should change their lifestyles and work at becoming gentle, hospitable, and above reproach. Guthrie (83) comments that society has often respected the "noble ideals of Christian character" but has always condemned hypocrisy in the church, especially in its leaders.

δέ, "and," carries only a weak adversative force. In contrast to those who fall prey to the judgment of the devil (v 6), it is necessary for an overseer to be above reproach. δεῖ, "it is necessary," is repeated from v 2 since v 7 begins a new sentence. ἔχειν, "to have," indicates a characteristic that should be possessed (cf. v 4). On καλός, "good," cf. *Comment* on 1 Tim 1:8. For a similar use of μαρτυρία, "reputation," to describe one person's opinion of another, cf. Titus 1:13; 1 John 5:9; 3 John 12 (cognates in 1 Tim 5:10; Luke 4:22; John 3:26; Acts 6:3; 13:22; 14:3; Heb 11:2, 4). τῶν ἔξωθεν, "those outside," is a normal Pauline expression for those who are outside the church (cf. 1 Cor 5:12, 13; Col 4:5; 1 Thess 4:12; cf. Matt 23:25; Mark 4:11; Luke 11:39–40; 2 Cor 4:16; although in these examples Paul uses the shorter ἔξω; here the article functions as a substantive [Wallace, *Greek Grammar*, 231–33]).

ὀνειδισμός, "reproach," is an extreme disgrace. Its cognates are used in the NT to describe the reproach that was heaped upon Jesus at the cross (Mark 15:32 [Matt 27:44]) and upon Jesus' disciples (Matt 5:11; Luke 6:22; 1 Pet 4:14; cf. Rom 15:3; Heb 10:33; 13:13). Jesus also pronounced a reproach on the unbelieving cities (Matt 11:20). In the LXX the cognate noun ὄνειδος, "disgrace," is often used in the context of a person's shame resulting from sin, and the verb ὀνειδίζειν, "to reproach," of the opponents reviling God, Israel, and the righteous, especially in the Psalms (J. Schneider, *TDNT* 5:238–39).

παγίδα τοῦ διαβόλου, "snare of the devil," is similar to the phrase κρίμα τοῦ διαβόλου, "judgment of the devil," in the preceding verse. There διάβολος was speaking not of human slanderers but of Satan, and this is true in v 7 as well. Bernard (56) argues that in both verses the word describes the pagan critic, saying that "plainly the context requires" it to be so. But according to the theology of the PE that sees Satan as active (cf. 1 Tim 1:20), it is easier to picture Satan setting a snare (cf. 1 Tim 4:1) rather than those outside the church. While nonbelievers may set snares (contra Hanson, [1983] 77), this particular idea is not present elsewhere in the PE. Dibelius-Conzelmann point out that ἐμπίπτειν εἰς παγίδα, "to fall into a snare," was a common expression (54; cf. Prov 12:13; Sir 9:3; Tob 14:10–11; 1QS 2:11–12, 17; CD 4:15, 17–18). The only remaining question is whether διαβόλου, "of the devil," is a subjective genitive (i.e., Satan sets the snare) or an objective genitive (i.e., the same snare into which Satan himself fell, namely, that of pride). If the similar phrase in v 6 is an objective genitive (i.e., the judgment into which Satan fell), then the phrase in v 7 would probably not be objective; otherwise this would be repetitious. The *former* possibility, a subjective genitive, is the only possible meaning of the same basic phrase in 2 Tim 2:26, where Paul says that the Lord's servant must correct the opponents gently so that "they may escape from the snare of the devil [ἐκ τῆς τοῦ διαβόλου παγίδος], after being captured by him to do his will."

παγίς, "snare," occurs in the PE elsewhere in Paul's description of the temptation, snare, and ruin that await those desiring to be rich (1 Tim 6:9; cf. Rom 11:9). As Robertson (*Word Pictures* 4:574) points out, Satan sets out for preachers many snares, many of which are enumerated throughout the PE: e.g., pride, money, women, ambition. The preceding καί is epexegetical: falling into reproach "which is" the devil's snare (BDF §442.9; BAGD, 393 ["explicative"]; cf. Matt 8:33; John 1:16; Acts 16:15; Rom 1:5; 1 Cor 3:5; 15:38). There is no question that Paul believed in the existence of a personal devil who interferes in the lives of individuals. Hanson ([1983] 77) misses the point when he says that this requirement for an overseer "would have disqualified Augustine, the converted profligate." This rule says nothing about the overseers' pre-Christian life but addresses the issue of how they have conducted themselves as Christians.

Explanation

The major problem in the Ephesian church was its leadership. From within the ranks of the church, a group of false teachers had sprung up who were perverting the gospel and teaching a message that ultimately stemmed from Satan. Not only was their theology erroneous, but their behavior was reprehensible. They were sexually promiscuous, lacked reserve and dignity, were teaching for financial gain, were drunkards, and looked down upon marriage. Those who were married were not managing their own households, much less the church. As a result, they were bringing reproach upon themselves, the church, and the cause of Christ.

It is the practical side of the problem that Paul addresses in chap. 3. Because the problem stems from bad leadership, any response to the problem must deal with the overseers. Timothy must be sure that they exhibit a high degree of moral fiber; they must be above reproach. The rest of the paragraph spells out what this entails. It is an official list, one that must be held to, but it is not exhaustive and is to be understood as an ad hoc list. Because its general thrust is to describe the character of an overseer, it is not easy to see what duties this office would entail. From reading between the lines and within the context of the PE, a few specifics can be gleaned. An overseer, as the name implies, was in charge of the general oversight of the church, including perhaps finances and official hospitality. The overseer had the primary responsibility of teaching the truth and refuting error. The atmosphere of this paragraph reminds one of the earlier days of the church when official functions were not yet clearly defined and it was necessary to spell out how problems were to be handled institutionally.

Bernard raises the issue of the normativeness of the requirements in this paragraph. Concerning the requirement that an overseer be a "one-woman man," which Bernard understands as being married only once, he comments,

It must be remembered that St. Paul is not enumerating here the "essential" characteristics of a bishop; he is dwelling upon certain moral and personal qualities which, in the Church of that day, it was desirable that he should possess. And it has been argued with considerable force that regulations of this nature cannot be regarded as of universal and permanent obligation, for circumstances may so change as to render them unwise or unnecessary. (53)

He then notes that the church has understood celibacy and remarriage among the bishops in different ways and concludes, "The sense of the church plainly is that this regulation [citing the marriage statement], at least, may be modified by circumstances." Concerning the necessity that an overseer be a skilled teacher, Bernard comments that this was, "perhaps, not part of the formal duty of the ἐπίσκοπος; it was a desirable qualification in view of the special circumstances of Ephesus and Crete" (54). As evidence he points out that the teaching responsibilities were assumed by the elders in the early church and that, according to 1 Tim 5:17, all elders did not teach. In a most astonishing comment, Bernard says that the prohibition against drunkenness would not be necessary in the present age, insofar as "each age has its own special sins to guard against" (54).

There is much in Bernard's comments that is based on an erroneous interpretation of the text, which has been covered above in the *Comment*. Paul is enumerating essential qualities of church leadership in 1 Tim 3:1-7. That is the whole point of the paragraph. As has been argued above, vv 2 and 4–5 do not demand marriage and children but say that an overseer must possess certain qualities among which are fidelity to his one wife (assuming he is married) and the ability to manage his children well (assuming he has children). In reference to Bernard's comments about teaching, it will be argued that the elders of chap. 5 are teaching overseers. Because the church came to interpret the posts of overseer and deacon in a certain fashion has no necessary relationship to the original intention of these verses. Being above reproach, clear-minded, self-controlled, dignified, hospitable, not violent but gracious, and not greedy are all qualities that should characterize any church leader of any culture at any time. If the phrase "one-woman man" is a call to fidelity, it is impossible to restrict this injunction to a specific culture; fidelity is always enjoined of all Christians. While it is necessary to interpret this paragraph in light of its historical context, this does not mean that what it says, or what the principles lying behind the text say, is necessarily limited to the original context. It is naive to believe that the problems that plagued the Ephesian church are no longer potential or actual in our day and age, and Paul's concerns apply to us with the same vigor. Certainly Bernard's comment about a supposed inapplicability of the injunction against drunkenness is naive. Then, as always, this has been a problem among the clergy as it has been with the laity (cf. Clement of Alexandria *Paed.* 2.2; *Apostolic Constitutions* 8.47.27).

One of the central issues in current discussions of 1 Tim 2:11–15 deals with the ad hoc nature of the instructions, and many are now arguing that these instructions are limited to Paul's day and age. But there is often a strange inconsistency when the same studies move to chap. 3 and it is assumed that the instructions there are not limited to Paul's day even though there does not appear to be any significant change in Paul's argument. In fact, as has been argued in *Form/Structure Setting* above, chap. 2 moves smoothly into chap. 3.

Two practical issues may be considered in conclusion. (1) The PE make it clear that the primary leadership is in the hands of the teachers. As Barclay notes, "It is perhaps a tragedy that what once was both an administrative and a teaching position has today often lost the latter. The leaders of the church should not only be able to administrate, but especially be able to teach the truth and refute error. This is the type of person whom the church needs" (73). Paul sees the church led by its teachers, those who can preach the truth and refute error; its primary leadership does not lie in the hands of administrators. (2) Because many Protestant churches today do not follow the organizational structure of the Ephesian church and are not small house churches, it is difficult to know which of their leaders correspond to the overseers in 1 Tim 3:1–7. To whom does the requirement that they be skilled teachers apply? The modern church needs to think through this issue if it desires to follow Paul's instructions.

Excursus: Bishops and Presbyters in the Postapostolic Church

An issue raised by 1 Tim 3:1–7 deals with the question of church structure, specifically the episcopate as it relates to the time of Ignatius. In this paragraph Paul has described what he considers to be some of the character traits necessary for a church leader. Because Paul's answer has the ring of institutionalism, it has been widely argued that the PE parallel Ignatius and his description of the monarchical episcopate. In Ignatius' day, the local church was ruled by one bishop who exercised complete authority over the elders, deacons, and laity in that city. The elders served the bishop (cf. *Form/Structure/Setting* above). This, it has been argued, is the same situation found in the PE with Timothy as the monarchical bishop or as one elder growing in significance over the other elders (often citing 1 Tim 5:17–25).

It is surprising that this position ever gained widespread popularity since a cursory reading of Ignatius reveals significant differences between the Bishop of Antioch and Timothy in the PE. In fact, the similarities are so superficial, and the differences so extreme, that this becomes one of the strongest arguments that the PE are not from the second century and in fact reflect a much earlier stage of the church's institutional development (see *Introduction*, "The Historical Problem"). In Ignatius, the bishop is distinct from the elders and is clearly the single Christian head over the city. For the sake of the unity of the church, all Christians must submit, absolutely and totally, to the teaching of the bishop. The bishop is to be regarded "as the Lord himself" (*Eph.* 6; citations from Lightfoot, *Apostolic Fathers*), having the "likeness of God" (*Magn.* 6), and therefore the church is to submit to the bishop just as they submit to God (*Magn.* 2). To disobey the bishop is to disobey "the Bishop of all . . . who is invisible" (*Magn.* 3). To be apart from the bishop is to be apart from the church (*Eph.* 5) and unclean (*Trall.* 7). Likewise, the council of elders is to be viewed as being "the likeness of the council of the Apostles" (*Magn.* 6) and the elders are to be obeyed in the same manner as one would obey "the law of Jesus Christ" (*Magn.* 2). Unity in the church is defined in terms of one's allegiance to the human institution, and therefore all people must "respect the bishop as being a type of the Father and the presbyters as the council of God and as the college of Apostles. Apart from these there is not even the name of a church" (*Trall.* 3). In other words, a Christian is to do nothing apart from the bishop or the elders (*Magn.* 7; *Trall.* 2). As Ignatius asserts, "For as many as are of God and of Jesus Christ, they are with the bishop; and as many as shall repent and enter into the unity of the Church, these also shall be of God, that they may be living after Jesus Christ. Be not deceived, my brethren. If any man followeth one that maketh a schism, 'he doth not inherit the kingdom of God'" (*Phil.* 3). Apart from the presence of the bishop, believers are not even to hold a baptism or love-feast (*Smyrn.* 8). Other writings indicate that engaged couples should even seek the consent of the bishop (Polycarp *Phil.* 5–6; cf. *1 Clem.* 42–45; see also the summary by Shepherd, *IDB* 1:441).

This is a completely different picture from the one we see in the PE (Spicq, 1:82). It is true that in the PE there are overseers who are to provide governance for the church and a slight form of institutionalism is seen as a partial key to the Ephesian problem. But Timothy and Titus are never pictured as the bishops of the Ephesian and Cretan churches (neither the title nor the function is applied to them). They are apostolic delegates, exercising Paul's authority over the churches, standing outside the formal structure of the church. The type of person defined in 1 Tim 3:1–7 is a person who is morally pure and is able to guide the church. This is a far cry from Ignatius' institutional hierarchy that equates obedience to the bishop with obedience to God. There is no equation between Timothy or Titus and God. Submission is to the true gospel as taught by Timothy and Titus, not to an office-bearer. The church is never defined in relationship to Timothy and Titus in Ignatius in reference to the bishop. Ignatius represents a significant development that deviates from the heart of the PE. He does see institutionalism as *the* key to preventing heresy; the PE see men of moral and Christian fiber who adhere to Paul's gospel as *a* key to preventing heresy. Another general difference is that in Ignatius the bishop and presbyters stand out directly from the laity. In the PE and the NT the leadership is much more part of the church. Fee comments on Phil 1:1, "The community as a whole is addressed, and in most cases therefore the 'overseers and deacons' are simply reckoned as being within the community. When they are singled out, as here, the leaders are not 'over' the church, but are addressed 'alongside of' the church, as a *distinguishable* part of the whole, but as *part of the whole*, not above or outside it" (*Philippians*, 67). L. T. Johnson adds that "1 Timothy lacks entirely the elaborate theological legitimation found in Ignatius" (147).

Caution is appropriate in postulating a consistency based on Ignatius' model across all of the early church too early in the second century. Ignatius' constant insistence on the centrality of church officials may point more to his desire to shape the church than to an explanation of what currently existed. The flexibility of using "overseer/bishop" and "elder/presbyter" interchangeably (see *Form/Structure/Setting* on 1 Tim 3:1–7; 5:17–25, and below) indicates that Ignatius' position may not have been the universally accepted structure in the first part of the second century. A. E. Harvey concludes,

> If there is any single item of progress to report from the immense amount of study which has been devoted to the early Christian ministry over the last half-century, it is probably the recognition that the church did not exhibit a uniform pattern of church order in all places to which the gospel had been carried during the first century or so of its existence. If, for instance, Ignatius of Antioch bears witness to the establishment of the threefold ministry in Asia Minor early in the second century, while other churches at the same period appear to have been organized somewhat differently, we no longer feel the need to force the evidence into harmony by making everything conform somehow to the Ignatian model or alternatively by casting doubt upon the value of Ignatius' evidence. (*JTS* n.s. 25 [1974] 331)

He refers to comments by W. A. Farrar, W. Bauer, and B. H. Streeter, who think that Ignatius exaggerated, indulged in wishful thinking, or was deluded, respectively.

The early Christian literature reveals more about the development of elders and deacons. In the *Didache* we see criteria similar to the PE for overseers/bishops and deacons, who work side by side with prophets and teachers:

> Appoint for yourselves therefore bishops and deacons worthy of the Lord, men who are meek and not lovers of money, and true and approved; for unto you they also perform the service of the prophets and teachers. Therefore despise them not; for they are your honourable men along with the prophets and teachers. (*Did.* 15; tr. Lightfoot, *Apostolic Fathers*, 234)

There is a two-tiered and not a three-tiered church structure.

In Polycarp there is the disturbing trend of equating the authority of the bishop with that of God:

> Wherefore it is right to abstain from all these things, submitting yourselves to the presbyters and deacons as to God and Christ. (*Phil.* 5; tr. Lightfoot, *Apostolic Fathers*, 179)

Polycarp also knows of a two-tiered and not a three-tiered structure; the bishop is not distinct from the presbyters. Polycarp specifies the characteristics of a presbyter, which should be equated with the overseer/bishop:

> And the presbyters [πρεσβύτεροι] also must be compassionate, merciful towards all men, turning back the sheep that are gone astray, visiting all the infirm, not neglecting a widow or an orphan or a poor man: but providing always for that which is honorable in the sight of God and of men, abstaining from all anger, respect of persons, unrighteous judgment, being far from all love of money, not quick to believe anything against any man, not hasty in judgment, knowing that we are all debtors of sin. (*Phil.* 6; tr. Lightfoot, *Apostolic Fathers*, 179)

That the titles continue to be used interchangeably is seen in *1 Clem.* 42, which also hints at what came to be known as apostolic succession, the apostles appointing their early converts after a testing period:

> The Apostles received the Gospel for us from the Lord Jesus Christ; Jesus Christ was sent forth from God. So then Christ is from God, and the Apostles are from Christ. Both therefore came of the will of God in the appointed order. Having therefore received a charge, and having been fully assured through the resurrection of our Lord Jesus Christ and confirmed in the word of God with full assurance of the Holy Ghost, they went forth with the glad tidings that the kingdom of God should come. So preaching everywhere in country and town, they appointed their first-fruits, when they had proved them by the Spirit, to be bishops [ἐπισκόπους] and deacons [διακόνους] unto them that should believe. And they did this in no new fashion; for indeed it had been written concerning bishops and deacons from very ancient times; for thus saith the scripture in a certain place, "I will appoint their bishops in righteousness and their deacons in faith." (tr. Lightfoot, *Apostolic Fathers*, 75)

In chap. 43 Clement continues by asking, "And what marvel, if they which were entrusted in Christ with such a work by God appointed the aforesaid persons?" He then cites the incident of Aaron's budding rod and concludes that Moses did this "that disorder might not arise in Israel." The theme of strife and the function of the bishop, which is the author's application of the OT account, continues in chap. 44. Evidently some church leaders had been "improperly" (in the author's view) removed from office.

> And our Apostles knew through our Lord Jesus Christ that there would be strife over the name of the bishop's office [ἐπισκοπῆς]. For this cause, therefore, having received complete foreknowledge, they appointed the aforesaid persons, and afterwards they provided a continuance, that if these should fall asleep, other approved men should succeed to their ministration. Those therefore who were appointed by them, or afterward by other men of repute with the consent of the whole church, and have ministered unblameably to the flock of Christ in lowliness of mind, peacefully and

with all modesty, and for long time have borne a good report with all—these men we consider to be unjustly thrust out from their ministration. For it will be no light sin for us, if we thrust out those who have offered the gifts of the bishop's office [ἐπισκοπῆς] unblameably and holily. Blessed are those presbyters [πρεσβύτεροι] who have gone before, seeing that their departure was fruitful and ripe: for they have no fear lest any one should remove them from their appointed place. For we see that ye have displaced certain persons, though they were living honourably, from the ministration which had been respected by them blameless. (tr. Lightfoot, *Apostolic Fathers*, 76)

"Bishop" and "presbyter" are used interchangeably. In chap. 47 the Corinthians' rebellion against their elders/presbyters is addressed.

It is shameful, dearly beloved, yes, utterly shameful and unworthy of your conduct in Christ, that it should be reported that the very stedfast and ancient Church of the Corinthians, for the sake of one or two persons, maketh sedition against its presbyters. And this report hath reached not only us, but them also which differ from us, so that ye even heap blasphemies on the Name of the Lord by reason of your folly, and moreover create peril for yourselves. (tr. Lightfoot, *Apostolic Fathers*, 77)

Even as late as Clement of Alexandria (A.D. 150–c. A.D. 211–20) the titles ἐπίσκοπος and πρεσβύτερος are used interchangeably. Clement of Alexandria reports that after John was released from Patmos and went to Ephesus,

he used to journey by request to the neighbouring districts of the Gentiles, in some places to appoint bishops [ἐπισκόπους], in others to regulate whole churches. . . . After he had set the brethren at rest on other matters, last of all he looked at him who held the office of bishop [ἐπισκόπῳ], and, having noticed a strongly built youth of refined appearance and ardent spirit, he said: "This man I entrust to your care with all earnestness in the presence of the church and of Christ as witness." When the bishop accepted the trust and made every promise, the apostle once again solemnly charged and adjured him in the same words. After that he departed to Ephesus; but the presbyter [πρεσβύτερος] took home the youth who had been handed over to him. (*Quis Dives Salvetur?* 4; tr. Butterworth, LCL, 357–59)

Irenaeus, the Bishop of Lyons (A.D. c. 130–c. 200), also uses πρεσβύτερος and ἐπίσκοπος of the same group in the past (*Adv. Haer.* 3.2.2; 3.3.1–3; cited below). This is especially significant because in his time the episcopate clearly existed. All this strongly urges caution in differentiating the terms "bishop/overseer" and "presbyter/elder" in the first century. It also cautions against seeing the strict three-tiered structure of Ignatius as being descriptive of the church everywhere at the beginning of the second century, especially in Alexandria.

In the fourth-century *Apostolic Constitutions* there is much about the bishop, especially in book 2. Perhaps the most startling change from the PE, a change already attested as early as Polycarp (see above), is the equating of the authority of the bishop with that of God.

For if Aaron, because he declared to Pharaoh the words of God from Moses, is called a prophet; and Moses himself is called a god to Pharaoh, on account of his being at once a king and a high priest, as God says to him, "I have made thee a god to Pharaoh, and Aaron thy brother shall be thy prophet"; why do not ye also esteem the mediators of the word to be prophets, and reverence them as gods? (2.4.29; ANF 7:411).

For now the deacon is to you Aaron, and the bishop Moses. If, therefore, Moses was called a god by the Lord, let the bishop be honoured among you as a god, and the deacon as his prophet. (2.4.30; ANF 7:411)

As to a good shepherd, let the lay person honour him, love him, reverence him as his lord, as his master, as the high priest of God, as a teacher of piety. For he that heareth him, heareth Christ; and he that rejecteth him, rejecteth Christ; and he who does not receive Christ, does not receive His God and Father. (2.3.20; ANF 7:404)

The bishop is the spiritual father and the laity are his children. (2.4.33; ANF 7:412)

For if the divine oracle says, concerning our parents according to the flesh, "Honour thy father and thy mother, that it may be well with thee"; and, "He that curseth his father or his mother, let him die the death"; how much more should the word exhort you to honour your spiritual parents, and to love them as your benefactors and ambassadors with God, who have regenerated you by water, and endued you with the fulness of the Holy Spirit, who have fed you with the word as with milk, who have nourished you with doctrine, who have confirmed you by their admonitions, who have imparted to you the saving body and precious blood of Christ, who have loosed you from your sins, who have made you partakers of the holy and sacred eucharist, who have admitted you to be partakers and fellow-heirs of the promise of God! Reverence these, and honour them with all kinds of honour; for they have obtained from God the power of life and death, in their judging of sinners, and condemning them to the death of eternal fire, as also of loosing returning sinners from their sins, and of restoring them to a new life. (2.4.33; ANF 7:412)

The *Apostolic Constitutions* also spells out the prescribed character of a bishop in language often reminiscent of the PE:

But concerning bishops, we have heard from our Lord, that a pastor who is to be ordained a bishop for the churches in every parish, must be unblameable, unreprovable, free from all kinds of wickedness common among men, not under fifty years of age; for such a one is in good part past youthful disorders, and the slanders of the heathen, as well as the reproaches which are sometimes cast upon many persons by some false brethren, who do not consider the word of God in the Gospel: "Whosoever speaketh an idle word shall give an account thereof to the Lord in the day of judgment." And again: "By thy words thou shalt be justified, and by thy words thou shalt be condemned." Let him therefore, if it is possible, be well educated; but if he be unlettered, let him at any rate be skilful in the word, and of competent age. But if in a small parish one advanced in years is not to be found, let some younger person, who has a good report among his neighbours, and is esteemed by them worthy of the office of a bishop,—who has carried himself from his youth with meekness and regularity, like a much elder person,—after examination, and a general good report, be ordained in peace. (2.1.1; ANF 7:396)

Evidently the *Apostolic Constitutions* would not accept Timothy, who most likely was considerably younger than fifty (cf. 1 Tim 4:12):

Let him therefore be sober, prudent, decent, firm, stable, not given to wine; no striker, but gentle; not a brawler, not covetous; "not a novice, lest, being puffed up with pride, he fall into condemnation, and the snare of the devil: for every one that exalteth himself shall be abused." Such a one a bishop ought to be, who has been the "husband of one wife," who also has herself had no other husband, "ruling well his own house." In this manner let examination be made when he is to receive ordination, and to be placed in his bishopric, whether he be grave, faithful, decent; whether he hath a grave and faithful wife, or has formerly had such a one; whether he hath educated his children piously, and has "brought them up in the nurture and admonition of the Lord"; whether his domestics do fear and reverence him, and are all obedient to him: for if those who are immediately about him for worldly concerns are seditious and disobedient, how will others not of his family, when they are under his management, become obedient to him?

Let examination also be made whether he be unblameable as to the concerns of this life; for it is written: "Search diligently for all the faults of him who is to be ordained for the priesthood." (2.1.2–3; ANF 7:396–97; cf. 2.2.3 and 2.2.5)

The bishop must not be greedy (*Apostolic Constitutions* 2.2.6) and must be above reproach (2.3.17). His role includes judging sinners (2.3.8–11, 21), restoring penitents (2.3.12, 14; 2.5.43; 2.6.44), and caring for the poor (2.4), and he plays the major role in the worship service (2.7.57):

The bishop, he is the minister of the word, the keeper of knowledge, the mediator between God and you in the several parts of your divine worship. He is the teacher of piety; and, next after God, he is your father, who has begotten you again to the adoption of sons by water and the Spirit. He is your ruler and governor; he is your king and potentate; he is, next after God, your earthly god, who has a right to be honoured by you. For concerning him, and such as he, it is that God pronounces, "I have said, Ye are gods; and ye are all children of the Most High." And, "Ye shall not speak evil of the gods." For let the bishop preside over you as one honoured with the authority of God, which he is to exercise over the clergy, and by which he is to govern all the people. (2.4.26; ANF 7:310)

The bishop is over the deacons; the latter are virtually unable to do anything without his permission (2.4.30–32; 2.4.26; 2.6.54; cf. *Explanation* on 1 Tim 3:8–13). The *Apostolic Constitutions* also regulates the ordination of the bishop (8.2; 8.3.16). It also spells out in greater detail the specifics of marriage:

We have already said, that a bishop, a presbyter, and a deacon, when they are constituted, must be but once married, whether their wives be alive or whether they be dead; and that it is not lawful for them, if they are unmarried when they are ordained, to be married afterwards; or if they be then married, to marry a second time, but to be content with that wife, which they had when they came to ordination. We also appoint that the ministers, and singers, and readers, and porters, shall be only once married. But if they entered into the clergy before they were married, we permit them to marry, if they have an inclination thereto, lest they sin and incur punishment. But we do not permit any one of the clergy to take to wife either a courtesan, or a servant, or a widow, or one that is divorced, as also the law says. (6.3.17; ANF 7:457)

The bishop's ministry began primarily as a liturgical function, presiding over the Eucharist. As time progressed, more power was given to the position. In Hippolytus, Cyprian, and Tertullian, the bishop is the chief "priest," presiding over the sacraments (Shepherd, *IDB* 1:442). As the passage of time saw the church become more institutionalized, there were attempts to read foreign ideas back into the PE, such as ordination and succession, in an attempt to justify the positions. Eventually the bishop was given control over large areas. Theodore of Mopsuestia (A.D. 350–428) says,

Those who had the authority to ordain, who are now called bishops, did not belong to a single congregation, but had authority over a whole province, and were called apostles. (cited in Dibelius-Conzelmann, 57)

Partially in response to new heresies, there emerged the monarchical episcopate, the singular bishop (ἐπίσκοπος) presiding over a city or province. Lightfoot's theory is that bishops/overseers and elders were synonymous, but eventually out of the college of elders (the presbyterate) developed the singular position of bishop. Sohm and others argue that bishops and elders were always two distinct groups, the former being responsible to appoint the latter (see Form/Structure/Setting, "The Development of Christian Ministry," above). With the rise of Gnosticism and its claim to esoteric knowledge given in "secret succession from the apostles" (Shepherd, IDB 3:391) and other teachings such as Montanism, eventually the church developed the doctrine of apostolic succession. Shepherd says, "The bishops were viewed in the church as the direct heirs of the authority of the apostles, in an unbroken continuity of office, and the primary preservers for the church of the apostolic faith" (Shepherd, IDB 1:441). This began as early as Clement of Rome (above) and is found in Tertullian, Cyprian, and Irenaeus (Adv. Haer. 3.2, 3, 4; ANF 1:415–16):

But, again, when we refer them to that tradition which originates from the apostles (and) which is preserved by means of the successions of presbyters in the Churches, they [the heretics] object to tradition, saying that they themselves are wiser not merely than the presbyters, but even than the apostles, because they have discovered the unadulterated truth. (Adv. Haer. 3.2.2)

It is within the power of all, therefore, in every Church, who may wish to see the truth, to contemplate clearly the tradition of the apostles manifested throughout the whole world; and we are in a position to reckon up those who were by the apostles instituted bishops in the Churches, and (to demonstrate) the succession of these men to our own times. (Adv. Haer. 3.3.1)

For it is a matter of necessity that every Church should agree with this Church [i.e., Rome], on account of its pre-eminent authority, that is, the faithful everywhere, inasmuch as the apostolical tradition has been preserved continuously by those (faithful men) who exist everywhere. (Adv. Haer. 3.3.2)

Having given the names of the twelve men who have been in succession since the apostles, Irenaeus concludes:

In this order, and by this succession, the ecclesiastical tradition from the apostles, and the preaching of the truth, have come down to us. And this is most abundant proof that there is one and the same vivifying faith, which has been preserved in the Church from the apostles until now, and handed down in truth. (Adv. Haer. 3.3.3)

For discussion on this topic see Kirk, Apostolic Ministry, and Ehrhardt, Apostolic Succession.

D. Deacons (1 Tim 3:8–13)

Bibliography

Ansorge, D. "Der Diakonat der Frau: Zum gegenwärtigen Forschungsstand." In *Liturgie und Frauenfrage: Ein Beitrag zur Frauenforschung aus liturgiewissenschaftlicher Sicht*, ed. T. Berger and A. Gerhards. St. Ottilien: EOS Verlag Erzabtei, 1990. 31–65. **Audet, J. P.** *Structures of Christian Priesthood: A Study of Home, Marriage, and Celibacy in the Pastoral Service of the Church*. Tr. R. Sheed. New York: Macmillan, 1968. 57–61. **Best, E.** "Bishops and Deacons." *SE* 4 [= TU 102] (1968) 371–76. **Beyer, H. W.** "διακονέω, διακονία, διάκονος." *TDNT* 2:81–93. **Blackburn, B. C.** "The Identity of 'the Women' in 1 Tim 3:11." In *Essays on Women in Early Christianity*, ed. C. D. Osburn. Joplin, MO: College Press, 1995. 1:303–19. **Borland, J. A.** "Women in the Life and Teachings of Jesus." In *Recovering Biblical Manhood and Womanhood*, ed. J. Piper and W. Grudem. Wheaton, IL: Crossway, 1991. 113–23. **Boulton, P. H.** "Διακονέω and Its Cognates in the Four Gospels." *SE* 1 [= TU 73] (1959) 415–22. **Caddeo, L.** "Le 'diaconesse.'" *RBR* 7 (1972) 211–25. **Clark, S. B.** *Man and Woman in Christ: An Examination of the Roles of Men and Women in Light of Scripture and the Social Sciences*. Ann Arbor, MI: Servant, 1980. **Colson, J.** "Der Diakonat im Neuen Testament." In *Diaconia in Christo*, ed. K. Rahner and H. Vorgrimler. Freiburg: Herder, 1962. 3–22. **Daniélou, J.** *The Ministry of Women in the Early Church*. Tr. G. Symon. New York: Faith, 1961. **Davies, J. G.** "Deacons, Deaconesses and the Minor Orders in the Patristic Period." *JEH* 14 (1963) 1–15. **Delling, G.** *Paulus' Stellung zu Frau und Ehe*. BWANT 108. Stuttgart: Kohlhammer, 1931. **Elchin, E. P.** *The Deacon in the Church: Past and Future*. Staten Island, NY: Alba, 1971. **Fitzgerald, K.** "The Characteristics and Nature of the Order of the Deaconess." In *Women and the Priesthood*, ed. T. Hopko. Crestwood, NY: St. Vladimir's Seminary Press, 1983. 84–89. **Galiazzo, D.** "Il diacono." *RBR* 7 (1972) 193–210. **Goerl, G.** "As Qualidades de Bispos, Presbiteros e Diaconos Segundo 1 Tim 3 e Tito 1." *Igreja Luterana* 19 (1958) 245–55. **Gryson, R.** *The Ministry of Women in the Early Church*. Tr. J. Laporte and M. L. Hall. Collegeville, MN: Liturgical Press, 1976. **Hick, L.** *Die Stellung des heiligen Paulus zur Frau im Rahmen seiner Zeit*. Köln: Amerikanisch-Ungarischer Verlag, 1957. **Hort, F. J. A.** *The Christian Ecclesia*. London: Macmillan, 1914. 171–88. **Huls, G.** *De dienst der vrouw in de kerk*. Wageningen: Veenman, 1951. **Kähler, E.** *Die Frau in den paulinischen Briefen*. Zürich: Gotthelf, 1960. **Kalsbach, A.** *Die altkirchliche Einrichtung der Diakonissen bis zu ihrem Erlöschen*. RQSup 22. Freiburg im Breisgau: Herder, 1926. **Kirk, K. E.**, ed. *The Apostolic Ministry: Essays on the History and the Doctrine of Episcopacy*. London: Hodder & Stoughton, 1946. 142–50, 216–27, 243–53. **Lauerer, H.** "Die 'Diakonie' im Neuen Testament." *NKZ* 42 (1931) 315–26. **Leclercq, H.** "Diaconesse." *DACL* 4:725–33. **Leenhardt, F. J.**, and **Blanke, F.** *Die Stellung der Frau im Neuen Testament und in der alten Kirche*. Zürich: Zwingli, 1949. **Lewis, R. M.** "The 'Women' of 1 Tim 3:11." *BSac* 136 (1979) 167–75. **Lietzmann, H.** "Zur altchristlichen Verfassungsgeschichte." *ZWT* 55 (1914) 97–153. **Lowrie, W.** *The Church and Its Organization in Primitive and Catholic Times: An Interpretation of Rudolph Sohm's Kirchenrecht*. New York: Longmans, Green, 1904. 371–83. **Lyonnet, S.** "Unius uxoris vir." *VD* 45 (1967) 3–10. **Martimort, A. G.** *Deaconesses: An Historical Study*. Tr. K. D. Whitehead. San Francisco: Ignatius, 1986. **McKee, E. A.** *John Calvin on the Diaconate and Liturgical Almsgiving*. Geneva: Libraire Droz, 1984. **Müller-Bardorff, J.** "Zur Exegese von 1 Timotheus 3, 3–16." In *Gott und die Götter*. FS E. Fascher, ed. H. Bardtke. Berlin: Evangelische Verlagsanstalt, 1958. 113–33. **Nugent, M. R.** *Portrait of the Consecrated Woman in Greek Christian Literature of the First Four Centuries*. Washington, DC: Catholic University of America Press, 1941. **Pantel, P. S.**, ed. *A History of Women in the West*. Vol. 1: *From Ancient Goddesses to Christian Saints*. Cambridge, MA: Belknap, 1992. **Peterson, E.** "Zur Bedeutungsgeschichte von παρρησία." In *Reinhold Seeberg Festschrift*. Vol. 1: *Zur Theorie des Christentums*, ed. W. Koepp. Leipzig: Scholl, 1929. **Reicke, B.**

Diakonie, Festfreude und Zelos in Verbindung mit der altchristlichen Agapenfeier. Uppsala: Lundequist, 1951. **Rengstorf, K. H.** "Die neutestamentliche Mahnungen an die Frau." In *Verbum dei manet in aeternum.* FS O. Schmitz, ed. W. Foerster. Witten: Luther-Verlag, 1953. 131–45. **Robinson, C.** *The Ministry of Deaconesses.* London: Methuen, 1898. **Schreiner, T. R.** "The Valuable Ministries of Women in the Context of Male Leadership." In *Recovering Biblical Manhood and Womanhood,* ed. J. Piper and W. Grudem. Wheaton, IL: Crossway, 1991. 209–24. **Schweizer, E.** *Church Order in the New Testament.* SBT 32. London: SCM Press, 1961. **Stiefel, J. H.** "Women Deacons in 1 Timothy: A Linguistic and Literary Look at 'Women Likewise' (1 Tim 3.11)." *NTS* 41 (1995) 442–57. **Swete, H. B.**, ed. *Essays on the Early History of the Church and the Ministry.* London: Macmillan, 1921. **Tucker, R. A.**, and **Liefeld, W.** *Daughters of the Church: Women and Ministry from New Testament Times to the Present.* Grand Rapids, MI: Zondervan, 1987. **Turner, C. H.** "Ministries of Women in the Primitive Church." In *Catholic and Apostolic: Collected Papers,* ed. H. N. Bate. London: Mowbray; Milwaukee: Morehouse, 1931. **Warfield, B. B.** "Some Exegetical Notes on 1 Timothy." *PresR* 8 (1921) 504–6. **Weinrich, W.** "Women in the History of the Church." In *Recovering Biblical Manhood and Womanhood,* ed. J. Piper and W. Grudem. Wheaton, IL: Crossway, 1991. 263–79. **Witherington, B.** *Women in the Earliest Churches.* SNTSMS 59. Cambridge: Cambridge UP, 1988. ———. *Women in the Ministry of Jesus.* SNTSMS 51. Cambridge: Cambridge UP, 1988.

For related bibliography on overseers/elders/bishops and Christian ministry in general, see *Bibliography* for 1 Tim 3:1–7.

Translation

[8]*Likewise, [it is necessary for] deacons [to be] dignified,*[a] *not gossips, not addicted to wine, not greedy for gain,* [9]*holding to the mystery of the faith with a clean conscience.* [10]*And they should also be tested first; then let them serve if they are found above reproach.* [11]*Wives likewise must be dignified, not slanderers, clear-minded, faithful in all things.* [12]*Deacons should be "one-woman" men, managing children and their own households well.* [13]*For those who serve well are acquiring a good standing for themselves and great confidence in faith, which [is] in Christ Jesus.*

Notes

א* *pc* omit σεμνούς, "dignified."

Form/Structure/Setting

Having finished his description of the type of person who can be an overseer, Paul moves to the type of person who can serve as a deacon. He lists nine qualities (counting v 11 as one) and concludes with a word of encouragement. Unlike the parallel lists of overseers (1 Tim 3:1–7) and elders (Titus 1:6–9), he does not begin with ἀνεπίλημπτος, "above reproach" (cf. 1 Tim 3:2; Titus 1:6 [ἀνέγκλητος]), although a synonym does occur later (3:10 [ἀνέγκλητος]). He begins with the admonition that deacons should be σεμνός, "dignified," an admonition that is repeated at the head of the requirements for their wives (v 11). V 11 raises the major exegetical question of the passage. If it refers to deaconesses, rather than to the wives of deacons, then the structure of the passage is disjointed with a return to the subject deacons in v 12.

The similarity of this list to the preceding one for overseers is striking (see table in *Form/ Structure/ Setting* on 1 Tim 3:1–7). Of the nine characteristics of a deacon, six are directly parallel to the characteristics of an overseer: dignified (although the actual words used are synonyms), not drunkards, not greedy for gain, blameless, "one-woman" men, and good managers of their households (cf. also the use of καλός, "good," in 3:1 and καλῶς, "well," in 3:13). Hanson ([1983] 79) argues that because these two lists are so similar they must have been drawn from the same source, which perhaps originally did not mention either overseer or deacon. But this misses the point of the lists, which are similar because they are describing not the functions of an office but the type of person who may fulfill that office. Both the office of church leader and the office of church worker require the same type of person: a mature Christian whose behavior is above reproach.

There are several differences between the list in 3:1–7 and the one in 3:8–13. (1) A deacon is not required to teach, whereas the official teaching duty is assigned to the overseers. However, this does not mean a deacon could not teach (see *Comment* on v 9). (2) As the title overseers implies and as v 5 states, this office is responsible for the general oversight of caring for the church; this is not the responsibility of the deacon. (3) Part of the examination of a deacon includes an examination of his wife's character (3:11). This may suggest that a deacon's wife was more involved with her husband's work than was the wife of the overseer (assuming that γυναῖκας is to be translated "wives"). If γυναῖκας is translated "deaconesses," then there are similarities between the qualifications of deaconesses and those of deacons and overseers (of the four qualities of a deaconess, the first three are paralleled in the other lists). (4) A deacon is not required to be hospitable (apart from the hospitality required of all Christians), suggesting that deacons were not responsible for official housing of guests. (5) A deacon is to be tested first, and then he is allowed to serve. However, Paul simply says that an overseer must not be a recent convert (1 Tim 3:6), although 1 Tim 5:22, 24–25 may assume a similar testing period for overseers. (6) There are a few other differences that seem to be generally virtues any Christian should have and thus do not help to differentiate the overseer from the deacon (see the table).

Much of what was said in *Form/Structure/Setting* on 1 Tim 3:1–7 applies here. Paul is giving an official, but not exhaustive, ad hoc description of the type of person who should be allowed to function as an official church worker, and most of the requirements stand in opposition to the opponents' behavior. They describe personal characteristics and not duties, although a reading between the lines gives some indication of the latter. While many of the qualities described are also lauded in contemporary secular literature, this does not keep them from being Christian ideals. For a discussion of διάκονος, "deacon," see *Comment* on v 8, and for the relationship of the deacon to overseers/elders as well as a general discussion of the development of Christian ministry, see *Form/Structure/Setting* on 1 Tim 3:1–7.

It is not clear what the duties of a deacon were. As their title implies, they were probably responsible for the serving duties (cf. use of διακονία, "service," throughout the NT). The requirements for a deacon suggest that there would be substantial contact with people: not double-tongued; a dignified wife; faithful in marriage; a well-managed family. The requirement that they not be greedy may suggest some responsibility for the church's purse, perhaps in the disbursement of funds to the poor. Their relationship to the overseer (see below) suggests that the deacons were more involved with the day-to-day needs of the community, but this distinctive should not be exaggerated since it was the overseers who provided official hospitality. It is tempting to compare deacons to the seven Hellenists who were appointed to deal with the practical needs of the early Christian community in Jerusalem (Acts 6), specifically the disbursement of food to widows. However, these Hellenists are never called διάκονοι, "deacons" (but a cognate noun and verb are used; see *Comment* on 1 Tim 3:8), and at least two of these seven were substantially more than table waiters. Stephen was a miracle worker (Acts 6:8) and preacher (Acts 6:8–10), and Philip was an evangelist (Acts 8:26–40; 21:8). Beyond these observations, it is not possible to determine with any certainty the duties of the deacons. This lack of definition probably indicates the embryonic state of the diaconate and the ad hoc nature of this list.

The relationship of deacons to overseers is also a difficult question. They represent two groups, as is also attested in Phil 1:1. In the PE, even though the lists of qualifications are similar, they are distinct, suggesting distinct functions. Never are the two titles interchanged in the NT in the same way as overseer and elder. In the postapostolic development of the offices, they are clearly distinct (see *Explanation*). Part of the problem is that this passage does not spell out the functions of a deacon but simply clarifies the type of person who qualifies to be a deacon. Overseers and deacons are distinct in function but similar in character. The TEV translates ἐπίσκοπος as "church leader" and διάκονος as "church helper," phrases that distinguish their functions. Hanson ([1983] 78) goes beyond the evidence when he says that "deacons are clearly by this time members of the ordained ministry."

There is no suggestion in the text that the deacon is subordinate to the overseer. Both performed vital functions in the church, and it is the deacon who is expressly told that a reward awaits those who serve well. As Ridderbos observes, "Paul speaks of deacons as servants of the church and their ministry as a *charisma* given to the church and not as servants or a *charisma* for the benefit of the apostles or bishops" (*Paul*, 460 n. 95). It is clear from Paul's teaching that the church is the body of Christ and that every part is important. The PE do not teach that a person would first become a deacon and then be elevated to the office of overseer (see *Comment* on v 13); otherwise, the requirement that an overseer not be a new convert (3:6) would be meaningless.

The question of the origin of the office is a difficult one that extends beyond the scope of this commentary. There does not seem to have been a parallel to the role of the deacon in secular society (cf. H. W. Beyer, *TDNT* 2:91–3). This is not surprising since the Christian ideals of sacrificial service and equality among all people were unusual. The term διάκονος was common in the Greek world, used to describe many different occupations. In Judaism there were officers of service, but there was no exact parallel to the Christian deacon. The ἀρχισυνάγωγος, "president of the synagogue," led the synagogue in its worship and was aided by the ὑπηρέτης, "assistant" (who was never called the διάκονος; cf. Luke 4:20; the Hebrew term was חזן *ḥazzān*), but their responsibilities extended only to worship; the remaining duties fell on the elders. There were hierarchies in the Qumran community, but these are not directly parallel. Even the appointment of the seven Hellenists to aid in διακονεῖν τραπέζαις, "waiting on tables" (Acts 6:2), cannot be the source (see above). The office of the deacon existed in Philippi as seen in Paul's greeting to the overseers and deacons (Phil 1:1). Elchin suggests that Epaphroditus may have been a deacon ("I have thought it necessary to send to you Epaphroditus my brother and fellow worker and fellow soldier, and your messenger and minister to my need. . . . So receive him in the Lord with all joy; and honor such men, for he nearly died for the work of Christ, risking his life to complete your service to me" [Phil 2:25, 29–30]) and concludes, "At a minimum Paul's greeting to different officers with different titles and his praise of Epaphroditus for help and companionship indicate that the diaconal function was gradually being structured even in the Pauline churches" (*Deacon*, 9–10). H. W. Beyer concludes,

> The creative power of the early Church was strong enough to fashion its own offices for the conduct of congregational life and divine worship. . . . Early Christianity took over words which were predominantly secular in their current usage and which had not yet been given any sharply defined sense. It linked these words with offices which were being fashioned in the community, and thus gave them a new sense which was so firmly welded with the activity thereby denoted that in all languages they have been adopted as loanwords to describe Christian office-bearers. (*TDNT* 2:91)

As is often the case, the origin of the office is seen in the dynamic and revolutionary teaching of Christ. The greatest serves. Who would be first must be last. A mark of true discipleship is the willingness to undergo sacrificial service to others, whether it be footwashing, serving in the common meal, or some other service. As the church began to grow, so did the need for guidance and structure. Much of the guidance came through those gifted to speak from the Lord, whether it be apostles, prophets, or others. But alongside these always existed the more "practically" oriented gifts of administration and service, gifts that enabled believers to deal with the day-to-day needs of the church in meeting the daily needs of the body. It is not surprising that those who excelled at serving came to be known as "servers," "deacons."

Comment

8 Διακόνους ὡσαύτως σεμνούς μὴ διλόγους, μὴ οἴνῳ πολλῷ προσέχοντας, μὴ αἰσχροκερδεῖς, "Likewise, [it is necessary for] deacons [to be] dignified, not gossips, not addicted to wine, not greedy for gain." The close connection between this paragraph and the preceding one is seen in its grammatical structure. V 8 assumes the δεῖ . . . εἶναι, "it is necessary for . . . to be," of v 2 (δεῖ is repeated in v 7). ὡσαύτως, "likewise," ties the requirements of a deacon to those of an overseer. Just as an overseer must be above reproach, likewise it is necessary for a deacon to be dignified. This use of ὡσαύτως is common in the PE (cf. 1 Tim 2:9; 3:11).

διάκονος, "server, deacon," and cognates (διακονεῖν, "to serve"; διακονία, "service") encapsulate an important Christian theme. The Greeks usually viewed serving others as a menial task; people were to rule, not serve, and the highest good was the development of the self, although service to the state was regarded as virtuous (H. W. Beyer, *TDNT* 2:81–82; but cf. Aristotle *Nic. Eth.* 9.81169a for the notion of sacrificial service). In Judaism, service was seen as something good, especially when it was directed toward God and the poor; however, service developed into a meritorious work that should be done not for the unworthy and unrighteous but only for the righteous (see H. W. Beyer, *TDNT* 2:82–93). The Essenes came closer to the Christian concept of sacrificial service (cf. K. Hess,

NIDNTT 3:545). In Jesus' teaching, service to others and to God was a mark of a true disciple (Luke 22:26), and this ideal was reflected in his own behavior as one who came not to be served but to serve (Matt 20:28; Mark 10:45). The Christian mandate for all disciples was sacrificial service (John 12:26). Neither Jesus nor Paul conceived of a follower or a believer who was not called to service.

The word group διακον- has three basic usages (cf. Hort, *Christian Ecclesia*, 202–8, 211; Trench, *Synonyms*, 53–58). The oldest and most common meaning is "to wait at table" and then more generally any type of service. Both these meanings are found in the NT. It is the literal use of waiting on tables that often provided Jesus a basis for his teaching on sacrificial service (John 13:1–20). It is one of the most distinctive elements of Jesus' teaching that the greatest should serve (Matt 23:11; Mark 9:35; 10:43). The third use of the word group is really a subset of the second: service within the Christian community. What gifts a believer may possess are to be used in service to others because believers are stewards of God's grace (1 Pet 4:10). διακονία, "service," is especially used in this regard. It is applied to the ministry of spiritual gifts (1 Cor 12:5), the apostolic office (Acts 1:17, 25; 2 Cor 4:1; 6:3) as carried out by Paul (Acts 20:24; Rom 11:13; 2 Cor 4:1; 6:3; 11:8; 1 Tim 1:12), the work of Timothy as an evangelist (2 Tim 4:5), Mark's ministry to Paul (2 Tim 4:11), the work of Archippus (Col 4:17), and the ministry performed by the household of Stephanas (1 Cor 16:15). It also describes the collection for the Jerusalem poor (Rom 15:25, 31; 2 Cor 8:4; 9:1, 12–13). διάκονος, "server," or "deacon," is used in this third sense as well. It describes the work of Timothy (1 Thess 3:2; cf. 1 Tim 4:6) as an evangelist (2 Tim 4:5), Erastus (Acts 19:22), Apollos (1 Cor 3:5), Paul (Rom 11:13; 1 Cor 3:5; 2 Cor 11:23; Col 1:23, 25), Tychicus (Col 4:7), the apostles (2 Cor 6:4), and false prophets as servants of Satan (2 Cor 11:15). (Cf. the similar use of the verb for Onesiphorus [2 Tim 1:18], Erastus [Acts 19:22], Onesimus [Phlm 13], and the prophets [1 Pet 1:10].) δοῦλος, "slave," is used in a similar manner in the NT, emphasizing submission and ownership.

Only four references in the PE describe official functionaries of the church: the noun is used in 1 Tim 3:8, 12 and the verb in 1 Tim 3:10, 13. Several other Pauline references might be interpreted thus: Paul addresses the "elders and deacons" of the Philippian church (1:1), which most think refer to two different groups within the church, although Hawthorne argues that Paul is referring to the elders who serve (*Philippians*, 10; but cf. Fee, *Philippians*, 66 n. 43). Phoebe is referred to as a διάκονος (Rom 16:1), which Cranfield (*Romans* 2:781) and many others argue is the office of deacon (ess) and not a description of her work as one who serves. Paul also addresses the γυναῖκας in Ephesus (1 Tim 3:11), who could be either the deacons' wives or the church's deaconesses. There is nothing unexpected about the use of this title in the PE to describe a church office; it was already part of the church's vocabulary, used to describe believers who were working within the church. On the origin of the title and office, and its relationship to the overseer, see *Form/Structure/Setting* above. On the postapostolic development of the office, see the excursus on "The Deacon and Deaconess in the Postapostolic Church" below.

To be σεμνός, "dignified," is required of deacons' wives (1 Tim 3:11) and older men (Titus 2:2; on its cognate noun, see *Comment* on 1 Tim 2:2). It occurs elsewhere in the NT only in Phil 4:8 in Paul's list of what is worthy of contemplation. Hawthorne comments that the word "has such a richness about it that it is impossible to equate it with any one English word," but suggests "noble," "worthy," and "esteemed." Because it was often associated with the divine, it also includes the ideas of "majesty, dignity and awe." He concludes that "it refers to lofty things, majestic things, things that lift the mind from the cheap and tawdry to that which is noble and good and of moral worth" (*Philippians*, 188). The word does not function as a title over the paragraph as ἀνεπίλημπτος, "above reproach," does in the preceding paragraph since what follows is not an elucidation of what it means to be dignified. It is somewhat synonymous with κόσμιος, "respectable," which is applied to overseers (1 Tim 3:2).

Paul adds to this positive quality three negative traits that should not characterize a deacon. Each calls for self-control, in speech, in drink, and in a desire for wealth. μὴ διλόγους, "not gossips," is a rare phrase, occurring elsewhere in Greek literature only in the second century A.D. (Pollux 2.118). There it means "repeating"; cf. its almost equally rare cognates διλογία, "repetition," and διλογεῖν, "to repeat" (cf. LSJ, 431; MM, 163). The closest form in the LXX is δίγλωσσος, "double-tongued," a person who reveals secrets in contrast to one who keeps secrets (Prov 11:3). The δίγλωσσος winnows with every wind and follows every path (Sir 5:9). δίλογος is a compound of δίς, "twice," and λόγος, "something said." Different suggested definitions are "repetitious," "gossips," "saying one thing and meaning another," or "saying one thing to one person but another thing to another person." Deacons thus must be the type of people who are careful with their tongues, not saying what they should not, being faithful to the truth in their speech. A similar requirement is applied to their wives in v 11 μὴ διαβόλους, "not slanderers."

μὴ οἴνῳ πολλῷ προσέχοντας, μὴ αἰσχροκερδεῖς, "not addicted to wine, not greedy for gain," are the next two requirements of a deacon. Both are also requirements for overseers. The first is mentioned in all three lists of church leaders (1 Tim 3:3; Titus 1:7), a fact that shows the severity of the problem in the Ephesian church. The verb προσέχοντας, "addicted," denotes a strong addiction such as the opponents' addiction to their myths (1 Tim 1:4) and Timothy's devotion to the public reading of Scripture (1 Tim 4:11). αἰσχροκερδής, "greedy," suggests that deacons would have some contact with the church's purse, possibly the disbursement of funds to the poor. This quality is also stipulated in all three lists for church workers (1 Tim 3:3; Titus 1:7). Kelly (81) says that this word in 3:8 is much stronger than its counterpart in 3:3. This requirement, combined with the fact that Paul's opponents are teaching for the sake of becoming rich (1 Tim 6:5), shows how serious the problem of professional religiosity had become. αἰσχροκερδής occurs elsewhere in the NT only in the similar list concerning elders (Titus 1:7; cf. variant at 1 Tim 3:3). It is a compound of αἰσχρός, meaning "shameful," "disgraceful" (BAGD, 25), and κέρδος, meaning "gain." Elsewhere Paul says that the opponents are teaching "for disgraceful gain" (αἰσχροῦ κέρδους χάριν; Titus 1:11; cf. 1 Pet 5:2).

9 ἔχοντας τὸ μυστήριον τῆς πίστεως ἐν καθαρᾷ συνειδήσει, "holding to the mystery of the faith with a clean conscience." The fifth requirement is that deacons have a firm grasp on the mystery of faith, which is the gospel, and that their consciences not be tainted with the guilt of sin. The opponents have shipwrecked the faith (1:19), and their consciences have been branded (4:2). This type of person is not to be allowed to serve in any official church capacity. Rather, church workers must understand the teaching of the gospel; and as that gospel works its way out in their lives, their consciences should not condemn them of sin. Once again the connection between faith and practice, so common throughout the PE, is brought to the forefront (cf. *Introduction,* "Themes in the PE"). Whereas much in this paragraph deals with outward behavior, this quality looks directly into the believer's heart.

ἔχοντας, "holding to, possessing" (cf. 1 Tim 1:19), describes the solid commitment to the true gospel. That they are to *hold* to the faith, rather than perhaps to *teach* the faith, combined with the absence of the requirement to be skilled teachers (v 2), implies that deacons are not responsible for the official instruction in the church. All Christians, including deacons, should be able to explain their beliefs (1 Pet 3:15), but the official teaching role belongs to the overseers.

μυστήριον, "mystery," is a significant word in Paul's theology, occurring twenty-one times throughout his writings. It refers to knowledge that is beyond the reach of sinners but has now been graciously revealed through the gospel. The emphasis of the concept is upon the fact that this information is now knowable, which explains its common association with words like ἀποκάλυψις, "revelation" (Rom 16:25; Eph 3:3), ἀποκαλύπτειν, "to reveal" (1 Cor 2:10; Eph 3:5), γνωρίζειν, "to make known" (Rom 16:26; Eph 1:9; 3:3, 5; Col 1:27), and φανεροῦν, "to make manifest" (Rom 16:26; Col 1:26 [cf. O'Brien, *Colossians,* 84]). In all but one occurrence of the term, the μυστήριον is the gospel (1 Cor 14:2 refers to the mysteries uttered by one speaking in tongues). The equation of mystery with the gospel is sometimes implicit (1 Cor 2:1; 2:7; 4:1) and sometimes explicit (Rom 16:25–26; Eph 6:19; Col 1:25–27). Sometimes μυστήριον refers to one particular aspect of God's redemptive plan such as the hardening of the Jews (Rom 11:25), the inclusion of the Gentiles into the church along with the Jews (Eph 3:3, 4, 9; Col 1:26–27), the change to be experienced by believers at the parousia (1 Cor 15:51), the union of all things in Christ (Eph 1:9), the nature of Christ (Col 2:2; 4:3), the relationship between Christ and his church (Eph 5:32), and the mystery of lawlessness that will be revealed at the parousia (2 Thess 2:7–8). This mystery that Paul proclaims is a revelation of God's plan, and yet without love this knowledge will avail a person nothing (1 Cor 13:2). For comments on the background to the word, see O'Brien (*Colossians,* 83–84) and G. Bornkamm (*TDNT* 4:802–28).

πίστις, "faith," could describe the deacon's personal faith or the Christian faith in a creedal sense (see *Introduction,* "Themes in the PE"). πίστεως, "of faith," could be a subjective (mystery produced by faith) or appositional (mystery, which is faith) genitive. Because μυστηριον refers to the gospel, Paul is probably saying that deacons must hold to the mystery, which is the Christian faith. The use of mystery in 3:16 also supports this interpretation; there Paul follows mention of the mystery with a description of its content.

A deacon's possession of the mystery of the faith is to be accompanied ἐν καθαρᾷ συνειδήσει, "with a clean conscience." It is not sufficient to have a grasp on the theological profession of the church; that knowledge must be accompanied with the appropriate behavior, in this case a conscience that is clear from any stain of sin. Once again Paul connects right belief with right behavior. Heresy and moral reprobation walk hand in hand (so Hanson, [1983] 79–80). On καθαρὰ καρδία, "cleansed heart," and ἀγαθὴ συνείδησις, "good conscience," see *Comments* on 1 Tim 1:5 and 19.

10   καὶ οὗτοι δὲ δοκιμαζέσθωσαν πρῶτον, εἶτα διακονείτωσαν ἀνέγκλητοι ὄντες, "And they should also be tested first; then let them serve if they are found above reproach." The sixth requirement for deacons is that they should be examined before being appointed. If this examination shows that they are above reproach, then they can serve in an official capacity. This requirement parallels the instruction that Timothy be slow in appointing elders because the sins of some are not immediately apparent but take time to surface (1 Tim 5:24; cf. v 25), and it addresses the problem of poor leadership in the Ephesian church. As Ignatius says, a deacon should "beware of blame as of fire" (*Trall.* 2.3). δέ has virtually no adversative force and in conjunction with καί here means "and . . . also," "and in the second place" (Ellicott, 45).

At a minimum the testing entailed some sort of formal examination: the candidate's background, reputation, and adherence to the mystery of the gospel would be checked. Anything less than this would not correct the Ephesian problem. Whether this examination involved a formal probationary period is more difficult to decide. Although 1 Tim 5:24 is dealing with elders/overseers, the observation that the sins of some people are not immediately apparent serves as a caution against cutting the time of examination too short. Since a large part of the problem in Ephesus had to do with improper conduct and damaging reputations, it seems feasible that what is being envisioned here is some sort of time period adequate to examine the applicant's character. The linear, rather than punctiliar, aspect of the two imperatives δοκιμαζέσθωσαν, "let them be tested," and διακονείτωσαν, "let them serve," also supports this conclusion. Clement says that the apostles "appointed their first-fruits, when they had proved them by the Spirit, to be bishops and deacons [δοκιμάσαντες τῷ πνεύματι, εἰς ἐπισκόπους καὶ διακόνους]" (*1 Clem.* 42; tr. Lightfoot, *Apostolic Fathers,* 75). The *Didache* also refers to appointing people who are "worthy of the Lord . . . and true and approved" (15:1). This is not to say, however, that the PE are describing the type of formal probationary testing found in later centuries (cf. *Explanation*). The length of time for testing would have varied from person to person.

In the choosing of the seven in Acts 6:3, it was the task of the church body to find "seven men of good repute." The Ephesian church as a whole also may have had some say in the election of their leadership. However, in a setting in which whole houses were being led astray, necessitating the sending of Timothy as an apostolic delegate with full authority, it is doubtful that the selection process would have been entrusted solely to the church body. It is also doubtful that Timothy himself was to be the sole arbiter since his time with the church would be temporary. While it is true that he is singled out in 1 Tim 5:21 as the person who is to hear the accusations against elders, it seems safe to assume that what was true for Timothy would also be true for the elders once Timothy had left Ephesus. The screening process would probably have involved the whole church with special responsibility falling on the overseers since they were responsible for the general oversight of the church and rebuking error (Titus 1:9).

While deacons were required to be tested, overseers were not. It may be that Paul inadvertently overlooked this in vv 1–7. But B. B. Warfield argues that the phrase καὶ οὗτοι δέ should be translated "But *these,* too," placing the emphasis on οὗτοι, "these," and understanding it as saying that "the deacons no less than the bishops (iii. 1–7) must be tried first" (*PresR* 8 [1921] 505). The reference would be to the requirement μὴ νεόφυτον, "not a recent convert," in v 6. Warfield, however, does not see this as a call to a testing period but instruction that "deacons must be chosen only from the tried and approved men of the Church."

δοκιμάζειν, "to test," can have the sense of "testing to see if something is true or genuine," such as the testing of metals, and in this case it carries the positive nuance that the object will pass the test and be shown to be true (H. Haarbeck, *NIDNTT* 3:809). Its other sense is of "approving" something that has already been shown to be true (cf. 1 Cor 16:3). It is the former meaning that is present here. MM say that in inscriptions the verb is almost a technical term for "passing as fit for a public office" (167). This is the word's only occurrence in the PE. The only cognate in the PE is δόκιμος, "approved," which occurs in Paul's admonition that Timothy present himself as approved to God, a worker who is not ashamed (2 Tim 2:15). The negative ἀδόκιμος, "unqualified," "worthless," describes Paul's opponents (Titus 1:16). The verb is used generally throughout the NT to describe testing of various kinds such as the testing of oneself (1 Cor 11:28; 2 Cor 13:5), one's works (Gal 6:4), and everything (1 Thess 5:21; cf. BAGD, 202; W. Grundmann, *TDNT* 2:255–60).

διακονεῖν, "to serve," here and in v 13, means "to serve as deacons" since the passage does not discuss serving in general. This, however, says nothing about the extent to which the church hierarchy is developed in the PE (contra Hanson, [1983] 80). It says that servers should be allowed to serve if they are found to be blameless. ἀνέγκλητος, "above reproach," is a synonym of ἀνεπίλημπτος, "above reproach," in 3:2 and occurs in a similar list for elders in Titus 1:6–7, where it stands as the leading requirement. ὄντες, "if they are," is conditional: let them serve if they are found above reproach.

11 Γυναῖκας ὡσαύτως σεμνάς, μὴ διαβόλους, νηφαλίους, πιστὰς ἐν πᾶσιν, "Wives likewise must be dignified, not slanderers, clear-minded, faithful in all things." Vv 11–12 form a significant unit. Having discussed some personal qualities, Paul turns to the candidate's home life and spells out what should characterize that part of his life. His wife is to be dignified, he is to be faithful to his wife, and his children and household are to be governed well (vv 11–12). These verses are somewhat parallel to the same stipulations for overseers in the previous paragraph, although there Paul does not raise the topic of the overseer's wife.

Because γυνή can mean both "wife" and "woman," it is not clear whether Paul is referring to the wives of deacons or to women workers, "deaconesses." The feminine form of the word διάκονος (διακόνισσα) had not yet been created. In Rom 16:1, Phoebe is called a διάκονος, the masculine form of the word. The first reference to διακόνισσα occurs in the fourth century in canon 19 of the Council of Nicea (Stählin, *TDNT* 9:464 n. 231; J. G. Davies, *JEH* 14 [1963] 1 n. 1). Whatever the specific interpretation of this verse may be, it is not related to the issue of women in leadership since the deacon(ess) does not provide authoritative leadership. There is no question that women were to play a significant role in serving the church. The NT is replete with such examples (see Spicq 1:76–77; and *Explanation* below), and deaconesses appear very early in church history. As is true of the requirements for overseers and deacons, the following four qualities, while desirable in and of themselves, are directed against the improper activities of the Ephesian women. The first three are also parallel to the requirements for overseers and deacons.

Arguments for the interpretation of γυναῖκας as "wives" are the following (Jerome; Calvin; Bengel; B. Weiss; von Soden; Moffatt tr.; Warfield, *PresR* 8 [1921] 505–6; Easton; Jeremias; Ridderbos, *Paul,* 461 n. 99; Knight; further references in McKee,

John Calvin, 162). (1) It would be awkward to discuss deacons in vv 8–10, switch to a different topic in v 11, and then return to deacons in vv 12–13 without a textual clue that the topic has changed. (On the force of ὡσαύτως, "likewise," see below.) This suggests the topic has not changed. (2) Vv 11 and 12 develop the common theme of the deacon's family: his wife must be blameless; he must be faithful in marriage; his children must be well-managed. These verses are thus dealing with the same topic and belong together. (3) B. B. Warfield suggests that v 10 is a semi-parenthetical explanation of v 9, v 11 follows closely on v 9, and v 11 assumes the verb ἔχοντας, "holding to," from v 9: "The deacon must have the mystery of faith in a pure conscience—and must not be accepted until his life has shown this possession—and a wife, like him grave, and full of other virtues" (*PresR* 8 [1921] 505, following Bengel). (4) If v 11 introduces a third office, one would expect more details, especially since women were so involved in the heresy. For example, in all three lists Paul raises the issue of marital fidelity (1 Tim 3:2, 12; Titus 1:6), and even in the case of widows (1 Tim 5:9). The problem is also dealt with elsewhere in the PE (1 Tim 2:9; 5:2, 11, 15; 2 Tim 3:6–9), and in light of Paul's readiness to repeat himself on this point, the omission of this qualification here is noteworthy. The requirements, if for a female deacon, are considerably lighter than for a male deacon, and this seems unlikely (unless Paul assumes vv 8–11, 13 carry over to the deaconesses). It could be argued that Paul did not want to repeat himself, but he has already repeated himself extensively as a comparison of the two paragraphs in this chapter shows. (Yet the concluding πιστὰς ἐν πᾶσιν, "faithful in all things," may be Paul's summary way of applying the qualities of a deacon to a deaconess.) (5) γυνή occurs in the very next verse where it must refer to the deacon's wife (cf. 3:2). (6) Paul shows a readiness, both in the PE and elsewhere, to create words to meet his needs. It would have been very easy for him to have written τὰς διακόνους or perhaps διακονίσσας and prevent what would be otherwise confusing if in fact he had changed topics. (7) Although it is an argument from silence, it may be significant that there are no clear references to the deaconess in the NT (see *Explanation* below). It has also been argued that γυναῖκας refers to women in general (Ambrosiaster; J. G. Davies, *JEH* 14 [1963] 2), but this seems out of place in a discussion of church offices (so Chrysostom).

Most argue for the translation "deaconess" (Theodore of Mopsuestia; Chrysostom; Theodoret; Ellicott; Holtzmann; Bernard; Wohlenberg; Hort, *Christian Ecclesia;* Lock; Spicq; Kelly; Audet, *Structures,* 57–61; Brox; Caddeo, *RBR* 7 [1972] 211–25; E. E. Ellis, "Paul and His Co-Workers," in *Prophecy and Hermeneutic in Early Christianity* [Grand Rapids, MI: Eerdmans, 1978] 3–22; Fee; Roloff; Oberlinner with reservations; L. T. Johnson). (1) The parallel use of ὡσαύτως, "likewise," in v 8 and v 11 as well as a mutual grammatical dependence on δεῖ . . . εἶναι, "it is necessary for . . . to be," from v 2 argues that v 11, like v 8, introduces a new category ("Likewise it is necessary for deacons to be. . . . Likewise it is necessary for deaconesses to be . . ."; cf. Spicq 1:460–61). Vv 12–13 then become an afterthought. However, the ὡσαύτως is as easily explained by saying that just as deacons are to be dignified so also are their wives. Also, because the content of v 12 is so significant, being repeated in all three lists (1 Tim 3:2, 4; Titus 1:6), it is doubtful that it is an afterthought. (2) It is often argued that if γυνή were "wife," one would also expect some word about the wife of the overseer (e.g., Roloff, 165). But not only is this an argument from silence, but it assumes that 1 Tim 3 is a formal list, which it is not. If Paul was developing an ad hoc list related to the problems prevalent at Ephesus, it might have been easy for him to overlook the qualities of the overseer's wife. Also, because a deacon presumably is more involved in activities such as visitation, it is more likely that his wife would be involved in his ministry than would the wife of an overseer. (Yet the overseers are responsible for hospitality, and hence their wives presumably would be involved.) B. B. Warfield adds that this is "explained by the circumstance that women could take no part either in ruling or in teaching (ii. 12), which constituted the functions of the bishop (v. 17)" (*PresR* 8 [1921] 506). (3) If γυνή refers to the deacon's wife, then some say there should be a qualifier such as αὐτῶν, "their," wives (cf. Spicq, 1:460; Roloff, 164). However, Paul may not have felt the same need to qualify γυναῖκας as do some modern editors. It could, on the other hand, be argued that if Paul switched topics, some qualifier such as "women who serve as deacons" or at least a specifier at the beginning of v 12 would be expected. (4) If γυνή refers to the deacon's wife, then some say a listing of household duties would be expected. But there are more important standards than household duties upon which to judge a woman. Also, the list in this chapter enumerates qualities, not duties. (5) Although the office of deaconess is found very early in church history, this tells us nothing necessarily about this verse. Guthrie (85) argues that v 11 is not sufficiently specific to construct an actual office of deaconess and that it refers to women in general who are involved in church ministry. The verse was used by the Montanists to support the ordination of women (as deaconesses), and much of the debate through the centuries has dealt with this issue. Lewis (*BSac* 136 [1979] 167–75) identifies γυναῖκας as unmarried female assistants, but one wonders whether Paul would have encouraged this type of relationship, a man working closely with a woman who was not his wife (cf. Knight, 171), especially in light of the Ephesian problem (cf. 1 Tim 2:9; 5:2, 3–16; 2 Tim 3:6–9).

Both interpretations have their strong points, and both are possible. However, the unnatural change of topics, twice in two verses without a clear transition, seems awkward. It is preferable to maintain the connection between v 11 and v 12 by translating γυνή as "wife." For a treatment of the exegetical history of this passage, see McKee, *John Calvin on the Diaconate*, 159–84. For a discussion of the postapostolic office of deaconess, see the excursus "The Deacon and Deaconess in the Postapostolic Church" below.

A deacon's wife must have four qualities (among others). (1) Like her husband, she too must be σεμνή, "dignified." This is the feminine form of the same adjective used of deacons in v 8 (see *Comment* on v 8 for a discussion of the word itself) and receives the force of the ὡσαύτως, "likewise." (2) She cannot be a διάβολος, "slanderer," a problem that was prevalent among the Ephesian women, some of whom are characterized as going about from house to house, learning to be idlers and gossips (1 Tim 5:13; on the word cf. 3:7). Just as her husband cannot be a gossip (δίλογος; 3:8), neither can she. (3) She must be νηφάλιος, "clear-minded" (the same word used in v 2; cf. Titus 2:2). The term carries the double nuance of being temperate in her use of alcohol and clear-minded in her judgments. (4) A deacon's wife must be πιστὰς ἐν πᾶσιν, "faithful in all things." This is a catch-all requirement in the list, stressing that she must be a fully trustworthy person. (On πιστός, see *Introduction*, "Themes in the PE.") The fact that Paul focuses on the deacon's wife shows that for the most part the deacons were men, but the passage does not require all deacons to be men, just as it does not require all deacons to have more than one child (cf. τέκνα, "children," in v 12). But there is nothing in this paragraph that would prohibit women from being deacons ("one-woman man" assumes male deacons but does not necessarily require it), and presumably in this case her husband's character would be examined. There always was a need for women to serve. When the female diaconate was finally formed, its basic sphere of ministry was service to women (see *Explanation* below).

12 διάκονοι ἔστωσαν μιᾶς γυναικὸς ἄνδρες, τέκνων καλῶς προϊστάμενοι καὶ τῶν ἰδίων οἴκων, "Deacons should be 'one-woman' men, managing children and their own households well." Paul continues his discussion of the family life of would-be deacons by insisting that they be faithful in marriage (cf. 1 Tim 3:2) and that their managerial abilities be proven in regard to their children in particular and their households in general (cf. 1 Tim 3:4–5). From the parallel passages we learn that this means the children are to be submissive to their parents, not recklessly extravagant, and faithful. The home is a microcosm of the church, and the qualities necessary for service in the church will be evident in the home. προϊστάναι, "to manage," carries the double nuance of leading by serving and is used of elders, deacons, and all believers applying themselves to good deeds. To do the task καλῶς, "well," includes not only achieving the proper results but doing it the right way by following Paul's instructions and not those of the opponents. These are the same stipulations required of overseers in the paragraph above; see v 2 and vv 4–5 for detailed discussion.

13 οἱ γὰρ καλῶς διακονήσαντες βαθμὸν ἑαυτοῖς καλὸν περιποιοῦνται καὶ πολλὴν παρρησίαν ἐν πίστει τῇ ἐν Χριστῷ Ἰησοῦ, "For those who serve well are acquiring a good standing for themselves and great confidence in faith, which [is] in Christ Jesus." Having completed his list of personal qualities that are essential for a deacon, Paul concludes on a note of encouragement similar to that with which he began his discussion of overseers, saying that anyone desiring to be an overseer is desiring a good thing. Far from being a menial task as some might surmise, providing daily service to the church has its rewards, and in summary Paul mentions two: deacons are building a good reputation within the community, and they are developing an even deeper confidence in their faith. All this is a far cry from Paul's opponents, whose reputation in the community is reprehensible and whose heretical behavior has shipwrecked the faith instead of increasing confidence in the church. The linear aspect of the verb, περιποιοῦνται, "are acquiring," indicates that Paul is describing an ongoing process. It is not so much that by being a good deacon a person will receive rewards; it is in the actual doing of the service that one daily acquires a better standing before the people and more confidence in one's personal faith. These rewards are not given to a believer at a certain time but rather are achieved during the process of service. While in later centuries the diaconate became a steppingstone to the episcopate, there is no suggestion of this type of hierarchy in 1 Timothy (so Easton, 134; Roloff, with some hesitation, 167–68; Oberlinner, 143).

γάρ, "for," is a decisive word in the interpretation of the verse. There is nothing in the content of v 12 that directly relates to v 13, so probably v 13 is acting as a summary of the whole paragraph of vv 8–12. By καλῶς διακονήσαντες, "serve well," Paul probably means that deacons should have these personal qualities when first entering the office and that they must be maintained throughout the exercise of the office. On the verb διακονεῖν, "to serve," see v 10. It refers to serving as a deacon.

Because the immediate concern is the reputation of the church before the world, it seems best to see the rewards of service within the earthly sphere. The opponents' behavior is bringing reproach on the church (3:2); however, if deacons are serving well they are acquiring just the opposite, βαθμὸν ἑαυτοῖς καλὸν, "a good standing for themselves," before the outside world, which is their first reward. This is not for vanity's sake; they would be correcting the problems created by the opponents, and consequently their ministry and the cause of the church would be enhanced.

βαθμός, "standing," has the concrete meaning of "step" (this is the only NT reference; cf. 1 Kgs 5:5 LXX), from which are derived different nuances. It can mean advancement of grade or rank. There are examples of βαθμός used in reference to advancement within the ranks of the army, in Clement of Alexandria to describe the advancement of the soul toward knowledge (*Strom.* 2.45.4), in the Hermetic writings for one's advancement toward heaven, and in philosophy for the gaining of wisdom (BAGD, 130; LSJ, 300–301; MM, 101; Kelly, 84–85). From this some derive the meaning that deacons who serve well are on their way to promotion within the clerical hierarchy (Chrysostom, "Homily 11" [NPNF 13:441–42]; Jerome), but evidence of this development does not occur until the second century, and even Hanson is hesitant to attribute such a developed sense to this verse. Paul says that the deacons acquire a καλός, "good," standing, not a κρείσσων, "better," standing. In Paul's mind the deacon is not under the overseer, but both offices are necessary for the well-being of the body of Christ. As Warfield asserts, "The Apostle makes no reference to the deacon progressing out of so desirable an office. His whole purpose is to enhance the value of the office, just as at iii.1 he enhanced the office of bishop" (*PresR* 8 [1921] 506). περιποιεῖν, "to acquire," occurs elsewhere only in Luke 17:33 and Acts 20:28.

The second reward received by a deacon who serves well is πολλὴν παρρησίαν ἐν πίστει τῇ ἐν Χριστῷ Ἰησοῦ, "great confidence in faith, which [is] in Christ Jesus." παρρησία, "confidence," is a common term for Paul, meaning "openness" or "clarity" of speech (saying what one really means), "publicly" in that what one is saying is open to all, or "courage" and "boldness" of speech. (NEB translates "the right to speak openly on matters of the Christian faith," but such a right should be for all believers and not only deacons.) As such it is often associated with someone standing before people of high rank or before God (BAGD, 630–31; cf. Eph 3:12; 1 John 3:21). The meaning here is that deacons who serve well will be bold in their faith and have courage in expressing what they believe. This boldness could be a confidence before God (cf. Eph 3:12), but because of the context here, it refers to one's relationship to the outside world and describes the deacon's boldness in public (cf. 2 Cor 3:12; Eph 6:19; Phil 1:20; Phlm 8; cf. Acts 4:13). As Barrett rightly comments, a deacon's confidence (which Barrett believes is before God) is "not *because* he is a good deacon, but because as a good deacon he knows well the meaning of faith in Christ Jesus" (63; cf. Peterson, "παρρησία").

πίστις, "faith," here probably refers to the deacon's individual faith that, as Paul continues, is rooted in Christ Jesus (cf. 2 Tim 3:15). In other words, the confidence that deacons build in the process of their service is a strengthening of their personal relationship with Jesus Christ, and consequently the proclamation of their faith becomes stronger and bolder (cf. similar use of παρρησία in Eph 6:19; cf. Acts 4:29, 31; 6:10). On the expression πίστις ἡ ἐν Χριστῷ Ἰησοῦ, "faith in Christ Jesus," see *Comment* on 1 Tim 1:14. On πίστις, see *Introduction*, "Themes in the PE."

Explanation

In 1 Tim 3:8–13 Paul has outlined the essential character and behavioral traits that must be found in the life of every deacon. He presents an official list in that it was intended to be followed, but it is not exhaustive, concentrating as it does on observable traits. It is, rather, an ad hoc list meant to combat the Ephesian heresy; yet in principle it is relevant today. It is a description of the type of person who can be a deacon, but a reading between the lines reveals hints regarding the deacon's duties. The paragraph is similar to the preceding one governing overseers because both offices require the same type of person: a mature Christian whose conduct is blameless.

In this paragraph Paul enumerates nine ingredients essential to the execution of the office. A deacon must be (1) dignified, (2) not a gossip or (3) drunkard or (4) mercenary. He must (5) hold firmly to the gospel message. In order to be sure that he fits these standards, he must (6) be examined; the length of this process would vary from person to person. A deacon's home life must be exemplary. His wife (7) must be of the same ethical and moral makeup. If married, he must (8) be faithful. His (9) managerial skills must have evidenced themselves in his home, both in the general running of his household and specifically in the conduct of his children. If a deacon meets these requirements, then he (for Paul envisions but does not require male deacons) will receive his rewards as he dutifully exercises the responsibilities of the office. He will be gaining a good reputation with those outside the church, an essential quality for someone in the position of deacon, and he will be gaining deeper confidence in his faith as he daily exercises it.

Paul is not concerned to enumerate the duties of the deacon and consequently reveals little information about this question. It may be surmised that a deacon was responsible for the daily serving required in the church. Deacons probably had daily contact with the people in visitation and disbursement of the funds for the poor. Although the burden of the official instruction in church did not lie directly on their shoulders, they were required to understand the gospel and be able to present its claims. Paul does not teach that the deacon is under the overseer; in the PE both overseer and deacon serve the church in different capacities.

Paul gives practical advice for the problems of daily living. (1) Throughout the PE, and specifically in v 9, Paul asserts the connection between correct belief and correct behavior. One is not sufficient in and of itself but always requires the other. It is not sufficient to hold to the mystery of the faith without at the same time maintaining a clean conscience. It is not sufficient to live an apparently moral life if one's belief is not in accord with the mystery that is the gospel. Belief and behavior go hand in hand, providing checks and balances for the believers as they attempt to live in a hostile world. Theology and morality cannot be separated without fatal damage to either or both. (2) V 13 shows also that the acquiring of benefits is a process that takes place within the context of service. It is in the serving that one develops a reputation and gains an ever deepening confidence in one's faith in Christ.

Excursus: The Deacon and Deaconess in the Postapostolic Church

Much of what was said in the excursus on "The Overseer/Bishop in the Postapostolic Church" (appended to the *Explanation* on 1 Tim 3:1–7) is relevant here as well. Along with the episcopate developed the diaconate. By the time of Ignatius—or at least in Ignatius' sphere of influence—it was a well-defined third member of the church's hierarchy with specific responsibilities. As is the case with the overseers/bishops, it is somewhat of a mystery how the system evolved from the time of the NT to the form we see in Ignatius. There are some early references that provide part of the picture.

Clement (d. A.D. 96), the bishop of the Roman church, wrote to the Corinthian church about their divisions and strife. Evidently they had disposed of their presbyters improperly, so Clement argues that because there was a succession from God to Christ to the apostles to the presbyters, the presbyters should not have been removed. Most of his emphasis is on the presbyters, but in the process of the argument he comments on deacons:

> So preaching everywhere in country and town, [the apostles] appointed their first-fruits, when they had proved them by the Spirit, to be bishops and deacons unto them that should believe. And this they did in no new fashion; for indeed it had been written concerning bishops and deacons from very ancient times; for thus saith the scripture in a certain place, "I will appoint their bishops in righteousness and their deacons in faith." (*1 Clem.* 42, citing Isa 60:17; Lightfoot, *Apostolic Fathers,* 75)

Polycarp also mentions deacons. The similarities with 1 Tim 3:8–13 suggest that Polycarp knew it, especially in his use of the rare δίλογος, "double-tongued."

> Deacons [διάκονοι] should be blameless [ἄμεμπτοι] in the presence of His righteousness, as deacons of God and Christ and not of men; not calumniators [διάβολοι], not double-tongued [δίλογοι], not lovers of money [ἀφιλάργυροι], temperate in all things, compassionate, diligent, walking according to the truth of the Lord who became a "minister [deacon] of all." (*Phil.* 5; Lightfoot, *Apostolic Fathers,* 178)

Later Polycarp gives the first hint of the radical change that finds its fulfillment in Ignatius, that of comparing the authority of church leaders and workers to God and Jesus, something Paul never did or intended for the church.

> Wherefore it is right to abstain from all these things, submitting yourself to the presbyters and deacons as to God and Christ. (*Phil.* 5.1; Lightfoot, *Apostolic Fathers,* 179)

Justin Martyr (c. A.D. 100–c. A.D. 165) says that deacons took the Eucharist to those who were not able to attend the assembly of the congregation:

> And on the day called Sunday, all who live in cities or in the country gather together to one place, and the memoirs of the apostles or the writings of the prophets are read, as long as time permits; then, when the reader has ceased, the president verbally instructs, and exhorts to the imitation of these good things. Then we all rise together and pray, and, as we said before, when our prayer is ended, bread and wine and water are brought, and the president in like manner offers prayers and thanksgivings, according to his ability, and the people assent, saying Amen; and there is a distribution to each, and a participation of that over which thanks have been given, and to those who are absent a portion is sent by the deacons. (*1 Apol.* 1.67; ANF 1:186)

The *Didache* joins overseers and deacons (unlike Ignatius, who firmly separates them). Its comparison of these offices to prophets and teachers (who were probably itinerant as opposed to deacons who served a local church) suggests that deacons shared in the teaching responsibilities. The *Didache* also suggests that deacons distributed the funds ("not lovers of money") and went through an examination ("true and approved"):

> Appoint for yourselves therefore bishops and deacons worthy of the Lord, men who are meek and not lovers of money, and true and approved; for unto you they also perform the service of the prophets and teachers. Therefore despise them not; for they are your honourable men along with the prophets and teachers. (15.1; Lightfoot, *Apostolic Fathers* 1:234)

The Shepherd of Hermas witnesses to the presence of deacons in Rome:

> Listen then concerning the stones which go into the building. The stones which are square and white and which fit into their joins are the Apostles and bishops and teachers and deacons who walked according to the majesty of God, and served the elect of God in holiness and reverence as bishops and teachers and deacons; some of them are fallen asleep and some are still alive. And they always agreed among themselves, and had peace among themselves, and listened to one another; for which cause their joins fit in the building of the tower. (*Vis.* 3.5; Lightfoot, *Apostolic Fathers* 2:37–39)

The *Similitudes* of the Shepherd shows that deacons dealt with the treasury; unfortunately some of them proved untrustworthy. It also appears that deacons were appointed for a set period of time:

> The ones with blemishes are deacons who served badly and stole the livelihood of widows and orphans and profited for themselves from the service which they received to perform. If, then, they persist in the same desire they are dead and there is no hope of life for them. But if they turn and sincerely complete their service they will be able to live. (*Sim.* 9.26.2; cited by Elchin, *Deacon*, 18)

The process begun in the NT, attested in Justin Martyr, Clement, and Polycarp, was altered by the time of Ignatius, or by Ignatius, where there is a clear division among the three branches of the clerical hierarchy that no longer serve the church as Paul had intended but possess institutional power. In Ignatius, the bishop is over the city (see excursus on "The Overseer/Bishop in the Postapostolic Church" after the *Explanation* on 1 Tim 3:1–7) and under him serve the presbyters and the deacons. This structure came to dominate the church.

Although the deacons exercised some authority, Ignatius' emphasis is on the fact that they were worthy of respect. He describes the deacons as walking after God (*Magn.* 13.1), "entrusted with the diaconate of Jesus Christ" (*Magn.* 6.1), and as his fellow servants (*Phld.* 4.1; *Smyrn.* 12.1). To the Trallians he says, "And those likewise who are deacons of the mysteries of Jesus Christ must please all men in all ways. For they are not deacons of meats and drinks but servants of the Church of God. It is right therefore that they should beware of blame as of fire" (*Trall.* 2.3; tr. of Ignatius from Lightfoot, *Apostolic Fathers*). They are worthy of respect (*Trall.* 3.1) and "have been appointed according to the mind of Jesus Christ" (preface to *Phld.*). The deacons are to be obeyed (*Pol.* 6.1; *Phld.* 7.1) with respect regarding God's commandments (*Smyrn.* 8.1): "In like manner let all men respect the deacons as Jesus Christ, even as they should respect the bishop as being a type of the Father and the presbyters as the council of God and as the college of Apostles. Apart from these there is not even the name of a church" (*Trall.* 3.1); "he that is within the sanctuary [i.e., the church] is clean; but he that is without the sanctuary is not clean, that is, he that doeth aught without the bishop and presbytery and deacons, this man is not clean in his conscience" (*Trall.* 7.2). There also is what almost appears to be the beginning of the office of archdeacon in that Ignatius can single out one deacon as "your deacon" (*Eph.* 2.1) or "the deacon" (*Magn.* 2.1; *Phld.* 11.1; cf. *Smyrn.* 10.1). Ignatius also requests that most of the churches send a deacon to the Syrian church in Antioch (*Phld.* 10.1; *Smyrn.* 11.2; *Pol.* 7.2). This shows the vast differences between the time of Ignatius and the time of the PE and also between Ignatius and the other early Christian writers. There is no hint in the PE of any sense of clerical hierarchy; the deacons are not "under" the overseers but perform a different function. There is no notion of authority associated with the position in the PE. In Paul the deacon is the server of the church; in Ignatius the deacon is over the church and serves the bishop.

Mention of the office of deacon continues throughout the writings of the church, especially in Hippolytus' third-century *Apostolic Tradition* and the third-century *Didascalia Apostolorum.* There deacons become servants to the bishop, providing the official link between him and the congregation. The bishop alone appoints the deacons (presbyters are appointed in conjunction with other elders). During the Eucharist over which the bishop presides, the deacons receive the offering, administer the sacraments, and read the lectionary. As the bishop's agents they visit the poor, disburse funds, and inform the bishop of needs. There is reference to the arrogance associated with the diaconate and stress that the position be fully subordinate to the bishop (cf. J. W. Charley, "Deacon," in *Dictionary of the Christian Church,* ed. J. D. Douglas, rev. ed. [Grand Rapids, MI: Zondervan, 1978] 285).

The fourth-century *Apostolic Constitutions* (ANF 7:421–22) contains passages on the development of the episcopate and diaconate. It compares the deacons to prophets (2.4.29) and demands obedience (2.4.30). The deacon can do nothing without the bishop's permission (2.4.31–32), the bishop alone can ordain (3.1.11; cf. 8.3.17–18), and the focus of the deacon's ministry is toward the bishop, not the church (2.6.44). There is also a description of the character of the person appointed to be a deacon (3.2.19) and the duties of the office (2.7.57). Elchin concludes, "Within the context of liturgy, word, and charity permanent deacons worked in close communion with the bishop. In the pre-Nicene period permanent deacons flourished in a golden age of diaconal service, until in the fourth century with the rise of sacerdotalism the gradual decline of the permanent diaconate began" (*Deacon,* 25). On subdeacons and acolytes, see Davies, *JEH* 14 (1963) 6–8. On the history of the diaconate, especially in light of the Reformation, see McKee, *John Calvin on the Diaconate,* 159–84.

While 1 Tim 3:11 was interpreted above to refer to deacons' wives, it is also possible that it refers to deaconesses, not so much as an established order but as women involved formally and officially in serving the church. It is therefore helpful to look at the evidence from the early church for a description of this developing function.

There is no clear reference to the office of deaconess in the NT. Phoebe is called a "deacon" (διάκονον) in Rom 16:1, but it is not certain whether this is an official title or a description of what she did. 1 Tim 5:3–16 discusses the role of widows in the early church, but this does not refer to an actual order of widows.

There are a few references to deaconesses prior to the third century. The first clear reference comes from Pliny, the governor of Bithynia, in his correspondence with the emperor Trajan (A.D. 112). He was unsure of how to deal with the Christians. If they would not renounce Christianity, Pliny normally executed them. But the numbers were so large that he tried to discover what Christianity taught. In this context he speaks about deaconesses:

> I thought it therefore the more necessary to try and find the truth of the matter by torture as well, (and that) from two female slaves [*ancillae*] who were called Deaconesses [*ministrae*]. I discovered nothing more than a perverse and contumacious superstition. (*Ep.* 10.96, cited in Robinson, *Ministry of Deaconesses,* 81–82)

Clement of Alexandria (c. A.D. 150–220) speaks of διακόνων γυναικῶν, "women deacons" or "ministering women," and συνδιάκονοι, "fellow deacons," who traveled with the apostles "not as wives but as sisters" (*Strom.* 3.6.1). In his commentary on Rom 16:1–2, Origin (A.D. 185–254) states that 1 Tim 3:11 shows "that women also were set in the ministry of the Church; in which office Phoebe was placed in the Church which is in Cenchreae" (cited in Robinson, *Ministry of Deaconesses*, 82–83). Beyond this the early Christian writers are silent. Tertullian does not discuss widows or virgins (see *Explanation* on 1 Tim 5:3–16). Even Ignatius, who almost constantly talks about the church hierarchy of bishop, presbyter, and deacon, has nothing to say about deaconesses. Polycarp is likewise silent.

The third-century *Didascalia Apostolorum* shows that the office of deaconess is fully intact. It gives the impression that deaconesses have been recognized for a long time. The *Didascalia Apostolorum* does embody traditional material, but the scarcity of evidence from the first two centuries urges caution. The basic picture is that deaconesses perform some of the functions of their male counterparts; yet their duties are restricted to serving the needs of women in the church, including baptism and anointing, teaching the newly baptized, and going "into the houses of the heathen where there are believing women, and to visit those who are sick, and to minister to them in that of which they have need, and to bathe those who have begun to recover from sickness" (*Didascalia Apostolorum* 16; cited by M. H. Shepherd, Jr., *IDB* 1:786). They are the conduit between the women in the church and the deacons and bishops. They supervise the seating of women in the worship service and keep men from entering the women's section in church. The motivating force seems to be the need for decency, especially in the East where the separation of the sexes was more important:

> For there are houses to which you [i.e., the bishop] cannot send a [male] deacon to the woman, on account of the heathen, but you may send a deaconess. (R. H. Connolly, *Didaskalia Apostolorum* [Oxford: Clarendon, 1929] 146)

In fact, the apparent absence of deaconesses in the West in the first four centuries (cf. Martimort, *Deaconesses*, 187–216) suggests that some of the development in the East was the result of social custom.

As the Eastern church grew it increasingly required women to serve other women, a function not open to men. The fourth-century *Apostolic Constitutions* repeats much of the *Didascalia Apostolorum* and adds to it.

> Let also the deaconess be honoured by you in the place of the Holy Ghost, and not do or say anything without the deacon; as neither does the Comforter say or do anything of Himself, but gives glory to Christ by waiting for His pleasure. And as we cannot believe on Christ without the teaching of the Spirit, so let not any woman address herself to the deacon or bishop without the deaconess. (2.4.26; ANF 7:410)

> Let the porters stand at the entries of the men, and observe them. Let the deaconesses also stand at those of the women, like shipmen. (2.7.57; ANF 7:421; fuller citation above)

> Let the deaconess be diligent in taking care of the women; but both of them [i.e., deacons and deaconesses] ready to carry messages, to travel about, to minister, and to serve. (3.2.19; ANF 7:432)

> Let the deaconess be a pure virgin; or, at the least, a widow who has been but once married, faithful, and well esteemed. (6.3.17; ANF 7:457)

A deaconess does not bless, nor perform anything belonging to the office of presbyters or deacons, but only is to keep the doors, and to minister to the presbyters in the baptizing of women, on account of decency. (8.3.28; ANF 7:494)

The fact that deaconesses are ordained shows the formal acceptance of their ministry. Their ordination is not to the full level of being clergy but rather to their well-defined tasks (cf. Tertullian *De exhort. cast.* 13.4; *De pud.* 13.7; *Ad uxor* 1.7.4). They could never become presbyters. The Synod of Laodicea (44) restricted deaconesses from taking the offering or even approaching the altar (3.2.16 [ANF 7:431]; 8.3.19–20 [ANF 7:492]). Robinson comments, "There is not in later writings the slightest hint of such a lapse and revival of the Order, nor any suggestion of a comparatively recent origin for the institution of the female diaconate at the time when the early rules which underlie the *Apostolic Constitutions* were framed" (*Ministry of Deaconesses*, 84).

The *Testament of Our Lord* (fifth century) gives widows the same rights/responsibilities as deaconesses and adds that they brought Communion to pregnant and ill women (2.20.7). Robinson concludes, "The office of Deaconess . . . is legislated for in two of the general Councils, and is mentioned by all the leading Greek Fathers and historians of the fourth and fifth centuries. Basil, Gregory of Nyssa, Epiphanius, Chrysostom, Theodoret and Sozomen all bear testimony to the flourishing condition of the Order. They have preserved to us the personal history of several of its members, and have shown how important was the position they occupied and the service they rendered in the Church" (*Ministry of Deaconesses*, 85). The order seems to have died out in the Middle Ages. For discussions related to the evidence, origin, and history of a deaconess order, see Davies, *JEH* 14 (1963) 1–15; Elchin, *Deacon*, 3–25; Robinson, *Ministry of Deaconesses*, 80–99; Clark, *Man and Woman;* W. Weinrich, "Women," 263–79; Gryson, *Ministry of Women*. For the role of the widows during these early centuries, see *Explanation* on 1 Tim 5:3–16. For a discussion of widows' duties, see *Explanation* on 1 Tim 5:3–16.

E. Heart of the Corpus   (1 Tim 3:14–16)

Bibliography

Baillet, M. "Les manuscrits de la grotte 7 de Qumrân et le Nouveau Testament." *Bib* 54.3 (1973) 340–50. **Benetti, L. de.** "La vita etica della comunità." *RB* 7 (1972) 259–84. **Benoit, P.** "Nouvelle note sur les fragments grecs de la grotte 7 de Qumrân." *RB* 80.1 (1973) 5–12. **Blair, H. A.** *A Creed before the Creeds.* London: Longmans, 1955. **Bover, J. M.** "El 'gran misterio de la piedad.'" *EstEcl* 21 (1947) 225–33. **Braun, R. A.** "Mysterium Pietatis seu in historiam interpretationis Eusebeias vocis Pastoralium Epistolarum, speciatim I T 3:16a inquisitio atque exegetica christologici hymni 1 T 3:16b explanatio." Diss., Pontifical Biblical Institute, Rome, 1956. **Cullmann, O.** *The Earliest Christian Confessions.* Tr. J. K. S. Reid. London: Lutterworth, 1949. **Deichgräber, R.** *Gotteshymnus und Christushymnus in der frühen Christenheit: Untersuchungen zu Form, Sprache und Stil der frühchristlichen Hymnen.* SUNT 5. Göttingen: Vandenhoeck & Ruprecht, 1967. 133–37. **Fee, G. D.** *God's Empowering Presence.* 761–68. **Fowl, S. E.** *The Story of Christ in the Ethics of Paul: An Analysis of the Function of the Hymnic Material in the Pauline Corpus.* JSNTSup 36. Sheffield: JSOT, 1990. 155–94. **Fowler, P. B.** "An Examination of 1 Tim 3:16b: Its Form, Language and Historical Background." Diss., University of Edinburgh, 1974. 155–94. **Gundry, R. H.** "The Form, Meaning and Background of the Hymn Quoted in 1 Timothy 3:16." In *Apostolic History and the Gospel.* FS F. F. Bruce, ed. W. W. Gasque and R. P. Martin. Grand Rapids, MI: Eerdmans, 1970. 203–22.

Guthrie, D. *New Testament Theology.* 358–60. **Hanson, A. T.** "An Academic Phrase: I Timothy 3.16a." In *Studies in the Pastoral Epistles.* 21–28. ———. "The Foundation of Truth: I Timothy 3.15." In *Studies in the Pastoral Epistles.* 5–20. **Hort, F. J. A.** "Lecture XI." In *The Christian Ecclesia.* 172–75. **Jaubert, A.** "L'image de la colonne (1 Timothée 3,15)." In *Studiorum Paulinorum Congressus Internationalis Catholicus 1961.* 2 vols. AnBib 17–18. Rome: Pontifical Biblical Institute, 1963. 2:101–8. **Klöpper, D. A.** "Zur Christologie der Pastoralbriefe (1 Tim. 3,16)." *ZWT* 45 (1902) 339–61. **Kremer, J.** "'Aufgenommen in Herrlichkeit' (1 Tim 3,16): Auferstehung und Erhöhung nach dem Zeugnis der paulinischen Schriften." *BK* 20 (1965) 33–37. **Lachenschmid, R.** "Geheimnis unseres Christseins: Das Christuslied aus 1 Tim 3,16." *GL* 39 (1966) 225–29. **Lülsdorff, R.** "ΕΚΛΕΚΤΟΙ ΑΓΓΕΛΟΙ: Anmerkungen zu einer untergegangenen Amtsbezeichnung." *BZ* 36 (1992) 104–8. **Manns, F.** "L'hymne judéo-chrétien de 1 Tim. 3,16." *ED* 32 (1979) 323–39 (digest in "Judeo-Christian Context of 1 Tim 3:16," *TD* 29 [1981] 119–22). **Massinger, M. O.** "The Mystery of Godliness." *BSac* 96 (1939) 479–89. **Metzger, W.** *Der Christushymnus 1 Timotheus 3,16: Fragment einer Homologie der paulinischen Gemeinden.* Arbeiten zur Theologie 62. Stuttgart: Calwer, 1979. **Micou, R. W.** "On ὤφθη ἀγγέλοις, I Tim. iii, 16." *JBL* 11 (1892) 201–4. **Müller-Bardorff, J.** "Zur Exegese von 1 Tim 3:3–16." In *Gott und die Götter.* FS E. Fascher, ed. H. Bardtke. Berlin: Evangelische Verlagsanstalt, 1958. 113–33. **Murphy-O'Connor, J.** "Redactional Angels in 1 Tim 3:16." *RB* 91 (1984) 178–87. **O'Callaghan, J.** "1 Tim 3,16; 4,1.3 en 7Q4?" *Bib* 53.3 (1972) 362–67. ———. "Notas sobre 7Q tomadas en el 'Rockefeller Museum' de Jerusalém." *Bib* 53.4 (1972) 517–33. ———. "Nota sobre 7Q4 y 7Q5." *SPap* 13.1 (1974) 61–63. ———. "Les papyri de la grotte 7 de Qumrân." *NRT* 95.2 (1973) 188–95. ———. "Sobre la identificación de 7Q4." *SPap* 13.1 (1974) 45–55. **O'Leary, A.** "The Mystery of Our Religion [1 Tim 3:16]." *Way* 21 (1981) 243. **Reicke, B.** "Les deux fragments grecs onciaux de 1 Tim. appelés 061 publiés." *ConNT* 11 (1947) 196–206. **Rovell, J. B.** "The Deity of the Lord Jesus Christ Vindicated." *BSac* 114 (1957) 70–77. **Salvoni, F.** "Qumrân e le Pastorali." *RBR* 7 (1972) 147–48. **Sanders, J. T.** *The New Testament Christological Hymns.* SNTSMS 15. Cambridge: Cambridge UP, 1971. **Schweizer, E.** "Two New Testament Creeds Compared: 1 Cor. 15,3–5 and 1 Tim. 3,16." In *Current Issues in New Testament Interpretation.* FS O. Piper, ed. W. Klassen and G. F. Snyder. London: SCM Press, 1962. 166–77. **Stanley, D. M.** *Christ's Resurrection in Pauline Soteriology.* AnBib 13. Rome: Pontifical Biblical Institute, 1961. 236–39. **Stenger, W.** "Der Christushymnus in 1 Tim. 3,16: Aufbau—Christologie—Sitz im Leben." *TTZ* 78 (1969) 33–48. ———. *Der Christushymnus 1 Tim. 3,16: Eine strukturanalytische Untersuchung.* RST 6. Frankfurt am Main: Lang, 1977. ———. "Textkritik als Schicksal (1 Tim 3,16)." *BZ* 19 (1975) 240–47. **Strange, J. F.** "A Critical and Exegetical Study of 1 Tim 3:16: An Essay in Traditionsgeschichte." Ph.D. Diss., Drew University, 1970. **Szczurek, T.** "*Ukazal sie aniolom* (Apparuit angelis)." *RevistB* 30 (1977) 195–98. **Towner, P. H.** *The Goal of Our Instruction.* 87–93. **Urban, A. C.** "Observaciones sobre ciertos papiros de la cueva 7 de Qumrân." *RevQ* 8.2 (1973) 233–51. **Verner, D. C.** *The Household of God.* **Villiers, J. L. de.** "Die Kerk en sy Lie (I Tim. 3:15–16)." *NGTT* 16 (1975) 292–306. **Warfield, B. B.** "Some Exegetical Notes on I Timothy: VI. The Progress of the Thought in I Timothy III. 14–IV. 5." *PresR* 8 (1921) 506–7. **Weiser, A.** "Die Kirche in den Pastoralbriefen: Ordnung um jeden Preis?" *BK* 46 (1991) 107–13. **Zachman, R. C.** "Jesus Christ as the Image of God in Calvin's Theology." *CTJ* 25/26 (1990–91) 45–62.

Translation

[14] *I am writing these things to you, even though I am hoping to come to you* [a] *quickly,* [b] [15] *but if I wait, in order that you may know how it is necessary [for people] to conduct themselves in the house of God, which is the church of the living God, a pillar and protector of the truth.* [16] *And undeniably* [c] *great is the mystery of godliness, who* [d]

> *was revealed in flesh,*
> *was vindicated in spirit,*
> *appeared to angels;*
> *was preached among the nations,*
> *was believed in the world,*
> *was taken up in glory.*

Notes

ᵃπρὸς σέ, "to you," is omitted by F G 6 1739 1881 *pc* vgᵐˢ sa.

ᵇτάχιον, "more speedily" (i.e., "than you might suppose from the fact that I am writing to you"; Bernard, 61), is read by ℵ (D²) F G 1739 1881 and TR. ἐν τάχει, "quickly," is read by A C D* P Ψ 33 81 *pc.*

ᶜD* 1175 *pc* separate ὁμολογουμένως, "undeniably," into ὁμολογοῦμεν ὡς, "we confess that."

ᵈThe identity of the subject of this hymn has been a topic of long discussion. Because of the theological significance of this question, discussion of this point has been reserved for the *Comment* except for the textual data (cf. *TCGNT*², 573–74).

ὅς, "who," has the best attestation, being read by ℵ* A* C* F G 33 365 442 2127 sy hᵐᵍ pal got aethᵖᵖ and some church fathers (Orˡᵃᵗ Epiph Jerome Theodore Eutherius [according to Theodoret] Cyr Liberatus), and refers to Jesus. It is a typical way to introduce a hymn (cf. Phil 2:6 and Col 1:15), and it is not necessary to locate an antecedent in the text.

The neuter ὅ, "which," in the Western text probably arose as an attempted correction of the ὅς, making μυστήριον, "mystery," the subject of the hymn. It therefore supports ὅς as the original reading. It is read by D* and almost all of the Latin tradition.

θεός, which makes God the subject of the hymn, is read by the Byzantine text and correctors (ℵᶜ Aᶜ C² D² Ψ). In majuscule script, ὅς is OC, and the abbreviation for θεός is Ō̄C, so one could be mistaken for the other. More likely, ὅς was changed to θεός in an attempt to glorify Christ as God. It is almost inconceivable that a scribe would change θεός to a pronoun. The pronoun is also more difficult because there is no antecedent.

Metzger concludes, "Thus, no uncial (in the first hand) earlier than the eighth or ninth century (Ψ) supports θεός; all ancient versions presuppose ὅς or ὅ; and no patristic writer prior to the last third of the fourth century testifies to the reading θεός" (*TCGNT*¹, 641). See also B. F. Westcott and F. J. A. Hort, "Notes on Select Readings," in *The New Testament in the Original Greek* (London: Macmillan, 1881) 132–34; Lock, xxxvi–xxxvii; W. Stenger, *BZ* 19 (1975) 240–47; G. D. Fee, "The Majority Text and the Original Text of the New Testament," *BT* 31 (1980) 116–18; id., *God's Empowering Presence*, 762 n. 30. Ellicott (49–50) was able personally to examine Alexandrinus and confirm that it clearly reads ὅς (100).

Form/Structure/Setting

It is now generally recognized that this paragraph is the heart of the Pastoral corpus (cf. Spicq, 1:464; Jeremias, 27), which puts the instructions of the corpus into proper perspective. Paul is hoping to visit Timothy soon; but because the possibility exists that he might delay, he writes to describe how believers should conduct themselves. (For those not accepting Pauline authorship, this passage shows that Paul's teaching is to replace his presence in the later church; so Roloff, 197.) The reason the church must accept Paul's teaching in this letter is that the church is "the house of God, which is the church of the living God, a pillar and protector of the truth." As God's house, it must protect God's gospel, and at precisely this point the Ephesian church is failing (cf. Spicq, 1:464, who explains these verses as describing the nature [the house of God] and the message [the incarnation] of the church). The leadership is sinful, and the church's reputation and ability to work in the world is being seriously hampered, and this must stop. 1 Tim 4:1 begins with δέ, "now" or "but," and contrasts true godliness (εὐσέβεια) with the demonic teaching of the opponents (see *Form/Structure/Setting* on 1 Tim 4:1–5).

This mandate is not optional. The church is the household of the living and judging God. It must maintain its sanctity because of its essential function as a guardian of the truth. When it ceases to perform its proper function, then the living God will act. So, for example, if an overseer is not a "one-woman" man, then he must be removed from office because the proclamation of the gospel is at stake.

Because 3:14–16 governs behavior in the church, Paul is thinking back to 1 Tim 2:1 where he begins discussing behavior. While chap. 1 has implications for behavior, its primary thrust is theological. 1 Tim 3:14–16 also shows that chaps. 2 and 3 are dealing with behavior in the church, and while principles expressed in these chapters may extend into other contexts, it is only by implication. For example, one would expect men always to pray without anger wherever or whenever they pray, but may women teach men outside of the church? There also is the interesting question of what exactly is the "church"? Is it analagous to our modern Sunday worship hour, or does it refer to any church and parachurch events?

The outstanding literary feature of the passage is the fragment of a christological hymn in v 16. The textual history (see *Note* d) shows both the significance of the hymn as well as the problem of deciding of whom it is speaking. Most agree that it speaks of Christ, spelling out what he did and the results of his actions. As such it clarifies the content of Christian theology, here called "the mystery of godliness." The rhythmical structure of the hymn is distinct. It has six lines, each beginning with a third-person-singular aorist passive verb followed by a prepositional phrase introduced by ἐν, "in," and a noun in the dative (except for the third line, which omits the preposition). The ὅς, "who," serves as an introduction to the hymn and is not part of it (see *Comment*). The themes that run through the hymn include *Heilsgeschichte* (a repeating of salvation history) and a humiliation/exaltation (or earth/heaven) motif. The hymn describes what Christ did on earth in his humbled state and how his actions were received on earth and in heaven. There also may be a chronology that runs throughout the hymn and distinct parallelisms. Because the hymnic structure is so pronounced, it is almost universally recognized as a fragment of a hymn.

Beyond this there are many questions: How many stanzas are there? Which lines are parallel? Is the chronology continuous throughout the whole hymn? Some of the words can have different meanings, and the possible interpretations seem almost endless. Hymns tend to be compact, and only a portion of the original hymn is cited, from which must be determined its original context. If the hymn is of non-Pauline origin, the words and ideas can only tentatively be compared with the Pauline literature.

Because it will be almost impossible to discuss the structure without considering the meaning, the following discussion is offered as a general guide to the more detailed exposition in the *Comment*. Decisions regarding structure are extremely subjective; for example, lines 1 and 2 as well as 4 and 5 appear to belong together on the basis of parallelism, but not all readers may perceive these connections. Another factor to be considered is the implied chronological relationship of the lines; it should have a role in the determination of the structure, but how significant should that role be, especially when the implied chronology seems to conflict with the parallelism? There are three basic configurations of the hymn. Possible meanings are listed in the right column although these interpretations are open to debate and the choices made are only possibilities.

(1) The first configuration sees the hymn as one stanza with six lines, emphasizing the continuous chronology of the hymn that describes Jesus' earthly ministry (Alford, *Greek New Testament;* Barrett). It ignores any apparent parallelism between the phrases and has difficulty with the sixth line, which seems to disrupt the chronology.

Who

was revealed in flesh,	incarnation
was vindicated in spirit,	baptism
was seen by angels,	during life
was preached among the nations,	early preaching
was believed in the world,	ensuing belief
was taken up in glory.	ascension/parousia

(2) The second arrangement sees two stanzas of three lines (Lock). This maintains the parallelism between "preached among the nations" and "believed on in the world." The first stanza is concerned with Christ's life and the second with the world's reception of him.

Who

was revealed in flesh,	incarnation
was vindicated in spirit,	resurrection
was seen by angels;	universal proclamation
was preached among the nations,	early preaching
was believed in the world,	ensuing belief
was taken up in glory.	present reign

Lock (45) sets the hymn up as follows and includes a poetic translation:

(i) *The Life of the Incarnate—*
    (a) as seen on earth,   ἐφανερώθη ἐν σαρκί
                                     ἐδικαιώθη ἐν πνεύματι
    (b) as watched from heaven,   ὤφθη ἀγγέλοις
(ii) *The Life of the Ascended Lord —*
    (a) as preached on earth,   ἐκηρύχθη ἐν ἔθνεσιν
                                       ἐπιστεύθη ἐν κόσμῳ
    (b) as lived in heaven.   ἀνελήμφθη ἐν δόξῃ

In flesh unveiled to mortals' sight,
Kept righteous by the Spirit's might,
    While angels watched him from the sky:
His heralds sped from shore to shore,
And men believed, the wide world o'er,
    When he in glory passed on high. (Lock, 42)

It is possible that the hymn is a chiasm with the pattern a b c — c' b' a'.

Who
a   was revealed in flesh,
   b   was vindicated in spirit,
      c   was seen by angels,
      c'   was preached among the nations,
   b'   was believed in the world,
a'   was taken up in glory.

The "a" sections provide the chronological bookends for Jesus ministry, antithetically contrasting flesh and glory. The "b" sections contrast the spirit world and the human world. The "c" sections contrast the invisible (angels) witnesses to the incarnation and glorification with the visible (nations) witnesses. Gundry ("Form, Meaning and Background") sees lines 1 and 6 as framing the hymn, and lines 2/3 and 4/5 as filling out the content. (See also E. W. Bullinger, *Figures of Speech Used in the Bible* [1898; repr. Grand Rapids, MI: Baker, 1968], esp. 379–80.)

(3) The third structure is three stanzas of two lines and is accepted by most (Spicq; Jeremias; Dibelius-Conzelmann; Kelly; Gundry, "Form, Meaning and Background"; Roloff; Oberlinner; Towner). This interpretation emphasizes the parallelism between "appeared in the flesh" and "vindicated in spirit" as well as a consistent chronology from one stanza to the next, but it breaks the parallelism between "preached among the nations" and "believed on in the world." It also possibly shows antithetical parallelism in each couplet (flesh–spirit; angels–nations; world–glory) in the chiastic pattern a–b, b–a, a–b.

Who
   was revealed in flesh,   incarnation
      was vindicated in spirit,   resurrection
   was seen by angels,   universal proclamation
      was preached among the nations,   early preaching
   was believed in the world,   ensuing belief
      was taken up in glory.   present reign

Jeremias thinks the hymn follows the enthronement ceremony of exaltation, presentation, and enthronement (27–29; cf. Spicq, 1:470). J. L. de Villiers says the progression is logical, not necessarily chronological, moving from salvation, to proclamation, to faith in the world and glory in heaven (*NGTT* 16 [1975] 292–306). Knight comments, "Even though there is not a strict chronology in the liturgical statement of v. 16, we may speak of a sense of theological direction. The first couplet speaks of the accomplishment of Christ's work, the second of the accomplishment made known, and the third of the response to the accomplishment made known" (186).

For the following reasons option (2) of two stanzas with three lines each appears to be the best configuration. (1) Although the parallelism of "appeared in the flesh" and "vindicated in the spirit" is patent, this does not mean that line 3 starts a new thought as required if there are three stanzas. (2) The strongest parallelism seems to be between lines 4 and 5: "preached among the nations" and "believed on in the world." Belief is the result of preaching, and viewing the hymn as having three stanzas breaks the relationship between these two lines. (3) If the hymn has two stanzas, then the first trilogy speaks of Christ's life and the second of the reception of his work. This is an attractive parallelism in which not only do the two trilogies compare to each other, but lines 1 and 4, 2 and 5, and 3 and 6 have points in common: Christ appeared in the flesh and is therefore preached to the nations; he was vindicated in the spirit and therefore is the object of faith; his vindication was not only witnessed to by angels, but as a result of people's belief he has been glorified throughout the world. (4) Most important, a two-stanza arrangement seems to fit the context best. The first stanza describes the mighty works of Christ: incarnation, resurrection, and ascension. The second stanza shows that the proper response is for the church to preach the gospel of Christ so people can come to faith, and as a result Christ will receive the glory he deserves. Unless the Ephesian church stops its sinning, the gospel will not be preached and people will not believe.

1 Tim 3:14–16 is often viewed as the conclusion to chaps. 2 and 3. However, as will be discussed later, 1 Tim 4:1–5 ties directly into chap. 3, showing that 3:14–16 is not a conclusion but merely a pause for Paul to put his instructions into perspective. The basic statement is that the church is the "house of God." Paul follows with four facts about the church, which strengthen his appeal to order it correctly: (1) it is the church of the living (and active) God; (2) it is a pillar of the truth; (3) it is a protector of the truth; and (4) it proclaims the great mystery of godliness. B. B. Warfield adds that 4:1–5 provides "an additional reason for the importance of rightly organizing the Church, drawn now not so much from the greatness of the truth it has to guard, as from the greatness of the danger which is impending over it" (*PresR* 8 [1921] 508).

Stenger (*TTZ* 78 [1969] 33–48) argues that the hymn comes from a Jewish-Christian milieu and can be understood only by someone thoroughly familiar with the OT. He sees the hymn referring specifically to OT ideas and sometimes specific events, e.g., comparing Jesus' ascent to those of Enoch and Elijah and Jesus' reign to the Danielic Son of man (see also Manns, *ED* 32.3 [1979] 323–39). O'Callaghan's proposal (*Bib* 53.3 [1972] 362–67) that 1 Tim 3:16 and 4:1–3 are found in fragments from 7Q4 has not been accepted; see critiques by Baillet (*Bib* 54.3 [1973] 340–50), Benoit (*RB* 80.1 [1973] 5–12), and Urban (*RevQ* 8.2 [1973] 233–51). Sanders identifies eight points of similarity among the NT christological hymns, including the redeemer, present with God, creating the world, descending and effecting redemption, and now exalted and enthroned (*New Testament Christological Hymns*, summary on 24–25), and allows that of all the christological hymns in the NT, only 1 Tim 3:16 has survived intact. W. Metzger attempts to reconstruct the entire hymn using 1 Tim 1:15a, 2:3b–6a, and 6:14–16 (*Christushymnus 1 Timotheus 3,16*, 136–42). Lock (45) suggests that it comes from the same hymn quoted in Eph 5:14, which provides ὁ Χριστός, "the Christ," as the subject of ὅς, "who."

Comment

14–15ab Ταῦτά σοι γράφω ἐλπίζων ἐλθεῖν πρὸς σὲ ἐν τάχει· ἐὰν δὲ βραδύνω, ἵνα εἰδῇς πῶς δεῖ ἐν οἴκῳ θεοῦ ἀναστρέφεσθαι, "I am writing these things to you, even though I am hoping to come to you quickly, but if I wait, in order that you may know how it is necessary [for people] to conduct themselves in the house of God." With an awkward Greek construction, Paul tells Timothy that he is hoping to visit him soon. But evidently there is a chance he will delay, and if this happens Paul wants Timothy to have the specific, official instructions on appropriate conduct in God's church. As discussed above, this paragraph is the heart of the PE corpus. In these three verses Paul pauses to put things in perspective for Timothy and the Ephesian church. These rules and instructions are to be followed not for their sake alone but because there is a greater reality at stake: the health of the gospel. The opponents are perverting the gospel, dragging the church's reputation down with them, and in so doing are damaging the proclamation of the gospel. Therefore, it is essential that these rules be followed. As Fee comments, "Such a statement of purpose hardly fits the 'church manual' approach to the letter" (92). Rather, the self-witness of the text is that Paul is addressing a specific historical situation. Oberlinner comes to the opposite conclusion, seeing v 14 as a key passage for post-Pauline authorship (153). For him, the underlying theme is continuity; the apostle from the past is present in the action of the current church teacher, providing a continuity of message into the second century.

Much has been made about the elementary nature of the instructions in the early chapters of 1 Timothy and how it would supposedly be inappropriate for Paul to write such instructions to Timothy (cf. Hanson, [1983] 82). However, the text does not demand that these rules be new to Timothy (so Jeremias, 27), and there have been several suggestions explaining why they would be repeated to him. It may be that Paul had to leave Timothy (cf. on 1 Tim 1:3 for the historical situation) before he had a chance to spell out the specific instructions. Perhaps Paul had covered these rules orally, and the letter is concrete confirmation of the specifics. Because of the semipublic nature of the corpus, these instructions could have been an official statement of policy made not for the benefit of Timothy but for the Ephesian church. Easton's (135) comment that Timothy's immaturity necessitated these elementary instructions is inconsistent with what we know of Timothy. Not only did Timothy act as Paul's emissary to other towns, but it is highly unlikely that Paul would send someone to Ephesus who did not know even the fundamentals of Christian behavior. Being somewhat timid is not the same as being ignorant.

Vv 14–16 put the whole of the epistle into perspective. The word ταῦτα, "these things," therefore refers to chaps. 1–3 and looks forward to 1 Tim 4:1–5. Using ταῦτα to summarize previous comments is common throughout the PE (1 Tim 4:6, 11, 15; 5:7, 21; 6:2, 11; 2 Tim 1:12; 2:2, 14; Titus 2:15; 3:8) and throughout Paul in general. ἐλπίζων, "hoping," is a concessive participle; even though Paul hopes to visit Timothy soon, he feels it is necessary to write the instructions. For a discussion of Paul's present whereabouts, see 1 Tim 1:3. βραδύνειν, "to wait," occurs elsewhere in the NT only in 2 Pet 3:9. Paul is not envisioning something stopping him permanently; he is allowing for the possibility that he would have to make a decision not to come as quickly as he would prefer (βραδύνω is active intransitive, "I wait," not passive as in most translations, "I am delayed"). Paul's reason for waiting probably would be the needs of his ministry elsewhere. The ἐάν, "if," clause is not followed by a "then" clause with a main verb, but the ἵνα, "in order that," conceptually, if not grammatically, tells of Paul's intent.

δεῖ, "it is necessary," is an important word in the PE. Of its nine occurrences, four of them are used to say that church leaders must be a certain type of person (see 3:2 for a discussion). Its occurrence here in 3:14 carries the strongest meaning of all nine passages. Paul is not saying that the behavior he is describing is optional; it is mandated because the church is the house of the living God, a protector of the truth, and it is therefore absolutely essential that its integrity be maintained. What is more problematic is the question of who or what is the implied subject of δεῖ. Some suggest that it is Timothy, who is the subject of the finite verb εἰδῇς, "you know," and his behavior is important. However, the instructions in chaps. 2 and 3 are addressed to the church and not to him personally. It is therefore more likely that the subject is the indefinite "one" or perhaps "people." Paul has been spelling out how the church as a whole should behave, specifically in its prayer life, worship, and leadership; now he tells them why this is important.

ἀναστρέφειν, "to conduct oneself" (reflexive sense in the passive; BAGD, 61), and its cognate noun (ἀναστροφή, "conduct") both refer not so much to individual actions as to general conduct, a person's way of life. The verb is used in the NT to describe a non-Christian's lifestyle (Eph 2:3; 4:22; 1 Pet 1:18; 2 Pet 2:7, 18) as well as the general conduct of Paul (2 Cor 1:12) and Christian wives (1 Pet 3:2). Christians are to be holy, just as God is holy, in all their conduct (1 Pet 1:15). Since the opponents and not Timothy are causing the problem, they and not Timothy are the focus of the verb, hence the translation " [for people] to conduct themselves," although this includes Timothy, who is to be an example (1 Tim 4:12). The verb does not occur again in the PE, but the noun is used once in Paul's admonition to Timothy that he set the believers "an example in speech and conduct [ἀναστροφῇ]" (1 Tim 4:12). Guthrie's definition as the "discharge of official duties (88)" is too narrow.

οἴκῳ θεοῦ, "house of God," is the first of several phrases in this passage that emphasizes the seriousness of Paul's injunctions. It is not as if the opponents were damaging a social organization. It is God's house that they are bringing into disrepute, and that constitutes a much more serious offense. (V 15cd continues with two further descriptions of the church that build on this note of seriousness.) οἶκος, "house," can mean either the household or the building (cf. 1 Tim 3:4 for discussion). (1) The imagery of the household has been used in 3:4–5 with an implicit connection made between an overseer's house and the church, and it has been repeated again for deacons in v 12. In 1 Tim 5:1–2 Paul tells Timothy to treat the different members of the Ephesian congregation as his fathers, mothers, brothers, and sisters (cf. Eph 2:19; Heb 3:5–6; 10:21; 1 Pet 4:17; οἰκεῖος, "member of the household," in Gal 6:10). (2) But the images of a στῦλος, "pillar," and ἑδραίωμα, "foundation," that follow in v 15cd suggest more the building aspect of οἶκος. The fact that Paul draws on both possible meanings within the chapter suggests that he intends both here: the church is God's temple, and as such it houses God's family. In Acts 16:34 οἶκος (and a cognate) is used with both meanings: "then he brought them up into his house [οἶκον] . . . and he rejoiced with all his household [πανοικεί]." Hanson's comment that "it is quite possible that the author did not know himself" ([1983] 82) is consistent with his opinion of the author but is hardly fair. There is no definite article before οἴκῳ θεοῦ, "house of God," suggesting that Paul is thinking not of the universal church but of each local congregation. This would be consistent with the context of chaps. 2 and 3. The anarthrous construction also prepares the way for the following phrases that also lack the definite article. But, on the other hand, articles are frequently absent in prepositional phrases (Robertson, *Grammar,* 791–92; Spicq, 1:466) and are used sparingly throughout the PE (Bernard, 61); so perhaps not too much emphasis should be placed on this point. Lock (43) unnecessarily limits the instructions to the Ephesian church; the lack of an expressed subject for ἀναστρέφεσθαι, "to conduct," the anarthrous constructions, and the central role of the paragraph in the corpus suggest that Paul is stating a general truth applicable to all churches.

Recently, the household metaphor has been proposed as having a dominating influence in the theology of the PE. For example, Verner argues that the use of οἶκος is to "bolster a hierarchical social structure in the church that is being threatened by disruptive forces. . . . [The author] responds by promoting an image of the church that legitimates the established hierarchical structure" (*Household of God,* 186; also Oberlinner, 155). This is tied to the idea that the household codes are also employed to enforce structure as a prevention of heresy. These issues are discussed in detail above in the *Introduction,* "The Response to the Heresy." However, the metaphor of the house is relatively minor in the PE and cannot bear the weight placed on it by Verner and others. The use of the *Haustafel* is too common in Paul to give it this special weight in the PE, as is the use of familial language for people in the church (1 Tim 5:1–2; 6:2; 4:6; 2 Tim 4:21; 1 Tim 1:2; Titus 1:4). Paul does ask Christian leaders to be stewards (1 Tim 1:5), and their management skills are first to be illustrated in their homes (1 Tim 3:4–5,12; Titus 1:6–7). The metaphor of a large house is also used as an encouragement to Timothy to cleanse himself and be of good use (2 Tim 2:20–21), though the house does not stand for the church. The language suggests the historical situation in which churches met in homes (Titus 1:11), but as was argued above, the house does not stand for the church. The metaphor is not a dominating force in the thought of the author and is not used to enforce a rigid structure on the Ephesian and Cretan churches. Neither is the author's intent to give institutional authority to enforce rules. Church leadership is composed of godly people who are serious and controlled, whose behavior does not bring reproach, whose management skills and Christian maturity are already visible, and in the case of overseers are able to teach the truth and refute error. Institutional authority structures are foreign to the text.

15c ἥτις ἐστὶν ἐκκλησία θεοῦ ζῶντος, "which is the church of the living God." In emphasizing how important it is that people conduct themselves properly in the household of God, Paul has already pointed out that the church is the house of God, understood as God's temple and his household. This phrase adds a further note of importance by emphasizing that God is the living God. This church does not worship a dead deity who can do nothing, but one who is alive. Within the context of the Ephesian situation and the urgency attached to the preceding instructions, Paul is probably saying that the living God can and will discipline those who damage his house (cf. 2 Tim 4:1). Oberlinner is right in emphasizing that the church is God's: "The community of those gathered in the house is not constituted by the will and the decision of those who are religiously likeminded, but it is based on the call of God" (155–56). This verse is also a statement against viewing the church in terms of static institutionalism.

The shift in imagery from οἶκος, "house," to ἐκκλησία, "church," here is the same as in 3:4–5 (cf. v 12) where Paul draws the connection between a person's leadership ability in the home and in the church. It is also similar to the shift in Eph 2:19–20 where Paul tells the Gentiles that they are now members of God's household, which is built upon the foundation of the apostles and prophets. (On ἐκκλησία, "church," cf. 1 Tim 3:5.) The lack of the definite article before ἐκκλησία indicates that Paul is thinking of the local church (cf. οἴκῳ above). ἥτις, "which," modifies the masculine οἴκῳ, "house," but is attracted to the gender of the feminine ἐκκλησία. The OT frequently describes God as ζῶντος, "living" (Deut 5:26; Josh 3:10; 1 Sam 17:26, 36; 2 Kgs 19:4, 16; Pss 18:46; 42:2; 84:2; Isa 37:4, 17; Jer 10:10; 23:26; Hos 1:10; Dan 6:26), and this usage carried over into the NT (Matt 16:16; 26:63; Acts 14:15; Rom 9:26 [quoting Hos 2:1]; 2 Cor 3:3; 1 Thess 1:9; Heb 9:14; 12:22; Rev 7:2; cf. John 6:57; Rev 15:7). The author of Hebrews uses the same imagery with much the same purpose: "Take care, brethren, lest there be in any of you an evil, unbelieving heart, leading you to fall away from the living [ζῶντος] God. But exhort one another every day, as long as it is called 'today,' that none of you may be hardened by the deceitfulness of sin" (Heb 3:12–13). Later he adds, at the end of a warning to his readers that they be obedient, "It is a fearful thing to fall into the hands of the living [ζῶντος] God" (Heb 10:31; cf. 2 Cor 6:16). Also significant for our passage is the OT phrase ζῶ ἐγώ, "as I live," when God uses it to take an oath of punishment (Num 14:21, 28; Deut 32:40; Zech 2:9). As surely as God lives, he will not allow the Ephesian opponents to destroy his house. Hort adds that not only does ζῶντος contrast God to dead idols but it also "implies a contrast with the true God made practically a dead deity by a lifeless and rigid form of religion; with the God in short in whom too many of the Jews virtually believed. Such is probably the force here as it evidently is in iv. 10" (*Christian Ecclesia*, 173–74).

15d στῦλος καὶ ἑδραίωμα τῆς ἀληθείας, "a pillar and protector of the truth." The third and crowning phrase that emphasizes the significance of the instructions to Timothy is that the church is a pillar and a protector of the gospel. (For ἀλήθεια, "truth," as a synonym of the gospel in the PE, cf. 1 Tim 2:4.) This is perhaps the most significant phrase in all the PE. It shows more clearly and more dramatically than anything else what is at stake in the Ephesian heresy and why it is essential that the church, especially the church leaders, conduct themselves properly. Not only is the Ephesian church a house of the living God, but one of its functions is to support and protect the proclamation of the gospel (cf. Spicq, 1:465–66). This is why it is essential that church leaders be of a certain caliber and that both men and women conduct themselves appropriately. This is why the church must understand that salvation is not through a mythical reinterpretation of the law available only to a select few, but through faith as seen in Paul, the chief example of a sinner saved by grace. It is not the church that is being protected but the gospel that is being protected by the church. Towner argues that by affirming "the stability or permanence of *the Church*" the imagery counteracts the impression that the current troubles in Ephesus are in fact destroying the church (*Goal*, 132). In Crete whole households were being upset (Titus 1:10); nevertheless, God's foundation stands firm (2 Tim 2:19).

This is a far cry from Ignatius in the second century (see excursuses on 1 Tim 3:1–7 and 1 Tim 3:8–13), for whom the clerical hierarchy was the protector of the church and the gospel. Here both στῦλος, "pillar," and ἑδραίωμα, "protector," are anarthrous. The church is only a part of God's defense. God is not dependent on the established church, in Ephesus or anywhere, to protect the proclamation of Christ. Hort comments, "There are few passages of the New Testament in which the reckless disregard of the presence or absence of the article has made wider havoc of the senses than this. To speak of either *an* Ecclesia or *the* Ecclesia, as being *the* pillar of the truth, is to represent the truth as a building, standing in the air supported on a single column" (*Christian Ecclesia,* 174).

στῦλος, "pillar," is used in the NT only in a figurative sense. In the Apocalypse, the legs of the angel with the small scroll are "like pillars of fire" (Rev 10:1). In his message to the church at Philadelphia, John says that those who endure the sufferings will be made into a pillar in God's temple and will never leave (Rev 3:12), the imagery stressing permanence. Closest to our passage is the statement that the leaders of the Jerusalem church are the pillars of the church (Gal 2:9). It is not so much that they are part of the structure (although this is to some extent true), but rather that they are part of the support and protection of the church (cf. Bruce, *Galatians,* 122–23). The church ceases to perform its function when its pillars crumble and can no longer be part of and aid in the proclamation of the truth. Unfortunately, this was happening in Ephesus.

ἑδραίωμα, "protector," is a more difficult term to define. It does not seem to occur in any other writings; there are no other references in BAGD (218), LSJ (478), or MM (181). (1) Hort argues that it means "stay" or "bulwark" on the basis of "the almost universal Latin rendering *firmamentum*" (*Christian Ecclesia,* 174). If "stay, support" is the correct translation, then both metaphors, pillar and support, have the same basic meaning and Paul is picturing the church as something that strengthens the gospel in its proclamation to the world. If "bulwark" is chosen, then the idea is that the church not only supports the church but also provides ramparts surrounding the gospel for protection, much like battlements protect a town. "Protector" does not carry the same image as "bulwark," but it makes the point more clearly. (2) The other suggested translation is "foundation." There is no example of ἑδραίωμα used with this meaning in any text (as is true of the previous translation). Hanson ([1983] 82–83) argues for this translation on the basis of the cognate noun ἕδρασμα, which means "foundation," and the Qumran concept of the community as the "foundation of truth." The only other cognate in the NT is ἑδραῖος, which means "firm" or "steadfast" (1 Cor 7:37; 15:58; Col 1:23), which could just as easily suggest the idea of pillar or protector.

Nothing in the PE supports the idea that the gospel is subordinate to the church (i.e., that the church is the foundation of the gospel) as developed in later centuries (cf. Roloff, 200–201). It is the gospel that takes preeminence (see *Introduction,* "Themes in the PE"). The church is a protector and a helper in the proclamation of the gospel. In the debate over the interpretation of the role of the church in this text, some refer to 1 Cor 3:10–11, where Paul says, "According to the grace of God given to me, like a skilled master builder I laid a foundation, and another man is building upon it. Let each man take care how he builds upon it. For no other foundation can anyone lay than that which is laid, which is Jesus Christ" (cf. Eph 2:20). It is argued that if ἑδραίωμα in 1 Tim 3:15 means "foundation," then the author of the PE is saying that the church is the foundation of the gospel, which would contradict 1 Cor 3:10–11. But this argument is not convincing, and even some who view the PE as non-Pauline recognize that the PE do not subordinate Scripture to the institution of the church (e.g., Roloff, 200-201). L. T. Johnson provides another solution, interpreting the phrase as following ἀναστρέφεσθαι, "to conduct themselves," not the relative clause, and calling it a "delayed apposition" (citing 1 Tim 1:7 and Paul's use of στῦλος, "pillar," in Gal 2:9 and ἑδραῖος, "steadfast," 1 Cor 15:58 in relation to people); believers should "live as a pillar and support of the truth in the church of the living God" (152).

The final question concerns the identity of the pillar and support. (1) Because στῦλος in the NT elsewhere always refers to people, some have argued that here it refers to Timothy, connecting the phrase with the verb εἰδῇς, "you may know," at the beginning of the verse. However, because there is so much distance between εἰδῇς and στῦλος, and because there is a closer word to which στῦλος καὶ ἑδραίωμα could refer, this interpretation is doubtful. It seems out of place to describe any one individual as a pillar and support of the church, even Timothy, especially when the significance of this paragraph is taken into account. (2) Another possibility is that the pillar and support are the mystery of godliness, which Paul spells out in the next verse. However, the mystery of godliness, which is the gospel (v 16), cannot be its own pillar and support (v 15). (3) The most likely interpretation identifies the pillar and support with the church. This has been the topic throughout the last two chapters. 1 Tim 3:14–16 is giving the reason that the preservation of the church is essential.

Identifying the pillar and support with the church also best explains the fact that the construction is anarthrous. The church is not ὁ στῦλος καὶ τὸ ἑδραίωμα, "the pillar and support," but is rather στῦλος καὶ ἑδραίωμα, "a pillar and support." This could mean that the Ephesian church is one of many supporting churches, or it could mean that the church is only one of several entities that support the gospel, another support possibly being Scripture. Even if the church fails in its task, the gospel will continue (2 Tim 2:9). That οἴκῳ, "house," and ἐκκλησία, "church," in the first part of the verse are also anarthrous emphasizes the point being made here (and also supports the identification of the pillar and support with the church). (For a summary and critique of Roloff's emphasis on 3:15 in formulating his view of the ecclesiology of the PE, see Towner, *TynBul* 46 [1995] 287–314.)

16 The instructions in the preceding chapters must be followed because the church is the house of God, the church of the living God, a pillar and protector of the truth, which is the gospel. Ultimately, it is the gospel that is at stake.

There appear to be several reasons that Paul quotes a hymn here. (1) Paul builds on the mention of ἀλήθεια, "truth," in v 15 by quoting a portion of a hymn that spells out some of the essentials of the truth. It tells of Christ's ministry and the ensuing work of the church: Christ came, and his person and message have been vindicated; the gospel is being proclaimed abroad, people are coming to faith, and as a result Christ is glorified as he sits in heaven. Great indeed is the mystery of godliness. (2) The hymn serves as a pivot between the two chapters. It looks back to the instructions in chaps. 2 and 3 by giving the reason that those rules must be followed, because one of the church's functions is to support and protect the gospel. As such, it defines the scope of chaps. 2 and 3 as being that of the church. It also looks ahead to the error of the opponents (1 Tim 4:1–5; cf. *Introduction,* "The Ephesian Heresy") from which the church must be protected, offering a contrast and explaining why it is wrong (Fee, 57) (3) This verse is key to Towner's understanding of the theological/ethical teaching of the PE (*Goal*, 87–93). The hymn presents the salvific Christ event and the demands for proper conduct that stem from it. V 16a ties this theological affirmation to εὐσέβεια, "godliness": the Christian life (εὐσέβεια, "godliness") flows from the Christ-event (μυστήριον, "mystery"). (4) The hymn emphasizes the centrality of Christ in the gospel. Murphy-O'Connor discusses how much of the Ephesian heresy is only words and concludes, "Although words are necessary (4:13), it would be futile to confront the adversaries merely with more words, even though they be the words of Christ (6:3). It was imperative to assert that God's truth was manifested in an historical person, and it is precisely this dimension that the hymn provides" (*RB* 91 [1984] 185). This stands in sharp contrast to the fictitious, nonhistorical myths created from genealogies (1 Tim 1:4; cf. L. T. Johnson, 157). (5) Murphy-O'Connor also emphasizes how the hymn shows Christ living an exemplary life, which acts as a practical guide of true godliness for Timothy (1 Tim 4:12), Titus (Titus 2:11–12), and all believers (2 Tim 1:14) as opposed to the opponents who only have a form of godliness (2 Tim 3:5). In a corpus that emphasizes practical answers to practical questions, this hymn presents pure theology upon which the practical aspects of ministry are based.

The structure of the hymn has been discussed in *Form/Structure/Setting* above. There the parallelisms and possible chronology that run throughout the hymnic fragment were noted. The conclusion was that the structure that gives the best sense to the parallelism and to the meaning of the phrases is two stanzas of three lines. The first stanza portrays Christ's work on earth while the second shows the results of his work. His incarnation, resurrection, and ascension are followed by preaching, belief, and glorification.

Who
    was revealed in flesh,
      was vindicated in spirit,
        appeared to angels;
    was proclaimed among the nations,
      was believed (on) in the world,
        was taken up in glory.

While it is easy to become lost in the exegetical minutiae of the hymn, its central purpose should not be lost: the gospel is about Christ, it is a mystery revealed, and the opponents are wrong. While there are many ways to interpret the hymn, the following are the basic options:

Revealed in flesh	Incarnation (Jesus' humanity)
	Earthly life
Vindicated in spirit	In spiritual realm (Jesus proven right)
	By the Holy Spirit (At baptism/resurrection)
	In Jesus' spirit
Appeared to angels	Seen as Christ's victorious ascent
	During Jesus' life

Proclaimed among the nations	Preaching by disciples before resurrection
	Preaching by apostles after resurrection
Believed on in the world	Result of preaching
Taken up in glory	Ascension
	Enthronement in heaven
	Parousia

There is such debate about the precise meaning of the phrases that caution is urged. If one removes the assumption that the six lines are chronological, the interpretation is easier. Lines 1 and 6 serve as the bookends of Jesus' earthly ministry, his birth and ascension. The remaining four lines can refer to events either before or after the ascension, spelling out aspects of Christ's earthly and risen life. For a detailed analysis of the hymn, see Gundry, "Form, Meaning and Background."

καὶ ὁμολογουμένως μέγα ἐστὶν τὸ τῆς εὐσεβείας μυστήριον, "And undeniably great is the mystery of godliness." Believers are of one voice in confessing that the mystery of godliness, which is the gospel, is indeed great. Paul does not use the phrase πίστος ὁ λόγος, "it is a faithful saying" (cf. 1:15), to introduce this hymn, but perhaps the grandeur of the hymn requires more than that simple introduction.

ὁμολογουμένως, "undeniably," occurs nowhere else in Scripture but is sufficiently attested outside the NT to give the meaning "undeniably," "confessedly" (BAGD, 569). It is an adverb from the participle ὁμολογούμενος, "confessing," and appears to have retained somewhat the same meaning. The basic idea is that all must confess that the gospel is indeed great; it is undeniable. This phrase is reminiscent of the cry μεγάλη ἡ Ἄρτεμις Ἐφεσίων, "Great is Artemis of the Ephesians" (Acts 19:28, 34; Spicq, 1:467, 475–82), and Kelly (89) says there is evidence that this was a common cultic cry throughout Ephesus in the first century. It is possible that Paul chooses a hymn that contrasts with the cultic language of Ephesian culture, claiming that what they worship in fact finds its true fulfillment in Christ and not in Artemis. Paul uses secular words and phrases throughout the PE, and this suggestion is more attractive than Hanson's ([1983] 84), who says that ὁμολογουμένως is a "highbrow" word used to impress the readers of 1 Timothy. The greatness does not lie in the secrecy of the mystery; μέγα . . . μυστήριον, "great . . . mystery," does not mean it is very mysterious. The hymn spells out the content of the mystery; there is no idea here that the mystery cannot be known. Rather, there is a note of awe as Paul reflects on the wonder and greatness of what Christ has done (cf. Eph 5:32).

μυστήριον, "mystery," is the gospel message, now made known through Christ (cf. "mystery of the faith," 3:9). In the NT the mystery is no longer hidden, concealed, or veiled but rather uncovered, revealed, and unveiled. Paul says elsewhere, "To whom [God's saints] God wished to make known how great are the riches of the glory of the mystery among the Gentiles, which is Christ in you, the hope of glory" (Col 1:27). εὐσέβεια, "godliness," is one of the main terms in the PE for the Christian faith, emphasizing the behavior appropriate to a believer (cf. 1 Tim 2:2), an emphasis in keeping with this context.

ὃς ἐφανερώθη ἐν σαρκί, "who was revealed in flesh." Most agree that the first line of the hymn refers to Christ's incarnation (cf. John 1:14; Rom 1:3; Phil 2:7–8). Although a doctrine of preexistence may not have been in the forefront of the author's mind, the use of this particular verb in the passive is compatible with the doctrine (cf. 1 Tim 1:15). ὅς, "who," probably is not part of the original hymn but introduces the hymnic fragment and acts as the subject. Presumably the subject was named earlier in the original hymn. Massinger suggests that "although there is grammatical irregularity in referring the masculine relative pronoun ὅς to the neuter pronoun μυστήριον, the result is a wonderful truth, namely that the mystery of godliness is Christ Himself; that godliness, hidden in ages past, has now been revealed, and is seen not to be an abstract ideal, a mere attribute of personality, but actually a person, the Lord Jesus Christ" (*BSac* 96 [1939] 481). On the variant θεός and the KJV "God," see *Note* d. Line 1 may contrast with line 6; he who appeared in flesh is now taken up in glory (bookends of Jesus' earthly career).

φανεροῦν, "to reveal," is a common term throughout the NT, sometimes used to describe Christ's coming into the world, often with the reason for his appearing stated (John 1:31; Heb 9:26; 1 Pet 1:20; 1 John 1:2; 3:5, 8). The word group occurs three other times in the PE. In another hymn the author says that the grace of God is visible through the appearing of Christ (2 Tim 1:10). Elsewhere Paul says that God has made eternal life visible through his preaching (Titus 1:3). Paul tells Timothy to immerse himself in his duties so that his progress will be visible to all (1 Tim 4:15). σάρξ, "flesh," refers not to sinful flesh but to Christ's humanity (cf. John 1:14; 6:51–59; Rom 8:3; Eph 2:15; Col 1:22; Heb 2:14; 5:7; 10:20; 1 Pet 3:18; 4:1; 1 John 4:2; 2 John 7; cf. Spicq, 1:472). It could also refer to the earthly sphere as opposed to the spiritual (Guthrie, 89). If the definite article were present (ἐν τῇ σαρκί, "in the flesh") we would be assured that it is a reference to Christ's earthly nature. However, definite articles are often omitted from prepositional phrases, and hymns tend to be compact, so the absence of the article may have no significance.

ἐδικαιώθη ἐν πνεύματι, "was vindicated in spirit." The second line is one of the more difficult lines in the hymn to interpret. δικαιοῦν could mean "to justify" or "to vindicate"; ἐν could mean "in" or "by"; πνεῦμα could mean Jesus' spirit, the spiritual sphere, or the Holy Spirit. These possibilities produce a seemingly endless number of combinations. This line seems to be parallel with the preceding, but even there σάρξ, "flesh," can be either humanity or the physical realm. A possible parallel is the statement in 1 Pet 3:18 that says that Christ died, θανατωθεὶς μὲν σαρκὶ ζωοποιηθεὶς δὲ πνεύματι, "being put to death in the flesh but made alive in (the) spirit." This passage suffers almost identical ambiguities with 1 Tim 3:16. Although lines 1 and 2 are parallel, this does not necessitate that the hymn have three stanzas of two lines. Lines 1 and 2 could be building to their climax in line 3.

Since the line most probably refers to the resurrection and what it effected, the translation "justified" can be placed aside. (Since Paul may not be the author of the hymn, this does not conflict with his normal use of the term.) The resurrection "vindicated" (i.e., proved correct; cf. Matt 11:19; Luke 7:35) the claims that Christ had made during his lifetime. This provides a parallel to the incarnation in line 1 and introduces the humiliation/exaltation theme. It may contrast with line 5; he who was vindicated in spirit was believed in the world as a result. Fee believes this statement is directed specifically toward the opponents' theology (especially their asceticism), which is about to be evaluated in 4:1–5. He says Christ's entering the spiritual sphere is not in contrast to his work in the physical realm, but rather is "the full vindication of his having been manifested in the flesh. That is, life in the flesh is not to be scorned; it is not to be separated from God, as the false teachers were plainly doing. The Spirit, therefore, in Pauline theology is not over against the physical world, as with so many of Paul's opponents. Rather, the Spirit, as God, affirms the created order" (*God's Empowering Presence*, 766).

If ἐν is the instrumental "by" then πνεύματι is the Holy Spirit, God's agent in Christ's resurrection (Rom 1:4; 8:11) who is mentioned in the next verse (4:1). The problem with this interpretation is that ἐν does not have this meaning in the other five lines of the hymn; the article or another modifier is missing (τῷ πνεύματι, "the Spirit"), and inconsistency in an otherwise highly developed structure would be surprising. Murphy-O'Connor believes the line refers "to the quality of Christ's life under the action of the Holy Spirit" (*RB* 91 [1984] 183).

If ἐν means "in," then πνεύματι can be (1) the spiritual realm of existence or (2) Christ's spirit as opposed to his flesh. (1) If πνεύματι refers to the spiritual realm, then the idea, according to Fee, is that "just as Christ when 'in the flesh' ministered in the power of the Spirit, so now Christ, by virtue of his resurrection, has entered the spiritual/supernatural realm, the realm of the Spirit, which is the final goal of those for whom the present gift of the Spirit is the ἀρραβών ('down-payment')" (*God's Empowering Presence*, 766). Towner likewise blends the two meanings of πνεύματι when he says it "is a reference to the supernatural realm which is characterized by the activity of the Holy Spirit" (99). This interpretation works best if the hymn has three stanzas. However, if there are two stanzas, then lines 2 and 3 must complement each other; and if line 3 ("seen by angels") refers to Christ's victorious ascension to which the spiritual world was witness, then lines 2 and 3 both speak of Christ's victory in the spiritual sphere, which is unnecessarily redundant. Therefore, if πνεύματι refers to the spiritual world, it seems best to view the hymn as having three stanzas. Lines 1 and 2 refer to Christ's appearing in the physical world and his vindication in the spiritual realm; lines 3 and 4 refer to his reception in heaven and on earth (in a chronological chiasm). (2) If πνεύματι refers to Christ's spirit as opposed to his σάρξ, "flesh" (line 1), then the structure of the hymn is not as significant. The hymn is contrasting Jesus' appearing in the flesh and his vindication in his spirit. Perhaps it is not helpful to separate options (1) and (2) too strictly. Any vindication of Christ's spirit would be wrought in the spiritual sphere. Parallel to this is Rom 1:3–4, which some have argued is an early creedal statement itself: Christ "was descended from David according to the flesh and designated Son of God in power according to the Spirit of holiness by his resurrection from the dead, Jesus Christ our Lord." However, here πνεῦμα is probably the Holy Spirit (cf. Cranfield, *Romans* 1:57–64). A problem with this interpretation of πνεύματι in 1 Timothy is that it makes an uncomfortable bifurcation of Christ's nature: human on the outside and divine on the inside, so to speak. And what does it actually mean to be vindicated in one's own spirit? Christ always knew who he was; it was the world that needed a revelation of his identity.

ὤφθη ἀγγέλοις, "appeared to angels," breaks the alliterative pattern by omitting the ἐν, "in." Why it is omitted is a mystery. Possibly the change in cadence signals the end of a stanza. Murphy-O'Connor argues that the third line is an interpolation—different number of syllables; verb is passive voice, but intransitive; absence of preposition—and the hymn thus does not divide into couplets (*RB* [1984] 180–81). This line is also difficult to interpret. The ἀγγέλοις could be the apostles who witnessed the resurrection (line 2; cf. Acts 2:22–36; 3:11–15; Rom 12:4), or demons who unhappily saw Christ's victorious ascent and victory (cf. Gal 4:3, 9; Col 2:8, 20; 1 Pet 1:12; cf. Eph 3:10; 6:12), or also angels who helped him during his life, watched him during his life, witnessed his resurrection, or now worship him (cf. Matt 4:11; 16:5–8; 28:2–7; Mark 1:13; Luke 2:9–14; John 20:12–13; Acts 1:10–11; Eph 3:10 [?]; Phil 2:10; Heb 1:6; 1 Pet 1:12; cf. *Asc. Isa.* 11:23). This latter interpretation seems the most likely since this is the most frequent use of ἄγγελος in the NT. If the hymn has three stanzas, the contrast in line 4 with ἔθνεσιν, "nations," implies that line 3 is speaking of supernatural beings. The passive of ὁράν means "to appear," used "mostly of beings that make their appearance in a supernatural manner" (BAGD, 578). Jesus did not appear in the sense of "presenting himself" to angels during his life, so the line refers to his victorious proclamation at the resurrection/ascension (cf. Phil 2:9–11; Col 2:15; 1 Pet 3:22).

A parallel question is the issue of time, and the structure of the hymn becomes important at this point. (1) If there is one stanza, then line 3 is not parallel with any of the others and the structure will be of little help in interpretation except if the chronology is consistent. Then the appearing would take place before the preaching (line 4). (2) If there are two stanzas, then line 3 is the climax of lines 1 and 2 and is parallel with line 6. The first trilogy would be expressing Christ's incarnation, resurrection, and glorification; the second trilogy would then express the results of Christ's work on earth. Just as Christ came in flesh and was vindicated in spirit, so also he was preached in and believed on in the world; just as he was glorified in his heavenly ascent, so the belief of the world results in a universal glorying in Christ. The parallelism is impressive, not only within each trilogy but between the two trilogies. (3) If there are three stanzas, then line 3 begins a new topic and is paired with line 4. The first stanza refers to the life of Christ, his appearing and vindication. The second speaks of the universal proclamation of his victory, extending from the angels in heaven to the people on the earth. The third stanza describes the results of this proclamation, the belief of the people and the glorification in heaven. Despite the parallelisms present in the three-stanza interpretation, the intricate and extensive parallelisms of the two-stanza interpretation are more impressive. Consequently, the third line is a reference to the victorious ascent of Christ that not only vindicated his claims (line 2) but was witnessed by angelic beings throughout the universe.

The meaning of ἐκηρύχθη ἐν ἔθνεσιν, "was preached among the nations," is straightforward. The only real question is the structure of the hymn and to which line it is parallel. If there are three stanzas, then it is parallel with "seen by angels" and marks the extent of the proclamation of Christ's vindication: those closest to the Lord (angels) and those farthest away (the Gentile nations; cf. Bernard, 63). If the hymn has two stanzas, then this line begins the second trilogy. Having described the work of Christ in the first three lines, the hymn now details the results of his ministry, beginning with the proclamation of the early church, perhaps contrasting human and angelic (line 3) responses to his vindication. Chrysostom ("Homily 11"; ANF 13:52) cites Ps 19:4, "yet their voice goes out through all the world." If line 6 is the ascension and a strict chronology is followed, the ἔθνεσιν, "nations," would be both Jews and Gentiles to whom Christ ministered during his earthly life and line 5 would refer to their belief in him. On κηρύσσειν, "to proclaim," cf. *Comment* on Titus 1:3. On ἔθνος, "nation, Gentile," cf. *Comment* on 1 Tim 2:7.

ἐπιστεύθη ἐν κόσμῳ, "was believed in the world." The meaning of this line is also straightforward. If the hymn has two stanzas, then this line details the results of the worldwide proclamation of Christ (line 4). It is parallel to the second line ("vindicated in spirit") in that the world's belief is in the risen savior. If Christ had not been raised (vindicated), people would not have believed. If the hymn has three stanzas, then line 5 begins the final couplet, which spells out the results of Christ's life (lines 1 and 2) and the proclamation of his vindication (lines 3 and 4). On earth, the result is that people believed the gospel. The belief described here is not exhaustive; it is not saying that everyone believed. Although κόσμος, "world," can refer to the created order, in this case it refers only to people since the created order is not capable of belief. There is also nothing evil about the world here as in the Fourth Gospel. This line would hold special significance to Paul insofar as he was the apostle to the Gentiles (cf. 1 Tim 2:7).

ἀνελήμφθη ἐν δόξῃ, "was taken up in glory," is the final line of the hymn. ἀναλαμβάνειν, "to take up," is used four times in the NT in reference to Christ's ascension (Mark 16:19; Acts 1:2, 11, 22; cf. Luke 9:51). If this is the case here and the chronology is consistent, then the hymn could be one stanza: "vindicated in spirit" would refer to Jesus' baptism; "seen by angels" would speak of times of angelic ministry such as the temptation or else to general oversight; "preached" and "believed" would refer to the preaching of Jesus and the disciples and the ensuing belief by those who heard; and "taken up in glory" would refer to the ascension. The strongest argument for this interpretation is that it makes the best and most obvious sense of this final line and the apparent chronology. But there are several problems. (1) In a hymn recounting the life of Christ, it is strange that no mention is made whatsoever of his death and resurrection. Only a fragment of the hymn may be cited here, and this topic may have been covered elsewhere in the hymn, but this omission remains significant. (2) If the author meant heaven, why was the word not used? Because the other parallels are so clear, one can reasonably expect some consistency at this point. If the hymn, however, has two stanzas in a chiastic arrangement, then line 6 contrasts with line 1, breaking the consistent chronology but providing the bookends of Jesus' ministry, his birth and ascension.

Kelly (91–92) argues that because δόξα, "glory," can be a technical term "for the dazzling brightness with which God's presence is encompassed," this line is saying that Jesus is now in the presence of God, ruling as the vindicated king. If Kelly is correct and the hymn has two stanzas, then this line serves as the summation of the preaching and belief that is progressing on earth: Christ is proclaimed and believed, and rightly so because he now sits in heaven. If the hymn has three stanzas, then it provides the heavenly counterpart to the fifth line: just as Christ came (first stanza), and his vindication was published abroad (second stanza), so now this results in belief on earth and his reigning presence in heaven.

Explanation

1 Tim 3:14–16, in connection with 1 Tim 1:3, plays a crucial role in the overall interpretation of the PE. Paul had already met once with Timothy about the problems in Ephesus. His intention is to visit Timothy soon. However, if his own ministry needs prevent him, he wants Timothy to have an official statement on proper behavior in the church. Timothy knows what type of behavior is appropriate, the types of people who should be in leadership positions, but the Ephesian church did not; so chaps. 2 and 3 serve as an official notice and perhaps an encouragement to Timothy.

The PE are often accused of being weak in theology (1 Tim 5). The PE never claim to be a theological treatise; they claim to clarify the issue of behavior. This is not to say that they are devoid of theology; it is to say that theology is not their central focus. But what is significant about this paragraph is that it goes beyond behavior and gives a glimpse of the theology behind the behavior. It is not a conclusion to chaps. 2 and 3 as if it were a church manual; rather it is a pause to put what Paul has been writing into perspective and to prepare the stage for 1 Tim 4:1–5. Paul's instructions about law, grace, his conversion, the opponents, the scope of salvation, men and women in church and in leadership, elders and deacons, all have one focus: to preserve the integrity of the gospel message. The church is one of the supporting pillars in the proclamation of the gospel. It is a protector, like a rampart built up around a city to protect it in time of battle. But those in the Ephesian church, rather than supporting and protecting the gospel, are bringing it into disrepute because of their sin. Their anger is so pronounced that even during times of prayer they will not keep peace. The women are dressing immodestly and trying to assume roles that Paul did not permit. Elders and deacons are behaving so poorly that their sins are destroying the reputation of the church. The Ephesian church is failing.

To emphasize why this misbehavior must stop, Paul reminds them of the true nature of the church. It is the household of the living God, a God who is not dead but alive and active, who will protect his church and punish those who assail its walls. The truth, the gospel that is Jesus Christ, must be protected. It is significant that Paul says the church is only "a" support and protector of the gospel since the preservation of the gospel is not dependent upon how the church performs its function. The gospel can never be destroyed (2 Tim 2:9), but the role of protection is one of the church's functions and one it must perform. To emphasize the greatness of the gospel, the greatness of the church's mission, Paul cites part of a hymn that was probably known by the Ephesian church. It describes first the work of Christ, his incarnation, resurrection, and ascension. Then it describes the ensuing obligation of the church to preach the gospel so people will believe and so Christ will receive the glory he deserves.

B. B. Warfield calls churches to take Paul's instructions seriously: "There is a right way to order God's house; nay, there is a way in which it must be ordered. . . . Is there or is there not a duty laid upon us of to-day to govern our Church services and conform our Church organization according to the pattern deductible from the two sections ii. 1–15, iii. 1–13, to which these solemn words refer? Is the Church still God's house, the Church of the living God? And is His or our way of ordering it best fitted to make it the pillar and ground of His great and inestimable truth?" (*PresR* 8 [1921] 507, 508).

The christological hymn played a significant role in Calvin's theology, as Zachman summarizes:

Calvin's understanding of Jesus Christ is rooted in the description of Christ found in the confession of faith in 1 Timothy: "God was manifested in the flesh" (1 Tim. 3:16). This confession lies behind Calvin's understanding of Jesus Christ both as the self-revelation of God the Father (Christ as the image of the invisible God) and as the mediator between God and humanity (Christ as prophet, king, and priest). Calvin begins his discussion of the person and work of Christ in the 1559 *Institutes* with the statement that is in accord with the definition of Chalcedon, but which Calvin interprets in light of 1 Timothy 3:16. "Now it was of the greatest importance for us that he who was to be our Mediator be both true God and true man *(verum esse et Deum et hominem)*." (*CTJ* 25/26 [1990–91] 46, citing *Institutes* 2.12.1)

F. The Source of the Heresy (1 Tim 4:1–5)

Bibliography

Ellis, E. E. "Traditions in the Pastoral Epistles." In *Early Jewish and Christian Exegesis*. FS W. H. Brownlee, ed. C. A. Evans and W. F. Stinespring. Atlanta: Scholars Press, 1987. 237–53. **Ford, J. M.** "A Note on Proto-Montanism in the Pastoral Epistles." *NTS* 17 (1970–71) 338–46. **Harris, R. J.** "The Background and Significance of the Polemic of the Pastoral Epistles." *JBL* 92 (1973) 549–64. **Haykin, M. A. G.** "The Fading Vision: The Spirit and Freedom in the Pastoral Epistles." *EvQ* 57 (1985) 291–305. **Lane, W. L.** "1 Tim 4:1–3: An Early Instance of Over-Realized Eschatology?" *NTS* 11 (1964) 164–67. **Lohse, E.** "Zu 1 Cor 10:26, 31." *ZNW* 47 (1956) 277–80. **Owen, E. C. E.** "δαίμων and Cognate Words." *JTS* 32 (1931) 133–53.

Translation

[1]*Now the Spirit clearly says that in the last times some of the faith will apostatize by being devoted to deceitful[a] spirits and teachings of demons,* [2]*by the hypocrisy of liars whose own consciences have been branded,[b]* [3]*forbidding to marry, demanding abstinence from foods that God created to be received with thanksgiving by those who are faithful and know the truth,* [4]*since all of God's creation is good, and nothing is unclean if it is received with thanksgiving;* [5]*for it is sanctified through [the] word of God and prayer.*

Notes

[a]The genitive singular πλάνης, "of deceit," is found in P Ψ 104 614 630 945 *al* lat.

[b]κεκαυστηριασμένων, "having been branded" (א A L *al;* Or), and κεκαυτηριασμένων (C D G I Ψ 33 1739 1881 TR; Cl Did Epiph) are two different spellings of the same word. A few MSS have καὶ καυ(σ)τηριασμένων, "and having been branded" (F 0241^vid *al* lat sy^p).

Form/Structure/Setting

1 Tim 4:1–5 does not begin a new topic. Paul, who has given his instructions on the true understanding of law, grace, and salvation (1:3–2:7) and on church behavior and leadership (2:8–3:13) and has paused to put his instructions into proper perspective (3:14–16), now concludes by pointing out that these types of problems should have been expected because the Holy Spirit had clearly prophesied their occurrence (4:1–5; cf. *Form/Structure/Setting* on 1 Tim 3:14–16). Paul does not deal with the opponents again until 6:3. There is a parallel between chap. 1 and chap. 4. In 1:3–17 Paul describes the Ephesian problem and then in 1:18–20 reminds Timothy of what he already knew—that he had the gifts necessary to perform this ministry—and encourages him to do the task. In 4:1–5 Paul tells Timothy more about the Ephesian heresy, and then in 4:6–16 he encourages Timothy to fight the good fight. The issue of asceticism also ties 4:1–5 together with 4:6–16. The opponents taught asceticism, abstention from marriage and certain foods; by contrast, Timothy is to train himself in godliness (v 8). Vv 1–5 therefore conclude the discussion begun in chap. 2 and are transitional in that they discuss the heresy and are followed by a personal encouragement for Timothy to deal with the problem.

Fee ties 4:1–10 even closer to 3:16, seeing the theology of the hymn as standing in direct conflict with the opponents in 4:1–5. He argues that (1) 3:14 is transitional, concluding all of the preceding, including the general conduct of the false teachers; (2) the δέ, "but," in 4:1 is a true adversative, connecting 3:16 with 4:1; and (3) "what holds this argument together (from 3:14) is the concern over εὐσέβεια ('godliness'); the hymn is intended to give content to εὐσέβεια; the pursuit of it is about to be urged on Timothy (4:6–10) in direct antithesis to the false teachers and their errors (4:1–5)" (*God's Empowering Presence,* 763).

Much is revealed about the opponents in these five verses. The opponents are hypocritical liars who know that what they are teaching is wrong and yet continue to teach, claiming to be Christians and yet bearing Satan's brand of ownership. Ultimately Satan lies behind their work and there is a reminder of the opponents' success. They are promoting asceticism, forbidding marriage, and enforcing dietary restrictions, but their asceticism is false and hypocritical. See the *Introduction,* "The Ephesian Heresy," for a comparison of this passage with the other descriptions of the opponents and their teaching.

The structure of this passage is somewhat cumbersome: it is one sentence with a series of clauses. Paul begins by saying that some believers have fallen away just as the Spirit said they would, and then he gives two reasons for the apostasy: they are devoted to spirits and their teachings, and they have given in to the hypocrisy of liars (vv 1–2). Then, building from the word ψευδολόγων, "liars," Paul describes their asceticism with a participial (κωλυόντων γαμεῖν, "forbidding to marry") and an infinitival (ἀπέχεσθαι βρωμάτων, "to abstain from foods") clause (v 3ab). Finally, Paul gives two reasons that no food is unclean: God's creative intentions and a believer's prayer of thanksgiving (vv 3c–5). Paul states each of these reasons three times, interweaving them together.

Comment

1a Τὸ δὲ πνεῦμα ῥητῶς λέγει ὅτι ἐν ὑστέροις καιροῖς ἀποστήσονταί τινες τῆς πίστεως, "Now the Spirit clearly says that in the last times some of the faith will apostatize." Timothy should not have been surprised at the problems he was having (1 Tim 2:1–3:13) because the Spirit clearly prophesied this apostasy. The emphasis is on the clarity of this prophecy. The same idea is repeated in 2 Tim 4:3–4, also in an eschatological context.

τὸ πνεῦμα, "the Spirit," refers to the Holy Spirit (cf. Acts 11:27–28 for a similar example of the Holy Spirit warning the church), but it is not clear through what medium the Spirit spoke about this apostasy. The idea of apostasy and a proliferation of evil in the end times is found throughout Jewish literature (Dan 12:1; *1 Enoch* 80:2–8; 100:1–3; *As. Mos.* 8:1; 4 Ezra 5:1–12; *2 Apoc. Bar.* 25–27; 48:32–36; 70:2–8; 1QpHab 2:5–10; 1QS 3:19–21; 1QH 4:9; CD 12:2–3), the Gospels (Mark 13), Paul (1 Cor 7:26; 2 Thess 2:1–12), the PE (2 Tim 2:16–18; 3:1–9, 13; 4:3–4), and elsewhere in the NT (2 Pet 3:3–7; 1 John 2:18; Jude 17–18). If this is the prophecy to which Paul refers, Timothy could have clearly known that it was coming, but perhaps he would have been somewhat surprised at its occurrence in Ephesus. It is also tempting to refer to Paul's prophecy in Acts 20:29–30 where he told the Ephesian church that "after my departure fierce wolves will come in among you, not sparing the flock; and from among your own selves will arise men speaking perverse things, to draw the disciples after them." This prophecy fits the context (see *Introduction,* "Historical Reconstruction from Acts").

At first glance it appears that the phrase ἐν ὑστέροις καιροῖς, "in the last times," refers to some time in the future, especially since the verb is a future tense (ἀποστήσονται, "will apostatize") and the phrase can be translated "in the later times." However, a closer examination shows that Paul sees Timothy and himself as being presently in the last times (cf. Spicq, 1:136; Towner, *NTS* 32 [1986] 427–48; Pfitzner, *Agon Motif,* 173). (1) This is required by the context. The purpose of 1 Tim 4:1–5 is to show that the problems Timothy is currently experiencing are not unexpected. (2) The actual phrase ἐν ὑστέροις καιροῖς does not occur again in the PE, but there is a similar phrase that employs a future verb although it refers to the present time: 2 Tim 3:1 says, "But know this, that in the last days [ἐν ἐσχάταις ἡμέραις] there will come [ἐνστήσονται] violent times"; as Paul continues his description he says, "Avoid [ἀποτρέπου] these people" (2 Tim 3:5b). The prohibition in 2 Tim 3:5b is linear in aspect: "Continually avoid"; "Continue to avoid" (cf. BDF §336). Paul concludes by discussing the present behavior of some of the opponents, not future behavior. (3) From the time of the experience of Pentecost the church viewed itself as being in the last days (Acts 2:17–21; Heb 1:2), and this expectation is throughout Paul. (4) ἀποστήσονται, "will apostatize," is future because Paul is probably looking at the prophecy from the perspective of the time it was originally given, a future that has now become present (cf. Lock, 47, citing 1 John 4:1–3). The gnomic present λέγει, "says," shows the abiding force of the prophecy.

δέ, "now," is not a strong adversative introducing a new topic but a gentle reminder that Timothy should not have been surprised at the opposition (cf. BAGD, 171). If there is any adversative force present, Paul's point is that despite the tremendous and significant role the church plays and the truth of the hymn (cf.

Form/Structure/Setting on 1 Tim 3:14–16), error can and has arisen (Bernard, 64). Ellicott (52) balances the adversative force against the mystery in 3:16. Despite the mystery of godliness, the Holy Spirit clearly speaks. The Spirit clearly, expressly, specifically, foretold this apostasy. ῥητῶς means "clearly, expressly," adding emphasis to the idea of the clarity of the prophecy (cf. MM, 564). It occurs nowhere else in the NT. ὕστερος functions as both a comparative ("later") and a superlative ("last"; cf. Wallace, *Greek Grammar,* 299) adjective (BAGD, 849; cf. BDF §62). Superlative forms in general were in decline in the Koine (BDF §60), and the superlative form ὕστατος, "last," does not occur in the NT.

There is a question regarding whether τῆς πίστεως, "of the faith," goes with τινές, "some," or with ἀποστήσονται, "will apostatize." Will "some of the faith apostatize" or will "some apostatize from the faith"? (In both cases πίστις, "faith," is used in the creedal sense; cf. *Introduction,* "Themes in the PE.") "Some of the faith will apostatize" seems preferable. (1) ἀφιστάναι, "to apostatize," occurs fourteen times in the NT. In ten of those times the verb is followed by the ablative ἀπό, "from," with the object of the preposition describing what they fell away from (Luke 4:13; 13:27; Acts 5:38; 12:10; 15:38; 19:9; 22:29; 2 Cor 12:8; 2 Tim 2:19; Heb 3:12). In every one of these instances, except in Acts 12:10, the preposition follows immediately after the verb. Of the other four instances (including 1 Tim 4:1), the verb is used absolutely with no object in Luke 8:13 (the seeds take root but in a time of temptation fall away [ἐν καιρῷ πειρασμοῦ ἀφίστανται]), with the ablative without a preposition in Luke 2:37 (Anna did not depart from the temple [ἀφίστατο τοῦ ἱεροῦ]), and with the accusative and a different preposition in Acts 5:37 (Judas the Galilean drew people away with him [ἀπέστησεν λαὸν ὀπίσω αὐτοῦ]). From this it can be seen that in the vast majority of cases if there is a recipient of the verb's action, it will most likely be indicated by a preposition and will immediately follow the verb. This suggests that τῆς πίστεως modifies τινές and not ἀποστήσονται. (2) τῆς πίστεως is closer to τινές than it is to ἀποστήσονται. (3) Historically, by the time of writing Christians were falling from the faith (cf. 1 Tim 1:6). (4) The people who were falling away were a different group from the opponents, those who were hypocritical liars whose consciences were seared. The context therefore envisions three groups: the opponents, the true believers, and those who had been part of the church but had since been lured away from the faith by the opponents. Paul commonly, but not always, refers to the opponents as τινές and not by name in the PE (cf. 1 Tim 1:3).

ἀποστήσονται, "will apostatize," refers to active rebellion against God and is so used in the LXX (BAGD, 126–27), achieving almost the status of a technical term (H. Schlier, *TDNT* 1:514–15; cf. Deut 32:15; Jer 3:14; Isa 30:1; Acts 5:37; 15:38; 19:9). Again we see an indication that the Ephesians are not being tricked into the heresy but are actively rebelling against God (cf. 1 Tim 1:6). The only other occurrence of ἀφιστάναι in the PE is in 2 Tim 2:19 where Paul uses its more basic meaning of "to depart" when he says, "Let every one who calls on the name of the Lord depart [ἀποστήτω] from unrighteousness."

καιρός, "time," occurs three times in the phrase καιροῖς ἰδίοις, "in the proper time," referring to the past manifestation of eternal life through Paul's preaching (Titus 1:3), the present applicability of the creed in 1 Tim 2:5–6a to the Ephesian situation (1 Tim 2:6b), and the future return of Christ (1 Tim 6:15). Therefore, there is nothing about the word καιρός that denotes a specific time period. καιρός also occurs by itself in 2 Tim 4:3 where Paul urges Timothy to continue his preaching, "For the time will come [ἔσται] when they will not put up with [ἀνέξονται] sound teaching," a use similar to that in 1 Tim 4:1. It also is used three verses later to refer to the time of Paul's death (2 Tim 4:6).

1b–2 προσέχοντες πνεύμασιν πλάνοις καὶ διδασκαλίαις δαιμονίων, ἐν ὑποκρίσει ψευδολόγων, κεκαυστηριασμένων τὴν ἰδίαν συνείδησιν, "by being devoted to deceitful spirits and teachings of demons, by the hypocrisy of liars whose own consciences have been branded." Not since 1 Tim 1:3–6 has such a clear picture been given of Paul's opponents. Here it is revealed that at the root of the Ephesian heresy lie Satan and his demons, leading people astray and teaching his own doctrines. The role of Satan has already been hinted at in 1 Tim 3:6–7, and it will appear again in 2 Tim 2:26 (cf. 1 Tim 1:20 for a discussion of Satan's role). It is also revealed that the opponents are hypocrites whose minds have been branded by Satan. Ultimately they know that what they were doing and teaching is wrong, and yet they persist. They are not honestly mistaken, but in fact carry Satan's brand of ownership on their consciences. This is the battle Timothy must fight, and this is his true enemy. Paul says elsewhere, "For we are not contending against flesh and blood, but against the principalities, against the powers, against the world rulers of this present darkness, against the spiritual hosts of wickedness in the heavenly places" (Eph 6:12).

The first clause, "by being devoted to deceitful spirits and teachings of demons," describes the force of the heresy upon the people (τινές). They were addicted to the demonic spirits and their teachings. Parallel to the participial clause is the prepositional clause "by the hypocrisy of liars whose own consciences have been branded." The Ephesians have also apostatized because of the work of Paul's opponents. Ellicott comments that a person "never stands isolated; if he is not influenced by [the Holy Spirit] . . . he at once falls under the powers of [the deceitful spirit]" (53).

Who were the πνεύμασιν πλάνοις, "deceitful spirits"? πνεῦμα, "spirit," elsewhere in the PE is always singular, referring to the Holy Spirit (1 Tim 4:1a; 2 Tim 1:14; Titus 3:5), Timothy's spirit (2 Tim 1:7; 4:22), and Jesus' spirit (1 Tim 3:16). The plural πνεύμασιν πλάνοις could be referring to Paul's opponents, but more likely, especially if the following phrase is to be translated "teachings of demons," it also refers to these same beings, the evil spirits who with Satan are assailing the Ephesian church (cf. 1 Tim 1:20), the spirits to whom the Ephesian church is devoting itself. προσέχοντες, "being devoted to," describes a strong attachment, a lifestyle (cf. 1 Tim 1:4). Those of the faith who have apostatized have become enamored with this new teaching. πλάνη, "deceitful," is a common term in both the LXX and the NT for religious error and is always bad. When people refuse to acknowledge God and are consumed with passion for each other, they bear the penalty for their error (πλάνη) in their own persons (Rom 1:27). Spiritually immature Christians are tossed to and fro by deceitful people (Eph 4:14). Paul's appeal to the Thessalonians comes not from deceit but from (it is implied) God (1 Thess 2:3). Because people refuse to love the truth, God will send a spirit of deceit so they will believe what is false (2 Thess 2:10–11). The term is used elsewhere in the NT to describe false teachers (2 Pet 2:18; 3:17; Jude 11), the spirit of error, which is the spirit of the antichrist (1 John 4:6), and sin resulting in damnation (Jas 5:20; cf. H. Braun, *TDNT* 6:228–53; BAGD, 665–66).

διδασκαλίαις δαιμονίων, "teachings of demons," has two interpretations: teachings taught by demons (subjective genitive) or teachings that are demonic in nature (attributive genitive). Both interpretations understand that Satan and his demons lie at the root of the heresy, although the former makes the connection more direct and almost personal. Because Satan is seen as having an active role in Ephesus, the stronger statement is preferred: at the heart of the problem lies the active teachings of demons. This agrees with 2 Tim 2:26, which states that the opponents have been ensnared by Satan to do his will. Although these two designations—deceitful spirits and teachings of demons—are closely related, they are not a hendiadys; the devotion is to the spirits and to the teaching. The term διδασκαλία, "teaching," is frequent in the PE, describing the gospel, and therefore its use here provides a startling contrast. As opposed to the sound teaching of Paul, the opponents are promulgating a sick, morbid heresy that is demonic in origin and spreading like gangrene (cf. 1 Tim 1:10). διδασκαλίαις δαιμονίων does not mean that the opponents themselves are demon possessed; if so we would expect Paul to say so. Rather, the phrase is saying that the opponents are the agents of demons (cf. 2 Cor 11:14–15: "Even Satan disguises himself as an angel of light. So it is not strange if his servants also disguise themselves as servants of righteousness").

Having accused the apostatized Christians of being devoted to demons and their teachings, Paul follows up with a second description of their woeful state. They have been led into apostasy by hypocritical "liars whose own consciences have been branded." This is in contrast to Paul who has, as a goal of his preaching, a good conscience (1 Tim 1:5). This phrase is important in the overall interpretation of the PE because it raises the question of the opponents' sincerity. The opponents have not been tricked; they do not deserve the benefit of the doubt. They know that what they are doing and teaching is wrong, and yet "they not only do them but approve those who practice them" (in the words of Rom 1:32). Ellicott (53) comments, "They knew the brand they bore, and yet with a show of outward sanctity . . . they strove to beguile and to seduce others, and make them as bad as themselves." They bear the brand of Satan on their conscience and yet pretend to be servants of God. Paul is justified in his condemnation of both their theology and their actions. ἐν, "by," indicates the intermediate means of the heresy; the ultimate source is the demons (v 1).

κεκαυστηριασμένων is capable of two translations. (1) The figurative translation is that their consciences "have been burned," as if pressed with a hot iron, so that they are no longer effective. This would be parallel to the concept of the hardened heart found throughout the NT (Matt 19:18; Mark 6:52; Rom 9:18; 11:7, 25; Eph 4:18; Heb 3:8, 13, 15; 4:7). The problem with this interpretation is that the imagery of a seared conscience does not fit with that of being a hypocritical liar: If a person's conscience has been seared, he or she cannot know the difference between truth and error, but the term ὑποκρίσει, "hypocrisy," implies that the opponents did know the difference.

(2) The nonfigurative translation is "brand with a red-hot iron" (BAGD, 425). The reference is to the ancient practice of branding criminals, runaway and disobedient slaves (Plutarch *Pericl.* 26), defeated soldiers (Lucian *Syr. dea* 59; Herodotus *Hist.* 2:113), people in certain religious cults, and people in other specific professions (J. Schneider, *TDNT* 3:643–45). This translation suggests that

Paul's opponents have had their consciences branded by Satan to mark his own-ership, somewhat like the "666" of the antichrist (Rev 13:16; cf. R. H. Mounce, *The Book of Revelation* [Grand Rapids, MI: Eerdmans, 1977] 261–62). There are several arguments for this interpretation. (a) The participle is passive, suggesting that Satan is the one who does the branding. This fits the context, which just mentioned his role in the heresy (v 1b). (b) It fits with the imagery of the sec-tion. Paul has just called the opponents hypocritical liars. For emphasis he points out that although they claim to be from God, they have the stamp of Satan on them, they are his agents. (c) This interpretation does not disagree with the de-scription of the opponents as hypocrites.

ὑπόκρισις, "hypocrisy," pretending to be what one is not, occurs elsewhere in the NT only in Gal 2:13 where Paul says that even Barnabas was carried away by Peter's hypocrisy. ψευδολόγος, "liar," occurs in the NT only here. It is a compound noun meaning "false word." Fee says it "has more to do with speaking falsehood as over against the truth of the gospel" (*God's Empowering Presence*," 768 n. 60). The perfect participle κεκαυστηριασμένων, "have been branded," emphasizes that they continue to carry the mark of their sin with them. This is the only occur-rence of the word in the NT. On συνείδησις, "conscience," cf. *Comment* on 1 Tim 1:5.

3ab κωλυόντων γαμεῖν, ἀπέχεσθαι βρωμάτων, "forbidding to marry, demand-ing abstinence from foods." The Ephesian heresy had to do with the law, myths, and genealogies (1 Tim 1:3–11). This verse gives the next clear indication of the content of the heresy. The opponents' desire to force all to obey the law includes the enforcement of asceticism (as also in Titus 1:15), specifically, dietary restric-tions and a forbidding of marriage (cf. Col 2:16–23 for a similar situation). The restrictions on marriage probably included everything associated with marriage, such as bearing children (discussed in 1 Tim 2:15). In light of the previous verses, which show that the opponents were hypocritical liars and agents of Satan, the as-ceticism of the opponents was surely feigned (cf. *Introduction*, "The Ephesian Heresy," for a fuller discussion of the heresy). Towner suggests that the opponents may have been attempting "to enact the life of resurrection paradise by following the model given in Genesis 1 and 2" (103–4), accounting for the prohibition against marriage and the vegetarianism. This would help to explain the use of Gen 2–3 in 1 Tim 2:13–15 as reflecting the opponents' teaching. It would also imply that the phrase "word of God" in 1 Tim 4:5 is God's statement on the goodness of creation and supports the identification of the "myths and genealogies" in 1 Tim 1:4 with the creation accounts (see *Introduction*, "The Ephesian Heresy").

Paul does not immediately deal with the issue of marriage. It has been raised in connection with bearing children (1 Tim 2:15) and will be discussed in more detail with the issue of widows in chap. 5. However, in the next several verses Paul deals with dietary restrictions and the goodness of food. Because marital and di-etary regulations are found in both Judaism (Josephus *J.W.* 2.8.2 §§119–21 [cf. 2.8.13 §§160–61]; *Ant.* 18.1.5 §§18–22; Pliny *Hist.* 5.17) and Gnosticism (Clem-ent of Alexandria *Strom.* 3.6; Irenaeus *Adv. Haer.* 1.22; cf. Oberlinner, 179), this passage does not help us in determining the source of the Ephesian heresy. The perversion of the gospel truth may have been the result of the philosophical du-alism present throughout the first-century world (cf. Spicq, 1:494–5; Jeremias, 32; W. L. Lane, *NTS* 11 [1964] 165 n. 1). Since there is nothing here beyond what we meet in Rom 14, Col 2:16–23, and Heb 13:4, 9, there is no reason to look beyond the first century (cf. Lock, 47). Because 1 Tim 4:1–5 is so closely tied in with chaps. 1 and 2 and because these five verses have nothing in common with the approach to interpreting the PE as a church manual, they give confirmation that the correct interpretation of the PE must take into account the historical situation. Lane argues that the opponents were teaching an over-realized eschatology in which the resurrection was past (2 Tim 2:18) and the new life of the age to come was present (cf. 4:8), a life in which there was no marriage (recalling Matt 22:30) and the food was fish or the honeycomb (recalling Luke 24:42–43; cf. John 21:9–14; Acts 10:41). But much of his argument assumes a closer connection between 4:1–5 and 4:8 than is warranted since v 6 starts a new section (albeit with some ties to the preceding), and it seems doubtful that Luke 24:42–3 is sufficiently significant to create a doctrine concerning dietary law in the eschatological kingdom.

Paul held a much higher view of marriage than did his opponents, encouraging women to bear children (1 Tim 2:15) and younger widows to remarry (1 Tim 5:11–15; cf. 1 Cor 7:8–9, 25–40). There was an obvious contradiction in the opponents' behavior: they eschewed marriage and childbearing, and yet Paul's statement that "For among them are those who make their way into households and capture weak women, burdened by sins and swayed by various impulses" (2 Tim 3:6) implies that they were sexually promiscuous. Paul has rightly called them hypocritical liars (1 Tim 4:2a). γαμεῖν, "to marry," occurs elsewhere in the PE only in 1 Tim 5 where Paul counsels the younger widows to remarry (vv 11, 14). Its only other occurrence in Paul is in 1 Corinthians where the same issue of marriage and remarriage is being discussed (1 Cor 7:8–16, 25–40).

Dietary restrictions were a common problem in the early church (cf. Acts 10:9–16; Rom 14:1–23; 1 Cor 10:23–33; Col 2:16, 21). Although Jesus had declared all foods clean (Mark 7:19), the restrictions persisted. Paul spends the next two and one-half verses explaining why food laws are wrong. There is a question whether the opponents forbade alcoholic drink; most likely they did not since they were well known for their excessive drinking (*Comment* on 1 Tim 3:3). Their asceticism also did not forbid financial gain (1 Tim 6:5). ἀπέχεσθαι, "to abstain," is "an intransitive middle that takes the genitive of the thing from which abstinence is required" (BAGD, 85). It is used elsewhere in the NT to enjoin abstinence from food offered to idols (Acts 15:29), from fornication (1 Thess 4:3), from every form of evil (1 Thess 5:22), and from the desires of the flesh (1 Pet 2:11). From these parallels it appears that the opponents are insisting very strongly that the church must follow their dietary restrictions. βρῶμα, "food," is used elsewhere with various shades of meaning. Paul uses it in his discussions of food being a stumbling block to "weaker" Christians (Rom 14:15, 20; 1 Cor 8:8, 13). Paul's contrasting of food with milk in his discussion of spiritual immaturity (1 Cor 3:2) suggests that βρῶμα is solid food. Paul interchanges it with κρέας, "meat," in similar discussions (Rom 14:15, 20, 21; 1 Cor 8:13: "If food [βρῶμα] is a cause of my brother's falling, I will never eat meat [κρέα]).

3c–5 ἃ ὁ θεὸς ἔκτισεν εἰς μετάλημψιν μετὰ εὐχαριστίας τοῖς πιστοῖς καὶ ἐπεγνωκόσι τὴν ἀλήθειαν. ὅτι πᾶν κτίσμα θεοῦ καλὸν καὶ οὐδὲν ἀπόβλητον μετὰ εὐχαριστίας λαμβανόμενον· ἁγιάζεται γὰρ διὰ λόγου θεοῦ καὶ ἐντεύξεως, "that God created to be received with thanksgiving by those who are faithful and know the truth, since all of God's creation is good, and nothing is unclean if it is received with thanksgiving; for it is sanctified through [the] word of God and prayer." Paul's opponents enforced cultic dietary restrictions on their converts. To show that they are wrong, Paul gives these two reasons: God created food good, and the prayer before the meal confirms the food's goodness.

The structure of these verses may seem confusing at first. Paul states both of his arguments three times, each time adding a little more to the argument, and weaves all six of these statements together, first referring to food's creative goodness and then to prayer. The first argument about God creating food to be good runs "that God created to be received . . . since all of God's creation is good . . . for it is sanctified through [the] word of God." The second argument about the power of prayer is "with thanksgiving by those who are faithful and know the truth . . . nothing is unclean if it is received with thanksgiving . . . for it is sanctified through . . . prayer." The interweaving may be a bit cumbersome, but the constant repetition drives the points home. Because all three statements of each argument help to interpret each other, the three statements arguing from the goodness of creation will first be analyzed, and then the three statements arguing from prayer.

ἃ ὁ θεὸς ἔκτισεν εἰς μετάλημψιν . . . ὅτι πᾶν κτίσμα θεοῦ καλόν . . . ἁγιάζεται γὰρ διὰ λόγου θεοῦ, "that God created to be received . . . since all of God's creation is good . . . for it is sanctified through [the] word of God." Paul's first argument is that God created the food, and since everything God creates is good, so also is all food allowed to be eaten. All food is inherently clean because of God's creative activity, and an insistence on cultic dietary restrictions is now wrong (cf. Titus 1:15). This is the same idea found elsewhere: "I know and am persuaded in the Lord Jesus that nothing is unclean in itself" (Rom 14:14). There is no room for the dualistic sense of an evil creation in the PE. God created the food, not a Gnostic demiurge as is met in the second century, and that goodness is still valid as the gospel declares, despite the Jewish laws. Again we see both Jewish and Gnostic tendencies in the Ephesian heresy.

The first statement of the argument asserts that it was God's intention to create food for human needs. To say that certain foods are not suitable for eating means that God's purposes have failed. εἰς, "to," indicates the purpose of the action (cf. BAGD, 229[4f]). The second statement of the argument says that everything created by God is good, καλόν, "good," being defined in this context as cultically pure. (On καλός, "good," cf. Comment on 1 Tim 1:8.) The third statement is more troublesome to interpret, but when it is seen side by side with the first two statements most issues are clarified. The usual Pauline sense of ἁγιάζειν, "to sanctify," as "to justify" (cf. 1 Cor 6:11) cannot be its meaning here. (The verb occurs elsewhere in the PE only in 2 Tim 2:21, where Paul says that if Timothy cleanses himself from that which is dishonorable, he will be "sanctified, useful for the master, prepared for every good work.") Since the context of this discussion is cultic, the more cultic, ritualistic meaning of the verb is intended. All food is made ritually pure because of the word of God, contra the opponents' ritualistic teachings (cf. Matt 23:17, 19; also Exod 29:27, 37, 44; Eph 5:26; Col 1:22; cf. O. Procksch, TDNT 1:112; BAGD, 8; Spicq, 1:499). Lock comments, "It becomes holy to the eater; not that it was unclean in itself, but that his scruples or thanklessness might make it so to him" (48; cf. Knight, 192). There is similarity with

Paul's injunctions in Rom 14: "Let every one be fully convinced in his own mind" (5b); "I know and am persuaded in the Lord Jesus that nothing is unclean in itself; but it is unclean for any one who thinks it unclean" (14); "The faith that you have, keep between yourself and God; happy is he who has no reason to judge himself for what he approves. But he who has doubts is condemned, if he eats, because he does not act from faith; for whatever does not proceed from faith is sin" (22–23).

λόγου θεοῦ, "[the] word of God," is that action (or "means" [Moule, *Idiom-Book*, 57]) of God whereby Paul's opponents are proven to be wrong. Five interpretations have been put forward. (1) In response to prayers (Paul's second reason), God pronounces the food clean. Spicq believes it is the divine blessing granted over the food in response to prayer and concludes that the verse is the most ancient attestation of a liturgical blessing placed on foods and objects for use by Christians (1:500). The problem with this is that God has already created the food good (1 Tim 4:4a); it does not become good in response to anything that is done. (2) "Word of God" refers to the use of the OT in mealtime prayers. The advantage of this interpretation is that it creates a hendiadys so that the word of God is the prayer, thus reinforcing the already close connection between these two arguments evident elsewhere in the context. The problem with this interpretation as well as others is that the two previous statements of this argument have set the context to be that of creation. (3) Hanson believes that these verses reflect a eucharistic prayer based on a comparison with *Did.* 9:19 (*Studies,* 97–109). But the similarities are at best superficial, and *Did.* 9:19 has no explicit discussion of the goodness of creation (it says that food and drink are for enjoyment), which is the thrust of 1 Tim 4:3–5.

(4) "Word of God" can be the gospel message, which includes the message that food laws are now passé. This interpretation has much to commend it. (a) It parallels the previous phrase, "by those who are faithful and know the truth" (1 Tim 4:3b), which refers to those who believe the gospel. (b) The phrase means the gospel when it is used elsewhere in the PE (2 Tim 2:9; 4:2; Titus 2:5; cf. similar expression in 1 Tim 5:6; 2 Tim 2:15) and Paul (1 Cor 14:36; 2 Cor 2:17; 4:2; Phil 1:14; Col 1:25; but in Rom 9:6 it is God's promise to Israel; cf. similar phrases in Col 3:16; 1 Thess 1:8; 2:13; 2 Thess 3:1). (c) The verb is in the present tense, suggesting an ongoing process. (5) The final interpretation is that "word of God" refers to God's statement that creation is good (Gen 1:4, 10, 12, 18, 21, 25, 31; cf. Sir 39:33), and this creation includes food. This is preferable to the previous interpretations because the context of this passage, specifically the two parallel statements of the argument, is creation: "God created food for receiving" (v 3a); "everything God created is good" (v 4a). Because the phrase "word of God" is the third repetition of the same argument, it too should be understood within the context of creation. When God looked over creation and pronounced it very good, all foods were declared clean. If Towner is correct that the opponents were trying to recreate the Garden of Eden with its lack of (formal) marriage and its vegetarianism, then Paul would be using one of their presumably key passages to argue against their teaching. It is perhaps possible to blend the final two interpretations. The gospel message reasserts what was true at the beginning: the fruit of the earth is good and available for consumption.

μετὰ εὐχαριστίας τοῖς πιστοῖς καὶ ἐπεγνωκόσι τὴν ἀλήθειαν, ὅτι . . . οὐδὲν ἀπόβλητον μετὰ εὐχαριστίας λαμβανόμενον· ἁγιάζεται γὰρ διὰ . . . ἐντεύξεως, "with thanksgiving by those who are faithful and know the truth, since . . . nothing is unclean if it is received with thanksgiving; for it is sanctified through . . . prayer." The second argument, thrice repeated and woven throughout this discussion, is that the opponents' dietary restrictions were wrong because of the prayer made before meals. This is the same argument found elsewhere: "If I partake with thankfulness, why am I denounced because of that for which I give thanks?" (1 Cor 10:30 [discussed below]; cf. Rom 14:6; Phil 4:6). Prayer before meals was a common practice in Judaism (b. Ber. 35a: "It is forbidden a man to enjoy anything of this world without a benediction" [cited in Fee, 100]) and during Christ's ministry (Mark 6:41; 8:6; 14:22–23; Luke 24:30).

But how does the prayer of thanksgiving sanctify the food, and what is the relationship between God's creative goodness (argument one) and the believers' prayers (argument two)? Nothing in the PE suggests that Paul sees prayers as having magical powers; the food is already clean by God's creative act and the gospel's reaffirmation of that fact. A prayer of thanksgiving merely confirms in the individual God's prior action of making food good for all. Paul's arguments regarding creation and prayer are closely related, which might explain his willingness to weave them together.

However, there is a conditional element implied in the relationship between God's creative goodness and a believer's prayer of thanksgiving. V 3 says that God created food for the purpose of having it received with thanksgiving, but v 4 makes the conditional element more pronounced: "if it is received with thanksgiving" (λαμβανόμενον, "being received," is a conditional participle). This is not to say that God's creative goodness in and of itself was ineffectual; it is to say that for believers the thankful recognition of the truth of the gospel, which renounces all stigma from foods formerly pronounced unclean, gives full assurance. (This note of thankfulness in prayer is also found in 1 Tim 2:1.) Without a belief in the gospel, a person has no assurance that the dietary laws still do not apply. (The argument does not work in reverse; if a person is not thankful, it does not make the food unclean.)

In 1 Cor 10:23–30 Paul voices a similar argument in a somewhat similar situation. All things are lawful, but not all things are helpful to the Christian community. A Christian is free to eat meat, not knowing if it has been offered to idols, because "the earth is the Lord's, and everything in it" (v 26, citing Ps 24:1). Barrett says that Ps 24:1 was used in Judaism to argue that grace should be said before meals, a prayer recognizing that "everything he eats is a gift from God" (240; citing m. Ber. 4.1 and E. Lohse, ZNW 47 [1956] 277–80). Several verses later in 1 Cor 10 Paul says, "If I partake with thankfulness, why am I denounced because of that for which I give thanks" (v 30). Paul's prayer of thankfulness before the meal was a recognition of the truth of Ps 24:1, a truth reiterated by the gospel message and one that the Corinthian (and Ephesian) church should have understood (cf. Fee, First Epistle to the Corinthians, 487).

εὐχαριστία, "thanksgiving," is a common Pauline term and has already been used to describe a prayer of thanksgiving (cf. 1 Tim 2:1). Its repetition emphasizes that the prayer is one of thankfulness. Not only is food intended to be received, but it is intended to be received with thanksgiving. τοῖς πιστοῖς, "those who are faithful" (cf. 1 Tim 4:10; 6:2), is a hendiadys with the following anarthrous phrase, ἐπεγνωκόσι τὴν ἀλήθειαν, "[those who] know the truth," i.e., Christians who fully know the gospel (cf. the similar combination of terms in Titus 1:1). The construction article-noun-καί-noun confirms this (BDF §276[3]) as well as the use of πιστός, "faithful," and ἐπιγινώσκειν τὴν ἀλήθειαν, "to know the truth," in the PE. ἐπιγινώσκειν, "to know," can be synonymous with γινώσκειν, "to know," and the perfective use of the preposition ἐπί can be felt—"know completely" (BAGD, 291). The perfective nuance would make Paul's statement stronger, and that would be appropriate for this context; the opponents claimed to know the truth, but believers fully understand the truth. κτίσμα, "creation," specifically refers to food, including those items restricted by the opponents. Although there is nothing specifically cultic about the word ἀπόβλητος, "unclean," the context gives it this nuance here. This is the word's only occurrence in the NT. Moffatt's translation (cited in Guthrie, 93) suggests "tabooed," which emphasizes the cultic context.

Explanation

1 Tim 4:1–5 is a transitional paragraph. It concludes the discussion in 2:1–3:13 and begins a topic that is carried over to 4:6–16. Paul has spelled out the rules for conduct in church, especially for the leadership, and concludes by telling Timothy that what is happening in Ephesus is not unexpected but is in line with the Spirit's prophecy. In the same style as he wrote in chap. 1, Paul describes the nature of the problem and then moves on to Timothy's role in dealing with it (4:6–16).

We learn much about the opponents and their heresy in this short paragaph. They were hypocritical liars, claiming to be believers but having capitulated to Satan, his demons, and his teachings. Their heresy included asceticism—a forbidding of marriage and certain foods (although probably not including drink or financial gain)—but their asceticism was feigned. Paul does not deal with the issue of marriage, having already touched on it in chap. 2, but waits until chap. 5 to deal with it again. He does, however, speak to the problem of food, arguing that God's creation of the world necessitates its goodness, a goodness reaffirmed by the gospel and restated every time a believer says table grace.

The issue of eating food was a continual thorn in Paul's side (cf. Rom 14:1–23; 1 Cor 8; 10:23–33; Col 2:16, 21). From these passages we can deduce several principles. (1) Food is indifferent, an *adiaphoron* (a matter of choice). To eat or not to eat is a personal decision. (2) Abstention may not be demanded, but it can be done voluntarily for the good of the community. This is the determining principle. (3) The one who abstains may not condemn the partaker (Rom 14:3,10; 1 Cor 10:29–30; Col 2:16), and the partaker must not look down upon the abstainer. (4) Once people make their decision, they must be consistent (Rom 14:22–23).

IV. Personal Notes to Timothy (1 Tim 4:6–16)

Bibliography

Baugh, S. M. "'Savior of All People': 1 Tim 4:10 in Context." *WTJ* 54 (1992) 331–40. **Brox, N.** "Προφητεία im ersten Timotheusbrief [1 Tim 1:18; 4:14]." *BZ* 20 (1976) 229–32. **Daube, D.** "Evangelisten und Rabbinen." *ZNW* 48 (1957) 119–26. ———. "The Laying on of Hands." In *The New Testament and Rabbinic Judaism*. London: Athlone, 1956. 244–45. **Duncan, J. G.** "Πιστὸς ὁ λόγος." *ExpTim* 35 (1922) 141. **Edwards, E.** "L'evangelizzatore biblico." *RBR* 7 (1972) 227–57. **Fee, G. D.** *God's Empowering Presence*. 771–76. **Haykin, M. A. G.** "The Fading Vision: The Spirit and Freedom in the Pastoral Epistles." *EvQ* 57 (1985) 291–305. **Hofius, O.** "Zur Auslegungsgeschichte von πρεσβυτέριον 1 Tim 4,14." *ZNW* 62 (1971) 128–29. **Jeremias, J.** "ΠΡΕΣΒΥΤΕΡΙΟΝ ausser christlich bezeugt." *ZNW* 48 (1957) 127–32. **Kilgallen, J. J.** "Reflections on Charisma(ta) in the New Testament." *Studia Missionalia* 41 (1992) 289–323. **Knight, G. W., III.** "1 Timothy 4:9 and Its Saying." In *The Faithful Sayings in the Pastoral Epistles*. 62–79. **Kretschmar, G.** "Die Ordination im frühen Christentum." *FZPT* 22 (1975) 35–69. **Lackmann, P. M.** "Paulus ordiniert Timotheus: Wie der katholische Bischof und Priesteramt entsteht [1 Tim 4:14]." *Bausteine* 12 (1963) 1–4; 13 (1964) 1–6; 14 (1964) 1–4; 15 (1964) 1–5; 16 (1964) 1–4; 15 (1965) 1–4; 16 (1965) 1–5. **Mantel, H.** "Ordination and Appointment in the Period of the Temple." *HTR* 57 (1964) 325–46. **Marshall, I. H.** "Universal Grace and Atonement in the Pastoral Epistles." In *The Grace of God, The Will of Man*, ed. C. Pinnock. Grand Rapids, MI: Baker, 1989. 51–69. **Martin, R. P.** "Aspects of Worship in the New Testament Church." *Vox Evangelica* 2 (1963) 6–32. **Møller, J. G.** "Melanchthon som fortolker af 1 Tim 4:13." *Kirkehistoriske Samlinger* 7 (1968) 520–54. **Oldfather, W. A.,** and **Daly, L. W.** "A Quotation from Menander [Adelphi 995] in the Pastoral Epistles [1 Tim 1:15; 4:9]." *CP* 38 (1943) 202–4. **Pfitzner, V. C.** *Paul and the Agon Motif*. 171–77. **Quinn, J. D.** "Ordination in the Pastoral Epistles." *ICR/C* (1981) 358–69. **Reid, M. L.** "An Exegesis of 1 Timothy 4:6–16." *Faith and Mission* 9 (1991) 51–63. **Schippers, R.** "1 Tim 4:15 ταῦτα μελέτα: Exeget. meditaties bij een pastorale opdracht." *Schriften uitleg.* FS W. H. Gispen, ed. D. S. Attema et al. Kampen: Kok, 1970. 179–94. **Skeat, T. C.** "'Especially the Parchments': A Note on 2 Timothy iv. 13." *JTS* n.s. 30 (1979) 173–77. **Spicq, C.** "Gymnastique et morale d'après 1 Tim. 4,7–8." *RB* 54 (1947) 229–42. **Swete, H. B.** "The Faithful Sayings." *JTS* 18 (1917) 1–7. **Wright, D. F.** "Ordination." *Themelios* 10 (1985) 5–9. **Young, J. R.** "Shepherds, Lead!" *Grace Theological Journal* 6 (1985) 329–35.

Translation

[6] *By placing these things before the brethren, you will be a good servant of Christ Jesus, being trained [daily] by the words of the faith and of the good teaching that* [a] *you have followed.* [b] [7] *But reject the profane and silly myths; rather train yourself for godliness;* [8] *for bodily exercise is of value for a little while, but godliness is of value for all things because it holds a promise for the present life and for the coming life.* [9] *Trustworthy is the saying and worthy of complete acceptance,* [10] *for with respect to this reason* [c] *we are toiling and struggling,* [d] *since*

We have placed [our] hope [e] *in the living God,*
who is the savior of all people,
particularly of those who believe.

[11] *Command these things and teach.* [12] *Let no one treat you contemptuously because of your youth, but be an example for the faithful in speech, in conduct, in love, in faith,[f] in purity.* [13] *Until I come, be devoted to the reading, to the exhortation, to the teaching.* [14] *Do not neglect the gift that is in you, which was given to you through prophecy with [the] laying on of the hands of the body of elders.[g]* [15] *Continually practice these things, immerse yourself in them, in order that your progress might be visible[h] to all.* [16] *Watch yourself and the teaching; be persistent in them; for by doing this you will save both yourself and those hearing you.*

Notes

[a]The dative ᾗ, "that," is replaced by the genitive ἧς, "of which," by A 365 *pc* because of attraction of the relative pronoun to its antecedent διδασκαλίας, teaching."

[b]The perfect-tense παρηκολούθηκας, "you have followed," is replaced by the aorist παρηκολούθησας, "you followed," in C F G *pc*. The perfect tense is better suited to the context: Timothy has followed the teachings of the gospel and should continue to do so.

[c]F G 1881 and TR insert καί, "both," before κοπιῶμεν, "we are toiling." It is omitted in ℵ A C D P Ψ 0241[vid] 6 33 81 365 1175 1739 *pc* lat sy; Ambst.

[d]ἀγωνιζόμεθα, "we are struggling," is replaced with ὀνειδιζόμεθα, "we suffer reproach," in ℵ[2] D 0241[vid] 1739 1881 TR latt sy co. However, the text used here has the better MS support (ℵ* A C F G K Ψ 33 104 326 1175 1505 *al*; Ambst), and the idea of struggle fits the context better. It makes a logical parallel to toil and continues the athletic metaphor from vv 7–8 (cf. Ellicott, 60; Lock, xxxvii; *TCGNT*[2], 574).

[e]The perfect-tense ἠλπίκαμεν, "we have placed [our] hope," is replaced by the aorist ἠλπίσαμεν, "we hoped," by D* 33.

[f]ἐν πνεύματι, "in spirit," is inserted before ἐν πίστει, "in faith," by TR, possibly owing to Col 1:8 (*TCGNT*[1], 642) or 2 Cor 6:2 (Ellicott, 62; cf. Fee, *God's Empowering Presence*, 771). Its omission is supported by ℵ A C D F G I Ψ 6 33 81 104 629 1175 1505 1739 1881 *pc* latt sy co; Cl.

[g]πρεσβυτερίου, "body of elders," is replaced with πρεσβυτέρου, "elder," by ℵ* 69* 1881[c], which would remove the apparent contradiction with 2 Tim 1:6 (see *Comment*), the elder probably being Paul.

[h]ἐν, "in," is inserted before πᾶσιν, "all," by D[2] Ψ 1881 TR vg[mss]. Its omission, possibly in imitation of Col 1:8, is supported by ℵ A C D* F G 6 33 81 104 1739 *pc* lat co.

Form/Structure/Setting

Paul established a pattern in chap. 1 that surfaces here and also in chap. 6. He first discusses the Ephesian heresy and what is wrong with it (1 Tim 1:3–17; 4:1–5; 6:2b–10) and then moves on to encourage Timothy to stand strong and continue the battle (1 Tim 1:18–20; 4:6–16; 6:11–16). He recognizes that a Christian mentor must both instruct and encourage (cf. L. T. Johnson, 168). 4:6–16 is a personal look at Paul's love and concern for Timothy with regard to both his ministry and his personal well-being. It is an admission that even Timothy must be careful not to fall prey to the wiles of the opponents. The opponents are never out of sight; many of the characteristics that Paul encourages Timothy to follow stand in contrast to the opponents' characteristics. Timothy is to be an example in speech (the opponents are babblers), conduct (the opponents have brought the church into disrepute), love (which they have abandoned), faith (which they have shipwrecked), and purity (which they have stained; see *Introduction*, "The Ephesian Heresy"). By reminding Timothy that he has the gifts for ministry, Paul cautions the opponents who are opposing Timothy (v 14). There is a sense of urgency throughout this passage in Paul's concern both for Timothy's personal well-being and for his ministry, but this should not be interpreted to indicate that Timothy has stopped ministering. This would not be in keeping with what is known of him elsewhere. Timothy evidently was meeting fierce opposition, was dispirited, and needed encouragement.

It is often pointed out that in the PE Paul attacks the opponents and not their teaching (cf. Karris, *JBL* 92 [1973] 549–64). However, while Paul does not deal with the nature of the heresy (although it is touched on in the preceding verses) in a positive tone, he does stress correct teaching and proper conduct, all the while implicitly drawing a contrast with the opponents' incorrect teaching and disgraceful conduct. Timothy is to follow Paul's instructions, making the gospel central to his personal life and his ministry. He is to pursue godliness because its goodness extends forever. Paul's God is the savior of all people, not just a select few with their myths. Timothy is to set an example for all and persevere. As Guthrie comments, "That the best refutation of error is a positive presentation of the truth is a principle which the Church in every age constantly needs to learn" (95).

Structurally two devices tie this section together. First, the term ταῦτα, "these things," occurs three times (vv 6, 11, 15; cf. αὐτοῖς, "in them," in v 16) referring to the previous instructions; its repetition gives a sense of flow throughout the eleven verses. Second, the most significant literary feature is the twelve imperatives, ten of them being paired together, giving seven distinct thoughts. (1) As the initial and overall theme of the passage, Paul tells Timothy that if he follows these instructions, being trained daily in the gospel and its doctrinal instructions, he will continue to be a good minister (v 6). (2) Timothy should avoid myths but exercise for the goal of godliness (vv 7–10). (3) He should command these instructions, and teach (v 11). (4) He should not let people look down on him because he is young but be a good example (v 12). (5) He should devote himself to Scripture (v 13). (6) He should not forget that he has the gifts for ministry (v 14). (7) He should continually practice these instructions, immerse himself in them, so that his progress will be visible to all (v 15). He should watch himself and the teaching, remain in them; for by persevering he will save himself and those who listen to him (v 16). One can view vv 6–16 as two paragraphs because in vv 11–16 there is a stronger personal element and a stronger concentration of imperatives (vv 6–10 contain a general saying and a "we" statement [v 10]). However, the pattern of parallel and contrasting imperatives found in v 11 and v 12 is also present in v 7, and the topic is basically the same, so it is best not to divide vv 6–16 too strictly. V 11 is a transitional verse that could be included with either the preceding or following paragraph. Since v 6a is a similar summary injunction, v 11 should be placed in the second paragraph so that it is structurally parallel to v 6a.

Stylistically, there are three other devices worth noting. (1) The imperatives are all linear in aspect, as is the participle in v 6, giving a sense of urgency to Paul's instructions. (2) Paul employs athletic imagery in the first several verses. Timothy is to exercise toward the goal of godliness because although physical exercise has some value for a while, godliness has value in all ways. Paul himself has toiled and struggled (the latter word continuing the imagery) in his ministry. L. T. Johnson points out that in fact much of the terminology employs "commonplace images for the moral life" (166). (3) Paul cites the third of the five faithful sayings. For a discussion of the faithful sayings in general, see *Form/Structure/Setting* on 1 Tim 1:12–17 and the *Bibliography* there. The formula of introduction in v 9 gives an indication that there is a quotation, but it is difficult to determine what the quotation actually is. The quotation is given in support of Paul's admonition that Timothy should avoid the heresy and train himself for godliness (v 7). The possibilities for identifying the quotation are v 8 (Ellicott, Lock, Barrett, Knight), v 8a (Towner), v 8b (NASB, Chrysostom, Bernard, Kelly, Fee, L. T. Johnson), v 10 (NEB, Roloff), or v 10b (NIV). Oberlinner believes it extends to the entire paragraph, v 8 and v 10, as a comment on εὐσέβεια, "godliness" (196). Hanson says the phrase simply "gives solemnity to the text as a whole when it seems to be growing too pedestrian" ([1983] 91) and identifies the saying with vv 11b–13. But the passage is not pedestrian, and the poetic structure of both v 8 and v 10 makes a quotation likely.

It is difficult to reach a decision on the issue of identifying the quotation because the criteria are subjective and because both v 8 and v 10 fit the criteria. (1) Neither verse has better parallel structure, but more important, only a portion of the saying may be given, and its parallelism may therefore not be apparent. (2) Both verses contain themes appropriate to a faithful saying. (3) Both verses fit the context of godliness (v 7). (4) Is v 10 a reflection and application of v 8, or is v 8 a preparatory statement for v 10? (5) Are the faithful sayings consistent among themselves, and if so, which of these verses best fits with the other sayings? Except for 1 Tim 3:1 all the other faithful sayings deal with the issue of salvation, which favors v 10b. Added to this is the fact that v 10b is similar to the faithful saying in 1 Tim 1:15. (6) Do either of these verses contain language foreign to the PE? (7) Perhaps Paul quotes the saying because the language is similar to what he has just said. For example, toil (v 10) may continue the athletic imagery of v 8 because v 10 is a reflection on the faithful saying in v 8, or Paul's use of the metaphor in v 8 may suggest the language of v 10a that leads to the faithful saying. (8) εἰς τοῦτο, "for this reason," can point forward or backward (see *Comment*), so it does not provide a clue. (9) V 8 is introduced by γάρ, "for," as is the faithful saying in 2 Tim 2:11, but v 10b is introduced with ὅτι as is the saying in 1 Tim 1:15.

With these problems noted, however, some tentative conclusions can be drawn. V 8b ("because it holds a promise for the present life and for the coming life") does not sound like a statement that would be transmitted as an independent saying, suggesting that v 8a is the saying and v 8b is Paul's comment on why the saying is true. V 8a contains two rare words: σωματικός, "bodily" (elsewhere in the NT only in Luke 3:22), and γυμνασία, "exercise" (only here in the NT), suggesting that the clause was not written by Paul, and yet v 8a also contains εὐσέβεια, "godliness," which is a dominant theme in the PE. It seems doubtful that v 10a is from a hymn or creed. It does not contain the same parallelism as does v 10b, the personal nature of the experience it describes does not lend itself to independent transmission, and εἰς τοῦτο γάρ . . . ὅτι, "for this reason . . . since," does not suggest that v 10a and v 10b originally belonged together. V 10b is more in line with the other faithful sayings because all except one (1 Tim 3:1) deal with the issue of salvation. It is similar to the ideas in 1 Tim 2:4–6, which might contain a creedal citation. V 10b gives the ultimate reason that Timothy should pursue godliness—salvation—and as such a hymnic citation would function well in supporting Paul's argument. Preference should thus be given to v 10a as Paul's comment on the introductory formula, enforcing the thought of v 9 and v 10b as the actual hymnic fragment. Paul affirms that the saying is trustworthy (v 9), and the saying explains why Paul labors at his missionary endeavors (v 10a), since:

> We have placed [our] hope in the living God,
>> who is the savior of all people,
>> particularly of those who believe.

ὅτι, "since," introduces the direct discourse and could be translated simply with quotation marks. μάλιστα πιστῶν, "particularly of those who believe," could be part of the hymn or it could be Paul's comment on the saying, making sure that no one misunderstood it to be teaching universal salvation. Both v 8a and v 10b are separated from the introductory formula (v 9), which is not the case with any of the other faithful sayings. The origin of the saying has little importance for the exegesis of these verses.

Comment

6a Ταῦτα ὑποτιθέμενος τοῖς ἀδελφοῖς καλὸς ἔσῃ διάκονος Χριστοῦ Ἰησοῦ, "By placing these things before the brethren, you will be a good servant of Christ Jesus." If Timothy continues to teach the gospel as Paul has been describing it, he knows that despite the opposition Timothy will encounter, he will be a good servant of Christ Jesus. The encouragement does not mean that Timothy has ceased ministering; Timothy was facing tremendous opposition and the encouragement was timely. This verse almost functions as the title of the section. It introduces the basic themes to be discussed: Timothy's role as a teacher; the place of Scripture and doctrine; concern for Timothy's personal and ministerial well-being; and an implicit contrast with the opponents.

ὑποτιθέμενος is usually understood as a conditional participle, "if you place." This might be suggested by the future-tense "you will be [ἔσῃ] a good servant," but from what is known of Timothy elsewhere, there is no reason to think he was not following Paul's earlier instructions. Translating it as a participle of means keeps the verse in line with Timothy's character; by continuing (the participle is linear in aspect) to put these instructions before the church, he will continue to be in the right, despite the opposition. ὑποτίθεσθαι has a range of meaning stretching from "to suggest" to "to order" (BAGD, 848). It occurs in the middle voice only here in the NT; it has a different meaning in the active voice ("to risk"; cf. Acts 16:4), and it is therefore difficult to fix a precise meaning here. As is the case elsewhere in the PE, Paul's language is stronger when thinking of the opponents (cf. 1 Tim 1:3) and milder when dealing with others (cf. 1 Tim 5:1). If he is here thinking of the Ephesian church in general, the positive translation "by suggesting these things" would be appropriate. But since ταῦτα, "these things," refers to the whole of the epistle (see below), which up to this point has been relatively harsh, Paul probably would not be characterizing his teaching as mere suggestions.

It is Paul's practice in the PE and elsewhere (cf. 1 Tim 3:4) to sum up a previous discussion through the use of ταῦτα, "these things." He does so three times in this section (1 Tim 4:6, 11, 15). Although 1 Tim 4:1–5 is an important part of the epistle, it is not so important as to warrant this threefold repetition, so Paul is probably thinking of the entire epistle up to this point. If Timothy continues to teach about law, grace, salvation, and conduct in the church, he will continue to be a good servant. ἀδελφοί, "brethren, brothers," is a common and primitive designation for the Christian community in the PE (1 Tim 6:2; 2 Tim 4:21; cf. 1 Tim 5:1) and in Paul (cf. H. F. von Soden, *TDNT* 1:145–46), which the NRSV translates "brothers and sisters" to make it inclusive. It continues the imagery of the church as a family from 3:15, imagery repeated in 5:1. On καλός, "good," see *Comment* on 1 Tim 1:8. διάκονος, "servant," is the same word used earlier to describe the office of deacon, but it is used here with the generic meaning of one who serves, a common use throughout Paul (cf. 1 Tim 3:8).

6b ἐντρεφόμενος τοῖς λόγοις τῆς πίστεως καὶ τῆς καλῆς διδασκαλίας ᾗ παρηκολούθηκας, "being trained [daily] by the words of the faith and of the good teaching that you have followed." As Timothy endeavors to do his work as God's minister, he is to draw his daily training from the gospel to which he has committed himself. This theme of relying on the gospel is enlarged later in this section (vv 13–16). The gospel is the backbone of Timothy's ministry, the standard against which the opponents are to be judged and found to be false.

ἐντρεφόμενος, "being trained," is a difficult word to translate. It does not occur again in the NT and is only rarely found in secular Greek. BAGD lists its range of meaning as "bring up, rear, train in τινί someth[ing]" (269; cf. LSJ, 577; Dibelius-Conzelmann, 68). Because ἐντρεφόμενος is linear in aspect, it describes not Timothy's past upbringing but his day-to-day habits (Chrysostom, "Homily 12"; NPNF 13:445). Most translators use a word such as "nourished," although usually no support is given for this translation (but the metaphor of teaching as food is used elsewhere; cf. 1 Cor 3:2; Heb 5:12–14). Because the context of this passage is one of doctrine, however, the metaphor "train" is to be preferred to that of "nourish." The issue is not one of sustenance but one of correct doctrine. 2 Tim 3:14–17 repeats a similar thought.

The primary source of Timothy's support is the gospel, but to make the point clear Paul distinguishes between the gospel itself (τοῖς λόγοις τῆς πίστεως, "the words of the faith") and the doctrine contained in that gospel (τοῖς λόγοις . . . τῆς καλῆς διδασκαλίας, "the words . . . of the good teaching"; cf. ὑγιαινούσῃ διδασκαλίᾳ, "healthy teaching," in 1 Tim 1:10). There are three passages in the PE that support this interpretation. Timothy is to honor elders who are involved in both preaching and teaching (ἐν λόγῳ καὶ διδασκαλίᾳ, "in word and teaching"; 1 Tim 5:17). If someone teaches another gospel (ἑτεροδιδασκαλεῖ) that does not agree with the healthy words (ὑγιαίνουσιν λόγοις) of Jesus Christ and the teaching (διδασκαλία) that is in accordance with godliness, he is conceited (1 Tim 6:3; the grammar does not allow λόγοις, "words," and διδασκαλία, "teaching," to be a hendiadys). An elder must hold firmly to the faithful word just as it has been taught (τοῦ κατὰ τὴν διδαχὴν πιστοῦ λόγου) so that he can instruct others in sound doctrine (ἐν τῇ διδασκαλίᾳ τῇ ὑγιαινούσῃ; Titus 1:9). From these three parallel passages it is clear that when λόγος, "word," and διδασκαλία, "teaching," are used together, they refer to different but related entities. Paul is differentiating between the basic gospel message ("the words of the faith") and the doctrinal teaching that comes out of it ("the good teaching"). This interpretation is confirmed later in chap. 4 where Paul separates preaching, exhortation, and doctrinal instruction (1 Tim 4:13; cf. 1 Tim 1:10). A reading of the gospel should always be accompanied by the correct interpretation or doctrinal understanding of the gospel. This emphasis on doctrine is similar to Paul's teaching elsewhere that Timothy must handle the gospel correctly (2 Tim 3:14–16). τῆς πίστεως, "of the faith," and τῆς καλῆς διδασκαλίας, "of the good teaching," both modify λόγοις, "words." For the creedal use of πίστις, "faith," cf. 1 Tim 1:2 and Reid, *Faith and Mission* 9 (1991) 52.

λόγος, "word," is used with three different meanings in the PE: it describes speech (1 Tim 4:12; Titus 2:8; cf. 2 Tim 2:17); it is used in the pronouncement formula for the faithful sayings (1 Tim 1:15; 3:1; 4:9; 2 Tim 2:11; 3:8); and it can be synonymous with the gospel (2 Tim 1:9; 2:15; 4:2, 15; Titus 1:9; 2:5; cf. 1 Tim 4:5, where it refers to God's word spoken over creation and its close relationship to the gospel), specifically Paul's gospel (2 Tim 1:13; 2:9; Titus 1:3). It is used several times in the construction ὑγιαίνοντες λόγοι, "healthy words" (1 Tim 6:3; 2 Tim 1:13; 2:17; cf. 2 Tim 4:3; Titus 1:9; and the discussion in the *Comment* on 1 Tim 1:10), a use that parallels the construction here. This verse is a typically Pauline appeal to correct doctrine. The phrase ᾗ παρηκολούθηκας, "that you have followed," is a reference to Timothy's long association with the gospel (cf. 2 Tim 1:5 and 2 Tim 3:10 of Timothy having followed Paul's life and teaching). BAGD (618–19) shows that παρακολουθεῖν can mean both "to follow" in the sense of "understanding, follow faithfully" (cf. 2 Tim 3:10) and "to investigate" (cf. Luke 1:3) with the dative of the thing followed or investigated. The idea of Timothy investigating the gospel is foreign to the PE while the idea of his continual adherence to it is not, so the interpretation "follow faithfully" is preferable.

7 τοὺς δὲ βεβήλους καὶ γραώδεις μύθους παραιτοῦ· γύμναζε δὲ σεαυτὸν πρὸς εὐσέβειαν, "But reject the profane and silly myths; rather train yourself for godliness." We meet here the first pair of imperatives so characteristic of this section (see *Form/Structure/Setting*); and just as in v 12, the imperatives balance each other. In contrast to following the gospel (v 6), Timothy must avoid the Ephesian heresy described here as "profane and silly myths" and exercise, much as an athlete does, for the goal of godliness. The athletic metaphor continues into the next verse, and the issue of whether Paul is calling Timothy to physical exercise or asceticism will be discussed there. The use of δέ, "but," and the word order make it clear that Paul is contrasting the gospel with the heresy (Jeremias; Pfitzner, *Agon Motif,* 173; Fee, 103), specifically contrasting godliness with myths. Timothy is to be trained by the gospel and its theology, but is to reject the silly and profane myths. Spicq discusses the role of exercise in the Greek educational process, emphasizing that the training included is not just physical but also moral and intellectual training (*RB* 54 [1947] 229–42). Pfitzner (*Agon Motif*) points out how Paul uses the imagery but with a significant difference in meaning.

The two occurrences of δέ ("but . . . rather") set up the contrasts made by this verse. The first δέ contrasts the gospel (v 6) with the opponents' myths (v 7a) while the second contrasts the myths with true godliness (v 7b). παραιτοῦ, "avoid," is perhaps too mild a translation. Timothy is to stay away from, actively "reject," the opponents' interpretation of the gospel. The linear aspect of the tense underlines the continual need for Timothy's attention at this point. The term is used elsewhere to tell Titus to avoid a factious person (probably the opponents; Titus 3:10) and to tell Timothy to refuse to enroll younger widows (1 Tim 5:11) and (in a similar passage) to avoid stupid and senseless controversies because they only give birth to quarrels (2 Tim 2:23). The presence of the article (τοὺς . . . μύθους, "the...

myths") indicates that Paul is thinking of the Ephesian heresy. βέβηλος, "profane," describes what is opposed to a holy God (cf. 1 Tim 1:9).

γραώδης, "silly," occurs in the NT only here. It refers to the stereotyped kind of stories bandied back and forth between gossipy women who have nothing better to do, conveying the idea of "limitless credulity" (Kelly, 99). Knight qualifies the metaphor by saying that it does not carry "any negative overtones about either age or sex (cf., e.g., 5:1 for Paul's own insistence that there be no negative attitudes relating to these matters)" (195; cf. Towner's similar comment about "no intentional chauvinism" [107 n.]). One wonders, however, whether Paul would have had the same sensitivity as a modern editor to this particular issue. Although the word is rare (LSJ, 360), the idea is a common sarcastic expression in philosophical argumentation (Epictetus *Diss.* 2.16.39; Strabo 1.2.2; Lucian *Philops.* 9). It contrasts with the disciplined training in godliness. This word, perhaps the harshest description of the opponents' theology, is important in an overall understanding of the PE. It shows that the theology of the opponents is vacuous, no better than prattle. It also explains why Paul does not spend more time arguing against the heresy itself; a person cannot argue against prattle (cf. *Introduction*, "Themes in the PE," and Reid, *Faith and Mission* 9 [1991] 52).

γυμνάζειν, "to train," is an athletic metaphor, contrasting Timothy's actions with those of the opponents. Rather than pursuing silly myths, Timothy should actively, rigorously pursue the true goal, godliness. The metaphor is continued into the next verse as Paul emphasizes the significance of this charge. The verb does not occur again in Paul (cf. Heb 12:11; 2 Pet 2:14) although the cognate noun (γυμνασία, "exercise") is used in the next verse. Paul uses athletic metaphors elsewhere as well (cf. 1 Tim 6:12; 2 Tim 2:5; cf. 1 Cor 9:24–27). πρός, "for," may indicate the goal of Timothy's exercise, but Knight thinks it indicates "that *in* which one exercises . . . as is evidenced by v. 8, where εὐσέβεια [godliness] is placed in parallel with σωματικὴ γυμνασία [bodily exercise] itself" (197). εὐσέβεια, "godliness," in the PE is a technical term for a life totally consecrated to God, carrying an emphasis on the observable aspects of this type of life (cf. 1 Tim 2:2; 3:16). Pfitzner emphasizes the difference between the imagery used of athletes and Paul's use:

> It is not the self-centred ascetic struggle of the individual for his own moral and religious perfection, but the training necessary for the unhindered pursuit of God's purposes. One can imagine Timothy's enemies have accused him of moral laxity since he refuses to follow their demands of abstention. But he too is to practise a γυμνασία, a vigorous development and application of all his strength and ability that he might serve the glory of God with every thought and action. Such exercise is not restricted to a negative physical asceticism, nor even to the self-disciplinary "enkrateia" of I Cor 9:25ff., but rather implies a positive developing of his strength nourished above all "by the words of faith" (v.6). (*Agon Motif,* 174–75)

8 ἡ γὰρ σωματικὴ γυμνασία πρὸς ὀλίγον ἐστιν ὠφέλιμος, ἡ δὲ εὐσέβεια πρὸς πάντα ὠφέλιμός ἐστιν ἐπαγγελίαν ἔχουσα ζωῆς τῆς νῦν καὶ τῆς μελλούσης, "for bodily exercise is of value for a little while, but godliness is of value for all things because it holds a promise for the present life and for the coming life." To support his statement in v 7a that Timothy should strive for/in godliness, Paul spells out the benefits of godliness and continues the imagery. Physical exercise has some value for this life, but godliness has value for both this life and the life to

come. Whereas the opponents' teaching is ungodly and silly, godliness has value
for all things. The two halves of the verse are parallel:

ἡ γὰρ	σωματικὴ	γυμνασία	πρὸς ὀλίγον	ἐστὶν ὠφέλιμος,
ἡ δὲ	εὐσέβεια		πρὸς πάντα	ὠφέλιμός ἐστιν.

They contrast bodily exercise, that which is outward and visible, with godliness,
that which is internal but yet eventually will show itself outwardly.

Many understand the basic argument to be that although physical exercise, or
perhaps asceticism, has some value, godliness has more value. The main problem
with this interpretation is that the text does not say that godliness has more value;
it says that godliness has value forever (v 8b). The issue is not how much value
exercise and godliness have, but how long they last. The difficult phrases are πρὸς
ὀλίγον, "for a little while," and πρὸς πάντα, "for all things." The profit gained by
godliness "holds a promise for the present life and for the coming life" (v 8b).
This is the primary significance of the passage, and it expresses a temporal concept (cf. Spicq, 1:507). Therefore, while πρὸς ὀλίγον can mean "for (only) a little,"
in this context it must also be temporal ("for a little while"). It does not exclude
the sense of "for a little" but clarifies that the relative value of bodily exercise is
primarily because of its temporal nature. The only other place this phrase occurs
is in Jas 4:14, where it also is temporal: "For you are a mist that appears for a little
time [πρὸς ὀλίγον] and then vanishes." ὀλίγον, "little," also occurs with other prepositions where the sense is temporal (ἐν ὀλίγῳ, "in a little while"; Acts 26:28; Eph
3:3; μετ' ὀλίγον, "after a little while," in nonbiblical Greek; cf. BAGD, 564, which
has other examples of πρὸς ὀλίγον in secular Greek with a temporal meaning).

The problem with this temporal interpretation is that the phrase πρὸς πάντα,
"for all things," which is in sharp contrast to πρὸς ὀλίγον, does not occur anywhere else in the NT, and πᾶς, "all," is not used elsewhere with any sense of time.
There are, however, several points to be taken into consideration. (1) V 8b indicates that the expression should be understood temporally. This is so clear that it
must be determinative. (2) The rarity of the πρὸς πάντα expression may be an
evidence that it is being used with an unusual meaning. (3) Paul may use this
specific construction (πρὸς πάντα) because he wants to emphasize the extreme
difference between bodily exercise and godliness. He could have said "but godliness has value both for this age and the age to come," which would have paralleled
the first half of the verse nicely (except that there would not have been an actual
parallel to πρὸς ὀλίγον). But the value of godliness extends far beyond temporal
limits, and to make that emphasis explicit Paul says "but godliness has value not
only for all time but also for all things." (The argument that uses v 8b to define
πρὸς ὀλίγον is less compelling if v 8a is the faithful saying and v 8b is Paul's comment on it. This would mean that v 8a was transmitted in isolation and that πρὸς
ὀλίγον, in contrast to πρὸς πάντα, would have meant "for a little." But the juxta-
position of v 8b with v 8a shows that as far as Paul is concerned πρὸς ὀλίγον means
"for a little while.")

There are three interpretations of σωματικὴ γυμνασία, "bodily exercise." (1)
Some argue that by physical exercise Paul means asceticism (Calvin; Ellicott; Ber-
nard; A. Oepke, *TDNT* 1:775–76; Easton; Jeremias; Dibelius-Conzelmann; Pfitzner,
Agon Motif, 172–73; Brox; Houlden; Towner, *NTS* 32 [1986] 433). He would be

saying that a little asceticism is good, with the emphasis on "little." Its goodness would not result from a dualism that sees the material world as evil, and the basic point would be to keep exercise and godliness in proportion. However, it seems unlikely that after condemning *in toto* the opponents' asceticism in vv 3–5, he would turn around and commend even a modified form of asceticism. Also, the word does not mean "asceticism"; it means "exercise" (cf. LSJ, 362; MM, 133). If v 8a is the faithful saying and is a rebuttal to excessive asceticism, it seems doubtful that it would have expressed the idea in these words. Looking at v 8a in isolation, there is nothing that suggests that asceticism is the issue.

(2) Others argue that σωματικὴ γυμνασία is a call for some physical exercise (Chrysostom, Lock, Falconer, Spicq, Gealy, Guthrie, Kelly). Reference is made to 1 Tim 5:23, where Paul says that Timothy should drink a little wine for his stomach's sake, assuming that a weak stomach is the result of a weak body requiring exercise, which is not necessarily a valid assumption. The verse does say exercise has profit, albeit for a short time. However, to say that Paul is commending exercise does not fit the context. There is nothing in this passage to suggest that Paul is concerned with Timothy's health; he is urging him to avoid the heresy and pursue godliness.

(3) The third interpretation sees the phrase "for bodily exercise is of value for a little while" merely as a literary foil against which Paul wants to say that "godliness is of value for all things." It is a poetic creation to balance the real emphasis: godliness. The phrase does assert the value of exercise, but the point of the phrase is not to encourage Timothy to exercise physically; that is foreign to the context.

ζωή, "life," denotes not mere existence but has a richer, fuller meaning, describing an abundant type of life that is promised to those in Christ (cf. *Comment* on 1 Tim 1:17). Significant is Knight's argument (*Faithful Sayings,* 74–76; id., *Pastoral Epistles,* 200) that the phrase means not "promise for life" but rather "promise of life," reading ζωῆς, "of life," as a qualitative or objective genitive indicating the content of the promise (cf. BAGD, 280). He cites the similar use of the genitive elsewhere (2 Tim 1:1; 2 Pet 3:4; Heb 9:15) and other passages with ἐπαγγελία, "promise," where the content of the promise is clarified (Rom 4:13; Heb 4:1; 1 John 2:25). Timothy is to train for godliness because only in it can one find true eschatological existence, abundant life.

σωματικός "physical, bodily," occurs elsewhere in the NT only in Luke 3:22. γυμνασία, "exercise," was evidently a significant part of the Ephesian youth culture (cf. Swete, *JTS* 18 [1917] 3; Spicq, *RB* 54 [1947] 229–42), and so this verse speaks directly to the historical situation. ὠφέλιμος, "valuable, advantageous, beneficial," occurs two other times in the NT, both in the PE: Scripture is God-breathed and profitable for teaching (2 Tim 3:16); applying oneself to good deeds is profitable for people (Titus 3:8). The commendation to physical exercise, although it is not the main point of the passage, may contain an implicit condemnation of the Ephesian heresy, if in fact it has Stoic influences, since Stoicism eschewed exercise (Dibelius-Conzelmann, 68 n. 4). It also contrasts with the extreme emphasis on physical exercise in the Greco-Roman world (cf. Spicq, *RB* 54 [1947] 229–42). By saying that physical exercise is of some value, there is an implicit limitation; it is only of some good.

ἔχουσα, "because it holds," is a causal participle explaining why godliness is of more value than exercise. ἐπαγγελία, "promise," is a common word in the NT;

with one exception (Acts 23:21) it refers to the promise of God (cf. 2 Tim 1:1). The theme of God as the author of life is explained in v 10, which describes God as the "living God." In Paul ἐπαγγελία refers to God's promise of salvation and all that entails; it often is used in contrast to the law (cf. J. Schniewind and G. Friedrich, *TDNT* 2:581–84; Gal 3). It therefore is not a reference to earthly riches. The phrase ἐπαγγελία ζωῆς, "promise of life," also occurs in 2 Tim 1:1.

The twofold promise, that godliness bears benefits both in this age and the age to come, parallels Jesus' promise that "there is no one who has left house or brothers or sisters or mother or father or children or lands, for my sake and for the gospel, who will not receive a hundredfold now in this time, houses and brothers and sisters and mothers and children and lands, with persecutions, and in the age to come eternal life" (Mark 10:29–30; cf. Matt 19:29). It is tempting to view v 8, especially if it is the faithful saying, as a reflection of Jesus' teaching (Lock, 51; Scott, 49–50; Kelly, 100–101; Knight, *Faithful Sayings*, 77). Others, assuming its independent existence from this text, see its origin in a philosophical critique of physical exercise (Dibelius-Conzelmann, 68), while yet others suggest the possibility of a Jewish origin (Lock; Gealy; cf. *m. Abot* 4.2). However, it is distinctly Christian in this context. ζωῆς τῆς νῦν, "present life," "life of the now," is a common use of νῦν, "now," to describe the present age (1 Tim 6:17; 2 Tim 4:10; Titus 2:12; cf. Rom 3:26; 8:18; 11:5; 2 Cor 8:14; Gal 4:25; cf. 2 Pet 3:7). ζωῆς . . . τῆς μελλούσης, "the coming life," "life of what is coming," is also a common use of μέλλειν, "to be about to," to describe the age to come (1 Tim 6:19; cf. Eph 1:21; cf. Matt 12:32; Heb 6:5; cf. Matt 3:7; Luke 13:9; Acts 24:25; Rom 5:14; 8:38; 1 Cor 3:22; Col 2:17; Heb 2:5; 13:14).

9 πιστὸς ὁ λόγος καὶ πάσης ἀποδοχῆς ἄξιος, "Trustworthy is the saying and worthy of complete acceptance." This introduces the third faithful saying in the PE (cf. discussion of the faithful sayings in *Form/Structure/Setting* on 1 Tim 1:12–17). This introductory formula is identical to that of the first saying in 1 Tim 1:15. See *Form/Structure/Setting* for the reasons for choosing v 10b as the saying.

10a εἰς τοῦτο γὰρ κοπιῶμεν καὶ ἀγωνιζόμεθα, "for with respect to this reason we are toiling and struggling." In order to emphasize the significance of the faithful saying (v 10b), Paul includes this phrase after the normal introductory formula (v 9). Not only is the faithful saying trustworthy and worthy of total acceptance, but it in fact expresses the focus of Paul's missionary labors. What Paul has worked on and struggled with is proclaiming the gospel of the living God who has offered salvation to all people. The "we" could refer to Paul and the apostles, to Paul and Timothy, or to Paul and his other coworkers. Owing to the personal nature of this passage, Paul is probably thinking of Timothy and himself. Hanson ([1983] 91–92) compares this passage to Col 1:29 and conjectures that 1 Tim 3:14–4:10 is a cc..1mentary on Col 1:24–29 because of the similarities of content and order. But the similarities are general and simply indicate that Paul repeats some of the same ideas from epistle to epistle.

γάρ, "for," looks forward to the faithful saying. εἰς τοῦτο, "with respect to this reason," is a common expression in the NT that can look back at the previous discussion (Mark 1:38; 1 Thess 3:3; 1 Pet 2:21) or look forward to the upcoming discussion (John 18:37 [2x]; Acts 9:21; 26:16; Rom 14:9; 2 Cor 2:29; 1 Pet 3:9 [?]; 4:6; 1 John 3:8; Jude 4). In this context it is looking forward: the reason Paul toils and struggles is that he has set his hope on the living God. κοπιῶμεν, "we are toiling," refers to hard labor. In the PE it describes hard-working elders (1 Tim 5:17) and farmers (2 Tim 2:6), and in Paul it is a common term describing the work of Christians (Rom 16:6, 12 [2x]; 1 Cor 16:16; 1 Thess 5:12; cf. 1 Cor 3:8; 15:58; 2 Cor 10:15; 1 Thess 1:3; also Gal 6:17; Eph 4:28; 2 Thess 3:8) and especially Paul's own missionary labors (1 Cor 4:12; 15:10; Gal 4:11; Phil 2:16; Col 1:29; cf. 2 Cor 6:5; 11:23, 27; 2 Thess 2:9; 3:5; cf. F. Hauck, *TDNT* 3:827–30; Spicq, 1:509; cf. ἐργάτης, "laborer," 2 Tim 2:15). From several examples it appears to refer to hard work, specifically manual labor: Peter toiled at fishing all night and caught nothing (Luke 5:5); Jesus rested at the Samaritan well because he was so wearied (John 4:6); Jesus invited all who were toiling to come to him, take his yoke, and find true rest (Matt 11:28); Paul set an example for the Ephesian church by toiling for his own living, which suggests tent making (Acts 20:35). This nuance of hard manual work strengthens the force of our passage; Paul agonized at his missionary work because God is the savior of all people. This verb and the following one are linear in aspect, emphasizing day-to-day labors. κοπιᾶν, "to toil," is also used in Phil 2:16 as an athletic metaphor, and perhaps its use here is intended to continue the athletic metaphor from vv 7–8. Since ἀγωνιζόμεθα, "we are struggling," in the next phrase contains athletic overtones as well, it probably is the case here.

Parallel to κοπιῶμεν is ἀγωνιζόμεθα, "we are struggling," which continues the imagery of vv 7–8 because it refers to the struggle of an athletic contest (BAGD, 15; Spicq, 1:509). This same imagery is continued when Paul tells Timothy to "fight the good fight" (1 Tim 6:12) and in his assessment of his own life when he says, "I have fought the good fight" (2 Tim 4:7). Conflict is part of Paul's (1 Thess 2:2) and Epaphras's (Col 4:12) lives, and all Christians struggle in a sinful world (Phil 1:30). κοπιᾶν, "to toil," and ἀγωνίζεσθαι, "to struggle," are joined again when Paul says, "For this I toil [κοπιῶ], striving [ἀγωνιζόμενος] with all the energy which he mightily inspires within me" (Col 1:29). See *Note* d for the variant "suffer reproach."

10b ὅτι ἠλπίκαμεν ἐπὶ θεῷ ζῶντι, ὅς ἐστιν σωτὴρ πάντων ἀνθρώπων μάλιστα πιστῶν, "since 'We have placed [our] hope in the living God, who is the savior of all people, particularly of those who believe.'" This is the third faithful saying in the PE. See *Form/Structure/Setting* for a discussion of the structure of the passage and why this verse has been chosen as the saying. This faithful saying is similar to the second, which says that God is our savior who "wishes all people to be saved and to come into a knowledge of [the] truth" (1 Tim 2:4). See there for a discussion of the teachings of God as savior and the universal offering of salvation, and also below on μάλιστα, "especially." Because God is living, he is the author of the promise of life (v 8).

The primary question is the relationship between the faithful saying and the immediate context. How does the proclamation of God's salvific plan fit into Paul's instructions to Timothy? The key word is εὐσέβεια, "godliness," and its contrast to the opponents. Timothy is instructed not to pursue silly myths but rather to train for godliness because the message of godliness is the message of the living God, the message that God is the savior of all people. It is this God, this gospel, this goal that Timothy is to pursue.

ὅτι, "since," is not part of the faithful saying but introduces it; Paul toils and struggles because, as the saying puts it (i.e., "since"), "We have placed our hope in the living God." ἐλπίζειν, "to hope," refers not to a future possibility that may or may not come true but to the believers' "confident anticipation of that which we do not yet see" (Cranfield, *Romans* 1:260; cf. 1 Tim 1:1). The perfect tense emphasizes the continuing assurance that a believer has, that this hope will be actualized; Paul does not mind toiling for the gospel because he knows that God is alive. ἐλπίζειν is used elsewhere in the PE to describe widows who have placed their hope in God (1 Tim 5:5) and in Paul's warning that the rich should not place their hope in riches but in God (1 Tim 6:17). It is used in 1 Tim 3:14 in a nontheological sense; Paul hopes to see Timothy soon. The description of God as the θεῷ ζῶντι, "living God," is a common theme in the Bible (cf. 1 Tim 3:15). Its use here emphasizes the certainty of Paul's hope: God is living and certainly will accomplish all he has planned to do.

The second line of the faithful saying closely parallels Paul's introduction to the second faithful saying (1 Tim 2:3–4) in its description of God as savior and as making the offer of salvation to all; see there for discussion of these ideas. There is no exclusivism in Paul's gospel, contrary to the opponents' teachings (cf. 1 Tim 2:1–7). This carries special weight if the heresy was primarily Jewish and was excluding Gentiles, the specific audience of Paul's calling (cf. 1 Tim 2:7). And as in 1 Tim 1:15, the ideas of election and predestination are foreign to this context; Paul is thinking only of the exclusivism of the opponents. But this line does add one new thought to that of the second saying: God is the savior of all people, μάλιστα πιστῶν, "particularly of those who believe." πιστῶν refers to "believers" (cf. 1 Tim 4:3). μάλιστα occurs twelve times in the NT with the meaning "especially" (e.g., Acts 20:38; 25:26; 26:3; Phlm 16; 2 Pet 2:10). It is used four other times in the PE: if someone does not provide for their relatives, especially their own family, they have denied the faith (1 Tim 5:8); the church should honor elders, especially (or namely) those who preach and teach (1 Tim 5:17); Paul asks Timothy to bring the cloak and books he left at Troas, and especially (or namely) the parchments (2 Tim 4:13); in describing the opponents, Paul says there are many deceivers, especially (or namely) the circumcision party (Titus 1:10). There are two other passages in Paul that approximate the use of μάλιστα in 1 Tim 4:10: "So then, as we have opportunity, let us do good to all people, and especially to those who are of the household of faith" (Gal 6:10); "All the saints greet you, especially those of Caesar's household" (Phil 4:22).

(1) Those who hold to the doctrine of universal atonement use this verse as one of the strongest scriptural supports for their position that God as savior has done something for all people, albeit more for believers (cf. M. E. Erickson, *Christian Theology* [Grand Rapids, MI: Baker, 1983] 2:834). The text is understood as teaching a potential, universal atonement: while the offer of salvation is open to all, the nature of God as savior is experienced in a special way by those who have accepted salvation by faith and experienced God's saving grace. Lock translates, "who is Saviour of all men, but, in the deepest sense, of those who put faith in Him" (49). (2) Those who hold to the doctrine of particular (limited) atonement often understand πάντων ἀνθρώπων, "all people," as "all kinds" or "all groups," interpreting the verse as reflecting the growth of the church from Judaism to the Gentile world. God's salvation includes not only Jews but also Gentiles, i.e., all groups of people. (3) Skeat translates μάλιστα as "to be precise," "namely," here and in 2 Tim 4:13 and Titus 1:10, based on the word's use in the papyri; the

second phrase is understood as repeating and filling out the first: "who is the savior of all people, that is, all who believe" (*JTS* n.s. 30 [1979] 174–75; followed by Marshall, "Universal Grace," 55). (4) Calvin and others hold that Paul is speaking not of salvation but of common grace, God's care for all people (cf. Ps 145:9; Matt 5:45; Acts 14:16–17). In a discussion of these four interpretations, Baugh shows from inscriptional evidence from Ephesus that the dead emperors were viewed as gods and saviors because they cared for Ephesus and Asia Minor (see excursus on 1 Tim 1:1): "Taken in this light, 1 Tim 4:10 is revealed to be a polemical aside aimed at the false veneration of men who were no longer living, yet who were publically honored as gods and saviors upon the Ephesian inscriptions" (*WTJ* 54 [1992] 338; cf. also Spicq, 1:368, 510; Grudem, *Systematic Theology*, 662, who defines σωτήρ as "one who preserves people's lives and rescues them from danger" [599 n. 38]). (5) There is no fifth option of universalism; the soteriology of the PE is fully Pauline (see *Comment* on 1 Tim 2:3–5).

11 Παράγγελλε ταῦτα καὶ δίδασκε, "Command these things and teach." These are the third and fourth imperatives within this section and start the second subsection (see *Form/Structure/Setting*). In light of the silly myths of the heresy, the goal of godliness, and the living God in whom Timothy has hoped, Paul once again encourages Timothy to stand firm in his preaching: he must continue commanding the opponents to cease teaching their heresy, and he must continue to teach true doctrine. Paul uses similar phrases throughout the PE to sum up what he has been saying and to call Timothy to continued action (1 Tim 5:7; 2 Tim 2:14; Titus 3:8b). The interjection could be a transitional statement as it is in 1 Tim 6:2b and Titus 2:15. Chrysostom makes the point that some situations require authoritative commands while others require teaching, and to use the wrong approach in a situation can create difficulties ("Homily 13"; NPNF 13:449).

παραγγέλλειν, "to command," is a term of authority, carrying connotations of a military or judicial order (cf. 1 Tim 1:3). Because it is a strong word, here it must be directed against the heresy. Especially when salvation is at stake (v 16), authoritative leadership can be appropriate. But the positive counterpart is that Timothy is also to teach. διδάσκειν, "to teach," can be used in an absolute sense without an object specified, which the word order suggests is the case here. Because the cognate noun διδασκαλία, "teaching," generally refers to Christian doctrine in the PE (cf. 1 Tim 4:6), it appears that Paul is contrasting the command to stop promulgating the heresy with the positive instruction to teach true doctrine. ταῦτα "these things," is Paul's usual term for summing up all that has preceded. It is used three times in this section and refers to all the instruction in the epistle (cf. 1 Tim 4:6).

12 μηδείς σου τῆς νεότητος καταφρονείτω, ἀλλὰ τύπος γίνου τῶν πιστῶν ἐν λόγῳ, ἐν ἀναστροφῇ, ἐν ἀγάπῃ, ἐν πίστει, ἐν ἁγνείᾳ, "Let no one treat you contemptuously because of your youth, but be an example for the faithful in speech, in conduct, in love, in faith, in purity." Ellicott translates: "Let the gravity of thy age supply the want of years" (61). These are the fifth and sixth imperatives in this section, and like those in v 7 they balance each other. On the one hand, Timothy should not allow himself to be despised (cf. similar injunction in 1 Cor 16:11) while, at the same time, he must be a good example. Both sides of the coin are necessary for a successful ministry. While in 4:6–16 Paul is speaking directly to Timothy, the historical situation at Ephesus is never far in the background;

between the lines can be seen a constant comparison between what the Ephesian church was doing wrong and what Timothy should do correctly. Every one of the five qualities enumerated in this verse is missing from the lives of the opponents.

On the one hand, Timothy is to let no one despise him because of his youth. The parallel imperative (v 12b) suggests that the way to do this is to be such a good example that accusations have no credence. καταφρονεῖν, "to despise, treat contemptuously," can be a strong word, denoting disgust and even hatred. Jesus said that no one can serve two masters; he will be devoted to and love one, and hate (μισεῖν) and despise (καταφρονεῖν) the other (Matt 6:24; Luke 16:13). Jesus also says not to despise little children (Matt 18:10). To the rich Corinthians who were abusing the Lord's Supper Paul says that by doing so they are despising the church and humiliating the poor (1 Cor 11:22). Peter describes those who "indulge in the lust of defiling passion and despise authority" (2 Pet 2:10). The only other occurrence of the word in PE is when Paul tells slaves not to despise their masters because they are Christians (1 Tim 6:2), although καταφρονεῖν does occur as a variant for περιφρονεῖν where Paul tells Titus not to let anyone disregard or despise him (Titus 2:15). The strong connotation that καταφρονεῖν carries helps to explain why throughout the PE Paul instructs Timothy on issues that Timothy already knows. Since Timothy was meeting extreme opposition, being ignored because of his age, this epistle must carry the apostle's full authority and transfer that authority to Timothy in the eyes of the Ephesians.

νεότης, "youth," occurs in the NT elsewhere only in the phrase "since my youth." The rich young ruler says that he had obeyed the commands since his youth (Mark 10:20; Luke 18:21), and Paul speaks of "my manner of life from my youth [ἐκ νεότητος] spent from the beginning [ἀπ' ἀρχῆς] among my own nation" (Acts 26:4). Paul was a youth when Stephen was stoned (cognate νεανίας: Acts 7:58; cf. Acts 20:9 [Eutychus]; Acts 23:17 [Paul's nephew]; cf. also the cognate νεανίσκος). The phrase ἐκ/ἀπὸ νεότητος, "from youth upwards," is common in extrabiblical Greek (MM, 424). The Didache says that "from their youth thou shalt teach them [i.e., sons and daughters] the fear of God" (4:9). These passages show that νεότης can refer to a very young person. LSJ (1170), moreover, cites several references where νεότης refers to young men of military or athletic age (e.g., Pindar Isth. Od. 8[7].75; Herodotus 4.3; 9.12; Thucydides 2.8, 20). Simpson (69) cites several secular references: Aulus Gellius (10.28) says soldiers are iuniores "up to forty-six"; Josephus notes that although Antonia "was still a young woman," she refused to marry; he calls Agrippa "youthful" when he was almost forty (Ant. 18.6 §§143–239); in describing Flaminus, Polybius says, "he was yet quite young, not being over thirty" (νέος ἦν κομιδῇ· πλείω γὰρ τῶν τριάκοντ' ἐτῶν οὐκ εἶχε; Hist. 18.12.5; LCL tr.). Irenaeus (Adv. Haer. 2.22.5) preserves a fragment from The Relics of the Elders that states "But that the age of thirty years is the prime of a young man's ability, and that it reaches even to the fortieth year, every one will allow" (tr. Lightfoot, Apostolic Fathers, 554). Timothy started serving with Paul during the second missionary journey about A.D. 49 (Acts 16:1). Allowing for that journey, the third journey, the imprisonments (including the Roman one), and the time required for a subsequent release and time spent in Ephesus (c. A.D. 62, assuming the historical reconstruction of the PE in the Introduction), thirteen years or so had passed. Combined with the fact that Timothy must have been old enough in Acts 16 to have been an effective helper, this suggests that Timothy was now in his late twenties to mid thirties.

The cognate νεόφυτος, "neophyte," "new convert," is found in the prohibition that neophytes should not be deacons (1 Tim 3:6), but this refers to spiritual and not physical age. W. M. Ramsay says that the cognate νέος, "new," was used of fully grown men of military age (*The Teaching of Paul in Terms of the Present Day* [London: Hodder and Stoughton, 1913] 41; cited in MM, 424). Ramsay also mentions the Νέοι, a social club of young men over twenty years old as distinct from the Ἔφηβοι (adolescents) and the Γερουσία ("Council of Elders"; "Senate"; "Sanhedrin"; *Cities and Bishoprics of Phrygia,* 2 vols. [Oxford: Clarendon, 1895, 1897] 1:110–11; cited in MM, 424). MM (424) cites a passage in which the νέοι are later described as ἀνδρῶν, "men" (Dittenberger, *Sylloge,* 524 [second century B.C.]). Polybius (18.12.5) describes Flaminius as young because he was thirty. Irenaeus (*Adv. Haer.* 2.22.5) says Jesus suffered when he was thirty, "being in fact still a young man." While there is a problem in using cognates to define related words, the meaning of νέος supports the conclusion that Timothy was in his late twenties to mid thirties. It is also true that the idea of youth is somewhat relative. Timothy was dealing with people whom Paul had personally evangelized many years earlier and who had been leaders in their church for some time. It would have been natural for them to have looked down on any younger person who was correcting them. There is no similar injunction to Titus, who was probably older than Timothy and did not have to deal with this particular problem.

Rather than giving the opponents the opportunity to despise him, Timothy must continually be (γίνου is linear in aspect) an example for the faithful (on πιστός, "faithful," designating Christians, cf. *Introduction,* " Themes in the PE"). Paul often sets himself up as an example for others and applies the same responsibility to others (cf. 1 Tim 1:16). τύπος, "example" (cf. discussion of the synonym ὑποτύπωσις, "example," in 1 Tim 1:16; also cf. Phil 3:17; 1 Thess 1:7; 2 Thess 3:9; 1 Pet 5:3), occurs elsewhere in the PE in Paul's injunction to Titus that he be an example of good deeds (Titus 2:7). It "denotes a mark made by striking, . . . an impression made by something, such as an impression used in its turn as a mould to shape something else" (Cranfield, *Romans* 1:283). The word picture it paints is not so much that Timothy is an example that others can emulate but that he is a mold that should be pressed into the lives of others so that they attain the same shape. The word is used similarly in 1 Pet 5:3 to describe the obligations of church leadership. Its only other use in the PE is when Paul says Timothy must follow the pattern of sound words that he has heard from Paul (2 Tim 1:13).

Paul now enumerates five specific areas in which Timothy is to be an example: speech, conduct, love, faith, and purity (cf. 2 Tim 2:22). The first two have an impact on his public ministry; the final three deal more with his personal life although what is true inwardly always shows itself outwardly (cf. 1 Tim 5:24–25). Love and faith are the inner qualities that motivate the outward manifestation of speech and conduct (so Ellicott, 61). Lock says the first two "give the sphere, and next three the qualities in which he is to be a model" (52). Even though vv 6–16 are personal, the Ephesian situation is never far in the background; each one of these qualities is sadly lacking in the opponents (see *Introduction,* "The Ephesian Heresy"). It is in contrast to them that Timothy is to maintain a good example. λόγος, "speech," refers to everyday speech (cf. 1 Tim 4:6); the opponents' speech was mere babble about what they did not know. ἀναστροφή, "conduct," is a general word referring to one's entire way of life, one's general conduct (cf. discussion on 1 Tim 3:15); the opponents' conduct was so reprehensible that it had brought disrepute to the church. On ἀγάπη, "love," see *Comment* on 1 Tim 1:5; the opponents had no love, just greed. πίστις, "faith," could refer to Timothy's personal faith (cf. *Introduction*, "Themes in the PE") or to his general trustworthiness; the opponents' faith was insincere (1 Tim 1:5).

Timothy is also to have ἁγνεία, "purity." This word occurs again in the PE only in 1 Tim 5:2, where Paul enjoins Timothy to treat younger women like they are his sisters ἐν πάσῃ ἁγνείᾳ, "in all purity," The word has sexual connotations, giving the meaning "chaste" (BAGD, 10; cf. the cognate ἁγνότης, which also has the nuance of "chastity"), which is definitely the case in 1 Tim 5:2, and these overtones are probably here as well. Paul was all too aware of the sexually perverse activities of the opponents (cf. 2 Tim 3:6) and of the problems with the younger widows in Ephesus (1 Tim 5:11–15). The cognate ἁγνός, "pure," occurs two other times in the PE. Timothy is not to be quick in appointing elders, lest he participate in their sins; he is to keep pure (1 Tim 5:22). Older women are to teach younger women to be pure, chaste (Titus 2:5). The sexual nuance of ἁγνός is present in 2 Cor 11:2: "I betrothed you to Christ to present you as a pure bride to her one husband."

13 ἕως ἔρχομαι πρόσεχε τῇ ἀναγνώσει, τῇ παρακλήσει, τῇ διδασκαλίᾳ, "Until I come, be devoted to the reading, to the exhortation, to the teaching." The seventh imperative tells Timothy that the focus of his attention as he ministers to the Ephesian church should be Scripture, its public reading, the exhortation for the people to follow its teaching, and the doctrinal exposition of its meaning. The definite article before each of the three words shows that all were "recognized items in the congregational meeting for worship" (Kelly, 105; cf. Spicq, 1:514; cf. τῇ διδασκαλίᾳ, "the teaching," in v 16). Each one is not sufficient in and of itself, but an effective ministry requires all three. Even the order of the three is significant. Timothy is to immerse himself in the biblical text, to encourage people to follow the text, and to teach its doctrines. The difference is not so much in terms of content as it is an issue of purpose: read, exhort, and understand (cf. Towner, 110–11). It also reflects the synagogue practice of appending exposition to the reading of Scripture. This same note of urgency is sounded in vv 15–16. Some have assumed that Paul is spelling out a liturgy and then have noted that many of the traditional elements of worship are missing: prayer (1 Tim 2:1–2; 1 Cor 11:2–16); singing (Col 3:16; 1 Cor 14:26); charismatic utterances (1 Thess 5:19–22; 1 Cor 2–16, 12–14); the Lord's Supper (1 Cor 11:17–34; cf. R. P. Martin, *Vox Evangelica* 2 [1963] 6–32, for a discussion of these different facets of worship). But the point of the passage is not to spell out a liturgy but to help Timothy protect himself from the doctrinal error of the heresy, for which Scripture is paramount. The emphasis on Scripture also contrasts with the empty prattle and silly myths of the opponents. Justin Martyr speaks of these three elements in his famous description of early Christian worship: "And on the day called Sunday, all who live in cities or in the country gather together to one place, and the memoirs of the apostles or the writings of the prophets are read, as long as time permits; then, when the reader has ceased, the president verbally instructs, and exhorts to the imitation of these good things. Then we all rise together and pray" (*1 Apol.* 1.67; ANF 1:186).

ἕως ἔρχομαι, "until I come," is a reference back to Paul's desire to visit Timothy, recognizing that he may delay his visit (1 Tim 3:14). Ellicott suggests that the use of the indicative, as opposed to the subjunctive (e.g., ἕως ἂν ἔλθω), "implies the strong expectation which the Apostle had of coming" (62). προσέχειν, "to be devoted to," is the same word used to describe the opponents' devotion to their teaching (1 Tim 1:4). Timothy's lifestyle is to be characterized as a devotion to, an immersion in, the biblical text. This desire for intensity of devotion is emphasized again in vv 15–16. Timothy's first duty is the ἀνάγνωσις, "public reading," of the biblical text (BAGD, 52–53). This was a common practice in the synagogue (Luke 4:16; Acts 13:15, 27; 15:21; 2 Cor 13:14; Knight [207] notes an inscription from a synagogue in Jerusalem: συναγωγὴν εἰς ἀνάγνωσιν νόμου, "synagogue for the reading of the law" [Hondius, *Supplementum* 8.170.1, 4]) that was carried over to the church, where Paul's writings were also read (Col 4:16; 1 Thess 5:27; cf. Rev 1:3). In the second century this duty was performed by the ἀναγνώστης, "[public] reader."

Timothy's second duty is to encourage and exhort people (τῇ παρακλήσει, "to the exhortation") to follow the message of the text (cf. similar use of the word in 1 Thess 2:3; Heb 12:5, which uses παράκλησις, "exhortation," to describe a quotation from Prov 3:11–12; 13:22, which describes the epistle as an exhortation; 1 Macc 12:9). Synagogue practice was to read the text aloud followed by a λόγος παρακλήσεως, "word of encouragement/exhortation" (Acts 13:15); the early church adopted the same pattern. Timothy's third duty is to teach doctrine. διδασκαλία, "teaching," has been a dominant concept throughout this section (cf. 1 Tim 4:6). The agenda Paul spells out for Timothy emphasizes the centrality of the text for theological correctness and includes not just a basic reading but a fuller awareness of the text's meaning that is gained through study, reflection, and devotion.

14 μὴ ἀμέλει τοῦ ἐν σοὶ χαρίσματος, ὃ ἐδόθη σοι διὰ προφητείας μετὰ ἐπιθέσεως τῶν χειρῶν τοῦ πρεσβυτερίου, "Do not neglect the gift that is in you, which was given to you through prophecy with [the] laying on of the hands of the body of elders." This is the second of the three references in the PE to Timothy's commissioning into ministry (cf. 1 Tim 1:18; 2 Tim 1:6). As is the case in these other passages, Paul is here using remembrance of this past event to encourage Timothy in his present work at Ephesus; he has the gifts to perform the task. It also provides a strong argument to the Ephesian leaders that Timothy's gifts were acknowledged by the body of elders, and now they stand under his authority as Paul's delegate. See the excursus after the *Comment* on 1 Tim 1:18 for a discussion of many of the issues raised by this passage. See *Explanation* on 1 Tim 1:18–20 for historical issues relating to ordination. The role of the body of elders is especially relevant now because Timothy is having to discipline them (Lock, 54).

The major question in this passage is the relationship between the two prepositions διά, "through," prophecy and μετά, "with," the laying on of hands. In 1 Tim 1:18 Paul says that he is entrusting these commands to Timothy κατὰ τὰς προαγούσας ἐπὶ σὲ προφητείας, "in accordance with the prophecies previously made about you"; in 2 Tim 1:6 he encourages Timothy to rekindle the gift of God ὅ ἐστιν ἐν σοὶ διὰ τῆς ἐπιθέσεως τῶν χειρῶν μου, "that is in you through the laying on of my hands"; here the gift was given "with [μετά] [the] laying on of the hands of the body of elders" (1 Tim 4:14). διά has a range of meaning extending from actual means (efficient cause), to agency, to attendant circumstances

(BAGD, 180; on attendant circumstances, see BDF §223; Moule, *Idiom-Book*, 57; M. J. Harris, *NIDNTT* 3:1182–83; cf. 1 Tim 2:15; cf. Rom 2:27; 4:11; 8:25; 14:20; 2 Cor 2:4; 5:7). μετά also carries the meaning of attendant circumstances (BAGD, 509; Moule, *Idiom-Book*, 61). An interesting parallel is Luke's statement that at the end of Paul's first missionary journey they appointed elders in every church, and with prayer and fasting (προσευξάμενοι μετὰ νηστειῶν) they were committed to the Lord (Acts 14:23; cf. also Matt 24:30, 31; Mark 10:30; 13:26; Luke 17:15, 20; 21:27; Acts 13:17; 25:23; 26:12; 27:10). The prophecy Paul refers to is not the efficient cause of Timothy's gifts; that is God's role. It is even doubtful that any idea of intermediate agency is intended since in the parallel passage (1 Tim 1:18) the prophecy simply indicates that Timothy possessed certain spiritual gifts. The variation of the prepositions is most likely stylistic, and they are used synonymously. This is supported by the fact that the same thought of laying on of hands is expressed elsewhere with both μετά (1 Tim 4:14) and διά (2 Tim 1:6). Paul is encouraging Timothy to make use of the gifts he possesses, gifts made evident at his commissioning into ministry, a commissioning that was accompanied by prophecy and by the ritual of laying on of hands.

As has been argued throughout this study, it seems doubtful that Timothy is the sort of person to give up. Verbs like ἀμελεῖν, "to neglect," can be understood as an encouragement to one who was becoming weary and perhaps faltering, but they do not necessitate that Timothy had given up. χάρισμα, "gift," refers to God's favor graciously and undeservedly bestowed through the working of his Holy Spirit. It can refer to a general blessing (Rom 1:11), God's blessing specifically on Israel (Rom 11:29) and on Paul (2 Cor 1:11), and God's saving grace in Christ (Rom 5:15, 16; 6:23), and in a very specific sense it can refer to spiritual gifts given to believers for ministry in the church (Rom 12:6; 1 Cor 1:7; 7:7; 12:4, 9, 28, 30, 31; 1 Pet 4:10). Its only other occurrence in the PE is in the parallel passage in 2 Tim 1:6, where it also refers to Timothy's spiritual gifts of ministry that enable him to continue his work at Ephesus. As is made clear in 1 Tim 1:18, the prophecies confirmed that Timothy was spiritually equipped for service. On the fact that προφητείας, "prophecy," here is singular but is plural in 1 Tim 1:18, see the excursus after the *Comment* on 1 Tim 1:18. On πρεσβύτεροι, "elders," see the discussion in *Form/Structure/Setting* on 1 Tim 3:1–7 and 1 Tim 5:17–25. The word here is πρεσβυτέριον, the "body of elders," used elsewhere of the Sanhedrin (Luke 22:66; Acts 22:5) although the usual word is συνέδριον. The translation "body of elders" has been chosen here so as not to confuse these elders with any second-century notion of a presbytery, and because πρεσβυτέριον is "always used of a body" (G. Bornkamm, *TDNT* 6:666 n. 92). It is a collective noun, the body of elders consisting of several elders (cf. Titus 1:5; Acts 14:23). Paul was evidently a member of the elders because in 2 Tim 1:6 he talks about his role in the laying on of hands. For the πρεσβυτέριον in early Christian writing, see G. Bornkamm, *TDNT* 6:654.

Another issue is the apparent contradiction between 2 Tim 1:6 and 1 Tim 4:14. In the former Paul says that he laid hands on Timothy, and here Paul refers to the body of elders laying hands on him. However, there is no contradiction since these two statements are not mutually exclusive. Daube argues that the phrase ἐπίθεσις τῶν χειρῶν τοῦ πρεσβυτερίου, "laying on of the hands of the body of elders," is a translation of the technical Hebrew phrase סמיכת זקנים *sĕmîkat zĕqēnîm*, meaning "the leaning on of hands on persons in order to make elders, Rabbis, of them" ("Laying on of Hands," 244–45; also id., *ZNW* 48 [1957] 125; Jeremias, *ZNW* 48 [1957] 130–31, who translates "Laying on of hands which confers presbyterial dignity"; suggested earlier by Ellicott, 63; criticized by Cousineau, *ScEs* 28 [1976] 160–61; G. Bornkamm, *TDNT* 6:666 n. 92; Hanson, [1983] 94). Because *sĕmîkat zĕqēnîm* refers not to the ordination of a specific rabbi but to ordination in general, Daube's argument is that in 1 Tim 4:14 Paul refers not to a group of elders but to the ordination process in general. But along with the inherent problems of dating rabbinic material, in neither of these passages in the PE is there the idea that Timothy is an elder. Prophecies have been made that Timothy has the gifts for ministry, and this was officially, publicly recognized when Paul and the elders laid hands on him. 1 Tim 4:14 sounds more like a commissioning along the line of Paul and Barnabas (Acts 13:3) than an ordination, and Paul is now referring to that public validation of his gift as a means of encouraging Timothy during this difficult time. Reference to the public role of the elders is appropriate to the public nature of 1 Timothy; throughout this passage there is an implicit censure of the Ephesian opponents. But 2 Timothy is a private letter, and Paul's personal role in Timothy's commissioning is appropriately mentioned there (cf. G. Bornkamm, *TDNT* 6:666 n. 92).

The practice of laying on of hands is found in the OT (Num 17:18–23; Deut 34:9). It was used in Judaism in the ordination of rabbis (E. Lohse, *TDNT* 9:429) and was associated with healing in the ministry of Jesus (Mark 1:31, 41; 3:10; 5:23; 6:5, 56; 7:32; 8:23, 25; 9:27; Luke 4:40; 6:19; 13:13; 14:4) and the early church (Acts 3:7; 5:12, 15; 9:12, 17; 19:11; 28:8). The ritual also signifies a blessing (Matt 19:13; Mark 10:13; cf. Heb 6:2), often associated with the Holy Spirit (Acts 8:17–18; 19:6). Most significantly, the laying on of hands is a ritual identifying a person's call to a specific task and as such is applied to Stephen and his colleagues (Acts 6:6), Paul and Barnabas (Acts 13:3), and in the PE to Timothy (1 Tim 1:18; 4:14) and elders (1 Tim 5:22; cf. E. Lohse, *TDNT* 9:428–34). There is nothing in the PE to suggest that the event to which v 14 refers was a second-century ordination to the monarchical episcopate (see *Explanations* on 1 Tim 1:18–20 and 3:1–7).

15–16 ταῦτα μελέτα, ἐν τούτοις ἴσθι, ἵνα σου ἡ προκοπὴ φανερὰ ᾖ πᾶσιν. ἔπεχε σεαυτῷ καὶ τῇ διδασκαλίᾳ, ἐπίμενε αὐτοῖς· τοῦτο γὰρ ποιῶν καὶ σεαυτὸν σώσεις καὶ τοὺς ἀκούοντάς σου, "Continually practice these things, immerse yourself in them, in order that your progress might be visible to all. Watch yourself and the teaching; be persistent in them; for by doing this you will save both yourself and those hearing you." These two verses contain the last four imperatives of this section and express perhaps the most intensely personal note in the epistle. Paul is concerned for Timothy and wants to impress upon Timothy that not even he is exempt from the temptation of the opponents. As Bishop Butler states, "Be more afraid of thyself than of the world" (cited in Bernard, 73). The continuous aspect of all four imperatives expresses Paul's urgency and concern: Timothy must continually, constantly, follow these instructions. The two verses are parallel in structure. Each employs two imperatives followed by a reason. Timothy must practice Paul's instructions so that his progress will be visible to all (v 15). Timothy must guard himself and the teaching so that he will save himself and those who hear and obey him (v 16). V 15 is an emphatic repetition of the charge in v 12 that Timothy be an example to believers in speech, conduct, love, faith, and purity. This is not the ultimate goal; v 16b shows what ultimately is at stake. Timothy should strive for visible progress in contrast to the opponents, whose sinful behavior is bringing disrepute upon the church.

προκοπή, "progress," is used elsewhere to describe the advancement of the gospel (Phil 1:12) and the Philippians' growth as a result of Paul's ministry (Phil 1:25; cf. Str-B 3:651–52). The cognate verb προκόπτειν, "to progress," is used to describe the passing of night as a reference to the coming of eschatological salvation (Rom 13:12), Jesus' growth in wisdom, stature, and favor (Luke 2:52), and Paul's progress in Judaism beyond those his own age (Gal 1:14). If this is the background to the word used here, then Paul's concern is that Timothy's adherence to the gospel be plainly seen as an example to the Ephesian church (cf. v 12). However, there is a possibility that Paul is intending more than this (cf. Fee, 109). Three times Paul uses the cognate verb to describe the opponents: they will not progress far because their folly is plain to all (2 Tim 3:9); evil men and deceivers will progress from bad to worse (2 Tim 3:13); and their heresy, which is godless chatter, will lead people into ungodliness (2 Tim 2:16). It is possible that this repetition of the verb in such a short space is an indication that the idea of progress is part of the opponents' teaching, and Paul is turning the term back upon them. In Stoicism, προκοπή referred to the advances made by a person in philosophy (G. Stahlin, *TDNT* 6:706–7, 717–19), and this might help explain the play on words and the nature of the heresy. L. T. Johnson argues that there was an ongoing debate in Greco-Roman moral teaching regarding "how susceptible virtue is to progress. Paul clearly aligns himself with those who consider it possible and visibly manifested" (166). If Paul is appropriating the opponents' terminology, then he is implying that true progress in religion is achieved not through adherence to myths but through following the true gospel as expounded by Timothy. However, this possible appropriation does not suggest that Timothy was advancing to a higher stage in Christian faith. The context puts the emphasis not on his personal achievement but on his role as an example to the Ephesians.

μελετᾶν, "to practice continually," can mean "to ponder," "to exercise oneself" (MM, 395), or "to practice" (BAGD, 500). The idea of Timothy meditating on these instructions reinforces the personal nature of these two verses. But meditation should always lead to action, and since an immediate goal is people seeing Timothy's spiritual progress, "practice" is the preferable translation (cf. Acts 4:25). It also continues the athletic metaphor from vv 7–8 and v 10. The linear aspect of the tense ("continually") emphasizes that this must be a day-to-day activity; it must become habitual. ταῦτα, "these things" (cf. 1 Tim 4:6), refers to the epistle as a whole. Because εἶναι, "to be," is linear in aspect, its use here as ἴσθι, "continually immerse yourself in them," strengthens the continuous notion. Although εἶναι does not mean "to immerse," this translation reflects Paul's intention more than the translation "remain" (cf. Matt 2:13).

V 16 repeats the same emphasis of v 15 while adding a few thoughts. Timothy is to ἔπεχε, "watch," both himself and the teaching. σεαυτῷ, "yourself," refers to his conduct (cf. v 12) and τῇ διδασκαλίᾳ, "the teaching," to the proclamation of biblical doctrine (cf. 1 Tim 4:6). The proclamation of the gospel cannot be separated from the character of the proclaimer. The difficult question of this verse is the meaning of σώσεις, "will save." It is tempting to translate σώσεις as "will be kept safe" and interpret the verse as saying that if Timothy follows the epistle, he and those with him will be kept safe from the Ephesian heresy. This would be in keeping with the context of this section where the topic of personal salvation sounds strange. However, when Paul means "to keep safe," he uses ῥύεσθαι and not σώζειν (cf. 1 Tim 2:15). Rather, we have here the Pauline idea of perseverance expressed in 1 Tim 2:15 (cf. Rom 11:22 [ἐὰν ἐπιμένῃς, "if you remain"]; 1 Cor 9:27; 15:1–2; Phil 2:12; Col 1:23 [εἴ γε ἐπιμένετε, "if indeed you remain"]). Later Paul will tell Timothy that "the Lord will rescue [ῥύσεται] me from every evil work and will save [σώσει] me for his heavenly kingdom" (2 Tim 4:18). (It is therefore unnecessary to speak of salvation being mediated through the church leader [contra Oberlinner, 214].) Although human responsibility is emphasized in the salvation process, it ultimately is the Lord who preserves and saves (see *Explanation*); the human agent is the intermediary (cf. Rom 11:14; 1 Cor 7:16; 9:22; Jas 5:20; Jude 23).

ἔπεχε, "watch," can mean to "hold fast" (cf. Phil 2:16 where the Philippians are to hold fast to the word of life) or to "aim at," to "fix one's attention on" (Acts 3:5), to "take notice" (Luke 14:7). Timothy must hold tightly to who he is and not allow himself to be caught by the teaching of the opponents. ἐπιμένειν, "to be persistent," can be synonymous with μένειν, "to remain" (cf. similar charge in 2 Tim 3:14: μένε, "remain"), but the context here requires that the perfective use of ἐπί (cf. John 8:7; Acts 12:16; Rom 6:1; 11:22, 23; Col 1:23) carry its full force; Timothy must persistently carry out Paul's instructions. Because v 16 reiterates v 15, αὐτοῖς, "them," refers back to ταῦτα, "these things," and τούτοις, "them," in v 15, encouraging Timothy to persist in following Paul's previous instructions. ποιῶν, "by doing," is an instrumental participle. τοῦτο, "this" (singular), is not the same as ταῦτα, "these things" (plural), used repeatedly throughout this section (cf. 1 Tim 4:6); τοῦτο refers to vv 15–16a. ἀκούοντας, "hearing," carries the nuance it sometimes does, not merely of sense perception but of response and obedience to that which is heard (e.g., "He who has ears to hear, let him hear" [Mark 4:9; Rev 2–3]; cf. G. A. Lee, *ISBE* 2:649–50). It is not those who merely hear Timothy's instructions but those who practice them who will be saved (cf. 2 Tim 2:14).

Explanation

Having described the Ephesian problem in 1 Tim 4:1–5, Paul continues the same pattern established in chap. 1 of encouraging Timothy in his task. In one of the most personal sections in all the NT Paul shows his deep concern for both Timothy's personal well-being and his ministry. This does not mean that Timothy has ceased ministering; it means that he needs encouragement in a difficult situation. The tone of this section is different from the rest of the epistle. Instead of merely debating the heresy or attacking the opponents, Paul shows that part of an effective approach is the positive presentation of correct doctrine and proper conduct. What follows comprises more than simple instructions to Timothy. These verses provide a paradigm of effective ministry for ministers of all ages and all times. The twelve imperatives form seven parts to Paul's paradigm of effective ministry.

(1) Personally, Timothy is daily to rely on Scripture and its teaching. This emphasis is repeated again in this section (cf. v 13) and is emphasized in Paul's second epistle to Timothy. (2) Timothy is to stay away from the heresy, as all ministers should stay away from silly and empty arguments about the meaning of words that produce nothing but controversy and have nothing to do with godliness.

While it is obvious that physical exercise is good, the goal of godliness is much more important because its fruits last forever. This is why Paul struggles so in his ministry, a ministry of the proclamation of salvation for all, a salvation that leads to godliness. (3) Timothy is to stand firm, commanding obedience to his instruction.

(4) The fourth part of the paradigm Paul is creating can well be described by the words of Elihu, the young friend of Job who did not speak at first out of respect for the older three friends. But as one whom God had blessed with wisdom, he was no longer able to keep silent: "I am young in years, and you are aged; therefore I was timid and afraid to declare my opinion to you. I said, 'Let days speak, and many years teach wisdom.' But it is the spirit in a man, the breath of the Almighty, that makes him understand. It is not the old that are wise, nor the aged that understand what is right" (Job 32:6b–9). Paul warns the Ephesians and Timothy about two excesses well guarded by Elihu. They must not look down on Timothy because he is younger than they, and Timothy must guard against the excesses of youth by being an example both in public and in private, thereby warranting their respect. It is not sufficient simply to demand respect; one's actions should prove oneself worthy. (5) Paul repeats again the emphasis of v 6 that Timothy must make Scripture, the text and its doctrine, central to his life and ministry. Ministry is to be biblically based. (6) Throughout the Psalms and the narrative texts in the OT the Israelites are told to reflect on God's goodness and faithfulness in the past and on the basis of this to learn to rely on him in the present. This is the same approach Paul takes in the sixth part of this paradigm. If Timothy would think back to the time of his public commissioning where it was apparent to all that he was gifted for ministry, that remembrance should encourage him now during this difficult time in Ephesus.

(7) Finally, Paul once again encourages Timothy to immerse himself in the things of God, recognizing that not even he is safe from the wiles of the opponents. He must continually, consciously, be on guard. As a result, the example of an effective minister will speak more loudly than words, and as a result both the minister and those listening will persevere and so be saved. True progress is not measured by the cleverness of words or the amount of worldly wisdom one may have to offer. True progress is seen in the simple proclamation of the crucified Christ (1 Cor 2:1–5) and obedience to his demands.

This call to perseverance again emphasizes human involvement in the salvation process. Ultimately it is the Lord who keeps and saves, but the continued perseverance of the believer is also required. The question of how these two doctrines can be balanced has bedeviled many centuries of church history. This is the same message Paul earlier sent to the Philippian church, telling them "work out your salvation with fear and trembling; for God is at work in you, both to will and to work for his good pleasure" (Phil 2:12–13; cf. Hawthorne, *Philippians*, 100, who cites Ridderbos: "Because God works and has worked, therefore man must and can work" [*Paul*, 255]). J. B. Phillips translates, "Be keener than ever to work out the salvation that God has given you with a proper sense of awe and responsibility. For it is God who is at work within you, giving you the will and the power to achieve his purpose" (*The New Testament in Modern English* [New York: Macmillan, 1958] 423–24).

This paradigm of Christian ministry, directed specifically to Timothy but applicable to ministers of all times, stands in judgment on those who neglect the teaching of Scripture, consume themselves with arguments about words devoid of godliness, bring reproach upon the church by their sinful lives, refuse to immerse themselves in the things of God, and as a result are destroying not only themselves but also those who listen and follow their example. Conversely, it is a word of encouragement and hope to those who are faithful to the apostolic example and teaching of the gospel.

V. How Timothy Is to Relate to Different Groups in the Church (1 Tim 5:1–6:2a)

A. People of Various Ages (1 Tim 5:1–2)

Bibliography

Burini, C. "Le 'vieillards,' 'nos parents' dans l'Église de Dieu—1 Tm 5,1–2." In *Paul de Tarse: Apôtre de notre temps*, ed. L. de Lorenzi. Rome: Abbaye de S. Paul, 1979. 697–720. Cousineau, A. "Les sens de *presbuteros* dans les Pastorales." *ScEs* 28 (1976) 147–62. Meier, J. P. "Prebyteros in the Pastoral Epistles." *CBQ* 35 (1973) 324–25. Spicq, C. "La place oule rôle des jeunes dans certaines communautés néotestamentaires." *RB* 76 (1969) 508–27. Winter, B. W. "Providentia for the Widows of 1 Timothy 5:1–16 [Acts 6:1–5]." *TynBul* 39 (1988) 83–99.

Translation

¹*Do not rebuke but encourage an older man as a father, younger men as brothers,* ²*older women as mothers, younger women as sisters with all purity.*

Form/Structure/Setting

There is a strong connection between these two verses and the preceding section, 1 Tim 4:6–16. In 4:12 Paul tells Timothy not to let people look down on his youthfulness but rather to be an example; 5:1–2 spells out one way to be an example to young and old alike. The last verse in chap. 4 refers to those who hear Timothy, and those people are the topic of chap. 5. 1 Tim 5:1–2 is directed specifically to Timothy as is chap. 4; in 5:3–6:19. Paul turns to the church as a whole. The pattern of two imperatives balancing each other in 4:7 and 4:12 resurfaces in 5:1; Timothy is not to rebuke but to encourage. The sense of ongoing responsibilities conveyed by the linear-aspect imperatives and the positive tone of describing correct conduct instead of debating the opposition are both present. And a concern for Timothy's personal life is readily visible when Paul says that Timothy is to treat younger women as sisters in all purity. The imagery of fellow believers as father, mother, brother, and sister goes back to 1 Tim 3:15 where the church is described as a family.

However, in the following paragraphs Paul discusses how Timothy should relate to different groups within the church: widows (5:3–16), elders (5:17–25), slaves (6:1–2a), and eventually the rich (6:17–19). Because 5:1–2 discusses how Timothy should relate to people of different ages and genders in the church, even though it does not address a distinct group as do the following sections, 5:1–2 is placed with the following paragraphs, recognizing that it also serves as a transitional passage. There is much in 1 Timothy that warrants the description "stream of consciousness" for Paul's writing style, and any attempt to outline the epistle often does an injustice to the flow of Paul's argument and use of imagery. Paul includes in his letter to Titus a similar discussion on how to deal with different age/gender groups in the Cretan church (Titus 2:2–10).

In these verses Paul is not thinking about the opponents. When dealing with them, Timothy is to be firm and commanding, a figure of authority (cf. 1 Tim 1:3). The gentle language of these verses and the qualification "do not rebuke but encourage" indicate that these instructions apply not so much to the refutation of heresy and the opponents as to Timothy's general conduct within the church. Stylistically, these two verses show a careful play on words and use of natural gender. πρεσβυτέρῳ, "older man," and πρεσβυτέρας, "older women," are the same word, one masculine and the other feminine, just as νεωτέρους, "younger men," and νεωτέρας, "younger women," are gender variations of the same word. Likewise, ἀδελφούς, "brothers," and ἀδελφάς, "sisters," are variations of the same word. Structurally, both verses are one sentence with the four age/gender groups grammatically dependent on παρακάλει, "encourage."

Comment

1–2 Πρεσβυτέρῳ μὴ ἐπιπλήξῃς ἀλλὰ παρακάλει ὡς πατέρα, νεωτέρους ὡς ἀδελφούς, πρεσβυτέρας ὡς μητέρας, νεωτέρας ὡς ἀδελφὰς ἐν πάσῃ ἀγνείᾳ, "Do not rebuke but encourage an older man as a father, younger men as brothers, older women as mothers, younger women as sisters with all purity." Continuing from 1 Tim 3:15 the imagery of the church as a household, Paul now says that Timothy should not take an adversarial role with the members of the Ephesian church (but not the opponents) but should treat them as family—fathers and mothers, brothers and sisters. This teaching not only builds on the social custom of the time that demanded a high degree of respect and honor for one's parents, but in a much more significant sense it is an extension of the gospel teaching that all believers are fathers and mothers, brothers and sisters (Mark 3:31–35). While it is true that the content of these verses is reminiscent of common Greek instruction (cf. esp. Plato *Rep.* 5.463c; cf. Wettstein, *Novum Testamentum Graecum;* MM, 535; Spicq, 1:522; Dibelius-Conzelmann, 72; Kelly, 110), the motivation and ultimate truth of the teaching is based not on social custom or etiquette but on the reality of the corporate nature of Christian salvation, that all who are in Christ are part of the same body (cf. Knight, 215).

ἐπιπλήσσειν, "to rebuke," is a strong, almost violent, term, occurring only here in the NT. Rather than standing over an older man and rebuking him, Timothy is παρακαλεῖν, "to encourage," him to follow the correct teachings. παρακαλεῖν is a common word in the PE (8x; cf. 1 Tim 1:3), used to describe Paul's encouragement that Timothy stay on at Ephesus (1 Tim 1:3) and to instruct Titus to encourage younger men to control themselves (Titus 2:6). Just as it is difficult for an older person to respect the teaching and leadership of a younger man (1 Tim 4:12), so also it is difficult for a younger man to know how to instruct and correct the older people in the church.

πρεσβύτερος, "older man" (cf. similar use in Luke 15:25; John 8:9; Acts 2:17), occurs in the feminine form in the next verse as πρεσβυτέρας, "older women," and elsewhere in the PE the word is used to mean an "elder" in the church (1 Tim 5:17, 19; Titus 1:5; cf. 1 Pet 5:5; see *Form/Structure/Setting* on 1 Tim 3:1 for a general discussion of this and related words). In Titus 2:2–3 Paul uses the cognates πρεσβύτης, "old man," and πρεσβῦτις, "old woman." Here πρεσβύτερος describes not the church office of elder but simply a man who is older (contra NEB). (1) It is parallel to πρεσβυτέρας, "older women," in the very next verse, and there was no position of "women elders" in the Pauline churches or in the second century. (2) The topic of this section is not church leadership but how Timothy is to treat people of different ages and genders. (3) The similarity to Hellenistic parallels suggests Paul is speaking of an older man (cf. Meier, *CBQ* 35 [1973] 324–25). (4) The command to encourage instead of rebuke is not appropriate if the audience is the elders since they are a large part of the problem and Paul uses harsher language with them. W. M. Ramsay feels that Paul is saying that Timothy should use the titles of father and mother in addressing those older than himself, and brother and sister for those of the same age ("Historical Commentary on the First Epistle to Timothy," *Exp* 9 [1910] 326–27). Within the social custom of that day and the biblical mandate (cf. Lev 19:32; Lam 5:12; Sir 8:6), to encourage an older man as a father would mean to treat him with respect, dignity, and honor. It would entail gentle persuasion rather than browbeating. The same would be true of Timothy's treatment of older women (cf. Rom 16:13). Using the term πρεσβύτερος, "old man," with its natural sense, which by the second century had a developed, technical meaning, suggests an early date for the composition of this letter.

νεωτέρους, "younger men," would be men not younger than Timothy but younger than the older men, hence men Timothy's own age and younger. Otherwise Paul would have no instructions for people Timothy's age in a passage that appears to cover people of all ages. J. H. Elliott ("Ministry and Church Order in the New Testament," *CBQ* 32 [1970] 367–91) sees νεώτεροι as "newly baptized men," but this seems out of place and breaks the natural parallels without a textual indication. When it comes to how Timothy is to treat younger women, Paul is a bit more explicit. (1) He appends the phrase ἐν πάσῃ ἁγνείᾳ, "with all purity." ἁγνεία, "purity" (cf. 1 Tim 4:12), carries the nuance of sexual chastity, which would be appropriate in light of the upcoming instructions about young widows (5:11–16) and the Ephesian problem in general (cf. 2 Tim 3:6; 1 Tim 2:9), and is accented with the emphatic πᾶς, "all," "complete." To treat younger women as sisters requires a careful examination of one's attitudes and a close watch on one's conduct as an example of ministerial integrity (cf. 1 Tim 4:12b). (2) Paul tells Titus that the day-to-day instruction of younger women should be carried out by the older women and not, it is implied, by Titus himself as a male minister (Titus 2:4). If this verse is used to clarify the present passage, to treat younger women as sisters means keeping some degree of separation, presumably to guard against the possibility of sin and the damaging of one's reputation and therefore that of the church. Chrysostom sees this as an admonition to avoid even the suspicion of sin ("Homily 13"; NPNF 13:450). Because ἁγνεία carries the idea of chastity, and because of the real dangers in the Ephesian situation, the phrase ἐν πάσῃ ἁγνείᾳ must modify the final νεωτέρας ὡς ἀδελφάς, "younger women as sisters," and not all four groups of people. Paul elsewhere uses the comparative of νέος, "young," in the masculine when referring to younger men (Titus 2:6) and in the feminine for younger women (1 Tim 5:2, 11, 14).

Explanation

Continuing the same tone and concern from chap. 4, Paul discusses how Timothy should relate to people of different ages and genders. The instruction grows directly out of the problem Timothy is having with the older elders (1 Tim 4:12) and out of Paul's concern that Timothy be on guard against the other problems evident in the Ephesian church. Timothy must treat all believers as members of the same family of God—fathers and mothers, brothers and sisters. His approach should not be one of domination but one of encouragement, including respect and honor. Especially when it comes to Timothy's ministry with younger women, he is to be careful, both for the sake of his personal well-being and for the sake of the ministerial example he is to set. As he did in 1 Tim 4:6–16, Paul encourages Timothy and thus ministers of later times to take special care in preserving the integrity of their ministry by avoiding those areas that so often are part of the downfall of both minister and church.

B. Widows (1 Tim 5:3–16)

Bibliography

Achelis, H., and **Flemming, J.,** eds. *Die syrische Didaskalia übersetzt und erklärt.* TU 25. Leipzig: Hinrichs, 1904. 247–88. **Bangerter, O.** "Les veuves des Épîtres pastorales: Modèle d'un ministère féminin dans l' Église ancienne." *FV* 83 (1984) 27–45. **Bartsch, H.-W.** *Die Anfänge urchristlicher Rechtsbildungen: Studien zu den Pastoralbriefen.* TF 34. Hamburg-Bergstedt: Reich, 1965. 112–43. **Bassler, J. M.** "The Widows' Tale: A Fresh Look at 1 Tim 5:3–16." *JBL* 103 (1984) 23–41. **Blanke, F.** "Die Frau als Wortverkündigerin in der alten Kirche." In *Die Stellung der Frau im Neuen Testament und in der alten Kirche,* ed. F. J. Leenhardt and F. Blanke. Zürich: Zwingli, 1949. **Bopp, L.** *Das Witwentum als organische Gliedschaft im Gemeinschaftsleben der alten Kirche: Ein geschichtlicher Beitrag zur Grundlegung der Witwenseelsorge in der Gegenwart.* Mannheim: Wohlgemuth, 1950. **Brauch, M. T.** "Worse Than an Unbeliever." In *Hard Sayings of the Bible.* Downers Grove, IL: InterVarsity Press, 1996. 671–73. **Campbell, R. A.** "ΚΑΙ ΜΑΛΙΣΤΑ ΟΙΚΕΙΩΝ—A New Look at 1 Timothy 5:8." *NTS* 41 (1995) 157–60. **Duncker, P.-G.** ". . . quae vere vidua est (1 Tim 5:3)." *Ang* 35 (1958) 121–38. **Ernst, J.** "Die Witwenregel des ersten Timotheusbriefes—Ein Hinweis auf die biblischen Ursprünge des weiblichen Ordenswesens?" *TGl* 59 (1969) 434–45. **Fridrichsen, A.** "Einige sprachliche und stilistische Beobachtungen." *ConNT* 2 (1936) 8–13; 6 (1942) 94–96. **Funk, H.** "Univira: Ein Beispiel heidnischer Geschichtsapologetik." JAC 8/9 (1965–66) 183–88. **Gryson, R.** *The Ministry of Women in the Early Church.* Collegeville, MN: Liturgical Press, 1976. **Hiebert, P. S.** "'Whence Shall Help Come to Me?' The Biblical Widows." In *Gender and Difference in Ancient Israel,* ed. P. L. Day. Minneapolis: Fortress, 1989. 125–41. **Leipoldt, J.** *Die Frau in der antiken Welt und im Urchristentum.* Leipzig: Koehler & Amelang, 1954. 205–10. **Lightman, M.,** and **Zeisel, W.** "Univira: An Example of Continuity and Change in Roman Society." *CH* 46 (1977) 19–32. **McKenna, M.** *Women of the Church: Role and Renewal.* New York: Kenedy, 1967. 35–63. **Müller-Bardorff, J.** "Zur Exegese von 1. Timotheus 5, 3–16." In *Gott und die Götter.* FS E. Fascher, ed. H. Bardtke. Berlin: Evangelische Verlagsanstalt, 1958. 113–33. **Or, A. d'.** "Varia Romana [de iure naturali in 1 Tim 5:8 etc.]." *AHDE* 26 (1956) 771–81. **Riesenfeld, H.**

"The Meaning of the Verb ἀρνεῖσθαι." In *In honorem Antonii Fridrichsen, sexagenarii*. ConNT 11. Lund: Gleerup, 1947. 207–19. **Sand, A.** "Witwenstand und Ämterstrukturen in den urchristlichen Gemeinden." *BibLeb* 12 (1971) 186–97. **Stahlin, G.** "χήρα." *TDNT* 9:440–65. **Thurston, B. B.** *The Widows: A Women's Ministry in the Early Church*. Minneapolis: Fortress, 1989. **Trummer, P.** "Einehe nach den Pastoralbriefen: Zum Verständnis der Termini μίας γυναικὸς ἀνήρ und ἑνὸς ἀνδρὸς γυνή." *Bib* 51 (1970) 471–84. **Verner, D. C.** *The Household of God: The Social World of the Pastoral Epistles*. SBLDS 71. Chico, CA: Scholars Press, 1983. 161–66. **Winter, B. W.** "Providentia for the Widows of 1 Timothy 5, 3–16." *TynBul* 39 (1988) 83–99. **Zscharnack, L.** *Der Dienst der Frau in den ersten Jahrhunderten der christlichen Kirche*. Göttingen: Vandenhoeck & Ruprecht, 1902. 47–50, 79–80.

See also the *Bibliography* on 1 Tim 3:9–13 for discussions of deaconesses and their possible overlap with widows.

Translation

³*Honor widows who are truly widows.* ⁴*But if a certain widow has children or grandchildren, let them learn* ᵃ *to show godliness first to their own household and to make some return to their parents; for this is* ᵇ*pleasing before God.* ⁵*But the true widow, who has been left totally alone, has set her hope on God* ᶜ *and continues in entreaties and prayers night and day.* ⁶*But the one having lived for pleasure, even though living, has died.* ⁷*Command these things as well, in order that they be above reproach.* ⁸*But if anyone does not care for* ᵈ *his own, especially [his] household members,* ᵉ *he has disowned the faith and is worse than an unbeliever.* ⁹*Let a widow be enrolled if she is not less than sixty years old, a "one-man" woman,* ¹⁰*being witnessed to by good deeds, if she raised children, if she showed hospitality, if she washed the feet of the saints, if she helped the afflicted, if she earnestly pursued every good work.* ¹¹*But refuse [to enroll] younger widows, for when they grow wanton against Christ, they desire to marry* ¹²*and come under judgment since they abandoned their former faith.* ¹³*But at the same time they also learn* ᶠ *to be idlers, flitting about among houses, but not only idlers but also gossips and busybodies, speaking about things that should not be spoken.* ¹⁴*Therefore I wish younger [widows] to marry, to bear children, to rule their households, to give the Accuser no occasion for slander,* ¹⁵*for some have already strayed after Satan.* ¹⁶*If any believing woman* ᵍ *has widows, let her care* ʰ *for them, and the church should not be burdened so that it may care for the true widows.*

Notes

ᵃThe singular μανθανέτω, "let her learn," is read by 945 *pc* d f m vg^d; Ambst Pel Spec.

ᵇκαλὸν καί, "good and," is inserted before ἀπόδεκτον, "pleasing," by analogy with 1 Tim 2:3 by 323 365 945 *pc* sa^ms bo.

ᶜἐπὶ θεόν, "on God" (C F G P Ψ 048 *pc* lat sy co), is altered to ἐπὶ τὸν θεόν, "on God" (ℵ² A D² 1739 1881 TR), ἐπὶ τὸν κύριον, "on the Lord" (ℵ* D* 81 *pc* vg^mss), and ἐπὶ κύριον, "on the Lord" (ℵ*).

ᵈThe active προνοεῖ, "care for" (ℵ² A C D² Ψ 33 1739 TR), is replaced by the middle προνοεῖται, "cause to be cared for," by ℵ* D* F G I K 104 1881 *pc*. Bernard, 76, compares 2 Cor 8:21 for a similar confusion of the active and middle. Cf. v 16 below.

ᵉτῶν, "the," is inserted before οἰκείων, "household members," by C D¹ 1881 TR (omitted by ℵ A D* F G I Ψ 048 1739 *pc*).

ᶠMoffatt's tr. and Jeremias conjecture an emendation, λανθάνουσιν, "they are unaware," although there is no textual support. See *Comment*.

ᵍThe reading πιστή, "believing woman," has the superior attestation (ℵ A C F G P 048 33 81 1175

1739 1881 *pc* m vg co; Ath). Others insert πιστὸς ἤ, "believing man or," before it (D Ψ TR a b vg^mss sy; Ambst; followed by Moffatt's tr., NEB, Easton, Guthrie). It is possible that a scribe skipped πιστὸς ἤ because of the similarity of πιστός and πιστή. But πιστή has better attestation and is the more difficult reading. It is more likely that a scribe did not understand why it would be the woman's task to care for widows and not the man's (cf. *TCGNT*², 574). There is therefore no reason to postulate as does Bartsch (*Anfänge*, 137) that this is evidence of a church document behind the emendation. Cf. also Ellicott, 76.

    ᵇThe active ἐπαρκείτω, "let her care for" (C D Ψ 048 1739 1881 TR), is replaced by the middle ἐπαρκείσθω, "let her have them cared for" (ℵ A F G 33 1175 *pc*).

Form/Structure/Setting

In 1 Tim 5:1–2 Paul began his discussion of how Timothy should deal with different groups within the Ephesian church. Vv 3–16 discuss issues relating to the financial support of the Ephesian widows. Interpretations of vv 3–16 fall into two camps. (1) Many (Ellicott, Bernard, Lock, Dibelius-Conzelmann, Kelly, Brox, Hanson [1983], Roloff, Oberlinner) feel that these verses spell out the duties of widows who have been enrolled in an order of widows, duties that include prayer, hospitality, pastoral house calls, and care for orphans. Most in this group argue for a formal order of widows (cf. Müller-Bardorff, "Exegese," 120–21; Bartsch, *Anfänge*, 121–23, 130–32; Verner, *Household of God,* 163–64). Lock paraphrases, "You must have an official list for widows in the service of the Church" (57). Ellicott speaks of the widows undertaking "the duties of the presbyteral office" (73; Bernard calls them πρεσβύτιδες, "women elders," 81). Ernest says they receive alms as a payment for their prayers (*TGl* 59 [1969] 434–45). Kümmel speaks of "the ecclesiastical office of the widows . . . whose essential task is continual prayer in connection with sexual abstinence" (*Introduction,* 382). While Guthrie does not believe Paul is discussing an order, he does see the passage as specifying both the characteristics and the duties of an enrolled widow (101–2). This group generally views the πρώτην πίστιν, "former faith," in v 12 as the pledge taken when entering the order, probably including a pledge of celibacy. However, those holding this position appear to have made assumptions based on the duties of widows in later centuries. Kelly says, "One of the big problems facing the early Church was the care of orphans (cf. Hermas, *Mand.* viii. 10; *Apost. Const.* III.iii.2; etc.); it seems likely that the official widows were given charge of these" (116–17), but the dates of his sources are late. Bassler agrees: "Yet this interpretation is based more on the later comments of the *Didascalia Apostolorum* (chaps. 14–15) than on this verse" (*JBL* 103 [1984] 40 n. 61).

(2) Others (Stählin, *TDNT* 9:457 n. 161; Sand, *BibLeb* 12 [1971] 186–97; Fee) argue that these verses do not discuss duties; rather the verses establish who should be enrolled to receive benefits as a widow and who should not. Consequently, there was no official order of widows beyond the formal recognition of who was truly alone (Towner, *Goal,* 183–85; Young, *Theology,* 116–20), and v 12 is not talking about the entrance pledge. The specific virtues, such as praying night and day, showing hospitality, etc., are not duties to be performed but indications of a widow's Christian maturity, which determined whether a widow should be enrolled. Kelly seems to accept both options, admitting that vv 9–10 deal with the qualifications for being enrolled but continuing to describe the specifics of the passage as "practical duties to perform in the community" (116). The text, however, never says it is describing

duties; rather it says that certain behaviors, such as prayer, are indications that a widow should be enrolled. (a) Whether a person has or does not have a family is not a duty, and yet this instruction is repeated three times throughout the passage (vv 4, 8, 10) and is a dominant theme. (b) "Having set her hope in God and continuing in prayer" (v 5) is never pictured as a duty as if an enrolled widow had to pray a certain number of hours per day. It describes what naturally happens when she sets her hope fully on God. It is evidence of the type of person she is and therefore indicates whether she should be enrolled. (c) Being at least sixty years old (v 9a) is not a duty. (d) Being faithful in marriage (v 9b) cannot be a duty of an enrolled widow. If she is currently faithful in marriage, she is not a widow. (e) The list of good deeds (v 10) has nothing to do with duties. The text states that a widow should be enrolled if she is witnessed to by good deeds such as hospitality, etc.; the good deeds are indications of her godly character. (f) Vv 11–16 describe the improper conduct of the younger widows, the thrust of which is to show why they should not be enrolled. The idea of duties is foreign to the text. The verse never calls for a vow of chastity, and Sand argues that such a vow is unknown in the NT and OT (*BibLeb* 12 [1971] 186–97). (g) Comparisons with Anna (Luke 2:36–37) and Tabitha (Acts 9:36–43) and Paul's request that older women teach the younger women (Titus 2:3–5) may be interesting, but they have no necessary connection with the current topic. Anna is not enrolled in the church, and neither Tabitha nor the older women in Titus are necessarily widows or work for the church. (h) While it is true that in later centuries the duties of widows were spelled out in detail (see *Explanation*), there is no historical evidence that such an order of widows existed at the time of the PE. Enrollment was a formal relationship between the church and the widow so that she could count on financial support (see *Comment* on v 3). There is no teaching in the text that she is married to Christ, celibate for life, or committed to working for the church. (i) While it is assumed that a godly woman would continue to do the same things after enrollment that she did before, this does not mean that this passage teaches duties. Paul is concerned not with duties but with the type of widow who should be enrolled.

The structure of this passage also confirms that Paul is not specifying duties but is enumerating the qualities that should characterize widows wishing to be enrolled. It comprises five structural units, and within each unit Paul contrasts those whom the church should support with those whom it should not.

(1) Honor widows who are truly widows (v 3), but those with families should be cared for by their families (v 4).
(2) The true widow is alone, has set her hope on God, and continues in prayer (v 5), but those living in self-indulgence are already dead (v 6).
(3) Command these things (v 7), but if someone does not listen, they have denied the faith and are worse than unbelievers (v 8).
(4) Let older godly women be enrolled (vv 9–10), but refuse to enroll younger ungodly widows who are likely to abandon their faith (vv 11–13).
(5) To sum up, the younger widows should remarry (vv 14–15), those who have families should receive support from them (v 16a), and the church should care for those who are truly widows (v 16b).

The repeated adversative δέ, "but" (vv 4, 6, 8, 11), separates the widows into two groups: those widows for whom the church should care and those who should rely on other resources. (Bernard argues that there were two groups of widows. All widows were deserving of honor and should benefit from the charity of the church [if they did not have family], but a special group was enrolled in the order of widows, received a stipend, and served the church [vv 9–10]. He feels that the conditions in vv 9–10 are too strict to have been applied to all widows, and therefore there must have been a special group. However, there is no clear indication that Paul shifts audiences in v 9, and the enrollment of widows over sixty did not mean that the church could not help younger widows who were truly in need.)

The implication of this passage is that the Ephesian church had committed itself to support some younger widows who, because of their age, idleness, and the Ephesian heresy, had turned against Christ and the church, were leaving the Christian faith, and were bringing reproach upon the church. To respond to this specific, historical situation Paul tells Timothy that the church should enroll only those widows who meet two qualifications. (1) They must be truly alone, without any family for support. This includes being at least sixty years old and not contemplating remarriage. (2) They must also be godly women. They must be the type of women who are committed to the Lord, having set their hope on him and constantly praying to him. Their past lives must show that they were faithful in marriage and busy at home.

Related to the issue of duties is the question of whether there was an order of widows in Ephesus as argued by Spicq (1:533) and others. By *order* is meant an actual organizational structure created to deal with widows that dictated the duties they performed and spelled out in detail the nature of the relationship between the church and the widow. This does not seem to be the case. The text is only concerned to describe the type of widow whom the Ephesian church could support and within the context of the Ephesian heresy the type of widow who was abusing the church's generosity and who should not be supported. There is nothing corresponding to an office of overseer (1 Tim 3:1). Unlike the case with overseers and deacons, there is no NT attestation for an office of widow. Enrollment meant that the widow had entered into a formal relationship with the church, but there is no evidence in the text that there was any organizational structure beyond meeting the widows' needs. Guthrie (102) argues that sixty was an excessively high age for entrance into a church order, considering the shorter average life spans in that day, and that this suggests that there was no ecclesiastical order. One would surmise that once a widow was enrolled, she would work for the church, but that is not the concern of this passage. Following the suggestion of E. Schüssler Fiorenza (*In Memory of Her*, 313–14), Oberlinner believes that some of the dangers that the author addresses were caused by rich women who lived together in community (*Frauengemeinschaften*) and had become influential (246). While much of the Ephesian situation is clouded in mystery, it is difficult to see such a community in this text. The subject of this section is not the influential and rich (except possibly in v 16) but the poor and unsupported.

Another issue in interpreting this passage is the nature of Paul's criteria for enrollment. Listing sixty as the minimum age gives the impression that the criteria were inflexible, but that would have led to the unavoidable and intolerable situation of the church not being allowed to care for a godly fifty-nine-year-old widow, or a godly sixty-year-old woman who had never been married (and hence was not a "one-man woman"). There are two factors that lessen this difficulty.

(1) For the most part, Paul's rules appear to be not a checklist but rather characteristics of the type of widow who should be supported. This would mean that he is not saying that she must have been married but rather that if she was married, she should have been faithful to her husband. This is like the requirements for elders and deacons in chap. 3 where Paul is not saying that a man must be married to be an elder; rather Paul is saying that if the man is married, he must be faithful and run his household well. The age of sixty was the commonly understood number of years denoting old age (see *Comment*), and Paul is saying that the widow must be elderly (although perhaps in this one requirement specificity is necessary).

(2) The second factor has to do with the precise nature of enrollment. It refers to a formal relationship between the church and the widow so that she knows she will be cared for until death. It is this type of relationship the younger Ephesian widows were not permitted to enter. However, presumably the church would still care for needy people even if they were widows younger than sixty years of age. The young widows should remarry, but until that happened the church certainly would have been free to help them financially if it so chose. What the church could not do was enter into a formal, permanent relationship with them that guaranteed their idleness. This is why Paul could set sixty as a specific age limit for what was to be considered *formally* as elderly.

Paul therefore groups widows in one of two categories (but cf. Spicq, 1:524). (1) Widows who should be supported by the church were totally alone and had set their hope on God as was evidenced by their constant prayer life. They had no one to care for them, and they were godly, mature Christians. To spell out what this means, Paul says a true widow is one who has been faithful to her husband (assuming she was married), who has busied herself with good works such as bearing children (assuming she had children, in contrast to the opponents' ban on marriage), has been hospitable, washed the feet of the saints, relieved the afflicted, and in every way been devoted to doing good things. In other words, she was the paradigm of Christian godliness. (2) Widows who should not be supported by the church included those who had other means of support such as family. This group also included many of the younger Ephesian widows who were the opposite of the first group. Rather than having set their hope on God and having been dedicated to him, they had grown wanton against Christ and were leaving the Christian faith. Rather than busying themselves with activities such as prayer, they were studying to be professional idlers, flitting about from house to house. They had become gossips and busybodies.

The older widows were paradigms of what the younger widows should be in the same way that Timothy was to be a good role model for the Ephesians (1 Tim 4:12). Almost every description of the younger widows carries an implicit contrast with the description of the godly widows. For example, godly widows had set their hope on God; the ungodly widows were abandoning their faith. In fact, Paul's response (v 14) was to encourage the younger, ungodly widows to become like the older, godly widows. The younger widows must recognize the importance of marriage and family, rule their own home, and not flit about from one place to another.

Part of the urgency of this passage results from Paul's concern for the pressing needs of the widows requiring support. Yet in the Ephesian setting there was another reason for urgency. Some of the widows were already turning against Christ, some believers were not caring for widows in their own family, and as a result the church was coming into disrepute. In fact, the situation was so extreme that Paul describes it as "death" (v 6) and a "going after Satan" (v 15). Those who were not following Paul's instructions had denied the faith and were worse than unbelievers (v 8). The problem had to be corrected immediately.

There are several important supplementary themes in this passage. (1) The first is the significance of family responsibility. Three times Paul states that it is the family's responsibility and not the church's to care for the widows in their own family. He begins (v 4) and ends (v 16) on this note. In the process he also expands the sphere of familial responsibility to include parents, grandparents, and even relatives in general. (2) Included in this is the theme that it is not the church's responsibility to care for everyone. The church must be discerning so that it can support those who are truly in need. (3) The church must care for those widows who are truly alone.

This passage also makes clear that the PE do not constitute a church manual independent of any historical situation but must be read in light of the Ephesian heresy. What Paul says in these fourteen verses is a reflection of what was happening in Ephesus and how Timothy had to deal with it.

According to Bassler's reconstruction (*JBL* 103 [1984] 23–41), the initial church was fully egalitarian, but by the time of the PE repressive patriarchalism was forced upon the church. Women were originally drawn to enrollment as widows because the church's call for celibacy freed them from patriarchal marriages. Bassler documents how through the centuries the freedom of asceticism has been attractive to women: "Indeed, widows were remarkably free of these ordinary restraints. Freed from the hierarchical dominance of either father or husband, freed from the demands of childbearing and rearing, freed even from pressing economic concerns, the 'widows' were granted a degree of freedom usually reserved for the *hetairai*, yet now enhanced by ecclesiastical respectability and esteem. The increased attractiveness of this office may rest as much on the freedom and equality it offered as on the esteem or dualistic influences" (36). Bassler's contention that the freedom and equality offered by Christianity were appealing to women seems reasonable, but her overall argument is based on the assumption that the PE represent a development from a supposedly fully egalitarian early church and also on the view that 1 Tim 5:3–16 teaches enrollment based on a vow of chastity, which is not supported by the text (see *Comment* on v 12). For a summary of the plight of widows in the OT with Hannah functioning as a paradigm, see Roloff, 285–86.

Comment

3 Χήρας τίμα τὰς ὄντως χήρας, "Honor widows who are truly widows." This verse is the title for the section, the phrase ὄντως χήρας, "truly widows," being repeated several verses later (v 5) and in the conclusion of the discussion (v 16). The theme of honor ties the section together as it applies to people of different ages (5:1–2), widows (5:3, 5, 16), elders (5:17), and masters (6:1; see *Form/Structure/Setting* on 1 Tim 5:1–2). This verse also begins the first of five contrasts between the widows who should be supported by the church and the ones who should not be (see *Form/Structure/Setting*). Paul's concern is that the Ephesian church take care of the widows who are truly in need but not burden itself with those who have other means of support. A true widow is not simply a woman whose husband is dead but one who deserves to be supported by the church. The following verses spell out two considerations for determining if a widow is truly deserving of support: she must be totally alone with no means of support (which includes the idea of being elderly and not desiring remarriage), and she must have shown exemplary Christian character throughout her life.

Care for widows plays an important role throughout the OT (Exod 22:22; Deut 10:18; 24:17, 19–21, 29; 24:17–21; 26:12–13; 27:19; Job 24:3; 29:13; Pss 68:5; 94:6; 146:9; Prov 15:25; Isa 1:17; Jer 7:6; 22:3; Mal 3:5; including levirate marriage [Deut 25:5–10]) and in early Christianity as reflected in the NT (Luke 2:37; Acts 6:1–6; 9:36, 39, 41; Jas 1:27) and the early church fathers (see *Explanation*). Repeatedly God is pictured as the provider and protector of widows and orphans (Exod 22:22; Deut 10:18; Pss 68:5; 146:9; Isa 1:17), Israel is called to defend widows (Deut 24:17–21; 25:5–9; 27:19; Jer 7:6; 22:3; Zech 7:10), and mistreatment of widows is often given as an example of sin (Job 24:21; Ps 94:6). The concern is derived from the fifth commandment and enlarged to be a community responsibility. Duncker (*Ang*35.2 [1958] 121–38) argues that throughout the ancient world (Semitic, Assyrian, Babylonian) widowhood was understood in the same way, not so much as a woman whose husband had died but as a woman deprived of any means of support. Bassler maintains that χήρα had a broader meaning than a person who was formerly married; rather, she says, the word designated "the life of renunciation of the bearer of the title more than her marital history" (*JBL* 103 [1984] 35), which allows for the enrollment of virgins. While this enlargement in the scope of the term might account for the large number of widows, the size can also be accounted for by the natural process of death and insufficient church funds as well as by the church's apparent willingness to support any widow whether or not she had other means. Stronger evidence must be offered to propose a definition other than the most usual one, "widow." See *Explanation* for the early church's involvement with widows.

There is a question regarding the precise meaning of τιμᾶν, "to honor," and the decision here affects the overall interpretation of the paragraph. At a minimum the word includes the idea of respect, making reference to the fifth commandment. This is how the cognate noun is used in 1 Tim 6:1: slaves must honor their masters. The verb is often used in reference to the fifth commandment (Eph 6:2; cf. Matt 15:4, 6; 19:19; Mark 7:10; 10:19; Luke 18:20). But although the type of widow described in v 5 and vv 9–10 is worthy of respect, in light of the overall thrust of the passage τιμᾶν must include the idea of caring for them since all godly widows, whether or not they are enrolled, are worthy of respect (cf. Lock, 57). But does caring include financial responsibility? (1) The verb τιμᾶν and the cognate noun τιμή, "honor," carry a financial nuance of setting a price, even an honorarium (cf. Matt 15:6; cf. BAGD, 817–8; J. Schneider, *TDNT* 8:1182). (2) The cognate noun is used in the next section for giving διπλῆς τιμῆς, "double honor," to elders who do their job well (v 17), referring to payment for services. (3) V 16 says that families should care for their own widows so that the church will not be burdened, and βαρεῖν, "to burden," most likely refers to financial burdens. (4) The thrust of this passage is that the church must care for the true widows because they have no one else. The most obvious interpretation is that these widows need money. As James says, "If a brother or sister is ill-clad and in lack of daily food, and one of you says to them, 'Go in peace, be warmed and filled,' without giving them the things needed for the body, what does it profit?" (Jas 2:15–16). (5) This is an allusion to the fifth commandment (Jeremias, 37), and the fifth commandment was understood to include financial support (Matt 15:5–6; Mark 7:11–12; cf. J. Schneider, *TDNT* 8:178–79). (6) Acts 6:1–6 shows that the church already had recognized its obligation to provide financial support for its widows (cf. also Matt 15:5–6). Easton comments on the appropriateness of the term τιμή, "honor," for this ministry: "Treat poverty not as something contemptible but as deserving honour" (152). τίμα is a second-person singular imperative addressed specifically to Timothy, and yet the following instructions expand to the entire church. (The verbs in v 4 and v 7 are plural. The indefinite τὶς, "any," in vv 4, 8, and 16 indicates that the verses are general rules. V 16 refers specifically to the church as a whole.) Paul probably started with the singular because the preceding vv 1–2 are directed specifically to Timothy, or else Paul was influenced by the second-person singular form of the fifth commandment (Knight, 216–17).

Winter adds another dimension to this topic as he discusses the legal *providentia*, the rules pertaining to a woman's dowry (*TynBul* 39 [1988] 83–99). The dowry was part of the legal requirement of marriage, and Greek and Roman laws were specific in how the dowry was to be managed after the husband's death. A person was placed in charge of the dowry, perhaps a son. The widow could remain in her husband's home or return to her parents' home along with the dowry. There were also laws requiring children to care for their parents (see Winter for references). From this background two points are clarified. (1) Some of the people in the Ephesian church who were responsible for a widow's dowry were evidently not doing their job. It is even possible that this was caused by the Ephesian heresy; see *Comment* on v 4. (2) Many of the widows may have come from the poor class, and their dowry was insufficient to support them (or there was no dowry). These widows would be the primary recipients of the church's generosity.

4   εἰ δέ τις χήρα τέκνα ἢ ἔκγονα ἔχει, μανθανέτωσαν πρῶτον τὸν ἴδιον οἶκον εὐσεβεῖν καὶ ἀμοιβὰς ἀποδιδόναι τοῖς προγόνοις· τοῦτο γάρ ἐστιν ἀπόδεκτον ἐνώπιον τοῦ θεοῦ, "But if a certain widow has children or grandchildren, let them learn to show godliness first to their own household and to make some return to their parents; for this is pleasing before God." In contrast to true widows (v 3; δέ, "but," is adversative), widows who have families should draw their support from them. Paul makes his point about showing godliness, defines godliness further ("to make some return to their parents"; καί, "and," is epexegetical), and then gives the ultimate reason for doing so ("for this is pleasing before God"). This is the first of three times Paul makes this point in the section (cf. vv 8, 16). People were not accepting their responsibilities, even those governed by secular law (cf. v 3). A. Padgett argues that it was the opponents who were urging the widows to refuse to support their parents and grandparents ("Wealthy Women at Ephesus: 1 Timothy 2:8–15 in Social Context," *Int* 41 [1987] 21). This agrees with v 15, which suggests that the widows were following the opponents.

This passage gives three reasons that caring for one's parents is important. (1) Stating the argument in a positive way, Paul says that such action is pleasing to God (v 4b; cf. 1 Tim 2:3). (2) Stating the argument negatively (cf. Brox, 187–89), Paul says that not to care for one's parents is to deny the faith and is to be worse than an unbeliever (v 8). One is reminded of Jesus' condemnation of those using the Jewish law of Corban (Mark 7:9–13) to avoid caring for their parents. (3) On the practical level, it is important to care for one's parents so that the church is not burdened (v 16b); for if the church spends resources on those who have other means of support, it cannot care for those who are truly in need. For Paul, Christianity begins at the home; and one's conduct in the microcosm of the home shows one's abilities, or lack of abilities, in the macrocosm of the church. This principle has already been observed in relation to church leaders (1 Tim 3:4–5, 12; Titus 1:6), and perhaps to the definition of a church leader managing his family well can be added the willingness to accept the responsibility of caring for widows in one's extended family. Caring for parents was held to be a virtue by non-Christian society (cf. Plato *Laws* 4.717), and Paul will compare Christian to non-Christian conduct on this point in v 8.

The translation interprets the subject of μανθανέτωσαν, "let them learn," to be τέκνα ἢ ἔκγονα, "children or grandchildren." Some, however, argue that the subject is the widows and that the point of the verse is that if a widow has children or grandchildren, she should not seek to be enrolled in the church but rather should show her godliness in her own home by taking care of her extended family (Chrysostom, Vulgate, Holtzmann, Jeremias). The argument for this interpretation is that the subject of the previous clause is χήρα, "widow," and since μανθανέτωσαν has no expressed subject, χήρα is the closest possible subject (for a variant reading, see *Note* a). Chrysostom comments, "Thou hast received from them great care. They are departed. Thou canst not requite them. For thou didst not not bring them forth, nor nourish them. Requite them in their descendants, repay the debt through the children" ("Homily 13"; NPNF 13:450). However, most commentators agree that the implied subject of the verb is τέκνα ἢ ἔκγονα and that the issue is not one of a widow choosing between house or church but of children taking care of parents (Bernard, Spicq, Dibelius-Conzelmann, Kelly, Brox, Hanson [1983]). (1) χήρα, "widow," is singular but μανθανέτωσαν, "let them learn," is plural, referring to the plural τέκνα ἢ ἔκγονα, "children or grandchildren." (2) The primary thrust of this whole passage is not the widows' duties in the church or home but the issue of which widows should be cared for (see *Form/Structure/Setting*). (3) τίμα, "honor" (v 3), and εὐσεβεῖν, "to show godliness" (v 4), read naturally as synonyms; the subject of τίμα, "honor," is the church, and its object is χήρας, "widows" (Dibelius-Conzelmann, 74). (4) If a widow is seeking enrollment, it suggests that she cannot provide for herself much less her mother or grandmother. (5) If the widows were the subject of μανθανέτωσαν, then Paul would be saying that by taking care of their own children they would be making some return to their parents, i.e., the children's grandparents. The logic of why this would be true, however, is not apparent. Rather, it is more natural to understand Paul saying that by taking care of a widowed mother or grandmother, the children are making some repayment to that mother or grandmother. (6) V 3 alludes to the fifth commandment, and v 4 is the practical extension of that commandment. Honoring one's parents means caring for a widowed mother who has no means of support.

The δέ, "but," that begins v 4 (omitted by the RSV and NRSV) is adversative: honor true widows, but those with families should be cared for by their families. ἔκγονον means "descendant," or specifically "grandchild" (BAGD, 238). This same range of meaning is also present with πρόγονος, which can mean "parent" or "ancestor" (BAGD, 704). πρόγονος is used elsewhere in the NT only in 2 Tim 1:3

where Paul says he served God as did his forefathers. This wide range of meaning shows that Paul is not thinking of the family as a small unit but is including at least three generations. εὐσεβεῖν, "to show godliness," is one of the key concepts in the PE, epitomizing total consecration to God (cf. 1 Tim 2:2) and describing conduct that comes from a godly person, an emphasis well illustrated by our passage. James combines many of these same thoughts: "Religion [θρησκεία] that is pure and undefiled before God and the Father is this: to visit orphans and widows in their affliction, and to keep oneself unstained from the world" (Jas 1:27). By πρῶτον, "first," Paul means that learning one's duty to parents is of primary importance. Throughout this epistle Paul uses οἶκος, "house(hold)," in both a metaphorical (1 Tim 3:15; cf. 5:1–2) and a concrete (1 Tim 3:4–5, 12) sense.

ἀμοιβὰς ἀποδιδόναι τοῖς προγόνοις, "to make some return to their parents," is an explanatory clause of what it means εὐσεβεῖν, "to show godliness." ἀμοιβή, "return, recompense," is a common term in honorary inscriptions (MM, 27), and F. Büchsel suggests that ἀμοιβὰς ἀποδιδόναι, "to make return," was a current formula for giving back to parents (*TDNT* 2:168, citing Dionysius [Hal.] *Ant. Rom.* 6.73; POxy 4.705.61). τοῦτο γάρ ἐστιν ἀπόδεκτον ἐνώπιον τοῦ θεοῦ, "for this is pleasing before God," is the ultimate reason that the children should care for their widowed mother, a reason almost identical to that given in 1 Tim 2:3 (see *Comment* there for discussion).

5 ἡ δὲ ὄντως χήρα καὶ μεμονωμένη ἤλπικεν ἐπὶ θεὸν καὶ προσμένει ταῖς δεήσεσιν καὶ ταῖς προσευχαῖς νυκτὸς καὶ ἡμέρας, "But the true widow, who has been left totally alone, has set her hope on God and continues in entreaties and prayers night and day." Vv 5–6 are the second set of verses contrasting the true widow and the one who has means of support. V 5 confirms our understanding of the true widow in v 3 as one who is totally alone, but the verse adds a second characteristic: a widow who deserves church support is one who has a godly character. She has fully set her hope on God, and this is seen publicly by her prayerful devotion to him as her provider. Her godliness contrasts with the behavior of the younger widows, who do not qualify for church support. This description of the godly widow is reminiscent of Anna the widowed prophetess, who "did not depart from the temple, worshiping with fasting and prayer night and day" (Luke 2:37). ἐλπίζειν, "to set one's hope on," is not a duty to be performed but rather a characteristic of a godly woman, and to hope in the Lord is common language in the Psalms (25:3, 5, 21; 33:18, 20, 22; 39:7; 42:5, 11; 43:5; 69:6; 119:43, 49, 74; 147:11).

On ὄντως χήρα, "true widow," see *Comment* on v 3. δέ, "but," sets the true widow apart from the widow with family in v 4. The Granville Sharp rule (concerning the use of the article with substantives linked by καί, "and") requires χήρα, "widow," and μεμονωμένη, "has been left alone," to express a unity, in this context an identity (cf. Wallace, *Greek Grammar,* 275). Three perfect-tense verbs clarify the passage. The godly widow μεμονωμένη, "has been left alone"; her destitute state is permanent and she is totally alone. She ἤλπικεν, "has set her hope on," God, emphasizing the finality and assuredness of her decision to rely fully on God and his provisions. In contrast, the self-indulgent widow has died (τέθνηκεν) and continues in that state (v 6). The biblical understanding of hope as confident assurance (cf. 1 Tim 1:1) strengthens the picture of the widow who is fully relying on God. The term ἐλπίζειν, "to set one's hope on," has already been used in 1 Tim 4:10 to describe Paul's attitude toward godliness and will be used to warn the rich in the

Ephesian church to set their hope not on riches, which are uncertain, but on God (1 Tim 6:17). The language is highly reminiscent of the poor in the OT, who have no earthly provisions of their own and have therefore turned to God for support and justice (cf. C. U. Wolf, *IDB* 3:843; E. Bammel, *TDNT* 6:889–92). Because the term ἐλπίζειν is used three times with no apparent difference in meaning (1 Tim 4:10; 5:4; 6:17), the fact that here it is followed by an accusative and elsewhere by the dative is merely a stylistic variation (so Hanson, [1983] 97; contra Bernard, 79).

She who hopes in God is the sort of person who prays continually. The perfective use of πρός in προσμένειν, "to continue" (Bernard, 79), the linear aspect of the verb (cf. Acts 13:43), and the further description νυκτὸς καὶ ἡμέρας, "night and day," all emphasize the true and constant godliness of the widow whom the church should support. δεήσεις, "entreaties," and προσευχαί, "prayers," occur together in 1 Tim 2:1, where any difference in meaning is minimal, but here the context preserves the difference in nuance. δεήσεις are prayers with specific requests (cf. 1 Tim 2:1), in this case probably prayers for provision since the issue of enrollment includes financial support. προσευχαί is a general, all-encompassing term. Kelly argues that the presence of the definite articles shows that Paul is thinking of prayers specifically during congregational meetings (114; cf. use of article in 1 Tim 4:13). If Paul were discussing the duties of the enrolled widow, such as participation in corporate prayer (as Kelly believes), this view of the article would have merit, but the emphasis is on her prayer life as illustrative of her godly character and not on duties. The order νυκτὸς καὶ ἡμέρας, "night and day," instead of the Western "day and night" shows the Semitic way of perceiving the beginning of a new day at sunset (Spicq, 1:528; cf. Gen 1; 1 Thess 2:9; 3:10; 2 Thess 3:8; 2 Tim 1:3; cf. Mark 5:5; Luke 2:37; Acts 20:31; 26:7). It emphasizes that the widow prays constantly (cf. 1 Thess 5:17). Ellicott (68) argues that the order is merely a personal preference. Since the dative is used simply to describe when something occurs, the use of the genitive (νυκτὸς καὶ ἡμέρας) here emphasizes the "kind of action" (BDF §186; Wallace, *Greek Grammar*, 124; cf. John 3:2 where Nicodemus came to Jesus νυκτός, "by night," as one who comes in the night). Widows worthy of church support are the type of people who are constantly in prayer, not those who merely pray at night and during the day.

6 ἡ δὲ σπαταλῶσα ζῶσα τέθνηκεν, "But the one having lived for pleasure, even though living, has died." In contrast to the godly widow who is alone and has set her hope on God (v 5), those widows who live not for God but for pleasure and who, even though they are physically alive, are spiritually dead (a "living corpse" [Simpson, 74]; cf. Str-B 3:652) should not be supported by the church. Lock (59) refers to Friar Alberigo in Dante's *Inferno* (33), whose soul Dante sees in hell although his body is still on earth. Wettstein (*Novum Testamentum Graecum*, 554) lists several parallels to this phrase in Hellenistic literature (e.g., Philo *Fug.* 55). The picture Paul paints in this verse is dramatic. These widows have lived not for God but for pleasure (σπαταλῶσα is a constative aorist), and even though they are alive (ζῶσα is a concessive participle), they in fact have died and continue in the finality of that state (τέθνηκεν is in the perfect tense). The perfect-tense τέθνηκεν, "has died," parallels the two perfect-tense verbs μεμονωμένη, "has been left alone," and ἤλπικεν, "has hoped," in the preceding verses, strengthening the contrast between the two types of widows.

σπαταλᾶν, "to live for pleasure," is a rare word, occurring in the NT elsewhere only in Jas 5:5 (cf. Ezek 16:49; Sir 21:15) in his condemnation of the self-indulgent rich person whose wealth is the result of cheating the workers. It is used to describe Sodom: "Nevertheless this is the transgression of Sodom, your sister: pride. She and her daughters were living for pleasure [ἐσπατάλων] in satiety of bread and in abundance of wine" (Ezek 16:49 LXX). Its basic meaning is to live a luxurious, self-indulgent life, given to pleasure (MM, 582; Ellicott, 68; cf. discussion of τρυφᾶν, "to live in luxury," by F. J. A. Hort on Jas 5:5, *The Epistle of St. James* [London: Macmillan, 1909] 107–9), an interpretation supported by the strong language of this verse, especially the final ζῶσα τέθνηκεν, "even though living, has died." Because these widows were seeking church support, σπαταλᾶν cannot here include the idea of wealth ("luxurious"); rather, σπαταλᾶν is the opposite of ἤλπικεν ἐπὶ θεόν, "have set their hope on God." Support from the church enables the younger Ephesian widows to live totally self-centered lives, given over to the pursuit of selfish pleasure, and they have grown wanton against Christ (cf. vv 11–13 where Paul spells out in more detail the specifics of their lifestyle). In fact, καταστρηνιᾶν τοῦ Χριστοῦ, "to become self-indulgent in contrast to Christ" (v 11), is synonymous with σπαταλᾶν. Easton (152) suggests that the widows have become prostitutes in order to support themselves (Hanson [1983], 97, says the word has sexual nuances but does not think it means prostitution); and while this would explain the strong language, if this were so, Paul would be expected to be more specific in his condemnation of their lifestyle as he is elsewhere with sexual sin (e.g., 1 Cor 5:1–5). The idea of a spiritual death is found elsewhere in Judaism (SB 1:489; 3:652) and Paul (Rom 7:10, 24; Eph 2:1, 5; 4:18; Col 2:13) and is roughly parallel to the angel's words to the church in Sardis: "I know your works; you have the name of being alive, but you are dead" (Rev 3:1b; cf. the words of the father concerning the prodigal son: "for this my son was dead, and is alive again" [Luke 15:24; cf. v 32]).

7 καὶ ταῦτα παράγγελλε, ἵνα ἀνεπίλημπτοι ὦσιν, "Command these things as well, in order that they be above reproach." After contrasting the two groups of widows (vv 3–4, vv 5–6), Paul gives this summary command: Timothy must insist that Paul's instructions in the preceding verses be followed so that the families will be without reproach. V 7 begins the third set of contrasts typical of this section, although the contrast between v 7 and v 8 is not as distinct as the contrasts in the preceding verses. It is common for Paul to use summary commands throughout this epistle (cf. discussion on 1 Tim 4:6). Far from being a "feeble connecting sentence" (Hanson [1983], 97), v 7 is an important verse. It adds a note of urgency to the situation, its brevity and strong language (on παραγγέλλειν, "to command," see *Comment* on 1 Tim 1:3) making the point clear.

There are two related questions in this verse. To what does ταῦτα, "these things," refer? Who are the "they" who are to be above reproach? Paul could be concerned about the responsibility of families to care for their own widows and not bring reproach on themselves. In this case ταῦτα, "these things," would refer to v 4 and the following v 8 (Ellicott, Fee, Knight). However, Paul could be speaking of the widows themselves, telling Timothy to command the instructions in vv 5–6 (Chrysostom, Bernard, Kelly). Guthrie generalizes v 7 to refer to both widows and their families. (1) The fact that Paul has just spoken of the widows in vv 5–6 suggests that they are the topic of v 7. However, v 8 continues by speaking of the families, suggesting that v 4 is still on his mind. (2) The description of widows in vv 5–6 is not something that can be commanded; but the instruction to families in vv 4, 8 can be commanded, suggesting that Paul is thinking of the families' responsibilities. (However, the force of παραγγέλλειν, "to command," could be directed toward the church, that they enroll the widow of v 5 and not the widow of v 6, and hence Paul could be thinking of the widows [vv 5–6]). Also, if v 4 speaks to widows and not the children, then certainly v 7 refers to vv 4–6 and the widows who are commanded in v 4. (3) Nowhere in the chapter does Paul directly address the widows; rather, he only describes them, so it seems unlikely he would be commanding them here. (4) The result of this specific command is that they be without reproach. Since vv 5–6 describe godly and ungodly widows, Paul is not speaking to them and hence is not speaking of their potential reproach. But if the command is to the church and its enrollment policies, it is not clear how commanding proper enrollment policies would result in the widows being above reproach. However, if families fail to follow the commands, it is clear that they would bring reproach on the themselves and on the church. In fact, v 8 can be read as Paul's clarification of what he means by ἀνεπίλημπτοι, "without reproach"; if a family does not care for its own widows, this family has "disowned the faith" and its members are "worse than an unbeliever." (5) Because the two themes of familial responsibility and true widows are intertwined throughout vv 3–16, it cannot be said that one group is necessarily being addressed here. Both groups must be above reproach, and both are capable of bringing reproach on the church. (6) Vv 7–8 form the third couplet in this section (see *Form/Structure/ Setting*). Since v 8 discusses the family, this suggests that Paul is here speaking of families. If Paul is thinking of familial responsibility, as is likely, the thought is as follows: children should care for their widows and mothers (v 4); a true widow has no family (v 5a); the topic shifts to a godly widow (vv 5b–6); and in vv 7–8 Paul comes back to the topic of vv 4–5a and concludes it before continuing with the theme of the godly widow in vv 9–15. Paul will close with a third reference to the family's responsibility (v 16).

The καί, "as well," refers the phrase ταῦτα, "these things," to 4:6, 11, and 15 (Bernard, 80; Kelly, 114); Timothy is to command the instructions in chap. 4, and he is to command the instructions here as well (καί). ἀνεπίλημπτος, "above reproach, blameless," occurs elsewhere in the titular description of elders (1 Tim 3:2) and in Paul's command that Timothy keep the commandment unstained (1 Tim 6:14). Being above reproach is one of the central themes in the PE (cf. *Comment* on 1 Tim 3:2). The Ephesians are evidently so spiritually immature that even after all the years of Paul's ministry he is not able to speak to them as mature Christians but still is dealing with the basics. It is a situation somewhat reminiscent of the Corinthian church to whom Paul said he could feed them merely milk rather than theological meat (1 Cor 3:1–2).

8 εἰ δέ τις τῶν ἰδίων καὶ μάλιστα οἰκείων οὐ προνοεῖ, τὴν πίστιν ἤρνηται καὶ ἔστιν ἀπίστου χείρων, "But if anyone does not care for his own, especially [his] household members, he has disowned the faith and is worse than an unbeliever." In contrast to those who are without reproach (v 7), those who do not care for their extended families, especially their immediate families, have denied their Christianity and do not even measure up to the socially accepted norms of familial responsibility. This is the second of three references in this section to the need for a family to care for its own and not to burden the church (cf. vv 4, 16). It is strong language. Evidently in Ephesus there was a serious problem of people not taking care of their parents, and the church was having to accept the responsibility; in turn the church was not able to care for those widows who were truly alone (v 16). Throughout the PE there is a concern that Christians be at least as good as pagan society (cf. *Form/Structure/Setting* on 1 Tim 3:1; cf. Rom 2:14; 1 Cor 5:1; Phil 4:8; cf. Philo *Decal.* 23; for further parallels, see Wettstein, *Novum Testamentum Graecum;* Lock, 58; Knight, 221, refers to the nonbelievers' innate knowledge of the law in Rom 2:14–5), and this is a situation in which the church is failing. Winter's comments about the control of a widow's dowry (cf. v 3) and evidence of secular and Jewish practices of caring for widows and others in need are helpful here (*TynBul* 39 [1988] 86–90). Of course, Paul uses strong language not merely because the Ephesians are not living up to the social norms. They are disobeying the teachings of the church, teachings going back to the fifth commandment, and their disobedience is the backdrop for this entire section (cf. v 3). This is why their negligence is worse than that of the nonbelievers: they are knowingly breaking God's law. Dibelius-Conzelmann (74) point out that in this verse there is an excellent example of the approach of the PE that intricately intertwines proper belief with godly behavior. The generalizing εἰ δέ τις, "but if anyone," shows that Paul is stating a general principle applicable to the entire church (cf. singular τίμα, "honor," in v 3).

The most significant exegetical issue in this verse is the meaning of ἀρνεῖσθαι, "to disown." It has a wide range of meanings, extending from "to refuse to do something" (Luke 8:45; John 1:20; Acts 4:16; 7:35) to a technical meaning of "to apostatize," as in a denial of Christ (Matt 10:33; Luke 12:9; Acts 3:13; 1 John 2:22, 23; 2 Pet 2:1; Jude 4). Between these two meanings is a denial that, while serious, falls short of apostasy, such as Peter's refusal to acknowledge Christ (Matt 26:70, 72; Mark 14:68, 70; Luke 22:57; John 13:38; 18:25, 27). This same range of meanings is evident in the PE. ἀρνεῖσθαι is used in the absolute sense of apostasy resulting in damnation in 2 Tim 2:12–13: "If we deny [him], he will also deny us; if we are faithless, he remains faithful, for he is not able to deny himself" (see *Comment* on 2 Tim 2:12). Titus 1:16 also belongs in this category: "They [the Cretans] profess to know God, but by their deeds they deny [him]." At the other end of the spectrum, ἀρνεῖσθαι is used to describe a refusal. God's grace trains believers to say "No" (ἀρνησάμενοι) to ungodliness (ἀσέβειαν; Titus 2:12). In the last days wicked people will "hold to the form of godliness but refuse [ἠρνημένοι] its power" (2 Tim 3:5). Between these two ends of the spectrum lies the meaning of 1 Tim 5:8. It cannot refer to apostasy; although ignoring one's familial responsibilities is reprehensible, it is not a damnable offense. Rather, for a person to claim to be a believer and yet not live up to even pagan standards of decency is virtually to deny the meaning of the Christian faith and live as an unbeliever. This is similar to 1 Cor 5:1: "It is actually reported that there is immorality among you, and of a kind that is not found even among pagans; for a man is living with his father's wife." But there may be a hint of something else: the believers who are not accepting their responsibility are doing more damage to the cause of the gospel than even an unbeliever could do. On τὴν πίστιν ἤρνηται, "he has disowned the faith," cf. A. Fridrichsen, *ConNT* 2 (1936) 8–13; 6 (1942) 94–96.

As is the case in vv 4, 6, 11, the δέ here is adversative: the church must be without reproach, "but" those not caring for their family have disowned the faith.

τὶς, "anyone," refers back to the children and grandchildren in v 4. The use of τῶν ἰδίων, "his own," and οἰκείων, "household members," also looks back to v 4, although here Paul is more specific: one's familial responsibility includes the extended family, but especially the immediate family, those living under the same roof. On μάλιστα, "especially," cf. *Comment* on 1 Tim 4:10. On the cognate οἶκος as referring to the household, cf. *Comment* on 1 Tim 3:15. πίστις, "faith," here can have both a personal and a corporate sense: those who do not accept familial responsibilities have disowned their own personal faith, and they have also disowned the Christian faith in that they have brought reproach upon it. The presence of the article (τὴν πίστιν) places the emphasis on the corporate sense (cf. *Introduction,* "Themes in the PE").

9–10a Χήρα καταλεγέσθω μὴ ἔλαττον ἐτῶν ἐξήκοντα γεγονυῖα, ἑνὸς ἀνδρὸς γυνή, ἐν ἔργοις καλοῖς μαρτυρουμένη, "Let a widow be enrolled if she is not less than sixty years old, a 'one-man' woman, being witnessed to by good deeds." Paul begins the fourth set of contrasts in this section: the church should enroll older godly widows (vv 9–10), but it must not enroll younger godless widows (vv 11–13). A widow must meet three qualifications to be enrolled: sixty years old and older; faithful in her marriage; well known for her good deeds (which Paul will spell out in detail). These verses are important for several reasons. (1) They confirm that the central purpose of vv 3–16 is to differentiate between the widows who should be cared for and those who should not, rather than to specify duties (see *Form/Structure/Setting*). Being sixty years old is not a duty, and being witnessed to by good works is a description not of what the widows will do but of what they have done. (2) These verses illustrate that the structure of vv 3–16 is one of contrast between older godly widows, who should be cared for, and younger widows, who should not receive the church's help. (3) They give additional details concerning who is a true widow (v 3).

καταλέγειν, "to enroll," has a range of meaning from "to regard as," "to count among" (Plato *Laws* 743e) to "to select" or "to enroll" as a member of a group. It is used for the enlistment of soldiers (BAGD, 413) and for joining the circle of the gods (Diodorus Siculus 4.39.4), the senate (Plutarch *Pomp.* 13.11), and the clergy (Tertullian *Ad uxorem* 1.7; cf. BGU 4.1073.10 [MM, 329]). While the word can refer to some type of enrollment, it does not specify the nature of the group into which the person is enrolled. It does not necessitate that Paul was envisioning an order of widows similar to the pattern of the later centuries. It means only that the widow was to enter into some type of formal relationship with the church. In fact, the absence of a description of any duties suggests that the relationship Paul is describing is much less formal than the later phenomenon.

The first requirement for entering into a formal relationship with the church is that the widow must be at least sixty years old. This specific age guaranteed that the widow would not be prone to the problems of youth and also that the problem of becoming self-indulgent in opposition to Christ (v 11), with its sexual overtones, would not be a factor. The age of sixty is in contrast to the younger age of the wanton widows (v 11), many of whom had been deceived by the opponents. Sixty seems to have been the age associated with becoming old (references in Spicq, 1:532–33; Str-B 3:653). *M. Abot,* in a discussion of what happens at various ages, says that old age creeps in at sixty (5.24). Because some of the sayings in this tractate may go back as far as the second century B.C. (Schürer, *History* 1:73), it may be that

Paul is reflecting Jewish custom. Paul uses πρεσβῦτις (cf. Titus 2:3) to address older women, and Philo uses the same word of women sixty years and older. Lock cites Plato's teaching that sixty was the age "for men and women to become priests and priestesses in his ideal state (*Laws*, p. 759 D)" and adds that it was "regarded by Orientals as the time for retiring from the world for quiet contemplation" (59, citing Ramsay, *Exp* [1910] 439). The fact that this requirement is listed first and is contrasted in v 11 shows that this was especially important to Paul. On the question of how strictly this age requirement was adhered to, see *Form/Structure/Setting*. ἔλαττον, "younger than," is the Attic form of ἔλασσον and is used as a comparative of μικρός, "small." γεγονυῖα is a conditional participle: "if she is."

The second requirement that a widow must fulfill before she can be officially recognized by the church is that she must have been faithful to her husband. ἑνὸς ἀνδρὸς γυνή, "one-man woman," is the reverse of the similarly unusual statement that each elder and deacon must be a "one-woman man" (μιᾶς γυναικὸς ἄνδρα; cf. *Comment* on 1 Tim 3:2, 12). The unusualness of the expression guarantees that it means the same thing in all three passages, but in reverse here. It also guarantees that "one-woman man" was not a prohibition of polygamy (contra Ellicott, 71) since polyandry (in contrast to a "one-woman man") was so rare that it hardly qualifies as one of the three basic requirements of widows. It appears that Paul is telling Timothy that a widow must either have been married only once (Ellicott, Bernard, Spicq, Guthrie, Kelly, Fee) or that she must have been faithful to her husband regardless of the number of times she had been married (Lock, Dibelius-Conzelmann). Fee (119) argues that the phrase "one-woman man" applied to elders refers to faithfulness in marriage, but "one-man woman" applied to widows is a prohibition of a second marriage. The NIV likewise is inconsistent in its interpretation: "husband of but one wife" (1 Tim 3:2, 12) and "faithful to her husband" (1 Tim 5:9). Although widows who refused to remarry were held in high esteem (references in Lock, 60; G. Delling, *Paulus' Stellung zu Frau und Ehe*, BWANT 108 [Stuttgart: Kohlhammer, 1931] 134; Dibelius-Conzelmann, 75 n. 18; Lightman and Zeisel, *CH* 46 [1977] 19–32), this is not sufficient argument to change the interpretation of the phrase in 1 Tim 5:9. The unusualness of the phrase argues for a consistent interpretation: what is true for elders and deacons should also be true for widows. This seems the best interpretation and therefore governs interpretation of the "one-woman man" phrase in 1 Tim 3:2, 12 (see *Comments* there).

Viewing the phrase "one-man woman" as describing faithfulness solves the possible conflict with the command in v 14 that younger widows remarry. If the phrase means one marriage, by urging remarriage for the younger widows Paul would be guaranteeing that, if they were to become widows again, when they were sixty, they would be ineligible for aid. However, it is also possible to remove any apparent contradiction by arguing that Paul is stating both the ideal (v 9) and what is realistic (v 14; Kelly, 116). Ideally the widow should remain single (vv 9–10); however, realistically it is best if she remarry (vv 11–14). This is much like Paul's teaching elsewhere on remarriage: it is ideal to stay single (1 Cor 7:8), but if this is not possible, then remarriage is recommended (1 Cor 7:2, 9, 39–40). Others have argued that Paul is referring to two groups of widows (Bernard, 80–81): vv 3–8 allow widows of all ages to be cared for, but vv 9–10 describe a special group of widows, older women who were entering into an order of widows with specific responsibilities to the church. While this suggestion might solve some of the difficulties, it does not appear that Paul is speaking to a different audience here from the one in the previous verses.

The third requirement for a widow to be enrolled is that her past life must show that she has been committed to doing good deeds. Paul continues by spelling out what he means by good deeds in v 10b: raising children, showing hospitality to strangers, washing the feet of the saints, and relieving the afflicted. In other words, she must have been a godly woman. This list completes the idea begun in v 5 that she be the sort of person who has set her hope on God. ἔργα καλά, "good works," is an important concept in the PE, illustrating the practical nature of Paul's instructions (cf. *Comment* on 1 Tim 2:10). These good deeds are not duties that an enrolled widow must perform in the church but are the types of things that she must have done in the past that currently testify that she is a godly person. One would expect, however, that an enrolled widow would continue doing the same activities she had always done but now in direct service to the church.

10b εἰ ἐτεκνοτρόφησεν, εἰ ἐξενοδόχησεν, εἰ ἁγίων πόδας ἔνιψεν, εἰ θλιβομένοις ἐπήρκεσεν, εἰ παντὶ ἔργῳ ἀγαθῷ ἐπηκολούθησεν, "if she raised children, if she showed hospitality, if she washed the feet of the saints, if she helped the afflicted, if she earnestly pursued every good work." Paul spells out in detail what he means by ἔργα καλά, "good works." These examples of good deeds are not a checklist that every widow must fulfill. Otherwise, godly widows who never had children would be excluded, which does not seem reasonable.

(1) She must have raised children. τεκνοτροφεῖν, "to raise children," occurs in the NT only here. Paul's opponents eschewed marriage (1 Tim 4:3) and probably child rearing (1 Tim 2:15). Not only does this show Paul's view of the importance of child rearing, but it is an implicit ban on the church's support of the opponents. Some argue the word should be translated "cared for children" (Kelly, 116–17), which would include the care of orphans (Dibelius-Conzelmann, 75) and allow for childless widows to be eligible for enrollment. Although one of the roles of widows in later centuries was the care of orphans (see *Explanation*), it is unnecessary to see this meaning in this verse. Paul's requirement that the widows have raised children is not a proscription of childless women (see *Form/Structure/Setting*). Dibelius-Conzelmann (75) point out that a widow who had children who could attest to their upbringing would be automatically disqualified because if she had children she would not be alone (v 4). But this misses the practical point that the children of some widows may not have been available or willing to help their mothers.

(2) She must have been the type of person who showed hospitality to people (ξενοδοχεῖν). Showing hospitality is one of the character requirements of elders (1 Tim 3:2) and all Christians (Rom 12:13). It is interesting that several of the character requirements of widows overlap with those of elders and deacons; all Christians should be godly people, especially if they are in any way officially connected to the church. Bernard (82), apparently reasoning that hospitality was costly, argues that this requirement shows that the widows being enrolled were not necessarily destitute. But the character trait of being hospitable would have been established while the widows were still married and had resources. Paul's statement does not mean widows have the responsibility of housing church guests. Chrysostom argues that these good deeds were not costly ("Homily 14"; NPNF 13:454).

(3) She must have been the type of person who willingly washed the feet of the saints. This is a mark of servanthood and humility (1 Sam 25:41; John 13:3–11, 14) and a custom necessary in a dry, dusty land (Str-B 3:653). It is performed for guests, husbands, parents (Barrett, *John*, 440), and teachers (*b. Ber.* 7b). A Jewish slave could not be forced to wash his master's feet although slaves of other nationalities could (*Mek.* on Exod 21:2). This does not refer to the later church ritual of foot washing (cf. Augustine *Letters* 55.33). Paul is not asking if the widow followed church ritual; he is asking if she was the type of person who had done good deeds throughout her life.

(4) She must have been the type of person who had helped the afflicted. θλίβειν, "to afflict," describes affliction in general or affliction from perse:ution as a Christian (H. Schlier, *TDNT* 3:143–48). The context does not suggest persecution, so Paul is probably thinking of a helping spirit toward all who are in need. ἐπαρκεῖν, "to help," occurs in the NT only here and in the conclusion of this passage (v 16).

(5) Paul concludes the list of types of good works with the all-inclusive "if she earnestly pursued every good work." The generality of this phrase confirms that these good deeds are not given as specific prerequisites to enrollment but are typical examples. This same use of a summarizing statement occurs in 1 Tim 1:10 at the end of the vice list: "liars, perjurers, and everything else that is contrary to healthy teaching." ἐπακολουθεῖν can mean "to follow after" as it does in 1 Tim 5:24, but the perfective use of ἐπί (cf. Robertson, *Grammar,* 600) is probably intended: "to devote oneself." It is not so much that the widow has done certain things but that she is the type of person who willingly, even joyfully, performed her tasks as a Christian wife and mother. V 10 ends on the same note as it began: the widow who should be enrolled by the church is the type of person who is fully committed to doing good deeds. Lock paraphrases, "if she has at all times thrown her whole heart into good deeds" (57).

11a νεωτέρας δὲ χήρας παραιτοῦ, "But refuse [to enroll] younger widows." In contrast to his approach to the older, godly widows (vv 9–10), Timothy must refuse to enroll younger widows. (καταλέγειν, "to enroll," is assumed from v 9.) Paul follows with two reasons. (1) Younger widows may desire to remarry and abandon their faith (vv 11b–12). (2) The younger widows are misbehaving in the extreme (v 13); their behavior is the opposite of the godly widows, and therefore they should not be enrolled.

As has been the case above (cf. vv 4, 6, 8), the δέ, "but," is adversative, separating the widows who should be enrolled from those who should not. παραιτεῖσθαι, "to refuse," is an emphatic term. Elsewhere Paul tells Titus to spurn the heretics (3:10) and Timothy to stay far away from the heresy (1 Tim 4:7; 2 Tim 2:23). It is with this same vigor that Timothy must ensure that the Ephesian church not enroll their younger widows. The problem is severe, as will be seen in Paul's description of their behavior (v 13). By νεωτέρας, "younger," Paul means at least younger than sixty (v 9), desirous of remarriage and able to bear children (v 14). This does not mean that the church cannot aid younger widows; it means that they must not be enrolled into a formal, ongoing financial relationship with the church. On νεώτερος as "younger," see *Comment* on 1 Tim 5:1.

11b–12 ὅταν γὰρ καταστρηνιάσωσιν τοῦ Χριστοῦ, γαμεῖν θέλουσιν, ἔχουσαι κρίμα ὅτι τὴν πρώτην πίστιν ἠθέτησαν, "for when they grow wanton against Christ, they desire to marry and come under judgment since they abandoned their former faith." The first reason that Timothy should not enroll younger widows is that their self-indulgent, self-centered lives outweigh their devotion to Christ. As a result, they wish to remarry, which in turn brings them into judgment because by remarrying they are abandoning their faith. The basic thrust of these verses is straightforward: these younger widows are turning against Christ. Beyond this, the specifics of the passage are difficult to interpret. What is there about their self-indulgence that is so horrific that remarriage becomes a sign of judgment and warrants unusually harsh language: "wanton against Christ"; "judgment"; "going after Satan" (vv 11–12, 15)? Contrary to Fee (120), this is not the same situation as in 1 Cor 7 where remarriage may not be preferred but is allowed. There is something in the Ephesian situation that makes remarriage wrong.

Paul's central concern is not remarriage. He cannot be condemning the widows for remarrying because he recommends remarriage two verses later. The real problem is that the younger widows have given themselves over to a self-centered, self-indulgent lifestyle and have followed after Satan (v 15). Their desire to remarry is symptomatic of their wantonness, and it is a wanton remarriage that Paul condemns.

καταστρηνιᾶν, "to become self-indulgent in opposition to," occurs in the NT only here. While it is difficult to be precise in defining this term, there are a few indications of its meaning. (1) BAGD (419; cf. Ps.-Ignatius *Ad Antioch* 11) defines it as "become wanton against" and suggests the translation "when they feel sensuous impulses that alienate them from Christ." LSJ (1654) defines the cognate στρηνιᾶν as "run riot, wax wanton," and στρῆνος as "insolence, arrogance, wantonness." (2) The simple forms στρηνιᾶν and στρῆνος occur in Rev 18:3–7 in the description of Babylon's destruction: "For all nations have drunk the wine of her impure passion, and the kings of the earth have committed fornication with her, and the merchants of the earth have grown rich with the wealth of her wantonness [ἐκ τῆς δυνάμεως τοῦ στρήνους]" (Rev 18:3); "As she glorified herself and played the wanton [ἐστρηνίασεν], so give her a like measure of torment and mourning. Since in her heart she says, 'A queen I sit, I am no widow, mourning I shall never see,' so shall her plagues come in a single day, pestilence with mourning and famine" (Rev 18:7–8). (3) The use of κατά to form the compound shows that this self-indulgence is directly opposed to Christ (cf. BDF §181). (4) The context of this chapter links καταστρηνιᾶν with σπαταλᾶν, "to live for pleasure" (v 6). (5) The following verse says that these widows have followed after Satan (v 15). From these five different hints and the general context, the situation appears to have been that some younger widows who had been enrolled were abusing the system (so Hanson [1983], 98). With the church caring for their physical needs, they had time to indulge themselves and live totally self-centered lives. Instead of maintaining their devotion to God, they were being captivated by their sensual desires and as a result wanted to remarry. Their lifestyles were so extreme that harsh language such as "judgment" and "going after Satan" was warranted. καταστρηνιᾶν does not necessarily contain any idea of sexual promiscuity, although the context suggests that it was part of the problem. Bernard (82) and Guthrie (103) both say that the word suggests an animal struggling to be freed from its yoke; unfortunately neither gives support. The widow's desire to remarry is interesting in light of the opponents' disregard of marriage (cf. 1 Tim 4:3) and the fact that the opponents have probably secured a following among these widows (cf. 2 Tim 3:6). This suggests that the Ephesian heresy was not a well-formulated doctrine but rather a collection of loosely associated ideas without internal consistency.

To complete the picture, we must understand that πρῶτος can mean both "first" and "former," the superlative used in place of the comparative (BDF §60[1]; W. Michaelis, *TDNT* 6:866). πίστις can mean both a "pledge" (cf. Polybius 8.2.5; 11.29.1; Diodorus Siculus 21.20) and a person's "faith" or Christian "faith" (cf. *Introduction*, "Themes in the PE"). Suggested interepretations of πρώτην πίστιν, "former faith," thus include (1) pledge of faithfulness to one's first husband (Holtz, 119–20; Brox, 194–95); (2) pledge of celibacy upon entrance to the order of widows (Ellicott, 73, who talks of their "engagement [συνθήκην, Chrys(ostom)] to Christ not to marry again"; Bernard, 83; apparently Dibelius-Conzelmann, 75; Guthrie, 103; Kelly, 117; Sand, *BibLeb* 12 [1971] 196; Hanson [1983], 98; Knight, 222; Oberlinner, 237); (3) pledge as part of the entrance into the order and equivalent to marriage to Christ (Roloff, 296); and (4) the widow's faith in Christ (Fee, 121). The preferred interpretation is the view that best explains the extremely harsh language.

It is doubtful that interpretation (1) is correct. Because Paul continues by encouraging remarriage in v 14 and elsewhere (1 Cor 7:39) and argues elsewhere that a wife is bound to her husband only as long as he lives (Rom 7:1–3), he does not view remarriage itself as breaking the vow to the first husband. (This would also require bringing the first husband into the discussion without any textual introduction, which seems unlikely.) Yet one is reminded of Malachi's judgment upon divorce when he says "So take heed to yourselves, and let none be faithless to the wife of his youth. For I hate divorce, says the LORD the God of Israel. . . . So take heed to yourselves and do not be faithless" (Mal 2:15–16). Option (2) is preferred by most. It assumes that the widows made a vow of celibacy when they were enrolled, and the desire to remarry is a breaking of that vow. Many comment that Christ is envisioned as a spiritual bridegroom (cf. 2 Cor 11:2; cf. J. Moffatt, *Love in the New Testament* [London: Hodder & Stoughton, 1929] 220–21; Jeremias, 39; Kelly, 117). By wanting to remarry, that pledge of faithfulness to Christ was broken. However, the major impediment to this interpretation is the harshness of the language. If a widow had pledged to remain single in order to be supported by the church and then later changed her mind, it is doubtful that this would have been classified as an act of a wanton woman, an act of judgment, an abandonment of her faith, and a following after Satan (v 15). Knight (226) translates κρίμα not as "condemnation" but as "censure" (citing the use of κρίνειν in 1 Cor 11:29, 31, 32, 34), making it less harsh. It can also be asked if a widow, in order to receive aid from the church, would have had to commit herself to lifelong celibacy (albeit she would have been at least sixty years old). This would seem to be too extreme and is more a reflection of a time later than the first or even the second century (cf. Sand, *BibLeb* 12 [1971] 196, who argues that a vow of celibacy by a sixty-year-old woman would make no sense). The text says nothing about spiritual marriage as in option (3). The most likely interpretation is that the widows were giving in to their sensual desires, turning against Christ, marrying non-Christians (Towner, 121; cf. 1 Cor 7:39), and abandoning their former faith, the Christian faith they had before they remarried (as in option [4]). (a) This interpretation alone explains the strong language of the verse. Simply wanting to remarry, even within the faith, or living a self-centered lifestyle, would not warrant the extreme language. (b) In addition, option (4) gives πίστις its normal meaning as "faith" and not as the unusual "pledge." (Even if τὴν πρώτην πίστιν, "the former pledge," referred to the pledge of being enrolled, this would still not be a pledge of celibacy. The problem is not primarily that of remarriage; rather the problem is self-indulgence and the resulting immorality.)

The case of Χριστοῦ, "Christ," is controlled by the compound verb. ἔχουσαι, "coming under," is technically a participle of attendant circumstance, but the context shows that it specifically includes the results of the widows' desire to remarry; they wish to remarry and therefore bring judgment down upon themselves. ἀθετεῖν as a transitive verb means "to declare invalid, nullify, set aside" (BAGD, 21). It is used elsewhere to describe the nullifying of the will of God (Gal 3:15), the commandment of God (Mark 7:9), the purposes of God (Luke 7:30), the law of Moses (Heb 10:28), the grace of God (Gal 2:21), and the cleverness of the clever (1 Cor 1:19). The idea of a spiritual marriage to Christ is present elsewhere in Paul (2 Cor 11:2) but not here.

13 ἅμα δὲ καὶ ἀργαὶ μανθάνουσιν περιερχόμεναι τὰς οἰκίας, οὐ μόνον δὲ ἀργαὶ ἀλλὰ καὶ φλύαροι καὶ περίεργοι, λαλοῦσαι τὰ μὴ δέοντα, "But at the same time they also learn to be idlers, flitting about among houses, but not only idlers but also gossips and busybodies, speaking about things that should not be spoken." The second reason that the Ephesian church should not enroll younger widows is that they lack true Christian character. This, combined with the fact that they have turned against Christ (vv 11b–12), is clear evidence that they are not true widows. Paul's main concern is that the younger widows have too much time on their hands (repeated twice; cf. Dibelius-Conzelmann, 75). As a result of their idleness, they have become gossips and busybodies. As Fee (122) points out, the younger widows lacked any constructive qualities and possessed several destructive ones.

Throughout vv 3–16 Paul has made implicit and explicit comparisons between the true widows who should be supported by the church and the widows who should not be supported. Here too the implicit comparison is made between the godly widow who dedicates herself to prayer and lives a life replete with good deeds (vv 5, 10) and the ungodly younger widows who use their freedom to waste time and become general nuisances. V 13 fills out the picture from v 12 since while they are desiring to remarry, ἅμα, "at the same time" (Moule, *Idiom-Book*, 81–82), they are learning to be idlers. The verse shows a distinct parallel structure: it contains two descriptions of these widows ("idlers"; "gossips and busybodies"), each of which is followed by an explanatory participial phrase ("flitting about among houses"; "speaking about things that should not be spoken"). This is intended as a description not of all young widows but of what is happening in the Ephesian church.

Paul's first description of their ungodly behavior, that they are learning to be idlers, is a sarcastic statement: "At the same time that they are turning against Christ, they are also studying hard to learn how to be idle." The sarcastic use of μανθάνειν, "to learn," is also found later in the PE where Paul describes his opponents as people who are "always learning [πάντοτε μανθάνοντα] and never able to come to the knowledge of the truth" (2 Tim 3:7). μανθάνειν governs both ἀργαί, "idlers," and φλύαροι καὶ περίεργοι, "gossips and busybodies." The construction is awkward: ἀργαὶ μανθάνουσιν, lit. "idlers they are learning." Several interpretations have been offered. (1) Moffatt's translation (310) and Jeremias (39) emend the verb to λανθάνουσιν (λανθάνειν, "to escape notice, be hidden"; BAGD, 466): "they become idle unconsciously." However, there is no textual support for this emendation, there is no reason to think that the widows were unknowingly caught up in their lifestyle of idleness, and there are other plausible suggestions for the construction. (2) Most assume an implicit εἶναι, "to be": "learn to be idlers" (cf. Dibelius-Conzelmann, 75; BDF §416[2]; and the use of the verb with an infinitive in 1 Tim 5:4; Titus 3:14; and Phil 4:11). (3) Lock (60–61) argues that μανθάνειν can be used idiomatically to describe preparation for a profession, with the profession being expressed in the nominative case (citing F. Field, *Otium Norvicense*, Part 3 [Cambridge, 1899]), which is affirmed by Kelly (118). If this is correct, then the sarcasm of the statement is heightened: "These widows are studying to become professional idlers."

ἀργαί, "idlers," occurs elsewhere in the PE only in Titus 1:12 in the quotation about Cretans: "Cretans are always liars, evil beasts, lazy [ἀργαί] gluttons." ἀργός means "unemployed, idle, lazy, useless, unproductive" (BAGD, 104). Elsewhere in the NT the word is used to describe every careless word for which people will give account on the day of judgment (Matt 12:36), unemployed laborers standing idly in the market place (Matt 20:3,6), and the vanity of faith without works (Jas 2:20). It also appears in the discussion of the virtues such as faith and self-control that keep a believer from becoming ineffective (ἀργούς) and unfruitful in the knowledge of Christ (2 Pet 1:8). ἀργαί here is the first of three adjectives used substantivally to describe the widows.

To spell out what this idleness entails, Paul adds the explanatory περιερχόμεναι τὰς οἰκίας, "flitting about among houses." Rather than busying themselves with prayer and good deeds as the godly widows had done, the younger widows were spending their free time going from house to house. It is difficult to see anything more specific in these verses. (1) Most assume that these verses describe the duties of the widow who has been enrolled, one of those duties being church visitation (Bernard, 83; Guthrie, 103; Kelly, 118; Brox, 195). Dibelius-Conzelmann say that this verse "refers to pastoral calls. The context clearly indicates that such calls were among widows' duties" (75). But Dibelius-Conzelmann have overstated their case, and it has been argued above that vv 3–16 have nothing to do with duties of an enrolled widow. (2) Kelly (118) argues that the widows were involved in witchcraft, and as they went from house to house they were performing magic (see below). This is based on the possible translation of περίεργος as "worker of magic" and the parallel use of περιέρχεσθαι, "to travel about," in Acts 19:13 to describe itinerant Jewish exorcists. For reasons listed below, however, magic is not the issue here, and in Acts 19:13 the verb has no necessary connection with magic since Luke felt it was necessary to add ἐξορκιστῶν, "exorcists." (3) It is doubtful that the widows were involved in much more than lazy idleness, except perhaps to spread the heresy; that is all the text will bear (cf. *Comment* on 2:11). περιέρχεσθαι describes moving from one place to another, such as Paul's trip from Syracuse to Rhegium (Acts 28:13; cf. variant in Acts 13:6), Jewish exorcists going from city to city (Acts 19:13), and OT martyrs going about in animal skins (Heb 11:37). The context here confirms that the goings and comings are the result of idleness, hence the translation "flitting." οἰκία, "house," idiomatically almost always occurs with the article.

The younger widows should not be enrolled in the church's care, not only because they are idlers but also because they are φλύαροι καὶ περίεργοι, λαλοῦσαι τὰ μὴ δέοντα, "gossips and busybodies, speaking about things that should not be spoken." φλύαροι, "gossips," and περίεργοι, "busybodies," are both substantival adjectives, parallel with ἀργαί, "idlers," and the predicate of the verb μανθάνουσιν, "they learn." φλύαρος occurs only here in the NT and means "gossipy, foolish" (BAGD, 862), "tattler, babbler" (LSJ, 1946), talking about something that does not concern oneself (Roloff, 297). The cognate verb φλυαρεῖν (cf. 3 John 10) means "to talk nonsense" (BAGD, 862). The problem is not so much that the widows were slandering people (although the verb can mean "to bring unjustified charges against" [BAGD, 862]) but that they were talking nonsense, the type of conduct one would expect from someone studying to be an idler. However, Fee says "the word means to 'talk foolishness' but not in the sense that 'gossipy' connotes. Rather, in most of its extant uses it means to prate on about something, either in a foolish manner or with foolish ideas. In the latter sense it is picked up in polemical contexts to refer to speaking what is foolish or absurd vis-à-vis the truth—precisely Paul's condemnation of the F[alse] T[eachers] in 1:6; 6:20; 2 Tim 2:23" (*JETS* 28 [1985] 148 n. 9).

The primary meaning of περίεργος is "meddlesome, a busybody" (BAGD, 646). It can describe behavior roughly analogous to φλύαρος, "gossipy." The problem in Ephesus was similar to that in Thessalonica, where members of the church were idle and creating a burden for the church (2 Thess 3:6–15). It is also possible to translate περίεργος as "pertaining to magic," used substantially for things used in the practice of magic, which Acts tells us was widespread in Ephesus (Acts 19:19; cf. Plutarch *Alexander* 2.5; Vettius Valens [index]; Aristaenetus 2.18.2; Deissmann, *Bible Studies*, 323). Kelly (118) says it was used in the magical papyri for "spells" or "magic arts" (cf. MM, 505). He argues that it was "discreetly veiled language," showing that the widows were using magic on the sick, and the following "speaking about things of which they should not speak" refers to casting spells (citing Titus 1:11; see also Paul's comparison of the opponents to the Egyptian magicians in 2 Tim 3:8 and Spicq, 1:104–6; *Introduction,* "The Ephesian Heresy"). Although an attractive suggestion, there does not seem to be sufficient evidence to require it. (1) The following phrase most naturally describes empty and senseless prattle, not magic. (2) Being parallel with φλύαροι, "gossips," suggests more the meaning "busybodies." (3) It is not clear why Paul would make a "discreetly veiled comment" rather than address the problem directly. If the problem was as serious as magic, a harsher and more direct condemnation would be expected.

λαλοῦσαι τὰ μὴ δέοντα, "speaking about things that should not be spoken," describes in more detail the nature of the gossip and meddlesome activities of the younger widows. δέοντα, "being necessary," the participle from δεῖ, "it is necessary," denotes that which is, or in this case is not, proper or necessary. δεῖ describes what is of necessity, such as a divine necessity, an unavoidable fate, a compulsion under duty, law, custom, or necessity, or that which is fitting or proper (BAGD, 172; W. Grundmann, *TDNT* 2:21–25; cf. *Comment* on 1 Tim 3:2). With the negative it describes what of necessity must not happen (cf. Luke 13:16; Acts 25:24). The Lord's servant must not be quarrelsome (2 Tim 2:24). The Ephesians' opponents must be silenced because they are teaching what must not be taught

(Titus 1:11). From this explanation it is apparent that the widows were not only discussing nonsense; they were talking about things that should not be discussed.

Fee (122) notes the similarity between this description of the widows' speech and that of the opponents' speech, which was foolish (1 Tim 1:6), empty (1 Tim 6:20), and betrayed ignorance of what they were teaching (1 Tim 1:6–7; 4:7; 6:3–4). The similar imagery suggests that it was the heresy that the widows should not discuss. This conforms to the earlier statement that the opponents were successful in recruiting women (cf. 2 Tim 3:6). It is also supported by an interpretation of v 15 that sees the "straying after Satan" as a euphemism for an acceptance of the heresy, which itself was demonic in origin (1 Tim 4:1).

14a βούλομαι οὖν νεωτέρας γαμεῖν, τεκνογονεῖν, οἰκοδεσποτεῖν, "Therefore I wish younger [widows] to marry, to bear children, to rule their households." The concern of vv 3–16 is how to differentiate the widows whom the church should support from those whom it should not support. Vv 14–16 are the conclusion to this discussion and repeat the answer in detail. Younger Ephesian widows were turning against Christ, and their idleness was leading to non-Christian behavior. Younger widows are therefore exhorted to remarry and fill up their time with their families and homes (vv 14–15). Families who had widows are required to care for their own so that the church can be free to care for widows who are truly alone (v 16).

οὖν, "therefore," introduces the response to the problems described in vv 11b–13: Paul's wish is that the younger widows remarry. This is the first of three activities Paul prescribes for the widows. βούλεσθαι, "to wish," a strong term in the PE, denotes Paul's authoritative judgment (cf. 1 Tim 2:8). Ellicott (74) compares this verse to v 11: the younger widows desire to remarry (γαμεῖν θέλουσιν) non-Christians; Paul desires (βούλομαι) that they should remarry and not be enrolled, but presumably remarry only in the Lord (cf. 1 Cor 7:39). Although Paul is not telling each individual widow that she must remarry, he is establishing church policy for the Ephesians on the issue of who should not be enrolled. This way the younger widows would not rely on the church for support, they would not be tempted to turn against Christ, and their time would be filled with family activities and not the idleness that leads to being gossips and busybodies. There is an implicit condemnation of the Ephesian heresy that forbade marriage (1 Tim 4:3). νεωτέρας, "younger," does not describe all young women, which would be out of context; χήρας, "widows," is assumed from v 11. Roman law required a widow under the age of fifty to remarry within two years of her husband's death (*lex Papia Poppaea,* A.D. 9; cited in Winter, *TynBul* 39 [1988] 85; cf. A. Wallace-Hadrill, "Family and Inheritance in the Augustan Marriage Laws," *Proceedings of the Cambridge Philological Society* n.s. 27 [1981] 59).

There is no conflict between Paul's prescription of remarriage and his earlier statement that a widow must have been a "one-man woman" to be enrolled (v 9). This phrase refers not to remarriage but to faithfulness within a marriage (see *Comment* on v 9). Hanson's statement that the author is "ambiguous on the issue of whether widows remarry" ([1983] 96) is built on a misunderstanding of the phrase. There also is no conflict between this statement and Paul's teaching to the Corinthian church (1 Cor 7:8–9, 39–40; cf. Knight, 228). Dibelius-Conzelmann (75–76) say that the approach in the PE is totally different from that in 1 Corinthians: there, it is claimed, Paul's approach is eschatologically determined while in the PE there is no hope in the imminence of Christ's return. In response to this position, it is not necessary to postulate, as does Kelly (119), that Paul's hope was dimming. Rather, the supposed conflict is remedied by seeing that in both epistles Paul differentiates between what is preferable and what is necessary in certain circumstances: to the Corinthian church Paul says that singleness is preferable, but if that is not possible then it is permissible to remarry; to the Ephesians he says that because of the problems caused by the Ephesian widows, it is best for them to remarry.

Paul adds that once the widows are remarried they are to bear children and run their households (τεκνογονεῖν, οἰκοδεσποτεῖν). This removes their idleness and the ensuing temptation to be gossips and busybodies. Bearing children is viewed as a good work in the PE (cf. 1 Tim 2:15) and is one of the qualifications for a widow to be enrolled for support by the church (5:10). Childbirth, along with marriage, was probably frowned upon by the opponents (1 Tim 2:15; 4:3). οἰκοδεσποτεῖν, "to rule a household," is a late word occurring nowhere else in the NT (but it does occur in secular writings; BAGD, 588; MM, 441), although its cognate noun οἰκοδεσπότης, "master of the house," is common in the Gospels. Lock points out that this verse illustrates "the new and improved position which was secured to women by the Gospel" (61, quoting Liddon), giving them the authority and requirement of ruling their households. S. M. Baugh shows that an Ephesian wife often had "extensive authority and management over domestic affairs" ("A Foreign World," in *Women in the Church,* ed. Köstenberger et al., 50–51). How this is balanced with the husband managing the home (1 Tim 3:5, 12) is not clarified.

14b   μηδεμίαν ἀφορμὴν διδόναι τῷ ἀντικειμένῳ λοιδορίας χάριν, "to give the Accuser no occasion for slander." Evidently the widows' behavior was bringing reproach upon the church, and a common theme throughout the PE is that the church must protect itself from unnecessary reproach (cf. 1 Tim 3:7; 6:1; Titus 2:5, 8).

The difficult question of this phrase is the identity of τῷ ἀντικειμένῳ, "the Accuser." ἀντίκεισθαι, "to oppose," indicates strong opposition such as the opposition Jesus received from the Jewish leaders and Paul received from his opponents in Corinth (cf. *Comment* on 1 Tim 1:10). (1) Some argue that it refers to human antagonists (Ellicott, Bernard, Dibelius-Conzelmann). This is the word's meaning in its other occurrences in the NT (Luke 13:17; 21:15; 1 Cor 16:9; Phil 1:28; 2 Thess 2:4; 1 Tim 1:10; the use of the word in Gal 5:17 speaks of the opposition between flesh and Spirit). (2) Others see it as referring to the Antagonist, Satan (Kelly, Hanson [1983], Fee; cf. use in *1 Clem.* 51:1; *Mart. Pol.* 17:1). (a) In our passage the word is singular whereas in the other passages discussing human antagonists it is usually plural. (In 2 Thess 2:4 it is singular referring to the antichrist, and in 1 Tim 1:10 it refers to anything that is opposed to healthy teaching.) (b) The presence of the article suggests a specific antagonist. (c) Throughout the PE Satan has been pictured as an active player in the events of the church (1 Tim 3:6–7). It is he who stands behind the Ephesian heresy, and it is he who has branded the opponents (1 Tim 4:1–2). In the next verse (v 15) Paul says that some of the widows have already followed after Satan. With either interpretation, Satan is involved, working through people either implicitly or explicitly.

ἀφορμή, "opportunity," is a common word in Paul (cf. Rom 7:8, 11; 2 Cor 5:12; 11:12; Gal 5:13). It originally described a "starting point or base of operations for an expedition, then gener. the resources used to carry through an undertaking"

(BAGD, 127; cf. G. Bertram, *TDNT* 5:472–74). The picture it paints is of the enemy gaining a toehold in the church because of the widows' misconduct, and from this toehold making his attack upon the church. Paul clarifies that the toehold gained is for the purpose of reproach. λοιδορία means "abuse, reproach" (BAGD, 479) and occurs in the NT elsewhere only in 1 Pet 3:9 (cognates in 1 Cor 4:12; 5:11; 6:10). χάριν, "for the sake of," is an improper preposition indicating a goal. It almost always follows its object, in this case λοιδορία (cf. Titus 1:5, 11; Luke 7:47; Gal 3:19; Eph 3:1, 14; 1 John 3:12; Jude 16). If the accuser is human opponents, then λοιδορία refers to the abuse they heap upon the church. If the accuser is Satan, then it refers to the abuse that comes as a result of his demonic activity within the church and through the opponents who teach demonic doctrine (1 Tim 4:1).

15 ἤδη γάρ τινες ἐξετράπησαν ὀπίσω τοῦ σατανᾶ, "for some have already strayed after Satan." V 15 adds a note of urgency to the situation. The younger widows have grown wanton against Christ (v 11), have started marrying non-Christians, and are leaving the faith (v 12); their idleness has led to a lifestyle of gossips and busybodies (v 13). To cap it off, they have even followed after Satan. The problem is serious, urgent, and must be dealt with immediately.

(1) The possibility of devil worship can probably be discounted. If the younger widows were actually worshiping Satan, Paul would be expected to have made that clear. (If this were the case, then v 13 would be translated, "At the same time they are learning to be idlers, practicing magic from house to house, but not only idlers but also gossips and magicians, speaking magical spells that should not be spoken" [see *Comment* above]). (2) Spicq (1:538) argues that ἐξετράπησαν ὀπίσω τοῦ σατανᾶ, "they have strayed after Satan," is a periphrastic way of saying that they had begun pursuing lives of immorality. Hanson ([1983] 99) believes the widows were becoming prostitutes, which is plausible. (3) Satan is pictured in the PE as being active throughout the Ephesian church, setting snares for elders (1 Tim 3:7), capturing the opponents (2 Tim 2:26; cf. 1 Tim 2:14), and punishing them (1 Tim 1:20). Most significantly, he is seen as the force behind the Ephesian heresy (1 Tim 4:1–2). Because Satan plays such an active role in the PE, the phrase "they have strayed after Satan" should be interpreted as a euphemism for acceptance of the demonic Ephesian heresy (Verner, *Household* [citing 1 Tim 1:6; 6:20; 2 Tim 4:4]; Bassler, *JBL* 103 [1984] 37 n. 51; Fee, 123; contra Brox, 197). Fee points out the similarity between Paul's description of desirable behavior for widows in v 13 and the opponents' teaching (see on v 13). If he is correct, then this interpretation is strengthened. The widows have accepted the false teaching, and as they have flitted from house to house, they have spread its doctrine.

The placement of the ἤδη, "already," is significant. The word does not refer to the age of the church as if Paul were expressing disbelief that after so few years the Ephesians were already dealing with this type of problem. It refers to what is already happening prior to the time of Paul's writing to Timothy, which must be dealt with immediately. On the general use of τινές, "some," to describe the opponents, see *Comment* on 1 Tim 1:3. ἐκτρέπειν, "to stray," is typical language in the PE (cf. 1 Tim 1:6). The problem came not from outside the church but from within the church, and people who once were participants in the truth are now falling away.

16 εἴ τις πιστὴ ἔχει χήρας, ἐπαρκείτω αὐταῖς καὶ μὴ βαρείσθω ἡ ἐκκλησία, ἵνα ταῖς ὄντως χήραις ἐπαρκέσῃ, "If any believing woman has widows, let her care for them, and the church should not be burdened so that it may care for the true widows." This is the third time Paul has mentioned the theme of family responsibility (vv 4, 8), showing that it extends beyond parents and grandparents and includes any widow in one's extended family. His concern in vv 3–16 is that the church care for widows who are truly widows, who have no one else to care for them and who have led godly lives. He also adds another concern that has only been implicit in the discussion. The church has an obligation to care for widows who truly are alone, but it cannot do this with its limited resources if families do not care for their own.

The textual tradition shows confusion on the identificaiton of πιστή, "believing woman," the feminine πιστή having been emended to πιστός, "believing man," or πιστὸς ἢ πιστή, "believing man or woman," although πιστή is certainly original (see *Note* g). (1) One interpretation reads πιστή as a prosperous woman, possibly a widow herself, who is encouraged to care for other widows (e.g., Roloff, 301; Young, *Theology*, 120). But if this is what Paul meant, he would surely have said so. Lock (57, 61) ties v 16 in with v 14: the young widows should marry, have children, govern their households (v 14), and if they have widows, they should care for them (v 16). But if a (young) widow needed to be enrolled, presumably for financial support, it is doubtful that she would have had the resources to provide for herself much less others. Once she was remarried, then she might have the resources, but v 16 appears to describe a current situation and not one that might be true in the future. (2) More likely this is another example of the practical focus of the PE. There was a problem in Ephesus with sexual impropriety (2 Tim 3:6), and Paul has already shown sensitivity to this issue (1 Tim 5:2). It would have been improper to ask a single man to care for widows; and if the man was married, the care of widows would most likely have been carried out by his wife (Kelly, 121). Paul was thinking of a Christian woman, either single or married, who had the financial resources to take widows into her home (especially mothers and grandmothers; cf. v 4; also Lydia [Acts 16:14–15] and Chloe [1 Cor 1:11]; cf. Knight, 229). These widows were to have been cared for by this believing woman and not by the church. This was especially important since younger widows could not be enrolled; their families had to accept responsibility. This verse also widens the scope of familial responsibility from children and grandchildren to the extended family.

ἐπαρκεῖν, "to care for," is used earlier to describe the true widow, one who has cared for the afflicted (v 10); the πιστή, "believing woman," is the type of woman who, if she is ever widowed after the age of sixty, will herself be eligible for enrollment. χήρας, "widows," is plural, referring to the mother, grandmother, and possibly mother-in-law and other relatives. βαρεῖν, "to burden," primarily describes a financial burdening and shows that τίμα, "honor" (v 3), includes financial support. βαρεῖν is not used elsewhere in the NT with financial overtones (cf. Matt 26:43; Luke 9:32; 21:34; 2 Cor 1:8; 5:4), but many references in secular writing support this meaning (G. Schrenk, *TDNT* 1:561). Its cognates in the NT carry a financial meaning (2 Cor 11:9 [ἀβαρής, "of no burden"]; 12:16 [καταβαρεῖν, "to be a burden to"]; 1 Thess 2:9 [ἐπιβαρεῖν, "to be a burden"]; 2 Thess 3:8 [ἐπιβαρεῖν]). Lightman and Zeisel cite this epitaph: "To well-deserving Regina her daughter nicely made this stone. Regina, mother, widow, who remained a widow sixty years and never burdened the Church; an univira who lived eighty years, five months, twenty-six days" (*CH* 46 [1977] 27).

Explanation

Paul's primary concern in this passage is to help Timothy distinguish between widows whom the church should support and those whom it should not. A serious problem had developed in the Ephesian church because widows had been enrolled who should not have been. Because of their idleness and the persuasiveness of the false teachers, they were turning against Christ and the church. On the other hand, the church's resources were stretched to the point that it was not able to care for those who truly needed and deserved financial help.

Paul teaches that the true widow, the widow who should be cared for, must be totally alone, unable to receive any family support, and unwilling to remarry. She must be a godly woman who has set her hope on God, a godliness made evident by her behavior, such as being diligent in her prayers, being faithful to her husband, raising children, showing hospitality, washing the feet of the saints, helping the afflicted, and being truly devoted to a life of good deeds. Also, because the problem in Ephesus involved the younger widows, Paul says that the widow must be at least sixty years old if she is to be enrolled. This does not mean that the church could ignore widows who did not fit these qualifications. It means that the church was not supposed to enter into a formal, lifelong relationship with widows who were not this type of person.

On the other hand, the widow who was not truly a widow, who should not be supported by the church, was a widow who failed to meet these qualifications. This included having family who could support her, being too young, and being ungodly, which excluded many of the widows in Ephesus who were causing the problems. They were self-indulgent, self-centered, physically alive but spiritually dead. They were turning against Christ, marrying outside the faith, and abandoning Christianity altogether. They were studying to be professional idlers, gossips, and busybodies. It is probable that many had been won over to the Ephesian heresy and were spreading it from house to house. Paul's response to this group is that they remarry, care for their own homes, and not bring reproach upon the church. They were probably eligible for some financial help from the church, but the church was not supposed to obligate itself for the long term.

Paul makes clear both the family's and the church's responsibility. The family must accept the primary responsibility. If a person has a widowed mother or grandmother, or even a widow in his or her extended family, he or she must provide the care. The Christian's responsibility extends beyond the immediate family. Not to accept one's responsibilities is to be worse than the unbelievers, to deny the faith, and to burden the church unnecessarily. On the other hand, the church is responsible to care for those who are totally alone and who have lived godly lives. In doing so, the church must be discerning concerning the recipients of its care, choosing those who are truly in need, the true widows.

Even though interpretation of this passage is tied to the historical situation at Ephesus (especially vv 11–13) and Acts 6:1–6 is the only other major discussion of widows in the NT (cf. 1 Cor 7:8; Jas 1:27), there is nothing in this passage that limits its application only to the Ephesian church. By making the reasons general (vv 4, 8, 16) Paul has expressed his desires for churches of all times. Paul would agree with the corporate enactment of James's principle, that "religion that is pure and undefiled before God and the Father is this: to visit orphans and widows in their affliction, and to keep oneself unstained from the world" (Jas 1:27).

D. M. Scholer is not alone in his comments about the relationship between 1 Tim 2:8–15 and this passage: "Certainly those who see the purpose of 1 Timothy as a 'timeless' church manual should hold that 1 Timothy 5:3–16 be applied as literally and absolutely as 2:11–12. Such inconsistency suggests that their agenda is much more than a concern for biblical authority and for accurate biblical teaching" ("1 Timothy 2:9–15 and the Place of Women in the Church's Ministry," in *Women, Authority and the Bible*, ed. A. Mickelsen [Downers Grove, IL: InterVarsity Press, 1986] 214; cf. G. D. Fee, *Gospel and Spirit* [Peabody, MA: Hendricksen, 1991] 59–60). While there is much with which to disagree in his statement—the PE do not constitute a church manual; lack of consistent application has no necessary connection with meaning; it is offensive to criticize motives when they cannot possibly be known—I believe and support James's statement (Jas 1:27) that true religion involves commitment to the socially disenfranchised and that churches of all time must care for godly widows who are truly alone.

Excursus: Widows in the Postapostolic Church

In the early centuries after the time of Paul, the development of a system for the care of widows can be observed, although there is much about this development that is unclear. By the time of Chrysostom the order of widows must have died out because he shows no knowledge of it. G. Stählin (*TDNT* 9:464) says that this order was called "deaconesses" from the fourth century on. But what we do know of this order of widows is that is was modeled on 1 Tim 5:3–16. For an excellent discussion of widows in the first several centuries of the church (as well as the biblical data), see Thurston, *Widows*.

Polycarp mentions widows in his epistle:

Our widows must be sober-minded as touching the faith of the Lord, making intercession without ceasing for all men, abstaining from all calumny, evil speaking, false witness, love of money, and every evil thing, knowing that they are God's altar, and that all sacrifices are carefully inspected, and nothing escapeth Him either of their thoughts or intents or any of the secret things of the heart. (Pol. *Phil.* 4; tr. Lightfoot, 125)

"God's altar" probably refers to receiving a stipend and offering prayers.

Ignatius, in a conclusion, states:

I salute the households of my brethren with their wives and children, and the virgins who are called widows [καὶ τὰς παρθένους τὰς λεγομένας χήρας]. (*Smyrn.* 13.1)

Bernard comments that "this may only mean that from the purity of their lives the enrolled widows might be counted virgins" (81) and adds that eventually even very young virgins were admitted into the order.

In his discussion of virgins Tertullian comments:

I know plainly, that in a certain place a virgin of less than twenty years of age has been placed in the order of widows! Whereas if the bishop had been bound to accord her any relief, he might, of course, have done it in some other way without detriment to the respect due to discipline; that such a miracle, not to say monster, should not be pointed at in the church, a virgin-widow! The more portentous indeed, that not even as a widow did she veil her head; denying herself either way; both as virgin, in that she is counted a widow, and as widow, in that she is styled a virgin. But the authority which licenses her sitting in that seat uncovered is the same which allows her to sit there as a virgin: a seat to which (besides the "sixty years" not merely "single-husbanded") (women)—that is, married women—are at length elected, but "mothers" to boot, yes, and "educators of children." (*Virg. Vel.* 9)

Justin shows that the church was actively involved in supporting widows and orphans. He explains that after worship and communion:

> there is a distribution to each, and a participation of that over which thanks have been given, and to those who are absent a portion is sent by the deacons [τῶν διακόνων]. And they who are well to do, and willing, give what each thinks fit; and what is collected is deposited with the president [τῷ προεστῶτι], who succours the orphans and widows, and those who, through sickness or any other cause, are in want, and those who are in bonds, and the strangers sojourning among us, and in a word takes care of all who are in need. (*1 Apol.* 67)

The *Apostolic Constitutions* refines who should be the recipient of the church's generosity:

> For if there be a widow who is able to support herself, and another woman who is not a widow, but is needy by reason of sickness, or the bringing up of many children, or infirmity of her hands, let him stretch out his hand in charity rather to the latter. But if any one be in want by gluttony, drunkenness, or idleness, she does not deserve any assistance, or to be esteemed a member of the Church of God. (2.2.4; ANF 7:397)

Eusebius refers to more than 1500 "widows and persons in distress" as being under the bishops, presbyters, and deacons (*Hist. Eccl.* 6.43.11; cf. Chrysostom *Hom. in Matt.* 66.3 [on Matt 20:29–30]; id., *De Sacer.* 3.16; *Didascalia* 3.4.2). Entrance into the order follows the guidelines Paul established. There must be a time period between the death of her husband and her enrollment (Hippolytus *Apost. Trad.* 10; *Testamentum Domini* 1.40; *Apostolic Constitutions* 8.25.2), and she should be married only once (Origen *Homilies in Luke* 17 [on Luke 2:33–38]; Tertullian *De exhort. cast.* 11.2). She is to have been a blameless wife (*Apostolic Constitutions* 8.25.2) and one who cared for her family (*Apostolic Constitutions* 8.25.2):

> Let the deaconess be a pure virgin; or, at the least, a widow who has been but once married, faithful, and well esteemed. (*Apostolic Constitutions* 6.3.17; ANF 7:457)

There is some controversy over the issue of the widow's age. The age limit of sixty established in the PE is maintained in the *Apostolic Constitutions* (3.1.1 and *Can. Bas.* 3). In *Didascalia* 3.1.1 it is lowered to fifty. The Council of Chalcedon (15) sets it at forty. The *Testamentum Domini* do not list an age (which is not necessarily indicative of a change in church policy).

The early church went beyond the teachings of Paul when it defined the widow's position in the church as being under the authority of the bishops who were responsible for them (Ignatius *Pol.* 4.1; *Didascalia* 2.4.1; *Apostolic Constitutions* 2.25.2; Chrysostom *De Sacer.* 3.16) along with the help of the presbyters and deacons (*Apostolic Constitutions* 8.47.41). For example: "Let the widows also be ready to obey the commands given them by their superiors, and let them do according to the appointment of the bishop, being obedient to him as to God" (*Apostolic Constitutions* 3.8). Eventually the responsibility for the care of widows fell to the state under Constantine (G. Stählin *TDNT* 9:461). There were also donations made for the sake of widows (Chrysostom *De Sacer.* 3.16; *Didascalia* 3.4.2 [cf. 2.27.3]; *Apostolic Constitutions* 4.6.6).

Unlike the PE, the early church laid out the responsibilities of widows, including prayer (*Mart. Pol.* 4:3; Hippolytus *Apost. Trad.* 23; *Didascalia* 3.7.6–7; *Testamentum Domini* 1.42–43 [which praises widows who pray literally night and day]), caring for the sick (Hippolytus *Apost. Trad.* 21; *Testamentum Domini* 1.40; *Canones Hippolyti* 9) and orphans (*Apostolic Constitutions* 3.1), teaching women converts (Origen *Homilies in Isaiah* 6.3 [on Isa 6:9]; *Testamentum Domini* 1.40), and fasting and prayer (Hippolytus *Apost. Trad.* 23; *Canones Hippolyti* 32; *Can. Bas.* 36; cf. G. Stählin, *TDNT* 9:464–65). The issue of remarriage is debated (cf. G. Stählin, *TDNT* 9:462). Some allowed it (*Testamentum Domini* 3.2.1; Epipanius *Haer.* 30.18.2; *Can. Bas.* 11) while others such as Tertullian argued that the widow is never free from the marriage vows, even if the husband dies (*De monog.* 10.2), going beyond Paul's instructions (Rom 7:1–3). There is much stronger language against third marriages (*Apostolic Constitutions* 3.2.2; *Can. Bas.* 11).

Most of the later information comes from a few sources. Hippolytus's *Apostolic Tradition* (3.1–3) comes from the early third century and shows the practices of the Roman church. It was a source for the fourth-century *Apostolic Constitutions* and the fourth- to fifth-century *Testamentum Domini* (40–43). The other major source is the early third-century *Didascalia Apostolorum*, which also served as a source for *Apostolic Constitutions*. It has several sections on widows, mostly from Book 3 (ANF 7:426ff.). These passages discuss the age of the widow, her character, and false widows. Widows are also discussed in detail by Chrysostom *De Sacer.* 3.16. For additional reading, see *Didascalia* 2.3; 3.5.1–11; Hippolytus *Apost. Trad.* 10; *Testamentum Domini* 1.40–43; *Can. Bas.* 36. On orphans, see Lucian *De morte Peregrini* 12. On the role of deaconesses, see *Explanation* on 1 Tim 3:8–13.

C. Payment and Discipline of Elders   (1 Tim 5:17–25)

Bibliography

Adler, N. "Die Handauflegung im Neuen Testament bereits ein Bußritus? Zur Auslegung von 1 Tim 5,22." In *Neutestamentliche Aufsätze.* FS J. Schmidt, ed. J. Blinzler, O. Kuss, and F. Mussner. Regensburg: Pustet, 1963. 1–6. **Bornkamm, G.** "πρεσβύτερος." *TDNT* 6:651–83. **Brauch, M. T.** "Wine for the Stomach?" In *Hard Sayings of the Bible.* Downers Grove, IL: InterVarsity Press, 1996. 673–74. **Cousineau, A.** "Les sens de *presbuteros* dans les Pastorales." *ScEs* 28 (1976) 147–62. **Ellis, E. E.** "Paul and His Co-Workers." *NTS* 17 (1971) 437–52. **Fuller, J. W.** "Of Elders and Triads in 1 Timothy 5.19–25." *NTS* 29 (1983) 258–63. **Galtier, P.** "La réconciliation des pécheurs dans la première Épître à Timothée." *RSR* 39 (1951) 317–20. ———. "La réconciliation des pécheurs dans Saint Paul." *RSR* 3 (1912) 448–60. **Kilpatrick, G. D.** "1 Tim. V. 22 and Tertullian *DE BAPTISMO* xviii. 1." *JTS* n.s. 16 (1965) 127–28. **Kirk, J. A.** "Did 'Officials' in the New Testament Church Receive a Salary?" *ExpTim* 84 (1972–73) 105–8. **Jeremias, J.** "ΠΡΕΣΒΥΤΕΡΙΟΝ außerchristlich bezeugt." *ZNW* 48 (1957) 127–32. ———. "Zur Datierung der Pastoralbriefe." *ZNW* 52 (1961) 101–4 (repr. in *Abba* [Göttingen: Vandenhoeck & Ruprecht, 1966] 314–16). **Lohfink, G.** "Die Normativität der Amtsvorstellungen in den Pastoralbriefen." *TQ* 157 (1977) 93–106. **MacArthur, J. S.** "On the Significance of ἡ γραφή in 1 Timothy v. 18." *ExpTim* 53 (1941–42) 37. **McKee, E.** "Les anciens et l'interpretation de 1 Tim 5:17 [l'ouvrier est digne de son salaire] chez Calvin: Une curiosité dans l'histoire de l'exégèse." *RTP* 120 (1988) 411–17. **Meier, J. P.** *"Presbyteros* in the Pastoral Epistles." *CBQ* 35 (1973) 323–45. **Michaelis, W.** *Das Ältestenamt der christlichen Gemeinde im Light der Heiligen Schrift.* Bern: Haller, 1953. 112–19. **Quinn, J. D.** "Tertullian and 1 Timothy 5:22 on Imposing Hands: Paul Galtier Revisited." *10th Patristic* 21 (1989) 268–70. **Schöllgen, G.** "Die διπλῆ τιμή von 1 Tim 5,17." *ZNW* 80 (1989) 232–39. **Spicq, C.** "1 Timothée 5:23." In *L'Évangile hier et aujourd'hui.* FS F.-J. Leenhardt. Geneva: Labor & Fides, 1968. 143–50. **Vliet, H. van.** *No Single Testimony: A Study on the Adoption of the Law of Deut. 19:15 Par. into the New Testament.* Studia theologica Rheno-Traiectina 4. Utrecht: Kemink & Zoon, 1958.

For bibliography on overseers, elders, and church ministry, see *Bibliography* on 1 Tim 3:1–7.

Translation

[17] *Let the elders who have been serving well be considered worthy of double honor, namely, those who are laboring hard at preaching and teaching.* [18]*For Scripture says, "Do not muzzle an ox that is treading out the grain,"* [a] *and, "Worthy is the worker of his wage."* [b] [19]*Do not accept an accusation against an elder, except on the basis of two or three witnesses.* [c] [20]*Confront* [d] *those who persist in sinning before everyone, in order that the rest might be in fear.* [21]*I solemnly charge [you] before God and Christ Jesus* [e] *and the elect angels that you keep these things without prejudging, doing nothing with partiality.* [f] [22]*Do not lay hands on anyone quickly or share in the sins* [g] *of others; keep yourself pure.* [23]*(No longer drink only water, but use a little wine, on account of [your]* [h] *stomach and your frequent illnesses.)* [24]*The sins of some people are evident, going before [them] into judgment, but they also follow after some.* [25]*In the same way* [i] *also the good works are evident, and those that are not are not able* [j] *to be hidden.*

Notes

[a]Some MSS change the order of the phrase to Οὐ φιμώσεις βοῦν ἀλοῶντα, "You shall not muzzle an ox treading out the grain," thus agreeing with the order of the LXX (A C I P Ψ 048 33 81 104 365 1175 *pc* [lat]; Or Ambst). D* follows our text's order except that it replaces φιμώσεις, "you shall muzzle," with κημώσεις, "you shall muzzle" (thus agreeing with the same quotation in 1 Cor 9:9). The order in our text is supported by ℵ F G D² 1739 1881 TR (it vg^ms); (Cl).

[b]τοῦ μισθοῦ, "wage," is apparently replaced by τῆς τροφῆς, "food," by ℵ* vid (a*); (Cl) in imitation of Matt 10:10. Cf. *TCGNT*², 575.

[c]ἐκτὸς εἰ μὴ ἐπὶ δύο ἢ τριῶν μαρτύρων, "except on the basis of two or three witnesses," is omitted by b; Ambst Pel. Cf. *TCGNT*², 575.

[d]The adversative δέ, "but," is inserted between τοὺς, "the [ones]," and ἁμαρτάνοντας, "sinning," by A D* (F G) 1175 *pc* it vg^mss; Ambst. Its omission.is supported by ℵ D² Ψ 048 33 1739 1881 TR r vg sy; Lcf. Its inclusion makes clear the implicit contrast between elders brought up on charges (v 19) and those who refuse to repent after that initial confrontation (v 20). Its absence is the more difficult reading.

[e]The texts exhibit the usual variations of the names of Jesus (cf. 1 Tim 1:1). κυρίου Ἰησοῦ Χριστοῦ, "Lord Jesus Christ," is read by D² TR sy. Ἰησοῦ Χριστοῦ, "Jesus Christ," is read by F Ψ 630 1175 1739 1881 *pc* bo^ms. The order of our text is supported by ℵ A D* G 33 81 104 365 629 *pc* latt co; Cl.

[f]πρόσκλισιν, "partiality" (ℵ F G K 81 630 1881 *al* latt sy; Cl), is replaced by πρόσκλησιν, "judicial summons," "invitation" (MM, 549), by ℵ D Ψ 33 1739 TR. Bernard suggests that the change was made through the "itastic interchange of ι and η" (77).

[g]Kilpatrick (*JTS* n.s. 16 [1965] 127–28) discusses the two readings in Tertullian for ἁμαρτίαις, "sins." Trecensis reads *amartiis*, and Mesnart reads *delicta*, which is the expected and more common form; *amartiis* is extremely rare and appears to be a transliteration from ἁμαρτία. (The current Vulgate

reads *peccatis,* which is also a common word.) Kilpatrick says that Mesnart "has been conformed to the Greek" (128) and therefore editors of the Greek text have preferred Trecensis.

ʰσου, "your," is inserted after στόμαχον, "stomach" (D² F G TR a vg sy; Cl), to smooth out the sentence since the wine was for "your stomach and your frequent illnesses." Our text is supported by ℵ A D* P Ψ 33 81 104 1739 1881 *pc* b m* r vgᵐˢˢ; Ambst.

ⁱδέ, "but," is inserted after ὡσαύτως, "in the same way," by A F G 81 *pc* a mᶜ vgᵐˢˢ. It is omitted in ℵ D Ψ 33 1739 1881 TR lat sy.

ʲThe plural δύνανται, "they are able," is changed to the singular δύναται, "it is able," by ℵ F G L 6 326 1241 1505 1739 *pm,* possibly because of the neuter plural subject. Whereas a plural verb is not found in classical Greek with a neuter plural subject, its use became frequent in the Koine and is the rule in modern Greek (Bernard, 77).

Form/Structure/Setting

Beginning in chap. 5 Paul addresses the concerns of different groups in the Ephesian church. He instructs Timothy on how he should treat people of different ages (1 Tim 5:1–2) and the widows (5:3–16), and now he deals with the issues relating to elders (5:17–25). He will continue with a discussion of slaves (6:1–2a) and eventually the rich (6:17–19). The discussion of elders has similarities with that of the widows. τιμή, "honor," is the key term in both discussions as it is throughout 5:1–6:2a (see *Form/Structure/Setting* on 1 Tim 5:1–2). True widows are to be honored by being enrolled; elders are to be given double honor. In both cases honor includes money. Much of the problem in Ephesus originated with the widows and the elders (cf. *Form/Structure/Setting* on 1 Tim 3:1–7 and 1 Tim 5:3–16). Since the elders possibly had converts among the widows (cf. 2 Tim 3:6), one would expect the discussions of these two groups to be related.

Some argue that Paul starts a new topic at v 20 (Galtier, *RSR* 39 [1951] 317–20; Hasler) or v 21 (Ellicott; Holtzmann; Lock; Easton; Dibelius-Conzelmann; G. Bornkamm, *TDNT* 6:666 n. 93; Hanson [1983]), switching from discussing elders to discussing sinners in general. They note that the charge in v 21 is transitional in nature (cf. 1:18; 3:14; 4:6); "sinning" (ἁμαρτάνοντας, v 20) is plural but "elder" (πρεσβυτέρου, v 19) is singular; it is unlikely that Timothy would be doing the commissioning alone if the topic were still elders; and Christians are often told to avoid sinners (e.g., 2 John 11 uses κοινωνεῖν, "to share," as does v 22; see summary in Meier, *CBQ* 35 [1973] 333). The "laying on of hands" in v 22 then refers to the ritual of reinstating a sinner into the congregation. V 23 does not necessarily bear any relationship to the verses before it, and vv 24–25 can refer back to the discussion of elders or the reinstatement of sinners.

However, the arguments are stronger that see vv 17–25 as a unit (Chrysostom; Jerome; Bernard; Jeremias; Guthrie; van Vliet, *No Single Testimony,* 88 n. 630; Adler, "Handauflegung"; Barrett; Kelly; Brox; Meier, *CBQ* 35 [1973] 325–27; Fee). (1) While these charges are often transitional in the PE, in 1 Tim 6:13–14 there is a similar charge that is not transitional and does not introduce a new topic. There is no other textual indication that Paul has switched topics. (2) While πρεσβύτερος, "elder," in v 19 is singular, it is plural in v 17, and the flow of the argument accounts for the change: honor all elders serving well; do not accept a charge against any specific elder without witnesses; rebuke all those who are sinning, without partiality. (3) The mention of "sins" in v 22 is a reference to the sinning elders in v 20, tying the verses together. (4) The urgency of v 21 is not appropriate to the content of vv 23–25, which would be the case if v 21 started a new topic. But its urgency and seriousness are appropriate if Paul is thinking of the need to confront and rebuke elders as discussed in vv 19–20. (5) Meier (*CBQ* 35 [1973] 323–25) argues that most of the participial uses of ἁμαρτάνειν, "to sin," are attributive or adverbial, suggesting in this passage that v 20 refers to v 19. (If Paul had meant "sinner" in general, his tendency would have been to use ἁμαρτωλός, "sinner.") (6) Meier (332) adds that viewing "those who persist in sin" as those who sin in general does not fit the context of 1 Tim 5:1–6:2a, which is dealing with different groups of people, and there is no evidence from the first century for an order of penitents that would fit the context. (7) Brox (202) points out how the consistent use of the participles suggests that the topic has not changed as Paul describes the elders as "ruling well" (οἱ καλῶς προεστῶτες, v 17), "laboring" (οἱ κοπιῶντες, v 17), and "sinning" (τοὺς ἁμαρτάνοντας, v 20). (8) Although the laying on of hands historically has been connected to many rituals (cf. J. Coppens, *L'imposition des mains et les rites conneves* [Paris: Gabalda, 1925]), in the NT it always has to do with leadership issues and never with the reinstatement of sinners. (9) Although the ritual was practiced in Africa in the third century (Meier, *CBQ* 35 [1973] 333; cf. Tertullian) and elsewhere (Eusebius *Hist. Eccl.* 8.2; Cyprian *Ep.* 74.12; *Apostolic Constitutions* 2.18), there is no evidence that it existed in the first century (admitted by Hanson, [1983] 103). (10) Fuller (*NTS* 29 [1983] 258–63) argues on the basis of Deut 19:15–20 that 1 Tim 5:19–21 is a single unit and discusses only one topic. He points out four similarities between the two passages (a desire for a fair examination; the effect of the process on those who watch [fear]; warning of not showing partiality; the triad of persons who ensure the fairness of the hearing). If 1 Tim 5:19–21 is drawing from Deut 19:15–20, since Deut 19:15–20 is discussing only one topic, so also is 1 Tim 5:19–21.

(11) The strongest argument that vv 17–25 form one discussion is that a common thread runs through the passage and adequately explains each verse: the payment (vv 17–18) and discipline (vv 19–25) of elders. Paul lays out four rules: (a) Elders who are doing their job well should receive not only the congregation's respect but also remuneration. This is based on the OT and accords with Jesus' teaching (vv 17–18). (b) When charges are brought against elders, they should not be acknowledged unless there are two or three witnesses. This is apparently a private confrontation (v 19). (c) If the elder is guilty of the accusation, and if he persists in sinning, Timothy must rebuke him before all the church so the rest of the elders will realize that they will be held accountable for their conduct. Timothy must be sure that while he is listening to these charges and confronting them, he makes judgment without discrimination or partiality. He is continually in the presence of God, Christ, and the elect angels, and they will hold him accountable (vv 20–21). (d) The fourth instruction deals with the appointment of elders, whether it be new elders or the reinstatement of those who after confrontation and repentance now wish to resume their duties (vv 22–25). Timothy must not be hasty in commissioning elders. If he appoints unworthy people and they sin, he is to some degree responsible. In all this Timothy must remain pure (v 22). (As an aside, Paul says that this call for purity does not mean that he approves of Timothy's decision to abstain totally from alcohol. In fact, Paul wishes that Timothy would use a little wine as necessary for his physical problems [v 23].) Paul concludes with two reasons that Timothy should not be hasty in commissioning elders. The first is that while the sins of some are evident and disqualify the sin-

ner from holding office, others' sins are less obvious. If elders are appointed too quickly, Timothy will find out after it is too late that they are not qualified for the office (v 24). The second reason is that while the good deeds of some people obviously attest that they should be elders, others' good deeds are not as visible. If Timothy is too hasty, he will miss the opportunity of appointing qualified people (v 25).

In any arrangement of these verses, Paul's comment about Timothy drinking wine (v 23) interrupts the flow of thought. But it can be seen as a digression based on v 22c. Vv 24–25 give the reason for v 22, and therefore v 23 should be viewed as part of the same discussion. Barrett (82) suggests that the discussion of elders extends to 6:2, in which the slaves are elders. This would provide an additional argument that 1 Tim 5:22–25 is discussing elders and not the readmission of a penitent sinner. But the ὅσοι, "whoever," in 6:1 suggests a change in topic; the context of chap. 5 shows that Paul is addressing various groups in the church; and the parallel discussions in the NT that deal with different groups often include slaves as one of the groups (Eph 6:5–9; Col 3:22–4:1; Titus 2:9–10; 1 Pet 2:18–25). See *Form/ Structure/Setting* on 1 Tim 6:12a for a further discussion. Meier (*CBQ* 35 [1973] 335–37) emphasizes the chiastic pattern of the passage as a-b-b´-a´.

a	positive	good elders	vv 17–18
	b	negative	sin and prevention	vv 19–22
		digression	v 23
	b´	negative	sin and prevention	v 24
a´	positive	good candidates	v 25

Stated more simply, Paul begins and ends on a positive note and deals with the negative issues in between.

Comment

17 Οἱ καλῶς προεστῶτες πρεσβύτεροι διπλῆς τιμῆς ἀξιούσθωσαν, μάλιστα οἱ κοπιῶντες ἐν λόγῳ καὶ διδασκαλίᾳ, "Let the elders who have been serving well be considered worthy of double honor, namely, those who are laboring hard at preaching and teaching." Paul begins the first of his four statements about elders on the same note with which he began and ended the preceding discussion of widows—honor—and in both cases honor involves money. The elders who were following his instructions and doing a good job not only were worthy of the peoples' respect but should also be paid for their work ("double honor"). He will continue in v 18 with his reason: workers should be paid. This was Paul's general rule (1 Cor 9:4–6; cf. Rom 13:7) although he himself often chose to earn his own living (cf. 1 Cor 4:12; 2 Cor 11:7–9; 1 Thess 2:9; cf. 2 Thess 3:7–9; Acts 18:3).

In *Form/Structure/Setting* on 1 Tim 3:1–7 the general issues relating to church leadership and structure were discussed as well as the various terms used for leadership, such as ἐπίσκοπος, "overseer," πρεσβύτερος, "elder," and διάκονος, "deacon." The conclusion was that Paul sees a two-level structure: overseers providing the general oversight of the church, distinguished from the deacons by their teaching ability, and not standing outside or above the church but serving within the church. Deacons were more involved in the day-to-day service needs of the church. It was also concluded that the flexibility of terminology and the need to define these roles give evidence of an early date in the development of church structure. The issue that needs to be discussed here is the relationship between the elder (πρεσβύτερος) and the overseer (ἐπίσκοπος). There are three options.

(1) "Elders" can be "elderly men" as in 1 Tim 5:1, the first use of πρεσβύτερος in 1 Timothy (cf. Luke 15:25; John 8:9; Acts 2:17; cf. πρεσβύτης, "elderly man," in Titus 2:2). Jeremias argues that v 17 means that double honor (respect plus payment) was to be given to the older men who accepted leadership responsibility and served faithfully. He also argues that their service was to be recognized by a doubling of their customary support (*der üblichen Unterstützung; ZNW* 52 [1961] 101–4). But (a) there is no evidence that the church was supporting elderly men (Kelly, 122). (b) There also is no clear evidence that the rulers of the church were necessarily drawn only from the ranks of the aged, although this may be suggested by the title, synagogue practice, and the culture's reverence for age (Spicq, 1:65–66). (c) Paul uses πρεσβύτερος, "elder," of church officials elsewhere (Titus 1:5; see below), and προϊστάναι, "to serve," is used five out of its eight occurrences in the NT in connection with church leadership (1 Tim 3:4, 5, 12; cf. Rom 12:8; 1 Thess 5:12; used of believers in general in Titus 3:8, 14). This limits "elders" to those functioning in that role; Jeremias's point is that these "elders" were "elderly men" functioning as church leaders. Few have followed him in this interpretation (cf. Meier for his summary and critique [*CBQ* 35 (1973) 343–44]).

(2) The second option sees two groups of elders, those "serving well" and those "laboring hard at preaching and teaching." The second group is either separate from the first or is a subset of the first. There are several ways to separate the two groups, but there are three objections that apply in general to seeing two groups regardless of how they are divided.

(a) 1 Tim 3:2 requires that all overseers be able to teach. If the elders here are the same group as the overseers in 1 Tim 3:1–7, it seems unlikely that there was such a person as a nonteaching elder/overseer (von Lips, *Glaube,* 114). Ridderbos qualifies this position by saying "for some the center of gravity was more general leadership, from which, however, one cannot dissociate the teaching aspect" (*Paul,* 458). (b) Especially in light of the Ephesian problem, it seems somewhat contradictory to speak of leaders who did not teach. More likely the leaders of the church were able and active in refuting error and encouraging the truth of the gospel (although this did not necessarily happen only at the corporate level but could have occurred at a personal level). (c) Paul says that double honor was due to elders who were serving well, not just to a subgroup who taught. If "double honor" was to be given to all elders serving well, in what way could double honor also have been given μάλιστα, "especially," to a subgroup who preached and taught? (Perhaps if "double honor" included a stipend and funds were low, Paul could have been saying that the elders who taught the community deserved the stipends first.)

There are several ways to see two groups of elders and still account for these three problems, but Paul does not distinguish between those serving and those serving well. All elders under consideration served well, and it seems highly unlikely, especially given the limited funds of the church (see discussion of widows above), that Paul would have allowed the church to give double honor to elders doing a poor or mediocre job.

(a) "Elder" could be a general term for anyone in church leadership, including overseers (who had to be able to teach) and deacons (who were not so required). Paul's use of the terminology is sufficiently flexible to allow for this. The problem with this is that elsewhere (see below) "elder" and "overseer" are used interchangeably of the same group, and it would be confusing to join two distinct groups under the same title without some contextual indication. (b) While asserting that all elders are able to teach, Paul could have based the division on those currently teaching and those who were not. Perhaps, as today, overseers would have had to vary the amount of time spent specifically on teaching because of other responsibilities, and this admonition would address those actively teaching. (c) "Serving well" could apply to gifted teachers who were currently leading in other ways (while still allowing for one-on-one teaching, both with the opponents and the other members of the church), and "laboring hard at preaching and teaching" could apply to those currently teaching the church as a whole. (d) The division could be based on those who were able to teach and those who were especially gifted to teach (Ellicott, Lock, Knight), dividing the elders on the basis of ability and giftedness and assuming that the more gifted did more of the corporate instruction. Meier (*CBQ* 35 [1973] 323–45) argues that three groups are envisioned here: elders who provided leadership, elders who were more involved with their ministerial responsibilities and were more successful, and those of the second group who led by preaching and teaching. It is this third group who are called "overseers" in 1 Tim 3:1–7. But this threefold division seems overly subtle and open to the problems associated with having just two groups.

(3) It appears best to interpret Paul's use of the terms "overseer" and "elder" as interchangeable references to the same group of church leaders. "Elder" may historically show that much of the leadership in the church was drawn from the older men, and "overseer" is more indicative of their function. (a) "Overseer" and "elder" are used interchangeably in Titus 1:5, 7, Acts 20:17, 28, and *1 Clem.* 44. The latter is especially significant in light of the closeness in date of Clement to Ignatius. προϊστάναι, "to shepherd," is used with all three terms, "elder" (πρεσβύτερος; 1 Tim 5:17), "overseer" (ἐπίσκοπος; 1 Tim 3:4, 5), and "deacon" (διάκονος; 1 Tim 3:12). By the time of the writing of the PE, these terms had not yet achieved the technical status that they would have in the second century, and so a degree of flexibility is expected. (b) The lists in 1 Tim 3:1–7 ("overseer") and Titus 1:5–9 ("elder/overseer") are very similar, suggesting that they are speaking of the same person/office. (c) It is possible to translate μάλιστα as "namely" rather than "especially" so that the second phrase clarifies the identity of the first; Paul is speaking of the elders, namely, all the overseers who teach (see *Comment*). This solves the problem of the meaning of "double honor" and maintains the two-level structure evidenced elsewhere in the early church. (d) Although eventually the overseer/bishop was elevated above the elders/presbyters and the two terms ceased referring to the same group (see *Form/Structure/Setting* on 1 Tim 3:1–7), there is clear evidence from the early church that originally both titles described the same office. *1 Clem.* 42:4–5 and *Didache* 15 speak of the apostles' appointment of overseers (ἐπίσκοποι) and deacons, not three groups. Polycarp (*Phil.* 5) and the Shepherd of Hermas also speak of two groups, not three. The Shepherd sim-

ply refers to the leaders as πρεσβύτεροι, "elders" (*Vis.* 3.1.8; 3.5.1). H. E. Dosker (*IDB* 1:516) cites Jerome's comment regarding Titus 1:7 that "the same is the presbyter, who is also the bishop," and adds that Augustine and the church fathers of the fourth and fifth centuries agreed.

τιμή, "honor," includes the idea of respect but may also imply remuneration (cf. 1 Tim 5:3; MM, 635; Spicq, 1:542 gives references from the NT, papyri, and inscriptions). This is made clear by v 18, which says that elders should receive double honor because the laborer is worthy of his wages. Ellis argues that there was a paid ministry in the apostolic church (*NTS* 17 [1971] 437–52), basing his argument on statements from Jesus (Matt 10:10; Luke 10:7; cf. 1 Cor 9:14), temple practice (1 Cor 9:13), Paul's teaching (Gal 6:6; Phil 4:15–19; 1 Thess 2:9), and statements from Paul's opponents (2 Cor 2:17). Kirk argues that while itinerant missionaries (such as the apostles) did receive payment, elders working in their local churches received not a salary but an honorarium "on a person-to-person and day-to-day basis, according to the circumstances, . . . [and] above all it is a free-will offering, the very antithesis to a regular paid salary" (*ExpTim* 84 [1972–73] 105–8, citing Hanson, [1966] 62). Kirk notes that (1) it is unlikely that the early church would have had sufficient funds to pay a regular salary; (2) 1 Tim 3:7 suggests that elders retained their jobs in the secular world; (3) τιμή means "honorarium" and never "regular salary"; and (4) "it does not seem likely that Paul would make a regular salary dependent on some sort of efficiency test . . . because of the sure threat of division it would bring" (107). Arguments (1) and (3) are the strongest. The issue of money lies near the heart of the Ephesian heresy; elders (1 Tim 3:3) and deacons (1 Tim 3:8) are exhorted not to love money, but the opponents have been teaching for financial gain (1 Tim 3:5). By calling for teaching elders to be paid, Paul does not contradict his later judgment that the love of money is a root of all kinds of evil (1 Tim 6:10). For the person who does not love money and is not greedy for gain, a double portion of respect and stipend does not cause a problem. To do a task καλῶς, "well," includes both the idea of efficiency and the notion of rightness of instruction (cf. 1 Tim 3:4).

What does διπλῆς τιμῆς, "double honor," mean? (1) The idea of "respect" is certainly part of it, but this alone does not explain the idea of "double." (2) "Double can be understood in a numerical sense as double what someone else is paid such as widows" (Lock, citing *Didache* 13; *Apostolic Constitutions* 2.28 [see *Explanation*]; and Wettstein's examples of double pay for good soldiers in *Novum Testamentum Graecum*) or nonteaching elders (Dibelius-Conzelmann; Meier [*CBQ* 35 (1973) 323–45]). But one wonders if the early church had sufficient funds to pay all elders and then pay double stipends to its teaching elders. (3) διπλῆ, "double," does not necessarily mean double the sum and can be used "without any definite numerical reference" (Bernard, 85) to mean "generously"; hence "double honor" can refer to respect and remuneration (Chrysostom, Lock). Elders who were carrying out Paul's instructions were not only supposed to receive their due respect from the church; they were also to be paid for their labor (Spicq, 1:541–42). This makes good sense of the double nuance of "respect" and "payment" present in both the meaning of τιμή, "honor," and the context. Michaelis (*Ältestenamt*, 112–19) argues that "double honor" does not refer to money since 1 Tim 3:4, 12 suggest that the church leaders kept their secular jobs. However, these two verses do not refer to a person's reputation in the workplace, and it is more likely that Paul was speaking of an honorarium than a set salary (Roloff, 308). Chrysostom adds that the passage not only requires the church to pay its teachers (making reference to the Levites) so that they are not distracted by worldly concerns; it also requires the teachers to work very hard: "See how he would have the teacher labor! . . . So that if any one lives in sloth and luxury, he is unworthy of it. Unless he is as the ox treading out the corn, and bearing the yoke, in spite of heat and thorns, and ceases not till he has carried the corn into the granary, he is not worthy" ("Homily 15"; NPNF 13:460; cf. Str-B 3:653–54).

προεστῶτες, "have been serving," carries the double nuance of leading and serving—servant leadership. It is used earlier to describe elders (1 Tim 3:4; see discussion there) and deacons (1 Tim 3:12) managing their households well (cf. Titus 3:8, 14). This is Paul's usual use of προϊστάναι, "to serve" (cf. Rom 12:8; 1 Thess 5:12; O. Cullmann, "Meditation," *CTM* 39.1 [1968] 6), and any supposed reference to an elder presiding at the Eucharist (so Hanson [(1983) 100–101], based on a later reference in Justin Martyr [*1 Apol.* 65]) is out of context and is read in from what elders did in the second century (see *Explanation* on 1 Tim 3:1–7).

ἀξιοῦν, "to consider worthy of," occurs only here in the PE and may have been suggested to Paul by the use of the cognate ἄξιος, "worthy," in v 18 (cf. 1 Tim 1:15). κοπιᾶν, "to work hard," is Paul's normal word for Christian labors and describes strenuous work (cf. 1 Tim 4:10). λόγος, "preaching," refers to the proclamation of the gospel in both Paul's other letters (1 Cor 14:36; 2 Cor 2:17; 4:2; Phil 1:14; Col 1:25) and the PE (2 Tim 2:9; Titus 2:5; cf. 1 Tim 5:6). διδασκαλία, "teaching," refers to the doctrinal instructions of the gospel (cf. *Comment* on 1 Tim 1:10).

18a λέγει γαρ ἡ γραφή, βοῦν ἀλοῶντα οὐ φιμώσεις, "For Scripture says, 'Do not muzzle an ox that is treading out the grain.'" V 18 gives two reasons for paying elders. The first is a citation of Deut 25:4 that prohibits the muzzling of an ox while it is working in the threshing process. In a similar passage where Paul is arguing that Christian workers deserve to be paid, he cites this same verse but continues with an explanation: "Is it for oxen that God is concerned? Does he not speak entirely for our sake? It was written for our sake, because the plowman should plow in hope and the thresher thresh in hope of a share in the crop. If we have sown spiritual good among you, is it too much if we reap your material benefits?" (1 Cor 9:9b–11). In other words, it is part of God's design that Christian workers be paid for their work. While much of the problem in Ephesus has to do with the love of money, that does not negate the right of Christian workers to be paid.

Threshing was the process of separating the husk from the kernel of grain. The threshing floor was usually hard-packed dirt surrounded by a curb so that the grain would not fall away. One method was for the ox to pull a sled over the grain to break the husks apart. The sled usually had bits of rock and metal attached to the underside with rocks or people on top for weight. γάρ, "for," shows that v 18 gives the justification for v 17. γραφή, "scripture," is the normal term used to refer to the OT (e.g., 2 Tim 3:16; Rom 4:3; 11:2), and "for Scripture says" is the normal Pauline citation formula (Rom 9:17; 10:11; Gal 4:30). The present tense λέγει, "says," shows the abiding authority of the OT for Paul (perfective present; cf. Wallace, *Greek Grammar*, 533).

18b καί, ἄξιος ὁ ἐργάτης τοῦ μισθοῦ αὐτοῦ, "and, 'Worthy is the worker of his wage.'" The second reason that elders should be paid is that Jesus so instructed. (Ellicott, 78, says that the second saying is not so much a second principle as it is an explanation of the first.) This same saying is recorded verbatim in Luke 10:7 (except for the connecting γάρ, "for"; cf. slightly different version in Matt 10:10, which substitutes τῆς τροφῆς, "food," for τοῦ μισθοῦ, "wage"; see *Note* b). In the parallel passage in 1 Cor 9 cited above, Paul does not quote this saying, but he does repeat its essence: "In the same way, the Lord commanded that those who proclaim the gospel get their living by the gospel" (1 Cor 9:14). Hanson ([1983] 102) notes that the same imagery is found in 2 Tim 2:6.

There are two related questions raised by this citation. (1) What is Paul's source? Is the citation from Luke's Gospel (Baur, *Pastoralbriefe;* Scott; Simpson; Knight), an earlier draft of Luke's Gospel (Spicq, 1:543), Q (MacArthur, *ExpTim* 53 [1941–42] 37, who argues that this has no effect on issues of authenticity), or another collection of Jesus' sayings (Barrett, Hanson [1983]), or is it part of the colloquial language, a common proverb picked up by Jesus and elevated to the rank of Scripture by Paul? (2) Why does Paul call the citation γραφή, "Scripture," when it appears that this term was used only of the OT until the end of the second century (cf. Fee's [134] argument, citing the examples of γραφή in Lampe's *Patristic Greek Lexicon* from *1 Clement,* Ignatius, Polycarp, Justin, etc.)? Suggestions regarding source are speculative, especially if one allows for any contact between Paul and Luke and the possibility that Luke acted as Paul's amanuensis (cf. *Introduction,* "The Linguistic Problem"). (Fee [129] does point out that the only other place where Paul cites Jesus [1 Cor 11:24–25] follows the Lukan pattern as it does here.) However, the problem of calling the citation "Scripture" is accounted for by recognizing that "Scripture" need only apply to Paul's first citation from the OT. This is similar to Mark 1:2–3 where the formula "as it is written in Isaiah the prophet" introduces three citations from Exod 23:20, Mal 3:1, and Isa 40:3 (cf. W. L. Lane, *The Gospel according to Mark,* NICNT [Grand Rapids, MI: Eerdmans, 1974] 45–46) and the citation formula need only apply to the one citation from Isaiah (cf. also Matt 15:4; Mark 7:10; Acts 1:20; Heb 1:8; 1 Pet 2:6, and esp. 2 Pet 2:22; cf. Knight, 234; J. A. Fitzmyer, "The Use of Explicit Old Testament Quotations in Qumran Literature and in the New Testament," in *Essays on the Semitic Background of the New Testament* [London: Chapman, 1971] 14–15). Yet it only seems natural that Paul would view the teaching of Jesus, his resurrected Lord, as on an equal par with the OT (cf. 1 Cor 7:10; 10:23–25).

19 κατὰ πρεσβυτέρου κατηγορίαν μὴ παραδέχου, ἐκτὸς εἰ μὴ ἐπὶ δύο ἢ τριῶν μαρτύρων, "Do not accept an accusation against an elder, except on the basis of two or three witnesses." Paul's second statement is designed to protect elders from malicious and unsubstantiated accusations. It is based on the OT rule in Deut 19:15 (cf. 17:6; 1QS 8), which was accepted by the church (Matt 18:16; John 8:16; 2 Cor 13:1; Heb 10:28). For an excellent discussion of the use Deut 19:15–20 in 1 Tim 5:19–25, see Fuller, *NTS* 29 (1983) 258–63. Chrysostom emphasizes that Paul is talking not about judgment but about accusation prior to judgment ("Homily 15"; NPNF 13:461).

There are a few hints regarding the nature of these accusations. κατηγορία, "accusation," occurs elsewhere in the PE only in Titus 1:6 where Paul tells Titus to appoint elders who are not open to the accusation of being "profligate or insubordinate" (cf. αἰτία, "reason," in Titus 1:13). The only other time the word occurs in the NT is in John 18:29 where Pilate asks the Jews what accusation they bring against Jesus. (The verbal cognate κατηγορεῖν, "to accuse," is a technical term for a formal court accusation; cf. Mark 3:2 [Matt 12:10; Luke 6:7]; 15:3, 4 [Matt 27:12; Luke 23:2]; Luke 23:10; John 5:45; Acts 22:30; 24:2, 8, 13, 19; 25:5, 11, 16; 28:19; Rev 12:10; cf. BAGD, 423; F. Büchsel, *TDNT* 3:637; αἰτία, "reason," in Titus 1:13.) It seems that Paul is addressing the situation of formal charges being brought against an elder, possibly charges of extravagance and insubordination. The "two or three witnesses" (cf. Matt 18:16; 2 Cor 13:1; Heb 10:28) most likely are two or three who themselves witnessed the extravagance and insubordination in accordance with the intent of Deut 19:15. If Paul is staying within the confines of Deut 19:15, the "two or three" must be actual witnesses; Deut 19:15 does not allow for the witnesses to hear a charge from a single person and then bring the matter to Timothy.

Two or three witnesses must attest to the charge, but who are they? Are they other elders or simply church members? This raises a question that is especially important in the exegesis of v 20, where Timothy is told to confront sinning elders in the presence of all so that the rest may fear. Who are the "all" and the "rest"? It may be concluded that the "all" are the church and the "rest" are the remaining elders who are to fear. If this is correct, then Paul is calling for a public hearing, and the "two or three witnesses" should not be limited to elders since there is no limitation on who the witnesses are in the other references to this principle in the NT.

ἐκτὸς εἰ μή, "except," is a pleonastic construction (Bernard, 86; cf. 1 Cor 14:5; 15:2; cf. Moule, *Idiom-Book*, 83). ἐπί, "on the basis of," introduces the basis for an action (BAGD, 286; Ellicott, 79; Knight, 235). The verse does not show the "beginnings of presbyterial discipline" (Bernard, 86) or "the beginnings of monepiscopacy" (Hanson, [1983] 102); it simply repeats the Deuteronomic law as accepted by the church and put into effect in Ephesus through Paul's apostolic authority.

20 τοὺς ἁμαρτάνοντας ἐνώπιον πάντων ἔλεγχε, ἵνα καὶ οἱ λοιποὶ φόβον ἔχωσιν, "Confront those who persist in sinning before everyone, in order that the rest might be in fear." This is the third statement about elders in this section and is a smooth progression from v 19. Timothy must protect elders from unsubstantiated accusations; but if those accusations prove true and the elders continue in sin, then they must be publicly rebuked before the church so that the rest of the elders may be fearful. As is the case with confrontation throughout the PE, rebuking always looks forward to a positive result (cf. 1 Tim 1:20), in this case to instill a healthy fear in other elders. Paul sees this as a serious issue; he wants to produce godly fear in the opponents' hearts (v 20b), and he feels it necessary to urge Timothy to carry out these instructions without prejudice or partiality and with God, Christ, and the elect angels as his witnesses (v 21).

What appears initially to be a straightforward verse actually has many exegetical problems. (1) Is Paul referring to sinners in general or to elders who are sinning? It was concluded above that Paul is still speaking about the problem of the Ephesian elders (see *Form/Structure/Setting*). (2) What is the force of the linear aspect of ἁμαρτάνοντας, "sinning"? Is it referring to elders who sin constantly as opposed to occasionally, or does it describe continuing sin after the initial confrontation described in v 19? These two options are not mutually exclusive. The linear aspect guarantees that Paul is discussing an elder living a life of sin, not an elder who commits an occasional sin. The linear aspect of ἔλεγχε, "confront," parallels the linear aspect of ἁμαρτάνοντας: Be in the habit of confronting those in the habit of sinning. If v 19 refers to a private confrontation of sin (see below), then it is probable that the linear aspect of ἁμαρτάνοντας in v 20 is a reference to those continuing in their sin despite this initial confrontation. The Greek word order is similar: "against an elder an accusation do not accept" (v 19); "those who persist in sinning before everyone confront" (v 20). Vv 19–20 contain two distinct ideas, but v 20 is a logical extension of v 19. (See *Note* d for the variant δέ, "but," inserted after τούς, "the [ones]," in v 20, reinforcing the connection with v 19.)

(3) ἐλέγχειν, "to confront," has a range of meanings, including "to expose," "to confront," "to rebuke," and "to discipline." It occurs four other times in the PE. Timothy is to rebuke the Cretans sharply (ἔλεγχε αὐτοὺς ἀποτόμως; 1:13), showing that Paul can use the term in its harshest sense. The other three occurrences pair it with παρακαλεῖν, "to exhort." Timothy is to preach the word, be prepared, confront (ἐλέγχειν), rebuke (ἐπιτιμᾶν), and exhort (παρακαλεῖν; 2 Tim 4:2). Elders must hold firmly to the gospel so they can give instruction (παρακαλεῖν) and argue against (ἐλέγχειν) those who oppose it (Titus 1:9). Titus is to exhort and reprove (παρακάλει καὶ ἔλεγχε) with all authority (Titus 2:15). The pairing of ἐλέγχειν and παρακαλεῖν is instructive; confrontation is remedial, done with an eye to encouraging proper behavior. This nuance agrees with the use of ἐλέγχειν throughout the NT, such as in the parallel discussion of church discipline in Matt 18:15, where restoration is the desired goal: "If he listens to you, you have gained your brother." The nuance is also visible in the verses using this word that demand repentance from sin, repentance being the positive goal of the confrontation (Luke 3:19; 1 Cor 14:24; Eph 5:13; Heb 12:5; Jas 2:9; variant reading in John 8:9). The word means "'to show someone his sin and to summon him to repentance . . . to point away from sin to repentance.' It implies educative discipline" (F. Büchsel, *TDNT* 2:474). See also the variant ἔλεγχος in 2 Tim 3:16, where Scripture is said to be profitable for "teaching, for rebuke [ἔλεγχος], for correction, and for training in righteousness."

(4) Does ἐνώπιον, "before," modify "those who persist in sinning" (i.e., public sin) or "confront" (i.e., public confrontation)? ἐνώπιον occurs eight times in the PE. Several considerations argue for the second interpretation. (a) The next verse has the construction διαμαρτύρομαι ἐνώπιον τοῦ θεοῦ, "I charge [you] before God," which is repeated verbatim in 2 Tim 2:14 and 4:1. The similar construction παραγγέλλω σοι ἐνώπιον τοῦ θεοῦ, "I charge you before God," appears in 1 Tim 6:13. Although in these cases ἐνώπιον follows the verb in word order, these parallels suggest that here ἐνώπιον modifies what follows (1 Tim 6:12). The similarity of the expressions ἐλέγχειν ἐνώπιον, "rebuke before," and διαμαρτύρεσθαι/παραγγέλλειν ἐνώπιον, "charge before," gives evidence that in 1 Tim 5:20 Paul is discussing a public rebuke: "confront before all." (b) If the procedure spelled out in Matt 18 was well known, it too would argue for this interpretation. V 19 corresponds to the private confrontation in Matt 18:15–16, and v 20 corresponds to the public hearing of Matt 18:17. (c) If οἱ λοιποί, "the rest," are the rest of the church (although this interpretation is not accepted in this commentary; see below), then the confrontation must take place in public so that the rest of the church will see it. (d) The similar structure of vv 19 and 20, ἐνώπιον being parallel in structure to κατά, "against," gives evidence that ἐνώπιον modifies what follows: "Against [κατά] an elder a charge do not accept; those sinning before [ἐνώπιον] all confront." (e) The Ephesian situation

also argues for this interpretation. The problems were advanced and public, apparently requiring an equally public confrontation.

(5) Related to the issue of ἐνώπιον, "before," is the identity of the πάντων, "everyone." Does it refer to all the elders or all the church? (6) Tied to this is the question of οἱ λοιποί, "the rest." Are they the rest of the elders or the rest of the church? (a) λοιπός means "rest of the same kind" (Fee, 130), but it could be referring to either ἁμαρτάνοντας, "those who persist in sinning," or πάντων, "everyone," so this is not decisive. (b) πάντων and οἱ λοιποί must refer to two different groups of people. It does not make sense to say that the confrontation must be before everyone so the rest will be in fear if everyone and the rest are the same group. (c) If πάντων refers to the other elders (Bernard, Lock), Paul is suggesting a private confrontation with the church leadership, and Kelly (127) argues that there is no other evidence that this sort of action was church policy. (d) If πάντων refers to the other elders, one would expect Paul to use οἱ λοιποί, "the rest," instead: "Rebuke those [elders] sinning in front of the rest [of the elders]" (Fee, 134). (e) In the Matthean account, the private confrontation is followed by public rebuking. If v 19 corresponds to the private confrontation, then v 20 is the public rebuking before the church. In light of the public nature of the Ephesian problem and the extent to which it had developed, it seems best to view πάντων as the church body (Calvin, Guthrie, Kelly, Fee, Knight) and the οἱ λοιποί as the rest of the elders (Bernard, Lock, Dibelius-Conzelmann, Kelly, Hanson [1983]). Sinning elders should be confronted before the whole church so that the remaining elders will become fearful and not follow in their sinful behavior. φόβος, "fear" (cf. Trench, Synonyms, 58–59), could be the fear of public rebuke, the fear of the consequences of sinning, or the "fear of God" (Fee, 130). φόβος does not occur elsewhere in the PE, so it is difficult to make a decision, but the fear discussed here is the result of a human confrontation and so it should include at least a human fear resulting from the knowledge that elders will be held accountable before the church for their actions. The use of public rebuke and ensuing fear is illustrated by the account of Ananias and Sapphira, who were publicly rebuked and as a result "great fear came upon the whole church, and upon all who heard of these things" (Acts 5:11).

Paul is therefore suggesting a twofold confrontation process. The first step is to accept an accusation only if there are two or three firsthand witnesses. This would supposedly be in private and include confrontation with the elder. If the accusation is valid and the sinning persists, then the elders should be confronted in public before the whole church so that the rest of the elders may fear, realizing that they will be held accountable for their own actions by the church and God, and presumably so that the sinning elder will repent.

21 Διαμαρτύρομαι ἐνώπιον τοῦ θεοῦ καὶ Χριστοῦ Ἰησοῦ καὶ τῶν ἐκλεκτῶν ἀγγέλων, ἵνα ταῦτα φυλάξῃς χωρὶς προκρίματος, μηδὲν ποιῶν κατὰ πρόσκλισιν, "I solemnly charge [you] before God and Christ Jesus and the elect angels that you keep these things without prejudging, doing nothing with partiality." V 21 does not start a new topic but adds a note of solemnity to the current topic before going on to the fourth statement about elders (see Form/Structure/Setting). As Timothy listens to charges against elders (v 19) and confronts those who refuse to repent (v 20), he must take pains to ensure that he not make up his mind before hearing the facts and that he not allow personal bias to affect his judgment.

Chrysostom enlarges the scope to chaps. 3–5, emphasizing the pride that can come with authority ("Homily 16"; NPNF 13:464). This note of seriousness is emphasized by the use of the very strong verb διαμαρτύρομαι, "I solemnly charge," and by Paul's reminder that Timothy is always in the presence of God, of Christ, and of the angels and therefore is accountable to them. The atmosphere of the verse is the law court: διαμαρτύρομαι carries the nuance of testifying under oath; φυλάξῃς, "keep," conveys the idea of keeping a law from being broken; and προκρίματος, "prejudging," is a legal term for making up one's mind before hearing the facts.

In two other places Paul repeats a similar solemn charge to Timothy: "In the presence of God who gives life to all things, and of Christ Jesus who in his testimony before Pontius Pilate made the good confession, I charge you [παραγγέλλω] to keep the commandment unstained and free from reproach" (1 Tim 6:13); "I solemnly charge [διαμαρτύρομαι] [you] before God and Christ Jesus who is about to judge [the] living and [the] dead, and [by] his appearing and [by] his kingdom: preach the word" (2 Tim 4:1–2a; cf. charge in 2 Tim 2:14 to the Ephesians using διαμαρτύρεσθαι, "to charge solemnly"). This does not necessarily mean that Paul has heard that Timothy was not being fair in his work in Ephesus. Paul is encouraging Timothy to be careful of accusations of unfairness, which can be difficult when a young person is being persecuted. If Paul recognized the possibility of failure even in himself (1 Cor 9:27), he surely knew the possibility existed for Timothy as well.

διαμαρτύρομαι, "I solemnly charge," expresses a formal charge, with διά, "through," adding intensity to the simple μαρτύρεσθαι, "to implore." It describes an emphatic demand or affirmation (1 Thess 4:6; 1 Tim 5:21; 2 Tim 2:14; 4:1; cf. H. Strathman, *TDNT* 4:512). It can have the meaning "to testify under oath" (BAGD, 186), and its nuance of formality and solemnity carries over into our context. διαμαρτύρεσθαι, "to charge solemnly," plays an interesting role in Acts. Luke uses it to describe Peter's sermon at Pentecost (Acts 2:40), Peter and John's ministry in Samaria (Acts 8:25), Peter at Cornelius's house (Acts 10:42), and the Lord's statement to Paul that he had witnessed in Jerusalem (Acts 23:11) and that he would witness in Rome (Acts 28:23; cf. also Acts 18:5; 20:21, 23, 24; and προμαρτύρεσθαι, "to testify in advance," in 1 Pet 1:11). The word stands at each major advance of the gospel, describing the proclamation of the gospel.

Paul makes this charge in the presence of God and Christ Jesus and the elect angels. He may be calling to mind the final judgment and Timothy's accountability to God at that time. The picture evokes the angels' participation in Christ's return and humanity's judgment (Dan 7:10; Matt 13:39–42; 16:27; 24:31; 25:31; Mark 8:38; Luke 9:26; 2 Thess 1:7; Heb 12:22–24; Rev 14:10, 14–20; 4 Ezra 16:67; *1 Enoch* 39:1; *T. Levi* 19) and also Christ's role as the final judge (2 Cor 5:10; cf. John 5:22, 27; Acts 17:31). However, the present tense of διαμαρτύρομαι, "I solemnly charge," indicates a present accountability, and this agrees with the use of παραγγέλλω, "I solemnly charge," in 1 Tim 6:13 (cf. also the use of the cognate μαρτυρήσαντος, "having witnessed"). Timothy must realize that as he does his ministerial duty in Ephesus, he does so in the unseen presence of God, Christ, and the angels (cf. 1 Cor 11:10; Gal 1:20; 1 Tim 6:13; 2 Tim 2:14; 4:1). Kelly joins the two time frames: "Timothy must exercise his judicial functions as their representative, and also as one who will himself be judged by them" (127). The Granville

Sharp rule does not apply here because "Christ Jesus" functions as a proper name (Wallace, *Greek Grammar,* 276).

The elect angels could be the unfallen as opposed to the fallen angels (cf. 2 Pet 2:4; Jude 6; *Odes Sol.* 4:8; cf. Ellicott, 80). But as Bernard (87) argues, the simple term ἄγγελοι, "angels," consistently refers to the angels who did not fall, so the use of ἐκλεκτός, "elect," would be superfluous. Rather, by "elect angels" Paul means those angels whom God chooses to do his special tasks (cf., e.g., 1 Cor 4:9; 1 Tim 3:16; Rev 2:1) and who will be part of the final judgment. This parallels the NT use of ἐκλεκτός to describe those chosen by God, such as Israel (e.g., 1 Chr 16:13; Pss 88:4; 104:6, 43; Isa 65:9, 15, 23), the Messiah (Luke 23:35; John 1:34 [*v.l.*]), and Christians (2 Tim 2:10; Titus 1:1; cf. Matt 24:22, 24, 31; Mark 13:20, 22, 27; Luke 18:17; Rom 8:33; Col 3:12; 1 Pet 1:1; 2:9; 2 John 1:13; Rev 17:14). Calling God as a witness is found elsewhere in Paul (cf. Rom 1:9; 2 Cor 1:23; Phil 1:8; 1 Thess 2:5–10). Fuller (*NTS* 29 [1983] 261–62; also Meier, *CBQ* 35 [1973] 332–33) argues that the triad here reflects the triad of Deut 19:17 in which the dispute must be settled "before the LORD, before the priests and the judges." While the Deuteronomic triad is specifically connected with the truthfulness of the witness and the triad in the PE is concerned with the judge, in both cases the intent is to ensure the fairness of the proceedings.

The ἵνα, "that," clause gives the content of the charge. φυλάσσειν, "to keep," can mean "to keep a law from being broken," such as the law regarding the Sabbath (Matt 19:20; Luke 11:28; 18:21; John 12:47; Acts 7:53; 16:4; 21:24; Rom 2:26; Gal 6:13; cf. BAGD, 868), and this parallels the legal nuance of διαμαρτύρομαι, "I solemnly charge." (It also can mean "to protect" [1 Tim 6:20; 2 Tim 1:12, 14; 4:15].) The seriousness and the legal context of the charge in v 21 suggest that ταῦτα, "these things," refers to vv 19–20 (Ellicott, Bernard, Fee) and not to vv 17–18 since vv 19–20 deal with accusation and judgment. The plural ταῦτα, "things," rather than the singular τοῦτο, "thing," suggests that both v 19 and v 20 are in view. πρόκριμα, "prejudging," occurs only here in the NT. It is a technical legal term for prejudging a case, making up one's mind before hearing the facts (BAGD, 708). In this case the meaning of the word's etymological roots has been maintained in the compound word: κρίμα, "judgment," plus πρό, "before." πρόσκλισις, "partiality," likewise occurs only here in the NT and is always used in early Christian literature with negative overtones (BAGD, 716; Ellicott, 80–81). It describes an inclination, a partiality. Paul is telling Timothy that he must be careful to weigh the facts before making a judgment regarding an elder (vv 19–20), and he must be sure not to allow personal biases to influence his judgment. This sentiment is somewhat paralleled by the next verse, which says that Timothy should do his task with all purity in an unbiased and fair manner.

22 Χεῖρας ταχέως μηδενὶ ἐπιτίθει μηδὲ κοινώνει ἁμαρτίαις ἀλλοτρίαις· σεαυτὸν ἁγνὸν τήρει, "Do not lay hands on anyone quickly or share in the sins of others; keep yourself pure." This is the fourth statement about elders in this section and is the logical progression from the previous three verses. When Timothy commissions ("lay hands on"; cf. 4:14 for a discussion of this process) an elder, whether it be a new elder or one who was caught in sin and repented (vv 19–21), he is not to do so quickly. The danger is that Timothy could be sharing in their sin. Vv 24–25 add that the sins of some and the good works of others are not readily apparent. Patience is therefore important, giving the sins and the good works time to surface, and hence avoiding sharing in sins. In saying this Paul repeats his earlier concern that elders not be recent converts (1 Tim 3:6) and that deacons undergo a testing period to confirm their character and Christian commitment (1 Tim 3:10). Moreover, Paul adds that Timothy must take pains in all this to maintain his own purity. ἐπιτιθέναι χεῖρας, "to lay hands on," does not refer to the later church ritual of reinstating a penitent sinner (see *Form/Structure/Setting* and *Explanation*). Chrysostom defines ταχέως, "quickly," not as a first, second, or even third trial; rather he urges that a decision be made "after frequent and strict examination and circumspection" ("Homily 16"; NPNF 13:464).

The remaining exegetical issue in this verse is the precise meaning of κοινώνει ἁμαρτίαις ἀλλοτρίαις, "share in the sins of others." (1) It could mean that Paul is concerned that Timothy not commit the sins that his opponents are committing. This would place a major break after ἐπιτίθει, "lay . . . on," and form a parallel between "share in the sins of others" and the final phrase: "Do not lay hands on anyone quickly; nor should you share in the sins of others [but] keep yourself pure." It is typical for Paul to follow up a statement about the sins of the Ephesian leaders with a warning to Timothy to be careful (cf. 1 Tim 4:6–16). It would also mean that this phrase introduces a new topic: Timothy must not commit the same sins as the opponents. (2) But it is preferable to place a major break after ἀλλοτρίαις, "others": "Do not lay hands on anyone quickly or share in the sins of others; keep yourself pure." Paul does not think that Timothy will start committing the same sins as the opponents; rather he is concerned that by commissioning a sinner to leadership Timothy may to some degree be responsible for their ministry and the sins they may commit, possibly because Timothy may appear to condone their sin and because a failure to punish sin may encourage others to sin. (a) μηδέ, "and not," is parallel with μηδενί, "on no one," which suggests that v 22a belongs with v 22b. (b) There is no adversative before σεαυτόν, "yourself," as would be expected in interpretation (1). (c) Elsewhere when Paul expresses concern for Timothy's spiritual well-being, he does not tell Timothy not to commit sins. Rather, Paul tells him to pay attention and be careful (e.g., 1 Tim 4:16). (d) Interpretation (2) makes better sense of vv 24–25. Timothy should be slow to commission new elders because the sins of some take time to surface while others' good character may not be immediately obvious. Timothy should therefore be cautious in commissioning elders lest he become culpable for their later sins (cf. 2 John 11 for a similar idea of sharing another's sins). (e) If v 22b introduces a new thought, especially one as serious as admonishing Timothy not to sin, some explanation or discussion or encouragement would be expected, but there is none. Rather, after a parenthetical comment (v 23), Paul continues to speak about commissioning elders. (f) The use of μηδέ, "and not," in the PE and in Paul's other letters supports the second interpretation and clarifies that "nor [μηδέ] share in the sins of others" does not introduce a new topic but rather specifies an analogous, almost identical, idea. Timothy is to charge the opponents neither to teach other doctrines nor (μηδέ) to occupy themselves with endless myths and genealogies (1 Tim 1:4; "endless myths and genealogies" is almost epexegetical, describing the nature of the "other doctrines"). The rich are neither to be haughty nor (μηδέ) to set their hope on uncertain riches (1 Tim 6:17; their riches are the cause of their haughtiness). Paul admonishes the Romans neither to let sin reign in their bodies nor (μηδέ) to yield their members to sin (Rom 6:13; the second

statement is synonymous with the first). Jacob and Esau had not been born nor
(μηδέ) had they done anything good or bad when God chose Jacob (Rom 9:11;
while the two halves of this statement are not synonymous they are intimately
related). The Ephesians are told to be angry but not to sin; this is to be accomplished by neither letting the sun go down on their anger nor (μηδέ) giving an
opportunity to the devil (Eph 4:27; the two phrases are closely related in that it is
by not letting the sun go down on one's sin that one does not give an opportunity
to the devil). Paul tells the Thessalonians that if they do not work, neither (μηδέ)
should they eat (2 Thess 3:10; this is perhaps the closest parallel to 1 Tim 5:22 in
that the second statement is the direct consequence of the first). It may be concluded that Paul is not introducing a new topic with the μηδέ clause but rather is
spelling out the consequences of commissioning elders too quickly.

To this warning Paul adds that Timothy must keep himself ἁγνόν, "pure," above
reproach, free from sin (cf. 2 Cor 7:11: ἁγνούς, "guiltless"; 1 John 3:3). V 22c is
related to v 22a–b in the same way that v 21 is related to vv 19–20. Timothy should
not accept a charge against an elder that is not properly witnessed, and he must
confront those who continue in their sin (vv 19–20). As he does this, he must
take pains to be sure that he does nothing through discrimination or partiality (v
21). In the same way Timothy is admonished to be cautious in commissioning
elders (v 22a–b) and in the process to keep himself pure (v 22c). ἁγνός, "pure,"
occurs elsewhere in the PE only in Titus 2:5 where the older women are encouraged to be pure. It can carry the sexual nuance of chaste (BAGD, 12), which is
present in Titus 2:5. This would parallel the use of ἁγνεία, "purity," in 1 Tim 5:2
where Timothy is instructed to treat younger women as sisters in all purity. The
lack of sexual propriety is a major issue in the Ephesian problem (cf. *Comment* on
1 Tim 2:9). However, in our passage Paul's warning is that Timothy should keep
himself pure as he commissions new elders. Since there is some overlap between
this verse and v 21, the notion of purity here is more the idea of keeping pure of
any accusation of discrimination or partiality. On τηρεῖν, "to keep," see *Comment*
on 2 Tim 4:7.

23 Μηκέτι ὑδροπότει, ἀλλὰ οἴνῳ ὀλίγῳ χρῶ διὰ τὸν στόμαχον καὶ τὰς πυκνάς
σου ἀσθενείας, "No longer drink only water, but use a little wine, on account of
[your] stomach and your frequent illnesses." At first glance it is difficult to see
how this verse fits into the flow of discussion, and as a result it has been viewed as
a gloss or displacement (e.g., Moffatt, *Introduction*, 402) despite the lack of any
textual evidence. Some have seen it as a personal comment Paul inserts in reference to Timothy's poor health (Guthrie, 108). However, many recognize that it is
a parenthetical, personal remark that Timothy is not to understand Paul's previous call to purity as an endorsement of Timothy's apparent decision to abstain
totally from alcohol. Vv 24–25 follow directly upon v 22. It is often pointed out
that the Ephesian opponents were ascetics (cf. 1 Tim 4:3), and Paul does not
want Timothy to appear as if he is following their ascetic practices. However, while
Paul's opponents did espouse asceticism, it appears that either their asceticism
did not include abstaining from alcohol or else they drank to excess despite their
teachings (cf. 1 Tim 3:3).

Paul tells Timothy to μηκέτι, "no longer," drink only water. It is interesting to
ask why Timothy was abstaining since it obviously was detrimental to his health.
The answer lies in the Ephesian situation. Paul's opponents were drunkards, and

to disassociate himself totally from them and their teaching, Timothy apparently had chosen to abstain to the point that it was hurting him physically. His abstinence was an example of not exercising his Christian liberty when it might damage another's faith (cf. 1 Cor 8:13; Rom 14:15, 21). While this was admirable, Paul did not want Timothy to think that the preceding statement was an endorsement of his decision to abstain, and in fact Paul thought that Timothy should change his habit and use a little wine because of his physical problems. If this is correct, then a different picture of Timothy emerges from this verse than is normally seen. For example, Fee comments that "the mention of Timothy's frequent illnesses helps to contribute to the picture of timidity that emerges from the various texts" (132). Yet physical weakness has no necessary connection with personal timidity, and it is hard to see Paul sending a timid person into the problems that existed in Ephesus (cf. *Introduction*, "Historical Reconstruction from the PE, B. 1 Timothy," for a picture of Timothy). Rather, this verse shows Timothy as a person of strong convictions, willing to do what was the best for the Ephesian community even though it hurt him physically. This is not the action of a timid person. Chrysostom wonders why Paul did not simply heal Timothy, "for he whose garment had raised the dead was clearly able to do this too" ("Homily 16"; NPNF 13:464). He concludes that as in the case of Paul (2 Cor 12:10), Timothy's afflictions kept him humble and helped other people see that he was only human despite his position and abilities.

ὑδροποτεῖν, "to drink only water," means to drink water to the exclusion of anything else (BAGD, 832). Paul is not telling Timothy not to drink water; he is advising him to drink something in addition to water. Bernard (88) adds that it means to abstain "habitually." This is the only occurrence of this word in the NT. The beneficial aspects of a little wine were common knowledge in the ancient world (cf. Prov 31:6; Hippocrates *Medic.* 13; Plutarch *De tuenda san.* 19; Pliny *Hist.* 2.19; 23.22; *b. Ber.* 51a; *b. B. Bat.* 58b; cf. Str-B 3:654–55; Spicq, 1:549). This verse has often been misused in popular exegesis as an endorsement of social drinking; the use of alcohol here is strictly medicinal. In the other occurrences of οἶνος, "wine," in Paul's letters, he urges caution in its use (Rom 14:21; Eph 5:18; 1 Tim 3:8; Titus 2:3). οἶνος, "wine," was a fermented drink; there is no evidence of non-alcoholic (pasteurized) wine in ancient times. For a discussion of alcohol and drunkenness, see *Comment* on 1 Tim 3:3. Paul does not specify the nature of Timothy's stomach problems and illnesses; cf. Spicq, "1 Timothée 5:23." Presumably Timothy's frequent illnesses were in addition to his stomach problems.

24 Τινῶν ἀνθρώπων αἱ ἁμαρτίαι πρόδηλοί εἰσιν προάγουσαι εἰς κρίσιν, τισὶν δὲ καὶ ἐπακολουθοῦσιν, "The sins of some people are evident, going before [them] into judgment, but they also follow after some." Having finished his parenthetical comment in v 23, Paul concludes his discussion of elders by pointing out why it is important that Timothy not be hasty in commissioning elders (v 22). It is obvious that some people are sinners and therefore not suited to be elders. However, other peoples' sins are not as readily apparent, and therefore Timothy must be cautious in his commissioning. Paul will conclude with the counterpart in v 25: the suitability of some people to be elders may be readily apparent, but there are others whose good deeds are not public and therefore may not appear to be qualified. A cautious attitude will help Timothy find these people as well. Thus v 24 and v 25 give both sides of the argument for caution. The use of the article here (αἱ ἁμαρτίαι, "the sins") balances and calls attention to the use of the article in the next verse (τὰ ἔργα τὰ καλά, "the good deeds"); the sins and the good deeds are the indications to Timothy of whether a person should be an elder.

There is some question regarding the time of the judgment mentioned here (present or future; cf. v 21) and who is to perform the judgment (God or Timothy). Most feel that the verse refers to God's judgment of these sinners at the final judgment. The idea is that although Timothy may not be able to see a person's sins, eventually God will reveal the sin when he judges each person. However, the context requires that the sins be obvious now so Timothy can make decisions about the leadership. The next verse must also refer to the same time of judgment. It may be that Timothy's present judgment is a precursor to God's judgment; Timothy sees the sins—which show that God's judgment rests, and will rest, on them—and on this basis does not commission elders.

The parallel structure of vv 24–25 is pronounced. Not only does v 24a contrast with v 24b, but v 24a parallels v 25a as v 24b parallels v 25b.

| Some sins | are visible; | the others | become visible later. | (v 24) |
| Some good deeds | are visible; | the others | cannot remain hidden. | (v 25) |

By ἁμαρτίαι, "sins," Paul is thinking back to his description of the sinning elders who refuse to repent after a confrontation (v 20). He may also be thinking ahead to what he will say in 1 Tim 6:3–10 since the sinners in 5:20 are most likely committing the sins described there. πρόδηλος, "evident," occurs elsewhere in the NT only in the next verse and in Heb 7:14; Bernard (89) defines it as "notoriously evident." On προάγειν, "to go before," see *Comment* on 1 Tim 1:18. The picture Paul creates is that of a person's sins as if they were a herald (Bernard's term, 89), going before and proclaiming a person to be a sinner and ineligible for the office of elder. εἰς, "into," indicates the result of the sins, that they lead to Timothy's and inevitably God's judgment. τισίν, "some," is a dative of reference referring back to ἀνθρώπων, "people," while the subject of ἐπακολουθοῦσιν, "follow after," is ἁμαρτίαι, "sins": "but [the sins of some people] follow after them." ἐπακολουθεῖν, "to follow after," occurs elsewhere in the NT only in 1 Tim 5:10, where it is used figuratively to mean "to devote oneself."

25 ὡσαύτως καὶ τὰ ἔργα τὰ καλὰ πρόδηλα, καὶ τὰ ἄλλως ἔχοντα κρυβῆναι οὐ δύνανται, "In the same way also the good works are evident, and those that are not are not able to be hidden." The counterpart to v 24 is that just as some sins are not immediately apparent, neither are some good works. If Timothy is hasty in commissioning elders, he may pass over some candidates who do not appear to be qualified but in fact are. He should therefore take time and observe.

The phrase τὰ ἄλλως ἔχοντα, "those that are not" (lit. "the things having otherwise"), has two interpretations. (1) It could refer to deeds that are not good (i.e., bad deeds), paralleling "sins" in v 24 and contrasting with "good deeds" in v 25a. Paul's argument would then be that the sins of some are obvious while others' sins are not; in the same way that good deeds are obvious (v 25a), bad deeds are not able to be hidden (v 25b). V 25b would repeat the gist of v 24b. (2) "Those that are not" could refer to good deeds that are not immediately visible, paralleling "going before [them] into judgment" in v 24. This is preferable. (a) V 24 points out the problem of accepting a bad elder; v 25 points out the danger of not appointing a good elder. Both halves of v 24 deal with bad deeds, and one would therefore expect v 25 to deal with good deeds in order to provide a suitable contrast. (b) ὡσαύτως, "in the same way," introduces a contrast with v 24, necessitating that the whole of v 25 deal with good deeds. (c) If "those that are not" refers to bad deeds, the logic of the comparison is not clear. How does the visibility of good deeds contrast with the fact that sins cannot remain hidden? A better contrast is achieved if the phrase refers to good deeds: some good deeds are immediately visible while others are not (but eventually will be), so Timothy should not turn anyone down hastily (v 25). On καλός, "good," see *Comment* on 1 Tim 1:8. On the role of τὰ ἔργα τὰ καλά, "good deeds," in the PE, see *Comment* on 1 Tim 2:10. ἄλλως, "otherwise," occurs only here in the NT.

Explanation

Many of the problems in Ephesus originated with the elders, their heretical teaching and their sinful behavior. It was therefore appropriate that Paul dealt with issues relating directly to them. Although much of the problem in Ephesus resulted from the Ephesians love of money, this did not negate the necessity of paying Christian workers as well as giving them the respect they were due. This was in line with both the OT instruction and Jesus' teachings. When a charge was brought against an elder, Timothy was supposed to be sure that there were witnesses, and if the elder was guilty and refused to repent, he would have to be dealt with in a public fashion as an example to the other elders. In this whole process Timothy must maintain seriousness. As he stood in the presence of the unseen God, Christ, and the angels, Timothy would have to be sure that his judgments were not clouded by prejudice or partiality. Finally, when appointing elders, Timothy would have to avoid being hasty. He would have to be patient and wait to see the true character of applicants because not only sin but also good deeds were not always immediately apparent. In the course of making this last point, Paul adds a parenthetical comment so Timothy will not misunderstand Paul's call for purity. He is not discussing ascetic purity in the sense of abstinence from alcohol, and Timothy should care for his physical needs.

The early church fathers very quickly called for treating the church leadership with honor, going far beyond Paul's intention:

My child, *thou shalt remember him that speaketh unto thee the word of God* night and day, and shalt honour him as the Lord; for whencesoever the Lordship abideth, there is the Lord. (*Didache* 4; Lightfoot, *Apostolic Fathers*, 230)

As to a good shepherd, let the lay person honour him, love him, reverence him as his lord, as his master, as the high priest of God, as a teacher of piety. For he that heareth him, heareth Christ; and he that rejecteth him, rejecteth Christ; and he who does not receive Christ, does not receive His God and Father. (*Apostolic Constitutions* 2.20; ANF 7:404)

Let the laity, therefore, pay proper honours in their presents, and utmost marks of respect to each distinct order. But let them not on all occasions trouble their governor, but let them signify their desires by those who minister to him, that is, by the deacons, with whom they may be more free. For neither may we address ourselves to Almighty God, but only by Christ. In the same manner, therefore, let the laity make known all their desires to the bishop by the deacon, and accordingly let them act as he shall direct them. For there was no holy thing offered or done in the temple formerly without the priest. (*Apostolic Constitutions* 2.28; ANF 7:411)

For if Aaron, because he declared to Pharaoh the words of God from Moses, is called a prophet; and Moses himself is called a god to Pharaoh, on account of his being at once a king and a high priest, as God says to him, "I have made thee a god to Pharaoh, and Aaron thy brother shall be thy prophet"; why do not ye also esteem the mediators of the word to be prophets, and reverence them as gods? (*Apostolic Constitutions* 2.29; ANF 7:411)

This type of divine veneration demands caution in comparing anything in the PE to the second century without first recognizing the significant development in thought. The church also interpreted "double" honor as double the stipend:

But as much as is given to every one of the elder women, let double so much be given to the deacons, in honour of Christ. Let also a double portion be set apart for the presbyters, as for such who labour continually about the word and doctrine, upon the account of the apostles of our Lord, whose place they sustain, as the counsellors of the bishop and the crown of the Church. (*Apostolic Constitutions* 2.28; ANF 7:411)

In 1 Tim 5:17–25 there are many principles governing the issue of church discipline, principles paralleling similar discussions elsewhere, such as in Matt 18. (1) Sin must be confronted. (2) Accusations must be supported by multiple witnesses. (3) It is not the occasional but the persistent sin that requires action. (4) Public rebuke should be preceded by personal confrontation. But when the confrontation is ineffective, the public rebuke must be carried out. (5) The purpose of public rebuke is not so much for punishment as it is to instill a healthy fear. (6) A person executing judgment, even someone of Timothy's stature, must strive to be as fair and pure in the process as possible. (7) The commissioning of elders is serious business, and there is a responsibility assumed by the one commissioning for the ones commissioned. (8) There is no substitute for caution and time. A person's true character and deeds are not always immediately visible.

The issue of church discipline has always been a difficult subject, not only to understand but especially to carry out. The history of the church, both ancient and modern, has been plagued by a refusal to follow the admonitions of Scripture (cf. *Comment* on 1 Tim 1:18–20). As Guthrie comments, "The abuse of discipline has often led to a harsh and intolerant spirit, but neglect of it has proved a danger almost as great. When faced with sinning elders a spineless attitude is deplorable" (106).

In his famous discussion of the church, Justin Martyr gives this instruction on church discipline:

In the same place also exhortations are made, rebukes and sacred censures are administered. For with a great gravity is the work of judging carried on among us, as befits those who feel assured that they are in the sight of God; and you have the most notable example of judgment to come when any one has sinned so grievously as to require his severance from us in prayer, in the congregation and in all sacred intercourse." (*1 Apol.* 39; ANF 7:46)

Book 2 of the *Apostolic Constitutions* (Sec. 3, chaps. 7ff.; ANF 13) devotes much discussion to how the church leadership should judge and treat repentant and nonrepentant sinners. It is worth reading the entire discussion, but the significant points are as follows:

Beloved, be it known to you that those who are baptized into the death of our Lord Jesus are obliged to go on no longer in sin; for as those who are dead cannot work wickedness any longer, so those who are dead with Christ cannot practise wickedness. We do not therefore believe, brethren, that any one who has received the washing of life continues in the practice of the licentious acts of transgressors. Now he who sins after his baptism, unless he repent and forsake his sins, shall be condemned to hell-fire. (2.7)

Upon this account, therefore, O bishop, endeavour to be pure in thy actions, and to adorn thy place and dignity, which is that of one sustaining the character of God among men, as being set over all men, over priests, kings, rulers, fathers, children, teachers, and in general over all those who are subject to thee: and so sit in the Church when thou speakest, as having authority to judge offenders. For to you, O bishops, it is said: "Whatsoever ye shall bind on earth shall be bound in heaven; and whatsoever ye shall loose on earth shall be loosed in heaven." (2.11)

Do thou therefore, O bishop, judge with authority like God, yet receive the penitent; for God is a God of mercy. Rebuke those that sin, admonish those that are not converted, exhort those that stand to persevere in their goodness, receive the penitent; for the Lord God has promised with an oath to afford remission to the penitent for what things they have done amiss. (2.12)

But if thou refusest to receive him that repents, thou exposest him to those who lie in wait to destroy. . . . Receive, therefore, without any doubting, him that repents. Be not hindered by such unmerciful men, who say that we must not be defiled with such as those, nor so much as speak to them: for such advice is from men that are unacquainted with God and His providence, and are unreasonable judges, and unmerciful brutes. (2.14)

When thou seest the offender, with severity command him to be cast out; and as he is going out, let the deacons also treat him with severity, and then let them go and seek for him, and detain him out of the Church; and when they come in, let them entreat thee for him. For our Saviour Himself entreated His Father for those who had sinned, as it is written in the Gospel: "Father, forgive them; for they know not what they do." Then order the offender to come in; and if upon examination thou findest that he is penitent, and fit to be received at all into the Church when thou hast afflicted him his days of fasting, according to the degree of his offence—as two, three, five, or seven weeks—so set him at liberty, and speak such things to him as are fit to be said in way of reproof, instruction, and exhortation to a sinner for his reformation, that so he may continue privately in his humility, and pray to God to be merciful to him, saying: "If Thou, O Lord, shouldest mark iniquities, O Lord, who should stand? For with Thee there is propitiation." (2.16)

Do not admit less evidence to convict any one than that of three witnesses, and those of known and established reputation; inquire whether they do not accuse out of ill-will or envy. (2.21)

But if any one returns, and shows forth the fruit of repentance, then do ye receive him to prayer, as the lost son, the prodigal, who had consumed his father's substance with harlots, who fed swine, and desired to be fed with husks, and could not obtain it. This son, when he repented, and returned to his father, and said, "I have sinned against Heaven, and before thee, and am no more worthy to be called thy son"; the father, full of affection to his child, received him with music, and restored him his old robe, and ring, and shoes, and slew the fatted calf, and made merry with his friends. Do thou therefore, O bishop, act in the same manner. And as thou receivest an heathen after thou hast instructed and baptized him, so do thou let all join in prayers for this man, and restore him by imposition of hands to his ancient place among the flock, as one purified by repentance; and that imposition of hands shall be to him instead of baptism: for by the laying on of our hands the Holy Ghost was given to believers. (2.41)

D. Slaves   (1 Tim 6:1–2a)

Bibliography

Bartchy, S. S. *ΜΑΛΛΟΝ ΧΡΗΣΑΙ: First-Century Slavery and the Interpretation of 1 Corinthians 7:21.* SBLDS 11. Missoula, MT: Scholars Press, 1973. **Berlendis, A.** "Esotazione agli schiavi." *RechBib* 7.2–3 (1972) 285–311. **Buckland, W. W.** *The Roman Law of Slavery.* Cambridge: Cambridge UP, 1970. **Finley, M. I.,** ed. *Slavery in Classical Antiquity.* Cambridge: Heffer, 1960. **Gayer, R.** *Die Stellung des Sklaven in den paulinischen Gemeinden und bei Paulus: Zugleich ein sozialgeschichtlich vergleichender Beitrag zur Wertung des Sklaven in der Antike.* Europaische Hochschul-Schriften 23.78. Bern: Lang, 1976. **Gülzow, H.** *Christentum und Sklaverei in den ersten drei Jahrhunderten.* Bonn: Habelt, 1969. **Klein, G.** "Christusglaube und Weltverantwortung als Interpretation—Probleme neutestamentlicher Theologie." *VF* 18 (1973) 47–54. **Laub, F.** *Die Begegnung des frühen Christentums mit der antiken Sklaverei.* Stuttgart: Katholisches Bibelwerk, 1982. **Lyall, F.** *Slaves, Citizens, Sons: Legal Metaphors in the Epistles.* Grand Rapids, MI: Zondervan, 1984. **Martin, D. B.** *Slavery as Salvation: The Metaphor of Slavery in Pauline Christianity.* New Haven, CT: Yale UP, 1990. **Schweizer, E.** "Zum Sklavenproblem im Neuen Testament." *EvT* 32 (1972) 502–6. **Spicq, C.** "Le vocabulaire de l'esclavage dans le Noveau Testament." *RB* 85 (1978) 201–26. **Westermann, W. L.** *The Slave Systems of Greek and Roman Antiquity.* 3rd ed. Philadelphia: American Philosophical Society, 1964. **Wiedemann, T.** *Greek and Roman Slavery.* London: Croom Helm, 1981. **Zeitlin, S.** "Slavery during the Second Commonwealth and the Tannaitic Period." *JQR* 53 (1962–63) 185–218.

For additional bibliography on slavery, see BAGD, 884, on χράομαι. For bibliography on other NT passages dealing with slaves and other members of the household, see O'Brien, *Colossians,* 214.

Translation

¹*As many as are under the yoke as slaves should consider their own masters as worthy of*

all honor in order that the name of God and the teaching might not be blasphemed. [2]*And let those who have believing masters not despise [them] because they are brothers; but let them serve all the more since those benefiting from [their] act of kindness are believers and beloved.*

Form/Structure/Setting

So far Paul has addressed three groups of people in the Ephesian church: people of different ages (5:1–2), widows (5:3–16), and elders (5:17–25). He now turns to a fourth group: slaves (6:1–2a). After discussing the Ephesian problems for the last time (6:2b–16), he will add one final group, the rich (6:17–19).

This paragraph repeats themes found elsewhere in the PE. (1) Honor is a central theme, as it is with all people in the church (5:1–2), widows (5:3,16) and hard-working overseers (5:17; cf. *Form/Structure/Setting* on 1 Tim 5:1–2). Lock paraphrases, "This duty of proper respect holds good also of the relation of slaves to their masters" (64–65). (2) The reputation of the church is a motivating factor for how people conduct themselves (3:15). It is essential that slaves respect their masters so that God's reputation and the gospel not be soiled (6:1b). (3) Although the idea of mutual servanthood is not explicitly stated, it underlies the teaching of v 2 (cf. Mark 10:43–45; 1 Cor 9:19; Gal 5:13; 1 Pet 2:16–17). A Christian slave must not despise his Christian master because the master is a fellow believer and beloved; the master should view the labors of the slave not as a demanded responsibility but as acts of kindness. The relationships that exist within the body of Christ transcend socially defined roles.

It may be asked why this discussion is included here. Fee (136–37) tentatively suggests that there was a conflict in the Ephesian church between slaves and masters. The discussions before and after 6:1–2a are directed specifically toward the excesses of the Ephesian heresy, and most of the PE is directed toward a specific historical situation. Believers' abuse of their newly found freedom in Christ proved to be an issue in other churches (cf. Rom 14:1–23; 1 Cor 11:2–16; 1 Pet 2:11–18), and 1 Tim 6:2 shows that in the Ephesian church slaves were taking advantage of their spiritual relationship to their believing masters. Chrysostom comments, "for do not suppose, because thou art a believer, that thou art therefore a free man: since thy freedom is to serve the more faithfully" ("Homily 16"; NPNF 13:465). While Fee's suggestion is probably correct, Paul has been specifying conduct for certain groups within the church, and within this type of context he often teaches about the responsibilities of Christian slaves to their masters (see *Explanation*). This is an appropriate place to repeat his normal instructions. However, Paul does not discuss other family relationships (e.g., husband, wife, children) as he does elsewhere, suggesting that he is not teaching in general but is addressing a specific Ephesian situation.

There are several issues relating to the structure of the passage worth noting. (1) Barrett (82) argues that these verses are part of the previous discussion, and therefore Paul is discussing slaves who are elders in the church. (a) But 1 Tim 6:1–2a is similar to the many other discussions of slaves in the NT (see *Explanation*). (b) Paul has been discussing different groups of people in the Ephesian church, and these verses naturally deal with another group. (c) There is nothing specific about elders in these two verses. (2) Some argue that v 1 is dealing solely with non-Christian masters while in v 2 the masters are Christian (see *Comment*). This interpretation of v 1 is to be rejected, however, and the two verses are to be seen as moving from a general statement about slaves (v 1) to the more specific situation of a slave's relationship to a Christian master (v 2). (3) V 2b can be viewed as part of vv 1–2a, in which case ταῦτα, "these things," may refer to the teaching to slaves. However, v 2b is similar to other statements in the PE that are transitional in nature, and ταῦτα can refer to the whole of 5:1–6:2a. (See *Form/Structure/Setting* on 6:2b–10 for a further discussion.)

Comment

1a Ὅσοι εἰσὶν ὑπὸ ζυγὸν δοῦλοι, τοὺς ἰδίους δεσπότας πάσης τιμῆς ἀξίους ἡγείσθωσαν, "As many as are under the yoke as slaves should consider their own masters as worthy of all honor." Paul knows that all people are equal in Christ, whether free or slave (Gal 3:28). But in keeping with his teaching elsewhere, Paul admonishes Christian slaves not to use their freedom as an excuse to treat their masters disrespectfully. As will be discussed in the *Explanation,* this may sound shortsighted and complacent to twentieth-century ears, but Paul has a different agenda from many today and has something more important than personal freedom in mind. As he goes on to say, what is at stake is the reputation of the gospel and God's reputation among the heathen. Paul's silence is not a tacit approval of slavery.

The exegetical question of this passage concerns the word ζυγός, "yoke." Paul does not say "the yoke of slavery" (ζυγῷ δουλείας) as he does in Gal 5:1. δοῦλοι, "slaves," must be the predicate, and ὑπὸ ζυγόν, "under the yoke," is added for emphasis: "As many as are slaves under the yoke." Some (Guthrie, Holtz, Hanson [1983], Knight) see the reference to the yoke as an indication that Paul is addressing slaves with non-Christian masters, those whose slavery is truly a yoke. The following verse then deals with slaves of Christian masters. (1) But slavery of any form, whether or not the master be Christian, is a yoke, so the distinction between two different classes of slaves does not seem to be correct. (2) ὅσοι, "as many as," is general, referring to all slaves. (3) "Yoke" is a common term for slavery (see below). It seems "needlessly subtle" (Kelly, 131) to read something else into the word. (4) Knight says "it is doubtful that a Christian master would regard his slave as 'under the yoke,' but a non-Christian might" (244), but this seems too idyllic. (5) The strongest argument that the masters in v 1 are nonbelievers is that the reason Paul gives for the slaves' honoring them is evangelistic: "in order that the name of God and the teaching might not be blasphemed." It can be argued this is applicable only to non-Christians. However, a disobedient slave, especially if the slave is a leader in the church, would bring reproach on the church regardless of the master. Rather, the phrase emphasizes that although slaves are oppressed, under the yoke, yet still they must consider their masters worthy of honor. V 1 is a general statement to slaves, and v 2 adds a further note to those with Christian masters.

ὑπό, "under," designates those under the "power, rule, sovereignty, command" (BAGD, 843[2b]) of something. ζυγός, "yoke," can be used in a positive sense as one under the yoke of the law (*m. Abot* 3.5; *y. Qid.* 1.2 [59d]; *m. Ber.* 2.2; cf. Bruce, *Galatians,* 226), of God (Jer 2:20), of wisdom (Sir 51:26; cf. 6:24–25), and of Christ

(Matt 11:29–30; cf. G. Bertram, *TDNT* 2:897–98). Most of the time it is used with negative connotations as in the yoke of political oppression (Gen 27:40; 2 Chr 10:4,10), foreign rule (Deut 28:48; Isa 9:4; 19:10; 14:29; 47:6; Dan 8:25; 1 Macc 8:18), slavery (Ezek 34:27; Sir 30:35), and the tongue (Sir 28:19; cf. K. H. Rengstorf, *TDNT* 2:898–901). ζυγός, "yoke," is used elsewhere in the NT in reference to the Jewish law (Acts 15:10) and slavery (Gal 5:1; cf. use as "balance" in Rev 6:5). δοῦλος, "slave," occurs three other times in the PE. In a metaphorical sense Paul describes the personal characteristics of the Lord's servant (2 Tim 2:24) and introduces himself as the slave of God (Titus 1:1; cf. Rom 1:1; Phil 1:1; Jas 1:1; 1 Pet 1:1; Jude 1). The word also occurs in the parallel discussion of slaves in Titus (2:9; cf. Trench, *Synonyms*, 53–58). δεσπότης, "master" (cf. Trench, *Synonyms*, 134–36), is the general term for a slave's master and is used in the discussion of useful vessels in the master's house (2 Tim 2:21) and in the parallel discussion in Titus (2:9). In the parallel passage in Eph 6:5 Paul uses κύριος, "lord," which fits Paul's argument that the slave is working "as to Christ," "as to the Lord" (ὡς τῷ κυρίῳ; Eph 6:7); "knowing that whatever good anyone does, he will receive again from the Lord, whether he is a slave or free" (Eph 6:8); and the masters (οἱ κύριοι) know "that he who is both their Master and yours is in heaven, and that there is no partiality with him" (Eph 6:9; cf. Col 3:24; 4:1). Paul does not make the same point here and hence uses the usual term. In a similar vein Paul calls the Roman church to obey the government, to pay taxes, and to give respect and honor to whom they are due (Rom 13:1–7) because authority ultimately stems from God (cf. Knight, 245; cf. 1 Pet 2:11–18). The Christian's relation to the government has already been raised in 1 Tim 2:2.

1b ἵνα μὴ τὸ ὄνομα τοῦ θεοῦ καὶ ἡ διδασκαλία βλασφημῆται, "in order that the name of God and the teaching might not be blasphemed." Slaves are to respect their masters not because slavery is a proper institution or because Paul supposedly has no social conscience. Rather, the success of the gospel is more significant than the lot of any one individual, and therefore slaves should behave in a way that does not bring reproach on the gospel. A similar statement occurs in Rom 2:24, where it is a quotation from Isa 52:5 (rather than being guides for the blind, the Jews are stealing, committing adultery and sacrilege, and dishonoring God by breaking the law; as a result, "the name of God is blasphemed among the Gentiles"). This is the same reason given in the parallel passage in Titus to explain why a slave should behave properly ("in order that they might adorn the teaching of God our savior in all things"; 2:10). This is significantly different from the reasons Paul gives for other earthly relationships: marriage is grounded in creation (1 Tim 2:13; 1 Cor 11:8–9; Eph 5:31); parent-child relationships are based on the fifth commandment (Eph 6:1–3). But not so with slavery. In fact, the verse can be read as a concession to culture without agreeing with it; the cause of Christ has priority. (This is not a cultural concession to the truth; Paul never says that slavery is correct in any circumstance. See discussions of 1 Cor 7:21 in Fee, *First Epistle to the Corinthians*, 315–18.) In the Prison Epistles Paul speaks of the slave's motivation for work as service for the Lord (Eph 6:5–8; Col 3:22–24); here the motivation is evangelistic (cf. Knight, 242–43).

The ὄνομα, "name," of God is equivalent to his reputation as is seen by its usage elsewhere (Rom 2:24; Rev 3:12; 16:9) and the frequent use of similar phrases such as "name of the Lord," "my name," and "your name" throughout Scripture,

especially in the Psalms. διδασκαλία, "teaching," can refer to the doctrinal exposition of the gospel (cf. 1 Tim 4:13), but here it is used synonymously with the
gospel. On βλασφημῆται, "be blasphemed," see *Comments* on 1 Tim 1:13, 20.

2aα   οἱ δὲ πιστοὺς ἔχοντες δεσπότας μὴ καταφρονείτωσαν, ὅτι ἀδελφοί εἰσιν,
"And let those who have believing masters not despise [them] because they are
brothers." Having given general instructions about slaves, Paul addresses one specific situation: slaves with Christian masters. The exegetical issue is whether the
ὅτι, "because," clause gives (1) the reason that the slaves are despising their Christian masters or (2) the reason that the slaves should not despise their masters. Is
this a situation where some slaves in Ephesus are treating their masters shame-
fully specifically because they are Christians, or is it the usual situation of the
natural tension between master and slave? The adversative ἀλλά, "but," gives evidence for option (1) because it can be seen as the major turning point of the
argument. Slaves should not despise their masters because they (i.e., the masters) are believers; rather (ἀλλά), they should serve them all the more because
the ones receiving the benefit of the slaves' service are believers. However, the
parallel structure of the following phrase argues for option (2). It is composed of
a command and a reason for the command: do not despise your masters because
they are believers; rather work harder since the ones receiving the benefit of your
work are believers. It is difficult for someone in a society in which there is no
slavery to understand the tension that must have existed between two believers
when one owned the other and how the internal contradiction must have chafed
against the slave's conscience and faith.

Evidently in the Ephesian church Christian slaves were taking advantage of
their relationship to their believing masters (see *Form/Structure/Setting*). This is a
different situation from Eph 6:9 and may account for the slightly different instructions in the Prison Epistles. The initial δέ is weakened to the point that it
means "and," introducing a related but slightly different topic from that in v 1.
πιστούς, "believing," is normal terminology for a Christian (cf. 1 Tim 4:3, 10, 12;
5:16), is parallel to ἀδελφοί, "brothers," and occurs again in the next phrase (as
πιστοί) parallel to ἀγαπητοί, "beloved." The normal meaning of καταφρονεῖν is
"to despise" (cf. 1 Tim 4:12). Kelly (131–32) prefers a weakened sense of "to treat
without the full consideration due to the other man's station," which fits the context well. On ἀδελφοί, "brothers," with the meaning "fellow Christians," cf. *Comment*
on 1 Tim 4:6.

2aβ   ἀλλὰ μᾶλλον δουλευέτωσαν, ὅτι πιστοί εἰσιν καὶ ἀγαπητοὶ οἱ τῆς εὐεργεσίας
ἀντιλαμβανόμενοι, "but let them serve all the more, since those benefiting from
[their] act of kindness are believers and beloved." Rather than despising their
masters, slaves should work even harder at their tasks because those who reap the
benefits of their kindness are fellow believers. This verse is more radical than it
may at first appear. Although Paul does not aggressively attack the institution of
slavery, his use of εὐεργεσία, "act of kindness," reminds the master that the slaves
ultimately are not slaves and should not be treated as such. This is similar to Paul's
statement to Philemon that he should receive Onesimus back "no longer as a
slave but more than a slave, as a beloved brother" (Phlm 16). Just as the slave
views his master as a fellow Christian and works all the more, so also the master
must realize that the slave is not ultimately a slave but a fellow Christian whose
labors are acts of kindness. As Paul says elsewhere, "through love be servants of

one another" (Gal 5:13). It is easy to see how a Christian slave might not work hard for a Christian master because of their relationship in the church. This verse calls for just the opposite: the slave should work μᾶλλον, "all the more," in a renewed vigor because of the bond between master and slave in Christ.

οἱ τῆς εὐεργεσίας ἀντιλαμβανόμενοι, "those benefiting from [their] act of kindness," could refer to (1) the masters who receive benefit from having Christian slaves ("Slaves should work all the more since the master who receives the benefit of their work is a believer and beloved"), which seems to be a more natural reading. (2) It could also refer to slaves who receive benefits from a Christian master ("Slaves should work all the more since their masters are believers and devote themselves to doing good deeds for the Christian slaves or in general"; cf. Towner, *Goal*, 179–80). This is an awkward reading of the verse and somewhat self-serving, lying outside Paul's instructions elsewhere that slaves should serve "as to the Lord" (see above). Hanson ([1983] 105) comments against option (1), saying that εὐεργεσία, "act of kindness," in profane Greek "never means a service done by an inferior [slave] to a superior [master]," but he goes on to say that "the author might be using the word deliberately in order to stress the ultimate equality of slaves and masters in God's eyes." (3) Lock thinks that εὐεργεσία refers to the divine act of kindness, which is redemption (66; cf. 2 Cor 9:15), the phrase repeating what Paul just said about the masters being believers.

ἀγαπητός, "beloved," is a standard term for a Christian (cf. Rom 1:7; 12:19; 1 Cor 15:58; 2 Cor 7:1; 12:19; Phil 2:12; 4:1). Because these masters are believers (πιστός), they are beloved. Dibelius-Conzelmann (82) argue that the term means "beloved by God" because "slaves who must be admonished to serve cannot, in the same injunction, be expected to act out of love for the masters." But as Fee (139) rightly comments, "besides taking quite a low view of the power of grace, that argues for a meaning of the word not found elsewhere in Paul." εὐεργεσία, "act of kindness," occurs elsewhere only in Acts 4:9; it refers to a good deed, an act of kindness (BAGD, 319). ἀντιλαμβάνειν, "to benefit," occurs elsewhere only in Luke 1:54 and Acts 20:35, where it has the different meaning of "to help, come to the aid of" (BAGD, 74). Lock (65) points out that some ancient writers were arguing that slaves deserved better treatment (Seneca *Ep.* 47; Epictetus 1.13; cf. S. Dill, *Roman Society from Nero to Marcus Aurelius*, 2nd ed. [London: Macmillan, 1905] 117; A. von Harnack, *The Mission and Expansion of Christianity in the First Three Centuries*, 2 vols., 2nd ed. [New York: Putnam, 1908] 1:208–11) and how slaves could "confer . . . freewill benefits upon their masters, Seneca, *De Benefic.* iii. 18–22," but one wonders how widespread this idea actually was.

Explanation

Having addressed issues relating to different groups within the Ephesian church, Paul concludes with these words to slaves. Despite the oppressiveness of slavery, slaves should still respect their masters so that God's reputation is not tainted and the cause of the gospel is not impeded. This is especially true if the master is a Christian. In this situation the slave should work all the more since the master who receives the benefit of the slave's kind deeds is a fellow believer. In the use of the word εὐεργεσία, "kind deed," is seen the theme expressed explicitly elsewhere (see below) that there is neither slave nor free for those in Christ.

While not condoning slavery or calling for its dissolution, Paul makes it clear that the deeper and more significant relationship is that between two believers rather than how society defines their relationship on the surface.

There must have been a large number of slaves in the early church since they receive instruction several times throughout the NT (1 Cor 7:20–24; Gal 3:28; 5:13; Eph 6:5–9; Col 3:22–25; Titus 2:9–10; Phlm 10–17; 1 Pet 2:18–25). Certain themes emerge from these passages. (1) Slaves are to be submissive and obedient to their masters, not fighting them but doing their best, even if their masters are evil and overbearing (Eph 6:5–9; Col 3:22–25; Titus 2:9–10; 1 Pet 2:18–25). (2) Masters also are obligated to treat their slaves well, recognizing that God is the master of all and his judgment is impartial (Eph 6:9; Col 3:25). Learning to view a slave's labor not as a duty but as an act of kindness (1 Tim 6:2a) is revolutionary.

(3) The issue of motivation is addressed regularly. (a) A slave should work especially hard for a Christian master since the person benefiting is a fellow believer (1 Tim 6:2a). (b) A slave's obedience should stem from the supreme importance of the gospel and recognition that its cause must not be damaged by the conduct of any one person (1 Tim 6:1; Titus 2:10). (c) Related to this is the realization that ultimately the slave is serving not the master but the Lord: "Slaves, be obedient . . . as to Christ . . . as servants of Christ, doing the will of God from the heart, rendering service with a good will as to the Lord and not to men" (Eph 6:5–7); "Slaves, obey in everything those who are your earthly masters . . . fearing the Lord. Whatever your task, work heartily, as serving the Lord and not men . . . ; you are serving the Lord Christ" (Col 3:22–24). (d) Slave and master must recognize that both will be judged by their works: "Knowing that whatever good any one does, he will receive the same again from the Lord, whether he is a slave or free. Masters, do the same to them . . . knowing that he who is both their Master and yours is in heaven, and that there is no partiality" (Eph 6:8–9); "Knowing that from the Lord you will receive the inheritance as your reward; you are serving the Lord. For the wrongdoer will be paid back for the wrong he has done, and there is no partiality" (Col 3:24–25). (e) Ultimately, the motivation for proper conduct grows out of the conviction that in Christ there is neither slave nor free (Gal 3:28), but in Christ believers transcend the confines of earthly relationships and relate to each other on an equal footing, all answering to the same God who judges without partiality. Social relationships, while significant, are secondary to the truth of the believers' union in the body of Christ and all that that entails: "You were called to freedom, brethren; . . . through love be servants of one another" (Gal 5:13); Philemon was to receive Onesimus back "no longer as a slave but more than a slave, as a beloved brother" (16). Consequently, as a general rule Paul urges people to remain as they were when they were called to Christ: "For he who was called in the Lord as a slave is a freedman of the Lord. Likewise he who was free when called is a slave of Christ" (1 Cor 7:22). These verses provide further illustration of Paul's eschatological view of reality that although believers exist in the here and now, they also exist in the age to come; they must be aware that what appears to be real on one plane is often illusory and that the truth is seen only on the higher plane.

Paul's refusal to condemn slavery has often been exploited by those who would use the text to argue for slavery. This is amply illustrated by antebellum writings in the American South. General arguments for the perpetuation of slavery included: (1) slaves do not have souls; (2) African slaves are suffering from the curse on Ham

(Gen 9:25); (3) Scripture does not prohibit slavery; (4) God ordains slavery, like marriage, and problems exist only because of poor administration; (5) slavery, along with the institutionalized church, is one of the stabilizing influences on society; and (6) owning slaves does not violate the spirit of the gospel.

> Now, unless Slavery is incompatible with the habitudes of holiness, unless it is inconsistent with the spirit of philanthropy or the spirit of piety, unless it furnishes no opportunities for obedience to the law, it is not inconsistent with the pursuit or attainment of the highest excellence. It is no abridgment of moral freedom; the slave may come from the probation of his circumstances as fully stamped with the image of God, as those who have enjoyed an easier lot—he may be as completely in unison with the spirit of universal rectitude, as if he had been trained on "flowery beds of ease." (J. H. Thornwell, *The Collected Writings of James Henley Thornwell* [1875; repr. Edinburgh: Banner of Truth Trust, 1974] 4:424)

See also R. L. Dabney, *A Defense of Virginia and the South* (Harrisonberg, VA: Sprinkle Publications, 1977); id., *Slavery Defended: The Views of the Old South*, ed. E. L. McKitrick (Englewood Cliffs, NJ: Prentice-Hall, 1963).

Arguments of this sort are not unique to American history but can be found, and most likely will continue to be found, throughout history. There are so many arguments that can be mustered against this exploitation of the gospel that space will not permit a full review, but many point out the following: (1) Nowhere does Paul say that slavery is good or acceptable. In fact, slave trading comes under the scope of the prohibition against kidnapping (1 Tim 1:9; see *Comment*). (2) Nowhere are masters told to demand submission from their slaves. The slaves are told to submit voluntarily. (3) Eph 6:10 asserts an equality of slave and master, both having the same impartial divine master. This idea is reflected here in Paul's assertion that master and slave are brothers (v 2; cf. Phlm 16). The gospel breaks down humanly defined structures (Gal 3:28). (4) Although slavery in any form is heinous, the slavery of Paul's day had many startling differences from that practiced in America. In Paul's day it was not racially based but resulted from war, poverty, and other social circumstances. It was not unusual to find people voluntarily submitting to slavery in exchange for economic security. (5) Although interpretation of 1 Cor 7:21 is difficult, it is most likely that Paul is admonishing slaves to take advantage of any proffered opportunity for freedom (cf. Fee, *First Epistle to the Corinthians*, 315–18). (6) The early church was convinced that the Lord would return very soon; consequently, the need to reform society naturally took a lesser place of importance to that of evangelism. (7) Paul's eschatological view of reality mentioned above sees that those in Christ transcend the bonds of social structures.

The fact of the situation is that Paul had a different agenda from what many have today. His ministry was governed by a passion to spread the gospel, and the cause of the gospel took precedence over all else. Given a different set of circumstances, Paul may have enlarged the scope of his ministry; his teaching to slaves must be understood within the larger picture of the needs of the gospel.

Ignatius gives these instructions to Polycarp about slaves:

> Despise not slaves, whether men or women. Yet let not these again be puffed up, but let them serve the more faithfully to the glory of God, that they may obtain a better

freedom from God. Let them not desire to be set free at the public cost, lest they be found slaves of lust. (*Pol.* 4; Lightfoot, *Apostolic Fathers*, 161)

The *Apostolic Constitutions* maintains somewhat the same balance as does Paul's recognizing the essential equality of slave and master while maintaining the social differences:

> But as to servants, what can we say more than that the slave bring a good will to his master, with the fear of God, although he be impious and wicked, but yet not to yield any compliance as to his worship? And let the master love his servant, although he be his superior. Let him consider wherein they are equal, even as he is a man. And let him that has a believing master love him both as his master, and as of the same faith, and as a father, but still with the preservation of his authority as his master: "not as an eye-servant, but as a lover of his master; as knowing that God will recompense to him for his subjection." In like manner, let a master who has a believing servant love him as a son or as a brother, on account of their communion in the faith, but still preserving the difference of a servant. (4.12; ANF 7:436)

The *Apostolic Constitutions* gives the following instruction on the baptism of a slave:

> Those, that first come to the mystery of godliness, let them be brought to the bishop or to the presbyters by the deacons, and let them be examined as to the causes wherefore they come to the word of the Lord; and let those that bring them exactly inquire about their character, and give them their testimony. Let their manners and their life be inquired into, and whether they be slaves or freemen. And if any one be a slave, let him be asked who is his master. If he be slave to one of the faithful, let his master be asked if he can give him a good character. If he cannot, let him be rejected, until he show himself to be worthy to his master. But if he does give him a good character, let him be admitted. But if he be a household slave to an heathen, let him be taught to please his master, that the word be not blasphemed. (8.32; ANF 7:494)

VI. Final Instructions   (1 Tim 6:2b–21)

A. The Final Discussion of the Opponents
(1 Tim 6:2b–10)

Bibliography

Brenk, F. E. "Old Wineskins Recycled: *autarkeia* in 1 Timothy 6:5–10." *Filología Neotestamentaria* 3 (1990) 39–50. **Burroughs, J.** *The Rare Jewel of Christian Contentment.* 1648. Repr. London: Banner of Truth Trust, 1964. **Byington, S. T.** "1 Timothy vi. 10." *ExpTim* 56 (1944–45) 54. **Dschulnigg, P.** "Warnung vor Reichtum und Ermahnung der Reichen: 1 Tim 6:6–10, 17–19 im Rahmen des Schlussteils 6:3–21." *BZ* 37 (1993) 60–77. **Halas, S.** "De cupiditate pecuniae sicut radice omnium malorum sec. 1 Tim 6:9–10." *RB* 40 (1987) 297–305. **Malherbe, A. J.** "Medical Imagery in the Pastoral Epistles." In *Texts and Testament: Critical Essays on the Bible and Early Church Fathers,* ed. W. E. March. San Antonio: Trinity UP, 1980. 19–35. **McEleney, N. J.** "The Vice Lists of the Pastoral Epistles." *CBQ* 36 (1974) 203–19. **Menken, M. J. J.** "῞Οτι en 1 Tim 6,7." *Bib* 58 (1977) 532–41. **Rönsch, H.** "Exegetisches zu 1 Tim 6,10." *ZWT* 27 (1884) 140–46. **Thurén, J.** "Die Struktur der Schlussparänese 1. Tim. 6,3–21." *TZ* 26 (1970) 241–53.

Translation

[2b] *Teach and urge these things.* [3] *If someone teaches a different doctrine and does not adhere* [a] *to the healthy words of our Lord Jesus Christ and the teaching that is according to godliness,* [4] *he is foolish, understanding nothing but having a sickly craving for speculations and fights about words out of which come* [b] *envy,* [c] *strife,* [d] *slanders, evil suspicions,* [5] *constant irritations among people who have been corrupted in their mind and have been robbed* [e] *of the truth, thinking that godliness is a means of profit.* [f]

[6] *Now godliness with contentment is a great profit.* [7] *For we brought nothing into the world, and* [g] *neither are we able to take anything out;* [8] *but having food* [h] *and clothing, with these we will be content.* [9] *But those wishing to be rich fall into temptation and a snare* [i] *and many foolish* [j] *and harmful passions that plunge the people into ruin and destruction.* [10] *For a root of all kinds of evils is the love of money, by reaching for which, some were led astray from the faith and have pierced themselves with many* [k] *pains.*

Notes

[a] προσέρχεται, "adheres to," is replaced by προσέχεται, "holds to," by ℵ* *pc* lat; Cyp. See *TCGNT*², 575; Lock, xxxvii.

[b] γίνεται, "come," is replaced by the more figurative γεννῶνται, "are born," by D*ᶜ lat.

[c] The singular φθόνος, "envy," is replaced by the plural φθόνοι, "envies" (D* *pc* latt bo), to match the plurals in the rest of the sentence. See *Note* d.

[d] The singular ἔρις, "strife" (ℵ A 048 33 1739 1881 TR syᵖ saᵐˢˢ; Cl), is replaced by the plural ἔρεις, "strifes"(D F G L Ψ 6 81 365 629 1175 *al* latt syʰ co saᵐˢˢ bo), to match the plurals in the verse. See *Note* c.

ᶜἀπεστερημένων, "having been robbed," is replaced by ἀπεστραμμένων ἀπό, "having been deprived from" (D*), and ἀπερριμμένων, "having been thrown away" (365).

ᶠOur text ends the sentence with εὐσέβειαν, "godliness" (א A D* F G 048 6 33 81 1175 1739 1881 *pc* lat co). Other MSS add ἀφίστασο ἀπὸ τῶν τοιούτων to the end, enjoining Timothy to "stay away from these things" (D² Ψ TR a b m vgᵐˢˢ sy; Cyp Lcf Ambst). Metzger says it is a "banal gloss" with inferior MS support, and there is no reason for its omission (*TCGNT²*, 575–76).

ᵍBecause of the confusion surrounding the two halves of v 7, there have been several alterations. ἀληθές, "true," is inserted before ὅτι, "that, because," by D* a b vgᵐˢˢ; Ambst Spec, and δῆλον, "clear," by א² D² Ψ TR (f m vg) sy. co; Hier omit ὅτι. The text here is supported by א* A F G 048 33 81 1739 1881 *pc* r; Did. See *TCGNT²*, 576; Lock, xxxvii.

ʰThe plural διατροφάς, "foods" (א A Ψ 33 1739ᵐᵍ ᵛⁱᵈ 1881 TR f vg syʰ), is replaced by the singular διατροφήν, "food," in D F G K P 048ᵛⁱᵈ 1739* ᶜ *al* it vgᵐˢˢ syᵖ co; Cyp Ambst.

ⁱThe insertion of τοῦ διαβόλου, "of the devil," after παγίδα, "snare," to agree with 3:7 is correct in its intent but late (D* F G [629] *pc* it vgᶜˡ; Spec). See *TCGNT²*, 576.

ʲἀνοήτους, "foolish," is replaced by ἀνονήτους, "useless," in 629 *pc* lat.

ᵏπολλαῖς, "many," is replaced by ποικίλαις, "various," in א* and H.

Form/Structure/Setting

1 Tim 6:2b–10 is Paul's final indictment of the false teachers in Ephesus. He still has a few words for the rich (vv 17–19), but this is the final, formal confrontation in this epistle. This passage has many similarities to 1 Tim 1:3–7, which was Paul's first confrontation with the opponents. Lock paraphrases, "I go back to the warning with which I began" (67). The opponents are teaching a different gospel, their teaching is not healthy, and they are ignorant, foolish, and given to speculations and arguments over words instead of preaching the message about Jesus Christ. The opposition has arisen from within the Ephesian church, not from without, and the opponents knowingly have given themselves to the error, thus causing self-inflicted wounds. Their motivation is tainted, desiring not only the respect of being teachers of the law but also money. Their teaching is devoid of almost any content and is rather a babbling about words. Consequently Paul cannot provide a point-by-point critique of their theology; instead he draws attention to their wicked behavior as evidence of their error, showing the strong connection between theology and ethics. A theology that produces improper behavior is poor theology. It is helpful to view all of vv 2b–21 as the conclusion to the epistle in that these verses repeat the two basic themes of the epistle: denunciation of the opponents and encouragement to Timothy (cf. also Thurén, *TZ* 26 [1970] 241–53).

There also is similarity between this passage and the one where Paul gives his requirements for overseers and deacons (1 Tim 3:1–13). The opponents are quarrelsome, slanderers, and greedy for money, and it is precisely these qualities that prohibit them from leadership positions in the church. Other themes found elsewhere in the corpus surface here as well. The "godliness with contentment" is not a Stoic defiance of nature but a trust in a merciful and gracious God who saves sinners (1 Tim 1:12–17). Satan is active in the Ephesian church, setting snares for those wishing to be rich (cf. 1 Tim 1:20).

The structure of the passage exhibits the same progression that is found elsewhere. Paul criticizes the opposition (1:3–11; 4:1–5; 6:2b–10) and follows with words of instruction and encouragement to Timothy (1:12–20; 4:6–16; 6:11–16). In the first of two paragraphs (vv 2b–5), Paul criticizes the opponents and the result of their teaching. He begins on a transitional note (v 2b): Timothy is to teach and urge these things, specifically Paul's instructions in the preceding chapter. In contrast to Timothy's teaching, the opponents' instructions are different (and therefore wrong) and do not produce godly living (vv 3–5). In the second paragraph (vv 6–10) Paul builds on the mention of their monetary motivation in v 5b and spells out what is right and what is wrong with their view of the profit of godliness. The opponents are right in so far as they think that godliness has great profit, but they should strive for a godliness with contentment, which means they must be satisfied with their financial condition and not fall in love with money. Paul generalizes that those loving money are susceptible to a unique set of temptations that apply only to them, and these temptations lead only to one place: Satan's snare, evil passions, and total ruin since the love of money lies at the root of all kinds of evil. Paul concludes by applying these general principles to the Ephesian situation. The opponents, who were infatuated with money, had abandoned the Christian faith and had inflicted grievous wounds on themselves.

Dibelius-Conzelmann fail to see this flow of thought (83–84). Because they find examples of this type of argument elsewhere in the secular literature, they conclude that it is "impossible to say with certainty" why the author attacked the opponents. Because they do not see the connection between the opponents' greed and the heresy, they conclude that vv 6–10 introduce a new topic not related to the preceding. These are the types of errors that occur when it is not realized how tightly related Paul's instructions in the PE are to their historical situation. Greed, which motivates the foolish and ignorant opponents, has already been introduced in chap. 3, and the topic must be addressed if Timothy is to be successful in stopping them. The flow of thought within the historical context is clear.

Much of the vocabulary of this section is rare in the NT. Much of the thought also parallels ideas in the Greek world. The goal of contentment, realizing that people are born and will die with no material possessions, learning to be content with food and clothing, and the dangers of the love of money, all find expression throughout the secular literature. But in every case, there are also parallels in the Gospels and in the rest of the NT. This should suggest caution in looking for either Greek or Christian sources for this passage. As he has been doing throughout the PE, Paul draws on imagery and concepts familiar to the Ephesian, Greek, and Christian alike.

There are several stylistic features worth noting. (1) Paul's use of transitional verses is found in two places. V 2b looks back to the preceding chapter of instructions and provides a contrast with the opponents' teaching in the next verse. (2) There is a possible pun on πορισμός, "profit," and πειρασμός, "temptation." The only profit the opponents gain is the pain of temptation. (3) Twice Paul graphically spells out the logical development of the opponents' teaching. (a) In 6:3–5, the opponents have chosen to teach a different gospel. They are therefore ignorant and foolish, having rejected the message of Christ and the healthy instruction of the gospel for a sickly craving for speculations and arguments about words. Within this atmosphere, envy and slander are soon to develop, and where they exist one is sure to find evil suspicions and constant irritation. The result of all this is corrupted minds and the loss of truth. It is a picture of the natural movement from intellectual error to moral corruption (Guthrie, 111). (b) In 6:9–10 there is a similar progression. The desire to be rich opens up a special set of temptations reserved just for that desire. The temptations lead to Satan's snare, which leads to many foolish and harmful passions. When these passions are brought to fruition, the result is total ruin. The lovers of money have left the faith and have inflicted grievous wounds on themselves. In both 6:3–5 and 6:9–10 Paul spells out logically and graphically the necessary results of certain actions. The implied message is that the people should never start down this course because once started there is only one possible end: corruption, a loss of truth, and pain.

Comment

2b Ταῦτα δίδασκε καὶ παρακάλει, "Teach and urge these things." This kind of statement serves as a transition throughout the PE (cf. 1 Tim 4:11). If it were part of 6:1–2a, then ταῦτα, "these things," would refer to the instructions for slaves. However, it is preferable to include it with the following verses. (1) This preserves the transitional nature of the sentence. (2) V 2b is closely linked to v 3 since it provides a contrast between Timothy's teaching and that of Paul's opponents: Timothy is to teach (διδάσκειν) these things; if people teach otherwise (ἑτεροδιδασκαλεῖν), they are conceited. ταῦτα therefore refers at least to the instructions in 5:3–6:2a. On παρακαλεῖν, "to urge," cf. *Comment* on 1 Tim 1:3. διδάσκειν, "to teach," is an authoritative act while παρακαλεῖν, "to urge," is gentler. Chrysostom says, "A teacher has need not only of authority, but of gentleness, and not only of gentleness, but of authority" ("Homily 17"; NPNF 13:467).

3 εἴ τις ἑτεροδιδασκαλεῖ καὶ μὴ προσέρχεται ὑγιαίνουσιν λόγοις τοῖς τοῦ κυρίου ἡμῶν Ἰησοῦ Χριστοῦ καὶ τῇ κατ᾽ εὐσέβειαν διδασκαλίᾳ, "If someone teaches a different doctrine and does not adhere to the healthy words of our Lord Jesus Christ and the teaching that is according to godliness." In contrast to what Timothy is to teach (v 2a), if others teach another doctrine, they are conceited. Paul begins his final indictment of the opponents by criticizing their teaching: it is different from Paul and Timothy's; it is not healthy; it does not center itself on the person of Christ; and it does not produce healthy and godly living. All of v 3 is the protasis ("if" clause) of a conditional sentence; vv 4–5 are the apodosis ("then" clause).

While much of Paul's critique of the opponents in the PE centers on their behavior, this verse deals with their teaching. Vv 4–5 will deal with their behavior, and vv 6–10 with their motivation. Much of what is said here is reminiscent of chap. 1. There too is given the content of the heresy, the effects of the heresy on people's behavior, and the motivation of the opponents. Much of our current passage is also reminiscent of chap. 3 where Paul is discussing the character of overseers and deacons. This reinforces the conclusion that the opponents had risen to power from within the church, which in turn forced Paul to disallow the opponents from being church leaders.

This verse gives a twofold test for orthodoxy. The first is whether the teaching agrees with that of Paul. If a person teaches otherwise, he or she is wrong. The second is an evaluation of the results produced by the teaching. Both ὑγιαίνουσιν, "healthy," and εὐσέβειαν, "godliness," have a decidedly practical, external aspect to them. ὑγιαίνειν, "to be healthy," is a medical term describing the physical effects of proper teaching (cf. 1 Tim 1:10). εὐσέβεια, "godliness," a key term in the PE, describes a life totally consecrated to God, with emphasis on how that consecration shows itself in the person's life (cf. 1 Tim 2:2). As throughout the PE, right teaching and right practice are inextricably bound together.

The use of the conditional sentence "if . . . then . . ." does not mean that this teaching is not occurring. First-class conditions assume the truth of the "if" clause for the sake of the argument (cf. BDF §372). τὶς, "someone," is Paul's common way of referring to the opponents (cf. 1 Tim 1:3), although in the PE he does become more specific than normal, actually naming a few of the opponents (cf. 1 Tim 1:20). In v 5 he is more specific in showing that he has the opponents in mind. ἑτεροδιδασκαλεῖν, "to teach a different doctrine," means to teach something that is essentially different, in this case different from what Timothy is to teach (v 2a). In 1 Tim 1:3, the only other occurrence of ἑτεροδιδασκαλεῖν in the NT, it is also used specifically of the opponents, confirming that Paul is speaking here of the opponents. This is the only passage in the NT where μή, "not," is used with an indicative verb (προσέρχεται, "adhere"), which is a classical pattern (BDF §428[1]; Moule, *Idiom-Book*, 148; Robertson, *Grammar*, 1011). προσέρχεσθαι, "to adhere to," usually means "to approach," but here it carries the meaning "to occupy oneself," thus having the nuance of agreeing (BAGD, 713). Kelly translates "give his mind to" (132).

The primary issue of the verse is the meaning of ὑγιαίνουσιν λόγοις τοῖς τοῦ κυρίου ἡμῶν Ἰησοῦ Χριστοῦ, "healthy words of our Lord Jesus Christ." (1) Some argue that the phrase refers to actual words of Christ (Ellicott, Knight) as found either in the Gospel of Luke (Spicq) or in the oral tradition. (2) Most agree that the phrase means "healthy words concerning Jesus" where τοῖς τοῦ κυρίου ἡμῶν Ἰησοῦ Χριστοῦ, "the [words] of our Lord Jesus Christ," defines the content of the words, which is equivalent to the gospel message about Christ. (a) This fits the context best since the problem in Ephesus is that the opponents have strayed from the teaching of the gospel (cf. 1 Tim 1:6) and have replaced Jesus with myths and legends (cf. 1 Tim 1:4). (b) This interpretation also provides a good parallel with the following phrase, where the gospel about Christ is equivalent to the teaching (διδασκαλία; cf. 1 Tim 1:11). (c) ὑγιαίνοντες λόγοι, "sound words," occurs elsewhere only in 2 Tim 1:13, where the phrase also refers to the gospel. ὑγιαίνειν, "to be healthy," and cognates also occur in conjunction with διδασκαλία, "teaching," and in every case refer to the doctrine of the gospel (1 Tim 1:10; 2 Tim 4:3; Titus 1:9; 2:1). The two phrases "sound words about Christ" and "teaching according to godliness" are synonymous, the first emphasizing the content of the proclamation and the second the effects of the proclamation. Paul's gospel, which produces true godliness (on εὐσέβεια, "godliness," cf. *Comment* on 1 Tim 2:2), stands in contrast to the opponents' false teaching, which, as Paul will say, is foolishness and produces a "sickly craving for speculations and empty words" (v 4). κατά, "according to," could indicate purpose or goal: the goal of the teaching is godliness (cf. BAGD, 406–7). It could also describe correspondence or conformity: the teaching that conforms to godliness (cf. BAGD, 407; M. J. Harris, *NIDNTT* 3:1200–1201). Knight (250) points out that Paul uses a full designation of Jesus' name ("Lord Jesus Christ") elsewhere in the PE when he addresses issues of authority and power (1 Tim 1:2, 12, 14; 6:14; 2 Tim 1:2; never in Titus).

4ab τετύφωται, μηδὲν ἐπιστάμενος, "he is foolish, understanding nothing." Having described the teaching of the opponents, Paul moves to the opponents themselves, describing their attitudes (vv 4–5a) and concluding by identifying their true motivation (vv 5b–10). If people teach differently from Timothy and do not adhere to healthy words and teaching that conforms to godliness, they are foolish and understand nothing. τυφοῦσθαι means either "to be conceited" or "to be foolish," and it is difficult in the PE to decide between the two (see *Comment* on 1 Tim 3:6). If it means "to be conceited," the participle ἐπιστάμενος, "understanding, knowing," would be concessive ("conceited even though they know nothing"). If it means "to be foolish," ἐπιστάμενος intensifies the statement ("foolish and know nothing"). The parallel with ἐπίστασθαι, "to understand, know," suggests that τυφοῦσθαι means "to be foolish." Malherbe ("Medical Imagery," 124 n. 7) says that τυφοῦσθαι can also describe mental illness (cf. ὑγιαίνουσιν, "healthy," in v 3). This theme of the opponents' ignorance was introduced in 1:7 and is found elsewhere in the corpus: the opponents wish "to be teachers of the law even though they do not understand either what they are saying or concerning the things they are so dogmatically asserting" (1 Tim 1:7; cf. Titus 1:16). The use of the perfect tense here (τετύφωται, "is foolish") and in v 5 (διεφθαρμένων, "have been corrupted"; ἀπεστερημένων, "have been robbed") emphasizes the established and seemingly permanent condition of the opponents' condition. Chrysostom says, "Presumption therefore arises not from knowledge, but from 'knowing nothing.' For he that knows the doctrines of godliness is also the most disposed to moderation" ("Homily 17"; NPNF 13:467).

In this statement and what follows there is a progression (see *Form/Structure/ Setting*). The opponents begin by rejecting the true gospel, that which is healthy and godly. They are foolish and know nothing. As a result they develop a sickly craving for speculations and spend their time arguing about words. Out of this atmosphere, envy and strife naturally develop; and whenever they are present, slander, evil suspicion, and constant irritation are soon to be found. Once these traits come to fruition, the only possible results are a corruption of the mind and a loss of the truth. As Guthrie comments, "this is a noteworthy example of the processes by which intellectual wrangling so often ends in moral deterioration" (111). This connection of intellectual error and its moral consequences provides a major theme throughout the PE. See the similar progression of thought in vv 9–10.

4c   ἀλλὰ νοσῶν περὶ ζητήσεις καὶ λογομαχίας, "but having a sickly craving for speculations and fights about words." In addition to being foolish and ignorant, the opponents replace a desire for truth with a sickly craving for speculations and arguing about words. νοσεῖν, "to have a sickly craving," is a rare word, occurring in the NT only here. It means to be sick, ailing (BAGD, 543), and it seems to refer to a serious illness (cf. MM, 430). It is parallel to the medical imagery of healthy words in the previous verse: whereas Paul and Timothy's proclamation comprises healthy words about Jesus and accords with godliness, the message of the opponents is sick. ἐπιστάμενος, "understanding," and νοσῶν, "having a sickly craving," are parallel, both modifying τετύφωται, "he is foolish." ζητήσεις, "speculations," is a common designation of the heresy (cf. 1 Tim 1:4 [ἐκζητήσεις, "speculations"]; 2 Tim 2:23–25; Titus 3:9). Rather than preaching the gospel of Jesus Christ, the opponents have filled their minds with idle speculations about myths and legends.

λογομαχία, "fight about words," is also a rare word (cf. 2 Tim 2:14; variant to Titus 3:9). It is a compound of λόγος, "word," and μάχη, "fight," and continues the meaning of its etymology. The opponents are arguing about words. (Luther translates literally with *Wortgefechte*.) Bernard (95) says it refers not to fighting about words but "a dispute in which words are the weapons" (also Lock, 68). NEB translates the word as "verbal quibbles." This too is a common description of the opponents (1 Tim 6:20; 2 Tim 2:14 [cognate verb], 17, 23; Titus 3:9). Paul even ends this letter to Timothy on this note: "Avoid the godless chatter and contradictions of what is falsely called knowledge" (1 Tim 6:20). The opponents' teaching, while having some content (cf., e.g., 1 Tim 1:7; 4:3), is mostly vacuous wrangling about words. It is not consistent or well formulated (see *Introduction*, "The Ephesian Heresy"). This is why Paul usually criticizes the opponents' lifestyle and not their theology. The fallacy of their teaching is confirmed by the lifestyle it produces, and hence Paul maintains the strong connection between right doctrine and right behavior throughout the PE.

4d–5a ἐξ ὧν γίνεται φθόνος ἔρις βλασφημίαι, ὑπόνοιαι πονηραί, διαπαρατριβαί, "out of which come envy, strife, slanders, evil suspicions, constant irritations." Out of the opponents' foolishness, ignorance, and craving naturally develop these evil qualities (ὧν, "of which," goes back to νοσῶν, "having a sickly craving"). As was mentioned above, this is a natural progression. Where there are speculations and word battles, one naturally finds envy and strife; envy and strife naturally develop into slander and evil suspicions, and where these are present there is constant irritation. The specifics that Paul is enumerating are an accurate depiction of the historical situation (contra Hanson, [1983] 106). Many of the qualities are repeated throughout the corpus. Paul "paints in lurid colors the pride from which it [the heresy] springs, the spirit of anti-social bitterness and suspicion which it sows in the church, and the moral degeneracy which it eventually produces" (Kelly, 135). On Paul's use of vice lists, see *Comment* on 1 Tim 1:9–10 and McEleney, *CBQ* 36 (1974) 203–19.

φθόνος, "envy, jealousy," and ἔρις, "strife, quarrel, contention," go hand in hand as seen by their frequent combination in Paul's writings. (ἔρις is joined with ζῆλος, "jealousy," in Rom 13:13; 1 Cor 3:3; 2 Cor 12:20; Gal 5:20; with φθόνος, in Rom 1:29 and Phil 1:15; and with σχίσμα, "division," in 1 Cor 1:10–11.) Paul also stipulates that overseers not be quarrelsome (1 Tim 3:3). On βλασφημία, "slander," see *Comment* on 1 Tim 1:13. In this case it is not slander against God but slander among people that fits the context best (cf. 1 Tim 1:20). ὑπόνοια, "suspicion," occurs only here in the NT (cf. BAGD, 846). Paul does not specify the content of the suspicions, but because of the association of the term with "slander," it can be assumed that he means the evil suspicions about people that arise because of slanderous statements. πονηρός, "evil," occurs two other times in the PE, describing wicked people who go from bad to worse in contrast to those wishing to live godly lives (2 Tim 3:13) and describing every evil deed from which Paul is assured that God will rescue him (2 Tim 4:18). διαπαρατριβή, "constant irritation," which occurs only here in the NT, is an intensive form of παρατριβή, "friction" (Bernard, 94), and describes a constant or mutual friction (BAGD, 187; on the compound cf. BDF §116[4]). Chrysostom comments that Paul can mean "that as infected sheep by contact communicate disease to the sound, so do these bad men" ("Homily 17"; NPNF 13:468). Dibelius-Conzelmann criticize Chrysostom's simile for being "much too learned," but the picture it creates is helpful. While Paul's opponents continue in their sickly craving, full of envy and strife, slandering and making evil accusations, they are a continual source of irritation as they rub shoulders one with another and with the Ephesian church. Malherbe ("Medical Imagery," 125 n. 9) agrees with Chrysostom and interprets the word as describing infected abrasions.

5b διεφθαρμένων ἀνθρώπων τὸν νοῦν, "among people who have been corrupted in their mind." ἀνθρώπων, "people," technically modifies διαπαρατριβαί, "constant irritations": "constant irritations among people." Following διαπαρατριβαί are three attributive participial phrases describing these people who are the source of constant irritation. The first two contain perfect participles describing what these people have become (continuing the use of the perfect from v 4), and the third participle is linear in aspect, emphasizing the ongoing motivation for their teaching. The first participial phrase states that they have been destroyed, ruined, and corrupted with reference to their minds. The use of διά, "through," in the compound διαφθείρειν, "to corrupt," parallels the use of διά in the compound διαπαρατριβή, "constant irritation," and intensifies the simple φθείρειν, "to corrupt." διαφθείρειν is used in a physical sense to describe the effect of rust on iron and moths on clothing, a ruined nation, and the bodies of starving people. It is also used in a moral sense to indicate corruption of the mind (cf. BAGD, 190). Elsewhere Paul describes his opponents as "people of corrupt [κατεφθαρμένοι] mind and counterfeit faith" (2 Tim 3:8) and as those whose "very minds and consciences are corrupted [μεμίανται]" (Titus 1:15). νοῦς, "mind," refers to a person's inner disposition, the moral and intellectual capacity to make a decision. It is this capacity that has been destroyed by their sickly cravings. διεφθαρμένων, "have been corrupted," and the following ἀπεστερημένων, "have been robbed," are both passives, possibly suggesting Satan as the agent, who elsewhere in the PE is recognized as active in the Ephesian church (cf. *Comment* on 1 Tim 1:20).

5c καὶ ἀπεστερημένων τῆς ἀληθείας, "and have been robbed of the truth." The second characteristic of these people is that the gospel has been taken from them. This same idea is repeated in Titus 1:14: the Cretans should not "give heed to Jewish myths or to commands of people who reject the truth [ἀποστρεφομένων τὴν ἀλήθειαν]." This does not mean that the opponents are the victims of someone else's thievery; the PE make it clear that the opponents know exactly what they are doing (cf. 1 Tim 1:6). The phrase creates a picture of people who have no participation in the gospel whatsoever. They do not teach an altered gospel; what they teach is wholly different (cf. 1 Tim 1:3). In the PE ἀλήθεια, "truth," is almost a technical term for the orthodox gospel (cf. 1 Tim 2:4). The opponents are often pictured as opposing the truth of the gospel (2 Tim 2:18; 3:7, 8; 4:4).

5d νομιζόντων πορισμὸν εἶναι τὴν εὐσέβειαν, "thinking that godliness is a means of profit." This phrase is a transitional statement, leading into the second paragraph (vv 6–10). Behind the opponents' facade, their supposed intellectualism and false piety, lies the real motivation for their ministry: they want to make money. Presumably they charged for their instructions (cf. 1 Tim 5:17; cf. Hanson, [1983] 107). This fact has already been hinted at when Paul says an elder (1 Tim 3:3; Titus 1:7) and deacon (1 Tim 3:8) must not be greedy for gain, but it finds its full discussion in this passage. Paul tells Titus that the opponents teach for shameful gain (Titus 1:11; cf. Jude 11). Paul has already commended paying for Christian services (1 Tim 5:17), so his concern is not that there is money involved. However, from vv 6–10 it is obvious that the love of money and the central place it holds in the opponents' lives constitute the real problem. This may be analogous to the situation in Thessalonica where Paul accused his opponents of using words as a cloak for greed (1 Thess 2:5). On εὐσέβεια, "godliness," see *Comment* on 1 Tim 2:2. In the NT πορισμός, "profit," occurs only here and in the next verse.

6 ἔστιν δὲ πορισμὸς μέγας ἡ εὐσέβεια μετὰ αὐταρκείας, "Now godliness with contentment is a great profit." Having introduced the topic of the opponents' greed in the previous verse, Paul enlarges his discussion in vv 6–10, the second paragraph of this section. In vv 6–8 he spells out what profit there is in godliness in Christian ministry. Then in vv 9–10 he shows why the opponents' view of profit is wrong. Godliness is of great value if it is accompanied by contentment. This means realizing that people will die as they were born: without any material goods. Is it not then irrational for them to pursue wealth? The godliness that is of great value is one that is accompanied by contentment, and this means being satisfied with food and clothing. But the godliness that the opponents pursued was not one of contentment. Rather, they wanted to be rich, and because of their desire they fell into snares that issued in their destruction. Their desire for riches had destroyed them, and they had abandoned the gospel. This is one of the most powerful condemnations in Scripture of the destructive lure of possessions. As Fee says, in light of Paul's teaching "Why would anyone want to get rich?" (145).

Paul begins by playing off his previous statement: the opponents thought that godliness was a means to profit (v 5); godliness has great profit, provided that it be the type of godliness that is characterized by contentment (v 6). Paul follows with his explanation of the great profit of contented godliness (vv 7–8). This passage is similar to 1 Tim 4:8 in both technique and structure: the opponents were ascetics, so Paul states that while bodily training has some little value, godliness has value in every way because it holds promise not only for this life but the life to come. πορισμός, "profit," and πειρασμός, "temptation," in v 9 are a pun.

What does αὐτάρκεια, "contentment," mean? (1) Context defines it not as pursuing riches but as being satisfied with food and clothing. This is the direct thrust of the next two verses. The context is so clear at this point that it must govern all other possible interpretations. (2) αὐτάρκεια occurs elsewhere in the NT only in 2 Cor 9:8, where it means "sufficient" or "adequate." The cognate αὐτάρκης, "content," occurs only in Phil 4:11 where Paul says "not that I complain of want; for I have learned, in whatever state I am, to be content [αὐτάρκης εἶναι]. I know how to be abased, and I know how to abound; in any and all circumstances I have learned the secret of facing plenty and hunger, abundance and want. I can do all things in him who strengthens me" (Phil 4:11–13). Paul has learned to be content not because he has an inner, Stoic, superhuman strength or because circumstances have been good to him. Paul's contentment is rooted in a faith that denies his own ability to perform his tasks and asserts the need for total reliance on the all-powerful God. The contentment that is of great profit is one that seeks its security not in worldly riches but in God. (3) This reliance on God is stressed elsewhere in the PE. In Paul's personal testimony he states that his own salvation is not the result of any merit on his part but is an act of grace on an undeserving sinner, a blasphemer, a persecutor, a totally insolent person. He was saved by God's mercy and grace to be an example to all who are to believe (1 Tim 1:12–17). (4) αὐτάρκεια is further defined in vv 7–8 as a willingness to be satisfied with food and clothing, and this idea also finds expression in the Gospels: Jesus' disciples were to seek God's kingdom, and the necessities such as food and clothing would be provided (Matt 6:25–34; cf. Burroughs, *Rare Jewel*).

(5) It is against this background that we can see why Paul uses αὐτάρκεια, which was also an important concept in Stoic and Cynic thought. For them it meant

"self-sufficiency," "that a man should be sufficient unto himself for all things, and able, by the power of his own will, to resist the force of circumstances" (Vincent, *Word Studies* 4:275; cf. Plato *Tim.* 33D; *Pss. Sol.* 5:18; Cynic references in A. J. Malherbe, *The Cynic Epistles,* SBLSBS 12 [Missoula, MT: Scholars Press, 1977] 124, l. 25; 176, l. 12; 244, l. 4; other references in Dibelius-Conzelmann, 84 n. 6, and Wettstein, *Novum Testamentum Graecum,* ad loc.). It is this quality that produces the stereotypical characterization of the proverbial Stoic, standing into the wind with a strong jaw, willing to face anything that circumstances and the Fates might send. Because the term is so important in Greek thought, many see the author of the PE using it here without redefining it (NEB, Dibelius-Conzelmann, Brox, Hanson [1983]). There is no question that Paul is playing off the Greek usage: the godliness that is profitable is not dependent upon circumstances, specifically riches. But godly contentment is not dependent upon a person's inner strength apart from Christ. Not to see that Paul has redefined the word's meaning is to ignore the immediate context, the context of the PE—especially 1 Tim 1:12–17— the context of Paul, and of the gospel message in general. Despite the popularity today of the saying from *Poor Richard's Almanac,* the gospel message does not declare that "God helps those who help themselves." G. G. Findlay says, "The self-sufficiency of the Christian is relative: an independence of the world through dependence upon God. The Stoic self-sufficiency pretends to be absolute. One is the contentment of faith, the other of pride. Cato and Paul both stand erect and fearless before a persecuting world: one with a look of rigid, defiant scorn, the other with a face now lighted up with unutterable joy in God. . . . The Christian martyr and the Stoic suicide are the final examples of these two memorable and contemporaneous protests against the evils of the world" (G. G. Findlay, *Christian Doctrine and Morals* [London: Kelly, 1894], quoted by Hawthorne, *Philippians,* 198– 99, who also cites O. Glombitza, "Der Dank des Apostels: Zum Verständnis von Phil. 4:10–20," *NovT* 7 [1964–65] 135–41; Sevenster, *Paul and Seneca,* 113–14). The Ephesians are reminded of both the Greek and the Christian associations as Paul intends, but the Christian redefining takes precedence.

7 οὐδὲν γὰρ εἰσηνέγκαμεν εἰς τὸν κόσμον, ὅτι οὐδὲ ἐξενεγκεῖν τι δυνάμεθα, "For we brought nothing into the world, and neither are we able to take anything out." This is an awkward sentence in Greek, but its basic thrust is understandable. It is Paul's reason (γάρ, "for") that contented godliness is of great profit: when people die, they leave all their earthly possessions behind, so the results of greediness are at best temporary. Why then pursue them at all? This sentiment is found in the OT (Job 1:21; Eccl 5:15; Wis 7:6), the NT (Luke 12:16–21), and early Christian (Hermas *Sim.* 1.6), Jewish (Philo *Spec. Leg.* 1.294–95; Str-B 3:655), and Greek literature (Seneca *Ep.* 102.24–25; Horace *Odes* 2.14.21; *Propert.* 4.4.13; cf. references in Wettstein, *Novum Testamentum Graecum;* Lock, 69; Dibelius-Conzelmann, 85 nn. 8–11; Spicq, 1:561). It is such a common idea that a person cannot point directly to its Greek or Jewish or Christian uses as the sole source, although for Paul the words of Jesus would have had primacy. Spicq (1:561–62) sees a slightly different nuance in the saying. For him it describes the transitory nature of life, how one begins with nothing and ends with nothing. The use of ἐκφέρειν, "to take out," and εἰσφέρειν, "to bring in," both sharing the same verbal root, makes an effective literary contrast appropriate for a proverbial saying.

What makes the verse difficult is the use of ὅτι, translated above as "and." The textual tradition evidences centuries of confusion at this point (see *Note* g). The context shows that the emphasis is on the second half of the statement, but what is its logical relationship to the first? (1) The most natural meaning of ὅτι is "because," but this gives a difficult, although not impossible, meaning: "We brought nothing into the world because we cannot take anything out." Lock paraphrases (inverting the order), "We can carry nothing with us when we leave the world, and that is why we brought nothing with us when we came into it" (67). Both ends of life attest to its transitory nature and the impermanence of earthly possessions. (2) Knight suggests that Paul omitted δῆλον, "clear" (ellipsis; see *Note* g for the *v.l.* that adds δῆλον), which, when added, would read "it is clear that": from our inability to bring anything into the world, it is clear that we also cannot take anything out. (3) Another possibility is that v 7b was a popular saying. ὅτι could have functioned as quotation marks (ὅτι *recitativum*), or ὅτι might have made sense in the original saying (cf. Kelly, 137) and Paul was not careful in how much of the saying he quoted. The problem is that v 7a would then not be part of the proverbial saying, and yet both halves of the verse read as if they belonged together, except for the ὅτι. (4) Menken (*Bib* 58 [1977] 532–41) argues that a ὅτι clause can give the reason for the preceding clause, and so the first statement was made in view of the second: "We brought nothing into the world, (and this is said) because we cannot take anything out of the world." (5) Most agree that Paul was using ὅτι in a weakened sense, meaning "and." Although there is no exact precedent for this use, ὅτι in certain circumstances was weakening in its causal sense (cf. BAGD, 589[3b]).

8 ἔχοντες δὲ διατροφὰς καὶ σκεπάσματα, τούτοις ἀρκεσθησόμεθα, "but having food and clothing, with these we will be content." Fee (143) says that this is the second reason Paul gives for v 6, but it reads more like a continuation of the reason in vv 6–7: it is because people leave this world empty-handed that they should learn to be content with the basics of life during their time in this world. As is the case with the preceding verses, this sentiment is found both in the words of Jesus (Matt 6:25–34; Luke 12:22–32) and in Stoicism (references in Wettstein, *Novum Testamentum Graecum;* Lock, 69; Dibelius-Conzelmann, 84 n. 15). To say that the author of the PE must be drawing more from the secular Greek than from the Christian background (Brox) is to make a judgment based more on one's general approach to the PE than on the text. Throughout the PE Paul has drawn on imagery from both sources.

This is a powerful verse, especially to an affluent church, and it is often ignored. By saying "we," Paul generalizes the truth to all believers. ἀρκεσθησόμεθα, "we will be content," can be a (Hebraic) imperatival future or simply a future that because of the speaker and the context carries an authoritative note (Bernard, 96); but in either case it carries the force of a command: "Believers must be content with merely the necessities of life." Jesus likewise stressed the sufficiency of the necessities (Matt 6:24–34; Luke 12:16–32; cf. Heb 13:5). Chrysostom goes one step further by saying that the believer should possess no more than the necessities: "So much ought we to eat, as will suffice to nourish us, and such things should we put on, as will cover us, and clothe our nakedness, and nothing more" ("Homily 17"; NPNF 13:468). He continues, as does Paul, by describing the plight of those who have more than the necessities. While vv 9–10 deal specifically with the love of money, in vv 17–19 Paul deals with the mere possession of wealth (see *Explanation*).

Both διατροφή, "food," and σκέπασμα, "clothing," occur only here in the NT. There is some question whether σκέπασμα means only "clothing" (Bernard, 95; Kelly, 137) or more generally "covering," including "shelter" (BAGD, 753; Dibelius-Conzelmann, 85; Guthrie, 113). It is common to find the two ideas joined, depicting the necessities of life (cf. Deut 10:18; Isa 3:7; Matt 6:25; cf. Diogenes Laertius 6.104; 10.131; references in Dibelius-Conzelmann, 85 n. 16). ἀρκεῖσθαι, "to be content" (cf. Luke 3:14; Heb 13:5; 3 John 10), is a term related to αὐτάρκεια, "contentment," in v 6, a nice literary touch pulling the argument together, and contrasts in the following verse with the opponents' desire to be rich.

9a οἱ δὲ βουλόμενοι πλουτεῖν ἐμπίπτουσιν εἰς πειρασμὸν καὶ παγίδα καὶ ἐπιθυμίας πολλὰς ἀνοήτους καὶ βλαβεράς, "But those wishing to be rich fall into temptation and a snare and many foolish and harmful passions." Having described what is profitable about godliness, Paul turns to the opponents and their understanding that the profit of godliness is measured in terms of wealth. He does not deal with the possession of wealth; that is discussed in vv 17–19. Rather, Paul argues that the strong desire to be rich, the desire that places wealth above all else, is exceptionally dangerous. There is a marked progression in his logic: the desire to be rich plunges a person into a special temptation; the temptation in turn leads one into the devil's snare; once caught in that snare, its inevitable end is foolish and harmful passions, and complete and total personal destruction. As Fee so aptly sums it up: "Why would anyone want to get rich? Wealth has nothing to do with one's eschatological existence in Christ; on the contrary, the desire leads to other desires that end up in ruin, of which truth the false teachers themselves are Exhibit A (v. 10)" (145; cf. *Form/Structure/Setting*).

Whereas Paul is speaking directly to his opponents in vv 6–8, in vv 9–10a he generalizes his discussion to anyone wanting to be rich. But in v 10b he comes back to the historical situation by summing up the sad condition of his opponents who do not recognize the special dangers of wanting to be rich. Warnings against riches abound throughout biblical and nonbiblical literature. The message is found in the Gospels (Matt 6:25–34; 13:22; 19:22–24), especially in Luke (1:53; 12:15–21; 16:14–15; 18:9–14, 18–27), and elsewhere in the NT (Heb 11:25–26; Jas 1:10–11; 2:1, 6–7; 5:3–5; Rev 2:9; 3:17–18; cf. F. Hauck and W. Kasch, *TDNT* 6:327–30).

δέ, "but," contrasts the contentment of one who has the necessities with the dissatisfaction of the opponents who want more. Bernard (96) says that βούλεσθαι, "to wish," is more definite than θέλειν, "to wish," the idea being that the people described here have their hearts set on being rich. (On the verb, cf. *Comment* on 1 Tim 2:8.) πλουτεῖν, "to be rich," and its cognate noun πλοῦτος, "riches," occur elsewhere in the PE only in Paul's final admonition to the rich (1 Tim 6:17–18). ἐμπίπτειν, "to fall," occurs earlier in the PE in a similar discussion of elders where Paul says that an elder must not be a recent convert lest he fall into the judgment of the devil and an elder must have a good reputation lest he fall into the snare set by Satan (1 Tim 3:6–7). The imagery in these verses is repeated in the following half of v 9.

Paul enumerates the consequences of the desire to be rich: temptation, a snare, and evil passions, which result in total ruin. Paul is saying more than that those wishing to be rich will be tempted because all people are tempted; he is saying that there is a special temptation (πειρασμός, "temptation," is singular), or perhaps set of temptations, that does not surface unless one is pursuing riches. In other words, the desire to be rich opens the door to a whole new set of temptations. No wonder that Paul's warnings to the rich are so strongly worded. Hanson ([1983] 108) mentions that Paul might have intended a pun on πορισμός, "profit" (v 6), and πειρασμός, "temptation" (v 9), and suggests the English equivalents of "gain" and "pain": the only profit the opponents gain is the pain of temptation.

Once people fall into temptation, they are susceptible to a snare. The text does not say that it is Satan's snare, but the other two times παγίς, "snare," is used in the PE, the snare is identified as Satan's (1 Tim 3:7; 2 Tim 2:26), and Satan is pictured as being active in the Ephesian church (cf. 1 Tim 1:20). The proximity of the word πειρασμός, "temptation," also supports the notion that the snare is set here by Satan to catch those desiring to be rich (Guthrie, 113). Once snared, the people fall into many foolish and harmful passions. The καί, "and," could be epexegetical, identifying the precise nature of the snare (the "snare" is "many foolish and harmful passions"; Fee, 145), but it could also be the third result of desiring to be rich and as such provides the next stage in the progression of sin. Although ἐπιθυμία, "passion," can describe something that is good, in the PE it always describes strong sinful desire (cf. discussion of its verbal cognate in the *Comment* on 1 Tim 3:1). In this case the passions are described as ἀνόητος, "foolish," and βλαβερός, "harmful." ἀνόητος occurs elsewhere only in Titus 3:3 where Paul describes the pre-Christian state of people as being foolish. It is the opposite of σοφός, "wise" (Rom 1:14), and is used elsewhere in the expression "O foolish Galatians/men" (Gal 3:1 [cf. 3:3]; cf. Luke 24:25). J. Behm adds that its emphasis here is more moral than intellectual (*TDNT* 4:962). βλαβερός occurs only here in the NT (cf. cognate verb in Luke 4:35; Mark 16:18).

9b αἵτινες βυθίζουσιν τοὺς ἀνθρώπους εἰς ὄλεθρον καὶ ἀπώλειαν, "that plunge the people into ruin and destruction." Paul adds this final note to his description of these evil passions, showing the ultimate end of those who desire to be rich. Their end is total annihilation. Chrysostom comments, "And to learn how true this is, the only way is to sojourn with the rich, to see how many are their sorrows, how bitter their complaints" ("Homily 17"; NPNF 13:468). βυθίζειν, "to plunge," is used to describe the sinking of ships (cf. Luke 5:7) and people into the sea, and is used figuratively of the total ruin of Sparta (BAGD, 148). It creates a picture of those wishing to be rich sinking further, inexorably, into the sea of ruin and destruction. τούς, "the," functions as a generic article categorizing people who desire wealth (cf. Bernard, 96; Wallace, *Greek Grammar,* 227–30), or it could be an anaphoric reference to οἱ . . . βουλόμενοι, "those wishing" (cf. BDF §252).

ὄλεθρος, "ruin," is a strong word denoting destruction, ruin, and death, always with religious overtones in early Christian literature (BAGD, 563; cf. 1 Cor 5:5; 1 Thess 5:3; 2 Thess 1:9). MM say that in biblical usage it depicts "the loss of all that gives worth to existence" (445). Relatively synonymous is ἀπώλεια meaning "destruction, annihilation." It is the standard term for the eternal destruction of the wicked (Job 21:30; Matt 7:13; Rom 9:22; Phil 1:28; 3:19; Heb 10:39; 2 Pet 2:1, 3; 3:7; Rev 17:8, 11) and is used in the expression "son of destruction" for Judas Iscariot (John 17:12) and the antichrist (2 Thess 2:3). Some argue that ὄλεθρος refers to the destruction of the material and ἀπώλεια to destruction of the spiritual (Spicq, Kelly, Dornier), or it could be that the repetition is meant to drive the point home that the ultimate destiny of those who pursue riches is complete and total ruin.

10a ῥίζα γὰρ πάντων τῶν κακῶν ἐστιν ἡ φιλαργυρία, "For a root of all kinds of evils is the love of money." This is a common proverb that Paul now quotes to strengthen his argument in v 9. The Ephesians should not be surprised that the pursuit of wealth leads to ruin and destruction, for (γάρ) the love of money lies at the root of all kinds of evils. This sentiment can be found throughout ancient literature. Diogenes of Sinope said that "the love of money is the mother-city of all evils [τὴν φιλαργυρίαν . . . μητρόπολιν πάντων τῶν κακῶν]" (Diogenes Laertius 6.50; cf. Sir 27:1–2; T. Jud. 19; Philo Spec. Leg. 4.65; Stobaeus Ecl. 3; cf. references in Wettstein, Novum Testamentum Graecum; Spicq, 1:564; Dibelius-Conzelmann, 85 nn. 18–19). Most commentators are quick to point out that the topic is not wealth but the love of wealth, the pursuit of wealth at all costs. While this is correct, it must be noted that especially the OT is clear that the mere possession of wealth has its own set of temptations (e.g., Pss 39:6; 49:6–10; 52:7; Prov 11:4, 16, 28; 23:4–5; Eccl 5:12–13).

ῥίζα, "root," is anarthrous. Paul is not claiming that the love of money is *the* singular root of all evils (contra KJV, RSV, NEB, Lock); it is *a* root (NASB, NIV), one among several. This helps in understanding the precise meaning of πάντων τῶν κακῶν, "all evils." (1) The love of money is not the root of every single, specific evil. Paul (e.g., Rom 7:13–25) and common sense make this clear. (2) BAGD shows that πᾶς can designate "everything belonging, in kind, to the class designated by the noun 'every kind of,' 'all sorts of'" (631[1aβ]), listing these examples among others: γέμουσιν . . . πάσης ἀκαθαρσίας, "they are full . . . of all kinds of uncleanness" (Matt 23:27); ἀπὸ παντὸς ἔθνους, "from every kind of nation" (Acts 2:5); πᾶσαν ἐπιθυμίαν, "[evil] desire of every kind" (Rom 7:8); and πᾶν ἁμάρτημα, "every kind of sin" (1 Cor 6:18). If this is applicable here, Paul is saying that every different category of sin, but not every specific sin, has a root in the love of money. The plural πάντων, "all," might also suggest that Paul is thinking of all types of sins (cf. Wallace, Greek Grammar, 265). (3) Knight rightly emphasizes the parallel with v 9, which says that those wishing to be rich fall into πολλάς, "many," foolish desires. Knight adds that Paul "does not assert that 'all' desires result from 'the will to be rich' but that 'many' do" (258; Knight also cites Paul's use of πᾶς for "all sorts of people" in 1 Tim 2:1b, 4, 6, and 4:10). Therefore, it would be unexpected for Paul to follow up by saying that all evil—not many evils—stems from the love of wealth. (4) It is the nature of proverbs to be inexact and often overstated, much like a hyperbole (Fee, 145; cf. Prov 26:4–5). Paul wants to drive home the dangers of a pursuit of wealth, and the proverb does precisely that with the inherent limitations of that genre. Hanson ([1983] 108) misses the context when he says that this verse is non-Pauline (citing Rom 7). Paul is not saying that the love of money is the one and only root of evil, or that it is the most significant one, but it is a serious stumbling block to the Ephesians, and the proverb is therefore appropriate in the Ephesian context. Byington states that "no reader would have thought of understanding anything else than 'the root of all evils'" and thinks Paul is quoting "a current quotation, perhaps from a comedy" without the same care he would give to a phrase he had coined (ExpTim 56 [1944–45] 54). But he gives no reason for the first statement, which can only be made by ignoring the absence of the article, and it seems doubtful that Paul would quote something unless he was in basic agreement. Lest the love of wealth be relegated to a minor consideration, Chrysostom's warnings are worth noting as he takes the position that the love of money is the root of all evils:

For what evil is not caused by wealth, or rather not by wealth, but by the wicked will of those who know not how to use it? . . . What evils then does it not cause! what fraudulent practices, what robberies! what miseries, enmities, contentions, battles! Does it not stretch forth its hand even to the dead, nay, to fathers, and brethren? Do not they who are possessed by this passion violate the laws of nature, and the commandments of God? in short everything? . . . It is a plague that so seizes all, some more, some less, but all in a degree. Like a fire catching a wood, that desolates and destroys all around, this passion has laid waste the world. ("Homily 17"; NPNF 13:469–70)

On the figurative use of ῥίζα, "root," see Matt 13:21 (Mark 4:17; Luke 8:13); Rom 11:16–18; Heb 12:15. φιλαργυρία, "love of money," is a compound of φιλία, "love," and ἀργύριον, "silver," which can have the general meaning of "money." φιλαργυρία occurs nowhere else in the NT (cf. 4 Macc 1:26; 2:15; cf. Trench, *Synonyms*, 117–19), but its cognate adjective φιλάργυρος, "fond of money," describes the love people will have for money in the last days (2 Tim 3:2) and the desire for money that the Pharisees had in Jesus' day (Luke 16:14). To love money more than anything is to break the first commandment.

10b ἧς τινες ὀρεγόμενοι ἀπεπλανήθησαν ἀπὸ τῆς πίστεως καὶ ἑαυτοὺς περιέπειραν ὀδύναις πολλαῖς, "by reaching for which, some were led astray from the faith and have pierced themselves with many pains." Paul returns from his generalizing in vv 6–10a to the specifics of the Ephesian situation (cf. vv 2b–5). The principles in v 9 have borne fruit in Ephesus. The lure of riches has tempted, ensnared, and destroyed Paul's opponents, and their final state is estrangement from the Christian faith and personal pain. Chrysostom states, "Two things he mentions, and that which to them might seem the more weighty he places last, their 'many sorrows.' And to learn how true this is, the only way is to sojourn with the rich, to see how many are their sorrows, how bitter their complaints" ("Homily 17"; NPNF 13:468).

ἧς, "which," refers back to φιλαργυρία, "love of money": it is the love of money for which some reach. The indefinite τινές, "some," is Paul's normal way of referring to the opponents (cf. 1 Tim 1:3); Timothy presumably knows who they are. On ὀρέγειν, "to reach for," see *Comment* on 1 Tim 3:1. It is used instrumentally to describe the love of money as the means by which they pierce themselves. The passive ἀπεπλανήθησαν, "were led astray," does not teach that the opponents were unknowingly led by another person into their present condition, although Satan was involved in their demise (cf. v 9). Paul goes on to say that they pierced themselves (ἑαυτούς), and this agrees with the picture of the opponents elsewhere in the PE (cf. 1 Tim 1:6). While others were involved in the promulgation of the heresy, the opponents knew what they were doing. ἀποπλανᾶν, "to lead astray," is used to describe the error of the false christs and prophets (Mark 13:22). The simple form πλανᾶν, "to deceive," describes evil people who are deceiving and being deceived (πλανῶντες καὶ πλανώμενοι; 2 Tim 3:13) and the pre-Christian state of all people (Titus 3:3). The words are often used in connection with religious error (cf. H. Braun, *TDNT* 6:242–51). On πίστις, "faith," see *Introduction*, "Themes in the PE."

Not only have these people been led astray from Christianity, but they have inflicted their own wounds. περιπείρειν, "to pierce," occurs only here in the NT. Chrysostom says, "Desires are thorns, and as when one touches thorns, he gores his hand, and gets him wounds, so he that falls into these lusts will be wounded by them, and pierce his soul with griefs. And what cares and troubles attend those who are thus pierced, it is not possible to express" ("Homily 17"; NPNF 13:469). ὀδύνη, "pain," describes the intense, continual pain Paul feels for his unrepentant nation (Rom 9:2). It appears as a variant in Matt 24:8, describing the pain of the last days. Its cognate verb ὀδυνᾶσθαι, "to be in great pain," describes the pain Jesus caused his parents by remaining behind in the temple (Luke 2:48), the pain of the rich man as he asked Lazarus for help (Luke 16:24–25), and the pain felt by the Ephesians when Paul told them that they would not see him again (Acts 20:38). The word group describes an intense, deeply felt pain. Because the opponents had fallen in love with money, they had, as it were, stabbed themselves with the sword of greed and bore the intense pain and grief of self-inflicted wounds. It can refer to the pangs of guilt, conscience, remorse, and the actual pains incurred by the sin itself.

Explanation

This is Paul's final, formal confrontation with his Ephesian opponents. He will follow as is his custom with a final note of instruction and encouragement to Timothy and then a final note to the rich. This passage is a powerful and graphically descriptive portrayal of the problems at Ephesus and the logical and necessary end of perverting the gospel and pursuing wealth. It is rich in vocabulary and imagery that can be understood from both the Greek and Christian spheres and is intended to appeal to both settings.

Timothy is to teach and urge the Ephesians to follow the instructions in chap. 5. But if someone does not listen to Timothy's instructions and insists on a message that does not produce a healthy lifestyle, that person is ignorant and knows nothing. Instead of preaching the gospel of Christ the opponents have chosen to fill their days with speculations and arguing about words. Once started down this road the end is inevitable. In come envy and strife that produce slander and evil accusations and from these develops mutual and constant irritation as these people rub shoulders with each other and the Ephesian church. These people are of corrupt mind, have been deprived of the truth, and are so far from the truth as to assume that Christian ministry is a source of wealth.

They are correct in that godliness is of great profit, but only godliness that is characterized by contentment is profitable. This stands to reason. People are born and will die penniless, so they should learn to be content with food and clothing. But there are those who will not listen to common sense. They insist on pursuing the love of wealth, and this opens up a whole new set of temptations that lead directly to Satan's snare. Once caught in the snare they are controlled by many harmful passions that plunge a person into the sea of despair and ruin. After all, a root of all kinds of evil is the love of money, so this development in Ephesus is no surprise. Those who have followed its path have abandoned the Christian faith and have, as it were, used the sword of greed to pierce their hearts with many pains. Why would anyone want to be rich?

Polycarp cites 1 Tim 6:7 in his letter to the Philippians:

> But the love of money is the beginning of all troubles. Knowing therefore that we brought nothing into the world neither can we carry anything out, let us arm ourselves with the

armour of righteousness, and let us teach ourselves first to walk in the commandment of the Lord. (*Phil.* 4; Lightfoot, *Apostolic Fathers,* 178)

In discussing riches Chrysostom argues as follows:

If we consider the vanity and the unprofitableness of wealth, that it cannot depart hence with us, that even here it forsakes us, and that whilst it remains behind, it inflicts upon us wounds that depart along with us. If we see that there are riches there, compared to which the wealth of this world is more despicable than dung. If we consider that it is attended with numberless dangers, with pleasure that is temporary, pleasure mingled with sorrow. If we contemplate aright the true riches of eternal life, we shall be able to despise worldly wealth. If we remember that it profits nothing either to glory, or health, or any other thing; but on the contrary drowns men in destruction and perdition. If thou consider that here thou art rich, and hast many under thee, but that when thou departest hence, thou wilt go naked and solitary. If we often represent these things to ourselves, and listen to them from others, there will perhaps be a return to a sound mind, and a deliverance from this dreadful punishment. ("Homily 17"; NPNF 13:470)

Chrysostom continues with a fascinating discussion about inherent value. His point is that if a person must be taught that something is beautiful, as opposed to possessing an inherent awareness of its beauty and worth, then it is not truly valuable; rather, people should pursue that which is of true worth—godliness and righteousness.

Is a pearl beautiful? yet consider, it is but sea water, and was once cast away in the bosom of the deep. Are gold and silver beautiful? yet they were and are but dust and ashes. Are silken vestments beautiful? yet they are nothing but the spinning of worms. This beauty is but in opinion, in human prejudice, not in the nature of the things. For that which possesses beauty from nature, need not any to point it out. If you see a coin of brass that is but gilded over, you admire it at first, fancying that it is gold; but when the cheat is shown to you by one who understands it, your wonder vanishes with the deceit. The beauty therefore was not in the nature of the thing. Neither is it in silver; you may admire tin for silver, as you admired brass for gold, and you need some one to inform you what you should admire. Thus our eyes are not sufficient to discern the difference. It is not so with flowers, which are much more beautiful. If you see a rose, you need no one to inform you, you can of yourself distinguish an anemone, and a violet, or a lily, and every other flower. It is nothing therefore but prejudice. And to show, that this destructive passion is but a prejudice; tell me, if the Emperor were pleased to ordain that silver should be of more value than gold, would you not transfer your love and admiration to the former? Thus we are everywhere under the influence of covetousness and opinion. And that it is so, and that a thing is valued for its rarity, and not for its nature, appears hence. The fruits that are held cheap among us are in high esteem among the Cappadocians, and among the Serians even more valuable than the most precious among us, from which country these garments are brought; and many such instances might be given in Arabia and India, where spices are produced, and where precious stones are found. Such preference therefore is nothing but prejudice, and human opinion. We act not from judgment, but at random, and as accident determines. But let us recover from this intoxication, let us fix our view upon that which is truly beautiful, beautiful in its own nature, upon godliness and righteousness. ("Homily 17"; NPNF 13:470)

B. Encouragement to Timothy (1 Tim 6:11–16)

Bibliography

Baldensperger, G. "Il a rendu témoignage devant Ponce Pilate." *RHPR* 2 (1922) 1–25, 95–117. **Fulford, H. W.** "St. Paul and Euripides [1 Tim. 6:12 comparatur cum Eurip., Alcestis 648]." *ExpTim* 31 (1919–20) 331. **Grossouw, W.** "Epiphaneia in de pastoralebrieven." *NKS* 49 (1953) 353–61. **Hasler, V.** "Epiphanie und Christologie in den Pastoralbriefen." *TZ* 33 (1977) 193–209. **Käsemann, E.** "Das Formular einer neutestamentlichen Ordinationsparänese." In *Neutestamentliche Studien für Rudolf Bultmann*, ed. W. Eltester. BZNW 21. Berlin: Töpelmann, 1954. 261–68 (repr. in *Exegetische Versuche und Besinnungen I* [Göttingen: Vandenhoeck & Ruprecht, 1960] 101–8). **Neufeld, V. H.** *The Earliest Christian Confessions.* Grand Rapids, MI: Eerdmans, 1963. **Nisbet, P.** "The Thorn in the Flesh [1 Tim 6:16]." *ExpTim* 80 (1968) 126. **Pax, E.** *Epifaneia: Ein religionsgeschichtlicher Beitrag zur biblischen Theologie.* Munich: Zink, 1955. **Pfitzner, V. C.** "The Agon Motif in the Pastoral Epistles." In *Paul and the Agon Motif.* 165–86. **Thurén, J.** "Die Struktur der Schlussparänese 1 Tim. 6:3–21." *TZ* 26 (1970) 241–53. **Turner, C. H.** "I Tim. 6:12,13: ἐπὶ Ποντίου Πιλάτου." *JTS* o.s. 28 (1927) 270–73.

For bibliography on doxologies, see *Bibliographies* for 1 Tim 1:12–17 and Titus 3:12–15.

Translation

[11] *But you, O man of* [a]*God, flee these things, but pursue righteousness, godliness, faith, love, endurance, gentleness.* [b] [12]*Fight the good fight of the faith. Seize hold of the eternal life, to which* [c]*you were called and confessed the good confession before many witnesses.* [13]*I urge [you],* [d] *before God* [e] *who gives life* [f] *to all things and Christ Jesus* [g] *who witnessed in the time of Pontius Pilate the good confession,* [14]*to keep the commandment unblemished [and] above reproach until the appearing of our Lord Jesus Christ,* [15]*which he will make known at the proper time. [To] the Blessed and only Sovereign, the King of kings and Lord of lords,* [16]*the only one having immortality, the one* [h] *dwelling in unapproachable light, whom no person has seen or is able to see, to him [be] honor and might forever, Amen.*

Notes

[a]τοῦ, "the," is inserted before θεοῦ, "God," by ℵ² D F G H Ψ TR. It is omitted by ℵ* A I 33 1739 1881 *pc.* See the same problem in v 13.

[b]πραϋπαθίαν, "gentleness" (ℵ* A F G H P^vid 81 630 1739 1881 *pc*), is replaced by the more common πρα(ό)τητα, "gentleness," in ℵ² D Ψ 33 TR with no change in meaning.

[c]καί, "both," is inserted before ἐκλήθης, "were called," by 81 1505 *pc* sy^h. The tradition is too weak to be considered, but it does correctly mark ἐκλήθης, "were called," and ὡμολόγησας, "confessed," as conveying parallel thoughts.

[d]σοι is omitted by ℵ* F G Ψ 6 33 1739 *pc* m sa^ms, and was the preferred reading in an earlier Nestle edition. Its inclusion is supported by ℵ² A D H 1881 TR lat sy sa^ms bo; Tert. It appears to be a later

insertion because of the difficulty of having the verbal idea begin with παραγγέλλω, "I urge," and not be completed until τηρῆσαί σε, "you to keep," in the next verse. Cf. *TCGNT*², 576.

ᶜThe article is omitted before θεοῦ, "God," in ℵ *pc*.

ᶠℵ and TR read the more common ζῳοποιοῦντος, "who gives life," instead of ζῳογονοῦντος, "who gives life" (A D F G H P Ψ 33 81 104 365 630 1175 1505 1739 1881 *pc*).

ᵍΧριστοῦ Ἰησοῦ, "Christ Jesus" (A D Ψ 33 1739 1881 TR latᵐˢ syʰ), is reversed to Ἰησοῦ Χριστοῦ, "Jesus Christ," by ℵ F G 326 *pc* syᵖ; Tert. See Elliott, "Appendix 1," in *Greek Text*, 199–202.

ʰκαί, "and," is inserted before φῶς, "light," by D* 629 a b m* vgᶜˡ; Tert Ambst.

Form/Structure/Setting

In chaps. 1 and 4 Paul establishes the pattern of criticizing his opponents (1:3–7; 4:1–5) and then following with words of encouragement to Timothy (1:18–20; 4:6–16), which include reference to Timothy's spiritual beginnings (1:18; 4:14). He repeats this same pattern here. In 6:2b–10 Paul attacked his Ephesian opponents. They were teaching incorrect doctrine and promoting unhealthy speculation, had a sickly craving for controversy, were corrupt in their minds and greedy for gain, had abandoned the faith, and wounded themselves. But Timothy, a man of God, is instructed to flee all these things, pursue righteousness, and keep the commandment pure, remembering the good confession he made before many witnesses at his baptism.

The predominant emphasis in this section is perseverance; Timothy must continue to flee evil and pursue good. Paul lists four reasons that Timothy must persevere. (1) He has been called to eternal life (v 12b). (2) This is the commitment he made before many witnesses (v 12c). (3) He should emulate Christ, who also persevered in making his own good confession (v 13b). (4) When Paul tells Timothy to persevere until the appearing of Jesus Christ that will come in God's own time and then moves into a grandiose doxology, extolling the power and transcendence of God (vv 15–16), he has really moved to the fourth and ultimate reason that Timothy must persevere: no matter how intense the opposition, how powerful his opponents, Timothy serves the God who is truly powerful, who is King over all kings and Lord over all lords, whose transcendent glory is overwhelming. Therefore, it is essential that Timothy persevere because, as biblical eschatology teaches, the fact that Christians serve the true God is motivation for ethical behavior here and now.

The structure of the passage only somewhat follows the flow of thought. (1) Paul begins with four imperatives: "flee," "pursue," "fight," and "take hold of" (vv 11–12). All four are linear in aspect, emphasizing the necessity of continual action. (2) He then admonishes Timothy to be true to his calling and commitments, just as Jesus was true to his confession (vv 13–14). (3) Finally, building from the eschatological reference that closes the previous thought, Paul breaks into a doxology (vv 15–16).

There are two parallels between this passage and other passages in the PE. (1) The charge that he delivers in vv 12–14 is similar to Paul's final words about himself in 2 Tim 4:6–8, except at the third point.

1 Tim 6:12–14	*2 Tim 4:6–8*
1. "Fight the good fight."	"I have fought the good fight."

2. "Keep the commandment pure."   "I have kept the faith."

3. Timothy is to follow the example   "There is laid up for me the crown of
   of Jesus, who also made the good   righteousness."
   confession.

4. Eternal life is held out as the   The Lord will reward Paul with a crown
   reward.   of righteousness.

5. Timothy must persevere until   God will give Paul his crown "on that
   the appearing of Jesus Christ.   day."

The similarities cannot be accidental. In 1:12–17 Paul also connects Timothy's ministry to his own. First, he retells his conversion in a way that connects the two. Then he assures Timothy that the God who strengthened Paul will also strengthen Timothy and that just as Paul's gifts are adequate for his work so are Timothy's. If God can transform a person like Paul, his powers are totally adequate for transforming the Ephesian church (see *Form/Structure/Setting* on 1 Tim 1:12–17).

(2) The second similarity is between the doxologies in 1:17 and 6:15–16.

1 Tim 1:17	*1 Tim 6:15–16*
King of ages	King of kings
Immortal	The only one having immortality
Invisible	Who dwells in unapproachable light,
	who no one has seen or is able to see
The only God	Only sovereign
Be honor and glory for ever and ever,	To him be honor and power forever,
Amen.	Amen.

Both doxologies also occur in the midst of a discussion and not at the end of a major discussion. Although all doxologies bear some degree of similarity, the substantial similarities here could attest to a common source, whether it be the Hellenistic synagogue or Paul's knowledge of the Hellenistic world, the needs of the Ephesian church, or his own literary genius.

The vocabulary of this section, especially the final three verses, draws heavily from the Hellenistic world and finds more parallels in the writings of Luke and Greek thought than in Paul's writings. Much of it seems to be composed in opposition to emperor worship, which explains Paul's motivation in using it: (1) the epiphany of Jesus is the true manifestation of divinity, not the appearance of the emperor; (2) God alone has immortality, not the dead emperor; (3) it is God and God alone who is the King over all who rule and Lord over all who would be lords; and (4) God is the only sovereign to whom alone belongs honor and might forever. This is another witness to the necessity of reading the PE in light of their historical background, the heresy in Ephesus, and the teachings that pervaded the city.

It is difficult to decide whether Paul's concern in these verses is for Timothy's own spiritual life or for his ministerial activity. This same ambiguity can be found in the similar discussions in 1 Tim 1:12–20, 1 Tim 4:6–16, and 2 Tim 4:6–8. Instead of trying to decide between the two, it seems best to view the ambiguity as intentional, realizing that Timothy's spiritual life and ministerial activities were inseparable.

Comment

11a Σὺ δέ, ὦ ἄνθρωπε θεοῦ, ταῦτα φεῦγε, "But you, O man of God, flee these things." This verse stands in contrast to the preceding section. σύ, "you," is emphatic, δέ, "but," is adversative, and these with the lengthened title "O man of God" all serve to set Timothy apart from those who want to be rich (v 9) and those who teach other doctrines (v 3). Paul repeats the thrust of the verse later when he tells Timothy to "flee [φεῦγε] youthful passions and pursue righteousness, faith, love, peace with those who call upon the Lord from a clean heart" (2 Tim 2:22). This is the first of four imperatives in this section and the introduction of the emphasis in the passage: a call to perseverance (the linear aspect of all four imperatives emphasizes the need for day-to-day action).

Paul often uses σὺ δέ, "but you" (2 Tim 3:14; 4:5; Titus 2:1; cf. 2 Tim 2:1, 3), to contrast Timothy and Titus with the opponents. The use of the interjection ὦ, "O," is Pauline (cf. 1 Tim 6:20; Rom 2:1, 3; 9:20; 11:33; Gal 3:1). The expression ἄνθρωπος (τοῦ) θεοῦ, "man of God," occurs sixty-eight times in the LXX. It is used as a title for Moses (e.g., Deut 33:1; Josh 14:6; 1 Chr 23:14), David (Neh 12:24), and prophets (e.g., Samuel [1 Sam 9:6, 10]; Elijah [1 Kgs 17:18, 24; 2 Kgs 1:10, 12]; Elisha [2 Kgs 4:7, 9]; unnamed [1 Kgs 13 (9x); 21:28]; and an angel [Judg 13:6–8]; cf. N. P. Bratsiotis, *TDOT* 1:233). It is used of Timothy (and other Christians by implication; cf. similar δοῦλον . . . κυρίου, "servant of God," in 2 Tim 2:24). Its use here is explained by the need to contrast Timothy with the opponents. They are people who teach incorrect doctrine, promote unhealthy instruction, have a sickly craving for controversy, are corrupt in the mind, are greedy for gain, have abandoned the faith, and have inflicted their own wounds. But Timothy is a man of God akin to the prophets of old with the authority to fight the false teachers of Ephesus.

Later Paul tells Timothy to flee (φεῦγε) from youthful passions (2 Tim 2:22; cf. 1 Cor 6:18; 10:14). The ταῦτα, "these things," from which he is to flee refer at least to the desire to be rich and the accompanying evils (vv 9–10). But since Paul has touched on a range of topics in vv 2b–10, ταῦτα may refer to everything wrong with the opponents.

11b δίωκε δὲ δικαιοσύνην εὐσέβειαν πίστιν, ἀγάπην, ὑπομονήν πραϋπαθίαν, "but pursue righteousness, godliness, faith, love, endurance, gentleness." Having referred to these things that Timothy should flee, Paul now tells Timothy what he should pursue, the δέ, "but," separating the two thoughts. This is the second of the four imperatives in this section and is reminiscent of Paul's "put off" and "put on" comments (Eph 4:22–24; Col 3:8–17).

διώκειν could mean "to persecute" as it does in 2 Tim 3:12, but in this context it carries the standard Pauline meaning of "to aspire, strive for, pursue" (cf. 2 Tim 2:22; Rom 9:30, 31; 12:13; 14:19; 1 Cor 14:1; 1 Thess 5:15). Elsewhere Paul talks about the pursuit of righteousness by Jews and Gentiles (Rom 9:30–31) and how Christians should pursue hospitality (Rom 12:13), love (1 Cor 14:1), goodness (1 Thess 5:15), and that which makes for peace and upbuilding (Rom 14:19; cf. Heb 12:14; 1 Pet 3:11). Paul specifies six qualities to pursue, which break down into three groups: right conduct (righteousness and godliness), the basic virtues of Christianity (faith and love), and endurance and gentleness. Lock (71) suggests that the order moves from virtues directed toward God to those directed toward people. He also refers to Ambrosiaster who "draws out the incompatibility of the love of money with each of these virtues." Ellicott suggests that they fall into three groups of paired terms "pointing to general conformity to God's law . . . the fundamental principles of Christianity . . . the principles on which a Christian ought to act toward" his opponents (92).

δικαιοσύνη, "righteousness," is used here in its ethical sense of the demands laid on a person who has been justified (2 Tim 2:22, 3:16, cf. discussion of the cognate δίκαιος, "righteous," in 1 Tim 1:9). εὐσέβεια, "godliness," is the technical term in the PE for a life fully consecrated to God (cf. 1 Tim 2:2). These two ideas are joined in Titus 2:11–12 where Paul says that God's grace teaches believers to renounce ungodliness (ἀσέβεια) and to live justly (δικαίως).

The trilogy of faith, love, and endurance occurs in Titus 2:2 in a similar injunction but directed to older men. πίστις, "faith," is used here in the standard Pauline sense of "trust" (cf. 1 Tim 1:2). ἀγάπη, "love," occurs eleven times in the PE. Its frequency attests to one of the basic problems in Ephesus: Paul's opponents are without love (cf. 1 Tim 1:5). In the PE, faith and love are almost always mentioned together (1 Tim 1:5, 14; 2:15; 4:12; 6:11; 2 Tim 1:13; 2:22; 3:10; Titus 2:2). The idea of pursuing love is similar to Paul's injunction to "make love your aim" (1 Cor 14:1). Although righteousness and faith are gifts from God, they are also Christian virtues that can be pursued (cf. 1 Tim 1:5; Gal 5:22; Paul's treatment of love in 1 Cor 14:1; and Introduction, "The Theological Problem").

ὑπομονή, "steadfastness, patience, endurance," occurs elsewhere in the PE in Paul's assessment of his ministry as being one of faith, patience, love, and steadfastness (2 Tim 3:10) and in his instructions that Titus should urge older men to be sound in faith, love, and steadfastness (Titus 2:2). Paul uses the verbal cognate ὑπομένειν, "to endure," to state that if believers endure they will also reign with Christ (2 Tim 2:12) and to describe his desire to endure everything for the sake of the elect (2 Tim 2:10). ὑπομονή is often presented within the context of suffering (cf. BAGD, 846). For Paul it is a Christian virtue resulting from faith and hope (Rom 8:25) and has strong connections with love (1 Tim 6:11; 2 Tim 3:10; Titus 2:2). It endures evil (Rom 12:2; 1 Cor 3:7) and suffering now (2 Thess 1:4), even to the point of realizing that the one enduring is called to suffer (2 Tim 2:10; cf. Acts 14:22), but it will result in character (Rom 5:3–4), reigning with Christ (2 Tim 2:11–12), and eternal life (Rom 2:7; cf. F. Hauck, TDNT 4:586–88).

πραϋπάθεια, "gentleness," or "meekness," is not easily defined. It is a rare word, occurring only here in the NT. It is basically synonymous with the simple form πραΰς, "gentle," which is more common, except that etymologically πραϋπάθεια is formed from πραΰς and a cognate of πάσχειν, "to suffer," and might therefore carry a nuance of gentleness in the midst of suffering. The cognate noun πραΰτης, "gentleness," occurs in 2 Tim 2:25 in the description of the Lord's servant being able to correct opponents with gentleness. Titus is also admonished to be gentle (Titus 3:2). Aristotle (Eth. Nic. 2.1108a) says gentleness is "the mean between excessive proneness to anger [ὀργιλότης] and incapacity for anger [ἀοργησία]" (Bruce, Galatians, 254). It contains the ideas of consideration for others and "a willingness to waive an undoubted right" (Martin, Colossians and Philemon, 111, citing 1 Cor

9:12–23) and should be understood against the OT backdrop of the poor who relied on God alone (L. H. Marshall, *The Challenge of New Testament Ethics* [London: Macmillan, 1947] 300; O'Brien, *Colossians*, 201). Greek culture interpreted meekness as servility, and deplored it. Bruce (*Galatians*, 254) comments:

> Moses was πραΰς σφόδρα, "very gentle" (Nu. 12:3), in the sense that, in [the] face of undeserved criticism, he did not give way to rage but rather interceded with God for the offenders. Jesus was "gentle [πραΰς] and lowly in heart" (Mt. 11:29) but was perfectly capable of indignation (Mk. 3:5). Paul entreats the Corinthians "by the meekness [πραΰτης] and gentleness [ἐπιείκεια] of Christ" (2 Cor. 10:1), but if the words that follow that entreaty are an expression of meekness and gentleness, one wonders what he would have said had he been unrestrained by these qualities. (There, as here, Paul's affectionate concern for his converts is matched by his fierce denunciation of those who troubled them.)

James adds that gentleness is the opposite of jealousy and selfish ambition (Jas 3:13–14; cf. F. Hauck and S. Schulz, *TDNT* 6:649–50; Spicq, *TLNT* 3:160–71; R. Leivestad, "'The Meekness and Gentleness of Christ,' II Cor. x.1," *NTS* 12 [1965–66] 156–64).

12a ἀγωνίζου τὸν καλὸν ἀγῶνα τῆς πίστεως, "Fight the good fight of the faith." This third imperative heightens Paul's call to daily perseverance. For the believer, life is a struggle against the world and flesh (Ellicott, 92) and ultimately "against the principalities, against the powers, against the world rulers of this present darkness, against the spiritual hosts of wickedness in the heavenly places" (Eph 6:12). The goal of the fight is eternal life. Paul has used athletic imagery earlier (1 Tim 4:10) and will use the phrase "I have fought the good fight" in the description of his life and ministry (2 Tim 4:7; cf. 2 Tim 2:2–4). Simpson (87–88) says it is a military metaphor as well, but most disagree (cf. Pfitzner, *Agon*, 178–81), thus avoiding a possible misconception that Timothy is to imitate an antagonistic action.

The primary question of this phrase is the precise meaning of τῆς πίστεως, "of the faith." Is it referring to Timothy's ministry within the Christian faith, or is it a call to personal perseverance, faithfulness? The subsequent phrase is a reference to his personal conversion, but v 12a could be a parallel or contrasting statement. In the similar 2 Tim 4:7–8, Paul is referring to both his personal life and his ministerial life. In the two other places where Paul is encouraging Timothy after denouncing the heresy as he is doing here (1 Tim 1:18–20; 4:6–16), he addresses both personal and ministerial concerns. It is therefore difficult to decide whether v 12a is referring to Timothy's personal life or to his ministry. Perhaps the ambiguity is intentional and instructive, for the life and the work of the minister are inextricably bound together. Pfitzner sees it as an appositional genitive: "Faith, by its very nature, demands a struggle on the part of the believer." (*Agon Motif*, 179). On πίστις, "faith," see *Introduction*, "Themes in the PE." On καλός, "good," see *Comment* on 1 Tim 1:8.

12b ἐπιλαβοῦ τῆς αἰωνίου ζωῆς, εἰς ἣν ἐκλήθης καὶ ὡμολόγησας τὴν καλὴν ὁμολογίαν ἐνώπιον πολλῶν μαρτύρων, "Seize hold of the eternal life, to which you were called and confessed the good confession before many witnesses." This fourth imperative continues the call to perseverance, holding out eternal life as the prize. "Seizing hold" is Timothy's response to God's prior act of "calling" him.

ἐπιλαμβάνεσθαι, "to seize hold of," is used of leading someone (Luke 9:47;

Acts 9:27; 17:19; 23:19; Heb 8:9), Jesus' healing touch (Mark 8:23; Luke 14:4), and mental comprehension (Luke 20:20, 26; cf. Heb 2:16). But ἐπί can also exert an intensifying force so that ἐπιλαμβάνεσθαι means "to grab tightly, hang on to." Jesus grabbed Peter before he sank beneath the waters (Matt 14:31), the slave owners seized Paul and Silas (Acts 16:19), the Jews seized Sosthenes and beat him (Acts 18:17), the mob seized Paul and tried to kill him in the temple (Acts 21:30), and Paul was then seized by the tribune (Acts 21:33). This nuance of seizing, grasping, fits our context well. Timothy is to make every effort to persevere in his life and ministry; he is to seize hold of the eternal life to which he was called. On αἰώνιος ζωή, "eternal life," see *Comment* on 1 Tim 1:16. As Fee (150) points out, this is an example of Paul's "already but not yet" eschatological view of reality, a theme that is enlarged in v 14.

Paul qualifies τῆς αἰωνίου ζωῆς, "the eternal life," with two thoughts. (1) The first is that Timothy was called to eternal life. As Paul will say later, God called believers with a holy calling (2 Tim 1:9) out of the sinful world into a life of holiness (cf. Titus 3:3–7). Being called by God is a common Pauline theme (1 Cor 1:9; 7:17–24; Gal 1:6, 15; 5:8, 13; 5:8, 13; Eph 4:1, 4; Col 3:15; 1 Thess 2:12; 4:7; 5:24; 2 Thess 2:14; cf. *Comment* on 2 Tim 1:9). This is the first of four reasons that Timothy should persevere: God has called him to eternal life. (2) The second qualifier is that Timothy made his good confession in reference to eternal life, and this in turn provides the second reason that Timothy should persevere. The question arises whether Timothy is being encouraged to persevere in his public ministry or in his personal salvation. (1) Thurén (*TZ* 26 [1970] 241–53; cf. Cullmann, *Earliest Christian Confessions*, 20ff.) argues that this refers to Timothy's confession before a tribunal, and this might be suggested by the parallel to Jesus' trial in v 13 and by the statement in Heb 13:23 that Timothy had been released from jail (also Baldensperger, *RHPR* 2 [1922] 1–25, 95–117). But there is no mention of an imprisonment in the PE, which would have been expected; it is based on a doubtful interpretation of "before Pilate" in v 13; and a trial can hardly be called a call to eternal life. (2) If Paul's concern is Timothy's public ministry, then this verse parallels the other references to Timothy's commissioning/ordination (1 Tim 1:18; 4:14) and the πολλῶν μαρτύρων, "many witnesses," would include the elders who laid hands on him in the ceremony (1 Tim 4:14; cf. 2 Tim 2:2; cf. Ellicott; Jeremias; Käsemann, "Ordinationsparänese," 261–68; Dibelius-Conzelmann; Barrett; Brox; Hasler; Hanson [1983]; Knight). (3) If Paul's concern is Timothy's personal life, then the confession could be a reference to his baptism and the public confession before the many witnesses of his conversion (Lock, Falconer, Spicq, Kelly, Holtz). (a) The verse shows that the call to eternal life occurred at the same time as Timothy's confession. A commission/ordination can hardly be termed a call to eternal life, but the conversion/baptism experience is precisely that: God's call on Timothy's life and Timothy's accompanying confession at his baptism. This is the decisive argument. (b) Paul has established a pattern of criticizing the Ephesian heresy and then encouraging Timothy (see *Form/Structure/Setting*), and in that encouragement he makes reference to Timothy's commissioning to service. 1 Tim 6:2b–16 follows this same pattern, which could suggest that Timothy's commissioning is also in view here. But even in the parallel passages Paul expresses a concern for Timothy's personal life as well. (c) Timothy's confession is parallel to Jesus' witness to the good confession in the next verse, but there is a question regarding the precise meaning of v 13 as well, so it is not necessarily helpful here. (d) If Paul is thinking of Timothy's confession at baptism, then Rom 6:1–14 is parallel where Paul reminds the Romans of their baptism and its implications for lifestyle. (Kelly discusses the use of "Pontius Pilate" in early baptismal confessions [143].) (e) The articular τὴν καλὴν ὁμολογίαν, "the good confession," implies that Timothy's confession was well known, but this could apply to either baptism or commissioning. (f) The notion of eternal life is a personal concept, and the verse reads more naturally as a call to personal perseverance, balancing the call to ministerial perseverance in v 12a. ὁμολογεῖν, "to confess," means "to declare publicly" (cf. Matt 7:23; Titus 1:16) and came to be a technical term for confessing Christ (Rom 10:9; cf. John 9:22; 1 John 4:2, 15). In similar passages, the author of Hebrews encourages his church to "hold fast our confession" (Heb 4:14); "let us hold fast the confession of our hope without wavering, for he who promised is faithful" (Heb 10:23; cf. O. Michel, *TDNT* 5:207–12, 215–17).

13 παραγγέλλω [σοι] ἐνώπιον τοῦ θεοῦ τοῦ ζῳογονοῦντος τὰ πάντα καὶ Χριστοῦ Ἰησοῦ τοῦ μαρτυρήσαντος ἐπὶ Ποντίου Πιλάτου τὴν καλὴν ὁμολογίαν, "I urge [you] before God, who gives life to all things and Christ Jesus who witnessed in the time of Pontius Pilate the good confession." Continuing his personal plea for Timothy's perseverance, Paul urges him to keep the commandment pure. The idea is begun in v 13, but before completing his thought, Paul adds a note of solemnity by appealing to God, Christ Jesus, and possibly the vow Timothy made at his baptism. He completes his thought in v 14 where he says that Timothy is to keep the commandment pure. It is also the third reason for Timothy's perseverance. This appeal is similar to statements in 1 Tim 1:19 and 4:12, 16 where Paul reminds Timothy of his earlier commitments as an encouragement to present perseverance. The thought of the verse is intentionally parallel with v 12, and yet there are a substantial number of exegetical questions raised by this parallelism. However, the basic thrust of the thought—just as Jesus persevered during his witness, so also Timothy must persevere during his ministry in Ephesus—is so clear that it must be the determining factor in interpreting the specifics of the verse.

On παραγγέλλειν, "to urge," see *Comment* on 1 Tim 1:3. Paul's solemn appeal to God and Christ is an echo of an earlier statement where he says "I solemnly charge before God and Christ Jesus and the elect angels, that you keep these things without prejudging, doing nothing with partiality" (1 Tim 5:21; see there for discussion). Paul's first appeal is to the God who gives life to all things. ζῳογονεῖν means both "to give life" and "to preserve or maintain life" (BAGD, 341; cf. Exod 1:17–18; Judg 8:19; 1 Kgs 8:19; Luke 17:33; Acts 7:19; cf. MM, 275). Fee (151) argues that the latter fits the context of perseverance better. If these words reflect a baptismal liturgy (see below), then the actual reference is to the new life given to the believer at conversion and symbolized in baptism. The linear aspect of ζῳογονοῦντος, "who gives life," emphasizes the continuing presence of God as a witness.

Paul's second witness is Christ Jesus and the good confession he made. There are several questions here. (1) To what extent does Paul intend to push the parallelism between Timothy's confession (v 12) and Jesus' (v 13) confession? The synonymous use of ὡμολόγησας, "confessed" (v 12), and μαρτυρήσαντος, "witnessed," and the similar use of τὴν καλὴν ὁμολογίαν, "the good confession," give assurance that there is an intended parallelism. The thrust is that just as Jesus persevered in giving the good confession, so also must Timothy. But this might be the only point of comparison, and the parallelism does not necessarily help to interpret the rest of the passage. The text does not require Timothy and Christ to have made the same confession.

(2) What is the precise meaning of ἐπί? (a) It can carry a spatial meaning of "before" (cf. Matt 28:14; Mark 13:9; Acts 23:30; 25:10; 1 Cor 6:1; 2 Cor 7:14), referring to Jesus' trial "before" Pilate and perhaps Pilate's actual question, "Are you king of the Jews?" (Matt 27:11; Mark 15:2; Luke 23:3; John 18:33–37). As such it is part of the terminology of lawsuits (BAGD, 286), which parallels the judicial use of ὁμολογεῖν, "to confess" (BAGD, 568). This interpretation is suggested by the parallel with ἐνώπιον, "before," in v 12. (b) ἐπί can also mean "in the time of" (Kelly; cf. Matt 1:11; Mark 2:26; Luke 3:2; 4:27; Acts 11:28; Rom 1:10; Eph 1:16; 1 Thess 1:2; Phlm 4; 1 Pet 1:20; 2 Pet 3:3; Jude 18). The confession could be either Jesus' life or perhaps his death, which occurred while Pilate was in power.

(3) Related to the meaning of ἐπί is the question of whether Jesus' confession was something he said, such as his admission before Pilate that he was king of the Jews, or something he did, such as dying. It seems more likely in this context that Paul is referring to Jesus' perseverance in his mission, not only in his life (cf. John 18:28–38; cf. Hasler) but especially in his death. This example of perseverance should inspire Timothy to continue in his own tasks and to be true to his commitment to Christ. This parallels the use of μαρτύριον, "testimony," in 1 Tim 2:6, which refers to Christ's death. Pfitzner says that the point of similarity between the two confessions is that both were made "over against a hostile world" (*Agon Motif,* 181).

Most agree that Paul is using creedal language. V 12 refers to a previous public commitment, most likely Timothy's baptism but possibly his commission to Christian service, and both those events would likely involve a creedal commitment (Kelly, 143). The articular τὴν καλὴν ὁμολογίαν, "the good confession" (v 12), suggests a well-known statement. Creedal statements recorded in Acts and the early fathers are somewhat similar, including reference to God, to Jesus and his death, and especially to Pontius Pilate (cf. Acts 3:13–15; 4:27; 13:28; Ignatius *Magn.* 11.11; *Trall.* 9.1; *Smyrn.* 1.2; Justin *1 Apol.* 13.3; 41.13). Kelly (143) goes into some detail on the form of the early baptismal vows, pointing out that the person being baptized was asked if he believed in God the Father "where 'Father' denoted the life-giving source of all reality," a parallel to our phrase "who gives life to all things." The Roman creed lying behind the Apostles' Creed also makes reference to Pilate. In these passages the form is ἐπὶ Ποντίου Πιλάτου, "in [the time of] Pontius Pilate," as it is here, thus fixing the passion in a particular historical setting. Hanson ([1983] 110–11) rightly criticizes Easton's objection that this reference to Timothy's baptism contradicts the later statement that Timothy knew the sacred Scriptures from an early age (2 Tim 3:15); Easton bases his objection on a questionable interpretation of 2 Tim 3:15 as teaching that Timothy was baptized as an infant. All that the verse requires is that Timothy knew the OT as was true of almost all Jewish children (cf. Kelly, 142). However, Hanson's objection that the author here omits any mention of the cross and the Holy Spirit and his conclusion that this shows "how far the author is from a Trinitarian concept of God" ([1983] 111) is unfounded. We have in v 13 but a mere snippet, meant to remind Timothy of his previous commitment. It is not a theological treatise in which omissions are significant.

14 τηρῆσαί σε τὴν ἐντολὴν ἄσπιλον ἀνεπίλημπτον μέχρι τῆς ἐπιφανείας τοῦ κυρίου ἡμῶν Ἰησοῦ Χριστοῦ, "[I urge] you to keep the commandment unblemished [and] above reproach until the appearing of our Lord Jesus Christ." Resuming the thought of παραγγέλλω, "I urge," in v 13, Paul continues his emphasis on perseverance by adding an eschatological note, the fourth reason for perseverance. Timothy must keep the commandment pure and above reproach until the Lord returns.

The primary question regarding the verse is the identity of the ἐντολήν, "commandment." There are many subtle variations offered as an answer, but they break into two basic divisions. (1) The "commandment" could be something specific, such as vv 11–12 (Easton), Timothy's baptismal (Bernard, Lock, Guthrie) or commission/ordination (Spicq, Barrett, Brox) vows, or the epistle as a whole (Calvin). (2) "Commandment" could also be something more general, such as the full intent of the vows referred to in vv 11–12 (Kelly), Timothy's faith and ministry (Scott; cf. 1 Tim 4:16), which is the "basic thrust of the letter" (Fee, 152), the gospel as the "rule of life" (Ellicott, 94; Knight), or the "deposit of faith" to which Paul is about to refer (1 Tim 6:20; cf. Dibelius-Conzelmann, Brox, Houlden, Hanson [1983]). Context ties v 14 in with vv 12–13, but the basic admonition is general: "fight the good fight of the faith." A similar verb, φυλάσσειν, "to guard" (in v 14 it is τηρεῖν, "to keep"), is used six verses later when Paul tells Timothy to guard what has been entrusted (παραθήκη), which summarizes the epistle as the true gospel in contrast to the Ephesian heresy. In 2 Tim 4:7 Paul uses τηρεῖν, "to keep," when he says "I have kept the faith," a summary statement of his life of ministry. The context of the command is serious, having summoned God, Christ, and those witnessing Timothy's confession, and therefore the commandment must be worthy of this degree of solemnity. The articular τὴν ἐντολήν, "the commandment," suggests something of independent existence that is well known. These considerations suggest that the commandment is more general, encompassing Timothy's commitment to Christ and his ministry, a commitment to preach the gospel that included righteousness, godliness, faith, love, endurance, and meekness in contrast to the opponents' teachings, and a commitment that demanded perseverance until the Lord returned. The commandment includes more than any one part of the immediate context and in fact encompasses it all.

To describe the commandment, Paul uses two words beginning with alpha privatives (cf. 1 Tim 1:9; 6:15, 16), the alliteration adding to the formality of the statement. ἄσπιλος, "unblemished," is a cultic concept, describing an unblemished animal appropriate for sacrifice (cf. Lev 4:3). Elsewhere in the NT it is used of Christ as a lamb without blemish (1 Pet 1:19) and of Christians (2 Pet 3:14; Jas 1:27; cf. Job 15:15; cf. A. Oepke, *TDNT* 1:502). ἀνεπίλημπτος, "above reproach," is one of the central themes in the PE. It is the primary requirement of an elder (1 Tim 3:2) and is required of families with widows (1 Tim 5:7). One of the problems in the Ephesian church is that their behavior had brought disrepute on the church and the gospel, and this must change (see *Form/Structure/Setting* on 1 Tim 3:1–7). It is possible that ἄσπιλον, "unblemished," and ἀνεπίλημπτον, "above reproach," modify σε, "you," i.e., Timothy (Guthrie). The two words are used in the NT in descriptions of people, and Paul elsewhere has expressed his desire for Timothy's personal purity (1 Tim 4:12; 5:2). But most agree that they modify ἐντολήν, "commandment." The words are closer to ἐντολήν than to σε, and there are secular examples of their application to nonpersonal objects such as apples (*Anthologia Palatina* 6.252.3), stones (*Inscriptiones Graecae II* 4:1054c; Dibelius-Conzelmann, 89), craftsmanship (Philo *Op.* 22; cf. 24.1), and actions (Polybius *Hist.* 14.2.14). Paul is calling Timothy to "contract no defilement, either of doctrine or of life" (so Chrysostom, "Homily 18"; NPNF 13:471).

The call to perseverance takes on eschatological dimensions as Paul urges Timothy to guard the commandment until Christ's second coming. ἐπιφάνεια, "appearance," was an important word in Hellenistic usage (cf. excursus in Dibelius-Conzelmann, 104). It denoted the intervention of God or a semidivine being. It described the person's birthday, a display of power, coronation or anniversary of such, or a return from abroad (R. Bultmann and D. Lührmann, *TDNT* 9:1–10; Dibelius-Conzelmann, 104; Kelly, 145). In Hellenistic Judaism it was used of a manifestation of God's power (2 Macc 2:21; 3:24; 3 Macc 5:78; *Ep. Arist.* 264; Josephus *Ant.* 2.16.2 §339; 3.14.4 §310). In the PE it describes Christ's incarnation (2 Tim 1:10) and his return (2 Tim 4:1, 8; Titus 2:13). The verbal cognate ἐπιφαίνειν, "to appear," describes Christ's first coming (Titus 2:11; 3:4) in passages that call the reader to obedience. Paul's use of ἐπιφάνεια with all its divine associations in speaking of Jesus Christ is an assault on the use of the word in emperor worship. This attack on emperor worship also plays a large role in the doxology in vv 15b–16. The only occurrence of ἐπιφάνεια elsewhere in the NT is in conjunction with the more common παρουσία, "coming," in 2 Thess 2:8. Its sparse use in the NT and frequent use in Hellenism shows that once again Paul is appropriating Hellenistic language to make his point. Its use in 2 Thess 2:8 shows Paul's acquaintance with the term; and although παρουσία is his most common term for Christ's return (1 Cor 15:23; 1 Thess 2:19; 3:13; 4:15; 5:23; 2 Thess 2:1, 8, 9), he exhibits sufficient diversity elsewhere that his use of ἐπιφάνεια is not problematic. Elsewhere Paul speaks of "the day of the Lord" (1 Cor 1:8; 5:5; 1 Thess 5:2), "the revelation of the Lord" (1 Cor 1:7; 2 Thess 1:7), and "the dawning of his appearance" (Bruce's [172] translation of 2 Thess 2:8).

It is often said that this verse shows that the author of the PE has no hope of an imminent parousia (e.g., Dibelius-Conzelmann, Brox, Hanson [1983]), but Paul tells Timothy to persevere until the Lord returns, expecting Timothy to experience the parousia firsthand. By saying that it will come "in his [i.e., God's] own time" (v 15), Paul is not saying anything that requires a significant change of opinion on his part. The PE show that Paul still saw himself living in the end times (1 Tim 4:1; 2 Tim 3:1; 4:1; see *Comments* on these verses). But even if Paul was coming to realize that he would not experience the Lord's return firsthand, this is only to be expected of a person who was growing in his understanding of God's ways, a person who always saw the future element in eschatology (cf. 1 Cor 1:7; 11:26; Phil 3:20–21; cf. Fee, 152).

15a ἣν καιροῖς ἰδίοις δείξει, "which he will make known at the proper time." Even though Paul has switched to a description of God's sovereignty, he is still dealing with the main topic of perseverance. Christ's appearing will most definitely come, but it will happen according to God's time table. And it is precisely because God is powerful that Timothy should persevere. The same God who gives life to all, who is the only sovereign, the King of kings and Lord of lords, the only one having immortality, who dwells in unapproachable light, whom no one has seen or can see, this is the God Timothy is serving and for whom he must faithfully perseーere. The expression καιροῖς ἰδίοις, "at the proper time," occurs two other placɛs in the PE: Christ's ransom was given at the proper time (1 Tim 2:6); eternal life was manifested by God through his word at the proper time (Titus 1:3; see *Coɔnment* on 1 Tim 2:6). It shows that the sovereign God is in control and does his wɔrk when he deems it best. The phrase could therefore be translated "in his timɛ."

15b ὁ ιακάριος καὶ μόνος δυνάστης, "[To] the Blessed and only Sovereign." Paul breaks into a doxology to describe God who will make known Christ's appearing. The language, drawn from the OT, the Hellenistic synagogue, and Hellenism, describes a mighty and transcendent God who deserves Timothy's loyalty. Some ɔf the language is directed against emperor worship, which had a center in Ephesuɛ, claiming that God and not the emperor possesses immortality, that God is the King over all kings and Lord over all lords, and that God alone possesses migllt. This continues the theme from v 14 that ἐπιφάνεια, "appearing," with its overtones of divine intervention belongs to God and not the emperor. This doxology bears many similarities to the one in 1 Tim 1:17 (see *Form/Structure/Setting*). There is no question that the language is borrowed from Hellenistic circles, although it has many parallels in the OT and may reflect the Hellenistic synagogue. This borrowing has been Paul's practice throughout the PE. While there is much discussion regarding the source of the actual phrases, Spicq notes that there is nothing here that could not be the result of Paul's own creative writing as he crew on current images and phrases. The similarities to the doxology in 1:17 support this. To dismiss this possibility out of hand as does Hanson on the basis of its non-Pauline style is not convincing. Hanson comments, "Spicq has persuaded himself that Paul carefully composed the seven phrases which make up vv. 15–16; to us they give the impression of being about as far from Paul's style and thougllt as anything in the Pastoral Epistles" ([1983] 112–13). Whatever its source, the doxology brings the discussion of perseverance to a fitting conclusion.

Here and in 1 Tim 1:11 are the only places μακάριος, "blessed," is used in the NT to desc ribe God, although the expression "Blessed is . . ." is common in the NT and in Greek literature such as Homer and Philo (see 1 Tim 1:11 for references and discussion). μόνος δυνάστης, "only Sovereign," repeats μόνῳ θεῷ, "the only God," of 1 Tim 1:17, the argument of 1 Tim 2:5, and the basic tenet of Judaism that the Lord God is one (Deut 6:4; cf. *Comment* on 1 Tim 2:5). This is the only time ἑυνάστης, "Sovereign," is used of God in the NT. It is used of God frequently in the LXX (Sir 46:5; 2 Macc 12:15; 15:3–4; 3 Macc 2:3; cf. *Sib. Or.* 3.719) and of people in the NT (Luke 1:52; Acts 8:27). Guthrie (116) says it describes not a derived power but one who inherently possesses power.

15c ὁ βασιλεὺς τῶν βασιλευόντων καὶ κύριος τῶν κυριευόντων, "the King of kings and Lord of lords." This second title places Timothy's God in direct opposition to the imperial cult (so Hanson [1983]). ὁ βασιλεὺς τῶν βασιλευόντων, "King of kings," is used to describe the Babylonian and Persian emperors (Ezek 26:7; Dan 2:37; Ezra 7:12) and is used of God in 2 Macc 13:4. κύριος τῶν κυριευόντων, "Lord of lords," is used in conjunction with the phrase θεὸς τῶν θεῶν, "God of gods," to assert Yahweh's absolute soノereignty (Deut 10:17; Ps 136:2–3; cf. Fee, 153). The two titles are joined in describirg Jesus in Rev 17:14 and 19:16 (cf. *1 Enoch* 9:4; cf. Str-B 3:656).

16a ὁ μόνος ἔχων ἀθανασίαν, "The only one having immortality." Some

(Guthrie, 117; Kelly, 146) comment that this claims not that God is the only immortal being but that he alone inherently possesses immortality: "He in whom immortality essentially exists, and who enjoys it neither derivatively nor by participation" (Ellicott, 96). ἀθανασία, "immortality," occurs here and in 1 Cor 15:53–54 in Paul's description of putting on immortality at the resurrection. It parallels the description of God as immortal (ἄφθαρτος; cf. variant ἀθάνατος) in 1 Tim 1:17. Since the emperor was viewed as immortal after death, this statement is aimed against emperor worship.

16b φῶς οἰκῶν ἀπρόσιτον, "The one dwelling in unapproachable light." This thought parallels the notion of God being invisible in 1 Tim 1:17 and emphasizes his transcendent majesty. The idea of God living in unapproachable light is probably based on the account of God's divine glory being visible as a fire on the top of the mountain (Exod 24:17). The theme of God's brilliance is continued throughout Jewish and Christian literature (1 Kgs 8:11; Ps 104:2; John 1:7–9; 3:19–21; 2 Cor 11:14; Col 1:12; 1 John 1:5–7; Philo *Mos.* 2.70 [3.2, in the account of Moses on Sinai]; Josephus *Ant.* 3.5.1 §76; see Str-B 3:656 for the rabbinic idiom. of unapproachable light). Ellicott notes, "In this sublime image God is represented, as it were, dwelling in an atmosphere of light, surrounded by glories which no created nature may ever *approach,* no mortal eye may ever *contemplate*" (96). Nisbet makes an interesting connection with Paul's "thorn in the flesh": if Paul suffered from intermittent or encroaching blindness,

> Paul's predilection for metaphors and similes dealing with light and brightness and his phrase "seeing through a glass darkly," all take on a sharper significance if one conceives of him as going blind. . . . In the great hymn of praise in I Timothy 6:16, Paul speaks of God "dwelling in the light which no man can approach unto." I have always considered that verse as the flash-point for Milton's wonderful Invocation to Light, which comes at the beginning of Book III "Paradise Lost"—". . . since God is light, And never but in unapproached light Dwelt from eternity." Milton knew what it was to live under the threat of developing blindness, and like-minded people with the same infirmity can recognize each other across the centuries. (*ExpTim* 80 [1968] 126; cf. 2 Cor 12:7; Gal 4:15; 6:11; 2 Thess 3:17; Phlm 19)

Both ἀπρόσιτον, "unapproachable," and the previous ἀθανασίαν, "immortality," are formed from alpha privatives (cf. v 14), the alliteration being appropriate to the lofty language of the doxology. ἀπρόσιτος, "unapproachable," occurs only here in the NT.

16c ὃν εἶδεν οὐδεὶς ἀνθρώπων οὐδὲ ἰδεῖν δύναται, "Whom no person has seen or is able to see." Continuing the idea of God dwelling in unapproachable light and his transcendence, Paul adds that no person has or is able to see him, a theme expressed in Moses' petition on Sinai (Exod 33:20; 33:17–23; cf. 34:30, 35; John 1:17–18; Col 1:15). God's invisible and unknowable nature is taught in the OT and in Greek thought, but with a significant difference. In Greek thought God is unknowable because he is spirit. In Jewish thought God's holiness separates him from creation (Exod 33:20; Judg 13:22; Isa 6:1–5; John 1:18; 6:46), although Jesus did promise that those who were pure in heart would see God (Matt 5:8; cf. Heb 12:14; 1 John 3:3; Rev 21:22–27). ἀνθρώπων, "of people," is a partitive genitive meaning that no one among humans, no person, can see God.

16d ᾧ τιμὴ καὶ κράτος αἰώνιον, ἀμήν, "To him [be] honor and might forever,

Amen." Paul closes the doxology in 1 Tim 1:17 with very similar words: "To the eternal king . . . [be] honor and glory forever and ever, Amen [τῷ δὲ βασιλεῖ τῶν αἰώνων . . . τιμὴ καὶ δόξα εἰς τοὺς αἰῶνας τῶν αἰώνων, ἀμήν]." The switch from δόξα, "glory" (1:17), to κράτος, "might," ends the passage, which emphasizes God's sovereignty on a note of strength. κράτος, "might," is never used of human strength in the NT. It is used once of Satan's power of death (Heb 2:14) and once of the mighty spread of God's word (Acts 19:20). Every other use describes God's supreme power (cf. W. Michaelis, *TDNT* 3:905–19; cf. Luke 1:51; Col 1:11; Eph 1:19–20; 6:10; 1 Pet 4:11; 5:11; Jude 25; Rev 1:6; 5:13). It is often part of doxologies (1 Pet 4:11; 5:11; Jude 25; Rev 1:6; 5:13; cf. *1 Clem.* 65:2).

It sounds as if Paul intended this to be the end of his letter but then realized that he still needed to address the issue of those who are rich (vv 17–19). But it is also common for Paul to break into this type of glorious praise even when he is not finished (cf. 1 Tim 1:17; Eph 3:20–21).

Explanation

Paul's opponents in Ephesus taught heresy, promoted unhealthy speculation, had a sickly craving for controversy, had corrupted minds, were greedy for gain, had abandoned the Christian faith, and had inflicted their own wounds. But true to his pattern established in 1:18–20 and 4:6–16, Paul follows his denunciation of the opponents with words of encouragement to Timothy, making reference to his spiritual beginnings and calling for perseverance. With a series of four imperatives, Paul urges Timothy, a man of God, to flee from these things, to pursue righteousness, godliness, faith, love, endurance, and meekness, to fight the good fight for the Christian faith, and firmly to grasp eternal life.

Then Paul spells out four reasons that Timothy should persevere. (1) He has been called to eternal life; it is God's desire that he stand firm. (2) At his baptism Timothy committed himself to Christ and to service, and this was witnessed by many people. (3) As Paul urges Timothy to keep the commandment, the Christian faith, pure and unblemished until the Lord returns, he calls God and Christ Jesus as witnesses. Just as Timothy has been called to remain true to his good confession, he is reminded that Jesus remained true to his good confession and gave his life in death. (4) The fourth and ultimate call to perseverance comes in the doxology extolling God's mighty power and transcendence. No matter what opposition Timothy meets, no matter what kind of pressures he feels from an erring church and heathen society known for its emperor worship, in language drawn from the Ephesian culture Paul extols the true God, the only blessed Sovereign, the King who rules over all kings, the Lord who is over all would-be lords, the only one who possesses immortality, the one who is unapproachable and separated from people, to whom belongs true honor and power forever. This is the God whom Timothy serves, who witnesses to Timothy's work, and who is in absolute control of the Ephesian situation.

These six verses are replete with significant theological truths. Even someone who bears the title "man of God" needs encouragement, to be called to persevere. The role of one's spiritual heritage is essential in the day-to-day labors of ministry, a reminder not only of one's prior commitments but of the God who witnesses one's actions and ultimately will prove victorious over evil. One's personal spiritual life and one's ministry are intricately interwoven, and to address the one is to deal with the other. Some day, when the sovereign God deems it appropriate, Jesus Christ will return. This God is a mighty God who is in absolute control, and to him alone belongs true honor and might. He will be victorious and, it is implied, will vanquish all his foes. Believers must live in the here and now with the conviction that eventually the enemy will be vanquished, and those who have persevered will receive their reward of eternal life.

C. Words to the Rich   (1 Tim 6:17–19)

Bibliography

Dschulnigg, P. "Warnung vor Reichtum und Ermahnung der Reichen: 1 Tim 6:6–10, 17–19 im Rahmen des Schlussteils 6:3–21." *BZ* 37 (1993) 60–77. **Furfey, P. H.** "PLOUSIOS and Cognates in the New Testament." *CBQ* 5 (1943) 241–63. **Hengel, M.** *Property and Riches in the Early Church: Aspects of a Social History of Early Christianity.* Tr. J. Bowden. Philadelphia: Fortress, 1974. **Olingdahl, G.** "Den kristne og jordisk rikedom: En formell och innehallslig analys av 1 Tim 6:17–19." Diss. lic., University of Uppsala, 1968. **Zeilinger, F.** "Die Bewertung der irdischen Güter im lukanischen Doppelwork und in den Pastoralbriefen." *BibLeb* 58 (1985) 75–80.

Translation

[17] *Urge the rich in the present age not to be haughty,[a] or to set [their] hope on [the] uncertainty of riches but on [b] God [c] who grants to us all things richly for [our] enjoyment,* [18]*to do good, to be rich in good deeds, to be generous, sharing,* [19]*laying up for themselves a good foundation [d] for the coming [age], in order that they might seize hold of what is truly [e] life.*

Notes

[a]ὑψηλοφρονεῖν, "to be haughty," is spelled ὑψηλὰ φρονεῖν, "to think high [things]," by ℵ I 048[vid] 33*; Or.

[b]Instead of the anarthrous ἐπὶ θεῷ, "on God" (ℵ D* F G; Or), many MSS insert τῷ, "the," before θεῷ, "God" (A I P Ψ 6 33 81 104 365 [629] 1175 1505 1739 1881 *pc*; Bas Did). ἐν τῷ θεῷ, "in the God," is read by D² TR. Cf. *TCGNT*², 576–77.

[c]In imitation of the phrase in 1 Tim 4:10 or 3:15, many MSS add τῷ ζῶντι, "the living," after θεῷ, "God" (D [the article is missing in D*] TR a b m vg[cl] sy bp[ms]; Ambst Spec). Its omission is supported by ℵ A F G I P Ψ 6 33 81 104 365 1175 1739 1881 *pc* vg[st ww] co; Or. See *TCGNT*², 576–77.

[d]Without any textual support, Moffatt's tr. emends θεμέλιον, "foundation," to θέμα λίαν, "amassing right good treasure" (following Lamb-Bos). Moffatt and Hanson ([1983] 114) say the emendation makes explicit a citation of Tob 4:9 (cf. Luke 12:33; 16:9; 18:22; cf. Matt 6:20). This avoids the mixed metaphor of laying up a foundation. κειμήλιον, "treasure," was conjectured by P. Junius. Although a mixed metaphor may not be pleasing to some literary tastes, that is no reason to conjecture a textually unsupported emendation. The thought of Tob 4:9 is similar to our passage, but so is the teaching of Jesus, which is a more likely source for Paul's thought.

[e]ὄντως, "truly" (ℵ A D* F G Ψ 81 104 365 1505 1739 *pc* latt sy), is replaced by αἰωνίου, "eternal" (D²

1881 TR bo^(ms)), and ὄντως αἰωνίου, "truly eternal" (1175 *pc;* a conflation of the two readings). These are attempts to clarify the meaning of ὄντως ζωῆς, "truly life," drawing from the parallel in 1 Tim 6:12. See *TCGNT*², 577.

Form/Structure/Setting

It can be argued that 1 Tim 6:17–19 fits more naturally after 6:2a as the fifth group within the Ephesian church that Paul addresses (those of different ages, 5:1–2; widows, 5:3–16; elders, 5:17–25; slaves, 6:1–2a). Some have argued that these verses are an interpolation, originally placed after v 2 or v 10, or added when wealth became a problem in the church (cf. A. von Harnack, *Geschichte* 1:482; Falconer; Easton). But there is no textual evidence supporting a transposition, and a good contextual argument can be made that the verses fit after v 16. Paul's opponents place the desire to be rich above all else, above their personal integrity, the Christian faith, and the spiritual lives of those they influence. This attitude deserves condemnation (vv 2b–10). After calling Timothy to persevere in his work with these people (vv 11–16), Paul balances his previous comments by saying that the mere possession of wealth is not wrong (as opposed to the love of wealth, which is wrong). He turns away from the opponents, faces the rich in the Ephesian church, and warns them not to trust in their wealth, for it will fail them; rather, they must place their hope in God (vv 17–19). The imagery of v 19 ties vv 17–19 into Paul's personal words to Timothy (vv 11–16) as it speaks of the reward of a good foundation (cf. v 12) and the dangers of (loving) wealth, has the same eschatological expectation (v 14), and admonishes the people to take hold of true life (v 19), which is eternal life (v 12). Vv 2b–19 therefore read as a consistent whole.

The major difficulty in this position, and what gives rise to speculations about interpolations, is the placement of the doxology in vv 15–16. But as is evidenced by 1 Tim 1:17 (see discussion there), Paul does not use doxologies solely as an indication of the end of a discussion. Vv 11–15a are an intense, personal admonition to a dear friend. As Paul's thoughts look forward to the end of time, as he encourages Timothy to persevere to the end, as he thinks about the Lord's appearing and all that entails, and as he contemplates the powerful and transcendent God who will bring all this about in his own time, he can but burst into glorious praise to God. Paul is a passionate person and far too creative to use doxologies merely as a way to end a paragraph.

The structure of the passage is simple. Paul gives six admonitions built around five imperatives: do not be haughty, do not set one's hope on riches but on God, do good, be rich in good works, be liberal and generous. He follows with the result of following these actions—the rich will lay a good foundation for the future—and concludes with the reason that they should do these things—in order to grasp true, eschatological, eternal life. Throughout this passage there is a play on the various forms of the word πλούσιος, "rich." Those who are rich (πλούσιος) should set their hope not on uncertain riches (πλοῦτος) but on God who richly (πλουσίως) gives all things. Rather they should be rich (πλουτεῖν) in good deeds. This is similar to the play on the word πίστις, "faith," in 1 Tim 1:12–17.

Comment

17a Τοῖς πλουσίοις ἐν τῷ νῦν αἰῶνι παράγγελλε μὴ ὑψηλοφρονεῖν, "Urge the rich in the present age not to be haughty." Chrysostom says, "And this advice he gives, knowing that nothing so generally produces pride and arrogance as wealth" ("Homily 18"; NPNF 13:472). Παραγγέλλειν in the PE means "to urge" rather than "to command" (cf. 1 Tim 1:3), and this confirms that Paul is speaking not to his opponents but generally to those in the church; his language is stronger when addressing the opponents. τῷ νῦν αἰῶνι, "the present age," is a normal idiom for the present (cf. 2 Tim 4:10; Titus 2:12 and the similar expressions in Rom 12:2; 1 Cor 2:6; 2 Cor 4:4) and is in contrast to the age that is to come (τὸ μέλλον) in v 19. ὑψηλοφρονεῖν, "to be haughty," is a rare word, occurring only here in the NT and as a variant in Rom 11:20. It is a compound of ὑψηλός, "haughty, lofty," and φρονεῖν, "to think," in the sense of a mindset, a disposition (cf. μὴ ὑψηλὰ φρόνει, "do not set your mind on haughty things [i.e., be proud]" [Rom 11:20]; μὴ τὰ ὑψηλὰ φρονοῦντες, "not setting your mind on haughty things [i.e., being proud]" [Rom 12:16]). Paul does not want the worldly rich to develop a mindset of superiority or of pride over the poor. That would be the opposite of realizing that all a person possesses is a gift from God (v 17b).

17b μηδὲ ἠλπικέναι ἐπὶ πλούτου ἀδηλότητι, "or to set [their] hope on [the] uncertainty of riches." When used with God as its object (1 Tim 4:10; 5:5), ἐλπίζειν, "to hope," signals a confident anticipation (cf. *Comment* on 1 Tim 1:1), but here it is the opposite. The rich are not to place their confidence in wealth, the perfect-tense ἠλπικέναι, "to set [their] hope," emphasizing in a negative sense the assuredness of their conviction. Although this section is addressed to the rich in general, one is reminded of the previous description of the opponents as being greedy for gain (6:5). ἀδηλότης, "uncertainty," occurs only here in the NT (cognates in 1 Cor 9:26; 14:8). The construction is the reverse order of the Hebrew construct state, equivalent to ἐπ᾽ ἀδήλῳ πλούτῳ, "on uncertain riches" (BDF §165). Riches are not a proper foundation for one's hope because they are uncertain, and riches are uncertain because they are of this age. The futility of setting one's hope on riches is a common theme throughout the Bible (Pss 52:7; 62:10; Prov 23:4-5; Eccl 5:8-20; Jer 9:23; Mark 10:17-27; Luke 12:13-21).

17c ἀλλ᾽ ἐπὶ θεῷ τῷ παρέχοντι ἡμῖν πάντα πλουσίως εἰς ἀπόλαυσιν, "but on God who grants to us all things richly for [our] enjoyment." Rather than setting one's hope on riches, the rich and everyone else should set their hope on God (1 Tim 4:10; 5:5). Whereas riches are uncertain, it is God who gives all things. This thought is similar to that in 1 Tim 4:3 where Paul argues that all foods can be eaten because they are given by God and are to be received with thanksgiving. πάντα, "all things," is not everything people could possibly want, as if God were obligated to fulfill every wish. 1 Tim 6:8 limits human needs to food and clothing, and therein lies God's obligation. πάντα means that everything a person has, whether it be food and clothing or more, is a gift from God. ἀπόλαυσις, "enjoyment," is a strong word denoting almost "sensual enjoyment" (Bernard, 102). It is used elsewhere of the temporary enjoyment of sin (Heb 11:25). Aggressive asceticism is wrong because it denies the goodness of God's creation and its intended purpose (1 Tim 4:3-5). On the other hand, the rich must not trust their own resources but trust God, who gives what is needed for enjoyment. It is enjoyable because God gives it and it is his intention. The time frame for this enjoyment is the present; Paul is speaking to the rich ἐν τῷ νῦν αἰῶνι, "in the present age," and παρέχοντι, "grants," is gnomic. (In v 19 Paul will move to the rewards in the future.) God does not give grudgingly; he gives πλουσίως, "richly." By using ἡμῖν, "to us," and not αὐτοῖς, "to them," Paul shows that he is stating a general truth applicable to all people, whether they are rich or not.

Fee (156) points out how similar this section is to Eccl 5:18–20: "Behold, what I have seen to be good and to be fitting is to eat and drink and find enjoyment in all the toil with which one toils under the sun the few days of his life which God has given him, for this is his lot. Every man also to whom God has given wealth and possessions and power to enjoy them, and to accept his lot and find enjoyment in his toil—this is the gift of God. For he will not much remember the days of his life because God keeps him occupied with joy in his heart" (Eccl 5:18–20). Throughout this passage there has been a wordplay on forms of the word πλούσιος, "rich." Those who are rich (πλούσιος) should set their hope not on uncertain riches (πλοῦτος) but on God who richly (πλουσίως) gives all things. This will be continued into the next verses where Paul says that they should be rich (πλουτεῖν) in good deeds. Any reflection of supposed Cynic or Stoic philosophy in 6:7–10 is nullified by this idea of God giving material things for personal enjoyment (cf. Gealy [457], who remarks on what he sees as a change in tone). For a treatment of πλούσιος, "rich," and its NT cognates, see Furfey, *CBQ* 5 [1943] 241–63.

18 ἀγαθοεργεῖν, πλουτεῖν ἐν ἔργοις καλοῖς, εὐμεταδότους εἶναι, κοινωνικούς, "to do good, to be rich in good deeds, to be generous, sharing." These final four actions are the natural result of realizing that all a person has is a gift from God. Paul starts with the general "do good" and moves to the more specific "be rich in good deeds," and then clarifies that by "good deeds" he means sharing generously with others. The three infinitives are grammatically dependent on παράγγελλε, "urge," in v 17.

ἀγαθοεργεῖν, "to do good," is a rare word, occurring only here and in Acts 14:17 (variant in Rom 13:3). πλουτεῖν, "to be rich," is the last of the wordplay on πλούσιος, "rich," that Paul started in v 17. To be truly rich is to give. ἔργοις καλοῖς, "good works," is a major theme in the PE, emphasizing the practical side of Christianity. There is no notion that people can earn their salvation, either in this (cf. *Comment* on 1 Tim 2:10) or the following phrase. Both εὐμετάδοτος, "generous," and κοινωνικός, "sharing," occur only here in the NT, but both convey the common idea in Paul that the rich should share with the poor (Rom 12:8, 13; 2 Cor 9:6–15). Bernard (102) says εὐμετάδοτος is limited to the "sharing of worldly goods." If the meaning of the cognate κοινωνία carries over to κοινωνικός, then this word refers to sharing on a much broader plane.

19 ἀποθησαυρίζοντας ἑαυτοῖς θεμέλιον καλὸν εἰς τὸ μέλλον, ἵνα ἐπιλάβωνται τῆς ὄντως ζωῆς, "laying up for themselves a good foundation for the coming [age], in order that they might seize hold of what is truly life." When the rich in the Ephesian church realize that what they have is a gift from God, they will stop thinking of their own abilities and possessions and instead learn to be rich in their generosity. The result of—not the reason for—doing this is that they will store up treasures for themselves, laying a good foundation, not for this world of uncertain riches but for the age to come. They should do this because, apart from a recognition that all things are from God, they may be able to grab on to

true life, not life of this world but of the world to come, eschatological life. There
is no suggestion that the rich can earn their way to heaven by doing these things;
Paul is spelling out the results of certain actions. Salvation in the PE is by God's
grace and mercy alone (cf. 1 Tim 1:12–17). There is an emphasis in the PE on
the practical outworking of Christianity such as the doing of good deeds (cf. 1
Tim 2:10; 6:18), but these actions are the result of one's faith and not attempts to
earn God's favor. The idea of devoting money to alms with an eye to a heavenly
reward is a theme in Jesus' preaching (Luke 12:33; 16:9; 18:22; cf. Matt 6:20),
and it is possible that Paul was thinking of that teaching (so Kelly). God gives
both for present enjoyment (v 17) and for the future.

The difficulty of the verse is the mixing of metaphors. ἀποθησαυρίζειν occurs
only here in the NT. It means "to store up, lay away" and "is about equal to 'treasure,' 'reserve'" (BAGD, 91). Kelly (149) says that it can refer to the amassing of
a treasure. But θεμέλιος means "foundation," used in the NT both literally of a
building and figuratively of the foundation built by a person's preaching of Christ
(Rom 15:20), the foundation of elementary theology (Heb 6:1), of Christ (1 Cor
3:11), and of the apostles and prophets (Eph 2:20) as the foundation of the church.
θεμέλιος is used elsewhere in the PE only in 2 Tim 2:19 where it refers to the
Ephesian believers as being firmly established, unable to be conquered by Paul's
opponents (see similar imagery in 1 Tim 3:15). The mixing of metaphors is somewhat confusing—Bernard (102) calls it "inexact brevity"—but the basic thrust is
clear. By being generous, the rich are not losing their wealth. Rather, they are
laying it away in heaven, and by doing so, they are establishing a firm foundation
for eternity, for life that is truly life. Lock translates, "in this way they store up
true treasures for themselves which form a firm foundation on which they can
build for the future" (73). Ellicott says there is no "confusion, but only a brevity
of expression which might have been more fully, but less forcibly, expressed by
ἀποθησαυρ. πλοῦτον καλῶν ἔργων ὡς θεμέλιον" (98). (See Note d for Moffatt's suggested emendation to avoid the mixed metaphors.)

Although the sharing of wealth profits those receiving the generosity, the emphasis here is on the benefits enjoyed by the giver. εἰς τὸ μέλλον, "for the coming
[age]," is parallel with ἐν τῷ νῦν αἰῶνι, "in the present age," of v 17; those who
are rich in the present age should use their wealth with a view to the coming age.
The articular participle τὸ μέλλον, "the coming," is often used of the coming age
(cf. 1 Tim 4:8). ἵνα, "in order that," goes back to παράγγελλε, "urge," explaining
why the rich should follow these six imperatives. ἐπιλαμβάνεσθαι, "to seize hold
of tightly," is used in 1 Tim 6:12 in Paul's admonition that Timothy grab on to
eternal life. This parallel helps interpret the phrase ὄντως ζωῆς, "truly life," as
eternal life, not life of this age but of the age to come. On the use of ὄντως,
"truly," see Comment on 1 Tim 5:3.

Explanation

After criticizing his opponents about their desire to be rich (6:2b–10) and encouraging Timothy (6:11–16), Paul finishes his instructions about wealth. While
the desire to be rich above all else is wrong and dangerous, the mere possession
of wealth is not inherently sinful. But those who are rich in this age must conduct
themselves in light of eschatological realities. What they have is a gift from God

given for their enjoyment; they must not be prideful. Because riches are a gift and of this age, they are uncertain and cannot bear the weight of a person's hope, which should be set on God. Those who fully realize this will turn to doing good, being rich in good deeds, in working out their Christianity in practical ways such as generously giving to others.

Believers live in an eschatological tension. They live in this age and must address themselves to the needs around them. But they also belong to the eschatological kingdom and must conduct themselves with an eye to what will be. By working out their salvation in practical ways such as sharing, they are transferring their riches to the coming age, establishing a firm foundation for them there. This is not the reason for sharing but the result. The reason for doing so, apart from recognizing one's true position in the present age as a recipient of God's gracious gifts, is the desire to grab on to life that is truly life: eschatological life, eternal life.

D. The Final Encouragement to Timothy (1 Tim 6:20–21)

Bibliography

Brun, L. *Segen und Fluch im Urchristentum.* Oslo: Dybwad, 1932. **Champion, L. G.** *Benedictions and Doxologies in the Epistles of Paul.* Oxford: Kemp Hall, 1934. **Doty, W. G.** *Letters in Primitive Christianity.* Guides to Biblical Scholarship, New Testament Series. Philadelphia: Fortress, 1973. 39–42. **Exler, F. X. J.** *The Form of the Ancient Greek Letter of the Epistolary Papyri.* Washington, DC: Catholic University of America, 1923. 69–77, 111–13. **Gamble, H. Y.** *The Textual History of the Letter to the Romans.* SD 42. Grand Rapids, MI: Eerdmans, 1977. 56–83. **Jewett, R.** "The Form and Function of the Homiletic Benediction." *ATR* 51 (1969) 18–34. **Horst, F.** "Segen und Fluch in der Bibel." *EvT* 7 (1947) 23–37. **Köster, H.** "Segen und Fluch: Im N.T." *RGG*[3] 5:1651–52. ———. "Um eine neue theologische Sprache: Gedanken zu 1 Tim 6,20." In *Wahrheit und Verkündigung.* FS M. Schmaus, ed. L. Scheffczyk, W. Dettloff, and R. Heinzmann. Munich: Paderborn; Vienna: Schoningh, 1967. 449–73. **Mullins, T. Y.** "Benediction as a New Testament Form." *AUSS* 15 (1977) 59–64. **Paramo, S. del.** "Depositum Custodi (1 Tim 6,20; 2 Tim 1,14)." *Sal Terrae* 50 (1962) 556–62. **Schlarb, E.** "Miszelle zu 1 Tim 6,20." *ZNW* 77 (1986) 276–81.

Translation

[20] *O Timothy, guard what has been entrusted* [a] *[to you], avoiding the unholy chatter* [b] *and contradictions of what is falsely named "knowledge,"* [21] *by professing which, some have departed from the faith.*

Grace [be] with you. [cde]

Notes

[a] TR reads παρακατάθηκην with no change in meaning.

ᵇA few MSS (F G lat; Irˡᵃᵗ) read καινοφωνίας, "'contemporary jargon,' unless this is simply a pho-netic variant, since in this period αι was pronounced as ε " (BAGD, 428). Bernard (91) says it was the result of itacism.

ᶜThe plural μεθ' ὑμῶν, "with you [pl.]" (ℵ A F G P 33 81 *pc* boᵐˢˢ), is replaced with the singular μετὰ σοῦ, "with you [sing.]" (D Ψ 048 1739 1881 TR lat sy boᵐˢ), because the letter appears to be written to one person. But there is good evidence that Paul wanted the letter read by the entire church, so the plural is appropriate (see *Comment*). Through accident, some versions and patristic witnesses omit the entire benediction (Lock, xxxvii; *TCGNT²*, 577).

ᵈἀμήν, "Amen," is added by some MSS (ℵ² D¹ Ψ TR 1739ᶜ TR vgᶜˡ ᵂᵂ sy bo; Ambst); this was a com-mon liturgical addition. Its omission has more textual support (ℵ* A D*F G 33 81 1739* 1881 *pc* it vgˢᵗ sa bpᵐˢˢ).

ᵉThe variants for the subscription are interesting, many of them identifying the location of writing. They reflect more tradition than fact. Some of the readings are πρὸς Τιμόθεον ᾱ, "To Timothy 1" (ℵ [D F G] Ψ 33 1739*); πρὸς Τιμόθεον ᾱ ἐγράφη ἀπὸ Λαοδικείας, "To Timothy 1, written from Laodicea" (A *pc*); πρὸς Τιμόθεον ᾱ ἐγράφη ἀπὸ Νικοπόλεως, "To Timothy 1, written from Nicopolis" (P); πρὸς Τιμόθεον πρώτη ἐγράφη ἀπὸ Λαοδικείας, ἥτις ἐστὶν μετρόπολις Φρυγίας τῆς Πακατιανῆς, "To Timothy, the first [letter], written from Laodicea, which is the capital of Phrygia Pacatiana" (TR); πρὸς Τιμόθεον ᾱ ἐγράφη ἀπὸ Μακεδονίας, "To Timothy 1, written from Macedonia" (boᵐˢ); πρὸς Τιμόθεον ᾱ ἐγράφη ἀπὸ Ἀθηνῶν διὰ Τίτου τοῦ μαθητοῦ αὐτοῦ, "To Timothy 1, written from Athens through Titus, his disciple"(boᵐˢ). Cf. *TCGNT²*, 577–78, and the *Introduction* for the question of location of writing.

Form/Structure/Setting

This conclusion may not sound as grand to some as the doxology in vv 15–16, but it provides a fitting end to the letter, making mention of the two primary themes in the PE: a call to personal perseverance and an attack on the Ephesian opponents. Positively, Timothy must guard the gospel that has been entrusted to him, and negatively, he must avoid the chatter of the opponents.

This section is shorter than most of Paul's conclusions, but the doxology in vv 15–16 may have reduced the need for a longer good-bye. It contains no real greet-ing, but this may attest to the urgency of the situation and the fact that Paul expected the Ephesian church to read it. Interestingly, the greeting also lacks Paul's usual words of encouragement and thankfulness. As Fee (162) points out, these omis-sions are also found in Galatians, and in both situations the problem was severe and required immediate action. Although there are a few significant and personal moments between Paul and Timothy, most of the epistle is "all business."

Paul always ends his letters with a benediction, usually some form of "may the grace of (our) Lord Jesus (Christ) (be with you)" (see *Comment*). Champion or-ganizes the benedictions into three groups: those at the opening of the letter, those at the closing, and those within the context of the letter. He describes the order as wish–divine source–recipient, allowing for variations, and sees its origin in the LXX and the synagogue. Jewett sees its origin in some portion of early Christian worship such as the sermon (*ATR* 51 [1969] 18–34). The usual ending in secular letters is ἔρρωσο, "Farewell" (cf. *v.l.* in Acts 23:30; cf. also ἔρρωσθε in Acts 15:29 and in Ignatius' letters).

Comment

20a Ὦ Τιμόθεε, τὴν παραθήκην φύλαξον, "O Timothy, guard what has been en-trusted [to you]." This is the fourth personal charge in the PE exhorting Timothy to persevere (cf. 1 Tim 1:18; 4:1–16; 6:11–16). It is the second time that Paul has called him tò guard what has been entrusted to him (1 Tim 1:18), a call that will be repeated at 2 Tim 1:14 and is similar to the summary calls to action peppered throughout the corpus (cf. 1 Tim 4:11). παραθήκη, "what has been entrusted," a "deposit," refers to valuable property entrusted to a person for safe keeping (cf. *Comments* on 2 Tim 1:12 and 1 Tim 1:18). In the PE it is always used in conjunction with φυλάσσειν, "to guard" (cf. 1 Tim 1:18; 2 Tim 1:14). Because this charge occurs in the conclusion to the epistle, παραθήκη refers at least to the epistle (and perhaps to the gospel and Timothy's ministry as a whole), which can be summed up, as it is in these two verses, as a call to guarding the truth of the gospel and avoiding the empty chatter of the heresy. It is somewhat analogous to the ἐντολή, "command-ment," in v 14 and synonymous with the concepts of ἡ πίστις, "the faith," and ἡ ἀλήθεια, "the truth," that play an important role in the PE. For the use of the inter-jection Ὦ, "O," cf. *Comment* on 1 Tim 6:11. The aorist φύλαξον, "guard," calls for immediate action (cf. shift of aspect in ἐκτρεπόμενος, "avoiding," below).

20b ἐκτρεπόμενος τὰς βεβήλους κενοφωνίας καὶ ἀντιθέσεις τῆς ψευδωνύμου γνώσεως, "avoiding the unholy chatter and contradictions of what is falsely named 'knowledge.'" In contrast to Paul's instruction to Timothy to guard the deposit, he now tells Timothy to avoid the teaching of the opponents. This teaching has nothing to do with God, is void of content, and is not what it seems, perhaps bearing a resemblance to knowledge but lacking any substance. This description of the opponents' teaching is similar to that in 1 Tim 1:6–7: the opponents are teaching babble, words without meaning, and speculations. It is no wonder that Paul had to deal more with the opponents' behavior than with their teachings (cf. *Introduction*, "The Ephesian Heresy"). Chrysostom comments, "for where there is not faith, there is not knowledge" ("Homily 18"; NPNF 13:472), and as Paul has hinted earlier, the opponents probably downplayed faith (cf. *Form/Structure/Setting* on 1 Tim 1:3–7 and 12–17).

ἐκτρεπόμενος, "avoiding," modifies Τιμόθεε, "Timothy," and bears the force of an imperative, paralleling φύλαξον, "guard!" (cf. 1 Tim 1:6 for the word). The change of tense is probably significant: Timothy must set his mind to guard the truth (aorist), which means that every day he must avoid (continuous) the godless chatter of the opponents. βέβηλος, "unholy," "profane," is a common description of the heresy (cf. 1 Tim 1:9). Because the article is not repeated before ἀντιθέσεις, "contradic-tions," βεβήλους, "unholy," modifies both κενοφωνίας, "chatter," and ἀντιθέσεις, "contradictions." κενοφωνία, "chatter," occurs elsewhere in the NT only in a similar description of the heresy in 2 Tim 2:16 in an identical phrase, βεβήλους κενοφωνίας, "unholy chatter," but it is roughly equivalent to other descriptions such as ματαιολογία, "senseless babble" (1 Tim 1:6; cf. BAGD, 428), γραώδης μύθους, "silly [old wives'] tales" (1 Tim 4:7), and λογομαχία, "fight about words" (1 Tim 6:4).

ἀντίθεσις, "contradiction," occurs only here in the NT. It is a technical term in debate for the counter proposition (Kelly, 151) and describes the heresy as self-defeating. It "crystallizes what Paul says elsewhere concerning the false teaching and those who are involved in it" (Knight, 277). Hort suggests that the word de-scribes "the endless contrasts of decisions, founded on endless distinctions, which played so large a part in the casuistry of the Scribes as interpreters of the Law. It would thus designate frivolities of what was called the Halacha" (*Judaistic Christian-ity*, 140). It (in the pl. form) is the title of Marcion's work (A.D. 150) in which he argues for the contradictions between the Jewish OT and the gospel message of

Jesus. In years past it was said that this verse was directed toward Marcion (Baur, *Pastoralbriefe,* 26–27; von Harnack, *Marcion,* 150–51; Bauer, *Orthodoxy,* 229; Easton, 170), but this view is rightly rejected today. It puts much too late a date on the PE (Easton says the one verse is an interpolation, with no textual support), and there is no discussion of typically Marcionite themes in the PE. The occurrence of the word may account for the omission of the PE from Marcion's canon (see *Introduction,* "Historical Reconstruction from Early Church Tradition"; Schlarb, *ZNW* 77 [1986] 276–81).

Paul continues by describing the heresy as τῆς ψευδωνύμου γνώσεως, "falsely named 'knowledge.'" Those holding to a later date for the PE and viewing the heresy as primarily Gnostic see in this word validation for their approach. While there is no doubt that Hellenistic thought played a role in the Ephesian heresy, there is nothing in the PE that gives evidence of second-century Gnosticism (see *Introduction,* "The Ephesian Heresy"), and the misuse of wisdom was already prevalent in Paul's day (1 Cor 1:10–4:21; 8:1–13; Col 2:1–10). This is also the only occurrence of γνῶσις, "knowledge," in the PE, which occurs only here at the next to last verse, an unexpected location if in fact the Gnostic teaching on knowledge is in view. Hort compares it to the Jewish scribes, often termed the wise ones, who had taken away the key of knowledge (Luke 11:52; cf. Rom 2:20–21; *Judaistic Christianity,* 141–43). γνῶσις occurs twenty-two times elsewhere in Paul; the characterization of a knowledge as something that puffs up (ἡ γνῶσις φυσιοῖ; 1 Cor 8:1) and as incomplete (1 Cor 8:2) sounds similar to the babbling of the Ephesian opponents (although the specifics of the content varies), who were arrogant and knew nothing (1 Tim 1:7) and whose "knowledge" was falsely named (1 Tim 6:20). The context defines the "knowledge" as being "unholy chatter and contradictions." Towner goes further by comparing this passage to 2 Tim 2:15–18, and on the basis of the similarities he includes the opponents' teaching on the resurrection as part of their esoteric knowledge (*JSNT* 31 [1987] 103–7; id., *Goal,* 29–33). Their "knowledge" had spiritualized the resurrection and claimed the benefits of the eschatological age for the present. ψευδώνυμος, "falsely named," occurs only here in the NT and carries its etymological meaning of ψευδής, "false," and ὄνομα, "name." "Knowledge" possibly mimics the opponents' terminology; they called their instruction "knowledge" (Roloff, 374).

21a ἥν τινες ἐπαγγελλόμενοι περὶ τὴν πίστιν ἠστόχησαν, "by professing which, some have departed from the faith." Repeating the same thought as in 1 Tim 1:6, Paul describes his opponents as people who were once part of the church but left because of their profession of this so-called knowledge. The attack comes from within the church and not from without. On referring to the opponents with the indefinite τινές, "some," see *Comment* on 1 Tim 1:3. ἐπαγγελλόμενοι, "professing," is instrumental, describing the means by which the people were removed from the church (see 1 Tim 2:10 for the verb). On ἀστοχεῖν, "to depart, fall short," see *Comment* on 1 Tim 1:6; on the creedal use of πίστις, "faith," see *Introduction,* "Themes in the PE"; and for why περὶ τὴν πίστιν, "from the faith," goes with ἠστόχησαν, "have departed," and not with ἐπαγγελλόμενοι, "professing," see *Comment* on 1 Tim 1:19.

21b Ἡ χάρις μεθ' ὑμῶν, "Grace [be] with you." It is usual for Paul to end with the word χάρις, "grace" (2 Cor 13:14; Gal 6:18; Eph 6:24; cf. Heb 13:25; Rev 22:21). He uses this same formula in 2 Tim 4:22 (but see variants) and Col 4:18, and a similar but lengthened form elsewhere (Titus 3:15; cf. Rom 16:20; 1 Cor 16:23; Phil 4:23; 1 Thess 5:28; 2 Thess 3:18; Phlm 25). In all of Paul's benedictions, χάρις is always articular, ἡ χάρις, "the grace," and he often adds "of (our) Lord Jesus (Christ)" (Rom 16:20; 1 Cor 16:23; 2 Cor 13:13; Gal 6:18; Eph 6:24; Phil 4:23; 1 Thess 5:28; 2 Thess 3:18; Phlm 3; not in Col 4:18; 2 Tim 4:22; Titus 3:15; cf. Quinn, 270, on the grace being from God). Greek often uses the article with abstract nouns, or the article here may be referring to the specific grace of Jesus. On the word χάρις, see *Comment* on 1 Tim 1:2. The usual Greek ending was ἔρρωσο or ἔρρωσθε, "be strong" (cf. Acts 15:29; Ignatius). The switch from the secular "be strong" to "(God's) grace" is perhaps a recognition on Paul's part that true strength comes only from the Lord (cf. 1 Tim 1:12–17; 2 Cor 12:9–10). The problem of the verse is that ὑμῶν, "you," is plural as it is in 2 Tim 4:22 and Titus 3:15. Several suggestions have been offered. (1) This is a horribly careless blunder on the part of a pseudepigrapher. However, it has been argued above (see *Introduction,* "Proposals regarding Authorship of the PE") that this is a self-defeating proposition in light of the supposed cleverness of the pseudepigrapher elsewhere. (2) Although Paul has written to Timothy, he intends the letter to be read to the church as a whole. This has been evident throughout the epistle and explains why much of 1 Timothy is directed not so much toward a trusted and informed coworker as to the troublesome Ephesian church (cf. *Introduction,* "Historical Reconstruction from the PE"). (3) Guthrie (119) argues that the papyri show evidence that one could conclude a letter to a single person with the plural. (4) Ellicott (100) thinks the plural pertains only to the benediction.

Explanation

Paul ends his first letter to Timothy by repeating the two main themes of the epistle. (1) Timothy must persevere and watch out for himself. He has been entrusted with the gospel and must guard it zealously. As Kelly says, "the Christian message . . . is not something which the church's minister works out for himself or is entitled to add to; it is a divine revelation which has been committed to his care, and which it is his bounden duty to pass on unimpaired to others" (152). This is not a wooden orthodoxy of a later century but a call for doctrinal purity, of teaching only what is true. (2) Timothy must also avoid the teaching of the opponents, which has nothing to do with God; it is mere babble and contradictions. It may bear the name of "knowledge," but it is not. Because Paul's opponents have professed this knowledge and this teaching, they have left the Christian faith. Paul then invokes God's grace on Timothy as he carries out the injunctions of this letter.

Titus

I. Salutation (Titus 1:1–4)

Bibliography

Metzger, B. M. "A Hitherto Neglected Early Fragment of the Epistle to Titus." *NovT* 1 (1956) 149–50.

On epistolary salutations, see *Bibliography* for 1 Tim 1:1–2.

Translation

[1] *Paul, a servant of God and an apostle of Jesus Christ,[a] for [the] faith of [the] elect of God and [the] knowledge of [the] truth that produces godliness,* [2] *for[b] the sake of the hope of eternal life, which the God who does not lie promised before times eternal,* [3] *but he revealed his word at the proper time in the proclamation, [with] which I was entrusted by the command of God our savior.* [4] *To Titus, a true son in a common faith.*
Grace and[c] peace from God [the] Father and Christ Jesus[d] our savior.

Notes

Metzger discusses a fifth-century transcription of Titus 1:4–6, 7–9 mentioned by G. Tseret'eli ("Un palimpseste grec du Vᵉ siècle sur parchemin [Epist. ad Fit (sic) 1. 4–6, 7–9]" *Bulletin de l'académie royale de Belgique* 18 [1932] 427–32). Sinaiticus is the only older MS (*NovT* 1 [1956] 149–50).

[a] The order of Ἰησοῦ Χριστοῦ, "Jesus Christ," is reversed by A 629 1175 a b vg^ms^ sy^h^; Ambst. D* omits Ἰησοῦ, "Jesus." Cf. Ellicott, 166.

[b] ἐπί, "for the sake of," is replaced with ἐν, "in," by F G H 365 *pc*. ἐπί is omitted in 33 *pc*.

[c] In an attempt to conform this greeting to those in 1 and 2 Timothy, some MSS include ἔλεος, "mercy." χάρις, ἔλεος, εἰρήνη, "grace, mercy, peace," is read by A C² sy^h^ bo^ms^. ὑμῖν, "to you," is inserted after χάρις, "grace," in 33. καί, "and," is omitted by 1739 1881 *pc* and is read by ℵ C* D F G P Ψ 088 365 629 1175 *pc* latt sy^p^ co; Chr. See *TCGNT*², 584.

[d] In typical fashion, some MSS enlarge the name of Jesus to κυρίου Ἰησοῦ Χριστοῦ, "Lord Jesus Christ" (-1175) D² F G TR sy. Our text is supported by ℵ A C D* Ψ 088 0240 33 81 365 629 *pc* lat; Ambst. The order is reversed in 1739 1881.

Form/Structure/Setting

See *Form/Structure/Setting* on 1 Tim 1:1–2 for a discussion of salutations in the PE, Paul's writings, and secular literature. The salutation to Titus follows the usual format: author, to recipient, greeting. As is typical of Paul, he has enlarged the first part of the greeting by describing the purpose of his apostleship. He is a servant of God and an apostle of Jesus Christ; his service is to bring the elect to faith, to an understanding of the gospel, and to godly living; his apostleship is to proclaim the Christian hope, which is part of God's eternal plan now made known through the proclamation of the gospel.

The salutation includes references to the major themes of the epistle. (1) Paul is the authoritative proclaimer of the gospel message, entrusted by the command of God; Titus is his legitimate spiritual son, bound together with him in a common faith. Although the issue of Paul's authority is not as central to the Cretan problem as it was in Ephesus, it is nonetheless present. (2) A believing response to the message of the gospel includes not only a full understanding of the content of the gospel but also godly behavior, a life fully consecrated to God (v 1b). (3) The salutation shows a high view of Christ as Paul pairs him with God in typical fashion. Paul is a servant of God and an apostle of Jesus Christ (v 1). Both God and Christ act as savior (vv 3–4), and both together grant grace and peace (v 4b; see *Comment*).

Comment

1a Παῦλος δοῦλος θεοῦ, "Paul, a servant of God." Paul introduces himself as God's δοῦλος, "servant" (δοῦλος also means "slave"). See *Comment* on 1 Tim 1:1–2 for a comparison of the different salutations in Paul's letters.

Slavery was widespread in the ancient world, and slaves were property with no freedom or rights. Why then do Paul and others use the term so frequently in a positive sense (cf. Quinn, 188–89, 204)? Part of the answer may lie in Paul's understanding of the power of sin. All people are in slavery to sin (cf. Rom 6:16; Gal 4:3, 8–9; Titus 3:3; cf. John 8:34) without choice. But once redeemed, they joyously become slaves of God (Rom 6:15–18, 20–23; 8:15; 1 Cor 7:22; Gal 4:4–5; cf. John 15:15) and are employed in his service (cf. K. H. Rengstorf, *TDNT* 2:273–77). "Slave of Christ" came to be a common designation. Paul uses it of himself (Rom 1:1; Gal 1:10; Phil 1:1, the first and last being in salutations), of Epaphras (Col 4:12), and of Timothy (2 Tim 2:24). Twice Paul says that Christians should behave as "slaves of Christ" (1 Cor 7:22; Eph 6:6). In the salutations in James, Jude, and 2 Peter, the authors use the same terminology of themselves. δοῦλοι, "slaves," is used elsewhere of all Christians (1 Pet 2:16) and especially in Revelation of the Christian prophets (Rev 1:1; 10:7; 11:18) and all Christians (Rev 7:3; 19:15; 22:3; cf. R. H. Mounce, *The Book of Revelation*, NICNT [Grand Rapids, MI: Eerdmans, 1977] 65). Elsewhere Paul calls himself and others a slave "of Christ" and not "of God" as he does here. The change may not be significant. Paul's expressions elsewhere show sufficient variety that a shift from God to Christ may not have been purposeful. It may have been a literary device to avoid repetition with the following phrase, "an apostle of Jesus Christ." However, "slave of God" is frequent in the OT as a designation for special people, including Abraham (Ps 105:42), Moses (Num 12:7; Neh 9:14; cf. Rev 15:3; Josephus *Ant.* 5.1.13 §39), David (Ps 89:3), Daniel (Dan 6:20), and the prophets (Jer 25:4; Ezek 38:17; Amos 3:7; Zech 1:6; cf. Quinn, 60–62). The shift from "of Christ" to "of God" may reflect Paul's appraisal of himself as a continuation of this OT theme (cf. R. F. Collins, "Image of Paul," *LTP* 31 [1975] 149; Hawthorne, *Philippians*, 4–5) and shows that "slave" was an honorific title, that he along with Abraham and others have a special relationship with God, and that he not only bore the responsibility of service to God ("slave") but also spoke with his master's authority ("servant"). The idea of "God's slave" being a positive title is similar to the idea of the yoke of the law being good (cf. 1 Tim 6:1).

1b ἀπόστολος δὲ Ἰησοῦ Χριστοῦ, "and an apostle of Jesus Christ." Paul writes as an authoritative messenger from Christ. Both δοῦλος, "servant," and ἀπόστολος, "apostle," carry a note of authority, although less pronounced than in the salutation to 1 Timothy (see there for discussion). The situation in Crete was different from that in Ephesus, and the issue of Paul's and Titus's authority was not so much in question. δέ, "and," is continuative, not adversative, and carries the meaning "and furthermore" (Bernard, 155), narrowing Paul's relationship from God's servant specifically to that of apostle. On ἀπόστολος, "apostle," see *Comment* on 1 Tim 1:1. On the order "Jesus Christ," see *Note* a.

1c κατὰ πίστιν ἐκλεκτῶν θεοῦ καὶ ἐπίγνωσιν ἀληθείας τῆς κατ' εὐσέβειαν, "for [the] faith of [the] elect of God and [the] knowledge of [the] truth that produces godliness." The main question is the precise meaning of the two occurrences of κατά, assuming there is a precise meaning. (1) The word can mean "in accordance with," in which case πίστις, "faith," is used in its creedal sense as a set of beliefs. But the anarthrous πίστις normally carries the subjective meaning of a believing response (see *Introduction*, "Themes in the PE"). More significantly, Paul's apostleship is not dependent upon the teaching of the church, regardless of the issue of authorship. (2) κατά therefore indicates purpose (cf. the following parallel use of ἐπί, "for the sake of"), and πίστις is the response of believers (Spicq, 2:592–93). The purpose for Paul's apostleship is to bring God's elect to faith. Similar is Paul's comment about his conversion where he says that he received mercy in order to be an example for all who will believe (1 Tim 1:16). Hidden away in this verse is the trilogy of faith, the intellectual understanding of the faith ("knowledge of the truth"), and the proper behavior that must come forth from faith ("godliness"). All three members of the trilogy are necessary elements in Christianity and constitute the goal of Paul's apostleship.

ἐκλεκτός, "elect," is a common description of Israel in the OT (1 Chr 16:13; Ps 105:6, 43; Isa 43:20; 45:4; 65:9, 15, 23; cf. 1QS 8:6; 1QH 2:13; cf. Quinn, 53–54) and continues to be used of believers in the NT (Matt 22:14; 24:22, 24, 31; Mark 3:20, 22, 27; Luke 18:7; Rom 8:33; Col 3:12; 1 Pet 1:1; 2:9; 2 John 1, 13; Rev 17:14; cf. Rom 16:13). It is used elsewhere in the PE of Christians (2 Tim 2:10) and of the elect angels who witness Timothy's activities (1 Tim 5:21). It continues the Pauline theme that the righteous remnant, the true people of God, comprises those who have faith (Rom 2:25–29), a theme significant in light of the Jewish nature of the problem in Crete (cf. Titus 1:10).

Paul's apostleship is not only for the faith of the believer but also for the understanding of the truth. ἐπίγνωσις, "knowledge," is not only intellectual apprehension but also a fullness of understanding, in this context the type of understanding that results from experience (cf. εὐσέβεια, "godliness," below). ἀλήθεια, "truth," is a technical term in the PE for the gospel, emphasizing the need to understand the content of the preached message. This balances the more subjective πίστις, "faith," while preparing the reader for the experiential element that follows. It also provides a contrast with the erroneous Cretan teaching that Paul is about to discuss (vv 9–16). ἐπίγνωσιν ἀληθείας, "knowledge of the truth," is a common phrase in the PE (cf. 1 Tim 2:4).

The final phrase, τῆς κατ' εὐσέβειαν, "that produces godliness," is difficult to translate because of the ambiguity of κατά. It defines the nature of the truth by saying either that the truth of the gospel is "in accordance with" godliness or that the purpose of the truth is "to produce" godliness. The latter repeats one of the more common themes in the PE, that right belief and right behavior are inseparable. As Bernard notes, "It is only in the life of godliness . . . that the 'knowledge of the truth' can be fully learnt" (155). This reference to godliness completes the trilogy of the verse. The goal of Paul's apostleship is the personal response of faith, a faith based on an accurate knowledge of the truth of the gospel, and a faith that naturally and necessarily shows itself in godly behavior. Paul has encapsulated his answer to the problem of the PE, felt more emphatically in Ephesus but also present in Crete, that Christianity is based on the truth of the gospel and demands the response of faith lived out in a godly life. While there are many similarities between 1 Timothy and Titus, Titus is more concerned with the basic ingredients of Christianity (e.g., faith and obedience; cf. *Introduction*, "Historical Reconstruction from the PE"), and the emphasis on the basics is highlighted from the beginning of the epistle. εὐσέβεια, "godliness," is a technical term in the PE for the total commitment of one's life to God with emphasis on the practical outworking of that faith (cf. 1 Tim 2:2).

2a ἐπ᾽ ἐλπίδι ζωῆς αἰωνίου, "for the sake of the hope of eternal life." ἐπί, "for the sake of," could modify ἀπόστολος, "apostle," and be parallel with the κατὰ πίστιν, "for [the] faith," phrase, or it could modify πίστιν, "faith," and ἐπίγνωσιν, "knowledge." Related to this is the question of its precise meaning. It can designate "that upon which a state of being, an action, or a result is based" (BAGD, 287; cf. especially the phrase ἐπ᾽ ἐλπίδι, "in hope," in Acts 2:26; 26:6; Rom 4:18; 8:20; 1 Cor 9:10), or it can describe purpose, goal, or result (cf. Gal 5:13; Eph 2:10; 1 Thess 4:7; 2 Tim 2:14). However, the hope of eternal life is not the basis of Paul's apostolic ministry (cf. 1 Tim 1:12–17). If it denotes purpose, ἐπί is parallel to κατά and spells out a second purpose of Paul's call to apostolic ministry. Paul is an apostle "for the sake of" (κατά) the faith of believers, for the gospel and its practical implications, and "for" (ἐπί) instilling the hope of eternal life. The variation of prepositions would be merely stylistic. ἐλπίς, "hope," is the confident anticipation of what the believer knows is to come (cf. 1 Tim 4:10). ζωή, "life," is more than physical existence; it is a fullness of life available now through Christ, which reaches its climax on the other side of the Lord's return (cf. 1 Tim 1:16). In the salutation to 2 Timothy Paul says that his apostolic ministry is "according to the promise of life that is in Christ Jesus" (2 Tim 1:1).

2b ἣν ἐπηγγείλατο ὁ ἀψευδὴς θεὸς πρὸ χρόνων αἰωνίων, "which the God who does not lie promised before times eternal." Paul follows with two descriptions of the Christian hope, both balancing each other and showing why the Christian hope is secure. The first is that before time, in the eternal purposes of God, God promised that it would be so. Paul's second reason (v 3a) will be that what was promised has now been revealed in the proclamation of the gospel. This eschatological contrast between the eternal purposes of God and their present fulfillment is a common Pauline theme and can be found throughout his writings (Rom 16:25–26; 1 Cor 2:6–10; Eph 1:9–10; 3:7–11; Col 1:25–27; 2 Tim 1:9–10; cf. Gal 4:4; Eph 1:4; cf. 1 Pet 1:20).

ἀψευδής, "who does not lie, truthful," is a compound of an alpha privative and ψευδής, "false, lying," hence "unlying, truthful, trustworthy" (BAGD, 129). It emphasizes the assuredness of the promise based on the character of God. It occurs only here in the NT but is always used of God in early Christian literature (cf. *Mart. Pol.* 14:2; Ignatius *Rom.* 8.2). The concept however is not unusual (Num 23:19; Wis 7:17; Rom 3:4; Heb 6:18). On ἐπαγγέλλεσθαι, "to promise," see *Comment* on 1 Tim 2:10. πρὸ χρόνων αἰωνίων, "before times eternal" (cf. Rom 16:25; 1

Cor 2:7; 2 Tim 1:9; cf. Acts 7:17; also Eph 1:4; the idiom is evidently plural), could refer to the time period of the OT (Brox, 280–81), in which case this verse would be parallel to Rom 1:2–4. Hanson ([1983] 170, following Hasler) introduces the foreign idea of salvation belonging "to the timeless eternal world" and also ignores the temporal context established by the next verse. In 2 Tim 1:9 the same phrase clearly refers to God's purposes before time but now made manifest, and this best fits the context here and conforms to the same idea in Paul (Bernard, Guthrie, Fee; see references above).

3a ἐφανέρωσεν δὲ καιροῖς ἰδίοις τὸν λόγον αὐτοῦ ἐν κηρύγματι, "but he revealed his word at the proper time in the proclamation." The second reason the Christian hope is sure is that not only was it promised by God but it has now been revealed in the proclamation of the gospel (cf. Quinn, 67, who fails to see the flow of thought, which he says "snaps" here). The grammar of the phrase in its relationship to the preceding relative clause is awkward, but its sense is clear. δέ, "but," establishes the temporal contrast between the two phrases. On φανεροῦν, "to reveal," see *Comment* on 1 Tim 3:16. καιροῖς ἰδίοις means "at the proper time," the time when God deemed it best (cf. 1 Tim 2:6 and discussion in Lock, 126). The classical distinction is that καιρός refers to a time period (cf. Rom 5:6; Gal 6:10) and χρόνος to a duration of time. Paul can distinguish between the two (1 Thess 5:1; cf. Mark 10:30; Luke 18:30), and the distinction is appropriate in this context where the two terms are in contrast. The plural is probably idiomatic (but cf. Lock, 126; Guthrie, 182). For a summary of the discussion between J. Barr and O. Cullmann on time, see Quinn, 65–66. The λόγον, "word," is the gospel (cf. 1 Tim 4:5), λόγον functioning grammatically as the direct object of ἐφανέρωσεν, "he revealed," and contextually as the content of the proclamation. κήρυγμα, "proclamation," and its cognate verb κηρύσσειν, "to proclaim," occur three other times in the PE. Paul quotes a hymn that speaks of the proclamation of the work of Christ among the nations (1 Tim 3:16), urges Timothy to preach the word (κήρυξον τὸν λόγον; 2 Tim 4:2), and credits the Lord for strengthening him so that the proclamation could be completed (ἵνα δι' ἐμοῦ τὸ κήρυγμα πληροφορηθῇ; 2 Tim 4:17). The word group primarily refers to the act of proclamation, but in the NT its content is almost always the gospel (cf. discussion of κῆρυξ, "herald," in *Comment* on 1 Tim 2:7; G. Friedrich, *TDNT* 3:683–718).

3b ὃ ἐπιστεύθην ἐγὼ κατ' ἐπιταγὴν τοῦ σωτῆρος ἡμῶν θεοῦ, "[with] which I was entrusted by the command of God our savior." The proclamation of this gospel, which has now been made known, was entrusted to Paul in accordance with the authoritative command of God who provides true salvation. Although the heresy was not as intense in Crete as it was in Ephesus, it was nonetheless present and receives comment from the beginning of the epistle. Paul's opponents may have been questioning his apostolic ministry and authority, but Paul carries divine authority (cf. 1 Tim 1:1, 12–17; on Paul's entrustment of the gospel, cf. *Comment* on 1 Tim 1:11; 2:7). He did not on his own decide to become an apostle but was commanded to accept the role. ἐπιταγή, "command," is a strong word, and the phrase κατὰ ἐπιταγήν, "by the command," is possibly a technical term meaning "by order of" (cf. 1 Tim 1:1). On σωτήρ, "savior," see *Introduction*, "Themes in the PE." Two of the dominant passages in Titus deal specifically with salvation (2:11–14; 3:3–8).

4a Τίτῳ γνησίῳ τέκνῳ κατὰ κοινὴν πίστιν, "To Titus, a true son in a common faith." In the second part of the salutation, Paul greets Titus in language similar to his address of Timothy, his γνησίῳ τέκνῳ ἐν πίστει, "true spiritual son" (1 Tim 1:2), his ἀγαπητῷ τέκνῳ, "beloved son" (2 Tim 1:2). See *Comment* on 1 Tim 1:2 for discussion. γνήσιος means "legitimate," carrying the notions of intimacy and authority. It could be that Titus was converted by Paul (Jeremias; Kelly; cf. Gal 2:1–3; *Introduction,* "The PE within the Framework of Paul's Life, Historical Reconstruction from Acts"), but it cannot be known for sure. κοινήν, "common," suggests to some that πίστιν, "faith," is used here in the sense of orthodoxy (cf. "common salvation" in Jude 3). But to others it has the usual Pauline sense of a believing response that binds Paul the Jew and Titus the Gentile together, a significant point in light of the Jewish nature of the heresy being taught in Crete (cf. 1:10, 14; on πίστις, "faith," cf. *Introduction,* "Themes in the PE"). It also shows that while Titus may have been Paul's spiritual son, they were both on equal footing in the arena of faith (so Chrysostom, "Homily 1"; NPNF 13:521–22). While Paul expected this letter to be read by the church as well (cf. especially 3:15), the salutation clearly designates the recipient as an individual, and the epistle asks to be interpreted primarily within that context.

4b χάρις καὶ εἰρήνη ἀπὸ θεοῦ πατρὸς καὶ Χριστοῦ Ἰησοῦ τοῦ σωτῆρος ἡμῶν, "Grace and peace from God [the] Father and Christ Jesus our savior." The third part of the salutation follows Paul's usual Christianized greeting. See *Comment* on 1 Tim 1:2 for a discussion of this phrase. Unlike the two letters to Timothy, Paul omits any reference to mercy. Hanson states that the "indiscriminate" application of σωτήρ, "savior," to either God or Christ shows "a rather muddled soteriology" ([1983] 171). Quite the contrary. The author's willingness to apply it to either God or Christ is calculated. As Kelly (229) points out, in the three places in Titus where Paul speaks of Christ as savior (Titus 1:4; 2:13; 3:6), Paul has just finished speaking of God and salvation (Titus 1:3; 2:11; 3:4; cf. 1 Tim 2:3–6). God and Christ work hand in hand in the process of salvation (see *Introduction,* "Themes in the PE"). This practice may account for the unique phrase "Christ Jesus our savior," which has no exact counterpart elsewhere in Paul (cf. 2 Tim 1:10; Titus 2:13; 3:6; cf. Phil 3:20; 2 Pet 1:1, 11; 2:20; 3:18) even though the idea is not unusual. Having called God σωτῆρος ἡμῶν, "our savior" (v 3), Paul wants to continue the comparison and replaces the usual "Christ Jesus our Lord" with "Christ Jesus our savior." The single preposition ἀπό, "from," governs both θεοῦ, "God," and Χριστοῦ, "Christ," and is common in Paul's writings, attesting to his high Christology (cf. 1 Tim 1:2).

Explanation

Paul begins his letter to Titus in usual fashion. He identifies himself as both a servant of God and an apostle of Jesus Christ and then enlarges on the purpose of his apostleship. His apostleship is to bring about the faith of the elect, to teach the content of the gospel and the necessity of living a life of godliness (a significant emphasis in the letter), and for sharing the certain hope of the gospel, which is eternal life. This gospel is part of God's eternal plan and now has been revealed in the proclamation of the gospel. Although Paul's authority was not in question in Crete to the degree that it was in Ephesus, he does address the issue. As God's servant, he not only is enslaved to God's service but also speaks as his servant. He is Jesus' apostle, sent with his mission and with his authority. Paul's proclamation of the gospel was entrusted to him by the authoritative command of God. Titus is his official representative to Crete, his true son who shares a common faith. Throughout the salutation Paul's high view of Christ and his relationship to God are apparent. Paul is God's slave and Christ's apostle. Both God and Christ are the savior, and both God and Christ together grant grace and peace. Although this theology is common in salutations, it will be shown that it addresses specific issues in Crete, where Titus was dealing with a Jewish influence that most likely downplayed Christ (cf. 1:10).

II. Qualities Necessary for Church Leadership (Titus 1:5–9)

Bibliography

For bibliography on virtue and vice lists, see *Bibliography* for 1 Tim 1:8–11. For bibliography on "overseers," "elders," and "presbyters," see *Bibliography* for 1 Tim 3:1–7 and for 1 Tim 5:17–25.

Translation

⁵*For this reason I left* ᵃ *you in Crete, in order that you might put right* ᵇ *the remaining things and appoint elders in every city, as I commanded you,* ⁶*if anyone is above reproach, a "one-woman" man, having believing children, not able to be accused of debauchery or rebellious.* ⁷*For it is necessary for an overseer to be above reproach as a steward of God, not arrogant, not quick-tempered, not a drunkard, not violent, not greedy for gain,* ⁸*but hospitable, loving what is good, self-controlled, just, holy, disciplined,* ⁹*holding fast to the trustworthy word that is in accordance with the teaching, in order that he might be able both to exhort with healthy doctrine* ᶜ *and to rebuke those who oppose [it].* ᵈ

Notes

ᵃThe aorist ἀπέλιπον, "I left" (ℵ* D* Ψ 81 365 1505 1739 1881 *pc*), is replaced by the imperfect ἀπέλειπον, "I was leaving" (A C F G 088 0240 33 1175 *pc*). Other MSS replace it with the more common κατέλιπον, "I left" (ℵ² D² TR), or the imperfect κατέλειπον, "I was leaving" (L P 104 326 *al*).

ᵇThe middle ἐπιδιορθώσῃ, "you might put right" (ℵ C D² 088 0240 33 1739 TR), is replaced with the active ἐπιδιορθώσῃς (A [D* F G] Ψ 1881 *pc*) with no change in meaning except that the middle may suggest that the burden is on Titus to set things right. Bernard (154) suggests that the variant is the result of assimilation to the following καταστήσῃς, "you might appoint." Cf. discussion by Ellicott (170) and Quinn (77–78).

ᶜA replaces ἐν τῇ διδασκαλίᾳ τῇ ὑγιαινούσῃ, "with healthy doctrine," with τοὺς ἐν πάσῃ θλίψει, "those in every affliction," which is reminiscent of 2 Cor 1:4.

ᵈThe minuscule 460 (a thirteenth-century trilingual MS [Greek, Latin, Arabic]) adds the following after v 9: μὴ χειροτονεῖν διγάμους μηδὲ διακόνους αὐτοὺς ποιεῖν μηδὲ γυναῖκας ἔχειν ἐκ διγαμίας· μηδὲ προσερχέσθωσαν ἐν τῷ θυσιαστηρίῳ λειτουργεῖν τὸ θεῖον. τοὺς ἄρχοντας τοὺς ἀδικοκρίτας καὶ ἅρπαγας καὶ ψεύστας καὶ ἀνελεήμονας ἔλεγχε ὡς θεοῦ διάκονος, "Do not appoint [those who have been] married twice, nor make them deacons, nor [those who] have wives from a second marriage; neither let them approach the altar for divine service. The rulers who are unjust judges and robbers and liars and merciless you should rebuke as a servant of God." The same MS has another major addition to v 11. This is typical of the early church's view, but it is foreign to Paul; see *Explanation* on 1 Tim 3:1–7. Cf. *TCGNT²*, 584.

Form/Structure/Setting

Paul begins the body of this epistle in much the same way as he does 1 Timothy. There are no usual words of thanksgiving, but he launches directly into the business at hand. Like 1 Timothy, this epistle is more official than personal, although it needs to be interpreted in light of the fact that it is addressed to an individual who is a close associate of Paul. In the PE, only 2 Timothy is overtly personal, although there are snippets of personal material throughout 1 Timothy. Paul and Titus possibly had a missionary tour through Crete after Paul's release from the first Roman imprisonment (see *Comment* on v 5 and *Introduction*, "Historical Reconstruction from the PE"), but Paul left before he was able to set the Cretan church in order. So Titus stayed to finish the task, which included the appointment of overseers. Titus's job was twofold: to complete the organization of the church in Crete and to preserve it from doctrinal contamination, the former being the first step toward the latter (Spicq, 2:600).

The list of qualifications is similar to those in 1 Tim 3. See *Form/Structure/Setting* there for a discussion. Paul is realistic in his expectations of the Cretan church, which was still young and existed in a culture Paul describes as full of liars, evil beasts, and lazy gluttons (1:12). At a minimum he wants them to live up to basic standards, and the emphasis is on observable, moral behavior, including the distinctly Christian virtues of holiness and adherence to the gospel. The terminology is rare for Paul as would be expected of vice and virtue lists that are Hellenistic in orientation, speaking to the church in language they could understand. The omission of a prohibition against the neophyte (1 Tim 3:6, 10) may suggest that the Cretan church was younger than the Ephesian church (Spicq, 2:600).

The structure of the passage is straightforward. Paul begins by stating the historical purpose (v 5), gives the summary charge to appoint elders who are above reproach (v 6a), and then spells out what this entails. Titus is instructed first to look at a man's home life since his management of this responsibility reveals his ability (or lack thereof) to be a steward in God's house. Paul then spells out five vices and seven virtues, qualities that parallel the lists in 1 Tim 3 and also contrast to the upcoming description of the Cretans. The seventh virtue is devotion to and competency in the gospel message, to teach the truth and refute error, and this leads directly into the next paragraph detailing what is being taught in Crete by the opponents.

The similarity of the list to that in 1 Tim 3:1–7, and the lack of any textual indication of change, suggests that Paul is discussing one office, not two, despite the shift from "elder" to "overseer." See *Comment* on v 7 and 1 Tim 5:17.

Comment

5a Τούτου χάριν ἀπέλιπόν σε ἐν Κρήτῃ, "For this reason I left you in Crete." Paul begins, as he does in 1 Timothy, without his usual thanksgiving. Except for 2:7–8 and 3:12–14, the epistle is devoid of personal comments; even 1 Timothy is peppered with a concern for Timothy's well-being. The conclusion of Titus is addressed to ὑμῶν, "you," plural: "Grace be with all of you" (3:15). This shows that despite its form as a personal epistle, it is written for public dissemination. Like 1 Timothy, it is an official validation of Titus's mission and a clarification of specific tasks. The lack of personal comments can also be accounted for by the historical situation. Titus may have been older, more mature, and therefore less prone to depression and the need for encouragement than was Timothy. The Cretan situation was also less serious, and Titus was in less danger.

Crete is mentioned only two times in Acts. There were Cretans in Jerusalem on the day of Pentecost (Acts 2:11), and it is perhaps because of them that the gospel initially spread back to Crete. The other reference is during Paul's journey to Rome as a prisoner (Acts 27:7–21). If Titus assumes an evangelistic journey through Crete that does not fit into the time frame of Acts, it is necessary to conclude either that the epistle is fictitious or that it refers to a time after the events recorded in Acts, after Paul's release from his first imprisonment and before the second imprisonment reflected in 2 Timothy (see *Introduction*, "Historical Reconstruction from the PE"). χάριν, "for," is an improper preposition that normally follows its object (cf. 1 Tim 5:14). τούτου, "this reason," looks forward to the ἵνα, "in order that," clause.

In this paragraph there are several indicators of the age of the Cretan church. (1) When Paul says that he ἀπέλιπον, "left," Titus in Crete, it suggests that Paul was with him, had left, and is asking Titus to finish the work and to appoint elders as was Paul's custom (Acts 14:21–23). Paul must have left before he could appoint any elders. (a) Most feel this suggests that Paul had a preaching trip through Crete sufficiently successful to require that elders be appointed in every city. This would mean that the church was quite young and that Paul had spent a significant amount of time there. (b) However, the text never says that Paul preached throughout Crete. It is also possible Paul went to Crete and found a struggling church that had perhaps originated when the converted Cretans returned home from Pentecost (Acts 2:11). Paul had started to help but had to leave, so he appointed Titus to finish the task. (c) Guthrie says that ἀπέλιπον "can be understood in the sense that Paul left Titus in Crete when he himself left Corinth" (*New Testament Introduction*, 612, citing de Lestapis, *L'Énigme*, 52–54; also suggested as a possibility by Robinson, *Redating*, 67–85), referring to an earlier missionary journey. This could apply equally to the time after the first Roman release. However, most feel that Paul was in Crete, "sent" being more appropriate than "left" if this third suggestion were followed. The nuance of being left behind may also be part of the word's meaning as is suggested by its two other occurrences in the PE (2 Tim 4:13, 20).

(2) The second indication of the church's age is that there is no discussion of the removal of bad elders (cf. 1 Tim 5:19–25). Titus is instructed to appoint elders where there previously were none, suggesting a young church. (3) The elders are required to have πιστά children (v 6). If πιστά means "believing" (see *Comment*), then sufficient time had passed for a pool of fathers with Christian children to be formed from which Titus could choose elders. If πιστά means "faithful," it is less significant as a time indicator. (4) However, unlike 1 Tim 3:6 (cf. v 10 on deacons), Titus is not warned against choosing a newly converted man to be an elder. Either this is assumed, or the church was so young that all the men were neophytes in the faith. (5) Titus is to appoint elders but not deacons, and it has been argued above that the pattern may have been to appoint elders first (cf. Acts 6:1–6; 14:23) and as the church grew to appoint deacons later as the need arose (see *Form/Structure/Setting* on 1 Tim 3:1–7). All of these indicators suggest that while there may have been Christians in Crete for some time, it seems doubtful that the church had thrived for very long (cf. Meier, *CBQ* 35 [1973] 338; Cousineau, *ScEs* 28 [1976] 159). (6) In light of the absence of any personal allusions in the epistle other than to Titus, it seems doubtful that the church was solely the result of Paul's ministry.

5b ἵνα τὰ λείποντα ἐπιδιορθώσῃ καὶ καταστήσῃς κατὰ πόλιν πρεσβυτέρους, "in order that you might put right the remaining things and appoint elders in every city." Unfortunately Paul does not specify the content of τὰ λείποντα, "the remaining things," but based on the content of the epistle, it can be assumed that these things included basic catechetical teaching on godly living. Titus is also instructed to appoint elders (plural) in every city (singular) in a land that was well known for its many cities. There is no monarchical episcopate, no singular bishop over a city or the country, in this epistle.

ἐπιδιορθοῦν, which occurs only here in the NT, means "to set right, correct," but the ἐπί can add the nuance of "to set in order further," "to correct in addition (to what has already been corrected)" (BAGD, 292). LSJ (631) says it means "to complete unfinished reform," which Hanson ([1983] 172) and Quinn (83) interpret as meaning that the problem in Crete was long term. But the word itself does not include the idea of reform. Bernard (157) suggests that the middle voice ἐπιδιορθώσῃ, "you might put right," shows that the task is Titus's alone (see *Note* b). Paul may be making a play on words as he tells Titus that he left him (ἀπέλιπον) in Crete to deal with the remaining things (τὰ λείποντα).

The appointment of elders could be a separate task from τὰ λείποντα, "the remaining things," or καί, "and," could carry the explicative meaning of "including" or "especially" (cf. BAGD, 393). On the office of elder (πρεσβύτερος), see *Form/Structure/Setting* on 1 Tim 3:1–7. Luke (Acts 14:23) records that it was Paul's practice from the beginning of his ministry to appoint elders for every church. καθιστάναι, "to appoint," does not mean "to ordain"; rather it means "to appoint, put in charge" (BAGD, 390; elsewhere in Paul only in Rom 5:19). BAGD lists "ordain, appoint" as a possible meaning, but none of the biblical references supports "ordain" (Luke 12:14; Acts 7:10, 27, 35; Titus 1:5; Heb 5:1; 7:28; 8:3) and the references in the church fathers are irrelevant. As is true of Timothy, Titus stands outside the structure of the Cretan church as an apostolic delegate; he is never identifed as an overseer or bishop. Quinn's comment that "Paul ordains Titus himself as bishop of Crete" (84) finds no basis in the text. In v 7 Paul refers to the same person with ἐπίσκοπος, "overseer" (see there). Jeremias (69) argues that πρεσβύτερος, "elder," is used in the same sense as in 1 Tim 5:1, where it refers to an elderly man. However, if this were the case, another accusative specifying the office to which the elderly man was appointed would be expected (Kelly, 122). There is also no evidence that the leadership of the church was drawn exclusively from the ranks of the elderly.

5c–6a ὡς ἐγώ σοι διεταξάμην, εἴ τίς ἐστιν ἀνέγκλητος, "as I commanded you, if anyone is above reproach." διατάσσειν, "to command," is a strong word denoting an authoritative command. It is used of the command given by the emperor Claudius (Acts 18:2) and that given by the military tribune Claudius Lysias (Acts 23:31), God's command to build the tabernacle (Acts 7:44), and the Lord's command that those who preach should make their living by the gospel (1 Cor 9:14). It may be that the command is directed toward Titus, just as Paul issues commands to Timothy (e.g., 1 Tim 4:11–16) and to all believers, or it may be directed toward Titus as a means of emphasizing his authority over the Cretan church. But the force of the verb could also be directed toward the necessity that an overseer be a certain type of person. As practical experience of any age confirms, adhering to these guidelines amidst the pressures that mount within the church can be difficult, and the strong language is appropriate.

Most of the following repeats Paul's instructions in 1 Tim 3. See there for detailed discussion. εἴ τίς, "if anyone," begins a conditional sentence that is never finished, but we can assume an apodosis such as "let them serve." ἀνέγκλητος, "above reproach," stands as the summary title and is Paul's primary concern. What follows are the specifics of how one is deemed above reproach. The problem in Crete, as in Ephesus, was partially the disrepute brought on the church by the conduct of its leadership. Titus is to appoint people who will keep the problem under control. As is the case in 1 Timothy, the requirements are not exclusively Christian. But the church was young, and Paul wants to ensure that at a minimum the office holders are decent people, living up to basic standards of Christianity and secular society, people who will conduct themselves properly and not soil the church's reputation. ἀνέγκλητος is a criterion for the appointment of elders (1 Tim 3:2). The word is repeated for emphasis in the next verse (Titus 1:7) and is synonymous with ἀνεπίλημπτος, "above reproach," which stands as the summary title of the list of requirements for overseers in 1 Tim 3:2. Quinn translates the word as "unimpeachable" and says it is "legal and forensic language" (78).

6b μιᾶς γυναικὸς ἀνήρ, τέκνα ἔχων πιστά, "a 'one-woman' man, having believing children." Paul now spells out what he means by being above reproach. μιᾶς γυναικὸς ἀνήρ, "a 'one-woman' man," is ambiguous, but the idea of fidelity in marriage is to be preferred, although it is possible that the term removes from consideration anyone who has been remarried after a divorce (cf. 1 Tim 3:2). As Chrysostom shows ("Homily 2"; NPNF 13:524), the early church viewed this as a prohibition against a second marriage for someone in church leadership. τέκνα ἔχων πιστά, "having believing children," repeats the general idea applied to both overseers and deacons in 1 Tim 3 that "the home is regarded as the training ground for Christian leaders" (Guthrie, 185; cf. Spicq, 2:602). There it is required that a church leader manage his household well (1 Tim 3:12), which includes having submissive children and maintaining fatherly dignity (1 Tim 3:4). This is not a requirement that an overseer have children, but if he does have children, they should be faithful. Knight notes that the implication of ἔχων, "having," children means that Paul is speaking "only about children who are still rightfully under their father's authority in his home" (289). While this is a helpful insight as one seeks to apply the passage to the church, it not dependent on ἔχων as much as on the overall context that evaluates a man's ability to lead by looking at his management of his home. Yet the criterion is based not so much on the character of the children, regardless of where they live, as on a man's ability to manage his home, the results of which can be seen in his children wherever they live.

πιστός could mean (1) "faithful, loyal," although it does not supply the content of their faithfulness—faithful to God, faithful to the family, faithful to a child's responsibilities, faithful to the church, etc.—an omission that argues against this option. However, the next qualifier emphasizes the children's behavior (as opposed to status; see below), and πιστός can have the meaning "submissive," "obedient," "trustworthy" (Matt 24:45; 25:21, 23; 1 Cor 4:2; cf. R. Bultmann, *TDNT* 6:175; secular references in Knight, 290). (2) In view of the use of πιστός in the PE, it could also mean "believer," "faithful to God" (Ellicott; Spicq; Quinn; Oberlinner, who says that it includes both the idea of being a believer and that of living a godly life as an example; cf. *Introduction,* "Themes in the PE"). This requirement would go one step beyond those listed in 1 Tim 3, where the qualifications for being a well-managed family do not require that the children be Christians. In this case Paul cites two basic requirements of the elder's children: their status (i.e., Christians) and their behavior (v 6b). It can be objected that a father has no direct control over his children's salvation, favoring the more neutral translation "faithful." However, if Paul is saying that elders must have believing children, this does not necessarily require fathers to have some control over their salvation. It may simply mean that a Christian leader should have Christian children (Spicq, 2:602). This would be a requirement for eldership that stands outside of the father's direct control. A decision is not easy.

Titus 1:5 seems to omit the rule from 1 Tim 3 that the person not be a new convert (1 Tim 3:6), but this verse implies that leadership tends to be drawn from those old enough to have believing/faithful children, implying that the father has been a believer for some time. This raises a question about the age of the church in Crete. It has been stated above that the church was relatively young, but this verse shows that it cannot have been too young, for there must have been time for fathers and their children to be converted (if πιστά is understood as "believing"). See *Comment* on v 5.

6c μὴ ἐν κατηγορίᾳ ἀσωτίας ἢ ἀνυπότακτα, "not able to be accused of debauchery or rebellious." This third set of requirements begins a negative list that continues through v 7, naming qualities that an overseer must not have. In 1 Tim 5:19 Paul uses κατηγορία, "accusation," to describe formal charges brought against an overseer. The genitive ἀσωτίας, "of debauchery," in Titus 1:6 gives the content of the accusation (cf. BDF §167). Elders are to be above even the suspicion of the following vices. μή, "not," may be used as the negation because there is perhaps an assumed ὤν, "being"; Ellicott says it is because these are the qualities an "*assumed model* bishop ought to have" (172). ἐν, "in," denotes the state of being charged with an accusation (cf. BAGD, 259 [I4d]). ἀσωτία, "debauchery," occurs elsewhere in lists of sins: "And do not get drunk with wine, for that is debauchery, but be filled with the Spirit" (Eph 5:18); "Let the time that is past suffice for doing what the Gentiles like to do, living in licentiousness, passions, drunkenness, revels, carousing, and lawless idolatry. They are surprised that you do not now join them in the same wild profligacy [εἰς τὴν αὐτὴν τῆς ἀσωτίας ἀνάχυσιν], and they abuse you" (1 Pet 4:3–4). Luke uses the cognate adverb (ἀσώτως) to describe the wild lifestyle of the prodigal son (Luke 15:13). The first two passages show a close association between ἀσωτία and drunkenness, but since the latter is specifically stated in the following verse, ἀσωτία here describes a wild, uncontrolled type of lifestyle in which a love of liquor is at home (cf. discussion of νηφάλιον, "clear-minded," in *Comment* on 1 Tim 3:2; cf. Trench, *Synonyms*, 83–87). ἀνυπότακτος means "undisciplined, rebellious, disobedient" (BAGD, 76). Paul uses it elsewhere to describe those for whom the law is intended (1 Tim 1:9) and in the following passage in his description of the Cretan opponents (Titus 1:10). It describes Eli's sons in Symmachus's version of 1 Sam 2:12 and 10:27 (LXX has λοιμοί, "pestilent ones").

7a δεῖ γὰρ τὸν ἐπίσκοπον ἀνέγκλητον εἶναι ὡς θεοῦ οἰκονόμον, "For it is necessary for an overseer to be above reproach as a steward of God." Paul shifts from the vice list to this explanation of why it is important for a church leader to be above reproach—because the church is the household of God and he is a steward in that house. This is reminiscent of 1 Tim 3:14–16, where Paul interrupts his train of thought to explain why it is important that Timothy carry out his instructions. There he says that the church is the household of God and it must protect the truth of the gospel. On δεῖ, "it is necessary," cf. 1 Tim 3:2.

The switch from πρεσβύτερος, "elder" (v 5), to the synonymous ἐπίσκοπος, "overseer," shows an early date of writing, at a time when the offices and terminology had not yet had time to solidify (contra Oberlinner, 17, who thinks the author is conflating two lists). The same fluctuation occurs in Acts 20:17, 28 (cf. 1 Pet 5:1–2, 5). As Ellicott notes, "The Apostle here changes the former designation into the one that presents the subject most clearly in his *official* capacity, the one in which his relations to those under his rule, would be most necessary to be defined" (171). It is significant that both here and in Acts 20 the men are first introduced as elders (Acts 20:17), but when the context shifts to the governing responsibilities, Paul switches to the designation overseer (Acts 20:28), the title that is more descriptive of their function. Knight calls it the "functional title" (290). The use of the singular ἐπίσκοπον, "overseer," does not denote a single bishop who has authority over a city; Paul shifts to the generic singular in v 6 ("if anyone is above reproach") and continues with the singular to the end of the passage. The force of γάρ, "for," is often missed; it ties the discussion together and argues against the suggestion that the overseers are distinct from the elders. An elder must be blameless since (γάρ) an overseer is God's steward. See *Form/Structure/Setting* on 1 Tim 3:1–7 for a discussion of the issues surrounding church leadership and the terminology, and see *Comment* on 1 Tim 5:17 for a discussion of the relationship between ἐπίσκοπος, "overseer, " and πρεσβύτερος, "elder." Unlike a good elder, the opponents are not doing their work as good stewards (1 Tim 1:4).

7b μὴ αὐθάδη, μὴ ὀργίλον, μὴ πάροινον, μὴ πλήκτην, μὴ αἰσχροκερδῆ, "not arrogant, not quick-tempered, not a drunkard, not violent, not greedy for gain." Paul follows with a list of five negative qualities a church leader should not possess. The list parallels both 1 Tim 3 (see table in *Form/Structure/Setting* on 1 Tim 3:1–7) and the following description of the Cretans (vv 10–11). αὐθάδης means "stubborn, arrogant, arbitrary" (cf. Prov 21:24; 2 Pet 2:10; cf. O. Bauernfeind, *TDNT* 1:508–9). Ellicott says it "implies a self-loving spirit, which in seeking only to gratify itself is regardless of others" (172). ὀργίλος, "quick-tempered," occurs only here in the NT (cf. Ps 17:49; Prov 21:19; 22:24; 29:22). πάροινος, "drunkard, addicted to wine," must indicate a serious problem in the Ephesian and Cretan church, and probably in contemporary society, since this vice surfaces in all three lists (cf. 1 Tim 3:3 [same word], 8). Surprisingly, Guthrie (185) says that this vice and the following two "probably had greater point in first-century Crete than in modern times" (cf. similar comments by Bernard on 1 Tim 3:3, discussed in the *Explanation* there). Surely this is an unrealistic, or at best an overly optimistic, evaluation of modern culture, in which alcoholism plays such a devastating role. πλήκτης, "violent, bully," occurs in the list in 1 Tim 3:3. Like the problem of alcoholism, a greediness for gain (αἰσχροκερδής) appears to have been one of the more pervasive problems among Paul's opponents since it too appears in all three lists (1 Tim 3:3, 8) and elsewhere (1 Tim 6:5–10; Titus 1:11). Barrett (129; followed by Fee, 174) argues that this refers to making a profit from Christian service. But Paul has already established that Christian workers should make a living from their labors (1 Tim 5:17–18), so Paul is referring to the desire to be rich beyond one's needs (cf. 1 Tim 6:5–10, 17–19; Titus 1:11).

8 ἀλλὰ φιλόξενον φιλάγαθον σώφρονα δίκαιον ὅσιον ἐγκρατῆ, "but hospitable, loving what is good, self-controlled, just, holy, disciplined." The adversative ἀλλά, "but," marks a change from vices to seven positive virtues a church leader must possess. On φιλόξενος, "hospitable," see *Comment* on 1 Tim 3:2. φιλάγαθος, "loving what is good," has kept its etymological meaning (φίλος, "loving" + ἀγαθός, "good"). It continues the compound use of φίλος from the previous word and occurs only here in the NT. This term is common in Aristotle and Philo and was used as a title of honor in the Greek societies (cf. excursus in Lock, 148–50; W. Grundmann, *TDNT* 1:18). It can refer to loving good people or good things, but because of the generality of the phrase, it probably encompasses both here. σώφρων, "self-controlled," occurs in 1 Tim 3:2 and is related to the idea of ἐγκρατής, "disciplined" (see below). δίκαιος, "just," is used in its ethical sense of just behavior (cf. *Comment* on 1 Tim 1:9 for discussion; similar use in 2 Tim 2:22; Titus 2:12; 3:5). Paired with it is ὅσιος, "holy" (cf. 1 Tim 2:8). Together they describe conduct appropriate toward people and God, respectively. The two ideas are paired elsewhere with this same duality (Luke 1:75; Eph 4:24; 1 Thess 2:10). ἐγκρατής means "self-controlled, disciplined" and can contain a sexual nuance (cf. cognate ἐγκρατεύεσθαι, "to exercise self-control," in 1 Cor 7:9; cf. BAGD, 216; σωφρονισμός, "self-control," in 2 Tim 1:7). It is one of the fruits of the Spirit (Gal 5:23; cf. Acts 24:25; 1 Cor 9:25; 2 Pet 1:6), was a cardinal virtue for Socrates, is found frequently in the writings of Aristotle and the Stoics, and is related to the idea of σώφρων, "self-controlled" (cf. excursus in Lock, 148–50; W. Grundmann, *TDNT* 2:339–42). The opposite trait, ἀκρατής, "lack of self-control," occurs in the vice list in 2 Tim 3:3.

9a ἀντεχόμενον τοῦ κατὰ τὴν διδαχὴν πιστοῦ λόγου, "holding fast to the trustworthy word that is in accordance with the teaching." This requirement of church leaders adds a theological dimension to a predominantly moral list of virtues, and this devotion provides the basis for exhortation and rebuke (v 9b). In a similar passage Paul requires this same devotion of Timothy so that he can exhort and rebuke (2 Tim 4:2). Lock comments that Titus is to be devoted "not to the law or the old covenant as a Jewish rabbi would . . . much less to commandments of men . . . but to the trustworthy . . . message . . . , which corresponds with the true teaching—the teaching of the Apostle himself . . . which is ultimately that of the Lord Himself (cf. I Ti 6³)" (131–32). Deacons also must hold the mystery of the faith with a good conscience (1 Tim 3:9). ἀντέχειν, "to hold fast, be devoted to" (cf. Bernard, 159), is synonymous with προσέχειν (cf. 1 Tim 1:4), which Paul uses in a similar passage to admonish Timothy to be devoted to the public reading of Scripture, to exhorting people to follow its teachings, and to the doctrinal exposition of its meaning (1 Tim 4:13). λόγος, "word," is the gospel (cf. 1 Tim 4:6), and πιστός, "trustworthy," is used not in the sense of a "faithful saying" (1 Tim 1:15) but to emphasize that the gospel is in fact trustworthy and therefore worthy of Titus's devotion (cf. *Introduction*, "Themes in the PE"). Chrysostom says it means the gospel is accepted by faith, not by "reasonings, or questionings" ("Homily 2"; NPNF 13:525), but this is not required by the use of πίστις, "faith," generally in the PE. διδαχή, "teaching," and its cognates in the PE refer to the doctrinal exposition of the gospel (cf. 1 Tim 4:6). The force of κατὰ τὴν διδαχήν, "that is in accordance with the teaching," looks forward to the Cretan problems spelled out in vv 10–16. The gospel is trustworthy if it corresponds to the apostolic preaching. If a particular presentation of the gospel does not correspond to the apostolic message, as is the case in Crete, then it is not trustworthy and is not the proper object of devotion.

9b ἵνα δυνατὸς ἦ καὶ παρακαλεῖν ἐν τῇ διδασκαλίᾳ τῇ ὑγιαινούσῃ καὶ τοὺς ἀντιλέγοντας ἐλέγχειν, "in order that he might be able both to exhort with healthy doctrine and to rebuke those who oppose [it]." The reason for the church leader to be devoted to the gospel as explained by the apostolic preaching is that this enables the leader to encourage people with the correct teaching and to reprove those who disagree. They must first accept the truth of the gospel personally and then out of their conviction confront error and teach truth. Implied is Paul's conviction that if they are not devoted, then they are not suitable for service. This spells out what Paul means when he tells Timothy that an overseer must be a "skilled teacher" (1 Tim 3:2). Leadership in the apostolic church was largely based on proper teaching (cf. 1 Tim 3:2). All this is said with an eye to the following description of the Cretans (note that v 10 begins with γάρ, "for"). When Paul tells Titus that the Cretan opponents must be muzzled, they are to be muzzled through the proper teaching of the gospel (1:11; cf. 1 Tim 4:11–16; 2 Tim 3:16–17). παρακαλεῖν, "to exhort," refers to encouragement, exhortation (cf. 1 Tim 1:3).

ὑγιαίνειν, "to be healthy," is a medical metaphor that sets the proper understanding of the gospel in contrast to the sick and morbid craving of Paul's opponents, more visible in Ephesus but also present in Crete (cf. 1 Tim 1:10), and it plays an ongoing role in this epistle (1:13; 2:1, 8; cf. 1 Tim 1:10). ἐλέγχειν, "to rebuke," denotes a strong rebuttal (cf. 1 Tim 5:20) as is made clear by the following charge, "rebuke them [the Cretans] sharply" (Titus 1:13). These two ideas are joined in Titus 2:15 where Paul instructs Titus to exhort and rebuke with all authority, and also in a similar discussion where Paul says that Scripture is inspired and therefore profitable for teaching (διδασκαλία), rebuking (ἐλεγμός), correcting, and training in righteousness (2 Tim 3:16). ἀντιλέγειν, "to speak against, oppose," occurs later in Paul's admonition to slaves that they not be disobedient (Titus 2:9) and is also used in Paul's quote from Isa 65:2, "All day long I have held out my hands to a disobedient and contrary people [πρὸς λαὸν ἀπειθοῦντα καὶ ἀντιλέγοντα]" (Rom 10:21; cf. Luke 2:34; 20:27; John 19:12; Acts 13:45; 28:19, 22).

Explanation

While written in the form of a personal letter addressed to an individual, the content of this letter is for public dissemination. Paul does not include his usual thanksgiving for the person to whom he is writing but gets right to business. The letter serves as an official endorsement of Titus's authority and his tasks. Titus and Paul may have made a missionary journey through Crete, where Paul had started to set things in order but had to leave before finishing, so Titus is given the job of completing the work.

Part of Titus's responsibility is to appoint church leaders. In Ephesus the church was older and the problems more serious, urgent, and ingrained. In Crete the problems were more those of a new church—no administrative structure, pressure from outside Jewish groups, evidence of sinful behavior. Titus does not have to remove bad elders; he must appoint good ones who can take care of potential and actual problems. Primarily, the overseers must be above reproach, which includes being faithful in their marriages, having proven their abilities in the home as witnessed by having believing children, being above any charge of debauchery, and not being rebellious. Paul interrupts his list by specifying why it is important that elders/overseers be above reproach (the alternation in terms showing an early date of writing before the offices of elder and overseer were separated). They are not watching over a human institution; they are stewards over God's house.

Paul continues with five vices and seven virtues that have parallels both with 1 Tim 3 and with the following description of the Cretan problem (Titus 1:10–16). Elders must not be arrogant, quick-tempered, addicted to wine, violent, or greedy for gain. The prohibitions against alcohol and monetary greediness are found in all three lists of qualifications for church leaders and constituted a substantial part of the problem in both Ephesus and Crete. On the positive side, the elders must be hospitable, loving what is good, self-controlled, just toward people, and holy in conduct toward God. If it sounds as if Paul is lowering his standards, that is only because he is being realistic in his approach to a new church in a hostile environment. Finally, elders must hold firmly to the gospel that agrees with the apostolic preaching as taught by Paul. If they do so, then they will be able to encourage the Cretans with doctrine that gives spiritual health and will also be able to rebuke those who are in disagreement. If elders are not devoted to Scripture, then they are not fit for service.

Chrysostom includes strong words for fathers wishing to be in church leadership:

> We should observe what care he bestows upon children. For he who cannot be the instructor of his own children, how should he be the Teacher of others? If he cannot keep in order those whom he has had with him from the beginning, whom he has brought up, and over whom he had power both by the laws, and by nature, how will he be able to benefit those without? . . . But if, occupied in the pursuit of wealth, he has made his children a secondary concern, and not bestowed much care on them, even so he is unworthy. For if when nature prompted, he was so void of affection or so senseless, that he thought more of his wealth than of his children, how should he be raised to the Episcopal throne, and so great rule? For if he was unable to restrain them it is a great proof of his weakness; and if he was unconcerned, his want of affection is much to be blamed. He then that neglects his own chidlren, how shall he take care of other men's? ("Homily 2"; NPNF 13:524–25)

III. Description of the Problem in Crete
(Titus 1:10–16)

Bibliography

Dimaratos, J. P. "Κρῆτες ἀεὶ ψεύσται." *Athena* 7 (1968) 95. **Ellis, E. E.** "Those of the Circumcision." *SE* 4 (1969) 390–99. **Folliet, G.** "Les citations des Actes 17,28 et Tite 1,12 chez Augustin." *Revue des Études Augustiniennes* 11 (1965) 293–95. **Galitis, G.** "The Disobedient in Crete and the Command of Obedience." *Deltion Biblikon Meleton* 5 (1977) 196–208. **Haensler, B.** "Zu Tit I, 15." *BZ* 13 (1915) 121–29. **Halkin, F.** "La légende crétoise de S. Tite." AnBoll 79 (1961) 241–56. **Harris, J. R.** "The Cretans Always Liars." *Exp* 7.2 (1906) 305–17. ———. "A Further Note on the Cretans." *Exp* 7.3 (1907) 332–37. **Lee, G. M.** "Epimenides in the Epistle to Titus (I 12)." *NovT* 22 (1980) 96. **Lemme, L.** "Über Tit. 1,12." *TSK* (1882) 13–144. **Plumpe, J. C.** "Omnia munda mundis." *TS* 6 (1945) 509–23. **Riverso, E.** "Il paradosso del mentitore." *Rassegna di Scienze Filosofiche* (1960) 3–32. **Sacchi, P.** "'Omnia munda mundis' (Tito 1:15): Il puro e l'impuro nel pensiero ebraico." *Pensiero di Paolo* (1983) 29–55. **Stegemann, W.** "Antisemitische und rassistische Vorurteile in Titus 1,10–16." *Kirche und Israel* 11 (1996) 46–21. **Thiselton, A. C.** "The Logical Role of the Liar Paradox in Titus 1:12, 13: A Dissent from the Commentaries in Light of Philosophical and Logical Analysis." *BibInt* 2 (1994) 207–23. **Zimmer, C.** "Die Lügner-Antinomie in Titus 1,12." *LB* 59 (1987) 77–99.

Translation

[10]*For there are many*[a] *rebellious people, senseless babblers and deceivers, especially those of the*[b] *circumcision.* [11]*It is [therefore] necessary to muzzle those who are upsetting entire households by teaching what is not proper for shameful gain.*[c] [12][d]*One of them, their own prophet, said, "Cretans are always liars, evil beasts, lazy gluttons."* [13]*This testimony is true, for which reason rebuke them sharply, in order that they may be healthy in*[e] *the faith,* [14]*not being devoted to Jewish myths and commandments*[f] *of people who are turning away from the truth.* [15]*All things*[g] *are clean to the clean, but to the defiled and unbelieving nothing is clean, but both their mind and conscience are defiled.* [16]*They profess to know God, but by their deeds they deny [him], being abominable and disobedient and*[h] *worthless for any good*[i] *work.*

Notes

[a]καί, "and," is omitted by earlier editions of Nestle-Aland, following the readings of ℵ A C P 088 81 104 365 614 629 630 *al* vg^ms sy co; Ambst. Its inclusion (D F G I Ψ TR 33 1739 1881 TR lat; Lcf Spec) forms a hendiadys (*TCGNT*[2], 584–85; cf. Quinn, 97–98).

[b]The article is omitted by A D[2] F G Ψ TR and included by ℵ C D* [c] I 088 33 81 104 365 1739 1881 *pc*. Shorter readings are generally uncharacteristic of the Byzantine text and therefore preferred here.

[c]460 adds the following to the end of v 11. τὰ τέκνα οἱ τοὺς ἰδίους γονεῖς ὑβρίζοντες ἢ τύπτοντες ἐπιστόμιζε καὶ ἔλεγχε καὶ νουθέτει ὡς πατὴρ τέκνα, "The children who abuse or strike their parents you must check and reprove and admonish as a father his children" (Metzger's translation: *TCGNT*[2], 585). It has no connection with the current text but might have originally been intended to appear in chap. 2 (Bernard, 154). The same minuscule makes another major addition to v 9 (see *Note* d on Titus 1:9 above).

ᵈAfter εἶπεν, "said," is inserted δέ, "but" (ℵ* F G 81 *pc*), and γάρ, "for"(103).

ℵ* *pc* omit ἐν, "in."

ᵉἐντολαῖς, "commandments," is replaced by ἐντάλμασιν, "commandments" (F G), and γενεαλογίαις, "genealogies" (075 1908 *pc*), the latter in imitation of 1 Tim 1:4.

ᵍμέν, "on the one hand," is inserted after πάντα, "all things," by ℵ² D² Ψ TR syʰ to make the parallelism with the following δέ, "but," clearer. γάρ, "for," is inserted in syᵖ boᵖᵗ, making the connection clearer between the falseness of ritual purity (v 15) and human commandments (v 14). The omission of both is supported by ℵ* A C D* F G P 6 33 81 1739 1881 *pc* latt sa boᵖᵗ.

ʰThe καί, "and," is omitted by ℵ*; Ambst.

ⁱἀγαθόν, "good," is omitted by ℵ* 81.

Form/Structure/Setting

These verses are the only real discussion of Paul's Cretan opponents (cf. 3:10–11). The situation in Crete appears to be similar to that in Ephesus, with a few important differences. The problem was real since their teaching was already upsetting whole households, and yet the Cretan opponents receive less attention, suggesting that the problem was not as developed as in Ephesus. The opponents were unqualified, rebellious, and inappropriate for positions of leadership in the church. In fact, vv 10–16 have the purpose of explaining why Titus must appoint only qualified people to church leadership (vv 5–9). The opponents were teaching senseless babble, words without meaning, myths. This passage clearly shows that the teaching was primarily Jewish and taught asceticism and guidelines for ritual purity and defilement. The opponents were part of the church but had left the truth of the gospel, and therefore they must be rebuked so that they and the church may become healthy in their faith. For the similarity between the teaching in Crete and Ephesus, see *Form/Structure/Setting* on 1 Tim 4:1–5, and on the similarity of the opponents' behavior in the two places, see *Form/Structure/Setting* on 1 Tim 1:3–7.

Titus 1:16 is the hinge verse of the entire epistle. The opponents claimed to know God, but their godless lives showed that they did not, and as a result they were not living our their salvation as God intended, pursuing good works. The essence of the Cretan theology was that they thought belief and practice could be separated, and Paul spends most of the rest of the letter arguing that God's salvific work and the believer's life of obedience must go hand in hand. Of course, this zeal for good works commended by Paul cannot earn salvation, but it is the necessary corollary to God's salvation and is in line with his original intent.

This passage includes one or possibly two citations. Paul cites a Cretan proverb to support his description of the opponents (v 12). See *Comment* for discussion. V 15 appears to some (Lock, Scott, Spicq) to be a citation, but it has many linguistic and ideological similarities with the context and with Paul's other writings, which suggests that it is his own creation.

Comment

10 Εἰσὶν γὰρ πολλοὶ [καὶ] ἀνυπότακτοι, ματαιολόγοι καὶ φρεναπάται, μάλιστα οἱ ἐκ τῆς περιτομῆς, "For there are many rebellious people, senseless babblers and deceivers, especially those of the circumcision." The γάρ, "for," shows the relationship between vv 10–16 and the preceding vv 5–9. Titus must appoint qualified people to church leadership because there are many wicked people in Crete who would destroy the church if they could. In v 9 Paul says Titus must appoint leaders who are devoted to Scripture so they can refute those who contradict the gospel, specifically those described in v 10 as rebels, senseless babblers, and deceivers (v 10).

ἀνυπότακτος, "rebellious," is part of Paul's description of what overseers' children should not be (v 6); the law was intended for such rebellious people (cf. 1 Tim 1:9). The word cannot refer to someone fighting church rule (contra Guthrie, 187) since there was no church structure yet in Crete (1:5). Rather, it speaks of a person who rebels against the gospel (v 9) as taught by Paul and Titus. ματαιολόγος describes someone who uses words that have no meaning, without substance, a "senseless babbler," and it is a common description of the problem in the PE (cf. cognate in 1 Tim 1:6). φρεναπάτης, "deceiver, misleader," occurs only here in the NT (cf. cognate in Gal 6:3).

Paul concludes this description with μάλιστα οἱ ἐκ τῆς περιτομῆς, "especially those of the circumcision." This is one of the clearest indications in the PE that the false teaching of Paul's opponents was primarily Jewish. In v 14 Paul calls it "Jewish myths." The heresy certainly had Hellenistic/gnostic elements in it, but its basic makeup was Jewish (cf. *Introduction,* "The Ephesian Heresy"). Oberlinner downplays the Jewishness of the opponents because of the lack of discussion concerning the law and because of his overall proposal of a Gnostic interpretation of the Christian faith in the PE (35). But the text is clear on the Jewishness of the opponents, and not all Jewish false teaching must have centered on the law, even though this was part of the false teaching in Ephesus.

ἐκ τῆς περιτομῆς, "of the circumcision," is a circumlocution for "Jewish." Paul uses it elsewhere of Jews (Rom 4:12) and Jewish Christians (Gal 2:7–9, 12; Col 4:11; cf. Acts 10:45; 11:2). This reference to circumcision, combined with other references to the law (e.g., 1 Tim 1:7), may suggest that circumcision played a role in the Ephesian heresy, although there is no other reference to this elsewhere in the PE. The phrase may mean nothing more than "Jewish." Outside sources indicate that there were large numbers of Jews in Crete (Josephus *Ant.* 17.12.1 §§23–25; *J.W.* 2.7.1 §§101–5; *Life* 48 §247; Philo *Leg.* 282). At first glance Paul's statement may imply that the opposition was coming from Jews outside the church as was the case throughout Paul's life (cf. Acts 13:45; 14:2, 19; 17:5). However, because the phrase is used so commonly as a periphrasis, Paul is probably referring to Jewish converts, and on this point most agree (cf. Spicq, 2:607–8). μάλιστα can mean both "especially" and "namely" (cf. Skeat, *JTS* 30 [1979] 173–77; *Comment* on 1 Tim 4:10). (1) The predominant meaning in Paul is "especially," which here would mean that the Jewish contingent in the church was one of the sources of conflict. (2) If it means "namely," then the Jewish converts were the problem and Paul is saying, "Make sure your appointees are qualified people, because there are already many insubordinates at work with their deceptions; I am referring in particular, as you know, to the converts from Judaism" (Fee, 178).

11a οὓς δεῖ ἐπιστομίζειν, οἵτινες ὅλους οἴκους ἀνατρέπουσιν, "It is [therefore] necessary to muzzle those who are upsetting entire households." Chrysostom ("Homily 2"; NPNF 13:526) uses this verse as an illustration of why it is important for qualified teachers to be able to refute error since the muzzling is to be done by instruction (so v 9; not by excommunication, contra Hanson, [1983] 175).

The etymological meaning of ἐπιστομίζειν (cf. στόμα, "mouth") is "to stop the mouth, silence" (BAGD, 301). Kelly says that it means "to put a muzzle, not simply a bridle, on an animal's mouth" (234). Unfortunately it is a rare word, occurring only here in the NT (MM, 246), so it is difficult to be precise in defining it, but its intent is clear. Although the situation in Crete was not as urgent as that in Ephesus, it was nonetheless real and required immediate attention. ἀνατρέπειν, "to upset," occurs in the same context in 2 Tim 2:18. Elsewhere in the NT it occurs only in John 2:15 in the description of Jesus overturning the money changers' tables. Paul is thinking of the effect on a family that is listening to the opponents' teaching, or of the internal struggle that occurs when some members of a family convert to the heresy.

11b διδάσκοντες ἃ μὴ δεῖ αἰσχροῦ κέρδους χάριν, "by teaching what is not proper for shameful gain." The opponents must be silenced because their teaching is wrong and their motives are sinful. The use of δεῖ, "it is proper," to describe what should not be done occurs elsewhere in the PE (cf. discussion at 1 Tim 3:2). The RSV translates as "they have no right to teach," and this is followed by Hanson ([1983] 175) as he comments that they had no right because they were not clergy, assuming a second-century clerical structure of authority. But there is no notion of right in this word. It describes what should not be and leaves the rest up to the context, which here emphasizes the content of their instructions. διδάσκειν, "to teach," can refer to both the act and the content of teaching as it does here (cf. 1 Tim 1:10).

The second reason they should be muzzled is that their motives are wrong; they were teaching for "shameful gain." This is to be expected of people who were "rebellious, senseless babblers and deceivers" (v 10). Elsewhere in the PE it is apparent that Paul believes Christian workers should be paid (1 Tim 5:17–18), so that was not the issue. The problem was that the opponents were greedy (Titus 1:7), their teaching was heretical, and their gain was therefore shameful. Their lust for financial power is one of the more obvious problems in the PE and calls for repeated discussion (cf. 1 Tim 3:3). αἰσχρός, "ugly, shameful, base" (BAGD, 25), occurs elsewhere in the NT only in the cognate compound αἰσχροκερδής, "greedy for shameful gain," in similar contexts (1 Tim 3:8; Titus 1:7). κέρδος, "gain," does not necessarily contain the idea of financial gain (cf. Phil 1:21), but its use in αἰσχροκερδής and the context assures that it does here. Tyndale's famous translation "filthy lucre" wrongly suggests to modern ears that it was the money itself that was wrong whereas it was their motives. Bernard (160) describes the situation as "a prostitution of the high gifts of a teacher." We know from historical sources that the Cretans had a reputation of loving money. Polybius (*Hist.* 6.46.3) says, "So much in fact do sordid love of gain and lust for wealth prevail among them, that the Cretans are the only people in the world in whose eyes no gain is disgraceful" (LCL tr.; cf. Livy, 44.45; Plutarch *Aemil. Paul.* 23; *Solon* 12).

12–13a εἶπέν τις ἐξ αὐτῶν ἴδιος αὐτῶν προφήτης, Κρῆτες ἀεὶ ψεῦσται, κακὰ θηρία, γαστέρες ἀργαί. ἡ μαρτυρία αὕτη ἐστὶν ἀληθής, "One of them, their own prophet, said, 'Cretans are always liars, evil beasts, lazy gluttons.' This testimony is true." To support his description of the Cretan opponents in v 10, Paul quotes a local prophet, generally believed to be Epimenides, a Cretan prophet of the sixth century B.C. who was highly regarded by his people (see below), and then adds his personal stamp of approval. Quinn poetically rephrases it: "Liars ever, men of Crete, / Nasty brutes that live to eat" (97). Paul obviously is not applying this saying to all Cretans; otherwise all Cretan Christians would fall under its condemnation, and Epimenides himself would also be a liar and therefore his saying false. Sweeping generalizations by nature do not always claim to be true in every situation; they are generally true. Paul is just trying to make a point.

This verse often appears in discussions of the logical fallacy known as the "liar's paradox" and has given rise to the colloquial use of "Cretan" to describe a reprobate person. For a discussion of the role of the "liar's paradox" and its philosophical background and development, see Thiselton, who argues that the saying does not make a generalization about Cretan society (*BibInt* 2 [1994] 207–23). Like v 10, it does include the Jewish Christians who are causing the problems, but one wonders if the description, like v 10, might also include non-Christian society in Crete. It certainly agrees with what is known of the reputation of the Cretan culture, which was renowned for its lack of ethics (see on "liars" below and "shameful gain" in v 11). Hanson ([1983] 176) points out that the verb κρητίζειν means "to lie," that the Cretans had a reputation for stealing, and that during the first century B.C. Crete became famous for housing robbers and pirates. Cicero states that "the Cretans . . . consider piracy and brigandage honourable" (*Republic* 3.9.15; LCL tr.; cf. also Josephus *Ant.* 17.5.5 §§117, 120; Polybius *Hist.* 6.46.3). If this is an accurate characterization, it is no wonder that Paul's requirements for church leaders (vv 5–9) are so basic. His statement of approval, "This testimony is true," is his way of giving apostolic authority to something said by a non-Christian. Quinn says that Crete was famous for not having any wild animals (108; citing Plutarch *De capienda* 86C; Pliny *Hist.* 8.83). This creates a powerful twist in the saying. While most countries had to deal with wild beasts, in Crete the same problem was posed by people who, in the absence of wild animals, assumed the role themselves.

Most attribute the saying to Epimenides, who lived about 600 B.C. He was known as a religious teacher and miracle worker, and respected as a prophet. There are legends that he lived to the age of 157 or 299 and that he slept fifty-seven years (*OCD*, 399). He supposedly predicted the failure of Persia to conquer Athens ten years before the event (Plato *Laws* 1.642d). Plato calls him a divine man and gives a description of his life (*Laws* 1.642d–e), and Aristotle says that "He used to divine, not the future, but only things that were past but obscure" (*The Art of Rhetoric* 3.17; LCL tr.). Diogenes Laertius (1.10.11) says that the Cretans sacrificed to him as if he were a god, and Plutarch calls him one of the seven wise men of Greece and says that the Cretans called him Κούρης νέος, "young Koures" (*OCD*, 399). Others (e.g., Theodore of Mopsuestia) attribute the saying to Callimachus in his *Hymn to Zeus* 8, but Callimachus appears to be quoting a known saying. Lock (134) adds that the dialect is Attic, not Cretan, and that Callimachus was from Cyrene. Lee (*NovT* 22 [1980] 96) cites G. L. Huxley's argument (*Greek Epic Poetry from Eumelos to Panyassis* [Cambridge, MA: Harvard UP, 1969] 81–82) that "Cretans are always liars" was actually said by a prophet of Delphi when denouncing Epimenides, which removes the perceived logical dilemma of a Cretan saying all Cretans are liars. Huxley's argument is either unknown or not followed, and the biblical text attributes the saying to a Cretan, not someone from Delphi. Unfortunately, the saying of Epimenides is known only through the citations of Clement of Alexandria (*Strom.* 1.59.2) and Callimachus (*Hymn to Zeus* 8, cited below; Hanson

[(1983) 176] also says it is cited by Jerome in his commentary on Titus and by Augustine). For what is known of Epimenides's writing, see H. Diels and W. Kranz, eds., *Fragmente der Vorsokratiker* (Zürich: Weidmann, 1966) 1:27–37; F. Jacoby, *Die Fragmente der griechischen Historiker* (Leiden: Brill, 1954–64) 457; G. S. Kirk and J. E. Raven, *The Presocratic Philosophers*, 2nd ed. (Cambridge: Cambridge UP, 1983) 23, 44–45.

Elsewhere Paul cites Menander (1 Cor 15:33) and Aratus (Acts 17:28). John views Caiaphas's words as prophetic by virtue of his office (John 11:51), and credence is given to the words of Balaam's ass in 2 Pet 2:16. Paul's use of the citation here, of course, does not mean that Paul accepts everything Epimenides taught, and the additional affirmation that "the testimony is true" is what gives the statement authority; the designation προφήτης, "prophet," is merely the common title given him. Chrysostom and other church fathers spend considerable time defending Paul's citation of a secular writer. Chrysostom raises the issue of why a secular writer should be cited and concludes, "It is because we put them most to confusion when we bring our testimonies and accusations from their own writers, when we make those their accusers, who are admired among themselves" (citing also 1 Cor 9:20–21; "Homily 3"; NPNF 13:528).

The repetition of αὐτῶν, "of them," is classical usage (Bernard, 176). By calling Epimenides a προφήτης, "prophet," Paul is adding weight to the saying and reflecting Cretan belief (see above). Cretans had such a reputation of being liars that the verb formed from their name, κρητίζειν, means "to lie" (cf. Dibelius-Conzelmann, 137 n. 14). In fact, the lie for which they were famous was their claim to have the tomb of Zeus. Callimachus, a Cretan poet of the third century B.C., wrote in his *Hymn to Zeus* (8–9), Κρῆτες ἀεὶ ψεῦσται· καὶ γὰρ τάφον, ὦ ἄνα, σεῖο Κρῆτες ἐτεκτήναντο· σὺ δ' οὐ θάνες· ἐσσὶ γὰρ αἰεί, "Cretans are always liars. For a tomb, O Lord, Cretans build for you; but you did not die, for you are forever" (cited in Dibelius-Conzelmann, 136; cf. also Athenagoras *Suppl.* 30; Lucian *Philopseudes* 3; id., *Timon* 6; *Anthologia Palatina* 7.275; Theodoret; Ovid *Amores* 3.10.19; id., *Ars amat.* 1.298; cf. Harris, *Exp* 7.2 [1906] 305–11; Dibelius-Conzelmann [137] also cite E. Rohde, *Psyche* [New York: Harcourt, Brace, 1925] 130–31). ψεύστης, "liar," occurs in the vice list for whom the law is intended (1 Tim 1:10). ἀργός, "lazy," also describes the lazy widows who should not be enrolled (1 Tim 5:13). It is somewhat surprising to find such a strong condemnation in the letter, offensive as it would have been to the Cretans. (1) This might suggest that Titus is more of a private letter albeit an impersonal letter that is all business, as opposed to 1 Timothy, which is to be read before the Ephesian church. (2) If the letter to Titus was intended to be read before the church, Paul could have assumed that the Cretans would interpret the saying in reference to Paul's opponents (in which case the strong language is parallel to the rest of the terminology in the PE), or as a just condemnation of their non-Christian society. Guthrie notes, "This principle has constant relevance, for every minister of the gospel must of necessity be cognizant with the character of his people, however distasteful the facts may be" (188).

13b δι' ἣν αἰτίαν ἔλεγχε αὐτοὺς ἀποτόμως ἵνα ὑγιαίνωσιν ἐν τῇ πίστει, "for which reason rebuke them sharply in order that they may be healthy in the faith." Because the Cretan opponents were such wicked people (v 10), as attested to by one of their own (v 12), and because they were upsetting whole households (v 11), Titus had to rebuke them and stop what they were doing. As is the case throughout the PE (cf. 1 Tim 1:20), Paul requires remedial discipline so that the opponents will be made healthy in the faith. The identity of αὐτούς, "them," is debatable. (1) Although the preceding condemnation is generally descriptive of Cretan society as a whole, Paul's concern in this letter is for the church, and the goal of being healthy in the faith confirms this. He is not speaking of non-Christian society. (2) From the beginning in v 10 and again in vv 14–16, Paul is speaking to the opponents, and they would be the most natural object of the rebuke in v 13b. The opponents are often the object of Paul's rebuke (cf. 1 Tim 5:20), and Paul holds out the possibility of their repentance and return to the faith (cf. 1 Tim 1:20; 2 Tim 2:25–26). Others (Ellicott, Knight) feel that Paul shifts to speaking of the believers who have been deceived by the opponents. The deceived families are mentioned in v 11, and vv 13–14 may distinguish between the church members who are to be rebuked (v 13) and the opponents who have turned away from the truth (v 14). Paul's intent would be that the Cretan church be rebuked so the heresy would not spread throughout it.

αἰτία can be a legal technical term like "accusation" (BAGD, 26), and that nuance would strengthen the sense of this verse. δι' ἣν αἰτίαν, "for which reason," occurs again in 2 Tim 1:6, 12 (cf. κατηγορία, "accusation," in 1 Tim 5:19; Heb 2:11). Hitchcock suggests that it is a Latinism (*ExpTim* 39 [1928] 350). On ἐλέγχειν, "to rebuke," see *Comment* on 1 Tim 5:20. In this verse Paul uses the verb in its strongest sense: "rebuke sharply." ἀποτόμως, "sharply," occurs elsewhere in the NT only in 2 Cor 13:10 where Paul says he is writing the letter so that when he returns to Corinth he will not have to be so severe in the use of his God-given authority. Chrysostom says, "Give them, he says, a stroke that cuts deep. . . . He does not here have recourse to exhortation. For as he who treats with harshness the meek and ingenious, may destroy them; so he who flatters one that requires severity, causes him to perish, and does not suffer him to be reclaimed" ("Homily 3"; NPNF 13:529). ὑγιαίνειν, "to be healthy," is a medical metaphor used throughout the PE to describe the proper interpretation of the gospel in contrast to the opponents' interpretation (cf. 1 Tim 1:10). The idea of the healthy gospel versus the opponents' teaching is continued in vv 10–11, 14 and carries into chap. 2 where Titus is instructed to urge the elderly men to be healthy in faith, love, and steadfastness. τῇ πίστει, "the faith," is probably the Christian faith (see *Introduction*, "Themes in the PE"), and yet if Titus does stop the spread of the opponents' teaching, the peoples' personal faith will be affected. Sometimes the creedal and personal use of πίστις, "faith," cannot be separated.

14 μὴ προσέχοντες Ἰουδαϊκοῖς μύθοις καὶ ἐντολαῖς ἀνθρώπων ἀποστρεφομένων τὴν ἀλήθειαν, "not being devoted to Jewish myths and commandments of people who are turning away from the truth." Paul spells out what it means to be healthy in the faith and why Titus must rebuke the opponents (v 13). This is another clear indication that the heresy is primarily Jewish, albeit with Hellenistic elements (cf. v 10).

On προσέχειν, "to be devoted to," see *Comment* on 1 Tim 1:4. The word μύθοις, "myths," refers to stories the opponents had created around minor OT characters, stories that contained their secret knowledge (cf. 1 Tim 1:4). The phrase ἐντολαῖς ἀνθρώπων, "commandments of people," "human commandments," as opposed to the healthy gospel of Jesus Christ, refers in part to the opponents' ascetic teachings (cf. 1 Tim 4:3–5), a ritualism that replaced true worship. This sets the stage for v 15 with its discussion of ritual, moral purity, and defilement. For the phrase ἐντολαῖς ἀνθρώπων, "human commandments," see Isa 29:13 (LXX, cited in Matt 15:9; Mark 7:7) and Col 2:22, which refer to human-made laws in distinction from what God intends. These human commandments were being promulgated by people who were busy turning themselves and others from the gospel. ἀποστρέφειν in the middle voice means "to turn away from" (cf. 2 Tim 1:15). In a similar passage Paul says that people will turn away from the truth and wander into myths (2 Tim 4:4). It is a common theme in the PE that the problem came from inside the church (cf. 1 Tim 1:6). ἀλήθεια, "truth," is a technical term in the PE for the gospel (cf. 1 Tim 2:4), but in this context Paul is thinking primarily of the ascetic practices of the opponents and the declaration of the gospel that all food is ritually clean (see next verse).

15a πάντα καθαρὰ τοῖς καθαροῖς, "All things are clean to the clean." The fact that Paul has been thinking of the opponents' ascetic teachings now comes to the forefront. To understand v 15 one must see that Paul is using καθαρός, "clean," in two different ways, referring to both ritual and moral purity. Here he says that "all things are [ritually] clean to the [morally] clean." The first "clean" (καθαρά) must refer to ritual purity since not all things are morally pure. The second "clean" (καθαροῖς) must refer to moral purity because ritual purity is inconsequential (Mark 7:7). This was the experience of Peter in Acts 10:15, 34–35 (cf. 15:9). Paul's Jewish Christian opponents would have been teaching that a morally pure person is still made unclean by eating unclean foods or by touching any defiled thing (cf. Hag 2:10–14; Philo *Spec. Leg.* 3.208–9). This topic has already been discussed in 1 Tim 4:1–5 where Paul asserts that all things are clean because God created them good, and the same topic is raised here for Titus's sake. For a discussion of the subsequent use of this statement in early church history, see Plumpe, *TS* 6 (1945) 509–23. Some (von Soden, Lock) suggest that it may have come from (or was "perhaps conditioned by" [Dibelius-Conzelmann]) Jesus, citing Luke 11:41 (cf. Rom 14:14, 20). It is found in the prophets (Hag 2:10–14) and was a common proverb in secular circles (citations in Spicq, 2:612). Jesus' and Paul's reason for the truth of the statement would presumably be substantially different from that in secular thought, for they would have grounded its goodness in God's creation and decree (cf. *Comment* on 1 Tim 4:3b–5).

15b τοῖς δὲ μεμιαμμένοις καὶ ἀπίστοις οὐδὲν καθαρόν, "but to the defiled and unbelieving nothing is clean." Paul's opponents were evidently teaching that one could attain ritual purity by following the ascetic laws. Paul asserts, rather, that those who are morally defiled and do not believe cannot be made acceptable to God even by ritual purity because everything about them is unclean. To the (morally) impure, all things are (ritually) impure. Their real problem is not ceremonial but moral. The perfect tense of μιαίνειν, "to defile," reflects the historical situation in which the opponents' defilement was an accomplished fact (cf. Heb 12:15; Jude 8; cf. Trench, *Synonyms*, 151). ἄπιστος, "unbelieving," is much too strong to be referring to weak Christians (contra Lock) but must refer to non-Christians (1 Tim 5:8; cf. *Introduction*, "Themes in the PE"). In v 16 Paul will continue the assonance of the initial α with four more words. The single article with μεμιαμμένοις, "defiled," and ἀπίστοις, "unbelieving," shows that these two words characterize the same group of people.

15c ἀλλὰ μεμίανται αὐτῶν καὶ ὁ νοῦς καὶ ἡ συνείδησις, "but both their mind and conscience are defiled." Ritual purity is inconsequential because purity and defilement come from within, from the heart and the conscience (cf. Mark 7:7). The opponents were defiled from within, having branded their consciences (1 Tim 4:2; cf. *Comment* on 1 Tim 1:5) and corrupted their minds (1 Tim 6:5; 2 Tim 3:8), thinking that ritual purity was essential. (For Greek parallels to the ethical component in Paul's argument, cf. Dibelius-Conzelmann, 138.) It is interesting to compare this passage with the parallel discussions in 1 Cor 8 and Rom 14:13–15:6. In those two passages the "strong," those who see that all things are pure to the pure, must recognize the weakness of those who have not been able to free themselves from their ritualistic background in Judaism or pagan worship. But in Titus the concept is expressed in black and white. Ritual is wrong. One can surmise that the historical background is significantly different. The Cretan opponents must have been teaching that ritual was essential, that it was part of the core of one's relationship with God. μιαίνειν, "to defile," occurs only here in the PE (cf. John 18:28; Heb 12:15; Jude 8), but the word is common in the LXX, where it is used to describe ritual and moral defilement (Job 31:11; Jer 2:7, 23, 33; 3:1–2; 7:30; Ezek 18:6, 11, 15; 22:11).

16a θεὸν ὁμολογοῦσιν εἰδέναι, τοῖς δὲ ἔργοις ἀρνοῦνται, "They profess to know God, but by their deeds they deny [him]." In Paul's final comment about these ritually and morally impure opponents, he says that despite their profession of knowing God, their lives prove that they do not. Paul will say the same thing of their Ephesian counterparts who hold to the form of religion but deny its power (2 Tim 3:5). As was the case in Ephesus, the Cretan opponents were insincere (cf. 1 Tim 1:6; cf. Barrett, 132–33).

As discussed in *Form/Structure/Setting*, v 16 is the hinge verse of the epistle. Paul has addressed the initial issues of the necessity of godly leadership and has called attention to the seriousness of the Cretan problem. In this verse he identifies a key issue: the opponents are teaching that what a person believes and how a person behaves are not related, and that godly living is not a necessary corollary to God's salvific plan and work. Then in the next two chapters, after giving instructions for different groups within the church, Paul will give Titus two creedal statements that show that obedience comes out of salvation and must come out of salvation, for it is a purpose for which salvation was provided.

Some (Easton, Dibelius-Conzelmann, Barrett) see here an indication of the Gnostic origin of the false teachings. Others (Bernard, Guthrie, Fee) are adamant that the opponents' professions come directly out of Judaism, which claimed exclusive knowledge of the one true God, and yet they did not live godly lives (John 8:54–55; Rom 2:17–18; Gal 4:8; 1 Thess 4:5; 2 Thess 1:18). The connection to Judaism has already been mentioned in v 14, which calls their teaching "Jewish myths" and "human commandments," suggesting Pharisaic oral tradition as it reinterpreted the Hebrew Scriptures. As was argued in the *Introduction*, throughout the PE there are words, phrases, and ideas that find a home in both Judaism and Hellenistic thought, and this dualism must be intentional although Jewish ideas were at the core of the heresy.

ὁμολογεῖν, "to confess," is a technical term for confessing Christ (cf. 1 Tim 6:12). Paul judges their profession to know God (see *Introduction*, "The Ephesian Heresy") to be only an appearance of religiosity produced by ascetic practices, an appearance that betrays a lack of true content. It is not clear whether the object of ἀρνοῦνται, "deny," is Jesus or their profession to know God; since ἀρνεῖσθαι, "to deny," elsewhere means a denial of Christ, that probably is its meaning here. See the hymn Paul quotes that says "If we deny him [i.e., Christ], he will also deny us" (2 Tim 2:12). In the words of James, "faith without works is dead" (Jas 2:14–17). ἀρνοῦνται continues the assonance of the initial a begun in v 15 and is repeated three more times in this verse.

16b βδελυκτοὶ ὄντες καὶ ἀπειθεῖς καὶ πρὸς πᾶν ἔργον ἀγαθὸν ἀδόκιμοι, "being abominable and disobedient and worthless for any good work." The opponents' ascetic facade failed to hide their true nature. βδελυκτός, "abominable, detestable" (BAGD, 138), occurs only here in the NT (cf. Prov 17:15; Sir 41:5; 2 Macc 1:27; cognate in Rom 2:22; Rev 21:8), but its cognate noun βδέλυγμα, "abomination," extremely common in the LXX, is used there to describe that which is detestable to God, especially idolatry (W. Foerster, *TDNT* 1:598–600). Paul may be using this word in an ironic sense; the opponents taught that myths and asceticism were the gateway to salvation, but they were idolatry, replacing the true worship of God with the idol of pseudo-asceticism. The falseness of the asceticism is made clear by their disobedience (ἀπειθής; cf. Titus 3:3; 2 Tim 3:2; cf. Rom 1:30; cf. Luke 1:17; Acts 26:19). ἀδόκιμος, "worthless," refers to the failure to stand the test, hence "worthless, unqualified" (cf. 2 Tim 3:8; cf. Rom 1:28; 1 Cor 9:27; 2 Cor 13:5–7; cf. Heb 6:8; W. Grundmann, *TDNT* 2:255–60). The test was their lifestyle, and they failed because they were idolaters and disobedient to the commands of God. This evaluation continues the PE theme of good works introduced in the first part of the verse; the opponents' behavior stands in contrast to God's true intention for believers, as is seen throughout the epistle. Jesus Christ gave himself to redeem sinners and "purify for himself a people of his own who are zealous for good deeds" (Titus 2:14; cf. Titus 2:7; 3:1, 8, 14; 2 Tim 2:21; 3:17; *Comment* on 1 Tim 2:10; for the positive use of δόκιμος, "approved," see 1 Tim 3:10 [δοκιμάζειν, "to approve"] and 2 Tim 2:15). In this context, the works that prove the opponents do not know God are their insistence on asceticism and possibly their lifestyle in general, a lifestyle of sin (v 10) and greed (v 11). Knight sees a progression in these three terms: "If one is 'detestable' because he judges the work of Christ inadequate for attaining true purity, and 'disobedient' because he rejects the good gifts of God's creation, then that person is also so 'disqualified' in God's sight that his unfitness extends to (πρός) anything and everything (πᾶν) that he does" (304).

Explanation

Having spelled out his instructions for appointing church leaders (vv 5–9), Paul clarifies why Titus must follow these instructions. There were many wicked people in Crete who, if they were to run the church, would do damage to the cause of the gospel. This is the only full discussion of Paul's Cretan opponents, although they are lying behind the surface elsewhere in the epistle. What is learned about them suggests that the situation in Crete was similar to that in Ephesus, although the problem in Crete was not as advanced. Paul's comments indicate that the heresy clearly had its roots in Judaism.

There were many rebellious people in Crete, especially the Jewish converts. They were actively promulgating their teachings, upsetting whole households, and had to be rebuked. They were teaching heresy, and their motivation was greed, pursuing "filthy lucre," in agreement with the worldwide reputation of the Cretans. To drive his point home Paul quotes the respected Epimenides that all Cretans are liars, evil beasts, lazy gluttons. The force of the quote was directed primarily toward the actual opponents but may also have included Cretan non-Christian society as a whole. After all, these were the people who claimed to possess Zeus's grave.

Therefore Titus must rebuke them sharply with the truth of the gospel so that the church may be healthy in its doctrine rather than devoted to Jewish myths and human commandments, the unhealthy asceticism and ritualism that were being taught. To the morally pure, all things are ritually pure; nothing from the outside can defile a person. But those who are morally defiled, who are impure inside, whose minds and consciences are defiled, defile everything they touch; no amount of ritual asceticism can make them acceptable to God. Despite the appearance of piety that asceticism seems to produce, the lives of the Cretan opponents showed that they did not know God, they were abominable to God, they had failed the test of life, and therefore they were unqualified for any good work that God desired.

IV. Instructions and Theological Basis for Godly Living (Titus 2:1–3:11)

A. Instructions (Titus 2:1–10)

Bibliography

Burini, C. "*Tē hygiainousē didaskalia:* Una norma di vita cristiana in Tito 2:1." *Vetera Christianorum* 18 (1981) 275–85. **Kee, H. C.** "The Linguistic Background of 'Shame' in the New Testament." In *On Language, Culture, and Religion.* FS E. A. Nida, ed. M. Black and W. A. Smalley. The Hague: Mouton, 1974. 133–47. **Lips, H. von.** "Die Haustafel als 'Topos' im Rahmen der urchristlichen Paränese: Beobachtungen anhand des 1. Petrusbriefes und des Titusbriefes." *NTS* 40 (1994) 261–80. **Mott, S. C.** "Greek Ethics and Christian Conversion: The Philonic Background of Titus II 10-14 and III 3–7." *NovT* 20 (1978) 22–48. **Padgett, A.** "The Pauline Rationale for Submission: Biblical Feminism and the *hina* Clauses of Titus 2:1–10." *EvQ* 59 (1987) 39–52. **Weiser, A.** "Titus 2 als Gemeindeparänese." In *Neues Testament und Ethik.* FS R. Schnackenburg, ed. H. Merklein. Freiburg: Herder, 1989. 397–414.

Translation

[1] *But you, speak what is fitting for healthy teaching.*

[2] *Older men [should] be clear-minded, dignified, self-controlled, healthy in faith, in love, [and] in steadfastness.*

[3] *Likewise [tell] elderly women [to be] reverent [a] in demeanor, not slanderers, and not [b] enslaved to much wine, teaching what is good* [4] *in order that they might encourage [c] the younger women to love their husbands [and] children,* [5] *[to be] self-controlled, pure, working at home, [d] kind, submissive to their own husbands in order that the word of God [e] may not be blasphemed.*

[6] *Urge the younger men likewise to be self-controlled* [7] *in all things, showing yourself [f] as an example of good works, pure [g] [and] dignified in your teaching,* [h] [8] *beyond reproach [in your] healthy instruction, in order that the opponent may be put to shame because [he] has nothing evil to say against us.* [i]

[9] *[Urge] slaves to be subject to their own masters [j] in all things, to be pleasing, not talking back,* [10] *not [k] pilfering but showing completely good faithfulness [l] in order that they might adorn the teaching of [m] God our savior in all things.*

Notes

[a] C 33 81 104 *pc* latt sy[p] sa; Cl read the dative singular ἱεροπρεπεῖ, "reverent," which modifies καταστήματι, "behavior." Most uncials and TR have the accusative plural, which makes ἱεροπρεπεῖς, "reverent," the predicate of the assumed εἶναι, "to be," from v 2.

[b] μή, "not," read by ℵ[2] D F G H Ψ 33 TR latt sy[h]; Cl, is replaced with μηδέ, "and not," by ℵ* A C 81 1739 1881 *pc* sy[p].

ᶜThe subjunctive σωφρονίζωσιν, "they might encourage" (א* C D Ψ 1739 1881 TR; Cl), is replaced with the indicative σωφρονίζουσι(ν), "they encourage," by א* A F G H P 104 326 365 1241 1505 *pc.* The indicative after ἵνα, "in order that," is unclassical, found but not common in Koine, and hence the harder reading. That א* reads the indicative is significant since some feel that it tends to correct the grammar.

ᵈοἰκουργούς, "working at home" (א* A C D* F G I Ψ 33 81 *pc*), is replaced with the more common οἰκουρούς, "staying at home, domestic" (BAGD), by א² D² H 1739 1881 TR, most of the church fathers, Latin and Syriac; cf. Bernard, 163. οἰκουργούς is the more difficult reading because of its rarity (cf. *1 Clem.* 1:3: τὰ κατὰ τὸν οἶκον σεμνῶς οἰκουργεῖν ἐδιδάσκετε, "you were teaching [them] to fulfill their household duties reverently"), but Bernard (167) prefers οἰκουρούς because it too, like many of the terms in this passage, was held up as a laudable quality in a wife by secular writers. Its textual evidence is widespread, and it does fit the discussion better. Cf. *TCGNT²*, 585.

ᵉAfter τοῦ θεοῦ, "of God," καὶ ἡ διδασκαλία, "and the teaching," is inserted by analogy to 1 Tim 6:1 by C *pc* vgᵐˢ syʰ.

ᶠBecause of the unexpected shift from discussing young men to addressing Titus, some MSS change πάντα σεαυτόν, "all things, yourself" (supported by א A C D² F G 1739 1881 TR lat), to πάντας ἑαυτόν, "all people, himself" (Ψ 33 104 326 *pc*), πάντα ἑαυτόν, "all things, himself" (D*), πάντας σεαυτόν, "all people, yourself" (*pc*), or πάντων σεαυτόν, "all, yourself" (P). The switch to the masculine πάντας, "all people," clarifies that Titus is to show himself a good model "on account of [περί] all people" and not "with reference to all things."

ᵍἀφθορίαν, "pure" (א* A C D* K P 33 [81] 104 1739 *al*), is replaced with the synonymous ἀδιαφθορίαν (א² D¹ Ψ TR) or ἀφθονίαν, "willingness" (𝔓³² F G 1881 *pc*). Cf. *TCGNT²*, 585.

ʰἀφθαρσίαν, "incorruptibility" (omitted by 𝔓³² ᵛⁱᵈ א A C D* F G P 33 81 365 1739 1881 *pc* latt co), is added to the end of the verse (D² Ψ TR syʰ), possibly borrowed from 2 Tim 1:10.

ⁱThe first-person ἡμῶν, "us," is switched to the second-person ὑμῶν, "you," by A *pc* a vgᵐˢˢ, missing the implication of corporate responsibility.

ʲThe order ἰδίοις δεσπόταις, "to their own masters" (א C F G Ψ 33 TR), is reversed by A D P 326 1739 1881 *pc.*

ᵏμή, "not," is replaced with μηδέ, "and not," by C² D* ᶜ F G 33 *pc* syᵖ.

ˡOur text, πᾶσαν πίστιν ἐνδεικνυμένους ἀγαθήν, "showing completely good faithfulness," is supported by א² A C D P 81 104 326 365 1505 1739 1881 *pc.* Ellicott (184) points out that in Paul (except in Eph 4:19), when πᾶς, "all," occurs with an abstract, anarthrous substantive, it always precede the noun. Its order is altered to πᾶσαν ἐνδεικνυμένους πίστιν ἀγαθήν (F G), πᾶσαν ἀγαθὴν πίστιν ἐνδεικνυμένους (629), πίστιν πᾶσαν ἐνδεικνυμένους ἀγαθήν (Ψ TR), or πᾶσαν ἐνδεικνυμένους ἀγαθήν (א*; 33 substitutes ἀγάπην, "love," for ἀγαθήν, "good"). Cf. Lock, xxxviii.

ᵐτήν, "the," is omitted by 1739 1881 TR but retained by א A C D F G Ψ 33 81 *pc.*

Form/Structure/Setting

Paul has been contrasting one group of people with another. He has listed the personal qualifications for church leaders (1:5–9), which contrast with the characteristics of the opponents (1:10–16). Paul now spells out how he wants Titus and different groups within the church to behave (2:1–10) and finally moves on to the ultimate reason that godly behavior is important (2:11–15). Most view vv 11–15 as a separate section. Yet v 11 begins with γάρ, "for," ana gives the theological basis for the instructions given in vv 1–10, so the chapter should be viewed as a whole. In fact, even a division between chap. 2 and chap. 3 is somewhat arbitrary since Paul continues many of the same topics and moves smoothly into chap. 3.

The structure of vv 1–10 is reminiscent of 1 Tim 5:1–2 because it breaks into segments based on the gender and age of his subjects. Paul begins with a summary command to Titus (v 1) and then gives instructions to older men (v 2) and older women (vv 3–4a). Because he perceives the older women's ministry to be directly related to younger women, he moves into a discussion of younger women without the expected "likewise younger women" (vv 4b–5). The fourth group is younger men (v 6), but instead of listing personal traits as he has been doing, he gives a summary description—"be self-controlled"—and moves into a few personal comments to Titus (vv 7–8). Titus himself may have been young, and the mention of younger men reminds Paul that he has a few things to say directly to Titus. Paul ends with instructions for slaves (vv 9–10). This breaks the pattern of discussing groups based on age and gender, but it could be that the slaves in Crete were causing a problem and this seemed to Paul the best place to discuss the issue.

There are several key thoughts woven throughout the discussion. (1) σώφρων, "self-controlled," and cognates appear four times as Paul asks older men (v 2), younger women (v 5), and younger men (v 6) to be self-controlled. The cognate verb σωφρονίζειν also occurs in the discussion of older women (v 4), but there it means "to encourage." (2) ὑγιαίνειν, "to be healthy," is another key term. In chap. 1 Paul said that church leaders must be able to instruct others in the healthy teaching and argue against those who oppose it (v 9). He then described the Cretan opponents and instructed Titus to rebuke them sharply so they would be sound in the faith (v 13). Paul begins chap. 2 by asking Titus to utter what is appropriate for healthy teaching (2:1), to urge older men to be healthy in faith, love, and steadfastness (v 2), and to keep the healthy word above reproach (v 8). Although the emphasis is on observable behavior, that behavior is based on healthy theology. (3) Three times Paul restates why the Cretans should behave in the way he has instructed them: the word of God must not be blasphemed (v 5); the opponent must be shamed by having nothing evil to speak against Paul and Titus (v 8); and the teaching of God our savior must be adorned (v 10). Each of these three statements occurs at the end of a set of instructions and tells the group why they must behave as Paul has instructed. As is the case throughout the PE, Paul requires the church members to meet, at a minimum, basic standards of decency so that their behavior will not bring reproach on the church. Given the proverbial wickedness of Cretan society, these basic standards cannot be determined by Cretan standards; and even though the stated reason has to do with the church's reputation, this is not necessarily the only reason for ethical behavior (see *Explanation*).

Lock has an excellent summary of the relationship between chap. 1 and chap. 2:

> The whole chapter is full of reminiscences of c. 1. Titus is to be in his teaching a model for the presbyters, to show them how to exhort and how to rebuke (cf. 2¹·¹⁵ with 1⁹). He is also to be a contrast to the false teachers: his teaching is to be sound, sincere, not able to be silenced (cf. 2⁷ with 1¹⁰): it is not to be aimless, but at all points to build up character (cf. 2¹ with 1¹⁰, 2¹⁴ with 1¹⁶): it is not to upset families but to build up a true family life on the basis of a willing subordination (cf. 2⁵·⁹ with 1¹⁰·¹¹). The 'evil beasts and idle bellies' are to be disciplined into self-control (cf. σώφρων, 2²·⁴·⁵·⁶·¹², with 1¹²): instead of attending to Jewish myths and ceremonial purifications, the Christians are to realize that *they* are now God's peculiar people, purified with a spiritual cleansing (cf. 2¹⁴ with 1¹⁴·¹⁵): instead of being useless for every good work, they are to be eager to stand out before the heathen world as models of excellence (cf. 2¹⁴ with 1¹⁶). (138)

There is some discussion on the source of these qualities. The emphasis on social standards (Dibelius-Conzelmann, 141) and the commonality of the terms in secular writings (Easton, 90–91) suggest to some that the author is drawing from secular lists. Quinn devotes a considerable amount of space to this topic (esp. 128). But as was argued regarding 1 Tim 3, Paul must be allowed to draw on the Hellenistic language of his audience and the needs of the historical situation. The similarity of the language here with that in 1 Tim 3 is explained by a common author, a common historical situation, and a closeness in the time of writing. The virtues stated here are referred to throughout the PE and are part of Paul's answer to the Cretan/Ephesian problem. As has been argued above (see *Introduction*, "Historical Reconstruction from the PE"), there are indications that Paul wrote 1 Timothy and Titus at the same time. There also are those who compare this passage to the so-called household codes found in Col 3:18–4:1, Eph 5:21–6:9, and 1 Pet 2:18–3:7. But as Fee argues (184), those codes are concerned more with relationships within the family, and our passage deals with relations in the church and a need to keep the church above reproach. The discussions regarding young women and slaves do overlap with the household codes, but they share the concern of the rest of the chapter: the church's reputation.

Comment

1 σὺ δὲ λάλει ἃ πρέπει τῇ ὑγιαινούσῃ διδασκαλίᾳ, "But you, speak what is fitting for healthy teaching." In contrast to the Cretans, who taught Jewish myths and human commandments (1:10–16), Titus must teach the true gospel. The content of that teaching is spelled out in the following verses. As is true throughout the PE, correct behavior (vv 2–9) is based on correct theology (v 1), and in vv 11–15 Paul will resume the theological discussion.

σύ, "you," is in an emphatic position, and δέ, "but," has its full adversative force. (See similar use of σὺ δέ in 1 Tim 6:11 and 2 Tim 3:10, 14; 4:5.) In this context λάλει, "speak," carries the meaning of "teach" (cf. 1 Tim 6:2) and is repeated in the conclusion to this section (v 15). πρέπει describes "what is appropriate, fitting" (cf. 1 Tim 2:10). ὑγιαινούσῃ διδασκαλίᾳ, "healthy teaching," is a common theme in the PE. Paul has just said that Titus must appoint church leaders who are devoted to the gospel so they can give healthy instruction (1:9), and then he describes the unhealthy teaching of the Cretans (1:10–11, 14). The same charge is repeated here to Titus, and in the next verse older men are told to be healthy in faith, love, and endurance (see *Form/Structure/Setting*). As is typical of Paul's instruction in the PE, Titus is told to λάλει, "speak, teach," what is fitting to the church while he is to ἔλεγχε . . . ἀποτόμως, "rebuke sharply" (1:13), the opponents.

2 πρεσβύτας νηφαλίους εἶναι, σεμνούς, σώφρονας, ὑγιαίνοντας τῇ πίστει, τῇ ἀγάπῃ, τῇ ὑπομονῇ, "Older men [should] be clear-minded, dignified, self-controlled, healthy in faith, in love, [and] in steadfastness." Paul first addresses the elderly men in the church. The language is reminiscent of his instructions for church leaders in 1 Tim 3, but πρεσβύτης, "older man," does not refer to a church office (πρεσβύτερος, "elder"). Paul is speaking to groups within the church based on gender and age just as he did in 1 Tim 5:1–2. πρεσβύτης occurs elsewhere in the NT in reference to Zechariah (Luke 1:18) and Paul (Phlm 9; but see the conjecture πρεσβευτής, "ambassador"; *TCGNT*[1], 657; O'Brien, *Colossians*, 290). Philo (*Opif.* 105) cites Hippocrates's discussion of the seven stages of life, the sixth being πρεσβύτης, which he identifies as being fifty to fifty-six years of age. Yet Paul appears to be addressing all the adult members in the Cretan church, so old and young are relative in reference to each other rather than to a time of life.

Paul may intend λάλει, "speak," in v 1 to be the governing verb for εἶναι, "to be"—"teach . . . older men to be . . ."—or the infinitive functions as an imperative (BDF §389; Moule, *Idiom-Book,* 126). In v 6 is the parallel phrase, παρακάλει σωφρονεῖν, "urge [them] to be self-controlled."

Paul follows with four qualities of older men. (1) νηφάλιος means "clear-minded, sober in judgment, self-controlled." It is used in the description of elders (1 Tim 3:2) and deacons' wives (1 Tim 3:11). (2) σεμνός means "dignified" and signifies that which lifts "the mind from the cheap and tawdry to that which is noble and good and of moral worth" (Hawthorne, *Philippians,* 188). It is part of Paul's description of deacons (1 Tim 3:8) and their wives (1 Tim 3:11). (3) σώφρων, "self-controlled," is the key term in this passage, occurring in the discussion of older women (v 4), younger women (v 5), and younger men (v 7; see *Form/Structure/Setting*). It is also a key term in the requirements for elders (1 Tim 3:2 [see discussion there]; Titus 1:8).

(4) The fourth quality enjoined upon elderly men is that they be healthy (cf. 1 Tim 1:10 and Titus 2:1) in the triad of faith, love (cf. 1 Tim 1:5), and steadfastness (cf. 1 Tim 6:11). The preceding list of ideals is not exclusively Christian, but this trilogy adds a decidedly Christian emphasis. When πίστις, "faith," is articular, it almost always means faith in the creedal sense of the Christian faith (cf. *Introduction,* "Themes in the PE"), but here it must refer to personal trust because it parallels the words for love and steadfastness. The other two members of the triad are personal, and this verse is parallel with 1 Tim 6:11, where the faith described is personal. This same trilogy occurs in 1 Tim 6:11, 2 Tim 3:10, and 1 Thess 1:3. Quinn argues that πίστις would have been understood by the Romans as *fides,* "loyalty to their pledged word" (132), a trait they held dear, but usage in the PE shows that this would not have been Paul's intention. The trilogy of "faith, hope [ἐλπίς], and love" is common and may have been a pre-Pauline formula (Hunter, *Paul and His Predecessors,* 33–35). Discussions of why Paul supposedly substituted steadfastness for hope are not always helpful (cf. Scott, 163; Hanson, [1983] 179). Both qualities are appropriate for older men. It is possible to view these qualities as general traits and not related to problems especially prevalent among older men. However, the qualities urged on younger men and women deal with issues especially relevant to them, and this might also be the case here. Chrysostom, for example, goes to great lengths to show that older men tend to lack these specific traits ("Homily 4"; NPNF 13:531).

3 πρεσβύτιδας ὡσαύτως ἐν καταστήματι ἱεροπρεπεῖς, μὴ διαβόλους μηδὲ οἴνῳ πολλῷ δεδουλωμένας, καλοδιδασκάλους, "Likewise [tell] elderly women [to be] reverent in demeanor, not slanderers, and not enslaved to much wine, teaching what is good." The second group Paul addresses is the older women, and again the discussion has similarities to 1 Tim 3, especially v 11 concerning deacons' wives. Paul lists four qualities and then gives his reason in v 4. λάλει . . . εἶναι, "speak . . . to be," is assumed from vv 1–2. ὡσαύτως, "likewise," is a usual way for Paul to link his thoughts (cf. 1 Tim 2:9; 3:8, 11; Titus 2:6). πρεσβῦτις, "elderly woman," occurs only here in the NT (cf. 4 Macc 16:14; Josephus *Ant.* 7.7.2 §142; 7.8.4 §186). Philo uses the word in reference to women over sixty years of age (*Spec. Leg.* 2.33), an interesting coincidence with the requirement that widows not be enrolled unless they are sixty or more years old (1 Tim 5:9). The text makes no connection between these older women and the enrolled widows in 1 Tim 5:3–16. The instructions here apply to all older women.

ἱεροπρεπής, "reverent," the first desirable quality of elderly women, occurs only here in the NT but is common in secular writing (G. Schrenk, *TDNT* 3:253–54; BAGD, 372). It refers to conduct appropriate to a temple (ἱερόν, "temple" + πρέπειν, "to be fitting"; cf. v 1). It is a shortened way of saying ὃ πρέπει γυναιξὶν ἐπαγγελλομέναις θεοσέβειαν, "what is fitting for women who claim to be godly" (1 Tim 2:10). It is frequently used in a cultic setting (cf. Dibelius-Conzelmann, 140 n. 6), but that is not the context here (but cf. ἁγνός, "pure," in v 5). G. Schrenk asserts, "The simple meaning is that we must take seriously the fact that we belong to God" (*TDNT* 3:254). κατάστημα refers to one's inner deportment, "demeanor." The word occurs only here in the NT (cf. 3 Macc 5:45).

Second, elderly women must not be slanderers (μὴ διαβόλους). This is also a requirement of deacons' wives (1 Tim 3:11), and slander was a characteristic of the young Ephesian widows that caused Paul to limit enrollment of widows in the church (1 Tim 5:13). Apart from 1 Tim 3:3, διάβολος, "slanderer," in the PE always refers to Satan (1 Tim 3:6, 7; 2 Tim 2:26; cf. *Comment* on 1 Tim 3:6). Third, elderly women must not be enslaved to much wine (μηδὲ οἴνῳ πολλῷ δεδουλωμένας). Alcoholism must have been a severe problem since it is a issue in the appointment of church leaders in every list (1 Tim 3:3, 8; Titus 1:7; cf. 1 Tim 5:23). While this is true in almost every culture (cf. 1 Cor 11:21 and *Comment* on 1 Tim 3:3), it was especially true in Crete; Spicq (2:618–19) lists epitaphs that view heavy drinking as a virtue. Chrysostom argues that this prohibition was included because of the weakness of age and its need for a little wine medicinally ("Homily 4"; NPNF 13:532) and not so much because of the heresy. The idea of being δεδουλωμένας, "enslaved," is found elsewhere in Paul (cf. Rom 6:18 [to righteousness], 22 [to God]; 1 Cor 7:15 [to an unbelieving partner]; 9:19 [to all people]; Gal 4:3 [to the elements of the world]; cf. 2 Pet 2:19 [slaves of corruption]; cf. *Comment* on 1:1).

The fourth and final characteristic is that elderly women must teach what is good (καλοδιδάσκαλος). This word occurs only here in Greek literature and may have been coined by Paul (cf. φιλάγαθος, "loving what is good," in Titus 1:8; on καλός, "good," see *Comment* on 1 Tim 1:8). Context shows that this refers not to an official teaching position in the church (1 Tim 2:11–12) but rather to informal, one-on-one encouragement (σωφρονίζωσιν [v 4]). It pictures the older women, those who were experienced in life, marriage, and child rearing, taking the younger women in the congregation under their care and helping them to adjust to their responsibilities. It is a blessed and needed ministry that cannot be accomplished by men (cf. 1 Tim 5:2b). This quality leads into the next section on young women as vv 4–5 spell out what the older women are to teach the younger ones.

4 ἵνα σωφρονίζωσιν τὰς νέας φιλάνδρους εἶναι, φιλοτέκνους, "in order that they might encourage the younger women to love their husbands [and] children." καλοδιδάσκαλος, "teaching what is good," in the previous verse provides the transition to the third group of people that Paul addresses: the younger married women. These instructions were probably not for married women as opposed to single women; rather they were for young women who Paul assumed were married, a normally safe assumption in that culture. Otherwise Paul omits any reference to single women in a discussion that appears to encompass the entire congregation. He lists seven qualities and a motivating reason. The discussion is reminiscent of the instructions for the young Ephesian widows (1 Tim 5:13–14) and was common in secular culture (see references in Spicq, 1:392–93). Fee suggests that the seven qualities in vv 4–5 are to be read in pairs with either ἀγαθάς, "good," modifying οἰκουργούς, "working at home," or ὑποτασσομένας, "being submissive," standing on its own. They all have to do with a woman's attitude and conduct toward her household. Just as the older Paul worked with the younger Timothy (1 Tim 1:2), so also the partnership of the old and young women should be beneficial to both parties. Paul ties together the discussions of older women and of younger women with a ἵνα, "in order that," clause rather than making a major break. This closely associates the younger and older women such that the older women teach what they already understand (so Knight, 307). Quinn mistakenly comments, "The older women are the ones who teach this virtue to their juniors, thus implying the practical advantages that accrue to such conduct. There is no appeal to its natural or legal necessity" (137). But there is no such statement in the text. While there is no ultimate reason given for the older women teaching the younger ones and the instruction does exhibit practical wisdom, that is all that should be adduced (see *Explanation*).

σωφρονίζειν, "to encourage," is the second use of this word group, which plays an important role in this passage (see *Form/Structure/Setting*), although this term does not carry the cognate's meaning of "to be self-controlled" (cf. v 6). It means "to encourage, advise, bring to their senses" (BAGD, 802). Our critical text accepts the subjunctive after ἵνα, "in order that"; the indicative is the harder reading and has a strong claim to authenticity (see *Note* c). νέας, "younger women," is used substantivally in contrast to older women. The first two qualities are that they are to "love their husbands" and "love their children." φίλανδρος, "loving one's husband," and φιλότεκνος, "loving one's children," are both compounds with φίλος, "loving," occurring only here in the NT and retaining their etymological meaning. Both qualities are common in inscriptions commending a good wife (cf. LSJ, 1931–32, 1940; Deissmann, *Bible Studies*, 255; Dibelius-Conzelmann, 140 n. 11). The former is especially appropriate in a culture where husbands were not chosen by the wife (Hanson, [1983] 180). The need to learn how to love is a lesson applicable in all ages (cf. Guthrie, 193), and it fills out Paul's instructions elsewhere to wives where he speaks of submission. These ideals, although not the words, lie behind Paul's concerns in 1 Tim 2:9–15 and 5:9–10, 14. Chrysostom emphasizes how love for one's husband is the chief point insofar as the other qualities flow from it ("Homily 4"; NPNF 13:532).

5a σώφρονας ἁγνάς οἰκουργούς ἀγαθάς, ὑποτασσομένας τοῖς ἰδίοις ἀνδράσιν, "[to be] self-controlled, pure, working at home, kind, submissive to their own husbands." σώφρονας, "self-controlled," is the third mention of this key term (see *Form/Structure/Setting*). Both it and the following term can carry nuances of sexual fidelity. ἁγνός means "pure, holy," often with cultic associations (see ἱεροπρεπής, "reverent," above). Originally it was an attribute of God but developed the transferred sense of moral behavior (cf. 1 Tim 5:22 and cognate ἁγνεία, "purity," in 1 Tim 5:2). When used of women, it often carries the meaning of "chaste, pure" (cf. 1 Tim 2:9). οἰκουργός, "working at home," contrasts with the conduct of the younger Ephesian widows who were lazy and ran from house to house (1 Tim 5:13). It is a rare word (BAGD, 561; see *Note* d for variant). It does not require a woman to work only at home (cf. Prov 31), but it does state that she does have duties at home. For issues of present-day relevance, see S. Foh, *Women and the Word of God* (Philadelphia: Presbyterian and Reformed, 1979) 190–91. ἀγαθάς, "good," could modify οἰκουργούς, "working at home" (Hanson, [1983] 180–81). This would disrupt the pairing of terms, as would the next phrase. ἀγαθάς could also stand on its own, meaning "kindly, benevolent" (Matt 20:15; Mark 10:17–18; 1 Pet 2:18), in this context referring to the young woman's kind treatment of those in her household. The final quality is that she be submissive to her own husband (ὑποτασσομένας τοῖς ἰδίοις ἀνδράσιν), which is a common instruction in Paul's writings (1 Tim 2:11 [see Comment]; Col 3:18; Eph 5:21–23; cf. 1 Pet 3:1). By specifying ἰδίοις, "one's own," Paul emphasizes that the submission is not of one gender to another but of the wife to her husband. In both the husband/wife and master/slave relationship, Paul does not allow the former to demand submission but instructs the latter to give it. This is a significant distinction.

5b ἵνα μὴ ὁ λόγος τοῦ θεοῦ βλασφημῆται, "in order that the word of God may not be blasphemed." This is the first of three times Paul shows that his concern for the Cretan church is the reputation the church has with non-Christians. It is also the justification he gives for his instructions to younger men (v 8) and to slaves (v 10). It is not his only reason for defining proper moral behavior, but it is a significant motivating factor that appears throughout the PE (cf. *Explanation*). If the scope of this phrase covers vv 2–5, the blasphemy Paul addresses is society's desecration of the church. However, Chrysostom sees the blasphemy as the response of an unbelieving husband toward his believing wife, the ἵνα, "in order that," clause referring just to vv 4–5: "For if thou gain nothing else, and do not attract thy husband to embrace right doctrines, yet thou hast stopped his mouth, and dost not allow him to blaspheme Christianity" ("Homily 4"; NPNF 13:532).

6–7a τοὺς νεωτέρους ὡσαύτως παρακάλει σωφρονεῖν περὶ πάντα, "Urge the younger men likewise to be self-controlled in all things." Paul moves to the third group, the younger men, and summarizes his desires using the key term of the passage—σωφρονεῖν, "to be self-controlled"—rather than listing several qualities as has been his pattern. This is the fourth and final use of this word group in this chapter (vv 2, 4, 5). Ellicott comments, "the repeated occurrence of this word in different forms in the last few verses, would seem to hint that 'immoderati affectus' were sadly prevalent in Crete, and that the Apostle had the best of reasons for his statement in I. 13, which De W[itte] and others so improperly and unreasonably presume to censure" (182).

ὡσαύτως, "likewise," joins this discussion to the previous one in usual fashion for the PE (cf. v 3). παρακάλει, "urge" (cf. 1 Tim 1:3), is stronger than its parallel λάλει, "speak," in v 1 and is the second imperative of the passage. The only difficult question is whether περὶ πάντα, "in all things," goes with the preceding (Jeremias, Dibelius-Conzelmann, Kelly, NEB) or the following (Bernard, RSV, GNB, NIV, and possibly Guthrie). σωφρονεῖν, "to be self-controlled," is such an important, all-encompassing term in the PE that περὶ πάντα, "in all things," reads naturally with it. ἐν πᾶσιν, "in all things," also occurs at the end of v 10 and goes with the preceding thought. If this is the case, σεαυτόν, "yourself," in the following verse is in an emphatic position, which is appropriate for what it is saying. J. H. Elliott's suggestion ("Ministry and Church Order in the New Testament," CBQ 32 [1970] 377–79) that νεωτέρους should be translated "newly baptized" is rightly rejected by Hanson ([1983] 181) because the discussion is based on physical age.

7b σεαυτὸν παρεχόμενος τύπον καλῶν ἔργων, "showing yourself as an example of good works." Mention of the younger men reminds Paul to address some personal concerns directly to Titus, who himself was probably young. Titus must not only teach what is true (vv 7c–8a), but he must be an example, a model to be followed: "Let the luster of thy life be a common school of instruction, a pattern of virtue to all" (Chrysostom, "Homily 4"; NPNF 13:533); "Because the heathen cannot see our faith, they ought to see our works, then hear our doctrine, and then be converted" (Luther on Titus 2:5 [*Luther's Works*, ed. J. Pelikan (St. Louis: Concordia, 1966) 29:57]; cited by Quinn, 142). This need for modeling is found throughout Paul (cf. 1 Tim 4:12; 1 Thess 1:7; 2 Thess 3:9; Phil 3:17) and contrasts with the behavior of the opponents (Titus 1:10–16). It is often suggested that Titus was older than Timothy because there are more comments to Timothy about his age and his need to persevere (cf. 1 Tim 4:12). Yet the situations in Ephesus and Crete are different, and therefore conclusions of relative age cannot be drawn with any assuredness. It can be assumed from this context that Titus was young, but it is not clear how young. This verse is one of the few personal passages in the epistle (cf. 2:15; 3:12–15). These words to Titus should not be interpreted as instructions to all young men (contra Jeremias, Dibelius-Conzelmann, Brox). (1) It is typical of Paul in the PE to imbed personal comments within a discussion (cf. 1 Tim 1:18–19; 4:6–16; 5:23; 6:11–16). (2) The discussion concerns Titus's teaching ministry, a topic not relevant to all young men. (3) His instructions bear similarity to his words to Timothy (cf. 1 Tim 4:12–16) and should be read as personal instructions to his apostolic delegate.

The participle παρεχόμενος, "showing," carries the force of an imperative, grammatically dependent on the preceding phrase but introducing a different topic. The grammar is not very clear, but the participle seems to govern the remaining accusatives: "showing yourself as an example of good works, pure [and] dignified in your teaching, beyond reproach [in your] healthy instruction." The force of the middle voice is emphasized by the reflexive pronoun σεαυτόν, "yourself." On the verb, see *Comment* on 1 Tim 1:4. On τύπος, "example," see *Comment* on 1 Tim 4:12. Titus is to be a mold into which others can be impressed and therefore bear a likeness to him. Once again the concept of good works, important throughout the PE and especially in Titus (cf. 1 Tim 2:10), is encountered. In this context Titus, who provides an example in his good works, contrasts with the opponents, who are unfit for any good work (Titus 1:16).

7c ἐν τῇ διδασκαλίᾳ ἀφθορίαν, σεμνότητα, "pure [and] dignified in your teaching." Continuing the force of παρεχόμενος, "showing," Paul tells Titus that as he teaches, he must maintain purity of motive (contra the opponents [Titus 1:7]) and a dignity in his behavior. Although διδασκαλία, "teaching," can refer to what is taught, here it refers primarily to the action of teaching since the qualities that follow apply more naturally to the action than to the content (cf. 1 Tim 1:10). The content of what is taught is picked up in the next verse in the phrase "healthy instruction." ἀφθορία, "pure," occurs only here in the NT. It means "soundness, uncorruptness, single-mindedness." σεμνότης, "dignified," is a quality all Christians, and especially elders (1 Tim 3:4), should possess (cf. *Comment* on 1 Tim 2:2).

8a λόγον ὑγιῆ ἀκατάγνωστον, "beyond reproach [in your] healthy instruction." In a grammatically awkward construction, Paul continues the force of παρεχόμενος, "showing" (v 7), and shifts his discussion from the act of teaching (διδασκαλία) to the content of the teaching (λόγος). ὑγιής, "healthy," is a common description of the apostolic gospel, and the concept plays a significant role throughout the PE (cf. 1 Tim 1:10). For Titus's part, his presentation of the apostolic gospel must be beyond reproach, another theme central to the PE (cf. 1 Tim 3:2; ἀκατάγνωστος, "beyond reproach," occurs only here in the NT [cf. 2 Macc 4:47]). This does not mean that Titus can somehow prevent society from criticizing the gospel. Context shows that the issue was Titus's behavior more than the content of his instruction. Bernard (169) says it means "not open to just rebuke," and both he and Guthrie (196) emphasize that the gospel will always be condemned by some. Indeed, all people who desire to live a godly life will be persecuted (2 Tim 3:12), and the gospel that stands in judgment of sin will always be condemned by a sinful world. In fact, it can be argued that if the gospel is not condemned by sinners then it is not the apostolic gospel. If the world hated Jesus, so it will hate his disciples (John 15:19–21). Paul is emphasizing that believers should behave in such a way that no charges can justifiably be brought against the message of the gospel.

8b ἵνα ὁ ἐξ ἐναντίας ἐντραπῇ μηδὲν ἔχων λέγειν περὶ ἡμῶν φαῦλον, "in order that the opponent may be put to shame because [he] has nothing evil to say against us." As Paul did in v 5, he again explains why Titus should be a good example. The desire for a good reputation is a motivating factor throughout the PE and especially in this discussion; it is the same reason given to young women (v 5) and slaves (v 10). And yet Paul goes considerably beyond appearances. The goal is not to have Cretan society think well of Christians; the goal is for Titus and other church members to behave so that no justifiable charges can be leveled against them (see *Explanation*).

ἐναντίος as an adjective means "opposite, against, contrary," but with ἐξ, "from," it forms an idiom meaning "opponent" (BAGD, 262; cf. Mark 15:39). The opponent was one who opposed Titus's ministry; that much is clear. What is confusing is the opponent's identity. (1) Chrysostom (and apparently no one else) suggests it was Satan. This accounts for the singular but does not fit the context. Satan would not be ashamed. (2) It could refer to the opponents within the Cretan church (Bernard, Brox), (3) or to non-Christians outside the church (Ellicott, Spicq). (4) Some allow for a combination of options (2) and (3) (Scott, Kelly, Hanson [1983], Fee). The latter seems preferable. The opposition was coming from within the church, especially from the Jewish converts (cf. 1:10), and yet throughout the PE Paul is concerned about what non-Christians think (cf. 1 Tim 3:2). Paul uses the singular because he is viewing the opposition as one entity, or else it is a generic singular, "whoever opposes." ἐντρέπειν in the passive means "to be put to shame" (cf. 2 Thess 3:14), to be shamed into silence. It could refer to shaming the opponents, which was their penalty, or to remedial shame (as discipline is throughout the PE; cf. 1 Tim 1:20), so that they would change their minds. This positive element is more apparent in the parallel reason in v 10. ἔχων, "having," is causal: because they have nothing evil to say, they will be ashamed. φαῦλος means "bad, evil, worthless" (cf. Rom 9:11; 2 Cor 5:10; cf. John 3:20; 5:29; Jas 3:16) and refers to one's actions (Bernard, 169; Fee, 189). Paul is therefore thinking of Titus's behavior, that it should be blameless. There is a change from singular to plural with an implication of corporate responsibility: Titus must behave properly so that the opponent has nothing bad to say about ἡμῶν, "us," the plural including Paul, the Cretan Christians, and probably all Christendom.

9a δούλους ἰδίοις δεσπόταις ὑποτάσσεσθαι ἐν πᾶσιν, "[Urge] slaves to be subject to their own masters in all things." Continuing the force of the imperative in v 6 (BDF §389), Paul turns to the sixth and final group addressed in this passage. Unlike the first four groups, this one is not based on gender and age, and what he says is similar to 1 Tim 6:1–2 (see there for discussion of δούλους ἰδίοις δεσπόταις, "slaves to their own masters"). In 1 Tim 6:1 Paul urges slaves to treat their masters as "worthy of all respect," and elsewhere he asks them to "obey" (ὑπακούετε) their masters (Eph 6:5; Col 3:22; cf. 1 Pet 2:18). Any differentiation between ὑπακούειν, "to obey," and ὑποτάσσεσθαι, "to be subject," seems overly subtle. For example, the holy women "were submissive [ὑποτασσόμεναι] to their husbands, as Sarah obeyed [ὑπήκουσεν] Abraham" (1 Pet 3:5–6). The middle-voice form of ὑποτάσσειν can carry the nuance of "to submit oneself" in the sense of willing submission. Chrysostom discusses extensively the generally perceived wickedness of slaves as a class and the influence of a slave's obedience on non-Christians: "So that it is not by chance or without reason, that Paul shows so much consideration for this class of men: since the more wicked they are, the more admirable is the power of that preaching which reforms them" ("Homily 4"; NPNF 13:533).

ἐν πᾶσιν, "in all things," could go with the preceding or the following. If ὑποτάσσεσθαι, "to be subject," stands as the head term and the following qualities clarify what it means to be subject (cf. Fee, 190, but see discussion below), then it would be most appropriate if ἐν πᾶσιν, "in all things," went with the preceding (cf. similar expression in Col 3:22: ὑπακούετε κατὰ πάντα, "obey in everything"). ἐν πᾶσιν occurs at the end of v 10, where it also goes with the preceding. The scope of πᾶσιν, "all," needs to be defined because Paul would not encourage a slave to follow mindlessly a non-Christian master's instructions that opposed the gospel. Fee (190) suggests that v 9 refers to Christian masters, as is true in 1 Tim 6:2, and yet the reason stated in v 10b implies that submissive behavior is required for the benefit of non-Christians. It is probable that the instructions are given to all Christian slaves regardless of their masters and that the limitation of Christian principles is always in the background of NT ethical instruction. Knight explains ἐν πᾶσιν, "in all things," as "in all aspects of their service that a Christian slave can render without sinning" (314).

9b–10a εὐαρέστους εἶναι, μὴ ἀντιλέγοντας, μὴ νοσφιζομένους, ἀλλὰ πᾶσαν πίστιν ἐνδεικνυμένους ἀγαθήν, "to be pleasing, not talking back, not pilfering but showing completely good faithfulness." Paul follows with four qualities, the first two general and the second two especially applicable to slaves. εὐάρεστος means "pleasing, acceptable," and everywhere in the NT except possibly here it refers to that which is pleasing to God (Rom 12:1, 2; 14:18; 2 Cor 5:9; Eph 5:10; Phil 4:18; Col 3:20; Heb 13:21; cf. BAGD, 318; W. Foerster, *TDNT* 1:456–57). Because of this near unanimous witness, it should not be quickly concluded that the masters are the only object, although they are the object of the other three qualities; Paul could be telling slaves to be pleasing to God. His instructions elsewhere to slaves are that they do their service not as to people but as to God (Eph 6:6–7; Col 3:22). If a slave does what is pleasing to God, the slave will usually be pleasing to the master. The only other use of ἀντιλέγειν, "to talk back," in the PE is in the description of the opponents speaking against the gospel (1 Tim 1:9). Here it refers to talking back to their masters or to slandering them behind their backs.

νοσφίζειν originally meant "to put aside for oneself, misappropriate" (BAGD,

543; Bernard, 170) and came to be a euphemism for petty theft (Kelly, 243). Its use to describe Ananias and Sapphira's withholding of money from the sale of their land (Acts 5:2–3) shows that it can describe more than petty thievery. The stereotype of thieving slaves is proverbial in the ancient world (references in Quinn, 149). But rather than stealing—the ἀλλά, "but," is strongly adversative—slaves must prove by their behavior that they are totally faithful. On ἐνδεικνύναι, "to show," cf. *Comment* on 1 Tim 1:16. Using πίστις as "faithfulness" is fully Pauline (cf. *Introduction*, "Themes in the PE"; Gal 5:22). On ἀγαθός, "good," cf. *Comment* on 1 Tim 1:8, and for a different translation, see Wallace, *Greek Grammar*, 188–89, 312–13.

10b ἵνα τὴν διδασκαλίαν τὴν τοῦ σωτῆρος ἡμῶν θεοῦ κοσμῶσιν ἐν πᾶσιν, "in order that they might adorn the teaching of God our savior in all things." Paul concludes this discussion by repeating for the third time his immediate concern for the reputation of the church, although this time his words are more positive than in v 8 (see *Explanation*). διδασκαλίαν, "teaching," refers to the gospel message (cf. 1 Tim 1:10). On τοῦ σωτῆρος ἡμῶν θεοῦ, "God our savior," cf. *Comment* on 1 Tim 1:1. κοσμεῖν, "to adorn," is used in 1 Tim 2:9 where Paul asks that the Ephesian women not concentrate on outward appearance but adorn themselves with what is fitting for godly women, with good deeds. Considering the presentation of the gospel in the PE, this cannot be an adornment apart from content but rather must be a clear presentation of the gospel that is enhanced by the slaves' behavior (contra A. Padgett, *EvQ* 59 [1987] 50). The slaves' motivation is to make the gospel as attractive as possible for those around them. While this may seem distasteful to some modern ears, it does show the emphasis Paul placed on the gospel and its effect on individuals (cf. 1 Tim 6:1). ἐν πᾶσιν, "in all things," repeats the same phrase in v 9 and emphasizes that the slaves' duty to the gospel encompasses everything around them.

Having described specific behavior in vv 1–10, in vv 11–15 Paul will move into the reason that this behavior is correct.

Explanation

With a list somewhat parallel to the qualifications for church leadership (1:5–9), Paul encourages Titus to teach the gospel message in a way that brings spiritual health. Titus's behavior and teaching should contrast with the behavior and teaching of the opponents, who are not fit for any good work (1:10–16). Paul emphasizes that Christians should be self-controlled and spiritually healthy, thereby enhancing the gospel's reputation.

For the most part, Paul speaks to different groups based on age and gender. Older men should be clear-minded, dignified, self-controlled, and healthy in faith, in love, and in steadfastness. Elderly women are to be reverent in demeanor, not slanderers, and not enslaved to much wine. The language is reminiscent of Paul's instructions both to deacons' wives (1 Tim 3:11) and to the young widows who were a part of the Ephesian problem (1 Tim 5:13–14). The older women are to teach what is good to the younger women, whom Paul assumes were married. This is not a formal function of the church but a personal, one-to-one teaching, a task that cannot properly be accomplished by men. They are to teach the younger women what they themselves know, to love their husbands and children, to be self-controlled, pure, working at home, kind, and submissive to their own husbands. Paul follows with the reason that the Cretans must follow his teaching: "in order that the word of God may not be blasphemed." Although there were other motivating factors, in this historical situation Paul's concern is for the church as a whole and its reputation.

The fourth group is young men, and Paul simply delivers the summary command: be self-controlled. But thinking of young men reminds him of one young man in particular, Titus, and he spells out a few particulars for him much in keeping with 1 Tim 4. Titus must show himself to be an example of good works, pure and dignified in how he teaches, and beyond reproach in what he teaches in order that the opposition might be silenced because they have nothing evil to say against the gospel.

The final group is slaves. This breaks the pattern of grouping people by age and gender and may signal a problem prevalent in Crete, although what Paul says is consistent with his instructions to Timothy and elsewhere. Titus must urge slaves to be subject to their own masters in all things, to be pleasing, not talking back, not pilfering but showing completely good faithfulness in order that they might adorn the teaching of God their savior in all things.

The thrice-repeated reason for these instructions has to do with their effect on society: "in order that the word of God may not be blasphemed" (v 5); "in order that the opponent may be put to shame because [he] has nothing evil to say against us" (v 8); "in order that they [i.e., the slaves] might adorn the teaching of God our savior in all things" (v 10). A. Padgett (*EvQ* 59 [1987] 39–52), following P. Lippert (*Leben als Zeugnis* [Stuttgart: Katholisches Bibelwerk, 1968]) and D. L. Balch (*Let Wives Be Submissive: The Domestic Code in 1 Peter* [Chico, CA: Scholars Press, 1981), argues that Titus 2:1–10 represents a "church-code," regulations governing conduct in the church in distinction from the household codes (cf. Eph 5:21–6:9; Col 3:18–4:1; 1 Pet 2:18–3:7) that "represent a standard Greek and Roman household ethic" (47). Padgett likens them to the household code in that one of their functions was "to reduce tension between society and the churches to stop the slander. Christians had to conform to the expectations of Hellenistic-Roman society so that society would cease criticizing the new cult" (47, quoting Balch, 88). Padgett summarizes Lippert's position as emphasizing not so much the issue of slander "as the missionary motive behind the call for irreproachable behavior" (47) and concludes, "The function of the church-codes (but *not* the house-codes) is a missionary one. . . . 'The author considers the civic virtues acknowledged in the Hellenistic world worthy of Christian imitation'" (47–48, quoting Barrett, 135). Speaking specifically of the younger women (v 5), Padgett writes, "the gospel of Jesus Christ is at stake in the actions of these young women. . . . They had to submit to their pagan husbands if the church was to survive" (49, 51). Padgett calls this "missionary accommodation" and concludes, "the rationales of the *hina* clauses of Tit. 2 demonstrate to me that Paul's concern was not to lay down a law for all time, but to give temporary marching orders for the church, so that the gospel could go forth to all peoples" (52).

It seems that if Padgett is correct, if the author of the PE believed that the gospel message would have been destroyed if egalitarianism were taught, if the Christian ethic was determined not by a deep awareness of what God had done in Christ (Rom 6), and if the author was not willing to confront Cretan society, which was characterized as "always liars, evil beasts, lazy gluttons" (1:12), then this is a teaching that is impossible to align with that of Paul and the rest of the NT. Yet it seems that Padgett has missed the point for the following reasons:

(1) Paul does not say that the *hina* clauses express his ultimate reason. They are a significant part of the overall picture throughout the PE; in a society renowned for its lack of ethics, Paul wants the church to stand out as a beacon. But Paul begins the discussion with his primary concern that Titus teach the apostolic message, that which "is fitting for healthy teaching" (v 1), and this topic is resumed in vv 11–15. Speaking the truth stands as the primary concern. Paul is also writing to one of his chief aids and rightfully assumes that Titus understands the fuller theological picture.

(2) Throughout the PE Paul's concern is not simply the avoidance of reproach because of what is taught. The apostolic gospel teaches that right actions are important, and it is sinful behavior (not words) that can cause the greatest damage. This is what Paul means in v 8 when he calls Titus to be "beyond reproach [in your] healthy instruction," both the act and the content, putting the opponent to shame "because [he] has nothing evil to say against us." If the Cretan Christians acted in accordance with the apostolic message, no unjust charge could be brought against them and hence the opponent would be put to shame. This is Paul's motivation, not a desire to get along with society. His desire is to stop the behavior that is wrong and that leads to slander.

(3) Of all the qualities enjoined on Titus and the Cretans in 2:1–10—to speak what is fitting, be clear-minded, dignified, self-controlled, healthy in faith, love, and steadfastness, reverent in demeanor, not slanderers or enslaved to wine, encouraging younger women to love, be pure, kind, being an example of good works, beyond reproach, pleasing, not talking back or pilfering, showing complete faithfulness— Padgett centers on two—wives being submissive and working at home—as being examples of missionary accommodation. This seems significantly arbitrary, suggesting that something other than the text is the issue. All the other qualities are intrinsically valuable, and most, if not all, are repeated throughout the PE and the NT (see Knight's comment on φαῦλος in v 8 being intrinsically a "moral evil" [317]). The text strongly suggests that Paul sees them all as intrinsically correct and valuable.

(4) While the issue of cultural accommodation is too large to discuss in detail here, it is hard to believe that the apostle Paul, if the picture of him in Acts and through his writings is to any degree accurate, would teach something that he believed was false. While he may voluntarily have altered his behavior, may have had Timothy circumcised but not Titus, may have become weak for the weak (1 Cor 9:22), this is different from teaching error. For example, while he instructs slaves to be obedient to their masters, he never teaches that slavery is right.

But that aside, especially in this letter it seems highly implausible that Paul would accommodate his teaching to Cretan culture. A person who says that Crete is full of liars, evil beasts, and gluttons (1:12) would not at the same time choose to accommodate to this culture in order to spread the gospel. Padgett comments, "The ethic of Tit. 2 is just what one would expect from the society of the day" (48); yet this was a society condemned by secular writers such as Cicero: "Moral principles are so divergent that the Cretans . . . consider highway robbery honorable" (*Republic* 3.9.15; see *Comment* on 1:12–13a). The Cretan social standards were evidently so low that there was, in essence, nothing to which Paul could accommodate.

(5) One of the strongest arguments against Padgett's proposed motive of missionary accommodation is the epistle to Titus itself. The fundamental teaching of the epistle is that the redemptive work of God in Christ (2:11–14; 3:3–7) must lead to changed lives (2:1–10; 3:1–2, 8–11), that Christ sacrificed himself to "redeem us from all lawlessness and cleanse for himself a special people, zealots for good works" (2:14), to "be intent on devoting themselves for good works" (3:8). God's foundation is firm; he knows who are his, and those who name his name must depart from wickedness (2 Tim 2:19). The motive for godly living does not stem from what would be a hypocritical and untruthful acceptance of secular thought; the motive comes from a full understanding of the nature and purpose of the atonement. There is no desire in the PE to change what the church taught so society would stop criticizing it.

While there is a strong emphasis in the PE on right behavior and the need to behave so that just reproach not be heaped on the church, at no time is the ethic ultimately determined by the secular mind. The idea of accommodating the truth of the gospel to the falsehood of a wicked society sounds oxymoronic. On this whole issue, see also Knight, 316–18.

B. Theological Basis for Godly Living (Titus 2:11–15)

Bibliography

Abbot, E. "On the Construction of Titus II.13." *JBL* 1 (1881) 3–19 (repr. in *The Authorship of the Fourth Gospel and Other Critical Essays* [Boston: Ellis, 1888] 439–52). **Berge, P. S.** "'Our Great God and Saviour': A Study of *Soter* as a Christological Term in Tit 2:11–14." Diss., Union Theological Seminary, Virginia, 1973. **Bover, J. M.** "Tit. 2:11–15: commentarium paraeneticum." *VD* 2 (1922) 10–14. **Harris, M. J.** *Jesus as God: The New Testament's Use of Theos in Reference to Jesus.* Grand Rapids, MI: Baker, 1992. 173–85. ———. "Titus 2:13 and the Deity of Christ." In *Pauline Studies.* FS F. F. Bruce, ed. D. A. Hagner and M. J. Harris. Grand Rapids, MI: Eerdmans, 1980. 262–77. **Hort, F. J. A.** *The Epistle of St. James.* London: Macmillan, 1909. 47, 103–4. **Moehlmann, C. H.** "The Combination *Theos Soter* as Explanation of the Primitive Christian Use of *Soter* as Title and Name of Jesus." Ph.D. diss., University of Michigan, 1920. **Mott, S. C.** "Greek Ethics and Christian Conversion: The Philonic Background of Titus 2:10–14 and 3:3–7." *NovT* 20 (1978) 22–48. **Ogara, F.** "Apparuit gratia Dei Salvatoris nostri." *VD* 15 (1935) 363–72. **Pesch, R.** "'Christliche Bürgerlichkeit' (Tit 2,11–15)." *ATW* 14 (1966) 28–33. **Reiser, M.** "Erziehung durch Gnade: Eine Betrachtung zu Tit 2,11–14." *Erbe und Auftrag* 69 (1993) 443–49. **Robertson, A.T.** "The Greek Article and the Deity of Christ." *Exp* 21 (1921) 182–88. **Romaniuk, K.** "L'origine des formules pauliniennes 'Le Christ s'est livré pour nous.' 'Le Christ nous a aimés et s'est livré pour nous.'" *NovT* 5 (1962) 55–76. **Schepens, P.** "De demonstratione divinitatis Christi ex epistula ad Titum II,13." *Greg* 7 (1926) 240–43. **Sisti, A.** "La pedagogia di Dio (Tito 2:11–15)." *BeO* 9 (1967) 253–62. **Spicq, C.** *L'Amour de père et du fils dans la sotériologie de saint Paul.* 2nd ed. AnBib 15A. Rome: Biblical Institute Press, 1974. 64–73. **Sullivan, K.** "The Goodness and Kindness of God Our Saviour." *TBT* 1 (1962) 164–71. **Vargha, T.** "Apparuit gratia Dei." *VD* 14 (1934) 3–6. **Wainwright, A. W.** "The Confession 'Jesus is God' in the New Testament." *SJT* 10 (1957) 274–99. **Wallace, D. B.** "The Article with Multiple Substantives Connected by καί in the New Testament: Semantics and Significance." Ph.D. diss., Dallas Theological Seminary, 1995. ———. *Greek Grammar beyond the Basics.* 270–90. ———. "Sharp *Redivivus?* A Re-Examination of the Granville Sharp Rule." Paper presented at the annual meeting of the Society of Biblical Literature, Philadelphia, November 1995. **Wendland, P.** "σωτήρ: Eine religionsgeschichtliche Untersuchung." *ZNW* 5 (1904) 335–53.

Translation

[11]*For the grace of God has appeared, bringing salvation* [a] *for all people,* [12]*teaching us that, having denied the ungodliness and the worldly passions, we should live in a self-controlled manner and justly and reverently in the present age,* [13]*waiting for the blessed hope and appearing of the glory of our great God and savior Jesus Christ,* [b] [14]*who gave himself for us in order that he might redeem us from all lawlessness and cleanse for himself a special people, a zealot for good works.*

[15]*Speak* [c] *these things and encourage and rebuke with all authority; let no one disregard* [d] *you.*

Notes

[a]Because σωτήριος, "bringing salvation," is anarthrous, it stands outside the noun group ἡ χάρις τοῦ θεοῦ, "the grace of God" (BAGD, 269 [3]; Bernard, 170), and must be in the predicate (see *Comment*). (C³) D² Ψ 33 1881 TR insert ἡ, "the," before σωτήριος, attaching it to the subject and resulting in the translation "the saving grace of God." Others change it to the noun σωτῆρος, "savior" (א* t vg^ms), or τοῦ σωτῆρος ἡμῶν, "our savior" (F G a b vg^cl ww co; Lcf). Our text is read by א² A C* D* 0278 1739 vg^st; Cl.

[b]The order of Ἰησοῦ Χριστοῦ, "Jesus Christ," is supported by א² A C D Ψ 0278 33 1881 TR lat sy; Cl Lcf Ambst Epiph. It is reversed by א* F G b. Cf. Quinn, 157.

[c]λάλει, "speak," is replaced with δίδασκε, "teach," by A, which clarifies the meaning.

[d]περιφρονείτω, "disregard," is replaced with καταφρονείτω, "despise," by P *pc* in imitation of 1 Tim 4:12.

Form/Structure/Setting

In a corpus that emphasizes the practical aspects of Christianity, these verses provide a firm theological foundation for right practice. Titus 1:16 sets the stage for this passage as it states that the opponents have separated theology from lifestyle, claiming to know God but denying him by their deeds; hence they are worthless for the very good works God intended in providing their salvation. After discussing different groups of people in 2:1–10, Paul now explains why this bifurcation is wrong. But vv 11–15 also have linguistic links to vv 1–10 through the common use of ἡμῶν/ἡμᾶς, "us" (vv 8, 12), πᾶσιν, "all" (vv 10, 11), θεοῦ, "God" (vv 10, 11), and "savior/saving" (vv 10, 13, σωτήρ; v 11, σωτήριος). Conceptually they are linked because vv 11–15 give the theological basis for the practical instructions in vv 1–10, and this is why v 11 begins with γάρ, "for," resuming the theological note begun in 2:1. While Paul sometimes moves from theology to behavior (e.g., Eph 1–3, 4–6), here and elsewhere (e.g., Phil 2:12–13) he moves from behavior to theology. The language is similar to that of Titus 3:4–7 and 2 Tim 1:8–10 (see table in *Form/Structure/Setting* on Titus 3:1–11) and presents a powerful claim that those saved by God's grace are required to respond in obedience (see *Explanation*). The obedience of the believer is based on and grows out of the gracious work of God in Christ (cf. Oberlinner, 125–26), and is a life lived in light of the eschatological awareness of the Lord's return.

The interchange of tenses is significant. God's grace ἐπεφάνη, "appeared" (aorist), daily παιδεύουσα, "teaching" (present), that ἀρνησάμενοι, "having made the decision to deny" (aorist), the world, believers ζήσωμεν, "should live" (ingressive aorist), their lives προσδεχόμενοι, "constantly expecting" (present), Christ's return. God ἔδωκεν, "gave" (aorist), himself, and Titus should λάλει, "constantly teach" (present), these truths. As has been pointed out, the language is decidedly Hellenistic because Paul is contrasting the appearance of the true savior with Hellenistic ideas, especially emperor worship (Spicq, 2:251–52; Dibelius-Conzelmann, 143–46; Mott, *NovT* 20 [1978] 22–48; Hanson, [1983] 186–88). Yet many of the terms and ideas are deeply rooted in the OT and Paul's own thought, and in firm contrast to the Hellenistic ideal of education resulting in virtue; the virtuous Christian life is firmly grounded in the redemptive work of Christ.

Vv 11–14 constitute one sentence with χάρις, "grace" (v 11), standing as its subject. There are several parallels and contrasts in these verses. Christ's first coming is a manifestation of God's grace (v 11); his second coming shows God's glory (v 13). Vv 11–12 spell out in detail the twofold aspect of Christ's coming: a denial of sinful ways and an appeal to live righteously. This same negative and positive presentation is repeated in v 14, which speaks of Christ giving himself to redeem believers from lawlessness and to cleanse a people who would be zealous for good works. We also see a threefold presentation of the time of salvation, which includes the past fact of Christ's appearance (vv 11, 14a), the present obligations of that salvation (vv 12, 14b), and the future hope of the Lord's return (v 13).

V 15 is a transitional verse that could be placed with 2:11–14, by itself, or with 3:1–11. Paul is tying the overall discussion together so tightly that it is difficult to separate it into sections without destroying his flow of thought. Titus 2:1–10 and 2:11–14 actually form a single unit, comprising a call to obedience and the theological basis of that call, and v 15 summarizes the teaching in its admonition to "speak these things," repeating the same command from v 1 (λάλει, "speak"). But v 15 also moves the reader smoothly into the instructions of chap. 3, the imperative ὑπομίμνησκε, "remind," of 3:1 continuing the flow of thought and style from the four imperatives in 2:15. The decision to include v 15 with vv 11–14 is somewhat arbitrary.

Comment

11 Ἐπεφάνη γὰρ ἡ χάρις τοῦ θεοῦ σωτήριος πᾶσιν ἀνθρώποις, "For the grace of God has appeared, bringing salvation for all people." The different groups of people in vv 1–10 must live godly lives, γάρ, "for," God's grace teaches them to deny ungodliness and live justly as they wait for his return. Proper behavior stems from proper theology (see *Form/Structure/Setting*).

Throughout this passage Paul uses Hellenistic language to create a polemic with the religious and philosophical thought of Crete, Ephesus, and the ancient world ("appeared," "teach," "godliness," "just," "self-control," "great God and savior"). Mott (*NovT* 20 [1978] 22–47) goes so far as to conclude that the PE are dependent upon "traditions represented by Philo" (47) as the source of Hellenistic philosophy in the PE. However, the language, or the ideas behind the language, are often found in the OT, LXX, and elsewhere in the PE. It would be a mistake to think that Paul is appropriating the language without redefining it within the context of the Christian faith. This passage shows this as well as any passage in the PE, for here the instructor is God's grace, which is revealed by the one true great God and savior, comes out of the redemptive work of the savior, and teaches that life is to be lived within the awareness of Christ's return; as a result believers, like ancient Israel, are a special people for God, zealous to do good. Apart from the words used, this is about as far from Hellenistic philosophy as one can get, a philosophy that looked within the self rather than outward to God (see v 13 below).

γάρ, "for," indicates that vv 11–14 give the reason behind the ethical injunctions of vv 1–10; the ethics in the PE grow out of an awareness of God's salvific work for the believer. χάρις, "grace," is a one-word summary of God's saving act in Christ, given freely to sinners who believe (cf. 1 Tim 1:2). The emphasis here is on the ongoing workings of the initial gift of grace, as it is in Rom 6 where it is stated that living under grace and not law necessitates one's obedience as a slave of Christ (Rom 6:14–23). Grace provides the ongoing empowerment for Paul to conduct himself "with holiness and godly sincerity" (2 Cor 1:12). At first glance it may appear that σωτήριος, "saving," modifies χάρις, "grace," which would mean "the saving grace of God has appeared to all people" (cf. KJV; cf. Note a), suggesting that all people have been exposed to God's saving grace. However, the anarthrous σωτήριος must be in the predicate (cf. Note a), and Simpson (107) shows that σωτήριος followed by the dative is a classical construction meaning "to bring deliverance." σωτήριος is a predicate nominative functioning adverbially, describing the effects of the appearing. (ἐπεφάνη, "has appeared," functions as an equative verb.) The thought then is that God's grace has appeared and in so doing has made deliverance available for all people. Moule translates "God's favor has appeared with saving power" (*Idiom-Book*, 114). This is not universalism but the PE theme that God's gift is available for all people, Jew or Gentile, slave or free (cf. *Comment* on 1 Tim 2:4).

ἐπιφαίνειν, "to appear," is common in secular thought denoting the appearance of a god, demigod, or king, and implicitly contrasts the epiphany of the true Christ with that of mere mortals (cf. *Comment* on 1 Tim 6:14). It picks up the mention of σωτῆρος, "savior," in v 10 that will be repeated in v 13. In the LXX ἐπιφαίνειν is frequently used of the appearing of God's face (Num 6:25; Pss 30:17; 66:2; 79:4, 8, 20; 117:27; 118:135). Here it refers to the totality of Christ's life: from the incarnation through the resurrection and redemption (cf. Titus 3:4; 2 Tim 1:9–10). In v 13 it will encompass his return. Fee (194) suggests that the time of Paul's ministry in Crete was the appearance of their salvation, but the generality of πᾶσιν ἀνθρώποις, "for all people," suggests that it is wider in scope. On σωτήριος, "bringing salvation," cf. *Introduction*, "Themes in the PE." Bernard (170) says that σωτήριος occurs only here in the NT, viewing the neuter σωτήριον, "salvation," as a noun and not a substantival adjective (Luke 2:30; 3:6; Acts 28:28; Eph 6:17; contra W. Foerster, *TDNT* 7:1023–24; BAGD, 802). Many (e.g., Lock, Knight) suggest that the πᾶσιν, "all," has the force of "all groups of people," referring specifically to the slaves in vv 9–10.

12 παιδεύουσα ἡμᾶς ἵνα ἀρνησάμενοι τὴν ἀσέβειαν καὶ τὰς κοσμικὰς ἐπιθυμίας σωφρόνως καὶ δικαίως καὶ εὐσεβῶς ζήσωμεν ἐν τῷ νῦν αἰῶνι, "teaching us that, having denied the ungodliness and the worldly passions, we should live in a self-controlled manner and justly and reverently in the present age." Not only has God's grace saved believers, but it has the ongoing task of teaching them to live righteously. In words reminiscent of the "Two Ways" found in Qumran and early Christian literature (*Did.* 1–6; *Barn.* 18–21), Paul spells out this task of grace in negative and positive terms. This verse, which emphasizes present-day obligations, contrasts with the next verse, which looks forward to the Lord's return. Its basic thrust is repeated in v 14. The verse deals a death blow to any theology that separates salvation from the demands of obedience to the Lordship of Christ (see *Explanation*). Nestle-Aland[27] places a comma after ἡμᾶς, "us," viewing the ἵνα, "that," clause as expressing purpose: the purpose of God's grace is that believers learn that they must deny ungodliness and live reverently. If the ἵνα clause is a content clause as it is translated here, it carries the same sense.

παιδεύειν, "to teach," and its cognate παιδεία, "training," occur four times in the PE, twice describing the correction of the opponents (1 Tim 1:20; 2 Tim 2:25) and twice the training in godly lives (Titus 2:12) and righteousness (2 Tim 3:16). παιδεύειν has two related meanings: in the OT it generally means "to discipline, teach by chastisement," while many feel in Greek thought it means "to educate" (cf. W. Jaeger, *Paideia: The Ideals of Greek Culture* [New York: Oxford UP, 1945]; W. Barclay, *Educational Ideals in the Ancient World* [Grand Rapids, MI: Baker, 1974]; G. Bertram, *TDNT* 5:597–603; cf. Trench, *Synonyms*, 152–56; Mott, *NovT* 20 [1978] 30–35). Paul uses it twice to mean "to discipline" (1 Cor 11:32; 2 Cor 6:9), and this is also its meaning in 1 Tim 1:20. But here in Titus it is argued by some that παιδεύειν means "to educate" since the following clause spells out the content of the education, thus betraying non-Pauline authorship (see *Introduction*, "Critical Questions about the PE within the Framework of Paul's Life; The Theological Problem"). (1) The word only occurs twice in Paul's writings outside the PE. It is not reasonable to draw a conclusion of Pauline style on the basis of two occurrences. (2) The cognate παιδευτής occurs in Rom 2:20 with the meaning "an educator" where the thought is "of the general influence of Jewish moral standards in the Gentile world" (Cranfield, *Romans* 1:167; but cf. Dunn, *Romans* 1:112–13). Paul also uses the cognate παιδαγωγός (Gal 3:24) with the Greek meaning "pedagogue." So Paul knows both meanings of the word group and uses both. (3) παιδεύειν is used in 2 Tim 2:25 meaning "to teach by correction," but in 2 Tim 3:16 the cognate παιδεία most likely refers to "teaching" (see *Comment*). (4) Luke uses both meanings of παιδεύειν to describe Jesus' whippings (Luke 23:16, 22; cf. Heb 12:6, 7, 10; Rev 3:19) and the education of Moses (Acts 7:22) and Paul (Acts 22:3, reportedly in Paul's own words). Because of the possibility of Luke's influence on the writing of the PE, these references are significant (see *Introduction*, "Proposals regarding Authorship of the PE, Amanuensis Hypothesis"). (5) There is nothing in our text that necessitates the meaning "to educate" rather than "to teach by discipline." It may seem more appropriate to some, but there is a fine line between teaching and teaching with discipline. In fact, Ellicott argues strongly that the word here means "to discipline": "Grace exercises its discipline on us (1 Cor. xi. 32, Heb. xii 6) before its benefits can be fully felt or thankfully acknowledged" (186). (6) Although the Jewish background to this word may emphasize the element of correction, the idea of education is often present (cf. G. Bertram, *TDNT* 5:603–6), especially in the Psalms (G. Bertram, *TDNT* 5:610). (7) Fee (199) shows that both meanings are present in the language of Hellenistic Judaism (Wis 6:11, 25; 11:19; Sir 6:32), and this is the milieu out of which Paul draws his terminology in the PE. (8) Quinn questions the premise of the distinction: "The education or schooling of the young designated by this cluster of terms was in the Hellenistic world so closely associated with whipping and cudgeling the refractory student that *paideuein* popularly designated corporal punishment as well as what a modern would call 'education' (see [H. I.] Marrou, [*A History of*] *Education [in Antiquity* (New York: Sheed and Ward, 1956)] pp. 158–159). Aristotle submitted as self-evident that learning occurs with pain" (163, citing *Politics* 8.1339a29 and Hesiod *Works and Days* 218). These arguments show that the ideas of education and discipline were not necessarily separated in Paul's mind and that he could use both meanings.

God's grace teaches believers that having denied ungodliness, they should live godly lives. It is not sufficient merely to "eschew evil," but believers must "pursue after integrity and holiness, with an outlook that embraces the future as well as the present" (Simpson, 109). Chrysostom comments, "See here the foundation of all virtue. He has not said 'avoiding,' but 'denying.' Denying implies the greatest difference, the greatest hatred and aversion" ("Homily 5"; NPNF 13:536). Much is often made of the significance of ἀρνησάμενοι, "having denied," suggesting that it refers to the person's renunciation of sin at baptism (e.g., Kelly, Brox, Hanson [1983], Quinn). But there is nothing in the verb itself that necessitates a reference to baptism; and because there supposedly was a renunciation of one's former life in baptismal liturgies, this does not mean that this is necessarily the case here. This is not a liturgical passage.

ἀσέβεια, "ungodliness," is the opposite of εὐσέβεια, "godliness," a key term in the PE (cf. 1 Tim 2:2) and mentioned in the next phrase (cf. 2 Tim 2:16; cf. Rom 1:18; 11:26 [Isa 59:20]; cf. Jude 15, 18, and the discussion of ἀσεβής, "ungodly," in the *Comment* on 1 Tim 1:9). κοσμικός, "worldly," occurs elsewhere in the NT only in Heb 9:1, but the idea of worldly in the sense of that which is opposed to the divine is frequent (cf. 1 Cor 1:21; cf. John 7:7; 1 John 2:16; cf. H. Sasse, *TDNT* 3:897–98). Although the word is morally neutral, in the PE ἐπιθυμία, "passion," always refers to evil passions (cf. 1 Tim 6:9).

The positive side of the teaching of God's grace is that σωφρόνως καὶ δικαίως καὶ εὐσεβῶς ζήσωμεν ἐν τῷ νῦν αἰῶνι, "we should live in a self-controlled manner and justly and reverently in the present age." ζήσωμεν, "live," may be ingressive, "begin to live," stating the positive turn in one's life that comes out of the denial of ungodliness. σωφρόνως, "in a self-controlled manner," continues the frequent use of the word group in vv 1–10 (cf. v 2). δικαίως, "justly," emphasizes the ethical obligations of one who has been justified (cf. 1 Tim 1:9; 1 Thess 2:10). εὐσεβῶς, "reverently," is the opposite of ἀσέβεια, "ungodliness," in the preceding phrase and is one of the key qualities required of Christians in the PE (cf. 1 Tim 2:2; on the phrase εὐσεβῶς ζῆν, "to live reverently," cf. *Comment* on 2 Tim 3:12). Some suggest that the three adverbs refer "to one's self, to one's relationships with other people, and to one's relationship with God" (Knight, 320; cf. Ellicott; Quinn). These qualities are three of the four cardinal virtues of Stoicism (see detailed discussion by Mott, *NovT* 20 [1978] 22–30), which shows again that Paul was consciously borrowing Hellenistic terminology but Christianizing it in the process (cf. the Christian traits of v 2). Quinn misses the point when he says "the form of the adverbial triad, the individual terms, and the way of life being signified are unabashedly Hellenistic . . . [and] living as a Christian . . . involves assimilating much of what Hellenistic culture valued in human life" (166), although he does later state that Christians were discriminating in their use of Hellenistic ethics (168). The entire thrust of vv 11–15 is that the Christian ethic stems not from what this present age teaches but from the revolutionary work of the redeeming God who has brought salvation by his mercy and grace (3:3–7), and it is conditioned by eschatological expectations. In the PE God's grace is the instructor, not Hellenistic philosophy (see above on ἐπεφάνη, "appeared"). ἐν τῷ νῦν αἰῶνι, "in the present age," contrasts with v 13 with its reference to the future return of Christ and shows a Jewish, not a Hellenistic, eschatology. On the phrase, cf. *Comments* on 1 Tim 6:17; 2 Tim 4:10.

13 προσδεχόμενοι τὴν μακαρίαν ἐλπίδα καὶ ἐπιφάνειαν τῆς δόξης τοῦ μεγάλου θεοῦ καὶ σωτῆρος ἡμῶν Ἰησοῦ Χριστοῦ, "waiting for the blessed hope and appearing of the glory of our great God and savior Jesus Christ." The Christian commitment involves not only a lifestyle obligation in the here and now (v 12) but also a hope for the future that is both an expectation and an obligation: an expectation of seeing the Lord and an implied obligation to stay true to one's commitment until that day. "For nothing is more blessed and more desirable than that appearing. Words are not able to represent it, the blessings thereof surpass our understanding," exclaims Chrysostom, and on that note he ceases writing ("Homily 5"; NPNF 13:537). Paul's eschatological expectations are as alive here as they have been at any time in his life. As is true throughout the NT, an expectation of the eschatological return of Christ encourages perseverance in the here and now. V 13 is parallel to v 11, based on the repetition of ἐπεφάνη, "appeared"/ ἐπιφάνειαν, "appearing." God's grace appeared at the incarnation; God's glory will appear with the coming of Jesus.

On μακάριος, "blessed," see *Comment* on 1 Tim 1:11. ἐλπίδα, "hope," refers not to the expectation so much as to what is hoped for, and the verse continues (καί, "and," can be epexegetical) by defining the content of the hope as the appearing of Jesus at his second coming. 1 Tim 1:1 personifies and identifies hope with Jesus. This is another NT example of hope meaning the believer's confident anticipation of what will surely come to pass (cf. 1 Tim 1:1). On the significance of ἐπιφάνεια, "appearing," and its associations with emperor worship, cf. *Comments* on v 11 and 1 Tim 6:14. This first καί, "and," is probably epexegetical: believers live their lives in the expectation of seeing the blessed hope, that is (καί), their great God and savior, Jesus Christ. τῆς δόξης, "of the glory," can have three meanings. (1) The phrase can be a Hebraic genitive and be translated "glorious appearance" (cf. Rom 8:21; 9:23; 2 Cor 4:6). (2) It can mean "the glory of God," "the awful radiance in which God dwells" (Kelly, 246). The synoptic Gospels teach that Christ's return will display God's glory (Matt 16:27; 24:30; 25:31; Mark 8:38; 13:26; Luke 9:26; 21:27; 24:26), which argues for this option. Paul elsewhere uses δόξα, "glory," followed by a genitive construction that refers to God (Rom 1:23; 3:23; 15:7; 1 Cor 10:31; 11:7; 2 Cor 4:6, 15; Phil 1:11; 2:11). If δόξης, "glory" (ἐπιφάνειαν τῆς δόξης τοῦ . . . θεοῦ, "appearing of the glory of . . . God"; v 13), parallels the substantival χάρις, "grace" (ἐπεφάνη . . . ἡ χάρις τοῦ θεοῦ, "the grace of God has appeared"; v 11), then it too is substantival, not adjectival. (3) Hort (*James*, 47, 103–4) suggests that it is a christological title: "The Glory of the Great God (who is) Jesus Christ" (see below).

Nowhere in the NT is μέγας, "great," applied to God or Jesus (but cf. Mark 13:26 [Luke 21:27]; Heb 2:3; 4:14; 10:21; 13:20), but ὁ θεὸς ὁ μέγας, "great God," is a common name for God in the LXX (Deut 10:17; Ezra 5:8; Neh 8:6; Isa 26:4; Jer 39:18, 19; Dan 2:45; 4:20, 23, 34, 37; 9:4; cf. Neh 1:5; 9:32; Pss 47:2; 76:14; 85:11; Mal 1:14) and 3 Maccabees (1:9, 16; 3:11; 4:16; 5:25; 7:2), and it was common in secular language, applied specifically to Claudius and Ptolemy I (see below). The feminine form is evidently part of the title of Artemis of the Ephesians (Acts 19:28, 34) and of Babylon (Rev 14:8; 16:19; 17:5 [cf. v 1]; 18:2, 10, 16, 19, 21). W. Grundmann (*TDNT* 4:538–40) shows that in both the OT and here in Titus 2 the phrase places God in contrast to the pagan gods. In light of the rarity of the expression in the NT, its use for Artemis in Ephesus, and the common use of the phrase "God and savior" to describe human beings (see below), it seems that Paul was choosing language that directly confronted the claims of the other religions. Jesus is the only great God and savior (see ἐπεφάνη, "appeared," in v 11). Chrysostom balances this when he argues that God's greatness is absolute, not relative: he is not greater than the other "gods"; he is great, and "after whom no one is great" ("Homily 5"; NPNF 13:537). ἡμῶν, "our," occurs after σωτῆρος, "savior," but if θεοῦ καὶ σωτῆρος, "God and savior," are a unit, then ἡμῶν may refer to both θεοῦ and σωτῆρος, justifying its placement before μεγάλου, "great," in the translation.

The key question regarding the verse is whether τοῦ μεγάλου θεοῦ καὶ σωτῆρος ἡμῶν Ἰησοῦ Χριστοῦ, "our great God and savior Jesus Christ," refers to two persons of the Godhead ("the great God [the Father] and our savior Jesus Christ") or just one ("our great God and savior, Jesus Christ"). If it refers to one person, Jesus, it is a direct statement of the divinity of Christ (but see Hort below for a variation). The doctrine of Christ's divinity does not rest on this verse (cf. Rom 9:5; 2 Pet 1:1; below). As Harris points out in detail, Christ's divinity is asserted when he is seen throughout the NT as the object of worship, the agent of salvation, the creator, the forgiver of sins, the final judge, the one to whom prayer is offered, the one who possesses the attributes of God, and the one who shares the OT names for God ("Titus 2:13," 271; cf. Cranfield, *Romans* 2:468). In the PE Paul joins the activity of God the Father and Jesus in such a way as is appropriate only if Jesus is divine (cf. 1 Tim 1:2). The question is whether in this verse Paul states what he knows to be true, that Jesus is God.

The arguments for Paul's identification of τοῦ μεγάλου θεοῦ . . . ἡμῶν, "our great God," and Ἰησοῦ, "Jesus," are impressive (cf. RV; Wey; RSV; NEB; NASB; JB; GNB; NIV; Bengel, *New Testament Word Studies;* Ellicott; Cremer, *Lexicon,* 279–81; Bernard; Moulton, *Grammar* 1:84; Robertson, *Exp* 21 [1921] 182–88; Lock; Robertson, *Grammar,* 786; Easton; Spicq; Simpson; Gealy; Guthrie; Hendriksen; Wainwright, *SJT* 10 [1957] 274–99; Moule, *Idiom-Book,* 109–10; Leaney; BDF §276[3]; Barrett; Turner, *Grammatical Insights,* 15–16; Ridderbos; Dornier; Houlden; Zerwick, *Biblical Greek,* 60; Hanson [1983]; Fee; Marshall, SNTU-A 13 [1988] 157–78; Knight; Wallace, *Greek Grammar,* 276; cf. Harris, "Titus 2:13," 264–77, esp. 276 nn. 69-72, for more references).

(1) θεοῦ, "God," and σωτῆρος, "savior," are both governed by the same article, and according to Granville Sharp's rule they therefore refer to the same person (Robertson, *Grammar,* 785–89; Zerwick, *Biblical Greek,* 59–60; Harris, "Titus 2:13," 267–69; Wallace, *Greek Grammar,* 270–90). For example, 2 Cor 1:2 speaks of ὁ θεὸς

καὶ πατήρ, "the God and Father," both terms referring to the same person. As Wallace clarifies Sharp's own qualifiers, the rule applies "*only* with personal, singular, and non-proper nouns" (*Greek Grammar,* 272) and indicates some degree of unity between the two words, possibly equality or identity (270). When understood as Sharp intended, there are no exceptions in the NT to the rule (although on theological grounds, not grammatical, the rule has been questioned here and in 2 Pet 1:1; cf. Wallace, *Greek Grammar,* 273 n. 50, and further bibliography at 273 n. 50 and 276 n. 55). If σωτῆρος referred to a second person, it would have been preceded by the article. However, this is not to make the mistake of modalism, which sees only one God appearing in different modes (cf. Grudem, *Systematic Theology,* 242). God the Father and God the Son are not identical in orthodox theology; the Son is God, but he is not the Father. Wallace and Robertson (*Exp* 21 [1921] 185–87) both describe the force of G. B. Winer's refusal (*A Grammar of the Idiom of the New Testament* [Andover, MA: Draper, 1869] 130) to accept Sharp's rule for theological and not grammatical reasons. Speaking of the same construction in 2 Pet 1:1, 11, Robertson is direct in his critique: "The simple truth is that Winer's anti-Trinitarian prejudice overruled his grammatical rectitude in his remarks about 2 Peter i. 1" (*Exp* 21 [1921] 185); and the influence that Winer exerted as a grammarian has influenced other grammarians and several generations of scholars.

The grammatical counterargument is that σωτήρ, "savior," like other technical terms and proper names, tends to be anarthrous; but θεός, "God" (Wallace, *Greek Grammar,* 272 n. 42), and σωτήρ (Harris, "Titus 2:13," 268) are not proper names. θεός is not a personal proper name because it can be made plural (θεοί, "gods"; cf. Wallace, *Greek Grammar,* 272 n. 42). Proper nouns are usually anarthrous since they are inherently definite, but θεός is almost always articular unless other grammatical rules require the article to be dropped in specific contexts. θεός occurs frequently in the TSKS (article-substantive-καί-substantive) construction to which Sharp's rule applies (Luke 20:37; John 20:27; Rom 15:6; 1 Cor 15:24; 2 Cor 1:3; 11:31; Gal 1:4; Eph 1:3; Phil 4:20; 1 Thess 1:3; 3:11, 13; Jas 1:27; 1 Pet 1:3; Rev 1:6), always in reference to one person (cf. Wallace, "Sharp *Redivivus?*" 46–47). In the PE σωτήρ occurs in eight other passages, seven of which are articular (1 Tim 2:3; 2 Tim 1:10; Titus 1:3, 4; 2:10; 3:4, 6). The only other anarthrous use of σωτήρ in the PE is in 1 Tim 1:1, where it is anarthrous in accordance with Apollonius's Canon (Wallace, *Greek Grammar,* 250). In other words, in the PE the articular construction is the rule, suggesting that there is a specific reason for its anarthrous state here. If the question is the grammatical meaning of this text, Sharp's rule is decisive. If Paul was speaking of two persons, it would have been easy to say so unambiguously (e.g., τοῦ μεγάλου θεοῦ καὶ Ἰησοῦ Χριστοῦ τοῦ σωτῆρος ἡμῶν, "the great God and Jesus Christ our savior," or τοῦ μεγάλου θεοῦ ἡμῶν καὶ τοῦ σωτῆρος Ἰησοῦ Χριστοῦ, "our great God and the savior Jesus Christ" [Harris, 269]). Instead he chose a form that most naturally reads as one person, Ἰησοῦ Χριστοῦ, "Jesus Christ," which is in apposition to τοῦ μεγάλου θεοῦ καὶ σωτῆρος ἡμῶν, "our great God and savior." To say it another way, if Paul did not believe that Jesus was God, it seems highly unlikely that he would have been so sloppy in making such a significant theological statement. If Paul did believe that Jesus was God, it is not a surprise to read this.

(2) The flow of the discussion argues that θεοῦ καὶ σωτῆρος, "God and savior," refers to one person and that the one person is Jesus Christ. (a) Paul begins by

saying "for the grace of God has appeared bringing salvation," associating God with salvation. Two verses later, without a change of subject, he speaks of θεοῦ καὶ σωτῆρος ἡμῶν, "our God and savior." The most natural reading is to continue the association between θεοῦ, "God," and σωτῆρος, "savior." However, since Ἰησοῦ Χριστοῦ, "Jesus Christ," most likely stands in apposition to σωτῆρος, "savior," because of their proximity, Jesus is that God and savior. (b) Since ἐλπίς, "hope," is personified in the PE as Jesus (see above), Paul begins the verse speaking of Jesus, not God the Father ("waiting for the blessed hope, which is the appearing of God, who is Jesus Christ"). (c) The following verse speaks of Jesus' saving activity. This does not mean that v 13 must be speaking of one person; Paul often changes subjects by adding a relative clause (e.g., Eph 1:7). However, since v 14 does discuss salvation, it strongly suggests that Paul is thinking of Jesus as savior. (This argues against Hort's position [below] that Ἰησοῦ Χριστοῦ, "Jesus Christ," refers back to τῆς δόξης τοῦ . . . θεοῦ, "the glory of God.") If God and savior refer to one person (below), and if savior refers to Jesus Christ, then so must God. Lock (145) also points out that the idea of ἵνα λυτρώσηται, "in order that he might redeem," which occurs in v 14, is used in the OT of God but here of Christ, implying an equation between the two.

(3) The phrase θεὸς καὶ σωτήρ, "God and savior," was a set phrase in Hellenistic language (P. Wendland, ZNW 5 [1904] 335–53; Moehlmann, *"Theos Soter";* Spicq, 1:249–51; 2:640; id., *Agape dans le Nouveau Testament,* 3 vols. [Paris: Gabalda, 1958–59] 3:31 n. 3) and always referred to one person, such as Ptolemy I (τοῦ μεγάλου θεοῦ εὐεργέτου καὶ σωτῆρος [ἐπιφανοῦς] εὐχαρίστου, "the great god, benefactor, and savior, [manifest one,] beneficent one" [GH §15; Moulton, *Grammar* 1:84]; σωτὴρ καὶ θεός, "savior and god" [Harris, "Titus 2:13," 263 n. 9, citing Wendland, ZNW 5 (1904) 335–53, and L. Cerfaux and J. Tondriau, *Le culte des souverains dans la civilisation gréco-romaine* (Paris: Desclée, 1957)]), Antiochus Epiphanes (θεὸς ἐπιφανής, "god manifest" [Harris, "Titus 2:13," 267, citing Cerfaux-Tondriau, *Le culte*]), and Julius Caesar (θεὸς καὶ σωτήρ, "god and savior" [Harris, "Titus 2:13," 267, citing Cerfaux-Tondriau, *Le culte*]; cf. L. R. Taylor, *The Divinity of the Roman Emperor* [Middletown, CT: American Philological Association, 1931], esp. "Appendix III: Inscriptions Recording Divine Honors," 267–83; Lock, 145; LSJ; BAGD). Moulton comments, "Familiarity with the everlasting apotheosis that flaunts itself in the papyri and inscriptions of Ptolemaic and Imperial times, lends strong support to Wendland's contention that Christians, from the latter part of i/A.D. onward, deliberately annexed for their Divine Master the phraseology that was impiously arrogated to themselves by some of the worst of men" (*Grammar* 1:84). It was also used by Hellenistic and Palestinian Judaism in reference to God (Dibelius-Conzelmann, 143–46). Since in Hellenism it was a set phrase referring to one person and Paul is using language that places his gospel in direct confrontation with emperor worship and Ephesian religion (Spicq, 2:251–2; Harris, "Titus 2:13," 267; *Comment* on v 11), the phrase most likely refers to one person in this context, not two. This is how it would have been understood in Cretan society. Wallace points out how rare this expression is in the LXX (Esth 5:1; Ps 61:1, 5, without the article; cf. 3 Macc 6:32; Philo *Leg. All.* 2.56; *Praem.* 163.5); the MT rarely has an analogous construction (singular article-noun-*waw*-noun), and when it does, the LXX uses a different construction in translation ("Sharp *Redivivus?"* 43). He cites O. Cullmann (*The Christology of the New Testament,* rev. ed. [Philadel-

phia: Westminster, 1963] 241) in concluding that "Hellenism accounts for the form, Judaism for the content of the expression" ("Sharp *Redivivus?*" 44).

(4) When Paul speaks of the "appearing of the glory of our great God," he ties "appearing" and "God" together. Yet ἐπιφάνεια, "appearing," in Paul always refers to Jesus' second coming and never to God. The appearance of God is therefore the appearance of Jesus (2 Thess 2:8; 1 Tim 6:14; 2 Tim 1:9–10; 4:1, 8; Titus 2:13). In fact 1 Tim 6:14 and 2 Tim 1:10 have much the same meaning as our passage and confirm this argument. Although God the Father is involved in the Son's return, he is not as involved as this would indicate if it refers to two people (Lock 145; Fee, 196). There are two related arguments. (a) If καί, "and," is epexegetical, ἐπιφάνειαν, "appearing," is a restatement of ἐλπίδα, "hope," and hope is a personification of Jesus, showing that the appearance is the appearance of Jesus. (b) ἐπιφάνειαν, "appearing" (v 13), parallels ἐπεφάνη, "appearance," in v 11, and since in v 11 Paul is speaking of Jesus' appearance, it is most likely here that he is speaking of Jesus' second appearance. The counterargument is that the cognate ἐπιφαίνειν, "to appear," occurs in Titus 2:11 and 3:4 as part of the description of God the Father; however, these verses speak of God sending Jesus the first time.

(5) Marshall (SNTU-A 13 [1988] 174–75) adds the following arguments: (a) Jesus, as Lord, is the judge, which is the sole prerogative of God (2 Tim 4:8); (b) Jesus and God are placed side by side (1 Tim 1:1–2; 5:21; 6:13; 2 Tim 4:1; Titus 1:1; 2:13); (c) both are given the title "savior" (1 Tim 1:15; 2 Tim 1:9; 4:18); (d) spiritual blessings come from both (2 Tim 1:3, 6, 18; 1 Tim 1:12, 14); and (e) both are "objects of the writer's service" (God: 2 Tim 1:3; 2:15; Titus 1:7; Jesus: 2 Tim 2:3, 24). If Jesus has the position and function of God, then he can "probably" be called God.

There are other arguments that are of questionable validity. (1) The early Greek church fathers are nearly unanimous in seeing "God and savior" as referring to Jesus, and it can be assumed that they would know the Greek idiom (not Justin Martyr [*1 Apol.* 61] and Ambrosiaster; cf. Lock, 145; Harris, "Titus 2:13," 271). The counterargument is that the early versions are nearly unanimous in seeing two persons in this passage (Latin, Syriac, Egyptian, Armenian, but not Ethiopic) and that the Greek church fathers tended to be controlled more by their theology than by the text itself. Bernard asserts, "The Fathers were far better theologians than critics. Their judgement on a point of doctrine may be trusted with much readier confidence than the arguments by which they support that judgement" (172). Moulton (*Grammar* 1:84) points out that this appears to be the interpretation of the seventh-century Christians as evidenced by the papyri (cf. ἐν ὀνόματι τοῦ κυρίου καὶ δεσπότου Ἰησοῦ Χριστοῦ τοῦ θεοῦ καὶ σωτῆρος ἡμῶν κ.τ.λ., "in the name of the Lord and master, Jesus Christ, our God and savior etc." [BGU 2:366, 367, 368, 371, 395]), but this is quite late. (2) The NT nowhere describes God as μέγας, "great," and it is argued that it would be tautological to call God great (Ellicott, 188; Guthrie, 200). But the use of μέγας, "great," distinguishes God from the pagan deities, and great is no more than a summary of what Paul says about him in 1 Tim 6:15–16. Harris lists other arguments that he feels are debatable ("Titus 2:13," 270–71).

There are also arguments for seeing two persons in the phrase τοῦ μεγάλου θεοῦ καὶ σωτῆρος ἡμῶν Ἰησοῦ Χριστοῦ, "the great God [= the Father] and our savior Jesus Christ," along with the counterarguments listed above (KJV; Moffatt's tr.; G. B. Winer, *A Grammar of the Idiom of the New Testament* [Andover, MA: Draper, 1869] 130 n. 2; Alford, *Greek New Testament;* Abbot, "Titus II. 13," 439–52; Huther; Hort, *James,* 4, 103–4; Parry; Scott; Jeremias; Dibelius-Conzelmann; V. Taylor, *The Person of Christ in New Testament Teaching* [London: Macmillan, 1958] 131–33; id., "Does the New Testament Call Jesus 'God'?" *ExpTim* 73 [1962] 116–18 [repr. in *New Testament Essays* (London: Epworth, 1970) 83–89]; Kelly; Holtz; Brox; Hasler; Roloff; Oberlinner; more references in Abbot, "Titus II. 13," 449–50).

(1) Nowhere else in the NT is Jesus directly called God (e.g., Oberlinner, 137). But this assumes a reading of Rom 9:5 and 2 Pet 1:1 (cf. Wallace, *Greek Grammar,* 276–77) that is unlikely (cf. Cranfield, *Romans* 2:464–70; Harris, *Jesus as God*). (There are textual problems with John 1:1, 18; Acts 20:28; 1 Tim 5:21; 2 Tim 4:1; Jude 4. 1 Tim 5:21; 2 Tim 4:1; 2 Thess 1:12; Eph 5:5 use the personal name "Jesus Christ" and therefore stand outside of Sharp's rule.) The reasons given for this decision are usually theological but can only be made at the expense of the grammar of Sharp's rule, which has no exceptions when his qualifications are followed. The issue is whether Paul believes that Jesus is God. If he does, then regardless of what he may or may not have said elsewhere, there is no contradiction if he does say it here. Harris argues that our passage and 2 Pet 1:1 show the first stage in the titular use of "God" for Christ that culminates in Ignatius. As he says, "there is an ever-present danger in literary research of making a writer's 'habitual usage' so normative that he is disallowed the privilege of creating the exception that proves the rule. Every NT writer must be permitted the luxury of some stylistic, verbal, or theological *hapax* (or *dis* or *tris*) *legomena*" ("Titus 2:13," 265).

(2) Throughout the PE, God the Father and Christ are separated (1 Tim 1:1, 2; 1:17; 2:3–5; 5:21; 6:13–16; 2 Tim 1:2, 8, 9; 4:1; Titus 1:1, 3, 4; 3:4–6), so it would be unexpected for them to be so closely associated here (Abbot, "Titus II. 13," 447–48). But just because Paul normally separates them does not mean that here, as he deems it appropriate to the context, he could not join them. Also, while Paul can distinguish God and Jesus, he does so in such a way as to assert their unique closeness (see *Explanation* on 1 Tim 1:1–2). It is a small but significant step from saying that God is the savior and he saved believers through Christ who is the savior (Titus 3:4–6) to saying that Christ is God. The nature of the relationship within the Godhead defies description in that it has no analogy. According to orthodox theology, God the Father and God the Son are not identical, and yet there is one God.

(3) Since θεοῦ, "God," in v 11 is God the Father, in v 13, which is part of the same sentence, it is unlikely that Paul would use the same word for another person, especially if v 11 and v 13 are parallel. Abbot argues, "As the first appearing of Christ was an *appearing* or visible manifestation of the *grace* of God, who sent him, so his second advent will be an *appearing* of the *glory* of God, as well as of Christ" ("Titus II. 13," 448). Harris's counterargument is that "short of coining a new theological term to denote deity, writers who believed in the divinity of Jesus were forced to employ current terminology or run the risk of being branded ditheistic" ("Titus 2:13," 265). It can likewise be argued that since in v 11 Paul speaks of God bringing salvation, in v 13 God should likewise be connected with σωτῆρος, "savior" (arguing against Abbot's position). Also, in the span of two verses (Titus 1:3–4), Paul uses σωτήρ, "savior," of both God the Father and of Jesus, showing that he is willing to be flexible in the meaning of the word.

Hort views θεοῦ καὶ σωτῆρος, "God and savior," as one person, God the Father, and places Ἰησοῦ Χριστοῦ, "Jesus Christ," in apposition to τῆς δόξης τοῦ . . . θεοῦ, "glory of God," which he sees as a christological title (citing 2 Cor 4:6; Eph 1:17; Heb 1:3; Jas 2:1; cf. 1 Pet 4:14; id., *James*, 47, 103–4; summarized by Lock [145–46] and followed by Parry, 81, and Fee, 196): "The appearing of [him who is] the Glory of our great God and Savior [= the Father], [which Glory is/that is] Jesus Christ." This view follows the PE usage of calling God σωτήρ, "savior" (1 Tim 1:1; 2:3; Titus 1:3; 2:10; 3:4). Similar would be a possible reading of Acts 7:55 in which Stephen sees "the glory of God, that is [καί], Jesus," viewing the καί as epexegetical. However, Hort's argument requires σωτῆρος, "savior," to refer to an antecedent several words back (which is possible but less probable). But since v 14 spells out the saving work of Jesus, it is more natural to associate Ἰησοῦ, "Jesus," with the closer σωτῆρος, "savior," and not with τῆς δόξης τοῦ . . . θεοῦ, "glory of God." σωτήρ, "savior," in the PE is also applied to Jesus (2 Tim 1:10; Titus 1:4; 3:6; cf. *Introduction*, "Themes in the PE"). It is also not undisputed that "glory of God" is in fact a christological title.

Fortunately the doctrine of Christ's divinity does not rest on this verse. But the question of what Paul is saying here is still important, and it seems that he is making a christological pronouncement on the divinity of Christ. This is the most natural reading of the text, is required by the grammar, concurs with Paul's use of ἐπιφάνεια, "appearing," accounts for the singular use of the phrase "God and savior" in secular thought, and fits the context well.

14 ὃς ἔδωκεν ἑαυτὸν ὑπὲρ ἡμῶν ἵνα λυτρώσηται ἡμᾶς ἀπὸ πάσης ἀνομίας καὶ καθαρίσῃ ἑαυτῷ λαὸν περιούσιον, ζηλωτὴν καλῶν ἔργων, "who gave himself for us in order that he might redeem us from all lawlessness and cleanse for himself a special people, a zealot for good works." Having described Jesus as σωτῆρος ἡμῶν, "our savior" (v 13), Paul spells out his salvific work of redemption and sanctification. This parallels 1 Tim 2:6 where Paul says that Jesus "gave himself as a ransom for all" (ὁ δοὺς ἑαυτὸν ἀντίλυτρον ὑπὲρ πάντων). It repeats the gist of v 11 and v 12, which discuss the appearance of salvation and the ensuing demands for godly living. V 14 also completes the threefold presentation of salvation as involving the past (v 12), the present (v 14), and the future (v 13).

On the phrases ὃς ἔδωκεν ἑαυτὸν ὑπὲρ ἡμῶν, "who gave himself for us," and ἵνα λυτρώσηται, "in order that he might redeem," see *Comment* on 1 Tim 2:6. They convey the normal Pauline thought of Christ's self-giving on behalf of and in place of sinners. The emphasis of the ransom metaphor here is on the cost of the redemption, Christ giving himself, and on the all-encompassing effects of his sacrifice "from all lawlessness." The language is reminiscent of Ezek 37:23b: "But I will save them from all the backslidings in which they have sinned, and will cleanse them; and they shall be my people, and I will be their God." καθαρίζειν, "to cleanse," occurs only here in the PE, but the thought is similar to Eph 5:25b–26: "Christ loved the church and gave himself up for her, that he might sanctify her, having cleansed her by the washing of water with the word [ὁ Χριστὸς ἠγάπησεν τὴν ἐκκλησίαν καὶ ἑαυτὸν παρέδωκεν ὑπὲρ αὐτῆς, ἵνα αὐτὴν ἁγιάσῃ καθαρίσας τῷ λουτρῷ τοῦ ὕδατος ἐν ῥήματι]."

λαὸς περιούσιος, "special people," is an expression used of the nation Israel in the OT (עַם סְגֻלָּה *'am sĕgullâ*). Because God chose Israel to be his special people, they must avoid idolatry (Deut 14:2) and keep his laws (Exod 19:5; 23:22 [LXX];

Deut 7:6; 14:2; 26:18). By using this expression of the church, Paul implies the biblical theme of the church being the new Israel (cf. Rom 2:25–29; Gal 6:16 [but cf. Bruce, *Galatians*, 273–75]; Phil 3:3; cf. 1 Pet 2:9–10). H. Preisker argues that סגלה, *sĕgullâ* means not just "property" but "rich possession" and describes God's people as "the people which constitutes the crown jewel of God" (*TDNT* 6:57–58, citing Debrunner). It is possible that עם סגלה *'am sĕgullâ* is cited in 1 Pet 2:9 (λαὸς εἰς περιποίησιν), but this could also be a quotation from Isa 43:21 (cf. Michaels, *1 Peter*, 109). On περιούσιος, "special," see J. B. Lightfoot et al., "Appendix II," in *The Revision of the English Version of the New Testament* (New York: Harper, 1873).

ζηλωτήν, "zealot," stands in apposition to λαόν, "people," acting as a title, and the word can be followed by the genitive of the person (Acts 22:3) or thing (Acts 21:20; 1 Cor 14:12; 1 Pet 3:13). The person who is a ζηλωτὴν καλῶν ἔργων, "zealot for good deeds," stands in contrast to the Cretan opponents, who are unfit for any good deed. The believer's zeal comes not from an intellectual acceptance of Hellenistic philosophy but from a full understanding of the redemptive work of Christ. ζηλωτής, "zealot," is used elsewhere of God being a zealous God (Exod 20:5; 34:14; Deut 4:24; 5:9; 6:15; Nah 1:2), of Paul's zeal for God (Acts 22:3) and the law (Acts 21:20; Gal 1:14; cf. Phil 3:6; cf. 2 Macc 4:2; 4 Macc 18:12), and of a Christian's zeal for spiritual gifts (1 Cor 14:12; cf. 14:1) and the good (1 Pet 3:13; cf. cognate noun ζῆλος, "zeal," and verb ζηλοῦν, "to manifest zeal"). Although awkward sounding in translation, the singular ζηλωτήν, "zealot," parallels the singular λαόν, "people." καλῶν ἔργων, "for good works," a significant theme in the PE, emphasizes the need for one's faith to have an impact on one's lifestyle (cf. 1 Tim 2:10).

15a Ταῦτα λάλει καὶ παρακάλει καὶ ἔλεγχε μετὰ πάσης ἐπιταγῆς, "Speak these things and encourage and rebuke with all authority." This verse provides the transition between chap. 2 and chap. 3 and as such could be included in the discussion of either chapter (see *Form/Structure/Setting*). It is a summary command typical of the PE, looking both forward and backward (cf. 1 Tim 4:11; 5:7, 21; 6:2b; Titus 3:8b). Paul uses second-person verb forms only fourteen times in this letter; four of them occur in 2:15–3:1. ταῦτα, "these things," could refer to 2:11–14 since the call to the godly lifestyle they espouse would be opposed by the Cretans. But more likely ταῦτα refers to the entire epistle. Paul started his discussion at 1:5, and each section is firmly tied to the next so that there is no natural break in thought.

λάλει, "speak," recalls the same command in 2:1. A textual variant interprets λάλει, "speak," as δίδασκε, "teach" (cf. *Note* c). This one verse contains three of the fourteen imperatives in Titus (attesting to the less urgent situation than in Ephesus). As is usual in the PE, Titus's words to the church in general are to be gentle; he is to teach and παρακάλει, "encourage" (cf. 1 Tim 1:3; 4:13; 2 Tim 4:2), them to follow his instructions. But in addressing the opponents his language must be much stronger; Titus must ἔλεγχε, "rebuke" (cf. 1 Tim 5:20; Titus 1:13; 2 Tim 4:2), with all authority. ἐπιταγή, "authority," denotes kingly or divine authority (cf. 1 Tim 1:1). These instructions are given to Titus, Paul's delegate, and he is to exercise his full delegated authority if necessary (cf. Guthrie, 202). One can assume that this strong language is intended more for the Cretan church than for Titus. These instructions are not given to all church leaders but just to Titus (contra Brox, 302) since the church leaders have not yet been appointed (Titus 1:5). μετὰ πάσης ἐπιταγῆς, "with all authority," is appropriate only for the command to rebuke, not the commands to encourage or to speak.

15b μηδείς σου περιφρονείτω, "let no one disregard you." Paul adds one of the few personal notes in the epistle (cf. 2:7–8; 3:12–15). As Titus carries out these instructions, he must not allow anyone to look down on him, to despise him. περιφρονεῖν, "to disregard," occurs only here in the NT and takes an object in the genitive (BAGD, 653). This personal concern is similar to Paul's words to Timothy that he must not allow anyone to treat him contemptuously (καταφρονεῖν, 1 Tim 4:12; see *Note* d). In Timothy's case Paul is concerned with his age, but there is no similar expressed concern for Titus. Most take this as an indication that Titus was older than Timothy. But care must be taken about drawing too strong a conclusion from this difference. The situation in Ephesus was more intense, more urgent, more difficult, and significantly different from the one in Crete. Why would Paul express concern for Titus? Perhaps because there was a natural opposition to authority, especially when that authority was demanding a change in behavior. Anyone in Titus's position, even Paul, would have been looked upon with disdain, especially considering Cretan culture.

Explanation

Having given a list of instructions for different people in the church, Paul lays down the theological basis for godly living. He argues that God's salvific workings intend more than salvation, that integral to the salvation is the recognition that the free gift of grace comes with a cost, that of obedience. To separate salvation from ensuing obedience was at the core of the opponents' "knowledge" (1:16) but is foreign to the PE and Paul as he makes abundantly clear in Rom 6.

In the past, God's grace appeared in the person of Christ, and through him salvation was made available to all people. But this same grace teaches believers that they must both remove themselves from ungodliness and worldly passions that are opposed to God and also live self-controlled, just, and reverent lives. Salvation is not concerned only with the present, for there is a day coming of blessed hope, the confident anticipation of the second appearance of the glory of the great God and savior, who is Jesus Christ. It is this same Jesus who gave himself for sinners to ransom them from lawlessness through his death and to cleanse for himself the new Israel who can be called by the name "zealot for good works." There is no suggestion of universalism or salvation by works in these verses. The offer is available for all people who hear, and once accepted, the free gift of grace teaches believers that the only acceptable response is the offering of a life pleasing to the Lord.

To the end of this theological discourse Paul appends a short personal note to Titus. He must continue to speak and encourage the Cretan church to accept these teachings, especially the obligatory nature of Christian obedience. He must strongly rebuke with full authority those who would oppose him. They will oppose him, look down on him, and despise him, but that is not to deter him in his task.

The emphasis on good works, present throughout Titus, receives no greater emphasis than here. It is stated in v 14. Believers are a special people, not to be occasionally interested in obedience but to carry the title "zealot for good works." It is God's grace that not only brought salvation but also teaches that the necessary outcome of salvation is to deny that which is ungodly and to pursue that which is godly. But not only does grace teach this; it is within the very purpose of the atonement not only to redeem but also to cleanse. This is not righteousness by works; it is the message of grace, the full message of grace that redeems and sanctifies.

Paul makes the same point in the next chapter. All people were at one time foolish sinners. But God saved believers, not because they deserved it but because of his goodness, philanthropy, and mercy through the work not of themselves but of Jesus Christ and the Holy Spirit. He did this to save them so they could receive their inheritance. The application of these truths is that believers be "intent on devoting themselves to good works" (3:8) and avoid false and harmful teaching and teachers, those who are self-condemned, perverted sinners (3:9–10). Paul will make the point again in his second letter to Timothy within the context of election: "The firm foundation of God stands firm, having this seal, 'The Lord knows those who are his,' and, 'Let everyone naming the name of [the] Lord depart from unrighteousness'" (2 Tim 2:19).

A popular debate today centers on the phrase "Lordship Salvation." While not everything that has been taught in connection with this concept has merit, its basic premise is proven true by Titus 2–3. Salvation never stops with redemption but always moves to sanctification. There is no salvation apart from discipleship. Paul is not teaching the annulment of grace; he is teaching the full measure of grace and the purpose of God, to cleanse for himself a *special* people, a *zealot* for good works, so that believers may "learn to be intent on good deeds" (2 Tim 3:14). Any teaching that removes obedience from the scope of salvation comes under the same condemnation as did the Cretan and Ephesian opponents.

C. Continued Call for Godly Behavior (Titus 3:1–11)

Bibliography

Beasley-Murray, G. R. *Baptism in the New Testament.* Exeter: Paternoster, 1962. **Boismard, M.-É.** "Une liturgie baptismale dans la Prima Petri." *RB* 63 (1956) 182–208; 64 (1957) 161–83. ———. *Quatre hymnes baptismales.* Paris: Cerf, 1961. **Büchsel, F.** "ἀναγεννάω." *TDNT* 1:673–75. ———. "γεννάω." *TDNT* 1:665–66, 668–75. ———. "παλιγγενεσία." *TDNT* 1:686–89. **Buonaiuti, E.** "Vorträge über die Symbolik der Wiedergeburt in der religiösen Vorstellung der Zeiten und Völker." *Eranos Jahrbuch* 7 (1939) 291–320. **Derrett, J. D. M.** "*Palingenesia* (Matthew 19.28)." *JTS* n.s. 20 (1984) 51–58. **Dey, J.** Παλιγγενεσία: *Ein Beitrag zur Klärung der religionsgeschichtlicher Bedeutung von Tit. 3,5.* NTAbh 17.5. Münster: Aschendorff, 1937. **Duncan, J. G.** "Πιστὸς ὁ λόγος." *ExpTim* 35 (1922) 141. **Englhardt, G.** "Erben des ewigen Lebens gemäss der Hoffnung (Tit 3:7)." *Liturgie und Mönchtum* 8 (1951) 58–78. **Fee, G. D.** *God's Empowering Presence.* 777–84. **Gennrich, P.** *Die Lehre von der Wiedergeburt: Die christliche Zentrallehre in dogmengeschichtlicher und religionsgeschichtlicher Beleuchtung.* Leipzig: Deichert, 1907. **Harnack, A. von.** *Der kirchengeschichtliche Ertrag der exegetischen Arbeiten des Origenes.* Part 1: *Die Terminologie der Wiedergeburt und verwandter Erlebnisse in der ältesten Kirche.* TU 42. Leipzig: Hinrichs, 1918.

97–143. **Irurvetagoyena, J. M.** "La gracia santificante en Tit 3:4–7." *Scriptorium Victoriense* (1956) 7–22. **Jacono, V.** "La παλιγγενεσία in s. Paolo e nel l'ambiente pagano." *Miscellanea Biblica* 1 (1934) 249–78. **Käsemann, E.** "Titus 3,4–7." In *Exegetische Versuche und Besinnungen*. Göttingen: Vandenhoeck & Ruprecht, 1964. 2:298–302. **Knight, G. W., III.** "Titus 3:8 and Its Saying." In *The Faithful Sayings in the Pastoral Epistles*. 80–111. **Le Déaut, R.** "Φιλανθρωπία dans la littérature grecque jusqu' au NT (Tite 3:4)." In *Mélanges Eugène Tisserant*. Vatican City: Biblioteca apostolica vaticana, 1964. 1:255–94. **Metzger, B. M.** "Considerations of Methodology in the Study of the Mystery Religions and Early Christianity." *HTR* 48 (1955) 1–20. **Mott, S. C.** "Greek Ethics and Christian Conversion: The Philonic Background of Titus 2:10–14 and 3:3–7." *NovT* 20 (1978) 22–48. **Mounce, W. D.** "The Origin of the New Testament Metaphor of Rebirth." Ph.D. diss., University of Aberdeen, 1981. **Nock, A. D.** *Conversion.* Oxford: Clarendon, 1933. ———. *Early Gentile Christianity and Its Hellenistic Background.* New York: Harper & Row, 1964. **Norbie, D. L.** "The Washing of Regeneration." *EvQ* 34 (1962) 36–38. **Procksch, O.** "Wiederkehr und Wiedergeburt." In *Das Erbe Martin Luthers*. FS I. Ihmels, ed. R. Jelke. Leipzig: Dörffling & Franke, 1928. 1–18. **Robinson, J. A. T.** "The One Baptism as a Category of New Testament Soteriology." *SJT* 6 (1953) 257–74. **Schweitzer, W.** "Gotteskindschaft, Wiedergeburt und Erneuerung im Neuen Testament und in seiner Umwelt." Diss., Eberhard Karls University, Tübingen, 1943. **Sjöberg, E.** "Wiedergeburt und Neuschöpfung im palästinischen Judentum." *ST* 4 (1950) 44–85. **Spicq, C.** "La philanthropie hellénistique, vertu divine et royale (à propos de *Tit.* III,4)." *ST* 12 (1958) 169–91. **Sullivan, K.** "The Goodness and Kindness of God Our Savior." *TBT* 3 (1962) 164–71. **Wagenvoort, H.** "'Rebirth' in Antique Profane Literature." In *Studies in Roman Literature, Culture and Religion*. Leiden: Brill, 1956. 132–49. **Wagner, G.** *Pauline Baptism and the Pagan Mysteries.* Tr. J. P. Smith. London: Oliver & Boyd, 1967. **Ysebaert, J.** *Greek Baptismal Terminology: Its Origins and Early Development.* Nijmegen: Dekker & Van de Vegt, 1962 (esp. Part 2, "Renewal, Re-Creation, and Rebirth," 85–154).

Translation

¹*Remind them to be subject to rulers,*[a] *to authorities, to be obedient,*[b] *to be ready for any good work,* ²*to blaspheme no one, to be peaceable, gracious, showing complete gentleness*[c] *toward all people.*

³*For formerly we ourselves also were foolish,*[d] *disobedient, being led astray, being enslaved by desires and various pleasures, living a life of evil and envy, detestable, hating one another.* ⁴*But when the goodness and philanthropy of God our savior appeared,* ⁵*not out of works of righteousness that*[e] *we did but in accordance with his mercy he saved us, through the washing of regeneration and renewal*[f] *of the Holy Spirit,* ⁶*whom he richly poured out for us through Jesus Christ our savior* ⁷*in order that having been justified by his grace, we might become*[g] *heirs according to [the] hope of eternal life.*

⁸*Trustworthy is the saying, and I want you to insist emphatically on these things in order that those who have believed in God might be intent on devoting themselves to good works. These are good*[h] *and profitable for people.* ⁹*But shun foolish speculations and genealogies*[i] *and strife*[j] *and quarrels about the law, for they are harmful and useless.* ¹⁰*Avoid the factious person after a first and second warning,*[k] ¹¹*knowing that such a person has been perverted and is sinning, being self-condemned.*

Notes

[a]καί, "and," is inserted after ἀρχαῖς, "rulers," by D² 0278 TR lat sy. Its omission is supported by ℵ A C D* F G Ψ 33 104 1739 1881 *pc* b. Its omission is the more difficult reading since it removes the

asyndeton; see discussion in *TCGNT²*, 586. Lock thinks it accidentally dropped out after ἀρχαῖς (xxxviii).

ᵇκαί, "and," is inserted before πειθαρχεῖν, "to be obedient," by F G to enhance readability (asyndeton). A inserts it after πειθαρχεῖν.

ℵ* replaces ἐνδεικνυμένους πραΰτητα, "showing complete gentleness," with ἐνδείκνυσθαι σπουδὴν τά (?), "to show earnestness with respect to the (?)." The shift to an infinitive is to parallel the previous infinitives. TR spells πραΰτητα, "gentleness," as πραότητα.

ᵈκαί, "and," is inserted before ἀπειθεῖς, "disobedient," by D a b t vg^mss sy^p; Lcf. See *Note* b above.

ᵉἅ, "that" (ℵ A C* D* F G 33 81 1739 *pc*; Cl), is replaced by the genitive ὧν, "that," in C² D² Ψ 1881 TR through attraction to ἔργων, "works." Cf. Ellicott, 192.

ᶠδιά, "through," is inserted before πνεύματος, "Spirit," by D* F G b vg^mss; Lcf. It is an attempt to clarify a difficult construction (see *Form/Structure/Setting*) and interprets διὰ πνεύματος ἁγίου, "through the Holy Spirit," as being epexegetical to διὰ λουτροῦ παλιγγενεσίας καὶ ἀνακαινώσεως, "through the washing of regeneration and renewal."

ᵍThe passive deponent γενηθῶμεν, "become" (ℵ* A C D* F G P 33 81 104 630 1739 1881 *pc*), is replaced with the middle deponent γενώμεθα, "become," by ℵ² D² Ψ TR.

ʰτά, "the," is inserted before καλά, "good," by D² Ψ TR. Its omission is supported by 𝔓⁶¹ ℵ A C D* F G I 0278 81 104 326 365 1505 1739 1881 *pc* co.

ⁱBy analogy with 1 Tim 6:4, F G replace γενεαλογίας, "genealogies," with λογομαχίας, "fights over words."

ʲThe plural ἔρεις, "strifes" (ℵ² A C I 1739 1881 TR latt sy co), agrees with the surrounding plurals. The singular ἔριν, "strife" (= ἔρειν), is read by ℵ* D F G Ψ *pc*; Ambst. ἔριν is the more difficult reading because one would expect the scribes to switch the singular to the plural because of the context, but the external evidence for the plural is stronger. See *TCGNT²*, 586; F. J. A. Hort, "Notes on Orthography," in *The New Testament in the Original Greek*, ed. B. F. Westcott and F. J. A. Hort (Cambridge: Macmillan, 1881) 2:157.

ᵏThe order is switched from καὶ δευτέραν νουθεσίαν, "and second warning" (𝔓⁶¹ ᵛⁱᵈ ℵ A C 0278 TR lat; Ir Or), to νουθεσίαν καὶ δευτέραν, "warning and second," by D (which apparently read δύο, "two," for δευτέραν, "second," by the original hand) Ψ 1505 1881*pc* sy^h. νουθεσίαν ἢ δευτέραν, "warning or second," is read by F⁻G. These variants do not affect the meaning of the verse; cf. Bernard, 175. καὶ δευτέραν, "and second," is omitted by 1739 b vg^ms; Ir^lat Tert Cyp Ambst, which does intensify Paul's command, telling Titus to avoid the factious person after only one warning. Cf. Lock, xxxviii.

Form/Structure/Setting

The structure of Titus 3:1–11 is similar to 2:1–14 as it spells out the nature of God's salvific plans and the implications of those plans for the lifestyle of believers as the following table shows. 2 Tim 1:9 is also similar. These passages discuss why God saved believers, the appearance of Christ, what he did, how he did it, its practical implications, and its eschatological consequences. All three passages are highly christological, especially in their use of σωτήρ, "savior."

Titus 2:11–15	*Titus 3:3–7*	*2 Tim 1:9*
	We were evil people.	
	Not because of our acts of righteousness.	Not because of our works but his purpose and grace.
Grace of God.	Goodness and philanthropy of God.	
	According to his mercy. Justified by his grace.	

Appeared.	Appeared.	Now visible through the appearing of our savior Christ Jesus.
Salvation of all people.	He saved us.	Who saved us and called us with a holy calling.
	Through regeneration and renewal.	
	Through the Holy Spirit given through Jesus Christ.	Given to us in Christ.
Training us to live godly lives.	Vv 1–2, 9–11	Timothy is not to be ashamed.
Who [i.e., Christ] gave himself to redeem us from iniquity and prepare a people, a zealot for good works.		Paul was appointed an apostle.
As we wait for the blessed hope, the appearing of the glory of our great God and savior Jesus Christ.	God our savior (v 4).	Our savior Christ Jesus.
	Jesus Christ our savior (v 6).	Christ abolished death and brought life and immortality through the gospel.
	We have an inheritance according to the hope of eternal life.	

Despite the similarity, it is difficult to draw many conclusions concerning their source with confidence. Titus 3:4–7 includes a faithful saying (see below) that is so replete with Paul's terminology that it is difficult to believe it is a citation.

The basic message of the statement is clear. It is not spelling out the involvement of believers in the salvation process. Its emphasis is on what God himself has provided through the work of Christ and the Holy Spirit, and the consequences of his actions on believers. If it is missing elements such as faith, this is to be expected. The passage speaks of God's actions, not the believers' (contra Knight, *Faithful Sayings*, 92). Conversion comes not because of human effort but because of God's goodness, love for people, and mercy. Justification is not achieved through human effort but through God's grace. Conversion consists of God's cleansing of the human heart and spiritual renewal accomplished through the Holy Spirit. The result is the believers' justification and an inheritance that will not disappoint. God is the initiator; people are the recipients. There is a chronological movement: appearance, possibility of salvation by God's mercy, the work of the Holy Spirit and Jesus, justification, and eschatological inheritance.

F. Chase (*Confirmation in the Apostolic Age* [New York: Macmillan, 1909] 100–101) argues for the corporate nature of the creed. The time frame of the creed is not an individual's appropriation of salvation but the offering of that salvation to all "when the goodness and philanthropy of God ... appeared" (v 4). The creed centers not on the individual appropriation of salvation but on God's overall plan of salvation actualized in the Christ event. The main thought is ἔσωσεν ἡμᾶς, "he saved us," and the rest of the creed is explanatory. The constant use of the plural "we" and "us" shows that the creed is speaking generally of all Christians, not any one individual. V 7 does not say that as a result of the washing and renewal a person is justified; it says that the purpose (ἵνα, "in order that") of the washing and renewal is that a person be justified (subjunctive) and become an heir. The Holy Spirit is poured out not on "you" but on "us." ἐξέχεεν, "he poured out" (v 6), may be a reflection of Pentecost and the outpouring of the Holy Spirit (see *Comment*), and this too shows that the author is thinking in general, corporate terms. While it is true that individual believers experience the benefit of being part of God's corporate plans, that is not the thrust of this passage. Its emphasis is on God's provision in Christ for his people, not on the individual's experience. This same corporate aspect is found in the parallel Titus 2:14: "who gave himself for us in order that he might redeem us from all lawlessness and cleanse for himself a special people, a zealot for good works." The corporate nature of the creed is often missed, mainly because it is often viewed as a baptismal hymn (see below). But the creed is a corporate description of what God has done.

One further clarification is necessary, and one that is almost universally missed: "when the goodness and philanthropy of God . . . appeared" (v 4) does not refer to the time when a person believes. The language is inappropriate for that event, and the corporate nature of the creed insists that it refer to the possibility of salvation accomplished by Christ's coming, his death, and resurrection. When the creed then speaks of "he saved us . . . poured out for us . . . having been justified . . . we might become heirs," the time frame has not shifted. These statements are to be interpreted in light of the time frame established by v 4. Despite the use of personal pronouns, they are not speaking of the individual's appropriation of salvation, a fact supported by the use of plural pronouns and the purpose clause rather than an indicative statement in v 7 (e.g., "and we were justified and we became heirs"). The plural personal pronouns personalize God's intentions, spelling out why he did what he did, but the focus is still on God and his labors and intentions. The focus should not be shifted to the believer.

On the relation of 3:1-2 with 2:15, see *Form/Structure/Setting* on Titus 2:11-15. Most view 3:8b-11 as a separate unit; however, there are good reasons not to divide 3:1-11. Paul begins in vv 1-2 by admonishing the Cretans to practice good behavior. In vv 3-8a he discusses the theological basis for salvation and behavior. The implicit argument is that God's love and mercy led him to save believers, and so believers should be led to obedience. V 8b draws this conclusion, and in fact the call to good deeds probably has in mind the people specified in vv 1-2 (or perhaps all people). If v 8b belongs with the preceding, and since vv 9-11 stand in contrast specifically to v 8b but also to those enjoying God's salvific work in vv 3-7, vv 1-11 form a single unit. There is also similarity between vv 9-11 and 1:10-16, both discussing the Jewish nature of the heresy (1:10, 14; 3:9) and the need to confront the opponents (1:11, 13-14; 3:10-11).

This is the fourth "faithful saying" in the PE. See *Form/Structure/Setting* on 1 Tim 1:12-17 for a general discussion. Most argue that the verses speak of baptism. In surprisingly strong language, Bernard (178) says, "It [baptism] is the instrument (διά) of salvation, the means, that is, through which we are placed in a 'state of salvation,' in union with the mystical Body of Christ." But as Paul makes abundantly clear through-out his writings—and Bernard holds to the authenticity of the PE—salvation comes apart from any human invention, especially a ritual. Quinn says, "The aorist repre-sented by 'saved' implies that a specific intervention by the Father in the historical lives of those who had come to believe brought them into a community. . . . That intervention was certainly in baptism, and thus sacramental" (217). But not only does the aorist not necessarily imply a "specific intervention" (cf. Wallace, *Greek Grammar,* 554–57), but nowhere in Paul or the PE does baptism save. Scott (176) is even fur-ther from the truth when he says that "the writer of the Pastorals seems to think of baptism as efficacious by itself." Scott misses the entire context of the faithful saying, which gives assurance that salvation is due to the direct work of God's goodness, love, mercy, the working of the Holy Spirit, and Jesus. He also misses the context of the PE as a whole with its orthodox presentation of salvation (see *Comment* on 1 Tim 1:14–16). Most important, the baptismal interpretation draws attention away from the real thrust of the creed: God's efforts in salvation and the demands they place on human lifestyles. It should therefore be concluded with Fee (204–5; id., *God's Empowering Presence,* 780–81) and others (Simpson, 115–16; Towner, *Goal,* 116–17) that the creed speaks of the regenerating power of the Godhead now available, and any use of bap-tismal imagery is secondary or foreign to the true thrust of the creed (cf. Acts 22:16; 1 Cor 6:11; Heb 10:22; J. A. T. Robinson argues that the baptism to which it is allud-ing is the "whole ministry of Jesus from Jordan to Pentecost, conceived as the great Baptism whereby 'he saved us'" [*SJT* 6 (1953) 269]). If baptism is in the author's mind at all (see below), then it is merely the event signifying what happens in conver-sion. As Kelly notes, "The sacrament was the outward and visible expression of the act of faith by which the Christian accepted Christ, and thus inaugurated the restored relationship with God which justification connotes" (254). Justification does not oc-cur at baptism; it occurs at conversion. Even though the NT views conversion and baptism as connected events, it does an injustice to Paul's theology and that of the PE to view baptism as the means of salvation.

Despite the current trend in scholarship to see references to the sacraments throughout the NT wherever water or cleansing is mentioned (see, for example, Beasley-Murray, *Baptism*), it is possible for the NT to use the imagery of cleansing without any reference to baptism, especially in this passage. (1) The creed is a corpo-rate praise of God's work and intentions. The time frame is not an individual's acceptance but the Christ event. (2) The only imagery of the creed that could indi-cate ties to baptism is λουτρόν, "washing." While λουτρόν is a suitable metaphor for baptism, it has many other uses. It is used to describe physical cleaning (Matt 6:17; Luke 5:2; Acts 16:33; 1 Tim 5:10; 2 Pet 2:22). In Cant 1:22 and 6:6 λουτρόν describes the washing of sheep, and these are two of the three occurrences of λουτρόν in the LXX (see *Comment*). λουτρόν denotes ritual purity (Matt 15:2 [Luke 11:38; cf. Mark 7:3–4]; 27:24; Acts 9:37; Heb 6:2; 9:10), and this is its meaning in Sir 34:25, which is the other occurrence of the word in the LXX. But most important, λουτρόν can de-scribe an inner cleansing apart from any cultic act (cf. entries under λούω in *PGL,* §C, 813, classified as "of spiritual cleansing without any direct allusion to baptism"). To interpret διὰ λουτροῦ παλιγγενεσίας, "by the washing of regeneration," as the inner cleansing effected in conversion is a plausible and natural reading of the text and emphasizes the true significance of the creed. Similarly, Eph 5:25–27 speaks of Christ loving the church and giving himself for her "that he might sanctify her, having cleansed her by the washing of water with the word [καθαρίσας τῷ λουτρῷ τοῦ ὕδατος ἐν ῥήματι]" (v 26). λουτρόν in this text in Ephesians refers not to an act of an individual but to an act of God on the church as a whole; it denotes the corporate cleansing of the church, not an individual's baptism (although this passage too could be interpreted baptismally; cf. F. F. Bruce, *The Epistles to the Colossians, to Philemon, and to the Ephesians*, NICNT [Grand Rapids, MI: Eerdmans, 1984] 387–89). Rev 7:14 and 22:14 also speak of a washing (πλύνειν) that is the result of the martyrs' perseverance, not baptism. (3) If Titus 3:4–7 is a baptismal hymn, one would expect more references to the sacrament than just the one metaphor of washing. (4) Although the Holy Spirit plays a role in baptism, he plays a role in many other activities, such as conversion (cf. Acts 10:45 [11:16; 15:3]; Rom 5:5). Acts 15:8–9 speaks of the gift of the Spirit and the cleansing of hearts without mentioning baptism. Other NT texts speak of the giving of the Spirit without any mention of baptism, although baptism is not necessarily excluded (Acts 2:4; 5:32; 2 Cor 1:22; 5:5; Gal 4:6; Eph 1:13; 4:30; 1 John 4:13). No argument should be based on the reference to washing here.

It remains to discuss the creedal nature of Titus 3:4–7, the verses of which make up the faithful saying, and the precise structure of v 5, which is the heart of the creed. The use of the faithful-saying formula suggests that here Paul is using traditional material (but see below). Most call it a hymn because of its structure, but its highly condensed theological content reads more like a creed. The unusual placement of ἔσωσεν ἡμᾶς, "he saved us," disrupts the proposed hymnic structure. The use of plural pronouns and the purpose clause in v 7 instead of an indicative (which would be appropriate for a hymnic confession) suggest a creed. And Fee (203) notes that many hymnic elements are missing. Of course, it is almost impossible to differentiate among a hymn, creed, and liturgical fragment with any degree of certainty, and doing so does not add appreciably to the understanding of the text.

As usual, commentators cannot agree on which verses are traditional and which are Paul's additions, especially because so many of the words throughout vv 4–7 are thoroughly Pauline (see references in Knight, *Faithful Sayings*, 108; id., *Pastoral Epistles*, 347–49). Options for traditional material include vv 3–7 (Dibelius-Conzelmann), vv 5b–6 (Kelly), vv 5–7 (Lock, who suggests that v 5 is the saying and vv 6–7 are Paul's comments on the creed; Spicq [contra Hanson (1983), who says Spicq views the verse following v 8 to be the faithful saying]; Guthrie; H. B. Swete, *The Holy Spirit in the New Testament* [London: Macmillan, 1921]), and vv 4–7, the majority choice (e.g., Bernard, Fee, Knight). Kelly (254) emphasizes that Paul could have woven his own material into the tradition. Jeremias argues that v 5a is a Pauline insertion, and Hanson ([1983] 193) thinks that the formula merely adds seriousness to the passage (cf. Dibelius-Conzelmann, 150).

V 3 does not appear to be hymnic or creedal and is parallel in form to vv 1–2, so it should not be considered part of the creed. Dibelius-Conzelmann argue that v 3 should be included because of the plural pronouns, but Paul uses plural pronouns in many passages without quoting traditional material, and the use of the plural here could be conditioned by the plurals in the creed he is about to quote. Knight (*Faithful Sayings*, 82) also notes that all the other faithful sayings are one sentence long. V 3 is one sentence, and vv 4–7 are a separate sentence.

V 4 contains ἐπεφάνη, "appeared," and τοῦ σωτῆρος ἡμῶν θεοῦ, "God our savior," two themes running throughout Titus, which may suggest that they are not traditional; however, Paul could have chosen such a traditional statement because it reinforced his themes. V 4 uses σωτῆρος, "savior," in connection with God, and v 6 uses it in connection with Jesus. It is typical in the PE to alternate between calling God σωτήρ, "savior," and calling Jesus σωτήρ (see *Introduction,* "Themes in the PE"), which is evidence that v 4 and v 6 are not part of the creed. But Paul could have called God σωτῆρος, "savior," in v 4 (nontraditional material) because he knew the creed would provide the counterpart in v 6. The creed itself could also include this alternation, just as the PE do. ἐπιφαίνειν, "to appear," is an important term in the PE, which suggests that v 4 is Paul's creation, but φιλανθρωπία, "loving kindness," is unusual, suggesting that v 4 is part of the creed.

The move from v 4 to v 5 is somewhat awkward, which may suggest that Paul is citing a source. δικαιοσύνη, "righteousness," in v 5 may be used in an un-Pauline sense (but cf. Eph 2:8–9) and balances Paul's usage in v 7. But it is difficult to tell whether this indicates a traditional formulation in v 5a or whether Paul uses δικαιοσύνη unconventionally in preparation for the contrast it provides with v 7. παλιγγενεσία, "regeneration," does not occur elsewhere in Paul. Jeremias argues that v 5a is a Pauline insertion. If v 7 were not part of the creed, then it would separate the creed from the formula, so v 7 probably belongs to the creed.

The fact of the matter is that the creed is so full of Pauline vocabulary and theology that it is virtually impossible to differentiate between traditional and Pauline material with any degree of certainty. If Paul is quoting a creed, it would be slightly preferable to see v 4 as Pauline and vv 5–7 as the creed because the language of v 4 is closely related to the discussion of the epistle (of course, that could be why Paul quotes the creed). Ultimately, discussions such as this are not helpful in determining meaning because they are subjective and uncertain. After all, Paul would not quote a source with which he did not agree. However, because the language is Pauline, it is difficult to view the passage as traditional (see, e.g., the graphical layout of the passages in Fee, *God's Empowering Presence,* 778–79, which shows it to be nonhymnic, creedal at best, and very typically Pauline). While Quinn feels that the creed is traditional, he points out the problems: "Still, there is no introductory formula, no word of praise or thanks for the God who is explicitly named, no regular pattern of syllables or accents per stich, a soft parallelism between the stichs, and no obvious chiasmic features, 'ring-composition,' or the like. If there was a baptismal hymn behind this passage . . . it has been freely reshaped in the tradition" (211). There is nothing in the passage that Paul (or the author of the PE) could not have written, and here Hanson ([1983] 193) may be correct in seeing the formula only as a means of adding solemnity to what the author is saying.

The structure of v 5 is difficult to determine. λουτροῦ, "washing," παλιγγενεσίας, "regeneration," ἀνακαινώσεως, "renewal," and πνεύματος ἁγίου, "Holy Spirit," are all genitives following διά, "through." There are two basic arrangements, and within each a number of possible variations.

	παλιγγενεσίας of regeneration	
Arrangement I	διὰ λουτροῦ through the washing	καὶ and
	ἀνακαινώσεως πνεύματος ἁγίου. renewal of the Holy Spirit.	

In this arrangement παλιγγενεσίας, "regeneration," and ἀνακαινώσεως, "renewal," are parallel, both governed by λουτροῦ, "washing" (Ellicott; Huther; H. B. Swete, *The Holy Spirit in the New Testament* [London: Macmillan, 1909] 247; Parry; Lock; possibly F. Büchsel, *TDNT* 1:688; A. Oepke, *TDNT* 4:304; Spicq; Jeremias; Gealy; Hendriksen; Beasley-Murray, *Baptism*, 210-11; Ysebaert, *Greek Baptismal Terminology*, 134; Barrett; Kelly; Schille, *Frühchristliche Hymnen*, 61; Knight, *Faithful Sayings;* Brox; Hanson [1983]; and most of the Greek church fathers and the Bohairic and Armenian versions [references in Bernard, 178]). Possible variations are as follows. (a) καί, "and," is copulative; regeneration and renewal are two different acts. (b) καί, "even," is resumptive; renewal defines the nature of regeneration. (c) πνεύματος ἁγίου, "Holy Spirit," can modify either ἀνακαινώσεως, "renewal" (as diagrammed above), or it could modify λουτροῦ, "washing," and thereby govern both παλιγγενεσίας, "regeneration," and ἀνακαινώσεως, "renewal" as diagrammed below.

	παλιγγενεσίας of regeneration	
διὰ λουτροῦ through the washing	καὶ and	πνεύματος ἁγίου. of the Holy Spirit
	ἀνακαινώσεως renewal	

Arrangement II is as follows.

	λουτροῦ παλιγγενεσίας the washing of regeneration
δὶα through	καὶ and
	ἀνακαινώσεως πνεύματος ἁγίου. the renewal of the Holy Spirit.

In this arrangement λουτροῦ, "washing," not παλιγγενεσίας, "regeneration," is parallel to ἀνακαινώσεως, "renewal," and both phrases are governed by διά, "through" (Syriac; Vulgate [in H. B. Swete, *The Holy Spirit in the New Testament* (London: Macmillan, 1921) 247]; Chrysostom; Jerome; Bengel, *New Testament Word Studies;* Alford, *Greek New Testament* 3:424-25; Bernard; Chase, *Confirmation*, 99; White, 4:198; Lenski; Dibelius-Conzelmann; Guthrie; Wuest, *Word Studies;* Knight, *Pastoral Epistles*, 343-44, changing his interpretation from *Faithful Sayings*, 96-97; see *Note* f for a *v.l.* repeating διά, "through," before ἀνακαινώσεως, "renewal," which also supports this arrangement).

It is difficult to decide between the two, and in many cases the distinctions are not that significant. For example, the argument is made that Arrangement II separates the work of the Holy Spirit from that of regeneration. But surely, even if grammatically πνεύματος ἁγίου, "Holy Spirit," is linked with ἀνακαινώσεως, "renewal," contextually it is linked with παλιγγενεσίας, "regeneration." Arrangement

II is to be preferred. (a) Regeneration is distinct from renewal even if they are contemporaneous events, and this is made clear by Arrangement II. (b) Renewal is never described as a washing, suggesting that ἀνακαινώσεως, "renewal," does not modify λουτροῦ, "washing." (c) The imagery of washing suggests a once-for-all cleansing. The context of the creed also requires ἀνακαινώσεως, "renewal," to be the believer's initial renewal (see *Comment*). If this is a correct understanding of the imagery, then regeneration and renewal describe the same event (conversion) from two different points of view (or the two halves of the one event), and Arrangement II is preferable. (d) Although style is a subjective evaluation, Arrangement II does maintain a better parallelism (see Jeremias, 74). However, if the traditional material is more creedal than hymnic, this is not a significant argument. (e) It is characteristic for Paul to omit the second preposition in a construction where a preposition governs a series of phrases connected by καί, "and." N. Turner (*Syntax*, vol. 3 of *A Grammar of New Testament Greek*, ed. J. H. Moulton [Edinburgh: T. & T. Clark, 1963] 275; cf. Robertson, *Grammar*, 565–67) counts twenty-four opportunities in the PE, and the preposition is repeated in only four of them. Its omission here is in line with Pauline style and suggests Arrangement II. But if the material is traditional, then this argument is not significant. (f) Although it is dangerous to say what an author should have written to make himself clear, if Arrangement I is correct, one might expect τοῦ, "the," or ὑπό,."by," before πνεύματος ἁγίου, "Holy Spirit," in order to set it off from ἀνακαινώσεως, "renewal," thereby joining παλιγγενεσίας, "regeneration," and ἀνακαινώσεως, "renewal," more closely. Since neither τοῦ nor ὑπό occurs, Arrangement II seems preferable. (g) Arrangement II does not teach justification by baptism (assuming washing refers to baptism), despite arguments to the contrary. The creed is meant to be read as a whole, and the context does not allow a magical understanding of washing. The core statement of vv 5–7 is "he saved us . . . so that we might . . . become heirs." V 5b is a description of how God saves, and this fact negates any possible view of magical baptismal regeneration (cf. Fee, *God's Empowering Presence*, 782–83). (h) Fee is correct in arguing that whatever arrangement is accepted, Paul is describing one event, not two (*God's Empowering Presence*, 781–83). παλιγγενεσία, "regeneration," and ἀνακαίνωσις, "renewal," are closely related in meaning (Fee says they are synonymous). The passage reflects Ezek 36:25–27, which speaks of one event.

Comment

1 ὑπομίμνησκε αὐτοὺς ἀρχαῖς ἐξουσίαις ὑποτάσσεσθαι, πειθαρχεῖν, πρὸς πᾶν ἔργον ἀγαθὸν ἑτοίμους εἶναι, "Remind them to be subject to rulers, to authorities, to be obedient, to be ready for any good work." Paul moves smoothly from his summary command in 2:15 to 3:1–11, the imperative ὑπομίμνησκε, "Remind!" (3:1), continuing the tone of λάλει, "Speak!" (2:15; see *Form/Structure/Setting* on Titus 2:11–15). Titus 3:1–11 is a repetition of 2:1–14. It is a call to obedience (3:1–2, 8b–11; 2:1–10) based on a theological understanding of the full purpose of salvation (3:3–8a; 2:11–14). Vv 1–2 contain seven commands, some concerned with the effects of a believer's behavior on outsiders, and others with personal virtues. Grammatically, the infinitives are dependent on ὑπομίμνησκε, "remind," with εἶναι, "to be" (v 2), governing both ἀμάχους, "peaceable," and ἐπιεικεῖς,

"gracious" (v 2), while the participle ἐνδεικνυμένους, "showing" (v 2), closes the list but performs the same function as the preceding infinitives.

Titus is to remind the Cretans of their obligations as Christians. The linear force of the imperative is to be felt, and its subject assumed from the context, an assumption so obvious that its omission is not an indication of a source (contra Houlden, Hanson [1983]). By saying that Titus is to remind them instead of, perhaps, to command them, Paul indicates that the members of the Cretan church knew their obligation and only needed encouragement. If Paul and Titus had a mission to Crete, it was of sufficient length to have included catechetical instruction. Quinn's discussion (183–85) of the supposed origin of the catechesis is highly speculative. (1) The first obligation is to be subject to the governing authorities. In light of the anti-emperor use of terminology in 2:11–14, Paul may have listed this obligation first to stem any possible misconception (Hanson, [1983] 189). While it was true that the true God and savior, the true epiphany, was not the emperor but was Jesus Christ, this did not mean that the Cretans could ignore the civil authorities. This instruction may also have carried special weight in light of the stereotyped rebellious character of the Cretans (cf. Polybius *Hist.* 6.46.1–47.6; Ellicott, 190). Quinn cites Polybius as saying that it was almost "impossible to find . . . personal conduct more treacherous or public policy more unjust than in Crete" (185; *Hist.* 6.47.5; cf. Ellicott, 190). If there were large numbers of Jews in Crete (cf. 1:10), this command may also have been directed specifically toward them. This injunction agrees with Paul's teaching in Rom 13:1–7 (cf. 1 Pet 2:13–17), although it is more cursory. Paul would not have wanted these instructions carried out regardless of what the governing authorities were telling the Cretans to do (cf. Acts 5:29). Paul was writing at a time when Rome was not aggressively attacking the church. But as is true throughout Paul and the NT, obedience to God overrides all other concerns, especially the evil demands of an ungodly government (cf. Fee, 201). On ὑποτάσσεσθαι, "to be subject," see Titus 2:5, 9 and the *Comment* on 1 Tim 2:11. ἀρχαί, "rulers," usually denotes angelic and demonic powers (Rom 8:38; 1 Cor 15:24; Eph 1:21; 3:10; 6:12; Col 1:16; 2:10, 15), but here it refers to earthly rulers (cf. Luke 12:11; 20:20; G. Delling, *TDNT* 1:482–84). The construction assumes a καί, "and," between ἀρχαῖς, "rulers," and ἐξουσίαις, "authorities" (asyndeton; see *Note* a).

(2) The second obligation is that the Cretans are πειθαρχεῖν, "to be obedient" (cf. Acts 5:29, 32; 27:21). While Paul begins the chapter by speaking of civil authorities, by v 3 he is no longer thinking solely of the believer's relationship to the state. The question is, at what point does he start to shift away from the thought of civil obedience? Here with the reference to obedience, or when speaking of "any good work" in v 2, or not until v 3? There is no expressed object of πειθαρχεῖν, "to be obedient," and its close association with the preceding implies that Paul is still thinking about being obedient to the governing authorities. (3) The third obligation is that they are πρὸς πᾶν ἔργον ἀγαθὸν ἑτοίμους εἶναι, "to be ready for any good work." Again the object of these good deeds is not expressed, and some have argued that Paul is enjoining the Cretans to be active in civic duties (Scott, Guthrie, Kelly). But good works is a prominent theme in the PE that might include civic deeds but is wider in scope (cf. 1 Tim 2:10). That Paul says πᾶν, "any," good deed confirms that he is speaking generally and not only of good civic deeds in relation to civil authorities. This theme has already occurred twice in the epistle

(Titus 1:16; 2:14) in a way that ties the discussions of chaps. 1 and 2 together, and its use here ties those chapters in with chap. 3.

2 μηδένα βλασφημεῖν, ἀμάχους εἶναι, ἐπιεικεῖς, πᾶσαν ἐνδεικνυμένους πραΰτητα πρὸς πάντας ἀνθρώπους, "to blaspheme no one, to be peaceable, gracious, showing complete gentleness toward all people." The lack of any specific mention of an object and the generality of πάντας ἀνθρώπους, "all people," and μηδένα, "no one," suggests that at least by v 2 Paul has shifted from the context of civil obedience in v 1, moving from Christians' obligations toward the governing authorities to their obligations toward all people (cf. 2 Tim 2:25; cf. Rom 13:1–7, 8–10; 1 Pet 2:13–16, 17). There is no contradiction with 1:10–16, and Quinn's conclusion "that even the apostolic work and teaching come in and through human work and teaching, marked by human limitations and sin" (186) is unnecessary. A refusal to blaspheme a person does not negate the need to confront sin and error. Jesus himself showed a balance between gentility and righteous anger. In 3:10 Paul tells Titus to warn a factious person two times, if necessary, and if there is no change to avoid that person. But in the previous verse Paul tells him to "shun foolishness and speculations." There is a time and place to avoid persons and teachings, and a time to confront both. As Knight observes, "Paul is not saying by this admonition that Christians must be naive and never correctly evaluate and speak about the evil that they see in anyone, since this is what he himself does in 1:10–16. Rather, he is urging Christians to restrain their natural inclination to say the worst about people" (333). Chrysostom differentiates between confronting those with whom there is hope of repentance and those who are set in their sin: "For when a man is perverted and predetermined not to change his mind, whatever may happen, why shouldest thou labor in vain, sowing upon a rock, when thou shouldest spend thy honorable toil upon thy own people" ("Homily 5"; NPNF 13:540).

(4) The fourth obligation of vv 1–2 is that Christians are not to blaspheme, not to slander others (cf. 1 Tim 1:13), which of course does not mean Christians cannot evaluate and criticize (cf. Rom 3:8; 14:16; 1 John 2:19; 4:1; *Comment* on 1 Tim 1:13). (5) They must also not be quarrelsome but be peaceable (ἄμαχος). Both this quality and the next (ἐπιεικής, "gracious") are required of Christian leaders (1 Tim 3:3). The simple form μάχας is used in v 9 for "quarrels" about the law. (6) The Cretans are to be ἐπιεικής, "gracious, gentle, kind" (cf. 1 Tim 3:3). (7) Finally, Paul enjoins the Cretans to demonstrate complete gentleness toward all people. πραΰτης, "gentleness" (2 Tim 2:25; cf. 1 Cor 4:21; 2 Cor 10:1; Gal 5:23; 6:1; Eph 4:2; Col 3:12), is virtually synonymous with πραϋπάθεια (cf. discussion at 1 Tim 6:11) and denotes a humility, a courtesy (BAGD, 699), a consideration of others without being servile. The force of πᾶσαν, "all," is variously translated ("perfect courtesy" [RSV]; "every consideration" [NASB]; "true humility" [NIV]) and conveys a sense of completeness with the following πάντας, "all." The force of πάντας ἀνθρώπους, "all people," Christians and non-Christians, is in agreement with the universal thrust of the PE (1 Tim 2:1, 4, 6) and Paul (Rom 13:17; Gal 6:10; Phil 4:5).

3 ἦμεν γάρ ποτε καὶ ἡμεῖς ἀνόητοι, ἀπειθεῖς, πλανώμενοι, δουλεύοντες ἐπιθυμίαις καὶ ἡδοναῖς ποικίλαις, ἐν κακίᾳ καὶ φθόνῳ διάγοντες, στυγητοί, μισοῦντες ἀλλήλους, "for formerly we ourselves also were foolish, disobedient, being led astray, being enslaved by desires and various pleasures, living a life of evil and envy, detestable, hating one another." Paul follows the ethical injunctions of vv 1–2 with the theological motivation for godly living. This is the same pattern he established in 2:1–10 and 2:11–14, and in fact much of 3:3–7 is parallel with 2:11–15 (see *Form/Structure/Setting* and Eph 2:3–7, which moves from who believers were to what God has done for them). It is because God has saved believers that they should be submissive to rulers and authorities, be obedient, etc. To separate salvation from obligatory obedience is to bifurcate unnaturally the plan of God (see *Explanation* on Titus 2:11–15). This also shows the primary instruction for godly living as a response to God's salvific work; other concerns such as the church's reputation (e.g., 2:6, 8, 10) are secondary. The sins listed here are not directed specifically toward Paul's opponents, who play a much less visible role in Titus than in 1 Timothy. These sins are more the sins of humanity in general (cf. Rom 1:29–31; 1 Cor 6:9–11; Gal 5:19–21; Eph 4:17–24). It is an accurate picture of the world as seen through God's eyes and those of the redeemed.

In typical fashion Paul joins himself with Titus (contra Quinn, 200; cf., e.g., Titus 2:11–14; Gal 1:4) and all believers (Wallace, *Greek Grammar,* 397–98), the emphatic use of καὶ ἡμεῖς, "we ourselves also," strengthening the contrast between what they were and what they have become. This same contrast is visible elsewhere in Paul's letters (Rom 6:17–18; 1 Cor 6:9–11; Eph 2:1–10; 4:17–18; Col 3:7–8). If Titus finds himself frustrated with the Cretans, he should remember that he too was once like them. γάρ, "for," makes the connection between vv 1–2 and vv 3–7 explicit. ποτέ, "formerly," refers to their pre-Christian years. ἀνόητος means "unintelligent, foolish," "without spiritual understanding" (Guthrie, 203), and is used elsewhere with ἐπιθυμία, "desire," to describe the foolish desires of those who want to be rich (1 Tim 6:9). ἀπειθής, "disobedient," is part of the description of Paul's opponents (Titus 1:16; cf. Acts 26:19; Rom 11:30) where it refers to disobedience toward God. Who is leading the Cretans away (πλανᾶν; cf. 2 Tim 3:13), or to what they are being led, is not stated. Fee (202) suggests that it is Satan (cf. discussion at 2 Tim 3:13), and Satan is active in this sort of activity (cf. 1 Tim 1:20). On δουλεύοντες, "being enslaved," cf. *Comment* on 1 Tim 6:2 and Quinn (188–89), and on ἐπιθυμίαις, "desires," see *Comment* on 1 Tim 3:1. Like ἐπιθυμία, ἡδονή, "pleasure," is a neutral term, but it usually describes evil pleasures, lusts (cf. Quinn, 189–90; G. Stählin, *TDNT* 2:909–26). διάγειν, "to live a life," describes a lifestyle (cf. 1 Tim 2:2, which supplies βίον, "life"). φθόνος, "envy," is a characteristic of Paul's opponents (1 Tim 6:4), but here the word is used of people in general (cf. Trench, *Synonyms,* 124–27). στυγητός, "hated, hateful, detestable," occurs only here in the NT (cf. *1 Clem.* 35:6; 45:7); it can be active ("hating God/people") or passive ("hated by God/people"). μισοῦντες is active ("hating"). The inclusion of ἀλλήλους, "one another," suggests a passive and active pairing: "detestable, hating one another." Chrysostom emphasizes that being "hateful and hating one another" is what "must necessarily happen, when we let loose every pleasure on the soul," by which he means the vices enumerated in the verse ("Homily 5"; NPNF 13:539).

4 ὅτε δὲ ἡ χρηστότης καὶ ἡ φιλανθρωπία ἐπεφάνη τοῦ σωτῆρος ἡμῶν θεοῦ, "But when the goodness and philanthropy of God our savior appeared." V 4 may begin the fourth faithful saying in the PE (or else the saying starts at v 5). See *Form/Structure/Setting* for a discussion of the structure of the creedal statement and its basic meaning. Despite (δέ, "but") their former condition (v 3), God's goodness and love did appear; or as Paul says elsewhere, "while we were yet sinners, Christ died for us" (Rom 5:8) and "We all once lived in the passions of our flesh. . . . But God, who is rich in mercy, out of the great love with which he loved us . . . made us alive" (Eph 2:3–5).

χρηστότης, "goodness, kindness, uprightness, generosity" (BAGD, 886; Knight, *Faithful Sayings*, 86), can mean human kindness (2 Cor 6:6; Gal 5:22; Col 3:12), but more often the word refers to the goodness of God toward people (Rom 2:4; 9:23 [*v.l.*]; 11:22; Eph 2:7), especially in the secular literature (K. Weiss, *TDNT* 9:489–91). It therefore forms a natural association with φιλανθρωπία, "philanthropy," which maintains its etymological meaning, a "love for people" (cf. Acts 28:2; cognate in Acts 27:3; cf. U. Luck, *TDNT* 9:111–12; Quinn, 214–15). Spicq shows how the word was used in Hellenistic thought of the love shown to people by the gods or kings ("Excursus VII," 2:657–76; id., *ST* 12 [1958] 169–91). When its subject is a person, the word refers to the kindness one has for someone in distress. When God is the subject, it speaks of his love for people in general. Lock (153) says it has associations with the ransoming of slaves. χρηστότης, "goodness," and φιλανθρωπία, "philanthropy," were commonly joined in secular writings as virtues for rulers and gods (F. Field, *Notes on the Translation of the New Testament* [Cambridge: Cambridge UP, 1899] 222–23). They refer here to the entire redemptive act of Christ (so Hanson [1983]): his life, death, and resurrection, the repeated articles (ἡ . . . ἡ) emphasizing their identity. Typical of the PE, σωτῆρος, "savior," is applied here to God the Father and to Jesus Christ in v 6, a variation with powerful christological implications (cf. *Comments* on 1 Tim 1:1; Titus 2:4, 13). ἐπεφάνη, "appeared," continues the imagery from 2:11, 13 as does σωτῆρος, "savior" (2:11, 13), and perhaps with them an implied contrast with emperor worship (cf. *Form/Structure/Setting* on Titus 2:11–15). ἐπιφαίνειν, "to appear," is always used in the NT of Jesus' appearing (cf. 2:11), so Paul probably sees Jesus as the embodiment of God the Father's goodness and philanthropy.

Spicq (2:651–52) comments that this passage has one of the most elegant descriptions of the Trinity in the NT. It shows the three members of the Godhead actively involved in the salvation of sinners: God the Father as the planner and initiator (v 4), Jesus Christ as the agent of redemption (v 6), and the Holy Spirit as the instrument of regeneration and renewal (v 5). This may lack specifically trinitarian language (so Hanson [1983]), but that is to be expected of a writing from the first century. Fee calls it an "inherent Trinitarianism . . . (cf. 1 Cor 12:4–6; Eph 1:3–14) that sees the Father, Son, and Spirit working co-jointly for our salvation" (206; cf. Bernard, 179; Kelly, 253; Knight, *Faithful Sayings*, 91). Ellicott speaks of the "principal," "meritorious," and "efficient" cause of the Father, Son, and Holy Spirit, respectively (195). Kelly (*Early Christian Creeds*, 13–29) argues that the process that results in Trinitarian creeds is evident in the NT and does not necessarily belong to a later date.

5a οὐκ ἐξ ἔργων τῶν ἐν δικαιοσύνῃ ἃ ἐποιήσαμεν ἡμεῖς ἀλλὰ κατὰ τὸ αὐτοῦ ἔλεος ἔσωσεν ἡμᾶς, "not out of works of righteousness that we did but in accordance with his mercy he saved us." This is the heart of the creedal statement. God saved believers not because they were deserving but because he is a merciful God. Believers were "foolish, disobedient, being led astray, being enslaved by desires and various pleasures, living a life of evil and envy, hateful, hating one another" (v 3). Their ἔργων τῶν ἐν δικαιοσύνῃ, "works of righteousness," had no

effect whatsoever on God's decision to save them. That this is a dominant theme
in the mind of Paul hardly needs mention (2 Tim 1:9; cf., e.g., Rom 3:21-28; 4:2-
6; 9:11; Gal 2:16; Eph 2:8-9; Phil 3:9). The two parts of this clause are parallel.
The salvation of believers is not due to ἔργων τῶν ἐν δικαιοσύνῃ, "works of righteousness," but to God's ἔλεος, "mercy," and the emphatic use of ἡμεῖς, "we,"
contrasts their attempts to earn salvation with αὐτοῦ, "his," mercy. As Quinn observes, "In the salvation of human beings God is wholly subject, men and women
are wholly objects" (217). Knight (*Faithful Sayings*, 94) rightly compares v 5a to
Eph 2:3-5, which teaches not only the same basic idea but also contains many of
the same specific themes.

δικαιοσύνη, "righteousness," refers either to a Pharisaic obedience to the law
(Guthrie, 204; Quinn, 216) or to "upright moral conduct in general" (Kelly, 251,
citing 1 Tim 6:11; 2 Tim 2:22; 3:16). The former seems out of context (Knight,
Faithful Sayings, 93). It will be balanced by v 7, which summarizes vv 4-6 by saying
δικαιωθέντες τῇ ἐκείνου χάριτι, "having been justified by his grace," a totally Pauline
thought. Hanson's ([1983] 191) comment that "Paul would never use *dikaiosune*
in this way" misses the point if Paul is quoting a source, and it is unreasonable to
insist that a person cannot quote a source where a word is used differently from
the way the person normally uses it. In addition, the thrust of the phrase is fully
Pauline, emphasizing the futility of human effort in contrast to the true righteousness from God by faith (v 7; cf. Phil 3:9). The contrasting use of the cognates
δικαιοσύνη, "righteousness" (v 5), and δικαιωθέντες, "justified" (v 7), makes a powerful play on words. On ἔλεος, "mercy," cf. *Comment* on 1 Tim 1:2. Here it is joined
with goodness and love as the motivating factors for God's salvific actions. In the
parallel passages Paul adds that our salvation is due to God's mercy (1 Tim 1:13,
16), grace (1 Tim 1:14; Titus 2:11; 3:7; 2 Tim 1:9), and purpose (2 Tim 1:9).

5b διὰ λουτροῦ παλιγγενεσίας καὶ ἀνακαινώσεως πνεύματος ἁγίου, "through
the washing of regeneration and renewal of the Holy Spirit." Having discussed
the "why" of salvation, the creed turns to the "how." The Holy Spirit both cleanses
believers through regeneration and fills them by a renewing, forming them into
a new creature. In *Form/Structure/Setting* it was argued that the correct arrangement of v 5b is two parallel clauses, both dependent on διά, "through," denoting
two different aspects of the same event. Conversion consists negatively of a cleansing and positively of a renewal brought about by the Holy Spirit. Although
grammatically the Holy Spirit is specifically the agent of renewal, by contextual
implication he is also the agent of regeneration. In contrast to almost all modern
writers (with the exception of Norbie [*EvQ* 34 (1962) 36-38] and possibly Fee),
the interpretation given here does not hold that the creed is thinking of baptism.
λουτρόν, "cleansing," is used many times of ceremonial cleansing with no thought
of the baptismal ritual. παλιγγενεσία, "regeneration," is not technically rebirth,
and therefore references to John 3 and 1 Peter are irrelevant. Although baptism
was certainly an important event in the first-century church (cf. Rom 6), nowhere
was it the agent of regeneration. The emphasis of the creed is on God's intentions and the implications for a believer's life. See *Form/Structure/Setting* for the
argument behind these conclusions.

λουτρόν, "washing," refers not to the laver but to the act of washing (Lock;
MM; A. Oepke, *TDNT* 4:295-30; Simpson; Guthrie; Knight, *Faithful Sayings*, 95;
cf. Eph 5:26; cf. Cant 4:2; 6:6; Sir 34:25) and as such is a metaphor of the cleans-

ing power of conversion. It occurs in the NT elsewhere only in Eph 5:26 (see *Form/Structure/Setting*). On the force of the imagery, Chrysostom comments, "For as when a house is in a ruinous state no one places props under it, nor makes any addition to the old building, but pulls it down to its foundations, and rebuilds it anew; so in our case, God has not repaired us, but has made us anew" ("Homily 5"; NPNF 13:538). It is possible that the καί, "and," is epexegetical so that the ἀνακαινώσεως, "renewal," is a commentary on παλιγγενεσίας, "regeneration"; it is preferable, however, to view καί as copulative, linking two aspects of the one event of conversion (see *Form/Structure/Setting*).

Despite the frequent assertions to the contrary (e.g., Oberlinner, 173–74), there is not one text that proves that the imagery of rebirth (παλιγγενεσία; ἀναγεννᾶν; *renascor*) was used in pre-Christian times for initiation into a mystery cult (see W. D. Mounce, "Origin"; Dey, Παλιγγενεσία; and W. Gunther, *Pauline Baptism and the Pagan Mysteries*, tr. J. P. Smith [London: Oliver & Boyd, 1967]). Even the frequent assertions about the taurobolium have no relevance for the origin of the Christian metaphor. Rather, the terminology of rebirth was frequent in philosophical writings and the common vernacular. For example, one occurrence in Philo's exposition of Stoic thought describes the re-creation of the world after its periodic destruction as ἀναγέννησις, "rebirth" (the normal term is ἀποκατάστασις, "restoration"; Philo *Aet.* 8). Pythagoreanism described transmigration as the rebirth of the soul (Pindar *Olympian Odes* 1.87–88). Cicero's and Claudius's returns from exile and Agrippa's release from prison were called their rebirths (Cicero *Ad Atticum* 6.6; Statius *Silvae* 3.3.154–69; Philo *Leg.* 324–25).

There are in fact only nine references to rebirth in all the literature about the mysteries; yet not one proves that the metaphor of rebirth was used by the mysteries in pre-Christian times. Tertullian's statement does not apply to the Eleusinian mysteries, and the terminology is probably of Christian origin (*De bapt.* 5). Apuleius's vocabulary was drawn from common speech and not from cultic terminology (*Metamorphoses* 11.6, 14, 16, 21; Lucius's initiation does not begin until 11.22). Plutarch's use of παλιγγενεσία, "regeneration," is derived from his philosophical heritage and has no relation to the fate of the mystery initiate (*De Iside* 35 [*Mor.* 364f–365a]; *De E* 9 [*Mor.* 388e–389a]). Because they are late and open to possible Christian influence, the taurobolium inscription (*CIL* 6.510 [6.1.976]) and the statement by Sallustius (*De deis et mundo* 4) are not trustworthy witnesses to the pre-Christian state of the Magna Mater and Mithras cults. A. Dieterich's "Mithras Liturgy" (*PGM* 1.66–181, lines 475–537a) is not Mithraic and therefore does not witness to the theology or the imagery of Mithraism.

The literature after the first century A.D. shows that the metaphor was used predominantly in Christian writings. Lampe's *Patristic Greek Lexicon* lists over 220 references under the headings of ἀναγεννάω, ἀναγέννησις, and παλιγγενεσία. Any use of the terminology by the mysteries, considering the evidence, the lateness of the texts, and the very nature of the mysteries as syncretistic, requires one to see the influence of Christianity upon the mysteries, not the reverse.

ἀνακαίνωσις, "renewal," occurs elsewhere only in Rom 12:2 (cognates in 2 Cor 4:16; Col 3:10; Heb 6:6) where Paul calls for the renewing of the mind. The context in Titus 3:5 requires that it be a once-for-all renewal because salvation is seen as an accomplished fact (although this is not learned from the aorist tense of ἔσωσεν, "he saved," which is not punctiliar but merely undefined [contra Kelly,

251]). Knight notes that most who see ἀνακαινώσεως, "renewal," as dependent
on διά, "through," view sanctification as progressive. But the creed views salvation
as an accomplished fact, so it must refer to positional sanctification (which may
by implication have an ongoing effect in the believer's life; cf. use of verbal cognate ἀνακαινοῦν, "to renew," in Rom 12:2; 2 Cor 4:16; Col 3:10). Conversion has
two halves, a negative cleansing and a positive re-creation. This thought is similar
to Col 3:5–10, which speaks of a punctiliar "putting off the old man," a punctiliar
"putting on the new," and the continuing renewing (ἀνακαινούμενον) of the believer, all within the context of a call to holiness in light of the Christian's previous
life of sin. The creed in Titus 3:4–7 is remarkably Pauline. πνεύματος ἁγίου, "the
Holy Spirit," is grammatically linked to ανακαινώσεως, "renewal," but the flow of
the creed assumes his activity also in regeneration. (If the καί, "and," is
epexegetical, then grammatically πνεύματος ἁγίου, "Holy Spirit," is tied to both
παλιγγενεσίας, "regeneration," and ἀνακαινώσεως, "renewal.") Quinn says that
the lack of the article before "Holy Spirit" may suggest that it is viewed as a name
(197); perhaps in light of the use and the non-use of the article before πνεῦμα,
"Spirit" (cf. Moule, *Idiom-Book,* 112–13), not much should be made of its absence
here. The creed has now brought two of the members of the Godhead into focus. The third member is introduced in the next verse.

6 οὗ ἐξέχεεν ἐφ᾽ ἡμᾶς πλουσίως διὰ Ἰησοῦ Χριστοῦ τοῦ σωτῆρος ἡμῶν, "whom
he richly poured out for us through Jesus Christ our savior." Paul moves to the
third member of the Godhead, the Holy Spirit (cf. John 14:26; 16:7; Luke 24:29;
Acts 2:33). οὗ, "whom" (attracted to the genitive case of ἁγίου, "holy"), is the Holy
Spirit. ἐκχεῖν, "to pour out," is the same word used to describe the outpouring of
the Holy Spirit at Pentecost (Joel 2:28–32 [MT 3:1–5]; Acts 2:17–18, 33; cf. 1 QS
4:21; cf. Rom 5:5). What was true then of the early church is true for every believer in salvation. God does not restrain himself in the giving of the Spirit but
gives him πλουσίως, "richly, abundantly" (cf. 1 Tim 6:17; cf. Col 3:16; 2 Pet 1:11).
The eschatological element of salvation that Hanson ([1983] 192) finds missing
is supplied by the next verse. It is once again significant that v 4 begins by applying the title of σωτῆρος, "savior," to God the Father and v 6 concludes by applying
the same title to Jesus Christ. There is no question that here, as well as elsewhere
in the PE, Paul holds to the full divinity of Christ (cf. discussion of σωτήρ, "savior," in *Introduction,* "Themes in the PE").

7a ἵνα δικαιωθέντες τῇ ἐκείνου χάριτι, "in order that having been justified by
his grace." Before moving on to the goal of God's salvific endeavors (v 7b), Paul
summarizes the discussion so far (vv 4–6), much in the same fashion that Rom
5:1 summarizes 3:21–4:24. δικαιωθέντες, "having been justified," stands in stark
contrast to δικαιοσύνη, "righteousness," in v 5. There it describes human attempts
to perform certain works and earn one's salvation; here it describes true justification, which can only be received as a result of God's graciousness and the believer's
faith (as v 8 adds; see similar phrase in Rom 3:24: δικαιούμενοι δωρεὰν τῇ αὐτοῦ
χάριτι, "being justified freely by his grace"). ἐκείνου, "his," refers to God the Father since Paul says elsewhere that it is God's grace that leads to the believer's
salvation (Titus 2:11; 2 Tim 1:9). The more difficult question is whether the ἵνα,
"in order that," continues the thought from ἐξέχεεν, "he poured out," or from
ἔσωσεν, "he saved us." Did God save believers in order that they might be heirs (v
7b), or was the Holy Spirit poured out so that they could become heirs? Because

these verses picture all three members of the Godhead actively involved in the salvific process, the question is more grammatical than theological. God initiates the process that is carried out through the work of Christ and the Spirit, and as a result believers become heirs.

Although the language appears to be purely Pauline, some still object to the precise wording of the phrase. Easton (100–101) thinks that the passage teaches that justification comes after baptism and not before, assuming that v 5 discusses the sacrament (cf. Scott, 176; Dibelius-Conzelmann, 150; contra Robinson, *SJT* 6 [1953] 269). Others are concerned by the lack of any mention of faith, thinking that Paul can only speak of justification by faith and not merely justification. (1) V 7 is possibly part of a creed Paul is quoting, and he is therefore not responsible for its precise wording. (2) The emphasis of the creed is on what God has done and the demands placed upon believers to maintain a godly lifestyle. To attribute the giving of justification to God's grace and not to mention the receiving of justification by faith is consistent with the emphasis of the creed. (3) To insist that Paul always mentions faith whenever he mentions justification borders on the absurd (cf. 1 Cor 6:11, where there is no mention of faith). The issue of faith does arise in the next verse.

7b κληρονόμοι γενηθῶμεν κατ᾽ ἐλπίδα ζωῆς αἰωνίου, "we might become heirs according to [the] hope of eternal life." The ultimate goal of God's initiative and Christ's and the Spirit's labors is that believers become heirs of eternal life (on ζωῆς αἰωνίου, "eternal life," see *Comment* on 1 Tim 1:16). The translation here continues the ambiguity of the phrase. (1) The genitive ζωῆς αἰωνίου, "of eternal life," can modify κληρονόμοι, "heirs." If this is the case, eternal life is that which believers will inherit. κατ᾽ ἐλπίδα, "according to hope," is a reminder that salvation is not the believers' in the fullest until the eschatological consummation of all things. But the Christian hope is secure, it is assured (cf. 1 Tim 1:1), so there is no question of the inheritance not being received. (2) ζωῆς αἰωνίου, "of eternal life," can also modify ἐλπίδα, "hope." In this case κληρονόμοι, "heirs," is used absolutely with no indication of the content of the inheritance (cf. Rom 4:14; 8:17; Gal 3:29), but the content of hope is specified as eternal life. While there is little theological difference between the two options, the word order suggests that ζωῆς αἰωνίου, "eternal life," modifies ἐλπίδα, "hope." The eschatological emphasis is pronounced in the passage, owing to the use of ἐλπίς, "hope," as it is used throughout the PE (1 Tim 1:16; 4:1; 6:14; 2 Tim 3:1–5). In the NT, κληρονόμος, "heir," is used once of Christ as the heir of all things (Heb 1:2) and several times to describe believers (Rom 4:13–14; 8:17; Gal 3:29; Heb 11:7; Jas 2:5). Guthrie (206–7) compares this passage to Gal 3, where Paul begins with the topic of justification and concludes with that of an inheritance (Gal 3:29).

8a Πιστὸς ὁ λόγος, "Trustworthy is the saying." This is the fourth of the five introductory formulas for the faithful sayings in the PE. See *Form/Structure/Setting* on 1 Tim 1:12–17 for the discussion of the faithful sayings in general and *Form/Structure/Setting* above for structural issues. Here it refers to the preceding verses, and as usual the saying is concerned with salvation. The only other saying where the introductory formula points backward is 1 Tim 4:9. In *Form/Structure/Setting* the difficulties of ascertaining the precise limits of the saying were discussed; vv 5–7 were proposed with some reservations.

8b καὶ περὶ τούτων βούλομαί σε διαβεβαιοῦσθαι, "and I want you to insist emphatically on these things." Most commentators separate vv 1–7 from vv 9–11, either at the beginning, the middle, or the end of v 8 (see *Form/Structure/Setting*). But as is true throughout Titus, Paul has not broken his discussion into units; the discussion flows smoothly from one thought into the next. τούτων, "these things," refers back at least to the creed in vv 5–7, but there is little in those verses that warrants the use of the strong διαβεβαιοῦσθαι, "to insist emphatically." It is the Cretans' poor behavior that is causing the problems. τούτων, "these things," therefore includes all of chap. 3 with the demands it places on lifestyle, specifically the qualities enumerated in vv 1–2 and perhaps recalling ταῦτα, "these things," in 2:15 (see *Form/Structure/Setting*). βούλομαι, "I want," is not forceful in this context because it is addressed to Titus (cf. 1 Tim 2:8), but διαβεβαιοῦσθαι, "to insist emphatically," is strong, being directed toward the Cretans. It is essential that they live out the practical implications of their theology as expressed by the creed. The only other occurrence of this verb in the NT is in Paul's description of his Ephesian opponents who were confidently asserting things about which they knew nothing (1 Tim 1:7).

8c ἵνα φροντίζωσιν καλῶν ἔργων προΐστασθαι οἱ πεπιστευκότες θεῷ, "in order that those who have believed in God might be intent on devoting themselves to good works." Titus must insist that the Cretans learn Christian theology and especially its demands on their lives so that they will vigorously pursue good works. This provides yet another illustration of the dominant theme in Titus, that right theology and right practice are inextricably bound together (on καλῶν ἔργων, "good works," cf. Titus 1:16; 2:14; *Comment* on 1 Tim 2:10). The perfect πεπιστευκότες, "having believed," carries the full sense of the completed action of belief with its continuing obligations. The word perhaps recalls the cognate πιστός, "faithful," earlier in the verse; those who believe accept the trustworthiness of the saying. With this word Paul supplies what some find lacking in v 7 (Knight, *Faithful Sayings,* 107). φροντίζειν, "to be intent on, concerned about" (BAGD, 866–67), occurs only here in the NT, and the full linear-aspect force of the verb is to be felt; an understanding of the full plan of salvation leads believers necessarily into a daily living out of their commitment to the Lord. To separate the two is nonsensical (cf. *Explanation* on Titus 2:11–15).

προΐστάναι can mean "to practice a profession," and this meaning is used by Moffatt's translation and the NEB ("Those who have come to believe in God should see that they engage in honourable occupations"). Analogous would be Paul's instructions to the Thessalonians (1 Thess 4:11) and the Ephesians (Eph 4:28) to work with their hands (Lock, 156). But good works is such a significant theme in the PE, referring to conduct in general, that most translate the verb as "to be concerned about, to care for" (BAGD, 707; cf. F. Field, *Notes on the Translation of the New Testament* [Cambridge: Cambridge UP, 1899]; Lock, 156; Fee, 209 n. 8), "to devote oneself to" (B. Reicke, *TDNT* 6:703). Paul's concern is for their behavior in general and not merely one aspect such as a profession. Its pairing with φροντίζειν, "to be intent on," makes the language strong; they must not merely be concerned about good works, but they must be intent on caring about good works. προΐστάναι is used elsewhere meaning "to rule" (1 Tim 3:4, 5, 12), and Paul may intend a play on words with the similar sounding περιιστάναι in the next verse.

8d ταῦτά ἐστιν καλὰ καὶ ὠφέλιμα τοῖς ἀνθρώποις, "These are good and profitable for people." Having pointed out the obligatory nature of obedience, Paul adds that it also is beneficial to believers, possibly even to non-Christians if ἀνθρώποις, "people," looks back to the same word in v 2. ταῦτα, "these," could refer back to τούτων, "these things," and thereby the entire chapter, or it could refer to καλῶν ἔργων, "good works"; the twofold repetition of "these" in one verse suggests the former. This phrase can be viewed as "mere banality" (Hanson, [1983] 194) only if it is decided that the personal benefits of godly living are banal, for that is Paul's argument. On καλός, "good," see *Comment* on 1 Tim 1:8. ὠφέλιμος, "profitable," occurs elsewhere in 1 Tim 4:8 (some physical exercise is beneficial) and 2 Tim 3:16 (Scripture is beneficial for teaching, etc.).

9a μωρὰς δὲ ζητήσεις καὶ γενεαλογίας καὶ ἔρεις καὶ μάχας νομικὰς περιΐστασο, "But shun foolish speculations and genealogies and strife and quarrels about the law." In contrast to the person who accepts the theology of the preceding discussion and puts it into practice, Paul encourages Titus to avoid those who disagree. V 10 adds that this shunning should be done after two warnings. The terminology μωρὰς ζητήσεις, "foolish speculations," is used elsewhere of Paul's opponents (1 Tim 1:3–7; 2 Tim 2:23), and most therefore assume that he is addressing the opponents here and not evil people in general. The similarity also suggests that the opponents in Ephesus and Crete were in basic agreement, although the Cretan opponents were considerably less troublesome. They have not been discussed since 1:10–16, and this is their last direct mention in this epistle. (It is possible to see an implied reference to them in vv 14–15.)

δέ, "but," establishes the contrast between the people of vv 1–8 and the opponents, as does the context. Paul lists four errors to avoid. (1) μωρός, "foolish, stupid," is a typical condemnation of the opponents' teaching (cf. 1 Tim 4:7; 2 Tim 2:23; see *Introduction,* "The Ephesian Heresy"). ζήτησις, "controversy, speculation" (cf. 1 Tim 6:4; 2 Tim 2:23; discussion of ἐκζήτησις, "speculation," in *Comment* on 1 Tim 1:4), emphasizes the lack of substance in the opponents' teaching and explains why Paul does not address the heresy theologically. It is vacuous, a quibbling about words. (2) The opponents view it as teaching drawn from the genealogies of the OT (cf. 1 Tim 1:4), but Paul views it as "Jewish myths" (Titus 1:14) that only produce (3) strife (cf. 1 Tim 6:4) and quarrels about the law. (4) μάχη, "quarrel," can be used of physical combat but in early Christian literature is always used of battles without weapons (BAGD, 496; cf. 2 Tim 2:23; cf. 2 Cor 7:5; Jas 4:1, and the discussion of ἄμαχος, "peaceable," which is a requirement of elders [1 Tim 3:3] and all Christians [Titus 3:2]). The law is the opponents' interpretation of the Jewish law (cf. 1 Tim 1:7, 8–11), their use of it to regulate daily life (Oberlinner, 185); the Jewish nature of the heresy has already been established (Titus 1:10,14). περιΐστάναι in the middle voice means "to go around so as to avoid, avoid, shun" (BAGD, 647) and is used in the same context in 2 Tim 2:16 (also used in the active voice in the physical sense of "to surround" in John 11:42 and Acts 25:7).

9b εἰσὶν γὰρ ἀνωφελεῖς καὶ μάταιοι, "for they are harmful and useless." It would have been helpful if Paul had clarified the opponents' misuse of the law as he did in 1 Tim 1:8–11, but as has been argued above, the heresy was not consistent; it comprised fables, silly stories, and arguments about words that produced conflicts within the church. These stories and arguments were ἀνωφελής, "harmful" (cf. Heb 7:18), and useless. It is no wonder Paul tells Titus simply to stay away from them (vv 10–11). μάταιος means "fruitless, useless, idle, without substance" (cf. Acts 14:15; 1 Cor 3:20;

15:17; Jas 1:26; 1 Pet 1:18; and the discussion of the μαται- word group in the *Comment* on 1 Tim 1:6). Elsewhere Paul calls the heresy ματαιολογία, "empty chatter" (1 Tim 1:6), and the opponents ματαιολόγοι, "empty chatterers" (Titus 1:10).

10 αἱρετικὸν ἄνθρωπον μετὰ μίαν καὶ δευτέραν νουθεσίαν παραιτοῦ, "Avoid the factious person after a first and second warning." To shun foolishness is only part of the answer (v 9). The person spreading foolishness should be confronted, and if there is no repentance, then that person should be avoided. The problem of a church separating into smaller divisions was common (cf. Acts 6:1–7). In Corinth the divisions were based on a party spirit. In Ephesus and Crete the divisions were along the lines of the heretical teaching of myths, genealogies, and asceticism. It is no wonder that Paul's instructions were so stringent. If people subscribe to what is described in v 9, Titus is to warn them once. If they do not listen, he is to warn them a second time. If they still do not listen, he is to have nothing to do with them. This is not as severe as the excommunication of the main opponents (1 Tim 1:20), but it is in line with Paul's teaching elsewhere that believers who live in sin must be socially ostracized to the point of not even eating with such a one (Rom 16:17; 1 Cor 5:11 [but cf. Fee, *Corinthians*, 226, who argues that this applies only to community meals and not private ones]; 2 Thess 3:14; cf. Matt 18:17). Paul is not spelling out in detail how to deal with the issue of church discipline; no significance should be attached to his silence here on related issues.

αἱρετικός, from which is derived the English *heretic*, originally meant "factious, causing divisions" (BAGD, 24; cf. use of cognate αἵρεσις, "division," in 1 Cor 11:19 and Gal 5:20). It also described the sects of the Sadducees (Acts 5:17) and the Pharisees (Acts 5:5; 26:5; cf. 24:5, 14; 28:22). By the second century it was used to mean "heretic" in the writings of Ignatius (*Eph.* 6.2; *Trall.* 6.1; cf. 2 Pet 2:1; cf. Quinn, 238, 248–49). Most writers (contra Hanson [1983]; KJV; NEB; cf. BAGD, 23–24) agree that the meaning "heretic" is too late and is not appropriate to the context. The term is defined by v 9 and is analogous to the description of their activity as "upsetting entire families" (Titus 1:11).

μία, though normally a numeral ("one"), can function as an ordinal ("first") as it does here. As is true throughout the PE, confrontation is done with the hope of restoration (cf. 1 Tim 1:20). νουθεσία, "warning, instruction," is used elsewhere in Paul's admonition that a father bring up his children in the discipline and instruction of the Lord (Eph 6:4), and that the account of the Exodus was written as a warning for the Corinthians (1 Cor 10:11). Unfortunately Paul does not specify any of the details of this warning, whether it is to be public or private (cf. 1 Tim 5:19–20; cf. Matt 18:15–17; cf. Trench, *Synonyms*, 152–56). If the sinners do not repent, Titus is to have nothing to do with them. παραιτοῦ, "avoid," carries its full linear-aspect force and is the same verb used to admonish Timothy to avoid godless and silly myths (1 Tim 4:7) as well as youthful passions (2 Tim 2:23; cf. Acts 25:11). These are instructions to Titus as the apostolic legate; they are not necessarily instructions to the church as a whole (contra Hanson, [1983] 195); but what was true for Titus may by implication be true for the church as a whole.

11 εἰδὼς ὅτι ἐξέστραπται ὁ τοιοῦτος καὶ ἁμαρτάνει ὢν αὐτοκατάκριτος, "knowing that such a person has been perverted and is sinning, being self-condemned." The result of a steadfast refusal to repent (v 10) is perversion and constant sin, and the sin condemns the sinner (hence, self-condemned). This not only gives Titus the encouragement to be strong in his task, but it also shows the seriousness of the problem. As is asserted throughout the PE, sinful behavior is an accurate indication of the condition of one's heart.

εἰδώς, "knowing," functions causally. The perfect tense of ἐξέστραπται, "has been perverted," shows the finality of this person's spiritual condition while the linear aspect of ἁμαρτάνει, "is sinning," spells out the day-to-day consequences of that perversion. αὐτοκατάκριτος bears its etymological meaning of "self-condemned" (αὐτός, "self" + κατάκριτος, "condemned"). It is not so much that Paul believed that the opponents really knew that what they were doing was wrong (see Bernard, 181, for a warning about such an evaluation); rather, it was their behavior, their steadfast refusal to listen to Titus, that condemned them as sinners. They claimed to know God but denied him by their deeds (Titus 1:16; cf. Luke 19:22), and therefore they were self-condemned (cf. Gal 2:11). αὐτοκατάκριτος occurs elsewhere only in a fragment from Philo (BAGD, 122) and in the church fathers, so it is possible that Paul coined the word for the occasion.

Explanation

Titus 3:1–11 continues the basic thought of 2:1–15, although many of the specifics are different. A full knowledge of salvation demands obedience to God. To separate salvation and discipleship is to miss the full intention of God's salvific plans. How can those who have died to sin still live in it (cf. Rom 6:1–14)?

Continuing the thought of 2:15, Paul urges Titus to remind the Cretans of their social obligations to the governing authorities and their neighbors. At one time Paul and Titus also were foolish and disobedient, but God's goodness and love appeared in order to save them. In language that places the gospel message in conflict with emperor worship, Paul spells out what God has done. The emphasis is on his actions and the change they effect in believers. The believers attempt to achieve righteousness to no avail. Rather, God's goodness and love through his mercy have brought salvation, which consists of a cleansing and an empowering by the Holy Spirit, who is given through Jesus Christ. As a result, having been justified by God's grace, believers now have an inheritance, a hope, which is eternal life. Throughout this process there is a threefold presentation of the Godhead, God the Father initiating the process, made possible through the work of the Son and actuated by the Holy Spirit. Because the faithful saying is theocentric and not anthropocentric, it discusses God's role in the process, not that of believers.

As a result of God's gracious work, believers are obligated to be intent on performing good works, not in order to earn salvation but as the necessary consequence of being recipients of God's graciousness. However, the opponents were divisive. If they continued in their error after confrontation, they were to be socially ostracized. This may not have been to the degree of the excommunication of the leaders, but it was serious. As Fee points out, "Unfortunately, all too often in the church the 'orthodox,' in ferreting out 'heretics' (i.e., people who hold different views from mine), have become the divisive ones!" (211). The believer must differentiate between personal preferences and the essentials of the faith and ministry.

V. Personal Comments and Final Greeting (Titus 3:12–15)

Bibliography

See *Bibliography* for 1 Tim 6:20–21.

Translation

[12] *When I send Artemas to you or Tychicus, do your best to come to me in Nicopolis, for I have decided to winter there.* [13] *Do your best to help Zenas the lawyer and Apollos on their journey, in order that they might lack [a] nothing.* [14] *And let our [people] learn to be devoted to good deeds, specifically the urgent needs, lest they be fruitless.* [15] *All those with me greet you. Greet [b] those who love us in faith. Grace [be] with all of you.[c d e]*

Notes

[a]The present subjunctive λείπῃ, "might be lacking," is replaced with the aorist λίπῃ, "might lack," by ℵ D* Ψ 1505 *pc.*

[b]The aorist singular imperative ἄσπασαι, "greet," is replaced by the plural ἀσπάσασθε, "greet," in A b.

[c]μετὰ πάντων ὑμῶν, "with all of you" (𝔓[61 vid] ℵ A C H Ψ 048 1739 1881 TR vg[mss] sy co), has undergone various changes owing to the lack of an object for χάρις, "grace" (τοῦ θεοῦ, "of God," is added by D F G 629 vg[mss] latt; τοῦ κυρίου, "of the Lord," by D b vg[mss]), and the problem of having the plural πάντων, "all," in a letter to one person. πάντων ὑμῶν, "all of you," is replaced with τοῦ πνεύματός σου, "your spirit," by 33 in imitation of 2 Tim 4:22. Uncial 81 conflates these two possibilities with πάντων ὑμῶν καὶ μετὰ τοῦ πνεύματος σου, "all of you and with your spirit" (cf. *TCGNT*[2], 586–87).

[d]ἀμήν, "Amen," is added after ὑμῶν, "of you," by ℵ[2] D[1] F G H Ψ 0278 TR lat sy bo. See *TCGNT*[2], 586–87.

[e]The subscriptions list Nicopolis of Macedonia (which cannot be correct because Paul was not yet there; cf. *Comment* on 3:12) as the location of Paul's writing, but these do suggest that the Nicopolis in Macedonia, and not the other Nicopolises, was historically seen as the location referred to in Titus 3:12. Several MSS call Titus the "first bishop of Crete" (H K L 101 462 1908 1927 TR sy[h]), but this cannot be correct because Titus was an apostolic delegate with no inherent power of his own. The Coptic version identifies Artemas as the bearer of the letter, but 3:12 shows that the letter preceded Artemas. The Syriac version says that Zenas and Apollos brought the letter. See *TCGNT*[2], 587, for details.

Form/Structure/Setting

Paul concludes the epistle by making a few personal comments (cf. Rom 16:1–23; 1 Cor 16:5–12; Col 4:7–9; 2 Tim 4:9–18), repeating a dominant theme in the epistle (cf. Rom 16:25–26; 2 Cor 13:11; Gal 6:17), sending greetings to the recipients from himself and those with him (cf. Rom 16:21–23; 1 Cor 16:19–21; 2 Cor 13:13; Eph 6:21–23; Phil 4:21–22; Col 4:7–18; 2 Tim 4:19), and finishing with a benediction (as in all his letters). The style is so Pauline that even Hanson thinks it is authentic. Hidden in v 14 and v 15 is a final warning that not all the Cretans who call themselves Christian are truly Christian. Quinn sees many literary affinities between 3:12–15 and 1:3–5 and discusses the structure of Greek letters of recommendation (261–63, following C.-H. Kim, *Form and Structure of the Familiar Greek Letter of Recommendation*, SBLDS 4 [Missoula, MT: Scholars Press, 1972]). On benedictions, cf. *Comment* on 1 Tim 6:20–21.

Comment

12 ὅταν πέμψω Ἀρτεμᾶν πρὸς σὲ ἢ Τυχικόν, σπούδασον ἐλθεῖν πρός με εἰς Νικόπολιν, ἐκεῖ γὰρ κέκρικα παραχειμάσαι, "When I send Artemas to you or Tychicus, do your best to come to me in Nicopolis, for I have decided to winter there." This is an important verse in ascertaining the situation of the epistle. It has already been noted that the epistle, except for the salutation and conclusion (and 2:7–8), is quite impersonal, containing few personal remarks to Titus such as are found in 1 Timothy (esp. 4:6–16) and throughout 2 Timothy. Now the situation becomes clear. Titus was left in Crete with the task of setting things right (1:5). After an undeterminable span of time, Zenas and Apollos (v 13) brought the letter with specific instructions for the Cretan church, and soon after that Titus was replaced by either Artemas or Tychicus. Therefore, the epistle is not so much for Titus as it is for the church. There is no contradiction between 1:5 and 3:12 (contra Hasler, Hanson [1983]).

Paul had not yet decided who Titus's replacement would be, whether Artemas or Tychicus. Nothing else is known of Artemas. A late tradition says that he was one of the seventy disciples (Lock, 158) and became bishop of Lystra (Bernard, 182). 2 Tim 4:12 says that Tychicus was sent to Ephesus, possibly to relieve Timothy, and this suggests that Artemas was eventually sent to Crete. His name is derived from the name of the Greek goddess Artemis (Roman name, Diana), the patron goddess of Ephesus (Acts 19:24, 27–28, 34–35), but it would be speculative to assume that Artemas was therefore from Ephesus. On the other hand Tychicus is the well-known traveling companion of Paul. He was an Asian (Acts 20:4) who carried Paul's letters to Ephesus and Colossae (Eph 6:21; Col 4:7). He did travel to Ephesus (2 Tim 4:12), possibly to relieve Timothy, but this is not specifically stated.

When either Artemas or Tychicus arrived, Titus was to do his best (σπουδάζειν; cf. cognate adverb σπουδαίως, "earnestly," and note in next verse; Gal 2:10; Eph 4:3; 1 Thess 2:17; 2 Tim 2:15; 4:9, 21; BAGD, 763; Quinn [264] says that the emphasis is more on determination than on speed) to meet Paul in Nicopolis. 2 Tim 4:10 says that Paul had sent Titus to Dalmatia. If this Nicopolis was the Nicopolis on the western shore of Macedonia (see below) and since Dalmatia was north of this Nicopolis, it can be assumed that Titus was able to join Paul. There were seven cities with the name Nicopolis in the ancient world (see Spicq, 2:690–91). Most agree that Paul refers to the Nicopolis in Epirus on the western coast of Achaia on the Ambracian Gulf off the Adriatic Sea. It was two hundred miles northwest of Athens and was the largest city on the coast. It was two hundred miles across the sea from Brindisi, Italy, from which the Via Appia went to Rome. It was also a stopping place for north-south travel. It had better weather than the Nicopolis in Cilicia (Kelly, 257; the Nicopolis in Thrace was north of Philippi; cf. *Introduction*, "Historical Reconstruction from the PE"). This Nicopolis was established by Augustus on his campsite after his defeat of Mark Anthony at Actium in 31 B.C. *Nicopolis* means "city of victory" (νίκη, "victory" + πόλις, "city"), which explains its popularity as a city name. This Nicopolis was an ideal location for Paul to continue meeting people and spreading the gospel. Its location to the

west of the lands Paul had evangelized may signal his intention to travel farther
west, perhaps to Spain (see *Introduction,* "Historical Reconstruction from the PE").
By saying that he had decided to winter ἐκεῖ, "there," and not ὧδε, "here," Paul
implies that he was not yet in Nicopolis. If Paul was making plans for winter, this
might suggest he was writing in midsummer, allowing Titus sufficient time to travel
from Crete to Nicopolis. It might also suggest that he currently was somewhere
in Achaia or Macedonia. But anything beyond this is overly speculative. Subscriptions of some MSS to both 1 Timothy and Titus incorrectly identify Nicopolis as
the location of writing (cf. *Note* e).

13 Ζηνᾶν τὸν νομικὸν καὶ Ἀπολλῶν σπουδαίως πρόπεμψον, ἵνα μηδὲν αὐτοῖς
λείπῃ, "Do your best to help Zenas the lawyer and Apollos on their journey, in
order that they might lack nothing." Apparently Zenas and Apollos were leaving
Paul on a journey that would take them through Crete. Presumably they brought
the epistle to Titus, and Titus in turn was to offer his best hospitality to them as
they prepared for their further journey, so that they would lack nothing. Their
ultimate destination is not revealed, but their direction and Apollos's association
with Alexandria in Egypt suggests that this might have been their goal. There are
two plays on words. Paul uses the verb σπουδάζειν, "to do one's best," in the previous verse and the cognate adverb σπουδαίως here, the latter meaning "diligently,
earnestly, zealously" (BAGD, 763). The translation "do your best" (Kelly's phrase)
emphasizes the wordplay. Paul also says that he will "send" (πέμπειν) Artemas or
Tychicus, and Titus is to speed (προπέμπειν) Zenas and Apollos on their journey.

προπέμπειν means to help on a journey by supplying food, clothing, etc. (BAGD,
709) and describes the hospitality required of all Christians (cf. Acts 15:3; 21:5;
Rom 15:24; 1 Cor 16:6,11; 2 Cor 1:16; 3 John 6; cf. Herodotus 1.111; 3.50; 1 Macc
12:4; *Ep. Arist.* 172), always in reference to Christian ministry. On the use of πρό,
"before," not designating time, see Moulton, *Grammar* 2:322. Nothing more is
known of Zenas, although there is a late tradition that he wrote the apocryphal
Acts of Titus (Bernard, 182) and became bishop of Diospolis. νομικός, "lawyer," in
the Gospels describes experts in the Jewish law (Matt 22:35; Luke 7:30; 10:25;
11:45–46, 52; 14:3), and this might be expected from his friendship with Apollos,
but Zenas is a Greek name, and it is also possible that he was a Roman lawyer
(Spicq). Apollos, the Alexandrian Jew trained by Priscilla and Aquila, ministered
in Corinth, and around him and others the Corinthian church divided (Acts 18:24;
19:1; 1 Cor 1:12; 3:4–6, 22; 4:6; 16:12). They are to go, lacking nothing, presumably nothing that is necessary (cf. Jas 2:15), or as 3 John 6 says, "send them on
their journey as befits God's service."

14 μανθανέτωσαν δὲ καὶ οἱ ἡμέτεροι καλῶν ἔργων προΐστασθαι εἰς τὰς
ἀναγκαίας χρείας, ἵνα μὴ ὦσιν ἄκαρποι, "And let our [people] learn to be devoted to good deeds, specifically the urgent needs, lest they be fruitless." Before
his final greeting, Paul emphasizes the theme of the epistle one last time. Christianity must manifest itself in practical ways. In light of Cretan society and the
young age of the church, this repetition is appropriate.

δὲ καί can mean "and once again [let me repeat myself]" or "and the Cretan
people as well as yourself" (v 13). Lock (158) suggests that it may mean "and the
Cretan Christians" in contrast to Cretan society, but this does not fit the context.
Quinn says it is the most common connective at this point in secular letters of recommendation (see *Form/Structure/Setting*), in which it has no adversative force but

is merely explanatory. For the same use of οἱ ἡμέτεροι, "our [people]," see Luke 16:12. It, as well as ἐν πίστει, "in faith," in v 15, separates the true and faithful Cretan Christians from Paul's opponents and their followers. μανθάνειν, "to learn," here refers not merely to intellectual acquisition (cf. 1 Tim 2:11) but to learning and putting what one has learned into practice (cf. 1 Tim 5:4). They learn by doing. καλῶν ἔργων προΐστασθαι, "to be devoted to good deeds," is exactly the same phrase as in v 8. This means not that Paul is running out of material or "inventiveness" (so Hanson, [1983] 197) but that he wants to drive home the central thrust of the epistle: the practical necessity of good deeds (cf. Titus 1:16; 2:7, 14; 3:8; *Explanation* on Titus 2:11–15). In what is proper Greek but awkward English, Paul clarifies that by good deeds he means "the necessary needs" (εἰς τὰς ἀναγκαίας χρείας; εἰς, "to," denoting reference). ἀναγκαίας, "necessary," could refer to the daily practical needs that everybody has, or it could refer to the urgent and pressing needs of others. Because Titus is asked to care for Zenas and Apollos in the preceding verse and the goal of the good deeds is that one not be fruitless (see below), ἀνακαίας, "necessary," here refers to the pressing needs of others. χρεία, "need," is used elsewhere by Paul to designate the necessities of life (Rom 12:13; Phil 2:25; 4:16). ἵνα μὴ ὦσιν ἄκαρποι, "lest they be fruitless," specifies the intended result of caring for the pressing needs of others. ἄκαρπος, "fruitless," used figuratively, means "useless, unproductive" (BAGD, 29; cf. Matt 13:22; Mark 4:19; 1 Cor 14:14; Eph 5:11; 2 Pet 1:8). Quinn comments on the metaphor, "The tree itself has no use for its fruit; the latter is meant to support the life of others. So the fraternal charity of the Cretan Christians helps sustain the life and missionary work of others for Christ and his church (see 2 Tim 2:6)" (268). Lock adds that "here the special reference seems to be to the Roman taunt that Christians were unprofitable to the State, as keeping apart from many trades" (159; citing Tertullian, *Apol.* 42).

15 ἀσπάζονταί σε οἱ μετ᾽ ἐμοῦ πάντες. ἄσπασαι τοὺς φιλοῦντας ἡμᾶς ἐν πίστει. ἡ χάρις μετὰ πάντων ὑμῶν, "All those with me greet you. Greet those who love us in faith. Grace [be] with all of you." Paul concludes the letter to his friend with his standard greeting. Paul often conveys greetings from his associates (Rom 16:21–23; 1 Cor 16:19–20; 2 Cor 13:12; Phil 4:22; Col 4:10–14; Phlm 25), usually without naming them (but cf. Rom 16:21–23; Col 4:10–14). ἐν πίστει could mean "within the sphere of (Christian) faith," or the anarthrous construction could suggest "faithfully" (cf. *Introduction,* "Themes in the PE"). In either case, Paul repeats the same veiled separation in v 14 when he says οἱ ἡμέτεροι, "our [people]." Paul does not wish to greet those who are being divisive in the Cretan church. On the final ἡ χάρις μετὰ πάντων ὑμῶν, "grace [be] with all of you," see *Comments* on 1 Tim 6:21 and 2 Tim 4:22. On χάρις, "grace," see *Comment* on 1 Tim 1:2. The plural πάντων, "all," suggests that despite its personal appearance, the epistle to Titus is more public than private, or that Paul recognizes that it eventually will become public. However, the same plural is found in the final greeting to his second epistle to Timothy (2 Tim 4:22), which is an intensely personal letter, so not too much should be made of the plural here.

Explanation

Paul ends his epistle to Titus in the normal fashion. He will be sending a replacement for Titus, either Artemas or Tychicus; most likely he sent Artemas.

When his replacement comes, Titus is to meet Paul in Nicopolis where he will be staying for the winter. From Nicopolis Titus eventually headed north to Dalmatia. Zenas and Apollos were coming to Crete, and Titus is to make sure that their needs are met. They probably brought the letter to Titus.

Before his final greeting, for the last time Paul emphasizes that Christianity must be practical, that all Christians must learn that good works, specifically those that provide for people with pressing needs, must be the logical and natural extension of submitting to the salvation and Lordship of Christ. Christians must not be fruitless. Paul then sends the greetings of his associates to Titus, asks Titus to greet the Cretan Christians who are truly Christian and faithful to Paul's gospel, and concludes by asking that God's grace be upon Titus and the Cretan church.

2 Timothy

I. Salutation   (2 Tim 1:1–2)

Bibliography

See *Bibliography* for 1 Tim 1:1–2.

Translation

¹*Paul, an apostle of Christ Jesus through [the] will of God according to [the] promise of life that [is] in Christ Jesus;* ²*to Timothy, beloved son: Grace, mercy, peace from God [the] Father and Christ Jesus* ᵃ *our Lord.*

Notes

ᵃThe order Χριστοῦ Ἰησοῦ is supported by the best MSS (א² A D F G I Ψ TR lat syʰ sa boᵖᵗ). The order is reversed in 629 1739 1881 *pc* vgᵐˢ, and κυρίου Ἰησοῦ Χριστοῦ, "Lord Jesus Christ," is read by א* 33 *pc* syᵖ.

Form/Structure/Setting

Paul begins his second epistle to Timothy in his usual manner: author, recipient, and greeting. His wording closely resembles the salutation in 1 Timothy except for the phrase "through [the] will of God according to [the] promise of life that [is] in Christ Jesus" and his use of "beloved" son rather than "true spiritual" son. See *Form/Structure/Setting* on 1 Tim 1:1–2 for a discussion of the salutations in the PE.

The tone of the salutation of 2 Timothy is different from 1 Timothy. There the statement that Paul's apostleship is the result of a command from God sets the authoritarian note for the entire epistle. While the note of Paul's authority is still present in 2 Timothy (see *Comment*), the tone of the salutation and the entire epistle is more personal, as in the address to Timothy as Paul's "beloved" son.

Comment

1a Παῦλος ἀπόστολος Χριστοῦ Ἰησοῦ διὰ θελήματος θεοῦ, "Paul, an apostle of Christ Jesus through [the] will of God." Paul begins by identifying himself by name and office. (See *Comment* on 1 Tim 1:1 for a discussion of the verse.) He follows with two clarifying phrases, the first being that his apostleship is due to the will of God (cf. similar statement in the salutations in 1 Corinthians, 2 Corinthians, Ephesians, and Colossians). While some may find it odd that Paul would call himself an apostle when writing to a friend (e.g., Easton), it is not inappropriate. (1) Paul was an apostle and out of habit, if nothing else, refers to himself as an apostle. (2) In the epistle Paul intertwines Timothy's and his own ministries, and therefore some of the authority of the apostle Paul carries over to Timothy, encouraging him and validating his work in Ephesus. (3) Although 2 Timothy is primarily personal, the closing plural ὑμῶν, "you" (4:22), suggests that

Paul expected the letter to be read by the Ephesian church; since parts of the second half deal with the Ephesian opponents (2:14–3:9; 4:3–4, 14–15), the letter functions as an authoritative rebuttal. However, this should not be overemphasized since the letter is so personal.

διὰ θελήματος θεοῦ, "through [the] will of God," shows Paul's view of his own ministry as defined by the Damascus-road experience (see 1 Tim 1:12–17). He did not choose to be an apostle, but God made his will known. Therefore the ultimate authority behind what Paul does is not Paul but God. διά, "through," denotes the efficient cause (BAGD, 180 [A III1d]); God's will caused Paul to become an apostle. θέλημα, "will," occurs sixty-two times in the NT, twenty-four in Paul. It is used mostly of God's will, or human will in contrast to God's (12x). In Paul it is used of God's will with four exceptions (1 Cor 7:37; 16:12; Eph 2:3; 2 Tim 2:26; cf. M. Limbeck, EDNT 3:52–62). Its only other use in the PE is in 2 Tim 2:26, which speaks of the devil's will to snare the Ephesians.

1b κατ' ἐπαγγελίαν ζωῆς τῆς ἐν Χριστῷ Ἰησοῦ, "according to [the] promise of life that [is] in Christ Jesus." Paul's second clarifying statement concerning his apostleship is that the intended goal (κατά, "according to"; BAGD, 406–7 [II4]) of his ministry is the fulfillment of God's promise, which is life in its fullest. (The promise is based not on law, a fact not understood by the Ephesian opponents [cf. 1 Tim 1:7–11], but on union "in Christ.") The promise of life is God's promise within the context of salvation to give life to believers. ζωῆς, "life," denotes not so much existence as it does a quality of life, life at its fullest, both on earth and in heaven. The gift of life comes from Christ Jesus to those who are in Christ Jesus (cf. discussion of a similar phrase in 1 Tim 4:8 and Titus 1:2; cf. also 1 Tim 1:14; Kelly, 154; Knight, 364).

2a Τιμοθέῳ ἀγαπητῷ τέκνῳ, "to Timothy, beloved son." The second part of the standard epistolary greeting is the identification of the recipient. In 1 Tim 1:2, where the emphasis is on Paul's authority and its transference to Timothy, Paul writes Τιμοθέῳ γνησίῳ τέκνῳ ἐν πίστει, "to Timothy, true spiritual son." In Titus 1:4 he writes, Τίτῳ γνησίῳ τέκνῳ κατὰ κοινὴν πίστιν, "To Titus, a true son in a common faith." While Paul's apostolic authority has its place in this letter (see on 2 Tim 1:1), the dominant note is Paul's friendship with Timothy. ἀγαπητῷ τέκνῳ, "beloved son," sets the stage for the argument in 2 Tim 1:3–2:13. Elsewhere Paul says Timothy is μοῦ τέκνον ἀγαπητὸν καὶ πιστὸν ἐν κυρίῳ, "my beloved and faithful child in the Lord" (1 Cor 4:17). ἀγαπητῷ τέκνῳ, "beloved son," could be in apposition to Τιμοθέῳ, "Timothy," functioning almost as a title (cf. Titus 1:4). ἀγαπητός, "beloved," occurs elsewhere in the PE in 1 Tim 6:2, where some slaves are reminded that their masters are beloved, i.e., Christian. See there for discussion. As such ἀγαπητός includes the meaning of ἐν πίστει, "in faith," found in the salutation in 1 Tim 1:2 and κατὰ κοινὴν πίστιν, "in a common faith," in Titus 1:4.

2b χάρις ἔλεος εἰρήνη ἀπὸ θεοῦ πατρὸς καὶ Χριστοῦ Ἰησοῦ τοῦ κυρίου ἡμῶν, "Grace, mercy, peace from God [the] Father and Christ Jesus our Lord." The third part of a standard salutation is a statement of greeting. As usual, Paul has enlarged and Christianized the greeting. The form here is identical to the greeting in 1 Tim 1:2 (see there for a discussion). Why Hanson complains that the author did not "associate the Spirit with the Godhead" ([1983] 119) is not clear since none of Paul's similar greetings makes the association.

Explanation

Paul begins his second letter to Timothy in usual fashion. The only significant shift from the salutation in 1 Timothy is the lack of emphasis on Paul's apostolic authority. Although the note of authority is present, the salutation sets the stage for a personal letter. Paul qualifies his apostolic position with two phrases. The first is that Paul's apostleship is the result of God's will and not his own, and therefore God stands behind the encouragement and instruction Timothy will read in this epistle. Second, the promise of life held out to Jew and Gentile alike is not through law (1 Tim 1:8–11) but only through being "in Christ."

II. Thanksgiving (2 Tim 1:3–5)

Bibliography

Elderen, B. van. "The Verb in the Epistolary Invocation." *CTJ* 2 (1967) 46–48. **Exler, F. X. J.** *The Form of the Ancient Greek Letter: A Study in Greek Epistolography.* 1923. Repr. Chicago: Ares, 1976. 102–11. **Hunt, A. S.**, and **Edgar, C. C.**, trs. *Select Papyri I.* LCL. Cambridge: Harvard UP, 1932. **Kowalski, B.** "Zur Funktion und Bedeutung der alttestamentlichen Zitate und Anspielungen in den Pastoralbriefen." STNU-A 19 (1994) 45–68. **Mansoor, M.** *The Thanksgiving Hymns.* Grand Rapids, MI: Eerdmans, 1961. **O'Brien, P. T.** *Introductory Thanksgivings in the Letters of Paul.* NovTSup 49. Leiden: Brill, 1977. 56–104. ———. "Thanksgiving and the Gospel in Paul." *NTS* 21 (1974–75) 144–45. **Read, D. H. C.** "Home-Made Religion." *ExpTim* 97 (1986) 307–8. **Sanders, J. T.** "The Transition from Opening Epistolary Thanksgiving to Body in the Letters of the Pauline Corpus." *JBL* 81 (1962) 348–62. **Schubert, P.** *Form and Function of the Pauline Thanksgivings.* BZNW 20. Berlin: Töpelmann, 1939. **Spicq, C.** "Epipothein, Désirer ou Chérir?" *RB* 64 (1957) 184–95. ———. "Loïs, ta grand-maman (II Tim. 1,5)." *RB* 84 (1977) 362–64. **White, J. L.** *The Form and Function of the Body of the Greek Letter: A Study of the Letter-Body in the Non-Literary Papyri and in Paul the Apostle.* SBLDS 2. Missoula, MT: Scholars Press, 1979.

For additional bibliography on epistolary salutations, see *Bibliography* for 1 Tim 1:3–7.

Translation

[3] *I continually thank God, whom I serve, as did my ancestors, with a clean conscience, as unceasingly I remember you in my prayers night and day,* [4] *yearning to see you, remembering your tears, in order that I may be filled with joy,* [5] *because I remember* [a] *your sincere faith, which dwelt first in your grandmother Lois and your mother Eunice, and I am confident that [it is] also in you.*

Notes

[a]The aorist ὑπόμνησιν λαβών, "having remembered" (ℵ* A C F G Ψ 33 104 1175 1739 [1881] *pc*), is replaced with the present ὑπόμνησιν λαμβάνων, "remembering," by ℵ² D (365) TR syʰ, bringing the tense into agreement with the other verbal forms.

Form/Structure/Setting

As is generally typical of Paul and ancient letter writing in general (cf. all of Paul's epistles except Galatians, 1 Timothy, and Titus), he follows the salutation with a statement of thanksgiving for the recipient. In it Paul introduces the themes that constitute the basis for his encouragement to Timothy (cf. O'Brien, *NTS* 21 [1974] 145–46) in 1:6–2:13, including Timothy's faith (1:13–14; 2:1, 3, 15, 22; 3:14), loyalty to Paul (cf. 1:8; 2:3; 3:10, 14), and perseverance in his ministry (cf. Fee, 221). Throughout the first half of the epistle Paul shows Timothy that their lives and ministries are intertwined and because of this Timothy can draw encouragement from Paul.

Vv 3–5 constitute a single sentence. The basic structure is "I give thanks (v 3) . . . because I remember your sincere faith" (v 5). V 3b contains two circumstantial modifiers ("whom I serve . . . as unceasingly I remember"), and v 4 is an affectionate parenthesis as Paul thinks about his dear friend and the last time they were together. Many who otherwise question the historicity of the PE feel that this passage with its personal references is historical. The fact that this statement of thanksgiving varies from similar statements elsewhere in Paul is of no real consequence (see *Introduction*, "Critical Questions, The Linguisitic Problem").

Comment

3a χάριν ἔχω τῷ θεῷ, ᾧ λατρεύω ἀπὸ προγόνων ἐν καθαρᾷ συνειδήσει, "I continually thank God, whom I serve, as did my ancestors, with a clean conscience." Paul begins by saying he is thankful to God, but it is not until v 5 that we learn why he is thankful: "because I remember your sincere faith." Vv 3b–4 give the circumstances surrounding Paul's thankfulness. (On χάριν ἔχω, "I continually thank," see *Comment* on the same phrase in 1 Tim 1:12.) The outstanding feature of this statement is Paul's attachment of his ministry to the work of God in the OT (λατρεύειν, "to serve"; see below) and to his Jewish ancestors. Paul sees his spiritual heritage not as one who broke with the past but as one who stands in the direct line of his Jewish ancestry as a worshiper of the God of Abraham, Isaac, and Jacob. He does this for several reasons. (1) He is preparing the way for his comments in v 5 about Timothy's spiritual heritage. (2) Paul and Timothy's union in a true spiritual heritage provides a condemning contrast to the error being taught by the opponents, who saw themselves as teachers of the law (1 Tim 1:7). (3) Also in these words can be seen the contemplative reflection of a man near death and his estimation of his life—one of ongoing service to God, in line with his spiritual heritage, the life of a man with a clear conscience.

Two important themes are introduced in this phrase, themes that play a central role as Paul encourages Timothy. (1) The first is that Paul and Timothy have much in common, and this commonality should encourage Timothy as both Paul and he suffer and persevere. Both have a godly heritage (1:3, 5; 3:15). Paul shared in Timothy's commissioning to ministry (1:6). They have both suffered, Paul in prison (1:8) and Timothy in Ephesus. Paul was called to be an apostle not because of what he had done but because of God's purpose and grace, and this call involved imprisonment and suffering (1:8–11). But Paul is not ashamed (1:12), and neither should Timothy be ashamed of Paul or the gospel (1:8). Paul trusts God (1:12), and so Timothy should continue to guard the gospel (1:13–14). Paul has been deserted by most of his associates, except for one faithful person (1:15–18). Timothy likewise should not be discouraged or feel abandoned. Rather he should be single-minded about the gospel and loyal to Paul's proclamation of it (2:1–7). Even though Paul is being treated like a criminal, the gospel is not chained and the elect will continue to be saved (2:8–10). Therefore Timothy should be strong, realizing that believers live with Christ, will reign with Christ, and can count on God's faithfulness in the face of their own faithlessness. Yet Timothy must be wary, and the opponents must be warned, because those who deny the God of Paul's gospel will themselves be denied on judgment day (2:11–13). Throughout the first half of the epistle Paul is constantly comparing *Timothy to*

himself, encouraging Timothy in the face of persecution and suffering in Ephesus.
The same argument continues throughout the second half of the epistle as well
(3:10–17; 4:6–8, 18; cf. 2 Cor 1:21–22) where Paul joins himself with the Ephesians.

(2) The second theme introduced in v 3 is the call to remember one's spiritual heritage. Paul's and Timothy's heritages are different. Paul served God as
did his Jewish ancestors. While Timothy's father was a Greek (Acts 16:1), his
mother and grandmother were believers. The point of the comparison is that
both have a rich spiritual heritage that functions as an encouragement. Timothy's
faith is sincere (1:5), and he has the spiritual gifts (1:6) and Spirit of power (1:7)
to accomplish his task in Ephesus and elsewhere. God's call on Timothy's life
includes a call to suffer (1:8–9). Timothy has heard the gospel from Paul, it has
been entrusted to him, and Timothy is to guard it not with his own power but by
the power of the Holy Spirit (1:13–14). Now it is time to pass this spiritual heritage and responsibility on to others (2:2). Even Paul's life of persecution and
rescue from suffering (3:10–11) serve as part of Timothy's spiritual heritage, encouraging him by showing that persecution is not a sign of God's displeasure but
is a necessary part of a godly life (1:12). Timothy has known the Hebrew Scripture from childhood and its ability to make believers mature, having learned it
from Paul, his mother, and his grandmother. He must continue in it (3:14–17).

These two themes—association with Paul and a spiritual heritage—form the
basis of Paul's encouragement in the first half of the epistle and are woven throughout the second half. They provide a personal look into Paul's heart and reveal his
love and concern for his good friend Timothy. λατρεύειν, "to serve" (with a dative object ᾧ, "whom"), is the usual word in the LXX for Israel's worship of God
(Exod 23:25; Deut 6:12; 10:12; Josh 22:27; cf. Strathmann, *TDNT* 4:58–61; Trench,
Synonyms, 171–74). It is always used in a religious sense, describing service to God
(except Deut 24:48), hence "worship" (δουλεύειν being the more general term
for "to serve"). Its linear aspect shows Paul's ongoing conviction of the rightness
of his gospel as the fulfillment of the OT promises. λατρεύειν occurs elsewhere in
Paul in Rom 1:9–10, 25 and Phil 3:3 (21x in the NT). "As did my ancestors" is a
loose translation of the awkward ἀπὸ προγόνων. πρόγονος can mean "parent,"
"grandparent," or "ancestor" (cf. 1 Tim 5:4). The use of ἀπό, "from," is unusual,
but its sense is sufficiently clear.

ἐν καθαρᾷ συνειδήσει, "with a clean conscience" (cf. 1 Tim 1:5; 3:9; Acts 23:1),
is a significant statement in light of the fact that Paul is chained as a criminal
ready to die (4:6–8). His refusal to be ashamed despite his seemingly constant
suffering echoes throughout this epistle, a tribute to the apostle who knows that
he and the gospel are right regardless of appearances. Timothy should not be
ashamed but should share in the suffering (1:9). Paul suffers not because he committed a crime but because he is an apostle (1:12), and like Onesiphorus (1:16)
Timothy also should not be ashamed but share in the suffering as a soldier for
Christ (2:3). Even if Paul suffers and is chained as a criminal, the gospel is not
chained (2:9–10). As Timothy reflects on Paul's life, his suffering and persecutions, he must recognize that God always rescued Paul. In fact all who are godly
will suffer (3:10–12). Timothy too should endure suffering (4:5). The believer's
life is necessarily bound up with suffering. Oberlinner points out an apparent
problem with Paul's emphasis on the continuity of service in which he stands,
contrasting this passage with the biographical sketch in 1 Tim 1:12–16 in which

Paul sees himself as a blasphemer and persecutor (vv 16–17). However, 1 Tim 1:12–16 is an evaluation only of himself, not his ancestors, and the phrase ἐν καθαρᾷ συνειδήσει, "with a clean conscience," can follow after ᾧ λατρεύω, "whom I serve," thus making ἀπὸ προγόνων, "as did my ancestors," grammatically parenthetical. Paul is not saying that the consciences of all Jews before him are clear. He is merely recognizing that he comes from within an ethnic continuity of service.

3b ὡς ἀδιάλειπτον ἔχω τὴν περὶ σοῦ μνείαν ἐν ταῖς δεήσεσίν μου νυκτὸς καὶ ἡμέρας, "as unceasingly I remember you in my prayers night and day." This is the second phrase qualifying the main verb χάριν ἔχω, "I continually thank." His thanks to God comes specifically during his regular prayer times. As a Pharisee, Paul would have followed a regular prayer schedule, and the habit probably carried over to his Christian walk. ἀδιάλειπος, "unceasing" (a neuter adjective used adverbially; see Rom 9:2 and the adverb ἀδιαλείπτως, "unceasingly," in Rom 1:9; 1 Thess 1:3, 13; 5:17), does not refer to nonstop prayer; rather it indicates that every time he prays, he remembers Timothy (cf. O'Brien, *Introductory Thanksgivings*, 56). ἔχω τὴν περὶ σοῦ μνείαν, "I have remembrance concerning you," is an usual way for Paul to refer to prayer (Rom 1:9; Eph 1:16; Phil 1:3; 1 Thess 1:2 [but not 3:6]; Phlm 4). δέησις, "prayer," refers specifically to prayer that expresses a need (cf. 1 Tim 2:1). νυκτὸς καὶ ἡμέρας, "night and day," was the normal Hebraic way of viewing time, the new day starting at sunset (cf. 1 Tim 5:5). Some punctuate so that νυκτὸς καὶ ἡμέρας goes with the following ἐπιποθῶν σε, "longing to see you" (cf. RV, Bernard, Moffatt's tr., RSV ["as I remember your tears, I long night and day to see you"]). However, it more naturally goes with the topic of prayer as it does elsewhere (1 Thess 3:10; cf. Luke 2:37), and Kelly (156) argues that it is "unnatural" to think of Paul longing night and day to see Timothy.

Elsewhere Paul says he prays because he has heard of a church's faith (Rom 1:8) and love (Eph 1:5; Col 1:4; 2 Thess 1:3; Phlm 4–5), and as he remembers their work (1 Thess 1:2–3). In 2 Tim 1:5 Paul says he prays for Timothy because of his sincere faith. Paul does not specifically discuss the content of his prayer for Timothy, although it can be surmised from the rest of the epistle that he prayed for Timothy's loyalty and perseverance (cf. Rom 1:8–12; 1 Cor 1:4–7; Eph 1:17–23; Phil 1:3–5; Col 1:9–12; 2 Thess 2:13; Phlm 4–6).

4 ἐπιποθῶν σε ἰδεῖν, μεμνημένος σου τῶν δακρύων, ἵνα χαρᾶς πληρωθῶ, "yearning to see you, remembering your tears, in order that I may be filled with joy." V 4 is the third parenthetical phrase between "I continually thank God" (v 3) and "because I am reminded of your sincere faith" (v 5). It can modify χάριν ἔχω, "I continually thank," or ἔχω τὴν περὶ σοῦ μνείαν, "I remember you" (v 3b). The participle ἐπιποθῶν, "yearning," could be causal ("because I yearn"), temporal ("when I yearn"), or circumstantial ("as I yearn"). Because v 5 explains why Paul gives thanks, it is doubtful that Paul means "I give thanks . . . because I yearn to see you." Also, it is doubtful that Paul's yearning is the basis for his giving thanks. It is preferable to see ἐπιποθῶν, "yearning," as a circumstantial participle modifying ἔχω τὴν περὶ σοῦ μνείαν, "I remember you." As Paul remembers Timothy during his prayer time, he is mindful of his intense desire to see Timothy. ἐπιποθεῖν, "to yearn," denotes a strong desire; it is a Pauline word (used in the NT only twice outside of Paul), always describing a good desire (Rom 1:11; 2 Cor 5:2; 9:14; Phil 1:8; 2:26; 1 Thess 3:6; cf. Spicq, *RB* 64 [1957] 184–95; id., *TLNT* 2:58–60). ἐπί, "upon," can make the form intensive: "to yearn" rather than "to desire" (cf.

Rom 1:11; 1 Thess 3:6). Ellicott (103) feels that it indicates direction—Paul's desire is toward Timothy—and points out that the simple ποθεῖν, "to desire," does not occur in the NT, so no comparison can be made.

μεμνημένος σου τῶν δακρύων, "remembering your tears," points to an unknown event in Paul and Timothy's life, most likely their last parting, which evidently ended in tears. Some see this as a reference to the tearful departing at Miletus (Acts 20:37; Bernard, Guthrie), although given the traditional historical reconstruction of the PE, this would mean that Paul had not seen Timothy for several years, which seems doubtful. It is probably the meeting referred to in 1 Tim 1:3, but beyond this, speculation is not helpful. In each of the following three verses Paul makes some mention of remembering, perhaps emphasizing "the apostle's reminiscent mood" (Guthrie, 124). The perfect-tense μεμνημένος, "remembering," from μιμνήσκεσθαι, "to remember," is used as a present tense and has a reflexive sense ("remind oneself, recall to mind" [BAGD, 522]), followed by the genitive of the thing remembered (τῶν δακρύων, "tears"). It is a clear look into a lonely man's heart, a man who loves Timothy and wants to see him (4:9–13) even though Timothy's work in Ephesus is not done (2:2).

Paul concludes the thought by adding that if he could see Timothy again, despite all the negative circumstances of his imprisonment (4:10–18) and knowing that his earthly life is nearly over (4:6–8), Timothy's presence would make his joy complete. Their relationship is special to Paul. The passive πληρωθῶ, "be filled" (aorist passive), could be a "divine passive," implying God as the agent of the filling, or the passive could simply describe the result of their friendship. Paul associates the ideas of sorrow and joy closely (cf. Phil 2:17; 2 Cor 7:8, 9). It may be no accident that δακρύων, "tears," and χαρᾶς, "joy," are separated by only one word (ἵνα, "in order that"). They are not mutually exclusive concepts.

5a ὑπόμνησιν λαβὼν τῆς ἐν σοὶ ἀνυποκρίτου πίστεως, "because I remember your sincere faith." V 5 completes the thought begun in v 3: "I continually thank God . . . because I remember your sincere faith." The NIV unfortunately starts v 5 as a new sentence, breaking the relationship between v 3 and v 5. Remembrance of the recipients' faith often occasions this same statement from Paul (Col 1:3–4, εὐχαριστοῦμεν . . . ἀκούσαντες, "we give thanks . . . having heard"; 2 Thess 1:3, εὐχαριστεῖν . . . ὅτι, "to give thanks . . . because"; Phlm 4–5, εὐχαριστῶ . . . ἀκούων, "I give thanks . . . hearing"; cf. Rom 1:8; Eph 1:15). In light of the desertions of those Paul considered brothers, both Demas (4:10) and others (4:16; cf. 1:15), people whose faith was evidently insincere, it is joyous for Paul to remember Timothy's sincere faith.

"Because I remember" is a loose translation of ὑπόμνησιν λαβών, "receiving remembrance." The fact that ὑπόμνησις, "remembrance," can refer to an external reminder has led some (Bengel, Bernard, Guthrie) to assume that Paul has just received an external reminder of Timothy's sincerity and that Paul's thankfulness is in reference to this. Onesiphorus would surely have updated Paul on Timothy's situation. Perhaps Timothy wrote Paul about his frustrations with the Ephesian church and his despondency about Paul's imprisonment. It would in fact be surprising if either or both of these did not occur. ὑπόμνησις, "remembrance," occurs elsewhere in the NT only in 2 Pet 1:13 and 3:1. There the word designates an external remembrance, namely, Peter causing his audience to remember. While this is possible in the present passage, it is not necessary. Paul's thanksgivings tend to be general in nature, and there is no further reference, explicit or implicit, to such an event. The aorist can be indefinite, which is its basic function, denoting Paul's remembrance in general. While ὑπόμνησις has the active sense of "the (act of) remembering" as seen in 2 Pet 1:13 and 3:1, it also has a passive sense of "receive a remembrance of" (BAGD, 846). Lock questions whether Hellenistic Greek maintains the same distinction (83, citing Mark 14:72 and Luke 22:61).

ἀνυπόκριτος, "sincere," means "genuine, without hypocrisy" (cf. 1 Tim 1:5). Scott (89) argues that πίστεως, "faith," must be reduced in meaning from Paul's usual concept of justifying faith (see *Introduction,* "Themes in the PE") to mean "religious feeling" since issues of sincerity are not appropriate to the inner relationship of a person to God. The same issue is raised in 1 Tim 1:5. This is an unnecessary conclusion at several points. (1) As Demas (4:10) and others (4:16) show, what may appear to be faith may in time be shown to be insincere. In contrast, Timothy's perseverance in the face of suffering shows that his faith was sincere, true (cf. Guthrie, 124). (2) While insincere faith may be no faith at all, using *sincere* in connection with faith emphasizes one aspect of faith as is appropriate to the historical context. (3) Timothy's sincere faith is emphasized in contrast to the faith of the opponents, who showed themselves to be insincere, hypocritical liars (ἐν ὑποκρίσει ψευδολόγων; 1 Tim 4:2; cf. 1 Tim 1:5).

5b ἥτις ἐνῴκησεν πρῶτον ἐν τῇ μάμμῃ σου Λωΐδι καὶ τῇ μητρί σου Εὐνίκῃ, πέπεισμαι δὲ ὅτι καὶ ἐν σοί, "which dwelt first in your grandmother Lois and your mother Eunice, and I am confident that [it is] also in you." Paul elaborates on Timothy's faith by reminding him of his spiritual heritage, a heritage that has carried over into Timothy's own life. By reminding Timothy of this and by implicitly comparing it to his own spiritual heritage (cf. 1:3), Paul begins his encouragement of Timothy, which becomes the dominant note throughout the first half of the epistle. The theme plays a major role in 3:14–15 in Paul's discussion of the trustworthiness of Scripture: Timothy learned Scripture not only from Paul but also from his mother and grandmother ("from childhood").

Paul uses ἐνοικεῖν, "to dwell in," when speaking of the Holy Spirit (Rom 8:11; 2 Tim 1:14), the word of Christ (Col 3:16), God (2 Cor 6:16), sin (Rom 7:17), and here faith (2 Tim 1:5). This is the only reference to Timothy's grandmother Lois. It is also the only mention of his mother by name, although she is referred to in Acts 16:1 when Paul meets Timothy during his second missionary journey: "Then he arrived at Derbe and Lystra. And behold a certain disciple was there named Timothy, [the] son of a certain Jewish woman [who was a] believer [γυναικὸς Ἰουδαίας πιστῆς] but [his] father [was] a Greek [πατρὸς δὲ Ἕλληνος]." μάμμη occurs only here in the NT and can mean "mother" or "grandmother" (BAGD, 490). Because Eunice is identified as his mother (μήτηρ), Lois must be his grandmother. Most assume that Lois was his maternal grandmother since his father was not a believer and she is mentioned with Timothy's mother. Some (Scott, 89) have argued that Lois and Eunice were Jewish believers, not Christians, and Paul is comparing Timothy's upbringing in a pious Jewish home with his own Jewish ancestry. But it is unnatural to read πιστῆς, "believer," in Acts 16:1 as anything other than a Christian believer. And Hanson ([1983] 12) is right that Timothy's upbringing could not have been in a pious Jewish home. His mother set herself outside of Judaism by marrying a Greek and by not having Timothy circumcised (Acts 16:3). Paul does not say that the faith dwelt first in Lois and then in Eunice; he says that both his mother and grandmother were Christians before he was. Many who doubt the historicity of the PE accept this fragment as trustworthy because of its personal nature.

Even less is known of Timothy's father. Acts 16:1, 3 state that he was a Greek and did not circumcise his son. From this it is assumed that he was not a believer, which probably explains why he is never mentioned again (Jeremias). A textual variant replaces Ἰουδαίας, "Jewish," with χήρας, "widow" (gig p vg^mss), in Acts 16:1, implying that his father had died. Hanson ([1983] 120) repeats the suggestion from K. Lake and H. J. Cadbury (in *The Beginnings of Christianity*, ed. F. J. Foakes Jackson and K. Lake [New York: Macmillan, 1933] 4:184) that the verb in "for his father *was* a Greek" (ὑπῆρχεν, not ἦν) in Acts 16:3 implies that he was dead at the time of Paul's visit. Hanson (1983) suggests that after the death of Timothy's father, both women reverted to Judaism and eventually converted back to Christianity; however, this is only supposition and no reason is given.

Paul is totally convinced that the faith of Lois and Eunice resides also in Timothy. δέ, "and," has no adversative force (BAGD, 171 [2]). πείθειν, "to convince," occurs one other time in the PE (2 Tim 1:12) and twenty other times in Paul. Its frequency provides insight into Paul's character. It has a wide range of nuances, from the usual "to persuade, convince" to "to trust, obey" (Heb 13:17; Jas 3:3; cf. A. Sand, *EDNT* 3:63). It is used frequently to express confidence, certitude, a confidence resulting in "quiet tranquility" (cf. esp. Phil 1:6, 25; *TLNT* 3:66–79). This meaning carries over to the perfect middle/passive form (Heb 6:9; Luke 20:6), the word often being followed by ὅτι, "that," as it is here (Rom 8:38; 14:14; 15:14; 2 Tim 1:12). Fee (223) points out how Paul tends to name people more frequently in his personal letters, twenty-two times in 2 Timothy and nine times in Philemon (evidently excluding the unusual sixteenth chapter of Romans).

Explanation

In his usual style, Paul follows the salutation with a statement of thanksgiving for the recipient, thanking God because of Timothy's sincere faith. At the end of a life that is marked with suffering and persecution, Paul is still able to assert that he faithfully worships God with a clean conscience, a worship that is in line with his Jewish ancestry. Timothy too has an ancestry, an ancestry of a godly mother and grandmother. Both Timothy and Paul are joined in the possession of a spiritual heritage that aids them in their own ministry, even though those heritages differ at several points. Paul thus begins encouraging Timothy to persevere in his work at Ephesus.

The thanksgiving also gives unusual insight into Paul. He knows he is at the end of his life, and what is important to him now is that his friend Timothy leave Ephesus, even before he is done with his work, and come to spend time with Paul. Their previous time together ended in painful tears, and in his regular praying Paul thanks God for Timothy and longs to see him again, so he may be filled with joy.

III. Encouragement to Timothy (2 Tim 1:6–2:13)

A. Call to Suffer without Shame (2 Tim 1:6–14)

Bibliography

Alpe, A. ab. "Paulus 'praedicator et Apostolus et magistar' (2 Tim 1, 11)." *VD* 23 (1943) 199–206, 238–44. **Barclay, W.** "Paul's Certainties VII: Our Security in God—2 Timothy i.12." *ExpTim* 69 (1958) 324–27. **Bauza, M.** "Ut resuscites gratiam Dei." *Semana Española de Teologia* (1969) 55–66. **Bius, C. L.** "Sei em quem pus a minha confiança." *Perspectiva Teológica* 3 (1971) 165–90. **Bover, J. M.** "Illuminavit vitam (2 Tim. 1,10)." *Bib* 28 (1947) 136–46. **Cipriani, S.** "La dottrina del 'depositum' nelle lettere pastorali." In *Studiorum Paulinorum Congressus Internationalis Catholicus 1961*. AnBib 17–18. Rome: Biblical Institute, 1963. 2:127–42. **Fee, G. D.** *God's Empowering Presence.* 785–89. **Gutzen, D.** "Zucht oder Besonnenheit? Bemerkungen zur Übersetzung von 2 Timotheus 1,7." *Die Bibel in der Welt* 21 (1985) 40–48. **Hall, D. R.** "Fellow-Workers with the Gospel." *ExpTim* 85 (1974) 119–20. **Kee, H. C.** "The Linguistic Background of 'Shame' in the New Testament." In *On Language, Culture, and Religion.* FS E. A. Nida, ed. M. Black and W. A. Smalley. The Hague: Mouton, 1974. 133–47. **Lemaire, A.** "Conseils pour le ministère: 2 Tim 1,6–8.13–14." *AsSeign* 58 (1974) 61–66. **Médebielle, A.** "Dépôt de la Foi." *DBSup* 2 (1934) 374–95. **Paramo, S. del.** "Depositum custodi [1 Tim 6:20; 2 Tim 1:14]." *Sal Terrae* 50 (1962) 556–62. **Saillard, M.** "Annoncer l'évangile c'est révéler le dessein de Dieu (2 Tim 1,8–10." *AsSeign* 15 (1973) 24–30. **Sohier, A.** "Je sais à qui j'ai donné ma foi (2 Tim. 1,12 et 4, 8)." *BVC* 37 (1961) 75–78. **Spicq, C.** "Saint Paul et la loi dépôts." *RB* 40 (1931) 481–502. **Stählin, G.** "Der heilige Ruf: 2 Timotheus 1,6–10." *TBei* 3 (1972) 97–106. **Stöger, A.** "Die Würzel priesterlichen Lebens: 2 Tim 1,6–14." *TPQ* 136 (1988) 252–57. **Thomas, W. D.** "Onesiphorus." *ExpTim* 96 (1984) 116–17.

Translation

[6]*For which reason I remind* [a] *you to fan into flame the gift of God,* [b] *which is in you through the laying on of my hands.* [7]*For God did not give us a spirit of cowardice but of power and of love and of self-control.* [8]*Therefore do not be ashamed of the testimony concerning our Lord or of me his prisoner, but share in suffering for the sake of the gospel according to the power of God,* [9]*who saved us and called us to a holy calling, not because of our works but because of* [his] *own purpose and grace, which was given to us in Christ Jesus before time eternal,* [10]*but now was made known through the appearing of our savior, Christ Jesus,* [c] *on the one hand, in order to abolish death and, on the other, to bring to light life and incorruptibility through the gospel,* [11]*to which I was appointed a herald and an apostle and a teacher,* [d] [12]*for which reason even* [e] *I am suffering these things; but I am not ashamed, for I know in whom I have trusted and I am fully convinced that he is able to guard my deposit until that day.* [13]*Hold to the pattern of healthy words that you have heard from me in* [the] *faith and* [the] *love that are in Christ Jesus.* [14]*Guard the good deposit by the Holy Spirit that indwells us.*

Notes

ᵃἀναμιμνήσκω, "I remind," is replaced with the basically synonymous ὑπομιμνήσκω (cf. Titus 3:1) by D Ψ 365 1505 *pc*.

ᵇθεοῦ, "of God," is replaced with Χριστοῦ, "of Christ," by A.

ᶜThe order Χριστοῦ Ἰησοῦ, "Christ Jesus" (ℵ* A D* 81 *pc* vgᵐˢˢ; Ambst), is reversed in ℵ² C D² F G Ψ 33 1739 1881 TR lat sy; Or. I possibly reads θεοῦ, "God."

ᵈκαὶ [– C P *pc*] διδάσκαλος ἐθνῶν, "and a teacher of the Gentiles" (ℵ² C D F G P Ψ 1739 1881 TR latt [*pc*] sy co), is in imitation of 1 Tim 2:7. The omission of ἐθνῶν, "of the Gentiles," is supported by ℵ* A I 1775 sy and a few other minuscules. 33 replaces διδάσκαλος, "teacher," with διάκονος, "servant." It is difficult to see why διδάσκαλος would have been dropped if it was original (*TCGNT*², 579).

ᵉκαί, "even," is omitted by ℵ* Ψ 1175 *pc* vgᵐˢˢ syᵖ.

Form/Structure/Setting

Vv 6–14 enlarge the theme of encouragement begun in vv 3–5. Because Timothy comes from a heritage of faith, a faith he personally possesses, Paul encourages him to use his spiritual gift in his work at Ephesus. Throughout this paragraph Paul weaves different themes together, all intended to encourage Timothy. (1) Paul identifies himself with Timothy. Paul was with Timothy when Timothy received his gift (v 6). The plural ἡμῖν, "us" (vv 7, 8, 9[2x], 10, 14), continually associates the two: God gave us a spirit of power, saved us not because of our works but because of his grace; the Holy Spirit too lives in us. Just as God gave Paul a spirit of power, called him to suffer without shame for the gospel, saved him to a life of holiness as a teacher of that gospel, and gave him the assurance that he would keep Paul safe, so also God has done, and will do, the same for Timothy. (2) Paul calls Timothy not to be ashamed of the gospel or of Paul himself (v 8). Paul is fully convinced that God can keep him safe and is therefore not ashamed (v 12), and neither should Timothy be. In the next paragraph Paul will remind Timothy of Onesiphorus, who was not ashamed and is therefore a model for Timothy (vv 16–18). (3) Paul encourages Timothy by calling him to share with him in suffering for the gospel (v 8); Timothy's suffering is not simply to be endured or viewed as a deterrent. (4) Paul reminds Timothy that God has not abandoned him in Ephesus but rather will empower him to do the work. The call to suffer with Paul for the gospel is "according to the power of God" (v 8), the same power that can keep Paul's deposit safe until judgment day (v 12). Likewise, as Timothy guards what God has given to him, he is to do this not in his own power but through the Holy Spirit that lives in him (v 14). (5) Finally, the description of the gospel itself serves as an encouragement to Timothy. The gospel to which Timothy is called to suffer and of which he is not to be ashamed is the very gospel that declares the salvation of God and a call to obedience, based not on human merit but on God's grace, the possession of which was Timothy's before time but is now revealed through Christ. No matter how difficult the situation becomes in Ephesus, Timothy can draw encouragement from a proper understanding of the gospel message.

The theme of suffering ties almost all of the epistle together. Paul is not ashamed to suffer (1:12; πάσχειν). Timothy should share in suffering (2:3; συγκακοπαθεῖν) as a good soldier. Paul suffers for the gospel (2:9; κακοπαθεῖν). Timothy is to take note of Paul's past sufferings (3:11; πάθημα) and persecutions, since all who wish to live godly lives will be persecuted (3:12; διώκειν), and be willing to endure suffering himself (4:5; κακοπαθεῖν).

It is difficult to break 1:3–2:13 into divisions. It is a consistent discussion with multiple themes and wordplays woven throughout. V 6 grows out of vv 3–5, but a break is suggested here after v 5 because in v 6 Paul starts to encourage Timothy explicitly. Vv 6–12 form a unit with the call to suffer and not be ashamed, the emphasis on the nature of the gospel, and a strong conclusion in v 12 (see *Comment*). It is true that the opponents are more visible in vv 13–14 than in vv 6–12, although they are present between the lines in the latter. To some this suggests a break after v 12. However, the sound words in v 13 are the gospel in vv 8–11, and the deposit Timothy is to guard in v 14 draws from the imagery in v 12. Although not explicitly stated, the gift of God (v 6) has strong associations with the Holy Spirit in Paul's writings; the Spirit is explicitly mentioned in v 14. Throughout there is a strong personal emphasis on ἐγώ, "I," and ἡμῖν, "us" (vv 7, 8, 9[2x], 10, 11, 12 [5x], 13, 14). Vv 15–18 are related to vv 6–14 in that they mention people who chose to be loyal to Paul and the gospel and those who abandoned Paul and the gospel; however, Paul shifts his emphasis from the personal to others, and so the passage is broken here after v 14, with vv 6–14 viewed as a unit of thought closely related to its surrounding verses and built around four basic admonitions. (1) Remember your gift (vv 6–7). (2) Do not be ashamed of Paul or the gospel but share in suffering for it (with an extended discussion of the nature of the gospel; vv 8–12). (3) Hold to the gospel (v 13). (4) Guard the gospel (v 14).

Many see vv 9–10 as a hymn or liturgical fragment used by Paul (cf. Hanson, [1983] 122). This, however, is doubtful (as also UBSGNT, Guthrie, Kelly, Fee). (1) Almost every word and the theology as a whole are so fully Pauline that the verses give no indication of a non-Pauline origin (see *Comment*). (2) There is nothing necessarily liturgical about the verses, and the parallelism could be the product of Paul's creative and Semitic mind (cf. Guthrie, *Mind of Paul*, 17–29). Parallelism by itself does not prove hymnic citation, and vv 7–8 have already established a pattern of parallelism ("not . . . of cowardice but of power . . . do not be ashamed . . . but share in suffering"). (3) Vv 9–10 fit the context perfectly, and in fact vv 8–12 form one sentence. Dibelius-Conzelmann (99) say, "they contain elements which are unnecessary to the context," which would support the idea that they are a hymn, but unfortunately Dibelius-Conzelmann do not identify the unnecessary elements, which are not apparent. (4) The play on the concept of savior, shifting between God as savior (v 9) and then Christ as savior (v 10) is characteristic of the PE. Vv 9–10 are Paul's words, Paul's theology, and fit tightly into Paul's grammar and argument.

Comment

6 δι᾽ ἣν αἰτίαν ἀναμιμνῄσκω σε ἀναζωπυρεῖν τὸ χάρισμα τοῦ θεοῦ, ὅ ἐστιν ἐν σοὶ διὰ τῆς ἐπιθέσεως τῶν χειρῶν μου, "For which reason I remind you to fan into flame the gift of God, which is in you through the laying on of my hands." Paul moves smoothly into the body of the letter. Because he knows Timothy's faith is sincere (v 5), he can remind Timothy to fan his spiritual gift of evangelism (2 Tim 4:5) into full flame to do battle with the Ephesian opponents.

What is the precise meaning of ἀναζωπυρεῖν, "to fan into flame"? It is a compound verb from ἀνά, "again," "up," and ζωπυρεῖν, "to kindle" a fire (cf. Moule, *Idiom-Book*, 87). It is possible that the preposition ἀνά should be given its full force of "again," hence "rekindle" (NRSV), "kindle afresh" (NASB). To most this implies that Timothy is failing to use his gift properly and needs to be admonished to start using it again, or that he is becoming weak in the faith. LSJ (104) list only the meaning "rekindle," never "kindle." The following verse may suggest that Timothy is timid, perhaps implying that he is prone to disappointment and failure. The problem with this interpretation is that it does not square with the general picture of Timothy, Paul's "right-hand man" upon whom Paul relied heavily on many occasions (see *Introduction*). ἀναζωπυρεῖν can also be translated "kindle" (BAGD, 54), "keep in full flame" (Abbott-Smith, *Lexicon*, 29), "fan into flame" (NIV), "stir up that inner fire" (Phillips), to "kindle *up*" (Ellicott, 104, citing usage in Wettstein, *Novum Testamentum Graecum*). In this case Paul is encouraging Timothy to continue on as he is doing, to keep his spiritual gift continually (ἀναζωπυρεῖν is linear in aspect) at its full potential (so Bernard, Guthrie, Kelly, Knight), perhaps to refresh it continually. The compound ἀναζωπυρεῖν may be an alliteration suggested by the prior ἀναμιμνῄσκω, "I remind," and the force of ἀνά is to be minimized. Unfortunately ἀναζωπυρεῖν occurs in the NT only here, and ζωπυρεῖν never occurs in the NT. "It does not necessarily imply an actual wavering or dying faith on Timothy's part" (Fee, 226), nor does it imply "anything more than a very natural anxiety on the part of the older man lest the younger one should faint under his heavy burden" (Bernard, 109). Ellicott suggests that Timothy had fallen into a state of despondency because of "the absence, trials, and imprisonment of his spiritual father in the faith" (104), and Paul's words are those of an encouraging father that he is all right and that Timothy should not be depressed. Chrysostom observes, "As fire requires fuel, so grace requires our alacrity, that it may be ever fervent" ("Homily 1"; NPNF 13:477). Just because people are encouraged by someone does not mean that they are failing. It can mean that they are being encouraged to continue despite the pressure.

The second issue in this verse is the event in Timothy's life to which it refers: the laying on of hands by Paul in recognition of Timothy's possession of his spiritual gift. See the excursus "Prophecies about Timothy" following the *Comment* on 1 Tim 1:20 for a detailed discussion of this verse and the event. The other two references to this event indicate that prophecies identified Timothy as possessing the necessary gift(s) to do his task (1 Tim 1:18), and this was confirmed by the corporate laying on of hands by the body of elders (1 Tim 4:14). As is discussed in the excursus, because of the personal nature of the passage, Paul here speaks only of his role in the commissioning ceremony. In all three passages Paul is reminding Timothy of this event as a means of encouragement to continue in his work despite the opposition. Guthrie comments, "Every Christian minister needs at times to return to the inspiration of his ordination, to be reminded not only of the greatness of his calling, but also of the adequacy of the divine grace which enables him to perform it. Indeed, every Christian worker engaged in however small a task requires assurance that God never commissions anyone to a task without imparting a special gift appropriate for it" (126).

δι' ἣν αἰτίαν, "for which reason," is an idiomatic causal phrase (cf. Titus 1:13; 2 Tim 1:12). The gender of ἥν, "which," is controlled by αἰτίαν, "reason" (cf. BDF §456[4]). While in Titus 1:13 αἰτία means "accusation," here it is the milder "cause, reason" (BAGD, 26). ἀναμιμνήσκω σε, "I remind you" (cf. Rom 15:15; 1 Cor 4:17; 2 Cor 7:15), is the third mention of remembering since v 4. While the simple μιμνῄσκειν has a reflexive sense, "to remind oneself" (BAGD, 522), the compound ἀναμιμνῄσκειν means "to remind" and in this context has moved to the idea of "to encourage." Although not specifically stated, Timothy's gift was given, as are all spiritual gifts (1 Cor 12:8), by the Holy Spirit (see next verse). Paul thus begins and ends (1:14) this paragraph on the same note: the role of the Holy Spirit in Timothy's life.

7a οὐ γὰρ ἔδωκεν ἡμῖν ὁ θεὸς πνεῦμα δειλίας, "for God did not give us a spirit of cowardice." Having reminded Timothy of the gift of God that he received for ministry (v 6), Paul clarifies the nature of that gift. It is not a gift characterized by cowardice, but through it the Holy Spirit gives power, love, and self-control, qualities essential for Timothy's ministry. V 7 draws out the implication of the event mentioned in v 6 in order to encourage Timothy. The two issues of the verse deal with the identity of πνεῦμα, "spirit," and what δειλίας, "cowardice," tells us about Timothy's character.

πνεῦμα here is generally understood as "spirit," a person's attitude or disposition, as opposed to "Spirit," the Holy Spirit. This is the more natural reading of the text, and Paul elsewhere uses πνεῦμα in this way (Rom 8:15, "spirit of slavery" [this is a literary foil]; 11:8, "spirit of stupor"; 1 Cor 4:21, "spirit of gentleness"; 2 Cor 4:13, "same spirit of faith"; Gal 6:1, "spirit of gentleness"; Phil 1:27, "stand fast in one spirit"; also 1 Cor 2:12; 5:3–4; 2 Cor 2:13; 7:13; 12:18). It is not quite the same as the use of πνεῦμα that designates the human spirit as separate from the body, but it is related (cf. Rom 1:9; 8:16; 1 Cor 5:3–5; 7:34; 14:14–16; 16:18; 2 Cor 7:1; Phil 3:3; Col 2:5; and in Paul's epilogues, Gal 6:18; Phil 4:23; 1 Thess 5:23; 2 Tim 4:22; Phlm 25).

Fee (226–27; *God's Empowering Presence,* 786–89) argues that πνεῦμα is the Holy Spirit. (1) V 7 is closely tied to v 6, which speaks of Timothy's gift (χάρισμα), and for Paul the gift and the Holy Spirit are closely connected (cf. 1 Cor 12:5, 7). This is especially true of the gift of Timothy's call to ministry (see "Excursus: Prophecies about Timothy" on 1 Tim 1:20). (2) δυνάμεως, "power," and ἀγάπης, "love," in the following phrase are associated with the Spirit. (3) The "not . . . but" construction parallels Rom 8:15 and 1 Cor 2:12. In these two verses the first half of the statement does not appear to be the Holy Spirit ("spirit of slavery," "spirit of the world"), but in the second clause it is clear that Paul is speaking of the Holy Spirit ("Spirit of adoption," "the Spirit who is from God"). Fee (227) translates, "For when God gave us his Spirit, it was not timidity that we received, but power, love, and self-discipline." (4) Ellicott (105) and Knight (371) add that Paul can speak of the πνεῦμα given by God (Rom 5:5; 1 Cor 12:7; 2 Cor 1:22; 5:5; 1 Thess 4:8; but not Rom 11:8) and received by people (Rom 8:15; 1 Cor 2:12), referring to the Holy Spirit.

However, while v 6 and v 7 are closely tied together, neither v 6 nor the other passages in the PE that discuss Timothy's commissioning explicitly cite the role of the Holy Spirit. While power and love can be associated with the Holy Spirit, this is not necessarily true in all cases (Rom 1:4, 16; 1 Cor 1:18, 24; 4:19–20; 2 Cor 4:7; 6:7; 12:9; 13:4; Eph 1:19; 3:7 [implicitly]; Col 1:11, 29; 2 Thess 1:11). The translation "For when God gave us his Spirit, it was not timidity that we received" is a difficult rendering of the genitive δειλίας, "of timidity." There is a middle road by which πνεῦμα is interpreted as a reference to a person's own spirit, a personal tendency toward cowardice, but the triad of "power, love, self-control" is understood as given by the Holy Spirit (Knight, 371–72).

It is preferable, however, to view all four qualities as relating to Timothy's spirit, recognizing that the gifts God gives to Timothy and all believers are given through the Holy Spirit. The emphatic position of οὐ, "not," is significant; in no way does God give a spirit of cowardice. Guthrie comments, "The power of the Holy Spirit within [the servant of God] has enabled many a naturally timid man to develop a boldness not his own when called in the name of God to fulfill a difficult ministry" (127). The aorist ἔδωκεν, "gave," could refer to a specific point in time: Timothy's commissioning or conversion. The plural ἡμῖν, "us," could be Paul and Timothy, or it could be all believers. The reference is probably to Timothy's conversion (v 4), speaking of what was given to Timothy by the Holy Spirit when he believed, and the plural ἡμῖν, "us," is Paul's tactful way of not singling out Timothy for undue criticism—and truthful since at conversion God did not give Paul a spirit of cowardice either. It is also in line with Paul's desire to join Timothy and himself as a means of encouraging Timothy (cf. v 3).

The second major issue of the verse regards what is learned about Timothy's character. Most translate δειλίας as "timidity," believing that v 6 along with other similar verses suggests that Timothy had a proclivity toward timidity. While this may have been true to a small degree, Timothy's supposed timidity has been overemphasized. δειλία occurs only here in the NT. However, there is good reason to question its translation as "timidity," and the translation here will affect one's view of Timothy's character. (1) The general picture of Timothy is not one of a shy, timid person who had to be constantly encouraged, who had ceased using his spiritual gifts and needed to be urged to relight the fire (v 6; see *Introduction*). (2) δειλία is better translated "cowardice" (Ellicott; Fee; cf. BAGD, 173; cf. Trench, *Synonyms*, 58–59), and even if Timothy may have been timid, he certainly was not a coward. δειλία occurs nine times in the LXX: Ps 54:5 speaks of the "terrors of death"; speaking of his enemies, Judas prayed that God would "fill them with cowardice [δειλίαν]; melt the boldness of their strength; let them tremble in their destruction" (1 Macc 4:32); when the Syrian Heliodorus came to Jerusalem to plunder the treasury, God "caused so great a manifestation that all who had been so bold as to accompany him were astonished by the power of God, and became faint with terror [δειλίαν] at the vision" (2 Macc 3:24; Heliodorus was struck down to the point of death, but raised up through Onias's sacrifice); when Eleazar refused to obey Antiochus and eat pork, he said it would be shameful to break the law for cowardice (δειλίᾳ; 4 Macc 6:20); δειλία is joined with fear (Sir 4:17) and confusion (3 Macc 6:19); if the Israelites disobey God, he will punish them severely (Lev 26:27–35), and he will make the heart of those who remain so fearful (δειλίαν) "that the sound of a windblown leaf will put them to flight" (Lev 26:36 [NIV]; cf. also Ps 89:40; Prov 19:15; and the cognate verb in Deut 1:21 and John 14:27).

These passages show that δειλία means "cowardice" and not the weaker "timidity," and it is highly doubtful that Paul is implying that Timothy was a coward. Also, if cowardice describes what Timothy was, "power," "love," and "self-control" would describe what Timothy was not, and this too seems unlikely. It is better to see Paul encouraging Timothy by calling him continually to act with power and love and self-control. Cowardice is merely a foil that serves to emphasize and define what Paul means by power (see Fee's discussion of the οὐ/ἀλλά, "not/but," construction in Paul in which "Paul's concern is always expressed in the ἀλλά ['but'] phrase or clause" [*God's Empowering Presence*, 788]). Chrysostom connects cowardice to God's activity in the OT: "For to many He [i.e., God] gives a spirit of fear, as we read in the wars of the Kingd[om]. 'A spirit of fear fell upon them.' [Ex. xv. 16?] That is, he infused terror into them. But to thee He has given, on the contrary, a spirit of power, and of love toward Himself" ("Homily 1"; NPNF 13:477).

7b ἀλλὰ δυνάμεως καὶ ἀγάπης καὶ σωφρονισμοῦ, "but of power and love and self-control." Instead of cowardice God gave Timothy a spirit of power, love, and self-control, spiritual abilities necessary for his task in Ephesus. δύναμις, "power," occurs elsewhere in the PE in 2 Tim 1:8 where Timothy is told to suffer hardship together (with Paul) for the gospel according to the power of God (who has saved and called believers), and in 2 Tim 3:5 where Paul says that the opponents have a mere form of godliness but deny its power. Timothy has been given power, a power from God through the Holy Spirit (cf. Rom 15:13, 19; 1 Cor 2:4; Eph 3:16, 20 [implicitly]; 1 Thess 1:5; cf. Luke 4:14; Acts 1:8) as evidenced by the gospel, a power that the opponents do not have. On ἀγάπη, "love," see *Comment* on 1 Tim 1:5. It is doubtful that the opponents, hypocritical liars that they were (1 Tim 4:2), could have been characterized as people of love. Paul does connect love with the Holy Spirit (Rom 5:5; 15:30; Col 1:8). σωφρονισμός, "self-control," occurs only here in the NT, but the word group σωφρον- is common in both the PE and Hellenism. See the discussion of σωφροσύνη, "moderation," in *Comment* on 1 Tim 2:9 (cf. also ἐγκράτεια, "self-control," in Gal 5:23; ἐγκρατεύεσθαι, "to exercise self-control," in 1 Cor 7:9 and 8:25; and ἐγκρατής, "self-controlled," in Titus 1:8). Paul's use here differs significantly from the proverbial, Stoic "stiff upper lip." It is not an innate ability that wells up from within a person but a supernatural gift from God.

8a μὴ οὖν ἐπαισχυνθῇς τὸ μαρτύριον τοῦ κυρίου ἡμῶν μηδὲ ἐμὲ τὸν δέσμιον αὐτοῦ, "Therefore do not be ashamed of the testimony concerning our Lord or of me his prisoner." οὖν, "therefore," shows the tight link between v 8 and vv 5–7. Because Timothy's faith is sincere and his spiritual gift is one of power, Timothy should not be ashamed. V 8 is the thesis statement of 2 Tim 1:3–2:13 as it calls for loyalty to Christ and the gospel as well as for loyalty to Paul himself. As has been argued with respect to vv 6–7, v 8 does not mean that Timothy is ashamed; the verse is a continual call to arms in the face of opposition. The possibility of failure and sin is always present and always merits close attention. Peter and Barnabas failed (Gal 2:11–13); Timothy could also fall (cf. 1 Tim 4).

ἐπαισχύνεσθαι, "to be ashamed," occurs elsewhere in the PE where Paul says that he is not ashamed because he knows Christ can guard him and the gospel (2 Tim 1:12) and also where Paul points out that Onesiphorus is not ashamed of Paul's imprisonment (1:16). It is the same sentiment seen in Paul's affirmation that he is not ashamed of the gospel, for it is the power of God for salvation (Rom 1:16; cf. Rom 6:21; cf. Mark 8:38; Luke 9:26; Heb 2:11; 11:16; and cognates in Luke 16:3; 2 Cor 10:8; Phil 1:20; 1 Pet 4:16; 1 John 2:28; A. Horstmann, *EDNT* 1:42; H. C. Kee, "The Linguistic Background of 'Shame,'" 133–47).

The specific object of shame is identified as τὸ μαρτύριον τοῦ κυρίου ἡμῶν, "the testimony of our Lord." μαρτύριον, "testimony," refers to the gospel message, or perhaps to the preaching (cf. 1 Tim 2:6; cf. 1 Cor 1:6; 2 Thess 1:10). The genitive τοῦ κυρίου, "of the Lord," could mean the "testimony borne by the Lord," i.e., his death (cf. 1 Tim 6:13). More likely it is an objective genitive: "the testimony concerning our Lord" (see the similar phrase in 1 Cor 1:6). This fits the historical context of Paul's imprisonment for the gospel. κυρίου, "Lord," is Christ, not God the Father (Knight, 372). From a human point of view, there was much in the gospel of which to be ashamed. It was the message of a failed prophet, rejected by his people, executed by the world's power, and preached by a collection of fishermen and other undesirables. The message they proclaimed was foolishness in the world's eyes (1 Cor 1:23), based on assumptions that ran counter to the generally accepted norms of Greek philosophy (Acts 17:32). And there was, on the surface, much to be ashamed about in reference to Paul, a man who met constant opposition (2 Cor 11:23–27) and was imprisoned in Rome. But Timothy was called not to be ashamed; in fact, he was called to share in suffering for this very gospel with Paul. The gospel is the power of God for salvation (Rom 1:16), and regardless of opposition, suffering, and shame, it is nothing to be ashamed of; rather it invites participation. One is reminded of Jesus' words, that "whoever is ashamed of me and of my words in this adulterous and sinful generation, of him will the Son of man also be ashamed, when he comes in the glory of his Father with the holy angels" (Mark 8:38).

Paul does not see himself as a prisoner of the emperor despite the apparent situation of his second imprisonment. Paul is αὐτοῦ, "his," i.e., Christ's, prisoner (cf. Eph 3:1; 4:1; Phlm 1, 9). Paul was not suffering as a criminal but was a messenger of the gospel, and Christ's purposes were not controlled by Rome but in fact superintended the emperor.

8b ἀλλὰ συγκακοπάθησον τῷ εὐαγγελίῳ κατὰ δύναμιν θεοῦ, "but share in suffering for the sake of the gospel according to the power of God." Rather than being ashamed, Timothy is called to embrace the gospel and suffer with others for its sake. But he is not called to do this on his own. Timothy has been given power by the Holy Spirit (v 7), and this same power from God will empower him while he suffers (v 8).

συγκακοπαθεῖν, "to share in suffering," occurs in the NT only here and in 2 Tim 2:3 in a similar context, the word possibly having been coined by Paul (cf. the simplified κακοπαθεῖν, "to suffer," in 2 Tim 2:9 where it is used of Paul's suffering for the gospel). The three morphemes give the meaning "suffer [πάσχειν] evil [κακός] with [σύν]," but the verb in 2 Tim 1:8 does not specify with whom or what (but see below). Because Paul's argument is based on Timothy identifying himself with Paul (cf. 1:3) and Paul is discussing his own suffering, the verb probably means to suffer with Paul. (It is an aorist imperative continuing the force of the negated aorist subjunctive μὴ . . . ἐπαισχυνθῇς, "do not be ashamed.") This must be understood in light of Paul's past life of suffering (2 Cor 4:7–15; Phil 1:12–14, 29; Col 1:24; 1 Thess 1:6; 2:14; 3:4), his current situation as a prisoner (2 Tim 1:12; 2:9; 3:10–13; 4:6–8), the call on Timothy's life (2 Tim 2:3; 4:5; cf. Heb 13:23; cf. 1 Clem. 5:4–7; cf. F. F. Bruce, ANRW 25.4 [1987] 3501 n. 43), and the fact that all believers share in suffering (2 Tim 3:12; Rom 8:17). Just as Timothy's call to ministry is based not on his innate abilities but on a gift from God (1:6), just as the power in Timothy's life is given by God (1:7), and just as Timothy is to draw his strength daily not from within himself but from God's grace (2:1), so also the call to suffering is based not on a natural ability but on God's power. Any teaching that denies the necessity of suffering is in direct opposition to Paul's gospel, which embraces suffering as a necessary part of the Christian experience.

εὐαγγελίῳ, "gospel," is a dative of advantage: "suffer for the sake of the gospel" (but cf. Hall [*ExpTim* 85 (1974) 120], who argues that this personifies the gospel such that Paul is calling Timothy to "suffer hardship along with the gospel"; this seems awkward). On εὐαγγέλιον, "gospel," see *Comments* on 1 Tim 1:11, 2 Tim 1:10; 2:8, and *Introduction*, "The Response to the Heresy." Mention of the gospel leads into vv 9–12, which discuss the content of the gospel and its relation to Paul's life. Timothy is not called to suffer on his own, but his suffering is in accordance with the power of God (κατὰ δύναμιν θεοῦ). On κατά, "according to," see BAGD, 406–7 (5), and 2 Tim 1:9. The power of God (cf. Rom 1:16; 1 Cor 1:18, 24; 2:5; 2 Cor 6:7; 13:4) is the same power given to Timothy (vv 6–7). Paul does not address the "why" of suffering until 4:12 where he says that everyone desiring to live a godly life will be persecuted. A clear presentation of the gospel places one in direct conflict with the world.

9a τοῦ σώσαντος ἡμᾶς καὶ καλέσαντος κλήσει ἁγίᾳ, "who saved us and called us to a holy calling." As Paul has been encouraging Timothy to share in the sufferings (v 8), mention of the gospel leads Paul to discuss it in more detail. The aspects of the gospel that are enumerated in vv 9–10—the sovereign call of God on Timothy's life based on God's purpose and grace, a salvation made available through Christ, God who has control over death and immortality—all serve as an encouragement to Timothy. As Lock notes, "Every word emphasizes the power which has been given to Christians: a power which has done what man could not do of himself, which has acted out of love for man, which has destroyed his chief enemy and given him life, which therefore calls for some return and gives strength to face suffering and death" (86; see also Chrysostom, "Homily 2"; NPNF 13:480). Whereas much of the PE concentrates on proper conduct, vv 9–10 give a solid theological foundation for righteous living.

As was argued in *Form/Structure/Setting*, the thought and vocabulary of vv 9–10 are so fully Pauline that they may be viewed as Paul's own discussion of the gospel. They are closely tied to his personal testimony in 1 Tim 1:12–17 and parallel Titus 2:11–14 and 3:4–7 (the latter may be a quotation of traditional material). The first of the two basic affirmations in vv 9–10 is that this God who will empower Timothy to suffer with Paul for the gospel (v 8) is the very God who has saved them and has called them away from a life of sin to a life of holiness. If God has been able to save Timothy, then he can empower Timothy as he lives out his holy calling in the midst of suffering. On the doctrine of salvation in the PE, see *Introduction*, "Themes in the PE." The plural ἡμᾶς, "us," could be Paul and Timothy, but inasmuch as vv 9–10 are general truths, Paul probably intends the word to include all Christians.

The idea of God calling (καλεῖν) is a fundamental doctrine for Paul. It expresses the belief in God's prior election based solely on his desire and grace, totally apart from human works, a call that drives believers toward a holy life. This same conjunction of two great truths—election and experiential sanctification—is found in 2 Tim 2:19: "But God's foundation stands firm, having this seal: 'He knows who are his,' and 'Let each one naming the name of the Lord depart from unrighteousness.'" κλῆσις, "calling," occurs only here in the PE (cf. Rom 11:29; 1 Cor 1:26; 7:20; Eph 1:18; 4:1, 4; Phil 3:14; 2 Thess 1:11), but the cognate verb καλεῖν, "to call," occurs in

1 Tim 6:12 ("Seize hold of the eternal life, to which you were called"; cf. also κλητός, "called," not in the PE). κλῆσις is used in early Christian literature almost exclusively in a religious sense. Paul uses it as a technical term. It almost always refers to a divine call—God calling believers through Christ through the gospel—emphasizing the divine initiative (cf. discussion and bibliography in J. Eckert, *EDNT* 2:240–44; K. L. Schmidt, *TDNT* 3:487–501; L. Coenen, *NIDNTT* 1:275–76; W. Grudem, *Systematic Theology*, 692–98).

Rom 8:28–30, better than any other passage, expresses Paul's understanding of God's calling: "And we know that for those who love God he works all things for good, for those who are called according to [his] purpose [τοῖς κατὰ πρόθεσιν κλητοῖς οὖσιν]. Because whom he foreknew [προέγνω], he also predestined to be conformed to the image of his son, in order that he would be the firstborn among many brethren; and whom he predestined, these he also called [ἐκάλεσεν]; and whom he called, these he also justified [ἐδικαίωσεν]; and whom he justified, these he also glorified [ἐδόξασεν]." Eph 1:4–5 is similar: "Just as he chose us in him before the foundation of the world for us to be holy and blameless before him in love, having predestined us to adoption as sons through Jesus Christ to him, according to the good pleasure of his will." The divine initiative is not due to believers' works or merits but to God's own purpose and grace (2 Tim 1:9; Gal 1:6, 15), so much so that God chose Jacob over Esau before their birth (Rom 9:7, 12; cf. 9:25–26). The call resides in God the Father and comes through the gospel of his Son (2 Thess 2:14). Paul was called (Rom 1:1; 1 Cor 1:1) as are believers (Rom 1:6, 7; 8:28; 1 Cor 1:2, 24; 7:20; 9:24; Gal 5:8) and the nation Israel (Rom 11:29). Sometimes when Paul speaks of God's call, he is looking back to conversion (e.g., 1 Cor 1:26), but more often he is looking forward. It is not so much that believers are called but that they are called to something: to the peace of Christ (Col 3:15), to know their hope (Eph 1:18; 4:4), to lead a life worthy of their calling (Eph 4:1; 1 Thess 2:12; 2 Thess 1:11; cf. Heb 3:1), to "press toward the goal for the prize of the upward call of God in Christ Jesus" (Phil 3:14; cf. 2 Pet 1:10), to eternal life (1 Tim 6:12), toward freedom (Gal 5:13), holiness (1 Thess 4:7), the unity of believers (Col 3:15), fellowship (1 Cor 1:9), and the glory of Christ (2 Thess 2:14). In other words, God's call is highly ethical: God does not just call believers; he calls them toward himself, toward holiness. (This call has little to do with social change; cf. 1 Cor 7:17–24.) This is precisely the point of our passage when it says that God saved believers and called them κλήσει ἁγίᾳ, "to a holy calling." In the face of shame and suffering (v 8), God has called Timothy to be holy, as God himself is holy (cf. 1 Pet 1:15–16). Paul says, "For God has not called [ἐκάλεσεν] us for uncleanliness but in sanctification [ἁγιασμῷ]" (1 Thess 4:7), and, "to the church of God that is in Corinth who have been sanctified [ἡγιασμένοις] in Christ Jesus, called [to be] saints [κλητοῖς ἁγίοις]" (1 Cor 1:2). In 2 Tim 1:9 ἁγίᾳ could be a dative of means, "with a holy calling" (cf. Eph 4:1), or a dative of interest, "to a holy life" (cf. 1 Thess 4:7), but most likely these two thoughts are inseparable. A holy God issues a holy call for believers to live a holy life (Knight, 374).

9b οὐ κατὰ τὰ ἔργα ἡμῶν ἀλλὰ κατὰ ἰδίαν πρόθεσιν καὶ χάριν, "not because of our works but because of [his] own purpose and grace." That salvation has nothing to do with human merit is so Pauline that it scarcely requires comment. Cf. Titus 3:5: "Not out of works of righteousness that we did but in accordance with his mercy he saved us." If salvation is based on works, then it can never be guaranteed (Rom

4:13–16) and it cannot serve as an encouragement to Timothy. But since Timothy's call is based on God's own purpose and grace, a grace that has obviously empowered Timothy (v 6: τὸ χάρισμα τοῦ θεοῦ, "the gift of God"), then Timothy can with full assurance meet the challenge of the Ephesian opponents. There is a strong emphasis on the practical outworking of Christianity in the PE, on doing good works (cf. 1 Tim 2:10), but never are those good deeds a means to salvation. They are based on the prior work of God in Christ, calling Timothy to a holy life.

ἰδίαν, "his own," emphasizes the sovereignty of God's decision. It probably modifies only πρόθεσιν, "purpose," since it contrasts with τὰ ἔργα ἡμῶν, "our works," and τὴν δοθεῖσαν, "which was given," modifies only χάριν, "grace" (see below). Of course, God's grace is his own by definition. πρόθεσις means "purpose," and in Paul is used of God's purpose in all cases except one (2 Tim 3:10; cf., e.g., Acts 11:23; 27:13). Rom 8:28 speaks of those "who are called [κλητοῖς] according to his purpose [πρόθεσιν]." Jacob's election was decided before birth, before he had done good or sinned, "in order that God's purpose [πρόθεσις] of election might continue, not because of works but because of his call [ἐκ τοῦ καλοῦντος]" (Rom 9:11–12). God works all things according to his will (Eph 1:11), and the mystery of God—the inclusion of the Gentiles with the Jews in God's kingdom—was made known to Paul in accordance with God's eternal purpose (Eph 3:11). Timothy's calling is in light of God's purpose through Christ and not through human effort (2 Tim 1:9). χάρις, "grace," as God's unmerited favor (cf. 1 Tim 1:2) is fully Pauline.

9c τὴν δοθεῖσαν ἡμῖν ἐν Χριστῷ Ἰησοῦ πρὸ χρόνων αἰωνίων, "which was given to us in Christ Jesus before time eternal." This phrase begins the second basic thought in vv 9–10, namely, Jesus' role in Timothy's salvation. Paul delves into the nature of the gospel as he attempts to encourage Timothy, reflecting on the fact of salvation (δοθεῖσαν, "was given") and the fact of Jesus' earthly existence and what he accomplished, by which Timothy should be strengthened in his Ephesian trials. Paul frequently speaks of grace being given (διδόναι, "to give"; Rom 12:3, 6; 15:15; 1 Cor 3:10; 15:57; 2 Cor 8:1; Gal 2:9; Eph 3:2, 7, 8; 4:7; 2 Thess 2:16; 2 Tim 1:9; cf. 1 Cor 1:4; 2 Cor 8:16; Eph 4:29; and his normal epistolary conclusion, "Grace be with you"). But what is especially important for Timothy is the time the gift was given. If Timothy has already received God's salvation and calling, the threat of the Ephesian opponents seems almost insignificant (cf. Ellicott, 107). The plural ἡμῖν, "to us," represents the same scope as it does earlier in the verse: Paul, Timothy, and by implication all believers. πρὸ χρόνων αἰωνίων, "before time eternal," is somewhat difficult to translate, the plural being idiomatic (see *Comment* on Titus 1:2). It cannot refer to the promise in Gen 3:15 (contra RSV ["ages ago"]; Guthrie) since the parallel verses show that this occurred before creation. It assumes a pre-existent Christ (Brox, 231; Marshall, SNTU-A 13 [1988] 171), one who like God is timeless, hence existing before time, "before the beginning of time" (NIV).

There is one final encouragement in these verses. The grace was given "in Christ Jesus," which, as v 10 clarifies, means that the grace was applied to Timothy through the earthly work of Christ, made available only to those who are "in Christ" (cf. 1 Tim 1:14). Furthermore, δοθεῖσαν, "was given," is a divine passive, God being the assumed agent of the giving. God was in Christ reconciling the world to himself (2 Cor 5:19), but even before that, before time began, Timothy was the recipient of God's grace and call. Timothy's current difficulties pale in comparison with this great truth.

10a φανερωθεῖσαν δὲ νῦν διὰ τῆς ἐπιφανείας τοῦ σωτῆρος ἡμῶν Χριστοῦ Ἰησοῦ, "but now was made known through the appearing of our savior, Christ Jesus." In contrast to the grace that "was given . . . before time eternal" (v 9), that same grace "now was made known." "The thought moves from eternity to time. Though the idea of God's eternal purposes of grace may be beyond comprehension, at least the fact of the incarnation is capable of being understood" (Guthrie, 142). Timothy is encouraged to suffer for the gospel because the reality of what God did before time has now been made clear through the gospel as it is the proclamation of Christ's life.

δὲ νῦν, "but now," contrasts with πρὸ χρόνων αἰωνίων, "before time eternal," while φανερωθεῖσαν, "was made known," parallels δοθεῖσαν, "was given." On νῦν, "now," see *Comment* on 1 Tim 4:8. The "then . . . now" contrast in Paul often places emphasis on the hiddenness of the mystery now revealed (cf. Col 1:26). While an element of mystery may be implicitly present, the contrast here is of the event accomplished and the full recognition of that event in the Incarnation. The divine passive φανερωθεῖσαν, "was made known," parallels the previous δοθεῖσαν, "was given," God being the ultimate cause of the revelation. The basic meaning of φανεροῦν is "to make visible," but in this context it moves beyond mere apprehension to actually accomplishing something concrete. God's grace is not just visible but effectual (cf. Kelly, 163). The second half of the verse explains what was effected. On ἐπιφάνεια, "appearing," see *Comment* on 1 Tim 6:14. It describes the appearance of a god or king, and in the Ephesian context sets Christ against pagan gods and emperor worship in hellenized language that would have been immediately recognized by the Ephesian church. As does v 9, this verse assumes the pre-existence of Christ. In the two parallel passages, one uses ἐπιφαίνειν, "to appear," in reference to the Incarnation (Titus 3:4–7), and the other uses the same verb in reference to Christ's second coming (Titus 2:11–14). On σωτήρ, "savior," see v 9 and *Introduction,* "Themes in the PE." It is significant that Paul switches from speaking of God (the Father) "saving us" (v 9) to "our savior Christ Jesus" (v 10). The fluctuation is common in the PE and illustrates Paul's view of the close relationship between God and Christ (cf. *Introduction,* "Themes in the PE").

10b καταργήσαντος μὲν τὸν θάνατον, "on the one hand, in order to abolish death." The grace that was made known in Christ has two effects on believers and the sinful world. The first is the destruction of death itself. Since believers still die, in what sense was death destroyed? (1) Paul could be thinking of the sting of death (1 Cor 15:54–56), its pain, now removed because beyond the grave lies life and incorruptibility. (2) He could also be thinking of death as the punishment for sin and hence the ultimate power in Satan's arsenal (cf. Heb 2:14–15). Death is not natural but is the divinely appointed punishment for sin (Rom 5:12). Since there is no condemnation for those in Christ Jesus (Rom 8:1), death cannot be a punishment for sin that has already been forgiven (Grudem, *Systematic Theology,* 810). (3) Paul may also be thinking of spiritual death, eternal separation from God. This is suggested by the following description of eternal life with God ("life and incorruptibility"), which stands in contrast to death. Perhaps this threefold division is overly subtle. The sting of death is gone because death is not a punishment for believers' sins and because true life with God is the believer's assured hope. This is the only occurrence of θάνατος, "death," in the PE, although it occurs forty-six other times in Paul. One is reminded of the apocalyptic picture in Revelation of the beast and false prophet (19:10), Satan (20:10; cf. Heb 2:14), people whose names are not in the book of life (20:15), and eventually death and Hades (20:14) all being cast into the lake of fire. Timothy can be encouraged to suffer for the gospel because one day the Lord "will swallow up death for ever" (Isa 25:8). While Timothy and all believers must wait until the final consummation to see death destroyed (1 Cor 15:26), in essence death has already been destroyed by Christ's work, and believers can live their lives in complete assurance of what has happened and what will happen (cf. Guthrie, 130). καταργεῖν occurs twenty-five times in Paul meaning "to make powerless" (Rom 3:3, 31; 4:14; Gal 3:17; 1 Cor 1:28; Eph 2:15) or the stronger "to abolish, wipe out" (e.g., 1 Cor 13:8, 10; 2 Cor 3:7, 11, 13; Gal 5:11; cf. BAGD, 417). Cf. 1 Cor 15:26: "The last enemy that is abolished [καταργεῖται] is death" (cf. Heb 2:14).

10c φωτίσαντος δὲ ζωὴν καὶ ἀφθαρσίαν διὰ τοῦ εὐαγγελίου, "and, on the other, to bring to light life and incorruptibility through the gospel." As a necessary corollary to the destruction of death, Christ's work also shows the incorruptible life as described in the gospel for which Timothy is called to suffer. As Paul says elsewhere, the Lord "will bring to light [φωτίσει] the hidden things of the darkness and will make clear [φανερώσει] the purposes of the hearts" (1 Cor 4:5; cf. Eph 1:18; 3:9). Paul is not saying that only Christians believe in eternal life; he is saying that only the gospel clearly shows the eternal life that comes through Christ from God, which is the only true eternal life (cf. Bernard, 111). Lock (88) cites S. R. Driver's powerful description of this verse: "The Gospel first gave to a future world clearness and distinctness, shape and outline; the Gospel first made it a positive district and region on which the spiritual eye reposes, and which stretches out on the other side the grave with the same solidity and extension with which the present world does on this side of it. The future life was not an image before the Gospel: the Gospel made it an image. It brought it out of its implicit form, and from its lower residence within the bosom of the great fundamental doctrine of true religion, into a separate and conspicuous position as a truth. This was a bringing to light, and a species of birth, compared with which the previous state of the doctrine was a hidden and an embryo state" (S. R. Driver, "Sermon 4," in *Sermons on Subjects Connected with the Old Testament* [London: Methuen, 1892]).

While Paul elsewhere does not make this same exact statement (so Hanson [1983]), it is of little consequence since all the ideas are fully Pauline. ζωή, "life," is a common Pauline topic (thirty-seven times), designating not mere physical life but a fullness of life that is a present experience of the eschatological existence promised to believers through Jesus Christ (2 Tim 1:1; cf. *Comment* on 1 Tim 1:16). While ἀφθαρσία, "incorruptibility, immortality" (BAGD, 125), is a Hellenistic concept, it is also fully Pauline, describing the resurrection body (1 Cor 15:42, 50, 53, 54). Eternal life will be awarded to those who seek glory, honor, and incorruptibility (Rom 2:7; cf. Eph 6:24). ἀφθαρσία, "incorruptibility," when joined with ζωή, "life," is synonymous with eternal life. See discussion of the word and cognates in *Comment* on 1 Tim 1:17. The final mention of "through the gospel" returns the discussion to Paul's beginning. Timothy is called to share in suffering for the gospel because only there is the saving grace of God made clear as it retells and explains the life and death of Christ.

11 εἰς ὃ ἐτέθην ἐγὼ κῆρυξ καὶ ἀπόστολος καὶ διδάσκαλος, "to which I was

appointed a herald and an apostle and a teacher." This verse is almost an exact
repetition of 1 Tim 2:7; see there for specific discussion. The two differences are
the omission of the phrases " I speak the truth; I do not lie" and "(teacher) of the
Gentiles in [the] faith and [the] truth." In 1 Tim 2:7 Paul is emphasizing his
divine call to preach authoritatively the gospel to the Gentiles, and so these phrases
are significant not for Timothy but for the Ephesian church. However, Paul's second epistle is more personal, and the issue of his apostolic authority is secondary
(contra Easton, Hanson [1983]). What is important is how v 11 encourages Timothy. Paul is encouraging Timothy to suffer for the gospel, to be loyal to it and to
Paul, and to see how Paul's and his own ministries are intertwined (cf. v 3). By
closely associating himself with the gospel, Paul shows Timothy that loyalty to
himself and to the gospel are in essence the same thing. As Paul suffers, so should
Timothy. V 11 not only looks backward but also forward to v 12, where Paul will
complete the argument.

   12a δι' ἣν αἰτίαν καὶ ταῦτα πάσχω, "for which reason even I am suffering
these things." V 12 brings the discussion to a close; almost every word in this
phrase, and several in the second half of the verse, are tied to the previous verses.
δι' ἣν αἰτίαν, "for which reason," is repeated from v 6. It is an idiomatic causal
phrase. πάσχω, "I suffer," recalls Paul's request that Timothy suffer with him
(συγκακοπάθησον; v 8). ταῦτα "these things," may refer back to τὸ μαρτύριον τοῦ
κυρίου ἡμῶν, "the testimony of our Lord" (v 8), but more likely the word refers to
Paul's imprisonment (v 8). Paul is encouraging Timothy by calling him to share
in the suffering for the gospel (v 8); Paul is suffering for it, and Timothy should
embrace his own suffering. καί, "even," could modify ταῦτα as the word order
implies ("I am suffering even these things"), but since the thrust of the passage is
Paul's own suffering as it compares to Timothy's, καί should be connected with
πάσχω: "even I am suffering these things." Finally, there is the issue of punctuation at the end of v 11 and after πάσχω. The phrase is so tightly connected to
both the preceding and the following (Paul's suffering brings no shame) that
commas are preferable in both places.

   12b ἀλλ' οὐκ ἐπαισχύνομαι, οἶδα γὰρ ᾧ πεπίστευκα, "but I am not ashamed,
for I know in whom I have trusted." Having encouraged Timothy not to be
ashamed of Paul as a prisoner (v 8), Paul now asserts that he is not ashamed. He
does not specify the object of his shame, but it is most likely his imprisonment.
Paul follows with two reasons (γάρ, "for"). The first is the nature of God, the God
in whom Paul has placed his trust.

   The second half of v 12—12b and 12c—is closely tied to the preceding, verbally and conceptually, and as such concludes the discussion. Paul's lack of shame
recalls his words in v 8. οἶδα, "I know" (chosen perhaps for its nuance of complete knowledge; cf. 1 Tim 1:8), continues the attitude of assuredness prevalent
throughout the discussion (e.g., πέπεισμαι, "I am confident" [v 5]; spirit "of power"
[v 7]; the fact of salvation in vv 9–10; Paul's divine appointment as an apostle [v
11: ἐτέθην, "I was appointed"]), an attitude strengthened by the following two
perfect-tense verbs: πεπίστευκα, "I have trusted" (and still do), and πέπεισμαι, "I
am fully convinced" (and still am). This phrase also continues the intensely personal nature of the discussion, starting with the emphatic ἐγώ, "I," in v 11 and
continuing through the six first-person verbs and one more first-person personal
pronoun, μοῦ, "my."

But the most important function of v 12 is to conclude the encouragement to Timothy. Paul calls Timothy to suffer with him for the gospel (v 8) and not to be ashamed of Paul or the gospel. Despite his own sufferings, Paul is not ashamed, and the reason he is not ashamed is as applicable to Timothy as it is to himself. Paul has placed his trust in the God who has saved him and appointed him to be an apostle, and despite the suffering he is still convinced that it was the right decision. ᾧ, "in whom," could refer to either God (v 9a) or Christ (vv 9b–10), but since God is pictured as the one who saves (vv 8–9a), the pronoun probably refers to him. ᾧ is masculine ("in whom," i.e., God), not neuter ("in which," i.e., the gospel), since Paul adds "he is able to guard." Therefore "I have believed" refers not to belief in a creedal sense (contra Easton) but is Paul's normal use of πιστεύειν, "to believe," to denote personal trust in God (see *Introduction*, "Themes in the PE").

12c καὶ πέπεισμαι ὅτι δυνατός ἐστιν τὴν παραθήκην μου φυλάξαι εἰς ἐκείνην τὴν ἡμέραν, "and I am fully convinced that he is able to guard my deposit until that day." This is Paul's second reason for not being ashamed. In light of Paul's imprisonment and his being near death (2 Tim 4:6–8), it is a marvelous witness to his faith and perseverance. The main question regarding the verse is the precise meaning of τὴν παραθήκην μου, "my deposit." παραθήκη means "deposit, property entrusted to another" (BAGD, 616). It is a common word in the vernacular, used literally and figuratively of money, people, and things (MM, 483–85). It was probably a technical commercial term describing money, documents, and wills, articles often left in a temple or with a friend for safekeeping (2 Macc 3:10, 15). Barclay comments, "The typical picture in the word is that of a man going upon a journey and depositing with, and entrusting to, a friend his most precious and valued possessions. . . . To be faithful to such a trust, and to return such a deposit unharmed, were amongst the highest and most sacred obligations which ancient thought recognized" (*ExpTim* 69 [1958] 324). Spicq notes that "the emphasis is always on the good faith and fidelity of the depositary," who in our passage is God (*TLNT* 3:26; id., *RB* 40 [1931] 481–502; cf. Oberlinner, 48 [bibliography on 54]; J. Ranft, "Depositum," *RAC* 3:778–84; C. Maurer, *TDNT* 8:163–64; Lock's extended note, 90–92; cf. Exod 22:7–13; Lev 6:2–7; 2 Macc 3:10–40). παραθήκη occurs elsewhere in the NT only twice, always with φυλάσσειν, "to guard." Timothy is told to "guard the deposit," i.e., the gospel, and to avoid the godless chatter of the opponents (1 Tim 6:20). Two verses after our current verse, Timothy is told to "guard the good deposit" (2 Tim 1:14), which again is the gospel (cf. cognates in 1 Tim 1:18 and 2 Tim 2:2). Paul uses a well-known custom, replete with its overtones of necessary faithfulness, to say that the gospel was given to Paul (1 Tim 2:7) and Timothy (1 Tim 1:18), was deposited into Timothy's care, and was to be deposited with faithful men (2 Tim 2:2) when Timothy left Ephesus. Just as God judged Paul faithful (1 Tim 1:12) and entrusted him with the gospel, so also God is able to guard what Paul has deposited into his care.

τὴν παραθήκην μου, "my deposit," is usually understood to be something God has entrusted to Paul, namely, the gospel message or perhaps his apostolic ministry ("he is able to guard what has been entrusted to me"). (1) The context is the gospel, referred to directly or indirectly in every verse since v 8. (2) Two verses later, as well as in 1 Tim 6:20, Paul uses the same term, παραθήκη, clearly in reference to the gospel. (3) It fits the flow of the argument. Paul was entrusted with the gospel, and now that he will suffer to the point of death, he is still convinced that God will continue to guard it. Because of the context, it is implied that God will guard the gospel by entrusting it to Timothy and other reliable men (2 Tim 2:2). Spicq comments, in light of its use to describe a person's deposit of a will in a temple, that παραθήκη "fits quite well in 1 and 2 Timothy, which are precisely Paul's last will and testament, instructing his favorite disciple to preserve intact and inviolable the wealth of teaching that he has passed on to him throughout his life" (*TLNT* 3:27).

τὴν παραθήκην μου, "my deposit," could also refer to something Paul has entrusted to God, namely, his life (e.g., NASB, NIV, Calvin, Lock, Fee, Knight). (1) In the other two passages, Timothy is the guard and not God, and here Paul states that it is "my" (μοῦ) deposit. These two differences set our passage apart from the others. (2) The eschatological orientation of guarding the deposit "until that day," the day of judgment, fits better with Paul's soul being kept safe than with the gospel being kept safe. (3) The previous phrase, "in whom I have trusted," suggests the idea of Paul placing something of his own ("faith," "my deposit") into God's care. (4) It also fits the flow of the passage as Paul encourages Timothy to share in suffering. Paul has suffered his share for the gospel, and despite his current imprisonment and certain death, he is fully convinced that God can continue to protect his life, even through death. Likewise Timothy should have no fear of his Ephesian opponents or of suffering for the gospel, for he too can trust that God is able to guard his life. Fee paraphrases, "Just as the gospel announces a salvation that God in grace initiated and effected, and through which he rendered death ineffective, so also the same God can be trusted to guard . . . for the End the life that has been entrusted to his care" (232; cf. Luke 23:46; 1 Pet 4:19). While the gospel plays a large role in Paul's discussion, the real point here is to encourage Timothy by showing him Paul's victory despite the appearance of suffering and defeat. The second view seems best to support this flow of thought and also is the most natural reading of "my deposit." Paul does not limit what he means by deposit, so there is no reason to limit it to just one item. Paul's deposit (singular) could be the sum total of all that Paul has entrusted to God, including his life, apostolic ministry, converts, etc. (so Lock, 88).

The perfect-tense πέπεισμαι, "I am fully convinced," emphasizes the completeness of Paul's belief and looks back to Paul's assurance of Timothy's faith in v 5. δυνατός, "able," looks back to the powerful God who can enable Timothy to suffer for the gospel and can save him (vv 8–9). On φυλάσσειν, "to guard," see *Comment* on 1 Tim 5:21. ἐκείνην τὴν ἡμέραν, "that day," is specific, Paul using both the demonstrative ἐκείνην, "that," and the article τήν, "the," and refers to the day of judgment. It occurs in 2 Tim 1:18; 4:8 and elsewhere in Paul (cf. 1 Cor 3:13: ἡ ἡμέρα, "the day"; 2 Thess 1:10: τῇ ἡμέρα ἐκείνῃ, "that day"; why Hanson [1983] says the phrase is not Pauline is not clear), and in the words of Jesus (Matt 7:22; Luke 10:12; 21:34) and in the OT (Zeph 1:15; cf. G. Delling, *TDNT* 2:951–53; BAGD, 347 [3bβ]).

13a ὑποτύπωσιν ἔχε ὑγιαινόντων λόγων, "Hold to the pattern of healthy words." While v 12 concludes the discussion of vv 6–11, vv 13–14 continue the series of Paul's instructions to Timothy, and so vv 13–14 are included with the preceding (see *Form/Structure/Setting*). Timothy is to fan his gifts into flame (v 6), not to be ashamed but to share in suffering (v 8), and now he is to hold on to the gospel (v 13) and guard it (v 14). Vv 13–14 are also related to the preceding verses by way of their content. The healthy words that Timothy is to hold on to and guard are the gospel for which Timothy is called to suffer, the gospel that tells of the God who saves through Christ.

While the gist of the phrase is clear, the first two words are somewhat difficult. ἔχε, "hold to," is a linear-aspect imperative meaning "keep, preserve" (BAGD, 332 [IIcβ]; cf. 1 Tim 3:9; cf. Mark 6:18; Rev 6:9; 12:17; 19:10). It is not exactly parallel with φύλαξον, "guard," in v 14; otherwise the verses would be overly repetitive. Paul is probably telling Timothy to hold on to the gospel ("sound words") in his own personal life as opposed to the more external guarding from heretical alterations. ὑποτύπωσις denotes a "sketch, model, or pattern" of something (cf. *Comment* on 1 Tim 1:16 where Paul says that he was an example of salvation by faith). It is also anarthrous, "a pattern," not "the pattern." Many writers (e.g., Guthrie; Kelly; even Hanson [1983]) assert that this means that Timothy is to view the gospel as taught by Paul (see the following phrase) as a basic sketch, a starting point, not as an established creed from which there can be no derivation or development. While this may be true, it should not be overemphasized. Any teaching that would fall outside Paul's sketch would surely draw instant criticism from him (cf. Gal 1:7). ὑγιαινόντων λόγων, "healthy words," is a theme in the PE emphasizing the correctness of Paul's gospel and the benefits it brings in contrast to the opponents' sick and morbid cravings (1 Tim 6:4) that spread like gangrene (2 Tim 2:16; cf. *Comment* on 1 Tim 1:10).

13b ὧν παρ' ἐμοῦ ἤκουσας, "that you have heard from me." Paul follows with two qualifying phrases. ὧν παρ' ἐμοῦ ἤκουσας, "that you have heard from me," qualifies ὑγιαινόντων λόγων, "healthy words," identifying the healthy words as those he has heard from Paul. Paul continues to identify loyalty to the gospel with loyalty to himself and his proclamation of the gospel. Once again Paul expresses the ongoing theme of the passing of the gospel from one trustworthy person to another: Paul was entrusted with the gospel (1 Tim 1:11; 2:7; Titus 1:3; 2 Tim 1:11; cf. 2 Tim 2:8–9; cf. 1 Cor 9:17; 11:2; Gal 1:1; 2:7; 2 Thess 2:15; 3:16); it was entrusted to Timothy (1 Tim 1:18; 2 Tim 1:13–14; 2:2; 3:14); and in turn Timothy is to entrust it to other trustworthy men as Paul is about to say (2 Tim 2:2). As was argued in the *Introduction,* this is not the formal transfer of power and creed that is found in the second century; it is an emphasis on preserving the true gospel, which is based on the teachings of Jesus and the apostolic interpretation of his life and death. While this emphasis is found elsewhere in Paul (Rom 16:17; Gal 1:12; Eph 4:21; Col 2:7; 2 Thess 2:15), it is natural that Paul would emphasize it as he nears the end of his life, realizing that his time of guarding the deposit is ending.

13c ἐν πίστει καὶ ἀγάπῃ τῇ ἐν Χριστῷ Ἰησοῦ, "in [the] faith and [the] love that are in Christ Jesus." The second qualifying phrase looks back to the imperative ἔχε, "hold to," and emphasizes two points. (1) It is not sufficient merely to hold to the gospel. How one holds to the gospel is also significant, and Timothy must be sure that his ministry is characterized by faith (cf. 1 Tim 1:2) and love (cf. 1 Tim 1:5, and especially 1:14). Rigid orthodoxy is insufficient. (2) Just as Timothy is called to suffer for the gospel not on his own strength but by the power of God (v 8), so also this faith and love are not inherent qualities but rather supernatural gifts given to those who are "in Christ Jesus" (cf. 1 Tim 1:14; 3:13). Paul continues this emphasis in the following verse where Timothy is told to guard the gospel "by the indwelling Holy Spirit." It is possible to connect this phrase with v 14, but this would negate the apparently emphatic position of τὴν καλὴν παραθήκην, "the good deposit," and Dibelius-Conzelmann (105) argue that expressions such as "in faith and love" tend to occur more often at the end of a clause.

14 τὴν καλὴν παραθήκην φύλαξον διὰ πνεύματος ἁγίου τοῦ ἐνοικοῦντος ἐν ἡμῖν, "Guard the good deposit by the Holy Spirit that indwells us." Paul continues the thrust of v 13 with terminology recalling v 12. Just as God can guard what Paul—and Timothy by implication—has deposited with God, so Timothy is to guard what God has deposited with him. And as Timothy is to hold to the pattern of Paul's gospel, empowered by the divine gifts of faith and love, so also Timothy is to guard the gospel not with his human abilities but empowered by the Holy Spirit (cf. v 7 and Spicq, 2:722) who lives within him. This is another reminder that the power to live out God's call on a believer's life does not come through human means but is only possible through the God who gives "you the will and the power to achieve his purpose" (Phil 3:13 [Phillips]; cf. 1 Tim 1:18–19; 2 Tim 1:5; cf. 1 Thess 1:5). When the Spirit calls believers to minister, the call is accompanied by supernatural empowerment (Spicq, 2:722). This same desire to guard the gospel has already been expressed in similar language in 1 Tim 6:20. The παραθήκην, "deposit," is the gospel, a different meaning from its use in v 12. Its emphatic position before the verb φύλαξον, "guard" (on which see v 12), and its description as καλήν, "good" (see 1 Tim 1:8), roughly paralleling ὑγιαινόντων λόγων, "healthy words," firmly separate it from the opponents' teachings.

τοῦ ἐνοικοῦντος, "that indwells," reminds us of the indwelling faith of Timothy, his mother, and his grandmother (v 5; cf. Rom 8:9–11). As has been true throughout this paragraph, Paul has been identifying himself with Timothy in order to encourage Timothy. Here the same Spirit who indwells Paul also indwells Timothy (ἡμῖν, "us") and, by implication, all believers. In the following paragraph, vv 15–18, Paul identifies two people who are not part of "us" and one person who is part of "us" and who serves as a model for Timothy. While some object that this view of the Spirit's work is too static for Paul (see *Introduction*, "The Theological Problem"), one wonders why a statement of the indwelling work of the Holy Spirit to empower believers in their ministry would place this verse outside the possible scope of what Paul could have said. As Fee observes, "Given the historical circumstances as they emerge in this letter—an especially onerous imprisonment, defections of people from whom he expected more, and the almost inevitable prospect of death—how else might one expect the apostle to speak to his closest and dearest companion in ministry? And what kind of prejudice is it, one wonders, which disallows beforehand that this combination of circumstances is possible for the apostle?" (*God's Empowering Presence*, 791 n. 149).

Explanation

Vv 6–14 not only afford a personal look into Paul's heart and his relationship with Timothy but also provide a paradigm of the nature of Christian encouragement. Timothy is reminded of the public acknowledgment of his gift and that the gift is not characterized by cowardice but by power. Rather than being ashamed of the gospel and Paul's imprisonment, he is encouraged to suffer with Paul for the gospel through God's power. In Paul's description of the gospel is a reminder of the suffering and persecution Timothy is facing in Ephesus. Contrary to the opponents' myths and devotion to the law, it is the gospel that clearly shows the message of salvation and sanctification, based not on works (such as obedience to the law) but on God's grace, revealed not through the law but through Christ Jesus. Regardless of what was being taught in Ephesus, death was defeated only through Christ, who alone brings life and incorruptibility. It is this gospel to which Paul was called, and yet he knows that his suffering is not a defeat of the gospel. Because he fully trusts God who can guard his life, he is not ashamed. Implied in all this is the need for Timothy, like Paul, not to be ashamed but rather to suffer for the gospel, to join Paul in his suffering as well as in his assurance. Finally, Timothy is to hold fast to Paul's gospel, characterized not by bitterness and quarreling but by faith and love. Since God can guard what Paul (and Timothy) has entrusted to him, Timothy should be able to guard what God has entrusted to Timothy, as always, through the power God gives him by the Holy Spirit.

At the core of Stoicism and many other philosophies and religions there was a message that was diametrically opposed to Paul's gospel. For Paul, belief entails a dying to oneself, a crucifixion with Christ, and a rising to a new kind of life in which strength and power come not from the sinful self but from a merciful God who empowers his children. While Paul may be using language often associated with Stoicism, he has fundamentally altered its meaning.

The guarding of the deposit, the transfer of tradition, was carried on by others as well as by Timothy. Clement writes,

> The Apostles received the Gospel for us from the Lord Jesus Christ; Jesus Christ was sent forth from God. So then Christ is from God, and the Apostles are from Christ. Both therefore came of the will of God in the appointed order. Having therefore received a charge, and having been fully assured through the resurrection of our Lord Jesus Christ and confirmed in the word of God with full assurance of the Holy Ghost, they went forth with the glad tidings that the kingdom of God should come. So preaching everywhere in country and town, they appointed their first-fruits, when they had proved them by the Spirit, to be bishops and deacons unto them that should believe. And this they did in no new fashion; for indeed it had been written concerning bishops and deacons from very ancient times; for thus saith the scripture in a certain place, "I will appoint their bishops in righteousness and their deacons in faith." (*1 Clem.* 42:1–5; tr. Lightfoot, *Apostolic Fathers,* 75)

> And our Apostles knew through our Lord Jesus Christ that there would be strife over the name of the bishop's office. For this cause therefore, having received complete foreknowledge, they appointed the aforesaid persons, and afterwards they provided a continuance, that if these should fall asleep, other approved men should succeed to their ministration. Those therefore . . . were appointed by them, or afterward by other men of repute with the consent of the whole church. (*1 Clem.* 44:1–3; tr. Lightfoot, *Apostolic Fathers,* 76)

B. Examples   (2 Tim 1:15–18)

Bibliography

Cabaniss, A. "The Song of Songs in the New Testament." *Studies in English* 8 (1967) 53–56. **Johnson, L.** "The Pauline Letters from Caesarea." *ExpTim* 68 (1956) 24–26. **Munk, P.** "Niels, Onesiforus [2 Tim. 1:16; 4:19]." *TT* 3.10 (1919) 193–200. **Ramsay, W. M.** "Notes on the 'Acta' of Martyrs." *ExpTim* 9 (1898) 495–97. **Wiles, G. P.** *Paul's Intercessory Prayers.*

Translation

¹⁵*You know this, that all those in Asia have deserted me, among whom are Phygelus and Hermogenes.* ¹⁶*May the Lord grant mercy to the household of Onesiphorus since often he refreshed me and was not ashamed of my chain,* ¹⁷*but being in Rome, he earnestly*^a *searched for me and found [me].* ¹⁸*May the Lord grant him to find mercy from [the] Lord on that day. And the services he performed*^b *in Ephesus you know very well.*

Notes

^aThe adverb σπουδαίως, "earnestly" (ℵ C D* F G P 6 33 81 104 1175 1739 1881 *pc* latt sy^p co; Or), is replaced with the comparative adjective σπουδαιότερον, "more earnest," by A D¹ Ψ TR sy^h (-ρως A 365 *pc*). The force of the comparative would be that Onesiphorus searched all the more when he realized that Paul was in captivity (see Ellicott, 112), implying that Onesiphorus did not realize when he set out for Rome that Paul was in prison.

^bThe implied μοι, "for me," is inserted after διηκόνησεν, "he performed services," as its object by 104 365 *pc* it vg^{cl} sy.

Form/Structure/Setting

Having encouraged Timothy not to be ashamed but rather to suffer for the gospel (vv 6–14), Paul follows with negative and positive examples. Lock paraphrases, "You know instances of both cowardice and of courage" (89). Everyone in Asia deserted Paul, but Onesiphorus was not ashamed of Paul and remained loyal to him. So should Timothy. Vv 15–18 therefore divide into two parts: the negative (v 15) and the positive (vv 16–18). The latter two verses divide into three segments: the two wish prayers (vv 16–17, v 18a) and v 18b. These verses are extremely personal. They create "a particularly vivid impression of authenticity, and also special difficulties for any theory of pseudonymity" (Kelly, 168). Some who see the PE as non-Pauline agree that vv 15–18 at least are an authentic fragment (Barrett, 98).

Comment

15a οἶδας τοῦτο, ὅτι ἀπεστράφησάν με πάντες οἱ ἐν τῇ Ἀσίᾳ, "You know this, that all those in Asia have deserted me." Evidently the situation in Ephesus and the surrounding province of Asia did not improve after the writing of the first epistle to Timothy. In what appears to be a mood of depression, Paul feels that all of Asia has abandoned him and he is facing trial and certain death alone. Later he will tell Timothy that his associate Demas has fallen in love with this world and has abandoned (ἐγκαταλείπειν) him (4:10) and that at his first defense everyone abandoned (same verb) him (4:16).

These verses show that Paul's current imprisonment was decidedly more severe than the one in Acts 28:23, 30–31. Other verses fill out the picture. When Onesiphorus came to Rome, he evidently had difficulty finding Paul and had to search diligently (1:17) for him, suggesting that Paul's prison was not an open house but was probably in a secure, remote location. Paul's eulogy in 4:6–8 and 4:18 show his awareness that his earthly life is over. His desire for Timothy to guard the deposit (1:14) and pass it on to reliable men (2:2) agrees with this picture. It is out of this situation that Paul writes, and it is out of this situation that the epistle must be interpreted. It colors Paul's statements, such as his lack of shame (1:8,12), call to suffering (1:8, 12; 2:3–7, 9), assurance of salvation and God's protection (1:9–11, 12; 2:11–13; 4:6–8, 17–18), call to ministry (1:11; 2:8–13), loyalty to the gospel and his ministry (1:11–12; 2:8–10; 3:10–11, 15–17; 4:6–8), and encouragement to Timothy to be strong and loyal and to persevere (1:8–14; 2:1–2, 3–7, 15; 3:14–17; 4:1–2, 5). All this paints an amazing picture of an amazing man: a life filled with suffering and persecution (as well as victories) and a life that was ending in what many would see as abandonment and defeat. Yet even within the darkness, or perhaps because of the darkness, the theme verses of the epistle stand out dramatically. Paul knew the God he had trusted and was convinced that this God would guard his life until the day of judgment (1:12). Despite the hopelessness of his case before Rome and the desertions of his friends and many of the people to whom he ministered, Paul still knew that the Lord would rescue him from every evil and would save him for heaven (4:18).

Within the context, v 15 serves as an illustration of those who did not guard the gospel as Timothy was called to do (v 14). There are two questions about this verse: who were the Asians, and what is the precise meaning of ἀπεστράφησαν, "have deserted"? (1) πάντες οἱ ἐν τῇ Ἀσίᾳ, "all those in Asia," cannot mean that every single person in Asia had deserted Paul; Onesiphorus (vv 16–18) and Timothy certainly had not. (2) Some argue that the Asians who were in Rome had not come to his defense and had deserted him, possibly at the time of his arrest (Jeremias, 52; Simpson, 128–29); perhaps they had returned to Asia (Lock, 89). The problem with this interpretation is that the text does not say those "from" (ἐκ) Asia but those "in" (ἐν) Asia. Spicq (2:732) works around this by postulating that the phrase is a Hebraism meaning "from," but he has not been followed at this point. (Oberlinner does suggest "from" as a possibility, postulating οἱ ἐκ τῆς Ἀσίας, "the ones from Asia," 58.) (3) Hendriksen (237–38) thinks Paul is referring to Christian leaders in Asia who were asked to come to Rome in Paul's defense but did not. However, the text says πάντες, "all," not "all of those summoned" or "all the leaders." (4) The easiest reading of the text remains that Paul means "all the Christians in Asia" in a statement that is slightly hyperbolic (Guthrie, 135). It appears that while Paul was victorious in Spirit (see above), he was also suffering the natural psychological depression of a person in his situation. "The defections in Asia have been so staggering" (Fee, 236). "He was writing with the exaggeration natural in depression" (Kelly, 169), thinking of what had happened when he was arrested (cf. Guthrie, 135). If ἀπεστράφησαν, "have deserted," refers to personal abandonment and not apostasy from the gospel, then this hyperbole is understandable.

ἀποστρέφειν can mean "to apostatize," deserting the gospel itself. This is how the verb is used in its two other occurrences in the PE (Titus 1:14; 2 Tim 4:4). Paul uses the verb only one other time, in an OT quotation (Rom 11:26). There is nothing in the word that requires εὐαγγέλιον, "gospel," to be its object (cf. BAGD, 100–101). In fact, the text states that the Asians had deserted με, "me," suggesting that Paul is describing a personal abandonment that stopped short of apostasy (cf. Dibelius-Conzelmann, Guthrie) and perhaps was true of Demas (4:10). Also, vv 16–18 provide a contrast to v 15, and in vv 16–18 Paul commends Onesiphorus's personal commitment to Paul, not to the gospel. This helps in understanding

the previous reference to "all those in Asia." While it is extremely doubtful that all
the believers in Asia apostatized from the gospel, it is plausible that almost all of
them disassociated themselves from Paul during his arrest and imprisonment. Paul
does not say why they did this. He attributes Demas's desertion to the love of this
world (4:10). It can only be assumed that the Asians did not want to be associated
with a state criminal, perhaps because they feared suffering the same fate or perhaps because of the natural desire many felt to separate themselves from
undesirables. On a passive verb with a direct object in the accusative (ἀπεστράφησάν
με, "have deserted me"), see Robertson (*Grammar*, 484–85) and BAGD, 100 (3).

οἶδας τοῦτο, "knowing this," shows that Timothy was already aware of the situation since he was currently in Asia. Paul does not need to explain it, and the
reader is therefore in the dark regarding the actual events. Ἀσία, "Asia," was the
Roman province covering the western half of Asia Minor. While it is difficult to
be precise about its exact boundaries (cf. F. D. Gealy, "Asia," *IDB* 1:257–59), it
included Mysia, Lydia, Caria, part of Phrygia, and the islands off the western coast.
It was bordered by Bithynia to the north, Galatia and Lycia to the east, and the
Aegean to the west. Ephesus was its principal city.

15b ὧν ἐστιν Φύγελος καὶ Ἑρμογένης, "among whom are Phygelus and
Hermogenes." Paul specifies two of the deserting Asians. Either they were leaders in the desertion or were friends whose desertion was particularly painful for
Paul, as was Demas's desertion (4:10). Nothing more is known of either Phygelus
(on spelling, cf. Moulton, *Grammar* 1:101) or Hermogenes (cf. MM, 255). The
latter is referred to as a coppersmith in the beginning paragraph of the second-
century *Acts of Paul and Thecla*. He and Demas, it says, "were full of hypocrisy and
flattered Paul as if they loved him" (Hennecke, *New Testament Apocrypha* 2:353;
see *Explanation*), but the account is apocryphal. While Paul generally does not
give specific names (cf. 1 Tim 1:18), he does so several times in the PE (1 Tim
1:20; 2:7; 4:10, 14–15).

16a δῴη ἔλεος ὁ κύριος τῷ Ὀνησιφόρου οἴκῳ, "May the Lord grant mercy to
the household of Onesiphorus." In vv 16–18 Paul provides for Timothy a positive
example of someone who did hold to the sound words (v 13) and did guard the
gospel (v 14). Onesiphorus refreshed Paul and was not ashamed of his imprisonment, conduct consistent with his behavior in Ephesus. V 16 is Paul's wish that
Onesiphorus's household be blessed with God's mercy. The verse is not a prayer,
nor is it necessarily addressed to God as if it were an intercessory petition. It does
not say, "Lord, grant them mercy." Rather it expresses Paul's wish in the style of
Rom 15:5 and 2 Thess 3:16 (cf. Wiles, *Paul's Intercessory Prayers*, 45–155). V 18
extends a similar wish to Onesiphorus himself.

Not much is known about Onesiphorus. He is mentioned only here (vv 15–
18) and his household again in 4:19, where it is revealed that he was from Ephesus,
hence an Asian who stood in contrast to Phygelus and Hermogenes (v 15). He
was active and prominent in Ephesus (v 18). He had also traveled to Rome, where
he evidently could not find Paul immediately. Nevertheless, he sought diligently
until he found Paul and repeatedly refreshed him, probably with both friendship
and physical sustenance. This he did with no shame of Paul's imprisonment (vv
16–17). A martyr with the same name died at Parium in Mysia sometime between
A.D. 102 and 114 (*Acta Sanctorum*, 662–66; Ramsay, *ExpTim* 9 [1898] 495–97; MM,
450), but no one appears to argue that the same person is intended here. The

second-century *Acts of Paul and Thecla* mentions an Onesiphorus, stating that his children were named Simmias and Zeno and his wife Lectra and that they entertained Paul on his journey from Antioch to Iconium (see *Explanation*), but the account is apocryphal and untrustworthy.

It is thought by most that Onesiphorus had died by the time of writing, a position argued against by Hendriksen (238–39) and Knight (386). (1) V 16 speaks of Onesiphorus's household, and the time frame is the present. This implies to some that Onesiphorus was no longer part of the household and that the wish is for mercy that they may continue without him. However, that Onesiphorus can be viewed as part of the household is proven possible by 1 Cor 1:16. (2) The wish of v 18 is directed specifically to Onesiphorus, and now the time frame has shifted to the future day of judgment. This may suggest that Onesiphorus had died and would next face judgment. However, Paul can pronounce an eschatological blessing on a church while the people are still alive (1 Thess 5:23) and can speak in general about "that day" without requiring the person to have died (1:12; 4:8). V 16 may be more of a general statement, but starting with the ὅτι, "since," clause Paul concentrates solely on Onesiphorus himself and what he did. It is therefore natural to single out Onesiphorus for blessing in v 18. It may also be possible that Onesiphorus was separated from his family (because he had just left Paul?) and Paul was therefore thinking of his family as they were currently without him. (3) The past-tense verbs throughout this passage suggest to some that Onesiphorus had since died, and yet each event was in the past from Paul's perspective as he wrote the epistle, and the tenses need not signify anything else. (4) The fourth reason for seeing Onesiphorus as having died is that in Paul's final greeting where he names everyone individually (except the concluding "and all the brethren"), instead of greeting Onesiphorus by name, Paul breaks the style and greets the household of Onesiphorus. Given the nature of their relationship, it is surprising that Paul did not greet Onesiphorus by name, if he was alive. However, there could be a historical situation in which this was appropriate (e.g., Onesiphorus did not return home immediately and the letter arrived at Ephesus before him, in which case greeting the household would be appropriate). Caution must also be exercised when arguing on the basis of what is considered to be consistent style when in fact Paul might not have conformed to a modern definition of consistency. (5) Fee argues that v 18a interrupts the flow, v 18b flowing naturally from v 17. But even if v 18a is an interjection, that still proves nothing. When all is said and done, these verses could reflect the possibility that Onesiphorus had died, but there is insufficient evidence to insist that this is necessarily the case (so Oberlinner, 61).

Based on the exegesis of v 18 below, κύριος, "Lord," in v 16 probably refers to Christ. δῴη, "may . . . grant," is an aorist active optative, expressing a wish (cf. Rom 15:5; Eph 1:17; 2 Thess 3:16; 2:25; J. K. Elliott argues that here and in v 18 the optative δῴη should be δῷη, a rare example of the jussive subjunctive ["ΔΙΔΩΜΙ in 2 Timothy," *JTS* 19 n.s. (1968) 621–23]; Wallace [*Greek Grammar*, 483] says that they are voluntative optatives expressing polite requests). On God giving (διδόναι; BAGD, 193 [1bβ]) mercy, see the cognate verb in Rom 9:15, 16, 18. On ἔλεος, "mercy" (neuter accusative), see *Comment* on 1 Tim 1:2.

16b ὅτι πολλάκις με ἀνέψυξεν καὶ τὴν ἅλυσίν μου οὐκ ἐπαισχύνθη, "since often he refreshed me and was not ashamed of my chain." The two immediate reasons

Paul wishes mercy on Onesiphorus's household are that when Onesiphorus found
Paul in Rome (v 17) he refreshed Paul and he was not embarrassed about Paul's
imprisonment. The key word in this verse is ἐπαισχύνθη, "was ashamed." Paul has
encouraged Timothy not to be ashamed (v 8), stated that he himself is not ashamed
(v 12), and now uses Onesiphorus as an example of someone who was not ashamed
(v 16). πολλάκις, "often," "frequently" (cf. Rom 1:13; 2 Cor 8:22; 11:23, 26, 27(2x);
Phil 3:18), is in an emphatic position. ἀναψύχειν, "to refresh," occurs only here in
the NT (cf. its cognate ἀνάψυξις, "refreshment," in Acts 3:20 and συναναπαύεσθαι,
"to have a time of rest with," in Rom 15:32). At a minimum Paul is refreshed because of his friendship and emotional support since personal allegiance is the
context set by v 15. It could also include physical aid (money, food, etc.) since pris-
oners were often responsible for their own keep. ἅλυσις, "chain," by metonymy can
refer to imprisonment in general (cf. BAGD, 41, and the only other reference in
Paul in Eph 6:20, ἐν ἁλύσει, "in chain"), which is preferable here because it is singular (as in Eph 6:20). In the nine other occurrences of the word in the NT, it is
always the chain(s) themselves that are being discussed (Matt 5:3, 4; Luke 8:29;
Acts 12:6, 7; 21:33; 28:20; Rev 20:1). If Paul means his physical chains, it heightens
the graphic image of Onesiphorus refusing to be ashamed.

17   ἀλλὰ γενόμενος ἐν Ῥώμῃ σπουδαίως ἐζήτησέν με καὶ εὗρεν, "but being in
Rome, he earnestly searched for me and found [me]." V 17 gives us the historical
situation behind Onesiphorus's actions described in v 16. γενόμενος ἐν can mean
"being in" Rome or "when he arrived in" Rome (cf. Acts 13:5), the latter perhaps
suggesting Onesiphorus traveled to Rome specifically to find Paul. This is the only
reference to the location of Paul's imprisonment, and proponents of a Caesarean
imprisonment as Paul's location when writing 2 Timothy must deal with this verse
(cf. L. Johnson, *ExpTim* 68 [1956] 24–26, and the *Introduction*). That Onesiphorus
has to seek for Paul σπουδαίως, "earnestly" (Titus 3:13; *Note* a on 2 Tim 1:17), and
the previous reference to lack of shame despite Paul's chain suggest that Paul's
current imprisonment was more severe than previous ones (cf. *Comment* on v 15
and "serious criminal" in 2:9) and was definitely different from the imprisonment
in Acts 28. καὶ εὗρεν, "and he found," without an expressed object (e.g., με, "me")
seems abrupt, but it may pave the way for the wordplay in v 18. The verbal similarity between ἐζήτησέν με καὶ εὗρεν, "he searched for me and found," and ἐζήτησα
αὐτὸν καὶ οὐχ εὗρον αὐτόν, "I sought him and did not find him" (Cant 3:1c), seems
at best coincidental since Paul is recounting a historical narrative and the phrase is
not unusual (contra Cabaniss, *Studies in English* 8 [1967] 53–56).

18a   δῴη αὐτῷ ὁ κύριος εὑρεῖν ἔλεος παρὰ κυρίου ἐν ἐκείνῃ τῇ ἡμέρᾳ, "May the
Lord grant him to find mercy from [the] Lord on that day." In a somewhat awkward manner Paul plays off the verb εὗρεν, "found," in v 17: "Onesiphorus found
Paul, and may he find mercy from God." The wish prayer is similar to the one in v
16 (see there for a discussion) except that it is for Onesiphorus himself and the
time frame has changed from the present to the future judgment day (i.e., "that
day"; cf. 1:12). Most agree that the first articular ὁ κύριος, "the Lord," is Christ
(Spicq, Kelly, Hanson [1983], Fee; cf. Rom 2:6; 3:6) and the second κυρίου, "Lord,"
is God the Father, following the LXX style, using κύριος without the article as a
name for God (G. Quell, *TDNT* 3:1058–59; Kelly, 170). δῴη, "may . . . grant," is a
late form of the optative; classical Greek used δοίη.

There is much discussion about whether this passage is the NT precedent for prayers for the dead, assuming Onesiphorus had died (cf. v 16; Bernard, Easton, Spicq, Jeremias, Hanson [1983]). Kelly says that prayers for the dead were part of Pharisaism following the events of 2 Macc 12:43–45 (171; see *Explanation*), and an inscription in Rome shows early acceptance of this practice by Christians (references in Bernard, 114; B. H. Throckmorton, Jr., "Onesiphorus," *IDB* 3:603). However, there are serious questions regarding whether Onesiphorus actually had died, so serious that it would be a mistake to base a theology of prayers for the dead on this passage. Second, as was mentioned, v 16 and v 18 are a far cry from any notion of intercessory or petitionary prayer. They are Paul's general wish for Onesiphorus and his family (Fee, 237; Knight, 386). See the *Explanation* for further discussion.

18b καὶ ὅσα ἐν Ἐφέσῳ διηκόνησεν, βέλτιον σὺ γινώσκεις, "And the services he performed in Ephesus you know very well." This idiomatic translation reflects an awkward Greek construction whose basic meaning is clear. Timothy was well aware of all the things Onesiphorus had done in Ephesus in service to the church. These actions, along with his ministry to Paul, formed the rationale for his wish in v 18a. They also showed Timothy that Onesiphorus's service for Paul was nothing unexpected but was in keeping with his lifestyle.

The meaning of ὅσα, "everything that" (i.e., "the services"), and its emphatic position stress the magnitude of Onesiphorus's actions. "Ephesus" tells us that Onesiphorus was an Asian. "Services he performed" brings out the significance of διηκόνησεν (cf. 1 Tim 3:10). Bernard suggests that the shift in verbs of knowing is significant, οἶδας, "you know" (v 15), expressing general knowledge, and γινώσκεις, "you know," describing personal knowledge. Perhaps the classical nuances of the verbs are present in as much as they fit the context. βέλτιον, "very well," is the neuter of βελτίων, which functions as the comparative of ἀγαθός, "good," used here adverbially (BAGD, 139; BDF §244; Robertson, *Grammar*, 665). It occurs only here in the NT (cf. Acts 10:28). It can mean "better," but better than who? Timothy had been in Ephesus for some time, so it could mean "you know better than Paul does." But Paul is intimately aware of Onesiphorus's past service, particularly because of his extended time in Ephesus (Acts 19:10). Most likely the comparative force has been lost and replaced with "a weak superlative" sense (Bernard, 115): "very well." This is a common occurrence in Hellenistic Greek, and "one of the functions of the superlative is elative," which is expressed in English with "very" (Turner, *Grammatical Insights*, 90).

Explanation

Vv 15–18 give us a close look into Paul's heart, the discouragement of being abandoned, and the joy of a friend who is not ashamed. Theologically the passage has played a role in the doctrines of prayers for the dead and purgatory (see Grudem, *Systematic Theology*, 817–18, 822, who cites L. Ott, *Fundamentals of Catholic Dogma*, ed. J. C. Bastible, tr. P. Lynch [St. Louis: Herder, 1955] 321–22, 482–85). The primary biblical passage is 2 Macc 12:39–45:

> On the next day, as by that time it had become necessary, Judas and his men went to take up the bodies of the fallen and to bring them back to lie with their kinsmen in the sepulchres of their fathers. Then under the tunic of every one of the dead they found sacred

tokens of the idols of Jamnia, which the law forbids the Jews to wear. And it became clear
to all that this was why these men had fallen. So they all blessed the ways of the Lord, the
righteous Judge, who reveals the things that are hidden; and they turned to prayer, be-
seeching that the sin which had been committed might be wholly blotted out. And the
noble Judas exhorted the people to keep themselves free from sin, for they had seen with
their own eyes what had happened because of the sin of those who had fallen. He also
took up a collection, man by man, to the amount of two thousand drachmas of silver, and
sent it to Jerusalem to provide for a sin offering. In doing this he acted very well and
honorably, taking account of the resurrection. For if he were not expecting that those
who had fallen would rise again, it would have been superfluous and foolish to pray for
the dead. But if he was looking to the splendid reward that is laid up for those who fall
asleep in godliness, it was a holy and pious thought. Therefore he made atonement for
the dead, that they might be delivered from their sin. (RSV)

Prayers for the dead can be found in early Christian epitaphs and liturgies (so
Lock, 90). In the second-century *Acts of Paul and Thecla,* it is related that the daugh-
ter of Tryphaena has died and speaks to her mother in a dream about Thecla:
"Mother, thou shalt have in my place the stranger, the desolate Thecla, that she
may pray for me and I be translated to the place of the just" (28; Hennecke-
Schneemelcher, 2:361).

For Roman Catholics, therefore, prayers for the dead historically become an
important means—along with good deeds of people still alive, the Mass, and in-
dulgences—whereby the duration and intensity of suffering in purgatory can be
shortened and lessened while the soul is being purified through suffering in preparation for going to heaven (cf. Berkhof, *Systematic Theology,* 686–87). But the verses
are of more theological significance for Roman Catholics than for Protestants
since the latter do not accept the OT Apocrypha as canonical or authoritative
and generally argue that the doctrine of purgatory is contrary to the teaching of
Scripture. If there is no purgatory, there is no reason for prayers for the dead.

There are too many significant problems in interpreting 1:16, 18 for these verses
to be the basis of a doctrine of prayers for the dead. It is not clear that Onesiphorus
has in fact died (so Oberlinner, 61), and the verses are more a general wish. They
fall short of being an intercessory prayer directed to God. For Protestants in general, the teaching of Scripture is that since a person's final destiny is determined
during the person's life, prayers after death will have no effect and only encourage false hopes among the living (Grudem, *Systematic Theology,* 822).

Outside of 2 Timothy nothing is known about Onesiphorus. He is used as a
secondary character in the second-century apocryphal *Acts of Paul and Thecla.*
The second and third paragraphs read as follows:

And a man named Onesiphorus, who had heard that Paul was come to Iconium, went
out with his children Simmias and Zeno and his wife Lectra to meet Paul, that he might
receive him to his house. For Titus had told him what Paul looked like. For (hitherto)
he had not seen him in the flesh, but only in the spirit. And he went along the royal
road which leads to Lystra, and stood there waiting for him, and looked at (all) who
came, according to Titus' description. And he saw Paul coming, a man small of stature,
with a bald head and crooked legs, in a good state of body, with eyebrows meeting and
nose somewhat hooked, full of friendliness; for now he appeared like a man, and now
he had the face of an angel. (Hennecke, *New Testament Apocrypha* 2:353–54)

The story is an interesting account that glorifies both Paul and Thecla and sees her saved from death twice, but it obviously has little basis in fact. This truly second-century writing is so different from the canonical writings that it helps to confirm the conviction that the PE have little to do with the second century (cf. *Explanations* for 1 Tim 3:1–7 and 1 Tim 5:3–16).

C. Continued Appeal to Timothy   (2 Tim 2:1–13)

Bibliography

Barclay, W. "Paul's Certainties VII: Our Security in God—2 Timothy i.12." *ExpTim* 69 (1958) 324–27. **Beasley-Murray, G. R.** *Baptism in the New Testament.* New York: Macmillan, 1962. 207–9. **Bornkamm, G.** "Das Wort Jesu vom Bekennen." *Monatsschrift für Pastoraltheologie* 34 (1938) 108–18. **Botha, F. J.** "The Word Is Trustworthy." *Theologia Evangelica* 1 (1968) 78–84. **Deiss, L.** "Souviens toi de Jésus Christ: 2 Tim 2,8–12." *AsSeign* 59 (1974) 61–66. **Driessen, E.** "'Secundum Evangelium meum' (Rom 2,16. 16,25. 2 Tim 2,8)." *VD* 24 (1944) 25–32. **Duncan, J. G.** "Πιστὸς ὁ λόγος." *ExpTim* 35 (1922) 141. **Elliott, J. K.** "ΔΙΔΩΜΙ in 2 Timothy." *JTS* n.s. 19 (1968) 621–23. **Fridrichsen, A.** "Einige sprachliche und stilistische Beobachtungen." *ConNT* 2 (1936) 8–13; 6 (1942) 96. **Harris, H. A.** *Greek Athletes and Athletics.* 3rd ed. Westport, CT: Cornwell UP, 1979. 170–78. **Harris, J. R.** "Pindar and St. Paul." *ExpTim* 33 (1921–22) 456–57. **Holzmeister, U.** "Assumptionis Deiparae mysterium verbis S. Pauli 2 Tim 2ff." *VD* 18 (1938) 225–26. **Javierre, A. M.** "'ΠΙΣΤΟΙ ΑΝΘΡΩΠΟΙ' (2 Tim 2:2): Episcopado y sucesión apostólica en el Nuevo Testamento." In *Studiorum Paulinorum Congressus Internationalis Catholicus.* AnBib 17–18. Rome: Biblical Institute, 1963. 2:109–18. **Knight, G. W., III.** "2 Timothy 2:11 and Its Saying." In *The Faithful Sayings in the Pastoral Letters.* 112–37. **Laconi, M.** "Se la parola non fosse incatenata." *Presbyteri* 21 (1987) 503–11. **Leege, W.** "Some Notes on 2 Tim. 2:1–13." *CTM* 16 (1945) 631–36. **Loh, I-Jin.** "A Study of an Early Christian Hymn in 2 Tim 2:11–13." Diss., Princeton Theological Seminary, 1968. **McCoy, B.** "Secure Yet Scrutinized: 2 Timothy 2:11–13." *Journal of the Grace Evangelical Society* 1 (1988) 21–33. **Ogara, F.** "'Apparuit gratia Dei Salvatoris nostri' (Tit. 2,11–15 et 3,4–7)." *VD* 15 (1935) 363–72. **Pfitzner, V. C.** *Paul and the Agon Motif.* **Roloff, J.** "Der Weg Jesu als Lebensnorm (2 Tim 2:8–13): Ein Beitrag zur Christologie der Pastoralbriefe." In *Anfänge der Christologie.* FS F. Hahn, ed. C. Breytenbach and H. Paulsen. Göttingen: Vandenhoeck & Ruprecht, 1991. 155–67. **Thompson, G. H. P.** "Ephesians iii. 13 and 2 Timothy ii. 10 in the Light of Colossians i. 24." *ExpTim* 71 (1960) 187–89. **Trummer, P.** "'Treue Menschen' (2 Tim 2:2): Amtskriterien damals und heute." In *Aufsätze zum Neuen Testament.* Graz: Institut für ökumenische Theologie und Patrologie, 1987. 95–135.

Translation

[1]*You, therefore, my child, be continually strengthened by the grace that is in Christ Jesus,* [2]*and what you have heard from me through many witnesses, entrust these things to faithful men, who will also be able to teach others.* [3]*Share* [a] *in suffering as a good soldier of Christ Jesus.* [4]*No one serving in the military* [b] *is entangled in the affairs of daily life so that he pleases the one who enlisted him.* [5]*Likewise, if anyone competes as an athlete, he does not receive a wreath unless he competes lawfully.* [6]*The hard-working farmer must be the first* [c] *to receive the fruit.* [7]*Reflect on what* [d] *I am saying, for the Lord will give* [e] *you insight in all this.*

⁸*Remember Jesus Christ, risen from [the] dead, from [the] seed of David, in accordance with my gospel,* ⁹*because of which I am suffering evil even to the point of imprisonment as a serious criminal, but the word of God is not bound;* ¹⁰*on account of this I am enduring all things for the sake of the elect, in order that they also may experience [the] salvation that is in Christ Jesus with eternal glory.*

¹¹*Trustworthy is the saying: for,*
> *If we died together,*
> > *we will also live together.*

¹²*If we endure,*
> > *we will also reign together.*

> *If we will deny* ᶠ *[Christ],*
> > *he will also deny us.*

¹³*If we are faithless,*
> > *he remains faithful,*
> > *for* ᵍ *he is unable to deny himself.*

Notes

ᵃσυγκακοπάθησον, "share in suffering" (ℵ A C* D* F G H* I P 33 81 104 365 1739 [1881*ᵛⁱᵈ] *pc* m syʰᵐᵍ bo), is replaced by σὺ οὖν κακοπάθησον, "you therefore suffer," in imitation of v 1 by C³ Dⁱ Hᶜ Ψ 1881ᶜ TR syʰ. It is simplified to κακοπάθησον, "suffer," by 1175 lat. Cf. Ellicott, 114–15; *TCGNT*², 579.

ᵇτῷ θεῷ, "for God," is inserted after στρατευόμενος, "serving in the military," by F G it vgᶜˡ ʷ; Cyp Ambst, making the spiritual nature of the metaphor explicit.

ᶜπρῶτον, "first," is replaced with πρότερον, "first," by ℵ*.

ᵈThe singular ὅ, "what" (ℵ* A C F G P 33 1739 *pc;* Epiph), is replaced with the plural ἅ, "what," by ℵ² D H Ψ 1881 TR lat syʰ, perhaps to emphasize that the call to reflection governs not just the last metaphor (v 6) but all the metaphors (vv 3–6) or all of Paul's instructions to this point.

ᵉThe future indicative δώσει, "will give" (ℵ A C* D F G 048 33 1175 1739, a few other minuscules, Latin, Epiph), is replaced with the aorist optative δῴη, "may give" (C³ H Ψ 1881 TR), showing less certainty on Paul's part that Timothy would come to understand the metaphors, and as such would be wholly inappropriate in this context. See J. K. Elliott, *JTS* n.s. 19 (1968) 621–23.

ᶠThe future ἀρνησόμεθα, "we will deny" (ℵ* A C Ψ 048 33 81 104 365 1175, a few other minuscules, Old Latin, Tert [F G: homoioteleuton]), is replaced by the present ἀρνούμεθα, "we deny" (ℵ² D 1739 1881 TR; Cyp Ambst), which forces the third line of the hymn to agree with the verbal tense of the second and fourth.

ᵍγάρ, "for" (ℵ* Aᵛⁱᵈ C D F G L P 048ᵛⁱᵈ 6 33 81 104 326 365 1175 1739 1881 sy bo), is omitted by ℵ² Ψ TR latt syʰ sa boᵐˢˢ; Tert.

Form/Structure/Setting

Vv 1–13 are held together by the theme of encouragement. Timothy is to be entirely devoted to his task in the face of suffering, encouraged by the example of Paul and God's faithfulness (Spicq, 2:737), and called to be loyal to Paul and the gospel. Some view 1:15–18 as a digression (e.g., Brox), but as will be seen, the Asians, Phygelus, Hermogenes, and Onesiphorus all play a role in Paul's forthcoming appeal because 2:1 continues the same discussion and 1:3–2:13 forms a single unit. (At 2:14 Paul turns his attention to the opponents, and in 3:10 through the end of the epistle Paul returns to Timothy.) It is possible to split this passage into two parts, 2:1–7 and 2:8–13. But the theme of both paragraphs is endurance in the face of suffering, and both form one unit. Much of 2 Timothy is stream of consciousness, and it is difficult and not always helpful to divide the letter into smaller divisions.

There are two literary issues in this passage. The first is the summation of Paul's gospel in v 8. Many argue that it is a creed quoted by Paul that is closely related to Rom 1:3–4 (Easton, Spicq, Jeremias, Dibelius-Conzelmann, Guthrie, Kelly, Brox, Hanson [1983]). Some of these also argue that the second statement—"from [the] seed of David"—is irrelevant to the context and hence indicates a citation. Others see it as a reference to Christ's incarnation, a polemic against Gnosticism, and hence another indication that it is a citation. But if it is irrelevant, it seems doubtful that it would have been cited since the text is only a fragment itself (see below). If Paul feels free to quote only part of a saying, it seems unlikely that he would include irrelevant material. As is often true of this type of discussion, there is no way to know with any degree of certainty whether it is a citation, and speculation about the source is irrelevant to its contextual meaning. The author who wrote Rom 1:3–4 could as easily have written 2 Tim 2:8, as the concluding "in accordance with my gospel" suggests. While the order "Jesus Christ" may be unique in 2 Timothy and hence an indication of a citation to some (Kelly, 177), it is not unique in the other two Pastoral letters (1 Tim 6:3, 14; Titus 1:1; cf. Titus 2:13; 3:6; which may be citations) and therefore not necessarily indicative of a citation.

The second literary issue is the fifth and final faithful saying in 2:11b–13. For a general discussion of the faithful sayings, see the *Form/Structure/Setting* on 1 Tim 1:12–17. There has been some discussion regarding the identity of the saying. Because of the γάρ, "for," in the first line, some feel that vv 11b–13 cannot be the saying, and the introductory formula therefore looks back to v 8 or v 9 (so Ellicott, 120; cf. Knight, *Faithful Sayings*, 112–15). Vv 11b–13 seem, however, to be the best candidate for the saying. (1) V 8 is far removed from v 11 with a significant amount of discussion between them. (2) Vv 9–10 are personal comments best understood within Paul and Timothy's historical context and within the flow of 1:2–2:13, and hence inappropriate for a citation. (3) Most of the faithful sayings deal with the topic of salvation, which is the theme of vv 11b–13. (4) Vv 11b–13 are structured like a hymn or creed (e.g., parallel structure, first person plural). (5) Vv 11b–13 illustrate what Paul means by "suffer" (v 9) and "endure" (v 10), and this would be an expected use of a hymnic citation. (6) γάρ, "for" (v 11b), can be Paul's insertion to link the hymn to the introductory formula (v 11a) and his discussion in vv 8–10, or it could be original, referring to the preceding part of the original hymn, which Paul does not cite.

The other structural issue of the faithful saying is the final line, which some believe is the author's comment on the hymn. But as is argued below, this line is essential in the argument of the supposed hymnic fragment, and without it the hymn breaks down. If vv 11b–13 are a hymn or creed, they most likely are only a fragment (see below), and what may seem to be an intrusion into the form of the hymn may in fact, if the hymn were to be seen as a whole, actually conform to the structure of the hymn (cf. Gealy, 484–87; Knight, *Faithful Sayings*, 134–35). If vv 11b–13 are not a fragment, the final line and its discussion of God's character are the focus of the hymn, and the irregular structure (i.e., an extra line) may serve to drive home the point. In either case, v 13c is a necessary and integral part of the hymn and not necessarily the author's addition.

Yet vv 11b–13 do not appear to be a citation of a hymn. (1) Paul is capable of writing in parallel structure using carefully worded language. (2) The use of the introductory formula for a faithful saying in 1 Tim 3:1 shows that it does not

always introduce a quotation but can merely call attention to what Paul is about
to say. (3) Most important, vv 11b–13 are so thoroughly Pauline—as even Hanson
([1983] 132) admits—that nothing in the passage suggests that the author is not
Paul. In fact, lines 1, 2, and 4 are very similar to verses in Romans. (Bernard and
Knight suggest that the supposed hymn was composed by the Roman church.
Line 3 appears to be a direct reference to the saying of Jesus recorded in Matt
10:33.) (4) Each line so closely parallels a previous theme in 2 Tim 1:1–2:11 (see
Comment) that one wonders if such a coincidence is in fact possible. If vv 11b–13
are a citation, they have been woven so tightly into the context that they should
only be interpreted in light of 2 Timothy as a whole. As Fee observes, "But if one
takes seriously the thoroughly Pauline nature of the poem, neither of these options [i.e., baptismal hymn, hymn of martyrdom] is necessary. The hymn, in all
of its parts, fits the context so well, that, whatever its origins or original setting, it
now *functions* to inspire loyalty to Christ" (252). If the saying is not a citation (so
Ridderbos, 196), then the introductory formula, like 1 Tim 3:1, only serves to
bring attention to the following verses. On Easton's position that the hymn extends only through v 12a, see the critique by Knight (*Faithful Sayings*, 132–34).
See also Knight's critique (*Faithful Sayings*, 136–37) of Spicq's position that Paul
utilizes a hymn both before and after the introductory formula in v 11a. Three
points suggest that the passage includes only a fragment of the supposed hymn.
(1) The text does not indicate to whom the prefix συν-, "together," refers. (2)
The object of ἀρνησόμεθα, "deny," is never identified. (3) The antecedent of
κἀκεῖνος, "he," in v 12b and ἐκεῖνος, "he," in v 13a is not given.

There are many parallels and contrasts in the saying.

	Line 1	Line 2	Line 3	Line 4
"if" clause				
introduction	if	if	if	if
tense	aorist	present	future	present
verb	συναποθνῄσκειν	ὑπομένειν	ἀρνεῖσθαι	ἀπίστειν
topic	conversion	perseverance	apostasy	faithlessness
type	encouragement	encouragement	warning	encouragement
"then" clause				
introduction	also	also	also (crasis)	
emphatic pronoun			ἐκεῖνος	ἐκεῖνος (crasis)
tense	future	future	future	present
verb	συζῆν	συμβασιλεύειν	ἀρνεῖσθαι	μένειν

The first two lines describe what will happen to believers in conjunction with
Christ. The last two describe what Christ will do to/for them. All four are first-
class conditional sentences; whether the conditional clause is assumed to be true
("since") or simply conditional ("if") is determined contextually. If the hymn is
confessional, then line 1 is assumed to be true ("since"). The final three are simply conditional ("if"), and hence the future-tense verbs in the "then" clauses in
the second and third lines are appropriate.

Comment

1 σὺ οὖν, τέκνον μου, ἐνδυναμοῦ ἐν τῇ χάριτι τῇ ἐν Χριστῷ Ἰησοῦ, "You, therefore, my child, be continually strengthened by the grace that is in Christ Jesus." Paul has been admonishing Timothy throughout chap. 1 with a series of imperatives (1:6, 8, 13, 14). Throughout chap. 1 Paul has also made it clear that Timothy is not to perform these tasks by his own strength (1:6, 7, 8, 9, 12, 13, 14). This verse, 2:1, brings these two thoughts together, continuing the series of commands to Timothy but stressing that Timothy is to work by the grace that comes from Christ Jesus. Whereas Gnosticism and Stoicism taught that behavior and salvation come from within the person, by knowing or doing certain things, the PE insist that Timothy's power comes from a daily empowering available only externally, from Christ.

σὺ οὖν, "you, therefore," is highly emphatic in both position and meaning. In contrast to Phygelus and Hermogenes (1:15), but following the examples of Paul (1:12) and Onesiphorus (1:16–18; contra Ellicott, 113), and remembering his own giftedness (1:6), Timothy is to do his work. But because of the general nature of the imperative—the command to be empowered and not to do something specifically—"you, therefore" also goes back to all the commands in chap. 1 (cf. 1 Tim 4:6 for the same idea). It is only through the daily empowering that comes from Christ that Timothy is "therefore" able to fan into flame his gift, not to be ashamed, etc. Lock suggests that Paul is thinking specifically of the empowerment necessary for Timothy to come to Rome (2 Tim 4:9). He paraphrases, "In that strength, come to me and, before you come, hand over the truths which you heard from me" (92). This has the advantage of emphasizing the connection of 1:13–14 with chap. 2, especially the repetition of the idea of passing on teaching (Paul to Timothy, 1:13; Timothy to others, 2:2) and the role of the gospel as something entrusted (1:14; 2:2). This would also suggest that Timothy's upcoming Roman trip is the context of the call to suffer in 2:3–7, a call not accepted by all the Asians, Phygelus, and Hermogenes (1:15), but one accepted by Onesiphorus (1:16–18). However, the charge is quite general, not as specific as Lock's suggestion may require, and it is separated from 2 Tim 4:9 by several verses.

τέκνον μου, "my child," repeats the personal nature of the epistle and Paul's affection for Timothy (cf. 1 Tim 1:2). All of 2 Tim 1:1–2:13 is clearly personal. The opponents surface only once (1:15; cf. 1:13–14; 2:8, 12–13), and the letter maintains throughout the tone of a personal appeal to a good friend. But this personal epistle must be understood in light of Timothy's historical situation. The opposition to Timothy is intense: perhaps his personality, like most, needs encouragement, and Paul wants Timothy to put his affairs in order and come to visit Paul in Rome as soon as possible.

ἐνδυναμοῦ, "be continually strengthened," is a present (linear) passive imperative, God being the agent of the empowerment. Unlike the other occurrences of the verb in the PE, which are aorists and look back to specific events (1 Tim 1:12; 2 Tim 4:17), Paul is speaking here of a daily empowerment (cf. Rom 4:20; Eph 6:10; Phil 4:13), an ongoing strengthening required to carry out the commands in chap. 1 (cf. 1 Tim 4:6 for the same idea). ἐν τῇ χάριτι, "by the grace" (on χάρις, "grace," see *Comment* on 1 Tim 1:2), could be locative ("in the grace"), indicating the "sphere in which all of Christian life is lived" (Fee, 239–40; cf.

Ellicott, 113; cf. Eph 6:10). But this makes the following phrase, "in Christ Jesus," somewhat repetitive since both would define the source of the power. It is preferable to see ἐν as instrumental (Kelly, Knight), "by the grace" being the means by which God empowers Timothy both to desire and to do God's pleasure (cf. Phil 2:13). Thus Paul continues his theme that the strength for the task comes not from within but from without. He also continues his emphasis on God's grace found throughout chap. 1 (vv 2, 3, 6, 9). This is the only time in Paul that the construction ἐν + article + χάρις occurs, except perhaps in Col 3:16. (It occurs without the article five times in Paul [Rom 5:15; 2 Cor 1:12; Gal 1:6; Col 4:6; 2 Thess 2:16].) It is common in prepositional phrases to drop the article, so its inclusion in this phrase is significant as Paul specifies that it is only "the" grace in Christ Jesus that empowers.

The source of this grace is Christ Jesus; it is available to those who are ἐν Χριστῷ Ἰησοῦ, "in Christ Jesus" (cf. 1:9b, 13; discussed in 1 Tim 1:14). As such, this same empowerment is available for all Christians, not only for some select group whose members think they are empowered by some special grace. This is similar to Paul's ongoing point that Timothy is to be enabled by the Holy Spirit (1:7, 9b, 14). This call to divine empowerment will be enlarged in the call to perseverance in vv 3–7 and theologized in vv 11–13. The repeated article (τῇ) before the phrase ἐν Χριστῷ Ἰησοῦ, "in Christ Jesus," shows that the phrase modifies χάριτι, "grace."

2 καὶ ἃ ἤκουσας παρ' ἐμοῦ διὰ πολλῶν μαρτύρων, ταῦτα παράθου πιστοῖς ἀνθρώποις, οἵτινες ἱκανοὶ ἔσονται καὶ ἑτέρους διδάξαι, "and what you have heard from me through many witnesses, entrust these things to faithful men, who will also be able to teach others." Paul is nearing the end of his life and wants Timothy to leave Ephesus, even before his work is done, so Paul can see Timothy one last time (4:9). In order to continue the work that Timothy began, it is essential that men of character continue to teach the true gospel, the same gospel Timothy learned from Paul. Timothy is to identify these men and entrust the gospel to them before he leaves, helping to ensure the integrity of the gospel message (Spicq, 2:738). Because teaching is the responsibility of elders (cf. 1 Tim 3:2), the faithful men are probably elders.

It is critical that v 2 be interpreted in light of the historical situation. It is not a formal institutionalizing of apostolic succession for the preservation of the Christian creed (contra, e.g., Oberlinner, 67–68, who says that the text requires that the people be installed into offices of church leadership). As W. G. Kümmel asserts, "There is no chain of *succession* constructed from Paul via his apostolic disciples to the holders of the office in the congregations—not even in II Tim 2:2" (*Introduction to the New Testament* [Nashville: Abingdon, 1975] 381–82). Paul wants Timothy to get his house in order before leaving Ephesus, and v 2 is a continuation of his concerns in 1:13–14 and 1 Tim 3. To see it as a second-century formalization of the transfer of power and creed is anachronistic and can only be done by ignoring the stated context of the epistle (contra Brox). (1) In v 2 Timothy is not told to hand over the reins to those in power as would be expected in an institutional structure. He is told to find men of good character. (2) He is not to entrust the gospel to others, who in turn will entrust the gospel to others, which would be expected if this is second-century institutionalism. Those entrusted with the gospel are to teach. (3) The context requires that v 2 be an instruction to Timothy. While it has ramifications for later Christian leaders, its historical meaning is set in Paul's desire to see Timothy. (4) Paul has always been interested in the transfer of tradition (cf. 2 Tim 1:13 and the *Introduction*, "Critical Questions, The Theological Problem"), an interest that one would expect to see heightened at the end of his life. (5) "Witnesses" is not "a natural description, in second-century idiom, for a succession of accredited teachers" (Kelly, 174). In the second century there were no witnesses; the church leaders passed on what they were told, not what they witnessed. (6) Although it is a subjective criterion, the second-century passages often cited as parallels (cf. *Explanation* below) sound significantly different from v 2. 2 Tim 2:2 is "clearly at a primitive stage . . . [where] no theory of apostolic succession is expounded. There is no suggestion of apostles as such passing on the faith to bishops and deacons, but we simply have Paul himself charging Timothy, and his interest is in the reliability rather than the status of the men Timothy will select" (Kelly, 174). 2 Tim 2:2 is a personal comment to a friend, and it seems anachronistic to use the translation "succession." D. A. Carson, D. J. Moo, and L. Morris (*An Introduction to the New Testament* [Grand Rapids, MI: Zondervan, 1992] 380) observe:

> In line with this, the apostle exhorts Timothy to pass the teaching on "to reliable men who will also be qualified to teach others" (2:2). There is a "given" about the Christian faith; it is something inherited from the very beginning of God's action for our salvation, and it is to be passed on as long as this world lasts. Paul is not arguing that believers should be insensitive to currents of thought and action in the world about them, nor is he saying that the Christian is a kind of antiquarian, interested in antiquity for its own sake. He is saying that there is that about the essence of the Christian faith that is not open to negotiation. God has said and done certain things, and Christians must stand by those things whatever the cost.

The key difficulty in v 2 is the phrase διὰ πολλῶν μαρτύρων, "through many witnesses." (1) One interpretation is that this phrase refers to a specific historical event. διά would mean "in the presence of" (Chrysostom; cf. Spicq, 2:738–39; for this meaning of διά, see Lock, 93; BAGD, 180 [AIII2a]; cf. also Moule, *Idiom-Book*, 57). The event would be Timothy's conversion, baptism, or commission to ministry (cf. 1 Tim 1:18), and the witnesses would be the elders or other people (perhaps his mother and grandmother; cf. 2 Tim 1:5) who watched or took part (cf. 1 Tim 4:14). They would have been witnesses to the truth of what Paul was teaching Timothy, or to the fact that the gospel was entrusted to Timothy (which Paul now wants Timothy to pass on to others). The only other occurrence of this phrase in the PE is in 1 Tim 6:12, which alludes to Timothy's good confession that he made ἐνώπιον πολλῶν μαρτύρων, "before many witnesses." Here the witnesses are probably people who were involved in Timothy's conversion (cf. 1:5). The major difficulty with interpreting the phrase as referring to one event is that regardless of which specific event Paul is referring to, it is improbable that Paul would have shared the entire gospel with Timothy at this one event (cf. Guthrie, 137–38). Yet it is precisely "what you [i.e., Timothy] heard from me" at this supposed event that Timothy is to entrust to others, and "what you heard" is required by the context to be a full expression of the gospel. To put it another way, it is doubtful that Paul is telling Timothy to entrust an encapsulated summary of the gospel to others so they can in turn teach others, and yet at best it would have been an encapsulated summary of the gospel that Timothy would have heard from Paul at his conversion, baptism, or commission to ministry.

(2) There are two other clues in the text suggesting another interpretation. The first is the two prepositions: the gospel is παρά, "from," Paul διά, "through," the witnesses. παρά denotes the person from whom something proceeds (cf. BAGD, 180 [AIII]). Unless Paul contradicts what he just said, διά cannot as well indicate the personal agent through whom Timothy received the gospel (cf. BAGD, 180 [AIII2a]). This negates any interpretation that sees the witnesses as authoritative bearers of the gospel coequal with Paul. It is doubtful that Paul would appeal to the authority of other people, and this would require καί, "and," before διά. The second clue is that the emphasis of the phrase is on πολλῶν, "many." Paul's concern is to emphasize that the gospel Timothy heard was not heard in secret from Paul alone but rather was heard from many people. This is not saying that Paul appeals to the authority of others. It is saying that in contrast to the Ephesian opponents with their myths and legends, the gospel is widely and publicly attested, and this is the gospel Timothy is to entrust to faithful Ephesians. In this case διά means "through" in the sense of being attested to, denoting the manner, attendant circumstance, or perhaps occasion of Timothy hearing the gospel repeatedly from Paul (cf. BAGD, 180 [AIII1b,c,e]). The witnesses then are all Christians, including Timothy, who have heard the gospel and are witnesses to the fact of Paul's sharing of the gospel with many other people.

ἃ ἤκουσας, "what you have heard," looks back to the similar phrase in 1:13 that speaks of the sound words that are the gospel (1:8–11). ταῦτα, "these things," likewise looks back to ἃ ἤκουσας, "what you have heard," the plural emphasizing that Paul is thinking of the gospel in its totality and not a summary of it. παράθου, "entrust" (BAGD, 623), is another imperative, but unlike ἐνδυναμοῦ, "be continually strengthened," in v 1, this one is aorist, signifying the need to find faithful men. Paul earlier said that he was entrusting his command to Timothy to stop the opponents (1 Tim 1:18), and he has just used the cognate noun to describe the deposit (παραθήκη) Timothy is to guard (1:14; cf. 1:12 and 1 Tim 6:20). As has been noted above, this is not a theology of institutional succession. Timothy is not to find people in positions of church authority and hand over the reins of power. He is to find believing men who are of trustworthy character.

πιστοῖς, "faithful," assumes that the people are believers (cf. Introduction, "Themes in the PE"), in contrast to the Ephesians who were pursuing myths, but its emphasis is on character, that they will be trustworthy as well as accurate in teaching the gospel (cf. Spicq, 2:739). This is how the word is used in the phrase "the saying is trustworthy" (cf. Form/Structure/Setting on 1 Tim 1:12–17), and it puts these men in contrast to those who will shortly be described (2 Tim 2:14). It also is a one-word summary of the condition for overseers and deacons in 1 Tim 3.

ἄνθρωπος, "man," is often used in a generic sense of "humankind," and there is no question that women played a vital role in Jesus' ministry and the spread of the gospel. But in light of the Ephesian problem and the limitation that Paul places on the Ephesian women (1 Tim 2:9–15) and widows (1 Tim 5:3–16), it seems unlikely that Paul is telling Timothy to entrust the gospel to men and women alike. It is more likely that Paul is thinking of male elders, who were repeatedly required to be able to teach (1 Tim 3:2; 5:17; cf. the use of ἄνθρωπος in, e.g., 1 Cor 7:1; Eph 5:31; 2 Tim 3:8; BAGD, 68 [2bα]) and who had to be able "to exhort with healthy doctrine and to rebuke those who oppose [it]" (Titus 1:9). However, there is nothing in the passage, or elsewhere, that limits teaching to elders alone.

The person's competency (ἱκανός; BAGD, 374 [2]) relates to the ability and gift-edness to teach (Spicq, 2:739). With the emphasis throughout the epistle on the source of Timothy's strength and ability lying outside himself (cf. 2:1), this competency must be viewed likewise (cf. 2 Cor 3:5). In classical Greek, ἕτερος meant "another" of two (duality) while ἄλλος meant "other" of many, but Hellenistic Greek was losing its sense of duality, and these two words were used interchangeably (Zerwick, *Biblical Greek*, §153). ἑτέρους, "others," could be other men but more likely refers to other people, i.e., instruction to the church as a whole.

3 Συγκακοπάθησον ὡς καλὸς στρατιώτης Χριστοῦ Ἰησοῦ, "Share in suffering as a good soldier of Christ Jesus." Empowered by the grace that is in Christ Jesus (v 1), Timothy is to entrust the gospel to others (v 2) and share in suffering (v 3). The key thought of v 3 is to "share in suffering." Paul compares Timothy to a good soldier, and in the next three verses he expands the comparison to an athlete and a farmer. Paul's call to reflection in v 7 shows that he realizes the points of the multiple metaphors may not be immediately apparent to Timothy, not so much in terms of understanding their meaning but in how to apply their truth in a concrete, practical way in his life. Paul may also be thinking specifically of the potential suffering that may await Timothy when he comes to Rome (cf. *Comment* on v 1).

Whatever the three metaphors mean, at a minimum they all illustrate Timothy's need to "share in suffering." There is also a development, the latter two metaphors emphasizing the idea of reward, which is not immediately apparent in the first metaphor.

		Share in Suffering	
metaphor	*soldier*	*athlete*	*farmer*
call to suffer	single-mindedness	to compete by the rules	to work hard
reward	to please one who enlists him	to win prize	to share crop

Although the main point is "share in suffering," each metaphor has its own special nuance. A soldier suffers by being forced to ignore civilian affairs. An athlete suffers by training properly. A farmer suffers by working hard. Through all of these metaphors the common theme of perseverance in the face of suffering is drawn. Each metaphor also has its own special reward: pleasing the one who enlists him; being able to compete and win the prize; being the first to receive a share of the crop. Paul has not yet specified what Timothy's reward will be, but in vv 8–13 Paul says he endures all suffering for the sake of the elect so that they can obtain salvation with its eternal glory (v 10). Paul lives with Christ and will reign with him (v 11). These too, by implication, are Timothy's rewards (cf. Matt 5:12; 13:43; 19:21). Beyond this, however, the metaphors should not be pressed. If an application moves beyond "share in suffering," it becomes suspect (see *Explanation*).

The same three metaphors are used in 1 Cor 9:7, 10 (cf. vv 24–27) to prove that Paul and Barnabas have the right to be paid for their Christian labors, and some have suggested that this emphasis on remuneration is present in the final two metaphors (Spicq, Dibelius-Conzelmann, Guthrie, Kelly, Hanson [1983]). Yet this sounds foreign to the Ephesian context and the flow of the discussion. Would Paul encourage Timothy to collect his wages on his way out of town as he travels to Rome? The flow of the discussion is that Timothy should expect suffering and share in that suffering, and it seems a base motive to be paid for suffering. Moreover, Paul continues the discussion by saying that he is willing to suffer for the eschatological goal of the salvation of the elect and the eternal glory of salvation (v 10) so that they will reign with Christ (v 12). This agrees with the eschatological flavor of the entire corpus (cf. 1 Tim 4:1–5; 3:1) and especially with 2 Tim 4:6–8 where Paul repeats the military (cf. 1 Tim 1:18–19) and athletic metaphors and concludes by looking forward to the crown of righteousness that he will receive on the eschatological day of judgment. Likewise, Timothy's reward is not remuneration but his own crown of righteousness given as he stands in the judgment at the end of time (cf. Fee, 244). It is not payment for services rendered. There is nothing incompatible between the metaphors and the concept of remuneration, but this does not appear to be the teaching of these metaphors in this context. On συγκακοπαθεῖν, "to share in suffering," see *Comment* on 2 Tim 1:8.

Pfitzner comments on the superficial similarities and significant differences this passage shares with the Stoics: "It is above all in this respect that Timothy's military service differs decisively from that of the Stoic sage. The latter also knows of the necessity to keep himself free from entanglement in the everyday affairs of life (Epict. III 22), but is, in the final analysis, responsible to himself alone. The Christian 'soldier' has only one goal and purpose—whole-hearted devotion to the given task in the effort to please his Lord" (*Agon Motif,* 169).

4 οὐδεὶς στρατευόμενος ἐμπλέκεται ταῖς τοῦ βίου πραγματείαις, ἵνα τῷ στρατολογήσαντι ἀρέσῃ, "No one serving in the military is entangled in the affairs of daily life so that he pleases the one who enlisted him." A good soldier (v 3) is single-minded, concentrating on his military task and hence not becoming involved in day-to-day civilian affairs. This single-mindedness is one way in which Timothy is called to suffer because no matter how difficult his task becomes, no matter how much suffering he endures, he cannot turn from his path of ministry. As such, the metaphor is a call to perseverance. The soldier's reward is the pleasure of the one who enlists him, who, if the metaphor is pressed, is God. For a discussion of the three metaphors in general, see *Comment* on v 3.

Does this call to single-minded devotion mean that the Christian minister can have nothing to do with secular life? Does it negate the possibility of being married or of working outside the church? Does it require a hermitlike existence, living separated from the world? While some in the church historically have interpreted the verse in these ways, the historical context and Paul's teaching elsewhere seem to disallow these options. While the gift of celibacy is highly valued by Paul (1 Cor 7:7), it is not the norm (1 Cor 7:9, 28, 36, 38). It would be contrary to the instructions in the PE for church leaders (1 Tim 3:2, 12; Titus 1:6) and widows (1 Tim 5:14), and the insistence on celibacy can in fact be based in demonic teachings (1 Tim 4:1–3). Paul and Barnabas worked outside their ministry (1 Cor 9:6), and their lives were anything but hermitlike (see further references from the early church in Lock, 94). The key is to realize that the purpose of the metaphor is to stress Timothy's call to suffer hardship, that regardless of the degree of suffering Timothy must, like a soldier, persevere in his ministry and by so doing please God. It is an issue of priorities, a "wholehearted devotion to his divine commanding officer" (Fee, 242). The text does not speak simply of involvement but says ἐμπλέκεται, "is entangled," in everyday affairs (cf. 2 Pet 2:20). When everyday life becomes an entanglement to ministry, when the pursuit of life apart from ministry results in God's displeasure, when believers are no longer willing to suffer the pain to which all godly people are called (3:12), then they, like Timothy, are no longer good soldiers and no longer please the one who enlisted them. This is an especially important distinction if the metaphor is intended to include not just leaders but all Christians as the relativizing οὐδείς, "no one," and the following ἐάν . . . τις, "if anyone" (v 5), imply. Obviously, Christians in general must have some involvement in day-to-day affairs, but they can never become entangled in them.

οὐδείς, "no one," turns the metaphor into a general maxim applicable not just to Timothy but to all Christian ministers and all believers (cf. Luke 8:14; 9:62). On στρατεύεσθαι, "to serve in the military," see *Comment* on 1 Tim 1:18 (cf. 1 Cor 9:7; 2 Cor 10:3). ἐμπλέκειν, "to entangle," occurs elsewhere in the NT only in 2 Pet 2:20, which speaks about becoming entangled in the corruptions of this world. It is used outside the NT in describing a sheep or hare being tangled in thorns (BAGD, 256), which creates a helpful picture for understanding this passage. BAGD notes that the verb is always passive in early Christian literature, but Knight (393) says the form here could be a reflexive middle, "entangle oneself." Lock cites Epictetus as using the word of the ideal Cynic (3.22.69). πραγματεία occurs only here in the NT and is always used in early Christian literature in the plural meaning of "business, affairs" (BAGD, 697). βίος is used here of "earthly life in its functions and its duration" (BAGD, 141; cf. *Comments* on 1 Tim 2:2 and 1 Tim 1:16 for how it differs from ζωή, "life"). Hanson ([1983] 129) suggests that the verse means that the Christian worker should not work for pay outside the church but should be content with wages from the church. But it is doubtful that the rewards of being a soldier, athlete, or farmer are viewed here as remuneration (cf. 2:3), and it would contradict Paul's well-known lifestyle as a tentmaker (1 Cor 9:6). ἀρέσκειν means "to please" (Rom 8:8; 15:1, 2, 3; 1 Cor 7:32, 33, 34; 10:33; Gal 1:10 [2x]; 1 Thess 2:4, 15; 4:1; cf. F. W. Danker, "Under Contract," in *Festschrift to Honor F. Wilber Gingrich*, ed. E. H. Barth and R. E. Cocroft [Leiden: Brill, 1972] 198). Whereas we might have expected "commander" (as the NIV mistakenly translates), στρατολογήσαντι is "the one who enlisted (him)" (BAGD, 770; MM, 592; Spicq, *TLNT* 3:300; O. Bauernfeind, *TDNT* 7:701–13). The emphasis is on the one who calls the soldier to his task, and hence the metaphor parallels God's call of Timothy to ministry (2 Tim 1:6–7).

Finally, Fee comments concerning Paul's use of military and athletic metaphors: "Here is a clear case of the 'authentic' Paul reflecting imagery in common with such contemporaries as Seneca and Philo, yet using it in a uniquely Christian way. The usage here, as Pfitzner convincingly demonstrates, reflects Pauline usage, not Hellenism or Hellenistic Judaism. This fact should cause one to be more cautious in describing other such metaphors, unique to these Epistles, as unPauline" (Fee, 244, citing Sevenster, *Paul and Seneca*, 162–64, and Pfitzner, *Agon Motif*, 157–86).

5 ἐὰν δὲ καὶ ἀθλῇ τις, οὐ στεφανοῦται ἐὰν μὴ νομίμως ἀθλήσῃ, "Likewise, if anyone competes as an athlete, he does not receive a wreath unless he competes lawfully." The second metaphor to help Timothy see the necessity of suffering with Paul is athletics (cf. 1 Tim 1:18; 4:7; 6:12; 2 Tim 4:7; 1 Cor 9:24–27; cf. Pfitzner, *Agon Motif*). Just as an athlete perseveres despite the suffering involved in training and competition, so also Timothy should willingly suffer. (His training is to

be in godliness [1 Tim 4:7].) Just as the athlete receives the reward of winning the victor's wreath, so also Timothy will receive his eschatological reward. On all three metaphors in general, see *Comment* on v 3.

δὲ καί, "likewise," introduces the second metaphor, which makes the same basic point as the first. The indefinite ἐάν . . . τις, "if anyone," generalizes the metaphor, so its application extends beyond Timothy to all Christian ministers and perhaps all Christians (cf. οὐδείς, "no one," in v 4). ἀθλεῖν, "to compete," occurs twice in this verse and nowhere else in the NT. Its second occurrence is modified by νομίμως, "lawfully" (cf. 1 Tim 1:8; cf. BAGD, 541; MM, 429). νομίμως ἀθλήσῃ, "competes lawfully," can mean competing in the actual contest according to the rules. It can also mean that athletes must properly prepare for the contest, reflecting the Greek rule that called for ten months of preparation before the games, an oath to Zeus that the preparation was done properly (Pausanius *Description of Greece* 5.24.9; cf. references in Wettstein, *Novum Testamentum Graecum* 2:357; J. H. Krause, *Die Gymnastik und Agonistik der Hellenen* [Leipzig: Barth, 1841] 1:362ff.; Bernard, 118; Lock, 94), and punishment if one lied (Spicq, 2:742–43; on athletic training, see Harris, *Greek Athletes,* 170–78). Does Paul view Timothy as preparing for the contest, participating in it, or both? Since Timothy is currently engaged in the struggle, the idea of participating is more relevent. οὐ στεφανοῦται, "does not receive a wreath," pictures the victor's wreath (cf. Heb 2:7) or a crown. Elsewhere Paul speaks of pursuing not a perishable but rather an imperishable wreath (1 Cor 9:25), and later in this epistle Paul writes of the crown of righteousness (4:8) he will receive.

6 τὸν κοπιῶντα γεωργὸν δεῖ πρῶτον τῶν καρπῶν μεταλαμβάνειν, "The hardworking farmer must be the first to receive the fruit." This third metaphor uses the image of a hard-working farmer to encourage Timothy to suffer with Paul. The emphatic position of κοπιῶντα, "hard-working," assures that this is the emphasis of the metaphor; God's call on Timothy's life and his willingness to suffer involve strenuous toil. More than the preceding two metaphors, this metaphor also emphasizes Timothy's reward: δεῖ, "it is necessary," that the farmer be the πρῶτον, "first," to benefit from the crop. For a discussion of the three metaphors in general, see *Comment* on v 3.

κοπιᾶν, "to work," describes hard work, often manual labor, and is frequently used by Paul figuratively of Christian ministry (cf. *Comments* on 1 Tim 4:10; 5:17; cf. Moule, *Idiom-Book,* 95, 104). This may explain why Paul includes this third metaphor. καρπός can refer to the "fruit" of trees or the "fruit" of the ground, i.e., crops (BAGD, 404). This is the only occurrence in Paul of γεωργός, "farmer, vine-dresser" (BAGD, 157; seventeen times elsewhere in the Gospels, and Jas 5:7). μεταλαμβάνειν, "to receive" (BAGD, 511), takes its object in the genitive (καρπῶν, "fruit"). πρῶτον, "first," modifies the infinitive μεταλαμβάνειν, "to receive," not καρτῶν, "fruit." While the metaphor of a farmer receiving his own crop as a return on his labor is consistent with the idea of a minister being paid for his work, this is not the emphasis of the metaphor in this context (cf. *Comment* on v 3).

7 νόει ὃ λέγω· δώσει γάρ σοι ὁ κύριος σύνεσιν ἐν πᾶσιν, "Reflect on what I am saying, for the Lord will give you insight in all this." Paul recognizes that the significance of the preceding three metaphors may not be fully apparent to Timothy, so he urges him to reflect, to mull over, what he says. Part of any possible confusion may be due to the additional emphasis on rewards, present in the latter two metaphors but not obvious in v 3. But the confusion involves more than meaning since the meaning is not that difficult and Paul knows that the Lord will give Timothy σύνεσιν, "insight," not just knowledge. V 7 is a call for Timothy also to reflect on the practical implications of these metaphors on his life, how he needs to suffer as a good soldier and what that means for his ministry in Ephesus. Lock paraphrases, "Think over the way in which this applies to you" (92). For a discussion of the doctrine of illumination, see the *Explanation*. There is no question in Paul's mind that the Lord δώσει, "will give," Timothy insight (see *Note* e; cf. 1 Cor 2:10). Along with the command of v 1, this verse shows Paul's view of God's deep involvement in Timothy's life and by implication in the lives of all ministers.

νοεῖν means "to reflect on, contemplate" (cf. 1 Tim 1:7; Eph 3:4, which also connects "reflection" [νοεῖν] with "insight" [σύνεσις]). The form in this verse is another imperative in a line of imperatives (cf. 2:1, 2, 3). ὃ λέγω, "what I am saying," probably refers back to the preceding metaphors since their meaning and personal application to Timothy may not be immediately clear (see J. R. Harris, *ExpTim* 33 [1921–22] 456–57, who finds that a "Pindaric formula underlies the language" of this expression). ὁ κύριος, "the Lord," could refer to God the Father (cf. παρὰ κυρίου, "from the Lord," in 1:18; cf. Eph 3:2–4) or Christ Jesus (cf. v 3; ὁ κύριος, "the Lord," in 1:16, 18). σύνεσις can move beyond "intelligence" to "insight" (cf. 1 Cor 1:19; Eph 3:4; Col 1:9; 2:2; cf. Mark 12:33; Luke 2:47; cf. BAGD, 788). The scope of ἐν πᾶσιν should be limited to Timothy's reflection, i.e., the three metaphors, and hence the translation "in all this."

8 μνημόνευε Ἰησοῦν Χριστὸν ἐγηγερμένον ἐκ νεκρῶν, ἐκ σπέρματος Δαυίδ, κατὰ τὸ εὐαγγέλιόν μου, "Remember Jesus Christ, risen from [the] dead, from [the] seed of David, in accordance with my gospel." Within the context of calling for Timothy's loyalty to Paul and the gospel, Paul defines that gospel: it is the account of Jesus the Messiah as the fulfillment of prophecy; it is also the account of Christ, raised from the dead. Perhaps ἐκ σπέρματος Δαυίδ, "from [the] seed of David," is the idea that just as Jesus Christ suffered and persevered, so also Timothy should willingly suffer and persevere.

In 1:8 Paul calls Timothy not to be ashamed of the gospel but to share in Paul's suffering. He continues by defining the gospel (1:9–10) for which they are suffering (1:11–12). The same process is visible in v 3 and vv 8–9. Paul calls Timothy to suffer together with him as a good soldier (v 3). Paul likewise is suffering for the gospel (v 9), which he summarizes in v 8. μνημόνευε, "continually remember" (present imperative), repeats the "remember" motif running throughout 2 Timothy (cf. 1:3; especially 1:13) and also continues the idea of thoughtful reflection (νόει) in the previous verse. Paul is not instructing Timothy but rather consoling and encouraging. Ellicott observes, "Timothy was to take courage, by dwelling on the victory over death and the glory of his Master,—his Master who was indeed once a man, yet, as the word of promise had declared, of the kingly seed of David" (117). On the name "Jesus Christ," see *Comment* on 1 Tim 1:1. In this passage it is doubtful that there is any significance to the order of the names. The order creates a chiasm with the following two phrases: earthly life ("Jesus . . . from [the] seed of David") and exaltation ("Christ, risen from [the] dead"). If the order of the names were reversed, they would parallel the order of the following phrases with no change in meaning.

The following two phrases summarize Paul's gospel for which Timothy and he have been called to suffer. It is similar in thought to Rom 1:3–4 (Oberlinner, 76, argues that it is based on the Romans text; Marshall argues that it is traditional and independent of Rom 1:3–4 [SNTU-A 13 (1988) 165–67]): "the gospel concerning his Son, who was descended from David according to the flesh and designated Son of God in power according to the Spirit of holiness by his resurrection from the dead." Discussions of the supposedly creedal origin of this gospel summary are not helpful in understanding the text (see *Form/Structure/Setting*).

ἐγηγερμένον ἐκ νεκρῶν, "risen from [the] dead," depicts the divine vindication of Jesus' earthly life in his resurrection. Although the primary significance of v 8 is to describe the gospel in preparation for v 9, one can also see the encouragement in the verse for Timothy's historical situation as it highlights Jesus' "eschatological victory" (Fee, 246) following Jesus' suffering on the cross (perhaps implied in the context; cf. Kelly, 396–97; Knight, 177). The God who raised Jesus is the same one who will daily empower Timothy (v 1). "Risen from [the] dead" in v 8 is firmly entrenched in the flow of the discussion. (1) The eschatological rewards of v 5 and v 6 encourage Timothy to suffer with Paul (v 3). (2) Christ's resurrection, and the benefits enjoyed by believers are the topics of the first stanza of the following hymn (v 11b). (3) Mention of Jesus' resurrection also prepares Timothy for Paul's condemnation of the opponents' theology, which teaches an incorrect view of the believers' resurrection (2:18). Towner argues that the nontemporal order—resurrection, incarnation—emphasizes the fact of Christ's resurrection in opposition to the opponents' realized eschatology:

> The sequence places the resurrection of Christ at the center of the apostolic gospel probably in answer to those who were instead emphasizing the already completed resurrection of believers. Similarly, inclusion of the saying of vv. 11b–13 in this context can be explained by its stress on the importance of faithful endurance in the present for a successful final outcome. Such a theme would have no place in the heretics' thinking alongside the realized belief referred to in v. 18. (*JSNT* 31 [1987] 106)

ἐγηγερμένον, "risen," is perfect tense, emphasizing its abiding significance to Timothy. It is another divine passive (cf. ἐνδυναμοῦ, "be continually strengthened," in v 1). The punctuation of UBSGNT[4]—no punctuation before ἐγηγερμένον, comma after νεκρῶν, "dead"—implies that the participle is adverbial, used in indirect discourse following μνημόνευε, "remember": "Remember that Jesus Christ has been raised from the dead" (Knight, 397; cf. Robertson, *Grammar*, 1041). Yet the following phrase (ἐκ σπέρματος Δαυίδ, "from [the] seed of David") reads as if it is parallel to the preceding participial phrase, and therefore ἐγηγερμένον should be viewed as adjectival, modifying Ἰησοῦν, "Jesus."

The second half of the gospel summary refers to Jesus' earthly life as the fulfillment of the prophecy in 2 Sam 7 that the Messiah would come from the lineage of David (cf. Marshall, SNTU-A 13 [1988] 166). Since this forms a necessary part of the gospel story, one need look no further for justification of its inclusion here. The bulk of the gospel story deals with Jesus' life, including his Davidic descent (cf., e.g., Matt 1:1; cf. Knight, 397), and his lineage played a role in the early kerygma (cf. R. H. Mounce, *The Essential Nature of New Testament Preaching* [Grand Rapids, MI: Eerdmans, 1960]; C. H. Dodd, *The Apostolic Preaching and Its Develop-*

ments [London: Hodder & Stoughton, 1944]). Jesus' lineage is therefore not irrelevant to a summary of the gospel, and his life does play a significant role in the parallel summary in 1:10. His lineage also stresses continuity with the past as the fulfillment of prophecy and as such parallels Paul's theme of Timothy's and his connection with their spiritual heritage (1:3, 5). Ellicott argues that it refers to "Christ's *human* nature, not a docetic reference to his human 'side'" (118). If the Ephesian opponents' denial of the resurrection (2 Tim 2:18) was based on docetism, the reference to Jesus' earthly lineage may also be intended as a rebuttal of their teaching. εὐαγγέλιόν μου, "my gospel" (cf. Rom 2:16; 16:25), refers to 2:2 and 1:14 as the gospel that was entrusted to Paul (cf. 1 Tim 1:11) and perhaps stands in contrast to what the Ephesian opponents were teaching, which is the next topic (2:14; cf. *Introduction,* "The Response to the Heresy").

9 ἐν ᾧ κακοπαθῶ μέχρι δεσμῶν ὡς κακοῦργος, ἀλλὰ ὁ λόγος τοῦ θεοῦ οὐ δέδεται, "because of which I am suffering evil even to the point of imprisonment as a serious criminal, but the word of God is not bound." Following the pattern established in 2 Tim 1:8–12, Paul defines the gospel (v 8) and then identifies it as the reason for his suffering. As is true throughout the epistle, Paul's suffering (1:8, 12) serves as an encouragement to Timothy.

The final phrase, "but the word of God is not bound," reads to some as a parenthesis, and yet it is key to what Paul is saying. Most writers comment that Paul recognizes that the gospel continues to be preached by others despite his imprisonment, referencing Phil 1:12–18. But v 10 continues by emphasizing the consequences of Paul's imprisonment; attention is not explicitly shifted to others. While the preaching by others is certainly part of Paul's assurance that the gospel is not bound (4:10b–12), he also sees the unleashed gospel still at work in his own life as he endures his suffering for the sake of the elect, that they themselves obtain salvation (v 10). He will later tell Timothy about his chance to share the gospel at his trial (4:16–17), and he may be thinking specifically of this event; even though imprisoned, Paul will stand before Caesar (Acts 27:24) and proclaim the gospel.

ἐν, "because of," indicates cause (BAGD, 261 [III3]); the relative pronoun ᾧ, "which," refers back to εὐαγγέλιον, "gospel." Because this makes good sense, there is no reason to find the antecedent in Ἰησοῦν Χριστόν, "Jesus Christ" (contra Simpson; NEB: "in whose service"). κακοπαθεῖν, "to suffer evil" (cf. 2 Tim 4:5; Jas 5:13), is a simplified form of συγκακοπαθεῖν, "to share in suffering," in v 3, a nice literary touch tying Paul's suffering to Timothy's. Paul uses the same verb later (4:5) explicitly to call Timothy to suffer evil. μέχρι, "even to the point of" (cf. Phil 2:8; Heb 12:4; cf. BAGD, 515), indicates the degree to which Paul's suffering has taken him. δεσμός can refer to an actual "bond, fetter" (Acts 26:29, 30; Heb 11:36; Jude 1:6; cf. ἅλυσις, "chain," 1:16), but it normally has a less concrete nuance. It is the bond that prevents a mute person from speaking (Mark 7:35) and what keeps a person sick (Luke 13:16). It is frequently used of imprisonment as it is here (cf. Phil 1:7, 13, 14, 17; Col 4:18; Phlm 10, 13; cf. Acts 23:39; cf. BAGD, 176).

Paul suffers not only to the point of being imprisoned but to the degree that he is treated like a κακοῦργος, "serious criminal," an adjective used substantivally, appearing in the NT elsewhere only as a description of the thieves crucified with Jesus (Luke 23:32, 33, 39). Etymologically it means "a worker [from the obsolete root ἔργειν] of evil [κακός]." Its meaning ranges from a "good-for-nothing" person (Spicq, *TLNT* 2:241–43) to "one who commits gross misdeeds and serious crimes" (BAGD, 398). Spicq gives many examples of this word's use, and most illustrate the harsher meaning of the word, referring to violent people without a conscience, mostly thieves, punished by arrest, torture, feet and hands cut off, and eyes gouged out. This is therefore another indication (cf. 1:17) that Paul's current imprisonment is much harsher than the one described in Acts 28. Since Paul was a serious criminal, it is no wonder that Onesiphorus had trouble finding him and that there is the potential for embarrassment (1:16–17). Bernard (119, see his critique) and Guthrie (143–44) refer to Ramsay's argument that "serious criminal" was the actual charge against Paul (*The Church in the Roman Empire* [London: Hodder & Stoughton, 1892] 249). Ramsay argues that being charged with criminal acts (*flasitiosi*) would have been an appropriate charge against a Christian under the Neronian persecution but not under the later Domitian persecution where simply being a Christian was sufficient charge. Ramsay uses this to argue for a first-century date for the writing of this epistle. Lock argues that ἐν ᾧ, "in which," "points to Christianity as the offense" (95).

ἀλλά, "but," has its full adversative force, setting the freedom of the gospel against Paul's imprisonment. The λόγος τοῦ θεοῦ, "word of God," is the gospel (cf. 1:13; 2:8; *Comment* on 1 Tim 4:5). οὐ δέδεται, "is not bound," is an intensive perfect, emphasizing the ongoing freedom of the gospel. They can bind the messenger but not the message. Fee (247) cites the words of Luther's hymn "A Mighty Fortress": "The body they may kill; God's truth abideth still; His kingdom is forever." The word δεῖν, "to bind," may have been chosen as a wordplay (paronomasia; BDF §488 [1]) with δεσμῶν, "imprisonment."

10a διὰ τοῦτο πάντα ὑπομένω διὰ τοὺς ἐκλεκτούς, "on account of this I am enduring all things for the sake of the elect." Paul is suffering as a serious criminal because of the gospel (vv 8–9). He is willing to do this because of what is at stake, the elect. Implied in this is the call to Timothy also to endure. The key word is ὑπομένειν, "to endure" (cf. Rom 12:12; 1 Cor 13:7). It continues the theme of perseverance throughout 1:3–2:13 and is the main link to the following faithful saying (vv 11–13); it is repeated in the second stanza. On ἐκλεκτός, "elect," see *Comments* on 1:9 and 2:19.

διά, "for the sake of" (BAGD, 181 [BII]), could mean that Paul is an encouragement or that he is making the gospel heard (cf. Phil 1:12–28). In this case ἐκλεκτούς, "elect," may refer to the elect who have not yet been saved. διά could also mean that Paul is thinking of the mystical idea of filling up what is lacking in the afflictions of Christ in his (i.e., Paul's) body (Col 1:24; cf. G. H. P. Thompson, *ExpTim* 71 [1960] 187–89). In this case ἐκλεκτούς, "elect," refers to all Christians and shows Paul's willingness to apply OT terms for Israel to the church (Titus 1:1; cf. Rom 8:33; 16:13; Col 3:12; cf. BAGD, 242 [1b]; cf. Hendriksen, 252–54; Fee, 247). διὰ τοῦτο, "on account of this," could refer back to v 9 and Paul's suffering, or forward to τοὺς ἐκλεκτούς, "the elect." There is no significant difference in meaning.

10b ἵνα καὶ αὐτοὶ σωτηρίας τύχωσιν τῆς ἐν Χριστῷ Ἰησοῦ μετὰ δόξης αἰωνίου, "in order that they also may experience [the] salvation that is in Christ Jesus with eternal glory." Paul now specifies what it is about the elect that makes him willing to endure suffering. His concern is that they, as well as he (note the emphatic καὶ αὐτοί, "they also"), might be saved. The fact that Paul includes himself—who is already saved—shows that he is thinking primarily of their eschatological salvation, the fullness of salvation that will be theirs at the consummation of God's kingdom. This eschatological emphasis, present throughout the epistle (cf. *Comment* on 4:6– 8), is confirmed by the final phrase, μετὰ δόξης αἰωνίου, "with eternal glory." This contrasts with the elect's present possession of salvation, but more important in this context it contrasts with Paul's and Timothy's present suffering, encouraging them to persevere by looking toward what waits for them (cf. 2 Cor 4:17).

τυγχάνειν means "to attain, find, experience" and takes its object in the genitive (BAGD, 829[1]; cf. Luke 20:35; Acts 24:2; 26:22; 27:3; Heb 8:26; 11:35). On σωτηρία, "salvation," see *Introduction*, "Themes in the PE." This salvation is available only for those who are ἐν Χριστῷ Ἰησοῦ, "in Christ Jesus" (cf. 1 Tim 1:14). μετὰ δόξης αἰωνίου, "with eternal glory," is an essential element of the verse (contra Hanson, [1983] 132) as it takes Timothy's attention off his present suffering and focuses it on what is to come. On δόξα, "glory," see *Comments* on 1 Tim 1:11 and Titus 2:13, where Paul again associates glory and salvation (cf. 2 Cor 4:17). The glory is God's glory, lost in sin (Rom 3:23), given to the elect in the eschatological kingdom (cf. Knight, 400; cf. Rom 5:1–2; 8:21–25; 2 Thess 2:13–14).

11a πιστὸς ὁ λόγος, "Trustworthy is the saying." To emphasize his call to endurance, Paul cites the fifth and final faithful saying. The key connection is ὑπομένειν, "to endure" (vv 10, 12; cf. Knight, 402), but much of vv 11–13 speaks to Timothy's historical situation. The hymn discusses conversion and how it works itself out in different lives. *Line 1:* As Paul previously reminded Timothy of his spiritual heritage (1:3, 5), so here Timothy is reminded of his baptism and his obligation to a new life. *Line 2:* As Paul endures suffering (v 10), so should Timothy as he imagines what it will be like to reign with Christ in eternal glory. *Line 3:* The punishment for apostasy is severe, as Timothy's opponents may one day experience it (1:15; 2:14). *Line 4:* Temporary faithlessness does not nullify the faithful God who always acts in accordance with his character. Lock (92) paraphrases the passage:

> Who shares Christ's death His life shall share:
> They reign with Him their cross who bear:
> Who Him deny He will deny:
> Though our faith fall, He cannot lie.
>
> Nay, He cannot be untrue to himself.

(Lock views v 13c as Paul's comment on the hymn.) All this should encourage Timothy to endure suffering as a good soldier of Christ Jesus. See *Form/Structure/ Setting* for discussion of the form of the saying and the argument that vv 11b–13 are the saying, and see the *Form/Structure/Setting* on 1 Tim 1:12–17 for a discussion of the faithful sayings in general. There are three compound words formed with σύν, "with," but the hymn does not identify the one with whom the believer dies, lives, and reigns. The object of the denial is also unidentified as is the antecedent of "he" (κἀκεῖνος, v 12; ἐκεῖνος, v 13). Presumably in both cases it is Jesus Christ, whom Paul identifies in v 10. If vv 11b–13 are a hymnic fragment, presumably Jesus would have been identified earlier in the hymn (cf. *Comment* on v 12b).

11b *Line 1: Conversion:* εἰ γὰρ συναπεθάνομεν, καὶ συζήσομεν, "For, if we died together, we will also live together." Most agree that this first line refers to a believer's baptism and the new life that follows. Most also agree that it is very similar to Rom 6:8: "But if we died with Christ, we believe that we also will live together with him" (εἰ δὲ ἀπεθάνομεν σὺν Χριστῷ, πιστεύομεν ὅτι καὶ συζήσομεν αὐτῷ). In fact, most interpretive issues in 2 Tim 2:11 are determined by the meaning of Rom 6. There Paul appeals to the Roman Christians' remembrance of baptism, what it signified, and how that affected their current behavior. Believers died (ἀπεθάνομεν, first person plural) to sin, so they should not live (ζήσομεν, future tense referring to the writer's present) in sin (Rom 6:2). In baptism believers were buried together (συνετάφημεν) with Christ into death so that they might walk in newness of life (περιπατήσωμεν; Rom 6:4). The Romans passage continues to use first-person plural verbs, compounds using σύν, "with," and future-tense verbs describing the present-day obligations of baptized believers. (They are future from the time of baptism but present relative to the time of Paul's writing; or else they are true futures, but eschatological futures that have come into the present.) Interpreted in light of this background, 2 Tim 2:11 calls Timothy to think back to his conversion/baptism experience and how it should affect his present life.

A few variations on this interpretation have been offered. Some see line 1 as a reference to martyrdom (Bernard; Hendriksen; Brox; cf. Knight, *Faithful Sayings*, 115–18), interpreting the aorist συναπεθάνομεν, "died together," as a "single definitive act of self-devotion" (Bernard, 121). (1) But in light of the chronological flow of the hymn, the aorist more naturally refers to a past event and not a future martyrdom. The next phrase speaks of endurance during one's life. (2) It is an unusual choice of word to express martyrdom, especially when the idea of "dying with" Christ in the NT always refers to conversion/baptism (Rom 6:8; Col 2:20 [cf. 3:1]; cf. Gal 2:19: συσταυροῦσθαι, "to be crucified with"; Col 2:12: συνθάπτειν, "to be buried together"). συζήσομεν, "will live together," could refer to life in heaven—it would have to if "died together" is martyrdom—but the use of the future-tense verbs in Rom 6 to refer to the present allows this as the meaning here. συζᾶν, "to live together," is the second of three verbal compounds formed with σύν, "with"; the ν is lost in formation (cf. *MBG*, §24.6). In a confessional hymn, the "if" clause is a call to the worshipers to confess the truth of the assertion for themselves.

12a   *Line 2: Perseverance:* εἰ ὑπομένομεν, καὶ συμβασιλεύσομεν, "If we endure, we will also reign together." The second line moves into the present life of the believer. It also provides the primary tie-in to the context. Paul endures all things (v 10), Timothy should also, and as a result they will reign together with Christ in the eschatological kingdom. The consequences of not enduring are covered in the next two lines. Context requires εἰ to be translated "if" (cf. *Form/Structure/Setting*), and consequently the verse is both a promise ("If we endure, then we will reign") and an implied warning ("If we endure, and this is not to say that we will, then . . ."). See Moule on the use of conditional sentences (*Idiom-Book*, 149).

ὑπομένειν, "to endure," occurs in the PE elsewhere only in v 10 and in Paul only in Rom 12:12 and 1 Cor 13:7 (cf. Matt 10:22; Mark 13:13; Heb 10:32; 12:7; Jas 1:12; 5:11; 1 Pet 2:20; cf. Knight, 404). Its rarity in Paul heightens the connection between v 10 and v 12. Although it is not stated, the object of endurance is faithfulness to Christ as is shown by the compound verbs with σύν, "with," the emphatic "he" (ἐκεῖνος) in lines 3 and 4, and the idea of denying (Christ) (cf.

Knight, 405, 407). Throughout the NT, the concept of endurance involves suffering and temptation, and as such provides a powerful reminder to Timothy to endure the suffering in Ephesus (cf. Knight, *Faithful Sayings*, 120–23).

συμβασιλεύειν, "to reign together," occurs elsewhere in the NT only in 1 Cor 4:8, although Paul frequently uses the simple βασιλεύειν, "to rule," both literally (of Christ, 1 Cor 15:25; of God the Father, 1 Tim 6:15) and figuratively (of death, Rom 5:14, 17, 21a; of grace, Rom 5:21b; of sin, Rom 6:12; of the Corinthians, 1 Cor 4:8 [2x]; see also Matt 19:28; Luke 22:29–30; 1 Cor 6:2; Rev 1:6; 3:21; 5:10; 20:4, 6; 22:5). The eternal glory (v 10) that awaits the elect is the rule of believers with Christ in the eschatological kingdom (συμβασιλεύσομεν, "will rule together," is future).

12b *Line 3: Judgment:* εἰ ἀρνησόμεθα, κἀκεῖνος ἀρνήσεται ἡμᾶς, "If we will deny [Christ], he will also deny us." The third line makes several significant shifts (see *Form/Structure/Setting*). The implied warning in line 2 is the primary thrust of line 3. If believers do not endure and do apostatize, then Christ will claim before the judgment seat that he never knew them. The shift to the future tense may indicate that the saying is directed toward a Christian and not a mixed audience since the denial is a future possibility. (If it were directed to a mixed audience, the denial of nonbelievers would be present tense.) ἀρνεῖσθαι, "to deny" (cf. Knight, *Faithful Sayings*, 123–25), has a range of meanings from a refusal to do something, to a temporary denial such as Peter's, to full-blown apostasy (see *Comment* on 1 Tim 5:8). Because the punishment is Christ's denial, because of the close similarity to the saying of Jesus in Matt 10:33, and because the fourth line refers to temporary unfaithfulness, line 3 speaks of apostasy in its fullest sense (cf. Titus 1:16). In its historical context it is a warning to the Ephesians, especially Hymenaeus, Philetus (2:17), and possibly the deserting Asians (1:15), that their apostasy has serious consequences. Since the force of 2:1–7 is directed toward Timothy, he would also be included in the warning along with Paul and all believers.

κἀκεῖνος is a crasis of καί and ἐκεῖνος. It therefore continues the pattern of the previous two "then" clauses that are introduced by καί, "also," and ἐκεῖνος, "he," and creates an emphatic contrast between the human and divine activity. Although the object of ἀρνησόμεθα, "will deny," is not stated, it must be Christ (cf. Matt 10:33). The future ἀρνήσεται, "will deny," looks forward to the day of judgment and hence reinforces the eschatological emphasis of the saying and the passage as a whole.

13ab *Line 4: Faithlessness:* εἰ ἀπιστοῦμεν, ἐκεῖνος πιστὸς μένει, "If we are faithless, he remains faithful." The basic question of this line is whether it is a warning, like line 3, or a promise, like lines 1 and 2. If it is a warning (Lock, 96), then it says that God is faithful to punish unbelief (ἀπιστεῖν), and the line is repetitive of the third line. However, it is more likely that line 4 is a promise. Having described the two extremes of present-day endurance and future apostasy, the saying pulls back to an intermediate position—present-day faithlessness—and describes what happens in this situation. (1) If line 4 is a warning, it is awkward language. (2) Discussion of God's faithfulness to believers usually leads into the benefits enjoyed by believers, not into punishment (cf. Knight, 406; id., *Faithful Sayings*, 128–30). (3) The tense shift from the future (line 3) to the present (line 4), especially as it parallels the present-tense ὑπομένομεν, "endure" (line 2), suggests a change in topic from line 3. (4) The simple form μένει, "remains," ties in with the promise of reigning for those who are enduring (v 12a). (5) The change of verb from ἀρνεῖσθαι, "to deny," to ἀπιστεῖν, "to be faithless," suggests a change in topic. (6) As a warning, line 4 would be highly repetitive of line 3. (7) It appears that the hymn is trying to deal with the different responses to conversion (line 1). If it does not cover the common occurrence of temporary faithlessness, then it has omitted a large part of the Christian experience. This suggests that line 4 deals with the present-day faithfulness of God. (On ἀπιστεῖν meaning "to be faithless" and not "to disbelieve," see Knight, *Faithful Sayings,* 126–27; the former translation is required by the context.)

For these reasons, most see line 4 as a promise of assurance to believers who have failed to endure (line 2) but not to the point of apostasy (line 3). Peter's denial of Christ (Matt 26:69–75; Mark 14:66–72; Luke 22:54–62; John 18:15–17, 25–27) and his repentance and forgiveness (John 21:15–19) are often used as an illustration. This message was especially significant in the Ephesian context since their opposition to Paul entailed faithlessness to God. If Timothy was feeling defeated, it would also serve to encourage him. It is not clear why Dibelius-Conzelmann (109) say line 4 is irrelevant to the context of 2 Tim 2.

Another issue is the scope of the audience to whom Christ remains faithful. (1) He could remain faithful to the one who is faithless. (2) Christ could also remain faithful to all the elect despite the faithlessness of a few (cf. Rom 3:3). The former is to be preferred. All four verbs are first person plural ("we"), and the first three refer to the same group, the elect. It would be awkward if the fourth verb referred to another group, the nonelect who deny Christ. ἀπιστεῖν can mean "to disbelieve," and if line 4 is a warning, this would be appropriate. But it can also mean "to be faithless" (Knight, 406), and since it is parallel to Christ's faithfulness (πιστός; see *Introduction,* "Themes in the PE") in the next verse, that is its meaning here. The next phrase also clarifies what it means for God to be faithful.

13c ἀρνήσασθαι γὰρ ἑαυτὸν οὐ δύναται, "for he is unable to deny himself." The one thing that God must do is be consistent with his character (see *Explanation*), and in this context it means being faithful despite faithlessness. As Fee observes, "Eschatological salvation is for Paul ultimately rooted in the character of God" (251). Or as Guthrie states, "The moral impossibility of self-contradiction in God forms the basis of His faithfulness" (146). The structure of the fourth line is different from the preceding three (see *Form/Structure/Setting*) because it introduces a paradox. While the movement from "died . . . live," "endure . . . reign," and "deny . . . deny" is expected, the fact that human faithlessness is met by God's faithfulness is unexpected. While in the first three lines the reason for the "then" clause is contained in the "if" clause, in the fourth line God's faithfulness (the "then" clause) is not explained by human faithlessness (the "if" clause). The final phrase (v 13c) is therefore required to make sense of the fourth line (cf. Knight, *Faithful Sayings,* 135). As such it becomes the highlight of the saying, the fact of God's faithfulness being buried deep inside the graciousness of the covenantal God who always acts in conformity to his nature, which is the point made by the final phrase. It seems best to limit the scope of this promise just to the fourth line because only it requires explanation (although God's consistency is the basis for all that he does and hence the basis for the entire hymn). For God to remain faithful (v 13b) means that he is faithful to his character (v 13c). It is a magnificient promise and comfort to believers struggling in their Christian walk.

With this hymn Paul ends the first major section of the epistle and his encouragement to Timothy that he remain loyal to Paul and the gospel, and that he share in suffering for the gospel. Paul next turns to Timothy's Ephesian opponents.

Explanation

2 Tim 2:1–13 completes Paul's appeal to Timothy that he began in 1:3. It is built around four imperatives and concludes with the fifth faithful saying. Throughout the passage Timothy's historical situation is apparent. Timothy is to draw his strength daily from the grace of Christ Jesus. As he prepares to leave Ephesus to visit Paul, Timothy is to find men of good character who will teach the gospel faithfully. Until he leaves, Timothy is called to suffer willingly for the gospel. To help him think through the full implications of this charge, Paul uses three metaphors. (1) Timothy should suffer as a soldier with single-minded devotion, not leaving his ministry, so that God, the one who enlists him, will be pleased. (2) Timothy should suffer as an athlete who competes according to the rules so that he will win the victor's wreath. (3) Timothy should suffer as a farmer, working hard so that he will be able to share in the crop. While the idea of reward is not clearly visible in the first metaphor, it grows in importance in the final two. Partly because the central point of each metaphor may not be clear, partly because the latter metaphors enlarge the emphasis on reward, and partly because it is not immediately clear how the metaphors affect Timothy's life practically, Paul encourages Timothy to reflect on the metaphors, confident that God will illuminate his mind. Paul then gives a two-part summary of the gospel, emphasizing that it is the reason for his imprisonment and asserting that he is not ashamed of his suffering because of the benefits received by the elect. Implied is a call to Timothy likewise to embrace suffering for the gospel.

Paul concludes with a magnificent hymn, which regardless of origin speaks directly to Timothy and his historical situation and includes a strong eschatological emphasis. (1) Conversion: those who have died with Christ in their conversion/baptism will live with Christ in their post-conversion life (sanctification). (2) Perseverance: if during their lives as believers they continue to be faithful to God and persevere, then they will surely reign with Christ in heaven. (3) Apostasy: however, if some deny Christ, if through their lives they deny knowing him by their word and deed, then before the judgment seat Christ will also deny knowing them. (4) Faithlessness: however, if a believer fails to persevere fully but yet stops short of apostasy, God will remain true to his character, true to his promises, and therefore will remain faithful to that person (immutability of God).

While it has been argued that v 2 reflects Paul's desire for Timothy to put his effects in order and come to Rome, the church did develop the concept of formalized succession. Hanson ([1983] 128–29) cites *1 Clem.* 42 and 44 as a parallel, not teaching the doctrine of succession of an "authorized office" but a succession of teaching, written later than the PE and evidence of the development of the doctrine. This passage has been cited in the *Explanation* on 2 Tim 1:6–14 above. It seems anachronistic to speak of succession of teaching (see *Comment*). Bernard (117) says that "entrust these things" is symbolized in his tradition by handing a Bible to a newly ordained minister.

The call to reflection in v 7 is similar to what became known as illumination.

John teaches that one of the Holy Spirit's functions was to teach the disciples and to bring things taught to their remembrance (14:26) and to guide them into truth (16:13). This parallels Jesus' promise that the Holy Spirit would tell the disciples what to say when they were on trial (Matt 10:19–20; Mark 13:11; Luke 12:11–12) and the frequent teachings about the Holy Spirit revealing specific facts to people (Luke 2:26; Acts 11:28; 20:23; 21:4, 11; 1 Cor 2:10, 12–15; 1 Tim 4:1; cf. Eph 1:17–19; and Grudem, *Systematic Theology*, 644–45). Most Reformed cessationists assert that the Holy Spirit illuminates the mind of believers as they read Scripture. Grudem defines illumination as "the Holy Spirit's enabling of Christians generally to understand, to recall to mind, to apply the Scriptures they have studied" (*Systematic Theology*, 1041, citing R. Reymond, *What about Continuing Revelations and Miracles in the Presbyterian Church Today?* [Phillipsburg, NJ: Presbyterian and Reformed, 1977] 28–29). He adds, "Often, too, what is seen as prophecy is actually a spontaneous, Spirit-worked application of Scripture, a more or less sudden grasp of the bearing that biblical teaching has on a particular situation or problem. All Christians need to be open to these more spontaneous workings of the Spirit" (1041, citing R. Gaffin, *Perspectives on Pentecost* [Phillipsburg, NJ: Presbyterian and Reformed, 1979] 120). While 2 Tim 2:7 is not a full-blown exposition of the doctrine of illumination, it certainly is a basis of the doctrine in germinal form.

The theological affirmations of the faithful saying are too rich to expound here in detail. If v 11b is read in light of Rom 6, then it expresses the doctrine of sanctification, that the conversion/baptism experience involves not only a dying to the old life but a rising to a new kind of life in which sin has no place (cf. Grudem, *Systematic Theology*, 709–21, 746–62). The call to endurance in the second line teaches the need for saints to persevere, reflecting Jesus' teaching that it is only those who endure to the end who will be saved (Matt 24:13; cf. Grudem, *Systematic Theology*, 788–809). The third line asserts the absolute seriousness of apostasy after one has professed faith in Christ, giving a reminder of the fact of final judgment. The fourth line teaches the marvelous faithfulness of God whose promises to people remain despite the temporary faithlessness of some.

Perhaps the most significant phrase of the hymn is the final one—"for he is unable to deny himself." The doctrine of the immutability of God affirms that God "does not change like shifting shadows" (Jas 1:17 NIV), and therefore the God who gives good gifts will continue to do so. As Hebrews affirms, "He also says, 'In the beginning, O Lord, you laid the foundations of the earth, and the heavens are the work of your hands. They will perish, but you remain; they will all wear out like a garment. You will roll them up like a robe; like a garment they will be changed. But you remain the same, and your years will never end'" (Heb 1:10–12 NIV, citing Ps 102:25–27); "Jesus Christ is the same yesterday and today and forever" (Heb 13:8). It is because "I the LORD do not change" that "you, O descendant of Jacob, are not destroyed" (Mal 3:6; cf. Num 23:19; Deut 7:9; Titus 1:2; cf. Grudem, *Systematic Theology*, 163–64). God will never change, will always be true to his character, and will continue to be faithful as he has promised regardless of the believer's faithlessness. God's omnipotence does not include the possibility of self-contradiction. God's divine faithfulness is immutable; for God not to be faithful would be to cease being himself (Spicq, 2:750–51). As is so often the case, Christian theology stems from the very character of God.

IV. Instruction for Timothy and the Opponents (2 Tim 2:14–4:8)

A. Timothy and Opponents Contrasted (2 Tim 2:14–26)

Bibliography

Arndt, W. F. "ἔγνω, 2 Tim. 2:19." *CTM* 21 (1950) 299–302. **Brown, E. F.** "Note on 2 Tim 2:15." *JTS* o.s. 24 (1922–23) 317. **Browne, F. Z.** "What Was the Sin of Hymenaeus and Philetus?" *BSac* 102 (1945) 233–39. **Bunn, L. H.** "2 Timothy ii. 23–26." *ExpTim* 41 (1929–30) 235–37. **Hanson, A. T.** *Studies in the Pastoral Epistles.* 29–41. **Lane, W. L.** "1 Tim 4:13: An Instance of Over-Realized Eschatology." *NTS* 11 (1965) 164–67. **Metzger, W.** "Die neôtérikai epithymíai in 2 Tim. 2,22." *TZ* 33 (1977) 129–36. **Penna, A.** "'In magna autem domo . . .' (2 Tim 2:20–21)." In *Studiorum Paulinorum Congressus Internationalis Catholicus 1961.* AnBib 17–18. Rome: Biblical Institute, 1963. 119–25. **Sellin, G.** "'Die Auferstehung ist schon geschehen': Zur Spiritualisierung apokalyptischer Terminologie im Neuen Testament." *NovT* 25 (1983) 220–37. **Skiles, J. W. D.** "2 Tim 2:15 and Sophocles, Antigone 1195." *IB* 204–5. **Weiser, A.** "Die Kirche in den Pastoralbriefen: Ordnung um jeden Preis?" *BK* 46 (1991) 107–13. **Wilson, J. P.** "The Translation of 2 Timothy 2:26." *ExpTim* 49 (1937–38) 45–46.

Translation

[14]*Remind [them] of these things, solemnly charging [them] before God [a] not to continue fighting about words,[b] [which result] in [c] nothing beneficial, in [the] ruin of those listening.* [15]*Be diligent to present yourself before God as one tried and true, an unashamed worker, correctly handling the word of truth.* [16]*But shun the unholy chatter,[d] for they will advance into greater and greater ungodliness* [17]*and their message will spread like gangrene, among whom are Hymenaeus and Philetus,* [18]*who have fallen short concerning the truth, saying the [e] resurrection has already occurred, and they are overturning the faith of some.* [19]*Nevertheless, the firm foundation of God stands firm, having this seal, "The Lord knew [f] those who were his," and, "Let everyone naming the name of [the] Lord depart from unrighteousness."*

[20]*And in a large house there are not only vessels of gold and silver but also of wood and clay, that is, some for honor and others for dishonor.* [21]*If, therefore, someone cleanses himself from these things, that person will be a vessel for honor, having been sanctified,[g] useful to the master, prepared for every good work.*

[22]*So flee from youthful passions, but pursue righteousness, faith, love, peace, with [h] those who call upon the Lord out of a clean heart.* [23]*But avoid the foolish and uneducated speculations, knowing that they give birth to quarrels.* [24]*But it is necessary that a servant of [the] Lord not be quarrelsome but be gentle [i] to all, skilled in teaching, patient even in the midst of evil,* [25]*in meekness instructing those who oppose [you], if perhaps God might grant [j] them repentance leading to a knowledge of [the] truth,* [26]*and they*

might return to soberness out of the snare of the devil (having been captured alive by him) in order [to do] his will.

Notes

ᵃθεοῦ, "God" (א C F G I 614 629 630 1175 *al* a vg^mss sy^hmg sa^mss bo^pt), is replaced by κυρίου, "Lord" (A D Ψ 048 1739 1881 TR b vg sy sa^ms bo^pt), and Χριστοῦ, "Christ" (206 *pc*). See additional evidence in UBSGNT⁴. θεοῦ agrees with 4:1 and 1 Tim 5:4, 21 (so *TCGNT*, 579).

ᵇThe infinitive λογομαχεῖν, "to continue fighting about words" (א C³ D F G I Ψ 33 1739 1881 TR sy; Cl), is replaced by the imperative λογομάχει, "continue to fight about words" (A C* 048 1175 *pc* latt).

ᶜἐπ', "in" (א* A C F G I P 048 33 1175 1241 *pc*), is replaced by εἰς, "into" (א² D Ψ 1739 1881 TR).

ᵈκενοφωνίας, "chatter," is replaced by καινοφωνίας, "novel speech" (F G b d; Lcf Spec).

ᵉThe article τήν, "the" (A C D Ψ 1739 1881 TR), is omitted by א F G 048 33 *pc*. See *TCGNT*², 579–80.

ᶠא* inserts πάντας, "all," before τοὺς ὄντας, "those who were."

ᵍκαί, "and," is inserted before εὔχρηστον, "useful," by א² C* D¹ Ψ 1739 1881 TR lat sy^h; Or; it is omitted by א* A C² D* F G 048 33 629 *pc* it; Ambst.

ʰπάντων, "all," is inserted before τῶν, "those," by F and G. πάντων is inserted and τῶν dropped by C F G I 048^vid 33 81 104 326 *pc* sy^h sa bo^pt. A has πάντων τῶν ἀγαπώντων, "all those who love." The translation here is supported by א D Ψ 1739 1881 TR lat sy^p bo^pt. Cf. *TCGNT* ¹, 648.

ⁱἤπιον, "gentle" (א A C D² Ψ 048 33 1739 1881 TR sy co), is replaced by νήπιον, "infant" (D* F G).

ʲUBSGNT⁴ prefers the stronger reading δώῃ, "might grant," a second aorist subjunctive (א* A C D* F G Ψ 81 104 *pc*; cf. J. K. Elliott, "ΔΙΔΩΜΙ in 2 Timothy," *JTS* n.s. 19 [1968] 621–23). This follows the classical rule that if the main verb is a primary tense, the verb in a dependent clause is subjunctive. If the main verb is a secondary tense, the verb in the dependent clause is optative.

The variant δῷ is subjunctive (BDF §95[2]). This reading has significantly less support (א² D² 33 1739 1881 TR) and is the Byzantine reading since the second correctors of א and D traditionally follow the Byzantine tradition. However, since iota subscripts were not indicated in the uncial MSS, δώῃ could be δώῃ as Bernard reads it, and δώῃ is optative. It is the Hellenistic form of δοίη (cf. Rom 15:5; 2 Thess 3:16; 2 Tim 1:16, 18). According to the classical rules, this could be a grammatical error. Yet if the optative is voluntative, and especially if v 25a is concluded with a period and μήποτε starts a new sentence (see *Comment*), δώῃ could be a correct use of the optative, stating a wish not likely to be fulfilled. While the optative was dropping out in the Koine, it would have been used correctly when employed.

The optative occurs three other times in the PE (2 Tim 4:16), twice in a wish (2 Tim 1:16,18), and the sense of the optative fits the context here. Paul holds out the possibility of the opponents repenting, but he is not hopeful. If the optative is to be read, then μήποτε should start a new sentence (see RSV). The external evidence, however, favors the subjunctive δώῃ.

Form/Structure/Setting

2 Tim 2:14–4:8 constitutes the second major division in the body of 2 Timothy. In 1:1–2:13 Paul has been speaking directly, personally, to Timothy. The faithful saying in 2:11–13 discusses faithlessness and apostasy, and from there Paul moves into a specific discussion of the Ephesian problem. However, while Paul is thinking of the opponents and their teaching, he is thinking primarily of Timothy and how he should conduct himself. Even in v 17, when Paul speaks of "their [αὐτῶν] message," there is no explicit antecedent. 2 Timothy is a personal letter; Paul does not appear to expect the church to read it as he did 1 Timothy (but cf. 2 Tim 4:22).

Vv 14–19 form a paragraph of instructions, vv 20–21 express a metaphor, and vv 22–26 comprise a series of commands explaining what v 21 means when it speaks of Timothy "cleansing himself." Both v 20 and v 22 begin with δέ, "and, so," showing the connection of thought among all three paragraphs. Vv 14–26 form a single unit. 2 Tim 3:1–9 continues the discussion of the opponents, and in 3:10 Paul turns back to his personal discussion with Timothy; perhaps 2:14–3:9 should not be split.

The three paragraphs are built around negative injunctions of what Timothy should not do (vv 14, 16–17, 22a, 23) and positive injunctions of what he should do (vv 15, 20–21, 22b, 24–26). Interspersed are a description of the heresy (v 18) and encouraging comments to Timothy. Despite the inroads made by the opponents, God's seal on the elect stands firm (v 18). Timothy, as a servant of the Lord, should strive for the positive qualities along with all who call on the name of the Lord; Timothy is not alone in his task. The intended goal of Timothy's instruction is that God give the opponents the gift of repentance (v 25); God is very much in control of the Ephesian situation. Lock (97) points out how the section contrasts work (vv 15, 21, 26) with mere talk (vv 14, 16, 18, 23), and true speech (vv 15, 24 [2x], 25) with false (vv 14, 16, 17, 18, 23).

Comment

14 ταῦτα ὑπομίμνῃσκε διαμαρτυρόμενος ἐνώπιον τοῦ θεοῦ μὴ λογομαχεῖν, ἐπ᾽ οὐδὲν χρήσιμον, ἐπὶ καταστροφῇ τῶν ἀκουόντων, "Remind [them] of these things, solemnly charging [them] before God not to continue fighting about words, [which result] in nothing beneficial, in [the] ruin of those listening." In light of the call to perseverance and the consequences of apostasy (2:11–13), Timothy is to charge the Ephesians to stop their senseless arguing about words. As elsewhere in the PE, the reason for the charge is the result of the heresy: nothing beneficial is produced; it results only in the ruin of those who listen to it. The same idea of prohibition and result is repeated in v 23. This passage, 3:1–9, and 4:14–15 contain the only significant references in 2 Timothy to the opponents and their teaching.

The scope of ταῦτα, "these things," is debated (cf. *Comment* on 1 Tim 4:11). (1) It could refer to all the letter to this point, but much of the preceding has been personal and what follows has all the Ephesians in mind, so ταῦτα is more limited in scope. (2) Knight (409–10) argues that it refers to the "faithful men" of 2:2, but v 2 is far removed from v 14 and in vv 3–13 Paul is speaking to Timothy personally; he does not continue to discuss the "faithful men." (3) The faithful saying (2:11–13) is closer to v 14 and fits the contextual needs of vv 14–26. ὑπομίμνῃσκε, "remind," in the active means to remind others (BAGD, 846), and most supply the object "them" for the imperative (as well as for the following phrase, "solemnly charge [them]"; cf. "them" in v 17). The verb takes the accusative of the thing remembered (Moule, *Idiom-Book*, 37). The linear aspect agrees with the linear aspect of μὴ λογομαχεῖν, "not to continue fighting about words," and contrasts with the linear aspect of τῶν ἀκουόντων, "of those listening." The verb reminds the reader of Paul's earlier reflective mood as he remembered Timothy's tears and spiritual heritage and reminded Timothy to use his spiritual gift (1:4–6). But in this passage it gains added strength by the following phrase: this reminding is to be done by solemnly charging the Ephesians before God. The use of διαμαρτύρεσθαι, "to solemnly charge" (1 Tim 5:21; 2 Tim 4:1), with the intensifying preposition διά along with the prepositional phrase ἐνώπιον τοῦ θεοῦ, "before God" (cf. the following verse and 1 Tim 5:21; 6:13; 2 Tim 4:1; cf. Gal 1:20), enforces the seriousness of the heresy and the necessity of Timothy's resolve to fight it. λογομαχεῖν, "to fight about words," occurs only here in the NT; its cognate noun λογομαχία, "fight about words," occurs two times in the PE in similar condemnations of the Ephesian and Cretan heresies (1 Tim 6:4; Titus 3:9). It is a compound verb (μάχεσθαι, "to fight," about λόγος, "word") meaning "to dispute about words, split hairs" (BAGD, 477; "word-warriors" [Lock, 97]). Knight gives too much credibility to the heresy by saying that these words were a "kind of serious dispute about the meaning and significance of words relating to the Christian faith" (410). If this were the case, Timothy would not have been told to avoid the dispute. Throughout the PE the Ephesian heresy is pictured as having little substance being merely a quibbling about words (see *Introduction* and 1 Tim 1:4). Paul is not saying that arguing is wrong; he is saying that Timothy should not argue about words, an arguing that results only in uselessness and ruin.

The reasons why Timothy should not argue about senseless words are given in two prepositional phrases. Both are introduced by ἐπί, "[which result] in," and indicate result (BAGD, 287 [II1bϵ]). χρήσιμος, "beneficial," occurs only here in the NT. The verse stands in contrast to Titus 3:8, which states that those who believe in God should devote themselves to good works and that the result of this is good and profitable. καταστροφή, "ruin, destruction," occurs elsewhere in the NT only in a questionable reading in 2 Pet 2:6, stating that God condemned Sodom and Gomorrah to ruin. Guthrie (147) says that etymologically it means "turning upside down" and hence is the antithesis of edification. ἀκούειν, "to listen," also carries the nuance of doing (cf. 1 Tim 4:16). Arguing about words ruins those who listen and participate in the arguments.

15 σπούδασον σεαυτὸν δόκιμον παραστῆσαι τῷ θεῷ, ἐργάτην ἀνεπαίσχυντον, ὀρθοτομοῦντα τὸν λόγον τῆς ἀληθείας, "Be diligent to present yourself before God as one tried and true, an unashamed worker, correctly handling the word of truth." Timothy is to take pains to present himself before God as one who has been tested and found to be genuine. This genuineness is shown by two characteristics: teaching and conduct. In contrast to the opponents' myths and misconduct, Timothy is to teach the true gospel and behave in accordance with its teachings, his teaching and conduct acting as a deterrent to the opponents.

The most difficult issue in the verse is the precise meaning of ὀρθοτομεῖν, "to handle correctly." However, while its specific nuance is debated, its general thrust is clear. In contrast to the opponents, perhaps with regard to both their beliefs and their behavior, Timothy is to deal correctly with the gospel message, perhaps both its teaching and the manner of life to which it calls (cf. Spicq, 2:755). ὀρθοτομεῖν occurs only here in the NT. It is a compound verb: τέμνειν, "to cut," ὀρθός, "straight." It is used in nonbiblical Greek in connection with ὁδός, "way," meaning "to cut a straight path." There has been much discussion of the precise nature of the metaphor: a mason cutting stone, a farmer cutting a straight furrow (Chrysostom), and other suggestions, with the emphasis on "the *straightness* with which the work of cutting or laying out is performed" (Ellicott, 123). Chrysostom emphasizes the idea of "to cut": to "cut away what is spurious, with much vehemence assail it, and extirpate it. With the sword of the Spirit cut off from your preaching, as from a thong, whatever is superfluous and foreign to it" ("Homily 5"; NPNF 13:493). ὀρθοτομεῖν occurs in the LXX in Prov 3:6; 11:5 (cf. 1QH 12:34), both in connection with ὁδός. However, ὁδός does not occur in this passage, and most agree that the imagery of the original metaphor has been lost

(Dibelius-Conzelmann, 11; H. Köster, *TDNT* 8:112) and that the emphasis is on the adjective ὀρθός (MM, 456), "straight," hence "right, correct" (see discussions in MM, 456–57; H. Köster, *TDNT* 8:111–12; BAGD, 580; *TLNT* 2:595; R. Klöber, *NIDNTT* 3:352). This is paralleled by the cognate adverb ὀρθῶς, "correctly," used to describe the answering of a question (Luke 10:28; 20:21), and by the similar verb ὀρθοποδεῖν, "to walk straight," a metaphor for correct behavior (Gal 2:14). The adjective ὀρθός can also mean "straight, correct" (BAGD, 580), and according to Klöber was used in secular Greek for "ethically correct behavior" and in the wisdom literature for "the kind of right attitude, speech, and action that accords with a proper relationship to Yahweh. It does not describe a virtue as much as a relationship" (*NIDNTT* 3:351).

From this are established two basic interpretations of ὀρθοτομεῖν. Both fit the contextual needs of Timothy's stance contrasted with the Ephesian myths and opponents. (1) "Right interpretation of the gospel." Here the primary contrast is between the rightness of the gospel as interpreted by Paul and Timothy and the wrongness of what is taught by the opponents arguing about words. This points in the direction of the cognate ὀρθοτομία and the related ὀρθοδοξία, which are used to indicate "orthodoxy" in later Christian writers (but see Köster, *TDNT* 8:112 n. 11). Spicq also mentions ὀρθοέπεια, "correct language," as the rule in Greek dialectic, "expressing oneself with exactness" (*TLNT* 2:595). (2) "Right behavior in line with the gospel." Here the emphasis is on Timothy's behavior, that it be in line with the gospel and that it be in contrast to the opponents. This agrees with the emphasis in the PE on the necessity of right conduct both in Paul's condemnation of the opponents' misconduct and in the repeated reminder to Timothy to observe his own conduct (cf. 1 Tim 4:6–16). It also agrees with the emphasis on conduct in this paragraph (2:14–18) and the repetition of the same ideas in 2:20–26. Perhaps the rarity of ὀρθοτομεῖν should serve as a caution against making too precise a distinction between the two options, especially in light of the theme in the PE that right belief and right conduct go hand in hand. Treating the gospel correctly cannot stop at right belief but must move into right conduct, and in fact vv 16–18 discuss both behavior and belief.

σπούδασον, "be diligent," describes a zeal or eagerness to do something (cf. Titus 3:12). The KJV's "study" is misleading in today's English. παραστῆσαι, "to present," combined with τῷ θεῷ, "before God," recalling the solemn warning before God in the previous verse, can move into the meaning "to make, render" and even "to prove, demonstrate" (cf. Acts 24:13; BAGD, 627 [1c,f]). To the Colossian Christians Paul says that Christ reconciled them by his death in order to present (παραστῆσαι) them holy and blameless and irreproachable before God (Col 1:22). In contrast, Paul tells the Corinthians that food does not commend (παραστήσει) them to God (1 Cor 8:8). δόκιμος carries the meaning of being tried and as a result of the test being found to be genuine, approved, hence "tried and true" (BAGD, 203; cf. Rom 16:10; 1 Cor 11:19; 2 Cor 10:18; 13:7). σεαυτόν, "yourself," contrasts Timothy with the opponents. ἐργάτης, "worker" (cf. 1 Tim 5:18), can be used figuratively for false apostles (2 Cor 11:13) and evil workers (Phil 3:2) and also for Christian workers (cf. συνεργός, "coworker" [Rom 16:21; 1 Thess 3:2], and κοπιᾶν, "to work" [1 Tim 4:10; 5:17; 2 Tim 2:6]). The language may remind Timothy of Paul's earlier words about the hard-working soldier, athlete, and farmer (2:3–7). Paul will use similar language to encourage Timothy to

work hard as an evangelist (4:5). ἀνεπαίσχυντος, "not ashamed," is formed with
an alpha privative (ἀν- before vowels; BDF §124). It could refer to shame of the
gospel, as in 1:8, but in this context it more likely refers to Timothy's conduct (cf.
Phil 1:20); Timothy is to do his ministry such that he will not be ashamed of it,
perhaps with the eschatological nuance of standing before God in the judgment
(see also E. F. Brown, *JTS* o.s. 24 [1923] 317). The λόγον τῆς ἀληθείας, "word of
truth," is the gospel (cf. *Comment* on 1 Tim 4:6); this is the only time in the PE
that the actual phrase occurs (but cf. Col 1:5 and Eph 1:13), but there are similar
phrases in the PE. On λόγος, "word," see *Comment* on 1 Tim 4:5, and on ἀλήθεια,
"truth," see *Comment* on 1 Tim 2:4.

16 τὰς δὲ βεβήλους κενοφωνίας περιΐστασο· ἐπὶ πλεῖον γὰρ προκόψουσιν
ἀσεβείας, "But shun the unholy chatter, for they will advance into greater and
greater ungodliness." Part of correctly handling the word of truth (v 15) is avoiding the Ephesian heresy, the arguing about words (v 14), which is really godless
chatter. One reason for doing so is that the opponents are moving toward ungodliness and will carry their followers with them. (The second reason comes in v
17.) Chrysostom emphasizes that what appears to be a single error will produce
multiple evils, hence "advancing. For it appears indeed to be a solitary evil, but
see what evils spring out of it" ("Homily 5"; NPNF 13:493).

βεβήλους κενοφωνίας, "unholy chatter," repeats the same phrase from 1 Tim
6:20 (on βέβηλος, "unholy," cf. *Comment* on 1 Tim 1:9), describing talk that is in
direct opposition to God. It is synonymous with ματαιολογίαν, "senseless babble"
(1 Tim 1:6), βεβήλους καὶ γραώδεις μύθους, "profane and silly myths" (1 Tim 4:7),
and λογομαχίας, "empty words" (1 Tim 6:4); they all describe the Ephesian heresy, emphasizing its lack of content, and as elsewhere Paul encourages Timothy
to stay away from it (cf. Titus 3:9). Their speech is "irreligious and frivolous hair-
splittings" (Lock, 97). The presence of the article τάς, "the," identifies the chatter
specifically as the Ephesian heresy (cf. ὁ λόγος, "the message," in v 7). Paul does
not discourage argumentation, nor is this a call for isolationism, but wisdom calls
for avoidance of fruitless discussion that only produces envy and strife. As Guthrie
comments on v 16b, "particular attention is paid to the devastating influence of
these godless chatterboxes, whose trivialities lead to increasing ungodliness" (148).

περιΐστασο, "shun" (cf. Titus 3:9; cf. ἐκτρεπόμενος, "avoiding," in 1 Tim 6:20),
is the Pauline parallel to Jesus' statement "Do not throw your pearls before swine"
(Matt 7:6) in that certain situations are best avoided. προκόπτειν, "to advance"
(cf. 2 Tim 3:9 [οὐ προκόψουσιν ἐπὶ πλεῖον, "they will not progress very far"]; 3:13;
and Gal 1:14), means "to go forward, make progress" for good or bad (followed
by the genitive; BAGD, 707–8; cf. cognate προκοπή, "progress," in 1 Tim 4:15)
and is sarcastic. The opponents think they are progressive, advancing in their
religion, but the only thing they are advancing in is ungodliness. There is no
expressed subject for προκόψουσιν, "they will advance," as there is no expressed
object twice in v 14, but the opponents can be supplied from the context, explicitly from αὐτῶν, "their," in v 17. Lock paraphrases, "Those who take part in them
will go forward—on a downward grade of impiety" (97). On ἀσέβεια, "ungodliness," see Titus 2:12 and the related words ἀσεβής, "godless" (1 Tim 1:9), and
εὐσέβεια, "godliness" (1 Tim 2:2). πλεῖον, as the comparative of πολύς, means
"more." Here it is used substantivally with a partitive genitive meaning "an even
greater [measure] of ungodliness" (BAGD, 689 [II2c]). The same basic phrase,

οὐ προκόψουσιν ἐπὶ πλεῖον, "they will not progress very far," occurs in a similar context in 3:9. To see developed Gnosticism in this verse goes beyond the text (contra Hanson, [1983] 135), the words all finding a natural meaning in the traditional Ephesian context.

17a καὶ ὁ λόγος αὐτῶν ὡς γάγγραινα νομὴν ἕξει, "and their message will spread like gangrene." The second reason Timothy and the Ephesians are to avoid the godless chatter of the opponents (v 16a) is because the sickening effects of their teaching will spread throughout the church as if it were gangrene in a body. The false teachers are advancing in ungodliness, and their teaching is eating away at the spiritual flesh of the church.

λόγος, "message," contrasts with the "word [λόγον] of truth" Timothy is to handle correctly (v 15). This contrast, along with the fact that the term is articular (cf. the articular τὰς . . . βεβήλους κενοφωνίας, "the unholy chatter," in v 16), gives assurance that Paul is speaking not of their speech in general (contra Bernard, 123) but of the heretical teaching itself. γάγγραινα is "gangrene, cancer of spreading ulcers" (BAGD, 149; contra Hanson, [1983] 135, who says it does not mean "ulcer" but cites no references; LSJ, 335, lists only "gangrene"). Bernard (123) says it is used of flesh-eating sores. It is a common medical term used as early as Hippocrates. It is used here figuratively, emphasizing the heresy's ability both to spread and to destroy. νομή is also a medical term. Its nonfigurative meaning is "pasture," and it is used figuratively for the "spreading" of disease (Galen *De simpl. medicam. temp. et fac.* 9, cited by Dibelius-Conzelmann, 111 n. 10; Bernard, 123; BAGD, 541), perhaps creating an image of sheep spreading over a pastureland. For the use of medical imagery in the PE, see *Comment* on 1 Tim 1:10.

17b ὧν ἐστιν Ὑμέναιος καὶ Φίλητος, "among whom are Hymenaeus and Philetus." Paul identifies two of the opponents by name (cf. 1 Tim 1:20) and will continue by describing their heretical instruction. Presumably they were leaders since they are singled out. Hanson ([1983] 135) feels that the two names are part of the reliable historical record, i.e., that they are actual opponents of Paul, but he gives no reason why they should be viewed as such, again illustrating the difficulty of any theory of reliable historical fragments supposedly woven into the text. Philetus is never mentioned again (MM, 670); because the name Hymenaeus is unusual, it may be assumed that he is the same person paired with Alexander and excommunicated by Paul in 1 Tim 1:20. Evidently the excommunication was not effective, and Hymenaeus was still opposing Paul and Timothy. Rather than indicating that 2 Timothy was written before 1 Timothy, these references show the difficulty in conducting church discipline over a long distance and the seriousness of the problem in Ephesus (cf. Kelly, 184; Fee, 258–59).

18 οἵτινες περὶ τὴν ἀλήθειαν ἠστόχησαν, λέγοντες [τὴν] ἀνάστασιν ἤδη γεγονέναι, καὶ ἀνατρέπουσιν τήν τινων πίστιν, "who have fallen short concerning the truth, saying the resurrection has already occurred, and they are overturning the faith of some." This is one of the few places in the PE where the content of the heresy is specified (see *Introduction*, "The Ephesian Heresy," for further discussion), and it functions as an example of the spread of the opponents' diseased teaching (v 17). The preaching of the bodily resurrection is a central element in Paul's theology. To deny the bodily resurrection is to deny Christ's resurrection, and if Christ is not raised, then the gospel message is empty (1 Cor 15:12–17). To deny the resurrection is to deny the truth of the gospel. But the doctrine came under early attack in Corinth (1 Cor 15:12) and elsewhere (2 Thess 2:1–2). Many suggest that Paul's teaching of spiritual death and rising to life (2 Tim 2:11; Rom 6:1–11; Col 2:20–3:4; cf. Eph 2:6; 5:14) had been perverted by replacing the bodily with the spiritual resurrection and hence denying the bodily resurrection (see also Lock, 7, 99; Scott, 56; Browne, *BSac* 102 [1945] 233–39; Spicq, 2:757–58; Lane, *NTS* 11 [1965] 164–67). This perversion would have been strengthened by the prevailing philosophical dualism that saw material as evil—cf. the Athenian ridiculing dismissal of any notion of a bodily resurrection (Acts 17:32)—and often resulted in asceticism or an indifference toward immorality. 1 Tim 4:3 shows that asceticism was part of the Ephesian heresy, which denied both marriage and the goodness of food, and the lack of morality is attested throughout the PE. The Ephesian problem may have been closer to that in Thessalonica than in Corinth since in the latter the fact of the resurrection was denied while in the former it was spiritualized (although these two positions can be merged more closely). Issues of the validity of the resurrection continued, and continue (e.g., Process Theology), to plague the church (see *Explanation*). While the heresy was a far cry from full-blown second-century Gnosticism, the opponents were headed in that direction (cf. Kelly, 185; Oberlinner, 98, who says this unambiguously confirms that the heresy was an early form of Gnosticism). Baur (*Pastoralbriefe*, 38) sees this as a reference of Marcion's teaching, and many Gnostics did argue that they would never die (citations in Lock, 99–100, who also cites the belief held by some that there was no resurrection but that people lived on through their posterity).

οἵτινες, "who," has no generalizing force (i.e., "whoever") because it refers to two specific people. It can be used synonymously for the relative pronoun or "qualitatively . . . to emphasize a characteristic quality, by which a preceding statement is to be confirmed," hence "insofar as" (BAGD, 587, which views it as equivalent to the relative pronoun; cf. Wallace, *Greek Grammar,* 343–45). ἀστοχεῖν means "to miss the mark, fall short" and is used elsewhere in the PE in the same context (cf. 1 Tim 1:6; 6:21). ἀλήθεια, "truth," is the true gospel message (cf. 1 Tim 2:4), correctly handled by Timothy (v 15) and contrasted with the godless chatter (v 16) of the opponents. The time element of γεγονέναι, "has occurred" (BAGD, 158–59 [I3]), is emphasized by the adverb ἤδη, "already." ἀνατρέπειν, "to overturn," occurs in the PE elsewhere only in Titus 1:11 in a similar context. Both of these verbs emphasize the present disastrous effects of the heresy and justify Paul's urgency. Although πίστιν, "faith," is articular, it means personal faith, as the addition τινῶν, "of some," clarifies (see *Introduction*, "Themes in the PE").

19a ὁ μέντοι στερεὸς θεμέλιος τοῦ θεοῦ ἕστηκεν, "Nevertheless, the firm foundation of God stands firm." Despite the success of Hymenaeus, Philetus, and the other opponents in leading some of the Ephesians astray (v 18), Timothy and Paul can be encouraged because the foundation of the elect (cf. v 10) will not be moved. θεμέλιος, "foundation" (cf. 1 Tim 6:19), is generally understood to refer to a corporate entity such as the church (1 Tim 3:15), the foundation consisting of the apostles (Eph 2:20) or Christ himself (1 Cor 3:11; cf. Hanson, [1983] 137). This is consistent with Paul's usage and with the following discussion of the usefulness of vessels in a house (vv 20–21). However, the emphasis in this passage is on individuals. (1) The firm foundation is in contrast to Hymenaeus, Philetus, and those (τινῶν) who have been led astray. (2) While θεμέλιος is singular, the first part of the following seal is the plural τούς, "those." (3) The second part speaks of "everyone naming the name of [the] Lord." (4) The discussion of vessels (vv 20–21) leads into Paul's admonition that Timothy, personally, remove himself from evil and the opponents. Therefore, it is preferable to see the foundation as the individuals who are firmly elect, not being swayed by the heresy.

μέντοι, "nevertheless," is adversative, separating the opponents from the true believers. στερεός means "firm, hard, solid, strong" (BAGD, 766; cf. Heb 5:12, 14; 1 Pet 5:9). στερεός is attributive (Robertson, *Grammar*, 656) and modifies θεμέλιος. The perfect tense of ἱστάναι is intransitive (BAGD, 382 [II2c]) and means "stand firm" (cf. Rom 11:20; 1 Cor 10:12), emphasizing the force of the previous στερεός.

19b ἔχων τὴν σφραγῖδα ταύτην, "having this seal." The firmness of God's foundation is described by the seal that God has placed on it. The metaphor is based on the practice of inscribing a seal on the foundation of a building in order to indicate ownership and sometimes the function of the building (cf. the seal of the twelve disciples on the foundation of the new Jerusalem in Rev 21:14). The following two phrases specify what the seal actually says; it was common to have the seal contain a motto or short phrase (Lyall, *Slaves*, 151).

σφραγίς, "seal" (cf. cognate verb σφραγίζειν, "to seal," and BAGD, 796), can indicate the seal itself or the mark made by the seal (Dan 6:17; Matt 27:66; especially the references in Rev 5:1, 2, 9; 6:1, 3, 5, 7, 9, 12; 7:2; 8:1; 9:4). It is often used figuratively as an indication of ownership, protection, and authentication (cf. Guthrie, 150; G. Fitzer, *TDNT* 7:939–53; R. Schippers, *NIDNTT* 3:497–501; O. Tufnell, *IDB* 4:255; Lyall, *Slaves*, 148–52). For example, the Holy Spirit is the seal, the guarantee of the promise given to all Christians (2 Cor 1:22; Eph 1:13). The Corinthians are the seal of Paul's apostleship (1 Cor 9:2). The sign of circumcision is Abraham's seal of his righteousness by faith (Rom 4:11; cf. also John 3:33; 6:27; Eph 4:30; Rev 7:3). Because the emphasis is on God's ownership and protection, it is unnecessary to place weight on the symbol itself as Hanson ([1983] 137) does by identifying the seal as baptism.

19c ἔγνω κύριος τοὺς ὄντας αὐτοῦ, "The Lord knew those who were his." This is a citation from Num 16:5 LXX. When Korah, Dothan, and the 250 leaders rebelled against Moses' leadership, he replied, "God has visited and known those who were his [ἔγνω ὁ θεὸς τοὺς ὄντας αὐτοῦ] and who were holy, and he brought [them] to himself, and whom he chose for himself he brought to himself." Paul has already introduced the topic of election in 1:9 and 2:10, and Arndt makes a good case that this is the meaning of ἔγνω, "knew," here (*CTM* 21 [1950] 299–302), citing R. Bultmann (*TDNT* 1:689–719; cf. 1 Cor 8:3; 13:12; and Gal 4:9). It is God's prior knowledge in election that assures Timothy that despite the success of the opponents the elect are safe. To read ἔγνω as a present tense is to treat it as a gnomic aorist, a rare use of the aorist that in fact some say does not occur in the NT (cf. Wallace, *Greek Grammar*, 562). It also seems doubtful that a single event (election) could be represented as gnomic.

19d καί· ἀποστήτω ἀπὸ ἀδικίας πᾶς ὁ ὀνομάζων τὸ ὄνομα κυρίου, "and, 'Let everyone naming the name of [the] Lord depart from unrighteousness.'" The second statement on the seal is one of the most strongly worded demands in Scripture, that obedience to the ethical demands of the gospel are mandatory, not optional. For Paul, to call on the name of the Lord *is* to depart from unrighteousness (see

Comment on Titus 2:11 and *Explanation* on Titus 2:11–15). The statement does not come from any one OT passage (but cf. Num 16:26). Most of the passages suggested as possible sources seem at best to be remote possibilities, and the idea of "depart from unrighteousness" is too general (cf. Ps 34:14; Prov 3:7; Isa 52:11). Lock (100) sees both statements coming from the account of Korah, but both modified by Jesus (citing Matt 7:23 and Luke 13:27): "Whatever false teachers may say, the solid foundation-stone of God's Temple has been fixed once for all; and on it are two inscriptions carved first by Moses and renewed by Our Lord: one tells of God's knowledge, 'The Lord knoweth them that are His own'; the other of man's duty, 'Let every one who worships the Lord depart from iniquity'" (97). ὀνομάζων τὸ ὄνομα, "naming the name," is roughly equivalent to "call(s) on the name" (e.g., 1 Kgs 18:24 [2x], 25; 2 Kgs 5:11; Ps 116:3, 17; Zeph 3:9; Acts 2:21; 1 Cor 1:2), "name" being metonymy for the Lord himself (cf. Isa 26:13). By emphasizing the necessity of righteous living, the seal disqualifies the opponents whose lives are filled with sin. Paul feels no tension, as is often the case in modern discussions, in placing the doctrines of election and sanctification side by side. ἀφιστάναι, "to depart," is used in the PE elsewhere only in 1 Tim 4:1, where it means "to apostatize." ἀδικία, "unrighteousness," occurs in the PE only here (cf. δίκαιος, "righteousness," in 1 Tim 1:9; 2 Tim 4:8; Titus 1:8; Rom 1:8; 2:8; 2 Thess 2:10–12).

20 ἐν μεγάλῃ δὲ οἰκίᾳ οὐκ ἔστιν μόνον σκεύη χρυσᾶ καὶ ἀργυρᾶ ἀλλὰ καὶ ξύλινα καὶ ὀστράκινα, καὶ ἃ μὲν εἰς τιμὴν ἃ δὲ εἰς ἀτιμίαν, "And in a large house there are not only vessels of gold and silver but also of wood and clay, that is, some for honor and others for dishonor." Building from the requirement of godly living established in v 19, Paul begins a new paragraph and urges Timothy to righteous conduct. V 20 is the metaphor, v 21 interprets the metaphor, and vv 22–26 spell out the specific terms of how Timothy is to behave. As is true throughout the letter, these injunctions are an encouragement for Timothy to "stay the course"; they do not indicate that Timothy has fallen into sin.

Paul has already used the metaphor of vessels in Rom 9:21–24. There he speaks of God's sovereignty in choosing certain vessels for honor (εἰς τιμὴν σκεῦος), vessels of mercy (σκεύη ἐλέους) prepared for glory (δόξαν), as well as vessels of wrath (σκεύη ὀργῆς) prepared for dishonor (εἰς ἀτιμίαν) and destruction (ἀπώλειαν). The emphasis is on God's sovereignty and the inappropriateness of a creature questioning the election by the creator. Jeremiah also speaks of God's freedom to do as he chooses, using the image of a potter and clay (Jer 18:1–11; cf. Wis 15:7). In 2 Cor 4:7 Paul uses σκεῦος, "vessel," to describe Christian ministers as ὀστρακίνοις σκεύεσιν, "earthen vessels," emphasizing that the transcendent power of the ministry belongs to God and not to them. (Paul's metaphor of the church as a body with many necessary parts is a somewhat related, and yet decidedly different, metaphor in both form and meaning.) Paul should not be expected to use the same metaphor with the same or related significance in 2 Tim 2:20. 2 Cor 4:7 shows that Paul willingly alters the force of the same imagery from context to context. The dominant note of God's sovereignty in Rom 9 is absent in 2 Tim 2 (cf. C. Maurer, *TDNT* 7:364). V 21 starts with οὖν, "therefore," insisting that it alone, not Rom 9, offers interpretation of the metaphor. If Paul had used the metaphor of vessel with more frequency, then perhaps it could be insisted that it have meaning in and of itself apart from the context. But he did not, and so primary interpretive significance is given to v 21.

δέ, "and," has no adversative force. σκεῦος, "vessel," denotes any object used for any purpose, but it is used especially of household vessels such as jars and dishes (BAGD, 754). Paul speaks of a μεγάλη, "large," house to create a picture of a house with a wide range of jars and dishes. Some vessels would have been made of gold (χρυσοῦς; cf. 1 Tim 2:9) or silver (ἀργυροῦς). These would have been the vessels for public meals. Other vessels were made of wood (ξύλινος; cf. Lev 15:12; Num 31:20; 35:18) and clay (ὀστράκινος, a word often used with σκεῦος, suitable to describe that which is breakable or ordinary [cf. 2 Cor 4:7; BAGD, 587]). These could be vessels used for private meals, or for less honorable uses such as for garbage or excrement, vessels often discarded with their contents. The καί, "that is," after ὀστράκινα, "clay," is epexegetical, further explaining these two categories. The gold and silver vessels are designed and function for honorable uses (εἰς τιμήν). The wood and clay vessels are for dishonorable uses (εἰς ἀτιμίαν).

At this point the metaphor ends. εἰς, "for," indicates the purpose of the metaphor (BAGD, 229 [4d]). τιμή, "honor," is used elsewhere of reverence toward God (1 Tim 1:17; 6:16), elders (1 Tim 5:17), and masters (1 Tim 6:1). Vessels that are εἰς τιμήν, "for honor," could mean that their designed purpose is honorable, or the phrase could describe their actual usage, i.e., for honorable functions. Perhaps the distinction is overly subtle. Within the context of the metaphor, honorable use refers to vessels set aside for the special use of public meals when gold and silver vessels would be appropriate. However, the choice of the term may also have been governed by the application of the metaphor in v 21. ἀτιμία, "dishonor," occurs only here in the PE but repeatedly in Paul (Rom 1:26; 9:21 [in a similar metaphor]; 1 Cor 11:14; 15:43; 2 Cor 6:8; 11:21).

21 ἐὰν οὖν τις ἐκκαθάρῃ ἑαυτὸν ἀπὸ τούτων, ἔσται σκεῦος εἰς τιμήν, ἡγιασμένον, εὔχρηστον τῷ δεσπότῃ, εἰς πᾶν ἔργον ἀγαθὸν ἡτοιμασμένον, "If, therefore, someone cleanses himself from these things, that person will be a vessel for honor, having been sanctified, useful to the master, prepared for every good work." Paul now interprets the metaphor of v 20. If Timothy wants to be a useful vessel for God, he must cleanse himself by fleeing lusts (v 22a), pursuing righteousness (v 22b), and avoiding the Ephesian heresy (v 23). As a servant of the Lord he must not be quarrelsome but be kind and gentle (v 24). This is how Timothy is to deal with his opponents (vv 25–26). Chrysostom emphasizes that here Timothy makes a choice while in 2 Cor 4:7 the same metaphor describes not volition but nature ("Homily 6"; NPNF 13:496). That this is the basic message of the metaphor is clear. However, two questions remain. How far is the metaphor to be pressed? To what extent, if any, does the metaphor relate to the metaphor in Rom 9?

As the metaphor is related to the Ephesian context, it makes a correspondence between honorable vessels of gold and silver and the role Timothy is to play if he cleanses himself. One of the questions, however, is the identity of the dishonorable vessels of wood and clay. Do they correspond to the opponents? Does the large house correspond to the church in which good and bad people coexist as in the parable of the net (Matt 13:24–30, 36–43)? Does the large house correspond to society in general in which there are believers (i.e., honorable vessels) and nonbelievers (i.e., dishonorable vessels) such as Hymenaeus and Philetus? Do the dishonorable vessels correspond to anything, or by insisting that they have a correspondence is the metaphor being pressed beyond the limits of what Paul intended? Perhaps the level of disagreement among writers and the lack of clarity at this point suggest that the metaphor is being pressed too far. Perhaps all Paul is doing is creating a picture in Timothy's mind of a large house with a wide variety of jars and dishes and telling him that if he wants to be like honorable vessels he must cleanse himself. The less honorable vessels of wood and clay only serve to emphasize the difference between the two types of vessels, somewhat as some details of a parable only help to create a picture but are not necessarily part of the application of the parable to real life. If the details of the metaphor are to be pressed, it should be emphasized that the metaphor does not say that the wood and clay vessels actually are of less honor. It says that they are for dishonorable uses.

The indefinite ἐὰν . . . τις, "if someone," makes the application of the metaphor applicable to all believers, much like the title "servant of the Lord" in v 24 and the "everyone naming the name of [the] Lord" in v 19. What is specifically meant by ἐκκαθαίρειν, "to cleanse" (cf. 1 Cor 5:7; also καθαρίζειν, "to cleanse," especially in 2 Cor 7:1), is spelled out by the imperatives in the following verses, which describe general spiritual purification as well as dealing specifically with the Ephesian opponents. The perfective ἐκ should be felt: "to cleanse thoroughly." The antecedent of τούτων, "these things," is not easily identified. The closest antecedent is the "vessels [σκεύη] of wood and clay . . . for dishonor." If the metaphor is to be pressed, in the Ephesian context the dishonorable vessels are the opponents and their teaching, perhaps as represented by Hymenaeus and Philetus (v 17). (To separate the teachers from the teaching is counter to the close association between the two expressed in the PE.) If this part of the metaphor is not to be pressed, then τούτων simply means that which dishonors.

What it means to be a σκεῦος εἰς τιμήν, "vessel for honor," is spelled out by three modifiers: (1) If ἡγιασμένον, "having been sanctified," is the result of Timothy cleansing himself (ἐκκαθάρῃ ἑαυτόν), then it cannot mean justification since it is the result of human effort. However, if ἡγιασμένον is equated with justification, then Timothy's cleansing of himself is the result of and is empowered by God's prior work. In 1 Tim 4:5 ἁγιάζειν, "to sanctify," is used of ceremonial cleansing, and that could be its nuance here (cf. Rom 15:16; 1 Cor 6:11; Eph 5:26). The passive voice (ἡγιασμένον) is in line with the usage of the word elsewhere in Paul to indicate that God is effecting sanctification (except 1 Cor 7:14). 1 Thess 4:3–4, which uses ἁγιασμός, "sanctification," is parallel in thought. Timothy cleanses himself, and in response God cleanses Timothy, the human and divine intertwined. (2) εὔχρηστον τῷ δεσπότῃ, "useful to the master," within the context of the metaphor refers to the master of the house, but in its application it refers to God. To be useful to God is a goal of Timothy and all believers (cf. v 15), and to be useful one must "flee from youthful passions" (v 22). On εὔχρηστος, "useful, serviceable" (BAGD, 329), see Comment on 2 Tim 4:11 and Phlm 11. δεσπότης, "master," is used elsewhere in the PE of masters of slaves (1 Tim 6:1–2; Titus 2:9), but here of God (cf. Luke 2:29; Acts 4:24; 2 Pet 2:1; Jude 4; Rev 6:10). (3) ἑτοιμάζειν, "to make ready, prepare," occurs ten times in the NT as a middle/passive (Matt 20:23; 25:34, 41; Mark 10:40; 2 Tim 2:21; Rev 9:7, 15; 12:6; 16:12; 21:2), always with God as the agent, and this could be the case with ἡτοιμασμένον, "prepared." However, because the emphasis of the context is on Timothy cleansing himself, ἡτοιμασμένον could be a reflexive middle, "having prepared himself." It would then be analogous to the call that Timothy be an unashamed workman, correctly handling the gospel message. εἰς, "for," is replaced by πρός, "for," in 3:17 with no apparent shift in meaning (Moule, *Idiom-Book*, 68). ἔργον ἀγαθόν, "good work," is a common theme in the PE, placing emphasis on the practical outworking of the gospel (cf. 1 Tim 2:10).

22 Τὰς δὲ νεωτερικὰς ἐπιθυμίας φεῦγε, δίωκε δὲ δικαιοσύνην πίστιν ἀγάπην εἰρήνην μετὰ τῶν ἐπικαλουμένων τὸν κύριον ἐκ καθαρᾶς καρδίας, "So flee from youthful passions, but pursue righteousness, faith, love, peace, with those who call upon the Lord out of a clean heart." This verse begins the third paragraph in this section. Having called on Timothy to purify himself (v 21), Paul gives two of the three imperatives that spell out specifically what that entails. By balancing the negative ("flee ... avoid") with the positive ("pursue"), Paul emphasizes that both are necessary parts of ministry. The verse should be viewed against the backdrop of the opponents, who do not exhibit these qualities.

The first δέ is difficult to translate. It is more than a simple connective because there is a contrast between being an honorable vessel (v 21) and fleeing from lusts (v 22). The context requires an inferential sense, "therefore, so." What follows is similar to 1 Tim 6:11: Σὺ δέ, ὦ ἄνθρωπε θεοῦ, ταῦτα φεῦγε· δίωκε δὲ δικαιοσύνην εὐσέβειαν πίστιν ἀγάπην ὑπομονὴν πραϋπαθίαν, "But you, O man of God, flee these things, but pursue righteousness, godliness, faith, love, endurance, gentleness." See there for a discussion of the words that occur in both verses. νεωτερικὰς ἐπιθυμίας, "youthful passions," could refer to the sensual lusts of youth (cf. 1 Tim 4:12; 5:2; Titus 2:6), but the following verses do not speak about this issue. While these may be included, the emphasis is more on Timothy's youthful temperament and the possible difficulty of avoiding arguments and being gentle in instruction (cf. Kelly, 188–89; Fee, 263, who translates "headstrong passions of youth," citing W. Metzger, *TZ* 33 [1977] 129–36). In this context, "youthful passions" include that which is contrary to "righteousness, faith, love, and peace" (v 22b). νεωτερικός, "youthful," occurs only here in the NT (cf. νεότης, "youth," in 1 Tim 4:12). On ἐπιθυμία, "passion," see *Comment* on 1 Tim 3:1.

In contrast (δέ, "but"), Timothy should pursue certain virtues. δικαιοσύνη, "righteousness," is used of the ethical demands placed on the person who has been made righteous, an unusual but yet not unknown use of the term in Paul (cf. *Comment* on 1 Tim 1:9). It is "the right conduct of man which follows the will of God and is pleasing to Him" (G. Schrenk, *TDNT* 2:198). To pursue πίστις, "faith," is to pursue the consequences of having faith, hence "faithfulness" (cf. 1 Tim 1:2). ἀγάπη, "love," is something a believer possesses (cf. 1 Tim 1:5) but also should be pursued (cf. Col 3:14). In this context it is love for one another, not for God. Likewise, εἰρήνη, "peace" (cf. 1 Tim 1:2), is a possession (cf. Rom 5:1; Paul's salutations and benedictions) but also something to be pursued (cf. Rom 8:6; 14:19; 1 Cor 7:15; 14:33; 16:11; 2 Cor 13:11; Gal 5:22; Eph 4:3; Col 3:15). The final prepositional phrase, μετὰ τῶν ἐπικαλουμένων τὸν κύριον ἐκ καθαρᾶς καρδίας, "with those who call upon the Lord out of a clean heart," modifies δίωκε, "pursue"; hence this call is true for all believers, in Ephesus and elsewhere. As such it ostracizes those whose hearts are not cleansed and whose behavior is contradictory to these virtues. "To call on the (name of the) Lord" is common terminology in the OT (Gen 12:8; 13:4; Judg 15:18; 1 Kgs 18:24; 2 Kgs 5:11; Pss 116:4, 13, 17; 118:5; Zeph 3:9; cf. Str-B 3:658). While it can be used of those who pray in the NT (Acts 2:21), it is normally broader in scope as it describes those who align themselves with the Lord (Acts 9:14, 21; 15:17; 22:16; Rom 10:12, 13, 14; 2 Cor 1:23; cf. 1 Cor

1:2). As such it is synonymous with the earlier phrase "everyone naming the name of [the] Lord" (v 19). κύριος, "Lord," specifically is Christ since the phrase is a description of Christians. But Timothy is joined not by all those who call on the Lord but by those whose call comes from a cleansed heart (see the same expression in 1 Tim 1:5). καθαρός, "clean," is a cognate of the key verb ἐκκαθαίρειν, "to cleanse," in v 21, confirming that vv 22–26 are the explanation of v 21.

23 τὰς δὲ μωρὰς καὶ ἀπαιδεύτους ζητήσεις παραιτοῦ, εἰδὼς ὅτι γεννῶσιν μάχας, "But avoid the foolish and uneducated speculations, knowing that they give birth to quarrels." This is the third imperative defining how Timothy should cleanse himself (v 21). In contrast to (δέ, "but") the positive δίωκε, "pursue," parallel with the negative φεῦγε, "flee," Timothy is παραιτεῖσθαι, "to avoid" (1 Tim 4:7; Titus 3:10), the Ephesian heresy. This verse is similar to the injunctions in 1 Tim 4:7 and Titus 3:9, which use many of the same words and also describe the effects of the heresy as the motive for avoiding them. Paul is not speaking about speculations in general, although pointless speculations that lead to quarrels would be included. He is speaking of "the [τάς] . . . speculations," the heresy. μωρός means "foolish, stupid" (cf. 1 Tim 4:7; Titus 3:9).

ἀπαίδευτος occurs only here in the NT. It means "uninstructed, uneducated" (BAGD, 79; Hanson, [1983] 141). Dibelius-Conzelmann show that in Epictetus it means "the man who has not learned to think" (113). In the LXX, it translates כְּסִיל kĕsîl, most often in the wisdom literature (Prov 8:5; 15:14; Abbott-Smith, Lexicon, 44), hence "foolish, undisciplined." Most suggest a meaning such as "illiterate, ill-informed, undisciplined, senseless." However, since the opponents saw themselves as teachers of the law even though they were ignorant of it (1 Tim 1:7), and because Paul is speaking specifically of the heresy, it is best to keep the etymological nuance of the word, "uneducated," and see it as an appraisal of the heresy and its proponents. This is also supported by the use of the cognate verb in v 25, παιδεύοντα τοὺς ἀντιδιατιθεμένους, "instructing those who oppose [you]." ζήτησις, "speculation" (cf. 1 Tim 6:4; Titus 3:9; ἐκζήτησις, "speculation," in 1 Tim 1:4), a common description of the heresy, emphasizes its lack of content. As usual, the reason Timothy should avoid the heresy is that (εἰδώς, "knowing," is causal) the heresy gives birth (see figurative use of γεννᾶν, "to give birth to," in 1 Cor 4:15; Phlm 10) to μάχας, "quarrels" (cf. Titus 3:9 and "fighting about words" [λογομαχία, 1 Tim 6:4; λογομαχεῖν, 2 Tim 2:14]), rather than divine stewardship (1 Tim 1:4).

24a δοῦλον δὲ κυρίου οὐ δεῖ μάχεσθαι, "But it is necessary that a servant of [the] Lord not be quarrelsome." Building on the statement in the previous verse that the heresy gives birth to quarrels (μάχας), Paul adds in contrast that Timothy must (δεῖ; cf. Comment on 1 Tim 3:2) not quarrel, using the cognate verb μάχεσθαι, "to be quarrelsome." He is to avoid controversies and to treat people gently. The qualities enumerated here and in v 25a are similar to the qualities required of church leaders in 1 Tim 3 and Titus 1.

δέ, "but," not only contrasts the opponents' behavior (which forms the backdrop to vv 22–23) with Timothy's behavior, but it helps contrast "quarrels" (v 23) with "not be quarrelsome" (v 24). Paul uses the general title "servant of [the] Lord" in keeping with the generalized terminology of v 21 (cf. Paul's self-designation as a "servant of God" in Titus 1:1). The indefinite δοῦλον, "a servant," and the parallel expression "servant of (Jesus) Christ" (Rom 1:1; 2 Cor 11:23; Gal 1:10; Eph 6:6;

Phil 1:1; Col 4:12; cf. 1 Cor 7:22; 2 Cor 4:5) describing Christian workers both show that the scope of the phrase extends beyond Timothy to Christian leaders in general (cf. the indefinite "if someone" [v 21] and "man of God" [1 Tim 6:11; 2 Tim 3:17]). It does not apply to the Christian laity since the following requirement, "skillful in teaching," is not appropriate for all Christians. κύριος, "Lord," probably refers to Jesus: κύριος in v 22 is Jesus; δοῦλος is most often associated with Christ (Knight, 423). Kelly (190) and Lock (101) suggest that the imagery is drawn from the servant songs of Isaiah (Isa 42:1–3; 53). μάχεσθαι, "to be quarrelsome" (cf. John 6:52; Acts 7:26; Jas 4:2), means "to fight with words" (BAGD, 496). The call not to quarrel is essentially the same as the previous charge to avoid the heresy (v 23) since the quarrels are specifically those caused by the speculations of the heresy. It is a requirement of church leaders that they not quarrel (1 Tim 3:3; cf. Titus 1:7).

24b ἀλλὰ ἤπιον εἶναι πρὸς πάντας, διδακτικόν, ἀνεξίκακον, "but be gentle to all, skilled in teaching, patient even in the midst of evil." ἀλλά, "but," establishes the contrast between "to be not quarrelsome" and the four positive injunctions that follow. Along with avoiding quarrels, Timothy is to conduct himself in a positive way that will also deal with the heresy. The following characteristics are to be understood not in general but against the backdrop of the opponents' misconduct.

(1) Timothy must be ἤπιος, "gentle, kind," just as Paul was gentle among the Thessalonians (1 Thess 1:7, a verse that also arises out of a context of conflict). But Timothy is to be kind to all, that is, not only to the faithful Ephesians but also to the opponents. In the next verse Paul will tell Timothy to be meek in his dealings with the Ephesians. Despite the difficult circumstances and the obvious tension, there is no call to stoop to their level; Timothy is to be gentle just as all church leaders are to be gentle (1 Tim 3:3; cf. Titus 1:7–8). Paul tells Titus that the Cretans are to show "complete gentleness [πραΰτητα] toward all people" (Titus 3:2). Chrysostom provides a helpful discussion of how Timothy and Titus are to balance their need to rebuke sharply with authority (1 Tim 4:12; Titus 1:13; 2:15): "A strong rebuke, if it be given with gentleness, is most likely to wound deeply: for it is possible, indeed it is, to touch more effectually by gentleness, than one overawes by boldness. . . . How is it then that he says, 'A man that is an heretic, after the first and second admonition, reject'? He speaks there of one incorrigible, of one whom he knows to be diseased beyond the possibility of cure" ("Homily 6"; NPNF 13:497).

(2) Timothy and the church leaders must be διδακτικός, "skilled in teaching," an ability required of all overseers (cf. 1 Tim 3:2), since the opponents saw themselves as teachers (1 Tim 1:7) and must be confronted with right doctrine. (3) A servant of the Lord must also be "patient even in the midst of evil." This periphrastic translation of ἀνεξίκακος (occurring only here in the NT) brings out the nuance of "bearing evil without resentment" (BAGD, 65). This word carries the nuance of patience within the context of adversity or pain as is suggested by its etymology (ἀνέξομαι, "I will endure" [future of ἀνέχομαι], and κακός, "evil"). This nuance is appropriate in the context of the conflict between Timothy and the opponents. Chrysostom emphasizes that patience is of supreme importance for a teacher, "for he that hears often will at length be affected" ("Homily 6"; NPNF 13:497).

25a ἐν πραΰτητι παιδεύοντα τοὺς ἀντιδιατιθεμένους, "in meekness instructing those who oppose [you]." The fourth positive characteristic of the Lord's servant is that he instruct those in opposition and that the instruction be characterized by πραΰτης, "humility, courtesy, meekness" (BAGD, 699). The Cretans are likewise encouraged to be gentle toward all people (πραΰτητα πρὸς πάντας ἀνθρώπους, Titus 3:2; cf. 2 Thess 3:15 and Gal 6:1, which is in a similar context of gentle correction).

παιδεύειν can mean "to instruct, educate" (cf. cognate noun in 3:16; Acts 7:22), which would be appropriate for the goal of having them repent concerning the "knowledge of [the] truth," a description of the gospel that emphasizes its cognitive element. It also reminds Timothy of the previous description of the heresy as ἀπαίδευτος, "uneducated" (v 23). However, παιδεύειν can also have the negative nuance of "to correct, discipline" as it does in 1 Tim 1:20 (cf. BAGD, 603–4), a nuance that would be appropriate within the context of a call to repentance. Because both nuances fit the immediate context, it is best to view both as present (see *Comment* on Titus 2:12).

ἀντιδιατιθεμένους is a rare word and therefore difficult to translate. It could be middle voice, "opposing oneself, being opposed" (BAGD, 74). As such Paul would be speaking about the opponents as he is in the similar phrase τοὺς ἀντιλέγοντας, "those who oppose" (Titus 1:9). ἀντιδιατιθεμένους could also be passive, "those adversely affected" (Bernard, 127), i.e., the laity affected by the opponents. Fee (267) argues that Paul uses other words for the leadership of the opposition and so follows Bernard. In this context of instructing and hoped-for repentance (vv 25b–26), is it more likely that Paul is speaking of the opponents or of their followers among the laity? The scope of "those who oppose [you]" can be defined by the previous "be gentle to all" (v 23), which is universal. However, v 25b discusses repentance, a goal held out for the opponents elsewhere in the PE (cf. 1 Tim 1:20). Because the language of being captured by Satan is strong (perhaps too strong for describing the laity) and elsewhere Satan is seen as active among the leaders of the opposition (cf. discussion at 1 Tim 1:20), ἀντιδιατιθεμένους should be viewed as middle voice ("those who oppose [you]") and as speaking of the opponents, and this verse should be seen as adding a further dimension to Timothy's manner of dealing with them. Although he has the authority to stand in judgment of them and rebuke them, he is to do so in meekness (see discussion of ἤπιος, "gentle," in *Comment* on v 24). Others may plant and water, but God effects the change (cf. 1 Cor 3:6).

25b μήποτε δώῃ αὐτοῖς ὁ θεὸς μετάνοιαν εἰς ἐπίγνωσιν ἀληθείας, "if perhaps God might grant them repentance leading to a knowledge of [the] truth." Paul spells out the two goals of Timothy's prescribed behavior. The first is the repentance of the opponents and their subsequent turning to the true gospel. As always in the PE, the goal of confrontation is remedial (cf. 1 Tim 1:20); punishment is not an end in itself. As an encouragement to Timothy, Paul emphasizes God's sovereign control over the Ephesian situation; it is God who gives repentance (cf. Acts 5:31; 11:18).

μήποτε, "if perhaps," can be a weak interrogative particle. Owing to the widening of the meaning of the subjunctive (δώῃ, "might grant"; cf. J. K. Elliott, "ΔΙΔΩΜΙ in 2 Timothy," *JTS* n.s. 19 [1968] 621–23; Moule, *Idiom-Book*, 157), the grammar does not give us a clue regarding whether Paul felt the opponents would repent. It is possible that v 25a should end in a period and μήποτε should introduce an independent sentence (cf. use in Matt 25:9; John 17:26; and possibly Acts 5:39), although normally μήποτε introduces a dependent clause. If δώῃ (subjunctive) should be read δῴη (optative, see *Note* j), then μήποτε should start a new sentence. αὐτοῖς, "them," looks back to τοὺς ἀντιδιατιθεμένους, "those who oppose [you]," the opponents.

μετάνοια, "repentance," is not a common word for Paul (cf. Rom 2:4; 2 Cor 7:9, 10; μετανοεῖν, "to repent," 2 Cor 12:21), but it is common elsewhere. It indicates a change of mind, a turning toward the knowledge of the truth. But repentance also demands a change of attitude and behavior (cf. Acts 20:21; 26:20; Heb 6:1; cf. BAGD, 512) in line with the demands of forgiveness (Matt 3:8; Spicq, *TLNT* 2:471–77). εἰς indicates a goal (cf. BAGD, 229 [4]), hence "leading to." ἐπίγνωσιν ἀληθείας, "knowledge of [the] truth," is commonly used in the PE for the gospel, emphasizing its cognitive, truthful, element, but it moves beyond a theoretical knowledge to fullness of knowledge gained by experience (cf. 1 Tim 2:4).

26a καὶ ἀνανήψωσιν ἐκ τῆς τοῦ διαβόλου παγίδος, "and they might return to soberness out of the snare of the devil." The second consequence of Timothy as the Lord's servant following Paul's instructions (vv 24–25a) is that the opponents would escape from the snare, set by the devil, in which they are trapped. Once again Satan is seen as active in the Ephesian heresy (cf. 1 Tim 1:20), specifically in setting snares (cf. 1 Tim 3:7), and the heresy is seen as the teachings of demons (1 Tim 4:1).

ἀνανήφειν means "to become sober," "to come to one's senses again" after drinking. It is often used figuratively in the spiritual/ethical realm (BAGD, 58). Although it occurs in the NT only here, the ideas of νηφάλιος, "temperate" (1 Tim 3:2, 11; Titus 2:2), and σεμνός, "serious," "sensible" (1 Tim 3:8; Titus 2:2, 7 [σεμνότης]), are present throughout the PE. Paul continues by speaking of the opponents being snared, and hence he mixes his metaphors. Most pass over the first metaphor, translating it with "escape," but Bernard's translation (127) is followed here. Paul does not specify the exact nature of the snare; in the similar phrase in 1 Tim 3:7 the snare is luring the Ephesians into behavior that would bring reproach on the church. On παγίς, "snare," see *Comment* on 1 Tim 3:7; on διάβολος, "devil," see *Comment* on 1 Tim 3:6.

26b ἐζωγρημένοι ὑπ' αὐτοῦ εἰς τὸ ἐκείνου θέλημα, "(having been captured alive by him) in order [to do] his will." In this section the final description of the ensnared opponents is that they have been captured—and held in captivity (ἐζωγρημένοι is perfect passive with emphasis on their present state of captivity)—by Satan's snare. ζωγρεῖν, "to capture alive" (BAGD, 340), occurs elsewhere in the NT only in Jesus' comment that Peter will catch people, not fish (Luke 5:10). On θέλημα, "will," see *Comment* on 2 Tim 1:1.

The major issue of the phrase is the antecedent of αὐτοῦ, "him," and ἐκείνου, "of that one" (cf. Wilson, *ExpTim* 49 [1937–38] 45–46). (1) Most ignore the fact that Paul uses different pronouns and refer both back to the closest possible antecedent, διαβόλου, "devil"; the opponents have been ensnared by Satan to do Satan's will. To do Satan's will is to bring reproach upon the church, among other things. Kelly says this option is the "least objectionable" (192). It has the advantage of finding its antecedent in the immediately preceding context. It has the disadvantage of ignoring the difference in the pronouns. When there were two possible antecedents in classical Greek, αὐτός referred to the nearer antecedent and ἐκεῖνος to the more remote, but this distinction was breaking down in the Koine, and ἐκεῖνος could substitute for the personal pronoun (BDF §291.6; Wallace, *Greek Grammar*, 329; Bernard; Easton; Kelly; Hanson, [1983] 143; most citing Wis 1:16). The variation can also be explained by a desire not to repeat αὐτοῦ (Dibelius-Conzelmann, 114; cf. also Hanson's discussion, [1983] 143). (2) The second interpretation sees αὐτοῦ as referring back to the δοῦλον κυρίου, "servant of [the] Lord" (v 24a), and ἐκείνου back to θεός, "God" (v 25b; so Bengel, Falconer, Lock). It requires that Paul now be speaking not of the opponents' present condition but of the future consequences of repentance. If the Lord's servant does his job, God may grant mercy to the opponents, who are ensnared by Satan but now have repented and are captured by the Lord's servant to do God's will. This interpretation has the advantage of differentiating between the two pronouns. But it would be unusual for αὐτοῦ to refer not to the closer antecedent but to the more remote one, and "servant of [the] Lord" is quite a few words back. It would be a strange concept to be captured by the Lord's servant (2 Cor 10:5 is not parallel). Most of all, the required shift to future repentance must be unnaturally inserted before the verse. (3) The third possibility sees αὐτοῦ as referring to the devil (as does the first option) and ἐκείνου to God (as does the second option; Bernard, Scott, Jeremias, Guthrie, Barrett). The opponents have been captured by the devil, but if Timothy does his task and the opponents repent, then the opponents will do the will of God. While this interpretation suffers some of the drawbacks of the second, it is more plausible in that it finds a much closer antecedent of αὐτοῦ. Also, instead of inserting the notion of repentance as does the second option, the participial phrase "having been captured by him" is viewed as parenthetical and the verse is seen as a continuation of the positive element of repentance in v 25. God might give them repentance, and they might escape the devil's snare (in which they are trapped) so that they might do God's will. This produces a smooth reading of the text and recognizes the change in pronouns as something more than stylistic. αὐτός and ἐκεῖνος occur in the same verse three other times in the PE, and in each case they refer to two different antecedents (2 Tim 1:18; 3:9; 4:8). 2 Tim 3:9 is especially helpful since it follows the classical rule of αὐτός referring to the near antecedent and ἐκεῖνος to the distant one.

Explanation

In light of the call to perseverance and the consequences of apostasy (2:11–13), Paul turns his attention to the opponents and instructs Timothy on how to deal with them and how he should conduct himself. As is true throughout the PE, it is the consequences of the heresy and the behavior of the opponents that are sufficient cause for Timothy not even to enter into debate with them but simply to avoid them. While there is some content to the heresy (it denies the resurrection), most of it is quibbling about words, and hence there is no way to deal with it in a substantial manner. The two leaders, Hymenaeus and Philetus, are identified by name, the former having already been excommunicated but still leading.

But avoidance is only half of the cure. Timothy must take pains to conduct himself properly. This involves being tested and found to be a true worker, unashamed of his work, correctly teaching and living the message of the gospel. It involves striving to be an honorable vessel for the master, fleeing youthful passions and pursuing those qualities not found in the opponents, qualities such as righteousness, faith, love, and peace.

There is much in this section to encourage Timothy. Despite the success of the opponents, Timothy can be assured that those who truly belong to God have a firm foundation and will not be swayed. One way to identify these people is to note their behavior since the elect are called to holiness. Therefore Timothy as the Lord's servant must not be quarrelsome as are the opponents but be gentle and patient as he deals with the problems, the ultimate goal being the opponents' repentance and inclusion back into the church. Even in this, Timothy can draw encouragement since God is in control, giving the gift of repentance so the opponents can escape from the power of Satan and once again do God's will. There is a reminder that the ultimate source of the heresy is Satan.

Despite the centrality of the bodily resurrection in Paul's theology and elsewhere (cf. Acts 2:32; 3:26; 4:2, 33; 17:18; 23:6; 26:6–8; Rom 10:9), the doctrine came under early and serious attack. As early as 1 Thessalonians there was at least some misconception about the doctrine (1 Thess 4:13–5:11). By the time of 2 Thessalonians (2:1–12) and 1 Corinthians (15:12–58) there were people denying the reality of the physical resurrection. This may have resulted from a misreading of Paul's doctrine of the believer's spiritual death and resurrection combined with the prevailing philosophical dualism and incipient Gnosticism. The fact of the resurrection could be simply asserted in the early writings of the church (cf. *Didache* 16:6; the Apostles' Creed ["I believe in . . . the resurrection of the body"]; the Nicene Creed ["I look for the resurrection of the dead"]). However, at times the church fathers wrote in defense of the reality of the bodily resurrection in such a way that it is clear that the doctrine continued to be denied.

1. Polycarp *Letter to the Philippians* 7.1–2 (c. A.D. 110).

For everyone "who does not confess that Jesus Christ has come in the flesh is antichrist"; and whoever does not acknowledge the testimony of the cross "is of the devil"; and whoever twists the sayings of the Lord to suit his own sinful desires and claims that there is neither resurrection nor judgment—well, that person is the first-born of Satan. Therefore let us leave behind the worthless speculation of the crowd and their false teachings, and let us return to the word delivered to us from the beginning; let us be self-controlled with respect to prayer and persevere in fasting, earnestly asking the all-seeing God "to lead us not into temptation," because, as the Lord said, "the spirit is indeed willing, but the flesh is weak." (tr. Lightfoot, *Apostolic Fathers*, 126–27)

2. *2 Clem.* 9:1–5 (c. A.D. 100–130).

And let none of you say that this flesh is not judged and does not rise again. Understand this: In what state were you saved? In what state did you recover your sight, if it was not while you were in this flesh? We must, therefore, guard the flesh as a temple of God. For just as you were called in the flesh, so you will come in the flesh. If Christ, the Lord who saved us, became flesh (even though he was originally spirit) and in that state called us, so also we will receive our reward in this flesh. (tr. Lightfoot, *Apostolic Fathers*, 72)

3. Justin *1 Apology* 26.4–5 (c. A.D. 150). Justin introduces the Samaritan magician Simon, who was viewed by many as a god but was actually demonically inspired. Then Justin introduces his disciple Meander.

And a man, Meander, also a Samaritan, of the town Capparetæa, a disciple of Simon, and inspired by devils, we know to have deceived many while he was in Antioch by his magical art. He persuaded those who adhered to him that they should never die, and even now there are some living who hold this opinion of his. (ANF 1:171)

Dialogue with Trypho 80

For if you have fallen in with some who are called Christians, but who do not admit this [truth], and venture to blaspheme the God of Abraham, and the God of Isaac, and the God of Jacob; who say there is no resurrection of the dead, and that their souls, when they die, are taken to heaven; do not imagine that they are Christians, even as one, if he would rightly consider it, would not admit that the Sadducees, or similar sects of Genistæ, Meristæ, Galilæans, Hellenists, Pharisees, Baptists, are Jews (do not hear me impatiently when I tell you what I think), but are [only] called Jews and children of Abraham, worshipping God with the lips, as God Himself declared, but the heart was far from Him. But I and others, who are right-minded Christians on all points, are assured that there will be a resurrection from the dead, and a thousand years in Jerusalem, which will then be built, adorned, and enlarged, [as] the prophets Ezekiel and Isaiah and others declare. (ANF 1:239)

4. *Acts of Paul* 3.11–14 (*Acts of Paul and Thecla;* c. A.D. 180). When Thecla refused to marry Thamyris, he found Demas and Hermogenes, who had already been introduced as pretending to love Paul but did not. It should be noted that the reference to the resurrection is not present in one Syriac and two Latin manuscripts or in the manuscript read by Ambrosiaster (Zahn, *Introduction* 2:129). Bernard (123) argues that it is based on the 2 Timothy passage and does not reflect reliable second-century information.

But Thamyris sprang up and went out into the street, and closely watched all who went in to Paul and came out. And he saw two men quarreling bitterly with one another, and said to them: "You men, who are you, tell me, and who is he that is inside with you, the false teachers who deceive the souls of young men and maidens, that they should not marry but remain as they are? I promise now to give you much money if you will tell me about him; for I am the first man of this city."

And Demas and Hermogenes said to him: "Who this man is, we do not know. But he deprives young men of wives and maidens of husbands, saying 'Otherwise there is no resurrection for you, except ye remain chaste and do not defile the flesh, but keep it pure.'" . . .

But Demas and Hermogenes said: "Bring him before the governor Castellius, on the ground that he is seducing the crowds to the new doctrine of the Christians, and so he will have him executed and thou shalt have thy wife Thecla. And we shall teach thee concerning the resurrection which he says is to come, that it has already taken place in the children whom we have, and that we are risen again in that we have come to know the true God." (Henneke-Schneemelcher, *New Testament Apocrypha*, 2:356–57)

5. Irenaeus *Against Heresies* (c. A.D. 190). In *Against Heresies* 2.31.2 Irenaeus describes false miracle-workers and authentic resurrection miracles.

They do not even believe this can possibly be done, [and hold] that the resurrection from the dead is simply an acquaintance with that truth which they proclaim. (ANF 1:407)

Cf. Irenaeus *On the Resurrection* (ANF 1:294–99) and Athenagoras (ANF 2:149–62). For additional references, see Zahn (*Introduction* 2:129–30 [§37 n. 17]).

B. The Presence of Eschatological Evil (2 Tim 3:1–9)

Bibliography

Bévenot, M. "An 'Old Latin' Quotation (II Tim. III,2) and Its Adventures in the MSS. of St. Cyprian's *De Unitate Ecclesiae.*" In *Studia Patristica,* ed. K. Aland and F. L. Cross. Berlin: Akademie, 1957. 249–53. **Burchard, C.** "Das Lamm in der Waagschale: Herkunft und Hintergrund und eines haggadischen Midrasches zu Ex 1:15–22." *ZNW* 57 (1966) 219–28. **Grabbe, L. L.** "The Jannes/Jambres Tradition in Targum Pseudo-Jonathan and Its Date." *JBL* 98 (1979) 393–401. **Koch, K.** "Das Lamm, das Ägypten vernichtet: Ein Fragment aus Jannes und Jambres und sein geschichtlicher Hintergrund." *ZNW* 57 (1966) 79–93. **McEleney, N. J.** "The Vice Lists of the Pastoral Epistles." *CBQ* 36 (1974) 203–19. **Metzger, B. M.** "Names for the Nameless in the New Testament: A Study in the Growth of Christian Tradition." In *New Testament Studies: Philological, Versional, and Patristic.* Leiden: Brill, 1980. **Pietersma, A.** "The Apocryphon of Jannes and Jambres." In *Congress Volume, Leuven, 1989,* ed. J. A. Emerton. VTSup 43. Leiden: Brill, 1991. **Sakkos, S.** "Ἰαννῆς καὶ Ἰαμβρῆς: Συμβολὴ εἰς τὴν εἰσαγωγὴν καὶ ἑρμηνείαν τῆς ΚΔ (2 Tim 3:8, cfr. Nu 25:14)." *EETT* 18 (1973) 253–311. **Sparks, H. F. D.** "On the Form Mambres in the Latin Versions of 2 Tim 3:8." *JTS* o.s. 40 (1939) 257–58. **Stephen, G.** "Parerga to 'The Book of Jannes and Jambres.'" *Journal for the Study of Pseudepigrapha* 9 (1991) 67–85.

Translation

[1] *But take note* [a] *of this, that in the last days there will be stressful times;* [2] *for the people will be lovers of self, lovers of money, braggarts, arrogant, abusive, disobedient to parents, ungrateful,* [b] *unholy,* [3] *unloving,* [c] *unforgiving, slanderous, uncontrolled, untamed, not loving the good,* [4] *treacherous, reckless, conceited, loving pleasure rather than loving God,* [5] *having the appearance of godliness but denying its power; and so avoid these people.*

[6] *For some of these are creeping into the homes and capturing* [d] *weak women* [e] *who have been burdened with sins, being led astray by various* [f] *passions,* [7] *always learning and never being able to come to a knowledge of [the] truth.* [8] *But just as Jannes and Jambres* [g] *opposed Moses, so also these men are opposing the truth, men who have been corrupted in the mind, worthless concerning the faith.* [9] *But they will not progress very far; for their folly* [h] *will be very clear to all, as also was the [folly] of those men.*

Notes

[a] The singular γίνωσκε, "take note," is replaced by the plural γινώσκετε, "take note" (A F G 33 *pc*), and γινωσκέτω, "let him take note" (1175; Ambst Spec), both being attempts to address the words to different audiences. Lock suggests that this was because these verses are more general than those preceding and following (xxxvii).

[b]ἀχάριστοι, "ungrateful," is replaced by ἄχρηστοι, "useless" (C* K *pc;* cf. Phlm 11).

[c]The order ἄστοργοι ἄσπονδοι, "unloving, unforgiving," is reversed by D 365 1175 *pc* (a) g m vg[ms]; Ambst. ἄστοργοι, "unloving," is omitted by א, and both are omitted by 431 sy[p].

[d]The Hellenistic αἰχμαλωτίζοντες, "capturing" (א A C [D*: εκμ-] F G P Ψ 6 33 81 104 365 1175 1505 1739 1881 *al*), is replaced by the Attic αἰχμαλωτεύοντες, "capturing" (D² TR; cf. Eph 4:8).

[e]The article τά, "the," is inserted before γυναικάρια, "weak women," by 2 *pc,* perhaps in imitation of the previous τὰς οἰκίας, "the homes."

[f]καὶ ἡδοναῖς, "and pleasures," is inserted before ποικίλαις, "various" (A 1505 *pc* sy[h]), to emphasize the bad lusts, the same phrase (ἐπιθυμίαις καὶ ἡδοναῖς) occurring in Titus 3:3.

[g]Ἰαμβρῆς is spelled Μαμβρῆς by F G it vg[cl ww]; Cyp. Cf. *TCGNT*², 580.

[h]ἄνοια, "folly," is replaced with διάνοια, "imagination, conceit" (BAGD, 187 [4]), by A.

Form/Structure/Setting

The second main division of the body of the epistle is 2:14–4:8, with 3:1–9 forming the second subdivision. Paul is still addressing Timothy and not the opponents directly, but the Ephesian situation is clearly in his mind, and these verses should be understood within the Ephesian context. The opponents will fade from view in 3:10, surfacing only briefly in 4:3–4 and 4:14–15. 2 Tim 3:1–9 breaks into two paragraphs. The vice list in 3:1–5 at first glance may appear to be general, but a closer look reveals the tight connection between the vices and the behavior of the opponents. This connection is made explicit in the second paragraph, 3:6–9, as Paul ties the behavior of the opponents to the eschatological prophecies and spells out the consequences of their sins. The connection between the two paragraphs also shows that the vices in the first paragraph are not overly pessimistic but an accurate description of the Ephesian situation. As Fee (270) states, "As always, such lists seem to come down a bit heavily on the human race and are the object of attack by those with humanistic tendencies. But unfortunately the list is only too realistic, reminding God's people over and again that these, too, are 'the last days'" (for further discussion of the vice lists in the PE, see McEleney, *CBQ* 36 [1974] 203–19, and *Comment* on 1 Tim 1:8–11).

This section continues the eschatological force of the epistle, showing Paul's belief that Timothy and he live in the last days and are seeing the fulfillment of eschatological prophecies. Even in the final days of his life Paul still holds this conviction. We also learn much about the heresy. Paul's day is part of the eschatological time of great sin. People have replaced the love of God with the love of self and the material world, having the facade of religiosity but denying the power of the true gospel. Specifically, the opponents have found success proselytizing women, with the implication that sexual sin is part of the problem. But Paul is convinced that eventually the heresy will fail because the opponents are living in obvious sin.

The use of vice lists is common for Paul, and they have been discussed in general in *Form/Structure/Setting* on 1 Tim 1:8–11. While there are similarities among this list, other lists in Paul, and other lists in religious and secular writings (cf. Spicq, 1:381–82, on Philo), almost every vice has a verbal or conceptual link to the Ephesian opponents, as will be shown in the *Comment*. While Paul may appear to be thinking in general terms in vv 1–4, both v 5 ("having the appearance of godliness") and the explicit connection made in vv 6–9 between the vices and the opponents (e.g., "some of these," v 6) show that Paul is not thinking about society in general (cf. the vice list in Rom 1:18–32). Rather he is thinking of the eschatological evil that has infiltrated the Ephesian church.

It is not helpful to speculate about the supposed source of the vice list. Hanson asserts that "we can say with confidence . . . that this list is modelled on Rom. 1:29–31" (144). Easton also sees Rom 1:29–31 as the source of the list here but emphasizes that it has been modified to fit the Ephesian historical context: "The modifications would be due to the fact that the author of the Pastorals was writing against very concrete adversaries. . . . He consequently selects terms that could be recognized as describing these people, and that led up to his more explicit characterization of them in the verses that follow" (*JBL* 51 [1932] 7). However, in Romans Paul describes all of the non-Christian world; here he describes one form of a heretical aberration of Ephesian Christianity. Also, since the vices are so closely tied to the Ephesian situation, any borrowed material has been so reworked that the source cannot be identified with any certainty, and knowing the source does not help to understand the meaning of the vices for Paul and Timothy.

While the structure of this vice list is not as predictable as the one in 1 Tim 1:9–10, which parallels the Decalogue, there are many literary patterns that tie the list together. (1) There are eighteen vices if v 5 is a summation. (2) Eleven words begin with alpha (usually alpha privative ἀ-, like the English "un-"), counting compound forms. (3) The list begins and ends with two sets of compound words formed with φίλος, "loving." φίλος also forms the compound ἀφιλάγαθοι, "not loving the good," the fourteenth vice. (4) The theme of self-centeredness permeates the list. It starts with the vice of "lovers of self," with the following vices flowing from this problem and the root problem being identified in the final vice, "not lovers of God." (5) Vices fifteen and sixteen are compounds formed with πρό, "before." (6) Many of the vices form pairs, either through assonance or through similarity of meaning. The pairs of vices that appear to belong together are discussed in the *Comment*. (7) Most of the vices are formed as masculine adjectives. (8) Several of the words are rare in the NT but are used in secular writings (see Fee, 269; Knight, 429). The compound words often continue their etymological meanings.

Comment

1 Τοῦτο δὲ γίνωσκε, ὅτι ἐν ἐσχάταις ἡμέραις ἐνστήσονται καιροὶ χαλεποί, "But take note of this, that in the last days there will be stressful times." In an attempt to place Timothy and his conflict at Ephesus in historical perspective, Paul reminds Timothy that he is living in the last days. In vv 2–5 Paul will describe in detail what χαλεποί, "stressful," involves, and in vv 6–9 he will apply this description of "moral decadence" (Guthrie, 156) to Timothy's opponents. The belief that moral decay will precede the day of the Lord is found throughout Judaism, the Gospels, and the rest of the NT. Timothy has already been reminded of this fact in a similar passage (1 Tim 4:1–5) and will be reminded again in 2 Tim 3:13. See *Comment* on 1 Tim 4:15 for a general discussion.

At first glance it appears that these ἐσχάταις ἡμέραις, "last days," are in Timothy's future. ἐνστήσονται, "there will be," and ἔσονται, "will be" (v 2), are both future tense. However, context requires that the vices of vv 2–5 and hence the "last days" of v 1 be in the present time for Timothy. (1) The imperative ἀποτρέπου, "avoid" (v 5), is present tense as are most of the verbal forms. Being nonindicative in mood, it has no time significance, and yet the context requires that this linear imperative refer to avoiding these people in the present. The use of the present-tense verb in v 6 assures that this is the case. "The people who will be lovers of self" (v 2) are the same as those who are (εἰσιν, v 6) currently entering Ephesian households. (2) In the parallel passage, 1 Tim 4:1–5, there is the same implication regarding time. The prophecy of apostasy in the last times originally referred to a future event, but the context shows that this prophecy is now in the present time for Timothy. (3) Although there is no prophecy explicitly mentioned in 2 Tim 3:1–9, the tenor of the passage and its parallel to 1 Tim 4:1–5 show that vv 1–2 are the future in which Timothy now finds himself embroiled. The future tense therefore does not exclude the present inception of the increasingly evil days to come.

δέ, "but," contrasts the preceding comment concerning the hope of repentance with the fact of evil in the last days. γίνωσκε, "take note of" (cf. BAGD, 161 [4]; the use of σὺ δέ, "but you," in 3:10, 14 acts as a transitional statement), τοῦτο, "this," refers to the following ὅτι, "that," clause, which is grammatically in apposition to τοῦτο (Wallace, *Greek Grammar*, 459). Paul is not telling Timothy new information but reminding him of what he already knows. ἐσχάταις ἡμέραις, "last days," refers to the time period between Christ's first and second coming (cf. 1 Tim 4:1; Acts 2:17; Jas 5:3; 2 Pet 3:3; Jude 18). ἐνιστάναι means "to impend, be imminent" (BAGD, 266). It can also mean "to be present" (Rom 8:38; 1 Cor 3:22, 7:26; Gal 1:4; 2 Thess 2:2 [possibly]; Heb 9:9; cf. A. Oepke, *TDNT* 2:544). The future tense requires the former meaning, "to be imminent," and yet the closeness of these two meanings accords well with the fact that the future apostasy is now present. χαλεπός means "hard, difficult" and can be used to describe that which is evil or dangerous (BAGD, 874; cf. Matt 8:28). In other words, the stress ("distressing times," NRSV) is caused by the presence of evil ("terrible times," NIV). καιροί, "times," indicates not the passage of time but a period of time (cf. 1 Tim 2:6).

2 ἔσονται γὰρ οἱ ἄνθρωποι φίλαυτοι φιλάργυροι ἀλαζόνες ὑπερήφανοι βλάσφημοι, γονεῦσιν ἀπειθεῖς, ἀχάριστοι ἀνόσιοι, "For the people will be lovers of self, lovers of money, braggarts, arrogant, abusive, disobedient to parents, ungrateful, unholy." The list of vices in vv 2–5 spells out why the last days will be stressful (v 1). While vice lists tend to be general, not addressing any one specific situation or audience, many of the vices mentioned here are parallel to descriptions of the opponents elsewhere in the PE (if not using the same words, then parallel in thought). This association will be specifically stated in v 6. For a discussion of the vice list in general and its structure, specifically the pairing of terms, see *Form/Structure/Setting*. The first eight vices are in v 2.

γάρ, "for," connects the vices in vv 2–4 with the "stressful times" in v 1. ἄνθρωποι, "people," is used generically of all people (cf. 1 Tim 2:1), οἱ, "the," emphasizing that the following description is true of most people (but not necessarily all). On the future tense ἔσονται, "will be," see *Comment* on v 1.

(1–2) φίλαυτοι, φιλάργυροι, "lovers of self, lovers of money." The first two vices are compound words formed with φίλος, "loving." It may not be accidental that they stand at the head of the list and in direct contrast with the final vice, φιλήδονοι μᾶλλον ἢ φιλόθεοι, "loving pleasure rather than loving God" (v 4), which likewise is expressed in compounds formed with φίλος. When one's love for God is replaced by love for oneself and the material world, then all the other vices naturally flow. As Guthrie observes, "Self-centeredness, and material advantages, when they become the chief objects of affection, destroy all moral values, and the subsequent list of vices is their natural fruit" (157). φίλαυτος, "lover of self," occurs only here in the NT (MM, 669). In earlier Greek literature it is used in a positive sense of "self-respect," but here it is used negatively of a self-centeredness that usurps God's rightful role (cf. Bernard, 129). φιλάργυρος, "lover of money, avaricious" (BAGD, 859; MM, 669), occurs in the NT elsewhere only in Luke 16:14 in a description of the Pharisees. Paul, however, has already taught that the love of money is a root of all kinds of evils (1 Tim 6:10); here he adds that behind the love of money is the love of self. The threefold repetition of the requirement for overseers (1 Tim 3:4) and deacons (1 Tim 3:8; cf. elders in Titus 1:7) that they not be greedy for financial gain shows that this was one of the basic problems in the Ephesian church, which is explicitly stated in Titus 1:11 concerning the situation in Crete (cf. 1 Tim 6:5–10).

(3–4) ἀλαζόνες, ὑπερήφανοι, "braggarts, arrogant." The classical distinction between these two words is that the former deals with behavior and the latter with feelings (Trench, *Synonyms*, 137–44; Kelly, 194). ἀλαζών, "braggart" (BAGD, 34), occurs elsewhere in Rom 1:30 and is one of two nouns in the vice list (see προδότης in v 4). ὑπερήφανος, "arrogant," occurs in Luke 1:51; Rom 1:30; Jas 4:6; 1 Pet 5:5 (the latter two citing Prov 3:34; cf. BAGD, 841; MM, 653; cf. the cognate ὑπερηφανία, "arrogance," in Mark 7:22). Both words are joined in Rom 1:30.

(5–6) βλάσφημοι, γονεῦσιν ἀπειθεῖς, "abusive, disobedient to parents." These two are not as closely related as the previous four, and yet abusiveness in general can lead to disobedience within the family. βλάσφημος (cf. MM, 112) probably means "abusive" in speech since the vices are generally directed toward people and not toward God. It occurs elsewhere in the PE in 1 Tim 1:13 (cf. there for discussion), but cognates occur five other times, showing that this was a common problem in Ephesus (cf. 1 Tim 6:4). γονεῦσιν ἀπειθεῖς, "disobedient to parents," breaks the pattern of single words, but ἀπειθεῖς, "disobedient," starts a pattern of vices beginning with alpha privative (ἀ-) that continues through v 4 with one exception (διάβολοι, "slanderous"). On ἀπειθής, "disobedient," see *Comment* on Titus 1:16. The same phrase occurs in Rom 1:30. A similar vice is listed in the vice list in 1 Tim 1:9 ("those who beat their fathers and mothers") and was evidently a problem in Ephesus in that people were not caring for their widowed mothers (1 Tim 5:8).

(7–8) ἀχάριστοι, "ungrateful" (BAGD, 128; MM, 99; cf. Luke 6:35), and ἀνόσιοι, "unholy," are the next two vices, their primary literary relationship being their formation with alpha privatives. On ἀνόσιος, "unholy," see *Comment* on 1 Tim 1:9; it describes conduct directly opposed to God. The ninth vice, ἄστοργοι, "unloving" (v 3), also has to do with family relations as perhaps does the tenth, ἄσπονδοι, "unforgiving."

3 ἄστοργοι ἄσπονδοι διάβολοι ἀκρατεῖς ἀνήμεροι ἀφιλάγαθοι, "unloving, unforgiving, slanderous, uncontrolled, untamed, not loving the good." (9) ἄστοργος, "unloving," also occurs in Rom 1:31. Bernard (130) defines it as "without natural affection." The positive στοργή (without alpha privative), which does not occur in the NT, means "love, affection" and is used "esp. of parents and children" but rarely of "sexual love" (LSJ, 1650). If the nuance of ἄστοργοι implies family love here, it is a reflection of the sixth vice, γονεῦσιν ἀπειθεῖς, "disobedient to parents."

(10) ἄσπονδος means "irreconcilable, unforgiving" (BAGD, 117; cf. Trench, *Synonyms*, 193–94; MM, 86). It occurs elsewhere in the NT only as a variant in Rom 1:31 following ἄστοργος, the previous vice in this list. MM give its basic meaning as "without treaty," commenting that "friends need no treaty, and implacable foes will not make one" (86). Guthrie defines it as "hostility that admits of no truce" (157; cf. LSJ, 260). The cognate σπονδή is a "drink-offering" that is poured out to the gods before drinking. It came to be used of a treaty or truce since the ceremony was concluded with a drink-offering (LSJ, 1629; cf. 2 Tim 4:6).

(11) διάβολοι, "slanderous," breaks the alliteration of the vices starting with alpha and the possible emphasis on vices within the family context. The word occurs six times in the PE and indicates a serious problem in Ephesus (cf. *Comment* on 1 Tim 3:6, 11; cf. Titus 2:3). Perhaps the choice of terms is designed to recall Paul's earlier comment that the opponents have been ensnared by the devil (διάβολος; 2 Tim 2:26).

(12) ἀκρατής, "uncontrolled, without self-control," occurs only here in the NT but expresses the opposite of the requirements for elders that they be "self-controlled" (ἐγκρατής, Titus 1:8), thus showing the connection of the vice to the historical situation of the PE. Bernard says it was used specifically of lack of controlling one's "bodily lusts" (130), which ties in with the Ephesian situation specified in 3:6.

(13) ἀνήμερος literally is "untamed," used figuratively as "savage, brutal" (BAGD, 66). MM (43) cite Epictetus's description (1.3.7) of those who forget their divine origin as being like lions, wild, savage, and untamed (ἀνήμεροι). It is somewhat synonymous with the previous vice, ἀκρατεῖς, "uncontrolled," and its antithesis, "not violent [πλήκτην] but gracious," is required of the Ephesian overseers (1 Tim 3:3) and the Cretan elders (Titus 1:7).

(14) ἀφιλάγαθος, "not loving the good," occurs only here in early Christian literature but is the antithesis of the requirement that elders "love what is good" (φιλάγαθος; Titus 1:8). It is the last vice beginning with alpha privative, and the opposites of both it and the preceding vice are found in the list of characteristics of elders in Titus 1.

4 προδόται προπετεῖς τετυφωμένοι, φιλήδονοι μᾶλλον ἢ φιλόθεοι, "treacherous, reckless, conceited, loving pleasure rather than loving God." (15) προδότης is one of two nouns in this list (the other is ἀλαζών, "braggart," in v 2) and means "traitor, betrayer" (BAGD, 704). It occurs elsewhere in the NT in reference to Judas (Luke 6:16) and the Jews (Acts 7:52). There is nothing in the Ephesian context suggesting that Christians are betraying Christians (contra Ellicott, Dornier) so the translation "treacherous" is chosen. This term pairs with the following vice in that both are compound words formed with πρό, "before."

(16) προπετής is always used figuratively in early Christian literature to mean "rash, reckless, thoughtless" (BAGD, 709), occurring elsewhere in the NT only in Acts 19:36. It is a compound word that pairs with the previous προδότης. Its verbal cognate is προπίπτειν, "to fall forward, headlong" (Abbott-Smith, *Lexicon*, 382), hence "reckless."

(17) τετυφωμένοι is the only participle in the vice list. It means "swollen with conceit" (RSV) and describes one of the serious problems of the Ephesian opponents (cf. 1 Tim 3:6; 6:4).

(18) φιλήδονοι μᾶλλον ἢ φιλόθεοι, "loving pleasure rather than loving God," the final vice, recalls the first in the list and provides a powerful conclusion. The people

in the last days will be lovers of themselves and of money (v 2). They will not love the good (ἀφιλάγαθος; v 3). They will love pleasure (φιλήδονος) rather than (μᾶλλον; BAGD, 489 [3]) love God (φιλόθεος). All five of these words are compounds using φίλος, "loving," the latter two occurring only here in the NT (although Paul does speak of δουλεύοντες . . . ἡδοναῖς, "being enslaved . . . to pleasures" [Titus 3:3]). φιλόθεοι, "lovers of God," reminds one of the Shema: "Hear, O Israel: The LORD our God is one LORD" (Deut 6:4; referred to in 1 Tim 2:5). When God is removed as the priority in life and is replaced with self, money, and pleasure, all the other vices naturally follow (see *Comment* on 3:2). Philo's similar statement is often cited: "lovers of self rather than lovers of God" (*Fug.* 81; Hanson, [1983] 144).

5a ἔχοντες μόρφωσιν εὐσεβείας τὴν δὲ δύναμιν αὐτῆς ἠρνημένοι, "having the appearance of godliness but denying its power." As a conclusion to the vice list and a stinging summary description of the hypocritical opponents, Paul describes them as perpetrating the myth of religiosity while their behavior proves that they are not what they appear to be, denying the power, the essence, of true Christianity by their sins. Fee observes, "They liked the visible expressions, the ascetic practices and the endless discussions of religious trivia, thinking themselves to be obviously righteous because they were obviously religious" (270). True Christianity consists not in the show of religiosity but in the powerful proclamation of the gospel accompanied by the life of obedience that conforms to the demands of the gospel. This fundamental assumption underlies Paul's statements to Timothy (cf., e.g., 1:8–9; 2:15, 21). It is the same sentiment expressed in Titus 1:16: "They profess to know God, but by [their] deeds they deny [him], being abominable, disobedient, and worthless for any good work."

V 5 shows that while the vice list may be applied to society in general, Paul is really thinking about certain people professing to be Christians in the last times; the people who were lovers of self (vv 2–4) have the veneer of godliness, and εὐσέβεια, "godliness," is a technical term in the PE for true Christianity (1 Tim 2:2). μόρφωσις, "appearance, form" (BAGD, 528), describes the mere shell, and the context shows that the shell has no correspondence to reality (contra W. Pöhlmann, *EDNT* 2:444; cf. J. Behm, *TDNT* 4:742–59). Their appearance of godliness (teaching the law, asceticism, etc.) is shown to be false because at the same time they love themselves, money, and pleasure rather than God. δέ, "but," is strongly adversative, separating the form from the reality. ἀρνεῖσθαι, "to deny" (cf. 1 Tim 5:8), describes their behavior (vv 2–4) as actively negating their claims of religious piety (cf. Titus 1:16). αὐτῆς, "its," refers back to εὐσεβείας, "godliness." Paul does not define what he specifically means by δύναμιν, "power." δύναμις, "power," occurs elsewhere in the PE twice: God gave Timothy a spirit of power (2 Tim 1:7), and therefore Paul calls on him to share in suffering for the gospel "according to the power of God" (2 Tim 1:8). In 2 Tim 1:12 Paul uses the cognate δυνατός, "able," to state that God is able to do what he has committed to do. In our context it is sinful behavior that denies the power of godliness. By referring to power Paul is thinking at least of the essential nature of the gospel, which includes the call to holy living and the close association between right belief and right behavior emphasized throughout the PE. But the opponents have replaced the true gospel with quibbling about words, the arrogant teaching of myths and fables, and a refusal to have their behavior controlled by the gospel. Hence their religiosity is an empty shell devoid of the power that comes from God that is meant to effect change in Timothy's life and others (cf. 1 Cor 4:20). Fee goes further and says that the power is in fact the Holy Spirit (which is also his view of πνεῦμα, "spirit," in 2 Tim 1:7; he cites 1 Cor 2:5 and 4:20 [*God's Empowering Presence*, 793]).

5b καὶ τούτους ἀποτρέπου, "and so avoid these people." καί, "and so," is somewhat awkward to translate, either as an explicative or as indicating contrast (BAGD, 393 [I3, II3]). Its function is to separate v 5b from vv 1b–4. τούτους, "these people," connects back with τοῦτο, "this," in v 1 (cf. τούτων, "of these," in v 6) and summarizes Paul's teaching about the kinds of people in vv 2–4: "Know this [τοῦτο γίνωσκε] . . . and avoid them [τούτους ἀποτρέπου]." ἀποτρέπεσθαι, "to avoid" (BAGD, 101), occurs only here in the NT, but it restates a common theme heard throughout the PE (cf., e.g., 1 Tim 6:20; 2 Tim 2:16, 23). Kelly says that it is a strong term indicating that "Timothy is to avoid them with horror" (195). The present linear aspect describes Timothy's ongoing behavior, confirming that the prophecies about the end times (vv 1–4) have now come true in Timothy's time.

6a ἐκ τούτων γάρ εἰσιν οἱ ἐνδύνοντες εἰς τὰς οἰκίας καὶ αἰχμαλωτίζοντες γυναικάρια, "For some of these are creeping into the homes and capturing weak women." Vv 6–9 are the second paragraph in this section. Having described the sinful Ephesians (vv 1–5), Paul centers on their proselytizing of women. This paragraph clarifies much of the historical picture. The opponents were deceptive, religious charlatans who, like many religious frauds, found disproportional success among the women (Justin *Apology* 1.26.3; Dibelius-Conzelmann, 116; Kelly, 195; Hanson, [1983] 145; Fee, 271, 273–74). Therefore this verse gives no necessary evidence of Gnosticism, which also found success among women (contra Baur, *Pastoralbriefe*, 36). The paragraph also helps to explain the emphasis on the Ephesian women and especially the widows throughout the PE (1 Tim 2:9–15; 3:11; 5:3–16).

γάρ, "for," introduces the reason why Timothy is to avoid the opponents (v 5b). ἐκ τούτων, "some of these," is partitive (cf. BAGD, 235–36 [4a]), identifying the opponents (v 6) as a subset of the evil people in the last days (vv 1–5), or identifying a subset of the opponents. The present tense εἰσίν, "are," makes explicit what is implicit in vv 1–5, that Timothy is living in the last times. ἐνδύνειν means "to go (in), enter, creep (in)" (BAGD, 263), suggesting the deceptive nature of the opponents' proselytizing, hence "worm their way" (Moffatt's tr.; NIV; cf. παρεισδύ[ν]ειν, "to infiltrate," Jude 4). The articular τὰς οἰκίας, "the homes," may suggest the well-known homes, either because Timothy knows the ones to which Paul is referring or because these women are especially rich and influential, capable of paying for the opponents' teaching (cf. 1 Tim 6:5–10). αἰχμαλωτίζειν means "to capture" in war (BAGD, 27; cf. Luke 21:24; cf. 2 Tim 2:26) and is used here figuratively (as in Rom 7:23 and 2 Cor 10:5; cf. cognate αἰχμάλωτος, "captive," in Luke 4:18; cf. Str-B 3:659), again suggesting their deceptive behavior. γυναικάριον, "little woman," is the diminutive of γυνή, "woman," used pejoratively of the Ephesian women who were falling prey to the opponents. The word occurs only here in the NT. The next phrase suggests that it is their lack of spiritual maturity ("burdened with sins") that causes Paul's disgust with them.

6b σεσωρευμένα ἁμαρτίαις, ἀγόμενα ἐπιθυμίαις ποικίλαις, "who have been burdened with sins, being led astray by various passions." Paul follows with three descriptions of these captured, weak women, expressed by four participles, all modifying γυναικάρια, "weak women." (1) They have been burdened (σωρεύειν) with sins. The perfect σεσωρευμένα, "have been burdened," describes the piling up of sins, its tense emphasizing the effects of their behavior. Their sins are not precisely defined. Most see them as the sins of their past that give the false teachers an opportunity to capture them. Possibly the opponents proclaimed a release from their sins or a hedonistic indifference to them. (2) As a result of their sins, the women were led by various passions. The tense shift to the present (ἀγόμενα, "being led astray") spells out the consequences of their established situation (σεσωρευμένα). Instead of being led by their passions, they should have controlled their passions. ἐπιθυμία, "passion," is used in the PE always of sinful desires (cf. 1 Tim 6:9). Among the ποικίλαις, "various" (cf. Titus 3:3), passions there is the possibility of sexual impurity. This is suggested by the picture of being captured in the privacy of their homes and by Paul's instructions to the younger widows (1 Tim 5): he wants them to remarry because some are "living for pleasure" (v 6), have grown "wanton against Christ," and desire to marry (v 11).

7 πάντοτε μανθάνοντα καὶ μηδέποτε εἰς ἐπίγνωσιν ἀληθείας ἐλθεῖν δυνάμενα, "always learning and never being able to come to a knowledge of [the] truth." (3) The third description of the weak women is that they are always appearing to learn but never able to arrive at the real truth of the gospel. It is a sarcastic description of "religious dilettantes" (Fee, 272; cf. Paul's description of the young widows "studying hard to learn how to be idle" [1 Tim 5:13]). One can imagine the cycle of instruction in senseless myths and quibblings about words, followed by payment, leading to more senseless babble. Because they are learning heresy and not the truth of the gospel, they "never really learn the truth that can make them free" (Knight, 434). Paul is not describing women in general but the specific women in Ephesus who were involved in the heresy.

The women's desire to learn, contrary to the learning prescribed in 1 Tim 2:11, is possibly due to idle curiosity, "a morbid love of novelty" (Ellicott, 137), or more likely due to the opponents' catering to them and proclaiming their freedom from cultural and religious restraints as in Corinth. It is not that the women would not but that they could not learn the truth, either because they were exposed only to the heresy or because prolonged exposure to the heresy had dulled their senses. ἐπίγνωσιν ἀληθείας, "knowledge of [the] truth," is a technical term in the PE for the true gospel (cf. 1 Tim 2:4), emphasizing the cognitive element in contrast to the theological error of the heresy. This disgust for learning but never knowing is shared by the philosophers (cf. Dibelius-Conzelmann, 116 n. 9).

8a ὃν τρόπον δὲ Ἰάννης καὶ Ἰαμβρῆς ἀντέστησαν Μωϋσεῖ, οὕτως καὶ οὗτοι ἀνθίστανται τῇ ἀληθείᾳ, "But just as Jannes and Jambres opposed Moses, so also these men are opposing the truth." Paul compares the opponents (who were creeping into women's homes, v 6) with two Egyptian magicians who opposed Moses (Exod 7:11, 22; 8:7, 18–19; 9:11). There are two points of comparison. Both groups opposed the true message (of Moses and of Timothy), and their failure was evident to all (as v 8b points out). The comparison also heightens the deceptiveness of the opponents and their folly. The magicians are not named in the OT, but Jewish and Christian tradition (cf. Acts 7:22–23, 53; 1 Cor 10:2, 4; Gal 3:19; Heb 2:2; Jude 9) developed the account of Moses, and within this development the names appeared. Perhaps this development was part of the opponents' fixation with Jewish myths and genealogies (1 Tim 1:4). It is possible that the opponents, like Jannes and Jambres, were practicing magic (cf. 1 Tim 5:13; cf. Ellicott, 138; Brox, 255–56), but the possibility has rarely been accepted (for further discussion see Grabbe, *JBL* 98 [1979] 393–401; Pietersma, "The Apocryphon of Jannes and Jambres," 383–95; Sparks, *JTS* o.s. 40 [1939] 257–58; Stephen, *Journal for the Study of Pseudepigrapha* 9 [1991] 67–85).

δέ, "but," contrasts the success of the opponents (v 6) with their Egyptian counterparts and leads into their failure (v 8b). ὃν τρόπον is idiomatic, meaning "the manner in which = (just) as" (BAGD, 827 [1]; cf. Matt 23:37; Luke 13:34; Acts 1:11; 7:28; 15:11; 27:25), and is balanced by the following οὕτως καί, "so also." Jewish tradition developed the names Jannes (from Johanna) and Jambres (also Mambres; see *Note* g). They are mentioned in the Qumran literature (CD 5:18, which attributes their behavior to Belial), in Jewish literature (*Tg. Ps.-J.* 1:3 [on Exod 1:15]; 7:2 [on Exod 7:11]; 40:6 [on Num 22:21–22, which says that they were Balaam's sons who were killed either in the Red Sea or after the golden-calf incident]; *b. Men.* 85a; *Exod. Rab.* on Exod 9:7), and by secular writers (Pliny *Natural History* 30.1.11; Apuleius *Apol.* 100.40; for further references, see Str-B 3:660–64; BAGD, 368; H. Odeberg, *TDNT* 3:192–93; A. Oepke, *TDNT* 3:990; Lock, 107; Dibelius-Conzelmann, 117; K. Koch, *ZNW* 57 [1966] 79–93, evaluated by C. Burchard, *ZNW* 57 [1966] 219–28; Hanson, *Studies*, 25–28). ἀνθιστάναι, "to oppose," is used twice, enforcing the comparison between the magicians (ἀντέστησαν, "opposed," aorist active) and the opponents (ἀνθίστανται, "are opposing," present middle). In early Christian literature the active voice has a middle-voice meaning, "to set oneself against" (BAGD, 67; followed by the dative, Μωϋσεῖ, "Moses"). It occurs in the NT twelve times in the active voice (cf. Alexander's opposition to Paul [2 Tim 4:15]) but only one other time in the middle voice, describing the opposition of the magician Elymas to Paul (Acts 13:8). καί, "also," strengthens οὕτως, "so," comparing the opposition of the magicians (v 8a) to that of the opponents (v 8b). οὗτοι, "these men," refers back to the opponents who "are creeping in" (οἱ ἐνδύνοντες; v 6). τῇ ἀληθείᾳ, "the truth," is the gospel (cf. 1 Tim 2:4), which the Ephesian women are not able to learn (2 Tim 3:7).

8b ἄνθρωποι κατεφθαρμένοι τὸν νοῦν, ἀδόκιμοι περὶ τὴν πίστιν, "men who have been corrupted in the mind, worthless concerning the faith." Paul gives two descriptions of the men who are opposing the true gospel. The first describes what happened to them, and the latter shows the consequences; they have been corrupted and are therefore worthless as far as Christianity is concerned. ἄνθρωποι, "men," is used here specifically of males (cf. 2 Tim 2:2) since the opponents appear to be males worming their way into women's homes. κατεφθαρμένοι is perfect passive, "have been corrupted, ruined, depraved" (cf. BAGD, 420), the agent of the corruption being the heresy or possibly Satan (cf. 1 Tim 4:1; 2 Tim 2:26). The verb occurs only here in the NT (variant in 2 Pet 2:12). This corruption is in the mind (νοῦς; cf. 1 Tim 6:5; Titus 1:15), thus affecting their moral and intellectual capacity to make a decision. It contrasts with the ἀλήθεια, "truth" (which is the gospel), a term emphasizing the cognitive element (cf. 1 Tim 2:4). As a result of this corruption, the opponents are ἀδόκιμοι, "worthless" (cf. Titus 1:16), as far as the faith (i.e., the Christian faith; cf. *Introduction*, "Themes in the PE") is concerned. They are contrasted with Timothy, who was tested and found to be true (δόκιμος; 2 Tim 2:15). The opponents' ascetic facade is betrayed by their sinful lives. Hanson ([1983] 147) sees a reflection of Rom 1:28: "And since they did not see fit [ἐδοκίμασαν] to acknowledge God, God gave them over to a debased mind [ἀδόκιμον νοῦν]." On the phrase περὶ τὴν πίστιν, "concerning the faith," cf. *Comment* on 1 Tim 1:19.

9 ἀλλ᾽ οὐ προκόψουσιν ἐπὶ πλεῖον· ἡ γὰρ ἄνοια αὐτῶν ἔκδηλος ἔσται πᾶσιν, ὡς καὶ ἡ ἐκείνων ἐγένετο, "but they will not progress very far; for their folly will be very clear to all, as also was the [folly] of those men." Despite the success of the opponents, Paul ends on a positive note of the eventual victory of the truth. Twice Paul uses the verb προκόπτειν, "to progress," sarcastically, first of the opponents' progress into ungodliness (2 Tim 2:16) and then of evil men progressing from bad to worse (2 Tim 3:13). Here he adds that their progress has its limits and they will eventually fail. Just as the magicians failed to copy Moses' miracle of the plague of gnats (Exod 8:18–19) and failed to deal with the boils (Exod 9:11), so also Timothy's opponents will eventually fail.

ἀλλ᾽, "but," sets off the positive hope of v 9 from the negative success of the opponents (v 8). The same phrase, ἐπὶ πλεῖον . . . προκόψουσιν, "they progress very far," occurs in 2 Tim 2:16; see *Comment* there for discussion. γάρ, "for," introduces the reason for Paul's optimism. ἄνοια, "folly" (BAGD, 70), occurs elsewhere in the NT only in Luke 6:11. ἔκδηλος, "very clear, quite evident, plain" (BAGD, 238), uses the perfective ἐκ to emphasize the clarity of the visibility; there will be no question that the opponents are foolish. In accordance with classical Greek rules (cf. 2 Tim 2:26), αὐτῶν, "their," refers to the closer antecedent (ἄνθρωποι, "men" [v 8b]) and ἐκείνων, "those," to the more distant one (Ἰάννης καὶ Ἰαμβρῆς, "Jannes and Jambres" [v 8a]). The definite article in the phrase ἡ ἐκείνων refers to the noun ἄνοια ("the [folly] of those men").

Explanation

As Paul has previously reminded Timothy (1 Tim 4:1–5), he now repeats that Timothy should not be surprised at the conflicts he is experiencing. They are living in the last days, and Jewish and Christian prophecy has been clear that evil will be on the rise. Rather than loving God, people will love themselves, and from that will flow love of the material world and the vices of self-centeredness that Paul lists in the first paragraph. These are not so much general sins as they are specific sins visible every day in Ephesus as Timothy deals with the false teachers who wear a veneer of piety but by their sin show that there is no substance, no power, to their religiosity.

As Paul reflects on the presence of eschatological evil in general and in the Ephesian church, he focuses on one specific form of evil: the false teachers are intent on deceiving women, probably rich and influential women who will pay for their teaching and yet be so burdened by their own sin that they can never learn the truth. Timothy must stay away from the opponents, not because he dislikes confrontation but because the utter folly of these sinners will become perfectly clear to the Ephesian church in time. For a discussion of the church viewing itself as living in the final days, see *Explanation* on 1 Tim 4:1–5.

C. Encouragement and Proclamation   (2 Tim 3:10–4:8)

Bibliography

Barton, J. M. T. "Bonum certamen certavi . . . fidem servavi: 2 Tim 4:7." *Bib* 40 (1959) 878–84. **Bennetch, J. H.** "2 Timothy 3,16a: A Greek Study." *BSac* 106 (1949) 187–95. **Borland, J. A.** "Re-Examining New Testament Textual-Critical Principles and Practices Used to Negate Inerrancy." *JETS* 25 (1982) 499–506. **Bover, J. M.** "Uso del adjectivo singular saq en San Pablo." *Bib* 19 (1938) 411–34. **Braun, R. A.** "Desempenha com perfeiçao o teu ministério."*Perspectivo Teológica* 2 (1970) 195–201. **Buis, H.** "The Significance of II Timothy 3:16 and II Peter 1:21 [as Illustrated from Calvin's Commentaries]." *Reformed Review* 14 (1961) 43–49. **Calvin, J.** "Sur l'inspiration biblique (Commentaire de Timothée 3,15–17)." *Revue Réformée* 34 (1983) 91–93. **Cook, D.** "Scripture and Inspiration: 2 Timothy 3:14–17." *Faith and Mission* 1 (1984) 56–61. ———. "2 Timothy 4:6–8 and the Epistle to the Philippians." *JTS* n.s. 33 (1982) 168–71. **De Virgilio, G.** "Ispirazione ed effcacia della Scrittura in 2 Tm 3,14–17." *RivB* 38 (1990) 485–94. **Dornier, P.** "Fréquentation de l'Écriture et proclamation de la parole: 2 Tm 3,14–4,2." *AsSeign* 60 (1975) 62–66. ———. "Paul au soir de sa vie: 2 Tim 4,6–8.16–18." *AsSeign* 61 (1972) 60–65. **Ferguson, S.** "How Does the Bible Look at Itself?" In *Inerrancy and Hermeneutic*, ed. H. M. Conn. Grand Rapids, MI: Baker, 1988. **Geisler, N.,** ed. "The Chicago Statement on Biblical Inerrancy." In *Inerrancy.* Grand Rapids, MI: Zondervan, 1980. 493–502. **Goodrick, E. W.** "Let's Put 2 Timothy 3:16 Back in the Bible." *JETS* 25 (1982) 479–87. **Hanson, A. T.** "Inspired Scripture: 2 Timothy 3.14–17." In *Studies in the Pastoral Epistles.* 42–55. **House, H. W.** "Biblical Inspiration in 2 Timothy 3:16." *BSac* 137 (1980) 54–63. **Jaeger, W.** *Paideia: The Ideals of Greek Culture.* New York: Oxford UP, 1945. **Jüngel, E.** "Bibelarbeit über 2 Timotheus 3,14–17." In *Erneuerung aus der Bibel,* ed. S. Meurer. Stüttgart: Deutsche Bibelgesellschaft, 1982. 93–106. **Karris, R. J.** "The Background and Significance of the Polemic of the Pastoral Epistles." *JBL* 92 (1973) 549–64. **Knight, G. W.** "The Scriptures Were Written for Our Instruction." *JETS* 39 (1996) 3–13. **Kowalski, B.** "Zur Funktion und Bedeutung der alttestamentlichen Zitate und Anspielungen in den Pastoralbriefen." SNTU-A 19 (1994) 45–68. **Langerak, A.** "Study of the Word: 2 Timothy 3:10–17—Mission in Faith [8th IAMS Conf., 1992]." *Mission Studies* 10 (1993) 230–31. **Malherbe, A. J.** "'In Season and Out of Season': 2 Timothy 4:2." *JBL* 103 (1984) 235–43. **McGonigal, T. P.** "'Every Scripture Is Inspired': An Exegesis of 2 Timothy 3:16–17." *SBT* 8 (1978) 53–64. **Miller, E. L.** "Plenary Inspiration and II Timothy 3:16." *LQ* 17 (1965) 56–62. **Moody, D.** "The Man of God (2 Tim 3,17)." *RevExp* 51 (1954) 495–507; 52 (1955) 44–54, 310–24. **Nicole, R.** "John Calvin and Inerrancy." *JETS* 25 (1982) 425–42. ——— and **Michaels, J. R.,** eds. *Inerrancy and Common Sense.* Grand Rapids, MI: Baker, 1980. **Nix, W. E.** "The Doctrine of Inspiration Since the Reformation." *JETS* 25 (1982) 443–54. **Oberlinner, L.** *Anpassung oder Widerspruch: Von der apostolishen zur nachapostolischen Kirche.* Freiburg: Herder, 1992. 66–91. **Peaston, M.** "First Sunday after Easter: Disengagement [Sermon on 2 Tim 4:6–8]." *ExpTim* 93 (1982) 180–82. **Pfitzner, V. C.** *Paul and the Agon Motif.* 182–85. **Pisero, A.** "Sobre el sentido de theopneustos 2 Tim 3:16." *Filologia Neotestamentaria* 1 (1988) 143–53. **Preus, R. C.** "Scripture: God's Word and God's Power: 2 Timothy 3:14–17." In *Can We Trust the Bible?* ed. E. Radmacher. Wheaton, IL: Tyndale, 1979. 57–71. **Prior, M.** *Paul the Letter-Writer.* **Reck, R.** "2 Tim 3,16 in der altkirchlichen Literatur: Eine wirkungsgeschichtliche Untersuchung zum Locus classicus der Inspirationslehre." *Wissenschaft und Weisheit* 53 (1990) 81–105. **Ridderbos, H. N.** *The Authority of the New Testament Scriptures.* Grand Rapids, MI: Baker, 1963. **Ro, B. R.** "The Inspiration of Scripture among the Seventeenth-Century Reformed Theologians." In *The Living and Active Word of God,* ed. M. Inch and R. Youngblood. Winona Lake, IN: Eisenbrauns, 1983. **Roberts, J. W.** "Every Scripture Inspired by God." *ResQ* 5 (1961) 33–37. ———. "Note on the Adjective after πᾶς in 2 Timothy 3:16." *ExpTim* 76 (1964) 359. **Sheriffs, R. J. A.** "A Note on a Verse in the New English Bible." *EvQ* 34 (1962) 91–95. **Spence, R. M.** "2 Timothy 3:15,16." *ExpTim* 8 (1896–97) 563–65. **Twomey, J. J.** "I Have Fought the Good Fight." *Scr* 10 (1958) 110–15. **Wallace, D. B.** "The Role of Adjective to Noun in Anarthrous Constructions in the New Testament." *NovT* 26 (1984) 128–67. **Warfield, B. B.** *The Inspiration and Authority of the Bible.* Philadelphia: Presbyterian and Reformed, 1948.

Translation

[10]*But you followed* [a] *my teaching, my way of life, my purpose, my faith, my patience, my love,* [b] *my steadfastness,* [11]*my persecutions, my sufferings, which happened* [c] *to me in Antioch,* [d] *in Iconium, in Lystra, which persecutions I endured, and out of all these the Lord rescued me.* [12]*And also all wishing to live godly [lives]* [e] *in Christ Jesus will be persecuted,* [13]*but wicked people and impostors will advance from bad to worse, deceiving and being deceived.*

[14]*But you, remain in what you have learned and have been convinced of, knowing from whom* [f] *you learned* [15]*and that from childhood you have known [the]* [g] *sacred writings, which are able to make you wise for salvation through faith that is in Christ Jesus.* [16]*All Scripture is God-breathed and* [h] *profitable for teaching, for reproof,* [i] *for correcting, for training in righteousness,* [17]*in order that the person of God be proficient,* [j] *fully equipped for every good work.*

[4:1]*I* [k] *solemnly charge [you] before God and Christ Jesus, who is about to judge* [l] *[the] living and [the] dead, and* [m] *by his appearing and by his kingdom:* [2]*Preach the word! Be prepared when it is opportune or inopportune! Confront! Rebuke! Exhort!* [n]*—with complete patience and teaching.* [3]*For a time will come when they will not put up with healthy teaching, but in accordance with their own lust* [o] *they will heap up teachers for themselves, having itching ears,* [4]*and they will turn away from listening to the truth and wander across to the myths.*

[5]*But you, be clear-minded in everything! Suffer evil!* [p][q] *Do the work of an evangelist! Complete your ministry!* [6]*For I am already being poured out like a drink offering, and the time of my departure* [r] *has arrived.* [7]*The good fight* [s] *I have fought, the race I have completed, the faith I have kept.* [8]*Now is reserved for me the crown of righteousness, which the Lord, the righteous judge, will give to me on that day, but not only to me but also to everyone* [t] *who has loved his appearing.*

Notes

[a]The aorist παρηκολούθησας, "you followed" (ℵ A C [F G: ηκ-] 33 *pc*), is replaced by the perfect παρηκολούθηκας, "you have followed" (D Ψ 1739 1881 TR), in an attempt to clarify the effect Paul's past persecution has had on Timothy. Cf. Ellicott, 140.

[b]τῇ ἀγάπῃ, "my love," is omitted by A *pc*.

[c]The singular ἐγένετο, "happened," is replaced with the plural ἐγένοντο, "happened," by A K 81 614 629 1881 *pc*.

[d]The copyist of 181 inserts ἅ διὰ τὴν Θέκλαν ἔπαθεν, "the things that he suffered on account of Thecla," before ἐν Ἰκονίῳ, "in Iconium." As Metzger points out, it should have read ἔπαθον, "I suffered" (*TCGNT²*, 580). The gloss sounds as if the editor was attempting to tie the apocryphal account of Paul and Thecla into the text; cf. *Explanation* on 2 Tim 1:15–18. The copyist of K inserts τοῦτ᾽ ἔστιν ἅ διὰ τὴν Θέκλαν πέπονθεν· ἐξ Ἰουδαίων πιστεύσασι εἰς Χριστόν, "that is, the things that he has suffered on account of Thecla, from Jews toward those who believed in Christ."

ᵉThe order εὐσεβῶς ζῆν, "in a godly manner to live" (C D F G Ψ 1881 TR lat[t]), is reversed in ℵ A P 33 104 365 1505 1739 *pc*.

ᶠThe plural τίνων, "whom," designating Timothy's mother, grandmother, Paul, and perhaps others as being his teachers (ℵ A C* F G P 33 81 1175 1505 1739 1881 *pc* b d; Ambst) is replaced by the singular τίνος, "whom" (C³ D Ψ TR lat), pointing specifically to Paul—not Timothy's mother, grandmother, and Paul—as his teacher (see *Comment;* Lock, xxxvii; *TCGNT²,* 580; additional references in UBSGNT⁴).

ᵍThe definite article is omitted by ℵ C²ᵛⁱᵈ D* F G 33 1175 *pc* co; Cl. Its inclusion is supported by A C* D¹ Ψ 1739 1881 TR. It is easy to see how the anarthrous use of ἱερὰ γράμματα, "holy writings," designating the OT, would invite the insertion of the article. As is discussed in the *Comment,* the meaning of the phrase is not substantially altered by the presence or absence of the article since the phrase had become somewhat technical and could stand on its own as a definite concept without the article. Nestle-Aland²⁷ puts the article in brackets.

ʰκαί, "and," is omitted in it vgᶜˡ syᵖ coᵇᵒ; Or Ambst with no significant change in meaning. Metzger says it was dropped because it was felt to "disturb the construction" (*TCGNT²,* 580).

ⁱἔλεγμόν, "reproof" (ℵ A C F G I 33 81 104 365 1175 1739 1881 *pc*), is replaced with ἔλεγχον, "reproof" (D Ψ TR; Cl), to enforce the parallelism with 2 Tim 4:2.

ʲἄρτιος, "proficient," is replaced with τέλειος, "perfect" (D* *ex* lat?), and with ὑγιὴς τέλειος, "soundly perfect" (104ᵐᵍ [a gloss]).

ᵏοὖν, "therefore" (Ψ 1505 *pc*), is inserted here to clarify the connection between the source of Scripture and the necessity of Timothy's proclamation (omitted by ℵ A C D* F G I P 6 33 81 104 365 1175 1739 1881 *pc* latt). ἐγώ, "I" (326*), and οὖν ἐγώ, "therefore I" (D¹ TR), also occur.

ˡThe present κρίνειν, "to judge," is replaced with the aorist κρῖναι, "to judge" (F G 6 33 81 1881 *pc*).

ᵐκατά, "according to," replaces καί, "and," in ℵ² D² Ψ 1881 TR vgᶜˡ (sy) sa (καί is in ℵ* A C D* F G 6 33 1175 1739 *pc* it vgˢᵗ ʷʷ bo), which produces an easier construction (*TCGNT²,* 580; additional references in UBSGNT⁴).

ⁿThe order is switched to παρακάλεσον ἐπιτίμησον, "Exhort! Rebuke!" by ℵ* F G 1739 1881 *pc* latt co.

ᵒTR changes τὰς ἰδίας ἐπιθυμίας, "their own lusts" (ℵ A C D F G P Ψ 33 81 104 365 1175 1505 1739 1881 *al*), to ἐπιθυμίας τὰς ἰδίας.

ᵖκακοπάθησον, "Suffer evil!" is omitted by ℵ* vgᵐˢ.

ᑫA inserts ὡς καλὸς στρατιώτης Χριστοῦ Ἰησοῦ, "as a good soldier of Christ Jesus," after κακοπάθησον, "Suffer evil!" referring back to 2 Tim 2:3–4.

ʳἀναλύσεώς μου, "my departure" (ℵ A C F G P 33 81 104 365 630 1175 1739 1881 *pc* b vgᶜˡ; Ambst), is replaced with ἐμῆς ἀναλύσεως (D Ψ TR a f t vgˢᵗ ʷʷ) with no change in meaning.

ˢτὸν καλὸν ἀγῶνα, "the good fight" (ℵ A C F G 33 81 104 629 1175 *pc;* Eus Did), is rewritten as ἀγῶνα τὸν καλόν by D Ψ 1739 1881 TR; Or.

ᵗπᾶσι, "to everyone," is omitted by D* 6 1739* 1881 *pc* lat syᵖ; Ambst. Metzger notes that copyists often added "all" "in order to heighten the account" (*TCGNT²,* 581), but the evidence for its inclusion is stronger.

Form/Structure/Setting

Having dealt with the issues of Timothy's treatment of the opponents and their heresy in 2:14–3:9, ending in a condemnation of the false teachers and their motives with a description of their ultimate ruin, and having located these teachers historically as part of the rise in evil in the end times, Paul returns to address Timothy. The dominant theme throughout the rest of the epistle is encouragement, and as such these verses bear a strong resemblance to 2 Tim 1:3–2:13. Paul calls Timothy to remember their times together, reflects on Timothy's spiritual heritage and the influences of the OT and the gospel, and continues the strong eschatological emphasis begun in 3:1–5. Just as Paul has called Timothy to look forward as he ministers in Ephesus, so Paul is an example of someone who has remained faithful and looks forward to what the Lord has in store for him, the same crown that awaits Timothy.

Another theme drawing these four paragraphs together is that of the OT and the gospel, which are sometimes joined in an awkward manner. This theme appears five times in this passage: Timothy has learned the OT and the gospel and is convinced of their truth (3:14); he has known the OT ("holy writings") from childhood (3:15); "Scripture" comes from God and is therefore sufficient to train Timothy fully for ministry (3:16–17; cf. 4:5); Timothy is to preach the word in season and out (4:2); Timothy's message is the truth, healthy instruction that the opponents are trading in for myths (4:4). Although Paul uses different terms to describe the OT and the gospel, they all refer to the message of God and need to be interpreted together. Timothy's ministry centers on Scripture: the OT and the gospel message.

There are different techniques that Paul uses to tie his discussion together. He begins and ends on the same note of personal reflection, looking back to the past and forward to the future (3:10–11; 4:6–8). Five times Paul speaks of the OT/gospel (see above). The eschatological reference in 3:13, building from 3:1–5, is continued in 4:6–8. These themes create a strong thread running throughout the section, which argues against breaking the passage into separate units. Most modern writers see a major break at 4:1, but this separates the charge that Timothy preach (4:1–2) from the ultimate reason that he is to do so (3:16–17; see *Note* k). It also disrupts the eschatological emphasis on persecution (3:10–13; 4:3–4, 6). Other writers view 4:6–8 as a separate section, but that downplays the connective in v 6 (γάρ, "for"), the continuation of the theme of the gospel ("evangelist" [v 5]) as seen in the fulfillment of Paul's ministry (esp. v 7), and the link between the personal comments in 3:10–11 and those in 4:6–8. Therefore 3:10–4:8 should be seen as a cohesive unit, tied closely to the following personal discussion in 4:9–22 and comprising four paragraphs. The first (3:10–13), second (3:14–17), and fourth (4:5–8) begin with the same phrase, σὺ δέ, "but you" (which Paul uses elsewhere as a section divider). 2 Tim 4:1–4 is set off by the nature of the charge, how it grows out of 3:16–11, and its discussion of the heresy.

Fee rightly emphasizes that Paul is here repeating many of the themes introduced in 1:3–2:13: Paul's relationship with Timothy (3:10–11; cf. 1:4, 6, 13); Paul as a model of loyalty (3:10–11; cf. 1:8, 11–12, 13; 2:9–10); the call to suffer (3:11–12; cf. 1:8, 16; 2:3–6, 11–12); the appeal directly to Timothy (3:15; cf. 1:6, 13–14; cf. also 2:2, 22, 24; 1 Tim 6:11; 4:12); spiritual heritage (3:15; cf. 1:5); and salvation (3:15; cf. 2:10–13). To Fee's list based on 3:10–17 can be added several other parallels. All three statements in v 7 have direct links to earlier admonitions to Timothy (see *Comment*). For example, just as a crown is held out to Timothy in 2:5, another is reserved for Paul in 4:8. Timothy is to guard the gospel (1:14) by preaching it (4:2). The sense of urgency throughout 1:3–2:13 is heightened by the eschatological perspective of 3:13 and 4:3–4, 8, and by the ten imperatives in 3:10–4:8 (nine in chap. 4).

2 Tim 4:6–8 paints the historical picture. Everything Paul says is to be understood within the historical framework of the Ephesian situation, especially the value of Scripture and the role it is to play in combating the false teachers. Paul also continues in his eschatological outlook, viewing the Ephesian opponents as examples of the prophecies concerning the rise of evil in the last days. In contrast to Acts 28, Paul is in a different, much harsher imprisonment that he knows will end in death.

Comment

10 Σὺ δὲ παρηκολούθησάς μου τῇ διδασκαλίᾳ, τῇ ἀγωγῇ, τῇ προθέσει, τῇ πίστει, τῇ μακροθυμίᾳ, τῇ ἀγάπῃ, τῇ ὑπομονῇ, "But you followed my teaching, my way of life, my purpose, my faith, my patience, my love, my steadfastness." Paul now turns back to Timothy and encourages him; Paul holds up his own life as an example for Timothy to emulate. This is not arrogance or an attempt to teach Timothy what he should already know. It is the act of a good friend and mentor encouraging his son in the faith by reflecting over their common experiences and calling Timothy to remember and be encouraged, and it parallels Paul's statements elsewhere that people should imitate him (cf. 1 Cor 4:16; 11:1; Phil 4:9; 2 Thess 3:7, 9). Almost every virtue that follows in v 10 appears elsewhere in the PE in an admonition to Timothy, either using the same word or the same concept (cf. especially 2 Tim 1:7; 2:2, 22, 24; 1 Tim 4:12; 6:11), and often is a characteristic that the opponents lack. For example, love is a characteristic of Paul's life (3:10); it should also be of Timothy's (1:7), but the opponents prefer speculations (1 Tim 1:4–5). This positive estimation of Paul's life balances the negative evaluation in 1 Tim 1:12–17 (cf. the other evaluations such as 2 Cor 6:4–10) and contrasts with the vices of the opponents in 3:1–9.

Paul lists nine items that Timothy has observed in Paul's life and from which he has learned. The article before each word is emphatic; these are the events in Paul's life of which Timothy knows and the significance of which he understands, hence the translation "my," looking back to the explicit μου, "my" (cf. Wallace, *Greek Grammar*, 215–16). The order of the terms is anything but "indiscriminate" (contra Hanson, [1983] 148). Paul begins with the most important items in that they offer the most visible and significant contrast to the opponents. Timothy knows Paul's doctrine and his manner of life, his conduct; the truth of a message can be connected to the character of the messenger (cf. 3:14). From these two flow Paul's purpose in ministry, his patience, and the three virtues of faith, love, and steadfastness. The final virtue, steadfastness, is especially significant in light of Paul's frequent persecutions and sufferings (vv 11–13; cf. Fee, 276).

σὺ δέ, "but you," contrasts Timothy and the following description of Paul's life with that of the opponents (3:1–9). The phrase occurs again in 3:14 (and 4:5) and as such sets off the first two paragraphs of the section—what Timothy knows and how he is to behave (see *Form/Structure/Setting*; cf. 1 Tim 6:11). παρακολουθεῖν means more than "to follow." It is used elsewhere of a disciple following his teacher, learning from him, and following his example (1 Tim 4:6; cf. Luke 1:3; cf. Kelly, 198). As Paul tells the Corinthians, "therefore I urge you, be imitators of me. For this reason I sent Timothy to you, who is my beloved and faithful child in the Lord, who will remind you of my ways [τὰς ὁδούς μου] in Christ" (1 Cor 4:16–17). 2 Tim 3:10 does not require Timothy to have been with Paul from the beginning of his ministry (cf. v 11). The variant reading παρηκολούθηκας, "you have followed" (see *Note* a), is perfect tense, making explicit what is implicit in the aorist παρηκολούθησας, "you followed"— that Timothy has known Paul's life and continues to follow his example (cf. Bernard, 133). The verb takes the dative of the thing and is followed by nine nouns in the dative. The prior placement of μου, "my," is emphatic in position, contrasting Paul's life with the opponents, and modifies the following nine nouns. The NRSV repeats "my" before each noun to make this clear.

(1) διδασκαλία, "teaching," and (2) ἀγωγή, "way of life," head the list as the two most significant aspects of Paul's ministry relative to Timothy's historical situation. The opponents' errant teaching (1 Tim 1:6–7) and aberrant behavior (2 Tim 3:6–9) are the main causes of Timothy's problems in Ephesus, and, as Paul repeatedly states, they are closely intertwined (see *Introduction,* "The Ephesian Heresy"). On διδασκαλία, see 1 Tim 1:10. ἀγωγή occurs only here in the NT (cf. BAGD, 14–15). Earlier Paul has encouraged Timothy to "be an example for the faithful in speech, in conduct [ἀναστροφῇ], in love [ἀγάπῃ], in faith [πίστει], in purity" (1 Tim 4:12). ἀγωγή is also similar to τὰς ὁδούς μου, "my ways," cited previously from 1 Cor 4:17. (3) πρόθεσις, "purpose," carries the idea of "resolve" (cf. BAGD, 706, which suggests "way of thinking"). It is used earlier of God's purpose in salvation; 2 Tim 3:10 is the only time in Paul that it is not used of God's purpose (cf. 2 Tim 1:9). (4) πίστις, "faith," begins the list of specific virtues that flow from correct doctrine and characterize a proper way of living. Timothy likewise is encouraged to pursue faith (cf. 2 Tim 2:22, cited above). Unlike most of the articular uses of πίστις in the PE, this one refers not to creedal faith but to "trust" (see *Introduction,* "Themes in the PE"). The article emphasizes Timothy's knowledge of the events in Paul's life (see above). (5) μακροθυμία, "patience" (cf. 1 Tim 1:16), is especially needed in the Ephesian context and elsewhere (2 Cor 6:6) and should be a quality of Timothy's life (2 Tim 4:2; cf. 2 Tim 2:24: "patient even in the midst of evil [ἀνεξίκακον]"). (6) ἀγάπη, "love" (cf. 1 Tim 1:5), is a virtue necessary in both Paul's life (2 Cor 6:6) and Timothy's (2 Tim 2:22) and is absent in the opponents' lives (cf. *Comment* on 1 Tim 1:5 and the general descriptions of their conduct, especially in 2 Tim 3:2–4). (7) ὑπομονή, "steadfastness," the ability to endure, to persevere, is required of Timothy (1 Tim 6:11) and older men (Titus 2:2). In all three of these occurrences, steadfastness is joined with love. The call to steadfastness is especially significant in light of the last two items in the list (v 11).

11a τοῖς διωγμοῖς, τοῖς παθήμασιν, οἷά μοι ἐγένετο ἐν Ἀντιοχείᾳ, ἐν Ἰκονίῳ, ἐν Λύστροις, οἵους διωγμοὺς ὑπήνεγκα, "my persecutions, my sufferings, which happened to me in Antioch, in Iconium, in Lystra, which persecutions I endured." The final two items in Paul's list are not virtues but rather events and their consequences in Paul's life that are known to Timothy (see *Form/Structure/Setting*). They illustrate why Paul needs "patience" (v 10). This shift is also highlighted by the change from singular to plural. Paul is reflecting back to his earliest persecutions, of which Timothy presumably knew. In Paul's first missionary journey he traveled to the south central part of Asia Minor. In Pisidian Antioch Paul was received well, but then the jealous Jews incited persecution, and Paul and Barnabas were expelled (Acts 13:14–52). In neighboring Iconium they spent considerable time, but Paul left when the Jews and Gentiles tried to stone them (Acts 14:1–5). Then in Lystra Paul and Barnabas were initially welcomed as gods, but eventually Paul was stoned and dragged out of the city (Acts 14:6–20). Acts 16:1–3 relates that Timothy was from this region and had a good reputation in the church (Acts 16:1–3). The PE also mention that Timothy was raised in a believing household (2 Tim 1:5; 3:15). From this it can be assumed that Timothy knew of Paul's earlier treatment in these cities, perhaps even having witnessed both the stoning and Paul's miraculous recovery (Acts 14:20).

Some writers have questioned the author's choice of these persecutions, assuming that Paul did not meet Timothy until his second missionary journey and that therefore Timothy did not witness or know of these earlier persecutions. It is argued that the real Paul would have mentioned the most recent persecutions, ones that he shared with Timothy. By referring to the earlier persecutions the author allegedly shows that he knows the book of Acts but not Paul. Hanson concludes, "It is (for me, at least) impossible to believe that the man who wrote those passages in 2 Corinthians [6:4–10; 11:22–33] also wrote 2 Tim. 3:10–17" ([1983] 149; cf. Easton, 67; Dibelius-Conzelmann, 119). However, to use this type of argument seems to be overly rigid and speculative, and ignores many plausible reasons, including the eight enumerated below, for why the author chose to reflect on these particular persecutions.

(1) Even if Paul did not personally meet Timothy until his second journey, there is no valid reason to assume that Timothy did not know of Paul or that he could not have witnessed the persecutions. Acts 16:1 does not say that Paul had just met Timothy. To say that the townspeople spoke well of Timothy (Acts 16:2) does not mean that this was Paul's first and only contact with him. But even if this were so, it is difficult to believe that Timothy would not have known how his home town had previously treated Paul. In fact, it can be argued that Paul's willingness to take Timothy on the second missionary journey assumes a longer period of acquaintance. (2) Paul has already appealed to Timothy's early spiritual heritage (2 Tim 1:5; 3:15), and a knowledge of these early persecutions is part of that heritage (Fee, 277). (3) Witnessing such ferocious persecutions at a young age could have made a considerable impact on Timothy (Kelly, 199), especially the remembrance of seeing Paul, presumably dead from stoning, get up and walk. (4) Timothy knew of these geographical areas, and the persecution by people from his home area could have had a considerable impact on him (cf. Chrysostom, who emphasizes that these trials are recorded only to encourage Timothy and not in praise of Paul). (5) It would be natural for an older person like Paul to reflect back on the events of his younger days, including the first days of his friendship with Timothy (Guthrie, 161). (6) By pointing out the earliest persecutions, Paul is emphasizing that Timothy has always known that persecutions are part of ministry and that therefore he should endure the work and persecutions now at Ephesus (Knight, 440). (7) Although Paul and Timothy would have experienced persecutions jointly, the first experience often carries the strongest memories. (8) Perhaps these persecutions were the most severe (Ellicott, 141). It is not possible to know why Paul chose to reflect on these persecutions and not others, but there are ample possibilities, and speculation at this point is unwarranted. It seems at best speculative to demand that the "real" Paul would have had to refer to the more recent persecutions rather than the earlier ones. Kelly (199) points out, furthermore, that if the author of the PE were simply borrowing uncritically from his sources, then why did he not draw from the events in Acts 16–17 where it is clear that Timothy was with Paul? (For other recountings of past persecutions, see 2 Cor 6:4–10; 11:22–33.)

διωγμός, "persecution," occurs twice in this verse and is its theme. The word is used specifically of religious persecution (BAGD, 201; cf. Rom 8:35; 2 Cor 12:10; 2 Thess 1:4; cf. Acts 8:1; 13:50; cf. Matt 13:21; Mark 4:17; 10:30). πάθημα, "suffering" (BAGD, 602; cf. Rom 7:5; 8:18; 2 Cor 1:5, 6, 7; Gal 5:24; Phil 3:10; Col 1:24), in this context is suffering due to persecution. οἷα, "which," according to classical rules, can "point to some definite things at hand" (BDF §304; BAGD, 562; 1 Thess

1:5), hence "which" and not "what sort of." Its antecedent is the neuter παθήμασιν, "sufferings." For ὑποφέρειν, "to endure," see 1 Cor 10:13 and 1 Pet 2:19.

11b καὶ ἐκ πάντων με ἐρρύσατο ὁ κύριος, "and out of all these the Lord rescued me." Paul ends his list begun in v 10 with an emphasis on the persecutions and sufferings he has experienced, especially those during his first missionary journey. But typical of Paul throughout this letter, he balances the good with the bad as he continues to encourage Timothy not only to join with him in suffering for the gospel (1 Tim 1:8) but to recognize God's sovereign control of the situation (2 Tim 2:19). The Lord rescued Paul out of all these persecutions, and he will care for Timothy in Ephesus. Later Paul will say that everyone deserted him at his first defense, except the Lord who stood by him and strengthened him to proclaim the gospel: "And I was rescued [ἐρρύσθην] from the lion's mouth. The Lord will rescue [ῥύσεται] me from every evil deed [ἀπὸ παντὸς ἔργου πονηροῦ] and will save [σώσει] [me] for his heavenly kingdom" (4:17b–18a). In this later passage Paul knows that he is going to die (4:6–8) but still sees the sovereign Lord at work, not keeping him from pain and suffering but bringing him through the pain and suffering and keeping him safe for heaven (cf. 1:12). Paul will continue in the next verse (v 12) by pointing out that persecution is an essential element in the life of Christians. It is necessary and should come as no surprise to Paul or Timothy (cf. *Comment* on 1 Tim 4:1). As such v 12 provides a powerful conclusion to the list of Paul's experiences as they call Timothy to loyalty both to Paul and to the gospel.

καί, "and," introduces Paul's positive evaluation (v 11b) of the aforementioned persecutions. ἐκ, "out of," shows Paul's awareness that he is not so much kept away from persecutions and sufferings as that God keeps him safe in the midst of them. πάντων, "all these," refers back to the persecutions and sufferings. The idea of God delivering people out of trouble is a common refrain in the OT, and caution is urged at seeing any one verse as the source of Paul's statement (but cf. Ps 34:19 [33:20 LXX]: καὶ ἐκ πασῶν αὐτῶν ῥύσεται αὐτούς, "and from them all he rescues them"; 34:20 MT: "and from them all the LORD [יהוה] rescues them"). ῥύεσθαι means "to save, rescue, deliver" (BAGD, 737). It is always used in the NT with God/Christ as the agent of deliverance (cf. H. Lichtenberger, *EDNT* 3:214–15). Its emphasis is not so much on salvation (as in σῴζειν, "to save"), although there can be some overlap, but on rescuing someone from danger of some sort (see O'Brien, *Colossians*, 27; discussion of σῴζειν in *Comments* on 1 Tim 3:15 and especially 2 Tim 4:18, where Paul uses both ῥύεσθαι and σῴζειν). On κύριος, "Lord," see *Comment* on 1 Tim 1:2, and on the identity of ὁ κύριος, "the Lord," see *Comment* on 2 Tim 1:18. 2 Tim 3:11 is not a discussion of an individual martyrdom as the next verse makes clear; persecution is part of the fate of all Christians striving for godliness.

12 καὶ πάντες δὲ οἱ θέλοντες εὐσεβῶς ζῆν ἐν Χριστῷ Ἰησοῦ διωχθήσονται, "And also all wishing to live godly [lives] in Christ Jesus will be persecuted." Vv 12–13 generalize the truth of Paul's experience of persecution and suffering, making it applicable to Timothy and all Christians. V 12 discusses those who are in Christ Jesus, and v 13 contrasts these with evil people, thereby calling Timothy to suffer with Paul for the gospel (2 Tim 1:8). The key words in vv 12–13 are εὐσεβῶς, "in a godly manner," and πονηροί, "wicked," as they contrast each other; Timothy is suffering because he is pursuing godliness, which stands in contrast to the sinful world, specifically Ephesus. The opponents are not being persecuted because they are pursuing evil. V 12 hammers the final nail into the coffin of any aberrant gospel that preaches an abundant life devoid of persecutions. Jesus also made it clear that his followers would experience the same suffering as their master (Matt 10:22–25; Luke 21:12; John 15:18–21) and would be blessed for it (Matt 5:10–12). Paul understood this well in both his experience and teaching (Rom 8:17; 2 Cor 12:9–10; Phil 1:29–30; 1 Thess 3:4).

καὶ . . . δέ, "and also" (cf. BAGD, 171 [2b]; 1 Tim 3:10), connects Paul's specific experience (v 11) to a general theological truth (v 12). πάντες . . . οἱ θέλοντες, "all wishing" (on θέλειν, "to wish," cf. *Comment* on 1 Tim 1:7), describes Christians whose desire to live a godly life is "not a mere passing desire, but the continual bent of the will" (Bernard, 134). εὐσεβῶς, "in a godly manner," is a technical term in the PE describing the goal of Christians to be totally consecrated to God with an emphasis on outward piety (cf. 1 Tim 2:2; on εὐσεβῶς ζῆν, "to live in a godly manner," see *Comment* on Titus 2:12). Paul continues by defining these people as being ἐν Χριστῷ Ἰησοῦ, "in Christ Jesus" (cf. 1 Tim 1:14); i.e., the Lordship of Christ is the sphere in which Christians exist. διωχθήσονται, "will be persecuted" (cf. 1 Tim 6:11), connects the persecution of Christians generally with that of Paul.

There is a significant exegetical decision relating to the prepositional phrase ἐν Χριστῷ Ἰησοῦ, "in Christ Jesus." (1) It could modify πάντες, "all," with οἱ θέλοντες εὐσεβῶς ζῆν, "wishing to live godly [lives]," being somewhat parenthetical and in apposition to πάντες: all those in Christ, i.e., those wishing to live godly lives, will be persecuted. By implication, this arrangement requires that all Christians experience persecution for their faith. Cf. Paul's statement that people are fellow heirs with Christ: "if, in fact, we suffer with him so that we may also be glorified with him [εἴπερ συμπάσχομεν ἵνα καὶ συνδοξασθῶμεν]" (Rom 8:17 NRSV). Persecution as a believer becomes a sign of one's salvation. (2) ἐν Χριστῷ Ἰησοῦ could also modify the closer εὐσεβῶς, "in a godly manner," defining it not as piety in general but as specifically Christian piety. In this case Paul is saying that everyone wishing to live a godly life, specifically Christian godliness, will be persecuted. This is probably the preferable reading since it links the prepositional phrase with the closer εὐσεβῶς. The persecution endured by Paul, Timothy, and others is a necessary consequence of striving for godliness; thus persecution functions as an indication of one's pursuit of godliness (and not so much as a necessary indication of one's salvation, as the first arrangement suggests). Timothy can therefore be encouraged that the troubles he is facing in Ephesus are the results of godliness and not some other cause.

13 πονηροὶ δὲ ἄνθρωποι καὶ γόητες προκόψουσιν ἐπὶ τὸ χεῖρον πλανῶντες καὶ πλανώμενοι, "but wicked people and impostors will advance from bad to worse, deceiving and being deceived." In contrast to those desiring to be godly and who are persecuted for it, evil people get worse and worse. Paul is continuing to reflect on the general prophetic message concerning the increase of evil in the last days (3:1–5; cf. 1 Tim 4:1–5), viewing the opponents as examples of this ever-increasing evil. The opponents avoid persecution not because they are right but precisely because they are not; they belong to this world, and so this world loves them (cf. John 15:19). This verse's relationship to v 9 is general to specific; as evil increases in general, the foolishness of the Ephesian opponents will eventually become obvious. The verses do not contradict each other. On the necessity of

Christians encountering trials and tribulations, Chrysostom comments, "One cannot be in combat and live luxuriously, one cannot be wrestling and feasting. Let none therefore of those who are contending seek for ease or joyous living. . . . The season for rest is not now, this is the time for toil and labor" ("Homily 8"; NPNF 13:506).

δέ, "but," contrasts the godly with the wicked (cf. 1 Tim 6:4 and 2 Tim 4:18 where Paul says God will rescue him from all evil). ἄνθρωποι is the generic "people" as it is in 3:2, although Paul is thinking specifically of the false teachers in Ephesus, who appear to have been men. These evil people are also γόητες, "impostors." The word originally meant "sorcerer" and connects these people with the magicians Jannes and Jambres who opposed Moses (3:8). Ellicott says it properly refers to "incantations by howling" (142). This confirms that in v 13 Paul is thinking specifically of the Ephesian opponents and not of evil people in general. In early Christian literature γόης is generally used to mean "swindler, cheat" (BAGD, 164; G. Delling, *TDNT* 1:737; Karris, *JBL* 92 [1973] 560), people who appear to be what they are not. Spicq says it is a term of insult in rhetorical vocabulary (1:105). In the next phrase, Paul confirms that the opponents are hypocrites. προκόπτειν, "to advance," is always used of the opponents in a negative sense in the PE (2 Tim 2:16; 3:9); rather than advancing into what is better, they advance into what is worse. In those passages προκόπτειν is modified by the idiomatic ἐπὶ πλεῖον, "even more," but here by the similar ἐπὶ τὸ χεῖρον, "to the worse." On ἐπί, "to a greater extent, further," see BAGD, 289 (III3). χείρων, "worse," is the comparative of κακός, "bad" (cf. 1 Tim 5:8). The translation "from bad to worse" emphasizes the idea of the verb προκόπτειν, "to advance": from one level of bad to the next.

Paul's final description is most telling: πλανῶντες καὶ πλανώμενοι, "deceiving and being deceived." The opponents know that what they are teaching is wrong, and yet they teach it (see *Introduction*, "The Ephesian Heresy"). But their deliberate decision to deceive comes back to affect them, and hence they are deceived. πλανώμενοι could be middle: "deceiving themselves." More likely it is passive with Satan being the agent of deception (cf. 2:26; 1 Tim 1:20; and especially 4:1). Deceiving others comes back upon the opponents, making them susceptible to Satan's deceptions, which leads them on a downward spiral, deceiving and being deceived to an ever-increasing degree. This twofold nature of deception is a common complaint in philosophical writings (references in Dibelius-Conzelmann, 119).

14a Σὺ δὲ μένε ἐν οἷς ἔμαθες καὶ ἐπιστώθης, "But you, remain in what you have learned and have been convinced of." In contrast to the deceiving opponents (v 13), Timothy is to remain steadfast in the gospel, the gospel he learned in the past and the gospel that experience has taught him is true. As Guthrie explains, "In contrast to the false teachers with their constant endeavor to advance to something new, Timothy may be satisfied with what he has already received" (162). Both objective learning and experiential validation are necessary parts of Timothy's growth as a believer.

There are two crucial exegetical points to be made. (1) In the next several verses Paul is discussing what Timothy has learned. In some places it appears that he is referring to the OT; in other places it appears that he is referring to the gospel message. Because of the flow of the discussion, it appears that Paul does not talk about the OT in distinction from the gospel message, or the gospel apart from its heritage in the OT. (2) ἐν οἷς, "in what," the first of these references, must include at least the gospel message. Paul would not call a Christian evange-list to depend solely on the OT, ignoring the specific gospel message of Jesus Christ. This means that at the beginning of the discussion Paul introduces the gospel, and its presence is felt throughout the rest of the discussion, even in those passages such as v 16 where it appears that Paul is talking specifically about the OT.

The gospel has been one of the dominant themes so far in this letter (see *Introduction,* "Themes in the PE"). Paul has called Timothy not to be ashamed of the gospel but to suffer willingly for the message of the God who saves believers according to his own desires (2 Tim 1:8–10). Paul was called to proclaim this gospel and therefore suffers as he does (1:11–12). So Timothy is to follow Paul's pattern of sound words (1:13), guard the gospel (1:14), and in turn entrust it to reliable men who will teach it when Timothy is gone (2:2). It is the word of truth (2:15, 25; 3:7) and that which Timothy is to teach (2:24). Within this context, and in light of Paul's earlier instructions to Timothy to preach the gospel (1 Tim 4:13–16), the call to steadfastness in 2 Tim 3:14 must deal with the gospel. οἷς, "what," however, is plural. Paul may be thinking of all the different parts that make up the whole gospel, or he may be thinking of the OT (see below) and the gospel message. He may also be preparing the way for the plural ἱερὰ γράμματα, "sacred writings" (v 15).

ἐν οἷς, "in what," is the first of six references to what Timothy has learned and is to proclaim, and like the following two references it is anarthrous. In v 15 Paul mentions ἱερὰ γράμματα, "sacred writings," which are the OT, and yet the expres-sion is somewhat unusual. It is also qualified by the phrase "through faith that is in Christ Jesus," necessarily expanding Paul's scope beyond the OT to the gospel of faith specifically in Jesus Christ. In v 16 Paul speaks of πᾶσα γραφή, "all Scrip-ture," using the NT term for the OT, but uncharacteristically it is anarthrous, and unlike the previous two references it is singular. These variations, plus the fact that all three expressions are talking about the same source(s) of instruction and confidence, are critical for understanding what Paul is saying. While the latter two expressions emphasize the OT, v 14 clearly includes the gospel as part of what Timothy has learned and in which he is called to persevere. This is con-firmed by the fourth reference, Paul's admonition in 4:2. Timothy has learned and has been convinced of the truth of the OT and the gospel message. He has had the OT from youth and understands it in light of the gospel message. The OT comes from God, and therefore in the presence of God and Christ Timothy is called to proclaim the word (4:2), the word of God. Paul is calling Timothy to proclaim not the OT alone but the whole counsel of God, which must include the apostolic message. Paul concludes with the common description of the gos-pel as "the healthy teaching" (v 3) and "the truth" (v 4). While each of these six references may have a different emphasis, they are to be viewed as a whole, speak-ing of the truth of all God's revelation, the Hebrew Scripture and the gospel.

σὺ δέ, "but you," makes a strong contrast with the previous verse. The present imperative μένε, "remain" (cf. 1 Tim 4:16 [ἐπίμενε, "immerse yourself"]), calls for daily steadfastness. οἷς, "what," is dative instead of accusative, having been attracted to the case of its unexpressed antecedent, which is the object of ἐν, "in." On ἔμαθες, "you have learned," see the discussion of its second use below. πιστοῦν, "to show oneself faithful, to be convinced" (BAGD, 665), occurs only here in the

NT. Paul appeals not only tc Timothy's schooling but also to the process by which that learning has proven .self to be true in his experience. Just as Paul believed in God and has become convinced of his character (2 Tim 1:12), so also Timothy has learned the gospel (1:5) and has become convinced that it is true (3:14).

14b–15a εἰδὼς παρὰ τίνων ἔμαθες, καὶ ὅτι ἀπὸ βρέφους [τὰ] ἱερὰ γράμματα οἶδας, "knowing from whom you learned and that from childhood you have known [the] sacred writings." Paul cites two sources of Timothy's confidence. The first is the character of those who taught him. In light of the fact that τίνων, "whom," is plural, that Paul has already made reference to Timothy's spiritual heritage that includes his mother and grandmother (1:5), and that Paul will next refer to Timothy's childhood (3:15), it may be assumed that among these teachers are his mother, Eunice, and grandmother, Lois. Because of Timothy and Paul's relationship, and in light of Paul's previous appeal to their joint experiences (3:10–11), Paul is also including himself among Timothy's teachers. The time frame, therefore, includes not only childhood (from family) but also young adult (from Paul) learning. Basing the reliability of the gospel message partly on the character of one's teachers is the positive counterpart to Paul's critique of the heresy based on the opponents' illicit behavior. This is not an anachronistic reference to the series of teachers leading into the second century (see *Introduction*, "Proposals regarding Authorship of the PE"). εἰδώς, "knowing," is causal and balances the following οἶδας, "you have known." Both the prepositional (παρά, "from") and the ὅτι, "that," phrases are dependent on εἰδώς. Rabbinic sources say that it was the responsibility of every father to instruct his sons in the Torah, starting at age five to six; evidently they began with Leviticus (Str-B 3:664–66).

The second source of Timothy's confidence is the ἱερὰ γράμματα, "sacred writings," that he has known since childhood. There are several issues relating to this expression, which occurs only here in the NT. The first issue is whether the article preceding it (τά, "the") is authentic. If it is not (see *Note* g), then what does the anarthrous "sacred writings" mean? The second is why γράμματα, "writings," is plural. Most writers are convinced that the sacred writings are the Hebrew Scripture. There is sufficient evidence in early Jewish literature that the anarthrous plural was a technical expression for the Hebrew Scripture (references in BAGD, 165 [2c]; G. Schrenk, *TDNT* 1:763–64; Bernard, 135; Dibelius-Conzelmann, 119 n. 6; Fee, 281). Technical phrases are often anarthrous in form but definite in meaning (cf. G. Schrenk, *TDNT* 1:765 n. 13; Dibelius-Conzelmann, 119–20). ἱερός, "sacred" (cf. with βίβλος, "book, scroll": 2 Macc 8:23; *1 Clem.* 43:1; with γραφαί, "writings": *1 Clem.* 45:2; 53:1), and γράμμα, "writing"(Rom 2:27, 29; 7:6; cf. 2 Cor 3:6), can be used in connection with the OT. Paul uses the more common γραφή, "Scripture," in the next verse with no major change in meaning. Since the time frame is Timothy's childhood, it supposedly would have been the Hebrew Scripture that played a vital role in Timothy's upbringing, even in the nontraditional household of a Jewish mother and a Greek father.

But the fact remains that the phrase is unusual for Paul and the NT, and one wonders if there is not something more in Paul's choice of the phrase (so Guthrie, 162). There are two suggestions. (1) More than the simple γραφή, "writing, Scripture," that Paul uses in the next verse, the expression ἱερὰ γράμματα, "sacred writings," stresses the recognized sanctity of the OT. This becomes the focus of attention in vv 16–17, which emphasize the sacred origin of Scripture and hence its applicability to Timothy. V 15 prepares Timothy for the encouragement of vv 10–17. (2) It is possible that this expression includes more than just the OT. The plural ἐν οἷς, "in what," in v 14 refers at least to the gospel message and prepares Timothy for the plural in v 15 by emphasizing either the plurality of doctrines that make up the gospel message or the combination of the OT and the gospel. In v 15b Paul describes the sacred writings as being able to make Timothy wise for salvation, a salvation specifically "through faith in Christ Jesus." While issues of faith and the message about a coming Messiah are part of the OT, it seems doubtful that Paul would say that the OT by itself could instruct Timothy in a salvation that was by faith in Christ Jesus; this would be anachronistic. In addition, vv 14–17 are yet another appeal that Timothy remain loyal to what he has learned, and earlier in this letter this means the gospel message (see discussion of ἐν οἷς, "in what," in *Comment* on v 14a). Of course, in his childhood Timothy would only have known the Hebrew Scripture. It may be concluded that the expression "sacred writings" is drawn solely from the vocabulary describing the Hebrew Scripture, but since Paul is thinking about the culmination of the scriptural hope realized through faith in Christ Jesus, he chooses the anarthrous plural construction to develop his argument in the direction of joining the Hebrew Scripture and the gospel. Kelly (201) reports that the NT writings are not formally classified as "Scripture" until Irenaeus (A.D. 180), although the process began earlier (cf. 2 Pet 3:15–16).

Despite the use of the aorist (ἔμαθες, "you learned"), the learning described is a process, begun in childhood (1:5) and continued by Paul, a process to which Paul repeatedly refers in this letter (1:13, 14; 2:2, 8–9, 15, 24). Moule classifies οἶδας, "you have known," as a "present of past action still in progress" (*Idiom-Book*, 8). Hanson's ([1983] 151) insistence that this learning did not start until Paul's missionary journey mistakenly separates the Hebrew Scripture and gospel messages and misses the full significance of the anarthrous plural "sacred writings" (see above). Acts 16:2 also reports that Paul received a good report of Timothy, suggesting that Timothy had already been a Christian for some time, enough time to allow for Christian maturing. βρέφος, "childhood," can refer to either an unborn baby (Luke 1:41, 44; 2:12, 16) or a newborn child (Luke 18:15; Acts 7:19; 1 Pet 2:2). Because the verse requires that Timothy be old enough to learn, the word has been translated "childhood," and yet the emphasis is on Timothy learning from the earliest age possible. Early rabbinic tradition gives the age of five as the starting time for education (*m. Abot* 5.21; cf. Sus 3; 4 Macc 18:9; Josephus *Ag. Ap.* 1.12 §60; 2.17–18 §§173–78; Str-B 3:664–66; S. Safrai, "Education and the Study of the Torah," in *The Jewish People in the First Century*, ed. S. Safrai and M. Stern [Philadelphia: Fortress, 1976] 2:945–70).

15b τὰ δυνάμενά σε σοφίσαι εἰς σωτηρίαν διὰ πίστεως τῆς ἐν Χριστῷ Ἰησοῦ, "which are able to make you wise for salvation through faith that is in Christ Jesus." Paul now spells out why the sacred writings are a source of confidence and instruction for Timothy. In them is the message that enables Timothy to be wise with a wisdom about salvation. However, Paul must add a qualifier: it is not the Hebrew Scripture alone that should instruct Timothy concerning salvation, but that Scripture understood through the faith of those who are "in Christ Jesus." This is implied in 3:14 and proclaimed in 4:2. It is not, however, to downplay the significance of the OT but to emphasize the completeness and clarity brought by the gospel message. δυνάμενα, "are able," is present linear aspect; the Hebrew Scripture is to play an ongoing role in Timothy's life, both in his childhood and in his adult ministry. Knight (443) speaks of the sacred writings as "having a certain innate ability." Because they are "God-breathed" (v 16), coming from the very mouth of God, they have been enabled to teach powerfully what is true concerning salvation.

σοφίσαι, "to make wise, teach, instruct" (BAGD, 760; cf. 2 Pet 1:16), contrasts Timothy with the opponents, who are not wise (3:9,13) and who teach not the sacred writings but human commandments (cf. Titus 1:14). It is not so much that salvation is the central teaching of the OT, as is pointed out by many modern writers (referencing Luke 24:25–27, 44–47; John 5:39, 46; Acts 17:2–3), but that the instruction of the OT specifically relevant to Timothy's situation is that concerning salvation (on σωτηρία, "salvation," cf. *Comment* on 2 Tim 2:10 and *Introduction*, "Themes in the PE") in contrast to the opponents' mythical reinterpretation of Hebrew genealogies and the law (1 Tim 1:3–4, 7). Because Paul is talking about a daily empowerment, σωτηρίαν, "salvation," refers either to the ongoing implications of salvation in Timothy's life or, more likely, to Timothy's continual work as an evangelist, which is the topic of vv 16–17. As always in the PE and Paul, salvation is by faith (cf. *Introduction*, "Themes in the PE") that is appropriated by those who are joined "in Christ" (cf. 1 Tim 1:14). The message of salvation begun in the OT has been fulfilled in the gospel, and this is what Timothy is to preach (2 Tim 4:2).

16a πᾶσα γραφὴ θεόπνευστος, "All Scripture is God-breathed." Through the centuries this verse has played a central role in the church's doctrine of the inspiration of Scripture. For the exegetical task it is essential to fit it firmly into the Ephesian context. There are a multitude of exegetical issues to be settled, and often one's decision on a single issue has a cascading effect on the others.

(1) The basic thrust of the passage is clear. Throughout the epistle Paul is calling Timothy to loyalty and perseverance in his proclamation of the true gospel. In 3:14–4:2 this is Paul's central focus; Timothy is to persevere in what he has learned and become convinced of (v 14); he learned from reliable people and was raised within the context of the OT (v 15; cf. 1:5). Paul will call on Timothy to preach the gospel (4:2), and Timothy can be fully assured that he is able to do this because the message he proclaims comes from God (v 16a), not from humans. Because it is God's word, it is therefore profitable for Timothy's ministry in Ephesus (v 16b) in that it can train Timothy to be a man of God, prepared for every good work (v 17). The opponents preach Jewish myths and human commandments (Titus 1:14), which stem ultimately from demons (1 Tim 4:1). By contrast, Timothy's message comes from God and is therefore profitable.

(2) While γραφή can refer to any "writing," within the context of the NT and also 2 Timothy it must refer at least to the OT. This is the case with every other occurrence of γραφή in the NT (used some forty-nine times). If πᾶσα is translated "each, every," then Paul could be saying that of all the world's writings, those coming from God are uniquely profitable for Timothy's ministry. But the consistent use of γραφή in the NT to refer to the OT argues against this possibility. Spence recalls Tertullian's position, that γραφὴ θεόπνευστος refers to "any writing which, in so far as it set forth truth, was, to that extent, an emanation from God, the sole source of truth" (*ExpTim* 8 [1896–97] 564).

(3) θεόπνευστος, "God-breathed," occurs only here in the Greek Bible, being found rarely in pre-Christian literature (MM, 287; E. Schweizer, *TDNT* 6:453–55).

It has generally been translated "inspired" (Vulgate, *inspirate*), but the NIV translation "God-breathed" accurately reflects the etymology of the compound word (θεός, "God" + πνεω [aorist *πνευ(σ)-], "to breathe" + verbal adjectival ending -τος) and its meaning as asserting the divine origin of Scripture. It denotes not the manner of the inspiration of Scripture but rather its source. Typical of words formed with -τος, it is passive ("Scripture is God-breathed") and not active ("Scripture emits God's breath," i.e., is inspiring; Robertson, *Grammar,* 157–58, 1095; Moulton, *Grammar* 1:222). Warfield's argument on this point seems to have been accepted nearly universally (Warfield, *Inspiration,* 245–96; contra Cremer, *Lexicon,* 730–32). Paul goes on to talk about the applicability of Scripture to Timothy's life, and although never stated, the assumption is that because Scripture comes from God, it is therefore true, and because it is true, it is therefore profitable. The closest parallel biblical passage is 2 Pet 1:20–21: "Above all, you must understand that no prophecy of Scripture came about by the prophet's own interpretation. For prophecy never had its origin in the will of man, but men spoke from God as they were carried along by the Holy Spirit" (NIV).

(4) Is the singular πᾶσα to be translated "each, every" or "all"? (a) When πᾶς modifies a singular noun, it is generally translated "each, every, any" (references in BAGD, 631 [1aα]; Moule, *Idiom-Book,* 94–95; Robertson, *Grammar,* 771–72; see also House, *BSac* 137 [1980] 54–56). BDF says, "πᾶς before an anarthrous substantive means 'everyone,' not 'each one' like ἕκαστος, but 'anyone'" (§275.3), citing Matt 3:10; 19:3; Acts 4:29; Jas 1:2. Translating πᾶσα as "every" requires θεόπνευστος, "God-breathed," to be an attributive adjective (see point [6] below): every inspired Scripture is profitable. Goodrick suggests that the plural "sacred writings" in the previous verse indicates that Paul is thinking of the different scrolls that made up the entire biblical text, and therefore the emphasis would have been on the reliability of each individual scroll (*JETS* 25 [1982] 480–81; cf. N. Turner, in Moulton, *Grammar* 3:199). (b) Others point out that πᾶς before a singular noun can be translated "all," which in 2 Tim 3:16 would view Scripture as a whole and γραφή as a technical term not requiring the article (Rom 11:26; Col 4:12; cf. Matt 28:18; Acts 2:36; possibly Eph 2:21; 3:15; cf. Robertson, *Grammar,* 772; Smyth, *Grammar,* 296; Moule, *Idiom-Book,* 94–95).

Either option is grammatically possible. The question is whether Paul is thinking of Scripture as a cohesive whole ("all") or as the sum total of its parts ("every"). Some argue that "every" suggests that only some portions of Scripture are God-breathed ("every Scripture that is inspired"), but this seems foreign to the text. Paul is encouraging Timothy to center his ministry on Scripture because it comes from God and will fully equip him for service. It is out of place within this context to introduce the note of the supposed unreliability of some of Scripture. Rather, translating πᾶς as "every" emphasizes that the origin of every single element of the OT comes from God. As stated by Ellicott, "Every separate portion of the Holy Book is inspired, and forms a living portion of a living and organic whole" (147; cf. Spicq, 2:787). Elsewhere in this passage it appears that Paul is viewing Scripture as a whole, and therefore the translation "all" is given. In its entirety Scripture comes from God, and therefore Timothy will be equipped to teach, reprove, correct, and train in righteousness.

(5) While γραφή refers to "Scripture," there is still the question of whether it refers to a single passage or all of the OT, or if it allows something in addition to

the OT (for bibliography cf. *EDNT* 1:260). The fact that it is singular and anarthrous makes this a difficult question. γραφή occurs fourteen times in Paul outside of this passage, and nowhere is γραφή used in a singular anarthrous construction. (In John 19:37 ἑτέρα γραφή, "another Scripture," introduces an OT citation, but ἑτέρα, "another," identifies γραφή much as the article does, and in the preceding verse another OT citation is introduced as ἡ γραφή, "the Scripture," the force of the article coming over to v 37. In 1 Pet 2:6 ἐν γραφῇ, "in Scripture," introduces an OT citation, but the article is often dropped in prepositional phrases.) Eight times in Paul γραφή is used in a singular articular construction (i.e., ἡ γραφή; 1 Tim 5:18; cf. Rom 4:3; 9:17; 10:11; 11:2; Gal 3:8, 22; 4:30). But in all cases except Gal 3:8, 22, Paul uses the phrase λέγει ἡ γραφή, "the Scripture says," to introduce an OT citation. To use the same formula, "the Scripture says," of multiple passages suggests that Paul thinks of Scripture as a whole, which contains different statements for different situations. This is especially true of Rom 11:2: "Don't you know what the Scripture says in the passage about Elijah [οὐκ οἴδατε ἐν Ἡλίᾳ τί λέγει ἡ γραφή]—how he appealed to God against Israel" (NIV). In Gal 3:8 Paul speaks of a section of the OT that is repeated in various places (cf. Longenecker, *Galatians*, 115). Gal 3:22 also uses ἡ γραφή to speak of all the OT, although it can be argued that Paul has a specific verse in mind (cf. Longenecker, *Galatians*, 115, 144). All this suggests that the singular γραφή can be used of the OT as a whole, not just one specific passage (cf. BAGD, 166 [2bβ]; Schrenk, *TDNT* 1:753–55; Warfield, *Inspiration*, 236–39). It should also be noted that the singular πᾶσα γραφή, "all Scripture," is parallel to the plural ἱερὰ γράμματα, "sacred writings," which refers to the entire OT.

γραφή also occurs in the plural with (Rom 15:4; 1 Cor 15:3, 4) and without (Rom 1:2; 16:26) the article. (a) When it is anarthrous, it occurs in a prepositional phrase, in which the article is frequently omitted, and with another specifier that performs somewhat the same function as the article (ἐν γραφαῖς ἁγίαις, "in the holy Scriptures" [Rom 1:2]; διὰ . . . γραφῶν προφητικῶν, "through the prophetic writings" [Rom 16:26]). In 2 Tim 3:16 πᾶσα, "all," might likewise be functioning as a specifier, and the article therefore is omitted as redundant. (b) Three times in Paul γραφή is used in a plural form with the article: having quoted an OT passage, Paul generalizes by saying that the Scriptures (τῶν γραφῶν) offer encouragement (Rom 15:4); in 1 Cor 15:3, 4 Paul speaks of the prophecies of Christ's death and resurrection being "according to the Scriptures" (κατὰ τὰς γραφάς), thinking either of various passages or of the OT as a whole (cf. Fee, *Corinthians*, 725). In Matt 21:42 Matthew uses the plural ἐν ταῖς γραφαῖς, "in the Scriptures," to introduce a citation from Ps 118:22–23. The pattern Paul reflects is basically the same found elsewhere in the NT (cf. references in BAGD; G. Schrenk, *TDNT* 1:742–73).

What then can be concluded about the anarthrous singular πᾶσα γραφή? The closest parallel is 2 Pet 1:20. It appears that the anarthrous construction is not significantly different from the articular one, although the latter is preferred. γραφή has achieved substantially technical status and can stand on its own, although the preceding anarthrous ἱερὰ γράμματα, "sacred writings" (v 15), and the force of πᾶσα, "all," may have encouraged the omission of the article. While the plural can emphasize the totality of Scripture or the multiplicity of passages cited by the author, the singular can carry the same force since it emphasizes the completeness of Scripture. It may be concluded that here πᾶσα γραφή refers to the entirety of the OT, Timothy's source of learning, which can instruct him for salvation, and out of which Timothy can teach, reprove, etc.

However, there is another issue relating to the scope of γραφή. While it certainly includes the OT, does it include more? If the usage elsewhere in the NT is the key, then the answer must be "No" since γραφή is used exclusively of the OT. But there are other factors, the most significant being the immediate context. As discussed in v 14, the fourfold reference to "in what" (v 14), "sacred writings" (v 15), "all Scripture" (v 16), and "the word" (4:2) suggests Paul is thinking of the OT in light of the gospel. ἐν οἷς, "in what," is plural, ἱερὰ γράμματα, "sacred writings," is plural and possibly anarthrous, πᾶσα γραφή, "all Scripture" is anarthrous and general in scope, and both "in what" and "the word" refer to the gospel. All this suggests that γραφή refers to both the OT and the gospel message (for the latter, its oral proclamation and perhaps parts that were written and disseminated by this time are to be included). While in extrabiblical literature reference to the NT writings as "Scripture" is not found until later, 2 Pet 3:15–16 shows that the shift started earlier (depending on one's dating of the epistle). Perhaps this is why Paul can introduce an OT citation and a saying of Jesus with the one formula, "Scripture says" (1 Tim 5:18). It is also an expected shift. Since the early church viewed the words of Jesus as fully authoritative, it would not have been a large step for the early Christians to accept the writings of his apostles as equally authoritative with the OT. While it cannot be asserted that γραφή in 2 Tim 3:16 includes Paul's correspondence, the door is open to enlarge the parameters of γραφή.

(6) The final issue in v 16a has to do with whether θεόπνευστος, "God-breathed," is an attributive adjective ("all God-breathed Scripture is also profitable") or a predicate adjective ("all Scripture is God-breathed and is profitable"). Grammatically both are possible and in the end not significantly different. Both assert two truths: Scripture comes from God; because it comes from God, it is useful in preparing Timothy for ministry.

If θεόπνευστος is an attributive adjective, "is" is inserted after "Scripture" and καί is adjunctive: "God-breathed Scripture *is also* profitable" (Syriac ["All scripture which by the Spirit is written is useful for teaching," cited in Sheriffs, *EvQ* 34 (1962) 94]; Origen ["Every Scripture, because it is theopneustic, is profitable," cited by Warfield, *Inspiration,* 293–94]; Vulgate; Wycliffe's tr.; Luther's tr.; Tyndale's tr.; H. Grotius, *Annotationum in Novum Testamentum,* 3 vols. [Paris, 1641–50]; Ellicott; RV; Spence, *ExpTim* 8 [1896–97] 563–65; Bernard; ASV; Spicq; Dibelius-Conzelmann; NEB; Sheriffs, *EvQ* 34 [1962] 91–95; Barrett; E. L. Miller, *LQ* 17 [1965] 56–62; Brox; GNB margin). καί is adjunctive in the sense that in addition to its divine origin Scripture is "also" profitable. (a) This construction emphasizes the parallelism between v 15 and v 16. The "writings" are "sacred"; "Scripture" is "God-breathed." The counterargument is that v 16 starts a new sentence and thus separates to some degree these two thoughts, a separation strengthened by the change from γράμματα, "writings," to γραφή, "Scripture." One might also expect v 16a to begin with a connective if it were so closely tied to v 15. Rather, v 16a can be read as a general truth out of which v 16b and, in a sense, v 15 flow. (b) Some argue that if θεόπνευστος were an attributive adjective, it would be expected to come first (Guthrie, 164; Kelly, 203). But there are many examples of an attributive adjective following the noun. Spence (*ExpTim* 8 [1896–97] 564) counts twenty-one NT passages in which "πᾶς and another adjective stand in connexion with the same substantive" and always finds the order πᾶς–substantive–adjective with the adjective being an attributive (Matt 7:17; 12:36; Acts 23:1; 2 Cor 9:8; Eph 1:3; 4:29; Col 1:10; 2 Thess 2:17; 2 Tim 2:21; 3:17; 4:18; Titus 1:16; 2:10; 3:1; Heb 4:12; Jas 1:17; 3:16; Rev 8:7; 18:2, 12; 21:19). Roberts summarizes Spence's argument and adds corroborating Septuagintal evidence (*ExpTim* 76 [1964–65] 359). He notes that the only exception appears to be 1 Tim 4:4, but this passage has an intervening word (πᾶν κτίσμα θεοῦ καλὸν καὶ οὐδὲν ἀπόβλητον, "every creation of God is good and nothing is rejected"). While an articular attributive adjective generally precedes the word it modifies, an anarthrous attributive adjective generally follows (BDF §251). The counterargument is that γραφή is a technical term and therefore does not require the article; its usage may be different from the passages cited. If θεόπνευστος is attributive, the verse does not read "every Scripture [that is] inspired is also profitable," suggesting that there are parts of the OT that are not inspired. "Every" would emphasize the inspiration of every part of Scripture: different passages, different books, different scrolls (see above).

If θεόπνευστος is a predicate adjective, "is" is inserted before "Scripture" and before ὠφέλιμος, "profitable," and καί is a regular copulative: "Scripture *is* God-breathed *and is* profitable" (Calvin; KJV; Weymouth's tr.; Goodspeed's tr.; Lock; Robertson, *Word Pictures* 4:627; Moffatt's tr.; RSV; Jeremias; Guthrie; Hendriksen; Kelly; Dornier; Holtz; NIV; House, *BSac* 137 [1980] 58–61; Goodrick, *JETS* 25 [1982] 483–86; Hanson [1983]; Fee; Oberlinner; Wallace, *Greek Grammar,* 313–14; Moule, *Idiom-Book,* 95). (a) This is the more natural reading of the text. When two adjectives follow the subject and are connected by καί, it is natural to treat them both the same way. (b) Instead of emphasizing the parallelism with "sacred writings" (but not ignoring it either), this construction emphasizes the parallelism between "God-breathed" and "profitable," which is more in line with Paul's argument. Because Scripture comes from God, it is profitable for Timothy's preparation for ministry. This arrangement also recognizes that v 16 starts a new sentence and states a general principle out of which v 15b and v 16b flow. (c) This does not mean that Timothy did not already know and accept this truth about Scripture. In fact, both arrangements assert the divine origin of Scripture; the second merely adds more emphasis to it. The entire context of the epistle is to remind Timothy of what he knows to be true and to encourage him in his battle with the Ephesians. (d) Wallace comments, "In the NT, LXX, in classical and Koine Greek, the overwhelming semantic force of an adj.–noun–adj. construction in an equative clause is that the first adj. will be attributive and the second will be predicate" (*Greek Grammar,* 314). He continues by formulating this rule: "In πᾶς + noun + adjective constructions in equative clauses the πᾶς, being by nature as definite as the article, implies the article, thus making the adjective(s) following the noun outside the implied article-noun group and, therefore, predicate" (*Greek Grammar,* 314). The only grammatical parallel to v 16a is 1 Tim 4:4, and there the adjective καλόν, "good," is in the predicate. (e) Bernard (137) and others argue that this construction makes the verse into a theological pronouncement on the doctrine of inspiration, which they feel is inappropriate to the context and is not being questioned by Timothy. Rather, they argue, the context requires the emphasis to be on the profitability of Scripture. But this is precisely what a theological pronouncement on the inspiration of Scripture accomplishes. The opponents are teaching commandments that come from demons (1 Tim 4:1) through people (Titus 1:14). Scripture, on the other hand, Paul says, comes straight from God, and therefore Timothy can trust it to equip and train him to do his work as an evangelist (cf. Kelly, 203). Often these two options are discussed as if they were mutually exclusive: the passage discusses either the inspiration of Scripture or its utility (e.g., E. L. Miller, *LQ* 17 [1965] 60). This is unnecessary; utility of Scripture flows out of its inspiration. The entirety of Scripture comes from the mouth of God. To read it is to hear him speak. It is therefore true, and it can therefore be trusted.

16b καὶ ὠφέλιμος πρὸς διδασκαλίαν, πρὸς ἐλεγμόν, πρὸς ἐπανόρθωσιν, πρὸς παιδείαν τὴν ἐν δικαιοσύνῃ, "and profitable for teaching, for reproof, for correcting, for training in righteousness." Because Scripture comes from God, it is profitable for Timothy in his task in Ephesus and ministry in general. The four prepositional phrases may form two groups, the first dealing with doctrine ("orthodoxy") and the second with behavior ("orthopraxy"). They are also chiastic in structure: (a) Scripture instructs positively in doctrine and (b) convicts heresy; likewise Scripture (b') corrects improper behavior and (a') educates positively in righteous behavior. Spicq (2:788–89) explains the four phrases as (a) Scripture is the only true source for pastoral and doctrinal teaching, (b) Scripture is the best ammunition for rebuking the false teachers, (c) Scripture will not only stop the deviations of the false teachers but straighten out and improve the condition, and (d) Scripture is necessary for the training of truly virtuous Christians. The list that follows is somewhat parallel to 2 Tim 4:2. As is stated elsewhere in the PE (1 Tim 4:6, 13, 16; 6:3), Timothy, and by implication every "person of God" (v 17), must be grounded in Scripture because it is what enables people for every good work.

On ὠφέλιμος, "profitable, useful," see *Comment* on 1 Tim 4:8. διδασκαλία, "teaching" (cf. 1 Tim 1:10), is a technical term in the PE for the doctrinal formulation of Scripture (cf. especially 1 Tim 4:13). It, not myths, is the basis of Timothy's ministry, as Paul emphasizes elsewhere (cf. Rom 15:4). ἐλεγμός, "reproof" (the only reference in the NT; cf. BAGD, 249, and its verbal cognate in 1 Tim 5:20 and 2 Tim 4:2), is the conviction of false doctrine. Scripture is the standard of truth, the pattern of truth (1:13). Timothy is to guard it (1:14) by using it to convict error. Shifting from doctrine to behavior, Paul says that Scripture is profitable for correcting improper behavior (ἐπανόρθωσις, "correcting," occurring only here in the NT; cf. BAGD, 283; MM, 229; H. Preisker, *TDNT* 5:450–51). Positively, Scripture is useful to train someone in righteousness since it provides not only the content of belief but also the guidelines for conduct. On παιδεία, "training," see *Comments* on Titus 2:12 and 2 Tim 2:25. δικαιοσύνη, "righteousness," is not only a gift bestowed but also a virtue to be sought (cf. 1 Tim 6:11; 2 Tim 2:22), the latter being emphasized in the PE owing to their practical emphasis.

17 ἵνα ἄρτιος ᾖ ὁ τοῦ θεοῦ ἄνθρωπος, πρὸς πᾶν ἔργον ἀγαθὸν ἐξηρτισμένος, "in order that the person of God be proficient, fully equipped for every good work." V 17 is not an afterthought tagged on to show the result of v 16b. ἵνα, "in order that," introduces the ultimate purpose of Scripture's inspiration. Scripture comes from God and is true; therefore it provides the content and direction necessary for Timothy, Christian leaders, and by implication all Christians to be fully equipped, enabled to do every good work, among which are teaching, reproving, correcting, and training in righteousness. It is difficult to bring the play on words into English. Paul says that Scripture makes the person of God proficient (ἄρτιος) and then uses the cognate verb (in a compound form with the perfective preposition) to emphasize that Timothy is fully equipped (ἐξαρτίζειν). The emphasis is on the sufficiency of Scripture to provide the knowledge and direction for Timothy's ministry (see *Explanation*). This is in line with Paul's affirmation elsewhere that the OT was written to instruct the believer (Rom 4:23–4; 15:4; 1 Cor 9:9–10; 10:11; cf. also Ellis, *Paul's Use of the Old Testament*, 10–11).

If ἵνα, "in order that," denotes result, it is linked to ὠφέλιμος, "profitable" (v 16), but in denoting purpose it goes back to θεόπνευστος, "God-breathed" (v 16). On ὁ τοῦ θεοῦ ἄνθρωπος, "person of God," see *Comment* on 1 Tim 6:11 and the δοῦλον ... κυρίου, "Lord's servant" (2 Tim 2:24). The phrase is directed specifically to Timothy, a "man of God" (1 Tim 6:11), and to all Christian leaders, but by implication to all Christians (hence, "person"). ἄρτιος occurs only here in the NT, meaning "complete, capable, proficient" (BAGD, 110), "thoroughly equipped" (NIV). But the following phrase defines the scope of preparedness: it is to be able to do every good work. ἐξηρτισμένος, "fully equipped" (BAGD, 273; Acts 21:5), is the verbal cognate of the previous ἄρτιος with the perfective preposition ἐκ added. The perfective form of this verb, the fact that it is in the perfect tense, and its connection to πᾶν, "every," all emphasize the completeness of Scripture's preparation. Timothy and all Christians can find in Scripture everything necessary to do good works. ἔργα ἀγαθά, "good works" (see *Comment* on 1 Tim 2:10), is a repeated theme in the PE, placing emphasis on the practical outworking of the gospel.

4:1 διαμαρτύρομαι ἐνώπιον τοῦ θεοῦ καὶ Χριστοῦ Ἰησοῦ τοῦ μέλλοντος κρίνειν ζῶντας καὶ νεκρούς, καὶ τὴν ἐπιφάνειαν αὐτοῦ καὶ τὴν βασιλείαν αὐτοῦ, "I solemnly charge [you] before God and Christ Jesus, who is about to judge [the] living and [the] dead, and by his appearing and by his kingdom." Paul starts the third paragraph in this section by creating a scene of solemnity against which Timothy is to understand the charge in v 2 to preach the gospel. As Timothy discharges his duties as an evangelist, he does so in full sight of God and of Christ, who is the eschatological judge, and in recognition of Christ's second coming and of the eschatological consummation of Christ's kingdom. This verse continues the theme of 3:16–17 and is the fourth reference to the message that Timothy is to proclaim (cf. 3:14).

The grammar is awkward. Paul starts with a prepositional phrase (ἐνώπιον ..., "before ...") but continues with two accusatives used as oaths; hence the inclusion of "by" in the translation ("I solemnly charge ... by ..."; cf. Wallace, *Greek Grammar*, 204; BDF §149; cf. Mark 5:7; Acts 19:13; 1 Thess 5:27; Jas 5:12). To swear by Christ's appearing and by his kingdom is to use the fact of these two future events as a basis for solemnity. Timothy's life is on display before God and Christ, and Christ will appear again and his kingdom will come in its fullness. In light of all this, Timothy is to preach the word (v 2). V 1 is also tied to v 8: at the end of his life Paul looks forward to the crown of righteousness he will receive from the Lord (ὁ κύριος), the righteous judge (κριτής), on judgment day, as will be true of everyone who has loved his appearing (ἐπιφάνεια).

διαμαρτύρεσθαι, "to solemnly charge," can be a technical term for taking an oath (cf. similar injunctions in 1 Tim 5:21, "I solemnly charge [you] before God and Christ Jesus and the elect angels" [see there for a discussion of the common words]; 1 Tim 6:13, "I urge [you] before God who gives life to all things and Christ Jesus who witnessed in the time of Pontius Pilate the good confession"; 2 Tim 2:14, "solemnly charging [them] before God"). Spicq (2:798) says that it can also be a technical term for the transfer of office, which is what is happening as Paul knows his life is ending and Timothy will have to shoulder the responsibility without him. It can be a technical term for judgment in a law court as well (BAGD, 452 [4b]). Cf. Paul's statement that God is the "living God" (1 Tim 3:15) and hence will not allow his church to be destroyed.

The use of the first person "I" expresses both a personal message and apostolic authority. μέλλοντος κρίνειν, "is about to judge," is a periphrastic future construction (1 Tim 1:16; 4:8; 6:19; BAGD, 500–501) and emphasizes the eschatological imminence of Christ's return (cf. 2 Tim 4:6–8, 18). One of Christ's eschatological duties will be to judge (Rom 2:16; 1 Cor 4:5; 2 Cor 5:10; John 5:22, 27; Acts 17:31) those who are alive (ζῶντας, "living," the older English "quick") at his return and those who have already died, that is, everyone (cf. 2 Cor 5:10; 1 Thess 4:16–17; cf. Acts 17:31). The phrase "the living and the dead" is used elsewhere in the NT (Rom 14:9, in reverse order; cf. Acts 10:42; 1 Pet 4:5; the latter two occurring in the context of final judgment) and became a creedal element in the early church (*Barn.* 7:2; Pol. *Phil.* 2.1; *2 Clem.* 1:1) as, for example, in the Apostles' Creed: "I believe in . . . Jesus Christ . . . who sits at the right hand of God the Father Almighty, ready to judge the quick and the dead." Although some say it is from a baptismal creed (Lock, Guthrie, Kelly), there is nothing about it that necessarily suggests baptism. On ἐπιφάνεια, "appearing," describing Christ's eschatological return, see *Comment* on 1 Tim 6:14 (also Titus 2:13 and 2 Tim 4:8). The emphasis is on αὐτοῦ, "his"; it is not the appearing of a world ruler (as the word is used in Hellenism; cf. 1 Tim 6:14) but that of Christ that is to be feared, and this is the basis for Paul's charge. Paul will soon say that a crown of righteousness awaits all who have loved his appearing (4:8). In reference to βασιλεία, "kingdom," Paul is thinking of its eschatological fulfillment (cf. 2 Tim 4:18 and the future aspect of the kingdom as seen in 1 Cor 6:9, 10; 15:24, 50; Gal 5:21; Eph 5:5; 1 Thess 2:12; 2 Thess 1:5). Paul generally calls it the "kingdom of God" (Rom 14:7; 1 Cor 4:20; 6:9–10; 15:24, 50; Gal 5:21; Eph 5:5; Col 4:11; 2 Thess 1:15), but he also calls it the "kingdom of his beloved Son" (Col 1:13), "his kingdom" (1 Thess 2:12), and "his heavenly kingdom" (2 Tim 4:18).

2 κήρυξον τὸν λόγον, ἐπίστηθι εὐκαίρως ἀκαίρως, ἔλεγξον, ἐπιτίμησον, παρακάλεσον, ἐν πάσῃ μακροθυμίᾳ καὶ διδαχῇ, "Preach the word! Be prepared when it is opportune or inopportune! Confront! Rebuke! Exhort!—with complete patience and teaching." Within the context of solemnity created by v 1, Paul delivers his charge to Timothy: Preach the gospel! Timothy learned the gospel (3:14) along with the OT (3:15); it is from God and is profitable for his ministry (3:16–17), and therefore Timothy must preach it. Once again Paul is repeating his central theme of the role Scripture and the gospel are to play in Timothy's ministry (cf. 1 Tim 4:6–16; 6:20; 2 Tim 1:13, 14). The anaphoric definite article identifies τὸν λόγον, "the word," specifically as the Scripture in 3:16–17 (cf. Wallace, *Greek Grammar*, 220) and strengthens the contrast with the heresy described in the following verses.

The verse is formed with five aorist imperatives, the aorist tense giving a serious tone appropriate for the pronouncements. The second imperative can function as a qualifier of the first—be prepared to preach—or it can stand on its own as a general call for preparedness to minister. The first, third, fourth, and fifth imperatives follow a logical sequence. Timothy is to preach the word. As it conflicts with the Ephesian heresy, he will need to confront the false teachers and their teaching, rebuke those who will not listen to him, and exhort those who will listen and follow the true gospel. The final prepositional phrase could modify the last three imperatives or all five. Especially in light of what the future holds (vv 3–4), Timothy must have complete and total patience, and his teaching must inform his preaching, confronting, rebuking, and exhorting. While Paul is thinking of Timothy in this verse, what he says is true for all Christian ministers, just as much of Paul's instruction elsewhere goes beyond Timothy.

κήρυξον, "preach" (constative aorist; Wallace, *Greek Grammar* 721; cf. noun cognate in 1 Tim 2:7), means to proclaim aloud. In the NT the term is usually used of the gospel. τὸν λόγον, "the word" (cf. 1 Tim 4:6), is the gospel (cf. 3:14); τόν, "the," is anaphoric (Wallace, *Greek Grammar,* 220), including the OT (3:15, 16–17). ἐπίστηθι, "be prepared," is a difficult word to translate. The aorist active is intransitive: "stand by or near," or "approach, appear" (cf. 1 Thess 5:3; BAGD, 330–31). The word occurs in v 6, but there it is perfect tense, "has arrived." The translations read "be prepared" (NIV), "be urgent" (RSV), "be ready" (NKJV; NASB; BAGD, 330 [1a]). The term is best defined by the following phrase. "When it is opportune or inopportune" is a loose translation of εὐκαίρως ἀκαίρως, a time that is suitable (εὐ-, "good, well," plus the adverb formed from καιρός, "time"; cf. BDF §117 [1]; εὔκαιρος, "well-timed, suitable"; εὐκαιρία, "favorable opportunity" [BAGD, 321]) and a time that is not suitable (the alpha privative ἀ-, "un-," plus the same adverb formed from καιρός, a word occurring only here in the NT; cf. ἄκαιρος, "untimely, ill-timed" [BAGD, 29; not occurring in the NT]). In other words Timothy is always to be prepared to preach and perform his ministry, in season and out of season. It can possibly be a military metaphor, "the Christian minister must always be on duty" (Guthrie, 166), although there is no indication in this text that it is so here (Kelly, 205–6). However, it is not clear whether the charge is directed toward Timothy or the opponents. Is Timothy to preach whether he is prepared or not (subjective), or is Timothy to preach whether the opponents are ready to hear it or not (objective)? The subjective interpretation would fit Timothy if he had a propensity toward timidity (2 Tim 1:7). Most prefer the objective interpretation in light of the opponents' opposition spelled out in vv 3–4, but these verses support the subjective as well since they encourage Timothy always to be willing to preach because one day it will become more difficult. The distinction is probably overly subtle; Timothy is to be about his task regardless of the situation (see also Malherbe, *JBL* 103 [1984] 235–43). The inopportune times (ἀκαίρως) are spelled out in vv 3–4 when Paul says a καιρός, "time," will come when people will not listen to the gospel.

The four main imperatives ("Preach! Confront! Rebuke! Exhort!") loosely parallel the four prepositional phrases in 3:16 ("profitable for teaching, reproof [ἐλεγμόν; cf. variant reading ἔλεγχον], correcting [ἐπανόρθωσιν], training in righteousness"), especially if "exhort" is encouragement to live out the gospel (i.e., "righteousness"). Kelly (206) says that these final three imperatives are often viewed as referring to reason, conscience, and the will, but he doubts that this is the case here. Rather, they seem to reflect a logical order of dealing with the opponents (see above). ἔλεγξον, "confront" (cf. 1 Tim 5:20, the variant reading ἔλεγχον, "reproof," in 3:16, and the pairing of the verb with παρακαλεῖν, "to exhort," as here, in Titus 1:9; 2:15), speaks of Timothy's confrontation of the false teachers and their heresy. Timothy is to ἐπιτίμησον, "rebuke" (BAGD, 303), those who do not listen. The word occurs twenty-nine times in the NT, but only here in Paul. It is a strong word, used of Jesus' rebuke of demons (Mark 3:12; 8:33; 9:25; Luke 9:55; 19:39–40; cf. E. Stauffer, *TDNT* 2:623–67; Trench, *Synonyms*, 31–34). But if they listen to Timothy, he is to παρακάλεσον, "exhort, encourage" (cf. 1 Tim 1:3), them to live out the gospel in a life of righteousness. It appears that the final prepositional phrase modifies not just παρακάλεσον, "exhort," but rather the final three imperatives or perhaps all five. All of Timothy's ministry is to be characterized by μακροθυμία, "patience" (cf. 1 Tim 1:16 where it occurs with ἅπας, "all"; 2 Tim 3:10; cf. 2 Cor 6:6), and a knowledge gained by διδαχή, "teaching," what is right (cf. Titus 1:9 where διδαχή is combined with παρακαλεῖν, "to exhort," and διδασκαλία, "teaching"). διδαχή can refer to what is taught or to the activity of teaching (cf. BAGD, 192 [1]; 1 Cor 14:6; Mark 4:2; 12:38), the latter seeming to be more appropriate here. However, it is the gospel, the word, that is taught. The emphasis on πάσῃ, "complete" (cf. BAGD, 631 [1aδ]), prepares Timothy for the difficulties described in vv 3–4 and the Ephesian situation.

3a ἔσται γὰρ καιρὸς ὅτε τῆς ὑγιαινούσης διδασκαλίας οὐκ ἀνέξονται, "For a time will come when they will not put up with healthy teaching." Vv 3–4 spell out the reason for the seriousness of v 1 and the urgency of v 2. Timothy is to be prepared to preach the gospel even when the time is not right (ἀκαίρως, "inopportune" [v 2]) because the καιρός, "time," is coming when people will not listen to the gospel. Although the verse is not stated as a prophecy of the increase of evil as the final day approaches, it is within that context that it should be understood, as 3:1–9 and 1 Tim 4:1–5 show. There too the prophecy is stated as a future reality but a future that has now been realized in Timothy's present. This is made clear in v 4 when Paul says they will wander into myths, and 1 Tim 1:4 indicates that the myths are currently being taught. The accumulation of teachers (v 4) also agrees with Paul's description of his opponents as those wanting to be teachers of the law (1 Tim 1:7). The subject of οὐκ ἀνέξονται, "they will not put up with," is never identified, the assumption being that it refers to the current Ephesians. Thus it need not be suggested that the author knew prophecies that were fulfilled in the second century in the time of the supposed pseudepigrapher (contra Dibelius-Conzelmann, 120–21). Paul sees himself living in the last days and sees the prophecies of increasing evil being fulfilled in Ephesus. The passage emphasizes once again the hypocrisy of the Ephesian church. They chose not to put up with correct teaching. The false teachers are chosen in accordance with their own evil desires. Rather than hearing one correct teacher, they build a wall of teachers as if the sheer number of teachers will make them right. What they really want is to have their itching ears tickled with the latest doctrinal fad. Paul's critique finds application during every stage of the church in the last days.

Vv 3–4 contain the fifth and sixth references to the gospel in this section (cf. 3:14). Rather than sound teaching, the Ephesians want teachers who will scratch their itching ears with doctrine that stems from their evil desires (v 3). Rather than listening to the truth, they will wander into myths (v 4). The emphasis of both verses is not so much on the false teachers as it is on those who choose to listen to them. On ὑγιαινούσης διδασκαλίας, "healthy teaching," as a synonym for the gospel, see *Comment* on 1 Tim 1:10. It continues the emphasis on the gospel. Paul often had to fight perversions of the gospel; the Ephesian heresy is just another form. ἀνέχεσθαι is always middle (deponent) in early Christian literature, meaning "to endure, put up with"; here it has the sense of being willing to hear or listen to something (followed by the genitive; BAGD, 65–66; H. Schlier, *TDNT* 1:359–60; cf. Heb 13:22).

3b ἀλλὰ κατὰ τὰς ἰδίας ἐπιθυμίας ἑαυτοῖς ἐπισωρεύσουσιν διδασκάλους κνηθόμενοι τὴν ἀκοήν, "but in accordance with their own lusts they will heap up teachers for themselves, having itching ears." The Ephesians are surrounding themselves with a wall of teachers who offer what their evil hearts want to hear rather than listening to Timothy and the gospel.

ἀλλά, "but," firmly separates the two parts of this verse. κατά, "in accordance with" (BAGD, 407 [II5]), modifies the following verb, identifying their true motivation. ἐπιθυμία, "lust," is always used in the PE of sinful desires (cf. 1 Tim 6:9 and discussion of the verbal cognate in 1 Tim 3:1). It stresses once again that a person's doctrine cannot be separated from behavior; because their actions are controlled by their lusts, the teaching is wrong (see *Introduction*, "The Response to the Heresy"). ἐπισωρεύειν, "to heap up," occurs only here in the NT (BAGD, 302; MM, 247). *Barn.* 4:6 speaks of "heaping up [ἐπισωρεύοντας] your sins," one on top of another. The image is of hypocritical people thinking that if they can find enough teachers, somehow they will be right and able to oppose Paul and Timothy. 1 Tim 1:7 indicates that these people want to be teachers of the law.

κνήθειν occurs only here in the NT. In the active voice it means "to scratch," and in the passive voice "to itch," used figuratively of curiosity (BAGD, 437). Bernard adds that it means "to be tickled" (141). The imagery is that their itching ears are tickled by the false teachers who teach whatever is sensational or novel but in the end what conforms to their evil lusts, specifically the myths of the Ephesian heresy, which people can always study but never gain in knowledge (3:7). ἀκοή is the faculty/act/organ of hearing, hence the "ear" (BAGD, 31; cf. Mark 7:35; Luke 7:1; Acts 17:20; Heb 5:11). The same word occurs in the next verse with reference to listening to truth. ἀκοήν, "ear," is singular, but idiomatic ("having itching ears") with the plural participle.

4 καὶ ἀπὸ μὲν τῆς ἀληθείας τὴν ἀκοὴν ἀποστρέψουσιν, ἐπὶ δὲ τοὺς μύθους ἐκτραπήσονται, "and they will turn away from listening to the truth and wander across to the myths." Enforcing the two actions in v 3, Paul repeats common themes found throughout the PE. This is the last mention of the heresy (although Paul will speak of Alexander and his opposition in 4:14–15), and Paul uses terms that are similar to his first reference to it (1 Tim 1:3–7) and to the reference in Titus 1:14. At one time the people believed the ἀλήθεια, "truth," the gospel (cf. 1 Tim 2:4), but they made a deliberate, conscious decision to turn from it. Paul tells Titus to rebuke the Cretans so that they will not be devoted to Jewish myths (μὴ προσέχοντες Ἰουδαϊκοῖς μύθοις) and turn from the truth (ἀποστρεφομένων τὴν ἀλήθειαν; Titus 1:14).

καί, "and," introduces v 4 as a repetition of v 3, and the verse is divided into two symmetrical parts, each having an introductory particle (μέν/δέ), a preposition (ἀπό/ἐπί) and its object, and a verb. They turned away from (ἀπό . . .

ἀποστρέφειν; cf. Titus 1:14) the truth and deliberately crossed over to (ἐπί . . . ἐκτρέπεσθαι; cf. 1 Tim 1:6; 5:15) the lie. The definite article before μύθους, "myths," identifies it specifically as τοὺς μύθους, "the myths," being taught in Ephesus, speculative reinterpretations of the OT (1 Tim 1:4), and sets it in contrast to τῆς ἀληθείας, "the truth," in v 4a. ἀκοήν is repeated from the previous verse ("having itching ears"), but here it refers to "listening."

5 Σὺ δὲ νῆφε ἐν πᾶσιν, κακοπάθησον, ἔργον ποίησον εὐαγγελιστοῦ, τὴν διακονίαν σου πληροφόρησον, "But you, be clear-minded in everything! Suffer evil! Do the work of an evangelist! Complete your ministry!" In contrast to the opposing Ephesians (vv 3–4) and in preparation for Paul's imminent death (vv 6–8), Timothy is to remain steadfast. The four imperatives all make this same point—perseverance (cf. 3:10). With this verse Paul ends his personal admonitions to Timothy. He began in 1:6 to encourage Timothy by comparing their ministries and calling him to loyalty to both himself and the gospel. This has been the dominant theme throughout the epistle.

(1) νήφειν, "to be clear-minded, sober" (cf. discussion of the cognate adjective in *Comment* on 1 Tim 3:2), in the historical context is a call to Timothy to "steer clear of the heady wine of heretical teaching" (Kelly, 207) but is also understood in a more general sense of clear-mindedness in all his ministry, ἐν πᾶσιν, "in everything" (cf. 2:7; 1 Tim 3:11; Titus 2:9–10). Paul uses the same verb to call all Christians to be sober as they await Christ's return (1 Thess 5:6, 8). The surrounding eight imperatives are all aorist; the shift to the linear aspect of the present tense here is appropriate for a general admonition.

(2) κακοπαθεῖν, "to suffer evil" (cf. 2 Tim 1:8; 2:9), is not a call to suffer evil in general. Paul willingly suffers evil (κακοπαθεῖν) for the gospel (2:9) and has already called Timothy to share in suffering (συγκακοπαθεῖν) for the gospel (1:8). Here Timothy is called to persevere in his ministry even if that entails suffering for it (cf. 2:3–7).

(3) While good works are a goal for all Christians (cf. 1 Tim 2:10), for Timothy specifically his good work is to do the work of an εὐαγγελιστής, "evangelist" (BAGD, 318); his good work stands in opposition to the myths of the opponents (v 4). This is Timothy's spiritual gift to which Paul previously referred (1:6; cf. 1 Tim 1:18). The emphasis of the word is on the task of one so gifted; it does not describe a church office (cf. Bernard, 142). The word occurs elsewhere as a description of Philip the evangelist (as distinguished from the apostle Philip; Acts 21:8), whose task was to preach the gospel (εὐαγγελίζεσθαι; Acts 8:4, 12, 35, 40) as was Paul's (1 Cor 1:17). It also occurs in a list of spiritual gifts ("apostles, prophets, evangelists, pastors, teachers"; Eph 4:11). Elsewhere Paul says that Timothy served him in the gospel (ἐδούλευσεν εἰς τὸ εὐαγγέλιον; Phil 2:22) and that Timothy is a servant of God in the gospel (διάκονον τοῦ θεοῦ . . . ἐν τῷ εὐαγγελίῳ; 1 Thess 3:2), both verses using cognates of the word "evangelist."

(4) The final imperative is general, as was the first. Timothy is to fulfill his ministry in the sense of persevering until his task is completed (πληροφορεῖν; BAGD, 670), until he fulfills his calling, his desire. Later Paul will say that the Lord strengthened him so that the proclamation (of the gospel) might be fulfilled (τὸ κήρυγμα πληροφορηθῇ) and all the Gentiles might hear (4:17; cf. Acts 12:25; Col 4:17, both of which speak of fulfilling the ministry in the sense of completing the task). Paul will soon die (vv 6–8); Timothy will have to carry on his task without him, and he

must be steadfast and loyal to that task (cf. 2 Tim 2:3–7). Just as Paul can give a confident assessment of his ministry (vv 6–8), so also Timothy must persevere so that he can do the same when he is about to die. In similar language Paul encourages Archippus to "fulfil [πληροῖς] the ministry which you have received in the Lord" (Col 4:17). διακονία, "ministry" (1 Tim 1:12; 4:11; cf. discussion of cognate διάκονος, "deacon," in 1 Tim 3:8) is the call to sacrificial service.

6 Ἐγὼ γὰρ ἤδη σπένδομαι, καὶ ὁ καιρὸς τῆς ἀναλύσεώς μου ἐφέστηκεν, "For I am already being poured out like a drink offering, and the time of my departure has arrived." Vv 6–8 are often called Paul's "Last Will and Testament." Paul knows he will die soon, and these verses express his spiritual legacy and his confident anticipation of his future with Christ. But he is not merely reciting his achievements. He is encouraging Timothy in the face of persecution to be steadfast, just as he has remained true despite sufferings and has completed his tasks. Chrysostom relates his struggles with the interpretation of the passage because it appears to be self-serving: "Often, when I have taken the Apostle into my hands, and have considered this passage, I have been at a loss to understand why Paul here speaks so loftily: 'I have fought the good fight.' But now by the grace of God I seem to have found it out. . . . He is desirous to console the despondency of his disciple, and therefore bids him be of good cheer, since he was going to his crown, having finished all his work, and obtained a glorious end" ("Homily 9"; NPNF 13:511).

Vv 6–8 form the final paragraph in this section, spelling out Paul's present (v 6), past (v 7), and future (v 8). They are a powerful conclusion to the third section of the epistle (3:10–4:8) as well as to the epistle as a whole. There remains but to send a few personal greetings and a final warning about one of the opponents. The emphasis of the paragraph is on the imminence of Paul's death. He is "already" (ἤδη) "being poured out" (σπένδομαι), his death is imminent (ἐφέστηκεν, "has arrived"), and his tasks have been completed (the three perfect-tense verbs in v 7). However, there is still time for Timothy to come to Paul before winter (v 21) and to bring some items such as warmer clothing (v 13). Paul sees his current imprisonment as a process that has begun and will most assuredly end in his death sometime in the following winter (see *Comment* on 4:9; for a discussion of the relationship between 2 Tim 4:6–8 and the letter to the Philippians, see Cook, *JTS* n.s. 33 [1982] 168–71).

ἐγὼ γάρ, "for I," contrasts with the previous σὺ δέ, "but you" (v 5), establishing three groups: the Ephesians (vv 3–4), Timothy (v 5), and Paul (vv 6–8). The verse gives the reason for the urgency of v 5; Timothy must persevere because Paul will soon be gone. σπένδειν means "to offer a libation or drink-offering" (BAGD, 761). The present tense here stresses that the process has begun, and the passive voice that God, not Rome, is still in control, despite appearances (the verb is always used in the passive in early Christian literature [BAGD, 761]). The background is the drink offering, the OT ritual of pouring out a drink before the altar as a sacrifice to God, often accompanied by other sacrifices. This practice was common throughout ancient cultures (O. Michel, *TDNT* 7:528–35; T. H. Gaster, *IDB* 4:150; Exod 29:38–42 [with the daily burnt offerings]; Lev 23:13; Num 15:5; 28:7). Lock compares it to the Greek ritual of pouring out a libation to Zeus at the end of a feast. He adds that "the metaphor rests on the Jewish belief in the sacrificial value of a martyr's death" (114).

Paul uses the same imagery in his letter to the Philippians, which is interesting in light of the fact that Timothy was with Paul when that letter was written (Phil 2:19–23). There Paul says of his current ministry, "I am being poured out [σπένδομαι] upon the sacrifice [θυσία] and service of your faith" (2:17). He earlier refers to his death as an ἀναλῦσαι, "loosing" (Phil 1:23), using the verbal cognate of ἀναλύσεως, "departure," in 2 Tim 4:6. Prior, however, argues that σπένδεσθαι, "to pour out like a drink offering," in Phil 2:17 refers not to Paul's death but rather to his "apostolic activity" and that the meaning of the same verb in 2 Tim 4:6 can only be determined by context (*Paul the Letter-Writer*, 92–98). He also maintains that the noun ἀνάλυσις, "departure," refers generally to a "loosing," and that in 2 Tim 4:6 it does not necessarily mean death; rather it means Paul's release from prison (98–103). Prior asserts that if Paul had meant "death," he would have used the more usual κοιμᾶσθαι or θάνατος (103). Prior is certainly correct that the terminology does not necessarily denote death, but the epistle's general context does imply that Paul is speaking of death. Moreover, Paul is under no obligation to use usual terminology. The use of the liturgical terminology is explained by Paul's view of death (that it is simply a passing into heaven) and his desire throughout the epistle to encourage Timothy. Hanson argues that 2 Tim 4:5–18 is a rewrite of Phil 2:12–30 "in the light of Paul's death as a martyr" ([1983] 155). But the similarities are at best coincidental—Timothy is with Paul, who is a prisoner—and superficial. Ellicott comments, "in the one case it is the trembling anxiety of the watchful, labouring minister, in the other, it is the blessed assurance vouchsafed to the toilworn, dying servant of the Lord" (154). The reuse of the imagery of Paul's life being a drink offering (Phil 2:17; 2 Tim 4:6) only shows that Paul can use the same imagery with different emphases (cf. Kelly, 208). This language parallels Paul's terminology elsewhere when he describes his ministry (λατρεύω, "I serve" [Rom 1:9]; λειτουργόν, "minister" [Rom 15:16]; cf. 2 Tim 1:3) and the ministry of Christians in general ("present your bodies a living sacrifice [θυσίαν]" [Rom 12:1]) with cultic language.

Paul has encouraged Timothy to perform his ministry in season and out of season (εὐκαίρως ἀκαίρως; v 2) because the time (καιρός; v 3) will come when people will not listen to the gospel. Paul is convinced that the time (καιρός) of his departure is at hand, but even in a difficult imprisonment (cf. 1:15–18) that will end in death, Paul is not defeated. He sees God's control even in the pouring out of his death as a libation, and thus his death is not a defeat but merely an ἀνάλυσις, "loosing," a "departure" from this life to the next. ἀνάλυσις occurs only here in the NT but is used of soldiers breaking camp or sailors loosing a ship from its moorings, and it is a known euphemism for death (cf. Peaston, *ExpTim* 93 [1982] 180–82; BAGD, 57). Its verbal cognate, ἀναλύειν, "to depart," occurs in Phil 1:23 also as a euphemism, emphasizing the passage from life through death to be with Christ. Spicq (2:803–4) cites an interesting analogy of sailors offering a libation before sailing, and ἀνάλυσις ("loosing, departure") is used of a ship loosing its anchor before setting sail; the libation is offered, and Paul's ship is setting sail for heaven. Paul now knows that he will have to face what he had hoped would not occur, a period of disembodied existence, separate from the body but present with the Lord (2 Cor 5:1–8). ἐφιστάναι in the perfect tense means "is imminent," which is different from its use in v 2 in the aorist tense (BAGD, 330–31).

7 τὸν καλὸν ἀγῶνα ἠγώνισμαι, τὸν δρόμον τετέλεκα, τὴν πίστιν τετήρηκα, "the good fight I have fought, the race I have completed, the faith I have kept." In view of his impending death Paul recites his spiritual legacy, not in a self-serving way but in a way that shows his perseverance as an encouragement to Timothy (see below). In fact, he uses imagery and words that elsewhere he uses to encourage Timothy. The parallel structure of the three clauses once again adds solemnity to the pronouncements. The objects are placed first to draw attention not to what Paul has done but to the fight, the race, and the faith that are the Lord's. This is emphasized by the use of the definite article "the" before each object. In fact, all three lines say basically the same thing: Paul faithfully completed his ministry. The perfect-tense verbs emphasize the finality of Paul's ministry and what the Lord has accomplished through him (cf. 1 Tim 1:12–17; 2 Tim 2:1).

(1) As an athlete, Paul has fought the good fight (cf. 2 Tim 1:8,12; 2:9–10; 3:11). It is not that he has fought well but that the fight of Christian ministry is inherently good and is worth the battle. So also Timothy is encouraged to struggle for the gospel (1 Tim 4:10; cf. his call to ministry in general in 1 Tim 4:11–16; 2 Tim 3:10–4:2) and share in the suffering (2 Tim 1:8; 3:12; 4:5). Chrysostom comments, "'The good fight'! There is no worthier than this contest. The crown is without end. This is not of olive trees. It has not a human umpire. It has not men for spectator. The theater is crowded with Angels" ("Homily 9"; NPNF 13:511). (2) Paul has completed the race, the course set out for him when God judged him faithful and called him to the task (1 Tim 1:12; cf. 2:7; Titus 1:3; 2 Tim 2:11). It is not that the race is won; otherwise Timothy's ministry would be unnecessary. It is that Paul has done his part: So also Timothy is called to compete as a single-minded athlete, not deterred by persecution (1 Tim 6:12; 2 Tim 2:5; cf. similar military imagery in 1 Tim 1:18; 2 Tim 2:3–4). (3) As a result of his faithfulness to the task, Paul can say that he has kept the faith (cf. 2 Tim 3:10). Likewise Timothy is called to keep the faith (1 Tim 6:14; cf. 1:19; 6:11; 2 Tim 1:13,14; 2:15, 22), to be nourished in the faith (1 Tim 4:6; 6:20; 2 Tim 2:1), to endure persecution and suffering for the faith (2 Tim 1:6–7, 13, 14; 2:1, 12–13), and to fight perversions of the faith (1 Tim 1:3–4; 4:1–5; 6:2b–10) as are the elders (1 Tim 3:2; 5:17; Titus 1:9) and older men (Titus 2:2) since the opponents are attacking the faith (1 Tim 1:19; 5:10; 6:20; Titus 1:13). V 8 will continue this same theme as Paul says that a crown of righteousness awaits him (cf. the future perspective in Titus 1:2; 2 Tim 1:12; 2:10; 4:18), and Timothy is elsewhere encouraged to compete lawfully as an athlete so that he will win the victor's crown/wreath (2 Tim 2:5; cf. 4:8). Paul does not say he looks forward to gaining "the crown of eternal life as a reward for one's righteousness on earth" (Hanson, [1983] 156). Paul says that he is looking forward to what lies ahead, using language that is consistent with the athletic metaphor in this passage.

(1) "The good fight I have fought." ἠγώνισμαι, "I have fought" (cf. 1 Tim 4:10 where it is used of the struggle in ministry of both Paul and Timothy), and ἀγῶνα, "fight," are cognates. Paul uses the same phrase to call Timothy to perseverance (1 Tim 6:12; see *Comment* there; on καλός, "good," see *Comment* on 1 Tim 1:8). Simpson (155–57) argues that it is a military metaphor (cf. 2 Tim 2:3–4), but most say it is an athletic metaphor because of the following two statements. (The following phrase does use athletic imagery, but Paul often varies his metaphors.) On the athletic metaphor in Paul, see 2 Tim 2:4–5 and *Comment* on 1 Tim 6:12 (cf. 1 Cor 9:24–27; Phil 3:12–14).

(2) "The race I have completed." What Paul has earlier anticipated (Phil 3:13–14) has now come to pass. δρόμος can mean "course" in general (BAGD, 206–7), but most believe it is specifically an athletic course, a race. Acts uses the word of

John the Baptist finishing his ministry (Acts 13:25) and of Paul's desire to finish his ministry (Acts 20:24). On the basis of this statement, most conclude that Paul knows his life will soon end (also 2 Tim 1:15–18; 4:16–18) and date this epistle as the last of Paul's writings. Paul has persevered and has brought his ministry to its intended end, its goal, its full completion, that all the Gentiles might hear the good news of the gospel (4:17; for τελεῖν, "to complete," cf. Rom 2:27; 13:6; 2 Cor 12:9; Gal 5:16).

(3) "The faith I have kept." While there is a question regarding the specific meaning of "the faith" (cf. Knight, 460, and below), the basic meaning of the clause is clear. Paul has remained true to his calling, his appointment as an apostle of Christ (1 Tim 1:12) and a proclaimer of the gospel (1 Tim 2:7; 2 Tim 1:11). Elsewhere Timothy is encouraged to keep (τηρεῖν) himself (1 Tim 5:22) and the commandment (1 Tim 6:14) pure (cf. 2 Tim 1:14). Despite their respective persecutions and suffering, they are to remain true to their calling and commitments. It is possible that "the faith" is to be understood in this subjective sense of remaining true to one's calling ("kept faith"; Bernard; Spicq; Dibelius-Conzelmann; Barton, *Bib* 40 [1959] 878–84; Brox; Pfitzner, *Agon Motif,* 183; Fee). Dibelius-Conzelmann (121 n. 18) and Fee (291) show that it is a common phrase with this meaning. Kelly argues that the context requires this general sense of "consistent loyalty throughout his ministry to his divine mandate" (209). However, when "faith" is preceded by the definite article, it generally means "the faith" in the objective, creedal sense of the Christian faith (cf. *Introduction,* "Themes in the PE"; Guthrie; Hanson [1983]). In this case Paul would be saying that he has safely guarded the deposit of the gospel (cf. 2 Tim 1:14), preserving it from attack ("kept the faith"). In favor of this understanding it is argued that the first two clauses of this verse point more to objective realities—the fight and race of Christian ministry. The objective understanding also agrees with the larger context of the epistle, in which Paul describes the Christian faith as being under attack (e.g., 1 Tim 1:19; 2 Tim 2:18, 25; 3:8) and gives encouragement to Timothy to protect the gospel (2 Tim 1:13, 14; 2:15). A dominant theme in 2 Tim 3:10–4:8 has also been the gospel (3:14, 15, 16–17; 4:2, 3, 4). It may be overly subtle to differentiate between these two options since for Paul keeping true to his call entails keeping the gospel message intact, and to keep the gospel requires personal perseverance in his call.

8a λοιπὸν ἀπόκειταί μοι ὁ τῆς δικαιοσύνης στέφανος, ὃν ἀποδώσει μοι ὁ κύριος ἐν ἐκείνῃ τῇ ἡμέρᾳ, ὁ δίκαιος κριτής, "Now is reserved for me the crown of righteousness, which the Lord, the righteous judge, will give to me on that day." Paul began his charge to Timothy to preach the gospel by calling up images of Christ the judge and the appearing of Jesus at his return (4:1). Paul uses some of the same images here to describe what lies ahead for himself now that he has completed his own ministry.

Much of the discussion of the authenticity of this verse misses the point. Dibelius-Conzelmann question whether Paul would "have spoken only of his success and not also of his weakness, whether he would have praised only his actions and not much rather God's actions" (121). But Paul is not spelling out what he has earned, what God has been forced to give him; he is not bugling his accomplishments and ignoring his failures; he is not emphasizing his actions and downplaying God's. His failures (1 Tim 1:12–17) and God's provision (2 Tim 2:1) have been clearly portrayed throughout the PE. The connection to v 1 is purposeful, and v 8 is a repetition of the most common theme in 2 Timothy—encouragement. Throughout the epistle, especially in chap. 1, Paul has been closely associating his ministry with Timothy's as he encourages him to persevere. V 7 is a sane, personal evaluation of his own ministry, one with which Timothy can identify and by which he can be encouraged. Besides, v 7 is a correct, sane, estimation of the life of the apostle to the Gentiles who bids people to imitate him (1 Cor 4:16; 11:1; Phil 4:9; 2 Thess 3:7, 9). These passages may not strike Hanson "as the sort of way in which Paul would in fact have expressed himself" ([1983] 156), but this level of skeptical subjectivity is not convincing (cf. Kelly, 210). Pfitzner comments specifically about Dibelius-Conzelmann's opinion that "such a statement robs the passage of its joyful certainty not in the achievement of Paul himself, but in the righteous judge" (*Agon Motif,* 184 n. 1; see Chrysostom's comments on v 6).

As Paul looks forward to what awaits him (v 8a), he acknowledges that the same awaits Timothy (v 8b); Paul and Timothy are joined in the same task, engaged in the same problems, and look forward to the same goal. While vv 7–8 are a personal estimation of Paul's life, they are not arrogant or boastful, but merely accurate. Timothy knows this, and sees himself as one of many believers who loves Christ's return and who will receive his crown of righteousness at the end of his life. Lock comments,

> With St. Paul there is always Χριστός behind the ἐγώ (Gal 2²⁰), always the thought of the grace which enables him who can do nothing by himself to do all things in his strength (1 Cor. 15¹⁰, Phil 4¹³, 1 Ti 1¹²); and to one who so recognizes the power which enables him to be what he is, there is a true self-confidence, a legitimate self-praise; especially when, as here, the purpose is to give confidence to a younger man to follow. (112)

Pfitzner adds,

> This is not the certainty of the man who, trusting and priding himself in the strength of his own achievement, now looks forward to the reward which he has merited. It is rather the certainty of faith and hope. He who has remained faithful to the end—and this of course includes the retention of his 'fides'—has fitted himself into God's plan of salvation, has given God the honour. His being crowned on the last day is God's own crowning act on that which He has created and perfected. . . . This amounts to a total absence of the agonistic thinking usually connected with the picture of the athlete. *Not the honour and glory of the 'spiritual athlete', but the honour of God Who has set the contest, is that which is sought in the good contest of faith for the faith.*" (*Agon Motif,* 184–85)

It is interesting that to some who deny Pauline authorship (e.g., Cook, *JTS* 33 [1982] 168–71; cf. Fee, 291), vv 6–8 sound like a reliable historical fragment, and to others who likewise deny Pauline authorship, they sound nothing like the real Paul (e.g., Hanson, [1983] 156).

Despite the use of the imagery of God giving Paul a crown, there is no suggestion that Paul is thinking of a specific reward beyond that of life with Christ. Paul speaks elsewhere of the reward of being able to preach the gospel free of charge and so not to hinder the spread of the gospel (1 Cor 9:17–18; Fee, *First Epistle to the Corinthians,* 420–21). He can speak of the reward of the laborers to emphasize "the servant nature of the workers" (1 Cor 3:8; Fee, *First Epistle to the Corinthians,* 133). In Rom 4:4 μισθός, "reward," is used in the negative sense of wages earned for labor as opposed to grace and the righteousness of faith. Paul can also speak of the reward one receives through the fire of judgment (1 Cor 3:14), but here it is a reward not earned but part of God's righteous gift and is possibly the final verdict of praise from God (1 Cor 4:5), "Well done, good and faithful servant" (Matt 25:21, 23; Fee, *First Epistle to the Corinthians*, 143 n. 42). Paul also looks forward to the prize at the end of the race of his life (1 Cor 9:24–27), although the exact nature of the reward is never identified; Fee simply calls it "the eschatological prize" (*First Epistle to the Corinthians*, 440). All of this is to say that the emphasis in 2 Tim 4:8 is not on God giving Paul a special reward in heaven for his work on earth. As an athlete completes the course and receives the crown, so Paul has completed his course, and his crown of life in heaven awaits.

τῆς δικαιοσύνης, "of righteousness," can have two meanings. (1) It can be an appositional genitive: Paul will receive the crown, which is righteousness. Other verses using στέφανος, "crown," followed by a genitive support this interpretation (1 Thess 2:19; Jas 1:12; 1 Pet 5:4; Rev 2:10; 21:1; especially 1 Cor 9:25; cf. G. Schrenk, *TDNT* 2:210; Pfitzner, *Agon Motif,* 184; Fee; Knight). While Paul generally views righteousness as the present possession of believers, he can also speak of eagerly awaiting the hope of righteousness (ἐλπίδα δικαιοσύνης ἀπεκδεχόμεθα; Gal 5:5). In this case Paul looks forward to "perfect righteousness as the crowning blessedness of those who have striven faithfully" (Kelly, 209, although he holds to the second interpretation listed here). (2) The genitive could also be possessive, stating that the victory crown will be given to everyone who is righteous (Bernard, Kelly). Those who are righteous and who live a life of righteousness (cf. 3:16) will indeed receive a crown. This fits better with the imagery of an athletic crown awarded to the winner and with the idea of it being held in store for Paul in heaven.

While λοιπόν, "now" (adverbial use of λοιπός), can possibly have an inferential sense, "therefore" (BAGD, 480 [3b]; cf. possibly 1 Cor 7:29; Moule, *Idiom-Book*, 161, 207), this would be unusual and not appropriate to this context since it would suggest that Paul's crown of righteousness has been earned by his life of obedience (v 7). The normal use of λοιπόν as an adverb of time, "from now on, in the future, henceforth" (BAGD, 480 [3a]), is more appropriate for the context. Paul has finished his earthly life, and the next major event of his Christian life is what lies ahead in heaven (cf. the use of λοιπόν to indicate the last in a series: Acts 27:20; 1 Cor 1:16; 2 Cor 13:11; Eph 6:10; Phil 3:1; 4:8; 1 Thess 4:1; 2 Thess 3:1; *EDNT* 2:360; Moule, *Idiom-Book*, 161). Death is not a factor (cf. *Explanation*). If λοιπόν is inferential, the crown still is not earned but is the result of Paul's obedience, his perseverence. The use of στέφανος, "crown/wreath" (cf. 2 Tim 2:5 where it is a reward held out to Timothy), continues the athletic imagery of v 7 and parallels Paul's usage elsewhere of a prize (βραβεῖον) held out as a goal (1 Cor 9:25; Phil 3:14). On δικαιοσύνη, "righteousness," cf. *Comments* on 1 Tim 6:11; 2 Tim 2:22 and the discussion of the cognate noun in *Comment* on 1 Tim 1:9. Timothy is to base his ministry on Scripture, which is profitable for training in righteousness (3:16); at the end of his ministry lies his crown of righteousness. ἀπόκειται, "is reserved" (BAGD, 92–93; Luke 19:20; Heb 9:27; especially Col 1:5 where Paul speaks of the "hope that is laid up for us in heaven"), was almost "technical in edicts of commendation, in which recognition was bestowed on someone by oriental kings" (Dibelius-Conzelmann, 121). Paul has entrusted his life to God (1:12), and God has Paul's crown safely in heaven, waiting for him. ὁ κύριος, "the Lord," is Christ since he is identified as the judge (4:1) and the context is his return (v 8b; cf. *Comment* on 2 Tim 2:19 for the use of the article with κύριος).

ἀποδιδόναι can mean "to reward" for both good (1 Tim 5:4) and bad (2 Tim 4:14) behavior; however, it can simply mean "to give" (BAGD, 90). Christ is ὁ δίκαιος κριτής, "the righteous judge" (cf. 2 Thess 1:5; cf. 2 Pet 2:23; Rev 16:5, 7; 19:2; cf. Ps 7:11), called as a witness to Timothy's ministry (2 Tim 4:1), who awards a crown of righteousness. Righteousness is inherently God's characteristic and his to give to Paul and Timothy. There may be an implicit comparison between the true judge, who will give Paul what is right, and the Roman judge, who is soon to pronounce the death sentence on him. ἐκείνῃ τῇ ἡμέρᾳ, "that day," is the day of judgment (cf. 2 Tim 1:12, 18; 4:1; cf. 2 Thess 1:10), which Paul will next refer to as his ἐπιφάνεια, "appearing" (v 8b).

8b οὐ μόνον δὲ ἐμοὶ ἀλλὰ καὶ πᾶσι τοῖς ἠγαπηκόσι τὴν ἐπιφάνειαν αὐτοῦ, "but not only to me but also to everyone who has loved his appearing." Paul now makes explicit what is implicit throughout the passage. Paul is encouraging Timothy by identifying their two ministries, and what awaits Paul awaits Timothy and everyone else who has longed for Christ's return. Paul thus ends his encouragement on a strongly eschatological note. Even at the end of his life Paul's orientation is expectant, looking forward to the future return of Christ, remaining true to his own teaching (1 Tim 4:8; 6:14; Titus 2:13; 2 Tim 1:12, 18; 2:10; 4:1, 18; cf. 1 Tim 4:1; 2 Tim 3:1; cf. 1 Cor 1:7; 16:22; Phil 3:20; 1 Thess 1:10; 5:6) and that of Jesus (cf. Matt 25:13). ἠγαπηκόσι, "has loved" (perfect tense of ἀγαπᾶν, "to love"; cf. cognate noun in 1 Tim 1:5; Trench, *Synonyms*, 65–71), carries the idea of "have longed for" (NIV), not merely as a periphrastic description of a Christian but as an emphasis on the expectant attitude Christians are to have, an expectancy often lost through Christian apathy and identification with the world, as was the case with Demas, who fell in love with the world (v 10). On ἐπιφάνεια, "appearing," cf. *Comments* on 2 Tim 4:1 and 1 Tim 6:14.

Explanation

Having briefly discussed the false teachers, their role in the rise of eschatological evil, and their eventual ruin, Paul returns to Timothy and completes the primary task of the epistle—encouragement. In language often similar to that in 1:3–2:13, Paul looks at his own life, his trials and victories, and through them reminds Timothy that while the righteous will suffer, God will rescue Timothy and all believers who desire to live godly lives. It is a call for Timothy to persevere, to suffer willingly for the gospel. It is not an arrogant recapitulation but the closing words of Timothy's good friend and mentor. Throughout the section Timothy can be visualized in Ephesus, knowing that his spiritual father is on trial for his life, and the turmoil this must have caused can only be imagined. Paul recognizes this and encourages Timothy to stay the course.

A large part of the encouragement is to remind Timothy of the role Scripture is to play in his life and ministry. While the opponents are proclaiming demonic myths that tickle the Ephesian's ears with their novelty, Timothy is to make Scripture central in his ministry. He had learned the Hebrew Scripture from childhood, had known the character of those who had taught it to him, had come to understand experientially that it was true, had recognized that its source was the very breath of God, had understood it within the context of the early Christian proclamation of Jesus Christ, and therefore had become convinced that it and it alone was able to equip him fully for the task of ministry. He is therefore to preach it at all times, whether or not he wants to, whether or not the Ephesians want to hear it. Though Timothy may have been tempted to rely on other sources, find other ways of arguing his case, Scripture is the means, Paul tells Timothy, by which he is to combat the Ephesian heresy and to train people in righteousness.

Timothy's reliance on Scripture is essential because soon Paul will be gone. Paul has finished the task laid before him, and while he knows that death awaits him on earth, all that he sees is the crown of righteousness that awaits him in heaven, the statement of praise from his God, "Well done, good and faithful servant." Death is merely a loosing, a passing from this life to the next.

Three themes stand out in this section. (1) The gospel does not proclaim the cessation of pain as the highest good. Christ suffered, Paul suffered, Timothy suffered, and all believers who seek to live godly lives will suffer. The proclamation of the true gospel will always stand in contrast to and in judgment of the message of the world, and since the world hated Christ, it will hate his followers. The absence of suffering is a sign that there is something wrong in a believer's life. But the good news of Paul and the gospel is that God is present with the believer in the midst of suffering, and Paul is convinced that God will rescue him out of it all. For Paul, pain is not something to be avoided at all costs; death is merely a loosing.

(2) Scripture is to play a central role in Timothy's ministry and by implication in the lives of all ministers. It is from God's mouth; it is therefore true, authoritative, able to equip fully the minister for ministry. As D. A. Hubbard asserts, "It has binding and absolute authority over what we believe and how we live" ("Christian Essentials: The Authority of the Bible," chapel address at Fuller Theological Seminary, Pasadena, 1976). The OT, understood more clearly through the apostolic proclamation, stands in contrast to all human and demonic teachings. No matter how many teachers of myths and human fables come against the gospel, with Scripture one is able to teach, reprove, correct, and train people in righteousness. This is reminiscent of Paul's earlier encouragement to Timothy in 1 Tim 4:6–16 to make Scripture central in his ministry: read it, exhort it, teach it. Ministers of all generations would do well to heed Paul's instruction, especially when encountering opposition or a desire to center one's ministry on something other than that which has come from the very mouth of God. Scripture is sufficient (cf. Grudem, *Systematic Theology*, 127–35).

(3) Paul's view of death is instructive. It scarcely is a factor in his life. He is on trial for his life, he knows that he will die, but from his perspective he is only departing life and all that awaits is his crown of righteousness. Death is a passage, a "loosing" from this world so that he can go on to the next and see his Lord face to face. What matters in his life is that he has stayed the course, has been true to God's call on his life, and has given his life as an offering to God. Rome has no power over him. This must have been difficult for Timothy to read. If leaving Paul for a short time led Timothy to tears (2 Tim 1:4), how much more so Paul's death? But even though this would have been difficult, Timothy could draw strength from Paul's spiritual courage.

V. Final Words to Timothy   (2 Tim 4:9–22)

Bibliography

Bojorge, H. "El poncho de san Pablo: Una posible alusión a la sucesión apostólica en II Timoteo 4,13." *Revista Bíblica* 42 (1980) 209–24. **Cadbury, H. J.** "Erastus of Corinth." *JBL* 50 (1931) 42–58. ———. "Roman Law and the Trial of Paul." In *The Beginnings of Christianity,* ed. F. J. Foakes Jackson and K. Lake. New York: Macmillan, 1933. 5:297–338. **Davies, T. W. L.** "Pauline Readjustments." *Exp* 5 (1921) 446–56. **Donfried, K. P.** "Paul as Skenopoios and the Use of the Codex in Early Christianity." In *Christus Bezeugen.* FS W. Trilling, ed. K. Kertelge et al. Leipzig: St. Benno, 1989. **Erbes, K.** "Zeit und Ziel der Grüße Röm 16,3–15 und der Mitteilungen 2 Tim 4,9–21." *ZNW* (1909) 128–47, 195–218. **Freeborn, J. C. K.** "2 Tim 4:11: 'Only Luke is with me.'" *SE* 6 (1969) 128–39. **Harnack, A.** "Probabilia über die Adresse und den Verfasser des Hebräerbriefs." *ZNW* 1 (1900) 16–41. **Josi, E.** "Pudente e Pudenziana." *Eastern Churches Quarterly* 10 (1953) 294. **Lee, G. M.** "The Books and the Parchments: Studies in Texts: 2 Tim 4:13." *Theology* 74 (1971) 168–69. **McGown, C. C.** "Codex and Roll in the NT." *HTR* 34 (1941) 219–50. **Meinertz, M.** "Worauf bezicht sich die πρώτη ἀπολογία?" *Bib* 4 (1923) 390–94. **Miller, W.** "Who Was Erastus?" *BSac* 88 (1931) 342–46. **Moffatt, J.** "Philippians ii,26 and II Tim. iv,13." *JTS* o.s. 36 (1917) 311–12. **Munk, P.** "Niels, Onesiforus." *Teologisk Tidsskrift* 3.10 (1919) 193–200. **Ryrie, C. C.** "Especially the Parchments." *BSac* 117 (1960) 242–48. **Skeat, T. C.** "Early Christian Book Production: Papyri and Manuscripts." In *The Cambridge History of the Bible,* ed. G. W. H. Lampe. Cambridge: Cambridge UP, 1969. ———. "'Especially the Parchments': A Note on 2 Timothy IV.13." *JTS* n.s. 30 (1979) 173–77. **Spicq, C.** "Pélerine et vêtements (A propos de 2 Tim 4:13 et Act 20:33)." In *Mélanges E. Tisserant I.* Vatican City: Biblioteca apostolica vaticana, 1964. 389–417. **Stevenson, J. S.** "2 Tim IV.13 and the Question of St. Paul's Second Captivity." *ExpTim* 34 (1922/23) 524–25. **Thomas, W. D.** "Demas the Deserter." *ExpTim* 95 (1983) 179–80. **Trummer, P.** "'Mantel und Schriften' (2 Tim 4,13): Zur Interpretation einer persönlichen Notiz in den Pastoralbriefen." *BZ* 18 (1974) 193–207.

On benedictions, see *Bibliography* for 1 Tim 6:20–21.

Translation

[9]*Do your best to come to me quickly,*[a] [10]*for Demas deserted*[b] *me because he loved the present age and has gone to Thessalonica, Crescens to Galatia,*[c] *Titus to Dalmatia.* [11]*Luke alone is with me. Get Mark [and] bring*[d] *[him] with you, for he is useful to me in service.* [12]*And I sent Tychicus to Ephesus.* [13]*Bring the cloak that I left*[e] *in Troas with Carpus when you come and the books,* [f]*especially the parchments.*

[14]*Alexander the coppersmith did me much harm; the Lord will repay*[g] *[him] according to his deeds,* [15]*[against] whom also you should be on your guard, for he vehemently opposed*[h] *our words.* [16]*At my first defense no one came forward*[i] *for me, but everyone deserted*[j] *me; may it not be held against them.* [17]*But the Lord stood by me and strengthened me, in order that through me the proclamation might be fulfilled, namely, all the Gentiles might hear,*[k] *and I was rescued from the mouth of a lion.* [18]*The Lord will rescue me from every evil deed and will save [me] into his heavenly kingdom, to whom be glory forever, Amen.*

[19] *Greet Prisca and Aquila* [m] *and the household of Onesiphorus.* [20]*Erastus remained in Corinth, and I left Trophimus behind* [n] *in Miletus because he was sick.* [21]*Do your best to come before winter. Eubulus greets you and Pudens and Linus and Claudia and all* [o] *the brethren.* [22]*The Lord* [p] *[be] with your spirit. Grace [be] with you all.*[q r s]

Notes

[a]ταχέως, "quickly," is replaced with τάχιον (I 33) and ἐν τάχει (442 *pc*) with no change in meaning.

[b]The aorist-tense ἐγκατέλιπεν, "deserted" (א [D*: κατελ-] I[vid] Ψ 1739 TR), is replaced by the imperfect-tense ἐγκατέλειπεν, "was deserting" (A C D² F G L P 33 81 1175 1881 *pc*), evidently to agree with the scribes' understanding of the historical circumstances of the passage. See similar change in *Notes* e, j, and n below and in *TCGNT*[1], 650–51.

[c]Γαλλίαν, "Gaul," is read by א C 81 104 326 *pc* vg[st ww] sa bo[pt]; Eus Epiph. See *TCGNT*[2], 581, for further MS evidence and another variant (Γαλιλαίαν, "Galilee"). See *Comment* for discussion.

[d]The present-tense ἄγε, "bring," is replaced with the aorist-tense ἄγαγε, "bring," by A 104 365 (1881*) *pc*.

[e]The same shift from the aorist-tense ἀπέλιπον, "left" (א D Ψ 1739 1881* TR), to the imperfect-tense ἀπέλειπον, "was leaving" (A C F G L P 33 104 326 1175 1881[c] *al*), is seen in vv 10, 16, 20 (*Note* b above).

[f]δέ, "and" (D* *pc* lat; Ambst), and καί, "and" (1175), are inserted after μάλιστα, "especially," suggesting that the books and the parchments are two different items.

[g]The future-tense ἀποδώσει, "will repay" (א A C D* [c] F G 6 33 81 104 365 630 1175 1739 1881 *pc* a vg[d]) is replaced with the optative ἀποδῴη, "may [the Lord] repay" (D² Ψ TR b vg[st ww]; Ambst), turning Paul's statement into a wish, an imprecation (see *Comment;* Ellicott, 160; cf. Lock, xxxviii; J. K. Elliott, "ΔΙΔΩΜΙ in 2 Timothy," *JTS* n.s. 19 [1968] 621–23). Internal evidence suggests that this is not correct since it would signal a decidedly different attitude from v 16.

[h]The aorist-tense ἀντέστη, "opposed" (א* A C D* F G 33 1175 *pc* lat; Ambst), is replaced with the perfect-tense ἀνθέστηκεν, "has opposed" (א² D² Ψ 1739 1881 TR a g vg[mss]).

[i]παρεγένετο, "came forward" (א* A C F G 33 326 1175 *pc* latt; Did [1739* uncertain]), is enlarged to συμπαρεγένετο, "came together," by א² D Ψ 1739[c] 1881 TR.

[j]The same shift from the aorist-tense ἐγκατέλιπον, "deserted" (א D* Ψ 1739 1881 TR), to the imperfect-tense ἐγκατέλειπον, "was deserting" (A C D¹ F G L P 33 104 326 1175 *al*), is seen in vv 10, 16, 20 (*Note* b above). Cf. *TCGNT*[1], 649–50.

[k]The plural ἀκούσωσιν, "might hear" (א A C D F G P 33 81 104 326 365 1175 1739 1881 *pc*), is replaced with the singular ἀκούσῃ by Ψ TR.

[l]καί, "and," is inserted at the beginning of the verse (D¹ F G Ψ TR sy) in an attempt to link the general truth of v 18 with the specific truth of Paul's experience in v 17. It is omitted by א A C D* 6 33 81 104 1175 1739 1881 *pc* lat.

[m]181 *pc* (eleventh century) and 1245 (thirteenth century) insert the following after Ἀκύλαν, "Aquila": Λέκτραν τὴν γυναῖκα αὐτοῦ καὶ Σιμαίαν καὶ Ζήνωνα τοὺς υἱοὺς αὐτοῦ, "Lectra his wife and Simmias and Zeno his sons." In the apocryphal *Acts of Paul and Thecla* 2, Lectra is Onesiphorus's wife and Simmias and Zeno are their sons. Metzger (*TCGNT*[2], 581) says that the gloss was originally in the margin and later moved into the text at the wrong location (cf. 2 Tim 1:16–18). Otherwise Aquila has two wives, Priscilla and Lectra.

[n]The same shift from the aorist-tense ἀπέλιπον, "left behind," to the imperfect-tense ἀπέλειπον, "was leaving behind" (C L P 33 104 323 326 365 1175 1241 *al*), is seen in vv 10, 16, 20 (*Note* b above).

[o]πάντες, "all," is omitted by א* 33 1739 1881 *pc*.

[p]Ἰησοῦς, "Jesus" (A 104 614 *pc* vg[st]), and Ἰησοῦς Χριστός, "Jesus Christ" (א² C D Ψ TR a b f vg[cl ww] sy bo; Ambst), are inserted after κύριος, "Lord," correctly identifying "Lord" as "Jesus." Enlargements on the name of Jesus are common in the MSS. The text used here is read by א* F G 33 1739 1881 *pc* sa. For more MS evidence, see *TCGNT*[2], 582. The shorter reading is preferred because it is unlikely that divine names would be dropped.

[q]Metzger (*TCGNT*[2], 582–83) lists eight variations on the benediction. The second-person ending ὑμῶν, "you all," is shifted to the first-person plural ἡμῶν, "us" (460 614 *pc* vg[st] bo), and singular σοῦ, "you" (sy[p] sa bo), because the epistle is written only to Timothy, not to the Ephesian church as well

(see *Comment*). ἔρρωσ(ο) ἐν εἰρήνῃ, "farewell in peace," is read by D* [1] a b; (Ambst), combining the standard Hellenistic greeting with the Jewish/Christian (ἐν εἰρήνῃ, "in peace"). The entire phrase is omitted in sa^{mss}.

ᵗἀμήν, "Amen," is added by ℵ² D Ψ 1739^C TR lat sy bo^{pt} and omitted by ℵ* A C F G 6 33 81 1739* 1881 *pc* b vg^{ms} sa bo^{pt}; Ambst. See *TCGNT²*, 582–83.

ᵗThere are several subscriptions, naming the recipient as Timothy, identifying this as the second letter, and saying that it had been written from Rome. Metzger (*TCGNT²*, 583) lists ten. πρὸς Τιμόθεον β̄, "to Timothy 2" ([-ℵ C] ℵ C [D F G] Ψ 33 *pc*). πρὸς (–1881) Τιμόθεον β̄ ἐγράφη ἀπὸ Ῥώμης, "to Timothy 2, written from Rome" ([Λαοδικείας, "Laodicea," A] A P 6 1739* 1881 *pc*). πρὸς Τιμόθεον β̄, τῆς Ἐφεσίων ἐκκλησίας ἐπίσκοπον πρῶτον χειροτονηθέντα, ἐγράφη ἀπὸ Ῥώμης, ὅτε ἐκ δευτέρου παρέστη Παῦλος τῷ καίσαρι Ῥώμης Νέρωνι, "to Timothy 2, first bishop appointed over the Church of the Ephesians, written from Rome, when Paul stood the second time before Caesar Nero of Rome" (1739^c TR). There is no subscription in 323 365 629 630 1505 *pc*.

Form/Structure/Setting

2 Tim 4:9–22 constitutes the last section of Paul's last letter to Timothy. It is an intensely personal passage centered around people—Paul, Timothy, and their friends—with secondary references to the problems at hand (vv 10, 14–15). A first-person form ("I," "we") occurs in every verse in vv 9–18 except v 15. Much is also revealed about the historical situation (vv 9–13, 16–17, 19–21). See *Comment* on v 9 and *Introduction*, "Historical Reconstruction from the PE," for a synthesis of the parts.

V 9 and its call for Timothy to come quickly to Rome is the theme of the section. Paul continues by talking about different people—Demas, Crescens, ¯itus, Luke, Mark, Tychicus, Alexander—who deserted Paul and about the Lord's sustaining presence. All this is shared not only for Timothy's information but also to encourage Timothy to come quickly. Paul is at the end of his life and is alone; he wants to see his friend before he dies.

Vv 9–22 may be arranged in three paragraphs. Vv 9–13 deal with Paul's inner circle, one of whom deserted him. Vv 14–18 deal with the opposition against Paul and how the Lord stepped in and rescued Paul. Vv 19–22 are the final greetings. Most view these last four verses as a separate section, but this decision has no effect on their meaning. They have been included here with the previous verses because they have close ties with vv 9–18, v 20 relates information on Timothy's friends just as vv 10–12 do, and v 21a repeats v 9. On benedictions, see *Comment* on 1 Tim 6:20–21.

Several writers see parallels between this passage and Ps 22 (see table in Lock, 116; Spicq, 2:809; J. Munck, *Paul and the Salvation of Mankind*, tr. F. Clarke [Atlanta: John Knox, 1977] 331–33; Hanson, [1983] 162; Fee, 297–98). There the psalmist cries out because it appears that God has forsaken him in his mortal illness (vv 1–2), and yet he expresses his trust in God (vv 3–5). The strongest point of comparison is that both writers speak of being saved from a lion's mouth (Ps 22:21). Also significant is the fact that the psalm is seen as prophetic of Christ's death. But the Psalms are replete with affirmations of trust despite difficult circumstances (cf. Pss 11:3–4, 7; 23:4; 27:1–3; 62:5–8; 91:3–8), Paul never felt abandoned by God as did the psalmist, and the metaphor of being saved from a lion is not that unusual. Perhaps as Paul approached the end of his life he thought of the psalm prophesying the end of Christ's life, but perhaps not.

Owing to the personal nature of this passage, many who hold to the Fragment

Hypothesis (see *Introduction*, "Proposals regarding Authorship of the PE") see some of these verses as reflecting authentic historical facts (e.g., P. N. Harrison, *The Problem of the Pastoral Epistles* [London: Oxford UP, 1921]; Hanson [1983]). But as always there is such a subjective element that the almost total lack of certainty is unsatisfying. Why do historical reminiscences strike some as having a claim to authenticity? Could they not be an imaginative attempt to apply a veneer of historicity to a pseudepigraphal work? Could they not be totally fabricated (e.g., R. Jewett, *Chronology*, 45; Hasler)? For example, Hanson views v 21 as "part of the author's epistolary trappings" ([1983] 163–64). But if this were the case, is it plausible that the writer would create these details? This is especially puzzling if Paul is a hero of the pseudepigrapher since it seems doubtful that he would have created verses describing his hero Paul as deserted, cold, and apparently lonely. Would he have made up verses that seem, to some, to contradict vv 6–8 (cf. Guthrie, 175)? There is such a commonness especially about v 13 that to many it is unlikely that the verse could be a fabrication, as can also be argued for Trophimus's illness in v 20 (Hanson, [1983] 163). It can also be argued that a pseudepigrapher conscious of being detected would not invent the defection of Demas (v 10), which is difficult to believe of a member of Paul's inner circle (cf. Kelly, 212–13). It is easier to accept these verses as authentic rather than a creation. But as has been argued in the *Introduction*, if the PE are not Pauline, then verses like these show that the pseudepigrapher is attempting to deceive his audience rather than write to a church that supposedly knows the PE are pseudepigraphal and accepts them as such. See the *Introduction* for a detailed discussion of authorship.

Comment

9 Σπούδασον ἐλθεῖν πρός με ταχέως, "Do your best to come to me quickly." Unlike the intent of 1 Timothy, the purpose of the Second Epistle is not to give instructions through Timothy to the Ephesian church (but cf. v 22b). Rather, it is meant to encourage Timothy and to ask him to leave Ephesus and visit Paul. Paul believes that his desire, expressed in 1:4, can be fulfilled. The same request is made in v 21, which although not using ταχέως, "quickly," does imply that if Timothy does not leave soon, the winter season will hinder his journey. There is no contradiction between this verse and Paul's awareness of his impending death. In vv 6–8, Paul does not say that he will die very soon; he implies that he will die in this imprisonment and that his ministry is over, and given the delays in the judicial system that Paul has already experienced (Acts 21:27–28:31), he assumes that there is sufficient time for the letter to get to Timothy and for Timothy to travel to Rome.

The sense of urgency is understandable. Paul and Timothy are good friends, and Paul wants to see him (1:4) even if this means that Timothy must leave Ephesus before his work is done and that associating with Paul may be dangerous (cf. 1:15–18; 4:10). Timothy is therefore to make every effort (σπουδάζειν, "to do one's best"; cf. v 21 and Titus 3:12) to come quickly. The persecutions that Timothy is undergoing must also have been felt by his friend Paul, who sent him to Ephesus in the first place. Many people have already deserted Paul (1:15; 4:10, 16), and others have left, perhaps for other ministries (4:10–12, 20). Paul's trial has begun, and no one has defended him (4:16). While the time of year when Paul wrote is not specified, it was such that if Timothy did not leave soon, the coming winter would affect his travel (4:21). Perhaps the presence of Luke the physician (4:11) and Paul's need for his cloak (4:13) hint at Paul's physical condition, sick and cold, and add to the urgency of the situation. (But Luke may have been there because they were friends.)

These verses also help to clarify the historical situation (cf. *Introduction,* "Historical Reconstruction from the PE"). Paul decided to winter in Nicopolis (Titus 3:12), sending Zenas and Apollos with his letter to Titus (Titus 3:13) and planning to send Artemas or Tychicus to relieve Titus (Titus 3:12). Evidently he actually sent Artemas because Tychicus went to Ephesus to relieve Timothy (2 Tim 4:12). Titus then came to Nicopolis, but later went north to Dalmatia (2 Tim 4:10). In order to determine the chronology of events, one must consider whether the winter in Nicopolis (Titus 3:12) is the winter Paul alludes to in 2 Tim 4:21. It is possible that Paul was arrested before going to Nicopolis. Titus therefore would have gone to Dalmatia, Paul's first defense in Rome would have been quick, and Timothy would have been asked to come before winter set in. If there does not seem to be sufficient time for all this to have occurred, then perhaps Paul did winter in Nicopolis. Titus then would have come, and in the spring he would have left for Dalmatia. Paul would have been arrested in Nicopolis or Troas (on his way to Ephesus?) in the spring or summer, and there would have been sufficient time for the letter and Tychicus to get to Ephesus and for Timothy to travel to Rome before the next winter. Given the time required to travel, perhaps the latter scenario is more likely.

10 Δημᾶς γάρ με ἐγκατέλιπεν ἀγαπήσας τὸν νῦν αἰῶνα καὶ ἐπορεύθη εἰς Θεσσαλονίκην, Κρήσκης εἰς Γαλατίαν, Τίτος εἰς Δαλματίαν, "for Demas deserted me because he loved the present age and has gone to Thessalonica, Crescens to Galatia, Titus to Dalmatia." Paul begins his list of six people by telling Timothy of three men who have left Rome. γάρ, "for," shows that v 10 gives the reason for the urgency of v 9. Grammatically the two final clauses are dependent on ἐπορεύθη, "has gone," but the departure of Crescens and Titus does not occur for negative reasons as does the departure of Demas.

Δημᾶς, "Demas" (BAGD, 178; MM, 144; BDF §125[1]), may be a shortened form of Δημήτριος, "Demetrius," but he is not to be identified with the Christian in 3 John 12 or the Ephesian silversmith (Acts 19:24, 38) of the same name. Demas is Paul's "fellow worker" mentioned in Col 4:14; Phlm 24 and listed in both places with Luke, as he is here. He is mentioned along with Hermogenes as a hypocritical friend of Paul in the apocryphal *Acts of Paul* (see *Explanation* on 2 Tim 1:15–18; *Acts of Paul* 1, 4, 12–14, 16) and elsewhere as an apostate (Epiphanius *Haer.* 51.6). The fact that Paul attributes his desertion to the love of this present age suggests that he apostatized from the faith (contra Spicq, 2:810–12) rather than the weaker meaning of disassociating himself from Paul along with the Asians (1:15; cf. Fee, 299, citing the use of the words by Polycarp *Phil.* 9.1–2). Paul uses ἐγκαταλείπειν, "to desert" (BAGD, 215; 2 Cor 4:9), to describe the abandonment by his friends at his first defense (v 16). It is a strong word; it is the same word Jesus uses to quote from Ps 21:1 (LXX) when he cries out on the cross, "My God, my God, why have you forsaken me?" (Mark 15:34; see *Form/Structure/Setting*). The suggestion is that Demas is a good friend and that his personal desertion is painful for Paul. The use of ἀγαπᾶν, "to love," contrasts with its use in v 8; a crown awaits those who love Jesus' return, but because Demas loved this age (ἀγαπήσας, "because he loved," is a causal participle), he deserted Paul. τὸν νῦν αἰῶνα, "the present age," is a common idiom (cf. 1 Tim 6:17; Titus 2:12; cf. Rom 12:2; 1 Cor 2:6; 2 Cor 4:4). Bernard (144) suggests that Demas is not a Jew, based on Col 4:11, 14, but rather a Thessalonian and is therefore returning home. In Phlm 24 Demas is listed with Aristarchus, who himself is a Thessalonian (cf. Acts 20:4; 27:2; cf. W. D. Thomas, *ExpTim* 95 [1983] 179–80).

Nothing more is known of Crescens. Tradition says that he went north from Rome into Gaul, founded the churches in Vienne and Mayence near Lyons (*Acta Sanctorum*, June 27; *Menologion*, May 30), and became the bishop of Chalcedon (*Chronicon Pasch.* 2.121). He had not ἐγκατέλιπεν, "deserted," Paul. Only Demas is the subject of that verb; Crescens and Titus are governed by ἐπορεύθη, "has gone." Crescens is a Latin name (BAGD, 450). There is an interesting textual history (see *Note* c for manuscript evidence); the best reading is Γαλατίαν, "Galatia." Normally in Paul, Galatia refers to the Roman province in Asia Minor, but this may be because that is where his journeys took him. Galatia can also refer to Gaul, modern-day France and northern Italy (Lightfoot, *Galatians*, 2–3; Spicq, 2:811–12; Kelly, 213), and often a qualifier such as "in Asia" is required to designate the Galatia in Asia Minor. This is suggested by the variant reading Γαλλίαν, which can only mean Gaul. Some of the early church fathers saw Γαλατίαν as Gaul to the north, and this could explain the shift to Γαλλίαν in an attempt to clarify the location (cf. Lock, xxxvii; it could also be due to reading the second alpha as a lambda [*TCGNT* ², 581]). If this is the case, then it is perhaps a slight indication that Paul was able to extend his ministry toward the west as he desired (Rom 15:24, 28), assuming Crescens was following Paul's trail of ministry.

Titus had gone to Dalmatia. Perhaps he wintered in Nicopolis on his return from Crete and then headed north (see discussion on v 9). Dalmatia was the southwestern part of Illyricum on the eastern shore of the Adriatic Sea (modern-day Yugoslavia, currently Croatia, Bosnia, and Herzegovina; cf. Pliny *Hist.* 3.26). Paul had gone as far as Illyricum in his journeys (Rom 15:19), so Titus may have been following up on Paul's missionary endeavors as he may have done in Crete.

11a Λουκᾶς ἐστιν μόνος μετ' ἐμοῦ, "Luke alone is with me." With Demas, Crescens, Titus (v 10), and Tychicus (v 12) gone, Luke is the only member of Paul's inner circle left with him. Dibelius-Conzelmann (122) say vv 10–11 depict Paul as "deserted by almost everyone" and therefore see a contradiction with v 21 with its greeting to Timothy from four people and "all the brethren." But when Paul says that "Luke alone is with me," perhaps he means that Luke is the only person of his inner circle who is with him, or perhaps that Luke is the only person staying with him day to day and the people listed in v 21 are Paul's friends in the Roman church (see further on v 21). Luke was a gentile physician, Paul's beloved friend and traveling companion (Col 4:14; Phlm 24; cf. Acts 20:6; 21:15; 24:23; 28:16), traditionally viewed as the author of the Third Gospel and Acts. Because he was the only person with Paul, it is most likely that he was the amanuensis of this epistle (and of 1 Timothy and Titus; cf. *Introduction*, "Historical Reconstruction from the PE").

11b Μᾶρκον ἀναλαβὼν ἄγε μετὰ σεαυτοῦ, ἔστιν γάρ μοι εὔχρηστος εἰς διακονίαν, "Get Mark [and] bring [him] with you, for he is useful to me in service." On his way from Ephesus to Rome, Timothy is to pick up Mark (ἀναλαμβάνειν, "to get"; BAGD, 57; cf. Acts 22:31; ἀναλαβών is a participle of antecedent action: "having gotten Mark, bring him"). John Mark was the son of Mary of Jerusalem and the cousin of Barnabas. He accompanied Paul and Barnabas on the first missionary journey as far as Pamphylia but then returned to Jerusalem (Acts 12:12, 25; 13:13). The circumstances were such that Paul did not want to take him on the second missionary journey, so Barnabas and Mark went to Cyprus and Paul took Silas (Acts 15:37, 39). Evidently there was a reconciliation because Mark was with Paul in his first Roman imprisonment and was called Paul's fellow worker (Col 4:10–11; Phlm 24; cf. 1 Pet 5:13). 2 Tim 4:11 is often seen as an acknowledgment that the reconciliation was complete, although this can be assumed from Paul's prior use of the title fellow worker. According to tradition, Mark wrote the Second Gospel based on Peter's teaching (Eusebius *Hist. Eccl.* 3.39.15) and died a martyr's death (B. H. Throckmorton, Jr., *IDB* 3:277–78). On εὔχρηστος, "useful," cf. *Comments* on 2 Tim 2:21 and Phlm 11. Paul has used διακονία, "service," of his ministry (1 Tim 1:12) and of Timothy's (2 Tim 4:5; on the word, cf. discussion of διάκονος, "deacon," in *Comment* on 1 Tim 3:8). This suggests that Paul is thinking of Christian ministry in general as is also suggested by the immediate context. Paul's coworkers have left, and the following δέ, "and" (v 12), ties Mark's usefulness directly to Tychicus's departure. Chrysostom sees Paul's request as a desire for Mark to help fill the ministerial void in Rome when Paul has died ("Homily 10"; NPNF 13:513). Paul could also be thinking of personal service to himself analogous to the service rendered by Onesiphorus (1:16–18; cf. 1 Cor 16:15).

12 Τύχικον δὲ ἀπέστειλα εἰς Ἔφεσον, "And I sent Tychicus to Ephesus." Tychicus is the final member of Paul's inner circle and has been sent to Ephesus to replace Timothy. If ἀπέστειλα, "sent," is an epistolary aorist (i.e., "I am sending"), Tychicus could have carried the letter to Timothy (Jeremias, 65), and this verse would be confirming the obvious (but maybe not so obvious to the Ephesian church; cf. vv 14–15), that Tychicus was Timothy's replacement. It is also possible that someone else carried the letter, and Tychicus was coming but was delayed because of some unknown situation. If ἀπέστειλα is not an epistolary aorist, it may suggest that Timothy has left Ephesus, but this runs counter to the general thrust of the letter and especially to 2:2.

Tychicus was a natural choice for this task. He was Asian and had been with Paul on his trip from Macedonia through Troas and Miletus (where Paul spoke with the Ephesian elders) and presumably on to Jerusalem. He had already carried Paul's letters to the Ephesian (and Colossian) church and remained to tell them how Paul was doing (Acts 20:4; Eph 6:21; Col 4:7; Titus 3:12). Paul calls him a beloved brother, a faithful servant (Eph 6:21), and a fellow slave in the Lord (Col 4:7). Later tradition says that he became the bishop of either Colophonia or Chalcedon (*Menologion*, Dec. 9). δέ, "and," makes Tychicus's leaving a reason for Timothy to bring Mark (see *Comment* on v 11).

13 τὸν φαιλόνην ὃν ἀπέλιπον ἐν Τρῳάδι παρὰ Κάρπῳ ἐρχόμενος φέρε, καὶ τὰ βιβλία μάλιστα τὰς μεμβράνας, "Bring the cloak that I left in Troas with Carpus when you come, and the books, especially the parchments." This is a personal comment, uncovering Paul's humanness, his daily and physical desires. It is assumed that he asks for the cloak because he is cold or in anticipation of the coming winter (v 21). Since there is no way to know the identity of the books and parchments, it is

not certain if the concern is legal (e.g., papers showing Roman citizenship), ministry oriented (e.g., blank writing material for further correspondence), or personal
and sentimental. The verse is so personal that even many scholars who deny Pauline
authorship of the PE assume its authenticity. If this verse was included by a
pseudepigrapher, he was clearly attempting to deceive his readership.

This verse helps to reconstruct the specific events behind Paul's final arrest.
Paul earlier told Timothy that he wanted to visit Ephesus (1 Tim 3:14), and the
continuing success of the Ephesian heresy, as seen in 2 Timothy, must have only
heightened the desire. Perhaps while going through Troas on the way to Ephesus,
Paul was arrested and forced to leave some items with Carpus (an otherwise unknown Christian), and was taken to Rome. If Timothy were to follow the usual
route, he would travel through Troas, pick up these items and meet John Mark
somewhere along the way, proceed through Macedonia on the Egnatian Way, sail
across the Adriatic to Brundisium on the eastern coast of Italy, and complete his
journey to Rome. Paul frequently visited Troas (Acts 16:8, 11; 20:5, 6; 2 Cor 2:12),
but since the PE as a whole do not fit into the framework of Acts (cf. *Introduction*,
"Historical Reconstruction from Acts"), this type of scenario may be assumed. It
is doubtful that Paul would have left items of such personal value behind during
the visits mentioned in Acts and only now ask for them.

φαιλόνης, "cloak," is a Latin loan word (cf. BAGD, 851; Ellicott, 159). It was a
circular, heavy garment with a hole in the middle for the head that was used for
warmth and protection from the elements. Lock (118) says that φαιλόνης could
also be "a woollen wrap for carrying books safely" (suggested as a possible meaning by Chrysostom ["Homily 10"; NPNF 13:514], who thinks the books were for
the Roman church, "who would retain them in place of his own teaching"), although this possibility has generally not been accepted.

βιβλίον, "book," is the diminutive of βίβλος and is a common word for books,
writings, or collections of writings such as in a library (G. Schrenk, *TDNT* 1:617–
18). It is used of secular writings, such as the certificate of divorce (Matt 19:7;
Mark 10:4), as well as of the writings in the OT (Luke 4:17, 20; Gal 3:10; Heb
9:19; 10:17) and the NT (John 20:30; 21:25; and the twenty-three references in
Revelation to the book, the scroll, and the book of life; cf. McGown, *HTR* 34
[1941] 219–50; Skeat, "Early Christian Book Production," 2:54–79). μεμβράνα is
a Latin loan word for "parchment," a writing material more expensive than papy-
rus, capable of being reused and more durable, made from the skins of sheep
and goats. Kelly (216) argues that the word was commonly used of a codex (as
opposed to a scroll). μάλιστα can mean "especially" (cf. discussion in *Comment* on
1 Tim 4:10), in which case the parchments are in addition to the books. It can
also be an identifier, "that is, namely, to be precise," in which case the books are
more closely defined as the parchments (Skeat, *JTS* n.s. 30 [1979] 173–77). Only
Paul, Carpus, and perhaps Timothy knew what they contained.

14   Ἀλέξανδρος ὁ χαλκεὺς πολλά μοι κακὰ ἐνεδείξατο· ἀποδώσει αὐτῷ ὁ κύριος
κατὰ τὰ ἔργα αὐτοῦ, "Alexander the coppersmith did me much harm; the Lord
will repay [him] according to his deeds." This is the last mention in the epistle of
any opposition to Paul. Because so little is known about the historical background,
what triggered Paul's memory of Alexander can only be guessed. While v 15 indicates that the harm he caused was through his opposition to "our words," it is not
clear in what way he opposed Paul and/or the gospel, whether it was in Ephesus,

Troas, Rome, or elsewhere, and whether it was general opposition to the gospel message or specific opposition against Paul at his trial as the aorist verbs ἐνεδείξατο, "did" (v 14), and ἀντέστη, "opposed" (v 15), may suggest as well as the immediately following discussion of Paul's first defense (vv 16–17). A possible historical reconstruction was sketched in the *Comment* on v 9. These verses add the possibility that Paul was arrested in Troas (cf. v 13) and that Alexander was instrumental in the arrest. Perhaps reflection on that time reminds Paul to warn Timothy to be careful when he travels through Troas. Alternatively Paul could be thinking of his first defense in Rome (vv 16–17) and Alexander's attack on him at that time, and hence warns Timothy to be wary of Alexander when he arrives in Rome. A third option is that Alexander was in Ephesus (especially if he is identified with the Alexander mentioned in 1 Tim 1:20; see below), and Timothy is to be especially careful of him until he leaves for Rome. The only thing that can be known for sure is that Timothy knew Alexander and needs to be careful.

Ἀλέξανδρος, "Alexander," was a common name, and a specific identification here is difficult. Most conclude that he was the same person excommunicated in 1 Tim 1:20. Because Alexander was still actively opposing Paul, it could be concluded that 2 Timothy was written before 1 Timothy. But the overall evidence for 2 Timothy being Paul's last letter seems overwhelming (cf. *Introduction*, "Historical Reconstruction from the PE"). The Ephesian church may or may not have followed Paul's (and presumably Timothy's) instructions to excommunicate Alexander, and an excommunicated person could oppose Paul just as one still in the church, especially if his opposition was a legal attack on Paul resulting in his arrest. It is a plausible scenario that Alexander's opposition was his personal vendetta against Paul because of the excommunication. There was another Alexander in Ephesus, a Jew who tried to speak to the crowd but was shouted down (Acts 19:33–34), but his relationship to Paul is not clear (cf. discussion at *Comment* on 1 Tim 1:20).

A χαλκεύς is a "coppersmith," but the word came to be used of a blacksmith or a metalworker in general (BAGD, 874). The aorist ἐνεδείξατο, "did," may point to a specific event; v 15 defines it as his opposition (another aorist) to "our words." Fee (295–96) argues that the specific event was Alexander's involvement in Paul's arrest, noting that ἐνδεικνύναι can be a legal term for "to inform against" (cf. Spicq, 2:316–17; LSJ, 558). This would be strengthened if Alexander's opposition to ἡμετέροις λόγοις, "our words," in v 15 refers to Paul's words of defense at his trial (Spicq, 2:817). Chrysostom notes that by avoiding Alexander, Timothy would be leaving vengeance to God ("Homily 10"; NPNF 13:514). The idea of the Lord (Jesus; cf. 4:1, 8) rendering judgment according to a person's deeds is fully Pauline (cf. Rom 2:6 [same quotation, as in Matt 16:27 and possibly Rev 2:23; cf. Cranfield, *Romans* 1:146]; 2 Cor 5:10; also Rom 14:12; 1 Cor 3:13; Eph 6:8; Col 3:25; Rev 20:12; 22:12), citing Ps 62:12 [61:13 LXX; cf. Ps 28:4; Prov 24:12]). While salvation is by God's grace through faith (1 Tim 1:14), elsewhere and especially in the PE Paul argues that belief and behavior are inextricably bound together so that one's deeds show one's heart (cf. *Introduction*, "The Response to the Heresy"). The text used in the *Translation* has the future ἀποδώσει, "will repay"; the variant ἀποδῴη, "may he repay" (optative), makes it an imprecation, a calling for God's judgment (cf. BDF §384; *Note* g). This is a different sentiment from the one expressed for people who deserted Paul at his preliminary hearing (v 16) and are not to be held accountable. Lock suggests that this repaying (ἀποδώσει) makes a "conscious contrast" (118) with v 8, where is stated that God will give (ἀποδώσει) Paul the crown of righteousness.

15 ὃν καὶ σὺ φυλάσσου, λίαν γὰρ ἀντέστη τοῖς ἡμετέροις λόγοις, "[against] whom also you should be on your guard, for he vehemently opposed our words." Although Alexander has done considerable harm to Paul, it is doubtful that Paul's primary motive in mentioning him is to call down God's judgment. It seems more likely that Paul's love and concern for Timothy prompt the warning. Plausible historical reconstructions for this verse have been discussed above in *Comment* on v 14. Timothy is to be on his continual guard (φυλάσσειν) for Alexander, and this becomes an example of why Timothy is to guard the gospel (1:13–14). The emphatic position of λίαν, "exceedingly, vehemently," stresses how aggressively Alexander opposed Paul. Paul earlier used ἀνθιστάναι, "to oppose," of Jannes and Jambres's opposition to Moses as a parallel to the opponents' opposition to the gospel (3:8). λόγοις, "words," could mean the words of Paul's defense at his trial (cf. Spicq, 2:817). This may be suggested by the aorist ἀντέστη, "opposed" (cf. the aorist ἐνεδείξατο, "did," in v 14), and the following two verses as they discuss the trial, as well as the use of the related ἀπολογία in v 16 to describe Paul's preliminary "defense." ἡμετέροις, "our," would have to be an editorial "we." In this case Alexander is in Rome and Paul is warning Timothy before he arrives. λόγοις could also be the gospel message as it frequently is used in the PE (2 Tim 1:13; 2:2, 9, 15; 4:2; Titus 2:5; *Comment* on 1 Tim 4:5), and a straightforward reading of "our" suggests that this is the case. The verse then does not help in historical reconstruction.

16 Ἐν τῇ πρώτῃ μου ἀπολογίᾳ οὐδείς μοι παρεγένετο, ἀλλὰ πάντες με ἐγκατέλιπον· μὴ αὐτοῖς λογισθείη, "At my first defense no one came forward for me, but everyone deserted me; may it not be held against them." As Paul reflects on his historical situation, on those who have opposed him, he tells Timothy that at his preliminary hearing no one came forward to support him or to argue his case. Everyone ἐγκατέλιπον, "deserted," him, just as Demas had deserted him (4:10; same verb) and all the Asian Christians had done (1:15). But in a gracious way reminiscent of Jesus (Luke 23:34) and Stephen (Acts 7:60), Paul does not want God to hold them accountable, and he even includes greetings from four leaders (presumably) of the Roman church in v 21. This is a somewhat different response from v 14 where he recognizes God's judgment on Alexander for his evil deeds (v 14; cf. 1 Tim 1:20). From this it may be assumed that the people who did not come forward have not apostatized, but rather want to distance themselves personally from Paul (cf. 1:15; 4:10), or perhaps are not qualified to help, or are unavailable. Paul's willingness to include greetings from four of them (v 21) suggests that the absence is not necessarily significant for all the absent people.

The primary question of the passage is the historical setting of the defense, namely, what was the πρώτῃ, "first," defense? (1) Historically it has been viewed as Paul's first imprisonment (Acts 24–28; Eusebius *Hist. Eccl.* 2.22.2–3; Theodoret 3.695–96; T. Zahn, *Introduction to the New Testament*, 3 vols. [repr. Grand Rapids, MI: Kregel, 1953 (tr. from 3rd German ed., 1909)] 2:7–8; Lock, 119). This interpretation takes οὐδείς, "no one," in the absolute sense, which solves the apparent contradiction with v 11 that says Luke is currently (i.e., in the second imprisonment) with Paul. It also gives full force to v 17a, which speaks of Paul's rescue from the mouth of the lion (i.e., a Roman judge), which in turn agrees with the implication that Paul's imprisonment in Acts 28 would end in release. But there are several difficulties with this view. In Acts 28 there is no hint of a universal abandonment, nor is there the sense of impending death as in 2 Tim 4:6–8. There is the question of why Paul would be telling Timothy about his first imprisonment since Timothy already knew about it and the sense of the passage is that Timothy is being informed. Most important, it is difficult to see why Paul would be reflecting on events several years in the past. Vv 16–17 appear to be in the same time frame as vv 14–15 and v 18, and it is difficult to see how reflections on a past event would apply to Paul and Timothy's current situation.

(2) Most modern writers see this first defense as the Roman *prima actio,* a public, preliminary hearing designed to gather basic information, which, if necessary, would be followed by a trial (see description by H. C. G. Moule, *The Second Epistle to Timothy: Short Devotional Studies on the Dying Letter of St. Paul* [Philadelphia: Union, 1905] 168–69). Spicq (2:818–19) points out that ἀπολογία, "defense," is a technical term for the reply of the defendant, requested by the magistrate, to accusations charged against him. This was one of the benefits of the Roman legal system, and the opportunity was frequently used to defend one's ideas rather than one's personal innocence. At this hearing Paul made his defense (cf. Acts 25:16; Phil 1:7). Either no friends came forward to encourage Paul as was the custom (Guthrie, 176; perhaps Luke [v 11] had not yet arrived), or Paul is again speaking in somewhat hyperbolic language typical of depression (cf. 1:15), or perhaps by παρεγένετο, "came forward," Paul is thinking not of friends but of someone making a formal defense for him. In Roman law, the *patronus* argued in defense of the prisoner; the *advocatus* gave counsel (Ellicott, 161). Perhaps the initial response to his *prima actio* was positive. Paul sees that there will be sufficient delay for Timothy to arrive (cf. the two-year delay in Acts 24:27; Spicq, 2:818), and for Paul this initial validation of his innocence and the ensuing delay is a rescue from a "lion's mouth" (v 17b). But this rescue is at best temporary because Paul still expects to die. More likely, v 17b is the recognition that even in death God will rescue him, not from death but by taking him to the heavenly kingdom (v 18). After all, Paul does not regard death as a major event; the only major thing he has ahead is his "crown of righteousness" (4:8). Most important, this interpretation fits the contextual needs of the verse. Paul is alone; Alexander is a serious threat, whom Timothy should avoid; Paul was deserted at his preliminary hearing; Timothy should take heart because God will rescue Paul and bring him to heaven. Alexander's opposition will have been to no avail.

παραγίνεσθαι means "to be present, come to the aid of" (BAGD, 613) and can be a technical term for a witness coming forward for a prisoner (Kelly, 218). λογίζεσθαι means to "to reckon, take into account; consider, ponder" (BAGD, 475–76), emphasizing the intellectual process. It can be "a technical term in commercial language for calculations, cost, debts, etc." (Cranfield, *Romans* 1:143 n. 4; used nineteen times in Romans; cf. also 2 Cor 5:19; H. W. Heidland, *TDNT* 4:284–92; J. Eichler, *NIDNTT* 3:824–26). μή, "not," with the optative expresses a negative wish (BDF §427 [4]).

17a ὁ δὲ κύριός μοι παρέστη καὶ ἐνεδυνάμωσέν με, ἵνα δι' ἐμοῦ τὸ κήρυγμα πληροφορηθῇ καὶ ἀκούσωσιν πάντα τὰ ἔθνη, "But the Lord stood by me and strengthened me, in order that through me the proclamation might be fulfilled, namely, all the Gentiles might hear." Even though Paul was deserted at his hearing (v 16), he was not alone for the Lord Jesus was by his side. Paul's ministry has come full circle. According to the account in Acts, Jesus told his disciples that they would be witnesses "to the ends of the earth" (Acts 1:8). After Paul was blinded on the Damascus road, Acts reports that the risen Jesus told Ananias that Paul "is a chosen vessel for me, to bear my name before the Gentiles and kings, and the sons of Israel" (Acts 9:15). Paul testifies that God considered him to be faithful as evidenced by appointing him to service (1 Tim 1:12) as a herald to the Gentiles (1 Tim 2:7; 2 Tim 1:11; Titus 1:3; cf. Rom 1:5; 16:25–26). Acts relates that the risen Jesus had already told Paul that he would keep him safe until he preached the gospel in Rome (Acts 23:11), and Paul confirms that he believed that God would keep him safe, to the point of being willing to suffer for the gospel (2 Tim 1:12). Paul now stands at the end of his life and ministry, having seen God's faithfulness to his promise and remained faithful to his call (1 Tim 1:12). Although friends and enemies alike have deserted him, he is not alone. God is faithful. His ministry of proclaiming the gospel to all Gentiles is now complete. (One is reminded of Jesus' promise that his followers would be brought to trial as a testimony to kings and the Gentiles, but that the Spirit of their Father would speak through them [Matt 10:17–20].) As Ellicott observes, "The κήρυγμα . . . was indeed *fully performed,* when in the capital of the world, at the highest earthly tribunal, possibly in the Roman forum . . . and certainly before a Roman multitude, Paul the prisoner of the Lord spoke for himself, and for the Gospel" (162). All that awaits for Paul is a visit from Timothy, the eternal kingdom (v 18), and his crown of righteousness (v 8). (If the "first defense" [v 16] is Paul's first Roman imprisonment, then the verse says that Paul was released [after Acts 28] and continued his ministry westward, thus proclaiming the gospel to all people.)

δέ, "but," contrasts human desertions (v 16) with the divine faithfulness (v 17). ὁ κύριος, "the Lord," is Jesus (cf. 4:1, 8). παριστάναι means "to be present, come to the aid of" (cf. Rom 16:2) and can be a technical term, "to bring before (a judge)" (BAGD, 628 [1e]; cf. 1 Cor 8:8; 2 Cor 4:14). Paul is always aware of God's presence and provision (cf. Acts 23:11; Phil 4:13). Just as Timothy is called to draw daily empowerment from the grace that is in Christ Jesus (ἐνδυναμοῦν, "to strengthen"; cf. 2 Tim 2:1), so also God empowers Paul at the beginning (1 Tim 1:12) and the end (2 Tim 4:17) of his ministry. The Lord is present with Paul, empowering Paul, and the end is the completion of Paul's ministry. δι' ἐμοῦ, "through me," is emphatic in placement and form, perhaps recalling Paul's wonder that God would use one such as he (1 Tim 1:12–17; note that both this passage and 1 Tim 1:12–17 have strong similarities, both closing in a doxology proclaiming the wonder of God's grace). At his first defense (2 Tim 4:16) Paul proclaimed the gospel (cf. Acts 24:1–21 and 26:1–32 for his speeches at his former defense). The emphasis of κήρυγμα, "proclamation," is on the act of proclamation (cf. Titus 1:3; discussion of cognate in *Comment* on 1 Tim 2:7), and in the NT it is usually the gospel that is being proclaimed (cf. 1 Cor 1:21; 2:4; 15:14; Titus 1:3). Earlier Paul called Timothy to complete his ministry, to persevere; he uses the same verb (πληροφορεῖν, "to fulfill") here to show that he too brought his ministry to its fulfillment, its completion. It is possible that ἵνα, "in order that," has two objects: the proclamation being completed and the Gentiles hearing the gospel. καί could also be epexegetical, i.e., "namely," so that the second phrase more precisely identifies the first. This makes good sense because Paul's mission (the first phrase) is to proclaim the gospel to the Gentiles (the second phrase).

There is a question concerning the phrase "all the Gentiles." Paul obviously has not preached to every single person in the non-Jewish world. It may have been that Paul sees his proclamation to the Roman court, at the center of the world's dominant empire, as being in essence a proclamation to all the Gentiles (Bernard; Spicq, 2:820–21). However, the phrase "all the nations/Gentiles" can mean "all groups of people," Jew and Gentile alike (translating ἔθνη as "nations," not "Gentiles"; Gal 3:8; cf. Matt 28:19; possibly Rom 1:5). This is presumably what Guthrie (177) and others (e.g., Kelly, 219) mean in speaking of the "cosmopolitan character of the audience." By proclaiming the gospel to the authorities in Rome, Paul has now preached to all groups and all types of Gentiles and therefore has fulfilled his ministry.

17b καὶ ἐρρύσθην ἐκ στόματος λέοντος, "and I was rescued from the mouth of a lion." Not only did the Lord stand by Paul; he also rescued him. In the discussion of v 16 above, the possible historical scenarios behind this verse were covered. The conclusion was that Paul made his defense at a preliminary hearing and instead of being condemned to immediate death was given a temporary reprieve, allowing sufficient time for Timothy to travel to Rome. It was also a victory in that Paul proclaimed the gospel in the Roman courts and received a somewhat positive hearing. It is this event that Paul terms a rescue from a lion's mouth. This does not mean that Paul believes he will be freed. He knows he is going to die (vv 6–8), and the temporary rescue (ἐρρύσθην, "was rescued") enjoyed now looks forward to the rescue (ῥύσεται, "will rescue" [v 18]) that will take him into God's heavenly kingdom. Paul does not envisage a rescue to freedom and extended earthly ministry.

ῥύεσθαι, "to rescue" (cf. 1 Tim 2:15; 2 Tim 3:11), denotes more an escape from danger than a salvation from sin. Ellicott says that the word means Paul "shall be removed from the sphere of evil in every form" (163). The lion was commonly used metaphorically of strength (Rev 5:5; cf. Gen 49:9) and danger (Pss 7:2; 22:21; 35:17; 1 Macc 2:60; Heb 11:33; 1 Pet 5:8; and the imagery in Rev 4:7; 9:8, 17; 10:3 [cf. Isa 31:4; Hosea 11:10; Amos 3:8]; cf. W. Michaelis, *TDNT* 4:252–53, especially 2:253 nn. 20, 21). The story of Daniel and the lion's den (Dan 6:19–23) would have encouraged the proverbial use of this imagery to denote rescue from any serious danger as Paul is doing here. Many have attempted to identify the lion specifically even though much subjectivity is required and the construction is anarthrous, λέοντος, "a lion," not "the lion." It is doubtful that Paul was literally saved from being thrown to the lions in the amphitheater (cf. the cry *Christianos ad leonem,* "Christians to the lion"; Bernard, 148). Knight (471) cites Robertson's assertion (*Word Pictures* 4:633) that this would not be a possible fate for a Roman citizen. Some identify the lion as Satan (cf. 1 Pet 5:8), the rescue being Paul's faithfulness and refusal to deny Christ (cf. 2 Tim 2:11–13) before the judge. The early Greek fathers identified the lion as the emperor (Chrysostom says it is Nero; "Homily 10"; NPNF 13:514). Herod Agrippa was told of Tiberius's death with the statement "The lion is dead" (Josephus *Ant.* 18.6.10 §228; cf. Prov 19:12; Ezek 19:1, 9). Several writers compare 2 Tim 4:17 to Ps 22:1, a psalm understood to be prophetic of Christ's death (especially vv 14, 16). There too the psalmist speaks of being deserted (v 1), but believers will be delivered by God (vv 4–5) as they cry out to be saved from the mouth of the lion (v 21; cf. *Form/Structure/Setting*). In the psalm it is rescue from death, which Fee (298) says is the meaning of "lion" in

2 Tim 4:17. But while Paul was delivered from immediate death, it was only a temporary stay of execution. It is preferable to see Paul speaking metaphorically of his rescue from immediate death, recognizing that while he will die in this imprisonment, God will rescue him from any serious danger and bring him safely to heaven (v 18).

18a   ῥύσεταί με ὁ κύριος ἀπὸ παντὸς ἔργου πονηροῦ καὶ σώσει εἰς τὴν βασιλείαν αὐτοῦ τὴν ἐπουράνιον, "The Lord will rescue me from every evil deed and will save [me] into his heavenly kingdom." Having reflected on three past events— the evil done by Alexander (vv 14–15), the desertions at his hearing (v 16), and the rescue from a lion's mouth (v 17)—Paul looks to the future (cf. Rom 5:9–10; cf. 2 Cor 1:10; 2 Tim 4:8) and draws out a general theological truth. ὁ κύριος, "the Lord" (i.e., Jesus; cf. 4:1, 8, 14, 17), ῥύσεται, "will rescue" (cf. *Comments* on 1 Tim 2:15; 2 Tim 3:11), him, not from death (4:6–8), not from a lion, but from any danger that would destroy Paul or his faith (interpreting ἔργου πονηροῦ, "evil deed," as spiritual, not physical). Stated positively this means that Jesus will save him and transport him out of the earthly realm of sin and Rome to the heavenly kingdom of God. Paul is absolutely confident (cf. 2 Cor 5:8; Phil 1:23; 1 Thess 4:17) that God is able to keep what Paul has entrusted to him (cf. 2 Tim 1:12).

To some writers, ἔργου πονηροῦ, "evil deed," is reminiscent of the Lord's Prayer, "but deliver [ῥῦσαι] us from evil [ἀπὸ τοῦ πονηροῦ]" (Matt 6:13; e.g., Lock). But the inclusion of ἔργου, "deed," argues against this, especially as it seems to refer back to Alexander and God's judgment according to his ἔργα, "deeds" (v 14). There have been many evil deeds against Paul; Alexander will be judged on the basis of his deeds, and Paul will continue to be rescued from each and every (παντός) evil deed, or "attack" (NIV). Paul holds to his eschatological view of reality to the very end, looking through death to God's βασιλεία, "kingdom" (cf. 2 Tim 4:1), and his crown of righteousness (v 8). This is the only appearance of ἐπουράνιος βασιλεία, "heavenly kingdom," although ἐπουράνιος, "heavenly" (cf. 1 Cor 15:40 [2x], 48, 49; Eph 1:3, 20; 2:6; 3:10; 6:12; Phil 2:10), is Pauline as is the future aspect of God's kingdom (cf. 1 Cor 6:9–10; 15:50; Gal 5:21; Eph 5:5; 1 Thess 2:12; 2 Thess 1:5). Perhaps it is intended to contrast with the earthly kingdom whose rulers will soon have Paul executed. The emperor, a "lion," has his kingdom and is soon to condemn Paul; God will save Paul for the true heavenly kingdom. The implicit comparison of both kings and kingdoms seems intentional.

18b   ᾧ ἡ δόξα εἰς τοὺς αἰῶνας τῶν αἰώνων, ἀμήν, "to whom [be] glory forever, Amen." Reflection on God typically drives Paul to ascribe glory to him in a doxology (cf. *Form/Structure/Setting* on 1 Tim 1:12–17 for a discussion of doxologies in the PE [1 Tim 1:17; 6:15–16] and in Paul in general [cf. especially Gal 1:5, which is exactly the same as this passage]). While most doxologies are addressed to God the Father, this doxology is addressed to Jesus (the antecedent of ᾧ, "to whom," is αὐτοῦ, "his," which goes back to ὁ κύριος, "the Lord," who is Jesus), God the Son, as is attested elsewhere (Matt 21:9; Rev 5:12; cf. Matt 23:39 [Mark 11:9; Luke 19:38]; cf. also doxologies to God that are offered "through Jesus Christ" [Rom 16:27; Heb 13:21; Jude 25] and "in Christ" [Eph 1:3; 3:21]). Perhaps this is a witness to a christological development in Paul's theology, possibly found in Rom 9:5 ("Christ, who is God over all, forever praised" [NIV]). See 1 Tim 1:17 for a discussion of δόξα, "glory," the idiom εἰς τοὺς αἰῶνας τῶν αἰώνων, "into the ages of ages," and ἀμήν, "Amen." Paul is calling for God's glory, glory that is his own, to be eternally seen and given back to him through the praise of those who agree with the communal "Amen."

19 ἄσπασαι Πρίσκαν καὶ Ἀκύλαν καὶ τὸν Ὀνησιφόρου οἶκον, "Greet Prisca and Aquila and the household of Onesiphorus." Paul usually ends his letters by greeting friends. See *Form/Structure/Setting* on Titus 3:12–15 for a general discussion, and *Form/Structure/Setting* above for why vv 19–22 are not viewed as a separate section. In v 21b Paul will send greetings from a group of believers. The imperative ἄσπασαι (cf. Titus 3:15) means "give greetings to"; the verb occurs forty times in Paul (twenty-one times in Rom 16), always at the end of a letter. Πρίσκιλλα, "Priscilla" (Acts 18:2, 18, 26, and as a *v.l.* in Rom 16:3 and 1 Cor 16:19), is the diminutive form of Πρίσκα, "Prisca" (Rom 16:3; 1 Cor 16:19). Aquila was a Jew from Pontus (northeast modern-day Turkey on the Black Sea). He and his wife, Priscilla, were expelled from Rome along with the rest of the Jews by Claudius, and they settled in Corinth (Acts 18:2). They were tentmakers, and Paul lived with them during his second missionary journey (Acts 18:3). They traveled with Paul to Ephesus and remained there when Paul continued on (Acts 18:18–19). Later they instructed Apollos (Acts 18:26). Eventually they returned to Rome, started a house church, and Paul calls them his "fellow workers in Christ Jesus, who risked their necks for my life, to whom not only I but also all the churches of the Gentiles give thanks" (Rom 16:3–4). Evidently they returned to Ephesus, perhaps to help Timothy (2 Tim 4:19). In four of the six times they are mentioned, always together, Priscilla is listed first. From this, writers have suggested that she was more active in Christian ministry (Fee, 300), had a higher social standing (cf. BAGD, 701), was more important (Harnack, *ZNW* 1 [1900] 16), had a more forceful personality (Kelly, 221), and was more active in Christian hospitality toward Paul; or the order of names reflects Christian courtesy (Knight, 475). The fact of the matter is that it is not clear why she is listed first four times, and no theory should be based on the order. For a discussion of Onesiphorus and the historical background, cf. 2 Tim 1:16–18. Some suggest Onesiphorus died after leaving Paul, and therefore he could not be greeted directly.

20 Ἔραστος ἔμεινεν ἐν Κορίνθῳ, Τρόφιμον δὲ ἀπέλιπον ἐν Μιλήτῳ ἀσθενοῦντα, "Erastus remained in Corinth, and I left Trophimus behind in Miletus because he was sick." Perhaps it is the mention of Prisca and Aquila, two of Paul's associates and possibly friends of Timothy (who twice had been in Ephesus), that prompts Paul now to tell Timothy about two of his other friends, Erastus and Trophimus, not only to relay information but as in vv 10–12 to show Timothy the urgency of coming quickly to Rome. Only Luke among Paul's inner circle is with him. The verbs ἔμεινεν, "remained," and ἀπέλιπον, "left behind" (cf. 2 Tim 4:13; Titus 1:3), may suggest that these two men have been accompanying Paul but have stopped along the way. It is not clear if this happened before or after Paul's arrest. For a discussion of the various historical scenarios, see *Comment* on v 9 and below.

Although Erastus, Corinth, Trophimus, and Miletus are all mentioned in Acts, it is doubtful that the events in v 20 refer to the time period of Acts since too much time had passed. For example, if Trophimus became sick during the events in Acts 20, the last time Paul is reported to have visited Miletus, then Paul is telling Timothy about an event that occurred at least three years earlier. It also appears that Timothy did not know of Trophimus's illness, and yet Miletus was only thirty-five miles south of Ephesus. It requires little imagination to see historical scenarios that would account for Paul's travels (after Acts 28) in this area with his close friends. Ephesus (vv 12 ,19), Miletus (v 20), and Troas (v 13) were close to each other and were on a main travel route on the western coast of Asia Minor. Timothy's ongoing work in Ephesus could have been the reason for Paul's desire to visit Ephesus again (cf. 1 Tim 3:14). Trophimus was an Ephesian (Acts 21:29), and it would be natural for him to have been included in another visit to that location.

Although the ordering of events is a mystery, it is conceivable that Paul was traveling to Ephesus and was arrested perhaps in Troas. Trophimus became ill before or after the arrest and stayed behind at Miletus, and Erastus accompanied the arrested Paul as far as Corinth. Most likely not much time had elapsed between Trophimus's illness and the writing of the Second Epistle to Timothy. Timothy and Trophimus were at least associates and perhaps friends, Timothy was in obvious need of support, Miletus was only thirty-five miles from Ephesus, and yet it appears from v 20 that Timothy did not know of Trophimus's illness. This suggests that the illness and Paul's arrest happened in close proximity; Paul was quickly taken to Rome (as would be expected of the leader of the Christian mission to the Gentiles) and given a preliminary hearing. Paul then wrote, asking Timothy to come quickly before winter and informing him of the whereabouts of these two friends.

There is an Erastus mentioned in Rom 16:23 as the οἰκονόμος τῆς πόλεως, "treasurer of the city," presumably of Corinth. There is an inscription found in Corinth with the words "Erastus, commissioner of public works, bore the expense of this pavement" (in H. J. Cadbury, *JBL* 50 [1931] 43; W. Miller, *BSac* 88 [1931] 345), although Cadbury concludes that he cannot be identified with any biblical characters with any probability. There also was another Erastus who worked with Paul (Acts 19:22), but this name was common (cf. Cadbury, *JBL* 50 [1931] 43–45; MM, 252) and there is no way to know if they were the same person, although the fact that Erastus remained in Corinth (v 20) may suggest that he too was a Corinthian. On Paul's third missionary journey after his two years in Ephesus, Paul decided to go through Macedonia and Achaia (Acts 19:21). He sent Timothy and Erastus ahead (Acts 19:22). Paul followed shortly thereafter and went to Greece (Acts 20:1–2). Timothy and Trophimus (an Asian [Acts 20:4] from Ephesus [Acts 21:29]) accompanied Paul through Macedonia and then went on ahead and waited for him in Troas (Acts 20:1–6). At least Trophimus continued with Paul to Jerusalem since the temple riot was caused by Jews accusing Paul of bringing the Gentile Trophimus into the temple (Acts 21:29). Knight (477) points out that while Paul could heal diseases (cf. Acts 14:9–10; 19:11–12; 20:10; 28:8–9), he evidently could not exercise the gift whenever he chose and hence was not able to heal Trophimus.

21a Σπούδασον πρὸ χειμῶνος ἐλθεῖν, "Do your best to come before winter." Paul repeats the essence of v 9 (see there for discussion) but specifies that by "quickly" (v 9) he means "before winter," when travel on the Adriatic was suspended (cf. Acts 27:20; Matt 24:20; Fee cites F. Braudel, *The Mediterranean and the Mediterranean World in the Age of Philip II* [New York: Harper & Row, 1972] 248–56). The urgency may also be related to Paul's need for his cloak (v 13) and the timing of the trial. See *Comment* on v 9 for a historical reconstruction.

21b ἀσπάζεταί σε Εὔβουλος καὶ Πούδης καὶ Λίνος καὶ Κλαυδία καὶ οἱ ἀδελφοὶ πάντες, "Eubulus greets you and Pudens and Linus and Claudia and all the brethren." Paul often sends greetings to the letter's recipient from those with him (cf. Titus 3:15). These four people are not mentioned elsewhere in the NT. The last three names are Latin, possibly suggesting Rome as the place of the letter's origin, and the fourth name is that of a woman. Most likely they were leaders in the Roman church and were known by Timothy. They were not part of Paul's inner circle and did not come forward at his preliminary hearing (vv 11, 16a). By including them here in a friendly manner, Paul puts feet to his request that God not hold their desertion against them (v 16). Tradition says that Linus became the first bishop of Rome (Irenaeus *Adv. Haer.* 3.3.3; cf. Eusebius *Hist. Eccl.* 3.2 [3.4.9]) and served for twelve years (Bernard, 151). A later tradition says that he was the son of Pudens and Claudia (*Apost. Const.* 7.46), and further "ingenuity" (Bernard, 151) traces them to the beginning of British Christianity. Paul concludes by sending greetings from all the Roman Christians (ἀδελφοί, "brethren," here refers to men and women; cf. 1 Tim 4:6; 1 Cor 16:20; 1 Thess 5:26, 27).

22 ὁ κύριος μετὰ τοῦ πνεύματός σου. ἡ χάρις μεθ' ὑμῶν, "The Lord [be] with your spirit. Grace [be] with you all." As Chrysostom comments, "There can be no better prayer than this. Grieve not for my departure. The Lord will be with thee" ("Homily 10"; NPNF 13:516). It is fitting that a personal epistle of encouragement end on the note of God's grace. The different subscriptions (see *Note* s) identify Timothy as the recipient and Paul as the author, specify the document as the second letter, and identify Rome as the place of writing.

Paul ends his letter to Timothy in a slightly different form from elsewhere. His final greeting is often "the grace of our Lord Jesus Christ be with you" (cf. *Comment* on 1 Tim 6:21). Here Paul may split the benediction into two parts. The first is addressed specifically to Timothy; σοῦ, "your," is singular. μετὰ τοῦ πνεύματός σου, "with your spirit" (Phil 4:23; Phlm 25; on πνεῦμα, "spirit," cf. *Comment* on 2 Tim 1:7), has roughly the same meaning as the plural μεθ' ὑμῶν, "with you" (cf. Rom 16:20; 1 Cor 16:23; 2 Cor 13:13; Gal 6:18; 1 Thess 5:28; 2 Thess 3:18; 1 Tim 6:21; Titus 3:15). The second part may be addressed to the Ephesian church; ὑμῶν, "you," is plural, hence "you all" (cf. *Comment* on 1 Tim 6:21, which also uses the plural, and the simplified benedictions in Titus 3:15; Eph 6:24; Col 4:18). Yet Paul ends his personal letter to Philemon with a plural ὑμῶν, "you" (25), so perhaps too much should not be made of the plural in 2 Timothy. Unlike the first epistle, Paul is not here addressing the church as a whole. The plural "you" may address Timothy's associates in Ephesus such as Priscilla, Aquila, and the household of Onesiphorus (v 19).

If the traditional historical reconstruction of the PE is correct, then these are the final recorded words written by Paul, apostle to the Gentiles. God's grace overflowed in his life with the faith and love that were in Christ Jesus (1 Tim 1:14). He lived a life characterized by the grace of God calling sinful men and women to Christ by faith. And he ends his ministry having fulfilled his calling (2 Tim 4:6–7) with χάρις, "grace," on his lips. Sometime that fall Timothy may have made the trip to Rome to see Paul one last time on earth. Paul lost his life most likely that winter. According to the Ostian Way tradition, Paul was beheaded at Aquae Salviae near the third milestone on the Ostian Way (F. F. Bruce, *Paul, Apostle of the Heart Set Free* [Grand Rapids, MI: Eerdmans, 1977] 450–51). Paul looked forward to his crown of righteousness (2 Tim 4:8), to being with the Lord (Phil

1:21, 23), to seeing him face to face, and to knowing God just as he is known (1 Cor 13:12). His wish was that Timothy and all who long for Christ's appearing be found as faithful.

Explanation

Paul was at the end of his life. The trial had begun and his ministry was somewhat validated, but Paul knew this would end in death, and he wanted to see his good friend Timothy one more time this side of heaven. Paul was lonely. He had been deserted by one good friend, Demas, and by most everyone else. The rest of his inner circle had left on their respective ministries; only Luke remained. As he came to Rome, Timothy was to get John Mark and Paul's cloak and his parchments. He was also to be careful of Alexander; he was a dangerous person, but vengeance was the Lord's.

In a remarkable but expected attitude of trust, Paul expresses his assuredness that the Lord is with him and will rescue him from any real harm by bringing him into heaven. His ministry was complete, he had faithfully proclaimed the gospel to all the nations, and his next stop would be heaven.

Paul concludes by greeting some of Timothy's friends in Ephesus, reporting on the whereabouts of Erastus and Trophimus. Once again he urges Timothy to come quickly. Little time was left, and Paul would not be alive in the spring. He concludes by sending greetings from four members of the Roman church. Although Paul could not be with Timothy any longer, the Lord would be, and his grace would be with Timothy.

It is difficult, if not impossible, to end this discussion of the PE following more than ten years of writing without breaking into praise of the God who in his love and mercy saves sinners, even sinners like Paul, and uses them for his purposes. May we be found as faithful as Paul when we meet our final hour. *The Lord be with your spirit. Grace be with you all. Amen.*

Index of Modern Authors

Index of Principal Topics

Index of Biblical and Other Ancient Sources

The Old Testament

The New Testament

3:8 227, 254
3:12 297
3:21 206
4:1-3 234
4:1 445
4:2 227, 357
4:6 236
4:13 440
4:14 cxxxiv
4:15 357
5:20 87
5:9 183

2 John

1 162, 379
3 9
7 227
11 304, 317
13 316, 379

3 John

1 162
2 41
5-10 173
6 458
8 173
10 294, 344
12 183, 589

Jude

1 327
3 xcv, cxxx, 382
4 37, 254, 285, 430, 532, 548
6 316, 513
8 401, 402
9 549
11 236, 340
15 37, 424
16 297
17-18 234
18 358, 424, 544
20 cxxx
23 265
24-25 48
25 cxxxiv, 9, 61, 62, 363, 598

Revelation

1:1 378
1:3 261
1:6 48, 62, 363, 427, 517
1:7 62
2-3 265
2:1-7 lxviii
2:1 316
2:9 69, 344
2:10 582
2:23 593
3:1b 283
3:9 69
3:12 223, 327
3:17-18 344
3:19 68, 423
3:21 517
4:4 162
4:7 597
4:9
4:10 162
4:11 61, 62
5:1 529
5:2 529
5:5 162, 597
5:6 162
5:8 162
5:9 529
5:10 517
5:11 162
5:12 61, 62, 598
5:13 48, 62, 363
5:14 162
6:1 529
6:3 529
6:5 327, 529
6:7 529
6:9 489, 529
6:10 532
6:12 529
7:2 222, 529
7:3 378, 529
7:11 162
7:12 61, 62
7:13 162
7:14 440
8:1 529
8:7 569
9:4 529
9:7 532
9:8 597
9:15 532
9:17 223
10:1 489
10:3 597
10:7 378
11:16 108, 162
11:18 378
12:6 532
12:7-17 182
12:10 312
12:17 489
13:16 238
14:3 162
14:8 175, 426
14:10 175, 315
14:14-20 315
15:3 60, 378
15:4 37, 108
15:7 222
16:5 37, 108, 583
16:7 583
16:9 327
16:12 532
16:19 175, 426
17:1 426
17:2 175
17:4 115
17:5 426
17:6 175
17:8 345
17:11 345
17:14 316, 361, 379
18:2 426, 569
18:3-7 290
18:3 175, 290
18:7-8 290
18:10 426
18:12 569
18:13 175
18:16 115, 426
18:19 426
18:21 426
19:2 583
19:4 162
19:10 485, 489
19:15 378
19:16 361
20:1 496
20:4 517
20:6 517
20:7-10 182
20:10 485
20:12 593
20:14 485
20:15 485
21:1 582
21:2 532
21:8 38, 403
21:14 529
21:19 569
21:22-27 362
22:3 378
22:5 517
593
22:14 440
22:15 38
22:18-19 xcv
22:20 62
22:21 372
2:12

Old Testament Apocrypha

Baruch
1:11 80
4:22 cxxxiv
5:4 117

4 Ezra
5:1-12 234
16:67 315

4 Kingdoms
17:15 26

1 Maccabees
2:60 597
4:32 478
7:33 80
8:18 327
12:4 458
12:9 261
14:21 62

2 Maccabees
1:27 403
2:21 360
3:10-40 487
3:10 487
3:15 487
3:20 108
3:24 360, 478
4:2 432
4:8 79
4:47 414
5:16 62
8:23 563

Pseudepigrapha and Early Jewish Literature

Dead Sea Scrolls

Josephus

Philo

Rabbinic Literature

Early Christian Literature

Greek and Latin Literature